READINGS IN THE PHILOSOPHY OF LANGUAGE

READINGS IN THE PHILOSOPHY OF LANGUAGE

Edited by Peter Ludlow

A Bradford Book
The MIT Press
Cambridge, Massachusetts
London, England

This book was set in Times Roman on the Monotype "Prism Plus" PostScript Imagesetter by Asco Trade Typesetting Ltd., Hong Kong, and was printed and bound in the United States of America.

First printing, 1997.

Library of Congress Cataloging-in-Publication Data

Readings in the philosophy of language / edited by Peter Ludlow.
        p.   cm.
   "A Bradford book."
   Includes bibliographical references and index.
   ISBN 0-262-12205-7 (alk. paper). — ISBN 0-262-62114-2 (pbk. : alk. paper)
   1. Language and languages—Philosophy. I. Ludlow, Peter, 1957–
P106.R385   1997
401—dc21   96-39198
                                                                        CIP

For Chiara Teodolinda Repetti-Ludlow

Contents

Preface   xiii

Acknowledgments   xvii

PART I

LANGUAGE AND MEANING   1

INTRODUCTION   3

Chapter 1
The Thought: A Logical Inquiry   9

Gottlob Frege

Chapter 2
Excerpt from *The Blue and Brown Books*   31

Ludwig Wittgenstein

Chapter 3
Translation and Meaning   49

Willard Van Orman Quine

Chapter 4
Utterer's Meaning and Intentions   59

Paul Grice

Chapter 5
Truth and Meaning   89

Donald Davidson

Chapter 6
What Model-Theoretic Semantics Cannot Do   109

Ernest Lepore

Chapter 7
What Is a Theory of Meaning?   129

Michael Dummett

Chapter 8
Elucidations of Meaning   157

James Higginbotham

Chapter 9
Knowledge of Meaning and Theories of Truth   179

Richard K. Larson and Gabriel Segal

PART II

LOGICAL FORM AND GRAMMATICAL FORM   201

INTRODUCTION   203

Chapter 10
Some Remarks on Logical Form   209

Ludwig Wittgenstein

Chapter 11
The Logical Form of Action Sentences   217

Donald Davidson

Chapter 12
Semantic Structure and Logical Form   233

Gareth Evans

Chapter 13
Deep Structure as Logical Form   257

Gilbert Harman

Chapter 14
Logical Form as a Level of Linguistic Representation   281

Robert May

PART III

DEFINITE AND INDEFINITE DESCRIPTIONS   317

INTRODUCTION   319

Chapter 15
Descriptions   323

Bertrand Russell

Chapter 16
On Referring   335

Peter F. Strawson

Chapter 17
Reference and Definite Descriptions   361

Keith S. Donnellan

Chapter 18
Speaker's Reference and Semantic Reference   383

Saul A. Kripke

Chapter 19
Context and Communication   415

Stephen Neale

Chapter 20
Referential and Quantificational Indefinites   475

Janet Dean Fodor and Ivan A. Sag

Chapter 21
Indefinite Descriptions: In Defense of Russell   523

Peter Ludlow and Stephen Neale

PART IV

NAMES   557

INTRODUCTION   559

Chapter 22
On Sense and Reference   563

Gottlob Frege

x   Contents

Chapter 23
Proper Names   585

John R. Searle

Chapter 24
Reference and Proper Names   593

Tyler Burge

Chapter 25
Lecture II of *Naming and Necessity*   609

Saul A. Kripke

Chapter 26
The Causal Theory of Names   635

Gareth Evans

PART V
_____

DEMONSTRATIVES   657

INTRODUCTION   659

Chapter 27
Truth and Demonstratives   663

Scott Weinstein

Chapter 28
Dthat   669

David Kaplan

Chapter 29
Frege on Demonstratives   693

John Perry

Chapter 30
Understanding Demonstratives   717

Gareth Evans

Chapter 31
Individuation and the Semantics of Demonstratives   745

Martin Davies

PART VI

ATTITUDE REPORTS   769

INTRODUCTION   771

Chapter 32
The Method of Intension   779
Rudolph Carnap

Chapter 33
On Synonymy and Indirect Discourse   793
Israel Scheffler

Chapter 34
Vagaries of Reference   801
Willard Van Orman Quine

Chapter 35
On Saying That   817
Donald Davidson

Chapter 36
Opacity and Scope   833
Barbara Partee

Chapter 37
Sententialist Theories of Belief   855
Stephen Schiffer

Chapter 38
A Puzzle about Belief   875
Saul A. Kripke

Chapter 39
Direct Reference, Propositional Attitudes, and Semantic Content   921
Scott Soames

Chapter 40
The Prince and the Phone Booth: Reporting Puzzling Beliefs   963
Mark Crimmins and John Perry

Chapter 41
Interpreted Logical Forms   993

Richard K. Larson and Peter Ludlow

Chapter 42
Intensional "Transitive" Verbs and Concealed Complement Clauses   1041

Marcel den Dikken, Richard K. Larson, and Peter Ludlow

Index   1055

This collection is a resource manual for persons interested in a particular research program in the philosophy of language, specifically, a program designed to use the tools of contemporary linguistic theory to help naturalize certain core problems in the philosophy of language. Each section of this reader is designed to provide some historical (twentieth-century) readings in each problem area and (where available) some of the recent attempts to apply the resources of contemporary linguistic theory to gain headway in those problem areas. My hope is that this will help show how the research program is firmly rooted in the leading questions of analytic philosophy, as well as how the program departs from traditional methods. But I also hope it will help to clarify the philosophical motivations of work that must look forbidding to the outsider.

This is not to say that all the readings in this collection represent examples of the naturalization-via-linguistics project. Most of these readings predate that project by years or decades. The older readings are here because they *inform* the current naturalization project and help lay the philosophical foundations for the project. Moreover, in my view the project cannot be fully understood without first understanding the issues in these papers.

Still, it is a central theme of this collection that the philosophy of language, or at least a core portion of it, has matured to the point where it is now being spun off into linguistic theory. If this is correct, then the philosophy of language is simply following in the tradition of other branches of philosophy that have been extruded into the natural sciences: physics, biology, and perhaps most recently, cognitive psychology.

There is admittedly a great deal of resistance to this view. Some philosophers seem reluctant to loosen their grip on the philosophy of language, or even admit that empirical evidence from linguistics might be relevant. The contrast with the situation in the philosophy of mind is marked.

Few philosophers of mind balk at the idea that what they are studying might have something to do with empirical research on vision or mental imagery or even the neuroanatomy of the brain. Yet philosophers of language continue to resist arguments that appeal to linguistic evidence.

I'm not sure why the situation is like this. Perhaps philosophers are willing to defer to sciences when it involves a domain that they cannot see (like the micro level in physics or the activity of the mind/brain in cognitive science) but are unwilling to be deferential when it involves a domain with which they have been fluent since childhood—language. If this is the subtext, then the fallacy is pretty obvious. Philosophers have likewise been "fluent" in thinking since childhood, but the best philosophers of mind do not thereby conclude that they are experts on the structure of their cognitive architecture.

On the other hand, perhaps the resistance to naturalizing the philosophy of language is simply due to the fact that philosophers are a skeptical lot and need to be shown that the philosophy of language really is ready to be transferred to the linguists. This is not an unreasonable position, and such philosophers are entirely justified in asking to be shown that the leading questions in the philosophy of language really are moving into the domain of linguistics. Specifically, they will want to see (1) how such research addresses the core problems in the philosophy of language, (2) the extent to which current research really does treat those problems as empirical, and (3) the extent to which the empirical research advances our understanding of those problems in ways that were not possible via the old techniques.

Answering the skeptical philosopher on all three points is a tall order, but the aim of this anthology is to do precisely that. I have selected six topic areas for examination:

1. Language and meaning
2. Logical form and grammatical form
3. Descriptions
4. Names
5. Demonstratives
6. Attitude reports

My aim in selecting the readings has been to show where these "classical" problems are currently being addressed with the help of linguistic theory (and where they aren't).

Of course, attempts to empiricize these problem areas are not new, and linguistic theory has not always been the supposed receiving science.

These abortive attempts have been catalogued here too, if only to show that the philosophy of language has for years had a metalevel research program whose goal is to spin off the contents of the philosophy of language into the sciences. The only question is whether current research is another false start or the research project that eventually naturalizes the philosophy of language. My intuition is that the latter is true.

An introduction to the technical part of this research program can be found in Richard Larson and Gabriel Segal's *Knowledge of Meaning* (also published by the MIT Press). I have cotaught that material with Richard on a number of occasions, and on each occasion we have supplemented the material with many of the readings in this volume. Richard and I were both of the opinion that these materials provided an important conceptual background not only to the mechanics of the theory but also for some of the philosophical claims made in *Knowledge of Meaning*. Accordingly, this collection can be seen as a kind of companion to the Larson and Segal effort.

Not only have I used these materials in graduate semantics courses, but I have also taught from these materials in the philosophy of language— indeed, *undergraduate* philosophy of language. Some might counsel that one should stay within the strict philosophy-of-language canon when teaching undergraduates, but I disagree completely. The canon has no direction. It has no theme. It is disembodied philosophy, sitting cold and lifeless and self-important. It stinks of death, and students have a keen sense of smell.

By contrast, whatever else you say about this collection, students can see that there is something happening here. They may not *agree* with what they see, but that is another matter. The whole project could crash tomorrow, but that is just part of the excitement. That is what *doing* real philosophy is all about, and students have a right to share in this experience.

While some of my friends have complained that the philosophy of language has become moribund or has been eclipsed by the philosophy of mind, my take on the situation is exactly the opposite. I won't say that the philosophy of language is about to enter another golden age, but I will say that it is entering an exciting period—one in which how we conduct philosophy of language could change in fundamental ways. If I am right, then this collection is not a final report on a mature line of philosophical inquiry but is merely the opening chapter in a drama that will feature a fundamental shift in how we conduct our inquiries into the nature of language.

Acknowledgments

A number of folks have helped make this project happen, some by introducing me to the philosophy-of-language/linguistics research program, others by helping me fine-tune the contents of this collection. James Higginbotham, Norbert Hornstein, and Robert May introduced me to the resources of generative grammar and showed me how they could be used to purchase insights into traditional philosophical problems. I am indebted to Paolo Leonardi and George Wilson for general discussions about pedagogy in the philosophy of language, many of which influenced the eventual composition of this reader. In addition, Paolo and I cotaught a course on descriptions at the University Venice in the fall of 1994, and that course had an important influence on the readings selected for section 3. I am also indebted to Noam Chomsky and Stephen Schiffer for useful comments on earlier incarnations of the proposed contents.

Most of my debt, however, is to friends and collaborators who have at some point drawn these readings to my attention, debated their merits with me, and shown how they might play a role in naturalizing the philosophy of language. In particular, I wish to thank Michael Devitt, Richard Larson, Stephen Neale, and Barry Schein, each of whom had a profound influence on this collection (whether they realize it or not).

Several of these readings were assigned in a semantics course that Richard Larson and I cotaught at SUNY Stony Brook and again at the 1991 Linguistic Society of America Summer Institute in Santa Cruz. Rather more of the readings made it into the assigned materials for my philosophy-of-language course at Stony Brook. In each case I have learned much from the students, and this collection is much stronger because of their feedback.

Finally, I want to thank my daughter, Chiara, for spurring me to finish this project. Her remarkable accomplishment in growing from a zygote to a fully functional baby within 9 short months showed me just how much one can accomplish in a short period of time. Her example encouraged me to get off my tail and finish this project (albeit four years behind schedule).

PART I
LANGUAGE AND MEANING

INTRODUCTION

Words and sentences mean things, or at least we can use them to mean things. But are there also meanings? Put another way, when we use a word so that someone understands us, are we successful by virtue of that word expressing a certain meaning? And if so, what are meanings? Are they objects in our heads? Are they something else?

Frege thought they were something else. As he argues in "The Thought," meanings can't be in our heads, for that would pose problems for our ability to communicate our thoughts. The possibility of communication implies that meanings must be public objects of some form or other. Moreover, Frege argues, meanings cannot be in the world, for we can express thoughts that bear no relation to the actual world. Instead, Frege concludes, meanings must be abstract objects that inhabit a third realm, neither psychological nor physical in nature.

Frege's proposal is ingenious but raises horrific epistemological problems. If meanings are off in some third realm—perhaps Plato's heaven—then how can we ever know that one of those meanings has been expressed? Wouldn't that involve our having some sort of acquaintance with these objects?

It seems that we are trapped in a dilemma. On the one hand, if meanings are in our heads, then meanings cannot be shared, and hence it is hard to understand how communication is possible. On the other hand, if we follow Frege and say that meanings are abstract objects, we appear to be in an epistemological quandary.

But perhaps it is a mistake to think that a theory of meaning requires that there be actual meanings, that is, meanings as entities to be apprehended and expressed. Perhaps we can have a theory of meaning without meanings. This, I think, was Wittgenstein's great insight, and it is an insight that is shared by the subsequent papers in this section.

In the excerpt from *The Blue and Brown Books*, Wittgenstein begins to develop a "use theory" of meaning, according to which words do not have meanings per se but rather can be used to perform certain tasks. Do you want to know what a word means? Well, what you really want to know is its use in a particular context.

Use theories are not the only way to avoid meanings. As Quine proposes in "Translation and Meaning," perhaps meanings can be reduced to classes of stimulations. So, for example, if I point in the direction of some object and say "gavagai," I am not expressing some determinate meaning. The most that we can say is that my assent to the term "gavagai" correlates with certain stimulations.

In "Utterer's Meaning and Intentions" Paul Grice takes yet another route. According to Grice, we might take the meaning of a proposition to be grounded in the intentions of the speaker. Along the way Grice is careful to draw a distinction between (among other things) what an utterance type x means and what the utterer U meant by x. One immediately sees that while Wittgenstein was right to say that use plays an important role in the theory of meaning, it cannot be the whole story. Indeed, it is only because propositions have certain stable meanings that we can successfully use them as we do. If it were nothing but use in a context, well, how would we ever learn to communicate? What would ground our rules of use?

If Grice divides the problem of meaning into more tractable parts, there remains the question of what could count as the core theory of meaning, particularly if we want to avoid meanings as abstract objects. In "Truth and Meaning" Donald Davidson offers a suggestion. Perhaps a theory of truth (or T-theory) can serve as a theory of meaning. That is, if someone knew a recursive characterization of truth for a language, perhaps that would be enough (given certain other constraints) to know for each sentence of the language what the meaning of that sentence is. Hence one could have a theory of meaning without meanings!

For Davidson this idea was not to be psychologized, but subsequent philosophers have not been so bashful. Perhaps there is a fact about the T-theory that an agent knows—indeed, a fact about the agent's psychology. Thus Gareth Evans (1981) holds that we could appeal to evidence from language acquisition and acquired language deficits to shed light on the T-theory that an agent is using in the comprehension of language. For example, given two T-theories that accurately characterize an agent's linguistic competence, there would arise the question of whether there is a fact about which of those T-theories the agent uses. According to Evans, one might look to facts about the development of the agent's linguistic competence, since that would shed light on which set of axioms were actually in play for the agent.

If T-theories are well designed to serve as meaning theories, other semantic theories allegedly are not. According to Ernest LePore in "What Model-Theoretic Semantics Cannot Do?" alternative semantic theories like structural semantics and model-theoretic semantics fail to provide the necessary language-world connections required if a semantic theory is really to serve as a theory of meaning. Thus, for example, while model-theoretic semantics is a perfectly respectable enterprise, perhaps even necessary for an account of logical inference, it is not particularly useful as part of a theory of meaning.

T-theories arguably play an important role in theories of meaning, but do they tell us enough? In "What Is a Theory of Meaning," Michael Dummett distinguishes between austere and robust theories of meaning and complains that the theories delivered by the Davidsonian program are of the austere variety. They tell us that "snow" refers to snow, and this is certainly informative (the word spelled s-n-o-w, after all, could have referred to something else), but we want more. We want to know what rules or procedures the agent exploits in identifying something as snow. That is, we want to know more about the agent's semantic knowledge than T-theories alone apparently deliver.

Can such information be added to Davidsonian T-theories? It is hard to see why not. In "Elucidations of Meaning" James Higginbotham sketches an approach to our semantic knowledge that embeds it within a scientific project to explore the nature of the lexicon. In this way he shows how even robust meaning theories might be naturalized.

The reading from Larson and Segal sketches a program for naturalizing the Davidson program within semantic theory. Like Gareth Evans, they hold that there is a fact of the matter about what rules the speakers are using, and they go on to explicitly argue that language users are hardwired to utilize T-theories as meaning theories. Ultimately, for them, the semantic project becomes a chapter of cognitive science, to be explored via the tools of the cognitive sciences.

Further Reading for Part I

On Frege's philosophy of language
Dummett, M. 1973. *Frege: Philosophy of Language*. London: Duckworth.

On the Gricean program

Black, M. 1973. "Meaning and Intention: An Examination of Grice's Views." *New Literary History* 4:257–279.

Grice, P. 1989. *Studies in the Way of Words.* Cambridge: Harvard University Press.

Schiffer, S. 1972. *Meaning.* Oxford: Oxford University Press.

Ziff, P. 1967. "On Grice's Account of Meaning." *Analysis* 28:1–8.

On possible-world semantics

Chierchia, G., and S. McConnell-Ginet. 1990. *Meaning and Grammar.* Cambridge: MIT Press.

Dowty, D., R. Wall, and S. Peters. 1981. *An Introduction to Montague Semantics.* Dordrecht: D. Reidel.

Lewis, D. 1972. "General Semantics." In D. Davidson and G. Harman (eds.), *Semantics of Natural Language.* Dordrecht: D. Reidel.

Lycan, W. 1979. "The Trouble with Possible Worlds." In M. Loux (ed.) *The Possible and the Actual.* Ithaca: Cornell University Press.

Montague, R. 1974. *Formal Philosophy: Selected Papers of Richard Montague.* Edited by R. Thomason. New Haven: Yale University Press.

Partee, B. 1973. "Some Transformational Extensions of Montague Grammar." *Journal of Philosophical Logic* 2:509–534.

Work stressing the importance of language-world connections

Barwise, J., and J. Perry. 1983. *Situations and Attitudes.* Cambridge: MIT Press.

Putnam, H. 1975. "The Meaning of 'Meaning'." In *Language, Mind, and Knowledge*, Minnesota Studies on the Philosophy of Science, no. 7. Minneapolis: University of Minnesota Press.

On truth-conditional semantics

Evans, G., and J. McDowell (eds.). 1976. *Truth and Meaning: Essays in Semantics.* Oxford: Oxford University Press.

Higginbotham, J. 1985. "On Semantics." *Linguistic Inquiry* 16:547–593.

Larson, R., and G. Segal. 1995. *Knowledge of Meaning: An Introduction to Semantic Theory.* Cambridge: MIT Press.

LePore, E. (ed.). 1986. *Truth and Interpretation: Perspectives on the Philosophy of Donald Davidson.* Oxford: Blackwell.

Platts, M. 1979. *The Ways of Meaning.* London: Routledge and Kegan Paul.

Schiffer, S. 1987. *Remnants of Meaning.* Cambridge: MIT Press.

On the issue of tacit knowledge of semantic rules

Davies, M. 1987. "Tacit Knowledge and Semantic Theory: Can a Five Per Cent Difference Matter?" *Mind* 96:441–462.

Evans, G. 1981. "Semantic Theory and Tacit Knowledge." In S. Holzman and C. Leich (eds.), *Wittgenstein: To Follow a Rule*. London: Routledge and Kegan Paul.

Wright, C. 1981. "Rule-Following, Objectivity, and Theory of Meaning." In S. Holzman and C. Leich (eds.), *Wittgenstein: To Follow a Rule*. London: Routledge and Kegan Paul.

Wright, C. 1986. "Theories of Meaning and Speaker's Knowledge." In S. G. Shanker (ed.), *Philosophy in Britain Today*. Albany: SUNY Press.

Chapter 1

The Thought: A Logical Inquiry

Gottlob Frege

Translated by A. M. and Marcelle Quinton

The word 'true' indicates the aim of logic as does 'beautiful' that of aesthetics or 'good' that of ethics. All sciences have truth as their goal; but logic is also concerned with it in a quite different way from this. It has much the same relation to truth as physics has to weight or heat. To discover truths is the task of all sciences; it falls to logic to discern the laws of truth. The word 'law' is used in two senses. When we speak of laws of morals or the state we mean regulations which ought to be obeyed but with which actual happenings are not always in conformity. Laws of nature are the generalization of natural occurrences with which the occurrences are always in accordance. It is rather in this sense that I speak of laws of truth. This is, to be sure, not a matter of what happens so much as of what is. Rules for asserting, thinking, judging, inferring, follow from the laws of truth. And thus one can very well speak of laws of thought too. But there is an imminent danger here of mixing different things up. Perhaps the expression 'law of thought' is interpreted by analogy with 'law of nature' and the generalization of thinking as a mental occurrence is meant by it. A law of thought in this sense would be a psychological law. And so one might come to believe that logic deals with the mental process of thinking and the psychological laws in accordance with which it takes place. This would be a misunderstanding of the task of logic, for truth has not been given the place which is its due here. Error and superstition have causes just as much as genuine knowledge. The assertion both of what is false and of what is true takes place in accordance with psychological laws. A derivation from these and an explanation of a mental process that terminates in an assertion can never take the place of a proof

Translated by A. M. and Marcelle Quinton. This translation first appeared in *Mind* 65 (1956): 289–311. Reprinted by permission of Oxford University Press.

of what is asserted. Could not logical laws also have played a part in this mental process? I do not want to dispute this, but when it is a question of truth possibility is not enough. For it is also possible that something not logical played a part in the process and deflected it from the truth. We can only decide this after we have discerned the laws of truth; but then we will probably be able to do without the derivation and explanation of the mental process if it is important to us to decide whether the assertion in which the process terminates is justified. In order to avoid this misunderstanding and to prevent the blurring of the boundary between psychology and logic, I assign to logic the task of discovering the laws of truth, not of assertion or thought. The meaning of the word 'true' is explained by the laws of truth.

But first I shall attempt to outline roughly what I want to call true in this connexion. In this way other uses of our word may be excluded. It is not to be used here in the sense of 'genuine' or 'veracious', nor, as it sometimes occurs in the treatment of questions of art, when, for example, truth in art is discussed, when truth is set up as the goal of art, when the truth of a work of art or true feeling is spoken of. The word 'true' is put in front of another word in order to show that this word is to be understood in its proper, unadulterated sense. This use too lies off the path followed here; that kind of truth is meant whose recognition is the goal of science.

Grammatically the word 'true' appears as an adjective. Hence the desire arises to delimit more closely the sphere in which truth can be affirmed, in which truth comes into the question at all. One finds truth affirmed of pictures, ideas, statements, and thoughts. It is striking that visible and audible things occur here alongside things which cannot be perceived with the senses. This hints that shifts of meaning have taken place. Indeed! Is a picture, then, as a mere visible and tangible thing, really true, and a stone, a leaf, not true? Obviously one would not call a picture true unless there were an intention behind it. A picture must represent something. Furthermore, an idea is not called true in itself but only with respect to an intention that it should correspond to something. It might be supposed from this that truth consists in the correspondence of a picture with what it depicts. Correspondence is a relation. This is contradicted, however, by the use of the word 'true', which is not a relation-word and contains no reference to anything else to which something must correspond. If I do not know that a picture is meant to represent Cologne Cathedral then I do not know with what to compare the picture to decide on its truth. A correspondence, moreover, can only be perfect if the corresponding things coincide and are, therefore, not distinct things at all. It is said to be possible to establish the authenticity of a banknote by comparing it stereoscopically with an authentic one. But it would be ridiculous to try to compare a gold piece with a twenty-mark note stereoscopically. It would only be possible to compare an idea with a thing if the thing were an idea too. And then, if the first did correspond perfectly with the second, they would coincide. But this is not at all what is wanted when truth is defined as the correspondence of an idea with something real. For it is absolutely essential that the reality be distinct from the idea. But then there can be no complete correspondence, no complete truth. So nothing at all would be true; for what is only half true is untrue. Truth cannot tolerate a more or less. But yet? Can it not be laid down that truth exists when there is correspondence in a certain respect? But in which? For what would we then have to do to decide whether something were true? We should have to inquire whether it were true that an idea and a reality, perhaps, corresponded in the laid-down respect. And then we should be confronted by a question of the same kind and the game could begin again. So the attempt to explain truth as correspondence collapses. And every other attempt to define truth collapses too. For in a definition certain characteristics would have to be stated. And in application to any particular case the question would always arise whether it were true that the characteristics were present. So one goes round in a circle. Consequently, it is probable that the content of the word 'true' is unique and indefinable.

When one ascribes truth to a picture one does not really want to ascribe a property which belongs to this picture altogether independently of other things, but one always has something quite different in mind and one wants to say that that picture corresponds in some way to this thing. 'My idea corresponds to Cologne Cathedral' is a sentence and the question now arises of the truth of this sentence. So what is improperly called the truth of pictures and ideas is reduced to the truth of sentences. What does one call a sentence? A series of sounds; but only when it has a sense, by which is not meant that every series of sounds that has sense is a sentence. And when we call a sentence true we really mean its sense is. From which it follows that it is for the sense of a sentence that the question of truth arises in general. Now is the sense of a sentence an idea? In any case being true does not consist in the correspondence of this sense with something else, for otherwise the question of truth would reiterate itself to infinity.

Without wishing to give a definition, I call a thought something for which the question of truth arises. So I ascribe what is false to a thought just as much as what is true.[1] So I can say: the thought is the sense of the sentence without wishing to say as well that the sense of every sentence is a thought. The thought, in itself immaterial, clothes itself in the material garment of a sentence and thereby becomes comprehensible to us. We say a sentence expresses a thought.

A thought is something immaterial and everything material and perceptible is excluded from this sphere of that for which the question of truth arises. Truth is not a quality that corresponds with a particular kind of sense-impression. So it is sharply distinguished from the qualities which we denote by the words 'red', 'bitter', 'lilac-smelling'. But do we not see that the sun has risen and do we not then also see that this is true? That the sun has risen is not an object which emits rays that reach my eyes, it is not a visible thing like the sun itself. That the sun has risen is seen to be true on the basis of sense-impressions. But being true is not a material, perceptible property. For being magnetic is also recognized on the basis of sense-impressions of something, though this property corresponds as little as truth with a particular kind of sense-impressions. So far these properties agree. However, we need sense-impressions in order to recognize a body as magnetic. On the other hand, when I find that it is true that I do not smell anything at this moment, I do not do so on the basis of sense-impressions.

It may nevertheless be thought that we cannot recognize a property of a thing without at the same time realizing the thought that this thing has this property to be true. So with every property of a thing is joined a property of a thought, namely, that of truth. It is also worthy of notice that the sentence 'I smell the scent of violets' has just the same content as the sentence 'it is true that I smell the scent of violets'. So it seems, then, that nothing is added to the thought by my ascribing to it the property of truth. And yet is it not a great result when the scientist after much hesitation and careful inquiry, can finally say 'what I supposed is true'? The meaning of the word 'true' seems to be altogether unique. May we not be dealing here with something which cannot, in the ordinary sense, be called a quality at all? In spite of this doubt I want first to express myself in accordance with ordinary usage, as if truth were a quality, until something more to the point is found.

In order to work out more precisely what I want to call thought, I shall distinguish various kinds of sentences.[2] One does not want to deny sense to an imperative sentence, but this sense is not such that the question of truth could arise for it. Therefore I shall not call the sense of an imperative sentence a thought. Sentences expressing desires or requests are ruled out in the same way. Only those sentences in which we communicate or state something come into the question. But I do not count among these exclamations in which one vents one's feelings, groaning, sighing, laughing, unless it has been decided by some agreement that they are to communicate something. But how about interrogative sentences? In a word-question we utter an incomplete sentence which only obtains a true sense through the completion for which we ask. Word-questions are accordingly left out of consideration here. Sentence-questions are a different matter. We expect to hear 'yes' or 'no'. The answer 'yes' means the same as an indicative sentence, for in it the thought that was already completely contained in the interrogative sentence is laid down as true. So a sentence-question can be formed from every indicative sentence. An exclamation cannot be regarded as a communication on this account, since no corresponding sentence-question can be formed. An interrogative sentence and an indicative one contain the same thought; but the indicative contains something else as well, namely, the assertion. The interrogative sentence contains something more too, namely a request. Therefore two things must be distinguished in an indicative sentence: the content, which it has in common with the corresponding sentence-question, and the assertion. The former is the thought, or at least contains the thought. So it is possible to express the thought without laying it down as true. Both are so closely joined in an indicative sentence that it is easy to overlook their separability. Consequently we may distinguish:

(1) the apprehension of a thought—thinking,
(2) the recognition of the truth of a thought—judgement,[3]
(3) the manifestation of this judgement—assertion.

We perform the first act when we form a sentence-question. An advance in science usually takes place in this way, first a thought is apprehended, such as can perhaps be expressed in a sentence-question, and, after appropriate investigations, this thought is finally recognized to be true. We declare the recognition of truth in the form of an indicative sentence. We do not have to use the word 'true' for this. And even when we do use it the real assertive force lies, not in it, but in the form of the indicative sentence and where this loses its assertive force the word 'true' cannot put it back again. This happens when we do not speak seriously. As stage thunder is only apparent thunder and a stage fight only an apparent fight, so stage assertion is only apparent assertion. It is only acting, only fancy.

In his part the actor asserts nothing, nor does he lie, even if he says something of whose falsehood he is convinced. In poetry we have the case of thoughts being expressed without being actually put forward as true in spite of the form of the indicative sentence, although it may be suggested to the hearer to make an assenting judgement himself. Therefore it must still always be asked, about what is presented in the form of an indicative sentence, whether it really contains an assertion. And this question must be answered in the negative if the requisite seriousness is lacking. It is irrelevant whether the word 'true' is used here. This explains why it is that nothing seems to be added to a thought by attributing to it the property of truth.

An indicative sentence often contains, as well as a thought and the assertion, a third component over which the assertion does not extend. This is often said to act on the feelings, the mood of the hearer or to arouse his imagination. Words like 'alas' and 'thank God' belong here. Such constituents of sentences are more noticeably prominent in poetry, but are seldom wholly absent from prose. They occur more rarely in mathematical, physical, or chemical than in historical expositions. What are called the humanities are more closely connected with poetry and are therefore less scientific than the exact sciences which are drier the more exact they are, for exact science is directed toward truth and only the truth. Therefore all constituents of sentences to which the assertive force does not reach do not belong to scientific exposition but they are sometimes hard to avoid, even for one who sees the danger connected with them. Where the main thing is to approach what cannot be grasped in thought by means of guesswork these components have their justification. The more exactly scientific an exposition is the less will the nationality of its author be discernible and the easier will it be to translate. On the other hand, the constituents of language, to which I want to call attention here, make the translation of poetry very difficult, even make a complete translation almost always impossible, for it is in precisely that in which poetic value largely consists that languages differ most.

It makes no difference to the thought whether I use the word 'horse' or 'steed' or 'cart-horse' or 'mare'. The assertive force does not extend over that in which these words differ. What is called mood, fragrance, illumination in a poem, what is portrayed by cadence and rhythm, does not belong to the thought.

Much of language serves the purpose of aiding the hearer's understanding, for instance the stressing of part of a sentence by accentuation or word-order. One should remember words like 'still' and 'already' too. With the sentence 'Alfred has still not come' one really says 'Alfred has not come' and, at the same time, hints that his arrival is expected, but it is only hinted. It cannot be said that, since Alfred's arrival is not expected, the sense of the sentence is therefore false. The word 'but' differs from 'and' in that with it one intimates that what follows is in contrast with what would be expected from what preceded it. Such suggestions in speech make no difference to the thought. A sentence can be transformed by changing the verb from active to passive and making the object the subject at the same time. In the same way the dative may be changed into the nominative while 'give' is replaced by 'receive'. Naturally such transformations are not indifferent in every respect; but they do not touch the thought, they do not touch what is true or false. If the inadmissibility of such transformations were generally admitted then all deeper logical investigation would be hindered. It is just as important to neglect distinctions that do not touch the heart of the matter as to make distinctions which concern what is essential. But what is essential depends on one's purpose. To a mind concerned with what is beautiful in language what is indifferent to the logician can appear as just what is important.

Thus the contents of a sentence often go beyond the thoughts expressed by it. But the opposite often happens too, that the mere wording, which can be grasped by writing or the gramophone does not suffice for the expression of the thought. The present tense is used in two ways: first, in order to give a date, second, in order to eliminate any temporal restriction where timelessness or eternity is part of the thought. Think, for instance, of the laws of mathematics. Which of the two cases occurs is not expressed but must be guessed. If a time indication is needed by the present tense one must know when the sentence was uttered to apprehend the thought correctly. Therefore the time of utterance is part of the expression of the thought. If someone wants to say the same today as he expressed yesterday using the word 'today', he must replace this word with 'yesterday'. Although the thought is the same its verbal expression must be different so that the sense, which would otherwise be affected by the differing times of utterance, is readjusted. The case is the same with words like 'here' and 'there'. In all such cases the mere wording, as it is given in writing, is not the complete expression of the thought, but the knowledge of certain accompanying conditions of utterance, which are used as means of expressing the thought, are needed for its correct apprehension. The pointing of fingers, hand movements, glances may belong here too. The same utterance containing the word 'I' will express different thoughts in the mouths of different men, of which some may be true, others false.

The occurrence of the word 'I' in a sentence gives rise to some questions.

Consider the following case. Dr. Gustav Lauben says, 'I have been wounded'. Leo Peter hears this and remarks some days later, 'Dr. Gustav Lauben has been wounded'. Does this sentence express the same thought as the one Dr. Lauben uttered himself? Suppose that Rudolph Lingens were present when Dr. Lauben spoke and now hears what is related by Leo Peter. If the same thought is uttered by Dr. Lauben and Leo Peter then Rudolph Lingens, who is fully master of the language and remembers what Dr. Lauben has said in his presence, must now know at once from Leo Peter's report that the same thing is under discussion. But knowledge of the language is a separate thing when it is a matter of proper names. It may well be the case that only a few people associate a particular thought with the sentence 'Dr. Lauben has been wounded'. In this case one needs for complete understanding a knowledge of the expression 'Dr. Lauben'. Now if both Leo Peter and Rudolph Lingens understand by 'Dr. Lauben' the doctor who lives as the only doctor in a house known to both of them, then they both understand the sentence 'Dr. Gustav Lauben has been wounded' in the same way, they associate the same thought with it. But it is also possible that Rudolph Lingens does not know Dr. Lauben personally and does not know that he is the very Dr. Lauben who recently said 'I have been wounded.' In this case Rudolph Lingens cannot know that the same thing is in question. I say, therefore, in this case: the thought which Leo Peter expresses is not the same as that which Dr. Lauben uttered.

Suppose further that Herbert Garner knows that Dr. Gustav Lauben was born on 13th September, 1875 in N. N. and this is not true of anyone else; against this, suppose that he does not know where Dr. Lauben now lives nor indeed anything about him. On the other hand, suppose Leo Peter does not know that Dr. Lauben was born on 13th September 1875, in N. N. Then as far as the proper name 'Dr. Gustav Lauben' is concerned, Herbert Garner and Leo Peter do not speak the same language, since, although they do in fact refer to the same man with this name, they do not know that they do so. Therefore Herbert Garner does not associate the same thought with the sentence 'Dr. Gustav Lauben has been wounded' as Leo Peter wants to express with it. To avoid the drawback of Herbert Garner's and Leo Peter's not speaking the same language, I am assuming that Leo Peter uses the proper name 'Dr. Lauben' and Herbert Garner, on the other hand, uses the proper name 'Gustav Lauben'. Now it is possible that Herbert Garner takes the sense of the sentence 'Dr. Lauben has been wounded' to be true while, misled by false information, taking the sense of the sentence 'Gustav Lauben has been wounded' to be false. Under the assumptions given these thoughts are therefore different.

Accordingly, with a proper name, it depends on how whatever it refers to is presented. This can happen in different ways and every such way corresponds with a particular sense of a sentence containing a proper name. The different thoughts which thus result from the same sentence correspond in their truth-value, of course; that is to say, if one is true then all are true, and if one is false then all are false. Nevertheless their distinctness must be recognized. So it must really be demanded that a single way in which whatever is referred to is presented be associated with every proper name. It is often unimportant that this demand should be fulfilled but not always.

Now everyone is presented to himself in a particular and primitive way, in which he is presented to no-one else. So, when Dr. Lauben thinks that he has been wounded, he will probably take as a basis this primitive way in which he is presented to himself. And only Dr. Lauben himself can grasp thoughts determined in this way. But now he may want to communicate with others. He cannot communicate a thought which he alone can grasp. Therefore, if he now says 'I have been wounded', he must use the 'I' in a sense which can be grasped by others, perhaps in the sense of 'he who is speaking to you at this moment', by doing which he makes the associated conditions of his utterance serve for the expression of his thought.[4]

Yet there is a doubt. Is it at all the same thought which first that man expresses and now this one?

A person who is still untouched by philosophy knows first of all things which he can see and touch, in short, perceive with the senses, such as trees, stones and houses, and he is convinced that another person equally can see and touch the same tree and the same stone which he himself sees and touches. Obviously no thought belongs to these things. Now can he, nevertheless, stand in the same relation to a person as a tree?

Even an unphilosophical person soon finds it necessary to recognize an inner world distinct from the outer world, a world of sense-impressions, of creations of his imagination, of sensations, of feelings and moods, a world of inclinations, wishes and decisions. For brevity I want to collect all these, with the exception of decisions, under the word 'idea'.

Now do thoughts belong to this inner world? Are they ideas? They are obviously not decisions. How are ideas distinct from the things of the outer world? First:

Ideas cannot be seen or touched, cannot be smelled, nor tasted, nor heard.

I go for a walk with a companion. I see a green field, I have a visual impression of the green as well. I have it but I do not see it.

Secondly: ideas are had. One has sensations, feelings, moods, inclinations, wishes. An idea which someone has belongs to the content of his consciousness.

The field and the frogs in it, the sun which shines on them are there no matter whether I look at them or not, but the sense-impression I have of green exists only because of me, I am its bearer. It seems absurd to us that a pain, a mood, a wish should rove about the world without a bearer, independently. An experience is impossible without an experient. The inner world presupposes the person whose inner world it is.

Thirdly: ideas need a bearer. Things of the outer world are however independent.

My companion and I are convinced that we both see the same field; but each of us has a particular sense-impression of green. I notice a strawberry among the green strawberry leaves. My companion does not notice it, he is colour-blind. The colour-impression, which he receives from the strawberry, is not noticeably different from the one he receives from the leaf. Now does my companion see the green leaf as red, or does he see the red berry as green, or does he see both as of one colour with which I am not acquainted at all? These are unanswerable, indeed really nonsensical, questions. For when the word 'red' does not state a property of things but is supposed to characterize sense-impressions belonging to my consciousness, it is only applicable within the sphere of my consciousness. For it is impossible to compare my sense-impression with that of someone else. For that it would be necessary to bring together in one consciousness a sense-impression, belonging to one consciousness, with a sense-impression belonging to another consciousness. Now even if it were possible to make an idea disappear from one consciousness and, at the same time, to make an idea appear in another consciousness, the question whether it were the same idea in both would still remain unanswerable. It is so much of the essence of each of my ideas to be the content of my consciousness, that every idea of another person is, just as such, distinct from mine. But might it not be possible that my ideas, the entire content of my consciousness might be at the same time the content of a more embracing, perhaps divine, consciousness? Only if I were myself part of the divine consciousness. But then would they really be my ideas, would I be their bearer? This oversteps the limits of human understanding to such an extent that one must leave its possibility out of account. In any case it is impossible for us as men to compare another person's ideas with our own. I pick the strawberry, I hold it between my fingers. Now my companion sees it too, this very same strawberry; but each of us has his own idea. No other person has my idea but many people can see the same thing. No other person has my pain. Someone can have sympathy for me but still my pain always belongs to me and his sympathy to him. He does not have my pain and I do not have his sympathy.

Fourthly: every idea has only one bearer; no two men have the same idea.

For otherwise it would exist independently of this person and independently of that one. Is that lime-tree my idea? By using the expression 'that lime-tree' in this question I have really already anticipated the answer, for with this expression I want to refer to what I see and to what other people can also look at and touch. There are now two possibilities. If my intention is realized when I refer to something with the expression 'that lime-tree' then the thought expressed in the sentence 'that lime-tree is my idea' must obviously be negated. But if my intention is not realized, if I only think I see without really seeing, if on that account the designation 'that lime-tree' is empty, then I have gone astray into the sphere of fiction without knowing it or wanting to. In that case neither the content of the sentence 'that lime-tree is my idea' nor the content of the sentence 'that lime-tree is not my idea' is true, for in both cases I have a statement which lacks on object. So then one can only refuse to answer the question for the reason that the content of the sentence 'that lime-tree is my idea' is a piece of fiction. I have, naturally, got an idea then, but I am not referring to this with the words 'that lime-tree'. Now someone may really want to refer to one of his ideas with the words 'that lime-tree'. He would then be the bearer of that to which he wants to refer with those words, but then he would not see that lime-tree and no-one else would see it or be its bearer.

I now return to the question: is a thought an idea? If the thought I express in the Pythagorean theorem can be recognized by others just as much as by me then it does not belong to the content of my consciousness, I am not its bearer; yet I can, nevertheless, recognize it to be true. However, if it is not the same thought at all which is taken to be the content of the Pythagorean theorem by me and by another person, one should not really say 'the Pythagorean theorem' but 'my Pythagorean theorem', 'his Pythagorean theorem' and these would be different; for the sense belongs necessarily to the sentence. Then my thought can be content of my consciousness and his thought the content of his. Could the sense of my Pythagorean theorem be true while that of his was false? I said that the word 'red' was applicable only in the sphere of my consciousness if it did not state a property of things but was supposed to characterize one of my sense-impressions. Therefore the words 'true' and 'false', as I understand them, could also be applicable only in the sphere of my consciousness, if they were not supposed to be concerned with something of which I was not the bearer, but were somehow appointed to characterize the content of my consciousness. Then truth would be restricted to the content of my consciousness and it would remain doubtful whether anything at all comparable occurred in the consciousness of others.

If every thought requires a bearer, to the contents of whose consciousness it belongs, then it would be a thought of this bearer only and there would be no science common to many, on which many could work. But I, perhaps, have my science, namely, a whole of thought whose bearer I am and another person has his. Each of us occupies himself with the contents of his own consciousness. No contradiction between the two sciences would then be possible and it would really be idle to dispute about truth, as idle, indeed almost ludicrous, as it would be for two people to dispute whether a hundred-mark note were genuine, where each meant the one he himself had in his pocket and understood the word 'genuine' in his own particular sense. If someone takes thoughts to be ideas, what he then recognizes to be true is, on his own view, the content of his consciousness and does not properly concern other people at all. If he were to hear from me the opinion that a thought is not an idea he could not dispute it, for, indeed, it would not now concern him.

So the result seems to be: thoughts are neither things of the outer world nor ideas.

A third realm must be recognized. What belongs to this corresponds with ideas, in that it cannot be perceived by the senses, but with things, in that it needs no bearer to the contents of whose consciousness to belong. Thus the thought, for example, which we expressed in the Pythagorean theorem is timelessly true, true independently of whether anyone takes it to be true. It needs no bearer. It is not true for the first time when it is discovered, but is like a planet which, already before anyone has seen it, has been in interaction with other planets.[5]

But I think I hear an unusual objection. I have assumed several times that the same thing that I see can also be observed by other people. But how could this be the case, if everything were only a dream? If I only dreamed I was walking in the company of another person, if I only dreamed that my companion saw the green field as I did, if it were all only a play performed on the stage of my consciousness, it would be doubtful whether there were things of the outer world at all. Perhaps the realm of things is empty and I see no things and no men, but have only ideas of which I myself am the bearer. An idea, being something which can as little exist independently of me as my feeling of fatigue, cannot be a man, cannot look at the same field together with me, cannot see the strawberry I am holding. It is quite incredible that I should really have only my inner world instead of the whole environment, in which I am supposed to move and to act. And yet it is an inevitable consequence of the thesis that only what is my idea can be the object of my awareness. What would follow from this thesis if it were true? Would there then be other men? It would certainly be possible but I should know nothing of it. For a man cannot be my idea, consequently, if our thesis were true, he also cannot be an object of my awareness. And so the ground would be removed from under any process of thought in which I might assume that something was an object for another person as for myself, for even if this were to happen I should know nothing of it. It would be impossible for me to distinguish that of which I was the bearer from that of which I was not. In judging something not to be my idea I would make it the object of my thinking and, therefore, my idea. On this view, is there a green field? Perhaps, but it would not be visible to me. For if a field is not my idea, it cannot, according to our thesis, be an object of my awareness. But if it is my idea it is invisible, for ideas are not visible. I can indeed have the idea of a green field, but this is not green for there are no green ideas. Does a shell weighing a hundred kilogrammes exist, according to this view? Perhaps, but I could know nothing of it. If a shell is not my idea then, according to our thesis, it cannot be an object of my awareness, of my thinking. But if a shell were my idea, it would have no weight. I can have an idea of a heavy shell. This then contains the idea of weight as a part-idea. But this part-idea is not a property of the whole idea any more than Germany is a property of Europe. So it follows:

Either the thesis that only what is my idea can be the object of my awareness is false, or all my knowledge and perception is limited to the range of my ideas, to the stage of my consciousness. In this case I should have only an inner world and I should know nothing of other people.

It is strange how, upon such reflections, the opposites collapse into each other. There is, let us suppose, a physiologist of the senses. As is proper for a scholarly scientist, he is, first of all, far from supposing the things he is convinced he sees and touches to be his ideas. On the contrary, he believes that in sense-impressions he has the surest proof of things which are wholly independent of his feeling, imagining, thinking, which have no need of his consciousness. So little does he consider nerve-fibres and ganglion-cells to be the content of his consciousness that he is, on the contrary, rather inclined to regard his consciousness as dependent on nerve-fibres and ganglion-cells. He establishes that light-rays, refracted in the eye, strike the visual nerve-endings and bring about a change, a stimulus, there. Some of it is transmitted through nerve-fibres and ganglion-cells. Further processes in the nervous system are perhaps involved, colour-impressions arise and these perhaps join themselves to what we call the idea of a tree. Physical, chemical and physiological occurrences insert themselves between the tree and my idea. These are immediately connected with my consciousness but, so it seems, are only occurrences in my nervous system and every spectator of the tree has his particular occurrences in his particular nervous system. Now the light-rays, before they enter my eye, may be reflected by a mirror and be spread further as if they came from a place behind the mirror. The effects on the visual nerves and all that follows will now take place just as they would if the light-rays had come from a tree behind the mirror and had been transmitted undisturbed to the eye. So an idea of a tree will finally occur even though such a tree does not exist at all. An idea, to which nothing at all corresponds, can also arise through the bending of light, with the mediation of the eye and the nervous system. But the stimulation of the visual nerves need not even happen through light. If lightning strikes near us we believe we see flames, even though we cannot see the lightning itself. In this case the visual nerve is perhaps stimulated by electric currents which originate in our body in consequence of the flash of lightning. If the visual nerve is stimulated by this means, just as it would be stimulated by light-rays coming from flames, then we believe we see flames. It just depends on the stimulation of the visual nerve, it is indifferent how that itself comes about.

One can go a step further still. This stimulation of the visual nerve is not actually immediately given, but is only a hypothesis. We believe that a thing, independent of us, stimulates a nerve and by this means produces a sense-impression, but, strictly speaking, we experience only the end of this process which projects into our consciousness. Could not this sense-impression, this sensation, which we attribute to a nerve-stimulation, have other causes also, as the same nerve-stimulation can arise in different ways? If we call what happens in our consciousness idea, then we really experience only ideas but not their causes. And if the scientist wants to avoid all mere hypothesis, then only ideas are left for him, everything resolves into ideas, the light-rays, nerve-fibres and ganglion-cells from which he started. So he finally undermines the foundations of his own construction. Is everything an idea? Does everything need a bearer, without which it could have no stability? I have considered myself as the bearer of my ideas, but am I not an idea myself? It seems to me as if I were lying in a deck-chair, as if I could see the toes of a pair of waxed boots, the front part of a pair of trousers, a waistcoat, buttons, part of a jacket, in particular sleeves, two hands, the hair of a beard, the blurred outline of a nose. Am I myself this entire association of visual impressions, this total idea? It also seems to me as if I see a chair over there. It is an idea. I am not actually much different from this myself, for am I not myself just an association of sense-impressions, an idea? But where then is the bearer of these ideas? How do I come to single out one of these ideas and set it up as the bearer of the rest? Why must it be the idea which I choose to call 'I'? Could I not just as well choose the one that I am tempted to call a chair? Why, after all, have a bearer for ideas at all? But this would always be something essentially different from merely borne ideas, something independent, needing no extraneous bearer. If everything is idea, then there is no bearer of ideas. And so now, once again, I experience a change into the opposite. If there is no bearer of ideas then there are also no ideas, for ideas need a bearer without which they cannot exist. If there is no ruler, there are also no subjects. The dependence, which I found myself induced to confer on the experience as opposed to the experient, is abolished if there is no more bearer. What I called ideas are then independent objects. Every reason is wanting for granting an exceptional position to that object which I call 'I'.

But is that possible? Can there be an experience without someone to experience it? What would this whole play be without an onlooker? Can there be a pain without someone who has it? Being experienced is necessarily connected with pain, and someone experiencing is necessarily connected with being experienced. But there is something which is not my idea and yet which can be the object of my awareness, of my thinking, I am myself of this nature. Or can I be part of the content of my consciousness while another part is, perhaps, an idea of the moon? Does this perhaps take place when I judge that I am looking at the moon? Then this first part would have a consciousness and part of the content of this consciousness would be I myself once more. And so on. Yet it is surely inconceivable that I should be boxed into myself in this way to infinity, for then there would not be only one I but infinitely many. I am not my own idea and if I assert something about myself, e.g. that I do not feel any pain at this moment, then my judgement concerns something which is not a content of my consciousness, is not my idea, that is me myself. Therefore that about which I state something is not necessarily my idea. But, someone perhaps objects, if I think I have no pain at the moment, does not the word 'I' nevertheless correspond with something in the content of my consciousness and is that not an idea? That may be. A certain idea in my consciousness may be associated with the idea of the word 'I'. But then it is an idea among other ideas and I am its bearer as I am the bearer of the other ideas. I have an idea of myself but I am not identical with this idea. What is a content of my consciousness, my idea, should be sharply distinguished from what is an object of my thought. Therefore the thesis that only what belongs to the content of my consciousness can be the object of my awareness, of my thought, is false.

Now the way is clear for me to recognize another person as well as to be an independent bearer of ideas. I have an idea of him but I do not confuse it with him himself. And if I state something about my brother I do not state it about the idea that I have of my brother.

The invalid who has a pain is the bearer of this pain, but the doctor in attendance who reflects on the cause of this pain is not the bearer of the pain. He does not imagine he can relieve the pain by anaesthetizing himself. An idea in the doctor's mind may very well correspond to the pain of the invalid but that is not the pain and not what the doctor is trying to remove. The doctor might consult another doctor. Then one must distinguish: first, the pain whose bearer is the invalid, second, the first doctor's idea of this pain, third, the second doctor's idea of this pain. This idea does indeed belong to the content of the second doctor's consciousness, but it is not the object of his reflection, it is rather an aid to reflection, as a drawing can be such an aid perhaps. Both doctors have the invalid's pain, which they do not bear, as their common object of thought. It can be seen from this that not only a thing but also an idea can be the common object of thought of people who do not have the idea.

So, it seems to me, the matter becomes intelligible. If man could not think and could not take something of which he was not the bearer as the object of his thought he would have an inner world but no outer world. But may this not be based on a mistake? I am convinced that the idea I associate with the words 'my brother' corresponds to something that is not my idea and about which I can say something. But may I not be making a mistake about this? Such mistakes do happen. We then, against our will, lapse into fiction. Indeed! By the step with which I secure an environment for myself I expose myself to the risk of error. And here I come up against a further distinction between my inner and outer worlds. I cannot doubt that I have a visual impression of green but it is not so certain that I see a lime-leaf. So, contrary to widespread views, we find certainty in the inner world while doubt never altogether leaves us in our excursions into the outer world. It is difficult in many cases, nevertheless, to distinguish probability from certainty here, so we can presume to judge about things in the outer world. And we must presume this even at the risk of error if we do not want to succumb to far greater dangers.

In consequence of these last considerations I lay down the following: not everything that can be the object of my understanding is an idea. I, as a bearer of ideas, am not myself an idea. Nothing now stands in the way of recognizing other people to be bearers of ideas as I am myself. And, once given the possibility, the probability is very great, so great that it is in my opinion no longer distinguishable from certainty. Would there be a science of history otherwise? Would not every precept of duty, every law otherwise come to nothing? What would be left of religion? The natural sciences too could only be assessed as fables like astrology and alchemy. Thus the reflections I have carried on, assuming that there are other people besides myself who can take the same thing as the object of their consideration, of their thinking, remain essentially unimpaired in force.

Not everything is an idea. Thus I can also recognize the thought, which other people can grasp just as much as I, as being independent of me. I can recognize a science in which many people can be engaged in research. We are not bearers of thoughts as we are bearers of our ideas. We do not have a thought as we have, say, a sense-impression, but we also do not see a thought as we see, say, a star. So it is advisable to choose a special expression and the word 'apprehend' offers itself for the purpose. A particular mental capacity, the power of thought, must correspond to the apprehension[6] of thought. In thinking we do not produce thoughts but we apprehend them. For what I have called thought stands in the closest relation to truth. What I recognize as true I judge to be true quite independently of my recognition of its truth and of my thinking about it. That someone thinks it has nothing to do with the truth of a thought. 'Facts, facts, facts' cries the scientist if he wants to emphasize the necessity of a firm foundation for science. What is a fact? A fact is a thought that is true. But the scientist will surely not recognize something which depends on men's varying states of mind to be the firm foundation of science. The work of science does not consist of creation but of the discovery of true thoughts. The astronomer can apply a mathematical truth in the investigation of long past events which took place when on earth at least no one had yet recognized that truth. He can do this because the truth of a thought is timeless. Therefore that truth cannot have come into existence with its discovery.

Not everything is an idea. Otherwise psychology would contain all the sciences within it or at least it would be the highest judge over all the sciences. Otherwise psychology would rule over logic and mathematics. But nothing would be a greater misunderstanding of mathematics than its subordination to psychology. Neither logic nor mathematics has the task of investigating minds and the contents of consciousness whose bearer is a single person. Perhaps their task could be represented rather as the investigation of the mind, of the mind not of minds.

The apprehension of a thought presupposes someone who apprehends it, who thinks. He is the bearer of the thinking but not of the thought. Although the thought does not belong to the contents of the thinker's consciousness yet something in his consciousness must be aimed at the thought. But this should not be confused with the thought itself. Similarly Algol itself is different from the idea someone has of Algol.

The thought belongs neither to my inner world as an idea nor yet to the outer world of material, perceptible things.

This consequence, however cogently it may follow from the exposition, will nevertheless not perhaps be accepted without opposition. It will, I think, seem impossible to some people to obtain information about something not belonging to the inner world except by sense-perception. Sense-perception indeed is often thought to be the most certain, even to be the sole, source of knowledge about everything that does not belong to the inner world. But with what right? For sense-impressions are necessary constituents of sense-perceptions and are a part of the inner world. In any case two men do not have the same, though they may have similar, sense-impressions. These alone do not disclose the outer world to us. Perhaps there is a being that has only sense-impressions without seeing or touching things. To have visual impressions is not to see things. How does it happen that I see the tree just there where I do see it? Obviously it depends on the visual impressions I have and on the particular type which occur because I see with two eyes. A particular image arises, physically speaking, on each of the two retinas. Another person sees the tree in the same place. He also has two retinal images but they differ from mine. We must assume that these retinal images correspond to our impressions. Consequently we have visual impressions, not only not the same, but markedly different from each other. And yet we move about in the same outer world. Having visual impressions is certainly necessary for seeing things but not sufficient. What must still be added is nonsensible. And yet this is just what opens up the outer world for us; for without this non-sensible something everyone would remain shut up in his inner world. So since the answer lies in the non-sensible, perhaps something non-sensible could also lead us out of the inner world and enable us to grasp thoughts where no sense-impressions were involved. Outside one's inner world one would have to distinguish the proper outer world of sensible, perceptible things from the realm of the non-sensibly perceptible. We should need something non-sensible for the recognition of both realms but for the sensible perception of things we should need sense-impressions as well and these belong entirely to the inner world. So that in which the distinction between the way in which a thing and a thought is given mainly consists is something which is attributable, not to both realms, but to the inner world. Thus I cannot find this distinction to be so great that on its account it would be impossible for a thought to be given that did not belong to the inner world.

The thought, admittedly, is not something which it is usual to call real. The world of the real is a world in which this acts on that, changes it and again experiences reactions itself and is changed by them. All this is a process in time. We will hardly recognize what is timeless and unchange-able as real. Now is the thought changeable or is it timeless? The thought we express by the Pythagorean theorem is surely timeless, eternal, un-changeable. But are there not thoughts which are true today but false in six months time? The thought, for example, that the tree there is covered with green leaves, will surely be false in six months time. No, for it is not the same thought at all. The words 'this tree is covered with green leaves' are not sufficient by themselves for the utterance, the time of utterance is involved as well. Without the time-indication this gives we have no complete thought, i.e. no thought at all. Only a sentence supplemented by a time-indication and complete in every respect expresses a thought. But this, if it is true, is true not only today or tomorrow but timelessly. Thus the present tense in 'is true' does not refer to the speaker's present but is, if the expression be permitted, a tense of timelessness. If we use the mere form of the indicative sentence, avoiding the word 'true', two things must be distinguished, the expression of the thought and the assertion. The time-indication that may be contained in the sentence belongs only to the expression of the thought, while the truth, whose recognition lies in the form of the indicative sentence, is timeless. Yet the same words, on account of the variability of language with time, take on another sense, express another thought; this change, however, concerns only the linguistic aspect of the matter.

And yet! What value could there be for us in the eternally unchangeable which could neither undergo effects nor have effect on us? Something entirely and in every respect inactive would be unreal and non-existent for us. Even the timeless, if it is to be anything for us, must somehow be implicated with the temporal. What would a thought be for me that was never apprehended by me? But by apprehending a thought I come into a relation to it and it to me. It is possible that the same thought that is thought by me today was not thought by me yesterday. In this way the strict timelessness is of course annulled. But one is inclined to distinguish between essential and inessential properties and to regard something as timeless if the changes it undergoes involve only its inessential properties. A property of a thought will be called inessential which consists in, or follows from the fact that, it is apprehended by a thinker.

How does a thought act? By being apprehended and taken to be true. This is a process in the inner world of a thinker which can have further consequences in this inner world and which, encroaching on the sphere of the will, can also make itself noticeable in the outer world. If, for example, I grasp the thought which we express by the theorem of Pythagoras, the consequence may be that I recognize it to be true and, further, that I apply it, making a decision which brings about the acceleration of masses. Thus our actions are usually prepared by thinking and judgement. And so thought can have an indirect influence on the motion of masses. The influence of one person on another is brought about for the most part by thoughts. One communicates a thought. How does this happen? One brings about changes in the common outside world which, perceived by another person, are supposed to induce him to apprehend a thought and take it to be true. Could the great events of world history have come about without the communication of thoughts? And yet we are inclined to regard thoughts as unreal because they appear to be without influence on events, while thinking, judging, stating, understanding and the like are facts of human life. How much more real a hammer appears compared with a thought. How different the process of handing over a hammer is from the communication of a thought. The hammer passes from one control to another, it is gripped, it undergoes pressure and on account of this its density, the disposition of its parts, is changed in places. There is nothing of all this with a thought. It does not leave the control of the communicator by being communicated, for after all a person has no control over it. When a thought is apprehended, it at first only brings about changes in the inner world of the apprehender, yet it remains untouched in its true essence, since the changes it undergoes involve only inessential properties. There is lacking here something we observe throughout the order of nature: reciprocal action. Thoughts are by no means unreal but their reality is of quite a different kind from that of things. And their effect is brought about by an act of the thinker without which they would be ineffective, at least as far as we can see. And yet the thinker does not create them but must take them as they are. They can be true without being apprehended by a thinker and are not wholly unreal even then, at least if they could be apprehended and by this means be brought into operation.

Notes

1. In a similar way it has perhaps been said 'a judgement is something which is either true or false'. In fact I use the word 'thought' in approximately the sense which 'judgement' has in the writings of logicians. I hope it will become clear in what follows why I choose 'thought'. Such an explanation has been objected to on the ground that in it a distinction is drawn between true and false judgements which of all possible distinctions among judgements has perhaps the least significance. I cannot see that it is a logical deficiency that a distinction is given with the explanation. As far as significance is concerned, it should not by any means be judged as trifling if, as I have said, the word 'true' indicates the aim of logic.

2. I am not using the word 'sentence' here in a purely grammatical sense where it also includes subordinate clauses. An isolated subordinate clause does not always have a sense about which the question of truth can arise, whereas the complex sentence to which it belongs has such a sense.

3. It seems to me that thought and judgement have not hitherto been adequately distinguished. Perhaps language is misleading. For we have no particular clause in the indicative sentence which corresponds to the assertion, that something is being asserted lies rather in the form of the indicative. We have the advantage in German that main and subordinate clauses are distinguished by the word-order. In this connexion it is noticeable that a subordinate clause can also contain an assertion and that often neither main nor subordinate clause express a complete thought by themselves but only the complex sentence does.

4. I am not in the happy position here of a mineralogist who shows his hearers a mountain crystal. I cannot put a thought in the hands of my readers with the request that they should minutely examine it from all sides. I have to content myself with presenting the reader with a thought, in itself immaterial, dressed in sensible linguistic form. The metaphorical aspect of language presents difficulties. The sensible always breaks in and makes expression metaphorical and so improper. So a battle with language takes place and I am compelled to occupy myself with language although it is not my proper concern here. I hope I have succeeded in making clear to my readers what I want to call a thought.

5. One sees a thing, one has an idea, one apprehends or thinks a thought. When one apprehends or thinks a thought one does not create in but only comes to stand in a certain relation, which is different from seeing a thing or having an idea, to what already existed beforehand.

6. The expression 'apprehend' is as metaphorical as 'content of consciousness'. The nature of language does not permit anything else. What I hold in my hand can certainly be regarded as the content of my hand but is all the same the content of my hand in quite a different way from the bones and muscles of which it is made and their tensions, and is much more extraneous to it than they are.

Chapter 2

Excerpt from *The Blue and Brown Books*

Ludwig Wittgenstein

What is the meaning of a word?

Let us attack this question by asking, first, what is an explanation of the meaning of a word; what does the explanation of a word look like?

The way this question helps us is analogous to the way the question "how do we measure a length?" helps us to understand the problem "what is length?"

The questions "What is length?", "What is meaning?", "What is the number one?" etc., produce in us a mental cramp. We feel that we can't point to anything in reply to them and yet ought to point to something. (We are up against one of the great sources of philosophical bewilderment: a substantive makes us look for a thing that corresponds to it.)

Asking first "What's an explanation of meaning?" has two advantages. You in a sense bring the question "what is meaning?" down to earth. For, surely, to understand the meaning of "meaning" you ought also to understand the meaning of "explanation of meaning". Roughly: "let's ask what the explanation of meaning is, for whatever that explains will be the meaning." Studying the grammar of the expression "explanation of meaning" will teach you something about the grammar of the word "meaning" and will cure you of the temptation to look about you for some object which you might call "the meaning".

What one generally calls "explanations of the meaning of a word" can, *very roughly*, be divided into verbal and ostensive definitions. It will be seen later in what sense this division is only rough and provisional (and that it is, is an important point). The verbal definition, as it takes us from one verbal expression to another, in a sense gets us no further. In

First appeared in *The Blue and Brown Books* (Oxford: Basil Blackwell, 1958). Reprinted by permission of Blackwell Publishers.

the ostensive definition however we seem to make a much more real step towards learning the meaning.

One difficulty which strikes us is that for many words in our language there do not seem to be ostensive definitions; e.g. for such words as "one", "number", "not", etc.

Question: Need the ostensive definition itself be understood?—Can't the ostensive definition be misunderstood?

If the definition explains the meaning of a word, surely it can't be essential that you should have heard the word before. It is the ostensive definition's business to *give* it a meaning. Let us then explain the word "tove" by pointing to a pencil and saying "this is tove". (Instead of "this is tove" I could here have said "this is called 'tove'". I point this out to remove, once and for all, the idea that the words of the ostensive definition predicate something of the defined; the confusion between the sentence "this is red", attributing the colour red to something, and the ostensive definition "this is called 'red'".) Now the ostensive definition "this is tove" can be interpreted in all sorts of ways. I will give a few such interpretations and use English words with well established usage. The definition then can be interpreted to mean:

"This is a pencil",
"This is a round",
"This is wood",
"This is one",
"This is hard", etc. etc.

One might object to this argument that all these interpretations pre-suppose another word-language. And this objection is significant if by "interpretation" we only mean "translation into a word-language".—Let me give some hints which might make this clearer. Let us ask ourselves what is our criterion when we say that someone has interpreted the ostensive definition in a particular way. Suppose I give to an Englishman the ostensive definition "this is what the Germans call 'Buch'". Then, in the great majority of cases at any rate, the English word "book" will come into the Englishman's mind. We may say he has interpreted "Buch" to mean "book". The case will be different if e.g. we point to a thing which he has never seen before and say: "This is a banjo". Possibly the word "guitar" will then come into his mind, possibly no word at all but the image of a similar instrument, possibly nothing at all. Supposing then I give him the order "now pick a banjo from amongst these things". If he picks what we call a "banjo" we might say "he has given the word 'banjo' the correct interpretation"; if he picks some other instrument—"he has interpreted 'banjo' to mean 'string instrument'".

We say "he has given the word 'banjo' this or that interpretation", and are inclined to assume a definite act of interpretation besides the act of choosing.

Our problem is analogous to the following:

If I give someone the order "fetch me a red flower from that meadow", how is he to know what sort of flower to bring, as I have only given him a *word?*

Now the answer one might suggest first is that he went to look for a red flower carrying a red image in his mind, and comparing it with the flowers to see which of them had the colour of the image. Now there is such a way of searching, and it is not at all essential that the image we use should be a mental one. In fact the process may be this: I carry a chart co-ordinating names and coloured squares. When I hear the order "fetch me etc." I draw my finger across the chart from the word "red" to a certain square, and I go and look for a flower which has the same colour as the square. But this is not the only way of searching and it isn't the usual way. We go, look about us, walk up to a flower and pick it, without comparing it to anything. To see that the process of obeying the order can be of this kind, consider the order *"imagine* a red patch". You are not tempted in this case to think that *before* obeying you must have imagined a red patch to serve you as a pattern for the red patch which you were ordered to imagine.

Now you might ask: do we *interpret* the words before we obey the order? And in some cases you will find that you do something which might be called interpreting before obeying, in some cases not.

It seems that there are *certain definite* mental processes bound up with the working of language, processes through which alone language can function. I mean the processes of understanding and meaning. The signs of our language seem dead without these mental processes; and it might seem that the only function of the signs is to induce such processes, and that these are the things we ought really to be interested in. Thus, if you are asked what is the relation between a name and the thing it names, you will be inclined to answer that the relation is a psychological one, and perhaps when you say this you think in particular of the mechanism of association.—We are tempted to think that the action of language consists of two parts; an inorganic part, the handling of signs, and an organic part, which we may call understanding these signs, meaning them, interpreting them, thinking. These latter activities seem to take place in a queer kind of medium, the mind; and the mechanism of the mind, the nature of which, it seems, we don't quite understand, can bring about effects which no material mechanism could. Thus e.g. a thought (which is such a mental process) can agree or disagree with reality; I am able to think of a man who isn't present; I am able to imagine him, 'mean him' in a remark which I make about him, even if he is thousands of miles away or dead. "What a queer mechanism," one might say, "the mechanism of wishing must be if I can wish that which will never happen".

There is one way of avoiding at least partly the occult appearance of the processes of thinking, and it is, to replace in these processes any working of the imagination by acts of looking at real objects. Thus it may seem essential that, at least in certain cases, when I hear the word "red" with understanding, a red image should be before my mind's eye. But why should I not substitute seeing a red bit of paper for imagining a red patch? The visual image will only be the more vivid. Imagine a man always carrying a sheet of paper in his pocket on which the names of colours are co-ordinated with coloured patches. You may say that it would be a nuisance to carry such a table of samples about with you, and that the mechanism of association is what we always use instead of it. But this is irrelevant; and in many cases it is not even true. If, for instance, you were ordered to paint a particular shade of blue called "Prussian Blue", you might have to use a table to lead you from the word "Prussian Blue" to a sample of the colour, which would serve you as your copy.

We could perfectly well, for our purposes, replace every process of imagining by a process of looking at an object or by painting, drawing or modelling; and every process of speaking to oneself by speaking aloud or by writing.

Frege ridiculed the formalist conception of mathematics by saying that the formalists confused the unimportant thing, the sign, with the important, the meaning. Surely, one wishes to say, mathematics does not treat of dashes on a bit of paper. Frege's idea could be expressed thus: the propositions of mathematics, if they were just complexes of dashes, would be dead and utterly uninteresting, whereas they obviously have a kind of life. And the same, of course, could be said of any proposition: Without a sense, or without the thought, a proposition would be an utterly dead and trivial thing. And further it seems clear that no adding of inorganic signs can make the proposition live. And the conclusion which one draws from this is that what must be added to the dead signs in order to make a live proposition is something immaterial, with properties different from all mere signs.

But if we had to name anything which is the life of the sign, we should have to say that it was its *use*.

If the meaning of the sign (roughly, that which is of importance about the sign) is an image built up in our minds when we see or hear the sign, then first let us adopt the method we just described of replacing this mental image by some outward object seen, e.g. a painted or modelled image. Then why should the written sign plus this painted image be alive if the written sign alone was dead?—In fact, as soon as you think of replacing the mental image by, say, a painted one, and as soon as the image thereby loses its occult character, it ceases to seem to impart any life to the sentence at all. (It was in fact just the occult character of the mental process which you needed for your purposes.)

The mistake we are liable to make could be expressed thus: We are looking for the use of a sign, but we look for it as though it were an object *co-existing* with the sign. (One of the reasons for this mistake is again that we are looking for a "thing corresponding to a substantive".)

The sign (the sentence) gets its significance from the system of signs, from the language to which it belongs. Roughly: understanding a sentence means understanding a language.

As a part of the system of language, one may say, the sentence has life. But one is tempted to imagine that which gives the sentence life as something in an occult sphere, accompanying the sentence. But whatever accompanied it would for us just be another sign.

It seems at first sight that that which gives to thinking its peculiar character is that it is a train of mental states, and it seems that what is queer and difficult to understand about thinking is the processes which happen in the medium of the mind, processes possible only in this medium. The comparison which forces itself upon us is that of the mental medium with the protoplasm of a cell, say, of an amoeba. We observe certain actions of the amoeba, its taking food by extending arms, its splitting up into similar cells, each of which grows and behaves like the original one. We say "of what a queer nature the protoplasm must be to act in such a way", and perhaps we say that no physical mechanism could behave in this way, and that the mechanism of the amoeba must be of a totally different kind. In the same way we are tempted to say "the mechanism of the mind must be of a most peculiar kind to be able to do what the mind does". But here we are making two mistakes. For what struck *us* as being queer about thought and thinking was not at all that it had curious effects which we were not yet able to explain (causally). Our problem, in other words, was not a scientific one; but a muddle felt as a problem.

Supposing we tried to construct a mind-model as a result of psychological investigations, a model which, as we should say, would explain the action of the mind. This model would be part of a psychological theory in the way in which a mechanical model of the ether can be part of a theory of electricity. (Such a model, by the way, is always part of the *symbolism* of a theory. Its advantage may be that it can be taken in at a glance and easily held in the mind. It has been said that a model, in a sense, dresses up the pure theory; that the *naked* theory is sentences or equations. This must be examined more closely later on.)

We may find that such a mind-model would have to be very complicated and intricate in order to explain the observed mental activities; and on this ground we might call the mind a queer kind of medium. But this aspect of the mind does not interest us. The problems which it may set are psychological problems, and the method of their solution is that of natural science.

Now if it is not the causal connections which we are concerned with, then the activities of the mind lie open before us. And when we are worried about the nature of thinking, the puzzlement which we wrongly interpret to be one about the nature of a medium is a puzzlement caused by the mystifying use of our language. This kind of mistake recurs again and again in philosophy; e.g. when we are puzzled about the nature of time, when time seems to us a *queer thing*. We are most strongly tempted to think that here are things hidden, something we can see from the outside but which we can't look into. And yet nothing of the sort is the case. It is not new facts about time which we want to know. All the facts that concern us lie open before us. But it is the use of the substantive "time" which mystifies us. If we look into the grammar of that word, we shall feel that it is no less astounding that man should have conceived of a deity of time than it would be to conceive of deity of negation or disjunction.

It is misleading then to talk of thinking as of a "mental activity". We may say that thinking is essentially the activity of operating with signs. This activity is performed by the hand, when we think by writing; by the mouth and larynx, when we think by speaking; and if we think by imagining signs or pictures, I can give you no agent that thinks. If then you say that in such cases the mind thinks, I would only draw your attention to the fact that you are using a metaphor, that here the mind is an agent in a different sense from that in which the hand can be said to be the agent in writing.

If again we talk about the locality where thinking takes place we have a right to say that this locality is the paper on which we write or the mouth which speaks. And if we talk of the head or the brain as the locality of thought, this is using the expression "locality of thinking" in a different sense. Let us examine what are the reasons for calling the head the place of thinking. It is not our intention to criticize this form of expression, or to show that it is not appropriate. What we must do is: understand its working, its grammar, e.g. see what relation this grammar has to that of the expression "we think with our mouth", or "we think with a pencil on a piece of paper".

Perhaps the main reason why we are so strongly inclined to talk of the head as the locality of our thoughts is this: the existence of the words "thinking" and "thought" alongside of the words denoting (bodily) activities, such as writing, speaking, etc., makes us look for an activity, different from these but analogous to them, corresponding to the word "thinking". When words in our ordinary language have prima facie analogous grammars we are inclined to try to interpret them analogously; i.e. we try to make the analogy hold throughout.—We say, "The thought is not the same as the sentence; for an English and a French sentence, which are utterly different, can express the same thought". And now, as the sentences are *somewhere*, we look for a place for the thought. (It is as though we looked for the place of the king of which the rules of chess treat, as opposed to the places of the various bits of wood, the kings of the various sets.)—We say, "surely the thought is *something*; it is not nothing"; and all one can answer to this is, that the word "thought" has its *use*, which is of a totally different kind from the use of the word "sentence".

Now does this mean that it is nonsensical to talk of a locality where thought takes place? Certainly not. This phrase has sense if we give it sense. Now if we say "thought takes place in our heads", what is the sense of this phrase soberly understood? I suppose it is that certain physiological processes correspond to our thoughts in such a way that if we know the correspondence we can, by observing these processes, find the thoughts. But in what sense can the physiological processes be said to correspond to thoughts, and in what sense can we be said to get the thoughts from the observation of the brain?

I suppose we imagine the correspondence to have been verified experimentally. Let us imagine such an experiment crudely. It consists in looking at the brain while the subject thinks. And now you may think that the reason why my explanation is going to go wrong is that of course the experimenter gets the thoughts of the subject only *indirectly* by being told them, the subject *expressing* them in some way or other. But I will remove this difficulty by assuming that the subject is at the same time the experimenter, who is looking at his own brain, say by means of a mirror. (The crudity of this description in no way reduces the force of the argument.)

Then I ask you, is the subject-experimenter observing one thing or two things? (Don't say that he is observing one thing both from the inside and from the outside; for this does not remove the difficulty. We will talk of inside and outside later.) The subject-experimenter is observing a correlation of two phenomena. One of them he, perhaps, calls the *thought*. This may consist of a train of images, organic sensations, or on the other hand of a train of the various visual, tactual and muscular experiences which he has in writing or speaking a sentence.—The other experience is one of seeing his brain work. Both these phenomena could correctly be called "expressions of thought"; and the question "where is the thought itself?" had better, in order to prevent confusion, be rejected as nonsensical. If however we do use the expression "the thought takes place in the head", we have given this expression its meaning by describing the experience which would justify the *hypothesis* that the thought takes places in our heads, by describing the experience which we wish to call "observing thought in our brain".

We easily forget that the word "locality" is used in many different senses and that there are many different kinds of statements about a thing which in a particular case, in accordance with general usage, we may call specifications of the locality of the thing. Thus it has been said of visual space that its place is in our head; and I think one has been tempted to say this, partly, by a grammatical misunderstanding.

I can say: "in my visual field I see the image of the tree to the right of the image of the tower" or "I see the image of the tree in the middle of the visual field". And now we are inclined to ask "and where do you see the visual field?" Now if the "where" is meant to ask for a locality in the sense in which we have specified the locality of the image of the tree, then I would draw your attention to the fact that you have not yet given this question sense; that is, that you have been proceeding by a grammatical analogy without having worked out the analogy in detail.

In saying that the idea of our visual field being located in our brain arose from a grammatical misunderstanding, I did not mean to say that we could not give sense to such a specification of locality. We could, e.g., easily imagine an experience which we should describe by such a statement. Imagine that we looked at a group of things in this room, and, while we looked, a probe was stuck into our brain and it was found that if the point of the probe reached a particular point in our brain, then a particular small part of our visual field was thereby obliterated. In this way we might co-ordinate points of our brain to points of the visual image, and this might make us say that the visual field was seated in such and such a place in our brain. And if now we asked the question "Where do you see the image of this book?" the answer could be (as above) "To the right of that pencil", or "In the left hand part of my visual field", or again: "Three inches behind my left eye".

But what if someone said "I can assure you I feel the visual image to be two inches behind the bridge of my nose";—what are we to answer him? Should we say that he is not speaking the truth, or that there cannot be such a feeling? What if he asks us "do you know all the feelings there are? How do you know there isn't such a feeling?"

What if the diviner tells us that when he holds the rod he *feels* that the water is five feet under the ground? or that he *feels* that a mixture of copper and gold is five feet under the ground? Suppose that to our doubts he answered: "You can estimate a length when you see it. Why shouldn't I have a different way of estimating it?"

If we understand the idea of such an estimation, we shall get clear about the nature of our doubts about the statements of the diviner, and of the man who said he felt the visual image behind the bridge of his nose.

There is the statement: "this pencil is five inches long", and the statement, "I feel that this pencil is five inches long", and we must get clear about the relation of the grammar of the first statement to the grammar of the second. To the statement "I feel in my hand that the water is three feet under the ground" we should like to answer: "I don't know what this *means*". But the diviner would say: "Surely you know what it means. You know what 'three feet under the ground' means, and you know what 'I feel' means!" But I should answer him: I know what a word means *in certain contexts*. Thus I understand the phrase, "three feet under the ground", say, in the connections "The measurement has shown that the water runs three feet under the ground", "If we dig three feet deep we are going to strike water", "The depth of the water is three feet by the eye". But the use of the expression "a feeling in my hands of water being three feet under the ground" has yet to be explained to me.

We could ask the diviner "how did you learn the meaning of the word 'three feet'?" We suppose by being shown such lengths, by having measured them and such like. Were you also taught to talk of a feeling of water being three feet under the ground, a feeling, say, in your hands? For if not, what made you connect the word 'three feet' with a feeling in your hand?" Supposing we had been estimating lengths by the eye, but had never spanned a length. How could we estimate a length in inches by spanning it? I.e., how could we interpret the experience of spanning in inches? The question is: what connection is there between, say, a tactual sensation and the experience of measuring a thing by means of a yard rod? This connection will show us what it means to 'feel that a thing is six inches long'. Supposing the diviner said "I have never learnt to correlate depth of water under the ground with feelings in my hand, but when I have a certain feeling of tension in my hands, the words 'three feet' spring up in my mind." We should answer "This is a perfectly good explanation of what you mean by 'feeling the depth to be three feet', and the statement that you feel this will have neither more, nor less, meaning than your explanation has given it. And if experience shows that the actual depth of the water always agrees with the words 'n feet' which come into your mind, your experience will be very useful for determining the depth of water".—But you see that the meaning of the words "I feel the depth of the water to be n feet" had to be explained; it was not known when the meaning of the words "n feet" in the ordinary sense (i.e. in the ordinary contexts) was known.—We don't say that the man who tells us he feels the visual image two inches behind the bridge of his nose is telling a lie or talking nonsense. But we say that we don't understand the meaning of such a phrase. It combines well-known words, but combines them in a way we don't yet understand. The grammar of this phrase has yet to be explained to us.

The importance of investigating the diviner's answer lies in the fact that we often think we have given a meaning to a statement P if only we assert "I *feel* (or I believe) that P is the case." (We shall talk at a later occasion of Prof. Hardy saying that Goldbach's theorem is a proposition because he can believe that it is true.) We have already said that by merely explaining the meaning of the words "three feet" in the usual way we have not yet explained the sense of the phrase "feeling that water is three feet etc." Now we should not have felt these difficulties had the diviner said that he had *learnt* to estimate the depth of the water, say, by digging for water whenever he had a particular feeling and in this way correlating such feelings with *measurements* of depth. Now we must examine the relation of the process of *learning to estimate* with the act of estimating. The importance of this examination lies in this, that it applies to the relation between learning the meaning of a word and making use of the word. Or, more generally, that it shows the different possible relations between a rule given and its application.

Let us consider the process of estimating a length by the eye: It is extremely important that you should realise that there are a great many different processes which we call "estimating by the eye".

Consider these cases:

(1) Someone asks "How did you estimate the height of this building?" I answer: "It has four storeys; I suppose each storey is about fifteen feet high; so it must be about sixty feet."
(2) In another case: "I roughly know what a yard at that distance looks like; so it must be about four yards long."
(3) Or again: "I can imagine a tall man reaching to about this point; so it must be about six feet above the ground."
(4) Or: "I don't know; it just looks like a yard."

This last case is likely to puzzle us. If you ask "what happened in this case when the man estimated the length?" the correct answer may be: "he *looked* at the thing and *said* 'it looks one yard long'". This may be all that has happened.

We said before that we should not have been puzzled about the diviner's answer if he had told us that he had *learnt* how to estimate depth. Now learning to estimate may, broadly speaking, be seen in two different relations to the act of estimating; either as a cause of the phenomenon of estimating, or as supplying us with a rule (a table, a chart, or some such thing) which we make use of when we estimate.

Supposing I teach someone the use of the word "yellow" by repeatedly pointing to a yellow patch and pronouncing the word. On another occasion I make him apply what he has learnt by giving him the order, "choose a yellow ball out of this bag". What was it that happened when he obeyed my order? I say "possibly just this: he heard my words and took a yellow ball from the bag". Now you may be inclined to think that this couldn't possibly have been all; and the *kind* of thing that you would suggest is that he imagined something yellow when he *understood* the order, and then chose a ball according to his image. To see that this is not *necessary* remember that I could have given him the order, "Imagine a yellow patch". Would you still be inclined to assume that he first imagines a yellow patch, just *understanding* my order, and then imagines a yellow patch to match the first? (Now I don't say that this is not possible. Only, putting it in this way immediately shows you that it need not happen. This, by the way, illustrates the method of philosophy.)

If we are taught the meaning of the word "yellow" by being given some sort of ostensive definition (a rule of the usage of the word) this teaching can be looked at in two different ways.

A. The teaching is a drill. This drill causes us to associate a yellow image, yellow things, with the word "yellow". Thus when I gave the order "Choose a yellow ball from this bag" the word "yellow" might have brought up a yellow image, or a feeling of recognition when the person's eye fell on the yellow ball. The drill of teaching could in this case be said to have built up a psychical mechanism. This, however, would only be a hypothesis or else a metaphor. We could *compare* teaching with installing an electric connection between a switch and a bulb. The parallel to the connection going wrong or breaking down would then be what we call forgetting the explanation, or the meaning, of the word. (We ought to talk further on about the meaning of "forgetting the meaning of a word").

In so far as the teaching brings about the association, feeling of recognition, etc. etc., it is the *cause* of the phenomena of understanding, obeying, etc.; and it is a hypothesis that the process of teaching should be needed in order to bring about these effects. It is conceivable, in this sense, that *all* the processes of understanding, obeying, etc., should have happened without the person ever having been taught the language. (This, just now, seems extremely paradoxical.)

B. The teaching may have supplied us with a rule which is itself involved in the processes of understanding, obeying, etc.; "involved", however, meaning that the expression of this rule forms part of these processes.

We must distinguish between what one might call "a process being *in accordance with a rule*", and, "a process involving a rule" (in the above sense).

Take an example. Some one teaches me to square cardinal numbers; he writes down the row

1   2   3   4,

and asks me to square them. (I will, in this case again, replace any processes happening 'in the mind' by processes of calculation on the paper.) Suppose, underneath the first row of numbers, I then write:

1   4   9   16.

What I wrote is in accordance with the general rule of squaring; but it obviously is also in accordance with any number of other rules; and amongst there it is not more in accordance with one than with another. In the sense in which before we talked about a rule being involved in a process, *no* rule was involved in this. Supposing that in order to get to my results I calculated 1×1, 2×2, 3×3, 4×4 (that is, in this case wrote down the calculations); there would again be in accordance with any number of rules. Supposing, on the other hand, in order to get to my results I had written down what you may call "the rule of squaring", say algebraically. In this case this rule was involved in a sense in which no other rule was.

We shall say that the rule is *involved* in the understanding, obeying, etc., if, as I should like to express it, the symbol of the rule forms part of the calculation. (As we are not interested in where the processes of thinking, calculating, take place, we can for our purpose imagine the calculations being done entirely on paper. We are not concerned with the difference: internal, external.)

A characteristic example of the case B would be one in which the teaching supplied us with a table which we actually make use of in understanding, obeying, etc. If we are taught to play chess, we may be taught rules. If then we play chess, these rules need not be involved in the act of playing. But they may be. Imagine, e.g., that the rules were expressed in the form of a table; in one column the shapes of the chessmen are drawn, and in a parallel column we find diagrams showing the 'freedom' (the legitimate moves) of the pieces. Suppose now that the way the game is played involves making the transition from the shape to the possible moves by running one's finger across the table, and then making one of these moves.

Teaching as the hypothetical history of our subsequent actions (understanding, obeying, estimating a length, etc.) drops out of our considerations. The rule which has been taught and is subsequently applied interests us only so far as it is involved in the application. A rule, so far as it interests us, does not act at a distance.

Suppose I pointed to piece of paper and said to someone: "this colour I call 'red'". Afterwards I give him the order: "now paint me a red patch". I then ask him: "why, in carrying out my order, did you paint just this colour?" His answer could then be: "This colour (pointing to the sample which I have given him) was called red; and the patch I have painted has, as you see, the colour of the sample". He has now given me a reason for carrying out the order in the way he did. Giving a reason for something one did or said means showing a *way* which leads to this action. In some cases it means telling the way which one has gone oneself; in others it means describing a way which leads there and is in accordance with certain accepted rules. Thus when asked, "why did you carry out my order by painting just this colour?" the person could have described the way he had actually taken to arrive at this particular shade of colour. This would have been so if, hearing the word "red", he had taken up the sample I had given him, labelled "red", and had *copied* that sample when painting the patch. On the other hand he might have painted it 'automatically' or from a memory image, but when asked to give the reason he might still point to the sample and show that it matched the patch he had painted. In this latter case the reason given would have been of the second kind; i.e. a justification *post hoc*.

Now if one thinks that there could be no understanding and obeying the order without a previous teaching, one thinks of the teaching as supplying a *reason* for doing what one did; as supplying the road one walks. Now there is the idea that if an order is understood and obeyed there must be a reason for our obeying it as we do; and, in fact, a chain of reasons reaching back to infinity. This is as if one said: "Wherever you are, you must have got there from somewhere else, and to that previous place from another place; and so on *ad infinitum*". (If, on the other hand, you had said, "wherever you are, you *could* have got there from another place ten yards away; and to that other place from a third, ten yards further away, and so on *ad infinitum*", if you had said this you would have stressed the infinite *possibility* of making a step. Thus the idea of an infinite chain of reasons arises out of a confusion similar to this: that a line of a certain length consists of an infinite number of parts because it is indefinitely divisible; i.e., because there is no end to the possibility of dividing it.)

If on the other hand you realize that the chain of *actual* reasons has a beginning, you will no longer be revolted by the idea of a case in which there is *no* reason for the way you obey the order. At this point, however, another confusion sets in, that between reason and cause. One is led into this confusion by the ambiguous use of the word "why". Thus when the chain of reasons has come to an end and still the question "why?" is asked, one is inclined to give a cause instead of a reason. If, e.g., to the question, "why did you paint just this colour when I told you to paint a red patch?" you give the answer: "I have been shown a sample of this colour and the word 'red' was pronounced to me at the same time; and therefore this colour now always comes to my mind when I hear the word 'red'", then you have given a cause for you action and not a reason.

The proposition that your action has such and such a cause, is a hypothesis. The hypothesis is well-founded if one has had a number of experiences which, roughly speaking, agree in showing that your action is the regular sequel of certain conditions which we then call causes of the action. In order to know the reason which you had for making a certain statement, for acting in a particular way, etc., no number of agreeing experiences is necessary, and the statement of your reason is not a hypothesis. The difference between the grammars of "reason" and "cause". is quite similar to that between the grammars of "motive" and "cause". Of the cause one can say that one can't *know* it but can only *conjecture* it. On the other hand one often says: "Surely *I* must know why I did it" talking of the *motive*. When I say: "we can only *conjecture* the cause but we *know* the motive" this statement will be seen later on to be a grammatical one. The "can" refers to a *logical* possibility.

The double use of the word "why", asking for the cause and asking for the motive, together with the idea that we can know, and not only conjecture, our motives, gives rise to the confusion that a motive is a cause of which we are immediately aware, a cause 'seen from the inside', or a cause experienced.—Giving a reason is like giving a calculation by which you have arrived at a certain result.

Let us go back to the statement that thinking essentially consists in operating with signs. My point was that it is liable to mislead us if we say 'thinking is a mental activity'. The question what kind of an activity thinking is is analogous to this: "Where does thinking take place?" We can answer: on paper, in our head, in the mind. None of these statements of locality gives *the* locality of thinking. The use of all these specifications is correct, but we must not be misled by the similarity of their linguistic form into a false conception of their grammar. As, e.g., when you say: "Surely, the *real* place of thought is in our head". The same applies to the idea of thinking as an activity. It is correct to say that thinking is an activity of our writing hand, of our larynx, of our head, and of our mind, so long as we understand the grammar of these statements. And it is, furthermore, extremely important to realize how, by misunderstanding the grammar of our expressions, we are led to think of one in particular of these statements as giving the *real* seat of the activity of thinking.

There is an objection to saying that thinking is some such thing as an activity of the hand. Thinking, one wants to say, is part of our 'private experience'. It is not material, but an event in private consciousness. This objection is expressed in the question: "Could a machine think?" I shall talk about this at a later point, and now only refer you to an analogous question: "Can a machine have toothache?" You will certainly be inclined to say: "A machine can't have toothache". All I will do now is to draw your attention to the use which you have made of the word "can" and to ask you: "Did you mean to say that all our past experience has shown that a machine never had toothache?" The impossibility of which you speak is a logical one. The question is: What is the relation between thinking (or toothache) and the subject which thinks, has toothache, etc.? I shall say no more about this now.

If we say thinking is essentially operating with signs, the first question you might ask is: "What are signs?"—Instead of giving any kind of general answer to this question, I shall propose to you to look closely at particular cases which we should call "operating with signs". Let us look at a simple example of operating with words. I give someone the order: "fetch me six apples from the grocer", and I will describe a way of making use of such an order: The words "six apples" are written on a bit of paper, the paper is handed to the grocer, the grocer compares the word "apple" with labels on different shelves. He finds it to agree with one of the labels, counts from 1 to the number written on the slip of paper, and for every number counted takes a fruit off the shelf and puts it in a bag.—And here you have a case of the use of words. I shall in the future again and again draw your attention to what I shall call language games. These are ways of using signs simpler than those in which we use the signs of our highly complicated everyday language. Language games are the forms of language with which a child begins to make use of words. The study of language games is the study of primitive forms of language or primitive languages. If we want to study the problems of truth and falsehood, of the agreement and disagreement of propositions with reality, of the nature of assertion, assumption, and question, we shall with great advantage look at primitive forms of language in which these forms of thinking appear without the confusing background of highly complicated processes of thought. When we look at such simple forms of language the mental mist which seems to enshroud our ordinary use of language disappears. We see activities, reactions, which are clear-cut and transparent. On the other hand we recognize in these simple processes forms of language not separated by a break from our more complicated ones. We see that we can build up the complicated forms from the primitive ones by gradually adding new forms.

Chapter 3

Translation and Meaning

Willard Van Orman Quine

FIRST STEPS OF RADICAL TRANSLATION

We have been reflecting in a general way on how surface irritations generate, through language, one's knowledge of the world. One is taught so to associate words with words and other stimulations that there emerges something recognizable as talk of things, and not to be distinguished from truth about the world. The voluminous and intricately structured talk that comes out bears little evident correspondence to the past and present barrage of non-verbal stimulation; yet it is to such stimulation that we must look for whatever empirical content there may be. In this chapter we shall consider how much of language can be made sense of in terms of its stimulus conditions, and what scope this leaves for empirically unconditioned variation in one's conceptual scheme.

A first uncritical way of picturing this scope for empirically unconditioned variation is as follows: two men could be just alike in all their dispositions to verbal behavior under all possible sensory stimulations, and yet the meanings or ideas expressed in their identically triggered and identically sounded utterances could diverge radically, for the two men, in a wide range of cases. To put the matter thus invites, however, the charge of meaninglessness: one may protest that a distinction of meaning unreflected in the totality of dispositions to verbal behavior is a distinction without a difference.

Sense can be made of the point by recasting it as follows: the infinite totality of sentences of any given speaker's language can be so permuted, or mapped onto itself, that (a) the totality of the speaker's dispositions

First appeared in *Word and Object* (Cambridge: MIT Press, 1960), pp. 26–35. Reprinted by permission of the MIT Press.

to verbal behavior remains invariant, and yet (b) the mapping is no mere correlation of sentences with *equivalent* sentences, in any plausible sense of equivalence however loose. Sentences without number can diverge drastically from their respective correlates, yet the divergences can systematically so offset one another that the overall pattern of associations of sentences with one another and with non-verbal stimulation is preserved. The firmer the direct links of a sentence with non-verbal stimulation, of course, the less that sentence can diverge from its correlate under any such mapping.

The same point can be put less abstractly and more realistically by switching to translation. The thesis is then this: manuals for translating one language into another can be set up in divergent ways, all compatible with the totality of speech dispositions, yet incompatible with one another. In countless places they will diverge in giving, as their respective translations of a sentence of the one language, sentences of the other language which stand to each other in no plausible sort of equivalence however loose. The firmer the direct links of a sentence with non-verbal stimulation, of course, the less drastically its translations can diverge from one another from manual to manual. It is in this last form, as a principle of indeterminacy of translation, that I shall try to make the point plausible in the course of this chapter. But the chapter will run longer than it would if various of the concepts and considerations ancillary to this theme did not seem worthy of treatment also on their own account.

We are concerned here with language as the complex of present dispositions to verbal behavior, in which speakers of the same language have perforce come to resemble one another; not with the processes of acquisition, whose variations from individual to individual it is to the interests of communication to efface. The sentence 'That man shoots well', said while pointing to an unarmed man, has as present stimulation the glimpse of the marksman's familiar face. The contributory past stimulation includes past observations of the man's shooting, as well as remote episodes that trained the speaker in the use of the words. The past stimulation is thus commonly reckoned in part to the acquisition of language and in part to the acquisition of collateral information; however, this subsidiary dichotomy can await some indication of what it is good for and what general clues there are for it in observable verbal behavior. Meanwhile what is before us is the going concern of verbal behavior and its currently observable correlations with stimulation. Reckon a man's current language by his current dispositions to respond verbally to current stimulation, and you automatically refer all past stimulation to the learning phase. Not but that even this way of drawing a boundary between language in acquisition and language in use has its fluctuations, inasmuch as we can consult our convenience in what bound we set to the length of stimulations counted as current. This bound, a working standard of what to count as specious present, I call the *modulus* of stimulation.

The recovery of a man's current language from his currently observed responses is the task of the linguist who, unaided by an interpreter, is out to penetrate and translate a language hitherto unknown. All the objective data he has to go on are the forces that he sees impinging on the native's surfaces and the observable behavior, vocal and otherwise, of the native. Such data evince native "meanings" only of the most objectively empirical or stimulus-linked variety. And yet the linguist apparently ends up with native "meanings" in some quite unrestricted sense; purported translations, anyway, of all possible native sentences.

Translation between kindred languages, e.g., Frisian and English, is aided by resemblance of cognate word forms. Translation between unrelated languages, e.g., Hungarian and English, may be aided by traditional equations that have evolved in step with a shared culture. What is relevant rather to our purposes is *radical* translation, i.e., translation of the language of a hitherto untouched people. The task is one that is not in practice undertaken in its extreme form, since a chain of interpreters of a sort can be recruited of marginal persons across the darkest archipelago. But the problem is the more nearly approximated the poorer the hints available from interpreters; thus attention to techniques of utterly radical translation has not been wanting. I shall imagine that all help of interpreters is excluded. Incidentally I shall here ignore phonematic analysis, early though it would come in our field linguist's enterprise; for it does not affect the philosophical point I want to make.

The utterances first and most surely translated in such a case are ones keyed to present events that are conspicuous to the linguist and his informant. A rabbit scurries by, the native says 'Gavagai', and the linguist notes down the sentence 'Rabbit' (or 'Lo, a rabbit') as tentative translation, subject to testing in further cases. The linguist will at first refrain from putting words into his informant's mouth, if only for lack of words to put. When he can, though, the linguist has to supply native sentences for his informant's approval, despite the risk of slanting the data by suggestion. Otherwise he can do little with native terms that have references in common. For, suppose the native language includes sentences S_1, S_2, and S_3, really translatable respectively as 'Animal', 'White', and 'Rabbit'. Stimulus situations always differ, whether relevantly or not; and, just because volunteered responses come singly, the classes of situations under which the native happens to have volunteered S_1, S_2, and S_3, are of course mutually exclusive, despite the hidden actual meanings of the words. How then is the linguist to perceive that the native would have been willing to assent to S_1 in all the situations where he happened to volunteer S_3, and in some but perhaps not all of the situations where he happened to volunteer S_2? Only by taking the initiative and querying combinations of native sentences and stimulus situations so as to narrow down his guesses to his eventual satisfaction.

So we have the linguist asking 'Gavagai?' in each of various stimulatory situations, and noting each time whether the native assents, dissents, or neither. But how is he to recognize native assent and dissent when he sees or hears them? Gestures are not to be taken at face value; the Turks's are nearly the reverse of our own. What he must do is guess from observation and then see how well his guesses work. Thus suppose that in asking 'Gavagai?' and the like, in the conspicuous presence of rabbits and the like, he has elicited the responses 'Evet' and 'Yok' often enough to surmise that they may correspond to 'Yes' and 'No', but has no notion which is which. Then he tries the experiment of echoing the native's own volunteered pronouncements. If thereby he pretty regularly elicits 'Evet' rather than 'Yok', he is encouraged to take 'Evet' as 'Yes'. Also he tries responding with 'Evet' and 'Yok' to the native's remarks; the one that is the more serene in its effect is the better candidate for 'Yes'. However inconclusive these methods, they generate a working hypothesis. If extraordinary difficulties attend all his subsequent steps, the linguist may decide to discard that hypothesis and guess again.[1]

Let us then suppose the linguist has settled on what to treat as native signs of assent and dissent. He is thereupon in a position to accumulate inductive evidence for translating 'Gavagai' as the sentence 'Rabbit'. The general law for which he is assembling instances is roughly that the native will assent to 'Gavagai?' under just those stimulations under which we, if asked, would assent to 'Rabbit?'; and correspondingly for dissent.

But we can do somewhat more justice to what the linguist is after in such a case if, instead of speaking merely of stimulations under which the native will assent or dissent to the queried sentence, we speak in a more causal vein of stimulations that will *prompt* the native to assent or dissent to the queried sentence. For suppose the queried sentence were one rather to the effect that someone is away tracking a giraffe. All day long the native will assent to it whenever asked, under all manner of irrelevant attendant stimulations; and on another day he will dissent from it under the same irrelevant stimulations. It is important to know that in the case of 'Gavagai?' the rabbit-presenting stimulations actually prompt the assent, and that the others actually prompt the dissent.

In practice the linguist will usually settle these questions of causality, however tentatively, by intuitive judgment based on details of the native's behavior: his scanning movements, his sudden look of recognition, and the like. Also there are more formal considerations which, under favorable circumstances, can assure him of the prompting relation. If, just after the native has been asked S and has assented or dissented, the linguist springs stimulation σ on him, asks S again, and gets the opposite verdict, then he may conclude that σ did the prompting.

Note that to prompt, in our sense, is not to elicit. What elicits the native's 'Evet' or 'Yok' is a combination: the prompting stimulation plus the ensuing query 'Gavagai?'

STIMULATION AND STIMULUS MEANING

It is important to think of what prompts the native's assent to 'Gavagai?' as stimulations and not rabbits. Stimulation can remain the same though the rabbit be supplanted by a counterfeit. Conversely, stimulation can vary in its power to prompt assent to 'Gavagai' because of variations in angle, lighting, and color contrast, though the rabbit remain the same. In experimentally equating the uses of 'Gavagai' and 'Rabbit' it is stimulations that must be made to match, not animals.

A visual stimulation is perhaps best identified, for present purposes, with the pattern of chromatic irradiation of the eye. To look deep into the subject's head would be inappropriate even if feasible, for we want to keep clear of his idiosyncratic neural routings or private history of habit formation. We are after his socially inculcated linguistic usage, hence his responses to conditions normally subject to social assessment. Ocular irradiation *is* intersubjectively checked to some degree by society and linguist alike, by making allowances for the speaker's orientation and the relative disposition of objects.

In taking the visual stimulations as irradiation patterns we invest them with a fineness of detail beyond anything that our linguist can be called upon to check for. But this is all right. He can reasonably conjecture that the native would be prompted to assent to 'Gavagai' by the microscopically same irradiations that would prompt him, the linguist, to assent to 'Rabbit', even though this conjecture rests wholly on samples where the irradiations concerned can at best be hazarded merely to be pretty much alike.

It is not, however, adequate to think of the visual stimulations as momentary static irradiation patterns. To do so would obstruct examples which, unlike 'Rabbit', affirm movement. And it would make trouble even with examples like 'Rabbit', on another account: too much depends on what immediately precedes and follows a momentary irradiation. A momentary leporiform image flashed by some artifice in the midst of an otherwise rabbitless sequence might not prompt assent to 'Rabbit' even though the same image would have done so if ensconced in a more favorable sequence. The difficulty would thus arise that far from hoping to match the irradiation patterns favorable to 'Gavagai' with those favorable to 'Rabbit', we could not even say unequivocally of an irradiation pattern, of itself and without regard to those just before and after, that it is favorable to 'Rabbit' or that it is not.[2] Better, therefore, to take as the relevant stimulations not momentary irradiation patterns, but evolving irradiation patterns of all durations up to some convenient limit or *modulus*. Furthermore we may think of the ideal experimental situation as one in which the desired ocular exposure concerned is preceded and followed by a blindfold.

In general the ocular irradiation patterns are best conceived in their spatial entirety. For there are examples such as 'Fine weather' which, unlike 'Rabbit', are not keyed to any readily segregated fragments of the scene. Also there are all those rabbit-free patterns that are wanted as prompting dissent from 'Rabbit'. And as for the patterns wanted as prompting assent to 'Rabbit', whole scenes will still serve better than selected portions might; for the difference between center and periphery, which is such an important determinant of visual attention, is then automatically allowed for. Total ocular irradiation patterns that differ in centering differ also in limits, and so are simply different patterns. One that shows the rabbit too peripherally simply will not be one that prompts assent to 'Gavagai' or 'Rabbit'.

Certain sentences of the type of 'Gavagai' are the sentences with which our jungle linguist must begin, and for these we now have before us the makings of a crude concept of empirical meaning. For meaning, supposedly, is what a sentence shares with its translation; and translation at the present stage turns solely on correlations with non-verbal stimulation.

Let us make this concept of meaning more explicit and give it a neutrally technical name. We may begin by defining the *affirmative stimulus meaning* of a sentence such as 'Gavagai', for a given speaker, as the class of all the stimulations (hence evolving ocular irradiation patterns between properly timed blindfoldings) that would prompt his assent. More explicitly, in view of the end of the last Section, a stimulation σ belongs to the affirmative stimulus meaning of a sentence S for a given speaker if and only if there is a stimulation σ' such that if the speaker were given σ', then were asked S, then were given σ, and then were asked S again, he would dissent the first time and assent the second. We may define the *negative* stimulus meaning similarly with 'assent' and 'dissent' interchanged, and then define the *stimulus meaning* as the ordered pair of the two. We could refine the notion of stimulus meaning by distinguishing degrees of doubtfulness of assent and dissent, say by reaction time; but for the sake of fluent exposition let us forbear. The imagined equating of 'Gavagai' and 'Rabbit' can now be stated thus: they have the same stimulus meaning.

A stimulus meaning is the stimulus meaning of a sentence for a speaker at a date; for we must allow our speaker to change his ways. Also it varies with the modulus, or maximum duration recognized for stimulations. For, by increasing the modulus we supplement the stimulus meaning with some stimulations that were too long to count before. Fully ticketed, therefore, a stimulus meaning is the stimulus meaning *modulo n* seconds of sentence S for speaker a at time t.

The stimulations to be gathered into the stimulus meaning of a sentence have for vividness been thought of thus far as visual, unlike the queries that follow them. Actually, of course, we should bring the other senses in on a par with vision, identifying stimulations not with just ocular irradiation patterns but with these and the various barrages of other senses, separately and in all synchronous combinations. Perhaps we can pass over the detail of this.

The affirmative and negative stimulus meanings of a sentence (for a given speaker at a given time) are mutually exclusive. Granted, our subject might be prompted once by a given stimulation σ to assent to S, and later, by a recurrence of σ, to dissent from S; but then we would simply conclude that his meaning for S had changed. We would then reckon σ to his affirmative stimulus meaning of S as of the one date and to his negative stimulus meaning of S as of the other date.

Yet the affirmative and negative stimulus meanings do not determine each other; for many stimulations may be expected to belong to neither. In general, therefore, comparison of whole stimulus meanings can be a better basis for translations than comparison merely of affirmative stimulus meanings.

What now of that strong conditional, the 'would' in our definition of stimulus meaning? Its use here is no worse than its use when we explain '*x* is soluble in water' as meaning that *x* would dissolve if it were in water. What the strong conditional defines is a disposition, in this case a disposition to assent to or dissent from *S* when variously stimulated. The disposition may be presumed to be some subtle structural condition, like an allergy and like solubility; like an allergy, more particularly, in not being understood. The ontological status of dispositions, or the philosophical status of talk of dispositions, is a matter which I defer to §46 of *Word and Object*; but meanwhile we are familiar enough in a general way with how one sets about guessing, from judicious tests and samples and observed uniformities, whether there is a disposition of a specified sort.

The stimulus meaning of a sentence for a subject sums up his disposition to assent to or dissent from the sentence in response to present stimulation. The stimulation is what activates the disposition, as opposed to what instills it (even though the stimulation chance to contribute somehow to the instilling of some further disposition).

Yet a stimulation must be conceived for these purposes not as a dated particular event but as a universal, a repeatable event form. We are to say not that two like stimulations have occurred, but that the same stimulation has recurred. Such an attitude is implied the moment we speak of sameness of stimulus meaning for two speakers. We could indeed overrule this consideration, if we liked, by readjusting our terminology. But there would be no point, for there remains elsewhere a compelling reason for taking the stimulations as universals; viz., the strong conditional in the definition of stimulus meaning. For, consider again the affirmative stimulus meaning of a sentence *S*: the class Σ of all those stimulations that *would* prompt assent to *S*. If the stimulations were taken as events rather than event forms, then Σ would have to be a class of events which largely did not and will not happen, but which would prompt assent to *S* if they were to happen. Whenever Σ contained one realized or unrealized particular stimulator event σ, it would have to contain all other unrealized duplicates of σ; and how many are there of *these*? Certainly it is hopeless nonsense to talk thus of unrealized particulars and try to assemble them into classes. Unrealized entities have to be construed as universals.

We were impressed in §3 of *Word and Object* with the interdependence of sentences. We may well have begun then to wonder whether meanings even of whole sentences (let alone shorter expressions) could reasonably be talked of at all, except relative to the other sentences of an inclusive theory. Such relativity would be awkward, since, conversely, the individual component sentences offer the only way into the theory. Now the notion of stimulus meaning partially resolves the predicament. It isolates a sort of net empirical import of each of various single sentences without regard to the containing theory, even though without loss of what the sentence owes to that containing theory. It is a device, as far as it goes, for exploring the fabric of interlocking sentences, a sentence at a time.

Between the notion of stimulus meaning and Carnap's remarks on empirical semantics[3] there are connections and differences worth noting. He suggests exploring the meaning of a term by asking the subject whether he would apply it under various imaginary circumstances, to be described to him. That approach has the virtue of preserving contrasts between such terms as 'goblin' and 'unicorn' despite the non-existence of contrasting instances in the world. Stimulus meaning has the same virtue, since there are stimulation patterns that would prompt assent to 'Unicorn?' and not to 'Goblin?'. Carnap's approach presupposes some decision as to what descriptions of imaginary circumstances are admissible; e.g., 'unicorn' would be not wanted in descriptions used in probing the meaning of 'unicorn'. He hints of appropriate restrictions for the purpose, mentioning "size, shape, color"; and my notion of stimulus meaning itself amounts to a firmer definition in that same direction. There remains a significant contrast in the uses the two of us make of subjunctive conditionals: I limit them to my investigator's considered judgment of what the informant would do if stimulated; Carnap has his investigator putting such conditionals to the judgment of the informant. Certainly my investigator would in practice ask the same questions as Carnap's investigator, as a quick way of estimating stimulus meanings, if language for such questions happened to be available. But stimulus meaning can be explored also at the first stages of radical translation, where Carnap's type of questionnaire is unavailable. On this score it is important that my theory has to do primarily with sentences of a sort and not, like Carnap's, with terms.

Notes

1. See Firth, *Elements of Social Organization*, p. 23, on the analogous matter of identifying a gesture of greeting.

2. This difficulty was raised by Davidson.

3. *Meaning and Necessity*, 2d ed., Suppl. D. See also Chisholm, *Perceiving*, pp. 175ff., and his references.

Chapter 4

Utterer's Meaning and Intentions

Paul Grice

1 SAYING AND MEANING

Let us take stock. My main efforts so far have been directed as follows:

(1) I have suggested a provisional account of a kind of nonconventional implicature, namely a conversational implicature; what is implicated is what it is required that one assume a speaker to think in order to preserve the assumption that he is observing the Cooperative Principle (and perhaps some conversational maxims as well), if not at the level of what is said, at least at the level of what is implicated.

(2) I have attempted to see to what extent the explanation of implicature is useful for deciding about the connection of some of the A-philosophical theses, listed in Essay 1 in *Studies in the Way of Words*.

A lot of unanswered questions remain:

(1) The reliance (without much exposition) on a favored notion of "saying" needs to be further elucidated.

(2) The notion of conventional force (conventional meaning) deserves more attention, and the notion itself needs to be characterized.

(3) The notion of conventional implicature requires attention, and the relation between what is conventionally implicated and what is said needs characterization.

(4) "Implicature" is a blanket word to avoid having to make choices between words like "imply," "suggest," "indicate," and "means." These words are worth analyzing.

First appeared in *Studies in the Way of Words* (Cambridge: Harvard University Press, 1989). Reprinted by permission of Harvard University Press. Copyright © 1989 by the President and Fellows of Harvard College.

(5) Also needed are a clarification of the notion of relevance, a more precise specification of when relevance is expected (filling out the maxim of relevance), and a further consideration of why there is a general expectation that this maxim (and indeed all maxims) be observed.

I doubt if I shall be able here to address myself to all of these questions. I shall, in the first instance, try to pursue question (1) further, which will carry with it some attention to questions (2) and (3).

What follows is a sketch of direction, rather than a formulation of a thesis, with regard to the notion of saying that p (in the favored sense of *say*).

I want to say that (1) "U (utterer) said that p" entails (2) "U did something x by which U meant that p." But of course many things are examples of the condition specified in statement (2) which are not cases of saying. For example, a man in a car, by refraining from turning on his lights, means that I should go first, and he will wait for me.

Let us try substituting, for (2), (2′):

"U did something x
(1) by which U meant that p
(2) which is of a type which means 'p'"(that is, has for some person or other an established standard or conventional meaning).

There is a convenient laxity of formulation here: quite apart from troubles about the quoted variable, "p" will be in direct speech and so cannot be a quotation of a clause following "U meant that". Again many things satisfy the condition mentioned in this example which are not cases of saying, such as hand-signaling a left turn.

We want doing x to be a linguistic act; with hideous oversimplification we might try the formulation:

"U did something x
(1) by which U meant that p
(2) which is an occurrence of an utterance type S (sentence) such that
(3) S means 'p'
(4) S consists of a sequence of elements (such as words) ordered in a way licensed by a system of rules (syntactical rules)
(5) S means 'p' in virtue of the particular meanings of the elements of S, their order, and their syntactical character."

I abbreviate this to:

"*U* did something *x*

(1) by which *U* meant that *p*

(2) which is an occurrence of a type *S* which means '*p*' in some linguistic systems."

This is still too wide. *U*'s doing *x* might be his uttering the sentence "She was poor but she was honest." What *U* meant, and what the sentence means, will both contain something contributed by the word "but," and I do not want this contribution to appear in an account of what (in may favored sense) *U* said (but rather as a conventional implicature).

I want here to introduce some such idea as that of "central meaning." I want to be able to explain or talk about what (within what *U* meant) *U* centrally meant, to give a sense to "In meaning that *p*, *U* centrally meant that *q*."

So "*U* said that *p*" may finally come out as meaning:

"*U* did something *x*

(1) by which *U* centrally meant that *p*

(2) which is an occurrence of a type *S* part of the meaning of which is '*p*'."

This leaves various questions to be pursued:

(1) How is "U meant that *p*" to be explicated?

(2) How is "*W* (word or phrase) means '...'" to be explicated, and how is this locution related to "*U* meant that *p*"?

(3) How is "*S* means (would mean) '*p*'" (also "*S* meant '*p*' here, on this occasion" and "*U* meant by *S* '*p*'") to be explicated, and how does this relate to the locutions mentioned in questions (1) and (2)?

(4) How is "*U* centrally meant that *p*" to be explicated?

2 VARIETIES OF NONNATURAL MEANING

Within the range of uses of the word "mean" which are specially connected with communication (uses, that is, of the word "mean" in one or another of what I have called "nonnatural" senses), there are distinctions to be made. Consider the following sentence (*S*):

"If I shall then be helping the grass to grow, I shall have no time for reading."

(1a) It would be approximately true to say that *S* means (has as one of its meanings) "If I shall then be assisting the kind of thing of which lawns are composed to mature, I shall have no time for reading." It would also perhaps be approximately true to say that S means (has as another of its meanings, in at least one version of English) "If I shall then be assisting the marijuana to mature, I shall have no time for reading." Such meaning-specification I shall call the specifications of the *timeless meaning(s)* of a "complete" utterance-type (which may be a sentence or may be a "sentence-like" nonlinguistic utterance-type, such as a hand-signal).

(1b) It would be true to say that the word "grass" means (loosely speaking) "lawn-material," and also true to say that the word "grass" means "marijuana." Such meaning-specifications I shall call the specifications of the *timeless meaning(s)* of an "incomplete" utterance-type (which may be a nonsentential word or phrase, or may be a nonlinguistic utterance-type which is analogous to a word or phrase).

(2a) Since a complete utterance-type x may have more than one timeless meaning, we need to be able to connect with a particular utterance of x just one of the timeless meanings of x to the exclusion of the others. We need to be able to say, with regard to a particular utterance of S, that S meant *here* (on this occasion) "If I shall be assisting the kind of thing of which lawns are composed to mature, I shall have no time for reading," and that "I shall then be assisting the grass to grow" meant *here* "I shall be assisting the kind of thing of which lawns are composed to mature." Such meaning-specifications I shall call specifications of the *applied timeless meaning* of a complete utterance-type (on a particular occasion of utterance). Such specifications aim to given one the correct reading of a complete utterance-type on a particular occasion of utterance.

(2b) Similarly, we need to be able to specify what I shall call the *applied timeless meaning* of an incomplete utterance-type; we need to be able to say, with respect to the occurrence of the word "grass" in a particular utterance of S, that *here*, on this occasion, the word "grass" meant (roughly) "lawn-material" and not "marijuana."

(3) It might be true to say that when a particular utterer U uttered S, *be meant by S* (by the words of S):

(i) "If a am then dead, I shall not know what is going on in the world," and possibly, in addition,

(ii) "One advantage of being dead will be that I shall be protected from the horrors of the world."

If it were true to say of U that, when uttering S, he meant by S (i), it would also be true to say of U that *he* meant *by the words*, "I shall be helping the grass to grow" (which occur within *S*), "I shall then be dead."

On the assumption (which I make) that the phrase "helping the grass to grow," unlike the phrase "pushing up the daisies," is *not* a recognized idiom, none of the specifications just given of what *U* meant by *S* (or by the words "I shall be helping the grass to grow") would be admissible as specifications of a timeless meaning or of the applied timeless meaning of *S* (or of the words constituting the antecedent in *S*). The words "I shall be helping the grass to grow" neither mean nor mean *here* "I shall be dead."

The kind of meaning-specification just cited I shall call the specification of the *occasion-meaning of an utterance-type*.

(4) The varieties of meaning-specification so far considered all make use of quotation marks (or, perhaps better, italics) for the specification of what is meant. The fourth and last type to be considered involves, instead, the use of indirect speech. If it were true to say of *U* that *he* meant by *S* (i) (and [ii]), it would also be true to say of him that when he uttered *S* (by uttering *S*) *he meant that* if he would then be dead he would not know what was going on in the world, and that when he uttered *S he meant that* (or *part of what he meant was that*) one advantage of being dead would be that he would be protected from the horrors of the world. Even if, however, when he uttered *S*, he meant, by the words "I shall then be helping the grass to grow," "I shall then be dead," it would not be true to say that he meant by these words *that* he would then be dead. To have meant that he would then be dead, *U* would have had to commit himself to its being the case that he would then be dead; and this, when uttering *S*, he has not done. This type of meaning-specifications I shall call specifications of *an utterer's occasion-meaning*.

We can, then, distinguish four main forms of meaning-specification:

(1) "*x* (utterance-type) means '...'" (Specification of *timeless meaning* for an utterance-type which is either [1a] complete or [1b] incomplete)
(2) "*x* (utterance-type) meant here '...'" (Specification of *applied timeless meaning* for an utterance-type which is either [2a] complete or [2b] incomplete)
(3) "*U* meant by *x* (utterance-type) '...'" (Specification of *utterance-type occasion-meaning*)
(4) "*U* meant by uttering *x* that ..." (Specification of *utterer's occasion-meaning*)

There is, of course, an element of legislation in the distinction between the four cited linguistic forms; these are not quite so regimented as I am, for convenience, pretending.

In Essay 6 of *Studies in the Way of Words* I consider in some detail the relations between timeless meaning, applied timeless meaning, and what I am now calling utterer's occasion-meaning. Starting with the assumption that the notion of an utterer's occasion-meaning can be explicated, in a certain way, in terms of an utterer's intentions, I argue in support of the thesis that timeless meaning and applied timeless meaning can be explicated in terms of the notion of utterer's occasion-meaning (together with other notions), and so ultimately in terms of the notion of intention. In that easy I do not distinguish utterance-type occasion-meaning from utterer's occasion-meaning; but once the distinction is made, it should not prove too difficult to explicate utterance-type occasion-meaning in terms of utterer's occasion-meaning. The following provisional definition, though inadequate, seems to provide a promising start in this direction.

Let "$\sigma(x)$" denote a complete utterance-type (σ) which contains an utterance-type x; x may be complete or incomplete, and may indeed be identical with σ. Let "ϕ" denote an utterance-type. Let "$\sigma(\phi/x)$" denote the result of substituting ϕ for x in σ. Then I propose for consideration the following loosely framed definition:

"By x, U meant ϕ iff ($\exists\sigma$) {U uttered $\sigma(x)$, and by uttering $\sigma(x)$ U meant that ... [the lacuna to be completed by writing $\sigma(\phi/x)$]}."

My task is, however, to consider further the assumption made in the essay to which I have been referring, that the notion of utterer's occasion-meaning is explicable, in a certain way, in terms of the notion of utterer's intention, and I shall now turn to that topic.

I shall take as a starting-point the account of nonnatural meaning which appears in Essay 14 in *Studies in the Way of Words*, treating this as an attempt to define the notion of utterer's occasion-meaning. To begin with, I shall take as my definiendum not the form of expression which is of primary interest, namely (1) "By uttering x, U meant that p," but rather another form of expression, discussed in my 1957 article, "meaning,"[1] namely (2) "By uttering x, U meant *something*." My 1957 account, of course, embodied the idea that an adequate definiens for (2) would involve a reference to an intended effect of, or response to, the utterance of x, and that a specification of this intended effect or response would provide the material for answering the question *what U meant by uttering x*.

Later, I shall revert to definiendum (1), and shall attempt to clarify the supposed link between the nature of the intended response and the specification of what U meant by uttering x.

I start, then, by considering the following proposed definition:

"U meant something by uttering x" is true iff, for some audience A, U uttered x intending:

(1) A to produce a particular response r
(2) A to think (recognize) that U intends (1)
(3) A to fulfill (1) on the basis of his fulfillment of (2).

Two explanatory remarks may be useful. I use the terms "uttering" and "utterance" in an artificially extended way, to apply to any act or performance which is or might be a candidate for nonnatural meaning. And to suppose A to produce r "*on the basis of*" his thinking that U intends him to produce r is to suppose that his thinking that U intends him to produce r is at least part of his reason for producing r, and not merely the *cause* of his producing r. The third subclause of the definiens is formulated in this way in order to eliminate what would otherwise be a counterexample. If, for subclause (3), we were to substitute:

(3a) A to fulfill (1) as a result of his fulfillment of (2)

we should have counterintuitively to allow that U meant something by doing x if (as might be the case) U did x intending:

(1) A to be amused
(2) A to think that U intended him to be amused
(3a) A to be amused (at least partly) as a result of his thinking that U intended him to be amused.

But though A's thought that U intended him to be amused might be a part-cause of his being amused, it could not be a part of his reason for being amused (one does not, indeed, have reasons for being amused). So the adoption of (3) rather than of (3a) excludes this case.

I shall consider objections to this account of utterer's occasion-meaning under two main heads: first, those which purport to show that the definiens is too weak, that it lets in too much; and second, those which purport to show that the definiens is too strong, that it excludes clear cases of utterer's occasion-meaning. To meet some of these objections, I shall at various stages offer redefinitions of the notion of utterer's occasion-meaning; each such redefinition is to be regarded as being superseded by its successor.

3   ALLEGED COUNTEREXAMPLES DIRECTED AGAINST THE SUFFICIENCY OF THE SUGGESTED ANALYSANS

(i)   J. O. Urmson in conversation

There is a range of examples connected with the provision by U (the utterer) of an inducement, or supposed inducement, so that A (the recipient or audience) shall perform some action. Suppose a prisoner of war is thought by his captors to possess some information which they want him to reveal; he knows that they want him to give this information. They subject him to torture by applying thumbscrews. The appropriate analysans for "They meant something by applying the thumbscrews (that he should tell them what they wanted to know)" are fulfilled:

(1) They applied the thumbscrews with the intention of producing a certain response on the part of the victim.
(2) They intended that he should recognize (know, think) that they applied the thumbscrews with the intention of producing this response.
(3) They intended that the prisoner's recognition (thought) that they had the intention mentioned in (2) should be at least part of his reason for producing the response mentioned.

If in general to specify in (1) the nature of an intended response is to specify what was meant, it *should* be correct not only to say that the torturers meant something by applying the thumbscrews, but also to say that they meant that he should (was to) tell them what they wished to know. But in fact one would not wish to say either of these things; only that they meant him *to* tell. A similar apparent counter-example can be constructed out of a case of bribery.

A restriction seems to be required, and one which might serve to eliminate this range of counterexamples can be identified from a comparison of the two following examples:

(1) I go into a tobacconist's shop, ask for a pack of my favorite cigarettes, and when the unusually suspicious tobacconist shows that he wants to see the color of my money before he hands over the goods, I put down the price of the cigarettes on the counter. Here nothing has been meant.
(2) I go to my regular tobacconist (from whom I also purchase other goods) for a pack of my regular brand X, the price of which is distinctive (say 43 cents). I say nothing, but put down 43 cents. The tobacconist recognizes my need and hands over the pack. Here, I think, by putting

down 43 cents, I meant something—namely, that I wanted a pack of brand X. I have at the same time provided an inducement.

The distinguishing feature of the second example seems to be that here the tobacconist recognized, and was intended to recognize, what he was intended to do from my "utterance" (my putting down the money), whereas in the first example this was not the case. Nor is it the case with respect to the torture example. So the analysis of meaning might be amended accordingly, in the first redefinition:

"*U* meant something by uttering *x*" is true iff:

(1) *U* intended, by uttering *x*, to induce a certain response in *A*

(2) *U* intended *A* to recognize, *at least in part from the utterance of x*, that *U* intended to produce that response

(3) *U* intended the fulfillment of the intention mentioned in (2) to be at least in part *A*'s reason for fulfilling the intention mentioned in (1).

While this might cope with this range of counterexamples, there are others for which it is insufficient.

(ii)   Stampe, Strawson, Schiffer

(a)   D. W. Stampe in conversation   A man is playing bridge against his boss. He wants to earn his boss's favor, and for this reason he wants his boss to win, and furthermore he wants his boss to *know* that he wants him to win (his boss likes that kind of self-effacement). He does not want to do anything too blatant, however, like telling his boss by word of mouth, or in effect telling him by some action amounting to a signal, for fear the boss might be offended by his crudity. So he puts into operation the following plan: when he gets a good hand, he smiles in a certain way; the smile is *very* like, but not *quite* like, a spontaneous smile of pleasure. He intends his boss to detect the difference and to argue as follows: "That was not a genuine giveaway smile, but the simulation of such a smile. That sort of simulation might be a bluff (on a weak hand), but this is bridge, not poker, and he would not want to get the better of me, his boss, by such an impropriety. So probably he has a good hand, and, wanting me to win, he hoped I would learn that he has a good hand by taking his smile as a spontaneous giveaway. That being so, I shall not raise my partner's bid."

In such a case, I do not think one would want to say that the employee had *meant*, by his smile (or by smiling), that he had a good hand, nor indeed that he had meant anything at all. Yet the conditions so far listed are fulfilled. When producing the smile:

(1) the employee intended that the boss should think that the employee had a good hand,

(2) the employee intended that the boss should think, at least in part because of the smile, that the employee intended the boss to think that the hand was a good one,

(3) the employee intended that at least part of the boss's reason for thinking that the hand was a good one should be that the employee wanted him to think just that.

(b)   To deal with an example similar to that just cited, Strawson[2] proposed that the analysans might be restricted by the addition of a further condition, namely that the utterer U should utter x not only, as already provided, with the intention that A should think that U intends to obtain a certain response from A, but also with the intention that A should think (recognize) that U has the intention just mentioned. In the current example, the boss is intended to think that the employee wants him to think that the hand is a good one, but he is *not* intended to think that he is *intended* to think that the employee wants him to think that the hand is a good one. He is intended to think that it is only as a result of being too clever for the employee that he has learned that the employee wants him to think that the hand is a good one; he is to think that he was supposed to take the smile as a spontaneous giveaway.

(c)   S. Schiffer in conversation   A more or less parallel example, where the intended response is a practical one, can be constructed, which seems to show the need for the addition of a fifth condition. U is in a room with a man A who is notoriously avaricious, but who also has a certain pride. U wants to get rid of A. So U, in full view of A, tosses a five-pound note out of the window. He intends that A should think as follows: "U wants to get me to leave the room, thinking that I shall run after the money. He also wants me to know that he wants me to go (so contemptuous was his performance). But I am not going to demean myself by going after the banknote; I shall go, but I shall go because he wants me to go. I do not care to be where I am not wanted." In this example, counterparts of all four of the conditions so far suggested for the analysans are fulfilled; yet here again I do not think that one would want to say that U had meant something by throwing the banknote out of the window—that he had meant, for example, that A was to (should) go away. The four conditions which are fulfilled are:

U uttered x (threw the banknote) with the intention

(1) that A should leave the room

(2) that A should think (at least partly on the basis of x) that U had intention (1)

(3) that A should think that U had intention (2)

(4) that in the fulfillment of intention (1), at least part of A's reason for acting should be that he thought that U had intention (1)—(that is, that intention (2) is fulfilled).

So unless this utterance is to qualify as having meant something, yet a further restriction is required. A feature of this example seems to be that though A's leaving the room was intended by U to be based on A's thought that U wanted him to leave the room, U did not intend A to *recognize* that U intended A's departure to be so based. A was intended to think that U's purpose was to get him to leave in pursuit of the five-pound note. So the needed restriction is suggested as being that U should intend:

(5) that A should think (recognize) that U intended that (4).

We can now formulate the general form of these suggested conditions, the second redefinition, version A:

"U meant something by x" is true iff U uttered x intending thereby:

(1) that A should produce response r

(2) that A should, at least partly on the basis of x, think that U intended (1)

(3) that A should think that U intended (2)

(4) that A's production of r should be based (at least in part) on A's thought that U intended that (1) (that is, on A's fulfillment of [2])

(5) that A should think that U intended (4).

A notable fact about this analysans is that at several points it exhibits the following feature: U's nth "sub-intention" is specified as an intention that A should think that U has his $(n-1)$th "sub-intention." The presence of this feature has led to the suggestion that the analysis of meaning (on these lines) is infinitely or indefinitely regressive, that further counter-examples could always be found, however complex the suggested analy-sans, to force the incorporation of further clauses which exhibit this feature; but that such a regress might be virtuous, not vicious; it might be as harmless as a regress proceeding from "Z knows that p" to "Z knows that Z knows that p" to "Z knows that Z knows that Z knows that p."

I am not sure just how innocent such a regress in the analysans would be. It certainly would not exhibit the kind of circularity, at least prima facie strongly objectionable, which would be involved in giving, for example, a definiens for "U meant that p" which at some point reintroduced the expression "U meant that p," or introduced the expression "U meant that q." On the other hand, it would not be so obviously harmless as it would be so suppose that whenever it is correct to say "it is true that p," it is also correct to say "it is true that it is true that p," and so on; or as harmless as it would be to suppose that if Z satisfies the conditions for knowing that p, he also satisfies the condition for knowing that he knows that p. In such cases, no extra conditions would be required for the truth of an iteration of, for example, "he knows that" over and above those required for the truth of the sentence with respect to which the iteration is made. But the regressive character of the analysans for "U meant something by x" is designed to meet possible counterexamples at each stage, so each additional clause imposes a restriction, requires that a further condition be fulfilled. One might ask whether, for example, on the assumption that it is always possible to know that p without knowing that one knows that p, it would be legitimate to define "Z super-knows that p" by the open set of conditions:

(1) Z knows that p.
(2) Z knows that (1).
(3) Z knows that (2), and so forth.

There is, however, the possibility that no decision is required on this question, since it might be that the threatened regress cannot arise.

It does not seem easy to construct examples which will force the addition of clauses involving further iterations of "U intended A to think that ..." The following is an attempt by Schiffer. U sings "Tipperary" in a raucous voice with the intention of getting A to leave the room; A is supposed to recognize (and to know that he is intended to recognize) that U wants to get rid of A. U, moreover, intends that A shall, in the event, leave because he recognizes U's intention that he shall go. U's scheme is that A should (*wrongly*) think that U intends A to *think* that U intends to get rid of A by means of the recognition of U's intention that A should go. In other words A is supposed to argue: "U intends me to *think* that he intends to get rid of me by the raucous singing, but he really wants to get rid of me by means of the recognition of his intention to get rid of me. I am really intended to go because he wants me to go, not because I cannot stand the singing." The fact that *A*, while thinking he is seeing through *U*'s plans, is really conforming to them, is suggested as precluding one from saying, here, that *U* meant by the singing that *A* should go.

But once one tries to fill in the detail of this description, the example becomes baffling. How is *A* supposed to reach the idea that *U* wants him to *think* that *U* intends to get rid of him by the singing? One might suppose that *U* sings in a particular nasal tone which he knows not to be displeasing to *A*, though it is to most people. *A* knows that *U* knows this tone not to be displeasing to *A*, but thinks (wrongly) that *U* does not know that *A* knows this. *A* might then be supposed to argue: "He cannot want to drive me out by his singing, since he knows that this nasal tone is not displeasing to me. He does not know, however, that I know he knows this, so maybe he wants me to think that he intends to drive me out by his singing." At this point one would expect *A* to be completely at a loss to explain *U*'s performance; I see no reason at all why *A* should then suppose that *U* really wants to get rid of him in some other way.

Whether or not this example could be made to work, its complexity is enormous, and any attempt to introduce yet further restrictions would involve greater complexities still. It is in general true that one cannot have intentions to achieve results which one sees no chance of achieving; and the success of intentions of the kind involved in communication requires those to whom communications or near communications are addressed to be capable in the circumstances of having certain thoughts and drawing certain conclusions. At some early stage in the attempted regression the calculations required of *A* by *U* will be impracticably difficult; and I suspect the limit was reached (if not exceeded) in the examples which prompted the addition of a fourth and fifth condition. So *U* could not have the intentions required of him in order to force the addition of further restrictions. Not only are the calculations he would be requiring of *A* too difficult, but it would be impossible for *U* to find cues to indicate to *A* that the calculations should be made, even if they were within *A*'s compass. So one is tempted to conclude that no regress is involved.

But even should this conclusion be correct, we seem to be left with an uncomfortable situation. For though we may know that we do not need an infinite series of "backward-looking" subclauses, we cannot say just how many such subclauses are required. Indeed, it looks as if the definitional expansion of "By uttering *x* U meant something" might have to vary from case to case, depending on such things as the nature of the intended response, the circumstances in which the attempt to elicit the response is made, and the intelligence of the utterer and of the audience. It is dubious whether such variation can be acceptable.

This difficulty would be avoided if we could eliminate potential counterexamples, not by requiring U to have certain additional ("backward-looking") intentions, but rather by requiring U *not* to have a certain sort of intention or complex of intentions. Potential counterexamples of the kind with which we are at present concerned all involve the construction of a situation in which U intends A, in the reflection process by which A is supposed to reach his response, *both* to rely on some "inference-element" (some premise or some inferential step) E *and* also to think that U intends A *not* to rely E. Why not, then, eliminate such potential counterexamples by a single clause which prohibits U from having this kind of complex intention?

So we reach the second redefinition, version B:

"U meant something by uttering *x*" is true iff (for some A and for some r):
(a) U uttered *x* intending
    (1) A to produce r
    (2) A to think U to intend (1)
    (3) A's fulfillment of (1) to be based on A's fulfillment of (2)
(b) there is no inference-element E such that U uttered *x* intending both (1′) that A's determination of r should rely on E and (2′) that A should think U to intend that (1′) be false.

(iii)   Searle[3]

An American soldier in the Second World War is captured by Italian troops. He wishes to get the troops to believe that he is a German officer, in order to get them to release him. What he would like to do is to tell them in German or Italian that he is a German officer, but he does not know enough German or Italian to do that. So he "as it were, attempts to put on a show of telling them that he is a German officer" by reciting the only line of German that he knows, a line he learned at school: "*Kennst du das Land, wo die Zitronen blühen.*" He intends to produce a certain response in his captors, namely that they should believe him to be a German officer, and he intends to produce this response by means of their recognition of his intention to produce it. Nevertheless, Searle maintained, it is false that when the soldier says "*Kennst du das Land*," what he means is "I am a German officer" (or even the German version of "I am a German officer"), because what the words mean is "Knowest thou the land where the lemon trees bloom." Searle used this example to support a claim that something is missing from my account of meaning; this would (I think he thought) be improved if it were supplemented as follows (my conjecture): "*U* meant something by *x*" means "*U* intended to produce in *A* a certain effect by means of the recognition of *U*'s intention to produce that effect, and (if the utterance of *x* is the utterance of a sentence) *U* intends *A*'s recognition of *U*'s intention (to produce the effect) to be achieved by means of the recognition that the sentence uttered is conventionally used to produce such an effect."

Now even if I should be here faced with a genuine counterexample, I should be very reluctant to take the way out which I suspect was being offered me. (It is difficult to tell whether this is what was being offered, since Searle was primarily concerned with the characterization of a particular speech-act [promising], not with a general discussion of the nature of meaning; and he was mainly concerned to adapt my account of meaning to his current purpose, not to amend it so as to be better suited to its avowed end.) Of course, I would not want to deny that when the vehicle of meaning is a sentence (or the utterance of a sentence), the speaker's intentions are to be recognized, in the normal case, by virtue of a knowledge of the conventional use of the sentence (indeed my account of nonconventional implicature depends on this idea). But as I indicated earlier, I would like, if I can, to treat meaning something by the utterance of a sentence as being only a special case of meaning something by an utterance (in my extended sense of utterance), and to treat a conventional correlation between a sentence and a specific response as providing only one of the ways in which an utterance may be correlated with a response.

Is Searle's example, however, a genuine counterexample? It seems to me that the imaginary situation is underdescribed, and that there are perhaps three different cases to be considered:

(1) The situation might be such that the only real chance that the Italian soldiers would, on hearing the American soldier speak his German line, suppose him to be a German officer, would be if they were to argue as follows: "He has just spoken in German (perhaps in an authoritative tone); we don't know any German, and we have no idea what he has been trying to tell us, but if he speaks German, then the most likely possibility

is that he is a German officer—what other Germans would be in this part of the world?" If the situation was such that the Italians were likely to argue like that, and the American knew that to be so, then it would be difficult to avoid attributing to him the intention, when he spoke, that they *should* argue like that. As I recently remarked, one cannot in general intend that some result should be achieved, if one knows that there is no likelihood that it will be achieved. But if the American's intention was as just described, then he certainly would not, by my account, be meaning that he is a German officer; for though he would intend the Italians to believe him to be a German officer, he would not be intending them to believe this on the basis of their recognition of his intention. And it seems to me that though this is not how Searle wished the example to be taken, it would be much the most likely situation to have obtained.

(2) I think Searle wanted us to suppose that the American hoped that the Italians would reach a belief that he was a German officer via a belief that the words which he uttered were the German for "I am a German officer" (though it is not easy to see how to build up the context of utterance so as to give him any basis for this hope). Now it becomes doubtful whether, after all, it is right to say that the American did not mean "I am a German officer." Consider the following example. The proprietor of a shop full of knickknacks for tourists is standing in his doorway in Port Said, sees a British visitor, and in dulcet tones and with an alluring smile says to him the Arabic for "You pig of an Englishman." I should be quite inclined to say that he had meant that the visitor was to come in, or something of the sort. I would not, of course, be in the least inclined to say that he had meant by the *words which he uttered* that the visitor was to come in; and to point out that the German *line* means not "I am a German officer" but "Knowest thou the land" is not relevant. If the American could be said to have meant that he was a Gernam officer, he would have meant that by saying the line, or by saying the line in a particular way; just as the Port Said merchant would have meant that the visitor was to come in by *saying* what he said, or by speaking to the visitor in the way he did.

(3) It has been suggested, however, that it makes a difference whether U merely intends A to think that a particular sentence has a certain meaning which it does not in fact have, or whether he also intends him to think of himself as supposed to make use of his (mistaken) thought that it has this meaning in reaching a belief about U's intentions. The Port Said mer-

chant is perhaps thought of as not intending the visitor to think of himself in this way; the visitor is not to suppose that the merchant thinks he can speak Arabic. But if A is intended to think that U expects A to understand the sentence spoken and is intended to attribute to it a meaning which U knows it does not have, then the utterer should not be described as meaning something by his utterance. I do not see the force of this contention, nor indeed do I find it easy to apply the distinction which it makes. Consider just one example, I was listening to a French lesson being given to the small daughter of a friend. I noticed that she thinks that a certain sentence in French means "Help yourself to a piece of cake," though in fact it means something quite different. When there is some cake in the vicinity, I address to her this French sentence, and as I intended, she helps herself. I intended her to think (and to think that I intended her to think) that the sentence uttered by me meant "Help yourself to some cake"; and I would say that the fact that the sentence meant and was known by me to mean something quite different is no obstacle to *my* having meant something by my utterance (namely, that she was to have some cake). Put in a more general form, the point seems to be as follows. Characteristically, an utterer intends an audience to recognize (and to think himself intended to recognize) some "crucial" feature F, and to think of F (and to think himself intended to think of F) as correlated in a certain way with some response which the utterer intends the audience to produce. It does not matter, so far as the attribution of the speaker's meaning is concerned, whether F is thought by U to be *really* correlated in that way with the response or not; though of course in the normal case U will think F to be so correlated.

Suppose, however, we fill in the detail of the "American soldier" case, so as to suppose he accompanies "*Kennst du das Land*" with gesticulations, chest-thumping, and so forth. He might then hope to succeed in conveying to his listeners that he intends them to understand the German sentence, to learn from the particular German sentence that the American intends them to think that he is a German officer (whereas really, of course, the American does not expect them to learn *that* way, but only by assuming, on the basis of the situation and the character of the American's performance, that he must be trying to tell them that he is a German officer). Perhaps in this case we should be disinclined to say that the American meant that he was a German officer and ready to say only that he meant them to think that he was a German officer.

How can this example be differentiated from the "little girl" example? I would like to suggest a revised set of conditions for "*U* meant something by *x*," the third redefinition, version A:

Ranges of variables
A: audiences
f: features of utterance
r: responses
c: modes of correlation (such as iconic, associative, conventional)

$(\exists A)(\exists f)(\exists r)(\exists c)$:
U uttered *x* intending
(1) *A* to think *x* possesses *f*
(2) *A* to think *U* intends (1)
(3) *A* to think of *f* as correlated in way *c* with the type to which *r* belongs
(4) *A* to think *U* intends (3)
(5) *A* to think on the basis of the fulfillment of (1) and (3) that *U* intends *A* to produce *r*
(6) *A*, on the basis of fulfillment of (5), to produce *r*
(7) *A* to think *U* intends (6).

In the case of the "little girl" there is a single feature *f* (that of being an utterance of a particular French sentence) with respect to which *A* has all the first four intentions. (The only thing wrong is that this feature is not *in fact* correlated conventionally with the intended responses, and this does not disqualify the utterance from being one by which *U* means something.)

In the "American soldier" case there is no such single feature *f*. The captors are intended (1) to recognize, and go by, feature f_1 (*x*'s being a bit of German and being uttered with certain gesticulations, and so forth) but (2) to think that they are intended to recognize *x* as having f_2 (as being a *particular* German sentence).

The revised set of conditions also takes care of the earlier bridge example. The boss is intended to recognize *x* as having *f* (being a fake smile) but not to think that he is so intended. So intention (2) on our revised list is absent. And so we do not need the condition previously added to eliminate this example. I think, however, that condition (7)—(the old condition (5) is still needed to eliminate the "banknote" example, unless it can be replaced by a general "antideception" clause. Such replacement may be possible; it may be that the "backward-looking" subclauses (2), (4), and (7) can be omitted and replaced by the prohibitive clause which figures in the second redefinition, version B. We have then to consider the merits of the third redefinition, version B, the definiens of which runs as follows:

$(\exists A)(\exists f)(\exists r)(\exists c)$:

(a) U uttered x intending

    (1) A to think x possesses f

    (2) A to think f correlated in way c with the type to which r belongs

    (3) A to think, on the basis of the fulfillment of (1) and (3) that U intends A to produce r

    (4) A, on the basis of the fulfillment of (3) to produce r,

and

(b) there is no inference-element E such that U intends both

    (1′) A in his determination of r to rely on E

    (2′) A to think U to intend (1′) to be false.

4 EXAMPLES DIRECTED TOWARD SHOWING THE THREE-PRONG ANALYSANS TOO STRONG

Let us (for simplicity) revert to the original analysans of "U means something by uttering x":

"U utters x intending A

(1) to produce r

(2) to think U intends A to produce r

(3) to think U intends the fulfillment of (1) to be based on the fulfillment of (2)."

Now abbreviate this to "U utters x M-intending that A produce r."

I originally supposed that the identification of *what* U meant by x would turn on the identification of the M-intended response or effect. In particular, I supposed that generic differences in type of response would be connected with generic differences within what is meant. To take two central examples, I supposed that "U meant by x that so-and-so is the case" would (roughly speaking) be explicated by "U uttered x M-intending to produce in A the belief that so-and-so," and that "U meant by x that A should do such-and-such" would be explicated by "U uttered x M-intending to produce in A the doing of such-and-such." Indicative or quasi-indicative utterances are connected with the generation of beliefs, imperative or quasi-imperative utterances are connected with the generation of actions.

I wish to direct our consideration to the emendation of this idea: to substitute in the account of imperative or quasi-imperative utterances, as the direct, M-intended response, "intention on the part of A to do such-and-such" (vice "A's doing such-and-such"). This has the advantages (1) that symmetry is achieved, in that the M-intended response will be proportional attitude in both cases (indicative and imperative), and (2) that it accommodates the fact that agreement ("yes," "all right") in the case of "The engine has stopped" signifies belief, and in the case of "Stop the engine" signifies *intention*. Of course action is the *ultimate* objective of the speaker. Cases of immediate response by acting are treatable, however, as special cases of forming an intention—namely, the intention with which the agent acts. Imperatives always call for *intentional* action.

Alleged counterexamples are best seen as attempts to raise trouble, not for the suggested analysis for U means *something* by uttering x," but for this analysis when supplemented by the kind of detail just mentioned, so as to offer an outline of an account of "By uttering x, U means (meant) that ..." In particular, it is suggested that to explicate "By uttering x, U meant that so-and-so is the case" by "U uttered x M-intending to produce in A the belief that so-and-so" is to select as explicans a condition that is too strong. We need to be able to say on occasion that U meant that so-and-so, without committing ourselves to the proposition that U M-intended to produce a belief that so-and-so.

The following examples seem to present difficulties:

Examinee

Q: "When was the Battle of Waterloo?"
A: "1815."

Here the examinee meant that the Battle of Waterloo was fought in 1815 but hardly M-intended to induce a belief to that effect in his examiner. The examiner's beliefs (whatever they may be) are naturally to be thought of by the examinee as independent of candidates' answers. The M-intended effect is (perhaps) that the examiner knows or thinks that the examinee thinks the Battle of Waterloo was fought in 1815, *or* (perhaps) that the examiner knows whether the examinee knows the correct answer to the question (perhaps the former is the direct, and the latter the indirect, intended effect).

Confession (some cases)

> *Mother:* "It's no good denying it: you broke the window, didn't you?"
> *Child:* "Yes, I did."

Here the child knows his mother already thinks he broke the window; what she wants is that he should say that he did. Perhaps the *M*-intended effect, then, is that the mother should think the child willing to say that he did (what does "say" mean here—how should it be explicated?) or that the mother should think the child willing not to pretend that he did not break the window (not to say things or perform acts intended to induce the belief that the child *did not* break the window). Confession is perhaps a sophisticated and ritual case.

Reminding

> *Q:* "Let me see, what was that girl's name?"
> *A:* "Rose" (or produces a rose).

The questioner is here presumed already to believe that the girl's name is Rose (at least in a dispositional sense); it has just slipped his mind. The intended effect seems to be that *A* should have it in mind that her name is Rose.

Review of facts

Both speaker and hearer are supposed already to believe that *p* (*q*, and so forth). The intended effect again seems to be that *A* (and perhaps *U* also) should have "the facts" in mind (altogether).

Conclusion of argument

p, *q*, therefore *r* (from already stated premises).

While *U* intends that *A* should think that *r*, he does not expect (and so intend) *A* to reach a belief that *r* on the basis of *U*'s intention that he should reach it. The premises, not trust in *U*, are supposed to do the work.

The countersuggestible man

A regards *U* as being, in certain areas, almost invariably mistaken, or as being someone with whom he cannot bear to be in agreement. *U* knows this. *U* says "My mother thinks very highly of you" with the intention that *A* should (on the strength of what *U* says) think that *U*'s mother has a low opinion of him. Here there is some inclination to say that, despite

U's intention that *A* should think *U*'s mother thinks ill of him, what *U* *meant* was that *U*'s mother thinks well of *A*.

These examples raise two related difficulties.

(1) There is some difficulty in supposing that the indicative form is *conventionally tied* to indicating that the speaker is *M*-intending to induce a certain belief in his audience, if there are quite normal occurrences of the indicative mood for which the speaker's intentions are different, in which he is not *M*-intending (nor would be taken to be *M*-intending) to induce a belief (for example, in reminding). Yet it seems difficult to suppose that the function of the indicative mood has *nothing to do* with the inducement of belief. The indication of the speaker's intention that his audience should act (or form an intention to act) is plausibly, if not unavoidably, to be regarded as by convention the function of the imperative mood; surely the function of the indicative ought to be analogous. What is the alternative to the suggested connection with an intention to induce a belief?

The difficulty here might be met by distinguishing questions about what an indicative sentence means and questions about what a *speaker* means. One might suggest that a full specification of sentence meaning (for indicative sentences) involves reference to the fact that the indicative form conventionally signifies an intention on the part of the utterer to induce a belief; but that it may well be the case that the speaker's meaning does not coincide with the meaning of the sentence he utters. It may be clear that, though he uses a device which conventionally indicates an intention on his part to induce a belief, *in this case* he has not this but some other intention. This is perhaps reinforceable by pointing out that *any* device, the primary (standard) function of which is to indicate the speaker's intention to induce a belief that *p*, *could* in appropriate circumstances be easily and intelligibly employed for related purposes—for example (as in the "examinee" example), to indicate that the *speaker* believes that *p*. The problem then would be to exhibit the alleged counterexamples as natural adaptations of a device or form primarily connected with the indication of an intention to induce a belief.

I think we want, if possible, to avoid treating the counterexamples as extended uses of the indicative form and to find a more generally applicable function for that form. In any case, the second difficulty is more serious.

(2) Even if we can preserve the idea that the indicative form is tied by convention to the indication of a speaker's intention to induce a belief, we should have to allow that the speaker's meaning will be different for different occurrences of the same indicative sentence—indeed, this is required by the suggested solution for difficulty (1). We shall have to allow this if differences in intended response involve differences in speaker's meaning. But it is not very plausible to say that if U says, " The Battle of Waterloo was fought in 1815"

(1) as a schoolmaster (intending to induce a belief)
(2) as an examinee
(3) as a schoolmaster in *revision class*,

U would mean something different by uttering this sentence on each of the three occasions. Even if the examinee M-intends to induce a belief that he (the examinee) thinks the Battle of Waterloo was fought in 1815, it does not seem attractive to say that when *he* said "Waterloo was fought in 1815," he meant that *he thought* that Waterloo was fought in 1815 (unlike the schoolmaster teaching the period for the first time).

We might attempt to deal with some of the examples (such as reminding and fact-reviewing) by supposing the standard M-intended effect to be not just a belief but an "activated belief" (that A should be in a state of believing that p and having it in mind that p). One may fall short of this in three ways: one may

(1) neither believe that p nor have it in mind that p
(2) believe that p but not have it in mind that p
(3) not believe that p, but have it in mind that p.

So one who reminds intends the same final response as one who informs, but is intending to remedy a different deficiency.

This (even for the examples for which it seems promising) runs into a new difficulty. If U says (remindingly) "Waterloo was fought in 1815," two of my conditions are fulfilled:

(1) U intends to induce in A the *activated* belief that Waterloo was fought in 1815.
(2) U intends A to recognize that (1).

But if the date of Waterloo was "on the tip of A's tongue" (as it might be), U cannot expect (and so cannot intend) that A's activated belief will be produced via A's recognition that U intends to produce it. If A already believes (though has momentarily forgotten) that Waterloo was fought in 1815, then the mention of this date will induce the activated belief, regardless of U's intention to produce it.

This suggests dropping the requirement (for speaker's meaning) that U should intend A's production of response to be *based* on A's recognition of U's intention that A should produce the response; it suggests the retention merely of conditions (1) and (2). But this will not do: there are examples which require this condition:

(a) Herod, showing Salome the head of St. John the Baptist, cannot, I think, be said to have meant that St. John the Bapstist was dead.
(b) Displaying a bandaged leg (in response to a squash invitation).

In (b) the displayer could mean (1) that he cannot play squash or (dubiously) (2) that he has a bad leg (the bandages might be fake) but not (3) that his leg is bandaged. The third condition seems to be required in order to protect us from counterintuitive results in these cases.

Possible remedies

(i) We might retain the idea that the intended effect or response (for cases of meaning that it is the case that p—indicative type) is activated belief, retaining in view the distinction between reaching this state (1) from assurance-deficiency and (2) from attention-deficiency, and stipulate that the third condition (that U intends the response to be elicited on the basis of a recognition of his intention to elicit that response) is operative *only* when U intends to elicit activated belief by eliminating *assurance-deficiency*, *not* when he intends to do so by elimination attention-deficiency. This idea might be extended to apply to imperative types of cases, too, provided that we can find cases of reminding someone to do something (restoring him to *activated* intention) in which U's intention that A should reach the state is similarly otiose, in which it is not to be expected that A's reaching the activated intention will be dependent on his recognition that U intends him to reach it. So the definition might read roughly as follows ($*_\psi$ is a mood marker, an auxiliary correlated with the propositional attitude ψ from a given range of propositional attitudes):

"U means by uttering x that $*_\psi p$" = "U utters x intending
(1) that A should actively ψ that p
(2) that A should recognize that U intends (1) and (unless U intends the utterance of x merely to remedy attention-deficiency)

(3) that the fulfillment of (1) should be based on the fulfillment of (2)."

This remedy does not, however, cope with (1) the "examinee" example, (2) the "confession" examples, or (3) the countersuggestible man.

(ii)   Since, when U does intend, by uttering x, to promote in A the belief that p, it is standardly requisite that A should (and should be intended to) think that U thinks that p (otherwise A will not think that p), why not make the *direct* intended effect not that A should think that p, but that A should think that U *thinks* that p? In many but not all cases, U will intend A to pass, from thinking that U thinks that p, to thinking that p himself ("informing" cases). But such an effect is to be thought of as indirect (even though often of prime interest).

We can now retain the third condition, since even in reminding cases A may be expected to think U's intention that A should think that U thinks that p to be relevant to the question whether A is to think that U thinks that p. We have coped, not only with the "reminding" example, but also with the "examinee" example and with the "countersuggestible man" (who is intended to think that U thinks that p, though not to think that p himself). And though the fact-review example is not yet provided for (since A may be thought of as already knowing that U thinks that p), if we are understanding "U believes that p" as "U has the activated belief that p," this example can be accommodated, too. A, though he is to be supposed to know that U believes that p, does not, until U speaks, know that U has it in mind that p.

But while a solution along these lines may be acceptable for indicative-type cases, it cannot be generalized to all non-indicative cases. Contrast:

(a) "You shall not cross the barrier."

(b) "Do not cross the barrier."

When uttering (a), U would characteristically intend A to think that U intends that A shall not cross the barrier; but it seems that a specification of U's meaning, for a normal utterance of (b), would be incompletely explicated unless it is stated that U intends A not merely to think that U intends that A shall not cross the barrier, but also himself to form the intention not to cross.

Let us then draw a distinction between what I might call "purely exhibitive" utterances (utterances by which the utterer U intends to impart a belief that he [U] has a certain propositional attitude), and utterances which are not only exhibitive but also what I might call "protreptic" (that is, utterances by which U intends, via imparting the belief that he [U] has a certain propositional attitude, to induce a corresponding attitude in the hearer).

We reach, then, the fourth redefinition, version A:

"By uttering x U meant that $*_\psi p$" is true iff
$(\exists A)(\exists f)(\exists c)$: U uttered x intending

(1)
(2)
(3)
(4)   } [as in the third redefinition, version A, with "ψ-ing that p"
(5)   substituted for "r"]
(6)
(7)

and (for some cases)
(8) A, on the basis of the fulfillment of (6), himself to ψ that p.

Whether a substitution-instance of subclause (8) is to appear in the expansion of a statement of the form represented in the definiendum will depend on the nature of the substitution for "$*_\psi$" which that statement incorporates.

We can also reach the fourth redefinition, version B, by adding what appears above as subclause (8) to the definiens of the third redefinition, version B, as subclause (a) (5), together with a modification of clause (b) of the third redefinition, version B, to take into account that the intended response r is now specified in terms of the idea of ψ-ing that p.

Whether either version of the fourth redefinition is correct as it stands depends crucially on the view to be taken of an imperatival version of the "countersuggestible man" example. Mr. A, wishing to be relieved of the immediate presence of Mrs. A, but regarding her as being, so far as he is concerned, countersuggestible, says to her, "Now, dear, keep me company for a little." Would it be correct to say that Mr. A, who clearly did not mean Mrs. A to keep him company, meant by his remark that she was to (should) keep him company? If the answer is "yes," the fourth redefinition is inadequate since, according to it, to have meant that Mrs. A was to keep him company, Mr. A would have had to intend that she form the intention to keep him company, an intention which he certainly did not have. Emendation, however, would not be difficult; we alter the new subclause from "*A*, on the basis of the fulfillment of (6), himself to ψ to that *p*" to "*A*, on the basis of the fulfillment of (6), *to think U to intend A* to ψ that *p*." If, however, the answer is "no," then the fourth redefinition is left intact.

5 UTTERER'S OCCASION-MEANING IN THE ABSENCE OF AN AUDIENCE

There are various examples of utterances by which the utterer could correctly be said to have meant something (to have meant that so-and-so), such that there is no actual person or set of persons whom the utterer is addressing and in whom he intends to induce a response. The range of these examples includes, or might be thought to include, such items as the posting of notices, like "Keep out" or "This bridge is dangerous," entries in diaries, the writing of notes to clarify one's thoughts when working on some problem, soliloquizing, rehearsing a part in a projected conversation, and silent thinking. At least some of these examples are unprovided for in the definitions so far proposed.

The examples which my account should cover fall into three groups:

(a) Utterances for which the utterer thinks there may (now or later) be an audience. *U* may think that some particular person, for example, himself at a future date in the case of a diary entry, may (but also may not) encounter *U*'s utterance; or *U* may think that there may or may not be some person or other who is or will be an auditor of his utterance.

(b) Utterances which the utterer knows not to be addressed to any actual audience, but which the utterer pretends to address to some particular person or type of person, or which he thinks of as being addressed to some imagined audience or type of audience (as in the rehearsal of a speech or of his part in a projected conversation).

(c) Utterances (including "internal" utterances) with respect to which the utterer neither thinks it possible that there may be an actual audience nor imagines himself as addressing an audience, but nevertheless intends his utterance to be such that it would induce a certain sort of response in a certain perhaps fairly indefinite kind of audience were it the case that such an audience was present. In the case of silent thinking the idea of the presence of an audience will have to be interpreted liberally, as being the idea of there being an audience for a public counterpart of the utterer's internal speech. In this connection it is perhaps worth noting that some cases of verbal thinking fall outside the scope of my account. When verbal thoughts merely pass through my head as distinct from being "framed" by me, it is inappropriate to talk of me as having meant something by them; I am, perhaps, in such cases more like a listener than a speaker.

I shall propose a final redefinition which, I hope, will account for the examples which need to be accounted for, and which will allow as special cases the range of examples in which there is, and it is known by the utterer that there is, an actual audience. This redefinition will be relatively informal; I could present a more formal version which would gain in precision at the cost of ease of comprehension.

Let "ϕ" (and "ϕ'") range over properties of persons (possible audiences); appropriate substituends for "ϕ" (and "ϕ'") will include such diverse expressions as "is a passerby," "is a passerby who sees this notice," "is a native English speaker," and "is identical with Jones." As will be seen, for U to mean something it will have to be possible to identify the value of "ϕ" (which may be fairly indeterminate) which U has in mind; but *we* do not have to determine the range from which U makes a selection.

The fifth redefinition is as follows:

"*U* meant by uttering x that $*_\psi p$" is true iff
$(\exists\phi)(\exists f)(\exists c)$:

I. *U* uttered x intending x *to be such that* anyone who has ϕ would think that

    (1) x has f
    (2) f is correlated in way c with ψ-ing that p
    (3) $(\exists\phi')$: *U* intends x to be such that anyone who has ϕ' would think, via thinking (1) and (2), that U ψ's that p
    (4) in view of (3), U ψ's that p;

and

II. (operative only for certain substituends for "$*_\psi$")
     U uttered x intending that, *should there actually be* anyone who has ϕ, he would via thinking (4), himself ψ that p;

and

III. It is not the case that, for some inference-element E, U intends x to be such that anyone who has ϕ will both

    (1') rely on E in coming to ψ^+ that p
    (2') think that $(\exists\phi')$: U intends x to be such that anyone who has ϕ' will come to ψ^+ that p *without* relying on E.

Notes:
(1) "ψ^+" is to be read as "ψ" if clause (II) is operative, and as "think that U ψ's" if clause (II) is nonoperative.
(2) We need to use both "ϕ" and "ϕ'," since we do not wish to require that U should intend his possible audience to think of U's possible audience under the same description as U does himself.

Explanatory comments

(1) It is essential that the intention which is specified in clause (II) should be specified as U's intention "that should there be anyone who has ϕ, he would (will) ..." rather than, analogously with clauses (I) and (II), as U's intention "that x *should be such that*, should anyone be ϕ, he would ..." If we adopt the latter specification, we shall be open to an objection raised by Schiffer, as can be shown with the aid of an example of the same kind as his. Suppose that, infuriated by an afternoon with my mother-in-law, when I am alone after her departure I relieve my feelings by saying, aloud and passionately, "Don't you ever come near me again." It will no doubt be essential to my momentary well-being that I should speak with the intention that my remark be such that were my mother-in-law present, she would form the intention not to come near me again. It would, however, be unacceptable if it were represented as following from my having this intention that I *meant that* she was never to come near me again, for it is false that, in the circumstances, I meant this by my remark. The redefinition as formulated avoids this difficulty.

(2) Suppose that in accordance with the definiens of the latest redefinition, $(\exists\phi)$: U intends x to be such that anyone who is ϕ will think ..., and suppose that the value of "ϕ" which U has in mind is the property of being identical with a particular person A. Then it will follow that U intends A to think ...; and given the further condition, fulfilled in any normal case, that U intends A to think that he (A) is the intended audience, we are assured of the truth of a statement from which the definiens of the fourth redefinition, version B, is inferrable by the rule of existential generalization (assuming the legitimacy of this application of E.G. to a statement the expression of which contains such "intensional" verbs as "intend" and "think"). I think it can also be shown that, for any case in which there is an actual audience who knows that he is the intended audience, if the definiens of the fourth redefinition, version B, is true then the definiens of the fifth redefinition will be true. If that is so, given that the fifth redefinition is correct, for any normal case in which there is an actual audience the fulfillment of the definiens of the fourth redefinition, version B, will constitute a necessary and sufficient condition for U's having meant that $*_\phi p$.

6 CONCLUSION

I see some grounds for hoping that, by paying serious attention to the relation between nonnatural and natural meaning, one might be able not only to reach a simplified account of utterer's occasion-meaning but also to show that any human institution, the function of which is to provide artificial substitutes for natural signs, must embody, as its key-concept, a concept possessing approximately the features which I ascribe to the concept of utterer's occasion-meaning. But such an endeavor lies beyond the scope of this essay.

Notes

1. Paul Grice, "Meaning," *Philosophical Review* 66 (1957): 377–388.

2. P. F. Strawson, "Intention and Convention in Speech Acts," *Philosophical Review* 73 (1964): 439–460.

3. John R. Searle, "What Is a Speech Act?" in *Philosophy in America*, ed. Max Black (Ithaca, N.Y., 1965), pp. 221–239.

Chapter 5

Truth and Meaning

Donald Davidson

It is conceded by most philosophers of language, and recently by some linguists, that a satisfactory theory of meaning must give an account of how the meanings of sentences depend upon the meanings of words. Unless such an account could be supplied for a particular language, it is argued, there would be no explaining the fact that we can learn the language: no explaining the fact that, on mastering a finite vocabulary and a finitely stated set of rules, we are prepared to produce and to understand any of a potential infinitude of sentences. I do not dispute these vague claims, in which I sense more than a kernal of truth. Instead I want to ask what it is for a theory to give an account of the kind adumbrated.

One proposal is to begin by assigning some entity as meaning to each word (or other significant syntactical feature) of the sentence; thus we might assign Theactetus to 'Theaetetus' and the property of flying to 'flies' in the sentence 'Theaetetus flies'. The problem then arises how the meaning of the sentence is generated from these meanings. Viewing concatenation as a significant piece of syntax, we may assign to it the relation of participating in or instantiating; however, it is obvious that we have here the start of an infinite regress. Frege sought to avoid the regress by saying that the entities corresponding to predicates (for example) are 'unsaturated' or 'incomplete' in contrast to the entities that correspond to names, but this doctrine seems to label a difficulty rather than solve it.

The point will emerge if we think for a moment of complex singular terms, to which Frege's theory applies along with sentences. Consider the expression 'the father of Annette'; how does the meaning of the whole depend on the meaning of the parts? The answer would seem to be that

First appeared in *Synthese* 17 (1967): 304–323. Reprinted with kind permission from Kluwer Academic Publishers.

the meaning of 'the father of' is such that when this expression is prefixed to a singular term the result refers to the father of the person to whom the singular term refers. What part is played, in this account, by the unsaturated or incomplete entity for which 'the father of' stands? All we can think to say is that this entity 'yields' or 'gives' the father of x as value when the argument is x, or perhaps that this entity maps people on to their fathers. It may not be clear whether the entity for which 'the father of' is said to stand performs any genuine explanatory function as long as we stick to individual expressions; so think instead of the infinite class of expressions formed by writing 'the father of' zero or more times in front of 'Annette'. It is easy to supply a theory that tells, for an arbitrary one of these singular terms, what it refers to: if the term is 'Annette' it refers to Annette, while if the term is complex, consisting of 'the father of' prefixed to a singular term t, then it refers to the father of the person to whom t refers. It is obvious that no entity corresponding to 'the father of' is, or needs to be, mentioned in stating this theory.

It would be inappropriate to complain that this little theory *uses* the words 'the father of' in giving the reference of expressions containing those words. For the task was to give the meaning of all expressions in a certain infinite set on the basis of the meaning of the parts; it was not in the bargain also to give the meanings of the atomic parts. On the other hand, it is now evident that a satisfactory theory of the meanings of complex expressions may not require entities as meanings of all the parts. It behoves us then to rephrase our demand on a satisfactory theory of meaning so as not to suggest that individual words must have meanings at all, in any sense that transcends the fact that they have a systematic effect on the meanings of the sentences in which they occur. Actually, for the case at hand we can do better still in stating the criterion of success: what we wanted, and what we got, is a theory that entails every sentence of the form 't refers to x' where 't' is replaced by a structural description[1] of a singular term, and 'x' is replaced by that term itself. Further, our theory accomplishes this without appeal to any semantical concepts beyond the basic 'refers to'. Finally, the theory clearly suggests an effective procedure for determining, for any singular term in its universe, what that term refers to.

A theory with such evident merits deserves wider application. The device proposed by Frege to this end has a brilliant simplicity: count predicates as a special case of functional expressions, and sentences as a special case of complex singular terms. Now, however, a difficulty looms if we want to continue in our present (implicit) course of identifying the meaning of a singular term with its reference. The difficulty follows upon making two reasonable assumptions: that logically equivalent singular terms have the same reference, and that a singular term does not change its reference if a contained singular term is replaced by another with the same reference. But now suppose that 'R' and 'S' abbreviate any two sentences alike in truth value. Then the following four sentences have the same reference:

(1) R

(2) $\hat{x}(x = x . R) = \hat{x}(x = x)$

(3) $\hat{x}(x = x . S) = \hat{x}(x = x)$

(4) S

For (1) and (2) are logically equivalent, as are (3) and (4), while (3) differs from (2) only in containing the singular term '$\hat{x}(x = x . S)$' where (2) contains '$\hat{x}(x = x . R)$' and these refer to the same thing if S and R are alike in truth value. Hence any two sentences have the same reference if they have the same truth value.[2] And if the meaning of a sentence is what it refers to, all sentences alike in truth value must be synonymous—an intolerable result.

Apparently we must abandon the present approach as leading to a theory of meaning. This is the natural point at which to turn for help to the distinction between meaning and reference. The trouble, we are told, is that questions of reference are, in general, settled by extra-linguistic facts, questions of meaning not, and the facts can conflate the references of expressions that are not synonymous. If we want a theory that gives the meaning (as distinct from reference) or each sentence, we must start with the meaning (as distinct from reference) of the parts.

Up to here we have been following in Frege's footsteps; thanks to him, the path is well known and even well worn. But now, I would like to suggest, we have reached an impasse: the switch from reference to meaning leads to no useful account of how the meanings of sentences depend upon the meanings of the words (or other structural features) that compose them. Ask, for example, for the meaning of 'Theaetetus flies'. A Fregean answer might go something like this: given the meaning of 'Theaetetus' as argument, the meaning of 'flies' yields the meaning of 'Theaetetus flies' as value. The vacuity of this answer is obvious. We wanted to know what the meaning of 'Theaetetus flies' is; it is no progress to be told that it is the meaning of 'Theaetetus flies'. This much we knew before any theory was in sight. In the bogus account just given, talk of the structure of the sentence and of the meanings of words was idle, for it played no role in producing the given description of the meaning of the sentence.

The contrast here between a real and pretended account will be plainer still if we ask for a theory, analogous to the miniature theory of reference of singular terms just sketched, but different in dealing with meanings in place of references. What analogy demands is a theory that has as consequences all sentences of the form '*s* means *m*' where '*s*' is replaced by a structural description of a sentence and '*m*' is replaced by a singular term that refers to the meaning of that sentence; a theory, moreover, that provides an effective method for arriving at the meaning of an arbitrary sentence structurally described. Clearly some more articulate way of referring to meanings that any we have seen is essential if these criteria are to be met.[3] Meanings as entities, or the related concept of synonymy, allow us to formulate the following rule relating sentences and their parts: sentences are synonymous whose corresponding parts are synonymous ('corresponding' here needs spelling out of course). And meanings as entities may, in theories such as Frege's, do duty, on occasion, as references, thus losing their status as entities distinct from references. Paradoxically, the one thing meanings do not seem to do is oil the wheels of a theory of meaning—at least as long as we require of such a theory that it non-trivially give the meaning of every sentence in the language. My objection to meanings in the theory of meaning is not that they are abstract or that their identity conditions are obscure, but that they have no demonstrated use.

This is the place to scotch another hopeful thought. Suppose we have a satisfactory theory of syntax for our language, consisting of an effective method of telling, for an arbitrary expression, whether or not it is independently meaningful (i.e. a sentence), and assume as usual that this involves viewing each sentence as composed, in allowable ways, out of elements drawn from a fixed finite stock of atomic syntactical elements (roughly, words). The hopeful thought is that syntax, so conceived, will yield semantics when a dictionary giving the meaning of each syntactic atom is added. Hopes will be dashed, however, if semantics is to comprise a theory of meaning in our sense, for knowledge of the structural characteristics that make for meaningfulness in a sentence, plus knowledge of the meanings of the ultimate parts, does not add up to knowledge of what a sentence means. The point is easily illustrated by belief sentences. Their syntax is relatively unproblematic. Yet, adding a dictionary does not touch the standard semantic problem, which is that we cannot account for even as much as the truth conditions of such sentences on the basis of what we know of the meanings of the words in them. The situation is not radically altered by refining the dictionary to indicate which meaning or meanings an ambiguous expression bears in each of its possible contexts; the problem of belief sentences persists after ambiguities are resolved.

The fact that recursive syntax with dictionary added is not necessarily recursive semantics has been obscured in some recent writing on linguistics by the intrusion of semantic criteria into the discussion of purportedly syntactic theories. The matter would boil down to a harmless difference over terminology if the semantic criteria were clear; but they are not. While there is agreement that it is the central task of semantics to give the semantic interpretation (the meaning) of every sentence in the language, nowhere in the linguistic literature will one find, so far as I know, a straightforward account of how a theory performs this task, or how to tell when it has been accomplished. The contrast with syntax is striking. The main job of a modest syntax is to characterize *meaningfulness* (or sentence-hood). We may have as much confidence in the correctness of such a characterization as we have in the representativeness of our sample and our ability to say when particular expressions are meaningful (sentences). What clear and analogous task and test exist for semantics?[4]

We decided a while back not to assume that parts of sentences have meanings except in the ontologically neutral sense of making a systematic contribution to the meaning of the sentences in which they occur. Since postulating meanings has netted nothing, let us return to that insight. One direction in which it points is a certain holistic view of meaning. If sentences depend for their meaning on their structure, and we understand the meaning of each item in the structure only as an abstraction from the totality of sentences in which it features, then we can give the meaning of any sentence (or word) only by giving the meaning of every sentence (and word) in the language. Frege said that only in the context of a sentence does a word have meaning; in the same vein he might have added that only in the context of the language does a sentence (and therefore a word) have meaning.

This degree of holism was already implicit in the suggestion that an adequate theory of meaning must entail *all* sentences of the form '*s* means *m*'. But now, having found no more help in meanings of sentences than in meanings of words, let us ask whether we can get rid of the troublesome singular terms supposed to replace '*m*' and to refer to meanings. In a way, nothing could be easier: just write '*s* means that *p*', and imagine '*p*' replaced by a sentence. Sentences, as we have seen, cannot name meanings, and sentences with 'that' prefixed are not names at all, unless we decide so. It looks as though we are in trouble on another count, however, for it is reasonable to expect that in wrestling with the logic of the apparently non-extensional 'means that' we will encounter problems as hard as, or perhaps identical with, the problems our theory is out to solve.

The only way I know to deal with this difficulty is simple, and radical. Anxiety that we are enmeshed in the intensional springs from using the words 'means that' as filling between description of sentence and sentence, but it may be that the success of our venture depends not on the filling but on what it fills. The theory will have done its work if it provides, for every sentence *s* in the language under study, a matching sentence (to replace '*p*') that, in some way yet to be made clear, 'gives the meaning' of *s*. One obvious candidate for matching sentence is just *s* itself, if the object language is contained in the metalanguage; otherwise a translation of *s* in the metalanguage. As a final bold step, let us try treating the position occupied by '*p*' extensionally: to implement this, sweep away the obscure 'means that', provide the sentence that replaces '*p*' with a proper sentential connective, and supply the description that replaces '*s*' with its own predicate. The plausible result is

(T) *s* is *T* if and only if *p*.

What we require of a theory of meaning for a language *L* is that without appeal to any (further) semantical notions it place enough restrictions on the predicate 'is *T*' to entail all sentences got from schema *T* when '*s*' is replaced by a structural description of a sentence of *L* and '*p*' by that sentence.

Any two predicates satisfying this condition have the same extension,[5] so if the metalanguage is rich enough, nothing stands in the way of putting what I am calling a theory of meaning into the form of an explicit definition of a predicate 'is *T*'. But whether explicitly defined or recursively characterized, it is clear that the sentences to which the predicate 'is *T*' applies will be just the true sentences of *L*, for the condition we have placed on satisfactory theories of meaning is in essence Tarski's Convention *T* that tests the adequacy of a formal semantical definition of truth.[6]

The path to this point has been tortuous, but the conclusion may be stated simply: a theory of meaning for a language L shows 'how the meanings of sentences depend upon the meanings of words' if it contains a (recursive) definition of truth-in-L. And, so far at least, we have no other idea how to turn the trick. It is worth emphasizing that the concept of truth played no ostensible role in stating our original problem. That problem, upon refinement, led to the view that an adequate theory of meaning must characterize a predicate meeting certain conditions. It was in the nature of a discovery that such a predicate would apply exactly to the true sentences. I hope that what I am saying may be described in part as defending the philosophical importance of Tarski's semantical concept of truth. But my defence is only distantly related, if at all, to the question whether the concept Tarski has shown how to define is the (or a) philosophically interesting conception of truth, or the question whether Tarski has cast any light on the ordinary use of such words as 'true' and 'truth'. It is a misfortune that dust from futile and confused battles over these questions has prevented those with a theoretical interest in language— philosophers, logicians, psychologists, and linguists alike—from seeing in the semantical concept of truth (under whatever name) the sophisticated and powerful foundation of a competent theory of meaning.

There is no need to suppress, of course, the obvious connection between a definition of truth of the kind Tarski has shown how to construct, and the concept of meaning. It is this: the definition works by giving necessary and sufficient conditions for the truth of every sentence, and to give truth conditions is a way of giving the meaning of a sentence. To know the semantic concept of truth for a language is to know what it is for a sentence—any sentence–to be true, and this amounts, in one good sense we can give to the phrase, to understanding the language. This at any rate is my excuse for a feature of the present discussion that is apt to shock old hands; my freewheeling use of the word 'meaning', for what I call a theory of meaning has after all turned out to make no use of meanings, whether of sentences or of words. Indeed, since a Tarski-type truth definition supplies all we have asked so far of a theory of meaning, it is clear that such a theory falls comfortably within what Quine terms the 'theory of reference' as distinguished from what he terms the 'theory of meaning'. So much to the good for what I call a theory of meaning, and so much, perhaps, against my so calling it.[7]

A theory of meaning (in my mildly perverse sense) is an empirical theory, and its ambition is to account for the workings of a natural language.

Like any theory, it may be tested by comparing some of its consequences with the facts. In the present case this is easy, for the theory has been characterized as issuing in an infinite flood of sentences each giving the truth conditions of a sentence; we only need to ask, in sample cases, whether what the theory avers to be the truth conditions for a sentence really are. A typical test case might involve deciding whether the sentence 'Snow is white' *is* true if and only if snow is white. Not all cases will be so simple (for reasons to be sketched), but it is evident that this sort of test does not invite counting noses. A sharp conception of what constitutes a theory in this domain furnishes an exciting context for raising deep questions about when a theory of language is correct and how it is to be tried. But the difficulties are theoretical, not practical. In application, the trouble is to get a theory that comes close to working; anyone can tell whether it is right.[8] One can see why this is so. The theory reveals nothing new about the conditions under which an individual sentence is true; it does not make those conditions any clearer than the sentence itself does. The work of the theory is in relating the known truth conditions of each sentence to those aspects ('words') of the sentence that recur in other sentences, and can be assigned identical roles in other sentences. Empirical power in such a theory depends on success in recovering the structure of a very complicated ability—the ability to speak and understand a language. We can tell easily enough when particular pronouncements of the theory comport with our understanding of the language; this is consistent with a feeble insight into the design of the machinery of our linguistic accomplishments.

The remarks of the last paragraph apply directly only to the special case where it is assumed that the language for which truth is being characterized is part of the language used and understood by the characterizer. Under these circumstances, the framer of a theory will as a matter of course avail himself when he can of the built-in convenience of a metalanguage with a sentence guaranteed equivalent to each sentence in the object language. Still, this fact ought not to con us into thinking a theory any more correct that entails ' "Snow is white" is true if and only if snow is white' than one that entails instead:

(S) 'Snow is white' is true if and only if grass is green,

provided, of course, we are as sure of the truth of (S) as we are of that of its more celebrated predecessor. Yet (S) may not encourage the same confidence that a theory that entails it deserves to be called a theory of meaning.

The threatened failure of nerve may be counteracted as follows. The grotesqueness of (S) is in itself nothing against a theory of which it is a consequence, provided the theory gives the correct results for every sentence (on the basis of its structure, there being no other way). It is not easy to see how (S) could be party to such an enterprise, but if it were—if, that is, (S) followed from a characterization of the predicate 'is true' that led to the invariable pairing of truths with truths and falsehoods with falsehoods—then there would not, I think, be anything essential to the idea of meaning that remained to be captured.[9]

What appears to the right of the biconditional in sentences of the form '*s* is true if and only if *p*' when such sentences are consequences of a theory of truth plays its role in determining the meaning of *s* not by pretending synonymy but by adding one more brush-stroke to the picture which, taken as a whole, tells what there is to know of the meaning of *s*; this stroke is added by virtue of the fact that the sentence that replaces '*p*' is true if and only if *s* is.

It may help to reflect that (S) is acceptable, if it is, because we are independently sure of the truth of 'Snow is white' and 'Grass is green'; but in cases where we are unsure of the truth of a sentence, we can have confidence in a characterization of the truth predicate only if it pairs that sentence with one we have good reason to believe equivalent. It would be ill advised for someone who had any doubts about the colour of snow or grass to accept a theory that yielded (S), even if his doubts were of equal degree, unless he thought the colour of the one was tied to the colour of the other.[10] Omniscience can obviously afford more bizzare theories of meaning than ignorance; but then, omniscience has less need of communication.

It must be possible, of course, for the speaker of one language to construct a theory of meaning for the speaker of another, though in this case the empirical test of the correctness of the theory will no longer be trivial. As before, the aim of theory will be an infinite correlation of sentences alike in truth. But this time the theory-builder must not be assumed to have direct insight into likely equivalences between his own tongue and the alien. What he must do is find out, however he can, what sentences the alien holds true in his own tongue (or better, to what degree he holds them true). The linguist then will attempt to construct a characterization of truth-for-the-alien which yields, so far as possible, a mapping of sentences held true (or false) by the alien on to sentences held true (or false) by the linguist. Supposing no perfect fit is found, the residue of sentences held true translated by sentences held false (and vice versa) is the margin for error (foreign or domestic). Charity in interpreting the words and thoughts of others is unavoidable in another direction as well: just as we must maximize agreement, or risk not making sense of what the alien is talking about, so we must maximize the self-consistency we attribute to him, on pain of not understanding *him*. No single principle of optimum charity emerges; the constraints therefore determine no single theory. In a theory of radical translation (as Quine calls it) there is no completely disentangling questions of what the alien means from questions of what he believes. We do not know what someone means unless we know what he believes; we do not know what someone believes unless we know what he means. In radical interpretation we are able to break into this circle, if only incompletely, because we can sometimes tell that a person accedes to a sentence we do not understand.[11]

In the past few pages I have been asking how a theory of meaning that takes the form of a truth definition can be empirically tested, and have blithely ignored the prior question whether there is any serious chance such a theory can been given for a natural language. What are the prospects for a formal semantical theory of a natural language? Very poor, according to Tarski; and I believe most logicians, philosophers of language, and linguists agree.[12] Let me do what I can to dispel the pessimism. What I can in a general and programmatic way, of course, for here the proof of the pudding will certainly be in the proof of the right theorems.

Tarski concludes the first section of his classic essay on the concept of truth in formalized languages with the following remarks, which he italicizes:

… *The very possibility of a consistent use of the expression 'true sentence' which is in harmony with the laws of logic and the spirit of everyday language seems to be very questionable, and consequently the same doubt attaches to the possibility of constructing a correct definition of this expression.* (165)

Late in the same essay, he returns to the subject:

… the concept of truth (as well as other semantical concepts) when applied to colloquial language in conjunction with the normal laws of logic leads inevitably to confusions and contradictions. Whoever wishes, in spite of all difficulties, to pursue the semantics of colloquial language with help of exact methods will be driven first to undertake the thankless task of a reform of this language. He will find it necessary to define its structure, to overcome the ambiguity of the terms which occur in it, and finally to split the language into a series of languages of greater and greater extent, each of which stands in the same relation to the next in which a formalized language stands to its metalanguage. It may, however be doubted whether the language of everyday life, after being 'rationalized' in this way, would still preserve its naturalness and whether it would not rather take on the characteristic features of the formalized languages. (267)

Two themes emerge: that the universal character of natural languages leads to contradiction (the semantic paradoxes), and that natural languages are too confused and amorphous to permit the direct application of formal methods. The first point deserves a serious answer, and I wish I had one. As it is, I will say only why I think we are justified in carrying on without having disinfected this particular source of conceptual anxiety. The semantic paradoxes arise when the range of the quantifiers in the object language is too generous in certain ways. But it is not really clear how unfair to Urdu or to Wendish it would be to view the range of their quantifiers as insufficient to yield and explicit definition of 'true-in-Urdu' or 'true-in-Wendish'. Or, to put the matter in another, if not more serious way, there may in the nature of the case always be something we grasp in understanding the language of another (the concept of truth) that we cannot communicate to him. In any case, most of the problems of general philosophical interest arise within a fragment of the relevant natural language that may be conceived as containing very little set theory. Of course these comments do not meet the claim that natural languages are universal. But it seems to me that this claim, now that we know such universality leads to paradox, is suspect.

Tarski's second point is that we would have to reform a natural language out of all recognition before we could apply formal semantical methods. If this is true, it is fatal to my project, for the task of a theory of meaning as I conceive it is not to change, improve, or reform a language, but to describe and understand it. Let us look at the positive side. Tarski has shown the way to giving a theory for interpreted formal languages of various kinds; pick one as much like English as possible. Since this new language has been explained in English and contains much English we not only may, but I think must, view it as part of English for those who understand it. For this fragment of English we have, *ex hypothesi*, a theory of the required sort. Not only that, but in interpreting this adjunct of English in old English we necessarily gave hints connecting old and new. Wherever there are sentences of old English with the same truth conditions as sentences in the adjunct we may extend the theory to cover them. Much of what is called for is to mechanize as far as possible what we now do by art when we put ordinary English into one or another canonical notation. The point is not that canonical notation is better than the rough original idiom, but rather that if we know what idiom the canonical notation is canonical *for*, we have as good a theory for the idiom as for its kept companion.

Philosophers have long been at the hard work of applying theory to ordinary language by the device of matching sentences in the vernacular with sentences for which they have a theory. Frege's massive contribution was to show how 'all', 'some', 'every', 'each', 'none', and associated pronouns, in some of their uses, could be tamed; for the first time, it was possible to dream of a formal semantics for a significant part of a natural language. This dream came true in a sharp way with the work of Tarski. It would be a shame to miss the fact that as a result of these two magnificent achievements, Frege's and Tarski's, we have gained a deep insight into the structure of our mother tongues. Philosophers of a logical bent have tended to start where the theory was and work out towards the complications of natural language. Contemporary linguists, with an aim that cannot easily be seen to be different, start with the ordinary and work toward a general theory. If either party is successful, there must be a meeting. Recent work by Chomsky and others is doing much to bring the complexities of natural languages within the scope of serious theory. To give an example: suppose success in giving the truth conditions for some significant range of sentences in the active voice. Then with a formal procedure for transforming each such sentence into a corresponding sentence in the passive voice, the theory of truth could be extended in an obvious way to this new set of sentences.[13]

One problem touched on in passing by Tarski does not, at least in all its manifestations, have to be solved to get ahead with theory: the existence in natural languages of 'ambiguous terms'. As long as ambiguity does not affect grammatical form, and can be translated, ambiguity for ambiguity, into the metalanguage, a truth definition will not tell us any lies. The chief trouble, for systematic semantics, with the phrase 'believes that' in English lies not in its vagueness, ambiguity, or unsuitability for incorporation in a serious science: let our metalanguage be English, and all *these* problems will be carried without loss or gain into the metalanguage. But the central problem of the logical grammar of 'believes that' will remain to haunt us.

The example is suited to illustrating another, and related, point, for the discussion of belief sentences has been plagued by failure to observe a fundamental distinction between tasks: uncovering the logical grammar or form of sentences (which is in the province of a theory of meaning as I construe it), and the analysis of individual words or expressions (which are treated as primitive by the theory). Thus Carnap, in the first edition of *Meaning and Necessity*, suggested we render 'John believes that the earth is round' as 'John responds affirmatively to "the earth is round" as an English sentence'. He gave this up when Mates pointed out that John might respond affirmatively to one sentence and not to another no matter how close in meaning.[14] But there is a confusion here from the start. The semantic structure of a belief sentence, according to this idea of Carnap's, is given by a three-place predicate with places reserved for expressions referring to a person, a sentence, and a language. It is a different sort of problem entirely to attempt an analysis of this predicate, perhaps along behaviouristic lines. Not least among the merits of Tarski's conception of a theory of truth is that the purity of method it demands of us follows from the formulation of the problem itself, not from the self-imposed restraint of some adventitious philosophical puritanism.

I think it is hard to exaggerate the advantages to philosophy of language of bearing in mind this distinction between questions of logical form or grammar, and the analysis of individual concepts. Another example may help advertise the point.

If we suppose questions of logical grammar settled, sentences like 'Bardot is good' raise no special problems for a truth definition. The deep differences between descriptive and evaluative (emotive, expressive, etc.) terms do not show here. Even if we hold there is some important sense in which moral or evaluative sentences do not have a truth value (for example, because they cannot be verified), we ought not to boggle at ' "Bardot is good" is true if and only if Bardot is good'; in a theory of truth, this consequence should follow with the rest, keeping track, as must be done, of the semantic location of such sentences in the language as a whole—of their relation to generalizations, their role in such compound sentences as 'Bardot is good and Bardot is foolish', and so on. What is special to evaluative words is simply not touched: the mystery is transferred from the word 'good' in the object language to its translation in the metalanguage.

But 'good' as it features in 'Bardot is a good actress' is another matter. The problem is not that the translation of this sentence is not in the metalanguage—let us suppose it is. The problem is to frame a truth definition such that ' "Bardot is a good actress" is true if and only if Bardot is a good actress'—and all other sentences like it—are consequences. Obviously 'good actress' does not mean 'good and an actress'. We might think of taking 'is a good actress' as an unanalysed predicate. This would obliterate all connection between 'is a good actress' and 'is a good mother', and it would give us no excuse to think of 'good', in these uses, as a word or semantic element. But worse, it would bar us from framing a truth definition at all, for there is no end to the predicates we would have to treat as logically simple (and hence accommodate in separate clauses in the definition of satisfaction): 'is a good companion to dogs', 'is a good 28-years old conversationalist', and so forth. The problem is not peculiar to the case: it is the problem of attributive adjectives generally.

It is consistent with the attitude taken here to deem it usually a strategic error to undertake philosophical analysis of words or expressions which is not preceded by or at any rate accompanied by the attempt to get the logical grammar straight. For how can we have any confidence in our analyses of words like 'right', 'ought', 'can', and 'obliged', or the phrases we use to talk of actions, events, and causes, when we do not know what (logical, semantical) parts of speech we have to deal with? I would say much the same about studies of the 'logic' of these and other words, and the sentences containing them. Whether the effort and ingenuity that have gone into the study of deontic logics, modal logics, imperative and erotetic logics have been largely futile or not cannot be known until we have acceptable semantic analyses of the sentences such systems purport to treat. Philosophers and logicians sometimes talk or work as if they were free to choose between, say, the truth-functional conditional and others, or free to introduce non-truth-functional sentential operators like 'Let it be the case that' or 'It ought to be the case that'. But in fact the decision is crucial. When we depart from idioms we can accommodate in a truth definition, we lapse into (or create) language for which we have no coherent semantical account—that is, no account at all of how such talk can be integrated into the language as a whole.

To return to our main theme: we have recognized that a theory of the kind proposed leaves the whole matter of what individual words mean exactly where it was. Even when the metalanguage is different from the object language, the theory exerts no pressure for improvement, clarification, or analysis of individual words, except when, by accident of vocabulary, straightforward translation fails. Just as synonymy, as between expressions, goes generally untreated, so also synonymy of sentences, and analyticity. Even such sentences as 'A vixen is a female fox' bear no special tag unless it is our pleasure to provide it. A truth definition does not distinguish between analytic sentences and others, except for sentences that owe their truth to the presence alone of the constants that give the theory its grip on structure: the theory entails not only that these sentences are true but that they will remain true under all significant rewritings of their non-logical parts. A notion of logical truth thus given limited application, related notions of logical equivealence and entailment will tag along. It is hard to imagine how a theory of meaning could fail to read a logic into its object language to this degree; and to the extent that it does, our intuitions of logical truth, equivalence, and entailment may be called upon in constructing and testing the theory.

I turn now to one more, and very large, fly in the ointment: the fact that the same sentence may at one time or in one mouth be true and at another time or in another mouth be false. Both logicians and those critical of formal methods here seem largely (though by no means universally) agreed that formal semantics and logic are incompetent to deal with the disturbances caused by demonstratives. Logicians have often reacted by downgrading natural language and trying to show how to get along without demonstratives; their critics react by downgrading logic and formal semantics. None of this can make me happy: clearly demonstratives cannot be eliminated from a natural language without loss or radical change, so there is no choice but to accommodate theory to them.

No logical errors result if we simply treat demonstratives as constants;[15] neither do any problems arise for giving a semantic truth definition. '"I am wise" is true if and only if I am wise', with its bland ignoring of the demonstrative element in 'I' comes off the assembly line along with '"Socrates is wise" is true if and only if Socrates is wise' with *its* bland indifference to the demonstrative element in 'is wise' (the tense).

What suffers in this treatment of demonstratives is not the definition of a truth predicate, but the plausibility of the claim that what has been defined is truth. For this claim is acceptable only if the speaker and circumstances of utterance of each sentence mentioned in the definition is matched by the speaker and circumstances of utterance of the truth definition itself. It could also be fairly pointed out that part of understanding demonstratives is knowing the rules by which they adjust their reference to circumstance; assimilating demonstratives to constant terms obliterates this feature. These complaints can be met, I think though only by a fairly far-reaching revision in the theory of truth. I shall barely suggest how this could be done, but bare suggestion is all that is needed: the idea is technically trivial, and in line with work being done on the logic of the tenses.[16]

We could take truth to be a property, not of sentences, but of utterances, or speech acts, or ordered triples of sentences, times, and persons; but it is simplest just to view truth as a relation between a sentence, a person, and a time. Under such treatment, ordinary logic as now read applies as usual, but only to sets of sentences relativized to the same speaker and time; further logical relations between sentences spoken at different times and by different speakers may be articulated by new axioms. Such is not my concern. The theory of meaning undergoes a systematic but not puzzling change; corresponding to each expression with a demonstrative element there must in the theory be a phrase that relates the truth conditions of sentences in which the expression occurs to changing times and speakers. Thus the theory will entail sentences like the following:

'I am tired' is true as (potentially) spoken by p at t if and only if p is tired at t.

'That book was stolen' is true as (potentially) spoken by p at t if and only if the book demonstrated by p at t is stolen prior to t.[17]

Plainly, this course does not show how to eliminate demonstratives; for example, there is no suggestion that 'the book demonstrated by the speaker' can be substituted ubiquitously for 'that book' *salva veritate*. The fact that demonstratives are amenable to formal treatment ought greatly to improve hopes for a serious semantics of natural language, for it is likely that many outstanding puzzles, such as the analysis of quotations or sentences about propositional attitudes, can be solved if we recognize a concealed demonstrative construction.

Now that we have relativized truth to times and speakers, it is appropriate to glance back at the problem of empirically testing a theory of meaning for an alien tongue. The essence of the method was, it will be remembered, to correlate held-true sentences with held-true sentences by way of a truth definition, and within the bounds of intelligible error. Now the picture must be elaborated to allow for the fact that sentences are true, and held true, only relative to a speaker and a time. Sentences with demonstratives obviously yield a very sensitive test of the correctness of a theory of meaning, and constitute the most direct link between language and the recurrent macroscopic objects of human interest and attention.[18]

In this paper I have assumed that the speakers of a language can effectively determine the meaning or meanings of an arbitrary expression (if it has a meaning), and that it is the central task of a theory of meaning to show how this is possible. I have argued that a characterization of a truth predicate describes the required kind of structure, and provides a clear and testable criterion of an adequate semantics for a natural language. No doubt there are other reasonable demands that may be put on a theory of meaning. But a theory that does no more than define truth for a language comes far closer to constituting a complete theory of meaning than superficial analysis might suggest; so, at least, I have urged.

Since I think there is no alternative, I have taken an optimistic and programmatic view of the possibilities for a formal characterization of a truth predicate for a natural language. But it must be allowed that a staggering list of difficulties and conundrums remains. To name a few: we do not know the logical form of counterfactual or subjunctive sentences; nor of sentences about probabilities and about causal relations; we have no good idea what the logical role of adverbs is, nor the role of attributive adjectives; we have no theory for mass terms like 'fire', 'water', and 'snow', nor for sentences about belief, perception, and intention, nor for verbs of action that imply purpose. And finally, there are all the sentences that seem not to have truth values at all: the imperatives, optatives, interrogatives, and a host more. A comprehensive theory of meaning for a natural language must cope successfully with each of these problems.

Notes

1. A 'structural description' of an expression describes the expression as a concatenation of elements drawn from a fixed finite list (for example of words or letters).

2. The argument derives from Frege. See A. Church, *Introduction to Mathematical Logic*, 24–5. It is perhaps worth mentioning that the argument does not depend on any particular identification of the entities to which sentences are supposed to refer.

3. It may be thought that Church, in 'A Formulation of the Logic of Sense and Denotation' (in *Structure, Method, and Meaning*, ed. P. Henle, H. M. Kallen, and S. K. Langer), has given a theory of meaning that makes essential use of meanings as entities. But this is not the case: Church's logics of sense and denotation are

interpreted as being about meanings, but they do not mention expressions and so cannot of course be theories of meaning in the sense now under discussion.

4. For a recent statement of the role of semantics in linguistics, see Noam Chomsky, 'Topics in the Theory of Generative Grammar' (in *Theoretical Foundations*, Current Trends in Linguistics, no. 3, ed. T. A. Sebeok). In this article, Chomsky (1) emphasizes the central importance of semantics in linguistic theory, (2) argues for the superiority of transformational grammars over phrase-structure grammars largely on the grounds that, although phrase-structure grammars may be adequate to define sentencehood for (at least) some natural languages, they are inadequate as a foundation for semantics, and (3) comments repeatedly on the 'rather primitive state' of the concepts of semantics and remarks that the notion of semantic interpretation 'still resists any deep analysis'.

5. Assuming, of course, that the extension of these predicates is limited to the sentences of *L*.

6. A. Tarski, 'The Concept of Truth in Formalized Languages', (in his *Logic, Semantics, Metamathematics*).

7. But Quine may be quoted in support of my usage: '. . . in point of *meaning* . . . a word may be said to be determined to whatever extent the truth or falsehood of its contexts is determined.' ('Truth by Convention', in his *Ways of Paradox*, 82.) Since a truth definition determines the truth value of every sentence in the object language (relative to a sentence in the metalanguage), it determines the meaning of every word and sentence. This would seem to justify the title Theory of Meaning.

8. To give a single example: it is clearly a count in favour of a theory that it entails ' "Snow is white" is true if and only if snow is white'. But to contrive a theory that entails this (and works for all related sentences) is not trivial. I do not know a wholly satisfactory theory that succeeds with this very case (the problem of 'mass terms').

9. Critics have often failed to notice the essential proviso mentioned in this paragraph. The point is that (*S*) could not belong to any reasonably simple theory that also gave the right truth conditions for 'That is snow' and 'This is white'. (See the discussion of indexical expressions below.) [Footnote added in 1982.]

10. This paragraph is confused. What it should say is that sentences of the theory are empirical generalizations about speakers, and so must not only be true but also lawlike. (*S*) presumably is not a law, since it does not support appropriate counter-factuals. It's also important that the evidence for accepting the (time and speaker relativized) truth conditions for 'That is snow' is based on the causal connection between a speaker's assent to the sentence and the demonstrative presentation of snow. For further discussion see Essay 12. [Footnote added in 1982.]

11. This sketch of how a theory of meaning for an alien tongue can be tested obviously owes it inspiration to Quine's account of radical translation in Chapter II of *Word and Object*. In suggesting that an acceptable theory of radical translation take the form of a recursive characterization of truth, I go beyond Quine. Toward the end of this paper, in the discussion of demonstratives, another strong point of agreement will turn up.

12. So far as I am aware, there has been very little discussion of whether a formal truth definition can be given for a natural language. But in a more general vein, several people have urged that the concepts of formal semantics be applied to natural language. See, for example, the contributions of Yehoshua Bar-Hillel and Evert Beth to *The Philosophy of Rudolph Carnap*, and Bar-Hillel's 'Logical Syntax and Semantics' (*Language* 30 [1954], 230–7).

13. The *rapprochement* I prospectively imagine between transformational grammar and a sound theory of meaning has been much advanced by a recent change in the conception of transformational grammar described by Chomsky in the article referred to above (note 4). The structures generated by the phrase-structure part of the grammar, it has been realized for some time, are those suited to semantic interpretation; but this view is inconsistent with the idea, held by Chomsky until recently, that recursive operations are introduced only by the transformation rules. Chomsky now believes the phrase-structure rules are recursive. Since languages to which formal semantic methods directly and naturally apply are ones for which a (recursive) phrase-structure grammar is appropriate, it is clear that Chomsky's present picture of the relation between the structures generated by the phrase-structure part of the grammar, and the sentences of the language, is very much like the picture many logicians and philosophers have had of the relation between the richer formalized languages and ordinary language. (In these remarks I am indebted to Bruce Vermazen.)

14. B. Mates, 'Synonymity', (in *Semantics and the Philosophy of Language*, ed. L. Linsky).

15. See W. V. Quine, *Methods of Logic*, 8.

16. This claim has turned out to be naïvely optimistic. For some serious work on the subject, see S. Weinstein, 'Truth and Demonstratives' (*Noûs* 8 [1974], 179–84). [Note added in 1982.]

17. There is more than an intimation of this approach to demonstratives and truth in J. L. Austin, 'Truth' (*Aristotelian Society*, suppl. vol. 24 [1950]).

18. These remarks derive from Quine's idea that 'occasion sentences' (those with a demonstrative element) must play a central role in constructing a translation manual.

Chapter 6

What Model-Theoretic Semantics Cannot Do

Ernest Lepore

It has frequently been argued that Structural Semantic theories (e.g., Katz [13, 14, 16, 18], Jackendoff [12], and some versions of Generative Semantics [1, 21, 27, 28]) are deficient in an essential way. Cresswell [3], Lewis [24], Partee [32], and Vermazen [39] (among others) all argue that Structural Semantic theories (hereafter, SS) do not articulate relations between expressions and the world, that they do not provide an account of the conditions under which sentences are true, and therefore, these theories are not really semantics. In their place, many philosophers and linguists endorse model-theoretic semantics (hereafter, MTS).[1] They do so because they believe that MTS compensates for what is deficient in SS. My aim in this discussion is to reconstruct the case against SS by demonstrating that the concept of truth is central to semantics and that a theory which issues in truth-conditions for sentences of a language L must be the heart of a semantic theory for L. But I will also argue that MTS theories by themselves, somewhat surprisingly, are inadequate in exactly the same way as SS theories. If I am correct, then the widespread view that MTS can provide either a theory of meaning or a theory of truth-conditions for the sentences of a natural language is mistaken.

1

SS theorists countenance properties and relations like synonymy, antinomy, meaningfulness, meaninglessness or semantic anomaly, redundancy, and ambiguity as a good initial conception of the range of semantics. They do so because, for them, a semantic theory for a language

First appeared in *Synthese* 54 (1983): 167–187. Reprinted with kind permission from Kluwer Academic Publishers.

L is a theory of meaning for L and they believe that properties and relations like these are central to our concept of meaning. Therefore, any theory which did not bear on all, or at least many, of these phenomena should be suspect as a semantic theory [8, 14].

Theories in the SS vein proceed by translating or mapping natural language expressions into (sequences or sets of) expressions of another language. There is no uniformity among SS theorists about the nature of this other language or about how these translations or mappings are to be effected.[2] For our purposes we beg no questions by restricting attention to Katz's suggestion, where the language translated or mapped into is "Semantic Markerese" [13, 14, 16, 18]. The culmination of the various translation rules and other apparatus within Katz's theory result in theorems like (A):

(A) "Barbara sekoilee" in Finnish translates into the language of
    Semantic Markerese as *S*.

Translations of this kind are constrained, and this is the reason for bringing them in along with the semantic markers in the first place, such that synonymous expressions of some language *L* translate into the same (sequence or set of) expressions of Semantic Markerese, ambiguous expressions of *L* translate into different expressions of Semantic Markerese, anomalous expressions of *L* translate into no expressions of Semantic Markerese at all, and so on. Facts about synonymy, ambiguity, anomaly, and other semantic properties and relations are accounted for through these representations, translations and semantic constraints (or definitions).

Some critics of Katz's theory charge that the phenomena he concerns himself with represent only a sample of the full range of facts semantics must ultimately deal with, and they argue that SS cannot in principle accommodate this full range. In particular, some argue that it is the construction of truth-conditions which should count as the central concern of semantics, not these other properties and relations, and that SS theories cannot provide truth-conditions.[3] This raises two questions: why can't SS theories provide truth-conditions and why should they? This second question is especially significant inasmuch as SS theorists have expressed bewilderment in the face of the criticism that their theories do not specify truth-conditions.

Katz, for one, agrees that his semantic theory leaves out the notion of truth, and therefore, does not specify truth-conditions, but, he goes on to say, "the subject matter to which 'truth' is central is not one that my semantic theory is or was ever intended to be about" [14:182]. If "semantics" is construed as having to do with meaning, then truth "is not central to semantics and so there can be no claim that my theory has left out something central" [14:182]. As Katz sees it, the criticism that his theory does not specify truth-conditions trades off an ambiguity of the term "semantics." For SS theorists the goal of a semantic theory is to construct a theory of meaning, whereas for their critics, the goal of a semantic theory is "to study relations between objects of one sort or another and the expressions of a language that speak about them" [14:183], relations which ultimately get spelled out through truth-conditions for sentences of this language. Therefore, if the criticism that SS theories do not specify truth-conditions is to carry any force with Katz, we must show that a semantic theory for a natural language which has as its goal the construction of a theory of meaning for this language must, in order to achieve this goal, specify truth-conditions for sentences of this language. This would have the effect of collapsing Katz's two senses of "semantics" into one. We take a step in this direction by asking, what should we expect from a semantic theory as a theory of meaning?

Traditional wisdom about meaning is that it is in virtue of knowing what a sentence means that we (in part) understand it. For example, it is in virtue of knowing what "Barbara sekoilee" means alone that I am warranted in believing that an assertive utterance of these words is an assertion that Barbara is confused. If I further know that these words are true on the occasion of utterance, then knowing their meaning warrants (in part) my believing that Barbara is confused as well.[4]

This illustration brings out nicely the two-sidedness of the concept of meaning. On the one hand, meaning is connected with a host of extensional concepts: satisfaction, denotation, truth and so on. This is reflected in the principle implicit in our example: if a sentence S is true, and if S means that p, then p. On the other hand, meaning is connected with a host of intensional concepts: indirect quotation, assertibility, and so on. This is reflected in the connection we just saw between meaning and indirect quotation: if someone assertively utters a sentence S, and S means that p, then this person says that p. Given the meaning of a sentence, this duality permits us to move in either of two directions. We can exploit the relationship between meaning and truth to infer something about the world beyond the speaker, or we can exploit the relationship between meaning and certain intensional notions to infer something about the speaker himself, what he asserted, queried, commanded, etc. With this wisdom in mind, we expect a semantic theory as a theory of understanding (or, as a theory of semantic competence) for a language L to at least specify the meanings of sentences of L.[5] SS theorists agree about this, but they have erred in assuming that any semantic theory which accounts for semantic properties and relations like ambiguity and synonymy in the manner suggested above will as a matter of course also specify meanings for sentences in an appropriate way.

Any SS theory which issues in (A) certainly entails (B):

(B) "Barbara sekoilee" means the same as S.

Therefore, any SS theory which issues in (A) can be said to specify the meaning of "Barbara sekoilee" but not in an appropriate way since (B) alone will not warrant its knower in believing that an assertive utterance of the sentence named on the left is an assertion that Barbara is confused. Nor would its knower be warranted in believing that Barbara is confused if he further knew that this sentence is true. Why not?

In the overall picture of SS there are three languages: the natural language, the language of Semantic Markers, and the translating language (which may be Semantic Markerese, the natural language, or some other language). Translation proceeds by correlating the first two of these using the third. But it is possible to understand (A) or (B) knowing only the translating language (in this case English) and not the other two. Put somewhat differently, we can know that a sentence translates, or means the same as, another without knowing what either means. We can know that (A) or (B), perhaps, on the basis of what Katz tells us, without knowing what either "Barbara sekoilee" or the Semantic Markerese sentence S means.

Of course, if someone understands Semantic Markerese, then he can no doubt use (B) to interpret the Finnish sentence; but this is because he brings to bear two things he knows that (B) does not state: that Semantic Markerese is a language he understands, and his particular knowledge how to interpret S. This latter knowledge is doing most of the work here—not the SS theory. And it is this knowledge we want an adequate semantic theory of meaning to characterize.

Nothing we have said so far, however, establishes either that a semantic theory as a theory of meaning should be concerned with truth-conditions, nor, for that matter, that SS theories cannot be used to assign truth-conditions. In fact, there is some prima facie evidence to think that SS theories can be used to assign truth-conditions to sentences. For, surely, if (A) holds, then it follows that (C):

(C) "Barbara sekoilee" is true in Finnish if and only if S is true in Semantic Markerese.

Since S's being true in semantic Markerese is one condition under which "Barbara sekoilee" is true in Finnish, shouldn't (C) count as providing truth-conditions for the Finnish sentence? It would seem that if there is a deficiency in SS theories with respect to truth-conditions, then something must be wrong with the kind of specification of truth-conditions (C) provides. To see that this is so, we must ask why a semantic theory as a theory of meaning should be concerned with truth-conditions in the first place.

We said before that someone who knows the meaning of "Barbara sekoilee" would, presumably, be warranted in believing that Barbara is confused if he further knew these words were true. But this is exactly what we would expect someone to be licensed to believe if he knew the conditions under which the sentence is true. The sentence is true if and only if Barbara is confused. That is to say, at least for a straightforward declarative sentence, in specifying the conditions that have to hold for it to be true, we are in effect characterizing a central aspect of its meaning.

Seen from another angle, suppose that someone knows the meaning of "Barbara sekoilee" and knows all the relevant facts (or, not to be tendentious, knows everything in the *world* there is to know), then this person will know whether the sentence is true. How could this be unless meaning determined truth-value throughout the relevant possible states of affairs? And, if meaning does determine truth-value in this way, then a theory of meaning for a language will have to specify truth-conditions. (Indeed, many semanticists would go so far as to say that knowledge of truth-conditions for a sentence *is* knowledge of its meaning cf., e.g., [3]. They do so because they believe that knowledge of truth-conditions warrants whatever knowledge of meanings has traditionally been thought to warrant.)

If the meaning of a sentence includes as a part (or is identical to) truth-conditions for this sentence, then any semantic theory for a language which purports to be a theory of meaning for this language must specify the truth-conditions for each sentence of the language. From this it does not follow that *any* semantic theory which provides a complete specification of truth conditions for sentences of this language is adequate. An SS theory which issues in theorems like (A) may entail (C), but (C) alone does not warrant its knower to believe that Barbara is confused if he further knows that "Barbara sekoilee" is true. This is because (C) does not specify truth conditions for "Barbara sekoilee" in an appropriate way.

What we have shown is that SS theories, though they may account for some aspects of our concept of meaning, cannot account for them all. For whatever knowing the meaning of an expression includes, it does not involve simply translating the expression into a semi-formal language, nor telling us which other sentence it means the same as, nor telling us which other sentence it has the same truth-conditions as. We turn now to MTS with an eye towards how it can compensate for what is deficient in SS; how is MTS able to provide an explicit characterization of what SS assumes and leaves unsaid?

2

Model theory has traditionally been used as a mathematical technique for investigating certain properties of formal systems such as consistency, completeness, the finite model property and having a decision procedure. There is now a growing impression among linguists and philosophers that model theory can provide a theory of meaning for natural languages. This view has greatly come into its own in the last few decades largely because of the work of Kripke [19, 20], van Fraassen [38], Hintikka [10], Montague [29, 30, 31], Lewis [24], and others. These authors have developed MTS for formal systems of many valued, sortal, free, tense, demonstrative, counter-factual and modal logics. These results have encouraged many researchers to believe that MTS may be sufficiently powerful to provide a theory of meaning for substantial fragments of natural language. There are many competing approaches; each, however, seeks to characterize (or define) a relativized concept of truth (at a world, time, or whatever other index is deemed relevant). Here I will focus discussion on Montague Grammar, in particular his theory in [31] (hereafter, PTQ). What I have to say about PTQ extends obviously to any MTS approach. Montague personally was not interested in a theory of understanding. My discussion, however, is directed not to Montague, but instead to those semanticists who are interested in formal semantics as a theory of understanding, and to those who have argued that MTS constitutes a real advance over SS. I focus on PTQ because it is familiar and because many semanticists who are interested in semantic competence employ the theory of PTQ or some variant of it [33].

In PTQ, Montague proposes a general theory of syntax and MTS. He treats a fragment of English which includes simple quantification and some intensional verbs. His theory involves three distinct phases: English expressions are assigned a syntactic analysis with respect to a categorial grammar. This syntax is translated into the syntax of a tensed intensional logic with various nonlogical constants. Finally, the expressions of this intensional logic undergo model-theoretic interpretation. This interpretation proceeds by linking linguistic entities with nonlinguistic entities in two ways: method of extension and method of intension.

The extension of an expression from some language L is determined relative to an interpretation A of L and a world w and time t in A (i.e., relative to the model $\langle A \langle w, t \rangle \rangle$ of L). In short, it is the object the expression denotes in A at w and t. The intension of this expression is the meaning, sense or concept correlated with the expression. Instead of treating intensions as basic, as some kind of ideal abstract entity or mental representation, Montague defines the intension of an expression as a function: it is the function which, for every possible world w and time t (in A), picks out exactly those objects in A which make up the extension of this expression in A at w and t. We need not go into any great detail. Suffice it to say that the culmination of the various definitions, translations, rules and other apparatus within PTQ result in theorems like the following:

(E) "Barbara sekoilee" is true in an interpretation A at a world w and a time t (in A) if and only if the extension picked out by the intension of "Barbara" in A at w and t is a member of the extension picked out by the intension of "sekoilee" in A at w and t.

(I) The intension of "Barbara sekoilee" in an interpretation A is a complex function from the set of possible worlds and times in A onto the set of truth values, true and false, where this complex function is arrived at by composing the intension of "Barbara" with the intension of "sekoilee." The intension of "Barbara" is a function from possible worlds and times (in A) to individuals in A. Similarly, the intension of "sekoilee" in A is a function from possible worlds and times (in A) to functions from individuals in A to truth values (alternatively, one can say, from possible worlds and times to classes of individuals). (Montague has different intensions for proper names and he treats predicate intensions as arguments of proper name intensions in composing the two functions. Neither of these points, however, affects the present discussion. I have chosen these intensions of expository purposes.)

It is held by many MTS theorists that there are important advantages PTQ offers over its SS competitors [cf. 3, 24, 29, 32]. It is distinguished from an SS approach inasmuch as instead of linking expressions of one language with expressions of another (i.e., instead of stopping at phase two in PTQ), PTQ links expressions to non-linguistic entities (the third phrase in PTQ). Our question is, Why should these links sign post an advance over SS? What advantages accrue to PTQ is virtue of having consequences like (E) and (I) that do not accrue to SS theories?

The PTQ embodies some very special claims about the fundamental nature of semantic interpretation, and about the way in which syntax and semantics systematically correlate. This correlation embodies the familiar Fregean principle of compositionality: stated crudely, this is the principle that "the meaning of the whole is a function of the meanings of its parts." The correlation is realized in Montague's work by giving the syntax the form of a simultaneous recursive definition of the sets of well-formed expressions of each syntactic category of the language, recursively building up larger phrases and clauses from smaller ones, and associating with each syntactic formation rule a semantic interpretation rule that specifies the interpretation of the constitutent phrases. Most semanticists argue that an adequate theory of meaning must embody this kind of compositionality; otherwise, it would be impotent to account for the obvious and essential fact that we can understand hitherto unencountered sentences.[6]

Evaluation of a semantic theory for some language is not limited to whether or not it embodies a principle of compositionality alone. It involves also, to some extent, evaluating how accurate a map the theory provides of the logical geography of the language, i.e., the logical consequences, truths, equivalences and other logical properties and relations. After all, part of understanding a language involves knowing which sentences stand in logical relationships (like logical consequence) to others. Someone who did not know that whenever a sentence of the form $\ulcorner P$ and $Q \urcorner$ is true, then sentence $\ulcorner Q \urcorner$ is true, cannot be said to understand English or at least one important word in English, "and." One important benefit MTS offers is a way to define these important logical notions. (If we consider a subset K of the models determined by an interpretation for some language, we can define a sentence O as K-valid if it is true in each of these models in K. If K is the set of models (determined by any interpretation) in which all the logical words of the language ("not," "or," "and," etc.) receive the extensions usually given by logicians to these words, then these will be the logically possible models for L. Then K validity is logical-validity. In PTQ, Montague effects this restriction by a set of meaning postulates. Meaning postulates are ways of placing restrictions on the interpretation of expressions. We could have a notion of logical validity based on the subset of models in which all of the meaning postulates are true [30:236; 31:263].)

Giving an account of compositionality and of logical consequence, therefore, are two central goals for PTQ. But—and this is a big "but"—these two goals are also central for SS. Katz seeks to embody a Fregean compositionality in his theory. His dictionary assigns a meaning ("lexical reading") to each basic expression of the language. Projection rules in his theory can be regarded as semantic operations, where there is a projection rule corresponding to each phrase structure rule. These projection rules combine recursively the readings for each node immediately dominating lower nodes [14, 18]. The more vital notion of entailment (and the family of notions definable in terms of it) Katz attempts to define not in terms of classes of models (nor in terms of inference in some formal deductive system), but rather in terms of containment of (parts of) one reading in another [14, 15, 17, 41].

None of the arguments in the critical literature shows that Katz's theory cannot in principle accommodate these two essential semantic features. And what's more important—and this is very important—the translation argument, the argument MTS theorists themselves have proferred in criticism of SS, was certainly not proferred to show that SS cannot account for compositionality or logical consequence. This is so because just as I can know that one sentence translates another without understanding either, I can know that the first entails the second without understanding either, without knowing what either means (though, perhaps, knowing that one sentence implies another is part of knowing what each sentence means). And, also, I can know how the parts of expressions combine to issue in the meanings of the larger expression without understanding this expression. If all we wanted from a semantic theory were to account for *these* two aspects of language, then no reason in principle has been proferred for preferring MTS over SS. Therefore, if SS is deficient in a way that MTS is not, then there must be another aspect of language that an adequate semantic theory must address which MTS addresses and SS does not.

The deficiency critics of SS emphasize is that SS fails to provide a connection between expressions and extralinguistic entities. Barbara Hall Partee, for example, writes:

Semantics [à la Montague and Thomason] has always been the study of the relations between expressions in a language and the non-linguistic subject matter that the expressions are about ... No amount of ... interlinguistic connections can serve to tie down the extralinguistic content of intensions. For that there must be some language-to-world ground [42].

Quotes of this sort can be produced ad infinitum. According to these authors, PTQ represents an advance over SS because it *requires* realizing a connection between expressions and extralinguistic entities. Contrary to SS, MTS proponents intend to break out of the "confines of language." Earlier we saw the importance of having a semantic theory that offered an explicit and general way of accounting for the relationships that hold between any sentence and a situation, where the sentence's truth conveys information about that situation. In virtue of understanding the sentence "Barbara sekoilee," I can come to have a belief about the nonlinguistic world, namely, the belief that Barbara is confused, upon hearing this utterance. A theory which never moves beyond mentioning language cannot accommodate this feature of language, for it is only by using language that we can talk about a nonlinguistic world. But, still, we must ask whether PTO issues in theorems which engineer transitions from utterances to assertions. We have no reason beforehand to assume that any linguistic/nonlinguistic link a theory forges will license ascriptions characteristic of language understanding. I will now argue that PTQ, like SS, does not provide enough to bridge the gap between utterance and assertion.

Suppose that Frank utters the words "Barbara sekoilee," and all I know about Frank's language is that (E') and (I') hold:

(E') "Barbara sekoilee" is true in Finnish if and only if whatever "Barbara" picks out is one of the things "sekoilee" is true of.

(I') The meaning of "Barbara sekoilee" in Finnish is the proposition which results from taking the meaning of "Barbara" as argument of the meaning of "sekoilee."

It would be quite remarkable if I were able to discern what Frank asserts when he utters "Barbara sekoilee," provided that (E') and (I') constituted the whole of my knowledge about Frank's language. Knowing that (E') or that (I'), at best warrants my believing that Frank asserted that something named "Barbara" has the expression "sekoilee" true of it. It would remain a mystery to me which thing it is, and exactly what is true of it.

Unless a sentence uttered is about language, reference to language must be eliminated entirely by any semantic theory which seeks to provide a theory of meaning; whatever we come up with has got to take its knower from the perception of the sequences of sounds to their characteristics. Once you understand the motivation for this condition you should see that PTQ, apart from whatever other riches it may yield, is as inadequate as SS. Both from the start take a wrong direction. We are never told straight out what the truth conditions or meanings of sentences are. Instead of fixing an interpretation of names and predicates, these are left open in PTQ. The notions of truth and denotation are defined relative to a given interpretation, which includes a given set of possible individuals, worlds, and times. (E) and (I) tell us how to derive the truth conditions of, and the proposition expressed by, the sentence "Barbara sekoilee" only relative to an interpretation A and a given world w and time t in A. In order to complete the disquotation and get at the actual truth conditions and propositions expressed by this sentence we need to specify (single out) the actual interpretation and the actual world and time. In this regard, it is illuminating to compare PTQ with Davidson's semantic theory.

Davidson's theory differs from PTQ in at least one important respect. Davidson [4] argues that the kind of structure needed to account for language understanding is either identical with or closely related to the kind given by a definition of truth along the lines first expounded by Tarski [36]. Such a theory (by means of a set of axioms) entails for every sentence in the language a statement of the conditions under which it is true, expressed by biconditionals of the form "S is true if and only if p." [S here refers to the sentence whose truth-conditions are being given, and p is that sentence itself. If the language in which these truth conditions are being stated does not include the language to which S belongs, then p will have to be a translation of S.] This condition of adequacy excludes MTS theories because these theories move in a direction different from that proposed by Davidson's conditions. Since MTS theories substitute a relational concept for the single place truth-predicate, such theories cannot carry through the last step of the recursion of truth (or satisfaction) which is essential to the quotation lifting feature of the truth-condition bi-conditionals [5].

Put somewhat differently, from a relativized truth-theory we cannot derive an absolute truth-theory. Thus, suppose, for example, language L consists of one sentence, "Barbara sekoilee." An MTS theory for L along the lines of PTQ would issue in a theorem something like:

(1) $(A)(p)$ ("Barbara sekoilee" is true in A at p iff the extension of "Barbara" in A at p satisfies "sekoilee" in A at p),

where "A" ranges over interpretations and "p" ranges over possible worlds. (We omit reference to times.) From a relativized truth-theory for L like (1) we cannot derive an absolute truth-theory for L like (2):

(2) "Barbara sekoilee" is true iff Barbara is confused.

The weakest addition to (1) we could make in order to derive (2) from it is the following:

(3) $(\exists A)(\exists p)(x)$ ((the extension of "Barbara" in A at p = Barbara) & (x satisfies "sekoilee" in A at p iff x is confused) & ("Barbara sekoilee" is true in A at p iff "Barbara sekoilee" is true))

The first two clauses in (3) essentially say that, in order to understand L, we must know, in addition to (1), the base clauses in an absolute truth-theory for L, i.e.,

(4) The extension of "Barbara" = Barbara,

(5) (x) (x satisfies "sekoilee" iff x is confused).

The last clause in (3), essentially says that we must further know that interpretation A is the actual interpretation and some world p in A is the actual world. Knowing that A is the actual interpretation and p is the actual world licenses us to infer that truth in A at p is absolute truth.

What can we conclude from the fact that (1) alone does not imply (2)? Hartry Field raises this question in other context [44]: he asks whether the facts that, for example, (6) contains a semantic term where (4) does not, give theories which employ base clauses like (4) an advantage over those which employ base clauses like (6).

(6) "Barbara" denotes what it denotes.

After a long investigation, in which he finds no adequacy condition on an absolute truth theory which rules out (6) but not (4), he concludes that there is unlikely to be any philosophical purpose or interest that theories which employ clauses like (4) serve better than those which employ clauses like (6). Partee endorses Field's conclusion. She writes [43], pp. 321–22:

As Hartry Field argues, a Tarskian truth definition has at its basis a listing of denotation conditions for the primitive terms in the form (7), and for the primitives we might just as well start with the form (8).

(7) "Snow" denotes snow.

(8) "Snow" denotes what it denotes.

Partee agrees with Field [44] (and Harman [9]) that:

The real work of the truth definition and similarly for a Montague-style possible world semantics, comes in the specifications of how the interpretations of the infinite set of sentences can be determined by a finite set of rules from the interpretations of the primitives.

The idea here is that truth-conditional semantics illuminates meaning not by assigning truth-conditions but through exhibiting the roles of logical words "and," "or," etc., in its recursive clauses. Partee sees Tarski-style truth theories and MTS style theories equally inadequate when it comes to specifying the meaning of lexical items.

One author, Richmond Thomason, taking an uncharacteristically Quinian line, goes further by arguing that we *cannot* reasonably expect semantic theories to tell us anything important about the meaning of lexical items. He writes:

The problems of a semantic theory should be distinguished from those of lexicography.... A central goal of (semantics) is to explain how different kinds of meanings attach to different syntactic categories; another is to explain how the meanings of phrases depend on those of their components.... But we should not expect a semantic theory to furnish an account of how any two expressions belonging to the same syntactic category differ in meaning. "Walk" and "run," for instance, and "unicorn" and "zebra" certainly do differ in meaning, and we require a dictionary of English to tell us how. But the making of a dictionary demands considerable knowledge of the word [37:48–9].

To ask the semanticist to give a specification of the meanings of words would be to ask too much, since it would require of him that he construct a world encyclopedia.

Each of these authors has gone wrong because he or she has failed to appreciate the differences between an absolute truth theory and MTS. First, this can be seen with regard to Partee's and Field's claim that there are no advantages in absolute truth theory with base clauses like (4) has over a theory, e.g. an MTS theory, with base clauses like (6). Simply note that if these authors were right, then a Davidsonian truth theory would tell us no more about lexical semantics than Montague's theory. But we have shown that this is false. Adding (6) to PTQ will not license the kinds of reasoning we have been probing, reasoning we have argued is characteristic of language understanding. Adding (4) will. (6) does not eliminate reference to language in ways that (4) does.

What about Thomason's argument that lexical semantics is not part of semantics proper since to distinguish the meanings of any two terms frequently requires more information than we can reasonably expect a semantic theory to provide us with? We cannot reply to him that a semantic theory which does not specify the meanings of the lexical items of a language L fails to specify the knowledge requisite for understanding L. Thomason's position apparently is that we cannot reasonably expect a semantic theory to specify all this knowledge. Semantics proper, according to him, is to specify the meanings of the connectives involved in inference. But Thomason is wrong here. Why should we think that the specification of the knowledge required for understanding lexical items in our language demands as much knowledge as Thomason thinks? Put somewhat differently, what do we expect to achieve by eliminating reference to language in the base clauses of PTQ? Again, we want a theory which will provide truth conditions (and/or meanings) of sentences of the language in such a way that someone who knows these truth conditions (or meanings) would be licensed to believe that the speaker asserted, or would be licensed in believing what the speaker asserted about the world. Our question is what do we need to know about the difference (to borrow Thomason's own example) between the words "run" and "walk" to guarantee such competence? Presumably clauses like (9) and (10):

(9) (x) (x satisfies the predicate "run" iff x runs).

(10) (x) (x satisfies the predicate "walk" iff x walks).

Someone who had this knowledge would be licensed to believe that Barbara runs when he hears the words "Barbara runs" uttered by a reliable speaker and he would be licensed to believe that Barbara walks when he hears the words "Barbara walks." This knowledge does not seem at all to require considerable nonlinguistic knowledge In fact, if anything, it seems to be paradigmatic of linguistic semantic knowledge.

What does all this add up to? One response is to say that our results are unsurprising since MTS is primarily valuable as a theory of logical consequence rather than as a theory of meaning. These two kinds of theory have different goals which have induced salient differences in approach. A theory of logical consequence is concerned with the validity of forms of argument, represented by inference schemas. Therefore, it must attend to a multiplicity of possible interpretations of a sentence schema: the notion it requires is that of truth under an interpretation. A theory of meaning, as we have portrayed it here, is concerned only with a single interpretation of a language, the correct or intended one: so its fundamental notion is that of meaning or truth—simpliciter.

However, despite their differences in goals, these two theories have been closely allied historically. Throughout the subsequent course of both subjects, theorists of meaning have borrowed from theorists of logical consequence many of the concepts devised by logicians: MTS being a primary example. The differences in goals between the two subjects raises the question, How far can the devices employed by logicians be made to serve the different purposes of semanticists of natural languages? The upshot of our investigation is that MTS can serve them no better than, and is consequently as deficient as, SS.

3

Many Montague grammarians and other proponents of MTS would agree with these last points but argue that in characterizing the collection of all interpretations of a language we also do specify a particular one, the actual interpretation, and that this specification of the actual interpretation also would involve specifying the actual world, thus enabling us to characterize absolute truth. After all, Tarski himself describes MTS as the general theory of which the absolute theory is a special case [36:156]. Montague showed no inclination to single out a unique interpretation of English, but he did note that "not all interpretations of Intensional Logic will be reasonable candidates for interpreting English" [PTQ:263]. And in EFL he says [29]:

> To be specific, a sentence would be considered true with respect to an analysis or a possible world i if it were true (in the sense given earlier) with respect to the actual model and i. This relativization to i would be eliminable in the same way once we were able to single out the actual world among all possible worlds.

The question we have been pursuing here is what *form* a semantic theory should assume, what kinds of procedures for presenting meaning and truth-conditions should a semantic theory take if it is to successfully characterize the linguistic knowledge which distinguishes speaker from nonspeaker. Montague apparently agrees here that his theories do not suffice for this purpose (although they may succeed in characterizing part of our semantic competence, e.g., our competencies to determine logical consequence, ambiguity, compositionality, etc.). To do a complete job, we need to go on to define the unrelativized sense of a sentence and the unrelativized truth conditions [cf. also 32]. In the above passage, Montague says that, if we adopt his approach, a complete job would involve singling out one interpretation to determine the meanings of the various sentences of the language, and in addition, one world in this interpretation to determine the truth conditions for these sentences. If an interpretation can be singled out and along with it the actual world, then presumably someone who understands PTQ can use it to interpret sentences from the fragment of English PTQ addresses itself to. But this is because he brings to bear his knowledge of what the actual interpretation of his language is and which world is the actual one. This is knowledge which PTQ does not state.

In our discussion of what we must add to an MTS theory (e.g., (1)) for L in order to derive from it an absolute truth theory (e.g., (2)) for L, we argued that the smallest addition would include adding the base clauses of an absolute truth-theory for L ("N" denotes N, "P" is true of P's, etc.), and, also, a statement that truth in some interpretation A (for L) at some world p in A is absolute truth. Put somewhat differently, a semantic theory for L must state that A and p are the actual interpretation and world respectively. Montague, however, seems to be recommending that we pass over the articulation of the base clauses—which would essentially involve constructing an absolute truth-theory for L—and instead single out the actual world and interpretation directly. Richmond Thomason, a proponent of Montague style semantics, seems to take a similar line. He agrees that Montague's theory is abstract in the sense that:

it not only allows a multiplicity of interpretation assignments, but a multiplicity of interpretation structures. That is, interpretations can differ in the material that are used to construct the space of possible denotations as well as in the particular semantic values they attach to basic expressions [37:50].

But Thomason thinks that:

in itself, this is not damaging; one might conclude that it is merely an *empirical matter* to construct an appropriate set of entities and possible worlds for one of Montague's fragments of English [37:50].

Both Thomason and Montague are over-zealous about what we can reasonably expect to accomplish by appeal to MTS. In conclusion, I will argue that the route Montague and Thomason apparently opt for will not work.

First, it is not clear how to go about specifying the actual interpretation. Returning to (E) and (I): singling out the actual interpretation would involve, e.g., determining which function "Barbara" denotes. But how would we specify this function? Is it the function which, given a possible world w as argument, has a value that "Barbara" denotes in world w? The trouble with this suggestion is that unless some further rule is laid down to deal with the notion expressed by the phrase "what 'Barbara' denotes in world w," we have not successfully eliminated reference to language, and therefore, we will not be able to derive theorems needed to do the intellectual work we are interested in. Perhaps we can specify the actual interpretation by saying that in it "Barbara" denotes the function which, given a possible world w as an argument, has as value the thing which is Barbara in world w. What in the world does this mean? Do we really need to understand it to understand the sentence "Barbara sekoilee?"

On the other side, Montague and Thomason seem to be saying that if we want to move from relativized truth conditions to absolute truth conditions we need to single out the actual world among all possible worlds. This certainly is no easy task either. How much about a world do we need to know before we can distinguish it from all other worlds? Presumably a lot. There presumably is a class of worlds in which the number of trees in Canada is even and one in which the number is odd. So far are we from being able to single out the actual world from all others that we do not even know which class it falls in. But do we need to distinguish the actual world from all others to understand our language? From the point of view of PTQ and MTS theories in general, what we are seeing is that in order to understand a language one must have enough knowledge to single out the actual world. And this—need it be said?—is more than any speaker knows. Indeed, Montague's semantics seems, for contingent sentences, to collapse the distinction between understanding a sentence and knowing whether it is true.

Notes

The idea for this paper derives from some comments Donald Davidson has made on model-theoretic semantics in several of his papers. I would like to thank him and John Wallace. I would also like to thank Bill Lycan, Paul Yu and John Biro for comments on earlier drafts of this paper.

1. Cf. [2], [24], [29], [30], [31], [32].

2. Cf. [8] for further discussions of these theories and their differences.

3. Cf. [3], [4], [5], [10], [24], [29], [31], [32], [35].

4. For arguments supporting these claims, cf. [22], [23].

5. One large issue that I will not address is the issue of whether the linguist's conception of a "competence theory" can be satisfied either by a structural semantics or a model-theoretic semantics. The problem is how to characterize what's in the "speaker's head." For MTS the issue is the status of the model theory; for SS, the issue is the status of the metalanguage in which the mappings are given. What is innately given or antecedently learned that enables a monolingual child in a monolingual community to learn the semantics of his language?

In another paper ('The Concept of Meaning and its Role in Understanding Language,' *Dialectica*, forthcoming), I argue that this issue is a non-issue. It arises only if, as many do, one views semantics as a subfield of psychology. If we assume that questions about knowledge and understanding of language are psychological questions, then semantics should be a subfield of psychology. However, I argue that semantics properly understood, is a subfield not of psychology but of epistemology. Since it is, we need not worry about what's in the speaker's head—whatever that may mean.

6. An exception to this compositionality principle is Game Theoretic Semantics. Cf. [11], [34], [40].

Bibliography

[1] Bach, Emmon: 1968, 'Nouns and Noun Phrases,' in Emmon Bach, and R. T. Harms (eds.), *Universals in Linguistic Theory*, Holt Rinehart and Winston, New York.

[2] Cresswell, M. J.: 1973, *Logics and Languages*, Methuen, London.

[3] Cresswell, M. J.: 1978, 'Semantic Competence,' in M. Guenthner Ruetter and F. Guenthner (eds.), *Meaning and Translation*, Duckworth, London.

[4] Davidson, D.: 1967, 'Truth and Meaning,' *Synthese* 17, 304–323. [Chapter 5 in this volume.]

[5] Davidson, D.: 1973, 'In Defense of Convention T,' in H. LeBlanc (ed.), *Truth Syntax and Modality*, North-Holland, Amsterdam.

[6] Dummett, M.: 1975, 'What Is a Theory of Meaning (pt. I)?,' in *Mind and Language*, ed. S. Guttenplan, Clarendon Press, Oxford. [Chapter 7 in this volume.]

[7] Fodor, J. A.: 1975, *Language of Thought*, Crowell, New York.

[8] Fodor, J. D.: 1977, *Semantics: Theories of Meaning in Generative Grammar*, Harvard Univ. Press, Cambridge, Mass.

[9] Harman G.: 1974, 'Meaning and Semantics,' in M. K. Munitz and P. Unger (eds.), *Semantics and Philosophy*, New York Univ. Press, New York.

[10] Hintikka, J.: 1969, 'Semantics for Propositional Attitudes,' in Davis, J. et al. (eds.), *Philosophical Logic*, D. Reidel, Dordrecht.

[11] Hintikka, J. and Carlson, L.: 1979, 'Conditionals, Generic Quantifiers and Other Applications of Subgames,' in *Meaning and Use*, Avishai Margalit (ed.), D. Reidel, Dordrecht.

[12] Jackendoff, R.: 1972, *Semantic Interpretation in Generative Grammar*, MIT Press, Cambridge Mass.

[13] Katz, J.: 1966, *The Philosophy of Language*, Harper, New York.

[14] Katz, J.: 1972, *Semantic Theory*, Harper, New York.

[15] Katz, J.: 1975, 'Logic and Language: An Examination of Recent Criticisms of Intensionalism,' in Gunderson, K. (ed.), *Language, Mind and Knowledge*, Univ. of Minnesota Press, Minneapolis.

[16] Katz, J. and Fodor, J. A.: 1963, 'The Structure of a Semantic Theory,' *Language* 39, 170–210.

[17] Katz, J. and Nagel, R.: 1974, 'Meaning Postulates and Semantic Theory,' *Foundations of Language* 11, 311–340.

[18] Katz, J. and Postal, P.: 1964, *An Integrated Theory of Linguistic Description*, MIT Press, Cambridge, Mass.

[19] Kripke, S.: 1963, 'Semantical Analysis of Modal Logic. I. Normal Propositional Calculi,' *Zeitschrift für mathematische Logik* 9, 67–96.

[20] Kripke, S.: 1963, 'Semantical Considerations on Modal Logic,' *Acta Philosophical Fennica* 16, 83–94.

[21] Lakoff, G.: 1972, 'Linguistics and Natural Logic,' in G. Harman and D. Davidson (eds.), *Semantics for Natural Languages*, D. Reidel, Dordrecht.

[22] LePore, Ernest: 1982, 'In Defense of Davidson,' *Linguistics and Philosophy* 5, 277–294.

[23] LePore, Ernest and Loewer, B.: 1981, 'Translational Semantics,' *Synthese* 48, 121–133.

[24] Lewis, D.: 1972, 'General Semantics,' in *Semantics for Natural Language* [see 21].

[25] Lewis, D.: 1973, *Counterfactuals*, Harvard Univ. Press, Cambridge, Mass.

[26] Lyons, J.: 1968, *Introduction to Theoretical Linguistics*, Cambridge Univ. Press, Cambridge.

[27] McCawley, J.: 1968, 'The Role of Semantics in Grammar,' in *Universals in Linguistic Theory* [see 1].

[28] McCawley, J.: 1971, 'Where Do Noun Phrases Come From?,' in Steinberg, J. and Jackobovits, L. (eds.), *Semantics*, Cambridge Univ. Press, Cambridge.

[29] Montague, R.: 'English as a Formal Language,' in [37].

[30] Montague, R.: 'Universal Grammar,' in [37].

[31] Montague, R.: 'The Proper Treatment of Quantification in Ordinary English,' in [37].

128 Ernest Lepore

[32] Partee, B.: 1975, 'Montague Grammar and Transformational Grammar,' in *Linguistic Inquiry* 6, 203–300.

[33] Potts, T.: 1975, 'Model Theory and Linguistics,' in *Formal Semantics for Natural Language*, ed. Keenan, E., Cambridge Univ. Press, Cambridge.

[34] Saarinen, E.: 1977, 'Game-Theoreitical Semantics,' *Monist* 60, 406–18.

[35] Stalnaker, R.: 1972, 'Pragmatics,' in *Semantics of Natural Language* [see 21].

[36] Tarski, A.: 1956, 'The Concept of Truth in the Languages of the Deductive Sciences,' in *Logic, Semantics, and Matamathematics*, Clarendon Press, Oxford.

[37] Thomason, R. (ed.): 1974, *Formal Philosophy: Selected Papers of Richard Montague*, Yale Univ. Press, New Haven, Conn.

[38] van Fraassen, B. C.: 1969, 'Presuppositions, Supervaluations and Free Logic,' in Lambert, K. (ed.), *The Logical Way of Doing Things*, Yale Univ. Press, New Haven, Conn.

[39] Vermazen, B.: 1967, 'Review of (13) and (18),' *Synthese* 17, 350–65.

[40] Hintikka, J.: 'Theories of Meaning and Learnable Languages,' forthcoming.

[41] Katz, J.: 1977, 'The Advantage of Semantic Theory over Predicate Calculus in the Representation of Logical Form in Natural Language,' *Monist* 60, 380–405.

[42] Partee, Barbara: 1980, 'Montague Grammar, Mental Representation, and Reality', *Midwest Studies in Philosophy*.

[43] Partee, Barbara: 1977, 'Possible World Semantics and Linguistic Theory,' *Monist* 60, 303–26.

[44] Field, Hartry: 1973, 'Tarski's Theory of Truth,' *Journal of Philosophy* 69, 347–75.

Chapter 7

What Is a Theory of Meaning?

Michael Dummett

According to one well-known view, the best method of formulating the philosophical problems surrounding the concept of meaning and related notions is by asking what form that should be taken by what is called 'a theory of meaning' for any one entire language; that is, a detailed specification of the meanings of all the words and sentence-forming operations of the language, yielding a specification of the meaning of every expression and sentence of the language. It is not that the construction of a theory of meaning, in this sense, for any one language is viewed as a practical project; but it is thought that, when once we can enunciate the general principles in accordance with which such a construction could be carried out, we shall have arrived at a solution of the problems concerning meaning by which philosophers are perplexed.

I share the belief that this is the most fruitful approach to the problems within this area of philosophy, although I should not feel capable of giving a demonstration that this was so to someone who denied it: but we can see some reasons for it if we contrast certain other cases. So far as I know, no one has ever suggested a parallel approach to the problems of epistemology: no one has proposed that the right way to go about tackling the philosophical problems relating to the concept of knowledge would be by considering how one might construct a theory of knowledge in the sense of a detailed specification of everything that any one individual, or community, can be said to know. The reason is, I think, that our grasp on the concept of knowledge is rather more secure than our grasp on the concept of meaning. We are in doubt about what ought to count as knowledge; we are even more in doubt about how to formulate the

First appeared in Samuel Guttenplan (ed.), *Mind and Language: Wolfson College Lectures, 1974* (Oxford: Oxford University Press, 1975). Reprinted by permission of Oxford University Press. © Oxford University Press, 1975.

principles we tacitly apply for deciding whether or not something is to count as knowledge; we also have some uncertainty about the semantic analysis of a sentence attributing knowledge of something to somebody: but at least we are quite certain *which* are the sentences whose logical form and whose truth conditions we are seeking to analyse. By contrast, while most of us, myself included, would agree that the concept of meaning is a fundamental and indispensable one, we are unclear even about the surface structure of statements involving that concept. What kind of sentence, of natural language, should be taken as the characteristic form for an attribution of a particular meaning to some given word or expression? Not only do we not know the answer to this: we do not even know whether it is the right question to ask. Perhaps it is impossible, in general, to *state* the meaning of an expression: perhaps we ought, rather, to inquire by what linguistic means, or possibly even non-linguistic means, it is possible to *convey* the meaning of an expression, otherwise than by explicitly stating it. Or perhaps even that is wrong: perhaps the question should be, not how we express that a particular expression has a certain meaning, but how we should analyse sentences which involve the concept of meaning in some different way. It is precisely because, in this area of philosophy, we know even less what it is that we are talking about than we do in other areas, that the proposal to approach our problems by considering how we might attempt to specify the meanings of the expressions of an entire language does not appear the waste of time that an analogous proposal would seem to be within epistemology.

As is well known, some, pre-eminently Quine, have preferred to circumvent this difficulty by investigating the principles underlying the construction not of a theory of meaning for a language, but of a translation manual from it into some known language. The advantage is that we know exactly what form a translation manual has to take, namely an effective set of rules for mapping sentences of the translated language into sentences of the language into which the translation is being made: we can therefore concentrate entirely upon the questions how we are to arrive at a system of translation as embodied in such a manual, and what conditions must be satisfied for such a system to be acceptable. The disadvantage is that, while the interest of such an inquiry must lie in the light it throws on the concept of meaning, we are unable to be certain what consequences the results of the inquiry into translation do have for the notion of meaning, just because they are stated without direct appeal to that notion. To grasp the meaning of an expression is to understand its role in the language: a complete theory of meaning for a language is, therefore, a complete theory of how the language functions as a language. Our interest in meaning, as a general concept, is, thus, an interest in how language works; a direct description of the way a language works—of all that someone has to learn to do when he learns the language—would, accordingly, resolve our perplexities in a way in which an indirect account, by means of a translation, cannot. It will quite rightly be said that the interest in the inquiry into translation attaches, not to the translation itself, but to the criteria proposed for judging the acceptability of a scheme of translation, and that these must relate to what can be observed of the working of the language to be translated. Indeed, it might plausibly be maintained that nothing short of a complete theory of meaning for the language—a complete account of the way it works—could be an adequate basis for judging the correctness of a proposed scheme of translation. I shall not attempt to adjudicate the soundness of this claim. If it is sound, then the apparent advantage of the approach via translation, rather than by asking outright what form a theory of meaning for the language should take, is wholly illusory. If it is unsound—and certainly the actual procedure of the principal practitioner of the approach via translation suggests that he takes it as unsound—then it follows that there is no immediate inference from results concerning translation to conclusions concerning meaning.

I have said that it is the job of a theory of meaning for a language to give an account of how that language works, that is, of how its speakers communicate by means of it: here 'communicate' has no more precise signification that 'do whatever may be done by the utterance of one or more sentences of the language'. And here I will repeat what I have maintained elsewhere, that a theory of meaning is a theory of understanding; that is, what a theory of meaning has to give an account of is what it is that someone knows when he knows the language, that is, when he knows the meanings of the expressions and sentences of the language. One question about the form which a theory of meaning should take is whether it should issue in direct ascriptions of meaning, that is, in propositions of the form 'The meaning of the word/sentence X is . . .' or of the form 'The word/sentence X means . . .' If the answer to this question is affirmative, then it may seem that such a theory of meaning will have no need to advert explicitly to the notion of knowledge: if the theory allows us to say that the meaning of a given word or sentence is something or other, say Q, then, presumably, we shall likewise want to say that someone knows the meaning of that word or sentence if he knows that Q is what that word or sentence means. We shall later see reason to doubt this; but for the present let us suspend judgement. If the theory of meaning allows us to derive such direct ascriptions of meaning, and if these direct ascriptions are such as to lead in this simple way to a characterization of what it is to know the meaning of each word or sentence in the language, then, indeed, my claim that a theory of meaning must be a theory of understanding is not intended in so strong a sense as to rule out such a theory, merely on the ground that it did not itself employ the notion of knowledge: it would be proper to accept such a theory as being a theory of understanding. If, on the other hand, although the theory of meaning allows the derivation of direct ascriptions of meaning, these ascriptions are so framed as not to permit an immediate characterization of what it is that a person knows when he knows the meaning of a given word or sentence, then, by hypothesis, the theory is inadequate to account for one extremely important type of context in which we are disposed to use the word 'meaning'. If, however, the theory of meaning does not issue in such direct ascriptions of meaning at all; and if, further, it does not contain within itself any overt account of what someone has to know in order to know or grasp the meaning of each expression of the language, but merely provides an explanation of other contexts in which we use the word 'meaning', such as 'X means the same as Y' or 'X has a meaning': then, it appears to me, it will again be inadequate for the construction out of it of any theory of understanding. That is, if it were possible to give an account of, for example, when two expressions have the same meaning, which did not overtly rely on an account of what it was to know the meaning of an expression, then it would not be possible to derive an account of knowledge of meaning from it. There is, indeed, good reason to suppose it impossible to give an account of synonymy save via an account of understanding, since it is a requirement on the former that whoever knows the meanings of two synonymous expressions must also know that they are synonymous: but I am saying merely that, if such an account of synonymy were possible, there would be no route from it to an account of understanding.

Any theory of meaning which was not, or did not immediately yield, a theory of understanding, would not satisfy the purpose for which, philosophically, we require a theory of meaning. For I have argued that a theory of meaning is required to make the workings of language open to our view. To know a language is to be able to employ a language; hence, once we have an explicit account of that in which the knowledge of a language consists, we thereby have an account of the workings of that language; and nothing short of that can give us what we are after. Conversely, it also appears to me that once we can say what it is for someone to know a language, in the sense of knowing the meanings of all expressions of the language, then we have essentially solved every problem that can arise concerning meaning. For instance, once we are clear about what it is to know the meaning of an expression, then questions about whether, in such-and-such a case, the meaning of a word has changed can be resolved by asking whether someone who understood the word previously has to acquire new knowledge in order to understand it now.

If a theory of meaning gives an account of the working of the language to which it relates, then, it seems, it must embody an explanation of all the concepts expressible in that language, at least by unitary expressions. We need not stop to inquire whether, or in what cases, someone who does not possess the linguistic means to express a concept, or who lacks a language altogether, may yet be said to grasp that concept: it is sufficient to acknowledge that the prototypical case of grasping a concept is that in which this grasp consists in the understanding of a certain word or expression, or range of expressions, in some language. Hence, if a theory of meaning is a theory of understanding, as I have claimed, it would appear to follow that such a theory of meaning must, in explaining what one must know in order to know the meaning of each expression in the language, simultaneously explain what it is to have the concepts expressible by means of that language.

The theory of meaning will, of course, do more than this: it plainly cannot merely explain the concepts expressible in the language, since these concepts may be grasped by someone who is quite ignorant of that particular language, but who knows another language in which they are expressible. Hence the theory of meaning must also associate concepts with words of the language—show or state which concepts are expressed by which words. And an alternative view will be that it is only this latter task which properly belongs to the theory of meaning: that to demand of theory of meaning that it should serve to explain new concepts to someone who does not already have them is to place too heavy a burden upon it, and that all that we can require of such a theory is that it give the interpretation of the language to someone who already has the concepts required. Let us call a theory of meaning which purports to accomplish only this restricted task a 'modest' theory of meaning, and one which seeks actually to explain the concepts expressed by primitive terms of the language a 'full-blooded' theory. One question which I wish to try to answer is whether a modest theory of meaning is possible at all, or whether anything to be ranked as a theory of meaning must be full-blooded.

If a well-known conception, propounded by Davidson, of the form which a theory of meaning ought to take be accepted, then, I think, it must be maintained that a modest theory of meaning is all that we have a right to ask for. On this conception, the core of the theory of meaning will be a theory of truth, framed on the model of a truth definition of Tarski's kind (the object-language not, in general, being assumed to be a fragment of the metalanguage): such a theory of truth will, however, lack the apparatus required for converting it into an explicit definition, and will not be serving to explicate the concept of truth in any way, but, taking it as already known, to give the interpretation of the object-language. The theory of truth will yield a T-sentence for each sentence of the object-language, viz. either a biconditional whose left-hand side is of the form 'The sentence S is true' or the universal closure of a biconditional whose left-hand side is of the form 'An utterance of the sentence S by a speaker x at a time t is true.' The notion of translation is not, however, appealed to in judging whether the T-sentences which the theory yields are the correct ones; rather, there are constraints which the theory must satisfy, to be acceptable, relating to the sentences held true by the speakers of the language (it being supposed that we can frame adequate criteria for whether a speaker holds a given sentence to be true): in the first place, that, by and large, the T-sentences derivable in the theory of truth state, on their right-hand sides, the conditions under which in fact the speakers hold true the sentences named on their left-hand sides.

The axioms of the theory of truth, when it forms part of the theory of meaning for a language under such a conception, will state the denotations of the proper names of the language, give the conditions for the satisfaction of the primitive predicates, etc. If a primitive predicate of the language expresses a certain concept, it would seem quite out of place to claim that a theory of meaning of this kind, or, in particular, the axiom of the theory of truth which governed that predicate, provided any explanation of that concept. Rather, the theory would be intelligible only to someone who had already grasped the concept. A Davidsonian theory of meaning is a modest theory.

I have already observed that a translation manual is to be contrasted with a theory of meaning, and cannot itself claim to be one. A theory of meaning describes directly the way in which the language functions, a translation manual merely projects that language on to another one, whose functioning must, if the translation is to be of practical use, be taken as already known. This point has equally been insisted upon by Davidson, who has put it by saying that the translation manual tells us only that certain expressions of the one language mean the same as certain expressions of the other, without telling us what, specifically, the expressions of either language mean; it would, he says, be in principle possible to know, of each sentence of a given language, that it meant the same as some particular sentence of another language, without knowing at all what meaning any of these sentences had. This objection to regarding a translation manual as itself constituting a theory of meaning is evidently just: but we may wonder why so heavy an emphasis is laid upon the distinction between a translation manual and a theory of meaning when the theory of meaning is required to be, not full-blooded, but only modest. A translation manual leads to an understanding of the translated language only via an understanding of the language into which the translation is made, an understanding which it does not itself supply; hence, we may say, it does not directly display in what an understanding of the translated language consists. But a modest theory of meaning, likewise, leads to an understanding of the object-language only via a grasp of the concepts expressed by its primitive expressions, which it does not itself explain; it seems, therefore, that we should similarly say that such a theory of meaning does not fully display in what an understanding of the object-language consists. Especially is this so since our best model—and, in many cases, our only model—for the grasp of a concept is provided by the mastery of a certain expression or range of expressions in some language. Thus a translation manual presupposes a mastery of some one other language—that into which the translation is made—if we are to derive from it an understanding of the translated language; but a modest theory of meaning presupposes a mastery of *some*, though unspecified, language, if we are to derive from it an understanding of the object-language. The significant contrast would, however, appear to be not between a theory which (like a translation manual) makes a specific presupposition and one which (like a modest theory of meaning) makes as heavy a presupposition, though less specific; but between theories which (like both of these) rely on extraneous presuppositions and those which (like full-blooded theories of meaning) involve no such presupposition at all.

Let us return to the question: should a theory of meaning issue in direct ascriptions of meaning? A theory of meaning should, of course, tell us, for each expression of the language, what it means: but it would be very superficial to conclude from this that it must therefore be possible to derive from the theory statements beginning 'The expression X means ...'. To give a trifling example, a successful theory of a crime, say a murder, should tell us the identity of the murderer: that does not entail that we should be able to derive from the theory a statement beginning, 'The identity of the murderer is ...'; indeed (where 'is' is the sign of identity) there are no well-formed statements beginning that way. As a more serious example, we may note that 'chemistry' is not itself a concept of chemical theory. We do indeed require, of chemical theory, that it enable us to say which properties of a substance are chemical properties, which interactions are chemical ones, etc.; likewise, it may be required of a theory of meaning that it enable us to say which properties of an expression are semantic ones, that is, depend on and only on its meaning: but we cannot require that 'meaning' itself be a concept of the theory of meaning, at least if this is taken as entailing that we are enabled by it to characterize the semantic properties of an expression by means of a statement beginning 'The meaning of the expression is ...' or 'The expression means ...'.

For expressions smaller than sentences, and particularly for connectives, prepositions, etc., there is some difficulty in framing even a grammatically correct form for a direct ascription of meaning (where, of course, we do not want to employ as the object of the verb 'means' a term denoting an expression, so that 'means' would become replaceable by 'means the same as'). However, it is not to my purpose to inquire how, or even whether, such difficulties may be resolved: we many restrict our attention to the case of sentences, for which the difficulty does not arise. Davidson himself allows that, from a theory of meaning of the kind he favours, a direct ascription of meaning will be derivable, at least for sentences. Given a T-sentence derivable from a theory of truth satisfying the required constraints, for instance the sentence '"La terra si muove" is true if and only if the Earth moves,' we may legitimately convert it into what we may call an M-sentence, in this instance '"La terra si muove" means that the Earth moves.' Now, earlier, we considered the question whether a theory of meaning which made no overt allusion to knowledge could nevertheless enable us to derive from it an account, for each expression, of what knowledge of the meaning of that expression consisted in; and, in particular, we supposed it argued that, if the theory allowed the derivation, for each expression, of a direct ascription of meaning, then it must also provide us with an account of what it was to know the meaning of a given expression, namely that this would be to know that was stated by the direct ascription of the meaning of the expression. But, now, if we are asked whether the M-sentence '"La terra si muove" means that the Earth moves' expresses what someone has to know in order to know what the Italian sentence 'La terra si muove' means, we can hardly do other than answer affirmatively: to know that 'La terra si muove' means that the Earth moves *is* just to know what 'La terra si muove' means, for that is precisely what it does mean. If, on the other hand, we are asked whether an adequate account of what a knowledge of the meaning of 'La terra si muove' consists in is given by saying that one must know what is stated by the relevant M-sentence, then, equally, we are impelled to answer negatively: for the M-sentence, taken by itself, is, though by no means uninformative, signally unexplanatory. If these reactions are correct, then it follows that the fact that a theory of meaning issues in direct ascriptions of meaning is not in itself a sufficient ground for claiming that it gives an adequate account of what knowledge of meaning consists in.

One of our as yet unresolved problems was to discover what advantage a modest theory of meaning could have over a mere translation manual. A translation manual will inform us, for example, that 'La terra si muove' means the same as 'The Earth moves': but the inadequacy of this was said to lie in the fact that someone could know the two sentences to be synonymous without knowing what either of them meant. In order to derive, from a knowledge that the two sentences are synonymous, a knowledge of what the Italian sentence means, what someone has to know in addition is, obviously, what the English sentence means. Equally obviously, what, in addition to knowing the two sentences to be synonymous, has to be known in order to know that the Italian sentence means that the Earth moves, is that that is what the English sentence means. It follows that if we were to hold that a knowledge of the meaning of the Italian sentence consisted in knowing that it means that the Earth moves, we must also hold that knowing what the English sentence, 'The Earth moves,' means consists in knowing that *it* means that the Earth moves. An M-sentence such as '"The Earth moves" means that the Earth moves,' for an object-language which is part of the metalanguage, appears totally unexplanatory because, this time, quite uninformative; although it still seems impossible to deny that someone knows what 'The Earth moves' means just in case he knows that it means that the Earth moves.

In this context, it is important to observe a distinction which, in many contexts, can be neglected: that between knowing, of a sentence, that it is true, and knowing the proposition expressed by the sentence. In using the phrase 'to know the proposition expressed by a sentence', I am intending no acknowledgement of propositions as entities, no commitment to an ontology of propositions: I employ the phrase simply as a convenient means of expressing the generalization of the distinction between, for example, saying of someone that he knows that the sentence '19 is prime' is true, and saying of him that he knows that 19 is prime. The reason why the M-sentence '"The Earth moves" means that the Earth moves' appears quite uninformative is that it could not possibly be maintained that a knowledge of the meaning of 'The Earth moves' consisted in the knowledge that that M-sentence was true; for anyone who has grasped the simplest principles governing the use of the verb 'to mean', and who knows that 'The Earth moves' is an English sentence, must know that that M-sentence is true, even though he may not know what, in particular, 'The Earth moves' means. The case is analogous with Kripke's example of the sentence, 'Horses are called "horses".' Kripke says that anyone who knows the use of 'is called' in English must know that that sentence expresses a truth, irrespective of whether he knows what horses are: plainly, all he needs to know is that 'horse' is a meaningful general term of English, and, equally plainly, the relevant sense of 'knowing what horses are' is that in which it is synonymous with 'knowing what "horse" means'. Kripke allows, however, that someone who does not know what horses are will not know *which* truth 'Horses are called "horses"' expresses. It seems reasonable to suppose that, by this concession, Kripke intends to deny that we could say of such a person that he knew that horses are called 'horses', although he is not explicit about this: that is, in my terminology, such a person may know that the sentence 'Horses are called "horses"' is true, without knowing the proposition expressed by that sentence.

It might be objected that someone who knows a sentence to be true must also know the proposition expressed by the sentence, on the ground that if he knows enough about the meaning of the word 'true' to be credited with the knowledge that the sentence is true, he must know the connection between knowing something and knowing it to be true (and between believing it and believing it to be true, etc.); a connection which is displayed by the T-sentences. For instance, he must know that 'Horses are called "horses"' is true if and only if horses are called 'horses': hence, since by assumption he knows that 'Horses are called "horses"' is true, he will, if he is capable of performing a simple inference, also be capable of knowing that horses are called 'horses'. But this objection derives its plausibility from ignoring in its premiss the distinction which it purported to demonstrate to be without substance, that, namely, between knowing that a sentence is true and knowing the proposition it expresses. We may justifiably credit someone who does not know what 'horse' means, but who knows that it is a meaningful general term, with the knowledge that the T-sentence, ' "Horses are called 'horses' " is true if and only if horses are called "horses" ', is true: but to assume, as the argument requires, that he knows that 'Horses are called "horses"' is true if and only if horses are called 'horses' is to beg the question.

To say of someone who does not know what 'The Earth moves' means, that he does not know that 'The Earth moves' means that the Earth moves, but only knows that the M-sentence is true, is not at all to say that he is not prepared to utter that M-sentence assertorically, but only the sentence, 'The sentence " 'The Earth moves' means that the Earth moves" is true.' It is not even to say that he could not give excellent grounds for the former utterance: on the contrary, he can give quite conclusive grounds, namely an appeal to the use of 'means' in English. But we have learned from Gettier's paradox that not every sound justification for a true belief is sufficient to entitle the holder of the belief to claim knowledge; the justification must be suitably related to what makes the belief true. A justification of an utterance of the M-sentence which would ground the ascription to the speaker of knowledge of the proposition expressed by that M-sentence would have to be one depending upon the specific meaning of the sentence of which the M-sentence treated, in our case the sentence, 'The Earth moves,' even though, in ordinary circumstances, no one would think of justifying such an utterance in so complicated a way.

All this shows that we were entirely right in our first inclination, to regard it as a necessary and sufficient condition of someone's knowing what 'The Earth moves' means that he know that it means that the Earth moves, that is, that he know the proposition expressed by the corresponding M-sentence. But it shows equally that we were also right to regard the M-sentence as being quite unexplanatory of what it is to know the meaning of the sentence, 'The Earth moves.' The simplest way we have to state its unexplanatory character is by observing that we have so far found no independent characterization of what more someone who knows that the M-sentence is true must know in order to know the proposition it expresses, save that he must know what 'The Earth moves' means: knowledge of that proposition cannot, therefore, play any part in an account of that in which an understanding of that sentence consists. And, if an M-sentence for which the metalanguage contains the object-language is unexplanatory, then an M-sentence for an object-language disjoint from the metalanguage is equally unexplanatory. In the latter case, the M-sentence does indeed provide some information: but the knowledge of the truth of such an M-sentence (as opposed to a knowledge of the proposition it expresses) does not require the possession of any information not also contained in the corresponding sentence from a translation manual.

The considerations about the connection between knowledge and justification which we saw to underlie the distinction between knowing the truth of a sentence and knowing the proposition expressed by it can be generalized to cases where it is not precisely this distinction which is in question. The expression 'knows that' is, of course, frequently used in everyday discourse, and in philosophical contexts in which attention is not focused on the concept of knowledge, merely as synonymous with 'is aware that'. Where 'knowledge' is used in a stricter sense, however, knowledge of a fact transcends mere awareness of it in that it involves that the awareness of it was arrived at in some canonical fashion, that is, that it was *derived* in some special way. If, then, we attempt to explain in what some capacity consists by saying that it consists in having a certain piece of knowledge, and if the plausibility of this account depends upon taking 'knowledge' in the strict sense, rather than as mere awareness, the attempted representation of the capacity will remain inadequate so long as it stops short at simply stating the *object* of knowledge—what it is that must be known, in the strict sense of 'know', for someone to have that capacity. To give an adequate explanation of the capacity in question, the account must do more than simply specify the fact that must be known: it must indicate how, in particular, awareness of that fact must have been attained, that is, what process of derivation is required for it to count as *knowledge*, in the strict sense.

It may be objected that no one has ever supposed that an adequate explanation of the meaning, or the understanding, of a sentence could be given by alluding merely to the M-sentence relating to it. In the terms in which I have just discussed the matter, the whole point of the theory of meaning is that it displays the canonical means by which the M-sentence is to be derived: only someone who was capable of so deriving it could be said to know it, in the strict sense, or, as I earlier expressed it, could be said to know the proposition it expresses. Such an objection is entirely just: my purpose in discussing M-sentences at such length was not to refute a thesis which no one has held, but to analyse the intuitive reasons we all share for rejecting such a thesis, in order to bring out some general points which we may apply elsewhere.

In order, then, to see in what, on a Davidsonian account, the knowledge of the meaning of a sentence consists, we must look to the way in which the M-sentence relating to it is derived in the theory of meaning. The M-sentence is, as we noted, obtained by replacing 'is true if and only if' in the corresponding T-sentence by 'means that': and the T-sentence is, in turn, derived from the axioms of the theory of truth governing the constituent words of the sentence and those governing the methods of sentence-formation exemplified by it. This, of course, entirely accords with our intuitive conviction that a speaker derives his understanding of a sentence from his understanding of the words composing it and of the way they are put together. What plays the role, within a theory of meaning of Davidson's kind, of a grasp of the meanings of the words is a knowledge of the axioms governing those words: in our example, these may be stated as '"The Earth" denotes the Earth' and 'It is true to say of something "It moves" if and only if that thing moves.' (This latter formulation of the axiom governing 'moves' eschews appeal to the technical device of satisfaction by an infinite sequence, and is only an approximate indication of what is wanted: but, if we are intending a serious representation of what is known by anyone able to speak English, we cannot literally credit him with an understanding of that technical device.)

It is not sufficient, for someone to know what the sentence 'The Earth moves' means, for him to know the M-sentence relating to it to be true; he must know the proposition expressed by that M-sentence. And the natural way to characterize what, in addition, someone who knows the truth of the M-sentence has to know in order to know the proposition it expresses is: the meanings of the component words. If, now, we explain an understanding of the component words as consisting in a knowledge of the axioms of the theory of truth which govern those words, the same question arises: is it sufficient for him to know those axioms to be true, or must he know the propositions which they express? The objection to requiring only that he know the axioms to be true is parallel to that we allowed in the case of the M-sentence: anyone who knows the use of 'denotes', and who knows that 'the Earth' is a singular term of English, must know that the sentence '"The Earth" denotes the Earth' is true, even if he does not know what, specifically, the phrase 'the Earth' means or what it denotes.

This might be objected to, however, on the ground that if we were to change the example from 'The Earth moves' to 'Homer was blind', it would become apparent that, in order to know that '"Homer" denotes Homer' is true, one must know more than that 'Homer' is a proper name: one must know also that it is not an empty name. Such an objection is ill taken, because, for any language in which the possibility that 'Homer' is an empty name is open, the relevant axiom of the theory of truth will not take the simple form '"Homer" denotes Homer'; at least, it will not do so if the name's being empty would deprive the sentence '"Homer" denotes Homer' of truth. It is only in a theory of truth for a language of a Fregean type, in which all singular terms are so understood as to be guaranteed a denotation, that the axiom governing each proper name will take that simple form. For languages of other types, the axiom governing such a name as 'Homer' will have to take a different form. For instance, for any language in which the predicate '. . . is Homer' was taken as true of the referent of 'Homer', if any, and false of everyone and everything else, the axiom could take the form, 'For every x, "Homer" denotes x if and only if x is Homer.' If, now, the language was Russellian, so that the presence of an empty name in an atomic sentence rendered that sentence false, suitable further axioms would yield the T-sentence, '"Homer was blind" is true if and only if Homer was blind.' If, on the other hand, the language was such that the presence of an empty name in a sentence, save when it followed the sign of identity, rendered that sentence neither true nor false, then we should not want that T-sentence to be derivable, since, if 'Homer' were an empty name, the left-hand side would be false while the right-hand side was not false. One would want, instead, the non-standard T-sentence, '"Homer was blind" is true if and only if, for some x, x is Homer and x was blind.' Hence the demand that, in order to be able to derive the T-sentence relating to 'Homer was blind,' one would first have to know whether or not 'Homer' was an empty name, is quite unjustified.

This could be denied only if it were held that in order to know the meaning of 'Homer', one must know whether or not there was in fact such a man as Homer: for the theory of truth is a part of the theory of meaning for the language, and will embody all and only what is required for an understanding of the language. But, clearly, in order to know the use of the name 'Homer' in our language, it is not necessary to know whether or not it has a denotation: the most that could be required is that one should know whether or not it is known whether the name has a denotation. That is, it might be held that for a name for which it is known that it has a denotation, this knowledge enters into the understanding of the name: if so, then, for such a name, say 'London', the axiom governing it will take the simple form ' "London" denotes London.' A knowledge of whether 'Homer' has a denotation or not, on the other hand, cannot be part of what is involved in knowing the use of that name, for the obvious reason that this knowledge is not possessed by the speakers of the language.

If it is supposed that anyone attempting a serious inquiry whether there was such a place as London would thereby show that he was not in command of the accepted use of the name 'London', then it will be true that someone who knows of the word 'London' only that it is a proper name cannot yet recognize the axiom governing it to be true: he must also know that it is a name of which we are certain that it is not empty. But, plainly, one could be informed of this fact, and hence conclude to the truth of the sentence ' "London" denotes London,' without knowing what, precisely, 'London' meant; and so we must still conclude that a knowledge of the truth of the axiom is insufficient for an understanding of the name. It would be wrong to argue against this that merely to be informed that 'London' is a name known for certain not to be empty is not to *know* that fact, that to know it, in the strict sense, involves knowing specifically how the name 'London' is used. If such an argument were correct, then Davidson's objection to considering a translation manual as a theory of meaning, that one could, for example, know that 'la terra' means the same as 'the Earth' without knowing what either of them meant, would be unsound: for one could, in the same way, argue that while someone might be informed of their synonymy, he could not, in the strict sense, *know* it without knowing what both words meant. The objection would run foul of the methodological principle we have adopted, namely not to accept as part of an explanation a requirement that some-one know something, where 'knowledge' is taken in the strict sense, as transcending mere awareness, but no account is given of what would constitute such knowledge.

It is essential to observe this principle if we are to avoid null or circular explanations. Suppose it true—doubtful as it seems to me—that one could not know, in the strict sense, that a name denotes a well-known object still in existence, without knowing the precise use of the name. This must be because, in order to count as *knowledge*, an awareness of the fact must be derived in a particular way. It is one of the merits of a theory of meaning which represents mastery of a language as the knowledge not of isolated, but of deductively connected, propositions, that it makes due acknowledgement of the undoubted fact that a process of derivation of some kind is involved in the understanding of a sentence. Where such a theory makes no appeal to any process of derivation is, naturally, in the recognition of the truth of the axioms. An insistence that such recognition amount to knowledge in the strict sense would, however, make a tacit appeal to a process by which their truth was derived, a process which the theory would fail to make explicit. It would, for example, be simply circular to say that an understanding of the name 'London' consisted in a knowledge, in the strict sense, of the truth of the sentence '"London" denotes London,' and then go on to say that a condition for having such knowledge was a grasp of the precise use of the name: what we were seeking was a characterization of what constituted a grasp of the use of such a name.

There is thus no possibility of holding that an understanding of the component words of a sentence consists just in an awareness of the truth of the axioms governing them: one would have to know the propositions expressed by those axioms. The theory of meaning must therefore be capable of explaining what differentiates a knowledge of the propositions expressed by those axioms from a mere awareness of their truth. Now Davidson himself has fully recognized the obligation upon a theory of meaning to yield a theory of understanding: he has been quite explicit about what, on his view, an understanding of a sentence consists in, namely in a knowledge both of the relevant T-sentence and of the fact that that T-sentence was derived from a theory of truth for the language which satisfies the constraints imposed upon such a theory for it to be acceptable. The analogue, for the understanding of a word, would presumably be a knowledge of the axiom governing it and also of the fact that that sentence was an axiom of a theory of truth satisfying those constraints. This time, therefore, the suggestion is that we may represent a knowledge of the propositions expressed by the sentences which serve as axioms as consisting in an awareness of their truth supplemented by certain background knowledge about those sentences.

It appears to me that only a very little consideration is needed to recognize that this appeal to background information cannot supply what we need. If someone does not know what 'the Earth' means, he will learn something from being told that the sentence '"The Earth" denotes the Earth' is true, provided that he understands the verb 'denotes': he will learn, namely, that 'the Earth' is a singular term and is not empty. But if, now, he asks to be told the specific meaning of the term, he will not be helped in the least by being told that the sentence in question is an axiom in a theory of truth for English satisfying certain particular constraints. Obviously, what tells him what, specifically, 'London' denotes is the *sentence* '"London" denotes London' itself, and, in particular, the object of the verb 'denotes' in that sentence, and not any extraneous information *about* that sentence. What is being attributed to one who knows English is not merely the awareness that that sentence (and others like it) is true, but that awareness taken together with an understanding of the sentence; in other words, a knowledge of the proposition expressed by the sentence. Of course, when we consider the degenerate case in which the metalanguage is an extension of the object-language, the requirement that the metalanguage be understood becomes circular; in order to derive from the axiom a knowledge of what 'London' denotes, one would have already to understand the name 'London'. But there is no requirement that the theory of truth be expressed in an extension of the object-language: if the axiom ran '"London" denota Londra,' then it would be an understanding of the term 'Londra' that was needed in order to learn the denotation of 'London', and there would be no circularity.

This is reasonable enough in itself, but it does not help us to understand what significant difference there is between a modest theory of meaning of this kind and a translation manual. It now appears clearly that we must ascribe to anyone able to use the theory of truth in order to obtain an interpretation of the object-language that he have a prior understanding of the metalanguage. This is even more apparent when we attribute to him an awareness that the theory of truth satisfies the required constraints, since these constraints allude to the conditions *stated* on the right-hand sides of the T-sentences, a notion which cannot be explained in terms of the formal theory, but presupposes an interpretation of it. Hence a theory of meaning of this kind merely exhibits what it is to arrive at an interpretation of one language via an understanding of another, which is just what a translation manual does: it does not explain what it is to have a mastery of a language, say one's mother tongue, independently of a knowledge of any other.

This conclusion could be avoided only if we could ascribe to a speaker of the object-language a knowledge of the propositions expressed by the sentences of the theory of truth, independently of any language in which those propositions might be expressed. If this is the intention of such a theory of meaning, it appears deeply dissatisfying, since we have no model, and the theory provides none, for what an apprehension of such propositions might consist in, otherwise than in an ability to enunciate them linguistically.

It may be replied that the apprehension of these propositions cannot be explained piecemeal, for each sentence of the theory of truth taken separately; but that a knowledge of the theory of truth as a whole issues, precisely, in an ability to speak and understand the object-language, so that there is no lacuna. What we are being given is a theoretical model of a practical ability, the ability to use the language. Since it is a theoretical model, the representation is in terms of the knowledge of a deductively connected system of propositions; and, since we can express propositions only in sentences, the model has to be described in terms of a deductively connected system of sentences. No presumption is intended that a speaker of the object-language actually has a prior understanding of the language in which those sentences are framed—that is why it is harmless to frame them in a language which is actually an extension of the object-language; but, equally, there is no undischarged obligation to say in what a grasp of the propositions expressed by the theory consists: it consists in that practical ability of which we are giving a theoretical model.

It is just here that the connection becomes apparent between a theory of meaning that proceeds via a theory of truth and a holistic view of language, a connection at first sight puzzling. A semantics which issues in a statement of truth conditions for each sentence, derived from finitely many axioms, each governing a single word or construction, appears at first as a realization of an atomistic conception of language, under which each word has an individual meaning and each sentence an individual content: the T-sentence for a given sentence of the language is derived from just those axioms which govern the words and constructions occurring in that sentence. But the connection between such a conception and the holistic view of language lies in the fact that nothing is specified about what a knowledge of the propositions expressed by the axioms, or by the

T-sentences, consists in: the only constraints on the theory are global ones, relating to the language as a whole. On such an account, there can be no answer to the question what constitutes a speaker's understanding of any one word or sentence: one can say only that the knowledge of the entire theory of truth issues in an ability to speak the language, and, in particular, in a propensity to recognize sentences of it as true under conditions corresponding, by and large, with those stated by the T-sentences.

Thus the appeal to the knowledge that the theory of truth satisfies the external constraints does not serve to explain a speaker's understanding of any individual word or sentence, to bridge the gap between his knowing an axiom or theorem of the theory of truth to be true and his knowing the proposition expressed by it: it mediates merely between his knowledge of the theory as a whole and his mastery of the entire language. Now the allure of a theory of meaning of this type is that it appears to refute the suspicion that a holistic view of language must be anti-systematic; since to speak a language is to have the capacity to utter sentences of it in accordance with their conventional significance, there appears no hope of any systematic account of the use of a whole language which does not yield an account of the significance of individual utterances. A Davidsonian theory of meaning, on the other hand, combines the basic tenet of holism with what purports to be an account of the way in which the meaning of each individual sentence is determined from the meanings of its constituent words. This appearance is, however, an illusion. The articulation of the theory of truth is not taken as corresponding to any articulation of the practical ability the possession of which is the manifestation of that knowledge of which the theory is presented as a theoretical model. A speaker's knowledge of the meaning of an individual sentence is represented as consisting in his grasp of a part of a deductive theory, and this is connected with his actual utterances only by the fact that a grasp of the whole theory is supposed to issue, in some manner of which no explanation is given, in his command of the language in its entirety; but no way is provided, even in principle, of segmenting his ability to use the language as a whole into distinct component abilities which manifest his understanding of individual words, sentences, or types of sentence. To effect any such segmentation, it would be necessary to give a detailed account of the practical ability in which the understanding of a particular word or sentence consisted, whereas, on the holistic view, not only cannot a speaker's command of his language be so segmented, but no detailed description of what it consists in can be given at all. Hence the

articulation of the theory plays no genuine role in the account of what
constitutes a speaker's mastery of his language.

Against this it may be objected that the theory of truth does tell us
something about the use of each individual sentence: for it states conditions under which a speaker will probably hold it to be true. Now it is
certainly the case that a theory of meaning based on a theory of truth
would reflect a molecular, rather than a holistic, view of language, if we
could take the right-hand sides of the T-sentences as stating conditions
under which speakers of the language invariably held true the sentences
named on the left-hand sides. This is not a possible way of construing the
theory, for two reasons. First, for any natural language, the conditions
stated on the right-hand sides of the T-sentences will not, in general, be
ones which we are capable of recognizing as obtaining whenever they
obtain. A molecular theory of meaning based on the notion of truth conditions must attribute to one who understands a sentence a knowledge of
the condition which must obtain for it to be true, not a capacity to recognize that sentence as true just in case that condition holds. Secondly,
such an account would leave no room for mistakes. In order to leave
room for them, we must claim that an acceptable theory of truth will give
the *best possible* fit between the conditions for the truth of a sentence and
the conditions under which it is held to be true, not a *perfect* fit: it follows
that a speaker's understanding of a sentence cannot be judged save in
relation to his employment of the entire language. (Indeed, it is somewhat
dubious whether an individual speaker's mastery of the language can be
judged at all. If we have identified a linguistic community from the outside, then a Davidsonian theory of meaning will give us a fairly good,
though necessarily imperfect, guide to which sentences its members will
hold to be true. There will be divergences on the part of the entire community—cases when we shall say, on the basis of that theory of meaning,
that the community shares a mistaken belief. There will also be disagreements between individual speakers. How are we to discriminate between
such a disagreement as may occur between two speakers who both tacitly
accept the same theory of meaning for their common language, and one
which reflects differing interpretations of that language? Presumably, if a
member of the linguistic community holds a divergent theory of truth for
the language, he will tend to diverge more in his judgements than most
speakers do from the majority. But, since no finite set of such divergences
will, in itself, reveal his reliance on a non-standard theory of truth, it is
hard to see how either he or the other speakers or we as observers could

ever detect this, or how, once discovered, it could be corrected. The difficulty arises precisely because there is no way of determining, within such a theory, the individual content with which any speaker endows a sentence.)

Davidson makes a virtue of necessity, and, as you heard in his brilliantly clear exposition in the first lecture in this series, uses the gap between the truth condition of a sentence and the condition under which it is held true to explain the genesis of the concept of belief. This is, however, an abnegation of what we are entitled to expect from a theory of meaning: such a theory ought to be able to distinguish between disagreements stemming from difference of interpretation and disagreements of substance (disagreements about the facts); it ought to be able to explain how it is possible for disagreement over the truth value of sentences to occur even when there is agreement over their meaning. We have, of course, been taught by Quine to regard this distinction with suspicion; and it is undeniably the case that the meanings of expressions of natural language are frequently fuzzy, and that the distinction becomes in consequence blurred. It is equally true that, as Davidson remarked in his lecture, we ought not lightly to assume that every disagreement over truth value, for instance of the sentence 'The Earth is round', should be regarded as one of substance rather than of interpretation. But a theory of meaning which denies in principle the viability of the distinction runs the risk of becoming solipsistic. A disagreement between individual speakers of the same language at the same time either cannot be accounted for at all, or should be explained by attributing to them divergent theories of truth for the language: and the same applies to a change of mind on the part of one individual. If the latter course is taken, we lose the conception of the linguistic community: a language, considered as determined by a theory of meaning, becomes something spoken by a single individual at a certain period.

The obvious fact of the matter is that the judgements which we make are not directly correlated with the states of affairs which render them true or false. Even if the correct theory of meaning for our language would represent our grasp of the meaning of each sentence as consisting in our knowledge of the condition which must hold for it to be true, we do not, in general, arrive at our evaluation of the truth of a sentence by direct recognition that the appropriate condition obtains, since, for the most part, that condition is not one we are capable of so recognizing. Should we therefore say that an adequate theory of meaning must be able to give an account not merely of what determines our judgements as correct or incorrect, but also of how we arrive at them, since this also depends upon the meanings we assign to the sentences whose truth value we are judging; and that this account must be able to show how, in the process, we are capable of going astray, even when we share with other speakers a common interpretation of the sentence? Whether we say this or not is partly a matter of taste, of how much we wish to reckon as belonging to a theory of meaning; such an account certainly belongs within a complete description of the workings of language. If a theory of meaning, based on a molecular view of language, enables a clear content to be given to an individual's associating a certain meaning with a sentence, a meaning which determines when that sentence may rightly be judged to be true, then we also have a clear criterion for when a judgement represents a mistake of fact; if we then choose to decree that an account of the processes leading to such mistakes does not belong to the theory of meaning, only a demarcation dispute is involved. But a theory of meaning based on a holistic view, which has no criterion for a speaker's associating a specific meaning with any one sentence, save his inclination to hold it true or false, and does not therefore purport to give an account of his understanding of that sentence, but only of the entire language, can give no determinate content to the notion of a mistake, which it invokes only to account for the lack of fit between the theory of truth and the judgements actually made by speakers. It would be absurd to expect a theory of meaning to ascribe to every expression a completely sharp meaning; I am arguing, however, that it is required that a place be left for a distinction between a disagreement of substance and a disagreement over meaning, a distinction which was not, after all, invented by misguided theorists, but is actually employed within our language. Any theory which associates sentences merely with truth conditions, without either attempting any account of the means by which we recognize or judge those truth conditions to be fulfilled, or providing any means of determining that an individual speaker, or even the whole community, associates a particular truth condition with a particular sentence, save a rough agreement between the truth conditions of all sentences under a given theory and the judgements made concerning them, is incapable of providing any place for such a distinction.

Now it could be replied that I am quite wrong in denying that Davidson can represent an individual speaker's grasp of the meaning of a particular sentence: in the lecture that inaugurated this series, he stated that an individual's understanding of a sentence consisted in his knowing, of the relevant T-sentence, that it was derivable from some theory of truth, satisfying the required constraints, for the language, without his having actually to know that theory of truth. But how is it to be judged that an individual knows this? What, indeed, is he to do with the information if he has it? It might be claimed that he will manifest this knowledge by judging that sentence to be true just in case the condition stated in the T-sentence obtains. But why should he do this? Well, it may be said, he knows that the theory of truth which yields what T-sentence achieves the best fit with the judgements made by other speakers, and he wants to maximize the agreement of his judgements with theirs. It is true, by hypothesis, that this theory of truth will achieve the best fit possible *for a theory of truth*: but since it will not achieve a perfect fit, he would do better, in maximizing agreement, not to be guided exclusively by any theory of truth. How can he know that he would not achieve a better agreement by disregarding the theory of truth in this instance? After all, it cannot be the case that other speakers all follow the policy of judging the truth values of sentences only in accordance with the given theory of truth, otherwise the fit *would* be perfect: so why should he? To this it can only be replied that the other speakers do try to follow that policy, but make mistakes in doing so. We have now come round once more to the question: what is a mistake? In attributing to the speakers a policy of conforming their judgements to a theory of truth, we have surreptitiously ascribed to them a capacity for judging whether the truth conditions of sentences are fulfilled—judgements which will not always be correct; but we have given no content to the notion of such a judgement, as distinct from a judgement as to the truth value of a sentence.

That we should appeal to the notion of a mistake in order to explain the lack of fit between a theory of truth and the actual judgements made by speakers of the language sounds plausible only because we find the notion of such a mistake already intelligible: we are familiar enough with the idea that someone may assign a determinate meaning to a sentence, and yet wrongly judge it to be true. But a theory which offers no explanation of how such mistakes occur has no right to appeal to this notion. We can see this plainly if we consider any theory which does not have language as its subject-matter, for instance, a physical theory. It would not be tolerable, for example, to say that a theory of the motions of the planets was one that achieved the best possible fit with their observed movements, any discrepancy being due to mistakes on the part of the planets. If all we had to go on, in constructing a theory of meaning, were judgements of speakers as to the truth or falsity of sentences, and the conditions prevailing when those judgements were made, then we should be entitled to demand, of any theory we were asked to accept, that the fit be perfect, save for small discrepancies assignable to errors of observation. Fortunately, this is not all that we have to go on.

The upshot of our discussion therefore, is this. If a theory of meaning of this type is taken literally, as relating to a theory of truth framed in actual sentences, it has no advantage over a translation manual, since it has to presuppose an understanding of the meta-language. If, on the other hand, it is construed as attributing to a speaker an unverbalized knowledge of the propositions expressed by the sentences of the theory, its explanatory force evaporates, since it provides no means whereby we can explain the ascription to an individual of a knowledge of the various distinct propositions and their deductive interconnection. That is to say: a modest theory of meaning either accomplishes no more than a translation manual, and hence fails to explain what, in general, someone knows when he knows a language; or it must be construed holistically, in which case its claim to give a systematic account of the mastery of a language is spurious, since a holistic view of language precludes the possibility of any such account.

We have noted that a theory of meaning, if it represents an understanding of an expression as consisting in the possession of a certain piece of knowledge, cannot rest content with specifying the object of this knowledge, and insisting that 'knowledge' must be taken in a strict sense; it must also display the way in which that knowledge had to be derived in order to qualify as knowledge. But our more recent considerations have related to a different point. In many contexts, we may take as unproblematic the ascription to someone of awareness of some fact, since we may credit him with an understanding of language, and the manifestation of his awareness will consist primarily in his ability to state the fact or his propensity to assent to a statement of it. But, where we are concerned with a representation in terms of propositional knowledge of some practical ability, and, in particular, where that practical ability is precisely the mastery of a language, it is incumbent upon us, if our account is to be explanatory, not only to specify what someone has to know for him to have that ability, but also what it is for him to have that knowledge, that is, what we are taking as constituting a manifestation of a knowledge of those propositions; if we fail to do this, then the connection will not be made between the theoretical representation and the practical ability it is intended to represent. I am not objecting to the idea of a theoretical representation of a practical ability as such, and certainly not to the representation of a mastery of a language by means of a deductive theory: I am saying only that such a representation is devoid of explanatory power unless a grasp of the individual propositions of the theory is explained in terms of a specific practical capacity of the speaker. I do not know whether this is possible; I do not know that holism is an incorrect conception of language. But I am asserting that the acceptance of holism should lead to the conclusion that any systematic theory of meaning is impossible, and that the attempt to resist this conclusion can lead only to the construction of pseudo-theories; my own preference is, therefore, to assume as a methodological principle that holism is false.

The next question that naturally arises is whether a full-blooded theory of meaning could be given in terms of the notion of the truth conditions of a sentence: you will be relieved to hear that I shall spare you the extended discussion that an answer would demand. But we are in a position to deal briefly with another question about the form which a theory of meaning should take, namely whether, in terminology which I borrow from Mr. John McDowell, it should be rich or austere. If the theory of meaning is given in terms of truth conditions, then, where a proper name is concerned, a rich theory will attribute to a speaker who understands the name a knowledge of the condition which must be satisfied by any object for it to be the bearer of the name, while an austere theory will simply represent him as knowing, of the object for which the name in fact stands, that it is the bearer. For this case at least, namely where the theory is framed in terms of truth conditions, the distinction appears to coincide with that between a full-blooded and a modest theory, although it is differently formulated. For a more verificationist type of theory, an austere theory will credit anyone who understands a name with a capacity to recognize its bearer when encountered, whereas a rich theory will, instead, represent him as ready to acknowledge whatever is taken as establishing, for any given object, that it is the bearer. In favour of the rich theory, it might be said: 'We don't *simply* recognize objects: we recognize them *by* some feature.' It might be replied, on behalf of the austere theory, that *how* we recognize an object is a psychological matter, irrelevant to a theory of meaning, and that, in any case, there does not have to be a means by which we recognize them; no one could give much of an account, for example, of the means by which he recognizes the predicate '. . . is red' as applying to something. So let us suppose that we encounter some rational but non-human creatures who have a language which contains what appear to be names of rivers: though they identify rivers under these names with remarkable accuracy, we cannot discover the means by which they make such identifications, nor can they give any account of this. It nevertheless remains that if one of these creatures has identified two distinct stretches of water by the same river-name, and it is subsequently proved, by tracing their course, that there is no flow of water from one to the other, then he must withdraw one or other identification; at least, if these creatures do not acknowledge this necessity, then their words cannot be taken as names *of rivers*. So-called theories of reference are theories about what, in problematic cases, we should take as establishing which object, if any, was the bearer of a given proper name, and hence should more accurately be called theories of sense for proper names: the fact that they are so disputable shows how inexplicit our grasp of our own use of proper names is. But if our imaginary creatures use names in such a way that, in a case of disagreement, they would not accept as settling the question which object was the bearer whatever we should in fact so accept, then they do not understand these names in the way that we understand ours. Such examples bring out sharply the merit of the idea that what determines the meaning of a word is not so much what in practice normally prompts its application as what is agreed on as conclusively establishing its correct application in cases of dispute: to argue that we do not need to rely, on ordinary occasions of use, on any principle guiding us to apply it, is to miss the point of this familiar idea.

I conclude, therefore, that a theory of meaning, if one is to be possible at all, must accord with an atomistic, or at least a molecular, conception of language, not a holistic one; that it must be full-blooded, not modest, and rich, not austere. It need not issue in any direct ascriptions of meaning; but it must give an explicit account, not only of what anyone must know in order to know the meaning of any given expression, but of what constitutes having such knowledge. As I remarked, the next step would be to ask whether such a theory of meaning should be based upon the notion of truth conditions or upon some other notion. When I began composing this lecture, I had the absurd idea that I should have the time to go on to discuss not only that, but also the question raised by Professor Strawson in his extremely interesting inaugural lecture, concerning the relation between theories of meaning as we have been discussing them and the account of meaning given by Grice, and so to conclude by examining the notion of a linguistic act and the relation between such acts and their interiorizations, for example between assertion and judgement. Only by treating of these topics could one claim to have answered the question I have taken as my title: but, you will be glad to know, I thought it best not to try to complete the answer now.

Chapter 8

Elucidations of Meaning

James Higginbotham

1 INTRODUCTION

Throughout this article, I am concerned with interactions between the meanings of words and the meanings of syntactic structures. A general point of view, articulated in this section, aims to set the stage for discussions tending to progressively finer detail in the sections that follow. In Section 2, I will elaborate further a thesis advanced in Higginbotham (1985), that reference to events is the appropriate way to view properties of subordinate clauses and modification, without the introduction of higher types. In Section 3, I consider some syntactic and semantic properties of raising and control, especially in connection with a modified form of the framework of Chomsky (1981), and the determination of the meaning of anaphoric connections. In both of these sections, the systematic elimination of what have come to the called 'semantic postulates' (or, in another way of looking at it, their reduction to the consequences of the ascription of meanings to words) will be emphasized. Section 4 treats some points of the semantics of the classical opaque contexts, following the method suggested in Higginbotham (1986), and brings out some connections with comprehension principles, recently brought into close consideration by the work of Bealer (1982) and Chierchia (1984). Taken altogether, the thrust of these investigations will be that one may clear the path to the principles of interpretation for complex syntactic structures, if only the meanings of words can be seen rightly. [Sections 3 and 4 are omitted here.—Ed.]

To speak and understand a language, one must know the meanings of its words, and also the semantic effects of combining those words in given

First appeared in *Linguistics and Philosophy* 12 (1989): 465–518. Reprinted with kind permission from Kluwer Academic Publishers. Abridged for this volume.

syntactic configurations. Our knowledge of meaning thus has two components, the lexical and the structural. In a conception of semantic theory whose aim is not only to describe meanings, but also to contribute to the explanation of how knowledge of meaning is acquired, it is natural to ask how these components of meaning come to be known, and how knowledge of each may serve as evidence for the other.

Words, at least, must be learned. Conversely, in view of the language-readiness of the learner, it is a natural conjecture that, once the syntax of a language is fixed, its words are all that must be learned in order to master it. If this view of semantics is correct, or close to correct, then one may reduce the burden on semantic theory, in the following sense: if the meanings of words are known, then the meanings of all phrases and sentences are known. The computation of structural meaning then follows a universal algorithm, the same for all human languages, and the learner's task in the apprehension of meaning is reduced to grasping the words.

However, the reduction, in the sense just described, of semantic theory to lexical meaning does not of itself simplify the task of language learning. For the meanings of words are not, and perhaps cannot be, simply *given* to the learner; rather, they must be extracted from the syntactic and semantic environment, and from the surrounding context, in the course of normal maturation. The perceptual features of that environment, both linguistic and non-linguistic, serve as evidence for what words may mean, and what people might intend by saying them. The problem is then to get from this evidence to knowledge of words. Lexical peculiarities abound, and must be stated in a full description of linguistic knowledge. But lexical meaning must in part be distilled from discernible structure, and its effects on the meanings of sentences.

Given the assumptions stated, a kind of dialectic is set up. We have the theoretical aim of deriving the meanings of whole sentences from the meanings of their words, given certain structural semantic principles P, presumed universal, or very nearly so. In this endeavor, much of the lexicon can be taken as known, or determinable to the fineness of detail needed for the investigation; the chief problem is to solve for P. But the language learner, for whom P is by hypothesis available as part of native endowment, has to derive the lexicon, initially completely unknown. Because P is nearly universal, a simple lexicon is not to be purchased at the cost of idiosyncratic structural rules, varying from language to language. But the lexicon is learnable, and it is therefore no advance to posit arbitrary lexical idiosyncrasy in the service of a universal account of structural meaning.

An adequate semantic theory for human languages will therefore exhibit deductive powers of two distinct sorts. First, we shall be able, given a string of words with known meanings, to deduce within the theory the syntactic structures that they admit, and the meanings of those structures. Second, we shall be able to deduce the central semantic characteristics of unknown words from the positions in which they are seen to occur.

Consider deductions of the first sort, of the meanings of sentences from the meanings of their words. If we are to trace meanings back through general principles of grammar to lexical items, then there must be some conception of what goes into our knowledge of the meaning of a word. What, for instance, is the meaning of the transitive verb 'cut', as it occurs in (1):

(1) I cut the fish (yesterday)?

To a first approximation, following Hale and Keyser (1985), it may be stated as follows:

(2) 'cut' is a V that applies truly to situations e, involving a patient y and an agent x who, by means of some instrument z, effects in e a linear separation in the material integrity of y.

The thematic structure of 'cut', following the notation in Higginbotham (1985), is $\langle 1, 2, E \rangle$, where 1 is designated for agent, 2 for patient, and E for the open position for events or situations.

It is to be verified by the careful sifting of examples that the clauses in (2) are each of them necessary to characterize cutting: for instance, you cannot be said to cut syrup at room temperature by passing a knife through it, because you cannot separate it by this means; you cannot cut a fish by punching a hole in it, or by stapling it to the wall, because the separation in the fish's body is not linear; if fish had zippers you couldn't cut them by unzipping them (any more than you can cut a briefcase by just unzipping it), since the fish's material integrity would not be disturbed thereby; and so on.

The information in (2) is needed to know what cutting is, or what 'cut' means. But this information is not to be dignified with the title of a *definition*. It does not even have the right form for that, since it does not provide a *synonym* for 'cut', but attempts to explain or to make clear what that word is *true of*. For this reason, an entry as in (2) I will call an *elucidation* of the meaning of a word.[1]

The value of an elucidation lies in what it implies for the meanings of sentences; that is, in what it does for the semantics of the whole language. What is shown in (2) will account, by familiar means, for the contribution of 'cut' to (1). The positions 1 and 2 of its thematic structure will be assigned to 'John' and 'the fish', respectively, thus discharging these positions in the terminology of Higginbotham (1985). The adjunct phrase 'yesterday', along with various other possible adjuncts, such as 'with a knife', 'along its back from head to tail', will find their place as well, as predicated of the position marked by E.

We have fairly good intuitions of meanings for some of the verbs, nouns, and adjectives, especially those whose reference is drawn from bodies and their actions on one another. The meanings of many other words are harder come by, particularly so if it is an aim to isolate their thematic structure. Nevertheless, I should like to conjecture that the method illustrated with the simple verb 'cut' deserves a wide application.

A general strategy might be outlined as follows: assuming (i) that all thematic positions are discharged in one or another of a limited set of ways, and (ii) that thematic discharge takes place only under highly restricted syntactic conditions, to assign thematic structures and elucidations of meaning to lexical items in such a way that the configurations into which those items enter will, by the specified means of thematic discharge, lead to a correct assignment of meanings to the sentences in which they occur. This is the strategy that I will follow and illustrate throughout.

If successful, the strategy may shed light not only on the characteristics of structural meanings, but also on the question how the thematic structure of a word is extracted from its syntactic environment. For, suppose now that a speaker is given (1), presumed to be a sentence, and that 'cut' is a new item for that speaker, the other items being known. From the knowledge (i) that English sentences have to have verbs, and that English VP is head-initial; (ii) that every thematic position in a V must be discharged; (iii) that NPs in a sentence must be assigned some role in its interpretation; (iv) that, taking 'yesterday' to be an adjunct, it must, to contribute to the interpretation, be predicated of the position E of a verb; and (v) that if there is an agent in (1), then the agent must be the subject NP, the learner will be able to infer (3):

(3)   'cut' is a transitive action verb in the past tense that applies truly to situations e involving objects y and x, appearing as internal and external arguments respectively, where x is agent, if anything is

—not an insignificant amount of information.

The little victory just shown, the partial determination of meaning on the basis of the slender evidence of a single sentence, was cheaply won, since we assumed that the other lexical items in (1) were already known. In the general case, the problems do not come one at a time, but all together, as in a system of simultaneous equations, of which our common knowledge of common words is one solution.

The meaning of a word, as I will understand that notion here, comprises that knowledge that is available about its reference or function, as shown through reflective explanation or through practice, to the competent speakers of a language. Room for experts may be provided as needed; but for most common words expert knowledge is not linguistically relevant, in that it neither reflects the linguistically central aspects of the meanings of sentences, nor makes the learner's task significantly easier or harder. It may be helpful further to see the notion of meaning that I will employ against a familiar background of philosophy and method.

In the positivist tradition, knowledge of meaning was constituted by such things as recognitional abilities and the grasp of synonymies, both of these being abilities of the individual speaker. Attributions of meaning were governed by the speaker's exercise of these cognitive powers. This conception leads to a strictly idiolectal notion of meaning.[2] In recent years, of a non-idiolectal view of meaning, and knowledge of meaning, has gained ground in philosophy.[3] Which, if either, is appropriate for linguistic theory?

Evidently, the meaning of a word in a speaker's environment is something that is to be apprehended by that speaker in the course of learning a language. Also, an individual can be *wrong* about what a word means, and can know only part of the meaning of a word (and be well aware that he or she is in this condition). The meaning of a word resents itself as objective, so that a misinformed or ignorant speaker can have a mistaken opinion or merely partial knowledge of meaning. But one is not ignorant, or at least not ignorant in this way, of one's own idiolect; that is, the meanings one is ignorant of are not one's *own* meanings. Must we therefore depart from the idiolectal conception? Not necessarily, since a number of cases of ignorance or misinformation, and perhaps all of them, can be thought of as ignorance about other people, or as involving conflicts between what one's own idiolect says the meaning of a word is, and one's intentions to speak as others do.

Of course, adopting an idiolectal conception as a proper framework for semantic theory does not require accepting the positivist tradition from which it sprung. In particular, it does not require assuming that recognitional and other abilities are constitutive of reference. To adapt an example due to Hilary Putnam, the words 'elm' and 'beech' in my grammar are not semantically distinguished except insofar as I know they refer to different things; the lexical entry for each is, approximately, "some kind of local (deciduous) tree." I cannot recognize elms or beeches, or tell them apart, without expert guidance: but I know that elms aren't beeches.

I have spoken of knowledge and elucidations of meaning; but I have not given a criterion distinguishing knowledge of meaning from knowledge of fact, or from what Quine (1960) calls attention to under the name of "widely shared collateral information." It is natural, therefore, to ask where meaning, strictly speaking, leaves off, and encyclopedic knowledge of the world begins. However, I doubt that a criterial demarcation of lexical and worldly knowledge is necessary, or even desireable, to pose the problems of knowledge and its acquisition that linguistic theory hopes to answer. For linguistic theory, the minimal condition of theoretical adequacy is that one gets the forms and interpretations of sentences, and the connections between them that are known routinely by native speakers, to come out right. A theory that accomplished this, and at the same time meshed with an empirically supported account of the path taken by the language learner, would not be thwarted by not having a criterion of meaning, strictly so-called.

Everything we know and can talk about is reflected somewhere in our language, in its "distribution of morphemes," to use the classical phrase. But linguistic theory is not just the whole theory of human knowledge. A traditional way of isolating linguistic knowledge from knowledge of other kinds is to formulate a sharp distinction between knowledge of meaning and worldly knowledge. However, what is crucial to the design of language is not some distinction, however drawn, between properly semantic information, on the one hand, and empirical or collateral information, on the other, but rather the distinction between information that has systematic grammatical effects and information that does not.

Children come rapidly to learn that knives are things you cut with. Should we regard this knowledge as analytic to the word 'knife'? The *linguistically* salient point is that instruments are promoted to subject-position in English, so that one has alongside sentences like "I cut the meat with a knife" also "The knife cut the meat." Instrumentality is not keyed to the preposition 'with': I can look at the moon with my father's binoculars, but they cannot look at the moon. So the instrumentality of knives in cutting is reflected in the grammatical function of the word 'knife', a fact that requires systematization and explanation. The analyticity or syntheticity of "Knives are for cutting" is simply an orthogonal question. (It is also orthogonal, for the same reason, whether "Knives are for cutting" is necessary or contingent.) Similarly, Hale and Keyser show that the acceptability of a variety of 'middle' constructions in English is governed by whether the object is to be considered physically altered by the action of the verb (that is, as altered in the course of the events of which the verb is true). Since cutting, as in (3) above, involves a linear separation along a surface, one has (4):

(4) The fish cuts easily.

but with verbs that do not involve physical alteration, middles are unacceptable, as in, "The fist pats easily" and the like. Again one may ask whether the facts about 'cut' that license (4) are analytic to that verb; and again the outcome seems orthogonal to the question how the language-learner comes to know these facts. It is not that distinctions between analytic and synthetic, or necessary and contingent, have to be regarded with grave suspicion; my skepticism in the present context comes from not seeing that they have a demonstrable theoretical use in the central issues of form and interpretation.

The above preliminary considerations are not, of ccourse, offered as arguments for the view I shall adopt; whatever may be right or wrong about it will have to emerge from the elaboration of the theory itself.

A final preliminary note to the reader: I am all too aware that my discussion, like any that attempts in relatively brief compass to do systematic justice to some central issues in semantics, has many a gap. In extenuation, I can plead (apart from lack of space) only that, since the picture that I wish to present differs, not just in detail but in many interconnected ways, from the one that has (if anything has) been standard in recent work, it seemed important to show how the view I will explore works out in detail in a number of typical, and critical, examples.

2 ADVERBIAL REFERENCES TO EVENTS

Davidson (1967) introduced the idea that ordinary predicates, specifically action verbs, contain, besides the positions assigned to overt arguments in the sentences in which they occur, also a position for events. This idea has been exploited in recent work by a number of authors, including T.

Parsons (1985), Croft (1984), Schein (1985), Higginbotham (1983, 1985, 1986), Vlach (1983), Sproat (1985), and references cited in those works. Since the outlines of Davidson's view are widely known, I will not rehearse it here. In this section, I will develop some applications of the view, mainly in connection with adverbials. Each of these applications involves the clarification of the meanings of lexical items. Some of the examples were prominent in the literature of generative semantics, and were not so much solved as set aside in later discussions.

A minimal Davidsonian account of events must regard them as the exemplary relata of causal relations. They have *participants*, whose connections with the events in which they participate are expressed in language through the assignment of thematic roles. In Higginbotham (1985) it was assumed that ordinary predicates, including stative verbs and adjectives, had an 'E-position', as I called it, in their thematic grids. A portion of the lexical entry for a verb like 'walk' might then be as in (5):

(5) 'walk', $(+V, -N)$, $\langle 1, E \rangle$, Actor (1)

The interpretation of this entry is: 'walk' is a binary verb, true of a thing x and an event e just in case e is a walking by the actor x. As in the case of (1), the positions 1 and E are discharged in such a manner as to give to simple sentences like 'John walks' the interpretation shown in (6) (ignoring tense):

(6) (Ee) walk (John, e)

The information given in (5) is obviously essential to knowing what 'walk' means. Further elucidation of its meaning, on a model analogous to that given above for 'cut', is needed to explain the proper role of adjuncts.[4]

A persistent feature of language that the E-position hypothesis explains is that of what I will call *root-related homonyms*. The basic case is illustrated by (7)–(8):

(7) John sprayed paint on the wall.

(8) John sprayed the wall with paint.

As Levin (1985) points out, these sentences are plainly not interchangeable: John may spray paint on the wall by writing his name, or by marking a spot on the wall with an 'X'; in such a case, it would be wrong to say that he sprayed the wall with paint. The object in (8) must be, as I shall say, *thoroughly involved* in the activity reported, in order that the report be true. The verbs in these sentences must be thematically distinguished, in that the PP in each can be dropped. They are homonymic, but different, and it seems obvious that they need not be learned independently. From what root meaning can these both be derived?[5]

Now, examples like Levin's go back to early studies in Case Grammar, and specifically to Fillmore's seminal article 'The Case for Case' (1968). Minimal pairs discussed by Fillmore include (9) (10):

(9)   The bees were swarming in the garden.

(10)   The garden was swarming with bees.

Fillmore suggested that both of these sentences had the underlying form (11):

(11)   Swarming [*locative* garden] [*dative* bees]

and that whichever argument became the subject lost its preposition. However, it is clear that, just as in Levin's examples, (9) and (10) are not synonymous: for the bees to be swarming in the garden, it is sufficient that a compact clot of bees have located itself in some corner of the garden, in which case the garden need not be swarming with them; and conversely, for the garden to be swarming with bees, it is sufficient that bees be found thickly-enough dispersed throughout the garden, in which case the bees need not form any clot that would count as a swarm of them.

The non-synonymy of (9) and (10) made a problem for Fillmore, given the assumption, general at the time, that underlying structure was determinate of meaning. We can, however, do justice to Fillmore's insight if we suppose that a basic predicate of events underlies both of the verbs 'swarm'; and similarly for Levin's example.

As Davidson observed, but recast into the resent terminology, the thematic relations that participants bear to events may be spelled out in terms of binary predicates, surfacing in the language as prepositions, or else indicated by positions in the argument structure. Thus, 'John walks' might be understood as in (12):

(12) $walks_0(e)$ & Actor(John, e)

But it would be wrong to suppose that the '$walks_0$' of (12) is the familiar 'walks' of English, given in (5); on the contrary, the latter verb has two argument positions, not one, and cannot appear without discharging the Actor thematic role. (We do not have sentences like "It walks," meaning that there is some walking going on.) So we must regard '$walks_0$' as a kind of theoretical construct. However, it and similar constructs enable us to characterize the root-related homonyms.

Suppose that the notion *spraying* is given first of all by a theoretical predicate 'spray$_0$'. This predicate applies to events of certain kinds, viz., the sprayings, and it is known of such events that they involve an actor, a medium (such as paint), and a direction (on the wall, in the air, sideways) in which the medium is dispersed by the activity of the actor. One might depict what is known about spraying by a diagram as in (13):

(13)

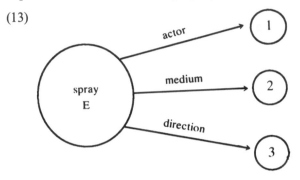

From the relations shown in the diagram, one may construct the verbs 'spray$_1$' and 'spray$_2$', among others, by means of the following explicit definitions:

(14) $\text{spray}_1(x, y, e) \leftrightarrow \text{spray}_0(e) \ \& \ \text{Actor}(x, e) \ \& \ \text{Medium}(y, e)$

(15) $\text{spray}_2(x, y, e) \leftrightarrow \text{spray}_0(e) \ \& \ \text{Actor}(x, e) \ \& \ \text{Direction}(y, e)$

The requirement of the thorough involvement of the denotation of the direct object may be expressed directly, by placing further conditions on the right-hand sides of (14)–(15) (in which case these definitions are not strictly correct as they stand), or it may be a semantic property that arises from the syntactic configuration in which the verbs are placed (in which case the definitions are correct, but a non-lexical feature of syntactic structure carries a meaning of its own). For present purposes, one may remain agnostic on the question which of these, if either, is the proper way to view things (see Levin, *op. cit.* for some discussion of similar cases). In any case, the mystery of root-related homonyms, and with it the notion 'optional argument,' disappears: the verbs 'spray' really are different, and at the same time both are derived from a single source.

The method just illustrated for 'spray' applies to Fillmore's cases, among many others. In (9)–(10), for instance, we have two root-related homonyms 'swarm', and the distinction in meaning between the sentences in which they occur is traceable to the requirement that the arguments of each, their subjects, be thoroughly involved in the event in question.

The upshot of the above discussion is that positing an E-position in the thematic grids of verbs, and the elucidation of verbal meaning in terms of a primary, although theoretical, classification of events, allows us to systematize an array of material pertaining to the semantics of simple sentences in a proper and uniform way. I turn now to the implication of events in adverbial modifications, via the E-position.

In (1985), I suggested that thematic discharge, or the elimination of open thematic positions in lexical items and in complex phrases, came in several varieties, all of them controlled by the configuration of *government* (mostly identifiable with sisterhood). The basic modes of discharge are as in (16):

(16)   a.   Theta-*marking*, exemplified by pairs consisting of a predicate and one of its arguments;

      b.   Theta-*binding*, exemplified by determiners or measure-words and their nominals, as in 'every dog', interpreted as 'for every x such that dog(x)';

      c.   Theta-*identification*, exemplified in simple adjectival modification, as in 'white wall' interpreted as 'white(x) and wall(x)'.

      d.   *autonomous* theta-marking, where the value assigned to the open position in the theta-marker is the attribute given by its sister constituent.

These modes of discharge are the primitive semantic operations, or the building-blocks of structural meaning, on the view taken here. Knowledge of the meaning of a word first of all requires knowledge of which combinations of (16a–d) it participates in. For further discussion and examples, the reader is referred to (1985).

The most elementary examples of modification are interpreted as simple conjunctions, and involve as their characteristic mode of discharge only theta-identification as in (16c). For concreteness, we rehearse this case. Given the syntactic structure (17):

(17) $[_{N'} [_A$ white, $\langle 1 \rangle] [_N$ wall, $\langle 1 \rangle]]$

we identify the open positions in modifier and modified, giving the complex N' the thematic grid $\langle 1 \rangle$, satisfied by a thing x that satisfies both adjective and noun. The identification discharges the open position in the modifier.

The color words are in many cases apparently *absolute*, that is, not relative to a choice of attribute or comparison class.[6] But many adjectives are relative to attributes. Adverbial modification is also attribute-relative, as discussed below.

Are there simple cases of adverbial modification, involving only theta-identification? It seems to me that one such is the adverb 'fatally', which came to my attention through the discussion of Cresswell (1985). Consider (18):

(18) Mary fatally slipped.

Analysis of this case will exemplify part of the approach taken here.

If Mary fatally slipped, then something happened to her, namely the slip, which was fatal to her. So we should assign to the adjective 'fatal' the thematic grid $\langle 1, 2 \rangle$, and the meaning that 1 is an event that killed 2, as 'a fatal wound', 'a fatal jump'. This meaning for 'fatal' gives the right interpretation to (19), for example:

(19) Mary slipped, and it (the slip) was fatal.

Indeed, this sentence is a paraphrase of (18) itself.

We make the prima facie simplest assumption, that an adverb derived from an adjective has the same thematic grid as that adjective. Then for 'fatally slipped' we shall have the structure (20):

(20) $[_{V'} [\text{fatally}, \langle \underline{1, 2} \rangle] [_{V'} \text{slipped}, \langle 1, E \rangle]]$

where thematic positions are identified as shown.[7] The interpretation is as in (21):

(21) slipped(*x*, *e*) & fatal(*e*, *x*)

Hence for (18) we derive truth-conditions in (22):

(22) (E*e*) slipped(Mary, *e*) & fatal(*e*, Mary)

Most adverbial modifications involve more than theta-identification. The following example, from an important article of McConnell-Ginet (1982), is representative:

(23) Lisa rudely departed.

The sentence is ambiguous as between the 'manner' reading (Lisa was free to depart, but did so without saying goodbye) and what I will call the *stative* reading (Lisa should not have departed when she did, and it was rude of her to have done so). McConnell-Ginet's own view of the ambiguity involves positing an extra place in the verb 'depart' under the manner reading, of which the adverb becomes an argument. For the stative reading, the adverb becomes an argument of another hypothetical verb, securing by postulate the effect of Thomason and Stalnaker (1973), who took VP as argument of the adverb.

McConnell-Ginet's discussion is confined to adverbs and VPs; but the properties of (23) carry over intact into nominals such as (24) and (25):

(24) Lisa's rude departure

(25) the rudeness of Lisa's departure

Thus (24) can purport to refer to a departure that was rude in manner, or to a departure that it was rude of Lisa to have made at all; similarly, the rudeness of her departure can consist in her having abruptly left without saying goodbye, or in her having left when she ought not have done so. In analogy with her discussion of adverbs, then, we would have to conclude that the adjective 'rude' may be an argument of the noun 'departure', and that the head noun 'rudeness' of (25) is semantically an argument of the embedded possessive NP, contradicting the intuitive semantics of such phrases.

Following the assumption that manner adverbials are attributive predicates of events, we would conceive of (23) in its manner interpretation as involving theta-identification and simple conjunction, together with autonymous theta-marking of the V′, comparable to adjectival modifications. The 'manner' reading of (24) follows along routinely, since departures are events; and we may hope to understand the abstract nominal (25) on a par with examples that involve no nominalizations of verbs, such as 'the hardness of this stone'. More precisely, we assign to the adjective 'rude', and to its adverbial form 'rudely', the grid $\langle 1, 2\rangle$, where 1 ranges over situations and 2 over attributes. Then, where the brackets '[¶ ... ¶]' are used for intensional abstraction, the V′ 'rudely departed' is interpreted as in (26):

(26) $depart(e, x)$ & $rude(e, [\P e': depart(e', x)\P])$

that is, "e is a departure by x, and it is rude (for a departure by x)."

Is the rudeness of something relative to the usual traits of the subject, as the slowness of something may be relative to the usual pace of its actor? Certainly we can say things like (27):

(27) Lisa departed rather graciously for her.

where the relativization of 'graciously', understood as a manner adverbial, to Lisa's usual ways is made explicit. However this may be, we can certainly appeal as above for 'slowly' to relativizations where the subject is not involved, for we have 'depart$_0$' as the basic predicate of events, from which the English verb 'depart' is constructed. We then get for the V′ not (26) but (28):

(28) depart(e, x) & rude$(e, [\P e': \text{depart}_0(e')\P])$

Now consider the stative interpretation of (23). It is obviously desirable to relate this to the paraphrase (29):

(29) For Lisa to have departed was rude of her.

as well as to other forms, such as (30)–(31):

(30) It was rude of Lisa [PRO to have departed]

(31) Lisa was rude in that she departed.

and so forth. For this case, following what we see in these adjectival constructions, we recognize an interpretation of 'rude', and of 'rudely', as three-place predicates with thematic grids $\langle 1, 2, 3 \rangle$ and the interpretation shown in (32):

(32) situation 1 is rude of actor 2 with respect to attribute 3

In application, for instance to (29), the attribute is of course the attribute mentioned in the very subject sentence that indicates the situation. The interpretation is to be as in (33):

(33) rude$(((\text{the } e) \text{ depart } (\text{Lisa}, e)), \text{Lisa}, [\P e': \text{depart}(\text{Lisa}, e'\P])$

that is, the departure by Lisa was rude of Lisa, as classified by that very attribute (of being a departure by Lisa).

Returning to (23), we take up the VP 'rudely departed' as in (34):

(34) rude$(e, x, [\P e': \text{depart}(e', x)\P])$ & depart(e, x)

The subject fills its usual role, and the sentence is completed by quantifying over the E-position in the usual way, giving (35):

(35) (Ee) rude$(e, \text{Lisa}, [\P e': \text{depart}(e', \text{Lisa})\P])$ & depart(e, Lisa)

that is, Lisa departed; and she was rude to have done so.[8]

McConnell-Ginet's discussion of the manner adverbial has the merit that it makes the factivity of the construction a matter of course; in other words, that it licenses the conditional (36) as obviously true, and a matter of logical form:

(36) If Lisa departed in a rude manner, then Lisa departed.

The present proposal has this property also. Moreover, we secure the factivity as well of (23), by a general rule that applies to constructions having the same form.

In my discussion of the stative interpretation of 'rudely', I have followed a version of the suggestion of Davidson (1967) for the adverb 'intentionally'. In the latter case, as Davidson notes, we have alongside sentences like (37) also (somewhat awkward) paraphrases such as (38)–(39):

(37) Oedipus intentionally married Jocasta.

(38) It was intentional of Oedipus that he married Jocasta.

(39) Oedipus's marrying Jocasta was intentional of him.

This example is important as showing the necessity of relativization to an attribute: it would be most unfair to Oedipus to conclude from any of the above that he intentionally married his mother. At the same time, the implications of each of these that Oedipus *did* marry Jocasta are appropriately trivial.

I have followed McConell-Ginet in assuming a lexical ambiguity in the adverb 'rudely'. Like other lexical ambiguities, this one calls for an explanation. In this respect, it is to be noted that some adverbs have no 'manner' interpretation at all. The adverb 'intentionally' itself is one. Returning to (27), repeated here:

(27) Lisa departed rather graciously for her.

we note that the explicit parenthetical relativization of the adverb to Lisa's usual ways forces the manner interpretation.[9] The parenthetical produces nonsense when combined with a stative adverb:

(40) Oedipus married Jocasta intentionally for him

thus underscoring the absence of a manner interpretation. Conversely, there are numerous adverbs for which no stative interpretation exists: we have, e.g., "John wrapped the meat loosely," but not "It was loose of John to wrap the meat." For the moment, then, there is no general way of tying the stative and manner adverbials together, except by comments on their individual meanings.

Another illustration of the fruitfulness of the E-position is provided by the word 'almost'. The ambiguity of sentences like (41), seen as giving evidence for lexical decomposition in generative semantics in McCawley (1973), ought to remain a puzzle even if lexical decomposition is rejected:

(41) John almost killed Bill.

The ambiguity, it will be recalled, is this: in one of its senses (41) has it that John did something that almost amounted to killing Bill (that he beat him within an inch of his life, for instance); in another, John need not have done anything to Bill, but is said to have been on the point of doing something that would have killed Bill had other circumstances not intervened (John was all set to shoot Bill, but his gun jammed); and there is also a third case, where John shot at Bill, and missed by a whisker. The ambiguity becomes more salient in pseudoclefted constructions, as (42)–(43):

(42) What John did to Bill was almost kill him.

(43) What John almost did to Bill was kill him.

McCawley argued, correctly, that if 'kill' is regarded as a simple binary predicate, then there is no room in the structure (41) for any ambiguity to arise.[10]

Syntactically, the qualifier 'almost' has something of a wild-card distribution. Its meaning we might elucidate as that of a two-place predicate true of an object and an attribute if the first came nigh unto the second.[11] Such is the meaning that we see in examples like (44)–(45):

(44) He ran almost a mile.

(45) He is almost a doctor.

A distance is almost a mile if it is nigh unto the attribute of being a mile long; a person is almost a doctor who is close to the attribute [¶x: doctor(x)¶]. In more detail, 'almost' is an adverb with a meaning that might be elucidated as in (46):

(46) 1 is a thing close to (having) the attribute 2.

(The ambiguity between reference to the attribute and reference to the subject's having it is considered further in Section 4 [omitted here— ed.].)

Consider the case (47):

(47) John almost fell down.

Significantly, it is not sufficient for the truth of (47) that something almost have happened that would have made John fall down had it occurred (say, my throwing a banana peel in John's path). In almost falling down, John must have tottered.

The semantic properties of (47) follow in a reasonable way from the assumption that 'fell down' has an E-position, and that among the objects that may be thought of as having, or coming near to having, one or another attribute are events. Following the method of Higginbotham (1985). I propose the thematic structure in (48):

(48) $[_{V'} [_{AdvP} \text{almost}, \langle 1, 2 \rangle] [_{V'} \text{fell down}, \langle 1, E \rangle], \langle 1, E \rangle]$

where the AdvP autonymously theta-marks the V' 'fell down', through position 2, and position 1 of the AdvP is identified with the E-position of that V'. In a more familiar notation (not, if I am right, the notation of English itself), we may say that the passage to the containing V' in (48) is made by welding the ordered pair of formulas (49) into the single formula (50):

(49) almost(x, y), fell down(z, e)

(50) almost$(e, [\P e': \text{fell down}(z, e' \P)])$

If this diagnosis is correct, it is clear why John must have tottered in order almost to fall down: something e must have happened to him that almost amounted to a falling-down. This case strongly argues that it will not do to lay the apparent ambiguity of (41) to mere lack of specificity; for then there would be no accounting for why (47) is unambiguous.

Returning to (41), we predict that, if there is an event which comes nigh to he attribute of being a killing of Bill, then John (in sone sense) almost killed Bill. What is it for an event to be so? It seems to me appropriate to group together the case where Bill is badly beaten with the case where John just missed hitting him with a bullet, since the latter interpretation is available in 'John almost shot Bill', where no question of causal consequences arises.[12]

The discussion so far leaves us with an account of two ways in which it can be true that John almost killed Bill, but not of the case where Bill was stopped from even attempting to kill Bill, because his gun jammed or the police intervened. The natural conjecture for this last is that, as a limiting case, the binary 'almost' may rate a proposition as almost being the case—that is, true. Let this be understood as follows:

(51) almost([¶(Ee) kill(John, Bill, $'e$)¶], [¶x: Tx¶])

This meaning would naturally be associated with assignment of sentential scope to the adverb. But then, why is that scope not available in (47)? A survey appears to suggest that the absence of ambiguity is correlated with the absence of the Actor thematic role. Thus in 'John almost arrived', we have the implication that John at least got close; not so in 'John almost went there'. Other cases with 'unaccusative' vs. agentive verbs seem to confirm the generalization. Again, we may imagine that (47) is evaluated in a context where falling down would be a deliberate action on John's part, as in a play or a game of football.[13] In those contexts, I think, we can easily understand (47) as conveying that John was on the point of falling down, but thought the better of it—so in those contexts he need not have tottered. I will have to leave the issue thus posed undeveloped here (one possibility that may be mentioned is some form of agent causation); in any case, I hope to have made the point that the ambiguities of 'almost' most plausibly stem from its being, not a higher-order operator of some sort, but a binary predicate, whose thematic structure and associated interpretation are in harmony with the general point of view here developed.

Among the modes of thematic discharge given in (16), I have considered here theta-identification and autonymous theta-marking. Binding is to be found also in adverbs, as in Lewis (1975). A single example may indicate how things are to go, assuming the E-position: a sentence like (52) will be understood as in (53), with the adverb binding that position:

(52) John never walks to work.

(53) [Never (e): $B(e)$] walks to work(John, e)

(where B expresses some background condition, such as John's travels to work). The intricacies of adverbial quantification would take us too far afield to be considered here.

I have assumed throughout this discussion that reference to events is incorporated in English and other languages in a very specific way, namely by argument positions. However, these positions are not, for the cases that we have been discussing, *assigned* to arguments: they are discharged, not by theta-marking, but by another device, existential closure. Hence it might be asked whether it is possible to relativize predicates and sentences to events, construed on one or another model that incorporates the obvious facts about the thematic relations of events to their participants, without going so far as to place an E-position in thematic or argument structures.

Besides various applications, such as those given here, there are two major reasons for thinking that references to events belong inside the thematic structures of words. The first, which has been repeatedly documented, is that there are a number of nominal locutions that show explicit reference to events, both as a matter of lexical semantics and, still more significantly, as a matter of morphological derivation.[14] Insofar as it is typical of morphological processes making nouns from verbs or adjectives to single out one among the available thematic positions as the position for the objects over which the noun is to range, we may take the existence of derived forms as strong evidence that reference to events is found within the thematic grid of the root. Even simple finite clauses can serve to refer to events, as in (54):

(54) John fell down after Bill hit him.

Cases like these yield readily to the semantics shown in (55):

(55) (Ee) [fell down(John, e) & after(e, (the e') hit(Bill, John, e'))]

In this case, the E-position in the V′ is the subject of the adjunct clause.

Second, although the E-position is in a way hidden in ordinary predicates, it does in fact surface in a number of special cases. One of these, discussed in Higginbotham (1986) with reference to work by Chierchia (1984), is the main verb 'do' of agency. When one does something, such as go to the movies, there is not, or at least there is no apparent reason to suppose that there is, in addition to the events of going to the movies to which one is related as actor or agent, also *another* event that is one's being the agent of the going: there is just the going. So the 'do' of agency would have a lexical entry as in (56):

(56) 'do', (+V, −N), $\langle 1, E \rangle$; Actor $(1, E)$

That is, there is no extra thematic relation of 1 to E in 'do', since that verb by itself *expresses* the actor relation. Hence in (57):

(57) John did that.

the verb is a binary predicate, both of whose thematic positions meet up with arguments.

What goes for 'do' goes also for 'undergo', as in examples discussed in Williams (1986b):

(58) John underwent an operation.

So this verb also has an E-position, filled by an internal argument. Similarly 'suffer', as in 'John suffered rejection'.

Finally, there is a reason why the E-position should surface only occasionally. Suppose that the basic account of lexical structure exhibited in (13) is correct. Then *e* is distinguished already from other potential arguments in that it is the thing to which thematic relations are borne, and not a bearer of relations.

Notes

An earlier draft of this article was circulated by the Lexicon Project of the MIT Center for Cognitive Science, with support provided by grants from the System Development Foundation and the Kapor Family Foundation. I am much indebted to Howard Lasnik, Richard Larson, Gabriel Segal, Scott Weinstein, Edwin Williams, and the students in my fall, 1985 classes for discussion. Comments from Gennaro Chierchia, Noam Chomsky, Alexander George, James McCawley, Sally McConnell-Ginet, and from anonymous reviewers, have also been very helpful.

1. I will not here undertake the task of rendering interpretations in the sense of (2) in a systematic and regimented form. While recognizing that the systematization of entries is a significant goal, it seems to me that the path toward this goal has to proceed from a better informal survey of the lexicon than we now possess.

2. See Burge (1986).

3. For a recent statement, see Dummett (1986).

4. It may be appropriate to clarify at once the use throughout this article of formulas like (6) above in spelling out interpretations. The formulas are not representations of English sentences at any linguistic level, but expressions of a regimented extension of English, that are to be provably equivalent to the truth of the English syntactic structures whose regimentations they are; it is for this reason that I write that they show the interpretations of English sentences. In a systematized semantics for English, or the fragment of it now under discussion, we would establish (i):

(i) 'John walks' is true $\leftrightarrow$ (Ee) walk(John, e)

This article is concerned with spelling out a view of what it is that is to be proved about the English sentences in question. Details of the methods of proof (straightforward for the cases in question) will be given in work now only in preparation. Finally, it should be noted that demonstrative elements are ignored throughout; I would add these following the method suggested in Burge (1974).

5. Sometimes the notion "optional argument" is used for the PPs in (7) and (8). This idea suffers from a general lack of coherence, in addition to being

inapplicable to the case at hand. For an optional argument must be represented in the thematic structure of the verb; and verbs that differ in their optional arguments are different. On the assumption that arguments are just what verbs assign thematic roles to, that there should be optional argument is even contradictory.

6. There are, of course, contextual effects: a wall is said to be white if it is white merely on its visible surface; but white ivory must be white through and through. Furthermore, as remarked in (1985) even the adjectives that are paradigmatic of relativity to an attribute, words like 'tall' or 'big', have contextually relative absolute uses. My assumption here is that context-relativity is distinct from linguistic relativity of an adjective to a comparison class.

7. I assume here that adverbs are Chomsky-adjoined to projections of V, if not at S-Structure, then at LF; for some discussion, see Chomsky (1986), Fukui (1986), and references cited in those works.

8. McConnell-Ginet notes paraphrases such as that of the stative interpretation of (23) and (30), expressing also some doubts about their evidential status; however, her semantic postulate on p. 155 in effect records just this sort of paraphrase.

9. I am indebted here to Sally McConnell-Ginet. See also Ernst (1986).

10. In fact, McCawley supposed that (41) was triply ambiguous. For some discussion of the possibilities, see Dowty (1979).

11. In the following discussion I am much indebted to Ewa Higgins, and use several observations from Higgins (1985).

12. Compare 'John almost shot Bill to death', which is ambiguous.

13. I am indebted here to James D. McCawley.

14. For a recent discussion, see Sproat (1985). Thomason (1984) gives a number of examples, at the same time expressing some skepticism that fully general rules can be found.

References

Bealer, G.: 1982, *Quality and Concept*, Clarendon Press, Oxford.

Burge, T.: 1974, 'Demonstrative Constructions, Reference, and Truth', *The Journal of Philosophy* 71, 205–23.

Chierchia, G.: 1984, *Topics in the Syntax and Semantics of Infinitives and Gerunds*, unpublished doctoral dissertation, University of Massachusetts, Amherst, Massachusetts.

Chomsky, N.: 1981, *Lectures on Government and Binding*, Foris Publications, Dordrecht, Holland.

Chomsky, N.: 1986, *Knowledge of Language*, Praeger Publications, New York.

Cresswell, M.: 1985, *Adverbial Modification*, D. Reidel, Dordrecht, Holland.

Croft, W.: 1984, 'Issues in the Logical Form of Adverbs and Adjectives', ms., Stanford University and SRI International.

Davidson, D.: 1967, 'The Logical Form of Action Sentences', in N. Rescher (ed.), *The Logic of Decision and Action*, University of Pittsburgh Press, Pittsburgh, Pennsylvania: Reprinted in Davidson (1980), pp. 105–48.

Dowty, D.: 1979, *Word Meaning and Montague Grammar*, D. Reidel, Dordrecht, Holland.

Ernst, T.: 1986, 'Manner Adverbs and the Sentence/Predicate Distinction', ms., The Ohio State University.

Fukui, N.: 1986, *A Theory of Category Projection and Its Applications*, unpublished doctoral dissertation, MIT, Cambridge, Massachustts.

Hale, K., and S. Keyser: 1985, 'The View from the Middle', ms., MIT, Cambridge, Massachusetts.

Higginbotham, J.: 1983, 'The Logical Form of Perceptual Reports: An Extensional Alternative to Situation Semantics', *The Journal of Philosophy* 80, 100–127.

Higginbotham, J.: 1985, 'On Semantics', *Linguistic Inquiry* 16, 547–93.

Higginbotham, J.: 1986, 'Linguistic Theory and Davidson's Program in Semantics', in E. LePore (ed.), *Truth and Interpretation: Perspectives on the Philosophy of Donald Davidson*, Basil Blackwell, Oxford, pp. 29–48.

Higgins, E.: 1985, 'On Adverbial Modification', ms., MIT.

Levin, B.: 1985, 'Lexical Semantics in Review: An Introduction', in B. Levin (ed.), *Lexical Semantics in Review*, MIT Lexicon Project Working Papers, 1, pp. 1–62.

Lewis, D.: 1975, 'Adverbs of Quantification', in E. Keenan (ed.), *Formal Semantics of Natural Language*, Cambridge University Press, Cambridge, pp. 3–15.

McCawley, J.: 1973, 'Syntactic and Logical Arguments for Semantic Structures', in O. Fujimura (ed.), *Three Dimensions in Linguistic Theory*. TEC Corp., Tokyo, Japan, pp. 259–376.

McConnell-Ginet, S.: 1982, 'Adverbs and Logical Form', *Language* 58, 144–84.

Parsons, T.: 1985, 'Underlying Events in the Logical Analysis of English', in E. LePore and B. McLaughlin (eds.), *Actions and Events: Perspectives on the Philosophy of Donald Davidson*, Basil Blackwell, Oxford, pp. 235–67.

Quine, W. V.: 1960, Word and Object, MIT Press, Cambridge, Massachusetts.

Schein, B.: 1985, *Event Logic and the Interpretation of Plurals*, unpublished doctoral dissertation, MIT, Cambridge, Massachusetts.

Sproat, R.: 1985, *On Deriving the Lexicon*, unpublished doctoral dissertation, MIT, Cambridge, Massachusetts.

Thomason, R., and R. Stalnaker: 1973, 'A Semantic Theory of Adverbs', *Linguistic Inquiry* 4, 195–220.

Thomason, R.: 1984, 'Some Issues Concerning the Interpretation of Gerundive and Derived Nominals', *Linguistics and Philosophy* 8, 73–80.

Vlach, F.: 1983, 'On Situation Semantics for Perception', *Synthese* 54, 129–52.

Chapter 9

Knowledge of Meaning and Theories of Truth

Richard K. Larson and Gabriel Segal

We have been pursuing semantics as a theory of the real but unconscious knowledge of speakers. We have argued that what is known by speakers is a set of rules and principles that are finite in number and compositional in form. These underlie our grasp of semantic facts, our capacity to make semantic judgments, and our ability to communicate with and understand others. Precisely what does this knowledge consist in? What kinds of rules and principles are known?

The idea we will adopt and develop in this book derives from the work of Donald Davidson, who proposes that the work of a semantic theory can be done by a particular sort of formal theory called a *truth theory*, or *T theory* for short.[1] A T theory for a particular language L is a deductive system that has the resources to prove something about the truth value of every sentence of L. More specifically, for each sentence of L it proves a theorem of the form in (T), where S is a name or description of the L sentence and p has the same truth value as the sentence referred to by S:

(T) S is true if and only if p.

The language from which S is drawn is typically referred to as the *object language*. It is the language that we are theorizing about. Here the object language is L. The language used to discuss the object language is typically referred to as the *metalanguage*. It is the language in which our theory is stated. Here the metalanguage is English. A T theory produces theorems that pair a sentence S of the object language L with a sentence p of the metalanguage. These two are paired together by the relation "is

First appeared in *Knowledge of Meaning* (Cambridge: MIT Press, 1995). Reprinted by permission of the MIT Press.

true if and only if" (hence-forth abbreviated "is true iff").[2] Theorems of the form (T) are called *T sentences* or *T theorems*.[3]

1 T THEORIES

The easiest way to understand the workings of a T theory is to examine a concrete instance. So let us consider a sample T theory for a small sublanguage of English that we will call PC, since it includes some elements of the propositional calculus. PC contains an infinite number of sentences, although they are all of a highly restricted form. In particular, PC contains the three elementary sentences *Phil ponders, Jill knows Kate*, and *Chris agrees*. PC also contains all sentences that can be produced from the basic three either by joining them together with one of the sentence conjunctions *and* or *or*, or by prefixing them with the negation *it is the case that*. For present purposes, we will assume that the elementary sentences are generated by the three rules in (1), and that the remainder are generated by the rules in (2). Rule (1a) may be read as saying that *Phil ponders* is a sentence (an S), and similarly for (1b, c). Rule (2a) may be read as stating that any two sentences (Ss) jointed by the word *and* is also a sentence, and similarly for (2b, c):[4]

(1) a. S → *Phil ponders*
    b. S → *Chris agrees*
    c. S → *Jill knows Kate*

(2) a. S → S *and* S
    b. S → S *or* S
    c. S → *It is not the case that* S

Under these rules PC will contain all of the example sentences in (3) (among infinitely many others):

(3) a. [$_S$ Phil ponders]
    b. [$_S$ Chris agrees]
    c. [$_S$ Jill knows Kate]
    d. [$_S$[$_S$ Phil ponders] or [$_S$ Chris agrees]]
    e. [$_S$[$_S$ Jill knows *Kate*] and [$_S$[$_S$ Phil ponders] or [$_S$ Phil ponders]]]
    f. [$_S$ It is not the case that [$_S$ Jill knows Kate]]
    g. [$_S$ It is not the case that [$_S$[$_S$ Phil ponders] or [$_S$ Chris agrees]]]

The *labeled brackets* in (3) depict the derivational histories of complex sentences. For example, (3g) is formed by our first connecting *Phil pon-*

ders and *Chris agrees*, using *or* to form a disjunction (as permitted by (2b)) and then attaching *it is not the case that* to form the negation of this disjunction (as permitted by (2c)). These derivations may be also depicted by means of familiar tree diagrams or *phrase markers.*[5] Thus (3d) can be associated with the tree in (4a). Likewise, (3f) can be represented with the tree in (4b):

(4) a.

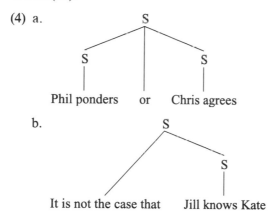

b.

The three elementary sentences *Phil ponders, Jill knows Kate*, and *Chris agrees* appearing as the leaves on these trees are treated as complex words in PC. That is, they are assigned no internal syntactic structure. Following standard terminology, we will refer to these elementary sentences as the *terminal nodes* in the tree. And we will refer to nodes with internal syntactic structure, for example, the built-up Ss in (3d–g), as *nonterminal nodes.*

A T theory for PC will allow us to derive a T theorem for each sentence of PC. The T theory we wish to explore consists of three basic parts. First, there are interpretation rules for the terminal nodes in the PC grammar. These assign a semantic contribution to the basic components of PC, as in (5):

(5) a. *Phil ponders* is true iff Phil ponders.
    b. *Chris agrees* is true iff Chris agrees.
    c. *Jill knows Kate* is true iff Jill knows Kate.

Second, there are interpretation rules for the nonterminal nodes. These allow us to derive T sentences for configurations with internal structure from the T sentences for their smaller component sentences. Thus for *any* sentences S, S_1, and S_2,[6]

(6) a. [$_S$ S_1 *and* S_2] is true iff both S_1 is true and S_2 is true
b. [$_S$ S_1 *or* S_2] is true iff either S_1 is true or S_2 is true
c. [$_S$ *It is not the case that* S] is true iff it is not the case that S is true
d. [$_S\alpha$] is true iff α is true (for any elementary sentence α)

Third and finally, there are *production rules*, which license inferences of certain specified kinds. These allow us to reason from the elementary and general semantic rules and to prove results using them. For PC we will adopt two production rules. The first is called substitution of equivalents, abbreviated (SE). This rule is defined as follows:

(SE) Substitution of equivalents

$$\frac{F(\alpha)}{\alpha \text{ iff } \beta}$$
$$\overline{F(\beta)}$$

According to (SE), if we have proved a statement involving α (i.e., $F(\alpha)$) and have proved that α is equivalent to β, (i.e., α iff β), then we may conclude the result of substituting β for α in the statement (that is, we may conclude $F(\beta)$). The second rule is universal instantiation, or (UI):

(UI) Universal instantiation

$$\frac{\text{For any S, } F(S)}{F(\alpha)}$$

Universal instantiation will allow us to apply the general rules in (6) to particular instances.

The three elements specified above may be viewed as jointly specifying a deductive system. The interpretation rules in (5) and (6) function as semantic axioms from which we can prove a T sentence for each sentence of PC, using the production rules (SE) and (UI).

1.1   A sample derivation

We can illustrate how this system works with example (3d). Recall this string of words receives the structure in (4a), which we represent with labeled bracketing as in (7):

(7) [$_S$[$_S$ Phil ponders] or [$_S$ Chris agrees]]

To derive the T sentence for this structure, we begin at the top (leftmost) S node and interpret it in terms of its subsentences. We do this by applying (UI) to the axiom in (6b):

(8) [s[s Phil ponders] or [s Chris agrees]] is true iff either
     [s Phil ponders] is true or [s Chris agrees] is true (by (6b), (UI))

The axiom in (6d) tells us how further to unpack each of the two disjuncts
on the right-hand side of "iff" in (8):

(9) a. [s Phil ponders] is true iff *Phil ponders* is true (by (6d), (UI))
     b. [s Chris agrees] is true iff *Chris agrees* is true (by (6d), (UI))

The clauses in (5a) and (5c) then tell us how to spell out the T sentence for
each of the two elementary sentences on the right-hand sides of the "iff"
connectors in (9):

(10) a. *Phil ponders* is true iff Phil ponders. (by (5a))
     b. *Chris agrees* is true iff Chris agrees. (by (5b))

To complete the T sentence for (3d), we now use the production rule (SE),
working our way back up the tree. Suppose that we let (9a) be $F(\alpha)$, "*Phil
ponders* is true" be α, and "Phil ponders" be β. By (10a), we have "α iff β,"
so we can use (SE) to conclude "[s Phil ponders] is true iff Phil ponders":

(11) [s Phil ponders] is true iff *Phil ponders* is true   (9a)

     Phil ponders is true iff Phil ponders   (10a)
     ―――――――――――――――――――――――――――――――――――――
     [s Phil ponders] is true iff Phil ponders

     (by (9a), (10a), (SE))

We now reapply the same strategy, this time letting (9b) be $F(\alpha)$, letting
"*Chris agrees* is true" be α, and letting "Chris agrees" be β. By (10b), we
have that "α iff β", so again, using (SE), we may conclude that (12b):

(12) a. [s Phil ponders] is true iff Phil ponders (by (9a), (10a), (SE))
     b. [s Chris agrees] is true iff Chris agrees (by (9b), (10b), (SE))

Next let (8) be $F(\alpha)$, let "[s Phil ponders] is true" be α, and let "Phil
ponders" be β. By (12a), we have "α iff β," so we can use (SE) to conclude
that (13):

(13) [s[s Phil ponders] or [s Chris agrees]] is true iff either
     Phil ponders or [s Chris agrees] is true (by (8), (12a), (SE))

Finally, let (13) be $F(\alpha)$, let "[s Chris agrees] is true" be α, and let "Chris
agrees" be β. By (12b), we have "α iff β," so, using (SE), we conclude that
(14):

(14) [s[s Phil ponders] or [s Chris agrees]] is true iff either
      Phil ponders or Chris agrees (by (13), (12b), (SE))

We have shown that the PC sentence *Phil ponders or Chris agrees* is true if
and only if Phil ponders or Chris agrees. Intuitively, of course, this is a
true outcome.

1.2   The nontriviality of T theories

Results like that in (14) are achieved by means of a formally precise
theory using explicit procedures. Nonetheless, they may appear entirely
trivial at first sight. After all, how informative is it to learn that *Phil ponders or Chris agrees* is true if and only if Phil ponders or Chris agrees? In
fact, such results are quite informative and the initial impression of triviality is really an illusion of sorts. It is important to locate the source of
this illusion and to dispel it.

Like other scientific statements, T theorems state facts or hypotheses
about certain phenomena, specifically, about linguistic phenomena. T
theorems thus make statements *in* a language *about* a language: language
is mentioned in the T theorem, and it is used to formulate the T theorem.
Given any object-language, there will be a vast array of languages in
which we can formulate T sentences for sentences of that object language.
We can give the truth conditions of a sentence of English using a T sentence formulated in Chinese. We can also give the truth conditions of a
sentence of English using a T sentence formulated in English. This is the
case with the T theory for PC. The object language, PC, is a small fragment of English. And the metalanguage in which we give our axioms,
production rules, and results is also English.

Now it is a simple fact about sentences and their truth conditions that
any sentence of a language *L* can be used to state its own truth conditions
in *L*. That is to say, T sentences of the following homophonic form are
(almost) always true for any sentence S of English:[7]

(T*) *S* is true if and only if S.

It is partly this fact that gives results like (14) their air of triviality. The T
sentence (14) mentions a sentence of English (*Phil ponders or Chris agrees*)
and then goes on to use this very sentence to state its truth conditions.
Part of what is obvious about T theorems like (14) is thus their truth.
Nonetheless, it is important to see that despite the obvious truth of (14),
this T sentence is far from trivial.

The general informativeness of truth theories can be seen most clearly when we consider examples where the object language and metalanguage diverge. For example, consider an alternative T theory for PC in which the metalanguage is German rather than English. Under this choice, (5) and (6) would be replaced by (5′) and (6′):

(5′) a. *Phil ponders* ist wahr genau dann wenn Phil nachdenkt.
   b. *Chris agrees* ist wahr genau dann wenn Chris zustimmt.
   c. *Jill knows Kate* ist wahr genau dann wenn Jill Kate Kennt.

(6′) a. [s S$_1$ *and* S$_2$] ist wahr genau dann wenn S$_1$ wahr ist und S$_2$ wahr ist.
   b. [s S$_1$ *or* S$_2$] ist wahr genau dann wenn S$_1$ ist wahr oder S$_2$ wahr ist.
   c. [s *It is not the case that* S] ist wahr genau dann wenn S nicht wahr ist.
   d. [sα] ist wahr genau dann wenn S wahr ist (fur jeden Elementarsatz α)

These results are evidently neither uninformative nor trivial. For a monolingual speaker of German, (5′) and (6′) will provide information about an infinite set of English sentences. Using these rules, the German speaker will be able to determine the truth conditions for all of the sentences comprising PC. However, (5′) and (6′) do not say anything different from what is said by the original (5) and (6). Indeed, they say just the same thing! They attribute the same truth conditions to the same elementary sentences of PC, and they provide the same rules for dealing with complex sentences of PC. It's just that they say these things in German, and so make them available to monolingual German speakers.

Why, then, do homophonic T sentences appear trivial? The answer is not too hard to find. If someone is in a position to understand a T sentence, then, obviously, they must understand the metalanguage, the language in which the T sentence is formulated. Or, more precisely, they must understand as much of the metalanguage as is used in the T sentence. For example, to understand any T sentence of the form of (14), it is necessary to understand as much English as is used in its formulation:

(15) S is true iff Phil ponders.

Understanding this includes understanding the RHS, "Phil ponders." Now anyone who understands the sentence *Phil ponders* knows that it is

Table 1
Truth table for the material biconditional, "iff"

p	q	p iff q
t	t	t
t	f	f
f	t	f
f	f	t

true if and only if Phil ponders. Understanding *Phil ponders* requires this at the very least. Consequently, anyone who is in a position to understand any T sentence of the form of (15) already knows what is stated by (5a): *Phil ponders* is true if and only if Phil ponders. But, of course, (5a) just is a T sentence of the form of (15). So anyone who understands (5a) must already know that it is true.

In a sense, then, homophonic T sentences are uninformative: anyone who is in a position to understand them already knows enough to know that they are true. But it certainly does not follow from this that what is stated by such a T sentence is not highly substantive. It is highly substantive, as we can see by the nonhomophonic cases. The purportedly unsubstantive (5a) says no more and no less than the evidently substantive (5'a).[8]

Although T sentences are not trivial, at the same time we should emphasize that by themselves they carry less information than one might think. In a T sentence the "if and only if" that appears is just the ordinary *material biconditional*, defined in standard logic texts by the truth table in table 1. According to this table, a sentence made up of two sentences p and q joined by "iff" is true whenever p and q are either both true or both false (and false otherwise). Since the "is true" in a T sentence is just the usual predicate "true," any T sentence in which the sentence on the left of "iff" has the same truth value as the RHS will be true. For example, (16) is perfectly true.

(16) *Snow is white* is true iff pigs have curly tails.

The upshot is that although T sentences carry nontrivial semantic information relating the truth value of a sentence to a worldly condition, the information they carry is somewhat limited. As we will shortly see, the issue of exactly how much information a T sentence carries is a central one.

2 T THEORIES AS THEORIES OF MEANING

We began our investigations by characterizing semantics as the study of linguistic meaning, more precisely, as the study of knowledge of meaning. From this perspective, it may seem quite puzzling to be told that knowledge of meaning amounts to knowledge of a T theory. After all, a T theory like the one for PC proves statements about the truth of sentences, for example, those in (17). It proves nothing directly about the meanings of sentences; it does not give results like (18):

(17) a. *Phil ponders* is true iff Phil ponders.

   b. *Phil ponders or Chris agrees* is true iff either Phil ponders or Chris agrees.

(18) a. *Phil ponders* means that Phil ponders.

   b. *Phil ponders or Chris agrees* means that either Phil ponders or Chris agrees.

But then what is the relation between the two? How are we to understand the claim that knowledge of the one might be responsible for our grasp of the other?

As a step toward clarifying the connection, note first that although our T theory for PC doesn't derive explicit statements of meaning, its results are similar to the latter in an important respect. Observe that while the sentences in (17) differ from those in (18) in involving the relation "is true iff" instead of the relation "means that," the two sets of statements are alike in pairing exactly the same object language sentences and metalanguage sentences together. That is, the relation "is true iff" defined by our truth theory for PC (that is, by (5), (6), (SE), and (UI)) is similar to the relation "means that" insofar as it associates an object-language sentence with a metalanguage sentence that intuitively gives its meaning. We will call a T theory that yields the same pairing as that given by "means that" an *interpretive T theory*. And we will call the T sentences yielded by an interpretive T theory *interpretive T sentences*.

We propose that knowledge of this special kind of T theory, an interpretive T theory, is what underlies our grasp of semantic facts, our ability to understand our language in the way that we do. That is, we propose the following empirical hypothesis about knowledge of meaning:

The T hypothesis   A speaker's knowledge of meaning for a language *L* is knowledge of a deductive system (i.e., a system of axioms and production rules) proving theorems of the form of (T) that are interpretive for sentences of *L*.

On this view, speakers who know the semantics of their language have internalized a system of rules like those in PC. The deliverances of this system, its (interpretive) T sentences, are what the speaker draws upon to encode and decode utterances, to make semantic judgments, and so on.

To explain the connection between interpretive T theories and semantic knowledge more fully and to show how the former could serve as a theory of meaning, it is useful to consider the T hypothesis in the light of two important questions that arise naturally in connection with it. First, under the T hypothesis, speakers are claimed to have internalized an interpretive T theory. But is it really possible to define such a T theory formally? Since "is true iff" and "means that" are different relations, is it possible to give a set of axioms and deductive principles for a natural language whose T theorems pair all and only those paired by "means that"? We call this the *extension question*.

Second, under the T hypothesis, knowledge of interpretive T theorems is claimed to provide the information that underwrites judgments about semantic facts. But would knowing an interpretive T theory be enough to tell you what the sentences of a language mean, to ground judgments about semantic properties and relations, and to account for the external and internal significance of language? Again, since "is true iff" and "means that" are two different relations that appear to talk about two very different things, truth versus meaning, a positive answer is by no means clear. We call this the *information question*.[9]

2.1 The extension question

There are two separate parts to the extension question. First, there is the question of whether we can give a T theory that's sufficiently productive, that is, one that proves an interpretive T theorem for every sentence of the object language. Second, there is the question of whether we can give a T theory that's not overproductive, that is, one that proves no uninterpretive results.

Both of these questions appear to be fundamentally empirical ones, to be answered by providing an interpretive T theory of the kind required. In subsequent chapters we will explore such theories for a wide variety of natural-language constructions, including such central ones as predicates, names, quantifiers, descriptions, anaphoric elements, modifiers, and embedded clauses. And there are other constructions not discussed here, such as comparatives, that have also been more or less satisfactorily dealt with. There remain, of course, elements of natural language that have so far resisted satisfactory T-theoretic treatment. Subjunctive conditionals are one well-known example. As we will see, however, the track record of T theories is a strong one—strong enough to warrant optimism about their power in principle to account for the full range of natural-language structures.

The second part of the extension question—whether it's possible to give a T theory that proves no uninterpretive results—is a bit more complex. As described earlier, a T theory consists of two basic parts: semantic axioms for interpreting lexical items and phrasal structures, and production rules for deducing results from the axioms. T theorems are the product of these components acting together, and including either the wrong axioms or the wrong production rules can yield uninterpretive results. For example, suppose that axiom (5c) (repeated below) were replaced with (19), or suppose that we simply added (19) to PC as it now stands:

(5c) *Jill knows Kate* is true iff Jill knows Kate.

(19) *Jill knows Kate* is true iff Jill knows Kate and 2 plus 2 equals 4.

Then we could obviously deduce uninterpretive T-theorems (including (19) itself). This is the case even though (19) is perfectly true, as are all the new T theorems that would result from its addition to the original theory.

A similar result holds with the production rules in the T theory for PC. This theory includes the highly restricted rule of substitution (SE) (repeated below). However, suppose that we replaced (SE) with the alternative rule (SE').

(SE) Substitution of equivalents

$$F(\alpha)$$
$$\alpha \text{ iff } \beta$$
$$\overline{F(\beta)}$$

(SE') Substitution of equivalents, version 2

For any formula β such that α iff β,

$$F(\alpha)$$
$$\overline{F(\beta)}$$

The two differ as follows: under (SE), we are allowed to substitute a formula β only if we have *proved* that it is equivalent to α as part of the derivation whereas under (SE'), we are allowed to substitute *any* β that is materially equivalent to α.[10] Such a change will once again yield uninterpretive results. For example, it is a fact of logic that the equivalence in (20) holds.

(20) Jill knows Kate iff Jill knows Kate and 2 plus 2 equals 4.

Accordingly, from this fact and interpretive axiom (5c), (SE') will allow us to prove an uninterpretive T theorem, as shown in (21):

(21) *Jill knows Kate* is true iff Jill knows Kate.   (5c)
   _____

   Jill knows Kate is true
   iff Jill knows Kate and 2 plus 2 equals 4.   (by (20), (21a), (SE'))

The original production rule (SE) blocks this result because it does not allow substitution of arbitrary equivalents but only βs that have been proven equivalent to α as part of the derivation. This feature essentially encapsulates the derivation, blocking the importation of extraneous results like (20). Hence uninterpretive consequences like (21) are not derivable.

The contrast between (SE) and (SE') illustrates a further important point. Readers familiar with logic will note that the alternative substitution rule (SE') is not a bizarre one in any sense but is just the rule for substitution of material equivalents standardly assumed in logic texts.[11] What we see, then, is that one of the standard inference rules of logic is not admissible in our semantic theory. This result is in fact quite general. If one were to add to our T theory for PC even the ordinary, truth-preserving rules of standard logical systems, one would easily be able to prove uninterpretive consequences, such as the T theorem in (22):[12]

(22) *Chris agrees and Jill knows Kate* is true iff it is not the case that
   either it is not the case that Chris agrees or it is not the case that
   Jill knows Kate.

That the inference rules of logic allow too wide a class of deductions for semantic theory is not an accidental fact but rather follows from the very different goals of logic and semantics, as conceived here. As Frege (1956 [1918]) succinctly put it, logic is the general theory of truth. The inference rules of logic are motivated by the conceptual or philosophical goal of characterizing the set of true inferences from a given set of axioms. By contrast, semantics is a theory of speaker knowledge. The production rules of semantics are motivated by the empirical goal of describing part of what speakers know about a language. On the assumption that what speakers know about meaning is an interpretive T theory, it is clear that semantic production rules cannot aim to yield T sentences that are merely true. Rather, they must yield T sentences that are both true and interpretive, since these are what underlie knowledge of meaning, according to the T hypothesis.[13]

Since most familiar logical systems are not adequate for the purposes of semantics, it is an interesting but, at present, largely unexplored question as to what rules or production procedures should be employed in their place. The semantic theory given for PC restricts the class of deductions from its (interpretive) lexical axioms to those derived by (UI) and (SE). As we will see in subsequent chapters, if the semantic axioms for the PC fragment are modified in even relatively simple ways, it becomes necessary to introduce additional production rules to prove the most basic interpretive results, and this immediately brings the risk of overgeneration. The production rules proposed in succeeding chapters do in fact produce only interpretive consequences. But there is no general theory at present of what formal procedures are best suited to the job of building interpretive T theories. This is an area of research that may ultimately draw on the resources of logic (proof theory) and psychology (reasoning and cognition).[14]

2.2   The information question

The T hypothesis not only assumes that it is possible to give an interpretive T theory for a language. It also asserts that knowledge of such a theory underlies judgments of actual meanings—that the information necessary for the latter is present in the former. This claim is strong and controversial. And, initially at least, it looks very dubious. The problem is that there just doesn't seem to be enough information in a T theory—even an interpretive one—to support judgments of meaning.

To see why this is so, consider the hypothetical situation in which you know no French but have at hand a T theory for French written out in English. Suppose that this theory is interpretive but that you don't know it is. You are now faced with the problem of finding out what certain French sentences mean, for example, the sentence in (23):

(23) Les oiseaux ont des plumes.

You can use the T theory to derive T theorems, such as (24):

(24) *Les oiseaux ont des plumes* is true iff birds have feathers.

But do you now know what any French sentence means? Do you know what *Les oiseaux ont des plumes* means? No. For (24) neither says nor implies (25), nor does anything else in the T theory.

(25) *Les oiseaux ont des plumes* means that birds have feathers.

The point here is a simple one. Since there are many true T theories for French in English that are not interpretive, you have no way of knowing in advance whether the particular theory before you is interpretive or not. And since you don't know that the theory is interpretive, you can't move from (24) to (25). What goes here for explicit theories would seem to go for tacit ones as well. If you had tacit knowledge of an interpretive T theory for French, then you would not seem to know enough to know what French sentences mean.

It is tempting to think that this problem might be solved by specifying some new additional theory that, if known, would allow speakers to discover whether their T theory were interpretive or not. If you had a second, independent theory permitting you to deduce that the T theory yielding (24) was interpretive, then you could indeed pass from (24) to (25). On reflection, however, this does not seem to be a promising strategy. After all, a theory allowing you to deduce that (24) is interpretive would be one telling you that "birds have feathers" gives the meaning of *Les oiseaux ont des plumes*. But this is just the job we want our T theory to do! We wanted the T theory to correlate sentences with their meanings. Hence it looks like we could succeed in this strategy only at the price of putting our T theory out of a job.

T theorems treated as interpretive   To motivate a more promising line on how a T theory might underlie judgments of meaning, let us recast the problem situation. In the previous little scenario, you had an interpretive T theory, but you didn't know that it was such. Because you didn't know this and couldn't deduce it, you didn't know you could use the theory to interpret French. Suppose, however, that because of your basic makeup you were compelled to take the T theory in your possession as interpretive, regardless of its actual status. Suppose, for example, that you are the kind of person who can't stand uncertainty, and to avoid it when dealing with Frenchmen, you simple decide to treat any T theory for French that comes into your hands as giving the meanings of French sentences. Whenever you are presented with a French sentence, you turn to your T theory, calculate a T sentence for it, and take whatever results on the RHS of the biconditional as giving its meaning.

Notice that in this circumstance, the knowledge gap noted earlier is still present: you still do not *know* that your T theory is an interpretive one, and the theory neither contains this information nor allows you to deduce it. Nonetheless, the T theory does underwrite judgments of meaning for you, since you use it to interpret and produce French sentences and you behave toward French speakers as if it rendered the meaning of their words. Given your constitution, you proceed as if the gap in question did not exist, as if you already knew your theory were interpretive. Notice furthermore that if the T theory coming into your hands were in fact interpretive, then all your judgments and acts would be appropriate: you would correctly render the meanings of French sentences, you would form correct beliefs about what French speakers were trying to say to you, you would plan actions correctly in accord with these beliefs, and so on. Thus a T theory could serve as a theory of meaning for you, and do so successfully, if you were constituted to treat any T theory as interpretive and if events conspired to bring an interpretive T theory into your hands.

We suggest this second scenario as our answer to the information question—as a picture of how T theories might successfully serve as semantic theories for human speakers despite containing no explicit information about the meanings of expressions. Suppose that as a matter of biological endowment (that is, of universal grammar), humans are designed to acquire T theories. These theories are not written out in some natural language in a book but rather are represented internally in the brain. In the course of learning a language, speakers fix axioms and production rules yielding T theorems as outputs. Suppose further that humans are designed to treat whatever T-theory they acquire as interpretive. That is, whenever they are called upon to produce or interpret their own sentences or the sentences of others, they draw on the results of their internalized T theory and treat its theories as interpretive: they take the RHS to give the meaning of the natural-language sentence mentioned on the LHS. Finally, suppose that events conspire to give speakers an interpretive T theory in the course of development. Then, although the T-theory contains no explicit information about the meanings of words and sentences, it would still be responsible for the semantic abilities of speakers. They would use it to make the judgments they do. The knowledge gap, though present, would be irrelevant to understanding or action, since speakers would proceed as if they already knew that their T theory were interpretive. Furthermore, since speakers would have learned an interpretive T theory as a matter of fact, all interpretations, beliefs, and actions undertaken in accordance with it would be appropriate ones. The use of the T theory as a theory of meaning would be successful.

The success of this proposal evidently turns on the correctness of its three central assumptions:

- Humans are designed to acquire a T theory.
- Humans are designed to treat any T theory they acquire as interpretive.
- In the course of development humans learn a T theory that is interpretive in fact.

About the first assumption we will say nothing more except that it is an obvious one, given our general approach. People acquire knowledge of meaning, and since we are assuming that a T theory underlies this knowledge, obviously we must assume that people acquire a T theory. As usual, checking the truth of such an assumption will be a highly indirect matter, involving the success of the larger enterprise as a whole.

The second assumption—that the mind treats T theorems as if they were interpretive—is also hard to spell out further here, given our present understanding of cognition and the brain. One potential way of conceptualizing the assumption is in terms of the familiar idea of the mind as computer. We might imagine the brain as manipulating an internal T theory that takes sentences of a natural language as input and computes T sentences for them in some "brain language" or "language of thought." Suppose that the outputs of these computations are passed to the various mental processors or modules responsible for inference, belief formation, planning of action, and suppose that these modules process the information to infer, form beliefs, plan, etc. The processors that need information about the literal meanings of sentences receive T theorems as their inputs and then proceed under the assumption that the RHSs of these T theorems give the meanings of what's mentioned on the left. In this way, information derived from a theory of truth is treated as information about meaning by the very way the mind passes information around—by the mind's functional architecture, so to speak.[15]

Our third assumption, that speakers acquire an interpretive T theory in the course of development, requires a bit more comment and involves a number of interesting subtleties. First of all, it's clear that this third assumption interacts strongly with the other two. If we are designed to acquire a T theory and to treat any T theory we acquire as interpretive, then we had better acquire the right one. If we somehow came to possess a noninterpretive T theory of French, then by assumption, we would necessarily apply it to the words of French speakers, misunderstanding them, forming wrong views about their beliefs, acting inappropriately toward them, and so on. How is it, then, that we acquire an interpretive T theory, and what *ensures* that the T theory we acquire *is* interpretive?

We suggest that nothing guarantees that the T theories we acquire are interpretive for those around us. Rather, this is a contingent result. That people do quite generally acquire an interpretive T theory is, we suggest, the product of two factors: universal grammar and the very context in which natural language is acquired. In the first chapter we observed that there must be principles of universal grammar heavily constraining the hypotheses that natural-language learners make about the meanings of words and phases. A child acquiring *rabbit*, for example, has available as hypotheses not only (26a) but also (26b), (26c), and an indefinite number of others:

(26) a. *Rabbit* refers to rabbits.
   b. *Rabbit* refers to undetached rabbit parts.
   c. *Rabbit* refers to rabbits, and either dogs are shaggy or dogs are not shaggy.

Similarly, a child acquiring the meaning of the structure [$_{NP}$ NP's N'] has available (27a) but also (27b), (27c), and an indefinite number of other hypotheses:

(27) a. *Rosa's book* refers to the book that Rosa has.
   b. *Rosa's book* refers to the book that Rosa is.
   c. *Rosa's book* refers to the book that Rosa has, and 2 is an even prime number.

Incorporating (26b, c), (27b, c), or any other equally wrong axioms into the T theory will produce uninterpretive T theorems for sentences containing *rabbit* or the possessive structure *Rosa's book*. Since we assume that UG constraints on lexical and phrasal acquisition play a role in excluding these candidates, UG will serve to guide learners to an interpretive T theory.

A second important factor in acquiring interpretive T theories, we believe, is the very situation in which natural language is acquired.

Languages are internalized in the context of communication—in the context of activities such as speaking and understanding. As T theory learners, we hypothesize and fix our rules while engaged in the practical tasks of trying to get our thoughts across to others and trying to grasp what others are trying to say to us. The primary data we use to fix semantic rules in the first place is thus speech produced in communicating with others. Semantic rules are, if you like, fundamentally hypotheses conjectured and tested so as to be interpretive of the speech of others, that is, so as to make sense of their meanings and to make our speech meaningful to them.

What is involved in testing such hypotheses? Briefly put, it seems that we try to see whether interpreting people's speech in the way we conjecture makes sense of their overall motions and interactions with the environment. That is, we try to see whether our interpretation of their speech makes their interactions appear *rational*. In the learning situations described above, for example, a child might plausibly decide between (26a) and (26c) on these grounds. If sentences containing *rabbit* are interpreted using (26a), then such sentences are simply about rabbits. If they are interpreted using (26c), however, then sentences containing *rabbit* are about rabbits and shaggy dogs. Presumably, a child or other learner would be able to determine by context whether shaggy dogs are under discussion or not, for example, by noting whether the person speaking held up a picture of a dog, made sounds like a dog, or in some other way introduced dogs into the subject matter. By examining the behavior of the speaker and making basic assumptions about the rationality of their actions, we can hypothesize about the meanings of their words. The principles of reasoning we are employing here are, of course, ones that apply not only to speech behavior but also to human action as a whole. We evaluate not only our hypotheses about the meaning of others' speech in this way but also our conjectures about their beliefs, motives, fears, etc. All are judged under the goal of trying to make maximal sense of their actions and behavior.

It is worth stressing, in conclusion, that our answer to the information question—our claims about how knowledge of T theorems might be capable of supporting judgments of meaning—is predicated on the assumption that there is a positive answer to the extension question. It remains a separate hypothesis that an interpretive T theory can actually be given for a full natural language. Our point here is that, on the assumption that such a T theory can be given, knowledge of this theory could account for judgments of actual meaning. In principle, then, judgments of actual meaning are within the scope of what T theories can explain.

Notes

1. See, in particular, Davidson 1965, 1967, 1968, 1970. Our view of the place of T theories in semantics departs significantly from Davidson's in a number of important respects. The formal notion of a T theory originates with Alfred Tarski (1944, 1956).

2. We use the term "relation" loosely. We do not intend to imply that the "p" on the right hand side of a T sentence names a state of affairs or proposition or anything that could be considered one relatum of a two-place relation.

3. Since we shall frequently be discussing T sentences and their various parts, it will be useful to introduce some abbreviatory terminology. We will use "LHS" to refer to what appears on the left hand side of the "if and only if" (i.e., "S is true") and "RHS" to refer to what appears on the right (what stands in the position occupied by "p" in (T)). We will also use "The S on the left" to refer to the object-language sentence named on the left. Also, we use italics to display words in the object language, the language under discussion, and we use quotation marks to mention words in the metalanguage, the language being used. In both cases we have language denoting language.

4. The rules in (1) and (2) are formally refereed to as *context-free phrase-structure rules*.

5. See chapter 3 of *Knowledge of Meaning* for a detailed discussion of phrase markers.

6. More properly, for any phrase markers S, S_1, S_2 whose root node is S.

7. The qualification "almost" is needed here for at least two reasons. First, some sentences of the form (T*) will be paradoxical rather than true, for example, (ii):

(i) (i) is false.

(ii) *(i) is false* is true iff (i) is false.

Second, object-language sentences with indexicals or demonstratives may falsify (T*) if those words refer to different things in their occurrences on the right- and the left-hand side of the "iff." For example, (iii) can be false if we take the two occurrences of "this sentence" to refer to different sentences:

(iii) *This sentence is on the left-hand side of a biconditional* is true iff this sentence is on the left-hand side of a biconditional.

8. For a different view of the informativeness of homophonic T theorems, see Higginbotham 1989.

9. This is one version of a problem that John Foster (1976) raised for Davidson's original version of the claim that a T theory could serve as a semantic theory.

10. We might also notate this with syntactic turnstiles "⊢" to indicate provability:

(SE) Substitution of equivalents

$$\frac{\vdash F(\alpha) \\ \vdash \alpha \text{ iff } \beta}{\vdash F(\beta)}$$

(SE') Substitution of equivalents, version 2

For any formula β such that α iff β,

$$\frac{\vdash F(\alpha)}{\vdash F(\beta)}$$

11. For logic texts especially directed toward toward linguistics studies, see Partee 1978 and Partee, ter Meulen, and Wall 1990.

12. Sine $[p \, \& \, q]$ is equivalent to $\neg[\neg p \lor \neg q]$.

13. Truth thus plays very different roles in logic and semantics, despite its central status in both. As Jason Stanley has observed to us, this point entails that it would be misleading to describe a semantic theory as a "logic" or its deductive procedures as "logical inference rules." Such a description would imply the goal of deducing true statements generally, which is not what we are concerned with in semantics. It is likely that a semantic theory will share two important features of standard logical systems: it will be be truth-preserving, and it will be a formal deductive system, in the sense that, for any set of sentences $\{S\}$ and any sentence k of the metatheory, it should be decidable whether k is a consequence of $\{S\}$.

14. Some theorists have addressed the problem of overgeneration by giving the T theory a full set of deductive rules, while permitting only a limited number to appear in the proofs of T theorems (see Davies 1981). This approach is unsuitable for our purposes, since it is not clear what it would mean for the semantic module to contain deductive rules that are never put to any use.

15. Since we know little about the nature of the processes that deploy the T theorems, we are unable to specify in detail what is involved in their treating the theorems as interpretive. One simple possibility is that the T theorems are fed into a processor that makes the brute inference in (i):

(i) $\dfrac{S \text{ is true iff } p.}{S \text{ means that } p.}$

The other processors involved in speech, understanding, etc., would receive the outputs of this processor. There are clearly more complex possibilities, however, and we will not speculate on the empirical question of which one is ultimately correct.

References

Davidson, D. (1965). "Theories of Meaning and Learnable Languages." In Y. Bar-Hillel (ed.), *Logic, Methodology, and Philosophy of Science*. Amsterdam: North-Holland, 383–394.

Davidson, D. (1967). "Truth and Meaning." *Synthese* 17:304–323.

Davidson, D. (1968). "On Saying That." *Synthese* 19:130–146. (Chapter 35 in this volume.)

Davidson, D. (1970). "Semantics for Natural Languages." In *Linguaggi nella Società e nella Technica*. Milano: Edizioni di Comunità.

Davies, M. (1981). *Meaning, Quantification, Necessity*. London: Routledge and Kegan Paul.

Foster, J. (1976). "Meaning and Truth Theory." In G. Evans and J. McDowell (eds.), *Truth and Meaning*. Oxford: Oxford University Press.

Frege, G. (1956). "The Thought: A Logical Inquiry." Trans. A. M. Quinton and M. Quinton. *Mind* 65:289–311. Originally published in 1918. (Chapter 1 in this volume.)

Higginbotham, J. (1989). "Knowledge of Reference." In A. George (ed.), *Reflections on Chomsky*. Oxford: Basil Blackwell, 153–174.

Partee, B. (1978). *Fundamentals of Mathematics for Linguists*. Dordrecht: D. Reidel Publishing Co.

Partee, B., A. ter Meulen, and R. Wall (1990). *Mathematical Methods in Linguistics*. Dordrecht: Kluwer.

Tarski, A. (1944). "The Semantic Conception of Truth." *Philosophy and Phenomenological Research* 4:341–375.

Tarski, A. (1956). "The Concept of Truth in Formalized Languages." In. A. Tarski, *Logic, Semantics, Metamathematics*. Oxford: Oxford University Press.

PART II
LOGICAL FORM AND GRAMMATICAL FORM

INTRODUCTION

In this section we turn to the relation between logical form and grammatical form—a key issue for anyone interested in naturalizing the philosophy of language. In the early part of the century important work on logical form was carried out by Bertrand Russell, Ludwig Wittgenstein, and Rudolph Carnap, among others. For the most part, however, their work was aimed not at elucidating the logical form of natural language but rather at artificial formal languages.

Why is the investigation of logical forms of interest? One source of interest is the possibility that such an investigation might allow us to develop ways of formally characterizing logical inferences. But there are other motivations as well. For example, Russell (1914) made the following remarkable claim about logical forms.

Some kind of knowledge of logical forms, though with most people it is not explicit, is involved in all understanding of discourse. It is the business of philosophical logic to extract this knowledge from its concrete integuments, and to render it explicit and pure.

In other words, the project of elucidating logical forms lies at the basis of the theory of meaning. It is doubtful that philosophers like Russell and Wittgenstein took their projects to be part of elucidating the logical form of natural language, but for a number of subsequent philosophers, that has been precisely the name of the game.

For example, Donald Davidson and Richard Montague have both taken the tools of logical analysis that were developed earlier in the century and applied them directly to the analysis of natural language. For Davidson in particular, one of the goals of this effort is to find ways of characterizing the form of natural language in a way that would allow building T-theories of the sort discussed in part I. But there are apparently other motivations for Davidson. In "The Logical Form of Action

Sentences" Davidson also develops an argument that shows the close link between the logical form of natural language and the inferences we routinely make.

As Davidson argues, the inference from (1) to (2) can be easily accounted for if we assume that in constructions like these there is an implicit quantification over events, so that the logical form of 'John buttered the toast quickly' is something akin to (3):

(1) John buttered the toast quickly.

(2) John buttered the toast.

(3) $(\exists e)$ [e is a buttering of the toast by John, and e was quick]

Then (2) follows by simple conjunction reduction.

Developments like these are particularly exciting for those interested in the project of naturalizing the philosophy of language. Not only does the application of the notion of logical form to natural language promise to be helpful in developing rigorous meaning theories, but it also promises eventually to yield a theory of natural logic—in the sense that logical inference might be defined over natural-language expressions under certain structural descriptions, rather than over artificial languages.

One commonly sees two routes in the analysis of logical entailment. The first route argues that entailment is well defined for certain formal languages and that we can make sense of it only insofar as we can squeeze natural language into these formal languages (for example, into first-order logic). The second approach argues that it is not form that is of interest in characterizing logical inference but rather a semantic notion of entailment that one finds in model-theoretic semantics. (If q is true in all models where p is true, then p entails q.) What I am suggesting here is a third route—one in which we need not translate into an artificial logical language nor rely on the resources of model theory, but in which we can define our rules of inference over the natural logical forms of natural-language expressions. This is a highly speculative suggestion, but many of the tools for executing the idea are in place.

If Davidson is to be credited both with the idea of a truth-conditional semantics and the idea that it might be profitable to investigate the logical form of natural language, Gareth Evans was one of the first to explore the connection between these two exercises. As Evans argues in "Semantic Structure and Logical Form," various natural language constructions (such as attributive adjectives) undermine the assumption that there is a close connection between logical form, motivated by entailment, and structure, motivated by theories of meaning.

With Evans's paper, we are already on the verge of naturalizing the investigation of the logical form of natural language, but certain other components have pushed the project along. Crucially important to the naturalization project has been work by Noam Chomsky that provides formal tools for describing natural languages and that also introduces the idea of a level of representation, which might be the input into semantic interpretation. The reading from Gilbert Harman is one of the first efforts to knit together Davidson's project with Chomsky's project. In it Harman makes the "Deep Structure" of Chomsky's Aspects theory serve the role of logical form as conceived by the philosophers in the first part of the century.

The project to identify logical form with grammatical form takes another interesting turn in the 1970s (after Chomsky's "Conditions on Rules of Grammar"). In this phase of the development of linguistic theory, the interface to semantic interpretation is not Deep Structure, but rather a level of representation called "LF," which, among other things, reflects the relative scope relations of quantified expressions. So, for example, the surface representation in (4) might yield two LF representations, corresponding to (5) and (6):

(4) Every man loves some woman.

(5) [every x: man x][some y: woman y](x loves y)

(6) [some y: woman y][every x: man x](x loves y)

Although Chomsky doubts that LF can serve as the logical form of the philosophers, the selection from Robert May explicitly makes the connection and offers a number of arguments about the way that scope relations are represented at LF (or logical form). What May does not do, however, is to argue for the thesis that such LFs might play a role in logical inferences. Rather, the LFs proposed by May seem to be motivated primarily by their role in a theory of semantic interpretation.

While the investigation into the linguistic representation LF has become quite robust, much work still remains. First and foremost, it is probably time for someone to extend theories of LF so that they can account for formal inferences in addition to their role in a theory of meaning. But in addition to this, there is also room for pressing the investigation of logical forms down into the sublexical level, since any thoroughgoing analysis of the logical form of natural language must find a way to elucidate the fine structure of grammatical elements like determiners (e.g., 'a', 'the', 'most', 'many'). To date, the properties of these elements have been well explored via model theory, but not as a function of their logical forms. Attempts to remedy this situation argue that an investigation into the fine structure of determiners can be quite illuminating—particularly as regards the light it can shed on the nature of logical inference. What remains to be accomplished, however, is the embedding of this theory within some version of contemporary grammatical theory.

The investigation into the logical form of natural language has made profound strides in the last 30 years, but there is much left to be done. In some cases the work undertaken thus far is so preliminary that it is impossible to predict what will develop only 10 years down the line. Rather, the work merely suggests the direction of future research. Some might consider this an unhappy situation, what with so much in flux and so little nailed down. In my view, however, this is simply the sign of a healthy and vibrant domain of research—one worthy of further exploration.

Further Reading on Part II

On Davidsonian event analyses of natural language
LePore, E., and B. McGlaughlin (eds.). 1985. *Actions and Events: Perspectives on the Philosophy of Donald Davidson.* Part 2. Oxford: Blackwell.

Parsons, T. 1990. *Events in the Semantics of English.* Cambridge: MIT Press.

Schein, B. 1993. *Plurals and Events.* Cambridge: MIT Press.

Criticism of formal and model-theoretic accounts of logical inference
Etchemendy, J. 1983. "The Doctrine of Logic as Form." *Linguistics and Philosophy* 6, 319–334.

Etchemendy, J. 1990. *The Concept of Logical Consequence.* Harvard: Harvard University Press.

On philosophical accounts of logical form
Lycan, W. 1984. *Logical Form in Natural Language.* Cambridge: MIT Press.

Russell, B. 1914. "Logic as the Essence of Philosophy." In *Our Knowledge of the External World*, London: George Allen and Unwin.

Sainsbury, R. M. 1991. *Logical Forms: An Introduction to Philosophical Logic.* Oxford: Basil Blackwell.

On the level of LF in generative grammar
Chomsky, N. 1976, "Conditions on Rules of Grammar." *Linguistic Analysis* 2:203–351.

Hoji, H. 1985. "Logical Form Constraints and Configurational Structures in Japanese." Unpublished dissertation, Dept. of Linguistics, University of Massachusetts at Amherst.

Hornstein, N. 1994. *Logical Form: From GB to Minimalism*. Oxford: Blackwell.

Huang, C.-T. J. 1982. "Logical Relations in Chinese and the Theory of Grammar." Unpublished dissertation, Dept. of Linguistics, MIT.

May, R. 1985. *Logical Form: Its Structure and Derivation*. Cambridge: MIT Press.

On the idea of natural logic
Sancez-Valencia, V. 1991. "Studies in Categorial Grammar and Natural Logic." Ph.D. Thesis, University of Amsterdam.

On the logical form of determiners
Ludlow, P. 1995. "The Logical Form of Determiners." *Journal of Philosophical Logic* 24:47–69.

Chapter 10

Some Remarks on Logical Form

Ludwig Wittgenstein

Every proposition has a content and a form. We get the picture of the pure form if we abstract from the meaning of the single words, or symbols (so far as they have independent meanings). That is to say, if we substitute variables for the constants of the proposition. The rules of syntax which applied to the constants must apply to the variables also. By syntax in this general sense of the word I mean the rules which tell us in which connections only a word gives sense, thus excluding nonsensical structures. The syntax of ordinary language, as is well known, is not quite adequate for this purpose. It does not in all cases prevent the construction of nonsensical pseudopropositions (constructions such as "red is higher than green" or "the Real, though it is an *in itself*, must also be able to become *a for myself*", etc.).

If we try to analyze any given propositions we shall find in general that they are logical sums, products or other truthfunctions of simpler propositions. But our analysis, if carried far enough, must come to the point where it reaches propositional forms which are not themselves composed of simpler propositional forms. We must eventually reach the ultimate connection of the terms, the immediate connection which cannot be broken without destroying the propositional form as such. The propositions which represent this ultimate connexion of terms I call, after B. Russell, atomic propositions. They, then, are the kernels of every proposition, *they* contain the material, and all the rest is only a development of this material. It is to them we have to look for the subject matter of propositions. It is the task of the theory of knowledge to find them and to understand their construction out of the words or symbols. This task is very difficult, and Philosophy has hardly yet begun to tackle it at some points. What method

First appeared in *Aristotelian Society*, suppl. vol. 9 (1929): 162–171. Reprinted by courtesy of the Editor of the Aristotelian Society; © 1929.

have we for tackling it? The idea is to express in an appropriate symbolism what in ordinary language leads to endless misunderstandings. That is to say, where ordinary language disguises logical structure, where it allows the formation of pseudopropositions, where it uses one term in an infinity of different meanings, we must replace it by a symbolism which gives a clear picture of the logical structure, excludes pseudopropositions, and uses its terms unambiguously. Now we can only substitute a clear symbolism for the unprecise one by inspecting the phenomena which we want to describe, thus trying to understand their logical multiplicity. That is to say, we can only arrive at a correct analysis by, what might be called, the logical investigation of the phenomena themselves, i.e., in a certain sense *a posteriori*, and not by conjecturing about *a priori* possibilities. One is often tempted to ask from an *a priori* standpoint: What, after all, *can* be the only forms of atomic propositions, and to answer, *e.g.*, subject-predicate and relational propositions with two or more terms further, perhaps, propositions relating predicates and relations to one another, and so on. But this, I believe, is mere playing with words. An atomic form cannot be foreseen. And it would be surprising if the actual phenomena had nothing more to teach us about their structure. To such conjectures about the structure of atomic propositions, we are led by our ordinary language, which uses the subject-predicate and the relational form. But in this our language is misleading: I will try to explain this by a simile. Let us imagine two parallel planes, I and II. On plane I figures are drawn, say, ellipses and rectangles of different sizes and shapes, and it is our task to produce images of these figures on plane II. Then we can imagine two ways, amongst others, of doing this. We can, first, lay down a law of projection—say that of orthogonal projection or any other—and then proceed to project all figures from I into II, according to this law. Or, secondly, we could proceed thus: We lay down the rule that every ellipse on plane I is to appear as a circle in plane II, and every rectangle as a square in II. Such a way of representation may be convenient for us if for some reason we prefer to draw only circles and squares on plane II. Of course, from these images the exact shapes of the original figures on plane I cannot be immediately inferred. We can only gather from them that the original was an ellipse or a rectangle. In order to get in a single instance at the determinate shape of the original we would have to know the individual method by which, *e.g.*, a particular ellipse is projected into the circle before me. The case of ordinary language is quite analogous. If the facts of reality are the ellipses and rectangles on plane I the subject-predicate and relational forms correspond to the circles and squares in plane

II. These forms are the norms of our particular language into which we project in *ever so many different ways ever so many different* logical forms. And for this very reason we can draw no conclusions—except very vague ones—from the use of these norms as to the actual logical form of the phenomena described. Such forms as "This paper is boring", "The weather is fine", "I am lazy", which have noting whatever in common with one another, present themselves as subject-predicate propositions, *i.e.*, apparently as propositions of the same form.

If, now, we try to get at an actual analysis, we find logical forms which have very little similarity with the norms of ordinary language. We meet with the forms of space and time with the whole manifold of spacial and temporal objects, as colours, sounds, etc., etc., with their gradations, continuous transitions, and combinations in various proportions, all of which we cannot seize by our ordinary means of expression. And here I wish to make my first definite remark on the logical analysis of actual phenomena: it is this, that for their representation numbers (rational and irrational) must enter into the structure of the atomic propositions themselves. I will illustrate this by an example. Imagine a system of rectangular axes, as it were, cross wires, drawn in our field of vision and an arbitrary scale fixed. It is clear that we then can describe the shape and position of every patch of colour in our visual field by means of statements of numbers which have their significance relative to the system of co-ordinates and the unit chosen. Again, it is clear that this description will have the right logical multiplicity, and that a description which has a smaller multiplicity will not do. A simple example would be the representation of a patch P by the expression "[6–9, 3–8]" and of a proposition about it, *e.g.*, P is red, by the symbol "[6–9, 3–8] R", where "R" is yet an unanalyzed term ("6–9" and "3–8" stand for the continuous interval between the respective numbers (figure 1). The system of co-ordinates here is part of the mode of expression; it is part of the method of projection by which the reality is projected into our symbolism. The relation of a patch lying between two others can be expressed analogously by the use of apparent variables. I need not say that this analysis does not in any way pretend to be complete. I have made no mention in it of time, and the use of two-dimensional space is not justified even in the case of monocular vision. I only wish to point out the direction in which, I believe, the analysis of visual phenomena is to be looked for, and that in this analysis we meet with logical forms quite different from those which ordinary language leads us to expect. The occurrence of numbers in the forms of atomic propositions is, in my opinion, not merely a feature of a special symbol-

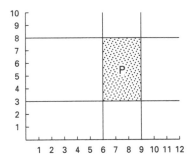

Figure 1

ism, but an essential and, consequently, unavoidable feature of the representation. And numbers will have to enter these forms when—as we should say in ordinary language—we are dealing with properties which admit of gradation, *i.e.*, properties as the length of an interval, the pitch of a tone, the brightness or redness of a shade of colour, etc. It is a characteristic of these properties that one degree of them excludes any other. One shade of colour cannot simultaneously have two different degrees of brightness or redness, a tone not two different strengths, etc. And the important point here is that these remarks do not express an experience but are in some sense tautologies. Every one of us knows that in ordinary life. If someone asks us "What is the temperature outside?" and we said "Eighty degrees", and now he were to ask us again, "And is it ninety degrees?" we should answer, "I told you it was eighty." We take the statement of a degree (of temperature, for instance) to be a *complete* description which needs no supplementation. Thus, when asked, we say what the time is, and not also what it isn't.

One might think—and I thought so not long ago—that a statement expressing the degree of a quality could be analyzed into a logical product of single statements of quantity and a completing supplementary statement. As I could describe the contents of my pocket by saying "It contains a penny, a shilling, two keys, and nothing else". This "and nothing less" is the supplementary statement which completes the description. But this will not do as an analysis of a statement of degree. For let us call the unit of, say, brightness b and let $E(b)$ be the statement that the entity E possesses this brightness, then the proposition $E(2b)$, which says that E has two degrees of brightness, should be analyzable into the logical product $E(b)$ & $E(b)$, but this is equal to $E(b)$; if, on the other hand, we try to distinguish between the units and consequently write $E(2b) = E(b')$ & $E(b'')$, we assume two different units of brightness; and then, if an entity possesses one unit, the question could arise, which of the two—(b') or (b'')—it is; which is obviously absurd.

I maintain that the statement which attributes a degree to a quality cannot further be analyzed, and, moreover, that the relation of difference of degree is an internal relation and that it is therefore represented by an internal relation between the statements which attribute the different degrees. That is to say, the atomic statement must have the same multiplicity as the degree which it attributes, whence it follows that numbers must enter the forms of atomic propositions. The mutual exclusion of unanalyzable statements of degree contradicts an opinion which was published by me several years ago and which necessitated that atomic propositions could not exclude one another. I here deliberately say "exclude" and not "contradict", for there is a difference between these two notions, and atomic propositions, although they cannot contradict, may exclude one another. I will try to explain this. There are functions which can give a true proposition only for one value of their argument because—if I may so express myself—there is only room in them for one. Take, for instance, a proposition which asserts the existence of a colour R at a certain time T in a certain place P of our visual field. I will write this proposition "R P T", and abstract for the moment from any consideration of how such a statement is to be further analyzed. "B P T", then, says that the colour B is in the place P at the time T, and it will be clear to most of us here, and to all of us in ordinary life, that "R P T & B P T" is some sort of contradiction (and not merely a false proposition). Now if statements of degree were analyzable—as I used to think—we could explain this contradiction by saying that the colour R contains all degrees of R and none of B and that the colour B contains all degrees of B and none of R. But from the above it follows that no analysis can eliminate statements of degree. How, then, does the mutual exclusion of R P T and B P T operate? I believe it consists in the fact that R P T as well as B P T are in a certain sense *complete*. That which corresponds in reality to the function "( ) P T" leaves room only for one entity—in the same sense, in fact, in which we say that there is room for one person only in a chair. Our symbolism, which allows us to form the sign of the logical product of "R P T" and "B P T" gives here no correct picture of reality.

I have said elsewhere that a proposition "reaches up to reality", and by this I meant that the forms of the entities are contained in the form of the proposition which is about these entities. For the sentence, together with the mode of projection which projects reality into the sentence, determines the logical form of the entities, just as in our simile a picture on plane II, together with its mode of projection, determines the shape of the figure on plane I. This remark, I believe, gives us the key for the explanation of the mutual exclusion of R P T and B P T. For if the proposition contains the form of an entity which it is about, then it is possible that two propositions should collide in this very form. The propositions, "Brown now sits in this chair" and "Jones now sits in this chair" each, in a sense, try to set their subject term on the chair. But the logical product of these propositions will put them both there at once, and this leads to a collision, a mutual exclusion of these terms. How does this exclusion represent itself in symbolism? We can write the logical product of the two propositions, p and q, in this way:—

P	Q	
T	T	T
T	F	F
F	T	F
F	F	F

What happens if these two propositions are R P T and B P T? In this case the top line "T T T" must disappear, as it represents an impossible combination. The true possibilities here are—

R P T	B P T
T	T
F	T
F	F

That is to say, there *is* no logical product of R P T and B P T in the first sense, and herein lies the exclusion as opposed to contradiction. The contradiction, if it existed, would have to be written—

R P T	B P T	
T	T	F
T	F	F
F	T	F
F	F	F

but this is nonsense, as the top line, "T T F," gives the proposition a greater logical multiplicity than that of the actual possibilities. It is, of course, a deficiency of our notation that it does not prevent the formation of such nonsensical constructions, and a perfect notation will have to exclude such structures by definite rules of syntax. These will have to tell us that in the case of certain kinds of atomic propositions described in terms of definite symbolic features certain combinations of the T's and F's must be left out. Such rules, however, cannot be laid down until we have actually reached the ultimate analysis of the phenomena in question. This, as we all know, has not yet been achieved.

Chapter 11

The Logical Form of Action Sentences

Donald Davidson

Strange goings on! Jones did it slowly, deliberately, in the bathroom, with a knife, at midnight. What he did was butter a piece of toast. We are too familiar with the language of action to notice at first an anomaly: the 'it' of 'Jones did it slowly, deliberately,...' seems to refer to some entity, presumably an action, that is then characterized in a number of ways. Asked for the logical form of this sentence, we might volunteer something like, 'There is an action x such that Jones did x slowly and Jones did x deliberately and Jones did x in the bathroom,...' and so on. But then we need an appropriate singular term to substitute for 'x'. In fact we know Jones buttered a piece of toast. And, allowing a little slack, we can substitute for 'x' and get 'Jones buttered a piece of toast slowly and Jones buttered a piece of toast deliberately and Jones buttered a piece of toast in the bathroom ...' and so on. The trouble is that we have nothing here we would ordinarily recognize as a singular term. Another sign that we have not caught the logical form of the sentence is that in this last version there is no implication that any *one* action was slow, deliberate, and in the bathroom, though this is clearly part of what is meant by the original.

The present Essay is devoted to trying to get the logical form of simple sentences about actions straight. I would like to give an account of the logical or grammatical role of the parts or words of such sentences that is consistent with the entailment relations between such sentences and with what is known of the role of those same parts or words in other (non-action) sentences. I take this enterprise to be the same as showing how the meanings of action sentences depend on their structure. I am not concerned with the meaning analysis of logically simple expressions in so far

First appeared in N. Rescher (ed.), *The Logic of Decision and Action* (Pittsburgh: University of Pittsburgh Press, 1967). Reprinted by permission of the University of Pittsburgh Press.

as this goes beyond the question of logical form. Applied to the case at hand, for example, I am not concerned with the meaning of 'deliberately' as opposed, perhaps, to 'voluntary'; but I am interested in the logical role of both these words. To give another illustration of the distinction I have in mind: we need not view the difference between 'Joe believes that there is life on Mars' and 'Joe knows that there is life on Mars' as a difference in logical form. That the second, but not the first, entails 'There is life on Mars' is plausibly a logical truth; but it is a truth that emerges only when we consider the meaning analysis of 'believes' and 'knows'. Admittedly there is something arbitrary in how much of logic to pin on logical form. But limits are set if our interest is in giving a coherent and constructive account of meaning: we must uncover enough structure to make it possible to state, for an arbitrary sentence, how its meaning depends on that structure, and we must not attribute more structure than such a theory of meaning can accommodate.

Consider the sentence:

(1) Jones buttered the toast slowly, deliberately, in the bathroom, with a knife, at midnight.

Despite the superficial grammar we cannot, I shall argue later, treat the 'deliberately' on a par with the other modifying clauses. It alone imputes intention, for of course Jones may have buttered the toast slowly, in the bathroom, with a knife, at midnight, and quite unintentionally, having mistaken the toast for his hairbrush which was what he intended to butter. Let us, therefore, postpone discussion of the 'deliberately' and its intentional kindred.

'Slowly', unlike the other adverbial clauses, fails to introduce a new entity (a place, an instrument, a time), and also may involve a special difficulty. For suppose we take 'Jones buttered the toast slowly' as saying that Jones's buttering of the toast was slow; is it clear that we can equally well say of Jones's action, no matter how we describe it, that it was slow? A change in the example will help. Susan says, 'I crossed the Channel in fifteen hours.' 'Good grief, that was slow.' (Notice how much more naturally we say 'slow' here than 'slowly'. But *what* was slow, what does 'that' refer to? No appropriate singular term appears in 'I crossed the Channel in fifteen hours.') Now Susan adds, 'But I swam.' 'Good grief, that was fast.' We do not withdraw the claim that it was a slow crossing; this is consistent with its being a fast swimming. Here we have enough to show, I think, that we cannot construe 'It was a slow crossing' as 'It was slow and it was a crossing' since the crossing may also be a swimming that was not slow, in which case we would have 'It was slow and it was a crossing and it was a swimming and it was not slow.' The problem is not peculiar to talk of actions, however. It appears equally when we try to explain the logical role of the attributive adjectives in 'Grundy was a short basketball player, but a tall man', and 'This is a good memento of the murder, but a poor steak knife.' The problem of attributives is indeed a problem about logical form, but it may be put to one side here because it is not a problem for action sentences alone.

We have decided to ignore, for the moment at least, the first two adverbial modifiers in (1), and may now deal with the problem of the logical form of:

(2) Jones buttered the toast in the bathroom with a knife at midnight.

Anthony Kenny, who deserves the credit for calling explicit attention to this problem,[1] points out that most philosophers today would, as a start, analyse this sentence as containing a five-place predicate with the argument places filled in the obvious ways with singular terms or bound variables. If we go on to analyse 'Jones buttered the toast' as containing a two-place predicate, 'Jones buttered the toast in the bathroom' as containing a three-place predicate, and so forth, we obliterate the logical relations between these sentences, namely that (2) entails the others. Or, to put the objection another way, the original sentences contain a common syntactic element ('buttered') which we intuitively recognize as relevant to the meaning relations of the sentences. But the proposed analyses show no such common element.

Kenny rejects the suggestion that 'Jones buttered the toast' be considered as elliptical for 'Jones buttered the toast somewhere with something at some time', which would restore the wanted entailments, on the ground that we could never be sure how many standby positions to provide in each predicate of action. For example, couldn't we add to (2) the phrase 'by holding it between the toes of his left foot'? Still, this adds a place to the predicate only if it differs in meaning from, 'while holding it between the toes of his left foot', and it is not quite clear that this is so. I am inclined to agree with Kenny that we cannot view verbs of action as usually containing a large number of standby positions, but I do not have what I consider a knock-down argument. (A knock-down argument would consist in a method for increasing the number of places indefinitely.)[2]

Kenny proposes that we may exhibit the logical form of (2) in somewhat the following manner:

(3) Jones brought it about that the toast was buttered in the bathroom with a knife at midnight.

Whatever the other merits in this proposal (I shall consider some of them presently) it is clear that it does not solve the problem Kenny raises. For it is, if anything, even more obscure how (3) entails 'Jones brought it about that the toast was buttered' or 'The toast was buttered' then how (2) entails 'Jones buttered the toast.' Kenny seems to have confused two different problems. One is the problem of how to represent the idea of *agency*: it is this that prompts Kenny to assign 'Jones' a logically distinguished role in (3). The other is the problem of the 'variable polyadicity' (as Kenny calls it) of action verbs. And it is clear that this problem is independent of the first, since it arises with respect to the sentences that replace 'p' in 'x brings it about that p'.

If I say I bought a house downtown that has four bedrooms, two fireplaces, and a glass chandelier in the kitchen, it's obvious that I can go on forever adding details. Yet the logical form of the sentences I use presents no problem (in this respect). It is something like, 'There is a house such that I bought it, it is downtown, it has four bedrooms, . . .' and so forth. We can tack on a new clause at will because the iterated relative pronoun will carry the reference back to the same entity as often as desired. (Of course we know how to state this much more precisely.) Much of our talk of action suggests the same idea: that there are such *things* as actions, and that a sentence like (2) describes the action in a number of ways. 'Jones did it with a knife.' 'Please tell me more about it.' The 'it' here doesn't refer to Jones or the knife, but to what Jones did—or so it seems.

'. . . it is in principle always open to us, along various lines, to describe or refer to "what I did" in so many ways,' writes Austin.[3] Austin is obviously leery of the apparent singular term, which he puts in scare quotes; yet the grammar of his sentence requires a singular term. Austin would have had little sympathy, I imagine, for the investigation into logical form I am undertaking here, though the demand that underlies it, for an intuitively acceptable and constructive theory of meaning, is one that begins to appear in the closing chapters of *How to Do Things with Words*. But in any case, Austin's discussion of excuses illustrates over and over the fact that our common talk and reasoning about actions is most naturally analysed by supposing that there are such entities.

'I didn't know it was loaded' belongs to one standard pattern of excuse. I do not deny that I pointed the gun and pulled the trigger, nor that I shot the victim. My ignorance explains how it happened that I pointed the gun and pulled the trigger intentionally, but did not shoot the victim intentionally. That the bullet pierced the victim was a consequence of my pointing the gun and pulling the trigger. It is clear that these are two different events, since one began slightly after the other. But what is the relation between my pointing the gun and pulling the trigger, and my shooting the victim? The natural and, I think, correct answer is that the relation is that of identity. The logic of this sort of excuse includes, it seems, at least this much structure: I am accused of doing b, which is deplorable. I admit I did a, which is excusable. My excuse for doing b rests upon my claim that I did not know that $a = b$.

Another pattern of excuse would have me allow that I shot the victim intentionally, but in self-defence. Now the structure includes something more. I am still accused of b (my shooting the victim), which is deplorable. I admit I did c (my shooting the victim in self-defence), which is excusable. My excuse for doing b rests upon my claim that I knew or believed that $b = c$.

The story can be given another twist. Again I shoot the victim, again intentionally. What I am asked to explain is my shooting of the bank president (d), for the victim was that distinguished gentleman. My excuse is that I shot the escaping murderer (e), and surprising and unpleasant as it is, my shooting the escaping murderer and my shooting of the bank president were one and the same action ($e = d$), since the bank president and the escaping murderer were one and the same person. To justify the 'since' we must presumably think of 'my shooting of x' as a functional expression that names an action when the 'x' is replaced by an appropriate singular term. The relevant reasoning would then be an application of the principle $x = y \rightarrow fx = fy$.

Excuses provide endless examples of cases where we seem compelled to take talk of 'alternative descriptions of the same action' seriously, i.e., literally. But there are plenty of other contexts in which the same need presses. *Explaining* an action by giving an intention with which it was done provides new descriptions of the action: I am writing my name on a piece of paper with the intention of writing a cheque with the intention of paying my gambling debt. List all the different descriptions of my action. Here are a few for a start: I am writing my name. I am writing my name on a piece of paper. I am writing my name on a piece of paper with the intention of writing a cheque. I am writing a cheque. I am paying my gambling debt. It is hard to imagine how we can have a coherent theory of action unless we are allowed to say that each of these sentences is made true by the same action. Redescription may supply the motive ('I was getting my revenge'), place the action in the context of a rule ('I am castling'), give the outcome ('I killed him'), or provide evaluation ('I did the right thing').

According to Kenny, as we just noted, action sentences have the form 'Jones brought it about that p.' The sentence that replaces 'p' is to be in the present tense, and it describes the result that the agent has wrought: it is a sentence 'newly true of the patient'.[4] Thus, 'The doctor removed the patient's appendix' must be rendered, 'The doctor brought it about that the patient has no appendix.' By insisting that the sentence that replaces 'p' describe a terminal *state* rather than an *event*, it may be thought that Kenny can avoid the criticism made above that the problem of the logical form of action sentences turns up within the sentence that replaces 'p': we may allow that 'The patient has no appendix' presents no relevant problem. The difficulty is that neither will the analysis stand in its present form. The doctor may bring it about that the patient has no appendix by turning the patient over to another doctor who performs the operation; or by running the patient down with his Lincoln Continental. In neither case would we say the doctor removed the patient's appendix. Closer approximations to a correct analysis might be, 'The doctor brought it about that the doctor has removed the patient's appendix' or perhaps, 'The doctor brought it about that the patient has had his appendix removed by the doctor.' One may still have a few doubts, I think, as to whether these sentences have the same truth conditions as 'The doctor removed the patient's appendix.' But in any case it is plain that in these versions, the problem of the logical form of action sentences does turn up in the sentences that replace 'p': 'The patient has had his appendix removed by the doctor' or 'The doctor has removed the patient's appendix' are surely no *easier* to analyse than 'The doctor removed the patient's appendix.' By the same token, 'Cass walked to the store' can't be given as 'Cass brought it about that Cass is at the store', since this drops the idea of walking. Nor is it clear that 'Cass brought it about that Cass is at the store and is there through having walked' will serve; but in any case, the contained sentence is again worse than what we started with.

It is not easy to decide what to do with 'Smith coughed.' Should we say 'Smith brought it about that Smith is in a state of just having coughed'? At best this would be correct only if Smith coughed on purpose.

The difficulty in Kenny's proposal that we have been discussing may perhaps be put this way: he wants to represent every (completed) action in terms only of the agent, the notion of bringing it about that a state of affairs obtains, and the state of affairs brought about by the agent. But many action sentences yield no description of the state of affairs brought about by the action except that it *is* the state of affairs brought about by that action. A natural move, then, is to allow that the sentence that replaces '*p*' in '*x* brings it about that *p*' may (or perhaps must) describe an event.

If I am not mistaken, Chisholm has suggested an analysis that at least permits the sentence that replaces '*p*' to describe (as we are allowing ourselves to say) an event.[5] His favoured locution is '*x* makes *p* happen', though he uses such variants as '*x* brings it about that *p*' or '*x* makes it true that *p*'. Chisholm speaks of the entities to which the expressions that replace '*p*' refer as 'states of affairs', and explicitly adds that states of affairs may be changes or events (as well as 'unchanges'). An example Chisholm provides is this: if a man raises his arm, then we may say he makes it happen that his arm goes up. I do not know whether Chisholm would propose 'Jones made it happen that Jones's arm went up' as an analysis of 'Jones raised his arm', but I think the proposal would be wrong because although the second of these sentences does perhaps entail the first, the first does not entail the second. The point is even clearer if we take as our example 'Jones made it happen that Jones batted an eyelash' (or some trivial variant), and this cannot be called progress in uncovering the logical form of 'Jones batted an eyelash.'

There is something else that may puzzle us about Chisholm's analysis of action sentences, and it is independent of the question what sentence we substitute for '*p*'. Whatever we put for '*p*', we are to interpret it as describing some event. It is natural to say, I think, that *whole* sentences of the form '*x* makes it happen that *p*' also describe events. Should we say that these events are the *same* event, or that they are different? If they are the same event, as many people would claim (perhaps including Chisholm), then no matter what we put for '*p*', we cannot have solved the *general* problem of the logical form of sentences about actions until we have dealt with the sentences that can replace '*p*'. If they are different events, we must ask how the element of agency has been introduced into the larger sentence though it is lacking in the sentence for which '*p*' stands; for each has the agent as its subject. The answer Chisholm gives, I think, is that the special notion of making it happen that he has in mind is intentional, and thus to be distinguished from simply causing something to happen. Suppose we want to say that Alice broke the mirror without implying that she did it intentionally. Then Chisholm's special idiom is not called for; buy we could say, 'Alice caused it to happen that the mirror broke.' Suppose we now want to add that she did it intentionally. Then the Chisholm-sentence would be: 'Alice made it happen that Alice caused it to happen that the mirror broke.' And now we want to know, what is the event that the whole sentence reports, and that the contained sentence does not? It is, apparently, just what used to be called an act of the will. I will not dredge up the standard objections to the view that acts of the will are special events distinct from, say, our bodily movements, and perhaps the causes of them. But even if Chisholm is willing to accept such a view, the problem of the logical form of the sentences that can replace 'p' remains, and these describe the things people do as we describe them when we do not impute intention.

A somewhat different view has been developed with care and precision by von Wright.[6] In effect, von Wright puts action sentences into the following form: 'x brings it about that a state where p changes into a state where q'. Thus the important relevant difference between von Wright's analysis and the ones we have been considering is the more complex structure of the description of the change or event the agent brings about: where Kenny and Chisholm were content to describe the result of the change, von Wright includes also a description of the initial state.

Von Wright is interested in exploring the logic of change and action and not, at least primarily, in giving the logical form of our common sentences about acts or events. For the purposes of his study, it may be very fruitful to think of events as ordered pairs of states. But I think it is also fairly obvious that this does not give us a standard way of translating or representing the form of most sentences about acts and events. If I walk from San Francisco to Pittsburgh, for example, my initial state is that I am in San Francisco and my terminal state is that I am in Pittsburgh; but the same is more pleasantly true if I fly. Of course, we may describe the terminal state as my having walked to Pittsburgh from San Francisco, but then we no longer need the separate statement of the initial state. Indeed, viewed as an analysis of ordinary sentences about actions, von Wright's proposal seems subject to all the difficulties I have already outlined plus the extra one that most action sentences do not yield a non-trivial description of the initial state (try 'He circled the field', 'He recited the *Odyssey*', 'He flirted with Olga').

In two matters, however, it seems to me von Wright suggests important and valuable changes in the pattern of analysis we have been considering, or at least in our interpretation of it. First, he says that an action is not an event, but rather the bringing about of an event. I do not think this can be correct. If I fall down, this is an event whether I do it intentionally or not. If you thought my falling was an accident and later discovered I did it on purpose, you would not be tempted to withdraw your claim that you had witnessed an event. I take von Wright's refusal to call an action an event to reflect the embarrassment we found to follow if we say that an act is an event, taking agency to be introduced by a phrase like 'brings it about that'. The solution lies, however, not in distinguishing acts from events, but in finding a different logical form for action sentences. The second important idea von Wright introduces comes in the context of his distinction between *generic* and *individual* propositions about events.[7] The distinction, as von Wright makes it, is not quite clear, for he says both: that an individual proposition differs from a generic one in having a uniquely determined truth value, while a generic proposition has a truth value only when coupled with an occasion; and that, that Brutus killed Caesar is an individual proposition while that Brutus kissed Caesar is a generic proposition, because 'a person can be kissed by another on more than one occasion'. In fact the proposition that Brutus kissed Caesar seems to have a uniquely determined truth value in the same sense that the proposition that Brutus killed Caesar does. But it is, I believe, a very important observation that 'Brutus kissed Caesar' does not, by virtue of its meaning alone, describe a single act.

It is easy to see that the proposals we have been considering concerning the logical form of action sentences do not yield solutions to the problems with which we began. I have already pointed out that Kenny's problem, that verbs of action apparently have 'variable polyadicity', arises within the sentences that can replace '*p*' in such formulas as '*x* brought it about that *p*'. An analogous remark goes for von Wright's more elaborate formula. The other main problem may be put as that of assigning a logical form to action sentences that will justify claims that two sentences describe 'the same action'. Our study of some of the ways in which we excuse, or attempt to excuse, acts shows that we want to make inferences such as this: I flew my spaceship to the Morning Star, the Morning Star is identical with the Evening Star; so, I flew my spaceship to the Evening Star. (My leader told me not to go the Evening Star; I headed for the Morning Star not knowing.) But suppose we translate the action sentences along the lines suggested by Kenny or Chisholm or von Wright. Then we have something like, 'I brought it about that my spaceship is on the Morning Star.' How can we infer, given the well-known identity, 'I brought it about that my spaceship is on the Evening Star'? We know that if we replace 'the Morning Star' by 'the Evening Star' in, 'My spaceship is on the Morning Star' the truth-value will not be disturbed; and so if the occurrence of this sentence in, 'I brought it about that my spaceship is on the Morning Star' is truth-functional, the inference is justified. But of course the occurrence can't be truth-functional: otherwise, from the fact that I brought about one actual state of affairs it would follow that I brought about every actual state of affairs. It is no good saying that after the words 'bring it about that' sentences describe something *between* truth-values and propositions, say states of affairs. Such a claim must be backed by a semantic theory telling us how each sentence determines the state of affairs it does; otherwise the claim is empty.

Israel Scheffler has put forward an analysis of sentences about choice that can be applied without serious modification to sentences about intentional acts.[8] Scheffler makes no suggestion concerning action sentences that do not impute intention, and so has no solution to the chief problems I am discussing. Nevertheless, his analysis has a feature I should like to mention. Scheffler would have us render, 'Jones intentionally buttered the toast' as, 'Jones made-true a that Jones-buttered-the-toast inscription.' This cannot, for reasons I have urged in detail elsewhere,[9] be considered a finally satisfying form for such sentences because it contains the logically unstructured predicate 'is a that Jones-buttered-the-toast inscription', and there are an infinite number of such semantical primitives in the language. But in one respect, I believe Scheffler's analysis is clearly superior to the others, for it implies that introducing the element of intentionality does not call for a reduction in the content of the sentence that expresses *what* was done intentionally. This brings out a fact otherwise suppressed, that, to use our example, 'Jones' turns up twice, once inside and once outside the scope of the intensional operator. I shall return to this point.

A discussion of the logical form of action sentences in ordinary language is to be found in the justly famed Chapter VII of Reichenbach's *Elements of Symbolic Logic.*[10] According to Reichenbach's doctrine, we may transform a sentence like

(4) Amundsen flew to the North pole

into:

(5) $(\exists x)$ (x consists in the fact that Amundsen flew to the North Pole).

The expression 'is an event that consists in the fact that' is to be viewed as an operator which, when prefixed to a sentence, forms a predicate of events. Reichenbach does not think of (5) as showing or revealing the logical form of (4), for he thinks (4) is unproblematic. Rather he says (5) is logically equivalent to (4). (5) has its counterpart in a more ordinary idiom:

(6) A flight by Amundsen to the North Pole took place.

Thus Reichenbach seems to hold that we have two ways of expressing the same idea, (4) and (6); they have quite different logical forms, but they are logically equivalent; one speaks literally of events while the other does not. I believe this view spoils much of the merit in Reichenbach's proposal, and that we must abandon the idea that (4) has an unproblematic logical form distinct from that of (5) or (6). Following Reichenbach's formula for putting any action sentence into the form of (5) we translate

(7) Amunsden flew to the North Pole in May 1926

into:

(8) $(\exists x)$ (x consists in the fact that Amundsen flew to the North Pole in May 1926).

The fact that (8) entails (5) is no more obvious than that (7) entails (4); what was obscure remains obscure. The correct way to render (7) is:

(9) $(\exists x)$ (x consists in the fact that Amundsen flew to the North Pole and x took place in May 1926).

But (9) does not bear the simple relation to the standard way of interpreting (7) that (8) does. We do not know of any logical operation on (7) as it would usually be formalised (with a three-place predicate) that would make it logically equivalent to (9). This is why I suggest that we treat (9) alone as giving the logical form of (7). If we follow this strategy, Kenny's problem of the 'variable polyadicity' of action verbs is on the way to solution; there is, of course, no variable polyadicity. The problem is solved in the natural way, by introducing events as entities about which an indefinite number of things can be said.

Reichenbach's proposal has another attractive feature: it eliminates a peculiar confusion that seemed to attach to the idea that sentences like (7) 'describe an event'. The difficulty was that one wavered between thinking of the sentence as describing or referring to that one flight Amundsen made in May 1926, or as describing a kind of event, or perhaps as describing (potentially?) several. As von Wright pointed out, any number of events might be described by a sentence like 'Brutus kissed Caesar.' This fog is dispelled in a way I find entirely persuasive by Reichenbach's proposal that ordinary action sentences have, in effect, an existential quantifier binding the action-variable. When we were tempted into thinking a sentence like (7) describes a single event we were misled: it does not describe any event at all. But if (7) is true, then there is an event that makes it true. (This unrecognized element of generality in action sentences is, I think, of the utmost importance in understanding the relation between actions and desires.)

There are two objections to Reichenbach's analysis of action sentences. The first may not be fatal. It is that as matters stand the analysis may be applied to any sentence whatsoever, whether it deals with actions, events, or anything else. Even '$2 + 3 = 5$' becomes '$(\exists x)$ (x consists in the fact that $2 + 3 = 5$)'. Why not say '$2 + 3 = 5$' does not show its true colours until put through the machine? For that matter, are we finished when we get to the first step? Shouldn't we go on to '$(\exists y)$ (y consists in the fact that $(\exists x)$ (x consists in the fact that $2 + 3 = 5$)'? And so on. It isn't clear on what principle the decision to apply the analysis is based.

The second objection is worse. We have:

(10) $(\exists x)$ (x consists in the fact that I flew my spaceship to the Morning Star)

and

(11) the Morning Star = the Evening Star

and we want to make the inference to

(12) $(\exists x)$ (x consists in the fact that I flew my spaceship to the Evening Star).

The likely principle to justify the inference would be:

(13) (x) (x consists in the fact that $S \leftrightarrow x$ consists in the fact that S')

where 'S'' is obtained from 'S' by substituting, in one or more places, a co-referring singular term. It is plausible to add that (13) holds if 'S' and 'S'' are logically equivalent. But (13) and the last assumption lead to trouble. For observing that 'S' is logically equivalent to '$\hat{y}(y = y \,\&\, S) = \hat{y}(y = y)$' we get

(14) (x) $(x$ consists in the fact that $S \leftrightarrow x$ consists in the fact that
$(\hat{y}(y = y \ \& \ S) = \hat{y}(y = y)))$.

Now suppose 'R' is any sentence materially equivalent to 'S': then '$\hat{y}(y = y \ \& \ S)$' and '$\hat{y}(y = y \ \& \ R)$' will refer to the same thing. Substituting in (14) we obtain

(15) (x) $(x$ consists in the fact that $S \leftrightarrow x$ consists in the fact that
$(\hat{y}(y = y \ \& \ R) = \hat{y}(y - y))$,

which leads to

(16) (x) $(x$ consists in the fact that $S \leftrightarrow x$ consists in the fact that $R)$

when we observe the logical equivalence of 'R' and '$\hat{y}(y = y \ \& \ R) = \hat{y}(y = y)$'. (16) may be interpreted as saying (considering that the sole assumption is that 'R' and 'S' are materially equivalent) that all events that occur ($=$ all events) are identical. This demonstrates, I think, that Reichenbach's analysis is radically defective.

Now I would like to put forward an analysis of action sentences that seems to me to combine most of the merits of the alternatives already discussed, and to avoid the difficulties. The basic idea is that verbs of action—verbs that say 'what someone did'—should be construed as containing a place, for singular terms or variables, that they do not appear to. For example, we would normally suppose that 'Shem kicked Shaun' consisted in two names and a two-place predicate. I suggest, though, that we think of 'kicked' as a *three*-place predicate, and that the sentence to be given in this form:

(17) $(\exists x)$ (Kicked (Shem, Shaun, x)).

If we try for an English sentence that directly reflects this form, we run into difficulties. 'There is an event x such that x is a kicking of Shaun by Shem' is about the best I can do, but we must remember 'a kicking' is not a singular term. Given this English reading, my proposal may sound very like Reichenbach's; but of course it has quite different logical properties. The *sentence* 'Shem kicked Shaun' nowhere appears inside my analytic sentence, and this makes it differ from all the theories we have considered.

The principles that license the Morning Star-Evening Star inference now make no trouble: they are the usual principles of extensionality. As a result, nothing now stands in the way of giving a standard theory of meaning for action sentences, in the form of a Tarski-type truth definition: nothing stands in the way, that is, of giving a coherent and constructive account of how the meanings (truth conditions) of these sentences depend upon their structure. To see how one of the troublesome inferences now goes through, consider (10) rewritten as

(18) $(\exists x)$ (Flew (I, my spaceship, x) & To (the Morning Star, x)).

which, along with (11), entails

(19) $(\exists x)$ (Flew (I, my spaceship, x) & To (the Evening Star, x)).

It is not necessary, in representing this argument, to separate off the To-relation; instead we could have taken, 'Flew' as a four-place predicate. But that would have obscured *another* inference, namely that from (19) to

(20) $(\exists x)$ (Flew (I, my spaceship, x)).

In general, we conceal logical structure when we treat prepositions as integral parts of verbs; it is a merit of the present proposal that it suggests a way of treating prepositions as contributing structure. Not only is it good to have the inference from (19) to (20); it is also good to be able to keep track of the common element in 'fly to' and 'fly away from' and this of course we cannot do if we treat these as unstructured predicates.

The problem that threatened in Reichenbach's analysis, that there seemed no clear principle on which to refrain from applying the analysis to every sentence, has a natural solution if my suggestion is accepted. Part of what we must learn when we learn the meaning of any predicate is how many places it has, and what sorts of entities the variables that hold these places range over. Some predicates have an event-place, some do not.

In general, what kinds of predicates do have event-places? Without pursuing this question very far, I think it is evident that if action predicates do, many predicates that have little relation to action do. Indeed, the problems we have been mainly concerned with are not at all unique to talk of actions: they are common to talk of events of any kind. An action of flying to the Morning Star is identical with an action of flying to the Evening Star; but equally, an eclipse of the Morning Star is an eclipse of the Evening Star. Our ordinary talk of events, of causes and effects, requires constant use of the idea of different descriptions of the same event. When it is pointed out that striking the match was not sufficient to light it, what is not sufficient is not the event, but the description of it—it was a *dry* match, and so on. And of course Kenny's problem of 'variable polyadicity', though he takes it to be a mark of verbs of action, is common to all verbs that describe events.

It may now appear that the apparent success of the analysis proposed here is due to the fact that it has simply omitted what is peculiar to action sentences as contrasted with other sentences about events. But I do not think so. The concept of agency contains two elements, and when we separate them clearly, I think we shall see that the present analysis has not left anything out. The first of these two elements we try, rather feebly, to elicit by saying that the agent acts, or does something, instead of being acted upon, or having something happen to him. Or we say that the agent is active rather than passive; and perhaps try to make use of the moods of the verb as a grammatical clue. And we may try to depend upon some fixed phrase like 'brings it about that' or 'makes it the case that'. But only a little thought will make it clear that there is no satisfactory grammatical test for verbs where we want to say there is agency. Perhaps it is a *necessary* condition of attributing agency that one argument-place in the verb is filled with a reference to the agent as a person; it will not do to refer to his body, or his members, or to anyone else. But beyond that it is hard to go. I sleep, I snore, I push buttons, I recite verses, I catch cold. Also others are insulted by me, struck by me, admired by me, and so on. No grammatical test I know of, in terms of the things we may be said to do, of active or passive mood, or of any other sort, will separate out the cases here where we want to speak of agency. Perhaps it is true that 'brings it about that' guarantees agency; but as we have seen, many sentences that do attribute agency cannot be cast in this grammatical form.

I believe the correct thing to say about *this* element in the concept of agency is that it is simply introduced by certain verbs and not by others; when we understand the verb we recognize whether or not it includes the idea of an agent. Thus, 'I fought' and 'I insulted him' do impute agency to the person referred to by the first singular term, 'I caught cold' and, 'I had my thirteenth birthday' do not. In these cases, we do seem to have the following test: we impute agency only where it makes sense to ask whether the agent acted intentionally. But there are other cases, or so it seems to me, where we impute agency only when the answer to the question whether the agent acted intentionally is 'yes'. If a man falls down by accident or because a truck knocks him down, we do not impute agency; but we do if he fell down on purpose.

This introduces the second element in the concept of agency, for we surely impute agency when we say or imply that the act is intentional. Instead of speaking of two elements in the concept of agency, perhaps it would be better to say there are two ways we can imply that a person acted as an agent: we may use a verb that implies it directly, or we may use a verb that is non-committal, and add that the act was intentional.

But when we take the second course, it is important not to think of the intentionality as adding an extra doing of the agent; we must not make the expression that introduces intention a verb of action. In particular, we cannot use 'intentionally brings it about that' as the expression that introduces intention, for 'brings it about that' is in itself a verb of action, and imputes agency, but it is neutral with respect to the question whether the action was intentional as described.

This leaves the question what logical form the expression that introduces intention should have. It is obvious, I hope, that the adverbial form must be in some way deceptive; intentional actions are not a class of actions, or, to put the point a little differently, doing something intentionally is not a manner of doing it. To say someone did something intentionally is to describe the action in a way that bears a special relation to the beliefs and attitudes of the agent; and perhaps further to describe the action as having been caused by those beliefs and attitudes. But of course to describe the action of the agent as having been caused in a certain way does not mean that the agent is described as performing any further action.

Notes

1. Anthony Kenny, *Action, Emotion and Will*, Ch. VII.

2. Kenny seems to think there is such a method, for he writes, 'If we cast our net widely enough, we can make "Brutus killed Caesar" into a sentence which describes, with a certain lack of specification, the whole history of the world, (op. cit., 160). But he does not show how to make each addition to the sentence one that irreducibly modifies the killing as opposed, say, to Brutus or Caesar, or the place or the time.

3. J. L. Austin, 'A Plea for Excuses' (in his *Philosophical Papers*), 148.

4. Kenny, op. cit., 181.

5. Roderick Chisholm, 'The Descriptive Element in the Concept of Action' (*Journal of Philosphy* 61 [1964], 613–24). Also see Chisholm, 'The Ethics of Requirement' (*American Philosophical Quarterly* 1 [1964], 1–7).

6. Georg Henrik von Wright, *Norm and Action*.

7. Op. cit., 23.

8. Israel Scheffler, *The Anatomy of Inquiry*, 104–5.

9. Donald Davidson, 'Theories of Meaning and Learnable Languages' (in *Proceedings of the 1964 International Congress of Logic, Methodology, and the Philosophy of Science*), 390–1. (Reprinted in his *Truth and Interpretation*.)

10. Hans Reichenbach, *Elements of Symbolic Logic*, sect. 48.

Chapter 12

Semantic Structure and Logical Form

Gareth Evans

The validity of some inferences is to be explained by reference to the meanings of the particular expressions occurring in them, while that of other inferences is due, rather, to the way in which the sentences are constructed out of their parts.[1] The inference from 'John knows that snow is white' to 'Snow is white' is given as an example of the first type of inference; for it is said to be explained by providing an analysis of the semantical primitive 'knows'. The inferences from 'John ran breathlessly' to 'John ran' and from 'John is a large man' to 'John is a man' may, tentatively, be taken to be examples of the second type.

The distinction I have gestured towards is not without its intuitive appeal, and for many years philosophers have been trying to provide a basis for it in harmony with what they took to be its importance. The debate centred upon, and eventually ran aground upon, the problem of identifying a set of expressions as the logical constants. For if we are determined to say that the inference from $\ulcorner P$ and $Q \urcorner$ to P is valid in virtue of structure, then the distinction between it and the detachment inference with 'knows' must reside in some difference between 'knows' and 'and'.

Donald Davidson has given the notion of structurally valid inference new life and importance by locating it within a highly suggestive theory of semantic theories. In his writings there appears to be support both for the conviction that there is an important difference between the two types of inference, and also for the view that, when an inference has been shown to be structurally valid, a deeper explanation of its validity will have been provided. He writes concerning one inference:

First appeared in G. Evans and J. McDowell (eds.), *Truth and Meaning: Essays in Semantics* (Oxford: Oxford University Press, 1976). Reprinted by permission of Oxford University Press. © Oxford University Press, 1976.

By saying exactly what the role of [a certain recurrent element] is and what the roles of the other significant features of the sentence are, we will have a deep explanation of why one sentence entails the other; an explanation that draws upon a systematic account of how the meaning of each sentence is a function of its structure[1].

My interest in the notion of structurally valid inference was awakened by these writings of Davidson, and like him I am ambitious to make precise that distinction which underlies the intuitions with which we began in such a way as would support the claim that, by showing an inference to be structurally valid, we thereby provide a deep explanation of its validity.

In the first part of this paper I shall examine the account of structurally valid inference which Davidson's writings suggest and try to indicate why I think that we have not there reached a finally satisfactory account of the matter. In the second part of the paper I shall sketch another approach to the idea with which I began. Finally from the vantage point provided by the sketch I shall look briefly at some recent and not so recent proposals concerning semantic structure.

I

We can distinguish two kinds of definition or explication in semantics which I shall label 'immanent' and 'transcendent'.

One provides an immanent definition of some semantical term W if one does not define it absolutely but rather defines the notion $\ulcorner e$ is W according to theory T$\urcorner$. One provides a transcendent definition when the definition contains no such relativity to a theory; when one says, rather, what a theory *ought* to treat as W.

Our pre-systematic theorizing about semantics has provided us with a set of terms not all of which may suitably be provided with transcendent definitions. Although some theories will be right to treat an expression e as W (for such a term), and some wrong, this will be because some theories are right or wrong overall. In so far as empirical considerations bear upon the correctness of the claim that an expression is W, they bear globally upon the theory according to which it is W, and cannot be brought into any more direct relation with that feature of the internal constitution of the theory in virtue of which it may be said to be treating e as W.

An example of such a semantical term might be 'is a designator'. If there is a theory of meaning, satisfying the global constraints upon such theories, which treats some expression *e* as a designator, and another such theory which does not, there is, perhaps, no sense to the question 'Is *e* really a designator?' because, perhaps, no evidence can additionally be brought to bear upon it.

However, this is not always the case. Consider the notion '*e* is (semantically) composite'. If the theories with which we are concerned are recursive definitions of truth, an immanent definition of this notion is readily obtainable:

e is semantically composite according to T iff
(i)   *e* is a semantical unit according to T and
(ii) there is no base or recursive axiom assigning *e* a semantical property in T.

But we should not rest content with such an immanent definition, since there is a consideration which bears directly upon the correctness of a theory's decision as to whether to treat an expression as semantically composite. It is this. Are the speakers of the language for which T is a semantical theory capable of understanding new expressions constructed in the way *e* is constructed, upon the basis of their understanding of the (syntactic) parts of those expression? This consideration provides materials for the construction of a transcendent definition of the notion '*e* is semantically composite'.

Clearly, a question which we must constantly keep in mind is whether the notion of structurally valid inference admits of a transcendent definition; whether there are considerations which bear directly upon the correctness of decisions concerning the structural validity of inferences.

I shall not attempt to answer this question now. My present concern is with the way in which Davidson has made the notion of structural validity precise. It seems evident that he has provided an immanent definition, which I shall now try to make explicit.

I shall assume familiarity with Davidson's conception of a theory of meaning as a theory of truth. It seems clear from his work that a semantic theory for any natural language would in his view have the following two tiers:

(1) a theory of truth, conforming to Tarski's Convention T, for a suitably chosen, regimented, but still interpreted, language, which will probably be, in large part, a fragment of the natural language, but could be a constructed language;

(2) a set of translation rules mapping any sentence of the natural language not provided with truth conditions at level (1) on to a sentence for which truth is defined directly.

Showing an inference to be structurally valid has a slightly different significance when the sentences concerned are in the fragment for which truth is directly defined and when they are not. I shall consider these in turn, starting with the fundamental case of sentences for which truth is directly defined.

Davidson writes: 'there is no giving the truth conditions of all sentences without showing that some sentences are logical consequences of others'.[2] This is explained as follows: 'A truth definition does not distinguish between analytic sentences and others except for sentences which owe their truth to the presence alone of the constants which give the theory its grip on structure.'[3] In a later paper he expands this idea: 'but it will be evident from a theory of truth that certain sentences are true solely on the basis of the properties assigned to the logical constants. The logical constants may be identified as those iterative features of the language which require a recursive clause (not in the basis) in the definition of truth or satisfaction.' He continues, in an explicit acknowledgement of the immanence of the definition: 'Logical form, on this account, will of course be relative to the choice of a metalanguage (with its logic) and a theory of truth'.[4]

Let us say that the conditional $\ulcorner$If S_1 is true,..., and S_{n-1} is true, then S_n is true$\urcorner$ is the *validating conditional* of the inference $S_1 \ldots S_{n-1} \vdash S_n$. I think Davidson's idea is that an inference is structurally valid according to a theory T if and only if its validating conditional is a *semantic* consequence of the theory's recursive clauses.

Thus to take a perhaps excessively simple case, a theory of truth which has the clause

for any sentences S and S', $S \frown$ 'and'$\frown S'$ is true if and only if S is true and S' is true

treats 'and' as a logical constant and attributes to it the semantic property of forming truths when and only when conjoining truths. It is a (semantic) consequence of this characterization, independent of the characterization of elements given in the base clause, that if $\ulcorner P$ and $Q\urcorner$ is true, then P is true. The theory thus treats the inference $\ulcorner P$ and $Q\urcorner \vdash P$ as a structural inference.

However, it appears possible to treat a great many expressions which are not typically regarded as logical constants in recursive clauses of the truth definition. (I ignore the fact that, on this view, the standard semantic treatment of identity shows it not to be a logical constant.) In particular, such a treatment appears possible for an attributive adjective, such as 'large'. The full details are given in the appendix, but the leading idea would be to have a clause in the definition of satisfaction along the lines of:

for all (possibly complex) monadic predicates ϕ, a satisfies 'large'$^\cap\phi$ if and only if a is a large satisfier of ϕ.

Such treatment takes seriously the grammatical status of 'large' as a predicate modifier. We will of course need some deductive machinery allowing for substitution within the scope of the metalinguistic modifier 'large', if the semantical material introduced into the right-hand side is to be eliminated and a homophonic biconditional thus to be derived. But an obviously valid rule permitting merely the substitution of predicates which are provably equivalent in the meta-language will suffice.

Then, such a theory will have shown the inference from 'X is a large man' to 'X is a man' to be formally valid. And if the theory were to treat 'small' in a parallel fashion, with *its* recursive clause, the same will hold for the inference from 'X is a large man' to 'X is not a small man', since it would be a semantic consequence of the two axioms taken together with the axiom for 'not' that if an object satisfies 'large man' it also satisfies 'not a small man'.

I am not claiming that this is an admirable semantical proposal. The point of the example is to cast doubt upon the idea that we have here captured the basis of the distinction with which we started, even in its application to those cases (e.g. the truth-functional connective and the quantifiers) for which the background theory is more orthodox. For we were surely encouraged to entertain hopes that a theory which showed an inference to be structurally valid would provide us with a kind of explanation of its validity which would *contrast* with those in which final appeal is made to the inferential properties of particular expressions. And the conviction that the recursive clause for 'large' provides us with no insight into why the detachment inference is valid is surely reinforced by the observation that an entirely parallel recursive treatment will suffice for such apparently heterogeneous modifiers as 'good' and 'breathlessly', and for 'fake', which does not even sustain the inference.

If you feel like saying that you have as yet no idea of what kind of semantic role 'large' is supposed to be playing in the recursive clause of the metalanguage, what kind of function from what kinds of elements to what kinds of elements it introduces, I must ask you to be patient in the knowledge that the drift of the paper is on your side. But you should also realize that you seem to be appealing to semantic notions richer than any Davidson appeals to in characterizing the notion of structurally valid inference.

I have interpreted Davidson's talk of a theory's *entailing* a validating conditional in terms of semantic consequence. But this is to render uninterpretable his own observation that what inferences count as structural will be relative to the *logic* of the metalanguage. I adopted this interpretation because to introduce mention of the deductive apparatus of the metalanguage simply invites the question: 'How much is relevant to determinations of structural validity?' In general, the inference pattern in the metalanguage which is necessary for proving the validating conditional with respect to a certain object-language pattern of inference is that very same pattern of inference. If the logic of the metalanguage contains the detachment inference for the metalinguistic modifier 'large' we can validate the detachment inference in the object language, if not, not.

Perhaps there is a limit upon metalinguistic logic which would save the notion of structurally valid inference, interpreted in terms of what consequences are provable from the axioms, from free-wheeling entirely. Count as logic for deducing the relevant validating conditionals just the logic the theory requires for deriving its T-sentence theorems.

Certainly this is far from arbitrary, but the results are meagre, since very little logic is necessary. It is known that an adequate theory of truth for a first-order language susceptible of a classical interpretation can be constructed in a metalanguage whose logic is intuitionistic, and so, on this account, not all classically valid inference patterns will be structural. Proof of the T-sentences requires, on the whole, substitution inferences; it is certain that, provided the biconditional is undefined, neither the detachment inference with 'and', nor that with 'large', will be required for such proofs.

Let us now turn to the other way in which an inference may, on Davidson's view, be shown to be formally valid; when the sentences concerned do not have their truth conditions defined directly by the theory of truth, but are mapped on to sentences which do. If $F(S)$ is the sentence in the fragment on to which S is mapped by the translation rules, then $S_1 \ldots S_{n-1}$ formally entail S_n iff $F(S_1) \ldots F(S_{n-1})$ formally entail $F(S_n)$.

Since this manoeuvre rests upon the idea of formally valid inference we have discussed it clearly inherits any difficulties we were able to point to in that idea. But there are additional questions and a slightly new perspective.

I do not think Davidson would want to claim that the methodology underlying this section of the semantic theory has been entirely worked out. What considerations should guide us in our choice of the background language which is to provide the kernel? Save for eschewing any commitment to first-order languages, little has been said about this. Does the chosen fragment even have to be a fragment of any natural language; and if not, what defence can be provided for, or significance attached to, the requirement that the semantics for a natural language be statable as a homophonic truth theory? Is the relation between S and $F(S)$ to be incorporated into the idea of a semantic theory as having something to do with how speakers understand a natural language, and if so, how?

However our immediate task is to consider the impact the construction of this additional tier of our theory has upon the notion of formally valid inference. It appears at first that it must reinforce the impression of arbitrariness which we brought away from our consideration of the leading idea.

For consider again the sentence 'John is a large man'. If we decide that our fragment is to be first-order, and thus without predicate modifiers, it appears that we have the choice of mapping our sentence either on to the sentence

Large-for (John, $\{y : \text{Man}(y)\}$)

or on to the sentence

Large-for* (John, $\{y : \text{Man}(y)\}$) & John $\in \{y : \text{Man}(y)\}$.[5]

If we adopt the first we determine that the detachment inference is to be accounted for by the analysis of the primitive relation 'Large-for', while if we adopt the second, using the primitive relation 'Large-for*', different in being satisfiable by objects and sets of which those objects are not members, the inference will be formally valid in virtue of the presence of the logical constant '&'. We may well wonder what is to stop someone adding $\ulcorner \ldots \& p \urcorner$ on to whatever translation his colleague provided for $\ulcorner X$ knows that $p \urcorner$, claiming to show thereby that the detachment inference with 'know' is formally valid.

However, I think a deeper and more sympathetic reading of Davidson's ideas would reveal that at least *this* charge of arbitrariness is unfair.

Davidson writes: '. . . we must uncover enough structure to make it pos-sible to state, for an arbitrary sentence, how its meaning depends upon its structure . . .'[6] and the suggested continuation is ' . . . and no more'. In 'On Saying That' he writes: 'For the purposes of the present paper, however, we can cleave to the most austere interpretation of logical consequence and logical form, those that are forced upon us when we give a theory of truth'.[7] We can discern the following plan. In order to provide for the sentence 'John is a white protestant American' a suitable sentence of, say, a first-order fragment with only a finite number of semantical primitives, we *have to* uncover a conjunctive structure. But the addition $\ulcorner \ldots \& p \urcorner$ adds nothing to the enterprise of providing a suitable translation for $\ulcorner X$ knows that $p \urcorner$, nor, incidentally, does the addition of the conjunct '. . . & John $\in \{y : \mathrm{Man}(y)\}$'. The only way in which we can incorporate $\ulcorner$John stopped ϕ-ing at $t \urcorner$ into a fragment with a finite number of semantical primitives (given that it is to contain no expression syntactically parallel to 'stopped') is to map it on to a sentence which contains ϕ occurring in its basic predicative role. Perhaps the only way to do that is to uncover the structure $\ulcorner$John ϕ-ed up to t and after t John did not $\phi \urcorner$. If and only if this is the situation, we shall have shown that the inference from $\ulcorner$John stopped ϕ-ing at $t \urcorner$ to $\ulcorner$John ϕ-ed before $t \urcorner$ is a formally valid one.

This certainly provides us with far from arbitrary account of what counts as revealing form and what as philosophical analysis. But there are still some grounds for reservation as to whether we have provided a finally satisfactory foundation for that distinction with whose allure we began.

First: it is not wholly nugatory to point to the fact that upon this con-ception the inference from 'John is a large man' to 'John is a man' will almost certainly not count as formally valid.

The second ground I have already mentioned. It is clear that what inferences come out as formally valid will vary radically, depending upon which language is used as the canonical fragment, and this imports an arbitrariness we might feel misplaced in a wholly explanatory account of the matter. Briefly, we miss transcendence.

Finally, and more seriously: it appears that the constraint upon how much structure to uncover will not, without considerable supplementa-tion, achieve the intended results.

Consider the two radically different kinds of attributive adjectives exemplified by 'large' and 'good'. 'Large'-type attributives sustain all the inferences 'good'-type attributives sustain, although the former in addi-tion sustain coextensive predicate substitution. Consequently, it is difficult to see why the general type of translation provided for 'good' will not also serve for 'large'. Suppose, merely for illustration, that we discerned a reference to the attribute 'being a man' in the sentence 'X is a good man', thus

Good-in $(X, \lambda y \, [\text{Man}(y)])$.

This would certainly also be a type of structure that would work for 'large'. From the point of view of merely being able to generate the T-sentences, the incorporation of reference to a set in the translation provided for the later attributive was as gratuitous as the incorporation of the additional conjunct.

This difficulty is quite general. Provided we have a scheme for the suitable translation of what are inferentially the weakest members of a certain grammatical category, we seem to be enjoined to run that scheme quite generally, treating the inferences which the inferentially stronger members sustain as being consequences of their analysis. It is obvious that the maxim 'Translate so as to maximize formally valid inferences' simply sends us back to wreck upon the shore of the superfluous conjunct.

It would be foolish to hold that no more refined criterion could be forthcoming, but I find it difficult to believe that it can be drafted without drawing upon the slightly richer conception of semantics which I shall develop in the next section. Before proceeding to that, I should like to draw the comments I have been making together by putting forward a more general observation.

Although Davidson's main conception of formally valid inference drew its inspiration from wholly novel considerations, it rests squarely within that tradition which distinguishes formally valid inferences as those which depend upon the presence of certain favoured words, the logical constants. The novelty lay in two points. First: in the idea that those words would receive a special treatment in any semantic theory through being recursive elements. Second, and, of course, connected, was the stress placed upon a profoundly important *necessary* condition for the inference from $\Sigma(e)$ to $\Sigma'(e)$ to be formally valid. This was the condition that e should be shown to occur as a semantical unit in both $\Sigma(e)$ and $\Sigma'(e)$. Davidson was at pains to point out that, although a syntactic transformation can easily be made to be sensitive to the occurrences of e in $\Sigma(e)$ and $\Sigma'(e)$, nevertheless unless e can be shown to occur there semantically, by some theory of truth, there will be no hope of showing that the transformation is valid, i.e. generally truth-preserving. For example, there is no difficulty whatever in writing a syntactic rule of inference which captures the inference pattern exemplified by

X is a tall man
Y is taller than X
Y is a man

Therefore Y is a tall man

But in the absence of a semantic theory which discerns 'tall' in 'taller than' (presumably by the construction of a recursive clause for the element '... er than'), we will have no hope of proving that each of the infinite number of inferences licensed by the syntactic rule is valid.

But, important though this second idea is, it does only provide us with a necessary condition. For even when a theory of truth has shown e to occur in $\Sigma(e)$, there is the additional question: 'Is the mode of containment $\Sigma(\ )$ by itself of a kind that warrants certain inferences, or are they rather due to certain special features of the particular constituents exemplifying that mode of containment?'

In addressing ourselves to that question, we have been following Davidson, and taking the way a theory of truth validates the inference from ⌐P and Q⌐ to P as the model of the way in which a semantic theory shows an inference to be structurally valid. But following that model with 'large' provided us with the very reverse of that explanation of which our original intuition seemed to encourage the expectation. The possibility that suggests itself is that this model is wrong. Perhaps there is a notion of structurally valid inference, for which we have been groping, which does not comprehend inferences which rely upon the logical constants, and which thus cannot be married with the traditional notion of logical validity without disappearing. If there is such a different conception, whatever its merits and whether or not anyone else has bee groping for it, we can only benefit by having it distinguished from its more traditional rival. It is this that I attempt in the next section.

II

Let us return to the intuition about structurally valid inferences with which we began. Surely the natural way of defending the claim that the inference from ⌐John knows that p⌐ to p is not structurally valid would not mention the logical constants at all, but would rather run as follows:

the inference cannot be a matter of structure, since the sentence ⌜John believes that p⌝ has precisely the same semantic structure as, is composed in exactly the same way out of the same types of semantic elements as, the sentence ⌜John knows that p⌝, and yet it does not sustain the inference.

We have here the idea of a contrast between inferences whose validity depends merely upon the *kind* of semantic elements out of which a sentence is constructed, and its manner of construction, on the one hand, and inferences whose validity depends upon the special variation a particular semantic element is playing upon the theme all expressions of its kind must play, on the other. Can we make anything of this idea?

The central task, if we are to make anything of it, will be to provide a way of telling when two expressions are of the same semantic category, and our hopes of doing this might appear rather dim. For we seem to be confronted with the following dilemma. If we are allowed to consider all the valid inferences involving some expression in determining the kind of semantic contribution it makes, there is nothing to stop us inventing a category of *factive attitudinatives*, unified in being like 'know' and sustaining the detachment inference. If we are not allowed to take all inferences into account, we will have to decide upon a partition amongst inferences as a preliminary to an enterprise whose object was the construction of just such a partition.

What makes a parallel problem in the taxonomy of natural kinds tractable is the conception of kinds as being differentiated by underlying structures from which the characteristics we use in classification may be regarded as flowing. To solve our problem for semantic kinds we need to find room for a parallel conception of something from which an expression's inferential properties may be regarded as flowing.

Just such a conception is provided by what I shall call an *interpretational semantics*. A semantic theory of that type specifies, for each kind of semantic expression, an entity—a set, a truth value, a function from sets to truth values, or whatever—which may appropriately be assigned to members of that kind upon an arbitrary interpretation of the language. We can regard the specification of the kind of assignment as a specification of the underlying real essence which a word has in common with many other words, and of which the validity of certain inferences involving it is a consequence. These will be the structurally valid inferences; inferences which are truth-preserving no matter how we permute assignments within the limits laid down as appropriate for members of that category.

Thus, to take a central but simple case, we justify the intuition that there is a unitary semantic category of n-place predicates, and provide a general characterization of their role, by stating that upon any admissible interpretation of the language each n-place predicate must be assigned a set of n-tuples of the domain, and by providing an adequate definition of truth upon an arbitrary interpretation using assignments of that type.

A slightly less obvious case is the following. We can justify the belief that there is a semantic category to which 'large', 'tall', 'expensive' and 'heavy' all belong (the extensional attributive adjectives), by showing that there is an assignment which may suitably be made to each (a function from sets to subsets of those sets, possibly satisfying certain additional conditions), and which provides the basis for an adequate definition of truth upon an interpretation. It is again clear that certain inferential features will flow from this underlying real essence. We see why the detachment inference is valid, why substitution of coextensive predicates within the scope of such adjectives is valid, and why commuting the adjectives will not in general be valid.

The metaphor of underlying essence suggests that we are attempting to *explain* why the expression has certain inferential properties, but is there any more justification in speaking of explanation here than there was when validation of the inference followed merely from the presence of the parallel inference in the metalanguage? Are we not merely restating, in set-theoretical terms, the various inferences we are concerned to explain?

I think this charge can be resisted. A certain, syntactically identified, patterns of inferential behaviour is a feature which can and does flow from many different underlying constitutions. For example, both standard adverbs—like 'breathlessly'—and intensional attributives—like 'good' in 'good (as a) king'—sustain a parallel detachment inference; yet it is clear that the 'restatement' we are supposed to have provided is inappropriate for both kinds of expressions. Neither can be seen as involving functions from sets to subsets of those sets. Davidson can be seen as providing a quite different explanation for the detachment inference in the case of adverbs (making assignments of sets of events to adverbs, and sets of $(n + 1)$-tuples, of events and n-tuples of objects, to verbs). No one yet knows how to provide an adequate explanation of the detachment inference for 'good'.

The requirement that one provide an account of an expressions's contribution by specifying an appropriate kind of assignment is not an easy one to meet, and certainly puts a quite different complexion upon the taxonomic problem. Some groupings of expressions upon the basis of shared inferential behaviour will be simply impossible, for no coherent kind of assignment to the members of the heterogeneous class which results will be available. While we are merely concerned with grouping expressions together in a way which imposes the best organization upon their inferential behaviour, we are bound to feel the force of a certain arbitrariness since it appears certain that an equally good scheme which organizes the data in another way can always be put together. Locating the taxonomic problem in the context of an interpretational semantics puts an end to this free-wheeling. What we expect, then, is the provision of the most determinate and yet economical statement of the kind of semantic contribution made by any expression of a given type, thereby making structurally valid as many inferences as possible. One hopes that this will not involve one restriction upon the assignment for every inference validated; we aim at the sort of illumination that can come from an economical axiomatization of the behaviour of groups of expressions. Then we can say: '*This* is the kind of expression *e* is, and that is why these inferences are valid.'

But this may simply be to raise another, deeper problem. I have spoken of making structurally valid as many inferences as possible. Does this not raise the old difficulty? For will we not be obliged to subdivide the class of attitudinatives, and discover a category of factive attitudinatives, the assignment to which differs from the assignment to their non-factive brothers solely in requiring the contained sentence to be true?

Now that we are working within the context of an interpretational semantics, I think we can quiet this worry. We should regard our construction of, and assignments to, categories in the following spirit: if two expressions behave in the same way but are in different categories, this is a lost generalization. If we regard the enterprise in this light, we will construct a new category out of an older and more comprehensive category only when we can make an assignment to members of the new category which provides a *different* explanation for the behaviour which members of the new category had in common with the old, the provision of which explanation would show that the apparent unity in the behaviour of members of the old category was deceptive, concealing deep differences of functioning. Only in this case will the discovery of a new category not lose us a significant generalization. By imposing this requirement we make the notion of structural validity transcendent.

Thus, to recognize a category of factive attitudinatives would require the provision of a different explanation, for its members, of the inferential properties they share with words like 'believe'; an explanation which would unify these properties with the detachment inference. It is by no means out of the question that just such an explanation ought to be provided. Zeno Vendler has provided arguments which cast doubt upon the apparent similarity of 'knows' and 'believes',[8] while the causal theory of knowledge provides us with a rationale for treating the contained sentence as designating a state of affairs with which the knower is stated to have come into epistemological contact. If we did so treat the contained sentence, this would be to treat 'know' like 'enjoy' in one of its uses, as introducing a function from states of affairs and persons to truth values. This is to provide an explanation of the detachment inference. And provided the identity conditions of states of affairs are sufficiently fine-gained, the explanation unifies that inference with the expression's other inferential properties, for example, its opacity.

If we are to preserve the promise in the notion of semantic structure, we have to steer between two courses. We must resist saying, with Montague, that no detachment inference with a predicate modifier is structurally valid, on the ground that the expression 'fake' must be regarded as belonging in that category.[9] But equally we must not allow the freedom to subdivide and form new categories to lead to that proliferation of categories which threatens our interest in the notion. We can steer this middle course only if we require that an appropriate assignment be provided for each category, and illuminatingly different assignments be provided for different categories.

The construction of an interpretational semantics for a natural language will doubtless follow a rather different course from that taken in the construction of such theories for artificial languages, not merely in the heterogeneity of entities assigned. In the first place, there is no reason for the different interpretations to have different domains. Secondly, instead of a single unsorted domain, it will be convenient to have a domain divided into fundamental sorts of objects: places, times, material objects, animate objects, events ... (This would enable us to describe the admissible assignment to an action verb, e.g., as 'a set of pairs of animate objects and times'.) Fundamental arguments can be expected on the question of how many, and which, sorts of objects we need, and on which we ought to take as primitive and which we can define. Is the sort of object,

Events, fundamental or can it be defined? Do we need *Facts*, or *States of affairs*, and if so can they be defined?

Argument can also be expected upon how we are to extend the programme to intensional areas of a natural language—how we are to represent meaning-sensitive functions. Perhaps by associating with each semantical primitive an intension and recursively defining intensions for complex expressions. But perhaps not.

All these are interesting, indeed fundamental, questions, but from the lofty viewpoint I have adopted in this paper, matters of detail. What is important is that we should have a general picture of the enterprise, and that it should be recognizable as a representation of at least part of what philosophers have been aiming at in their exploration of the semantic structure of sentences of natural languages. They are seen to have been asking questions like: 'What kind of element is this? Does it introduce a class?' (cf. Davidson's remark 'Intentional actions are not a class of actions'[10]), 'Can vague predicates introduce classes?', 'If what this expression introduces is a function, what are its inputs and outputs?'

It seemed that questions of this kind were not necessarily answered by the construction of a truth theory (except in a mildly perverse way, when the background language is taken to be first-order). More interestingly, the answers have little to do with the logical constants.

How do standard inferences involving the logical constants fare? In any interpretational semantics for English the propositional connectives, 'not', 'and', 'or', and so on, would surely fall into a common semantic category, to which, on the classical conception, there would be assigned functions from truth values to truth values. In the definition of satisfaction upon an arbitrary interpretation, I, we would have a clause for any sentence involving any n-ary connective θ (possibly joining open sentences), and for any infinite sequence s:

$\text{Sats}_I \ (s, \theta \ (S_1 \ldots S_n)) \leftrightarrow$
$\quad \text{Assig}_I \ (\theta) \ [\langle \text{Val}_I \ (s, S_1) \ldots \text{Val}_I \ (s, S_n)\rangle] = \text{T}$

where

$\text{Val}_I \ (s, S_1) = \text{T} \leftrightarrow \text{Sats}_I \ (s, S_1).$

Consequently, with the exception of inferences involving substitution of sentences with the same truth value, none of the standard inferences involving the sentential connectives is structurally valid. Briefly, the sentences $\ulcorner P$ and $Q \urcorner$ and $\ulcorner P$ or $Q \urcorner$ have the same semantic structure; the former's entailing P is due to the special variation the word 'and' plays upon a theme it has in common with 'or'.[11]

In view of this, it is not surprising that we found the manoeuvrings necessary for validating the inference from $\ulcorner P$ and $Q\urcorner$ to P an unilluminating model, and it is clear why, when we followed it with 'large', the distinction we were trying to capture between structurally valid inferences and those requiring proper axioms petered out into nothing. To put the point succinctly, there *is* no deep explanation of why $\ulcorner P$ and $Q\urcorner$ entails P.[12]

Quantifiers are more complicated but they too can be seen as falling into a single semantic category. There is work by Lindstrom and Mostowski on generalized quantifiers in which the characterization of the category is attempted.[13]

It is now time to deal with something I have left unclear up to this point. I spoke of the structural inferences as being those whose validity was due to the types of semantic element involved *and* the significance of their construction. What is meant by the semantic significance of a grammatical construction?

An interpretational semantics must not only provide appropriate assignments to expressions; it must also provide an adequate definition of truth upon an arbitrary interpretation making use of those assignments.[14] Each clause in that definition can be regarded as making explicit the significance of one kind of grammatical construction, and certain inferential consequences will follow from the significance thus characterized.

To understand this idea consider the following simple example. Suppose we have a language like English in that attributive adjectives can be stacked, yet unlike English in that from 'John is a strong tall man' it follows both that John is a strong man and also that John is a tall man, and the former sentence is entailed by these taken together. One way of capturing these facts is by making (to such attributive adjectives) the assignments we have earlier suggested (functions from sets to subsets), and writing the following clause in the definition of satisfaction upon an interpretation:

Where M, M' ... range over object-language attributive modifiers, ϕ over object-language monadic (possibly complex) predicates, and 'Var$_I$' designates the ith object-language variable, for any infinite sequence of elements s,

$$\text{Sats}_I \ (s, \ M(M'(\phi))^\cap \text{Var}_n) \leftrightarrow$$
$$\quad \text{Sats}_I \ (s, \ M(\phi)^\cap \text{Var}_n) \text{ and } \text{Sats}_I \ (s, \ M'(\phi)^\cap \text{Var}_n).$$

A consequence of this clause will be that upon the designated interpretation,[15] 'John is a large strong man' is true iff John is a large man and John is a strong man.

If what has gone before is correct, it would be a mistake to try to render explicit the semantical potential lodged in the construction of stacking modifiers by saying that our original sentence has the same semantic structure as some sentence containing the connective 'and'. For such a sentence achieves what is admittedly the same net effect by means of different semantic elements and different constructions.

Just as one can never dispense with rules of inference by enriching one's axioms (though a limited trade-off is possible) so, no matter how interlocking the assignments to interacting expressions are made, one can never obviate the need for *some* semantic potential to be lodged in the grammatical constructions—even if it is merely that concatenation signifies functional applications.[16]

The need for the distinction between inferences whose validity is due to the semantic significance of grammatical constructions and those which depend upon the logical words would certainly evaporate if we could see our way to accepting Quine's suggestion[17] that the logical constants should be regarded as 'absorbed into the constructions' they signalize. But, as Quine recognizes, we lack a clear reason for distinguishing them in this way.

It is not part of the thesis of this paper that no satisfactorily transcendent account of the logical constants can be produced, nor, consequently, that there is no well defined notion of logical form, logical consequence, and logical validity. It is merely that there is another, deeper notion, of semantic structure and of structural validity, from which those notions should be distinguished.

Does it follow from what has gone before that we are only interested in relative truth—truth upon an interpretation (truth$_I$)—and not simple truth? Certainly not: no theory of meaning which fails to state the actual truth conditions of sentences of a language is worthy of the name. But since an interpretational semantics will comprise a definition of 'true$_I$' there is a very natural way of modulating to truth by specifying, for each semantical primitive of the language, what assignment it is to receive on the designated interpretation, I^*, and thus enabling us to derive for each sentence of the language its truth$_{I^*}$ (= truth) conditions.[18] In other words, we require not merely that we are told what *kind* of function 'large' is, but *which* function of that kind it is. Thus we will expect the specification of I^* to include such clauses as

$$\text{Assig}_{I^*} \, (\text{'large'}) = \{\langle \alpha, \beta \rangle : a \in \beta \leftrightarrow \text{large } \hat{y}[y \in \alpha]a\};$$

i.e. on the designated interpretation 'large' is to be assigned that function from sets to sets such that an object is a member of the output set iff is a large member of the input set.

When the whole weight of the notion of structurally valid inference was being placed upon them, we found clauses like these—clauses in which a term is used to state its own semantic contribution—threateningly trivial. But now that the structurally valid inferences are fixed without their help, they can play their part, for it is an essential one.

Such a modulation to absolute truth is not merely desirable, it is necessary. For it is only by testing consequences of this kind generated by an interpretational semantic theory that we can impose any criterion of adequacy upon such theories. The truth$_I$-conditions of a sentence will necessarily be stated in rich semantical and set-theoretical notation, and in that condition they are immune from empirical control. We must bring an interpretational semantics down to earth by insisting that it should meet just the constraints that Convention T imposes; that it generate for each sentence of the language under consideration a true sentence of the form

$$\ulcorner S \text{ is true}_{I^*} \text{ iff } p \urcorner$$

where p is a translation of the sentence S names.[19] This means *at least* that p should be no richer in conceptual content or ontology, and thus should contain no semantic terms not obviously present in the original.

To summarize, then, an *interpretational semantics for a language L* is a theory consisting of three main parts:

(i) a definition of an *admissible interpretation of L*, which proceeds, in part, by stating, for each grammatical category of semantical primitives of L, what constitutes an appropriate assignment to a member of that category;

(ii) a definition of *truth upon an arbitrary interpretation of L*;

(iii) a definition of the *intended or designated interpretation of L*, which identifies, for each semantical primitive of L, which of all the appropriate assignments it is to receive on the designated interpretation.

It is important to observe that we can now allow the deductive apparatus of the metalanguage in which we state the interpretational semantics to comprise any *complete* proof theory for expressions of that language, without the danger of trivializing the notion of structurally valid inferences.

Now let us say that a phrase-structure grammar, G, is adequate for an interpretational semantics of L iff it generates a structural description of every sentence of L such that:

(a) There is an effective procedure for determining, upon the basis of this description of any sentence S, which clauses of the definition of truth$_I$ are to be used in deriving the truth$_I$ conditions of S, and in what order. (This is needed to deal with scope.)

(b) Where a *penultimate non-terminal node* is a node directly dominating only a terminal node (i.e. a lexical item of L): at each *penultimate non-terminal node* of each tree generated by G is a symbol for a category an appropriate assignment to the members of which is given by the definition of an admissible interpretation of L.

Then we may say: two sentences have the same semantical structure relative to an interpretational semantics iff the grammar adequate to that semantics assigns them structural descriptions which agree up to all non-terminal nodes.

The effect of this definition is that two sentences have the same semantical structure iff they are composed out of elements of the same semantic categories in the same way—where 'composed in the same way' means that they will trace exactly parallel courses through the definition of truth$_I$ in the generation of their truth$_I$ conditions.

And finally let us say that an inference from $S_1 \ldots S_{n-1}$ to S_n is structurally valid iff S_n is true upon every admissible interpretation on which $S_1 \ldots S_n$ are true; or more strictly, for every interpretation, every sequence which satisfies $S_1 \ldots S_{n-1}$ upon that interpretation also satisfies S_n upon that interpretation.

III

A logically perfect language would have one-to-one correspondence between its semantic and syntactic categories. I see no reason to suppose that natural languages are logically perfect, at any level.[20] There can be a breakdown of the one-to-one correspondence in either direction. We may find it necessary to subdivide a syntactically unitary category, so that, for example, even if 'It is certain that ...' and 'It is not the case that ...' were everywhere substitutable *salva congruitate*, they could be members of different semantic categories. And equally we may find it convenient to make assignments of the same kind to expressions of different syntactic categories. Thus we might find it convenient to assign to an adverb and also an adjective a set of events (indeed, if they stand in some morphological relationship, we may even require that they be assigned the same set of events). We do not have to gerrymander the grammar to get the two expressions into the same syntactic position; we have room for the idea of one and the same semantic element's being realized by expressions of different syntactic categories, no one of which is basic in a transformational sense.

In addition, logical constants will appear only when they appear to appear. We leave the clauses in the theory of truth$_l$ to capture the semantic significance of the construction.

These features taken together mean that the structures we regard as exhibiting semantic structure can be relatively close to object-language syntactic structures; close, that is, relative to some recent proposals concerning semantic structure. A good example is provided by Davidson's proposal that the semantic structure of 'John ran breathlessly' is that of 'There is an event *e* such that John ran *e* and *e* was breathless'.

Now there is no doubt that proposals of this kind have tended to mystify people. I quote James Cargile as a representative example:

First: we might think that this sentence ['Shem kicked Shaun'] consisted of two names and a two-place relation ... But this is wrong! Wrong? Yes, wrong! Second: the sentence really is of a three-place relational form, with two names and an existential quantifier. An existential quantifier? Where is it?[21]

It is not difficult to make sense of proposals such as Davidson's from the standpoint of the theory we have been developing, if we regard the sentence which is claimed to exhibit the semantic structure of a natural-language sentence as doing two related things. First, it indicates to what semantic category an expression is to be regarded as belonging, by representing it by an expression in the new sentence which belongs to a grammatical category of a canonical syntax, the admissible assignments to which are taken to be well understood. Secondly, it makes explicit with logical constants the semantic significance of the grammatical constructions employed in the original sentence.

Thus, instead of saying that 'breathlessly' should be assigned a set of events, we say that it is *really* a predicate, and instead of saying that to 'runs' should be assigned a set of pairs of agents and events, we say that *really* it is a two-place predicate.

This is a perfectly natural way to proceed; indeed, there has been a long tradition of representing intuitions about semantic functioning as intuitions about syntactic position (in some, admittedly rather mysterious, level of syntax). For example, philosophers have said that 'John feels a pain' has the form 'John feels painfully' (the 'adverbial analysis'), that 'carelessly' is a sentential adverb, that 'before' is not a sentential connective, that 'exists' is not a predicate, that definite descriptions are not terms, and so on.[22] It was natural to present semantic proposals in this way since it represented, before the development of formal semantic theories, one way of registering one's intuition that two expressions did or did not belong to the same semantic category.

Thus I think we can understand proposals like Davidson's as involving much more than claims to mere logical equivalence or regimentation without being mystified by them. The theorist is representing in a favoured, logically perfect, notation the types of semantic element which figure in the original sentence, and representing as explicitly as possible the significance of the construction which it exemplifies.

However, there is no need to make semantic proposals in this way; and if one is going to go for it one must be sure that one has a canonical syntax rich enough to accommodate all the types of semantic element one wishes to discover, and that one has an interpretational semantics for the language specified by the canonical syntax. It would seem preferable to short-circuit the canonical language, constructing an interpretational semantics for the natural language directly, where this is possible.

I said earlier that translation into a first-order language did force one to confront the right questions, but led one to answer them in a mildly perverse way. I want to end by explaining why I think that this is so.

We have put into the center of the picture Frege's idea that some expressions can be regarded as introducing functions. This means that we are obliged to ask, concerning the functions introduced by some expression like 'fake' or 'carelessly', 'What are its inputs and outputs?' Now if we translate such expressions into first-order languages, we will probably represent them as relational expressions whose terms designate objects of the type determined to be suitable as inputs. Thus instead of introducing a function from sets, 'large' becomes the relational expression 'large-for' holding between individuals and sets. In a way we register the extensionality of the function, but it is a different way.

Why is it perverse? The perversity lies in the fact that we attribute to the speakers of the language the ontological commitments which properly belong to the *theorist*. We are in fact no more justified in holding that the speakers' ontology encompasses sets, on the basis of the existence of expressions of theirs which introduce functions on sets, than we are in supposing that they require an ontology of truth values in order to have expressions for the truth functions. Delicacy on this issue will pay off when we come to consider intensional areas of language.

Notes

An earlier version of this paper was read at a weekend conference on 'Language and Meaning' at Cumberland Lodge, in November 1973. I would like to thank the following for their help and encouragement: D. Davidson, D. Isaacson, J. H. McDowell and P. F. Strawson. Special thanks are due to B. Taylor for help with both technical and theoretical problems.

1. D. Davidson, 'Action and Reaction', *Inquiry* xiii (1970), 144.

2. D. Davidson, 'Semantics for Natural Languages' in *Linguaggi nella Società e nella Tecnica* (Edizioni di comunità, Milan, 1970), pp. 184–5.

3. D. Davidson, 'Truth and Meaning', *Synthese* xvii (1967), 318. [Chap. 5, p. 103, in this vol.]

4. D. Davidson, 'In Defense of Convention T', in H. Leblanc (ed.), *Truth Syntax and Modality* (North-Holland, Amsterdam, 1973), p. 81. This way of identifying the logical constants is also to be found in M. A. E. Dummett, *Frege* (Duckworth, London, 1973), p. 22.

5. This latter is a suggestion found in S. C. Wheeler, 'Attributives and their Modifiers', *Noûs* vi (1972), 310.

6. D. Davidson, 'The Logical Form of Action Sentences', in N. Rescher (ed.), *The Logic of Decision and Action* (University of Pittsburgh Press, Pittsburgh, 1967), p. 82. [Chap. 11, p. 218, in this volume.]

7. D. Davidson, 'On Saying That', in D. Davidson and J. Hintikka (eds.), *Words and Objections* (D. Reidel, Dordrecht, 1969), pp. 160–1. [Chap. 35, p. 819, in this vol.]

8. 'On What One Knows', in Z. Vendler, *Res Cogitans* (Cornell University Press, Ithaca, 1972), p. 89.

9. R. Montague, 'English as a Formal Language', in *Linguaggi nella Società e nella Tecnica*, pp. 212–4.

10. 'The Logical Form of Action Sentences', p. 94. [Chap. 11, p. 232, in this vol.]

11. 'One might surely have expected that if any pair of non-synonymous expressions exhibit non-difference of type or category, "or" and "and" would be one such pair and "all" and "some" another.' P. F. Strawson, 'Categories', in O. P. Wood and George Pitcher (eds.) *Rely* (Macmillan, London, 1970), p. 184.

12. It is worth observing that intuitionistic sentential connectives cannot be regarded as representing truth functions in any finite many-valued logic. See K. Gödel, 'Zum intuitionistischen Aussagenkalkül', *Ergebnisse eines mathematischen Kolloquiums*, iv, 1933, pp. 34–38.

13. Per Lindstrom, 'First Order Predicate Logic with Generalized Quantifiers', *Theoria xxxii* (1966), A. Mostowski, 'On a Generalization of Quantifiers', *Fundamenta Mathematicae* lxiv (1957).

14. What constitutes adequacy will be considered later, see pp. 250–251.

15. For an explanation of the notion of the designated interpretation see below, p. 250.

16. As it does in the system put forward in D. K. Lewis, 'General Semantics', in D. Davidson and G. Harman (eds.), *Semantics of Natural Languages* (D. Reidel, Dordrecht, 1972), p. 169.

17. W. V. Quine, *Philosophy of Logic* (Prentice-Hall, Englewood Cliffs, 1970), pp. 28–30.

18. See Montague, op. cit., p. 211.

19. Given what I have said about clauses in the definition of truth$_I$ stating, with the use of logical constants, the significance of grammatical constructions not containing such expressions, I cannot require homophonic truth$_I$*-biconditionals. How important a difference this is between myself and Davidson depends upon the view one takes of the significance of requiring a homophonic truth theory merely for the regimented fragment, and allowing sentences of the natural language to be mapped on to sentences of the fragment which are very different.

20. Here, it seems to me, I depart from D. K. Lewis (op. cit.).

21. J. Cargile, 'Davidson's Notion of Logical Form', *Inquiry* xiii (1970), pp. 137–8.

22. See, for example, G. Ryle's notion of 'adverbial verbs' (including 'hurry' and 'think') in 'Thinking and Reflecting', *Collected Papers*, vol. ii (Hutchinson, London, 1971), p. 467.

APPENDIX

Fragment of a homophonic truth theory for a regimented language containing extensional attributive adjectives as predicate modifiers.

The syntax is as for standard first-order theories save, in addition: where A is any one-place open sentence, $\hat{x}_i[A]$ is a one-place predicate abstract. A complex predicate of degree one is any one-place predicate abstract possibly preceded by one or more modifiers $M, M', \ldots$. If ϕ is a complex predicate of degree one, ϕx_j is a wff.

We let $a, b, \ldots$ be metalinguistic variables over objects, and $s, s', \ldots$ metalinguistic variables over infinite sequences, and we write '$s \underset{i}{\approx} s'$' for '*s* differs from *s'* in at most the *i*th place'. We presuppose the standard two-place function * from infinite sequences and object-language variables to objects such that $s^*(x_i) = $ the *i*th member of *s*.

The recursive definition of the two-place relation of satisfaction ('Sats') holding between sequences and object-language expressions is enriched by the following clauses:

$\text{Sats}(s, \phi x_i) \leftrightarrow \text{SAT}(s^*(x_i), s, \phi)$.

$\text{SAT}(a, s, \text{'large'}^\cap \phi) \leftrightarrow \text{large } \hat{b} \, [\text{SAT} \, (b, s, \phi)] \, a$.

$\text{SAT}(a, s, \hat{x}_j[A]) \leftrightarrow (s')[(s' \underset{j}{\approx} s \,\&\, s'^*(x_j) = a) \leftrightarrow \text{Sats}(s', A)]$.

Note

We are obliged to define satisfaction for modified wffs by way of the three-place relation SAT for the following reason. If we attempted the most direct manoeurve

$\text{Sats}(s, \text{'large'}^\cap \phi x_j) \leftrightarrow \text{large } \hat{b} \, [\text{Sats}(b, \phi)] \, s^*(x_j)$

then the predicate abstract $\hat{b}[\text{Sats}(b, \phi)]$ would have to be true of individuals, not sequences. But in general ϕ cannot be assumed to be replaced by an expression which an individual can be regarded as satisfying directly. For we need to keep relativity to the sequence *s* to deal with any free variables which the predicate abstract replacing ϕ may contain.

Chapter 13

Deep Structure as Logical Form

Gilbert Harman

I

A *transformational derivation* of a sentence is a sequence of labeled phrase structure trees. The last tree in the sequence represents the *surface structure* of the sentence. The first tree represents the *deep structure* of the sentence.[1] Each later tree is derived from its predecessor via the application of exactly one transformational rule. The surface structure tree represents that syntactic structure relevant to the way in which the sentence is pronounced. It will be assumed here that the deep structure tree is a full semantic representation of the sentence.[2]

Until recently, transformational grammarians assumed that deep structures took the form *subject phrase followed by predicate phrase*. But considerable simplification results if deep structure takes the form *predicate followed by one or more arguments*. If the auxiliary verb is ignored (as it will be throughout this paper), the difference is given in Figure 1.

On the new analysis, transformations such as passive, indirect-object inversion, and extraposition can move around the NPs that follow the V. Later, the first NP that ends up following the V is moved in front of the V and raised into a higher S. The result of such *subject raising* is shown in Figure 2.

This sort of surface structure is just like what one had on the old analysis, except that the node that was labeled VP on the old analysis is labeled S on the new.

This points to one advantage the new analysis has over the old. It had been known that verb phrases in surface structure have the properties of

First appeared in D. Davidson and G. Harman (eds.) *Semantics of Natural Language* (Dordrecht: D. Reidel, 1972). © D. Reidel, Dordrecht, 1972. With kind permission from Kluwer Academic Publishers.

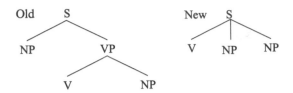

Figure 1

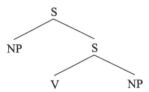

Figure 2

embedded sentences. The relabeling permits a simplified statement of the relevant facts. A good example is *backwards pronominalization*, where a pronoun precedes its antecedent. In many dialects this can occur when the pronoun is in either a subordinate clause, or a verb phrase, that does not also contain its antecedent. In my dialect, there can be backwards pronominalization in (1) and (2) but not in (3).

(1)   When she smiled, Bob kissed Mabel.

(2)   Bob kissed her, when Mabel smiled.

(3)   *She kissed Bob, when Mabel smiled.

There is backwards pronominalization into a subordinate clause in (1) and into a verb phrase in (2). There can be no backwards pronominalization in (3) because the pronoun is in neither a subordinate clause nor a verb phrase. When verb phrases are labeled S, they become subordinate clauses in surface structure. Instead of saying that backwards pronominalization can occur in either of two circumstances, into subordinate clauses and also into verb phrases, we can simplify the rule: backwards pronominalization can occur into subordinate clauses.

More importantly, various transformations are simpler on the new analysis than they were on the old. For example, on the old analysis, the passive transformation moved the subject of the sentence to the end of the verb phrase and then put the object where the subject used to be. (This

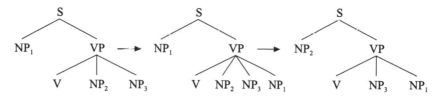

Figure 3

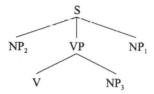

Figure 4

way of putting things assumes that all NPs contain prepositions that may later get deleted. The subject contains the preposition *by*, the object *of*, the indirect object *to*, etc.) (Figure 3).

A problem for the old analysis arose from the assumption that transformations can be rather simply represented. Passive might have been written like this:

$$NP_1 - V - NP_2 - X \rightarrow NP_2 - V - X - NP_1$$

(Introduction of the verb *to be* is here ignored as are other considerations involving the auxiliary verb.) Given the accepted limitations imposed on the statement of transformations, it was not clear why the original subject should end up inside the VP rather than following it and attached directly to S, as shown in Figure 4.

Eventually, a rather *ad hoc* solution to this problem was adopted. It was assumed that the deep structure of a passive sentence was different from that of its corresponding active version in that it contained within the VP a constituent labeled 'PASSIVE' (Figure 5).

The passive transformation applied only to structures containing that special constituent. The subject NP would then be substituted for PASSIVE, and this was to explain how it ended up in the VP.[3]

The new view avoids this *ad hoc* treatment of passive. The passive transformation occurs before subject raising and moves NPs so that they remain within the same clause. After subject raising, this clause represents

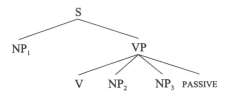

Figure 5

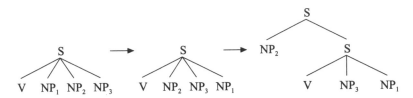

Figure 6

the verb phrase and contains what would have been the subject had passive not been used (Figure 6).

A further advantage of the new analysis is that passive is no longer represented as two operations—moving subject, then moving object—but as one—moving first argument to the end of the clause.

But the full power of the new analysis does not really emerge until other transformations are considered. Extraposition is a good example. Extraposition yields sentences like

(4) It had surprised him that Bob was sick.

from a structure that could also yield

(5) That Bob was sick had surprised him.

Notice that *him* can refer to Bob in (5) but not in (4). To account for the impossibility of backwards pronominalization in (4), it must be supposed that the extraposed sentence 'that Bob was sick' occurs within the verb phrase. On the old analysis, extraposition would have to move the extraposed sentence from subject position outside the verb phrase into predicate position within the verb phrase. That raises the same problem for the old analysis that its treatment of passive does. And the new analysis permits the same sort of simplification. Extraposition moves the extraposed sentence to the end of the clause, leaving an 'it' behind. That 'it' may later be raised into subject position (Figure 7).

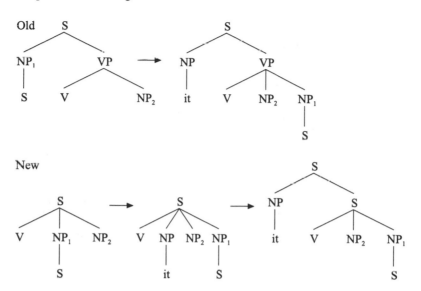

Figure 7

Infinitival clause separation is a kind of extraposition appropriate to infinitive clauses. It leaves behind, not 'it', but whatever was in subject position. For example,

(6) Bob is believed by her to love Mary.

comes from a structure that could also have yielded

(7) *(For) Bob to love Mary is believed by her.

except that (7) is not well formed, for reasons not relevant to this discussion. The impossibility of backwards pronominalization in (6) shows that the phrase 'to love Mary' is contained within the verb phrase. Therefore, infinitival clause separation raises the same problem for the old analysis that passive or extraposition does; and the new analysis offers a similar simplification.

Actually, the simplification afforded is much greater than so far indicated. Both extraposition and infinitival clause separation can apply when the clause to be extraposed or separated does not appear in subject position. That means the old analysis will have to provide two quite different statements of these transformations, whereas only one statement of each is needed on the new analysis.

For example, infinitival clause separation must be used to obtain

(8) I believe myself to be honest.

For this sort of reflective pronominalization (yielding 'myself') is possible only if the item thus pronominalized is separated out of the embedded sentence. Compare

(9) *I believe that myself am honest.

Furthermore, infinitival clause separation applies after passive, since (10) but not (11) is well formed.

(10)   Bob is believed by me to be honest.

(11) *Bob is believed to be honest by me.

If passive could apply after infinitival clause separation, (11) would be well formed. Therefore, on the old analysis, infinitival clause separation must sometimes apply to clauses in subject position, in order to get (10), and sometimes to clauses not in subject position, in order to get (8). And that means there will have to be two different statements of infinitival clause separation on the old analysis.

A similar duplication must arise on the old analysis of extraposition, since a clause not in subject position may be extraposed. Compare

(12) I know it well.

(13) I know well that Bob is honest.

All such duplication is avoided on the new analysis. Extraposition and infinitival clause separation apply possibly after passive and before subject raising to move something to the end of the clause.

Many years ago philosophers went beyond an Aristotelian subject-predicate logic to develop a logic of relations. The distinction between subject and predicate was seen to be a matter of surface form, of no logical importance. For logic, the important distinction became that between a predicate and its arguments. It is interesting to observe that what holds for logic holds for deep structure as well. Here is a first example of benefits to be derived through the identification of deep structure with logical form.

II

For philosophers, the logical form of a sentence is given by a paraphrase into quantification theory. This leads one to wonder whether anything in deep structure corresponds to the quantifiers of logic. Work by the linguist James McCawley and by the philosopher John Wallace suggests the following answer.

Quantifiers in deep structure differ from the familiar quantifiers of modern logic in their variety of type and in the restrictions they carry with them. First, there are many more kinds of quantifiers than the simple universal and existential quantifiers mentioned in discussions of quantification theory. Types of quantifiers are roughly indicated by what linguists sometimes call the *determiners* of noun phrases, words such as *any, every, all, each, a, the, some, few, a few, several, many, much, most, one, seven,* etc. Second, the quantifiers in a natural language have a varying range whereas quantifiers used in logic are usually associated with a fixed range: the universe of discourse. Occasionally, a logician will let certain quantifiers range over one universe while others range over other universes, depending on the style of variable employed. In that case, a small number of different sorts of quantifier are envisioned with fixed ranges. On the other hand, the quantifiers in a natural language have a varying range, where this is determined by a restricting phrase that follows the word indicating quantifier type. For example, the quantifier represented by the noun phrase 'many arrows' ranges over arrows and not over all things in the universe of discourse. How many count as many depends on that restricting phrase. If there are not many green arrows, then many of the green arrows will not be many of the arrows: many of the green arrows can hit the target without many of the arrows hitting the target.

Consider

(14) Many arrows didn't hit the target.

(15) The target wasn't hit by many arrows.

On the old analysis, (14) and (15) are corresponding active and passive. Since (14) does not mean what (15) means, at least in some dialects, the old analysis must permit transformations to change meaning. If quantifiers are represented in deep structure, (14) and (15) can be assigned different deep structures. For example, (14) might be assigned a deep structure as shown in Figure 8 whereas (15) might be assigned a deep structure as given in Figure 9.

The relative scopes of *many arrows* and *not* are different in (14) and (15). These scopes are determined by the deep structure: the scope of a constituent in deep structure includes whatever is dominated by the constituent immediately dominating it.

(14) is derived from its deep structure by the following transformations in this order: subject raising, not-placement (changing *hit* to *didn't hit*), NP-placement (substituting *many arrows* for *y*), and another NP-

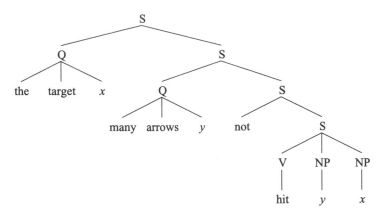

Figure 8

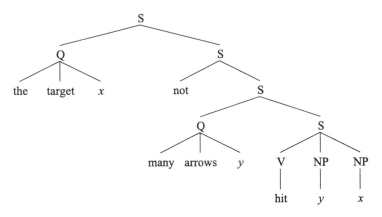

Figure 9

placement (substituting *the target* for *x*). The order of these operations is determined by the *cyclic nature of transformational rules* which are to apply to more deeply embedded sentences before they apply to less deeply embedded sentences. Similarly, (15) is derived from its deep structure by passive, subject raising, NP-placement, not-placement, and a final NP-placement.

(14) and (15) cannot be derived from each other's deep structure because of some general constraints on derivations that have been discussed by George Lakoff. In particular, for many operators, including certain quantifiers and negation, if in deep structure the scope of one

includes a second, then in later stages of the derivation the first must precede the second whenever the second *commands* the first. (X commands Y if all S's dominating Y also dominate X.) This constraint would be violated with respect to *not* and *many* if (14) or (15) were derived from the other's deep structure.[4]

Quantifiers are variable binding operators. Sometimes a variable bound by a quantifier is replaced by the relevant noun phrase. Bound variables in deep structure that do not get replaced with noun phrases become pronouns:

(16) If any arrow is green, it will hit the target.

(17) If it is green, any arrow will hit the target.

(17) can be read as an instance of backwards pronominalization, in which case it is equivalent to (16). On the old view, pronominalization occurred when a noun phrase was 'identical' with its antecedent. (18) was supposed to have come from (19):

(18) If this arrow is green, it will hit the target.

(19) If this arrow is green, this arrow will hit the target.

(16) or (17) would have come from

(20) If any arrow is green, any arrow will hit the target.

Since (20) does not mean what (16) or (17) means, this provides another instance in which transformations do not preserve meaning on the old analysis.

A series of difficulties eventually undermined the old theory. One was that it could not account for the fact that

(21) Everyone loves everyone.

does not reduce via obligatory reflexive pronominalization to

(22) Everyone loves himself.

Another was that the theory sometimes seemed to lead to infinite regress.

(23) A boy who was fooling her kissed a girl that loved him.

According to the old theory, both *her* and *him* represent full NPs that are identical with their antecedents. (23) might come from

(24) A boy who was fooling a girl that loved him kissed a girl that loved a boy who was fooling her.

Even apart from the fact that (24) is not equivalent to (23), there is the added problem that it contains pronouns which—according to the old theory—represent full noun phrases identical with their antecedents. Obviously an infinite regress results. The old theory cannot account at all for sentences like (23).[5]

When semantic considerations are brought in, it becomes clear how linguistic theory benefits from the introduction of quantifiers and variables into deep structure. The *they* in

(25) If any arrows are green, they will hit the target.

cannot be the result of identical NP pronominalization, since (25) is not equivalent to

(26) If any arrows are green, any arrows will hit the target.

But *they* in (25) is easily taken as the trace of a variable:

(27) (Any arrows x) (if x are green, x will hit target).

Furthermore, then quantifiers appear in deep structure, ambiguity of scope becomes a form of syntactic ambiguity. The sentence

(28) Jones believes someone to be a spy.

may mean that there is someone in particular that Jones believes is a spy or it may mean that Jones believes there is at least one spy. On the new theory, this difference is reflected in there being two possible deep structures for (28): Roughly

(29) (Someone x) (Jones believes (x is a spy)).

(30) (Jones believes (Someone x) (x is a spy)).

Notice that in

(31) Someone is believed by Jones to be a spy.

the scope of *someone* cannot be read as confined to the embedded sentence, although it can be read that way in (28). We can account for this difference between (31) and (28) by supposing that the infinitival clause separation transformation can move only variables and sentences. For then (31) could be derived only from (29) and not from (30). Infinitival clause separation could not apply if *someone* has already been substituted for the relevant variable by NP-placement. Only a variable could be separated out from the rest of the infinitival clause. If *someone* has narrow scope, NP-placement will have to apply before infinitival clause separation can, this preventing the latter operation. If *someone* has wide scope, infinitival clause separation can apply before NP placement. Therefore, (31) can only be read with *someone* having wide scope, although (28) can be read either way.[6]

III

Improved grammars result from the identification of deep structure with logical form. Two points have been mentioned so far, the replacement of the subject-predicate form with predicate plus arguments and the introduction of quantifiers and variables. But mention of sentences like (28) and (31) suggests a problem about the analysis of *statements of propositional attitude*. Can the deep structure of such sentences be identified with their logical form?

Here are two sentences of propositional attitude:

(32) Jones believes that Ortcutt is a spy.

(33) Sam wants Ortcutt to be a spy.

Deep structures usually cited for such sentences contain as an embedded sentence, expanded in the usual way:

(34) Ortcutt is a spy.

But the most familiar philosophical analyses of the logical form of (32) or (33) suppose that (34) cannot appear as an embedded sentence in (32) or (33).

The problem is this. (34) and

(35) Ortcutt is the president of the local bank.

logically entail

(36) The president of the local bank is a spy.

But (32) and (35) do not logically entail

(37) Jones believes that the president of the local bank is a spy.

And (33) and (35) do not logically entail

(38) Sam wants the president of the local bank to be a spy.

(36) follows from (34) and (35) by the *substitutivity of identity*. The problem is to explain why contexts of propositional attitude block the substitutivity of identity.

One philosophical answer supposes that in (32) and (33) the word 'Ortcutt' does not refer to the same thing it refers to in (34). According to Frege, words that appear in a context of propositional attitude do not have the same meaning and reference they have outside that context. In (34) the word 'Ortcutt' refers to Ortcutt. In (32) and (33) it refers not to Ortcutt but to something else, e.g. to itself, or to the usual meaning of the word 'Ortcutt', or perhaps to the mental word 'Ortcutt'. What corresponds to (34) in (32) and (33) does not function semantically as a sentence but rather serves to refer to a sentence, a proposition, or a propositional attitude. Substitutivity of identity permits one to substitute one reference to a thing for another reference to the same thing. Given (35), 'Ortcutt' and 'the president of the local bank' refer to the same thing, but only in ordinary contexts. In a context of propositional attitude these phrases do not refer to the same thing, since e.g. they refer to the meaning of 'Ortcutt' and the meaning of 'the president of the local bank' respectively; so the substitutivity of identity does not authorize the replacement of one with the other.

An alternative answer, due to Donald Davidson, permits Ortcutt to have its usual reference in (32) and (33). But (32) and (33) are not taken to be sentences that contain (34) embedded within them. What corresponds to (34) in (32) and (33) is not taken to be part of the original sentence at all. Instead it accompanies the original sentence as an example or illustration referred to by that sentence. More perspicuously written, (32) and (33) would look like this:

(39) Jones believes that. Ortcutt is a spy.

(40) Sam wants (that). Ortcutt (is) to be a spy.

When someone asserts (39) or (40), he asserts the first sentence, not the second. In uttering the second sentence he produces an example of the sort of thing referred to in his first sentence. Similarly in (32) or (33). In uttering the words 'Ortcutt is a spy' or 'Ortcutt to be a spy', one gives an example of what one's assertion refers to. These words are not part of what one says when one utters (32) or (33) but are rather part of what one is talking about. In one's example, the word 'Ortcutt' does refer to Ortcutt; but substitutivity of identity cannot be applied to (32) or (33) with respect to 'Ortcutt' since that word does not occur in these sentences. It only occurs in something that accompanies them and to which they refer.

Neither of these philosophical answers to the problem of failure of substitutivity in these contexts fits in with the idea that deep structure is logical form. Deep structure is supposed to provide a full semantic representation of a sentence. There seems to be no syntactic alternative to the assumption that the deep structure of (34) appears embedded in the deep structures of (32) and (33). These philosophical answers would have us suppose that something that must function syntactically in deep structure as an embedded sentence does not function semantically as an embedded sentence. And that seems to violate at least the spirit of the idea that deep structure is full semantic representation. Thus, on Davidson's analysis, a structure that behaves syntactically as an embedded sentence in deep structure is semantically a sentence but is not semantically embedded. On Frege's analysis, that structure is semantically embedded but it is not semantically a sentence, although it behaves syntactically as a sentence. So both analyses conflict with the idea that at the deepest level syntactic and semantic structure coincide.

However, there is a way to account for the failure of substitutivity of identity in sentences such as (32) and (33) without supposing that syntactic and semantic structure diverge at the level of deep structure. The analysis of noun phrases and quantification already sketched above will do the trick. On that analysis all noun phrases come from quantifiers and therefore have a certain scope in deep structure. If the principle of the substitutivity of identity is stated so as to apply only when the noun phrase in question has wide scope, it will automatically fail to apply in contexts of propositional attitude.

If (32) is understood like this

(41) Jones believes ((Ortcutt x) (x is a spy)).

then from (32) and (35) one cannot infer (37), because 'Ortcutt' does not have wide scope in (32). On the other hand, (32) can be understood like this

(42) (Ortcutt x) (Jones believes (x is a spy)).

In that case (32) and (35) do entail (37) because 'Ortcutt' has wide scope and substitutivity of identity applies.

Philosophers sometimes argue that an adequate analysis of logical form must permit a truth characterization. So it is important that a truth characterization of sentences of propositional attitude can be given if deep structure is identified with logical form. Into a Tarski-type theory of truth one might add principles for the denotation of names. Then one might take the representation of the object of a propositional attitude—which includes in deep structure an embedded S plus something more—to denote the embedded S itself or alternatively the proposition S expresses. The embedded S and its constituents retain their usual meaning. What is syntactically an embedded sentence is semantically an embedded sentence.[7]

IV

Finally, it is useful to consider what sort of theory results if deep structure is identified with logical form in the analysis of action sentences and causal sentences. Here there are competing philosophical theories of logical form as well as competing syntactic theories about the proper deep structures. Furthermore, all these theories are in a state of flux and development. The subject is too complex for detailed consideration here. All that can be done is to present a rather crude version of a theory of logical form that is being developed by Donald Davidson and then to compare that theory with standard grammatical analyses involving embedded sentences.

Consider these sentences:

(43) Jack opened the door with the key at ten o'clock.

(44) Fear caused Jack to open the door with the key at ten o'clock.

A semantic analysis of such sentences must account for the fact that (43) entails

(45) Jack opened the door with the key.

(46) Jack opened the door at ten o'clock.

(47) Jack opened the door.

One must also account for the fact that (44) and the following sentences can be understood so that (44) entails them.

(48) Fear caused Jack to open the door with the key.

(49) Fear caused Jack to open the door at ten o'clock.

(50) Fear caused Jack to open the door.

The problem is made more difficult by the fact that an indefinite number of adverbial phrases can occur in the verb phrase of (43). So it does not seem that one can account for the first set of entailments by supposing that e.g. (47) is a reduced form of

(51) Jack opened the door with something at some time...

One might attempt to account for the second set of entailments in terms of the first set along with the principle that, if *P* entails *Q*, then *X causes P* entails *X causes Q*. But there is a difficulty here.

(52) A house that Jack built burned down.

entails

(53) Jack built a house that burned down.

but

(54) A short circuit caused a house that Jack built to burn down.

does not entail

(55) A short circuit caused Jack to build a house that burned down.

This does not refute the principle in question, since a defender of that principle can reply that the scopes of the noun phrases in (54) and (55) are wide, so that (52) and (53) do not actually occur in (54) and (55). But then the problem becomes that of explaining why (54) and (55) cannot be understood in such a way that the relevant noun phrases have narrow scope and (52) and (53) do occur in them.

Davidson analyzes all these sentences as containing implicit quantification over events or actions. There is talk of Jack's opening of the door where that is a particular event related in various ways to Jack, the door, the key, and ten o'clock. That event is caused by fear. In order to get a rough idea of the structure of his analysis, consider the following abbreviations:

(*Ex*) for *there is an event x such that*
Ox for *x is an opening (of something by someone)*
Bxy for *x is done by y* or *y is the agent of x.*
Fxy for *x is of (or done to) y* or *y is the object of x*
Wxy for *x is (done) with y* or *y is the instrument used in doing x*
Axy for *x is (done) at the time y*
Cxy for *x causes y*
j for *John*
d for *the door*

k for *the key*
t for *ten o'clock*
f for *fear*

Then Davidson's analyses of (43)–(50) are respectively

(56) (*Ex*) (*Ox* & *Bxj* & *Fxd* & *Wxk* & *Axt*).

(57) (*Ex*) (*Ox* & *Bxj* & *Fxd* & *Wxk* & *Axt* & *Cfx*).

(58) (*Ex*) (*Ox* & *Bxj* & *Fxd* & *Wxk*).

(59) (*Ex*) (*Ox* & *Bxj* & *Fxd* & *Axt*).

(60) (*Ex*) (*Ox* & *Bxj* & *Fxd*).

(61) (*Ex*) (*Ox* & *Bxj* & *Fxd* & *Wxk* & *Cfx*).

(62) (*Ex*) (*Ox* & *Bxj* & *Fxd* & *Axt* & *Cfx*).

(63) (*Ex*) (*Ox* & *Bxj* & *Fxd* & *Cfx*).

On these analyses, the fact that (43) entails (45), (46), and (47) is represented by the fact that (56) entails (58), (59), and (60) in elementary quantification theory. The fact that (44) entails (48) (49) and (50) is represented
by the fact that (57) entails (61), (62), and (63). If with Davidson one
treats these sentences as involving implicit quantification over events, one
can give a perfectly straightforward account of the relevant entailments.

However, if Davidson's analyses are accepted, the semantic representation of (44) cannot contain embedded within it the semantic representation of (43). The semantic materials out of which (43) is constructed are
also used in the construction of (44) but these materials are put together
differently, so that (43) itself is not used in the construction of (44). The
point stands out if the relevant materials are underlined when (56) is
compared with (57):

(56) <u>(*Ex*) (*Ox* & *Bxj* & *Fxd* & *Wxk* & *Axt*)</u>.

(57) <u>(*Ex*) (*Ox* & *Bxj* & *Fxd* & *Wxk* & *Axt*</u> & *Cfx*).

What corresponds to (56) in (57) is not quite a sentence: it lacks a right
parenthesis—or, perhaps, it contains a gap right before its right parenthesis. That lack or gap is enough to keep (56) from appearing in (57). So,
if Davidson's analysis is accepted and if deep structure is identified with
logical form, one cannot say that the deep structure of (43) is embedded in
that of (44) and the usual syntactic analyses of these sentences must be
rejected.

As noted already, the situation is complicated by the existence of alternatives to Davidson's analysis and to the usual syntactic analyses. All analyses, including Davidson's, are in the process of being developed, elaborated, and modified. It is not possible to say at this time what the end result will be. It is to be expected that that result will be compatible with the identification of deep structure with logical form.

APPENDIX: PRONOMINALIZATION PROBLEMS

How is one to analyze (23)?

(23) A boy who was fooling her kissed a girl that loved him.

It is true that in some sense (23) is equivalent to

(64) (A boy x) ((a girl y) (x was fooling y and x kissed y and y loved x)).

But the quantifiers in (64) range over all boys and all girls respectively, while that does not seem true in (23). Karttunen makes an analogous point by considering the presuppositions of a sentence like

(65) The boy who was fooling her kissed the girl who loved him.

This sentence presupposes that there is exactly one pair consisting of a boy and a girl and such that he was fooling her and she loved him. Such presuppositions ought to be reflected in restrictions on appropriate quantifiers. This would not be so if (65) were analyzed as

(66) (The boy x) ((the girl y) (x was fooling y and x kissed y and y loved x)).

One needs something like

(67) (The boy x such that x was fooling y) ((the girl y such that y loved x) (x kissed y)).

But (67) is not correct since the first occurrence of y is not bound by the relevant quantifier.

The same problem emerges in clearer form in

(68) A boy who was fooling them kissed many girls who loved him.

Since *many* here must be associated with a narrower scope than that associated with the *a* of *a boy*, one is tempted to try:

(69) (A boy x such that x was fooling y) ((many girls y such that y loved x) (x kissed y)).

Again the first occurrence of y has not been bound by the relevant quantifier. Since the major quantifier ranges over boys who are fooling many girls who love them, one is tempted to try this:

(70) (A boy x: (many girls y: y loved x) ((x was fooling y)) (x kissed y).

[Here the colon is used for 'such that' introducing the restriction on a quantifier.] But now the final occurrence of y remains unbound by the relevant quantifier. If all occurrences of y are to be bound by a single quantifier, that quantifier will have to have wider scope. But, if *many* is given wide scope, the wrong meaning results; for then one is quantifying over girls who love some boy or other, not necessarily the same one.

One might consider a mixed analysis. For example, one might suppose that (68) comes from

(71) A boy who was fooling many girls who loved him kissed many
       girls who loved him

via identical NP pronominalization, whereas the pronouns in (71) are traces of bound variables. But this conflicts with the point noted in the main body of this paper, namely that identical NP pronominalization does not in general preserve meaning. Thus (68) and (71) are not equivalent. A boy who was fooling many girls who loved him might kiss many other girls who loved him. In that case (71) would be true but (68) could be false.

Indeed, it is not very clear what to logical form of (68) could be. It seems at least roughly equivalent to

(72) A boy who was fooling many girls who loved him kissed and was
       fooling many girls who loved him.

That suggests a deep structure roughly like this:

(73) (A boy x: (many girls y: y loved x) (x was fooling y)) ((many girls
       z: z loved x) (x was fooling z and x kissed z)).

But it is not at all obvious what transformations would be used to get (68) from (73).

An example that raises a similar problem is due to Geach:

(74) Almost every man who borrows a book from a friend eventually
       returns it to him.

A possible deep structure for (74) might be this:

(75) (Almost every man x: (a book y) ((a z: z is a friend of x) (x borrows y from z))) ((a book w: (a u: u is a friend of z) (x borrows w from u)) ((a v: v is a friend of x and x borrows w from v) (x eventually returns w to v))).

This would be to treat (74) as somehow a reduced form of

(76) Almost every man who borrows a book from a friend eventually returns a book that he has borrowed from a friend to a friend from whom he has borrowed it.

Again it is not clear that this gets the meaning right nor is it easy to see what transformations should be postulated to get (74) from (75). That suggests these analyses are wrong: but it is unclear what an alternative would be.

Here is an apparently similar problem which does seem to have a plausible solution. Recall that the *they* in

(25) If any arrows are green, they will hit the target.

represents the trace of a variable in

(27) (Any arrows x) (if x are green, x will hit target).

Notice that

(77) If some arrows are green, they will hit the target.

can be read as equivalent to (25). Here too *they* cannot be the result of identical NP pronominalization, since (77) is not equivalent to

(78) If some arrows are green, some arrows will hit the target.

Furthermore, there seems to be no way to analyze *they* as the trace of a variable bound by *some arrows*. Thus

(79) (Some arrows x) (if x are green, x will hit the target).

gives a reading of (77) but not the intended reading on which (77) is equivalent to (25). Nor can we simply confine the scope of *some arrows* to the antecedent of the conditional, for then the *they* in the consequent would not fall under its scope:

(80) If (some arrows x) (x are green), x will hit the target.

A similar problem arises if *some* in (77) is replaced with *several, many, a few, two, seven*, etc.

One might try to argue that a third kind of pronominalization is at work here. (77) is equivalent with

(81) If some arrows are green, those arrows will hit the target.

Furthermore, one might take (81) as transformationally derived from

(82) If some arrows are green, those arrows that are green will hit the target.

by deleting *that are green.*

However, the problem with this solution is that the phrase *those arrows* in (81) would seem itself to be more a kind of pronoun, a variant of *they*, than a reduced version of *those arrows that are green*. Compare (81) with

(83) If some arrows are such that those arrows are green, those arrows will hit the target.

The phrase *those arrows* seems to have the same function in (81) and in both of its occurrences in (83). But (83) cannot be read as

(84) If some arrows are such that those arrows that are green are green, those arrows that are green will hit the target.

So it is doubtful that in (81) *those arrows* represents a reduced form of *those arrows that are green.*

Similarly, consider

(85) Any arrows are such that, if those arrows are green, those arrows will hit the target.

Here *they* may replace *those arrows* on each of its occurrences without change of meaning. Furthermore, *those arrows* has the same function on each of its occurrences, and its occurrence in the antecedent is obviously not a reduced version of *those arrows that are green*. One can best account for these cases by assuming that bound variables that are not replaced by the NP of the quantifier binding them can become, not only pronouns, but also NPs of the form *the, these,* or *those Fs*, where *F* is a possibly reduced form of the restriction on the relevant quantifier.[8]

How then is one to account for the pronominalization in (77)? One plausible solution is to suppose that the deep structure quantifier in (77) is not *some arrows* but is rather *any arrows*. This is to suggest that both (25) and (77) have the same analysis:

(25) If any arrows are green, they will hit the target.

(77) If some arrows are green, they will hit the target.

(27) (Any arrows x) (if x are green, x will hit the target).

One must also suppose that *any* can sometimes be changed to *some* during NP-placement. This can only happen when an NP is placed into certain contexts, e.g. the antecedent of a conditional; however, it is not clear how one might give a general characterization of the relevant contexts.

This theory explains the otherwise puzzling difference between (77) and

(86) If they are green, some arrows will hit the target.

If *they* is treated as (cross) referring to the relevant arrows, (77) is ambiguous in a way that (86) is not. In (77) *some arrows* can be read as coming from an underlying *some arrows*, with wide scope, or from *any arrows*. In (86), since *some arrows* appears in the consequent, it can come only from an underlying *some arrows*, and not from *any arrows*.

This suggestion can be extended to examples in which *some* in (77) is replaced by *several, many, a few, two, seven*, etc. For example,

(87) (Any seven arrows x) (if x are green, x will hit the target

can become any of the following:

(88) If any seven arrows are green, they will hit the target.

(89) If some seven arrows are green, they will hit the target.

(90) If seven arrows are green, they will hit the target.

So, the second problem seems solvable in a completely satisfactory way. Whether an analogous trick will take care of the first problem remains unclear.

Notes

Work reported here was supported in part by the National Science Foundation.

1. The notion 'deep structure' is sometimes defined differently.

2. This assumption is accepted by James McCawley, Paul Postal, Emmon Bach, Charles Fillmore, John Ross, George Lakoff, and Pieter A. M. Seuren. The presentation here is (selectively) based on their work, especially McCawley's. Noam Chomsky defends a theory not discussed here in which deep structure trees are not full semantic representations.

3. PASSIVE appeared in the VP because it was taken to be a form of manner adverbial which appears in the VP. Thus, many manner adverbial phrases contain the preposition *by* which the subject is assigned when put into passive position. And verbs that take passive also take manner adverbial—and vice versa.

4. Lakoff points out that these constraints are weak and vary from person to person, so (14) or (15) or both may be ambiguous for some readers.

5. Not that such sentences are easy to handle on any theory. For more discussion, see the Appendix.

6. Generalizing the movement constraint here placed on infinitival clause separation may shed light on movement constraints discussed by Ross and by Postal; but this point cannot be pursued here.

7. The preceding paragraphs generalize points made by Smullyan. I am indebted here to John Wallace.

8. Quine makes roughly this point.

Bibliography

Bach, Emmon, 'Nouns and Noun Phrases' in *Universals in Linguistic Theory* (ed. by E. Bach and R. Harms), Holt, Rinehart, and Winston, New York, 1968, pp. 90–122.

Chomsky, Noam, 'Deep Structure, Surface Structure, and Semantic Interpretation in *Semantics: An Interdisciplinary Reader in Philosophy, Linguistics, Anthropology and Psychology* (ed. by Leon Jakobovits and Danny Steinberg), Cambridge University Press, Cambridge, 1970.

Davidson, Donald, 'Causal Relations', *The Journal of Philosophy* 64 (1967) 691–703.

Davidson, Donald, 'The Logical Form of Action Sentences' in *The Logic of Decision and Action* (ed. by Nicholas Rescher), University of Pittsburgh Press, Pittsburgh, Penn., 1968.

Fillmore, Charles J., 'The Case for Case' in *Universals in Linguistic Theory* (ed. by E. Bach and R. Harms), Holt, Rinehart, and Winston, New York, 1968.

Geach, P. T., 'Quine's Syntactical Insights', *Synthese* 19 (1968–69) 118–129.

Karttunen, Lauri, *Problems of Reference in Syntax*, Indiana University doctoral dissertation, 1969.

Lakoff, George, 'On Generative Semantics' in *Semantics: An Interdisciplinary Reader in Philosophy, Linguistics, Anthropology and Psychology* (ed. by Leon Jakobovits and Danny Steinberg), Cambridge University Press, Cambridge, 1970 (to appear).

McCawley, James D., 'Where Do Noun Phrases Come From' in *Readings in English Transformational Grammar* (ed. by Roderick Jacobs and Peter S. Rosenbaum), Blaisdell, Boston, 1970.

McCawley, James D., 'English as a VSO Language', *Language* 46 (1970), 286–299.

Postal, Paul M., 'Cross-Over Phenomena', in *Specification and Utilization of a Transformational Grammar* (Scientific Report No. 3), IBM Research Center, Yorktown Heights, New York, 1968.

Ross, John R., *Constraints on Variables in Syntax*, M.I.T. doctoral dissertation, 1967.

Quine, W. V., *Word and Object*, M.I.T. Press, Cambridge, Mass., 1960.

Seuren, Pieter A. M., *Operators and Nucleus*, Cambridge University Press, Cambridge, 1969.

Smullyan, A. F., 'Modality and Description', *Journal of Symbolic Logic* 13 (1948) 31–37.

Smullyan, Raymond M., 'On Languages in Which Self Reference Is Possible', *Journal of Symbolic Logic* 22 (1955) 55–67.

Wallace, John, *Philosophical Grammar*, Stanford University doctoral dissertation, 1964.

Chapter 14

Logical Form as a Level of Linguistic Representation

Robert May

What is the relation of a sentences's *syntactic* form to its *logical* form? This issue has been of central concern in modern inquiry into the semantic properties of natural languages, at least ever since Frege and Russell's disagreement over definite descriptions. Frege was at pains to show how natural language deviated from the logical perfectability of his *Begriffschrift*, holding, for example, that the grammar of natural language did not properly represent the semantic structure of quantified sentences. Russell concurred with this assessment and extended the point to definite descriptions, arguing that their logical form was obfuscated by the grammar even more thoroughly, so as to require their 'elimination' in logical representation. Frege, however, maintained otherwise; descriptions were not so much akin to quantifiers, but rather to arguments, syntactically and semantically comparable, aside from their presuppositions, to proper names. Hence, in this case, for Frege the relation of form and interpretation was rather direct, in that the grammar revealed more or less transparently the logical structure of description, but not so to Russell, who felt that the grammar disguised their true semantic nature.

Since that time it has become a common and traditional supposition in discussions of the relation of linguistic form to its interpretation that the grammar of a natural language, in ultimately mediating between sound and meaning, provides for a mapping from syntactic structures onto logical representations, the latter the objects of formal semantic analysis. As Donald Davidson puts it, 'It would be strange if the structure essential to an account of truth were not effectively tied to the patterns of sound we

First appeared in *Logical Form: Its Structure and Derivation* (Cambridge: MIT Press, 1985).

use to convey truth.' In this paper, I will be introducing a particular
approach to this view, in which the role of the grammar in characterizing semantically relevant structural properties of natural languages is
explicated in terms of formal levels of grammatical representation, an
approach expressed in the earliest discussions of transformational grammar, for example in Chomsky's *Syntactic Structures* (p. 87):

> What we are suggesting is that the notion of 'understanding a sentence' will be
> explained in part in terms of the notion of 'linguistic level'. To understand a sen-
> tence, then, it is first necessary to reconstruct its analysis on each linguistic level;
> and we can test the adequacy of a given set of abstract linguistic levels by asking
> whether or not grammars formulated in terms of these levels enable us to provide
> a satisfactory analysis of the notion of 'understanding'.

What I will propose is that the levels of linguistic representation be
articulated so as to include a level of representation, *Logical Form* (LF)
related to (more precisely, derived from) other linguistic levels in specified
ways. Logical Form, in the sense to be developed, will then simply be that
level of representation which interfaces the theories of linguistic form and
interpretation. It represents, in this view, whatever properties of syntactic
form are relevant to semantic interpretation; those aspects of semantic
structure which are expressed syntactically. Succinctly, the contribution of
grammar to meaning.

Two basic questions immediately arise. First, exactly how this semantically relevant level of representation is to be formally defined. Second,
how structures at this level are assigned 'meanings'; for our purposes,
loosely put, under what conditions a logical representation can be said to
truthfully describe, or correspond to, some appropriately individuated
aspect of the world, or perhaps more accurately, of our knowledge and
belief about the world. Of course, the answers to these questions are intimately intertwined, but conceptually the former, syntactic issue is prior: If
there are no representations, then there is nothing to be interpreted, at
least in the sense of a formal semantic interpretation. Indeed, the more
highly articulated the syntactic properties of logical representations—to
us, representations at Logical Form—the more highly determined will be
the interpretations such representations receive. Moreover, the more
highly determined semantic structure is by syntactic structure, the more
'transparent' the relation of form and interpretation will be. The question
then is just how much of the semantic structure of a natural language is
manifest in its syntax? In giving an answer to this, we must consider in
detail the first issue posed above.

Since the earliest work in generative grammar, an empirical goal has been to provide a class of descriptive levels for grammatical analysis, each constituted by a class of formal representations, well-formed with respect to individually necessary and collectively sufficient conditions on class membership. A *grammar* is understood as a function which specifies for each sentence of a language its formal description at each level of representation. A grammar (strongly) *generates* a class of *structural descriptions*, whose members are sets of representations $\{a_1, \ldots, a_n\}$, where each a_j, $(1 \leqslant j \leqslant n)$, is a representation at level A_j. A 'grammatical' sentence, then, is one that is assigned a structural description each of whose members are well-formed; an ungrammatical sentence one which is assigned a structural description with at least one ill-formed member. A sentence is n-ways grammatically ambiguous if it is assigned n-many distinct well-formed structural descriptions.

Uncovering the properties of any hypothesized level centers around three basic concerns. One has to do with the formal nature of representations at that level, the second with how these representations are derived and the third with constraints on their well-formedness. Though the answers to these questions will be deeply interconnected for any given level, only with respect to specified assumptions as to rules, representations and conditions can levels be initially individuated and their empirical content—what they represent—be ultimately determined.

Let us take an example of the sort of approach I have in mind. D(eep)-Structure is the level of representation projected from lexical properties in accordance with certain conditions determining well-formedness, for example, $\overline{X}$-theory (Chomsky, 1981). S(urface)-Structure is then that level of representation derived by rules having D-Structure phrase structure representations as their input. From a further assumption, namely that these rules effect a transformational mapping, it follows that S-Structure is a level of *phrase-structure* representation, since transformations map phrase-markers onto phrase-markers. Among the well-formedness conditions applying to S-Structure is Case-theory, in the sense of Chomsky (1980, 1981), Rouveret & Vergnaud (1980) and others, from which it follows that lexical noun phrases may occur only in positions of Case assignment. This differentiates *It is unclear what Bill is doing* from the ungrammatical **It is unclear what Bill to do*; subjects of tensed clauses are assigned nominative Case, but subjects of infinitives are usually assigned no Case at all. Thus the grammar only assigns a well-formed structural description to the former sentence. Representations at S-Structure are, in turn, phonologically interpreted—assigned phonetic values—by rules which are, in part, sensitive to structural properties of this level. To take a well-known example, the possibility of phonologically contracting *want* and *to* to form *wanna*, as in *Who do you wanna visit*? has been argued to depend upon properties of syntactically represented empty categories, and in particular upon the Case properties assigned to these categories at S-Structure (Jaeggli, 1980). In this regard, S-Structure properties in part determine the sound structure assigned to a sentence and S-Structure may be thought of as the contribution of the theory of linguistic form (that is, the syntax) to the theory of linguistic sounds.

In part, then, Universal Grammar (UG) specifies the constitution of the 'core' levels of syntactic representation, now considered to include, in addition to D-Structure and S-Structure, a level of Logical Form. Extending our mode of inquiry to this latter level, we proceed as before by fixing its syntactic properties and the type of interpretations assigned to its representations. As a point of departure, then, let us suppose that representations at LF are derived by rules having S-Structure representations as their input, so that the core levels of representation are as depicted in (1), comprising the syntactic component of what has been called 'sentence grammar':

(1) D-Structure—S-Structure—Logical Form

D-Structure is projected from the lexicon; it represents syntactically the basic functional and structural properties associated with lexical items. S-Structure is derived by a (possibly null) set of applications of transformational rules, and in turn maps onto LF, the latter level consisting of a class of fully indexed phrase markers. In May (1977) it was proposed that this latter mapping is also transformational. From this it follows that LF is a level of phrase-structure representation as well, consisting of a class of bracketings labeled with linguistic categories, a consequence of the structure-preserving nature of transformational mappings. By hypothesis, S-Structure representations are assigned phonological interpretations, while it is to LF-representations that semantic interpretations are assigned.

To be more specific about the nature of transformational mappings, I will assume, following Chomsky (1981), that there is but one transformational rule, 'Move α': Displace an arbitrary constituent to any other structural position. Among the structures which may be derived is (2), derived by movement of the *wh*-phase to COMP:

(2) [$_{S'}$ [$_{COMP}$ who$_2$] [$_S$ did John see [$_{NP}$ e_2]]]

The functioning of 'Move α' will in all cases leave a *trace* (designated by '*e*'), which is a category devoid of lexical content coindexed with, and hence bound to, the moved phrase. Turning to LF, 'Move α' chiefly figures in its derivation in transforming the S-Structure representations of quantified sentences like *John saw everyone* onto LF-representations like (3):

(3) [$_S$[$_{NP}$ everyone$_2$] [$_S$ John saw [$_{NP}$ e_2]]]

(3) is derived by (Chomsky)-adjunction of the S-Structure object NP to the S node.[1] This central case of LF-movement, which I will refer to as QR, following the usage of May (1977), derives representations that structurally overlap in certain important ways with *wh*-constructions like (2). In particular, both contain traces coindexed with phrases displaced to positions outside the predicate's argument positions. These positions will be referred to as Ā-positions, as opposed to A-positions (roughly those bearing grammatical relations). Given this, we can recognize both (2) and (3) as containing (logical) variables, which, at a first approximation, are simply those traces contained within A-positions which are Ā-bound (that is, coindexed with phrases in Ā-positions; see Borer (1981), Chomsky (1981)). In turn, the structural properties of (2) and (3) allow us to syntactically characterize certain semantically relevant concepts. Thus *scope* can be defined as follows:[2]

(4) The scope of α is the set of nodes which α c-commands at LF

Thus, in a structure like (5a), (=(2)),

(5) a.

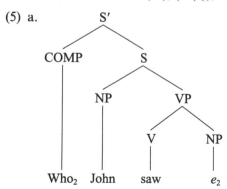

b.

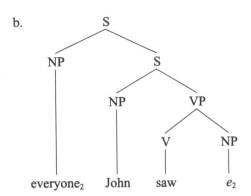

the *wh*-phrase in COMP has scope over all the nodes it c-commands, that is, S and all the nodes S dominates. This includes the trace of *who*; hence, we may take this variable as a *bound* variable as it lies within the scope of a coindexed *wh*-phrase, interpreted here as a quasi-quantifier.[3] Parallel comments hold for representations in which the binding phrase is a true quantified phrase, as in (5b) (= (3)).

The grammar, then, provides for a direct representation of quantificational structure, arguing on syntactic grounds for a particular way of representing natural language quantification, although other types of representation giving rise to the same class of interpretations can be easily imagined. This is afforded to a large extent through the mediation of trace theory. As a result, it becomes possible to explain a range of phenomena by appeal to general principles of syntactic well-formedness which interact to determine the distribution and binding of lexically empty categories, where, in part, this generality is expressed by their holding of LF-representations. To take a simple example, it is a consequence of trace theory of movement rules that 'downgrading' movements are proscribed (Fiengo, 1977; May, 1981). Thus, even though relevant subcategorization restrictions are satisfied, (6) is ill-formed, since the trace is not c-commanded by the *wh*-phrase with which it is coindexed:

(6) *[$_S$ e_2 wondered [$_{S'}$ who$_2$ [$_S$ Angleton suspected Philby]]]

Similarly, QR could apply so as to downgrade a phrase:

(7) *[$_S$ e_2 believed [$_S$ someone$_2$ [$_S$ Angleton suspected Philby]]]

However, (7) is ill-formed for just the same reason as (6)—the trace is not c-commanded by its antecedent.[4] This allows us to explain why *Someone believed Angleton suspected Philby* may not be construed with the quantifier understood as outside the scope of *believe*; it only has the well-formed logical form in (8):

(8) [$_S$ someone$_2$ [$_S$ e_2 believed [$_S$ Angleton suspected Philby]]]

This is an indication of the initial plausibility of proposing that Universal Grammar makes available a class of conditions that determine in part not only the properties of overt movements such as *wh*-movement, but also the properties of 'LF-movements' like QR that also derive structures containing traces.

The extended degree of structural articulation found at LF allows as well for the statement of generalizations not apparently manifest at other syntactic levels. One rather widely discussed case is 'weak crossover' phenomena: the impossibility of construing the pronoun as anaphoric in either *Who did his mother see?* or *His mother saw everything*, although such a construal is possible with a non-quantified antecedent: *His mother saw John*. Given that the relevant representations are as in (9);

(9) a. [$_{S'}$ who$_2$ [$_S$ did his mother see e_2]]
    b. [$_S$ everyone$_2$ [$_S$ his mother saw e_2]]
    c. [$_S$ his mother saw John]

a descriptive generalization is apparently that a trace cannot be the antecedent of a pronoun to its left; see Chomsky (1976), Higginbotham (1980), and, for somewhat different approaches, Reinhart (1983), Koopman & Sportiche (1983) and Safir (1984). In (9a) the trace arises as a result of application of 'Move α' in the mapping from D-Structure to S-Structure; in (9b), from 'Move α' applying from S-Structure to LF. To (9c) 'Move α' has not applied at all, so, in the relevant respects, its representations at D-Structure, S-Structure, and LF are non-distinct. Since the object NP is a full lexical NP, it is not proscribed from being the antecedent of the pronoun by the generalization in question. Notice that the S-Structure representations of (9a)–(9c) would not afford the relevant generalization, since the S-Structure of (9b), like that of (9c), contains not a trace but a lexical object.

Having spelled out to some degree our syntactic assumptions, we now sketch the semantic assumptions underlying our primarily syntactic investigations, so as to be able to isolate those semantic properties that will intersect with the syntax of LF-representations, in particular with our notions of variable and scope. Simplifying from the approach developed

in Higginbotham & May (1981a), suppose there is a (non-null)) domain
D. A quantifier Q is interpreted by a *quantification* **Q** on D, a function
from subsets of **D** onto $\{1,0\}$, i.e., truth and falsity.[5] *Restricted quantifi-*
cations on D, which are typically found in natural languages, differ in that
they are functions from the Cartesian product of the power set D on to
$\{1,0\}$. Restricted quantifications of the form

$$\mathbf{Q}(X, Y) = 1 \quad \text{iff } \psi$$
$$= 0 \quad \text{otherwise}$$

where ψ is some function from X and Y onto subsets of D, interpret representations at LF of the form

$$[_\alpha Q - X_i^n [_\beta \dots e_i \dots]]$$

where Q ranges over quantifier elements like *every, some, few, several, so,*
the, a, no, two, etc, X^n is an n-level projection of a lexical category and β
an open sentence containing e_i free. That β is the maximal domain containing e_i free follows from assuming the coincidence of a quantifier's
scope with its c-command domain. A quantification, then, effects a partitioning of the universe, its application to an LF-representation containing
a quantifier Q being fixed by simple rule; the value of X is determined
on the basis of X^n, that of Y on the basis of β. Supposing that there is
an (extensional) category-type correspondence such that both X^n and β
denote subsets of the domain, then **Q** establishes that relationship that
must hold between X and Y, the sets so denoted, for truth to obtain.
Multiple quantification sentences, whose syntax we will turn to below,
will be treated in the usual way via truth relative to assignment of values
to variables.[6]

As an example, consider the sentence *No Russian is a spy*, which has the
logical form (10) in the relevant respects:

(10) $[_S [_{NP}$ No $[_{N''}$ Russian$]]_i [_S e_i$ is a spy$]]$

This is interpreted by a quantification in which ψ is an intersective function on subsets of D:

$$\mathbf{No}(X, Y) = 1 \quad \text{iff } X \cap Y = \varnothing$$
$$= 0 \quad \text{otherwise}$$

When applied to (10) the value of X will be defined as

$$\{x | \text{Russian}(x)\}$$

while that of Y will be

$\{y|\text{spy}(y)\}$.

(10) will be true, then, just in case the set of Russians and the set of spies have no members in common, and false otherwise. Similarly, the truth conditions for other quantifiers can be specified. *Every* will be interpreted by the intersective quantification

$$\textbf{Every}(X, Y) = 1 \quad \text{iff } X = X \cap Y$$
$$\qquad\qquad\quad = 0 \quad \text{otherwise}$$

while *some* will be interpreted by

$$\textbf{Some}(X, Y) = 1 \quad \text{iff } X \cap Y \neq \varnothing$$
$$\qquad\qquad\quad\; = 0 \quad \text{otherwise}$$

which is also intersective. Numerals will be interpreted by quantifications of the form

$$\textbf{n}(X, Y) = 1 \quad \text{iff } |X \cap Y| = n$$
$$\qquad\qquad = 0 \quad \text{otherwise.}$$

This interprets the 'exactly' sense of numerical quantifiers; the 'at least' sense is arrived at by substituting '$\geqslant$', the 'at most' sense by substituting '$\leqslant$'. All three quantifications apply equally well (in the absence of any pragmatic constraint), to the LF-representation of *Three professors left*, which will then be true under three related, but distinct, interpretations pertaining to the cardinality of the intersection of the set of individuals who are professors and left. *The* will be interpreted by

$$\textbf{The}(X, Y) = 1 \quad \text{iff } X = X \cap Y = \{a\}, \text{ for } a \in D$$
$$\qquad\qquad\quad = 0 \quad \text{otherwise}$$

which embeds the existence and uniqueness properties of definite descriptions, found invariantly under alternative scopes:

(11) The president of every public authority in New York is a crook

Although on the preferred construal of (11) *the* has narrower scope, it can also have broader scope, a construal facilitated by substituting *Robert Moses* for *a crook*. On the former interpretation (11) entails that each authority has one, and only one, president; on the latter it entails that there is exactly one person who is president of all the public authorities. This is as expected, as these properties of interpretation do not accrue to *the* in virtue of its scope. We are thus distinguishing properties of quantifiers traceable to structural sources from those which are lexically inherent, expressed as aspects of quantifications. Indeed, this can be the only source of inherent properties of quantifiers, since syntactic rules, and in particular, transformational mappings, including those onto LF, are context-free, and hence blind to lexical governance. This precludes the possibility of marking quantifiers for specified scopes, although inherent properties may be more consonant with certain scopes. For example, *each* often preferentially takes broad scope. But whatever the source of this preference, we would not want to maintain that it is an obligatorily broad scope quantifier, as it can have narrow scope as well, as in (12), in which it stands inside of the embedded quantifier in logical form:

(12) Each person in some midwestern city voted for Debs in the '08 election

Thus the theory sharply distinguishes the general grammatical properties of quantifiers—their scope—from their lexical properties, expressed semantically by quantifications.

The interpretation of quantifiers just sketched constitutes an hypothesis as to the semantic component of our linguistic knowledge of quantification. Now, of course, our syntactic assumptions do not uniquely determine the sort of semantics just outlined; one could imagine other interpretive systems wedded to the structural aspects of Logical Form. But whatever the exact system of semantic interpretation assumed, insofar as it characterizes notions that interact with grammatically determined semantic structure, we will have an argument that linguistic theory should countenance a formal semantic component with those properties. To take an example, the notion of quantification adumbrated above allows us to classify quantifiers as either monotone increasing or decreasing, depending upon whether they warrant upward or downward entailments among pairs like (13a)/(13b) and (13a)/(13c) (Barwise & Cooper, 1981):

(13) a. Every man left
      b. Every father left
      c. Every man left early

(13a) entails (13b); this is a downward entailment since it runs from a superset, the set of men, to a subset, the set of fathers. On the other hand, the entailment relation between (13a) and (13c) is upward entailing, as it runs from a subset, the set of individuals who left early, to a superset, the set of individuals who left. Thus, we will say that the quantifier *every*, interpreted by the quantification given above, is monotone decreasing for argument X and monotone increasing for Y. (What I am calling 'monotone increasing/decreasing for X', Barwise & Cooper (1981) call persistent/ antipersistent, reserving the term monotone for what I have referred to as monotonicity for Y.) All other quantifiers can be classified by their monotone properties; for example, *no* is monotone decreasing for both X and Y, *some* monotone increasing for both, for example.

Monotone properties of quantifiers afford a number of interesting generalizations with syntactic consequences. To mention one, apparently it is only those quantifiers that are monotone decreasing for Y which can be moved to COMP in S-Structure:[7]

(14) Only/no/few spies that he trusts would Dulles send inside Russia

This contrasts with quantifiers which minimally differ from those in (14) in being monotone increasing for this argument:

(15) *Even/all/many spies that he trusts would Dulles send inside Russia Russia

Another very interesting case is discussed in Ladusaw (1981). He argues that a necessary condition on the occurrence of polarity *any* is that it occur within the scope of a monotone decreasing operator. He points to examples like (16), which under the assumptions here have the LF-representations in (17):

(16) a. No student who ever read anything about phrenology attended Gall's lecture
   b. No student who attended Gall's lecture had ever read anything about phrenology

(17) a. No student who ever read anything about phrenology$_2$ [e_2 attended Gall's lecture]
   b. No student who attended Gall's lecture$_2$ [e_2 had ever read anything about phrenology]

In deriving (17) it has been assumed that QR applies to the entire restrictive relative clause, and not just its head. This is just as with *wh*-movement; thus *Which book that John likes did he give to Mary to read* contrasts with *Which book did he give that John likes to Mary to read*. Thus, in (17a) the polarity item *anything* is included within that part of the logical form which fixes the value of X in the quantification interpreting *no*, in (17b) that part which fixes the value of Y. Since *no* is monotone decreasing for both arguments, occurrence of polarity items is warranted in either constituent in the LF-representation. On the other hand, both (18a) and (18b) are ungrammatical, since *some* is fully monotone increasing:

(18) a. *Some student who ever read anything about phrenology attended Gall's lecture
     b. *Some student who attended Gall's lecture had ever read anything about phrenology

In contrast to (16) and (18), Ladusaw points to examples like (19):

(19) a.   Every student who ever read anything about phrenology attended Gall's lecture
     b. *Every student who attended Gall's lecture had ever read anything about phrenology

Since *every* is monotone decreasing for X and increasing for Y, the polarity item can only occur within that part of the LF-representation corresponding to the former argument; thus (19a) is well-formed, but not (19b).

The 'pied-piping' property of QR, whose importance we have just observed in describing the properties of polarity items, has a number of other consequences. For example, VP-deletion is possible, in general, if neither the missing verb nor its antecedent c-commands the other. This will clearly always hold when VP-deletion applies across sentential conjuncts or members of a discourse. But consider (20), the case of antecedent contained deletion discussed in Sag (1976) and elsewhere.

(20) Dulles suspected everyone who Angleton did

This seems to violate the condition, as *suspected* c-commands *did*. But as Sag (1976) and Williams (1977) have argued, the constraints on VP-deletion are properly stated over logical representation, and indeed, the LF-representation of (20) will be consistent with the c-command constraint, as now there is no c-command relation between the verb phrase headed by *suspected* and the missing VP.

(21) [everyone who Angleton did$_2$ [Dulles suspected e_2]]

I will suppose, along with Williams, that VP-deletion involves a reconstruction of the missing VP in the place of the pro-form, respecting certain identity conditions. While matters are in actuality somewhat more complex, for our purposes it will do to simply assume that it is the syntactic VP which is copied; the resulting structure will be as in (22):

(22) [[everyone who Angleton suspected e_2]$_2$ [Dulles suspected e_2]]

This represents just the desired interpretation, namely that Angleton and Philby suspected all the same people. Note that in (22) *who* now properly binds an empty category, presuming that it is normally coindexed with the head of the relative. A comparable substitution of VP in the S-Structure of (20), however, would lead to a reconstructive regress, as substitution of the VP *everyone who Angleton did* would lead to a structure still containing a deleted VP, which itself would have to be reconstructed, and so on. That such a regress is a cause of ungrammaticality can be summized from the deviance of (23), with a non-restrictive relative substituted; compare *Dulles suspected Philby, who Angleton did too*:

(23) *Dulles suspected Philby, who Angleton did

Here, since LF-movement affects only quantified phrases, there is no possibility of deriving the structure which properly permits reconstruction. Needless to say, the contrast of (20) and (23) provides strong evidence for a level of Logical Form, and for movement operations onto that level which single out quantified phrases. This is reinforced by the account of examples like (24):[8]

(24) *Dulles suspected everyone who knew Philby, who Angleton did

It might be thought that substitution of an antecedent VP in a non-restrictive relative would be possible if it were moved as part of another phrase, so as to avoid the regress just described for (23). This is so, but, it turns out, a well-formed LF-representation is still not derivable. Application of QR gives (25a); subsequent substitution of the VP, (25b):

(25) a. [everyone who knew Philby, who Angleton did^2 [Dulles suspected e_2]]
     b. [[everyone who knew Philby, who Angleton suspected e_2]$_2$ [Dulles suspected e_2]]

The problem with (25b) is that the embedded *wh*-phrase binds no empty category. That is, the two *wh*-phrases will bear distinct indices, but the index of the empty category contained in the reconstructed VP must be that of the higher occurrence of *who*, as only it is coindexed with the phrase which undergoes LF-movement. Thus the ungrammaticality of (24) can be attributed to its LF-representation (25b) containing an operator which binds no variable. Note that the analysis further predicts that *Dulles suspected everyone who knew some agent who Angleton did* is grammatical, but only with an interpretation under which the deleted phrase is understood as the embedded VP, that headed by *knew*.

The grammar, then, provides sufficient structure so that at Logical Form the application of quantifications can be transparently determined. This structure arises from assuming that LF-representations of quantified sentences are derived by transformational mappings, exploiting a notion of logically bound variable which receives grammatical foundation through trace theory. Such mappings, note, do not 'translate' between the *sentences* of some language and those of some other formal representational system; rather, they are mappings wholly within the formal representational system for natural language. Indeed, the assumption that LF is derived in this way adds nothing to linguistic theory which need not otherwise be assumed as provided by UG. Whatever theoretical apparatus is needed to properly characterize the syntactic properties of *wh*-constructions like *Who does Angleton suspect?* will be sufficient, I am arguing, to properly characterize the syntactic properties of the LF-representation of *Angleton suspected everyone*, giving a general theory of the representation of quantificational binding without introducing any special types of rules or principles. This is an important point, and it should be emphasized. Assuming that there is a level of Logical Form derived by 'Move α' does not entail any extension of the formal expressiveness of linguistic theory—that is, there is no extension of the types of grammatical rules or representations which it countenances—although it does extend the range of phenomena which, *prima facie*, fall under its descriptive and explanatory purview. Insofar, then, as this approach can be seen to be empirically motivated, it will represent the best possible circumstance for incorporating a theory of logical representation within the grammar.

We now turn to the logical syntax of multiple quantification. As a point of departure consider the following analysis, that of May (1977), of the class of structures derived by application of QR to (26), an S-Structure containing two quantified phrases:

(26) [s[NP every spy] [VP suspects [NP some Russian]]]

A single application of QR to either NP in (26) yields the structures in (27):

(27) a. [$_S$[$_{NP}$ every spy]$_2$ [$_S$ e_2 suspects [$_{NP}$ some Russian]]]
       b. [$_S$[$_{NP}$ some Russian]$_3$ [$_S$[$_{NP}$ every spy] suspects e_3]]

Since QR is a (Chomsky)-adjunction, each of these structures now contains two S nodes to which further application of QR can attach phrases, allowing for the derivation of the distinct structures in (28):[9]

(28) a. [$_S$[$_{NP}$ every spy]$_2$ [$_S$ [$_{NP}$ some Russian]$_3$ [$_S$ e_2 suspects e_3]]]
       b. [$_S$[$_{NP}$ some Russian]$_3$ [$_S$ [$_{NP}$ every spy]$_2$ [$_S$ e_2 suspects e_3]]]

(28a) and (28b) represents the ambiguity of *every spy suspects some Russian* as a matter of quantifier scope. Since in (28a) *every spy* c-commands *some Russian*, but not vice versa, the former has broader scope. The opposite holds in (28b), in which *some Russian* has been adjoined at a higher position from which it has broader scope over *every spy*. Thus, simply given the free application of QR, (and the usual sort of assumptions as to the recursive assignment of truth-conditions), it is possible to represent certain ambiguities of multiple quantification, so that an S-Structure such as (26) will count as grammatically disambiguated with respect to its logical form.

Bear in mind that the issue which concerns us here is to what degree the class of *possible* interpretations which can be assigned to a given syntactic structure is a function of its grammatical properties. This is not to say, however, that every *sentence* of a given form will exhibit every possible interpretation; even less to say a sentence will exhibit every possible interpretation on every use. Which construal or construals will be preferred on a given occasion of use is a matter which goes beyond grammar *per se*, taking into account various properties of discourse, shared knowledge of the interlocutors, plausibility of description, etc.[10] To conflate these matters would be to confuse the grammatical issue—to what degree does a sentence's structure fix its meaning—with an issue ultimately of use. And to do so would undoubtedly not lead to a clear understanding of the content of either topic.

Sentences of mixed universal and existential quantification, such as *Everybody loves somebody*, have the property that one of the interpretations represented by their logical forms entails the other, a matter of logic, just as it is a matter of logic that the interpretations represented by the logical forms of *Everyone loves everyone* are equivalent. Regardless of these logical relations, however, both sentences are assigned two structurally distinct representations at LF; their equivalence or disequivalence simply amounts to the claim that distinct modes of composition either do or do not lead to identical interpretations. From the logical relations of such sentences, however, another moral can be drawn, namely that there is no need to represent both scope orders, but rather only one, the other to be seen as following in virtue of some logical (or perhaps pragmatic), relation. For instance, with sentences of mixed universal and existential quantifiers, there would be only a representation of the interpretation in which the existential has broader scope, as this entails the other interpretation, in which the universal has broader scope. In a sense, this is to take the logical laws of quantification theory as generative, rather than interpretive, as they derive the interpretations not given by the grammar. On this view, however, it would seem that it remains necessary to reserve multiplicity of representation for any sentence whose interpretations are logically independent, as otherwise there would be no way to derive all its interpretations. Just this is found in sentences such as (29), which on one construal is true in case everyone is a lover, on the other just in case everyone is loved:[11]

(29) Nobody loves nobody

Assuming that *no* is logically glossed as the negation of the existential quantifier, the interpretations of these structures can be schematically represented as follows:

(30) a. $\neg \exists x \, \neg \exists y \, P(x, y) \leftrightarrow \forall y \, \exists y \, P(x, y)$ (Everyone is a lover)
       b. $\neg \exists y \, \neg \exists x \, P(x, y) \leftrightarrow \forall x \, \exists x \, P(x, y)$ (Everyone is loved)

But if it is necessary to countenance an ambiguity of representation for *Nobody loves nobody*, as a matter of grammar, it is hard to see how a parallel ambiguity can be disallowed for *Everybody loves somebody*, given that they have identical S-Structure constituencies. One could invoke some sort of semantic or syntactic constraint to obtain this result, but it is unclear how the former would avoid the ill effect of constraining the functioning of grammatical rules not formally but on the basis of a sentence's meaning,[12] while the latter would have to be quite complicated in order to pick out a constant representation under varying surface positions of the particular lexical quantifiers, to which the condition would have to overtly refer. Even if some such approach were feasible, however, it would obscure the possibility of ambiguities of composition accrueing to sentences by virtue of their syntactic construction, and would fail to recognize the role of general syntactic rules and principles in grammatically expressing such ambiguities. But assuredly this is a proposition we wish to entertain, within the context of particular grammatical theories.

For multiple quantification sentences, then, representation at LF disambiguates their interpretations. Ambiguities of multiple quantification, therefore, are syntactic ambiguities, grammatically disambiguated, a 'constructional hononymity'. Such disambiguation as we find at LF, under our syntactic characterization of this level, will clearly be relevant in determining logical consequence in natural language (with respect to a specified semantic interpretation), although since LF does not represent, for instance, contextually assigned values of indexical elements, or the knowledge, beliefs and intentions of the interlocutors, matters which transcend the grammatical, it will only contribute part of the overall characterization of the structure of inference in natural language. (This is not to say that inferences involving non-grammatical factors will not make reference to LF, only to say that they will not be *represented* at this level.) LF will constitute just the grammatical component of this overall system, contributing a notion of consequence following in virtue of syntactic constituency and grammatical form. Note that there can be no *a priori* judgment as to just which inferences fall in this latter class; this is an empirical matter which can be adjudged only with respect to a fixed nexus of assumptions as to the nature of syntax and its relation to semantic interpretation. For instance, it is by no means necessary to hold that ambiguities of multiple quantification are represented at any syntactic level, eschewing the assumption that the representation of quantifier scope involves movement, and maintaining rather that insofar as this is represented, it is within the semantic, not syntactic, component. Part of the appeal of such a view is that it might allow for a seemingly simpler 'surface' syntax; cf Cooper (1983) for an account along these lines.[13] But as pointed out above this may very well be illusory, as assuming movement onto a syntactic level of Logical Form does not extend the formal structure of the theory. Moreover, the motivation for LF does not arise solely from its being disambiguated, to whatever degree, but to a large extent because it extends the empirical domain of syntax so as to afford uniform accounts of a number of generalizations which might otherwise only be describable, in a theory which eschews this assumption, via a disjunction of heterogeneous properties. To take an example, consider certain basic properties of *wh*-questions. As it well-known, the verbs *believe, wonder* and *know* form a paradigm when taking finite complement clauses; *believe* takes only declarative complements, *wonder* interrogative and *know* either. Since *believe* takes only declaratives, **Philby believed who Angleton suspected*, containing an indirect question is ungrammatical, although direct questions with *believe* are possible: *Who did Philby believe that Angleton suspected. Wonder*, on the other hand, requires an interrogative complement. Hence we have *Philby wondered who Angleton suspected* but not **Who did Philby wonder (that) Angleton suspected*. By contrast, *know* takes both types of complements, as witnessed by the grammaticality of the direct question *Who did Philby know that Angleton suspected* as well as the indirect question *Philby knows who Angleton suspected*. Now suppose, as is usual, that predicates subcategorize for declarative or interrogative clauses inclusively. Marking COMP with the feature [±WH] as a convenient method for registering this, the well-formed cases just noted will have the representations in (31) through (33):[14]

(31) Who did Philby believe [$_{S'}$[$_{COMP}$ –WH that] [$_S$ Angleton suspected *e*]]

(32) Philby wondered [$_{S'}$[$_{COMP}$ +WH who] [$_S$ Angleton suspected *e*]]

(33) a. Who did Philby know [$_{S'}$[$_{COMP}$ –WH that]
　　　　[$_S$ Angleton suspected *e*]]
　　 b. Philby knows [$_{S'}$[$_{COMP}$ +WH who] [$_S$ Angleton suspected *e*]]

As a first approximation, we can account for these observations on the basis of the following principle:

(34) *Wh*-Criterion
　　(i)　Every [+WH] COMP must dominate a *wh*-phrase
　　(ii)　Every *wh*-phrase must be dominated by a [+WH] COMP

(32) and (33b) are consistent with the *Wh*-Criterion, since they contain [+WH] COMPs filled by *wh*-phrases. (31) and (32a) also satisfy this condition, since they contain [–WH] COMPs. If a *wh*-phrase were to move into the complement COMP in either case the resulting structures would be ruled out, since they would contain *wh*-phrases not governed by [+WH]. The effect, then, of the *Wh*-Criterion is to require *wh*-movement whenever there is a [+WH] COMP, since only then can there be the requisite containment in COMP.[15]

The examples discussed so far are neutral as to whether the *Wh*-criterion holds of S-Structure or LF. If it holds of the latter, then not only is movement of the *wh*-phrase obligatory in (32) and (33b), but also in multiple questions like (35).

(35) [$_{S'}$ which spy$_2$ [$_S$ *e*$_2$ suspects [$_{NP}$ which Russian]]]

Only if the *wh*-phrase not in COMP in S-Structure is moved there in LF will the *Wh*-Criterion be satisfied. This can be accomplished by assuming that LF-movement applies to quantified expressions in general, including the quasi-quantificational *wh*-phrases found in direct and indirect questions, moving them when unmoved at S-Structure into COMP at LF. Then at LF (36) can be derived from (35):

(36) [$_{S'}$ which Russian$_3$ which spy$_2$ [$_S$ e_2 suspects e_3]]

As both *wh*-phrases now occur in COMP, the *Wh*-Criterion, now taken as a condition on LF, is satisfied, and (37) can be properly interpreted as a multiple question. If movement is into a COMP to which an interrogative interpretation is not assigned, the result is deviant; thus (37) stands in violation of the *Wh*-Criterion, as there is no [+WH] COMP into which it can move at LF:

(37) *The spy who suspects which Russian is Angleton

The analysis of (36) and (37) assumes that LF-movement of a *wh*-phrase is to COMP, as in S-Structure, and as opposed to movement of other (non-*wh*) quantified phrases, which adjoin to S. This may simply reflect the more general fact, in part formally expressed by the *Wh*-Criterion, that COMP is a selected position, which can be occupied only by phrases satisfying its selectional restrictions, others being excluded.

The role of LF-movements in accounting for properties of *wh*-constructions gains further support from observations of Huang (1982). He notes that in Chinese interrogatives, there is no overt *wh*-movement at S-Structure.[16] Thus we find examples like (38) through (40) which are syntactically identical, aside from choice of matrix verb:

(38) Zhangsan xiang-zhidao [ta muqin kanjian shei]
              wonder   his mother see   who
      "Zhangsan wondered who his mother saw"

(39) Zhangsan xiangxin [ta muqin kanjian shei]
              believe   his mother see   who
      "Who does Zhangsan believe his mother saw?"

(40) Zhangsan zhidao [ta muqin kanjian shei]
              know   his mother see   who
      (i) "Who does Zhangsan know his mother saw?"

      (ii) "Zhangsan knows who his mother saw"

Huang points out that the interpretations of these examples are identical to their English counterparts. Thus, (38) can only be understood as a direct question, (39) as an indirect question, while (40) is ambiguous between these construals, as indicated by the glosses.

The explanation for this, Huang argues, follows from holding that Chinese differs minimally from English in that unary questions are derived by *wh*-movements confined to the mapping from S-Structure onto LF. What is apparently constant in Chinese and English are the sub-categorization properties of the relevant predicates. Thus, 'believe' only takes [−WH] complements, 'wonder' only [+WH] and 'know' either. Given that the *Wh*-Criterion applies at LF, it now follows that the LF representations of the Chinese examples (38) through (40) will be structurally non-distinct from their English counterparts in (31) through (33). That movement is in fact involved here is further evidenced by the fact, observed in Higginbotham (1980), that the pronouns in (38) through (40) cannot be construed as variables bound by *shei*; that is, they display weak crossover effects. As noted above, as a generalization, a variable cannot serve as antecedent of a pronoun to its left. If the derivation of the LF-representations in (38) through (40) involves movement, then the weak crossover effects can be accounted for on exactly the same grounds as their English counterparts. By assuming, then, that *wh*-phrases can—and, in fact, given the *Wh*-Criterion, must—be moved to COMP in LF, the properties of LF afford a general explanation of the apparent universality of *wh*-complementation. Thus, we find identity of interpretation, even though only in English are direct and indirect questions structurally distinguished at S-Structure.

Huang's observations, provide, I believe, a very strong *prima facie* case for the existence of LF movements and, hence, for the level itself. Another example to the same point can be made on the basis of properties of crossing coreference:

(41) Every pilot who shot at it hit some Mig that chased him

As is well-known, sentences like (41) allow for a construal in which the antecedent of *it* is taken as *some Mig that chased him* simultaneously with *him* being understood as having *every pilot who shot at it* as antecedent. The property of these sentences which interests us here is how this pattern of crossed binding of the pronouns is to be represented at LF. First, however, it is important to take note of some special properties of the anaphoric relation illustrated in (42):

(42) Every Mig destroyed its target

As many authors have pointed out,[17] the pronoun in (42) is most properly construed as a bound variable; since its antecedent is not referential, anaphora here clearly cannot be explicated through co- or overlapping reference. In our terms, we may represent this construal by (43):

(43) [$_S$ every Mig$_2$ [$_S$ e_2 destroyed its$_2$ target]]

The pronoun is (properly) bound by the trace arising from movement of the quantifier phrase. Notice that there is no particular reason to suppose that the pronoun is replaced by a variable at LF, since semantically its interpretation will be wholly determined by the nature of the interpretation of the element which ultimately binds it, here a quantifier.

Now consider a somewhat more complicated example:

(44) Every pilot hit some Mig that chased him

Like other simple transitive clauses discussed above, (45) exhibits a scope ambiguity; either quantifier may be understood as having broader scope over the other. Interestingly, the construal of the pronoun *him* varies according to the scope relations—*him* can be bound by *every pilot* only if *every pilot* is understood as having broader scope than *some Mig that chased him*. The LF representations derivable from the S-Structure of (44) are those in (45):

(45) a. [every pilot$_2$ [[some Mig that chased him]$_3$ [e_2 hit e_3]]]
     b. [[some Mig that chased him]$_3$ [every pilot$_2$ [e_2 hit e_3]]]

Consider (45a). Here the pronoun resides within the scope of the c-commanding quantifier phrase *every pilot*, and hence can be construed as a bound variable. In (45b), on the other hand, *him* is not within the scope of *every pilot*; the c-command domain of this latter phrase is solely the most deeply embedded S. When *some* is assigned broader scope, the pronoun is carried along to a position outside the scope of *every*. Hence, in this structure, no bound variable construal of the pronoun is possible.

The relevant property of LF-representations which accounts for the range of interpretations available to (44) can be stated as follows:

(46) A pronoun is a bound variable only if it is within the scope of a coindexed quantifier phrase

This properly accounts for the availability of a bound construal in (45a), and for its absence in (45b). That this principle holds of LF can be garnered by the availability of a bound variable construal of the pronoun in *Somebody in every city despises it*. If the principle on bound variable anaphora held at S-Structure, we would not expect this to be possible. At LF, however, the embedded quantified phrase must be extracted to a position in which in has broadest scope, a position from which it will c-command, and hence bind, the object pronoun; see May (1977).

Now reconsider the case of crossed binding, the 'Bach–Peters' example in (41), *Every pilot who shot at it hit some Mig that chased him*. Given our assumptions so far, QR can derive two structures from the S-Structure representation of this sentence:

(47) a. [[every pilot who shot at it]$_2$ [[some Mig that chased him]$_3$
    [e_2 hit e_3]]]
b. [[some Mig that chased him]$_3$ [[every pilot was shot at it]$_2$
    [e_2 hit e_3]]]

We are now faced with a problem. In (47a), while *him* can be construed as a bound variable, as it is c-commanded by the *every*-phrase, *it* cannot be construed in this way, since it is not c-commanded by the *some*-phrase. Just the inverse circumstance obtains in (47b); here only *it* can be a bound variable. It would seem, then, that it is not possible to represent the simultaneous binding of the two pronouns.

In Higginbotham & May (1981a, b) it is argued that crossed binding sentences are to be properly analyzed as containing 'binary quantifiers'. The idea developed there is that among the rules applying to LF is *Absorption*, whose effect can be characterized as in (48):

(48) ... [NP$_i$ [NP$_j$ ... → ... [NP$_i$ NP$_j$]$_{i,j}$ ...

Structurally, Absorption takes structures in which one NP immediately c-commands another NP and derives structures in which they form something like a conjoined constituent:

(49))

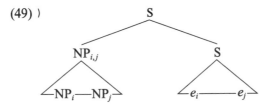

Notice that in the absorbed structure (49), NP$_i$ c-commands NP$_j$ and vice versa. Semantically, such structures are interpreted by binary (actually *n*-ary) quantifications, derived from pairs (*n*-tuples) of unary quantifications, defined as functions from the powerset of the Cartesian product of **D** onto {0, 1}. This is for unrestricted binary quantifiers. Restricted binary quantifiers are functions from $P(D \times D) \times P(D \times D)$. If the binary quantification is made up of 'intersective' quantifiers, that is, those that are defined in terms of intersections of subsets of D, then it can be proven that the absorbed and non-absorbed LF-representations lead to equivalent interpretations, with the further proviso that the narrower scope quantifier contains no occurrence of x free. Thus just the same truth conditions will be ascribed to *Everybody loves someone*, regardless of whether it is represented at LF with absorbed quantifiers or not. Where binary quantifiers differ is that they apply to all variable positions simultaneously. So they are particularly suited for the treatment of crossed binding (Bach-Peters) sentences. Both of the representations (47) satisfy the structural description of Absorption, deriving (50)

(50) a. [[every pilot who shot at it]$_2$ [some Mig that chased him]$_3$]$_{2,3}$
[e_2 hit e_3]

b. [some Mig that chased him]$_3$ [[every pilot who shot at it]$_2$]$_{2,3}$
[e_2 hit e_3]

In both of these structures, the syntactic condition on bound variable anaphora is satisfied, because the *every*-phrase c-commands *him* and the *some*-phrase c-commands *it*. Focusing on (50a) we see that it is interpreted by the binary quantification

Every, Some$(R, S) = 1$ iff $x \in dom\ R \to (R \cap S)'x \neq \emptyset$
$\qquad\qquad\qquad = 0$ otherwise.

In the notation of Higginbotham & May (1981a), *dom R* denotes the domain of a relation R on D, and $R'x$ stands for

$\{y \in D | \langle x, y \rangle \in R\}$.

Applying this quantification to (50a), we set R equal to

$\{\langle x, y \rangle | x$ is a pilot who shot at y and y is a Mig that chased $x\}$

and S equal to

$\{\langle x, y \rangle | x$ hit $y\}$.

(50a) is then true iff for any pilot who shot at a Mig that chased him, there is at least one such Mig that he hit, and these truth conditions accord with our intuitive judgment about such sentences, cf Higginbotham & May (1981a) for a detailed formal development of the semantics of binary quantifiers.

From the syntactic side, an important property of this analysis of crossed binding is that it assumes that absorption can apply only to local pairs of quantifiers. Absorption, so to speak, takes two quantifier phrases *A* and *B* such that *A* immediately c-commands *B*, but not vice-versa, into a structure in which *A* and *B* c-command each other. As with *wh*-complementation, the approach assumes that there is LF movement, and moreover, that the relevant properties will also be found where there is overt S-Structure movement. That is, the application of Absorption, it is assumed, is blind to whether quantifier *A* came to c-command quantifier *B* via application of overt movements (i.e., those onto S-Structure), covert movements (i.e., those onto LF) or some combination thereof. That this is in fact the case is borne out by the following, all of which exhibit crossed binding:

(51) a. Which pilot who shot at it hit which Mig that chased him
      b. Which pilot who shot at it some Mig that chased him
      c. Which Mig that chased him did every pilot who shot at it hit

Wh-movement has applied in each of these cases, so the initial *wh*-phrase occurs in COMP. In each case, further application of QR gives a representation to which Absorption applies; in (51a) this movement is of another *wh*-phrase, in (51b) and (51c) a quantifier phrase. The contrast between (51b) and (51c) shows that crossed binding is possible regardless of whether the *wh*-phrase in COMP has been moved from subject or object. This is just as we would expect, given the analysis here.

The possibility of crossed binding in these examples contrasts with a similar class of cases, brought out by Jacobson (1977), which differ in that they do not contain quantified phrases. (52) is an example:

(52) His wife saw her husband

Unlike the previous cases, this sentence cannot receive a crossed interpretation: *his* cannot be taken as dependent upon *her husband* simultaneously with *her* being dependent on *his wife*. This is all the more odd, given the possibility of coreference in both *His wife saw John* and *Mary saw her husband*. Higginbotham & May (1981b) argue that the reason for this is that fixing the values of the pronouns in (52) turns on a particular property of reference, namely that it must be fixed in a definite, non-circular fashion. This is not possible for (52); the reference of *his* is given by *her husband*, which in turn contains a pronoun *her*, whose reference is given by *his wife*, which contains *his*, whose reference is given by *her husband*, etc. Thus the 'chain of reference' associated with this sentence is

circular and unending, leading to no definite determination of reference at
all. If some other phrase is available to which the referential chain can
lead that does not contain a pronoun, this sort of vicious circularity is
avoided; thus there is no problem interpreting either *His wife, Mary saw
her husband* or *His wife saw Jack, her husband.*

Assuming that there are distinct devices for the establishment of referential, as opposed to bound variable, anaphora, it is possible to account
for certain cases which appear to be crossover environments, but in which
an anaphoric interpretation can be easily obtained. So consider the difference between the non-restrictive relatives in the (a) examples, and the
free relatives in the (b) examples:

(53) a. John, who his mother admires, . . .
      b. Whoever his mother admires . . .

(54) a. Stieglitz, whose picture of O'Keefe he took while she was lying
          supine, . . .
      b. Whoever's picture of O'Keefe he took while she was lying
          supine, . . .

That an anaphoric interpretation cannot be obtained for the pronouns in
the free relatives is not surprising; these are simply cases of crossover.
What is surprising is that in the non-restrictive relatives, an anaphoric
interpretation *is* possible, since the *wh*-phrase, its trace and the pronoun
all stand in the same structural relation as in the free relative. An account
is forthcoming once it is recognized that there is an alternative route to
anaphora available for the non-restrictive not found with the free relative.
Let us suppose that the semantics of this construction require that the
reference of the head NP is identical to the individuals who satisfy the
relative clause; note that this will be a singleton, as the head is a singular
referring expression. Now strictly speaking the pronoun in (53a), for
instance, cannot be a bound variable, as this would violate the crossover
constraint. This constraint, however, does not bar the pronoun from
being referential and from picking up its reference in the manner described above for such pronouns. In particular, there is nothing to stop its
picking up the reference of the head of the relative, *John*, which, after all,
is an independent referring expression. But then the mechanisms of reference will specify the same value for the pronoun as the mechanisms of
quantification, (i.e., assignments of values) specify for the variable the
wh-phrase binds. These critical properties of reference are not available,
however, for free relatives, simply because they are headless. Rather they
can avail themselves solely of the mechanisms of quantification and

bound variables, which preclude anaphora in the configuration under consideration.

Thus we see from these latter cases, as well as from the distinction in crossed binding sentences between the sensible *Every pilot who shot at it hit some Mig that chased him*, and the non-sensical *His wife saw her husband*, that there is a fundamental distinction between those pronouns which are assigned their values via interpretation of quantification as opposed to the interpretation of reference. Thus the analysis of these cases rests on the assumption, as has all the discussion to this point, that at LF quantified and non-quantified phrases are distinguished, not only in their interpretation, but also in those aspects of their syntax to which the rules of interpretation are sensitive. In this regard the position differs from that found in Montague (1974), for instance, in which quantified and non-quantified phrases are assimilated under a uniform syntactic and semantic treatment. Now insofar as the phenomena we have been discussing turn on distinguishing these types of expressions, it argues against such a conflation of categories, at least from the syntactic perspective. Indeed, given the validity of the analyses, the phenomena we have considered can be employed as a diagnostic of quantificational status. For instance, consider definite phrases, those containing *the*; are they quantified phrases? We have assumed that they are; cf the semantic treatment of definite descriptions above. This is corroborated by their having interacting scope relations, seen in sentences such as *Every man admires the woman he loves*[18] and *The president of every public authority is a crook*, by their allowing VP-deletion in relatives, as seen in *Dulles suspected the agents who Philby did*, by their occurrence in crossed binding sentences such as *The pilot who shot at it hit the Mig that chased him*, and by the differential distribution of *any*, seen in the contrast of *The students who had ever read anything about phrenology attended Gall's lecture* with **The students who attended Gall's lecture had ever read anything about phrenology*. Thus, insofar as the explanation of these phenomena turn on the assumption that there is LF-movement, and insofar as LF-movement is sensitive to whether phrases are quantificational, then it follows that *the*, at least on the uses exemplified in the above examples, is a quantifier, as otherwise we would expect to find quite a different complex of properties. And it is the fact that we do find these contrasting complexes of properties that argues for the fundamental distinction of logical syntax which forms the basic presupposition of our inquiries. In this regard out position agrees with that of the line of thinking from Frege to Tarski, in which quantified phrases where taken to require treatment quite distinct from that of proper names.

Once we take the distinction in semantic type between quantificational and referential expression as basic, then the syntactic paradigms we find at LF can be seen as consequences of requirements on the mapping of argument structure onto logical form. Following Chomsky (1981), we will suppose that the relation of arguments to their structural manifestations in argument positions of predicates at LF is mediated by the θ-Criterion, which requires that they stand in a one-one correspondence:

(55) θ-Criterion
   (i) Every θ-role must be assigned to just one argument chain
   (ii) Every argument chain must be assigned just one θ-role

The θ-roles characterize the argument positions of a predicate, specified as part of its lexical structure. Argument positions can differ in the semantic roles which their arguments must fulfil; thus subjects may be agents or themes and objects may be themes, goals, patients, etc (Jackendoff, 1972). Lexical items, such as proper names, can normally stand as arguments bearing θ-roles, and so can certain empty categories, in particular those which are Ā-bound and function as variables. An 'argument chain' is any sequence of arguments which bear occurrences of a given index. The structures in (56) are associated with degree 1 chains containing the traces as their members. It is these arguments which bear the θ-roles (here theme) assigned to the subject positions, and not the operators which bind them:

(56) a. Which agent$_2$ [e_2 is a spy]
     b. Every agent$_2$ [e_2 is a spy]

Given that variables can stand as arguments of predicates, reinforcing the coincidence of the syntactic and semantic notions, we might also hold, inversely, that quantified phrases do not themselves count as arguments, at least with respect to their normal interpretation via quantification theory.[19] Then, we might speculate, on the presumption that the θ-criterion applies just to LF-representations, the fact that movement to Ā-positions is usually reserved for phrases that are 'nonreferential' (in some sense), follows, as there is no interpretation available for such phrases in argument positions, since they are not legitimate bearers of θ-roles.[20] The point is more general; no phrase which is functionally an operator can occur in an Ā-position at LF, by the θ-criterion, if this line of reasoning is correct. Thus, *wh*-movement is just as well required in relative clauses, as in *wh*-questions.

In effect, then, the θ-criterion makes LF-movement obligatory, although the rule itself would apply optionally. Obtaining this result turns on the assumption that quantified phrases can only be properly interpreted as operators, and are unable to bear semantic roles in argument positions. While to a large extent this assumption is intuitive and uncontroversial, one need not make it. It is not held, for instance, in Montague (1974), who allows quantified phrases, in addition to being interpreted in operator positions, to be interpreted in their surface positions as denoting intensions, functions from possible worlds to familes of properties of individuals. The utility of this bifurcation is argued to be found in the treatment of *John seeks a unicorn*. Leaving technical details aside, on this view *seek* is a relation between individuals and intensions, functions from possible worlds to denotations. Assuming that *a unicorn* translates as such a function, then the *de dicto* construal is just where this phrase is interpreted as an argument of the predicate. On this interpretation, the truth of *John seeks a unicorn* requires only that John is seeking something with the appropriate properties, properties that in some possible world, distinct from the actual, pick out unicorns in their extension. Thus, *John seeks a unicorn* may be true, on this interpretation, even though John's search is a chimerical one. The *de re* construal, on the other hand, is to be represented by quantifying in, so that its truth requires that there is a unicorn, in the actual world, and John is seeking it. One can construct accounts of this ambiguity, however, which do not turn on assuming that *John seeks a unicorn* has any LF-representation different from that in (57):

(57) a unicorn$_2$ [John seeks e_2]

Suppose, following Parsons (1980), that the domain of objects is populated by both actual and non-actual objects. Parsons' idea is that any class of what he calls 'nuclear' properties defines a distinct object; on this view, 'being a book about linguistics', just as much characterizes an object as 'being a golden mountain' or 'being a unicorn'. The domain of such objects is then further partitioned by what Parsons calls 'non-nuclear' properties, of which existence is the central case, so that our quantifiers are existential only insofar as they are restricted to subsets of existent objects. Now if we take verb selection, in the sense of Chomsky (1965), to be sensitive to this partitioning in terms of non-nuclear properties, the difference between an intensional verb like *seek* and an extensional one like *buy* can be reduced to the former ambiguously selecting, for the object NP, either positively or negatively for existence, while the latter only selects positively. Thus, *John seeks a unicorn* will be false if *seek* positively selects, as then the quantifier will range only over that subpart of the domain containing existent objects, but true if it negatively selects, since then the quantifiers will range over the non-existent objects, which includes unicorns. If these conjectures are along the right track, then it means that ambiguities of multiple quantifier scope are of a different sort than the ambiguities of intensional transitive verbs, the former being structural, the latter not.[21]

The θ-Criterion will play other roles in insuring that LF-representations containing $\bar{\text{A}}$-binding properly express argument structure. For instance, it will insure that in multiple quantified sentences that each empty category will correspond to a distinct variable. This is because if there is an *n*-tuple of coindexed empty categories they will form an argument chain which must be assigned only one thematic role. This accounts for the contrast of *$*John_i$ admired e_i* with *$John_i$ was admired e_i*. Each of these is associated with the degree 2 chain $\langle John, e_i \rangle$, but it only satisfies the θ-Criterion with respect to the latter structure. This is because in the former the chain is associated with two θ-roles; those of the subject and object positions. But in the latter, passive, sentence, the chain is only associated with a single θ-role, that of the object, as passive subjects, by hypothesis, are dethematized (Chomsky, 1981). Turning to multiple quantification structures, since we are assuming that assignment of indices under movement is free, distinct application of QR can assign the same index, deriving something like (58):

(58) [every professor$_2$ [some student$_2$ [e_2 admires e_2]]]

But this violates the θ-Criterion, the relation between the empty categories being no different than that found in improper movement structures like *$*Who_2$ e_2 admires e_2*. That is, the pair of traces forms a chain, and it is associated with two θ-roles, as above. Only if the empty categories in (58) bear different indices will each trace correspond to a distinct variable, and hence qualify as distinct argument chains with respect to the θ-Criterion. Because the grammar then requires that each LF-movement to an $\bar{\text{A}}$-position give rise to a distinct variable, it now follows, for instance, that *Everybody admires everybody* entails, but is not equivalent to *Everybody admires himself*, in which the subject and object positions can be legitimately coindexed, (reflexive pronouns qualifying as independent arguments for the θ-Criterion). For the same reason *Who did he admire* does not ask a reflexive question, to wit, which persons are self-admirers. This would be the interpretation if *he* and the trace of *wh* could be coindexed; but to do so would violate the θ-Criterion, for it would result once again in the illicit coindexing of thematic subject and object positions. Given the θ-Criterion, then, the distinctness of variables in LF-representations is no isolated matter, but rather has as its cause the same principle which accounts for improper movement and strong crossover phenomena.

In beginning this paper, I characterized Logical Form as that level of linguistic representation interfacing the theories of linguistic form and interpretation. I have outlined one way to turn this from an operational to a formal (that is, syntactic) definition, and an examination of some of the basic consequences of the principles and conditions embedded in that definition. I have constructed the assumptions as to the nature of the rules and representations of LF so as to extract the syntactic aspects of semantic interpretation—the 'semantic structure'—and to unify it, in very basic ways, with certain 'overt' aspects of syntactic structure. This reduction has been afforded in part by the hypothesis that the rules mapping onto LF share certain fundamental properties with rules mapping onto S-Structure, in particular *wh*-movement. Thus both are movements to non-argument ($\bar{\text{A}}$) positions and leave empty categories which can be structurally defined as variables, both 'pied-pipe', of importance in the analysis of polarity items and VP-deletion, movement by either can derive structures which accord with the *Wh*-Criterion, give rise to crossover violations, or be input to Absorption, and the output of each obeys general conditions on proper binding and argument structure. Just as *wh*-movement is a well-defined mapping, applying to phrases of a particular type, and giving rise to a specifiable class of S-Structure representations, so too is QR, in giving rise to a definable class of LF-representations. What the commonality of these 'rules' suggests is that the clusters of properties referred to as *wh*-movement and QR are reflections of deeper, more general, properties of grammar; that is, both are just aspects of 'Move α', their divergent properties being attributable to differential principles and conditions on S-Structure and Logical Form. The sorts of discrepancies we do observe between *wh*-movement and QR—in particular in that the range of movement possibilities for LF-movement is broader than for movements onto S-Structure—indicate that movement in LF is, in a sense, less restricted, applying unencumbered by conditions which more severely limit the derivation of *wh*-constructions in S-Structure. LF-movements are subject only to more general conditions on Logical Form, which are applicable as well to structures derived by S-Structure movements. The formal properties, then, of LF-movement can be thought of as the result of factoring out the conditions, universal and particular, holding just of the rules deriving, or the representations at, S-Structure.

What is left are the conditions on Logical Form, specified ultimately by Universal Grammar, which determines the core properties of logical representations, for example, that natural language quantification is represented in operator-variable notation. To a large extent these properties of LF will be invariant from language to language, although one could imagine a range of differences as a function of independently varying properties of the S-Structure input to the rules deriving LF, for instance. Thus we do not want to preclude the possibility that given construction types may give rise to differential classes of interpretations from language to language (although this is not to say that languages will differ in the class of propositions they can express, given the unboundedness of paraphrase). But insofar as the nature of logical representation follows from principles of UG directly, the child will need no evidence from his or her environment to determine its properties; they will be consequences of 'hard-wired' aspects of the language faculty. Indeed, it is difficult to imagine what would be a sufficiently structured environment to provide evidence for a child to 'learn' the various aspects of the syntax of logical form we have been considering thus far. Plausibly, a child learning English might induce the relevant structural properties on the basis of *wh*-constructions, generalizing its formal properties to a class of semantically related elements, and thus inferring that representation involving trace binding extends to the broader class of quantified sentences. The child learning English would be, in this regard, rather fortunate, having evidence available that a child learning Chinese, which does not have overt *wh*-movement, would not. What then would serve as the evidentiary basis for the induction that quantification is represented at LF, in Chinese as well as in English, by variable binding? What this suggests is that the grounding of our knowledge of the logical form of language as represented at Logical Form arises from Universal Grammar, and constitutes, in the final analysis, part of our innately specified knowledge of language.

Notes

1. Chomsky-adjunction of a constituent to a node yields structures either of the form '$[_\alpha \beta \; [_\alpha \ldots]]$' (left Chomsky-adjunction) or '$[_\alpha \; [_\alpha \ldots]\beta]$' (right Chomsky-adjunction). In what follows the difference between right and left adjunction will turn out to be immaterial, since they manifest the identical hierarchical constituent

structures, but the convention will be adhered to of representing QR as affecting a left adjunction.

2. α c-commands β iff the first branching node dominating α dominates β (and α does not dominate β). This definition is essentially that proposed originally in Reinhart (1976).

3. Cf Higginbotham & May (1981a) for a formal analysis of the semantics of questions in this framework.

4. Note that assuming trace theory to apply generally to movement operations rules out the possibility of deriving something like S-Structure from something like LF by 'lowering' quantified phrases, since such movements would give rise to structures containing unbound traces. Thus the approach here is materially distinct from that found in Lakoff (1971), for example.

5. With the further requirement that such functions assign the same value to $X \subset D$ as to automorphisms of X.

6. Restricted quantifiers, in the defined sense, can be shown to have a number of properties. For instance, as shown in Higginbotham & May (1981a), they respect only the size of sets, and not the identity of their membership. Also, because such quantifiers encode effectively the same semantic information as the generalized quantifiers of Barwise & Cooper (1981), many of the results obtained there will carry over. Also see van Benthem (1983).

7. This generalization apparently holds in other languages as well; it also characterizes, for instance, the class of S-Structure preposable phrases in Hungarian, as discussed in Kiss (1981).

8. This example was brought to my attention by a reviewer.

9. Actually, there will be derived two equivalence classes of structures.

10. Linear order has often been claimed to strongly affect preferential order of interpretation. I am doubtful, however, of the overall importance of this factor. In part this is because linear order is easily conflated with topic–comment relations; in most languages the subject precedes the object and corresponds to the discourse topic. And since topics take prominence in discourse, it is not surprising that when they are quantified phrases, they will have preferentially broad scope. Also, examples which purport to show the importance of linear order seem to me less than convincing. For instance, it is often held that in sentences with universal and negative quantifiers, scope is a function of precedence; cf Halvorsen (1983) for a recent discussion. Examples like *No student admires every professor* and *Every professor is admired by no student* are taken to support this contention. But the latter example is considerably less than well-formed, and the former is interpretively suppletive with *No student admires any professor*. And it is rather these latter observations, it seems to me, which are in need of explanation.

11. These cases were pointed out to me by J. Higginbotham. Notice that such examples have a third interpretation, on which no one is either loved or a lover. This is an independent, or branching, interpretation. Note that this interpretation is also logically independent of either of the dependent interpretations; thus for

those who find one or the other of the latter construals difficult to obtain, the argument in the text will till go through substituting the independent interpretation.

12. A semantically based filter would also be inappropriate here. If the grammar generates a class of representations each expressing, under an interpretation, correct truth-conditions, it would be otiose to filter some just to reconstruct them elsewhere in the system.

13. See May (forthcoming) for a discussion of Cooper's approach.

14. I have ignored, for exposition, traces of cyclic movement in the embedded COMPs of the direct questions.

15. I have left aside the relation of this condition to the application of *wh*-movement in other constructions such as relative clauses and clefts.

16. We can capture this difference by maintaining that for English, but not Chinese, clause (i) of the *Wh*-Criterion must also be satisfied at S-Structure. There are also languages, such as Polish and Czech, which require that clause (ii) be satisfied at S-Structure, and which consequently allow multiply filled COMPs at this level (Toman, 1981).

17. For instance, Bach & Partee (1980), Evans (1980), Higginbotham (1980) and Lasnik (1976).

18. This is pointed out in Heim (1982). There is, however, more here than meets the eye, as only a broad scope interpretation is possible for this sentence if the pronoun is taken nonanaphorically, or a proper name is substituted, as in *Every man admires the woman John loves*.

19. Note that it is not precluded that types of phrases may cross-classify, as has been argued for indefinite phrases. See Fodor & Sag (1982) for discussion.

20. Care is needed in clarifying just what is meant by 'non-referential', as it must be taken to denote a type of phrase, and not whether tokens, in fact, make reference to actual objects. Thus, *Pegasus* does not refer in the latter sense, but it is a referential phrase.

21. Thanks are due to P. Ludlow for discussion of this point.

References

Bach, E., & Partee, B., Anaphora and Semantic Structure. In J. Kreiman & N. Odeja (Eds), *Papers from the Parasession on Pronouns and Anaphora*. Chicago, Illinois: University of Chicago, 1980.

Barwise, J., & Cooper, R., Generalized Quantifiers and Natural Language. *Linguistics and Philosophy*, 1981, 4, 159–219.

Bentham, J. van, Determiners and Logic. *Linguistics and Philosophy*, 1983, 6, 447–478.

Borer, H., On the Definition of Variables. *Journal of Linguistic Research*, 1983, 1, 3, 17–40.

Chomsky, N., *Aspects of the Theory of Syntax*. Cambridge, MA: MIT Press, 1965.

Chomsky, N., Conditions of Rules of Grammar. In N. Chomsky, *Essays on Form and Interpretation*. New York: North-Holland, 1976.

Chomsky, N., On Binding. *Linguistic Inquiry*, 1980, 11, 1–46.

Chomsky, N., *Lectures on Government and Binding*. Dordrecht: Foris Publications, 1981.

Cooper, R., *Quantification and Syntactic Theory*. Dordrecht: Reidel, 1983.

Evans, G., Pronouns. *Linguistic Inquiry*, 1980, 11, 337–362.

Fiengo, R., On Trace Theory *Linguistic Inquiry*, 1977, 8, 35–61.

Fodor, J. D., & Sag, I., Referential and Quantificational Indefinites. *Linguistics and Philosophy*, 1982, 5, 355–398.

Halvorsen, P.-K., Semantics for Lexical-Functional Grammar. *Linguistic Inquiry*, 1983, 14, 567–615.

Heim, I., The Semantics of Definite and Indefinite Noun Phrases. Doctoral dissertation, Amherst, MA: University of Massachusetts, 1982.

Higginbotham, J., Pronouns and Bound Variables, *Linguistic Inquiry*. 1980, 11, 679–708.

Higginbotham, J., & May, R., Questions, Quantifiers and Crossing. *The Linguisic Review*, 1981a, 1, 41–79.

Higginbotham, J., & May, R., Crossing, Markedness, Pragmatics. In A. Belleti, L. Brandi & L. Rizzi (Eds), *Theory of Markedness in Generative Grammar*. Pisa: Scuola Normale Superiore, 1981b.

Huang, C.-T. J., Move WH in a Language without *Wh*-Movement. *The Linguistic Review*, 1982, 1, 369–416.

Jacobson, P., The Syntax of Crossing Coreference Sentences. Doctoral dissertation, Berkeley, CA: University of California, 1977. (Distributed by Indiana University Linguistics Club.)

Jackendoff, R., *Semantic Interpretation in Generative Grammar*. Cambridge, MA: MIT Press, 1972.

Jaeggli, O., On Some Phonologically-null Elements in Syntax. Doctoral dissertation, Cambridge, MA: MIT, 1980

Kiss, K., Structural Relations in Hungarian, a 'Free' Word Order Language. *Linguistic Inquiry*, 1981, 12, 185–213.

Koopman, H., & Sportiche, D., Variables and the Bijection Principle. *The Linguistic Review*, 1982, 2, 139–161.

Ladusaw, W., On the Notion *Affective* in the Analysis of Negative-Polarity Items. *Journal of Linguistic Research*, 1981, 1, 2, 1–16.

Lakoff, G., On Generative Semantics. In D. Steinberg & L. Jakobovits (Eds), *Semantics*. Cambridge: Cambridge University Press, 1971.

Lasnik, H., Remarks on Coreference. *Linguistic Analysis*, 1976, 2, 1–22.

May, R., The Grammar of Quantification. Doctorial dissertation, Cambridge, MA: MIT, 1977. (Distributed by Indiana University Linguistics Club.)

May, R., Movement and Binding. *Linguistic Inquiry*, 1981, 12, 215–243.

May, R., Review of R. Cooper *Quantification and Syntactic Theory*. To appear in *Language* (forthcoming).

Montague, R., The Proper Treatment of Quantification in Ordinary Englsh. In R. Thomason (Ed), *Formal Philosophy: Selected Papers of Richard Montague*. New Haven, CT: Yale University Press, 1974.

Parsons, T., *Nonexistent Objects*. New Haven, CT: Yale University Press, 1980.

Reinhart, T., The Syntactic Domain of Anaphora. Doctoral dissertation, Cambridge, MA: MIT, 1976.

Reinhart, T., *Anaphora and Semantic Interpretation*. London: Croon Helm, 1983.

Rouveret, A., & Vergnaud, J.-R., Specifying Reference to the Subject: French Causatives and Conditions on Representations. *Linguistic Inquiry*, 1980, 11, 97–202.

Safir, K., Multiplc Variable Binding. *Linguistic Inquiry*, 1984, 15, 603–638.

Sag, I., Deletion and Logical Form. Doctoral dissertation, Cambridge, MA: MIT, 1976.

Toman, J., Aspects of Multiple *Wh*-Movement in Polish and Czech. In R. May & J. Koster (Eds), *Levels of Syntactic Representation*. Dordrecht: Foris Publications, 1981.

Williams, E., Discourse and Logical Form. *Linguistic Inquiry*, 1977, 8, 101–139.

PART III
DEFINITE AND INDEFINITE DESCRIPTIONS

INTRODUCTION

One of the archimedian points in the philosophy of language during this century has been the proper analysis of definite and indefinite descriptions. What turns on the analysis of simple words like 'a' and 'the'? Consider first the metaphysical consequences.

If expressions must refer in order to be contentful, then serious questions arise about descriptions, like 'the present King of France', that are perfectly contentful yet apparently fail to refer. There are several routes one can take here. First, one can "bite the bullet" and argue that expressions like 'the present King of France' do in fact refer, albeit to nonexistent objects. Another route is to reject the idea that the contentful use of a term requires that it hook up with the world somehow. Whatever might be said on behalf of this solution, it certainly seems to run counter to one of the central threads of part I—that a theory of meaning needs to provide language-world relations. Bertrand Russell is credited with a third route, arguing that descriptions are not "referring" expressions but rather are "denoting" expressions. A great deal of semantic literature uses the terms 'denotation' and 'reference' interchangeably, which is unfortunate, for it ignores some very important considerations—considerations that, for example, were central in the dispute between Russell's position in "On Denoting" and Strawson's in "On Referring."

Following Evans (1982), and Neale (1990), one can understand the distinction between referring and denoting by considering Russell's theory of psychology. Russell (1911) distinguished knowledge by acquaintance from knowledge by description, arguing that to have knowledge of a certain object by acquaintance, one must be directly acquainted with the object. Alternatively, to have knowledge of a certain object by description, one need not be acquainted with the object but need only know the object as the unique satisfier of a certain description.

These two species of knowledge are in fact quite different on Russell's view. A belief about some object known by acquaintance is a belief in a singular proposition that has that object as a constituent. So, for example, my belief that my neighbor is tall is a singular proposition having my neighbor as a constituent. It is a belief *about* my neighbor. On the other hand, I might believe that the thief who stole my computer is tall, and the thief may even be my neighbor, but unless I know that my neighbor is the thief and unless I saw the thief stealing my computer, my belief will be not a singular proposition but rather a general one. It will not be a belief *about* my neighbor (or anyone else), but rather the object of my belief will be a general proposition about the world, essentially that the world is such that there is a unique thief of my computer and that he or she is tall.

The same point can be extended easily to the semantics of natural language. Applied here, the question is whether there is a semantic difference between a sentence containing a description that uniquely determines some individual (e.g., 'the third planet from the sun') and a sentence containing a referring expression (e.g., 'the Earth'). For Russell, descriptions are never referring expressions in the sense just outlined. Rather, indefinite descriptions are simply existential quantifiers; definite descriptions are somewhat more complex. The description 'the F' has the underlying logical form '$(\exists x)[F(x) \& (\forall y)(F(y) \to y = x)]$'. An expression like 'The F is G' has the underlying form $(\exists x)[F(x) \& (\forall y)(F(y) \to y = x) \& G(x)]$.

Russell noted that 'The present King of France is bald' is perfectly sensible despite the fact that there is no present King of France, since it is not about any unique individual. Rather, it is a general claim to the effect that there is a unique present King of France and he is bald.

Peter F. Strawson takes issue with Russell on a number of points, in particular, the uniqueness claim in Russell's analysis of descriptions. Is it really the case that 'The present King of France is bald' is false? Strawson argues that on the contrary it has no determinate truth value. It is neither true nor false, and perhaps it fails to even express a determinate proposition (or so Strawson appears to argue in some places). The explanation for this, according to Strawson, is that descriptions are referring expressions, and when they fail to refer, the result is a kind of an incomplete proposition—one in which the thing being talked about remains unidentified.

Keith Donnellan argues that while on some occasions definite descriptions are clearly quantificational, on other occasions they are referring expressions. So, for example, if Jones is charged with the murder of Smith and we witness the strange behavior of Smith at the trial, when I turn to you and say "The murderer of Smith is insane," the description I use is a referring expression. On the other hand, if we are detectives at the scene of the crime and have no idea as to the identity of the murderer but are shocked by what we find at the murder scene, when I turn to you and say "The murderer of Smith is insane," the description I use is no longer a referring expression. Donnellan distinguishes these two uses of descriptions as the referential and attributive uses respectively and appears to suggest (although this is not completely clear) that there is a kind of referential/attributive ambiguity in the expression 'the murderer of Smith'.

In "Speaker's Reference and Semantic Reference," Saul Kripke cautions against the use of Donnellan-type arguments to support an ambiguity thesis about descriptions. As Kripke notes, while it is certainly the case that there are referential *uses* of descriptions, it does not follow that descriptions must sometimes refer. On the contrary, it is entirely possible that a general proposition can be used to communicate a singular one.

In "Context and Communication," Stephen Neale takes up the general Kripkean line about speaker's reference and semantic reference and attempts to elucidate the Gricean mechanisms by which a general proposition may be used to communicate a singular proposition about some individual. In addition, Neale takes up a number of other arguments that have been advanced against the Russellian theory, including the argument from improper descriptions.

If most of the action in the philosophy of language has been with *definite* descriptions, *indefinite* descriptions have generated their share of attention in the linguistic community. One such line of argument is found in the paper "Referential and Quantificational Indefinites," by Janet Fodor and Ivan Sag. They observe that indefinite descriptions, like definite descriptions, have both referential and quantificational uses. Fodor and Sag then enlist a number of linguistic arguments (e.g., from facts about scope ambiguities to facts about verb-phrase ellipsis) to show that some indefinite descriptions are not only used to refer but are actually genuine referring expressions.

Fodor and Sag's argument is taken up in Ludlow and Neale's "Indefinite Descriptions: In Defense of Russell." Ludlow and Neale wade into linguistic waters in an effort to refute the arguments marshalled by Fodor and Sag. In addition, they attempt to clarify what they see as several uses of descriptions that have been run together in the literature, pointing out along the way that using an expression with a particular individual in mind is not the same thing as referring to that individual.

Further Reading for Part III

Devitt, M. 1981. "Donnellan's Distinction." In P. A. French, T. E. Uehling Jr., and H. K. Wettstein (eds.), *The Foundations of Analytic Philosophy*, Midwest Studies in Philosophy, no. 6. Minneapolis: University of Minnesota Press.

Donnellan, K. 1968. "Putting Humpty Dumpty Back Together Again." *Philosophical Review* 77:203–215.

Donnellan, K. 1978. "Speaker Reference, Descriptions, and Anaphora." In P. Cole (ed.), *Pragmatics*, Syntax and Semantics, no. 9. New York: Academic Press.

Evans, G. 1982. *Varieties of Reference*. Oxford: Oxford University Press.

King, J. 1988. "Are Indefinite Descriptions Ambiguous?" *Philosophical Studies* 53:417–440.

Linsky, L. 1977. *Names and Descriptions*. Chicago: University of Chicago Press.

Neale, S. 1990. *Descriptions*. Cambridge: MIT Press.

Recanati, F. 1981. "On Kripke on Donnellan." In H. Parrett, M. Sbisa, and J. Verschueren (eds), *Possibilities and Limitations of Pragmatics*. Amsterdam: John Benjamins.

Recanati, F. 1989. "Referential/Attributive: A Contextualist Proposal." *Philosophical Studies* 56:217–249.

Russell, B. 1905. "On Denoting." *Mind* 14:479–493.

Russell, B. 1911. "Knowledge by Acquaintance and Knowledge by Description." In *Mysticism and Logic*. London: George Allen and Unwin, 1917.

Salmon, N. 1982. "Assertion and Incomplete Definite Descriptions." *Philosophical Studies* 42:37–45.

Schiffer, S. 1995. "Descriptions, Indexicals, and Belief Reports: Some Dilemmas (But Not the Ones You Expect)." *Mind* 104:107–131.

Sharvey, R. 1980. "A More General Theory of Definite Descriptions." *Philosophical Review* 89:607–624.

Soames, S. 1986. "Incomplete Definite Descriptions. *Notre Dame Journal of Formal Logic* 27:349–375.

Wettstein, H. 1981. "Demonstrative Reference and Definite Descriptions." *Philosophical Studies* 40:241–257.

Wilson, G. 1984. "On Definite and Indefinite Descriptions." *Philosophical Review* 87:48–76.

Chapter 15

Descriptions

Bertrand Russell

We dealt in the preceding chapter with the words *all* and *some*; in this chapter we shall consider the word *the* in the singular, and in the next chapter we shall consider the word *the* in the plural. It may be thought excessive to devote two chapters to one word, but to the philosophical mathematician it is a word of very great importance: like Browning's Grammarian with the enclitic δε, I would give the doctrine of this word if I were "dead from the waist down" and not merely in a prison.

We have already had occasion to mention "descriptive functions," *i.e.* such expressions as "the father of *x*" or "the sine of *x*." These are to be defined by first defining "descriptions."

A "description" may be of two sorts, definite and indefinite (or ambiguous). An indefinite description is a phrase of the form "a so-and-so," and a definite description is a phrase of the form "the so-and-so" (in the singular). Let us begin with the former.

"Who did you meet?" "I met a man." "That is a very indefinite description." We are therefore not departing from usage in our terminology. Our question is: What do I really assert when I assert "I met a man"? Let us assume, for the moment, that my assertion is true, and that in fact I met Jones. It is clear that what I assert is *not* "I met Jones." I may say "I met a man, but it was not Jones"; in that case, though I lie, I do not contradict myself, as I should do if when I say I met a man I really mean that I met Jones. It is clear also that the person to whom I am speaking can understand what I say, even if he is a foreigner and has never heard of Jones.

But we may go further: not only Jones, but no actual man, enters into my statement. This becomes obvious when the statement is false, since

First appeared in *Introduction to Mathematical Philosophy* (London: George Allen and Unwin, 1919). Reprinted by permission of the Bertrand Russell Peace Foundation.

then there is no more reason why Jones should be supposed to enter into the proposition than why anyone else should. Indeed the statement would remain significant, though it could not possibly be true, even if there were no man at all. "I met a unicorn" or "I met a sea-serpent" is a perfectly significant assertion, if we know what it would be to be a unicorn or a sea-serpent, *i.e.* what is the definition of these fabulous monsters. Thus it is only what we may call the *concept* that enters into the proposition. In the case of "unicorn," for example, there is only the concept: there is not also, somewhere among the shades, something unreal which may be called "a unicorn." Therefore, since it is significant (though false) to say "I met a unicorn," it is clear that this proposition, rightly analysed, does not contain a constituent "a unicorn," though it does contain the concept "unicorn."

The question of "unreality," which confronts us at this point, is a very important one. Misled by grammar, the great majority of those logicians who have dealt with this question have dealt with it on mistaken lines. They have regarded grammatical form as a surer guide in analysis than, in fact, it is. And they have not known what differences in grammatical form are important. "I met Jones" and "I met a man" would count traditionally as propositions of the same form, but in actual fact they are of quite different forms: the first names an actual person, Jones; while the second involves a propositional function, and becomes, when made explicit: "The function 'I met x and x is human' is sometimes true." (It will be remembered that we adopted the convention of using "sometimes" as not implying more than once.) This proposition is obviously not of the form "I met x," which accounts for the existence of the proposition "I met a unicorn" in spite of the fact that there is no such thing as "a unicorn."

For want of the apparatus of propositional functions, many logicians have been driven to the conclusion that there are unreal objects. It is argued, *e.g.* by Meinong,[1] that we can speak about "the golden mountain," "the round square," and so on; we can make true propositions of which these are the subjects; hence they must have some kind of logical being, since otherwise the propositions in which they occur would be meaningless. In such theories, it seems to me, there is a failure of that feeling for reality which ought to be preserved even in the most abstract studies. Logic, I should maintain, must no more admit a unicorn than zoology can; for logic is concerned with the real world just as truly as zoology, though with its more abstract and general features. To say that unicorns have an existence in heraldry, or in literature, or in imagination, is a most pitiful and paltry evasion. What exists in heraldry is not an animal, made of flesh and blood, moving and breathing of its own initiative. What exists is a picture, or a description in words. Similarly, to maintain that Hamlet, for example, exists in his own world, namely, in the world of Shakespeare's imagination, just as truly as (say) Napoleon existed in the ordinary world, is to say something deliberately confusing, or else confused to a degree which is scarcely credible. There is only one world, the "real" world: Shakespeare's imagination is part of it, and the thoughts that he had in writing Hamlet are real. So are the thoughts that we have in reading the play. But it is of the very essence of fiction that only the thoughts, feelings, etc., in Shakespeare and his readers are real, and that there is not, in addition to them, an objective Hamlet. When you have taken account of all the feelings roused by Napoleon in writers and readers of history, you have not touched the actual man; but in the case of Hamlet you have come to the end of him. If no one thought about Hamlet, there would be nothing left of him; if no one had thought about Napoleon, he would have soon seen to it that some one did. The sense of reality is vital in logic, and whoever juggles with it by pretending that Hamlet has another kind of reality is doing a disservice to thought. A robust sense of reality is very necessary in framing a correct analysis of propositions about unicorns, golden mountains, round squares, and other such pseudo-objects.

In obedience to the feeling of reality, we shall insist that, in the analysis of propositions, nothing "unreal" is to be admitted. But, after all, if there *is* nothing unreal, how, it may be asked, *could* we admit anything unreal? The reply is that, in dealing with propositions, we are dealing in the first instance with symbols, and if we attribute significance to groups of symbols which have no significance, we shall fall into the error of admitting unrealities, in the only sense in which this is possible, namely, as objects described. In the proposition "I met a unicorn," the whole four words together make a significant proposition, and the word "unicorn" by itself is significant, in just the same sense as the word "man." But the *two* words "a unicorn" do not form a subordinate group having a meaning of its own. Thus if we falsely attribute meaning to these two words, we find ourselves saddled with "a unicorn," and with the problem how there can be such a thing in a world where there are no unicorns. "A unicorn" is an indefinite description which describes nothing. It is not an indefinite description which describes something unreal. Such a proposition as "*x* is unreal" only has meaning when "*x*" is a description, definite or indefinite;

in that case the proposition will be true if "x" is a description which describes nothing. But whether the description "x" describes something or describes nothing, it is in any case not a constituent of the proposition in which it occurs; like "a unicorn" just now, it is not a subordinate group having a meaning of its own. All this results from the fact that, when "x" is a description, "x is unreal" or "x does not exist" is not nonsense, but is always significant and sometimes true.

We may now proceed to define generally the meaning of propositions which contain ambiguous descriptions. Suppose we wish to make some statement about "a so-and-so," where "so-and-so's" are those objects that have a certain property ϕ, *i.e.* those objects x for which the propositional function ϕx is true. (*E.g.* if we take "a man" as our instance of "a so-and-so," ϕx will be "x is human.") Let us now wish to assert the property ψ of "a so-and-so," *i.e.* we wish to assert that "a so-and-so" has that property which x has when ψx is true. (*E.g.* in the case of "I met a man," ψx will be "I met x.") Now the proposition that "a so-and-so" has the property ψ is *not* a proposition of the form "ψx." If it were, "a so-and-so" would have to be identical with x for a suitable x; and although (in a sense) this may be true in some cases, it is certainly not true in such a case as "a unicorn." It is just this fact, that the statement that a so-and-so has the property ψ is not of the form ψx, which makes it possible for "a so-and-so" to be, in a certain clearly definable sense, "unreal." The definition is as follows:—

The statement that "an object having the property ϕ has the property ψ"

means:

"The joint assertion of ϕx and ψx is not always false."

So far as logic goes, this is the same proposition as might be expressed by "some ϕ's are ψ's"; but rhetorically there is a difference, because in the one case there is a suggestion of singularity, and in the other case of plurality. This, however, is not the important point. The important point is that, when rightly analysed, propositions verbally about "a so-and-so" are found to contain no constituent represented by this phrase. And that is why such propositions can be significant even when there is no such thing as a so-and-so.

The definition of *existence*, as applied to ambiguous descriptions, results from what was said at the end of the preceding chapter. We say that "men exist" or "a man exists" if the propositional function "x is human" is sometimes true; and generally "a so-and-so" exists if "x is so-and-so" is sometimes true. We may put this in other language. The proposition "Socrates is a man" is no doubt *equivalent* to "Socrates is human," but it is not the very same proposition. The *is* of "Socrates is human" expresses the relation of subject and predicate; the *is* of "Socrates is a man" expresses identity. It is a disgrace to the human race that it has chosen to employ the same word "is" for these two entirely different ideas—a disgrace which a symbolic logical language of course remedies. The identity in "Socrates is a man" is identity between an object named (accepting "Socrates" as a name, subject to qualifications explained later) and an object ambiguously described. An object ambiguously described will "exist" when at least one such proposition is true, *i.e.* when there is at least one true proposition of the form "x is a so-and-so," where "x" is a name. It is characteristic of ambiguous (as opposed to definite) descriptions that there may be any number of true propositions of the above form—Socrates is a man, Plato is a man, etc. Thus "a man exists" follows from Socrates, or Plato, or anyone else. With definite descriptions, on the other hand, the corresponding form of proposition, namely, "x is the so-and-so" (where "x" is a name), can only be true for one value of x at most. This brings us to the subject of definite descriptions, which are to be defined in a way analogous to that employed for ambiguous descriptions, but rather more complicated.

We come now to the main subject of the present chapter, namely, the definition of the word *the* (in the singular). One very important point about the definition of "a so-and-so" applies equally to "the so-and-so"; the definition to be sought is a definition of propositions in which this phrase occurs, not a definition of the phrase itself in isolation. In the case of "a so-and-so," this is fairly obvious: no one could suppose that "a man" was a definite object, which could be defined by itself. Socrates is a man, Plato is a man, Aristotle is a man, but we cannot infer that "a man" means the same as "Socrates" means and also the same as "Plato" means and also the same as "Aristotle" means, since these three names have different meanings. Nevertheless, when we have enumerated all the men in the world, there is nothing left of which we can say, "This is a man, and not only so, but it is *the* 'a man,' the quintessential entity that is just an indefinite man without being anybody in particular." It is of course quite clear that whatever there is in the world is definite: if it is a man it is one definite man and not any other. Thus there cannot be such an entity as "a man" to be found in the world, as opposed to specific men. And accordingly it is natural that we do not define "a man" itself, but only the propositions in which it occurs.

In the case of "the so-and-so" this is equally true, though at first sight less obvious. We may demonstrate that this must be the case, by a consideration of the difference between a *name* and a *definite description*. Take the proposition, "Scott is the author of *Waverley*." We have here a name, "Scott," and a description, "the author of *Waverley*," which are asserted to apply to the same person. The distinction between a name and all other symbols may be explained as follows:—

A name is a simple symbol whose meaning is something that can only occur as subject, *i.e.* something of the kind that we defined as an "individual" or a "particular." And a 'simple" symbol is one which has no parts that are symbols. Thus "Scott" is a simple symbol, because, though it has parts (namely, separate letters), these parts are not symbols. On the other hand, "the author of *Waverley*" is not a simple symbol, because the separate words that compose the phrase are parts which are symbols. If, as may be the case, whatever *seems* to be an "individual" is really capable of further analysis, we shall have to content ourselves with what may be called "relative individuals," which will be terms that, throughout the context in question, are never analysed and never occur otherwise than as subjects. And in that case we shall have correspondingly to content ourselves with "relative names." From the standpoint of our present problem, namely, the definition of descriptions, this problem, whether these are absolute names or only relative names, may be ignored, since it concerns different stages in the hierarchy of "types," whereas we have to compare such couples as "Scott" and "the author of *Waverley*," which both apply to the same object, and do not raise the problem of types. We may, therefore, for the moment, treat names as capable of being absolute; nothing that we shall have to say will depend upon this assumption, but the wording may be a little shortened by it.

We have, then, two things to compare: (1) a *name*, which is a simple symbol, directly designating an individual which is its meaning, and having this meaning in its own right, independently of the meanings of all other words; (2) a *description*, which consists of several words, whose meanings are already fixed, and from which results whatever is to be taken as the "meaning" of the description.

A proposition containing a description is not identical with what that proposition becomes when a name is substituted, even if the name names the same object as the description describes. "Scott is the author of

Waverley" is obviously a different proposition from "Scott is Scott": the first is a fact in literary history, the second a trivial truism. And if we put anyone other than Scott in place of "the author of *Waverley*," our proposition would become false, and would therefore certainly no longer be the same proposition. But, it may be said, our proposition is essentially of the same form as (say) "Scott is Sir Walter," in which two names are said to apply to the same person. The reply is that, if "Scott is Sir Walter" really means "the person named 'Scott' is the person named 'Sir Walter,'" then the names are being used as descriptions: *i.e.* the individual, instead of being named, is being described as the person having that name. This is a way in which names are frequently used in practice, and there will, as a rule, be nothing in the phraseology to show whether they are being used in this way or *as* names. When a name is used directly, merely to indicate what we are speaking about, it is no part of the *fact* asserted, or of the falsehood if our assertion happens to be false: it is merely part of the symbolism by which we express our thought. What we want to express is something which might (for example) be translated into a foreign language; it is something for which the actual words are a vehicle, but of which they are no part. On the other hand, when we make a proposition about "the person called 'Scott,'" the actual name "Scott" enters into what we are asserting, and not merely into the language used in making the assertion. Our proposition will now be a different one if we substitute "the person called 'Sir Walter.'" But so long as we are using names *as* names, whether we say "Scott" or whether we say "Sir Walter" is as irrelevant to what we are asserting as whether we speak English or French. Thus so long as names are used *as* names, "Scott is Sir Walter" is the same trivial proposition as "Scott is Scott." This completes the proof that "Scott is the author of *Waverley*" is not the same proposition as results from substituting a name for "the author of *Waverley*," no matter what name may be substituted.

When we use a variable, and speak of a propositional function, ϕx say, the process of applying general statements about x to particular cases will consist in substituting a name for the letter "x," assuming that ϕ is a function which has individuals for its arguments. Suppose, for example, that ϕx is "always true"; let it be, say, the "law of identity," $x = x$. Then we may substitute for "x" any name we choose, and we shall obtain a true proposition. Assuming for the moment that "Socrates," "Plato," and "Aristotle" are names (a very rash assumption), we can infer from the law of identity that Socrates is Socrates, Plato is Plato, and Aristotle is

Aristotle. But we shall commit a fallacy if we attempt to infer, without further premisses, that the author of *Waverley* is the author of *Waverley*. This results from what we have just proved, that, if we substitute a name for "the author of *Waverley*" in a proposition, the proposition we obtain is a different one. That is to say, applying the result to our present case: If "x" is a name, "$x = x$" is not the same proposition as "the author of *Waverley* is the author of *Waverley*," no matter what name "x" may be. Thus from the fact that all propositions of the form "$x = x$" are true we cannot infer, without more ado, that the author of *Waverley* is the author of *Waverley*. In fact, propositions of the form "the so-and-so is the so-and-so" are not always true: it is necessary that the so-and-so should *exist* (a term which will be explained shortly). It is false that the present King of France is the present King of France, or that the round square is the round square. When we substitute a description for a name, propositional functions which are "always true" may become false, if the description describes nothing. There is no mystery in this as soon as we realise (what was proved in the preceding paragraph) that when we substitute a description the result is not a value of the propositional function in question.

We are now in a position to define propositions in which a definite description occurs. The only thing that distinguishes "the so-and-so" from "a so-and-so" is the implication of uniqueness. We cannot speak of "*the* inhabitant of London," because inhabiting London is an attribute which is not unique. We cannot speak about "the present King of France," because there is none; but we can speak about "the present King of England." Thus propositions about "the so-and-so" always imply the corresponding propositions about "a so-and-so," with the addendum that there is not more than one so-and-so. Such a proposition as "Scott is the author of Waverley" could not be true if *Waverley* had never been written, or if several people had written it; and no more could any other proposition resulting from a propositional function x by the substitution of "the author of *Waverley*" for "x." We may say that "the author of *Waverley*" means "the value of x for which 'x wrote *Waverley*' is true." Thus the proposition "the author of *Waverley* was Scotch," for example, involves:

(1) "x wrote *Waverley*" is not always false;
(2) "if x and y wrote *Waverley*, x and y are identical" is always true;
(3) "if x wrote *Waverley*, x was Scotch" is always true.

These three propositions, translated into ordinary language, state:

(1) at least one person wrote *Waverley*;
(2) at most one person wrote *Waverley*;
(3) whoever wrote *Waverley* was Scotch.

All these three are implied by "the author of *Waverley* was Scotch." Conversely, the three together (but no two of them) imply that the author of *Waverley* was Scotch. Hence the three together may be taken as defining what is meant by the proposition "the author of *Waverley* was Scotch."

We may somewhat simplify these three propositions. The first and second together are equivalent to: "There is a term c such that 'x wrote *Waverley*' is true when x is c and is false when x is not c." In other words, "There is a term c such that 'x wrote *Waverley*' is always equivalent to 'x is c.'" (Two propositions are "equivalent" when both are true or both are false.) We have here, to begin with, two functions of x, "x wrote *Waverley*" and "x is c," and we form a function of c by considering the equivalence of these two functions of x for all values of x; we then proceed to assert that the resulting function of c is "sometimes true," *i.e.* that it is true for at least one value of c. (It obviously cannot be true for more than one value of c.) These two conditions together are defined as giving the meaning of "the author of *Waverley* exists."

We may now define "the term satisfying the function ϕx exists." This is the general form of which the above is a particular case. "The author of *Waverley*" is "the term satisfying the function 'x wrote *Waverley*.'" And "the so-and-so" will always involve reference to some propositional function, namely, that which defines the property that makes a thing a so-and-so. Our definition is as follows:

"The term satisfying the function ϕx exists" means:
    "There is a term c such that ϕx is always equivalent to 'x is c.'"

In order to define "the author of *Waverley* was Scotch," we have still to take account of the third of our three propositions, namely, "Whoever wrote *Waverley* was Scotch." This will be satisfied by merely adding that the c in question is to be Scotch. Thus "the author of *Waverley* was Scotch" is:

"There is a term c such that (1) 'x wrote *Waverley*' is always equivalent to 'x is c,' (2) c is Scotch."

And generally: "the term satisfying ϕx satisfies ψx" is defined as meaning:

"There is a term c such that (1) ϕx is always equivalent to 'x is c,' (2) ψc is true."

This is the definition of propositions in which descriptions occur.

It is possible to have much knowledge concerning a term described, *i.e.* to know many propositions concerning "the so-and-so," without actually knowing what the so-and-so is, *i.e.* without knowing any proposition of the form "x is the so-and-so," where "x" is a name. In a detective story propositions about "the man who did the deed" are accumulated, in the hope that ultimately they will suffice to demonstrate that it was A who did the deed. We may even go so far as to say that, in all such knowledge as can be expressed in words—with the exception of "this " and "that" and a few other words of which the meaning varies on different occasions—no names, in the strict sense, occur, but what seem like names are really descriptions. We may inquire significantly whether Homer existed, which we could not do if "Homer" were a name. The proposition "the so-and-so exists" is significant, whether true or false; but if a is the so-and-so (where "a" is a name), the words "a exists" are meaningless. It is only of descriptions—definite or indefinite—that existence can be significantly asserted; for, if "a" is a name, it *must* name something: what does not name anything is not a name, and therefore, if intended to be a name, is a symbol devoid of meaning, whereas a description, like "the preset King of France," does not become incapable of occurring significantly merely on the ground that it describes nothing, the reason being that it is a *complex* symbol, of which the meaning is derived from that of its constituent symbols. And so, when we ask whether Homer existed, we are using the word "Homer" as an abbreviated description: we may replace it by (say) "the author of the *Iliad* and the *Odyssey*." The same considerations apply to almost all uses of what look like proper names.

When descriptions occur in propositions, it is necessary to distinguish what may be called "primary" and "secondary" occurrences. The abstract distinction is as follows. A description has a "primary" occurrence when the proposition in which it occurs results from substituting the description for "x" in some propositional function ϕx; a description has a "secondary" occurrence when the result of substituting the description for x in ϕx gives only *part* of the proposition concerned. An instance will make this clearer. Consider "the present King of France is bald." Here "the present King of France" has a primary occurrence, and the proposition is false.

Every proposition in which a description which describes nothing has a primary occurrence is false. But now consider "the present King of France is not bald." This is ambiguous. If we are first to take "x is bald," then substitute "the present King of France" for "x," and then deny the result, the occurrence of "the present King of France" is secondary and our proposition is true; but if we are to take "x is not bald" and substitute "the present King of France" for "x," then "the present King of France" has a primary occurrence and the proposition is false. Confusion of primary and secondary occurrences is a ready source of fallacies where descriptions are concerned.

Descriptions occur in mathematics chiefly in the form of *descriptive functions*, *i.e.* "the term having the relation R to y," or "the R of y" as we may say, on the analogy of "the father of y" and similar phrases. To say "the father of y is rich," for example, is to say that the following propositional function of c: "c is rich, and 'x begat y' is always equivalent to 'x is c,'" is "sometimes true," *i.e.* is true for at least one value of c. It obviously cannot be true for more than one value.

The theory of descriptions, briefly outlined in the present chapter, is of the utmost importance both in logic and in theory of knowledge. But for purposes of mathematics, the more philosophical parts of the theory are not essential, and have therefore been omitted in the above account, which has confined itself to the barest mathematical requisites.

Note

1. *Untersuchungen zur Gegenstandstheorie und Psychologie*, 1904.

Chapter 16

On Referring

Peter F. Strawson

I

We very commonly use expressions of certain kinds to mention or refer to some individual person or single object or particular event or place or process, in the course of doing what we should normally describe as making a statement about that person, object, place, event, or process. I shall call this way of using expressions the 'uniquely referring use'. The classes of expressions which are most commonly used in this way are: singular demonstrative pronouns ('this' and 'that'); proper names (e.g. 'Venice', 'Napoleon', 'John'); singular personal and impersonal pronouns ('he', 'she' 'I', 'you', 'it'); and phrases beginning with the definite article followed by a noun, qualified or unqualified, in the singular (e.g. 'the table', 'the old man', 'the king of France'). Any expression of any of these classes can occur as the subject of what would traditionally be regarded as a singular subject-predicate sentence; and would, so occurring, exemplify the use I wish to discuss.

I do not want to say that expressions belonging to these classes never have any other use than the one I want to discuss. On the contrary, it is obvious that they do. It is obvious that anyone who uttered the sentence, 'The whale is a mammal', would be using the expression 'the whale' in a way quite different from the way it would be used by anyone who had occasion seriously to utter the sentence, 'The whale struck the ship'. In the first sentence one is obviously *not* mentioning, and in the second sentence one obviously *is* mentioning, a particular whale. Again if I said, 'Napoleon was the greatest French soldier', I should be using the word 'Napoleon' to

First appeared in *Mind* 59 (1950): 320–344. Reprinted by permission of Oxford University Press.

mention a certain individual, but I should not be using the phrase, 'the greatest French soldier', to mention an individual, but to say something about an individual I had already mentioned. It would be natural to say that in using this sentence I was talking *about* Napoleon and that what I was *saying* about him was that he was the greatest French soldier. But of course I *could* use the expression, 'the greatest French soldier', to mention an individual; for example, by saying: 'The greatest French soldier died in exile.' So it is obvious that at least some expressions belonging to the classes I mentioned *can* have uses other than the use I am anxious to discuss. Another thing I do not want to say is that in any given sentence there is never more than one expression used in the way I propose to discuss. On the contrary, it is obvious that there may be more than one. For example, it would be natural to say that, in seriously using the sentence. 'The whale struck the ship', I was saying something about both a certain whale and a certain ship, that I was using each of the expressions 'the whale' and 'the ship' to mention a particular object; or, in other words, that I was using each of these expressions in the uniquely referring way. In general, however, I shall confine my attention to cases where an expression used in this way occurs as the grammatical subject of a sentence.

I think it is true to say that Russell's Theory of Descriptions, which is concerned with the last of the four classes of expressions I mentioned above (i.e. with expressions of the form 'the so-and-so') is still widely accepted among logicians as giving a correct account of the use of such expressions in ordinary language. I want to show, in the first place, that this theory, so regarded, embodies some fundamental mistakes.

What question or questions about phrases of the form 'the so-and-so' was the Theory of Descriptions designed to answer? I think that at least one of the questions may be illustrated as follows. Suppose someone were now to utter sentence, 'The king of France is wise.' No one would say that the sentence which had been uttered was meaningless. Everyone would agree that it was significant. But everyone knows that there is not at present a king of France. One of the questions the Theory of Descriptions was designed to answer was the question: how can such a sentence as 'The king of France is wise' be significant even when there is nothing which answers to the description it contains, i.e., in this case, nothing which answers to the description 'The king of France'? And one of the reasons why Russell thought it important to give a correct answer to this question was that he thought it important to show that another answer which might be given was wrong. The answer that he thought was wrong, and to which he was anxious to supply an alternative, might be exhibited as the conclusion of either of the following two fallacious arguments. Let us call the sentence 'The king of France is wise' the sentence S. Then the first argument is as follows:

(1) The phrase, 'the king of France', is the subject of the sentence S. Therefore (2) if S is a significant sentence, S is a sentence *about* the king of France.
But (3) if there in no sense exists a king of France, the sentence is not about anything, and hence not about the king of France.
Therefore (4) since S is significant, there must in some sense (in some world) exist (or subsist) the king of France.

And the second argument is as follows:

(1) If S is significant, it is either true or false.
(2) S is true if the king of France is wise and false if the king of France is not wise.
(3) But the statement that the king of France is wise and the statement that the king of France is not wise are alike true only if there is (in some sense, in some world) something which is the king of France.
Hence (4) since S is significant, there follows the same conclusion as before.

These are fairly obviously bad arguments, and, as we should expect, Russell rejects them. The postulation of a world of strange entities, to which the king of France belongs, offends, he says, against 'that feeling for reality which ought to be preserved even in the most abstract studies'. The fact that Russell rejects these arguments is, however, less interesting than the extent to which, in rejecting their conclusion, he concedes the more important of their principles. Let me refer to the phrase, 'the king of France', as the phrase D. Then I think Russell's reasons for rejecting these two arguments can be summarized as follows. The mistake arises, he says, from thinking that D, which is certainly the *grammatical* subject of S, is also the *logical* subject of S. But D is not the logical subject of S. In fact S, although grammatically it has a singular subject and a predicate, is not logically a subject-predicate sentence at all. The proposition it expresses is a complex kind of *existential* proposition, part of which might be described as a 'uniquely existential' proposition. To exhibit the logical form of the proposition, we should rewrite the sentence in a logically appropriate grammatical form; in such a way that the deceptive similarity of S to a sentence expressing a subject-predicate proposition would disappear, and we should be safeguarded against arguments such as the bad ones I outlined above. Before recalling the details of Russell's analysis of S, let us notice what his answer, as I have so far given it, seems to imply. His answer seems to imply that in the case of a sentence which is similar to S in that (1) it is grammatically of the subject-predicate form and (2) its grammatical subject does not refer to anything, then the only alternative to its being meaningless is that it should not really (i.e. logically) be of the subject-predicate form at all, but of some quite different form. And this in its turn seems to imply that if there are any sentences which are genuinely of the subject-predicate form, then the very fact of their being significant, having a meaning, guarantees that there *is* something referred to by the logical (and grammatical) subject. Moreover, Russell's answer seems to imply that there are such sentences. For if it is true that one may be misled by the grammatical similarity of S to other sentences into thinking that it is logically of the subject-predicate form, then surely there must be other sentences grammatically similar to S, which *are* of the subject-predicate form. To show not only that Russell's answer seems to imply these conclusions, but that he accepted at least the first two of them, it is enough to consider what he says about a class of expressions which he calls 'logically proper names' and contrasts with expressions, like D, which he calls 'definite descriptions'. Of logically proper names Russell says or implies the following things:

(1) That they and they alone can occur as subjects of sentences which are genuinely of the subject-predicate form;
(2) that an expression intended to be a logically proper name is *meaningless* unless there is some single object for which it stands: for the *meaning* of such an expression just is the individual object which the expression designates. To be a name at all, therefore, it *must* designate something.

It is easy to see that if anyone believes these two propositions, then the only way for him to save the significance of the sentence S is to deny that it is a logically subject-predicate sentence. Generally, we may say that Russell recognizes only two ways in which sentences which seem, from their grammatical structure, to be about some particular person or individual object or event, can be significant:

(1) The first is that their grammatical form should be misleading as to their logical form, and that they should be analysable, like S, as a special kind of existential sentence;

(2) The second is that their grammatical subject should be a logically proper name, of which the meaning is the individual thing it designates.

I think that Russell is unquestionably wrong in this, and that sentences which are significant, and which begin with an expression used in the uniquely referring way, fall into neither of these two classes. Expressions used in the uniquely referring way are never either logically proper names or descriptions, if what is meant by calling them 'descriptions' is that they are to be analysed in accordance with the model provided by Russell's Theory of Descriptions.

There are no logically proper names and there are no descriptions (in this sense).

Let us now consider the details of Russell's analysis. According to Russell, anyone who asserted S would be asserting that:

(1) There is a king of France.
(2) There is not more than one king of France.
(3) There is nothing which is king of France and is not wise.

It is easy to see both how Russell arrived at this analysis, and how it enables him to answer the question with which we began, viz. the question: How can the sentence S be significant when there is no king of France? The way in which he arrived at the analysis was clearly by asking himself what would be the circumstances in which we would say that anyone who uttered the sentence S had made a true assertion. And it does seem pretty clear, and I have no wish to dispute, that the sentences (1)–(3) above do describe circumstances which are at least *necessary* conditions of anyone making a true assertion by uttering the sentence S. But, as I hope to show, to say this is not at all the same thing as to say that Russell has given a correct account of the use of the sentence S or even that he has given an account which, though incomplete, is correct as far as it goes; and is certainly not at all the same thing as to say that the model translation provided is a correct model for all (or for any) singular sentences beginning with a phrase of the form 'the so-and-so'.

It is also easy to see how this analysis enables Russell to answer the question of how the sentence S can be significant, even when there is no king of France. For, if this analysis is correct, anyone who utters the sentence S today would be jointly asserting three propositions, one of which (viz. that there is a king of France) would be false; and since the conjunction of three propositions, of which one is false, is itself false, the assertion as a whole would be significant, but false. So neither of the bad arguments for subsistent entities would apply to such an assertion.

II

As a step towards showing that Russell's solution of his problem is mistaken, and towards providing the correct solution, I want now to draw certain distinctions. For this purpose I shall, for the remainder of this section, refer to an expression which has a uniquely referring use as 'an expression' for short; and to a sentence beginning with such an expression as 'a sentence' for short. The distinctions I shall draw are rather rough and ready, and, no doubt, difficult cases could be produced which would call for their refinement. But I think they will serve my purpose. The distinctions are between:

(A1) a sentence,
(A2) a use of a sentence,
(A3) an utterance of a sentence,

and, correspondingly, between:

(B1) an expression,
(B2) a use of an expression,
(B3) an utterance of an expression.

Consider again the sentence, 'The king of France is wise.' It is easy to imagine that this sentence was uttered at various times from, say, the beginning of the seventeenth century onwards, during the reigns of each successive French monarch; and easy to imagine that it was also uttered during the subsequent periods in which France was not a monarchy. Notice that it was natural for me to speak of 'the sentence' or 'this sentence' being uttered at various times during this period; or, in other words, that it would be natural and correct to speak of *one and the same* sentence being uttered on all these various occasions. It is in the sense in which it would be correct to speak of one and the same sentence being uttered on all these various occasions that I want to use the expression (A1) 'a sentence'. There are, however, obvious differences between different *occasions of the use* of this sentence. For instance, if one man uttered it in the reign of Louis XIV and another man uttered it in the reign of Louis XV, it would be natural to say (to assume) that they were respectively talking about different people; and it might be held that the first man, in using the sentence, made a true assertion, while the second man, in using the same sentence, made a false assertion. If on the other hand two different men simultaneously uttered the sentence (e.g. if one wrote it and the other spoke it) during the reign of Louis XIV, it would be natural to say (assume) that they were both talking about the same person, and, in that case, in using the sentence, they *must* either both have made a true assertion or both have made a false assertion. And this illustrates what I mean by *a use* of sentence. The two men who uttered the sentence, one in the reign of Louis XV and one in the reign of Louis XIV, each made a different use of the same sentence; whereas the two men who uttered the sentence simultaneously in the reign of Louis XIV, made the same use[1] of the same sentence. Obviously in the case of this sentence, and equally obviously in the case of many others, we cannot talk of *the sentence* being true or false, but only of its being used to make a true or false assertion, or (if this is preferred) to express a true or a false proposition. And equally obviously we cannot talk of *the sentence* being *about* a particular person, for the same sentence may be used at different times to talk about quite different particular persons, but only of a *use* of the sentence to talk about a particular person. Finally it will make sufficiently clear what I mean by an utterance of a sentence if I say that the two men who simultaneously uttered the sentence in the reign of Louis XIV made two different utterances of the same sentence, though they made the same *use* of the sentence.

If we now consider not the whole sentence, 'The king of France is wise', but that part of it which is the expression, 'the king of France', it is obvious that we can make analogous, though not identical distinctions between (1) the expression, (2) a use of the expression and (3) an utterance of the expression. The distinctions will not be identical; we obviously cannot correctly talk of the expression 'the king of France' being used to express a true or false proposition, since in general only sentences can be used truly or falsely; and similarly it is only by using a sentence and not by using an expression alone, that you can talk about a particular person. Instead, we shall say in this case that you *use* the expression to *mention* or *refer to* a particular person in the course of using the sentence to talk about him. But obviously in this case, and a great many others, the *expression* (B1) cannot be said to mention, or refer to, anything, any more that the *sentence* can be said to be true or false. The same expression can have different mentioning-uses, as the same sentence can be used to make statements with different truth-values. "Mentioning', or 'referring', is not something an expression does; it is something that someone can use an expression to do. Mentioning, or referring to, something is a characteristic of *a use* of an expression, just as 'being about' something, and truth-or-falsity, are characteristics of *a use* of a sentence.

A very different example may help to make these distinctions clearer. Consider another case of an expression which has a uniquely referring use, viz. the expression 'I'; and consider the sentence, 'I am hot'. Countless people may use this same sentence; but it is logically impossible for two different people to make *the same use* of this sentence; or, if this is preferred, to use it to express the same proposition. The expression 'I' may correctly be used by (and only by) any one of innumerable people to refer to himself. To say this is to say something about the expression 'I': it is, in a sense, to give its meaning. This is the sort of thing that can be said about *expressions*. But it makes no sense to say of the *expression* 'I' that it refers to a particular person. This is the sort of thing that can be said only of a particular use of the expression.

Let me use 'type' as an abbreviation for 'sentence or expression'. Then I am not saying that there are sentences and expressions (types), *and* uses of them, *and* utterances of them, as there are ships *and* shoes *and* sealing-wax. I am saying that we cannot say *the same things* about types, uses of types, and utterances of types. And the fact is that we do talk about types; and that confusion is apt to result from the failure to notice the differences between what we can say about these and what we can say only about the *uses* of types. We are apt to fancy we are talking about sentences and expressions when we are talking about the uses of sentences and expressions.

This is what Russell does. Generally, as against Russell, I shall say this. Meaning (in at least one important sense) is a function of the sentence or expression; mentioning and referring and truth or falsity, are functions of the use of the sentence or expression. To give the meaning of an expression (in the sense in which I am using the word) is to give *general directions* for its use to refer to or mention particular objects or persons; to give the meaning of a sentence is to give *general directions* for its use in making true or false assertions. It is not to talk about any particular occasion of the use of the sentence or expression. The meaning of an expression cannot be identified with the object it is used, on a particular occasion, to refer to. The meaning of a sentence cannot be identified with the assertion it is used, on a particular occasion, to make. For to talk about the meaning of an expression or sentence is not to talk about its use on a particular occasion, but about the rules, habits, conventions governing its correct use, on all occasions, to refer or to assert. So the question of whether a sentence or expression *is significant or not* has nothing whatever to do with the question of whether the sentence, *uttered on a particular occasion*, is, on that occasion, being used to make a true-or-false assertion or not, or of whether the expression is, on that occasion, being used to refer to, or mention, anything at all.

The source of Russell's mistake was that he thought that referring or mentioning, if it occurred at all, must be meaning. He did not distinguish B1 from B2; he confused expressions with their use in a particular context; and so confused meaning with mentioning, with referring. If I talk about my handkerchief, I can, perhaps, produce the object I am referring to out of my pocket. I can't produce the meaning of the expression, 'my handkerchief', out of my pocket. Because Russell confused meaning with mentioning, he thought that if there were any expressions having a uniquely referring use, which were what they seemed (i.e. logical subjects) and not something else in disguise, their meaning must *be* the particular object which they were used to refer to. Hence the troublesome mythology of the logically proper name. But if someone asks me the meaning of the expression 'this'—once Russell's favourite candidate for this status— I do not hand him the object I have just used the expression to refer to, adding at the same time that the meaning of the word changes every time it is used. Nor do I hand him all the objects it ever has been, or might be, used to refer to. I explain and illustrate the conventions governing the use of the expression. This *is* giving the meaning of the expression. It is quite different from giving (in any sense of giving) the object to which it refers; for the expression itself does not refer to anything; though it can be used, on different occasions, to refer to innumerable things. Now as a matter of fact there is, in English, a sense of the word 'mean' in which this word does approximate to 'indicate, mention or refer to'; e.g. when somebody (unpleasantly) says, 'I mean you'; or when I point and say, 'That's the one I mean'. But *the one I meant* is quite different from *the meaning of the expression* I used to talk of it. In this special sense of 'mean', it is people who mean, not expressions. People use expressions to refer to particular things. But the meaning of an expression is not the set of things or the single thing it may correctly be used to refer to: the meaning is the set of rules, habits, conventions for its use in referring.

It is the same with sentences: even more obviously so. Everyone knows that the sentence, 'The table is covered with books', is significant, and everyone knows what it means. But if I ask, 'What object is that sentence about?' I am asking an absurd question—a question which cannot be asked about the sentence, but only about some use of the sentence: and in this case the sentence hasn't been used, it has only been taken as an example. In knowing what it means, you are knowing how it could correctly be use to talk about things: so knowing the meaning hasn't anything to do with knowing about any particular use of the sentence to talk about anything. Similarly, if I ask: 'Is the sentence true or false?' I am asking an absurd question, which becomes no less absurd if I add, 'It must be one or the other since it's significant.' The question is absurd, because the *sentence* is neither true nor false any more than it's *about* some object. Of course the fact that it's significant is the same as the fact that it *can* correctly be used to talk about something and that, in so using it, someone will be making a true or false assertion. And I will add that it will be used to make a true or false assertion *only* if the person using it *is* talking about something. If, when he utters it, he is not talking about anything, then his use is not a genuine one, but a spurious or pseudo-use: he is not making either a true or a false assertion, though he may think he is. And this points the way to the correct answer to the puzzle to which the Theory of Descriptions gives a fatally incorrect answer. The important point is that the question of whether the sentence is significant or not is quite independent of the question that can be raised about a particular use of it, viz. the question whether it is a genuine or a spurious use, whether it is being used to talk about something, or in make-believe, or as an example in philosophy. The question whether the sentence is significant or not is the question whether there exist such language habits, conventions or rules that the sentence logically could be used to talk about something; and is hence quite independent of the question whether it is being so used on a particular occasion.

III

Consider again the sentence, 'The king of France is wise', and the true and false things Russell says about it.

There are at least two true things which Russell would say about the sentence:

(1) The first is that it is significant; that if anyone were now to utter it, he would be uttering a significant sentence.
(2) The second is that anyone now uttering the sentence would be making a true assertion only if there in fact at present existed one and only one king of France, and if he were wise.

What are the false things which Russell would say about the sentence? They are:

(1) That anyone now uttering it would be making a true assertion or a false assertion;
(2) That part of what he would be asserting would be that there at present existed one and only one king of France.

I have already given some reasons for thinking that these two statements are incorrect. Now suppose someone were in fact to say to you with a perfectly serious air: 'The king of France is wise.' Would you say, 'That's untrue'? I think it's quite certain that you wouldn't. But suppose he went on to *ask* you whether you thought that what he had just said was true, or was false; whether you agreed or disagreed with what he had just said. I think you would be inclined, with some hesitation, to say that you didn't do either; that the question of whether his statement was true or false simply *didn't arise*, because there was no such person as the king of France.[2] You might, if he were obviously serious (had a dazed astray-in-the-centuries look), say something like: 'I'm afraid you must be under a misapprehension. France is not a monarchy. There is no king of France.' And this brings out the point that if a man seriously uttered the sentence, his uttering it would in some sense be *evidence* that he *believed* that there was a king of France. It would not be evidence for his believing this simply in the way in which a man's reaching for his raincoat is evidence for his believing that it is raining. But nor would it be evidence for his believing this in the way in which a man's saying, 'It's raining' is evidence for his believing that it is raining. We might put it as follows. To say, 'The king of France is wise' is, in some sense of 'imply', to *imply* that there is a king of France. But this is a very special and odd sense of 'imply'. 'Implies' in this sense is certainly not equivalent to 'entails' (or 'logically implies'). And this comes out from the fact that when, in response to his statement, we say (as we should) 'There is no king of France', we should certainly *not* say we were *contradicting* the statement that the king of France is wise. We are certainly not saying that it's false. We are, rather, giving a reason for saying that the question of whether it's true or false simply doesn't arise.

And this is where the distinction I drew earlier can help us. The sentence, 'The king of France is wise', is certainly significant; but this does not mean that any particular use of it is true or false. We use it truly or falsely when we use it to talk about someone; when, in using the expression, 'The king of France', we are in fact mentioning someone. The fact that the sentence and the expression, respectively, are significant just is the fact that the sentence *could* be used, in certain circumstances, to say something true or false, that the expression *could* be used, in certain circumstances, to mention a particular person; and to know their meaning is to know what sort of circumstances these are. So when we utter the sentence without in fact mentioning anybody by the use of the phrase, 'The king of France', the sentence doesn't cease to be significant: we simply *fail* to say anything true or false because we simply fail to mention anybody by this particular use of that perfectly significant phrase. It is, if you like, a spurious use of the sentence, and a spurious use of the expression; though we may (or may not) mistakenly think it a genuine use.

And such spurious uses are very familiar. Sophisticated romancing, sophisticated fiction,[3] depend upon them. If I began, 'The king of France is wise', and went on, 'and he lives in a golden castle and has a hundred wives', and so on, a hearer would understand me perfectly well, without supposing *either* that I was talking about a particular person, *or* that I was making a false statement to the effect that there existed such a person as my words described. (It is worth adding that where the use of sentences and expressions is overtly fictional, the sense of the word 'about' may change. As Moore said, it is perfectly natural and correct to say that some of the statements in *Pickwick Papers* are *about* Mr Pickwick. But where the use of sentences and expressions is not overtly fictional, this use of 'about' seems less correct; i.e. it would not *in general* be correct to say that a statement was about Mr X or the so-and-so, unless there were such a person or thing. So it is where the romancing is in danger of being taken seriously that we might answer the question, 'Who is he talking about?' with 'He's not taking about anybody'; but, in saying this, we are not saying that what he is saying is either false or nonsense.)

Overtly fictional uses apart, however, I said just now that to use such an expression as 'The king of France' at the beginning of a sentence was, in some sense of 'imply', to imply that there was a king of France. When a man uses such an expression, he does not *assert*, nor does what he says *entail*, a uniquely existential proposition. But one of the conventional functions of the definite article is to act as a *signal* that a unique reference is being made— a signal, not a disguised assertion. When we begin a sentence with 'the such-and-such' the use of 'the' shows, but does not state, that we are, or intend to be, referring to one particular individual of the species 'such-and-such'. *Which* particular individual is a matter to be determined from context, time, place and any other features of the situation of utterance. Now, whenever a man uses any expression, the presumption is that he thinks he is using it correctly: so when he uses the expression, 'the such-and-such', in a uniquely referring way, the presumption is that he thinks both that there is *some* individual of that species, and that the context of use will sufficiently determine which one he has in mind. To use the word 'the' in this way is then to imply (in the relevant sense of 'imply') that the existential conditions described by Russell are fulfilled. But to use 'the' in this way is not to *state* that those conditions are fulfilled. If I begin a sentence with an expression of the form, 'the so-and-so', and then am prevented from saying more, I have made no statement of any kind; but I may have succeeded in mentioning someone or something.

The uniquely existential assertion supposed by Russell to be part of any assertion in which a uniquely referring use is made of an expression of the form 'the so-and-so' is, he observes, a compound of two assertions. To say that there is a ϕ is to say something compatible with there being several ϕs; to say there is not more than one ϕ is to say something compatible with there being none. To say there is one ϕ and one only is to compound these two assertions. I have so far been concerned mostly with alleged assertion of existence and less with the alleged assertion of uniqueness. An example which throws the emphasis on to the latter will serve to bring out more clearly the sense of 'implied' in which a uniquely existential assertion is implied, but not entailed, by the use of expressions in the uniquely referring way. Consider the sentence, 'The table is covered with books.' It is quite certain that in any normal use of this sentence, the expression 'the table' would be used to make a unique reference, i.e. to refer to some one table. It is a quite strict use of the definite article, in the sense in which Russell talks on p. 30 of *Principia Mathematica*, of using the article '*strictly*, so as to imply uniqueness'. On the same page Russell says that a phrase of the form 'the so-and-so', used strictly, 'will only have an application in the event of there being one so-and-so and no more'. Now it is obviously quite false that the phrase 'the table' in the sentence 'the table is covered with books', used normally, will 'only have an application in the event of there being one table and no more'. It is indeed tautologically true that, in such a use, the phrase will have an application only in the event of there being one table and no more *which is being referred to*, and that it will be understood to have an application only in the event of there being one table and no more which it is understood as being used to refer to. To use the sentence is not to assert, but it is (in the special sense discussed) to imply, that there is only one thing which is *both* of the kind specified (i.e. a table) *and is being referred to* by the speaker. It is obviously not to assert this. To refer is not to say you are referring. To say there is *some table or other* to which you are referring is not the same as referring to a particular table. We should have no use for such phrases as 'the individual I referred to' unless there were something which counted as referring. (It would make no sense to say you had pointed if there were nothing which counted as pointing.) So once more I draw the conclusion that referring to or mentioning a particular thing cannot be dissolved into any kind of assertion. To refer is not to assert, though you refer in order to go on to assert.

Let me now take an example of the uniquely referring use of an expression not of the form, 'the so-and-so'. Suppose I advance my hands, cautiously cupped, towards someone, saying, as I do so, 'This is a fine red one.' He, looking into my hands and seeing noting there, may say: 'What is? What are you talking about?' Or perhaps, 'But there's nothing in your hands.' Of course it would be absurd to say that in saying 'But you've got nothing in your hands', he was *denying* or *contradicting* what I said. So 'this' is not a disguised description in Russell's sense. Nor is it a logically proper name. For one must know what the sentence means in order to react in that way to the utterance of it. It is precisely because the significance of the word 'this' is independent of any particular reference it may be used to make, though not independent of the way it may be used to refer, that I can, as in this example, use it to *pretend* to be referring to something.

The general moral of all this is that communication is much less a matter of explicit or disguised assertion than logicians used to suppose. The particular application of this general moral in which I am interested is its application to the case of making a unique reference. It is a part of the significance of expressions of the kind I am discussing that they can be used, in an immense variety of contexts, to make unique references. It is no part of their significance to assert that they are being so used or that the conditions of their being so used are fulfilled. So the wholly important distinction we are required to draw is between:

(1) using an expression to make a unique reference; and
(2) asserting that there is one and only one individual which has certain characteristics (e.g. is of a certain kind, or stands in a certain relation to the speaker, or both).

This is, in other words, the distinction between

(1) sentences containing an expression used to indicate or mention or refer to a particular person or thing; and
(2) uniquely existential sentences.

What Russell does is progressively to assimilate more and more sentences of class (1) to sentences of class (2), and consequently to involve himself, in insuperable difficulties about logical subjects, and about values for individual variables generally: difficulties which have led him finally to the logically disastrous theory of names developed in the *Enquiry* and in *Human Knowledge*. That view of the meaning of logical-subject-expressions which provides the whole incentive to the Theory of Descriptions at the same time precludes the possibility of Russell's ever finding any satisfactory substitutes for those expressions which, beginning with substantival phrases, he progressively degrades from the status of logical subjects.[4] It is not simply, as is sometimes said, the fascination of the relation between a name and its bearer, that is the root of the trouble. Not even names come up to the impossible standard set. It is rather the combination of two more radical misconceptions: first, the failure to grasp the importance of the distinction (Section II above) between what may be said of an expression and what may be said of a particular use of it; second, a failure to recognize the uniquely referring use of expressions for the harmless, necessary thing it is, distinct from, but complementary to, the predicative or ascriptive use of expressions. The expressions which can in fact occur as singular logical subjects are expressions of the class I listed at the outset (demonstratives, substantival phrases, proper names, pronouns): to say this is to say that these expressions, together with context (in the widest sense) are what one uses to make unique references. The point of the conventions governing the uses of such expressions is, along with the situation of utterance, to secure uniqueness of reference. But to do this, enough is enough. We do not, and we cannot, while referring, attain the point of complete explicitness at which the referring function is no longer performed. The actual unique reference made, if any, is a matter of the particular use in the particular context; the significance of the expression used is the set of rules or conventions which permit such references to be made. Hence we can, using significant expressions, pretend to refer, in make-believe or in fiction, or mistakenly think we are referring when we are not referring to anything.

This shows the need for distinguishing two kinds (among many others) of linguistic conventions or rules: rules for referring, and rules for attributing and ascribing; and for an investigation of the former. If we recognize this distinction of use for what it is, we are on the way to solving a number of ancient logical and metaphysical puzzles.

My last two sections are concerned, but only in the barest outline, with these questions.

IV

One of the main purposes for which we use language is the purpose of stating facts about things and persons and events. If we want to fulfil this purpose, we must have some way of forestalling the question, 'What (who, which one) are you talking about?' as well as the question, 'What are you saying about it (him, her)?' The task of forestalling the first question is the referring (or identifying) task. The task of forestalling the second is the attributive (or descriptive or classificatory or ascriptive) task. In the conventional English sentence which is used to state, or to claim to state, a fact about an individual thing or person or event, the performance of these two tasks can be roughly and approximately assigned to separable expressions.[5] And in such a sentence, this assigning of expressions to their separate roles corresponds to the conventional grammatical classification of subject and predicate. There is nothing sacrosanct about the employment of separable expressions for these two tasks. Other methods could be, and are, employed. There is, for instance, the method of uttering a single word or attributive phrase in the conspicuous presence of the object referred to; or that analogous method exemplified by, e.g. the painting of the words 'unsafe for lorries' on a bridge, or the tying of a label reading 'first prize' on a vegetable marrow. Or one can imagine an elaborate game in which one never used an expression in the uniquely referring way at all, but uttered only uniquely existential sentences, trying to enable the hearer to identify what was being talked of by means of an accumulation of relative clauses. (This description of the purposes of the game shows in what sense it would be a game: this is not the normal use we make of existential sentences.) Two points require emphasis. The first is that the necessity of performing these two tasks in order to state particular facts requires no transcendental explanation: to call attention to it is partly to elucidate the meaning of the phrase, 'stating a fact'. The second is that even this elucidation is made in terms derivative from the grammar of the conventional singular sentence; that even the overtly functional, linguistic distinction between the identifying and attributive roles that words may play in language is prompted by the fact that ordinary speech offers us separable expressions to which the different functions may be plausibly and approximately assigned. And this functional distinction has cast long philosophical shadows. The distinctions between particular and universal, between substance and quality, are such pseudo-material shadows, cast by the grammar of the conventional sentence, in which separable expressions play distinguishable roles.

To use a separate expression to perform the first of these tasks is to use an expression in the uniquely referring way. I want now to say something in general about the conventions of use for expressions used in this way, and to contrast them with conventions of ascriptive use. I then proceed to the brief illustration of these general remarks and to some further applications of them.

What in general is required for making a unique reference is, obviously, some device, or devices, for showing both *that* a unique reference is intended and *what* unique reference it is; some device requiring and enabling the hearer or reader to identify what is being talked about. In securing this result, the context of utterance is of an importance which it is almost impossible to exaggerate; and by 'context' I mean, at least, the time, the place, the situation, the identity of the speaker, the subjects which form the immediate focus of interest, and the personal histories of both the speaker and those he is addressing. Besides context, there is, of course, convention—linguistic convention. But, except in the case of genuine proper names, of which I shall have more to say later, the fulfilment of more or less precisely stateable contextual conditions is *conventionally* (or, in a wide sense of the word, *logically*) required for the correct referring use of expressions, in a sense in which this is not true of correct ascriptive uses. The requirement for the correct application of an expression in its ascriptive use to a certain thing is simply that the thing should be of a certain kind, have certain characteristics. The requirement for the correct application of an expression in its referring use to a certain thing is something over and above any requirement derived from such ascriptive meaning as the expression may have; it is, namely, the requirement that the thing should be in a certain relation to the speaker and to the context of utterance. Let me call this the contextual requirement. Thus, for example, in the limiting case of the word 'I' the contextual requirement is that the thing should be identical with the speaker; but in the case of most expressions which have a referring use this requirement cannot be so precisely specified. A further, and perfectly general, difference between conventions for referring and conventions for describing is one we have already encountered, viz. that the fulfilment of the conditions for a correct ascriptive use of an expression is a part of what is stated by such a use; but the fulfilment of the conditions for a correct referring use of an expression is never part of what is stated, though it is (in the relevant sense of 'implied') implied by such a use.

Conventions for referring have been neglected or misinterpreted by logicians. The reasons for this neglect are not hard to see, though they are hard to state briefly. Two of them are, roughly: (1) the preoccupation of most logicians with definitions; (2) the preoccupation of some logicians with formal systems. (1) A definition, in the most familiar sense, is a specification of the conditions of the correct ascriptive or classificatory use of an expression. Definitions take no account of contextual requirements. So that in so far as the search for the meaning or the search for the analysis of an expression is conceived as the search for a definition, the neglect or misinterpretation of conventions other than ascriptive is inevitable. Perhaps it would be better to say (for I do not wish to legislate about 'meaning' or 'analysis') that logicians have failed to notice that problems of use are wider than problems of analysis and meaning. (2) The influence of the preoccupation with mathematics and formal logic is most clearly seen (to take no more recent examples) in the cases of Leibniz and Russell. The constructor of calculuses, not concerned or required to make factual statements, approaches applied logic with a prejudice. It is natural that he should assume that the types of convention with whose adequacy in one field he is familiar should be really adequate, if only one could see how, in a quite different field—that of statements of fact. Thus we have Leibniz striving desperately to make the uniqueness of unique references a matter of logic in the narrow sense, and Russell striving desperately to do the same thing, in a different way, both for the implication of uniqueness and for that of existence.

It should be clear that the distinction I am trying to draw is primarily one between different roles or parts that expressions may play in language, and not primarily one between different groups of expressions; for some expressions may appear in either role. Some of the kinds of words I shall speak of have predominantly, if not exclusively, a referring role. This is most obviously true of pronouns and oridnary proper names. Some can occur as wholes or parts of expressions which have a predominantly referring use, and as wholes or parts of expressions which have a predominantly ascriptive or classificatory use. The obvious cases are common nouns; or common nouns preceded by adjectives, including participial adjectives; or, less obviously, adjectives or participial adjectives alone. Expressions capable of having a referring use also differ from one another in at least the three following, not mutually independent, ways:

(1) They differ in the extent to which the reference they are used to make is dependent on the context of their utterance. Words like 'I' and 'it' stand at one end of this scale —the end of maximum dependence—and phrases like 'the author of Waverley' and 'the eighteenth king of France' at the other.

(2) They differ in the degree of 'descriptive meaning' they possess: by 'descriptive meaning' I intend 'conventional limitation, in application, to things of a certain general kind, or possessing certain general characteristics'. At one end of this scale stand the proper names we most commonly use in ordinary discourse; men, dogs and motor-bicycles may be called 'Horace'. The pure name has no descriptive meaning (except such as it may acquire *as a result of* some one of its uses as a name). A word like 'he' has minimal descriptive meaning, but has some. Substantival phrases like 'the round table' have the maximum descriptive meaning. An interesting intermediate position is occupied by 'impure' proper names like 'the Round Table'—substantival phrases which have grown capital letters.

(3) Finally, they may be divided into the following two classes: (i) those of which the correct referring use is regulated by some *general* referring-cum-ascriptive conventions. To this class belong both pronouns, which have the least descriptive meaning, and substantival phrases which have the most; (ii) those of which the correct referring use is regulated by no general conventions, either of the contextual or the ascriptive kind, but by conventions which are *ad hoc* for each particular use (though not for

each particular utterance). Roughly speaking, the most familiar kind of proper names belong to this class. Ignorance of a man's name is not ignorance of the language. This is why we do not speak of the meaning of proper names. (But it won't do to say they are meaingless.) Again an intermediate position is occupied by such phrases as 'The Old Pretender'. Only an old pretender may be so referred to; but to know which old pretender is not to know a general, but an *ad hoc*, convention.

In the case of phrases of the form 'the so-and-so' used referringly, the use of 'the' together with the position of the phrase in the sentence (i.e. at the beginning, or following a transitive verb or preposition) acts as a signal *that* a unique reference is being made; and the following noun, or noun and adjective, together with the context of utterance, shows *what* unique reference is being made. In general the functional difference between common nouns and adjectives is that the former are naturally and commonly used referringly, while the latter are not commonly, or so naturally, used in this way, except as qualifying nouns; though they can be, and are, so used alone. And of course this functional difference is not independent of the descriptive force peculiar to each word. In general we should expect the descriptive force of nouns to be such that they are more efficient tools for the job of showing what unique reference is intended when such a reference is signalized; and we should also expect the descriptive force of the words we naturally and commonly use to make unique reference to mirror our interest in the salient, relatively permanent and behavioural characteristics of things. These two expectations are not independent of one another; and, if we look at the difference between the commoner sort of common nouns and the commoner sort of adjectives, we find them both fulfilled. These are differences of the kind that Locke quaintly reports, when he speaks of our ideas of substances being *collections* of simple ideas; when he says that 'powers make up a great part of our ideas of substances'; and when he goes on to contrast the identity of real and nominal essence in the case of simple ideas with their lack of identity and the shiftingness of the nominal essence in the case of substances. 'Substance' itself is the troublesome tribute Locke pays to his dim awareness of the difference in predominant linguistic function that lingered even when the noun had been expanded into a more or less indefinite string of adjectives. Russell repeats Locke's mistake with a difference when, admitting the inference from syntax to reality to the extent of feeling that he can get rid of this metaphysical unknown only if he can purify language of the referring function altogether, he draws up his programme for 'abolishing particulars'; a programme, in fact, for abolishing the distinction of logical use which I am here at pains to emphasize.

The contextual requirement for the referring use of pronouns may be state with the greatest precision in some cases (e.g. 'I' and 'you') and only with the greatest vagueness in others ('it' and 'this'). I propose to say nothing further about pronouns, except to point to an additional symptom of the failure to recognize the uniquely referring use for what it is; the fact, namely, that certain logicians have actually sought to elucidate the nature of the variable by offering such *sentences* as 'he is sick', 'it is green', as examples of something in ordinary speech like a *sentential function*. Now of course it is true that the word 'he' may be used on different occasions to refer to different people or different animals: so may the word 'John' and the phrase 'the cat'. What deters such logicians from treating these two expressions as quasi-variables is, in the first case, the lingering superstition that a name is logically tied to a single individual, and, in the second case, the descriptive meaning of the word 'cat'. But 'he', which has a wide range of applications and minimal descriptive force, only acquires a use as a referring word. It is this fact, together with the failure to accord to expressions used referringly the place in logic which belongs to them (the place held open for the mythical logically proper name), that accounts for the misleading attempt to elucidate the nature of the variable by reference to such words as 'he', 'she', 'it'.

Of ordinary proper names it is sometimes said that they are essentially words each of which is used to refer to just one individual. This is obviously false. Many ordinary personal names—names par excellence—are correctly used to refer to numbers of people. An ordinary personal name, is, roughly, a word, used referringly, of which the use is *not* dictated by any descriptive meaning the word may have, and is *not* prescribed by any such general rule for use as a referring expression (or a part of a referring expression) as we find in the case of such words as 'I', 'this' and 'the', but is governed by *ad hoc* conventions for each particular set of applications of the word to a given person. The important point is that the correctness of such applications does not follow from any *general* rule or convention for the use of the word as such. (The limit of absurdity and obvious circularity is reached in the attempt to treat names as disguised description in Russell's sense; for what is in the special sense implied, but not entailed, by my now referring to someone by name is simply the existence of someone, *now being referred to*, who is *conventionally referred to* by that name.) Even this feature of names, however, is only a symptom of the purpose for which they are employed. At present our choice of names is partly arbitrary, partly dependent on legal and social observances. It would be perfectly possible to have a thorough-going *system* of names, based e.g. on dates of birth, or on a minute classibication of physiological and anatomical differences. But the success of any such system would depend entirely on the convenience of the resulting name-allotments for the purpose of making unique references; and this would depend on the multiplicity of the classifications used and the degree to which they cut haphazard across normal social groupings. Given a sufficient degree of both, the selectivity supplied by context would do the rest; just as is the case with our present naming habits. Had we such a system, we could use name-words descriptively (as we do at present, to a limited extent and in a different way, with some famous names) as well as referringly. But it is by criteria derived from consideration of the requirements of the referring task that we should assess the adequacy of any system of naming. From the naming point of view, no kind of classification would be better or worse than any other simply because of the kind of classification—natal or anatomical—that it was.

I have already mentioned the class of quasi-names, of substantival phrases which grow capital letters, and of which such phrases as 'the Glorious Revolution', 'the Great War', 'the Annunciation', 'the Round Table' are examples. While the descriptive meaning of the words which follow the definite article is still relevant to their referring role, the capital letters are a sign of that extra-logical selectivity in their referring use, which is characteristic of pure names. Such phrases are found in print or in writing when one member of some class of events or things is of quite outstanding interest in a certain society. These phrases are embryonic names. A phrase may, for obvious reasons, pass into, and out of, this class (e.g. 'the Great War').

V

I want to conclude by considering, all too briefly, three further problems about referring uses:

(a) Indefinite references

Not all referring uses of singular expressions forestall the question 'What (who, which one) are you talking about?' There are some which either invite this question, or disclaim the intention or ability to answer it. Examples are such sentence-beginnings as 'A man told me that ...' The orthodox (Russellian) doctrine is that such sentences are existential, but not uniquely existential. This seems wrong in several ways. It is ludicrous to suggest that part of what is asserted is that the class of men or persons is not empty. Certainly this is *implied* in the by now familiar sense of implication; but the implication is also as much an implication of the *uniqueness* of the particular object of reference as when I begin a sentence with such a phrase as 'the table'. The difference between the use of the definite and indefinite articles is, very roughly, as follows. We use 'the' either when a previous reference has been made, and when 'the' signalizes that the same reference is being made; or when, in the absence of a previous indefinite reference, the context (including the hearer's assumed knowledge) is expected to enable the hearer to tell what reference is being made. We use 'a' either when these conditions are not fulfilled of when, although a definite reference could be made, we wish to keep dark the identity of the individual to whom, or to which, we are referring. This is the *arch* use of such a phrase as 'a certain person' or 'someone'; where it could be expanded, not into 'someone, but you wouldn't (or I don't) know who' but into 'someone, but I'm not telling you who'.

(b)   Identification statements

By this label I intend statements like the following:

(i.a)   That is the man who swam the channel twice on one day.
(ii.a) Napoleon was the man who ordered the execution of the Duc D'Enghien.

The puzzle about these statements is that their grammatical predicates do not seem to be used in a straightforwardly ascriptive way as are the grammatical predicates of the statements:

(i.b)   That man swan the channel twice in one day.
(ii.b) Napoleon ordered the execution of the Duc D'Enghien.

But if, in order to avoid blurring the difference between (i.a) and (i.b) and (ii.a) and (ii.b), one says that the phrases which form the grammatical complements of (i.a) and (ii.a) are being used referringly, one becomes puzzled about what is being said in these sentences. We seem then to be referring to the same person twice over and either saying nothing about him and thus making no statement, or identifying him with himself and thus producing a trivial identity.

The bogey of triviality can be dismissed. This only arises for those who think of the object referred to by the use of an expression as its meaning, and thus think of the subject and complement of these sentences as meaning the same because they could be used to refer to the same person.

I think the differences between sentences in the (a) group and sentences in the (b) group can best be understood by considering the differences between the circumstances in which you would say (i.a) and the circumstances in which you would say (i.b). You would say (i.a) instead of (i.b) if you knew or believed that your hearer knew or believed that *someone* had swum the channel twice in one day. You say (i.a) when you take your hearer to be in the position of one who can ask: 'Who swam the channel twice in one day?' (And in asking this, he is not saying that anyone did, though his asking it implies—in the relevant sense—that someone did.) Such sentences are like answers to such questions. They are better called 'identification-statements' than 'identities'. Sentence (i.a) does not assert more or less than sentence (i.b). It is just that you say (i.a) to a man whom you take to know certain things that you take to be unknown to the man to whom you say (i.b).

This is, in the barest essentials, the solution to Russell's puzzle about 'denoting phrases' joining by 'is'; one of the puzzles which he claims for the Theory of Descriptions the merit of solving.

(c)   The logic of subjects and predicates

Much of what I have said of the uniquely referring use of expressions can be extended, with suitable modifications, to the non-uniquely referring use of expressions; i.e. to some uses of expressions consisting of 'the', 'all the', 'all', 'some', 'some of the', etc. followed by a noun, qualified or unqualified, in the *plural*; to some uses of 'they', 'them', 'those', 'these'; and to conjunctions of names. Expressions of the first kind have a special interest. Roughly speaking, orthodox modern criticism, inspired by mathematical logic, of such traditional doctrines as that of the Square of Opposition and of some of the forms of the syllogism traditionally recognized as valid, rests on the familiar failure to recognize the special sense in which existential assertions may be implied by the referring use of expressions. The universal propositions of the fourfold schedule, it is said, must *either* be given a negatively existential interpretation (e.g. for A, 'there are no Xs which are not Ys') *or* they must be interpreted as conjunctions of negatively and positively existential statements of, e.g., the form (for A) 'there are no Xs which are not Ys, and there are Xs'. The I and O forms are normally given a positively existential interpretation. It is then seen that, whichever of the above alternatives is selected, some of the traditional laws have to be abandoned. The dilemma, however, is a bogus one. If we interpret the propositions of the schedule as neither positively, nor negatively, nor positively *and* negatively, existential, but as sentences such that *the question of whether they are being used to make true or false assertions does not arise except when the existential conditions is fulfilled for the subject term,* then all the traditional laws hold good together. And this interpretation is far closer to the most common uses of expressions beginning with "all" and 'some' than is any Russellian alternative. For these expressions are most commonly used in the referring way. A literal-minded and childless man asked whether all his children are asleep will certainly not answer 'Yes' on the ground that he has none; but nor will he answer 'No' on this ground. Since he has no children, the question does not arise. To say this is not to say that I may not use the sentence, 'All my children are asleep', with the intention of letting someone know that I have children, or of deceiving him into thinking that I have. Nor is it any weakening of my thesis to concede that singular phrases of the form 'the so-and-so' may sometimes be used with a similar purpose. Neither Aristotelian nor Russellian rules give the exact logic of any expression of ordinary language; for ordinary language has no exact logic.

Notes

1. This usage of 'use' is, of course, different from (a) the current usage in which 'use' (of a particular word, phrase, sentence) = (roughly) 'rules for using' = (roughly) 'meaning'; and from (b) my own usage in the phrase 'uniquely referring use of expressions' in which 'use' = (roughly) 'way of using'.

2. Since this article was written, there has appeared a clear statement of this point by Mr Geach in *Analysis*, 10:4 (March 1950), 84–8.

3. The unsophisticated kind begins: 'Once upon time there was . . .'.

4. And this in spite of the danger-signal of that phrase, '*misleading* grammatical form'.

5. I neglect relational sentences; for these require, not a modification in the principle of what I say, but a complication of the detail.

Chapter 17

Reference and Definite Descriptions

Keith S. Donnellan

I

Definite descriptions, I shall argue, have two possible functions.[1] They are used to refer to what a speaker wishes to talk about, but they are also used quite differently. Moreover, a definite description occurring in one and the same sentence may, on different occasions of its use, function in either way. The failure to deal with this duality of function obscures the genuine referring use of definite descriptions. The best-known theories of definite descriptions, those of Russell and Strawson, I shall suggest, are both guilty of this. Before discussing this distinction in use, I will mention some features of these theories to which it is especially relevant.

On Russell's view a definite description may denote an entity: "if 'C' is a denoting phrase [as definite descriptions are by definition], it may happen that there is one entity x (there cannot be more than one) for which the proposition 'x is identical with C' is true.... We may then say that the entity x is the denotation of the phrase 'C.'"[2] In using a definite description, then, a speaker may use an expression which denotes some entity, but this is the only relationship between that entity and the use of the definite description recognized by Russell. I shall argue, however, that there are two uses of definite descriptions. The definition of denotation given by Russell is applicable to both, but in one of these the definite description serves to do something more. I shall say that in this use the speaker uses the definite description to *refer* to something, and call this use the "referential use" of a definite description. Thus, if I am right, referring is not the same as denoting and the referential use of definite descriptions is not recognized on Russell's view.

First appeared in *The Philosophical Review* 77 (1966): 281–304. In the public domain.

Furthermore, on Russell's view the type of expression that comes closest to performing the function of the referential use of definite descriptions turns out, as one might suspect, to be a proper name (in "the narrow logical sense"). Many of the things said about proper names by Russell can, I think, be said about the referential use of definite descriptions without straining senses unduly. Thus the gulf Russell thought he saw between names and definite descriptions is narrower than he thought.

Strawson, on the other hand, certainly does recognize a referential use of definite definitions. But what I think he did not see is that a definite description may have a quite different role—may be used non-referentially, even as it occurs in one and the same sentence. Strawson, it is true, points out nonreferential uses of definite descriptions,[3] but which use a definite description has seems to be for him a function of the kind of sentence in which it occurs; whereas, if I am right, there can be two possible uses of a definite description in the same sentence. Thus, in "On Referring," he says, speaking of expressions used to refer, 'Any expression of any of these classes [one being that of definite descriptions] can occur as the subject of what would traditionally be regarded as a singular subject-predicate sentence; and would, so occurring, exemplify the use I wish to discuss."[4] So the definite description in, say, the sentence "The Republican candidate for president in 1968 will be a conservative" presumably exemplifies the referential use. But if I am right, we could not say this of the sentence in isolation from some particular occasion on which it is used to state something; and then it might or might not turn out that the definite description has a referential use.

Strawson and Russell seem to me to make a common assumption here about the question of how definite descriptions function: that we can ask how a definite description functions in some sentence independently of a particular occasion upon which it is used. This assumption is not really rejected in Strawson's arguments against Russell. Although he can sum up his position by saying, " 'Mentioning' or 'referring' is not something an expression does; it is something that someone can use an expression to do,"[5] he means by this to deny the radical view that a "genuine" referring expression *has* a referent, functions to refer, independent of the context of some use of the expression. The denial of this view, however, does not entail that definite descriptions cannot be identified as referring expressions in a sentence unless the sentence is being used. Just as we can speak of a function of a tool that is not at the moment performing its function, Strawson's view, I believe, allows us to speak of the referential function of a definite description in a sentence even when it is not being used. This, I hope to show, is a mistake.

A second assumption shared by Russell's and Strawson's account of definite descriptions is this. In many cases a person who uses a definite description can be said (in some sense) to presuppose or imply that something fits the description.[6] If I state that the king is on his throne, I presuppose or imply that there is a king. (At any rate, this would be a natural thing to say for anyone who doubted that there is a king.) Both Russell and Strawson assume that where the presupposition or implication is false, the truth value of what the speaker says is affected. For Russell the statement made is false; for Strawson it has no truth value. Now if there are two uses of definite descriptions, it may be that the truth value is affected differently in each case by the falsity of the presupposition or implication. This is what I shall in fact argue. It will turn out, I believe, that one or the other of the two views, Russell's or Strawson's, may be correct about the nonreferential use of definite descriptions, but neither fits the referential use. This is not so surprising about Russell's view, since he did not recognize this use in any case, but it is surprising about Strawson's since the referential use is what he tries to explain and defend. Furthermore, on Strawson's account, the result of there being nothing which fits the description is a failure of reference.[7] This too, I believe, turns out not to be true about the referential use of definite descriptions.

II

There are some uses of definite descriptions which carry neither any hint of a referential use nor any presupposition or implication that something fits the description. In general, it seems, these are recognizable from the sentence frame in which the description occurs. These uses will not interest us, but it is necessary to point them out if only to set them aside.

An obvious example would be the sentence "The present king of France does not exist," used, say, to correct someone's mistaken impression that de Gaulle is the king of France.

A more interesting example is this. Suppose someone were to ask, "Is de Gaulle the king of France?" This is the natural form of words for a person to use who is in doubt as to whether de Gaulle is king or president of France. Given this background to the question, there seems to be no presupposition or implication that someone is the king of France. Nor is the person attempting to refer to someone by using the definite description. On the other hand, reverse the name and description in the question and the speaker probably would be thought to presuppose or imply this. "Is the king of France de Gaulle?" is the natural question for one to ask who wonders whether it is de Gaulle rather than someone else who occupies the throne of France.[8]

Many times, however, the use of a definite description does carry a presupposition or implication that something fits the description. If definite descriptions do have a referring role, it will be here. But it is a mistake, I think, to try, as I believe both Russell and Strawson do, to settle this matter without further ado. What is needed, I believe, is the distinction I will now discuss.

III

I will call the two uses of definite descriptions I have in mind the attributive use and the referential use. A speaker who uses a definite description attributively in an assertion states something about whoever or whatever is the so-and-so. A speaker who uses a definite description referentially in an assertion, on the other hand, uses the description to enable his audience to pick out whom or what he is talking about and states something about that person or thing. In the first case the definite description might be said to occur essentially, for the speaker wishes to assert something about whatever or whoever fits that description; but in the referential use the definite description is merely one tool for doing a certain job—calling attention to a person or thing—and in general any other device for doing the same job, another description or a name, would do as well. In the attributive use, the attribute of being the so-and-so is all important, while it is not in the referential use.

To illustrate this distinction, in the case of a single sentence, consider the sentence, "Smith's murderer is insane." Suppose first that we come upon poor Smith foully murdered. From the brutal manner of the killing and the fact that Smith was the most lovable person in the world, we might exclaim, "Smith's murderer is insane." I will assume, to make it a simpler case, that in a quite ordinary sense we do not know who murdered Smith (though this is not in the end essential to the case). This, I shall say, is an attributive use of the definite description.

The contrast with such a use of the sentence is one of those situations in which we expect and intend our audience to realize whom we have in mind when we speak of Smith's murderer and, most importantly, to know that it is this person about whom we are going to say something.

For example, suppose that Jones has been charged with Smith's murder and has been placed on trial. Imagine that there is a discussion of Jones's odd behavior at his trial. We might sum up our impression of his behavior by saying, "Smith's murderer is insane." If someone asks to whom we are referring, by using this description, the answer here is "Jones." This, I shall say, is a referential use of the definite description.

That these two uses of the definite description in the same sentence are really quite different can perhaps best be brought out by considering the consequences of the assumption that Smith had no murderer (for example, he in fact committed suicide). In both situations, in using the definite description "Smith's murderer," the speaker in some sense presupposes or implies that there is a murderer. But when we hypothesize that the presupposition or implication is false, there are different results for the two uses. In both cases we have used the predicate "is insane," but in the first case, if there is no murderer, there is no person of whom it could be correctly said that we attributed insanity to him. Such a person could be identified (correctly) only in case someone fitted the description used. But in the second case, where the definite description is simply a means of identifying the person we want to talk about, it is quite possible for the correct identification to be made even though no one fits the description we used.[9] We were speaking about Jones even though he is not in fact Smith's murderer and, in the circumstances imagined, it was his behavior we were commenting upon. Jones might, for example, accuse us of saying false things of him in calling him insane and it would be no defense, I should think, that our description, "the murderer of Smith,' failed to fit him.

It is, moreover, perfectly possible for our audience to know to whom we refer, in the second situation, even though they do not share our presupposition. A person hearing our comment in the context imagined might know we are talking about Jones even though he does not think Jones guilty.

Generalizing from this case, we can say, I think, that there are two uses of sentences of the form, 'The ϕ is ψ." In the first, if nothing is the ϕ then nothing has been said to be ψ. In the second, the fact that nothing is the ϕ does not have this consequence.

With suitable changes the same difference in use can be formulated for uses of language other than assertions. Suppose one is at a party and, seeing an interesting-looking person holding a martini glass, one asks, "Who is the man drinking a martini?" If it should turn out that there is only water in the glass, one has nevertheless asked a question about a particular person, a question that it is possible for someone to answer. Contrast this with the use of the same question by the chairman of the local Teetotalers Union. He has just been informed that a man is drinking a martini at their annual party. He responds by asking his informant, "Who is the man drinking a martini?" In asking the question the chairman does not have some particular person in mind about whom he asks the question; if no one is drinking a martini, if the information is wrong, no person can be singled out as the person about whom the question was asked. Unlike the first case, the attribute of being the man drinking a martini is all-important, because if it is the attribute of no one, the chairman's question has no straightforward answer.

This illustrates also another difference between the referential and the attributive use of definite descriptions. In the one case we have asked a question about a particular person or thing even though nothing fits the description we used; in the other this is not so. But also in the one case our question can be answered; in the other it cannot be. In the referential use of a definite description we may succeed in picking out a person or thing to ask a question about even though he or it does not really fit the description; but in the attributive use if nothing fits the description, no straightforward answer to the question can be given.

This further difference is also illustrated by commands or orders containing definite descriptions. Consider the order, "Bring me the book on the table." If "the book on the table" is being used referentially, it is possible to fulfill the order even though there is no book on the table. If, for example, there is a book *beside* the table, though there is none *on* it, one might bring that book back and ask the issuer of the order whether this is "the book you meant." And it may be. But imagine we are told that someone has laid a book on our prize antique table, where nothing should be put. The order, "Bring me the book on the table" cannot now be obeyed unless there is a book that has been placed on the table. There is no possibility of bringing back a book which was never on the table and having it be the one that was meant, because there is no book that in the sense was "meant." In the one case the definite description was a device for getting the other person to pick the right book; if he is able to pick the right book even though it does not satisfy the description, one still succeeds in his purpose. In the other case, there is, antecedently, no "right book" except one which fits the description; the attribute of being the book on the table is essential. Not only is there no book about which an order was issued, if there is no book on the table, but the order itself cannot be obeyed. When a definite description is used attributively in a command or question and nothing fits the description, the command cannot be obeyed and the question cannot be answered. This suggests some analogous consequence for assertions containing definite descriptions used attributively. Perhaps the analogous result is that the assertion is neither true nor false: this is Strawson's view of what happens when the presupposition of the use of a definite description is false. But if so, Strawson's view works not for definite descriptions used referentially, but for the quite different use, which I have called the attributive use.

I have tried to bring out the two uses of definite descriptions by pointing out the different consequences of supposing that nothing fits the description used. There are still other differences. One is this: when a definite description is used referentially, not only is there in some sense a presupposition or implication that someone or something fits the description, as there is also in the attributive use, but there is a quite different presupposition; the speaker presupposes of some *particular* someone or something that he or it fits the description. In asking, for example, "Who is the man drinking a martini?" where we mean to ask a question about that man over there, we are presupposing that that man over there is drinking a martini—not just that *someone* is a man drinking a martini. When we say, in a context where it is clear we are referring to Jones, "Smith's murderer is insane," we are presupposing that Jones is Smith's murderer. No such presupposition is present in the attributive use of definite descriptions. There is, of course, the presupposition that someone *or other* did the murder, but the speaker does not presuppose of someone in particular—Jones or Robinson, say—that he did it. What I mean by this second kind of presupposition that someone or something in particular fits the description—which is present in a referential use but not in an attributive use—can perhaps be seen more clearly by considering a member of the speaker's audience who believes that Smith was not murdered at all. Now in the case of the referential use of the description, "Smith's murderer," he could accuse the speaker of mistakenly presupposing both that someone or other is the murderer and that also Jones is the murderer, for even though he believes Jones not to have done the deed, he knows that the speaker was referring to Jones. But in the case of the attributive use, he can accuse the speaker of having only the first, less specific presupposition; he cannot pick out some person and claim that the speaker is presupposing that that person is Smith's murderer. Now the more particular presuppositions that we find present in referential uses are clearly not ones we can assign to a definite description in some particular sentence in isolation from a context of use. In order to know that a person presupposes that Jones is Smith's murderer in using the sentence "Smith's murderer is insane," we have to know that he is using the description referentially and also to whom he is referring. The sentence by itself does not tell us any of this.

IV

From the way in which I set up each of the previous examples it might be supposed that the important difference between the referential and the attributive use lies in the beliefs of the speaker. Does he believe of some particular person or thing that he or it fits the description used? In the Smith murder example, for instance, there was in the one case no belief as to who did the deed, whereas in the contrasting case it was believed that Jones did it. But this is, in fact, not an essential difference. It is possible for a definite description to be used attributively even though the speaker (and his audience) believes that a certain person or thing fits the description. And it is possible for a definite description to be used referentially where the speaker believes that nothing fits the description. It is true—and this is why, for simplicity, I set up the examples the way I did—that if a speaker does not believe that anything fits the description or does not believe that he is in a position to pick out what does fit the description, it is likely that he is not using it referentially. It is also true that if he and his audience would pick out some particular thing or person as fitting the description, then a use of the definite description is very likely referential. But these are only presumptions and not entailments.

To use the Smith murder case again, suppose that Jones is on trial for the murder and I and everyone else believe him guilty. Suppose that I comment that the murderer of Smith is insane, but instead of backing this up, as in the example previously used, by citing Jones's behavior in the dock, I go on to outline reasons for thinking that *anyone* who murdered poor Smith in that particularly horrible way must be insane. If now it turns out that Jones was not the murderer after all, but someone else was, I think I can claim to have been right if the true murderer is after all insane. Here, I think, I would be using the definite description attributively, even though I believe that a particular person fits the description.

It is also possible to think of cases in which the speaker does not believe that what he means to refer to by using the definite description fits the description, or to imagine cases in which the definite description is used referentially even though the speaker believes *nothing* fits the description. Admittedly, these cases may be parasitic on a more normal use; nevertheless, they are sufficient to show that such beliefs of the speaker are not decisive as to which use is made of a definite description.

Suppose the throne is occupied by a man I firmly believe to be not the king, but a usurper. Imagine also that his followers as firmly believe that he is the king. Suppose I wish to see this man. I might say to his minions, "Is the king in his countinghouse?" I succeed in referring to the man I wish to refer to without myself believing that he fits the description. It is not even necessary, moreover, to suppose that his followers believe him to be the king. If they are cynical about the whole thing, know he is not the king, I may still succeed in referring to the man I wish to refer to. Similarly, neither I nor the people I speak to may suppose that *anyone* is the king and, finally, each party may know that the other does not so suppose and yet the reference may go through.

V

Both the attributive and the referential use of definite descriptions seem to carry a presupposition or implication that there is something which fits the description. But the reasons for the existence of the presupposition or implication are different in the two cases.

There is a presumption that a person who uses a definite description referentially believes that what he wishes to refer to fits the description. Because the purpose of using the description is to get the audience to pick out or think of the right thing or person, one would normally choose a description that he believes the thing or person fits. Normally a misdescription of that to which one wants to refer would mislead the audience. Hence, there is a presumption that the speaker believes *something* fits the description—namely, that to which he refers.

When a definite description is used attributively, however, there is not the same possibility of misdescription. In the example of "Smith's murderer" used attributively, there was not the possibility of misdescribing Jones or anyone else; we were not referring to Jones nor to anyone else by using the description. The presumption that the speaker believes *someone* is Smith's murderer does not arise here from a more specific presumption that he believes Jones or Robinson or someone else whom he can name or identify is Smith's murderer.

The presupposition or implication is borne by a definite description used attributively because if nothing fits the description the linguistic purpose of the speech act will be thwarted. That is, the speaker will not succeed in saying something true, if he makes an assertion; he will not succeed in asking a question that can be answered, if he has asked a question; he will not succeed in issuing an order that can be obeyed, if he has issued an order. If one states that Smith's murderer is insane, when Smith has no murderer, and uses the definite description nonreferentially, then one fails to say anything *true*. If one issues the order "Bring me Smith's murderer" under similar circumstances, the order cannot be obeyed; nothing would count as obeying it.

When the definite description is used referentially, on the other hand, the presupposition or implication stems simply from the fact that normally a person tries to describe correctly what he wants to refer to because normally this is the best way to get his audience to recognize what he is referring to. As we have seen, it is possible for the linguistic purpose of the speech act to be accomplished in such a case even though nothing fits the description; it is possible to say something true or to ask a question that gets answered or to issue a command that gets obeyed. For when the definite description is used referentially, one's audience may succeed in seeing to what one refers even though neither it nor anything else fits the description.

VI

The result of the last section shows something to be wrong with the theories of both Russell and Strawson; for though they give differing accounts of the implication or presupposition involved, each gives only one. Yet, as I have argued, the presupposition or implication is present for a quite different reason, depending upon whether the definite description is used attributively or referentially, and exactly what presuppositions or implications are involved is also different. Moreover, neither theory seems a correct characterization of the referential use. On Russell's there is a logical entailment: "The ϕ is ψ" entails "There exists one and only one ϕ." Whether or not this is so for the attributive use, it does not seem true of the referential use of the definite description. The "implication" that something is the ϕ, as I have argued, does not amount to an entailment; it is more like a presumption based on what is *usually* true of the use of a definite description to refer. In any case, of course, Russell's theory does not show—what is true of the referential use—that the implication that *something* is the ϕ comes from the more specific implication that *what is being referred to* is the ϕ. Hence, as a theory of definite descriptions, Russell's view seems to apply, if at all, to the attributive use only.

Russell's definition of denoting (a definite description denotes an entity if that entity fits the description uniquely) is clearly applicable to either use of definite descriptions. Thus whether or not a definite description is used referentially or attributively, it may have a denotation. Hence, denoting and referring, as I have explicated the latter notion, are distinct and Russell's view recognizes only the former. It seems to me, moreover, that this is a welcome result, that denoting and referring should not be confused. If one tried to maintain that they are the same notion, one result would be that a speaker might be referring to something without knowing it. If someone said, for example, in 1960 before he had any idea that Mr. Goldwater would be the Republican nominee in 1964, "The Republican candidate for president in 1964 will be a conservative," (perhaps on the basis of an analysis of the views of party leaders) the definite description here would *denote* Mr. Goldwater. But would we wish to say that the speaker had referred to, mentioned, or talked about Mr. Goldwater? I feel these terms would be out of place. Yet if we identify referring and denoting, it ought to be possible for it to turn out (after the Republican Convention) that the speaker had, unknown to himself, referred in 1960 to Mr. Goldwater. On my view, however, while the definite description used did *denote* Mr. Goldwater (using Russell's definition), the speaker used it *attributively* and did not *refer* to Mr. Goldwater.

Turning to Strawson's theory, it was supposed to demonstrate how definite descriptions are referential. But it goes too far in this direction. For there are nonreferential uses of definite descriptions also, even as they occur in one and the same sentence. I believe that Strawson's theory involves the following propositions:

(1) If someone asserts that the ϕ is ψ he has not made a true or false statement if there is no ϕ.[10]

(2) If there is no ϕ then the speaker has failed to refer to anything.[11]

(3) The reason he has said nothing true or false is that he has failed to refer.

Each of these propositions is either false or, at best, applies to only one of the two uses of definite descriptions.

Proposition (1) is possibly true of the attributive use. In the example in which "Smith's murderer is insane" was said when Smith's body was first discovered, an attributive use of the definite description, there was no person to whom the speaker referred. If Smith had no murderer, nothing true was said. It is quite tempting to conclude, following Strawson, that nothing true *or* false was said. But where the definite description is used referentially, something true may well have been said. It is possible that something true was said of the person or thing referred to.[12]

Proposition (2) is, as we have seen, simply false. Where a definite description is used referentially it is perfectly possible to refer to something though nothing fits the description used.

The situation with proposition (3) is a bit more complicated. It ties together, on Strawson's view, the two strands given in (1) and (2). As an account of why, when the presupposition is false, nothing true or false has been stated, it clearly cannot work for the attributive use of definite descriptions, for the reason it supplies is that reference has failed. It does not then give the reason why, if indeed this is so, a speaker using a definite description attributively fails to say anything true or false if nothing fits the description. It does, however, raise a question about the referential use. Can reference fail when a definite description is used referentially?

I do not fail to refer merely because my audience does not correctly pick out what I am referring to. I can be referring to a particular man when I use the description "the man drinking a martini," even though the people to whom I speak fail to pick out the right person or any person at all. Nor, as we have stressed, do I fail to refer when nothing fits the description. But perhaps I fail to refer in some extreme circumstances, when there is nothing that *I* am willing to pick out as that to which I referred.

Suppose that I think I see at some distance a man walking and ask, "Is the man carrying a walking stick the professor of history?" We should perhaps distinguish four cases at this point. (a) There is a man carrying a walking stick; I have then referred to a person and asked a question about him that can be answered if my audience has the information. (b) The man over there is not carrying a walking stick, but an umbrella; I have still referred to someone and asked a question that can be answered, though if my audience sees that it is an umbrella and not a walking stick, they may also correct my apparently mistaken impression. (c) It is not a man at all, but a rock that looks like one; in this case, I think I still have referred to something, to the thing over there that happens to be a rock but that I took to be a man. But in this case it is not clear that my question can be answered correctly. This, I think, is not because I have failed to refer, but rather because, given the true nature of what I referred to, my question is not appropriate. A simple "No, that is not the professor of history" is at least a bit misleading if said by someone who realizes that I mistook a rock for a person. It may, therefore, be plausible to conclude that in such a case I have not asked a question to which there is a straightforwardly correct answer. But if this is true, it is not because nothing fits the description I used, but rather because what I referred to is a rock and my question has no correct answer when asked of a rock. (d) There is finally the case in which there is nothing at all where I thought there was a man with a walking stick; and perhaps here we have a genuine failure to refer at all, even though the description was used for the purpose of referring. There is no rock, nor anything else, to which I meant to refer; it was, perhaps, a trick of light that made me think there was a man there. I cannot say of anything, "That is what I was referring to, though I now see that it's not a man carrying a walking stick." This failure of reference, however, requires circumstances much more radical than the mere nonexistence of anything fitting the description used. It requires that there be nothing of which it can be said, "That is what he was referring to." Now perhaps also in such cases, if the speaker has asserted something, he fails to state anything true or false if there is nothing that can be identified as that to which he referred. But if so, the failure of reference and truth value does not come about merely because nothing fits the description he used. So (3) may be true of some cases of the referential use of definite descriptions; it may be true that a failure of reference results in a lack of truth value. But these cases are of a much more extreme sort than Strawson's theory implies.

I conclude, then, that neither Russell's nor Strawson's theory represents a correct account of the use of definite descriptions—Russell's because it ignores altogether the referential use, Strawson's because it fails to make the distinction between the referential and the attributive and mixes together truths about each (together with some things that are false).

VII

It does not seem possible to say categorically of a definite description in a particular sentence that it is a referring expression (of course, one could say this if he meant that it *might* be used to refer). In general, whether or not a definite description is used referentially or attributively is a function of the speaker's intentions in a particular case. "The murderer of Smith" may be used either way in the sentence "The murderer of Smith is insane." It does not appear plausible to account for this, either, as an ambiguity in the sentence. The grammatical structure of the sentence seems to me to be the same whether the description is used referentially or attributively: that is, it is not syntactically ambiguous. Nor does it seem at all attractive to suppose an ambiguity in the meaning of the words; it does not appear to be semantically ambiguous. (Perhaps we could say that the sentence is pragmatically ambiguous: the distinction between roles that the description plays is a function of the speaker's intentions.) These, of course, are intuitions; I do not have an argument for these conclusions. Nevertheless, the burden of proof is surely on the other side.

This, I think, means that the view, for example, that sentences can be divided up into predicates, logical operators, and referring expressions is not generally true. In the case of definite descriptions one cannot always assign the referential function in isolation from a particular occasion on which it is used.

There may be sentences in which a definite description can be used only attributively or only referentially. A sentence in which it seems that the definite description could be used only attributively would be "Point out the man who is drinking my martini." I am not so certain that any can be found in which the definite description can be used only referentially. Even if there are such sentences, it does not spoil the point that there are many sentences, apparently not ambiguous either syntactically or semantically, containing definite descriptions that can be used either way.

If it could be shown that the dual use of definite descriptions can be accounted for by the presence of an ambiguity, there is still a point to be made against the theories of Strawson and Russell. For neither, so far as I can see, has anything to say about the possibility of such an ambiguity and, in fact, neither seems compatible with such a possibility. Russell's does not recognize the possibility of the referring use, and Strawson's, as I have tried to show in the last section, combines elements from each use into one unitary account. Thus the view that there is an ambiguity in such sentences does not seem any more attractive to these positions.

VIII

Using a definite description referentially, a speaker may say something true even though the description correctly applies to nothing. The sense in which he may say something true is the sense in which he may say something true about someone or something. This sense is, I think, an interesting one that needs investigation. Isolating it is one of the by-products of the distinction between the attributive and referential uses of definite descriptions.

For one thing, it raises questions about the notion of a statement. This is brought out by considering a passage in a paper by Leonard Linsky in which he rightly makes the point that one can refer to someone although the definite description used does not correctly describe the person:

> ... said of a spinster that "Her husband is kind to her" is neither true nor false. But a speaker might very well be referring to someone using these words, for he may think that someone is the husband of the lady (who in fact is a spinster). Still, the statement is neither true nor false, for it presupposes that the lady has a husband, which she has not. This last refutes Strawson's thesis that if the presupposition of existence is not satisfied, the speaker has failed to refer. [13]

There is much that is right in this passage. But because Linsky does not make the distinction between the referential and the attributive uses of definite descriptions, it does not represent a wholly adequate account of the situation. A perhaps minor point about this passage is that Linsky apparently thinks it sufficient to establish that the speaker in his example is referring to someone by using the definite description "her husband," that he *believe* that someone is her husband. This will only approximate the truth provided that the "someone" in the description of the belief means "someone in particular" and is not merely the existential quantifier, "there is someone or other." For in both the attributive and the referential use the belief that someone *or other* is the husband of the lady is very likely to be present. If, for example, the speaker has just met the lady and, noticing her cheerfulness and radiant good health, makes his remark from his conviction that these attributes are always the result of having good husbands, he would be using the definite description attributively. Since she has no husband, there is no one to pick out as the person to whom he was referring. Nevertheless, the speaker believed that *someone or other* was her husband. On the other hand, if the use of "her husband" was simply a way of referring to a man the speaker has just met whom he assumed to be the lady's husband, he would have referred to that man even though neither he nor anyone else fits the description. I think it is likely that in this passage Linsky did mean by "someone," in his description of the belief, "someone in particular." But even then, as we have seen, we have neither a sufficient nor a necessary condition for a referential use of the definite description. A definite description can be used attributively even when the speaker believes that some particular thing or person fits the description, and it can be used referentially in the absence of this belief.

My main point, here, however, has to do with Linsky's view that because the presupposition is not satisfied, the *statement* is neither true nor false. This seems to me possibly correct *if* the definite description is thought of as being used attributively (depending upon whether we go with Strawson or Russell). But when we consider it as used referentially, this categorical assertion is no longer clearly correct. For the man the speaker referred to may indeed be kind to the spinster; the speaker may have said something true about that man. Now the difficulty is in the notion of "the statement." Suppose that we know that the lady is a spinster, but nevertheless know that the man referred to by the speaker is kind to her. It seems to me that we shall, on the one hand, want to hold that the speaker said something true, but be reluctant to express this by "It is true that her husband is kind to her."

This shows, I think, a difficulty in speaking simply about "the statement" when definite descriptions are used referentially. For the speaker stated something, in this example, about a particular person, and his statement, we may suppose, was true. Nevertheless, we should not like to agree with his statement by using the sentence he used; we should not like to identify the true statement via the speaker's words. The reason for this is not so hard to find. If we say, in this example, "It is true that her husband is kind to her," *we* are now using the definite description either attributively or referentially. But we should not be subscribing to what the original speaker truly said if we use the description attributively, for it was only in its function as referring to a particular person that the definite description yields the possibility of saying something true (since the lady has no husband). Our reluctance, however, to endorse the original speaker's statement by using the definite description referentially to refer to the same person stems from quite a different consideration. For if we too were laboring under the mistaken belief that this man was the lady's husband, we could agree with the original speaker using his exact words. (Moreover, it is possible, as we have seen, deliberately to use a definite description to to refer to someone we believe not to fit the description.) Hence, our reluctance to use the original speaker's words does not arise from the fact that if we did we should not succeed in stating anything true or false. It rather stems from the fact that when a definite description is used referentially there is a presumption that the speaker believes that what he refers to fits the description. Since we, who know the lady to be a spinster, would not normally want to give the impression that we believe otherwise, we would not like to use the original speaker's way of referring to the man in question.

How then would we express agreement with the original speaker without involving ourselves in unwanted impressions about our beliefs? The answer shows another difference between the referential and attributive uses of definite descriptions and brings out an important point about genuine referring.

When a speaker says, "The ϕ is ψ," where "the ϕ" is used attributively, if there is no ϕ, we cannot correctly report the speaker as having said *of* this or that person or thing that it is ψ. But if the definite description is used referentially we can report the speaker as having attributed ψ to something. And *we* may refer to what the speaker referred to, using whatever description or name suits our purpose. Thus, if a speaker says, "Her husband is kind to her," referring to the man he was just talking to, and if that man is Jones, we may report him as having said *of Jones* that he is kind to her. If Jones is also the president of the college, we may report the speaker as having said *of the president of the college* that he is kind to her. And finally, if we are talking to Jones, we may say, referring to the original speaker, "He said of you that *you* are kind to her." It does not matter here whether or not the woman has a husband or whether, if she does, Jones is her husband. If the original speaker referred to Jones, he said of him that he is kind to her. Thus where the definite description is used referentially, but does not fit what was referred to, we can report what a speaker said and agree with him by using a description or name which does fit. In doing so we need not, it is important to note, choose a description or name which the original speaker would agree fits what he was referring to. That is, we can report the speaker in the above case to have said truly of Jones that he is kind to her even if the original speaker did not know that the man he was referring to is named Jones or even if he thinks he is not named Jones.

Returning to what Linsky said in the passage quoted, he claimed that, were someone to say "Her husband is kind to her," when she has no husband, *the statement* would be neither true nor false. As I have said, this is a likely view to hold if the definite description is being used attributively. But if it is being used referentially it is not clear what is meant by "the statement." If we think about what the speaker said about the person he referred to, then there is no reason to suppose he has not said something true or false about him, even though he is not the lady's husband. And Linsky's claim would be wrong. On the other hand, if we do not identify the statement in this way, what is the statement that the speaker made? To say that the statement he made was that her husband is kind to her lands us in difficulties. For we have to decide whether in using the definite description here in the identification of the statement, we are using it attributively or referentially. If the former, then we misrepresent the linguistic performance of the speaker; if the latter, then we are ourselves referring to someone and reporting the speaker to have said something of that person, in which case we are back to the possibility that he did say something true or false of that person.

I am thus drawn to the conclusion that when a speaker uses a definite description referentially he may have stated something true or false even if nothing fits the description, and that there is not a clear sense in which he has made a statement which is neither true nor false.

IX

I want to end by a brief examination of a picture of what a genuine referring expression is that one might derive from Russell's views. I want to suggest that this picture is not so far wrong as one might suppose and that strange as this may seem, some of the things we have said about the referential use of definite descriptions are not foreign to this picture.

Genuine proper names, in Russell's sense, would refer to something without ascribing any properties to it. They would, one might say, refer to the thing itself, not simply the thing in so far as it falls under a certain description.[14] Now this would seem to Russell something a definite description could not do, for he assumed that if definite descriptions were capable of referring at all, they would refer to something only in so far as that thing satisfied the description. Not only have we seen this assumption to be false, however, but in the last section we saw something more. We saw that when a definite description is used referentially, a speaker can be reported as having said something *of* something. And in reporting what it was of which he said something we are not restricted to the description he used, or synonyms of it; we may ourselves refer to it using any descriptions, names, and so forth, that will do the job. Now this seems to give a sense in which we are concerned with the thing itself and not just the thing under a certain description, when we report the linguistic act of a speaker using a definite description referentially. That is, such a definite description comes closer to performing the function of Russell's proper names than certainly he supposed.

Secondly, Russell thought, I believe, that whenever we use descriptions, as opposed to proper names, we introduce an element of generality which ought to be absent if what we are doing is referring to some particular thing. This is clear from his analysis of sentences containing definite descriptions. One of the conclusions we are supposed to draw from that analysis is that such sentences express what are in reality completely general propositions: there is a ϕ and only one such and any ϕ is ψ. We might put this in a slightly different way. If there is anything which might be identified as reference here, it is reference in a very weak sense—namely, reference to *whatever* is the one and only one ϕ, if there is any such. Now this is something we might well say about the attributive use of definite descriptions, as should be evident from the previous discussion. But this lack of particularity is absent from the referential use of definite descriptions precisely because the description is here merely a device for getting one's audience to pick out or think of the thing to be spoken about, a device which may serve its function even if the description is incorrect. More importantly perhaps, in the referential use as opposed to the attributive, there is a *right* thing to be picked out by the audience and its being the right thing is not simply a function of its fitting the description.

Notes

1. I should like to thank my colleagues, John Canfield, Sydney Shoemaker, and Timothy Smiley, who read an earlier draft and gave me helpful suggestions. I also had the benefit of the valuable and detailed comments of the referee for the paper, to whom I wish to express my gratitude.

2. "On Denoting," reprinted in *Logic and Knowledge*, ed. by Robert C. Marsh (London, 1956), p. 51.

3. "On Referring," reprinted in *Philosophy and Ordinary Language*, ed. by Charles C. Caton (Urbana, 1963), pp. 162–163. [Chap. 16 in this volume.]

4. *Ibid.*, p. 162.

5. *Ibid.*, p. 170.

5. Here and elsewhere I use the disjunction "presuppose or imply" to avoid taking a stand that would side me with Russell or Strawson on the issue of what the relationship involved is. To take a stand here would be beside my main point as well as being misleading, since later on I shall argue that the presupposition or implication arises in a different way depending upon the use to which the definite description is put. This last also accounts for my use of the vagueness indicator, "in some sense."

7. In a footnote added to the original version of "On Referring" (*op. cit.*, p. 181) Strawson seems to imply that where the presupposition is false, we still succeed in referring in a "secondary" way, which seems to mean "as we could be said to refer to fictional or make-believe things." But his view is still that we cannot refer in such a case in the "primary" way. This is, I believe, wrong. For a discussion of this modification of Strawson's view see Charles C. Caton, "Strawson on Referring," *Mind*, LXVIII (1959), 539–544.

8. This is an adaptation of an example (used for a somewhat different purpose) given by Leonard Linsky in "Reference and Referents," in *Philosophy and Ordinary Language*, p. 80.

9. In "Reference and Referents" (pp. 74–75, 80), Linsky correctly points out that one does not fail to refer simply because the description used does not in fact fit anything (or fits more than one thing). Thus he pinpoints one of the difficulties in Strawson's view. Here, however, I use this fact about referring to make a distinction I believe he does not draw, between two uses of definite descriptions. I later discuss the second passage from Linsky's paper.

10. In "A Reply to Mr. Sellars," *Philosophical Review*, LXIII (1954), 216–231, Strawson admits that we do not always refuse to ascribe truth to what a person says when the definite description he uses fails to fit anything (or fits more than one thing). To cite one of his examples, a person who said, "The United States Chamber of Deputies contains representatives of two major parties," would be allowed to have said something true even though he had used the wrong title. Strawson thinks this does not constitute a genuine problem for his view. He thinks that what we do in such cases, "where the speaker's intended reference is pretty clear, is simply to amend his statement in accordance with his guessed intentions and assess the amended statement for truth or falsity; we are not awarding a truth value at all to the original statement" (p. 230).

The notion of an "amended statement," however, will not do. We may note, first of all, that the sort of case Strawson has in mind could arise only when a definite description is used referentially. For the "amendment" is made by seeing the speaker's intended reference. But this could happen only if the speaker had an intended reference, a particular person or thing in mind, independent of the description he used. The cases Strawson has in mind are presumably not cases of slips of the tongue or the like; presumably they are cases in which a definite description is used because the speaker believes, though he is mistaken, that he is describing correctly what he wants to refer to. We supposedly amend the statement by knowing to what he intends to refer. But what description is to be used in the amended statement? In the example, perhaps, we could use "the United States Congress." But this description might be one the speaker would not even accept as correctly describing what he wants to refer to, because he is misinformed about the correct title. Hence, this is not a case of deciding what the speaker meant to say as opposed to what he in fact said, for the speaker did not mean to say "the United States Congress." If this is so, then there is no bar to the "amended" statement containing any description that does correctly pick out what the speaker intended to refer to. It could be, e.g., "The lower house of the United States Congress." But this means that there is no one unique "amended" statement to be assessed for truth value. And, in fact, it should now be clear that the notion of the amended statement really plays no role anyway. For if we can arrive at the amended statement only by first knowing to what the speaker intended to refer, we can assess the truth of what he said simply by deciding whether what he intended to refer to has the properties he ascribed to it.

11. As noted earlier (n. 7), Strawson may allow that one has possibly referred in a "secondary" way, but, if I am right, the fact that there is no ϕ does not preclude one from having referred in the same way one does if there is a ϕ.

12. For a further discussion of the notion of saying something true *of* someone or something, see sec. VIII.

13. "Reference and Referents," p. 80. It should be clear that I agree with Linsky in holding that a speaker may refer even though the "presupposition of existence" is not satisfied. And I agree in thinking this an objection to Strawson's view. I think, however, that this point, among others, can be used to define two distinct uses of definite descriptions which, in turn, yields a more general criticism of Strawson. So, while I develop here a point of difference, which grows out of the distinction I want to make, I find myself in agreement with much of Linsky's article.

14. Cf. "The Philosophy of Logical Atomism," reprinted in *Logic and Knowledge*, p. 200.

Chapter 18

Speaker's Reference and Semantic Reference[1]

Saul A. Kripke

I am going to discuss some issues inspired by a well-known paper of Keith Donnellan, "Reference and Definite Descriptions,"[2] but the interest—to me—of the contrast mentioned in my title goes beyond Donnellan's paper: I think it is of considerable constructive as well as critical importance to the philosophy of language. These applications, however, and even everything I might want to say relative to Donnellan's paper, cannot be discussed in full here because of problems of length.

Moreover, although I have a considerable interest in the substantive issues raised by Donnellan's paper, and by related literature, my own conclusions will be methodological, not substantive. I can put the matter this way: Donnellan's paper claims to give decisive objections both to Russell's theory of definite descriptions (taken as a theory about English) and to Strawson's. My concern is *not* primarily with the question: is Donnellan right, or is Russell (or Strawson)? Rather, it is with the question: do the considerations *in Donnellan's paper* refute Russell's theory (or Strawson's)? For definiteness, I will concentrate on Donnellan versus Russell, leaving Strawson aside. And about this issue I will draw a definite conclusion, one which I think will illuminate a few methodological maxims about language. Namely, I will conclude that the considerations in Donnellan's paper, *by themselves*, do *not* refute Russell's theory.

Any conclusions about Russell's views *per se*, or Donnellan's, must be tentative. If I were to be asked for a tentative stab about Russell, I would say that although his theory does a far better job of handling ordinary discourse than many have thought, and although many popular arguments

First appeared in P. A. French, T. E. Uehling Jr., and H. K. Wettstein (eds.), *Studies in the Philosophy of Language*, Midwest Studies in Philosophy, no. 2 (Minneapolis: University of Minnesota Press, 1977). Reprinted by permission of Saul Kripke.

against it are inconclusive, probably it ultimately fails. The considerations I have in mind have to do with the existence of "improper" definite descriptions, such as "the table," where uniquely specifying conditions are not contained in the description itself. Contrary to the Russellian picture, I doubt that such descriptions can always be regarded as elliptical with some uniquely specifying conditions added. And it may even be the case that a true picture will resemble various aspects of Donnellan's in important respects. But such questions will largely be left aside here.

I will state my preference for one substantive conclusion (although I do not feel completely confident of it either): that unitary theories, like Russell's, are preferable to theories that postulate an ambiguity. And much, though not all, of Donnellan's paper seems to postulate a (semantic) ambiguity between his "referential" and "attributive" uses. But—as we shall see—Donnellan is not entirely consistent on this point, and I therefore am not sure whether I am expressing disagreement with him even here.[3]

1 PRELIMINARY CONSIDERATIONS

Donnellan claims that a certain linguistic phenomenon argues against Russell's theory. According to Russell, if someone says, "The x such that $\phi(x)$ ψ's," he means that there is an x which uniquely satisfies "$\phi(x)$" and that any such x satisfies "$\psi(x)$." (I.e., $(\exists x) (\phi!(x) \wedge \psi(x))$, where "$\phi!(x)$" abbreviates "$\phi(x) \wedge (y)(\phi(y) \supset y = x)$"). Donnellan argues that some phenomenon of the following kind tells against Russell: Suppose someone at a gathering, glancing in a certain direction, says to his companion,

(1) "The man over there drinking champagne is happy tonight."

Suppose both the speaker and hearer are under a false impression, and that the man to whom they refer is a teetotaler, drinking sparkling water. He may, nevertheless, be happy. Now, if there is no champagne drinker over there, Russell would regard (1) as false, and Frege and Strawson would give it a truth-value gap. Nevertheless, as Donnellan emphasizes, we have a substantial intuition that the speaker said something true of the man to whom he referred in spite of his misimpression.

Since no one is really drinking champagne, the case involves a definite description that is empty, or vacuous, according to both Russell and Frege. So as to avoid any unnecessary and irrelevant entanglements of the present question with the issues that arise when definite descriptions are vacuous, I shall modify this case (and all other cases where, in Donnellan's paper, the description was vacuous).[4] Suppose that "over there," exactly one man *is* drinking champagne, although his glass is not visible to the speaker (nor to his hearer). Suppose that he, unlike the teetotaler to whom the speaker refers, has been driven to drink precisely by his misery. Then *all* the classical theories (both Russellian and Fregean) would regard (1) as false (since exactly one man over there is drinking champagne, and he is *not* happy tonight). Now the speaker has spoken *truly* of the man to whom he refers (the teetotaler), yet this dimension is left out in all the classical analyses, which would assign falsehood to his assertion solely on the basis of the misery of *someone else* whom *no one* was talking about (the champagne drinker). Previously Linsky had given a similar example. He gave it as an empty case; once again I modify it to make the description non-vacuous. Someone sees a woman with a man. Taking the man to be her husband, and observing his attitude towards her, he says, "Her husband is kind to her," and someone else may nod, "Yes, he seems to be." Suppose the man in question is not her husband. Suppose he is her lover, to whom she has been driven precisely by her husband's cruelty. Once again both the Russellian analysis and the Fregean analysis would assess the statement as false, and both would do so on the basis of the cruelty of a man neither participant in the dialogues was talking about.

Again, an example suggested to me by a remark of L. Crocker: suppose a religious narrative (similar, say, to the Gospels) consistently refers to its main protagonist as "The Messiah." Suppose a historian wishes to assess the work for *historical accuracy*—that is, he wishes to determine whether it gives an accurate account of the life of its hero (whose identity we assume to be established). Does it matter to this question whether the hero really was the Messiah, as long as the author took him to be so, and addressed his work to a religious community that shared this belief? Surely not. And note that it is no mere "principle of charity" that is operating here. On the contrary, if someone other than the person intended were really the Messiah, and if, by a bizarre and unintended coincidence, the narrative gave a fairly true account of *his* life, we would not for that reason call it "historically true." On the contrary, we would regard the work as historically *false* if the events mentioned were false of its intended protagonist. Whether the story happened to fit the true Messiah—who may have been totally unknown to the author and even have lived after the time the work was composed—would be irrelevant.

Once again, this fact seems inconsistent with the positions both of Frege and of Russell.

On the basis of such examples, Donnellan distinguishes two uses of definite descriptions. In the "attributive" use, a speaker "states something about whoever or whatever is the so-and-so." In the "referential" use, a speaker "uses the description to enable his audience to pick out whom or what he is talking about and states something about that person or thing. In the first [attributive] case, the definite description might be said to occur essentially, for the speaker wishes to assert something about whatever or whoever fits that description; but in the referential use the definite description is merely one tool for ... calling attention to a person or thing ... and ... any other device for doing the same job, another description or name, would do as well."[5] For example, suppose I come upon Smith foully murdered. The condition of Smith's body moves me to say, "Smith's murderer is (must be) insane." Then we have an *attributive* use: we speak of the murderer, whoever he may be. On the other hand, suppose that Jones is on trial for Smith's murder and that I am among the spectators in the courtroom. Observing the wild behavior of the defendant at the dock, I may say, "Smith's murderer is insane." (I forgot the defendant's name, but am firmly convinced of his guilt.) Then my use is referential: whether or not Jones was the real murderer, and even if someone else was, if Jones accused me of libel, his failure to fit my description would give me no defense. All of the previous cases, (the teetotaling "champagne" drinker, the lover taken for a husband, the false Messiah), are all referential in Donnellan's sense.

An intuitive mark of the attributive use is the legitimacy of the parenthetical comment, "whoever he is." In the first case, we may say "Smith's murderer, whoever he is, is insane," but not in the second. But we should not be misled: a definite description may be used attributively even if the speaker believes that a certain person, say, Jones, fits it, provided that he is talking about *whoever* fits, and his belief that Jones in fact fits is not relevant. In the case where I deduce the murderer's insanity from the condition of Smith's body, I use the description attributively even if I suspect, or even am firmly convinced, that Jones is the culprit.

I have no doubt that the distinction Donnellan brings out exists and is of fundamental importance, though I do not regard it as exclusive or exhaustive. But Donnellan also believes that Russell's theory applies, if at all, only to attributive uses (p. 371), and that referential uses of definite descriptions are close to proper names, even to Russell's "logically proper" names (see p. 362 and Section IX). And he appears to believe that the examples of the referential uses mentioned above are inexplicable on Russell's theory. It is these views that I wish to examine.

2   SOME ALLEGED APPLICATIONS OF THE DISTINCTION

Some alleged applications of Donnellan's distinction have entered the oral tradition, and even to an extent, the written tradition, that are not in Donnellan's paper. I will mention some that I find questionable. Unfortunately I will have to discuss these applications more briefly than the issues in question really deserve, since they are ancillary to the main theme.

2a   De dicto–de re

Many able people, in and out of print, have implied that Donnellan's distinction has something to do with, can be identified with, or can replace, the *de dicto–de re* distinction, or the small scope-large scope distinction in modal or intensional contexts.

"The number of planets is necessarily odd" can mean two things, depending on whether it is interpreted *de dicto* or *de re*. If it is interpreted *de dicto*, it asserts that the proposition that the number of planets is odd is a necessary truth—something I take to be false (there might have been eight planets). If it is interpreted *de re*, it asserts that the actual number of planets (nine) has the property of necessary oddness (essentialists like me take this to be true). Similarly, if we say, "Jones believes that the richest debutante in Dubuque will marry him," we may mean that Jones's belief has a certain content, viz., that the richest debutante in Dubuque will marry him; or we may mean that he believes, *of* a girl who is (in fact) the richest in Dubuque, that she will marry him. The view in question suggests that the *de dicto* case is to be identified with Donnellan's *attributive* use, the *de re* with the *referential*.

Any such assimilation, in my opinion, is confused. (I don't think Donnellan makes it.) There are many objections; I will mention a few. First, the *de dicto* use of the definite description cannot be identified with either the *referential* or the *attributive* use. Here the basic point was already noticed by Frege. If a description is embedded in a (*de dicto*) intensional context, we cannot be said to be talking *about* the thing described, either *qua* its satisfaction of the description or *qua* anything else. Taken *de dicto*, "Jones believes that the richest debutante in Dubuque will marry him," can be asserted by someone who thinks (let us suppose, wrongly) that there are *no* debutantes in Dubuque; certainly then, he is in no way talking about the richest debutante, even "attributively." Similarly, "It is possible that (France should have a monarchy in 1976, and that) the king of France in 1976 should have been bald" is true, if read *de dicto*; yet we are not using "the king of France in 1976" attributively to speak of the king of France in 1976, for there is none. Frege concluded that "the king of France in 1976" refers, in these contexts, to its ordinary sense; at any rate, if we wish to speak of "reference" here, it cannot be to the non-existent king. Even if there were such a king, the quoted assertion would say nothing about *him*, if read *de dicto*: to say that *he* might have been bald, would be *de re* (indeed, this *is* the distinction in question).

Second, and even more relevantly, Donnellan's referential use cannot be identified with the *de re* use. (I think Donnellan would agree.) Suppose I have no idea how many planets there are, but (for some reason) astronomical theory dictates that that number must be odd. If I say, "The number of planets (whatever it may be) is odd," my description is used attributively. If I am an essentialist, I will also say, "The number of planets (whatever it may be) is necessarily odd," on the grounds that all odd numbers are necessarily odd; and my usage is just as attributive as in the first case. In "Smith's murderer, whoever he may be, is known to the police, but they're not saying," or, more explicitly, "The police know concerning Smith's murderer, whoever he is, that he committed the murder; but they're not saying who he is," "Smith's murderer" is used attributively, but is *de re*.

Finally: Russell wished to handle the *de dicto–de re* distinction by his notion of the *scope* of a description. Some have suggested that Donnellan's referential-attributive distinction can replace Russell's distinction of scope. But *no* twofold distinction can do this job. Consider:

(2) The number of planets might have been necessarily even.

In a natural use, (2) can be interpreted as true: for example, there might have been exactly eight planets, in which case the number of planets would have been even, and hence necessarily even. (2), interpreted as true, is neither *de re* nor *de dicto*; that is, the definite description neither has the largest nor the smallest possible scope. Consider:

(2a) $\Diamond \Box (\exists x)$ (There are exactly x planets and x is even)
(2b) $(\exists x)$ (There are exactly x planets and $\Diamond \Box$ (x is even)).
(2c) $\Diamond (\exists x)$ (There are exactly x planets and $\Box$ (x is even)).

(2a)–(2c) give three alternative Russellian analyses of (2). (2a) gives the description the smallest possible scope (*de dicto*); it says, presumably falsely, that it might have been necessary that there was an even number of planets. (2b) gives the description the largest possible scope (*de re*); it says, still falsely, of the actual number of planets (viz., nine) that it might have been necessarily even. (2c) is the interpretation which makes (2) true. When intensional operators are iterated, intermediate scopes are possible. Three analogous interpretations are possible, say, for "Jones doubts that Holmes believes that Smith's murderer is insane"; or (using an indefinite description) for "Hoover charged that the Berrigans plotted to kidnap a high American official." (I actually read something like this last in a newspaper and wondered what was meant.)[6] This may mean: (a) there is a particular high official such that Hoover charged that the Berrigans plotted to kidnap him (largest scope, *de re*, this was the interpretation intended); or (b) Hoover charged that the Berrigans plotted as follows: let's kidnap a high official (smallest scope, *de dicto*); or (c) Hoover charged that there was a high official (whose identity may have been unknown to Hoover) whom the Berrigans planned to kidnap (intermediate scope).

As intensional (or other) constructions are iterated, there are more and more possible scopes for a definite description. No *twofold* distinction can replace Russell's notion of scope.[7] In particular, neither the *de dicto–de re* distinction nor the referential-attributive distinction can do so.

2b   Rigid definite descriptions

If definite descriptions, $\imath x\phi(x)$, are taken as primitive and assigned reference, then the conventional non-rigid assignment assigns to such a description, with respect to each possible world, the unique object, if any, which would have ϕ'd in that world. (Forget the vacuous case, which requires a further convention.) For example, "the number of planets" denotes eight, speaking of a counterfactual situation where there would have been eight planets (and "the number of planets is even" is true of such a situation). Another type of definite description, $\imath x\phi x$, a "rigid" definite description, could be introduced semantically by the following stipulation: let $\imath x\phi x$ denote, with respect to all possible worlds, the unique object that (actually) ϕ's (then "the number of planets is odd," as interpreted, expresses a necessary truth). Both kinds of definite descriptions can obviously be introduced, theoretically, into a single formal language, perhaps by the notations just given. Some have suggested that definite descriptions, in English, are *ambiguous* between the two readings. It has further been suggested that the two types of definite descriptions, the nonrigid and the rigid, are the source of the *de dicto–de re* distinction and should replace Russell's notion of scope for the purpose. Further, it has been suggested that they amount to the same thing as Donnellan's attributive-referential distinction.[8]

My comments will be brief, so as to avoid too much excursus. Although I have an open mind on the subject, I am not yet convinced that there is any clear evidence for such an ambiguity. Being a twofold distinction, the ambiguity alleged cannot replace Russell's notion of scope, for the reasons given above. Once Russell's notion is available, it can be used to handle the *de dicto–de re* distinction; a further ambiguity seems unnecessary. More relevantly to the present context, the "rigid" sense of a definite description, if it exists, cannot be identified with Donnellan's "referential" use. I take it that the identification of the referential use with the rigid definite description was inspired by some line of reasoning like this: Donnellan holds that referential descriptions are those close to proper names, even to Russell's "logically proper names." But surely proper names, or at least, Russellian "logically proper names," are rigid. Hence Donnellan's referential descriptions are just the rigid definite descriptions.

If we assume that Donnellan thinks of names as rigid, as I think of them, his referential definite descriptions *would* most plausibly be taken to refer rigidly to their referents. But it is not clear that he does agree with me on the rigidity of such reference.[9] More important, a rigid definite description, as defined above, still determines its referent via its unique satisfaction of the associated property—and this fact separates the notion of such a description from that of a referential description, as Donnellan defines it. David Kaplan has suggested that a demonstrative "that" can be used, in English, to make any definite description rigid. "That bastard—the man who killed Smith, whoever he may be—is surely insane!" The subject term rigidly designates Smith's murderer, but it is still attributive in Donnellan's sense.[10]

2c

In "Naming and Necessity,"[11] one argument I presented against the description (or cluster-of-descriptions) theory of proper names concerned cases where the referent of a name, the person named by the name, did not satisfy the descriptions usually associated with it, and someone else did. For example, the name "Gödel" might be taken to mean "the man who proved the incompleteness of arithmetic"; but even if Gödel had been a fraud, who had proved nothing at all and had misappropriated his work from an unknown named "Schmidt," our term "Gödel" would refer to the fraud, not to the man who really satisfied the definite description. Against this it has been said that although the argument does succeed in its main purpose of refuting the description theory as a theory of reference (that is, it shows that the descriptive properties cited do not determine the referent), it does nothing to show that names are not abbreviated definite descriptions, because we could take the descriptions in question to be referential in Donnellan's sense. Referential descriptions can easily refer to things that fail to satisfy the descriptions; nothing in my argument shows that names are not synonymous with such descriptions.[12]

My reaction to such an argument may become clearer later. For the moment, (too) briefly: In the case of "Her husband is kind to her," and similar cases, "her husband" can refer to her lover, as long as we are under the misapprehension that the man to whom we refer (the lover) *is* her husband. Once we are apprised of the true facts, we will no longer so refer to him (see, for example, pp. 376–377 of Donnellan's paper). Similarly, someone can use "the man who proved the incompleteness of arithmetic," as a referential definite description, to refer to Gödel; it might be so used, for example, by someone who had forgotten his name. If the hypothetical fraud were discovered, however, the description is no longer usable as a device to refer to Gödel; henceforth it can be used only to refer to Schmidt. We would withdraw any previous assertions using the description to refer to Gödel (unless they also were true of Schmidt). We would *not* similarly withdraw the *name* "Gödel," even after the fraud was discovered; "Gödel" would still be used to name Gödel, not Schmidt. The name and the description, therefore, are not synonymous. (See also note 27 below).

3   THE MAIN PROBLEM

3a   A disagreement with Russell?

Do Donnellan's observations provide an argument against Russell's theory? Do his *views* contradict Russell's? One might think that if Donnellan is right, Russell must be wrong, since Donnellan's truth conditions for statements containing referential definite descriptions differ from Russell's. Unfortunately, this is not so clear. Consider the case of "Her husband is kind to her," mistakenly said of the lover. If Donnellan had roundly asserted that the quoted statement is true if and only if the *lover* is kind to her, regardless of the kindness of the husband, the issue between him and Russell would be clearly joined. But Donnellan doesn't say this: rather he says that the speaker has referred to a certain person, the lover, and said of *him* that he is kind to her. But if we ask, "Yes, but was the statement he made true?", Donnellan would hedge. For if *we* are not under the misimpression that the man the speaker referred to was her husband, *we* would not express the same assertion by "Her husband is kind to her." "If it ['her husband'] is being used referentially, it is not clear what is meant by 'the statement.' ... To say that the statement he made was that her husband is kind to her lands us in difficulties. For we [in so reporting what the speaker said must use the definite description] either attributively or referentially. If the former, then we misrepresent the linguistic performance of the speaker; if the latter, then we ourselves are referring to someone," and ordinarily we can refer to someone as "her husband" only if we take him to be her husband.[13]

Since Donnellan does not clearly assert that the statement "her husband is kind to her" ever has non-Russelian truth conditions, he has *not*, so far, clearly contradicted Russell's theory. His argument, as he presents it, that there is a problem in reporting "the statement" is questionable, in two ways.

First, it uses the premise that if we say, "Jones said that her husband is kind to her," we ourselves must use the description attributively or referentially; but, as we saw, a definite description in indirect discourse is *neither* referential nor attributive.[14]

Second, there is an important problem about the nature of the referential-attributive distinction. Donnellan says that his distinction is neither syntactic nor semantic:

The grammatical structure of the sentence seems to me to be the same whether the description is used referentially or attributively: that is, it is not syntactically ambiguous. Nor does it seem at all attractive to suppose an ambiguity in the meaning of the words; it does not appear to be semantically ambiguous. (Perhaps we could say that the sentence is pragmatically ambiguous: the distinction between roles that the description plays is a function of the speaker's intentions.) These, of course, are intuitions; I do not have an argument for these conclusions. Nevertheless, the burden of proof is surely on the other side.[15]

Suppose for the moment that this is so. Then if the referential-attributive distinction is pragmatic, rather than syntactic or semantic, it is presumably a distinction about speech acts. There is no reason to suppose that in making an indirect discourse report on what someone else has said I myself must have similar intentions, or be engaged in the same kind of speech act; in fact, it is clear that I am not. If I say "Jones said the police were around the corner," Jones may have said it as a warning, but *I* need not say it as a warning. If the referential-attributive distinction is neither syntactic nor semantic, there is no reason, without further argument, to suppose that my usage, in indirect discourse, should match the man on whom I report, as referential or attributive. The case is quite different for a genuine semantic ambiguity. If Jones says, "I have never been at a bank," and I report this, saying, "Jones denied that he was ever at a bank," the sense I give to "bank" must match Jones's if my report is to be accurate.

Indeed, the passage seems inconsistent with the whole trend of Donnellan's paper. Donnellan suggests that there is no syntactic or semantic ambiguity in the statement, "Her husband is kind to her." He also suggests that Russell may well give a correct analysis of the attributive use but not of the referential use. Surely this is not coherent. It is not "uses," in some pragmatic sense, but *senses* of a sentence which can be analyzed. If the sentence is *not* (syntactically or) semantically ambiguous, it has only *one* analysis; to say that it has two distinct analyses is to attribute a syntactic or semantic ambiguity to it.

Donnellan's arguments for his refusal to give a truth value to the speaker's assertion, "Her husband is kind to her," seem to be fallacious. My own suggested account of the matter below—in terms of a theory of speech acts—creates no problem about "the statement"; it is simply the statement that her husband is kind to her. But Donnellan's cautious refusal to say, under the circumstances mentioned, that "Her husband is kind to her" is true, seems nevertheless to be intuitively correct. The man to whom the speaker refers is—let us suppose—kind to her. But it seems hard for us to say that when he uttered, "Her husband is kind to her," it expressed a truth, if *we* believe that her husband is unkind to her.

Now Donnellan thinks that he has refuted Russell. But all he has clearly claimed, let alone established, is that a speaker can refer to the lover and say, of him, that he is kind to her by saying "Her husband is kind to her." So, first, we can ask: *If* this claim is correct, does it conflict with Russell's views?

Second, since Donnellan's denial that he advocates a semantic ambiguity in definite descriptions seems inconsistent with much of his paper, we can try ignoring the denial, and take his paper to be arguing for such an ambiguity. Then we may ask: has Donnellan established a (semantic) ambiguity inconsistent with Russell's theory?

3b   General remarks: apparatus

We need a general apparatus to discuss these questions. Some of the apparatus is well known, but I review it for its intrinsic importance and interest. First, let us distinguish, following Grice,[16] between what *the speaker's words meant*, on a given occasion, and what *he meant*, in saying these words, on that occasion. For example, one burglar says to another, "The cops are around the corner." What *the words meant* is clear: the police were around the corner. But *the speaker may well have meant*, "We can't wait around collecting any more loot: Let's split!" That is not *the meaning of the words*, even on that occasion, though that is *what he meant in saying those words, on that occasion*. Suppose he had said, "The cops are inside the bank." Then on that occasion, "bank" meant a commercial bank, not a river bank, and this is relevant to what the *words* meant, on that occasion. (On other occasions, the same words might mean that the police were at a river bank.) But, if the speaker *meant* "Let's split," this is no part of the *meaning of his words*, even on that occasion.

Again (inspired by an example of Grice)[17]: A magician makes a hand-kerchief change color. Someone says, recalling the trick, "Then he put the red handkerchief on the side of the table"; and someone else interjects, cautiously, "It *looked* red." The words meant, on that occasion, that the object referred to (the handkerchief) looked red. What we speak of when we speak of the meaning of his words, on that occasion, includes a disambiguation of the utterance. (Perhaps, on some occasions, where "it" refers to a book, a phonetically identical utterance might mean, "it looked read," well-thumbed and well-perused). But the speaker meant, on this occasion, to suggest that perhaps the handkerchief wasn't really red, that perhaps the trick relied on some kind of illusion. (Note that, on this occasion, not only do the *words* "it looked red" mean what they mean, but also the *speaker* means that it looked red, as well as that it may not have been red. On the other hand, the speaker has no intention of producing a belief in the hearer that the handkerchief looked red, or a belief in the hearer that he (the speaker) believed it looked red. Both facts are common knowledge. The same *could* hold for "The cops are around the corner."[18] Do these examples contradict Grice's analysis of "meaning"? Grice's theory has become very complex and I am not quite sure.)

The notion of what words can mean, in the language, is semantical: it is given by the conventions of our language. What they mean, on a given occasion, is determined, on a given occasion, by these conventions, together with the intentions of the speaker and various contextual features. Finally what the speaker meant, on a given occasion, in saying certain words, derives from various further special intentions of the speaker, together with various general principles, applicable to all human languages regardless of their special conventions. (Cf. Grice's "conversational maxims.") For example, "It looks red" replaced a categorical affirmation of redness. A plausible general principle of human discourse would have it that if a second speaker insists that a stronger assertion should be replaced by a weaker one, he thereby wishes to cast doubt on the stronger assertion; whence, knowing the semantics of English, and the meaning of the speaker's words on this occasion, we can deduce what was meant (the Gricean "conversational implicature").[19]

Let us now speak of speaker's reference and semantic reference: these notions are special cases of the Gricean notions discussed above. If a speaker has a designator in his idiolect, certain conventions of his idiolect[20] (given various facts about the world) determine the referent in the idiolect: that I call the *semantic referent* of the designator. (If the designator is ambiguous, or contains indexicals, demonstratives, or the like, we must speak of the semantic referent on a given occasion. The referent will be determined by the conventions of the language plus the speaker's intentions and various contextual features.)

Speaker's reference is a more difficult notion. Consider, for example, the following case, which I have mentioned elsewhere.[21] Two people see Smith in the distance and mistake him for Jones. They have a brief colloquy: "What is Jones doing?" "Raking the leaves." "Jones," in the common language of both, is a name of Jones; it *never* names Smith. Yet, in some sense, on this occasion, clearly both participants in the dialogue have referred to Smith, and the second participant has said something true about the man he referred to if and only if Smith was raking the leaves (whether or not Jones was). How can we account for this? Suppose a speaker takes it that a certain object a fulfills the conditions for being the semantic referent of a designator, "d." Then, wishing to say something about a, he uses "d" to speak about a; say, he says "$\phi(d)$." Then, he said, of a, on that occasion, that it ϕ'd; in the appropriate Gricean sense (explicated above), he *meant* that a ϕ'd. This is true even if a is not really the semantic referent of "d." If it is not, then *that a ϕ's* is included in what he meant (on that occasion), but not in the meaning of his words (on that occasion).

So, we may tentatively define the speaker's referent of a designator to be that object which the speaker wishes to talk about, on a given occasion, and believes fulfills the conditions for being the semantic referent of the designator. He uses the designator with the intention of making an assertion about the object in question (which may not really be the semantic referent, if the speaker's belief that it fulfills the appropriate semantic conditions is in error). The speaker's referent is the thing the speaker referred to by the designator, though it may not be the referent of the designator, in his idiolect. In the example above, Jones, the man named by the name, is the semantic referent. Smith is the speaker's referent, the correct answer to the question, "To whom were you referring?"[22]

Below, the notion of speaker's reference will be extended to include more cases where existential quantification rather than designation is involved.

In a given idiolect, the semantic referent of a designator (without indexicals) is given by a *general* intention of the speaker to refer to a certain object whenever the designator is used. The speaker's referent is given by a *specific* intention, on a given occasion, to refer to a certain object. If the speaker believes that the object he wants to talk about, on a given occasion, fulfills the conditions for being the semantic referent, then he believes that there is no clash between his general intentions and his specific intentions. My hypothesis is that Donnellan's referential-attributive distinction should be generalized in this light. For the speaker, on a given occasion, may believe that his specific intention coincides with his general intention for one of two reasons. In one case (the "simple" case), his specific intention is simply to refer to the semantic referent: that is, his specific intention *is* simply his general semantic intention. (For example, he uses "Jones" as a name of Jones—elaborate this according to your favorite theory of proper names—and, on this occasion, simply wishes to use "Jones" to refer to Jones.) Alternatively—the "complex" case—he has a specific intention, which is distinct from his general intention, but which he believes, as a matter of fact, to determine the same object as the one determined by his general intention. (For example, he wishes to refer to the man "over there" but believes that he *is* Jones.) In the "simple" case, the speaker's referent is, *by definition*, the semantic referent. In the "complex" case, they may coincide, if the speaker's belief is correct, but they need not. (The man "over there" may be Smith and not Jones.) To anticipate, my hypothesis will be that Donnellan's "attributive" use is nothing but the "simple" case, specialized to definite descriptions, and that the "referential" use is, similarly, the "complex" case. If such a conjecture is correct, it would be wrong to take Donnellan's "referential" use, as he does, to be a use of a description as if it were a proper name. For the distinction of simple and complex cases will apply to proper names just as much as to definite descriptions.

3c   Donnellan's argument against Russell: methodological and substantive considerations

In the light of the notions just developed, consider the argument Donnellan adduces against Russell. Donnellan points to a phenomenon which he alleges to be inexplicable on a Russellian account of English definite descriptions. He accounts for it by positing an ambiguity. Alternatively, we wish to account for the phenomenon on pragmatic grounds, encapsulated in the distinction between speaker's reference and semantic reference. How can we see whether Donnellan's phenomenon conflicts with a Russellian account?

I propose the following test for any alleged counterexample to a linguistic proposal: If someone alleges that a certain linguistic phenomenon in English is a counterexample to a given analysis, consider a hypothetical language which (as much as possible) is like English except that the analysis is *stipulated* to be correct. Imagine such a hypothetical language introduced into a community and spoken by it. *If the phenomenon in question would still arise in a community that spoke such a hypothetical language (which may not be English), then the fact that it arises in English cannot disprove the hypothesis that the analysis is correct for English.* An example removed from the present discussion: Some have alleged that identity cannot be the relation that holds between, and only between, each thing and itself, for if so, the nontriviality of identity statements would be inexplicable. If it is conceded, however, that such a relation makes sense, and if it can be shown that a hypothetical language involving such a relation would generate the same problems, it will follow that the existence of these problems does not refute the hypothesis that "identical to" stands for this same relation in English.[23]

By "the weak Russell language," I will mean a language similar to English except that the truth conditions of sentences with definite descriptions are *stipulated* to coincide with Russell's: for example, "The present King of France is bald" is to be true iff exactly one person is king of France, and that person is bald. On the weak Russell language, this effect can be achieved by assigning semantic reference to definite descriptions: the semantic referent of a definite description is the unique object that satisfies the description, if any; otherwise there is no semantic referent. A sentence of the simple subject-predicate form will be true if the predicate is true of the (semantic) referent of its subject; false, if either the subject has no semantic referent or the predicate is not true of the semantic referent of the subject.

Since the weak Russell language takes definite descriptions to be primitive designators, it is not fully Russellian. By "the intermediate Russell language," I mean a language in which sentences containing definite descriptions are taken to be abbreviations or paraphrases of their Russellian analyses: for example, "The present king of France is bald" *means* (or has a "deep structure" like) "Exactly one person is at present king of France, and he is bald," or the like. Descriptions are not terms, and are not assigned reference or meaning in isolation. The "strong Russell language" goes further: definite descriptions are actually *banned* from the language and Russellian paraphrases are used in their place. Instead of saying "Her husband is kind to her," a speaker of this language must say "Exactly one man is married to her, and he is kind to her," or even (better), "There is a unique man who is married to her, and every man who is married to her is kind to her," or the like. If Russell is right, long-windedness is the only defect of these versions.

Would the phenomenon Donnellan adduces arise in communities that spoke these languages? Surely speakers of these languages are no more infallible than we. They too will find themselves at a party and mistakenly think someone is drinking champagne even though he is actually drinking sparkling water. If they are speakers of the weak or intermediate Russell languages, they will say, "The man in the corner drinking champagne is happy tonight." They will say this precisely because *they think, though erroneously, that the Russellian truth conditions are satisfied.* Wouldn't we say of these speakers that they are referring to the teetotaler, under the misimpression that he is drinking champagne? And, if he is happy, are they not saying of him, *truly*, that he is happy? Both answers seem obviously affirmative.

In the case of the weak Russell language, the general apparatus previously developed seems fully adequate to account for the phenomenon. The semantic referent of a definite description is given by the conditions laid down above: it is a matter of the specific conventions of the (weak)

Russell language, in this case that the referent is the unique object satisfying the descriptive conditions. The speaker's referent, on the other hand, is determined by a general theory of speech acts, applicable to all languages: it is the object to which the speaker wishes to refer, and which he believes fulfills the Russellian conditions for being the semantic referent. Again, in asserting the sentence he does, the speaker means that the speaker's referent (the teetotaler) satisfied the predicate (is happy). Thus the rough theoretical apparatus above accounts fully for our intuitions about this case.

What about the other Russellian languages? Even in the strong Russell language, where explicit descriptions are outlawed, the same phenomena can occur. In fact, they occur in English in "arch" uses of existential quantification: "Exactly *one person* (or: *some* person or other) is drinking champagne in that corner, and I hear he is romantically linked with Jane Smith." The circumlocution, in English, expresses the delicacy of the topic, but the speaker's reference (in quite an ordinary sense) may well be clear, even if he in fact is drinking sparkling water. In English such circumlocutions are common only when the speaker wishes to achieve a rather arch and prissy effect, but in the strong Russell language (which of course isn't English), they would be made more common because the definite article is prohibited.

This example leads to an extension of the notion of speaker's reference. When a speaker asserts an existential quantification, $(\exists x)(\phi x \wedge \psi x)$, it may be clear which thing he has in mind as satisfying "ϕx," and he may wish to convey to his hearers that that thing satisfies "ψx." In this case, the thing in question (which may or may not actually satisfy "ϕx") is called the "speaker's referent" when he makes the existential assertion. In English, as I have mentioned, such cases ("arch" uses) are rather rare; but they can be carried off even if the existential quantification is expressed in a highly roundabout and apparently nonreferring fashion. "Not *everyone* in this room is abstaining from champagne, and any such nonabstainer...."[24]

If the notion of speaker's reference applies to the strong Russell language, it can apply to the intermediate Russell language as well, since the speaker's referent of "$\psi(\imath x\phi(x))$" is then the thing he has in mind as uniquely instantiating "$\phi(x)$" and about which he wishes to convey that it ψ's.

Since the phenomenon Donnellan cites *would* arise in all the Russell languages, if they *were* spoken, the fact that they *do* arise in English, as *actually* spoken, can be no argument that English is not a Russell language.

We may contrast the Russell languages with what may be called the D-languages. In the D-languages the apparent ambiguity between referential and attributive definite descriptions is explicitly built into the semantics of the language and affects truth conditions (The D-languages are meant to suggest "Donnellan," but are not called the "Donnellan languages," since Donnellan, as we have seen, is "ambiguous" as to whether he posits a semantic ambiguity.) The *unambiguous D-language* contains two distinct words, "the" and "ze" (rhymes with "the"). A statement of the form "... the *F* ..." is true iff the predicate represented by the dots is true of the unique object fulfilling F (we need not specify what happens if there is no such thing; if we wish to follow Russell, take it to be false). A statement of the form "... ze F ..." is to be true iff the predicate represented by the dots is true of the unique thing the speaker thinks F is true of. (Once again, we leave free what happens if there is no such thing.) *The ambiguous D-language* is like the unambiguous D-language except that "the," ambiguously, can be interpreted according to the semantics either of "the" *or* of "ze." The general impression conveyed by Donnellan's paper, in spite of his statement at one point to the contrary, is that English is the ambiguous D-language; only on such a hypothesis could we say that the "referential use" (really, referential *sense*) diverges from Russell's theory. The truth-conditions of statements containing "ze," and therefore of one sense of "the" in the ambiguous D-language, *are* incompatible with Russell's theory.[25]

We have two hypotheses: one says that English is a Russell language, while the other says that English is the ambiguous D-language. Which hypothesis is preferable? Since, as we have argued, the phenomena Donnellan adduces would arise in a hypothetical society that spoke any of the Russell languages, the existence in English of such phenomena provides no argument against the hypothesis that English is a Russell language. If Donnellan had possessed a clear intuition that "Her husband is kind to her," uttered in reference to the kind lover of a woman married to a cruel husband, expressed the literal truth, then he *would* have adduced a phenomenon that conforms to the ambiguous D-language but is incompatible with any Russell language. But Donnellan makes no such assertion: he cautiously, and correctly, confines himself to the weaker claim that the speaker spoke truly of the man to whom he referred. This weaker claim, we have seen, *would* hold for a speaker of a Russell language.

So Donnellan's examples provide, in themselves, no evidence that English is the ambiguous D-language rather than a Russell language. Granting that this is so, we can ask whether there is any reason to favor the Russell language hypothesis over the D-language hypothesis. I think there are several general methodological considerations that are relevant.

The Russell language theory, or any other unitary account (that is, any account that postulates no semantic ambiguity), accounts for Donnellan's referential-attributive phenomenon by a general pragmatic theory of speech acts, applicable to a very wide range of languages; the D-language hypothesis accounts for these same phenomena by positing a semantic ambiguity. The unitary account appeals to a general apparatus that applies to cases, such as the "Smith-Jones" case, where it is completely implausible that a semantic ambiguity exists. According to the unitary account, far from the referential use constituting a special namelike use of definite descriptions, the referential-attributive distinction is simply a special case of a general distinction, applicable to proper names as well as to definite descriptions, and illustrated in practice by the (leaf-raking) Smith-Jones case. And anyone who compares the Smith-Jones case, where presumably no one is tempted to posit a special semantic ambiguity, with Donnellan's cases of definite descriptions, must surely be impressed by the similarity of the phenomena.[26]

Under these circumstances, surely general methodological principles favor the existing account. The apparatus of speaker's reference and semantic reference, and of simple and complex uses of designators, is needed *anyway*, to explain the Smith-Jones case; it is applicable to all languages.[27] Why posit a semantic ambiguity when it is both insufficient in general and superfluous for the special case it seeks to explain?[28] And why are the phenomena regarding proper names so similar to those for definite descriptions, if the one case involves no semantic ambiguity while the other does?

It is very much the lazy man's approach in philosophy to posit ambiguities when in trouble. If we face a putative counterexample to our favorite philosophical thesis, it is always open to us to protest that some key term is being used in a special sense, different from its use in the thesis. We may be right, but the ease of the move should counsel a policy of caution: Do not posit an ambiguity unless you are really forced to, unless there are really compelling theoretical or intuitive grounds to suppose that an ambiguity really is present.

Let me say a bit more in defense of this. Many philosophers, for example, have advocated a "strong" account of knowledge according to which it is very hard to know anything; stiff requirements must be satisfied. When such philosophers have been confronted with intuitive counterexamples to such strong requirements for knowledge they either have condemned them as popular and loose usages or they have asserted that "know" is being used in a different "weak" sense. The latter move —distinguishing two or more "strong" and "weak" senses of "know"— strikes me as implausible. There *are* different senses of "know," distinguished in German as "kennen" and "wissen," and in French as "connaître" and "savoir"; a person is usually known in the one sense, a fact in the other. It is no surprise that other languages use distinct words for these various senses of "know"; there is no reason for the ambiguity to be preserved in languages unrelated to our own. But what about the uses of "know" that characteristically are followed by that-clauses, knowing that *p*? Are these ambiguous? I would be very surprised to be told that the Eskimos have two separate words, one for (say) Hintikka's "strong" sense of "know," another for his "weak" sense. Perhaps this indicates that we think of knowledge as a unitary concept, unlikely to be "disambiguated" by two separate words in any languages.

We thus have two methodological considerations that can be used to test any alleged ambiguity. "Bank" is ambiguous; we would expect the ambiguity to be disambiguated by separate and unrelated words in some other languages. Why should the two separate senses be reproduced in languages unrelated to English? First, then, we can consult our linguistic intuitions, independently of any empirical investigation. Would we be surprised to find languages that used two separate words for the two alleged senses of a given word? If so, then, to that extent our linguistic intuitions are really intuitions of a unitary concept, rather than of a word that expresses two distinct and unrelated senses. Second, we can ask empirically whether languages are in fact found that contain distinct words expressing the allegedly distinct senses. If no such language is found, once again this is evidence that a unitary account of the word or phrase in question should be sought.

As far as our main question is concerned, the first of these two tests, that of our intuitive expectation, seems to me overwhelmingly to favor a unitary account of descriptions, as opposed to the ambiguity postulated in the ambiguous D-language. If English really is the ambiguous D-language, we should expect to find other languages where the referential and attributive uses are expressed by two separate words, as in the *unambiguous* D-language. I at least would find it quite surprising to learn that say, the Eskimo, used two separate words "the" and "ze," for the attributive and referential uses. To the extent that I have this intuition, to that extent I think of "the" as a unitary concept. I should have liked to be able to report that I have reinforced this guess by an actual empirical examination of other languages—the second test—but as of now I haven't done so.[29]

Several general methodological considerations favor the Russell language (or some other unitary account) against the ambiguous D-language as a model for English. First, the unitary account conforms to considerations of economy in that it does not "multiply senses beyond necessity." Second, the metalinguistic apparatus invoked by the unitary account to explain the referential-attributive distinction is an apparatus that is needed in *any case* for other cases, such as proper names. The separate referential sense of descriptions postulated by the D-language hypothesis, is an idle wheel that does no work: if it were absent, we would be able to express everything we wished to express, in the same way. Further, the resemblance between the case of descriptions and that of proper names (where presumably no one would be tempted to postulate an ambiguity) is so close that any attempt to explain the cases differently is automatically suspect. Finally, we would not expect the alleged ambiguity to be disambiguated in other languages, and this means we probably regard ourselves as possessing a unitary concept.

Aside from methodological considerations, is there any direct evidence that would favor one of our two rival accounts? As I remarked above, if we had a direct intuition that "Her husband is kind to her" could be true even when her actual husband is cruel, then we would have decisive evidence for the D-language model; but Donnellan rightly disclaims any such intuition. On the other hand, I myself feel that such a sentence expresses a falsehood, even when "her husband" is used referentially to refer to a kind man; but the popularity of Donnellan's view has made me uncertain that this intuition should be pressed very far. In the absence of such direct intuitions that would settle the matter conclusively, it would seem that the actual practice of English speakers is compatible with either model, and that only general methodological considerations favor one hypothesis rather than another. Such a situation leaves me uneasy. If there really is no direct evidence to distinguish the two hypotheses, how are they different hypotheses? If two communities, one of whom spoke the ambiguous D-language and the other of whom spoke the (weak) Russell language, would be able to intermingle freely without detecting any linguistic difference, do they really speak two different languages? If so, wherein is the difference?

Two hypothetical communities, one of which was explicitly taught the ambiguous D-language and the other of which was taught the (weak) Russell language (say, in school), would have direct and differing intuitions about the truth-value of "Her husband was kind to her"; but it is uncertain whether English speakers have any such intuitions. If they have none, is this a respect in which English differs from both the Russell language and the D-languages, and thus differentiates it from both? Or, on the contrary, is there a pragmatic consideration, deriving no doubt from the fact that the relevant rules of language are not explicitly taught, that will explain why we lack such intuitions (if we do) without showing that neither the D-language nor the Russell language is English?

Some commentators on the dispute between Russell and Frege and Strawson over sentences containing vacuous definite descriptions have held that no direct linguistic phenomena conclusively decide between the two views: we should therefore choose the most economical and theoretically satisfying model. But if this is so, are there really two views, and if there are, shouldn't we perhaps say that neither is correct? A hypothetical community that was explicitly taught Russellian or Frege-Strawsonian truth-conditions for sentences containing vacuous definite descriptions would have no difficulty producing direct intuitions that decide the Russell-Strawson dispute. If the commentators in question are correct, speakers of English have no such intuitions. Surely this fact, too, would be a significant fact about English, for which linguistic theory should give an account. Perhaps pragmatic considerations suffice for such an account; or, perhaps, the alleged lack of any such intuition must be accounted for by a feature built into the semantics of English itself. In the latter case, neither the Russellian nor the Frege-Strawsonian truth-conditions would be appropriate for English. Similar considerations would apply to the issue between Donnellan and Russell.[30]

I am uncertain about these questions. Certainly it would be best if there were directly observable phenomena that differentiated between the two hypotheses. Actually I can think of one rather special and localized phenomenon that may indeed favor the Russellian hypothesis, or some other unitary hypothesis. Consider the following two dialogues:

Dialogue I
A "Her husband is kind to her."
B "No, he isn't. The man you're referring to isn't her husband."

Dialogue II
A "Her husband is kind to her."
B "He is kind to her, but he isn't her husband."

In the first dialogue the respondent (B) uses "he" to refer to the semantic referent of "her husband" as used by the first speaker (A); in the second dialogue the respondent use "he" to refer to the speaker's referent. My tendency is to think that both dialogues are proper. The unitary account can explain this fact, by saying that pronominalization can pick up *either* a previous semantic reference or a previous speaker's reference.[31,32] In the case of the two contrasting dialogues, these diverge.

If English were the ambiguous D-language, the second dialogue would be easy to explain. "He" refers to the object that is both the semantic referent and the speaker's referent of "her husband." (Recall that the notions of speaker's reference and semantic reference are general notions applicable to all languages, even to the D-languages.[33]) The first dialogue, however, would be much more difficult, perhaps impossible, to explain. When A said "her husband," according to the D-language hypothesis he was using "her husband" in the referential sense. Both the speaker's referent and the semantic referent would be the kind lover; only if B had misunderstood A's use as attributive could he have used "he" to refer to the husband, but such a misunderstanding is excluded by the second part of B's utterance. If the first dialogue is proper, it seems hard to fit it into the D-language model.[34]

4 CONCLUSION

I said at the beginning that the main concern of this paper was methodological rather than substantive. I do think that the considerations in this paper make it overwhelmingly probable that an ultimate account of the phenomena behind Donnellan's distinction will make use of the pragmatic ambiguity between "simple" and "complex" uses, as I defined them above, rather than postulating an ambiguity of the D-language type. But any ultimate substantive conclusion on the issue requires a more extensive and thorough treatment than has been given here. First, I have not here examined theories that attempt to explain Donnellan's distinction as a *syntactic* ambiguity, either of scope or of restrictive and non-restrictive clauses in deep structure.[35] Both these views, like the line suggested in the present paper, are compatible with a unitary hypothesis such as the hypothesis that English is a Russell language. Although I am not inclined to accept either of these views, some others have found them plausible and unless they are rebutted, they too indicate that Donnellan's observations cannot be taken as providing a conclusive argument against Russell without further discussion.

Second, and most important, no treatment of definite descriptions can be complete unless it examines the complete range of uses of the definite article and related linguistic phenomena. Such a treatment should attempt, as I have argued above, to make it clear why the same construction with a definite article is used for a wide range of cases. It would be wrong for me not to mention the phenomena most favorable to Donnellan's intuitions. In a demonstrative use such as "that table," it seems plausible, as I have mentioned above,[36] that the term rigidly designates its referent. It also seems plausible that the reference of such a demonstrative construction can be an object to which the descriptive adjectives in the construction do not apply (for example, "that scoundrel" may be used to refer to someone who is not, in fact, a scoundrel) and it is not clear that the distinction between speaker's reference and semantic reference should be invoked to account for this. As I also said above, it seems to me to be likely that "indefinite" definite descriptions[37] such as "the table" present difficulties for a Russellian analysis. It is somewhat tempting to assimilate such descriptions to the corresponding demonstratives (for example, "that table") and to the extent that such a temptation turns out to be plausible, there may be new arguments in such cases for the intuitions of those who have advocated a rigid vs. non-rigid ambiguity in definite descriptions, or for Donnellan's intuitions concerning the referential case, or for both.[38]

Because I have not yet worked out a complete account that satisfies me, and because I think it would be wrong to make any definitive claim on the basis of the restricted class of phenomena considered here, I regard the primary lessons of this paper as methodological. They illustrate some general methodological considerations and apparatus that I think should be applied to the problems discussed here and to other linguistic problems. They show in the present case that the argument Donnellan actually presents in his original paper shows nothing against a Russellian or other unitary account, and they make it highly probable to me that the problems Donnellan handles by semantic ambiguity should instead be treated by a general theory of speech acts. But at this time nothing more definitive can be said. I think that the distinction between semantic reference and speaker's reference will be of importance not only (as in the present paper) as a critical tool to block postulation of unwarranted ambiguities, but also will be of considerable constructive importance for a theory of language. In particular, I find it plausible that a diachronic account of the evolution of language is likely to suggest that what was originally a mere speaker's reference may, if it becomes habitual in a community, evolve into a semantic reference. And this consideration may be *one* of the factors needed to clear up some puzzles in the theory of reference.[39,40,41]

Notes

1. Versions of this paper—not read from the present manuscript—were given from 1971 onward to colloquia at New York University, M.I.T., the University of California (Los Angeles), and elsewhere. The present version was written on the basis of a transcript of the M.I.T. version prepared by the editors of this volume. Donnellan himself heard the talk at U.C.L.A., and he has a forthcoming paper, "Speaker Reference, Descriptions and Anaphora," that to a large extent appears to be a comment on considerations of the type mentioned here. (He does not, however, specifically refer to the present paper.) I decided *not* to alter the paper I gave in talks to take Donnellan's later views into account: largely I think the earlier version stands on its own, and the issues Donnellan raises in the later paper can be discussed elsewhere. Something should be said here, however, about the pronominalization phenomena mentioned on p. 405 below. In his forthcoming paper, Donnellan seems to think that these phenomena are incompatible with the suggestion that speaker's reference is a pragmatic notion. On the contrary, at the end of the present paper (and of the talk Donnellan heard), I emphasize these very phenomena and argue that they support this suggestion. See also note 31 below.

2. *The Philosophical Review* 75 (1966): 281–304, [chap. 17 in this vol.; page references are to this vol.]. See also Keith S. Donnellan, "Putting Humpty Dumpty Together Again," *The Philosophical Review* 77 (1968): 203–215.

3. In his later paper mentioned above in note 1, Donnellan seems more clearly to advocate a semantic ambiguity; but he hedges a bit even in the later paper.

4. I will also avoid cases of "improper" descriptions, where the uniqueness condition fails. Such descriptions may or may not be important for an ultimate evaluation of Donnellan's position, but none of the arguments in this paper rest on them.

5. "Reference and Definite Descriptions," p. 365. My discussion in this paragraph and the next is based on Donnellan's paper, pp. 365, 368–69.

6. At the time, it had not yet been revealed that Kissinger was the official in question.

7. In fact, no *n*-fold distinction can do so, for any fixed *n*. Independently of the present writer, L. Kartunnen has argued similarly that no dual or *n*-fold distinction can replace scope distinctions. I discussed the matter briefly in "Identity and Necessity," *Identity and Individuation*, ed. M. Munitz (New York, 1972), p. 149, n. 10.

8. See the papers of Stalnaker and Partee in *The Semantics of Natural Language*, ed. D. Davidson and G. Harman (Dordrecht, 1971) for such suggestions and also for some of the views mentioned in the previous section. I should emphasize that most of the stimulating discussion in these papers can be made independent of any of the identifications of Donnellan's distinction with others which are rejected here.

9. See his paper "The Contingent *A Priori* and Rigid Designators," *in Contemporary Perspectives in the Philosophy of Language*, ed. P. A. French, T. E. Uehling, and H. K. Wettstein, 45–60. In that paper, Donnellan asks whether I think proper names (in natural language) are *always* rigid: obviously, he thinks, proper names *could* be introduced to abbreviate nonrigid definite descriptions. My view is that proper names (except perhaps, for some quirky and derivative uses, that are not uses as *names*) *are* always rigid. In particular this applies to "Neptune." It would be logically possible to have single words that abbreviated nonrigid definite descriptions, but these would not be *names*. The point is not merely terminological: I mean that such abbreviated nonrigid definite descriptions would differ in an important semantical feature from (what we call) typical proper names in our actual speech. I merely state my position and do not argue it; nor can I digress to comment on the other points raised in Donnellan's paper in this volume.

10. See Kaplan's paper "Dthat" [chap. 28 in this vol.]. In that paper, however, he also has some tendency to confuse rigidity with Donnellan's referentiality.

11. In the Davidson-Harman volume mentioned in note 8.

12. For this view, see Jerrold J. Katz, "Logic and Language: An Examination of Recent Criticisms of Intensionalism," in *Minnesota Studies in the Philosophy of Science*, vol. VII (Minneapolis, 1975), pp. 36–130. See especially sections 5.1 and 5.2. As far as proper names are concerned, Katz thinks that *other* arguments tell against the description theory even as a theory of meaning.

13. See Donnellan, "Reference and Definite Descriptions," p. 378.

14. So I argued in the talks, and rightly, if Donnellan is taken literally. See note 25 below, however, for a more charitable reading, which probably corresponds to Donnellan's intent. We must, however, take descriptions to be *semantically* ambiguous if we are to maintain the reading in question: see the point raised immediately after this one.

15. "Reference and Definite Descriptions," p. 374.

16. For Grice, see the following papers, which I follow loosely in a good deal of the discussion at the beginning of this section: "The Causal Theory of Perception," *Proceedings of the Aristotelian Society*, supplementary vol. 35 (1961); "Logic and Conversation" (unpublished lectures); "Meaning," *Philosophical*

Review 66 (1957): 377–88; "Utterer's Meaning, Sentence-Meaning and Word-Meaning," *Foundations of Language* 4 (1968): 225–42; "Utterer's Meaning and Intentions," *Philosophical Review* 78 (1969): 147–77 [chap. 4 in this vol.].

17. In "The Causal Theory of Perception."

18. Suppose the second burglar is well aware of the proximity of the police, but procrastinates in his greed for more loot. Then the first burglar imparts no *information* by saying what he does, but simply urges the second burglar to "split."

19. Although conversational principles are applicable to *all languages*, they may apply differently to *different societies*. In a society where blunt statement was considered rude, where "it looks red" replaced "it is red" just because of such a custom, "it looks red" might carry different conversational implicatures from our own. This might be the case even though the members of the society spoke *English*, just as we do. Conversational principles are matters for the psychology, sociology, and anthropology of linguistic communities; they are applicable to these communities no matter what language they may speak, though the applicable principles may vary somewhat with the communities (and may even, to some extent, be conditioned by the fact that they speak languages with certain structures.) Often, of course, we can state widely applicable, "cross-cultural," general conversational principles. Semantic and syntactic principles, on the other hand, are matters of the conventions of a language, in whatever cultural matrix it may be spoken. *Perhaps* sometimes it is difficult to draw the line, but it exists in general nonetheless.

20. If the views about proper names I have advocated in "Naming and Necessity" are correct (Donnellan, in fact, holds similar views), the conventions regarding names in an idiolect usually involve the fact that the idiolect is no mere idiolect, but part of a common language, in which reference may be passed from link to link.

As the present paper attests, my views on proper names in "Naming and Necessity" have no special connection with the referential-attributive distinction.

21. "Naming and Necessity," p. 343, n. 3.

22. Donnellan shows in his paper that there are "referential" uses, of a somewhat exceptional kind, where the speaker, or even both the speaker and the hearer, are aware that the description used does not apply to the thing they are talking about. For example, they use "the king," knowing him to be a usurper, but fearing the secret police. Analogous cases can be given for proper names: if Smith is a lunatic who thinks he is Napoleon, they may humor him. Largely for the sake of simplicity of exposition, I have excluded such both from the notion of speaker's reference and from Donnellan's "referential" use (and the "D-languages" below). I do not think that the situation would be materially altered if both notions were revised so as to admit these cases, in a more refined analysis. In particular, it would probably *weaken* the case for a semantic ambiguity if these cases were allowed: for they shade into ironical and "inverted commas" cases. "He is a 'fine friend'," may be ironical (whether or not inverted commas are used in the transcription). "'The king' is still in power"; "'Napoleon' has gone to bed" are

similar, whether or not explicit inverted commas are used. It is fairly clear that "fine friend," "brillant scholar," etc., do not have ironical and inverted commas *senses*: irony is a certain form of speech act, to be accounted for by pragmatic considerations. The case for a semantic ambiguity in definite descriptions is similarly *weakened* if we include such cases as referential uses.

In ordinary discourse, we say that the speaker was referring to someone under a wide variety of circumstances, including linguistic errors, verbal slips, and deliberate misuses of language. (If Mrs. Malaprop says, "The geography teacher said that equilateral triangles are equiangular," she *refers* to the geometry teacher.) The more such phenomena one includes in the notion of speaker's reference, the further one gets from any connection of the notion with semantical matters.

23. See the discussion of "schmidentity" in "Naming and Necessity," p. 310.

24. Or, using variables explicitly, "There is a person x such that ..." Notice that in an utterance of "$(\exists x)(\phi x \wedge \psi x)$," as long as it is clear *which* thing allegedly satisfying "ϕx" the speaker has in mind, there can be a speaker's referent, even if both the speaker and the hearer are aware that many things satisfy "ϕx."

25. This description of the D-languages specifies nothing about semantical features more "intensional" than truth conditions. It is plausible to assume that "ze F" is a *rigid* designator of the thing believed to be uniquely F, but this is not explicitly included in the extensional truth conditions. Nor has anything been said about the behavior of "ze F" in belief and indirect discourse contexts. *If* we stipulate that "ze F," even in such contexts, designates the thing the speaker believes uniquely F's, then indeed "Jones said that ze man she married is kind to her," will not be a proper way of reporting Jones's utterance "Ze man she married is kind to here" (even if Jones and the speaker happen to have the same belief as to who her husband is; the difficulty is more obvious if they do not.) No doubt it is this fact that lies behind Donnellan's view that, in the referential case, it is hard to speak of "the statement," even though his exposition of the matter seems to be defective. Such implications, which are not present in the Russell language, lend only further implausibility to the supposition that English is the ambiguous D-language.

To repeat note 22, actually there are many other ways, other than taking something uniquely to satisfy "F," that might be included under referential uses of "the F." The best short way to specify the semantics of "ze F" would seem to be this: "ze F" refers, in the unambiguous D-language, to what would have been the speaker's referent of "the F" in the weak Russell language (under the same circumstances)! But this formulation makes it very implausible that the ambiguous D-language is anything but a chimerical model for English.

26. There is one significant difference between the case of proper names and that of definite descriptions. If someone uses "Jones" to refer to Smith, he has *misidentified* Smith as Jones, taken Smith for someone else. To some extent I *did* think that *Jones* was raking the leaves. (I assume that "Jones" is already in his idiolect as a name of Jones. If I am introduced to an impostor and am told, "This man is none other than Albert Einstein," if I am fooled I will have *taken* him, falsely, to be Einstein. Someone else, who has never heard of Einstein before, may merely be mistaken as to the impostor's name.) On the other hand, if I think that someone is

"her husband" and so refer to him, I need not at all have confused two people. I merely think that one person possesses a property—that of being married to her—that in fact he lacks. The real husband is irrelevant.

27. In terms of this apparatus, I can sharpen the reply to Katz, p. 391 above. If Schmidt had discovered the incompleteness of arithmetic but I had thought it was Gödel who did so, a complex ("referential") use of the description has a semantic reference to Schmidt but a speaker's reference to Gödel. Once I am apprised of the true facts, speaker's reference and semantic reference will coincide thereafter and I will no longer use the description to refer to Gödel. The name "Gödel," on the other hand, has Gödel as its *semantic* referent: the name will always be applied to Gödel in the presence of correct information. Whether a term would be withdrawn in the presence of correct information (without changing the language) is a good intuitive test for divergence of semantic reference and speaker's reference disregarding the cases in note 22).

28. There is another problem for any theory of semantic ambiguity. Donnellan says that if I say "Smith's murderer is insane," solely on the basis of the grizzly condition of Smith's body, my use of "Smith's murderer" is attributive (even if I in fact have a belief as to who the murderer is), but if I say it on the basis of the supposed murderer's behavior at the dock, my use is referential. Surely, however, my reasons can be mixed: perhaps neither consideration would have sufficed by itself, but they suffice jointly. What is my use then? A user of the unambiguous D-language would have to choose between "the" and "ze." It seems very implausible to suppose that the speaker is confused and uncertain about what sense he gives to his description; but what else can we say if we suppose that English is the ambiguous D-language? (This problem arises even if the man at the dock is guilty, so that in fact there is no conflict. It is more obvious if he is innocent.)

A pragmatic theory of the referential-attributive distinction can handle such cases much more easily. Clearly there can be borderline cases between the simple and the complex use—where, to some extent the speaker wishes to speak of the semantic referent and to some extent he wishes to speak of something he believes to be the semantic referent. He need not sort out his motives carefully, since he thinks these things are one and the same!

Given such mixed motives, the speaker's reference may be partially to one thing and partially to another, even when the semantic reference is unambiguous. This is especially likely in the case of proper names, since divergences between speaker's referent and semantic referent are characteristically *misidentifications* (see note 26). Even if the speaker's referent of "Jones" in "Jones is raking the leaves" is Smith, to some extent I have said *of Jones* that he is raking the leaves. There are gradations, depending on the speaker's interests and intentions, as to what extent the speaker's reference was to Jones and to what extent it was to Smith. The problem is less common in the case of descriptions, where misidentification need not have occurred.

29. Of course these tests must be used with some caution. The mere fact that some language subdivides the extension of an English word into several subclasses, with their own separate words, and has no word for the whole extension, does not show

that the English word was ambiguous (think of the story that the Eskimos have different words for different kinds of snow). If many unrelated languages preserve a single word, this in itself is evidence for a unitary concept. On the other hand, a word may have different senses that are obviously related. One sense may be metaphorical for another (though in that case, it may not really be a separate sense, but simply a common metaphor). "Statistics" can mean both statistical data and the science of evaluating such data. And the like. The more we can explain relations among senses, and the more "natural" and "inevitable" the relationship, the more we will expect the different senses to be preserved in a wide variety of other languages.

The test, therefore, needs further exploration and refinement. It is certainly wrong to postulate an ambiguity without any explanation of some connection between the "senses" that explains why they occur in a wide variety of languages. In the referential-attributive case, I feel that any attempt to explain the connection between the referential and the attributive uses will be so close to the kind of pragmatic account offered here as to render any assumptions of distinct senses inplausible and superfluous.

30. That is, the *concept* of truth conditions is somehow inappropriate for the semantics of English.

The vague uneasiness expressed in these paragraphs expresses my own rather confused occasional doubts and is ancillary to the main theme. Moore's "paradox of analysis" may be a related problem.

Quine's philosophy of language characteristically is based on a naturalistic doubt about building any "rules" or "conventions" into a language that are not recoverable from actual linguistic practices, even if such rules may be necessary to stipulate the language. In this sense, the uneasiness expressed is Quinean in spirit. I find Quine's emphasis on a naturalistic approach to some extent salutary. But I also feel, that our intuitions of semantic rules as speakers should not be ignored cavalierly.

31. Geach, in his book "Reference and Generality," emended edition (Ithaca, 1970), and elsewhere, has argued vigorously against speaking of pronominalization as picking up a previous reference. I do not wish to argue the extent to which he is right here. I use the terminology given in the text for convenience, but to the extent Geach's views are correct I think the example could presumably be reformulated to fit his scheme. I think the views expressed in this paper are very much in the spirit of Geach's remarks on definite descriptions and speaker's reference in the book just cited. See Geach's discussion, e.g., on p. 8.

32. Donnellan, in his paper "Speaker Reference, Descriptions and Anaphora," thinks that the fact that pronouns can pick up a previous semantic reference somehow casts doubt on a view that makes speaker's reference a nonsemantical notion. I don't see why: "he," "she," "that," etc., can, under various circumstances, refer to anything salient in an appropriate way. Being physically distinguished against its background is a property that may make an object salient; having been referred to by a previous speaker is another. In "Naming and Necessity," footnote 3, I suggested tentatively that Donnellan's "remarks about reference have little to

do with semantics or truth conditions." The point would be put more exactly if I had said that Donnellan's distinction is not itself a semantical one, though it is relevant to semantics through pronominalization, as many other non-semantical properties are.

Pronominalization phenomena are relevant to another point. Often one hears it argued against Russell's existential analysis of *indefinite* descriptions that an indefinite description may be anaphorically referred to by a pronoun that seems to preserve the reference of the indefinite description. I am not sure that these phenomena do conflict with the existential analysis. (I am not completely sure there are some that don't, either.) In any event, many cases can be accounted for (given a Russellian theory) by the facts that: (i) existential statements can carry a speaker's reference; (ii) pronouns can refer to the speaker's referent.

33. The use of "ze" in the unambiguous D-language is such that the semantic reference automatically coincided with the speaker's reference, but nevertheless, the notions are applicable. So are the notions of simple and complex uses of designators. However, speakers of the unambiguous D-language might be less likely ever to use "the" in a complex case: for, one might be inclined to argue, if such are their intentions, why not use "ze"?

34. Various moves might be tried, but none that I can think of seem to me to be plausible. It has been suggested to me that sometimes the respondent in a dialogue deliberately feigns to misunderstand an ambiguous phrase used by the first speaker, and that, given the supposed ambiguity of "her husband" in the ambiguous D-language, the first dialogue can be interpreted as such a case. For example, the following dialogue: "Jones put the money in a bank." "He put the money in one all right, but it wasn't a commercial bank; he was so much afraid it would be discovered that he hid it near the river." It seems implausible to me that the first dialogue in the text fits into such a very jocular model. But notice further that the joke consists in a mock *confirmation* of the first speaker's assertion. It would be rather bizarre to respond, "He didn't put the money in the bank, and it wasn't a commercial bank." The first dialogue would have to conform to such a bizarre pattern on the hypothesis in question.

Alternatively, it might be suggested that B uses "he" as a pronoun of laziness for A's "her husband," taken in the supposed referential sense. This move seems to be excluded, since B may well be in no position to use "her husband" referentially. He may merely have heard that she is married to a cruel man.

35. I believe that Kartunnen has advocated the view that the referential-attributive distinction arises from a scope ambiguity; I do not know whether this has been published. Since the referential-attributive "ambiguity" arises even in simple sentences such as "Smith's murderer is insane," where there appears to be no room for any scope ambiguity, such a view seems forced to rely on acceptance of Ross's suggestion that all English assertive utterances begin with an initial "I say that," which is suppressed in "surface structure" but present in "deep structure."

For the view that derives the referential-attributive "ambiguity" from a distinction of restrictive and non-restrictive clauses in "deep structure," see J. M. Bell, "What is Referential Opacity?", *The Journal of Philosophical Logic* 2

(1973): 155–180. See also the work of Emmon Bach on which Bell's paper is based, "Nouns and Noun Phrases," in *Universals in Linguistic Theory*, ed. E. Bach and R. T. Harms (New York, 1968), pp. 91–122. For reasons of space I have not treated these views here. But some of my arguments that Donnellan's distinction is pragmatic apply against them also.

36. See p. 390 above; also see note 10 above.

37. The term is Donnellan's. See 'Putting Humpty Dumpty Together Again," p. 204, footnote 5.

38. I believe that when Donnellan heard the present paper, he too mentioned considerations of this kind. The cases are mentioned briefly in Donnellan's paper, "Putting Humpty Dumpty Together Again," *ibid*. Donnellan's paper mentioned in note 1 above also makes use of the existence of such incomplete descriptions but I do not find his arguments conclusive.

39. See the Santa Claus and Madagascar cases in "Naming and Necessity." See "Naming and Necessity," pp. 300–302 for the Santa Claus case the pp. 768–9 of the "Addenda" to that paper for the Madagascar case.

40. It seems likely that the considerations in this paper will also be relevant to the concept of a supposed "±Specific" distinction for indefinite descriptions, as advocated by many linguists.

41. I should like to thank Margaret Gilbert and Howard Wettstein for their assistance in the preparation of this paper.

Chapter 19

Context and Communication

Stephen Neale

1 INTRODUCTORY REMARKS

As we saw in the last chapter, *prima facie* there is a case to be made for the view that descriptions may, on occasion, function more like referring expressions than quantifiers. Consequently, if Russell's theory is to serve as a *general* account of the semantics of descriptive phrases, an explanation of what is going on in such cases must be provided. And this means taking into account the powerful effects of *context* on the interpretation of utterances.

This breaks down into two distinct tasks. First, we need an account of context-sensitive expressions like indexicals and demonstratives, if only for the reason that definite descriptions—indeed quantifiers quite generally —may contain such expressions as *constituents*. Second, we need, at least in broad outline, a general framework within which to discuss the relationship between the genuinely semantical features of an expression ζ and those features of the use of ζ that issue, at least in part, from non-semantical facts about the context of utterance and from constraints governing rational discourse. In particular, we need a framework within which we can provide a reasonably clear and precise characterization of the intuitive Gricean distinction between the *proposition expressed* by an utterance and the proposition (or propositions) the speaker seeks to communicate by it, what we might call *the proposition(s) meant* by the speaker.

In section 2, I shall make some preliminary remarks about the history and nature of the referential challenge to the Theory of Descriptions. In section 3, I begin the examination of the effects of context on the

First appeared in *Descriptions* (Cambridge: MIT Press, 1990), chapter 3, pp. 62–117. Reprinted by permission of the MIT Press.

interpretation of descriptions with the aid of a standard theory of indexicality. Section 4 is primarily an exegetical discussion of various strands of Grice's work on meaning and implicature, which will be put to use in section 5. (Grice's own machinery and terminology will be modified slightly to suit the present discussion, but this section can still be skipped by those familiar with Grice's program.) In section 5, I attempt to spell out the details of the Gricean response to the referential challenge. In section 6, I turn to the problems apparently raised by so-called "incomplete" descriptions like 'the table'.

2   THE REFERENTIAL CHALLENGE

In the 1960s, several philosophers published papers in which they pointed to apparently *referential* "uses" or "functions" of definite descriptions. Marcus (1962), for example, noted a namelike use of descriptions. As she puts it, over a period of time a description may come to be used rather like a proper name (as "an identifying tag") its descriptive meaning "lost or ignored." Marcus suggests that 'the evening star' and 'the Prince of Denmark' are examples of this sort. Similarly, Mitchell (1962) distinguished between two "functions" of descriptions, one of which is to *identify* an individual in much the same way as a name does.[1] And Rundle (1965) argued for a genuinely referential interpretation of descriptions that could be put to use in modal contexts. According to Rundle, the *prima facie* ambiguity in a sentence like

(1) The first person in space might not have been Gagarin

should be seen as the product of an ambiguity in the definite article: the definite description 'the first man in space' is ambiguous between Russellian and referential interpretations.[2]

In 1966, Keith Donnellan published an influential paper in which he distinguished between what he called *attributive* and *referential* uses of descriptions; he then argued that Russell's theory did not provide an accurate account of sentences containing descriptions used referentially. To illustrate his distinction, Donnellan asks us to consider a sentence like

(2) Smith's murderer is insane

as used in the following two scenarios:

(i) A detective discovers Smith's mutilated body and has no idea who has killed him. Looking at the body, the detective exclaims, "Smith's murderer is insane."

(ii) Jones is on trial for Smith's murder, and you and I are convinced of his guilt. Seeing Jones rant and rave in court, I say to you, "Smith's murderer is insane."

On Donnellan's account, in case (i) the description 'Smith's murderer' is being used attributively; in case (ii) it is being used referentially. In the attributive case, Russell's analysis may well provide an accurate account of the proposition expressed. That is, in this situation the detective plausibly expresses the descriptive proposition that whoever it was that uniquely murdered Smith is insane. But in the referential case, Donnellan urges, the description functions like a referring expression not a quantifier phrase, and the proposition expressed is not faithfully captured by Russell's quantificational analysis. According to Donnellan, I will, by my use of 'Smith's murderer', be *referring to* Jones, and hence I will be saying something *about him*, viz., that he (Jones, that man in the dock) is insane.[3]

Grice (1969) noted a similar distinction:

(1) A group of men is discussing the situation arising from the death of a business acquaintance, of whose private life they know nothing, except that (as they think) he lived extravagantly, with a household staff that included a butler. One of them says "Well, Jones' butler will be seeking a new position."

(2) Earlier, another group has just attended a party at Jones' house, at which their hats and coats were looked after by a dignified individual in dark clothes with a wing-collar, a portly man with protruding ears, whom they heard Jones addressing as 'Old Boy,'' and who at one point was discussing with an old lady the cultivation of vegetable marrows. One of the group says "Jones' butler got the hats and coats mixed up" (p. 141).

Grice points to two important features of case (2) that are not shared by case (1). First, only in case (2) has some particular individual been "'described as', 'referred to as', or 'called', Jones' butler by the speaker" (p. 141). Second, in case (2), someone who knew that Jones had no butler and who knew that the man with the protruding ears, etc. was actually Jones' gardener "would also be in a position to claim that the speaker had *mis*described that individual as Jones' butler" (p. 142).[4] As a preliminary convenience, let us take the first of these features to be characteristic of *referential* usage (a more useful and precise characterization will be provided in section 5).

Unlike Donnellan, Grice did *not* feel that there was a problem for Russell here. On Grice's account, the intuitive distinction between case (1) and case (2) is quite consistent with the view that "descriptive phrases have no relevant systematic duplicity of meaning; their meaning is given by a Russellian account" (1969, p. 143). If one is to understand what is going on in case (2), Grice suggests, one needs to invoke an independently motivated distinction between what a speaker *says* (in a certain technical sense) and what he or she *means* (also in a technical sense)—or, as I shall put it in sections 4 and 5, between the *proposition expressed* and the *proposition(s) meant*.[5]

Those influenced by Donnellan have tended to see things rather differently. Despite some early equivocation, in the 1970s a very simple and exact claim emerged:

(A1) If a speaker S uses a definite description 'the F' referentially in an utterance u of 'the F is G', then 'the F' functions as a referring expression and the proposition expressed by u is *object-dependent* (rather than descriptive).[6]

I shall take this claim (or pair of claims) to entail the view that there is a semantically distinct referential interpretation of definite descriptions. On this view, descriptions are *semantically ambiguous* between Russellian and "referential" interpretations, i.e., the definite article is lexically ambiguous.[7] One of the main aims of the present chapter is to compare the view that definite descriptions are ambiguous with the Gricean view that referential usage is a nonsemantical phenomenon.

For convenience, let us treat as interchangeable the locutions (a) "the proposition expressed by S's utterance u of ϕ," (b) "the proposition S expressed by S's utterance u of ϕ," and (c) "the propositions S expressed by uttering ϕ," where S is the speaker, u is a particular dated utterance, and ϕ is a sentence of English. Let's now define what we might call *a basic case* of a referential use of a definite description 'the F' as it occurs in a particular utterance u of 'the F is G' made by a sincere speaker S. In the basic case four conditions obtain:

(a) There is an object b such that S knows that b is uniquely F;
(b) It is b that S wishes to communicate something about;
(c) 'The F' occurs in an extensional context;[8]
(d) There are no pronouns anaphoric on this occurrence of 'the F'.

According to the "referentialist," if these four conditions are satisfied, the proposition expressed by u is true if and only if b is G. Thus the proposition expressed by u will be true on the referential interpretation if and only if it is true on the Russellian interpretation. So unless the referentialist can provide an argument that demonstrates beyond any doubt that one must entertain an object-dependent proposition about *b* in order to grasp the proposition expressed by *u*, he or she is forced to move away from the basic case in order to provide a convincing case for an ambiguity. (There is still, of course, an onus on the Russellian to explain how a referential use of a description can arise from general pragmatic principles.)

To the best of my knowledge, no one has ever provided the requisite argument for an ambiguity in the basic case. However, there are, in the literature, four quite distinct arguments for a non-Russellian interpretation that involve departing from the basic case in one way or another. The first such argument I shall call the "Argument from Misdescription." This argument involves toying around with conditions (a) and (b) in order to produce cases in which the Russellian and referential analyses yield propositions that differ in truth-value. The referentialist then urges that our ordinary intuitions favor the referential interpretation.

The second argument for a non-Russellian interpretation I shall call the "Argument from Incompleteness." This involves relaxing condition (a) in order that 'the *F*' may be an "incomplete" definite description like 'the table', which seems to resist Russell's analysis on account of not being uniquely-denoting. Again, an interpretation of such descriptions as referring expressions is supposed to get things right.

The third type of argument involves dispensing with condition (c) in order to examine sentences in which definite descriptions occur in nonextensional contexts, such as those created by modal and temporal operators and psychological verbs. Here a variety of interconnected considerations about scope, variable-binding, and opacity seem to have convinced some philosophers that the postulation of a referential (or otherwise non-Russellian) interpretation of descriptions will circumvent technical difficulties that arise for a unitary quantificational analysis. For example, it is sometimes claimed that so-called *de re* readings of sentences containing definite descriptions and nonextensional operators either lie beyond (or else stretch the plausibility of) Russell's theory because of semantical or syntactical constraints on quantification into nonextensional contexts. Arguments that are based on such considerations I shall call versions of the "Argument from Opacity."

The fourth type of argument for an ambiguity involves dispensing with condition (d) in order to allow for pronouns that are anaphoric on 'the *F*'.

It is then argued that certain anaphoric relations cannot be accounted for if the description is analyzed in accordance with Russell's theory. This argument comes in several different forms, some of which interact in interesting ways with versions of some of the other arguments. I shall call the general form of the argument the "Argument from Anaphora."

Before looking at *any* of the arguments, however, we need to say a little about the role of context in the interpretation of utterances.

3   CONTEXT AND THE PROPOSITIONS EXPRESSED

Russell rarely invokes the intuitive distinction between sentences and *utterances* of sentences. However, once the philosophical underpinnings of the Theory of Descriptions are in focus, it is clear that Russell is concerned with the propositions expressed by particular utterances of sentences containing descriptive phrases; he is *not* primarily concerned with the more abstract notion of the linguistic meaning of sentence-*types*.

To facilitate discussion, let's distinguish between what we can call *meaning* and *value*; that is, between the *linguistic meaning of an expression* ζ, and the *semantical value of a particular dated utterance u of* ζ. Expressions have meanings; utterances of expressions have values.[9] The semantical value of an utterance of a sentence ϕ is a *proposition*. The semantical value of an utterance of a subsentential expression α is whatever the utterance of α contributes to the identity of the proposition expressed by the utterance of the sentence ϕ of which α is a constituent. For the purposes of this chapter, it will be convenient to adopt Russell's talk of object-dependent propositions containing their "subjects" as constituents. (The reason is that this way of characterizing object-dependent propositions is utilized by several philosophers who have argued for a semantically distinct referential interpretation of definite descriptions. I will be addressing two of their official arguments later in this chapter, and working with the same conception of a proposition will make it easier to focus on the relevant issues and avoid orthogonal engagements. My use of this notion of a proposition should not be confused with any sort of commitment to its overall philosophical utility.)

On this account, the semantical value of an utterance of a *referring* expression is just the expression's *referent*. The characteristic property of an utterance of an *indexical* expression is that its semantical value depends, in a systematic way, upon the *context of utterance*. Thus the characteristic property of an utterance of an *indexical referring* expression is that its referent depends, in a systematic way, upon the context of utterance.

Consider the first person singular pronoun 'I', as it occurs in the sentence 'I am cold'. If I utter this sentence right now, I will be the referent of my utterance of 'I'. But if you utter the very same sentence right now, you will be the referent of your utterance of 'I'. It is clear then, that distinct utterances of 'I' may receive distinct individuals as their respective semantical values. But this does not mean that the *linguistic meaning* of the expression-type 'I' changes from occasion to occasion, or person to person. To know the linguistic meaning of the word 'I' is to know something constant across utterances, roughly that the referent is the individual using the word. Similarly for 'you': the referent is the addressee (or addressees).

The same distinction needs to be made for demonstrative noun phrases such as 'this', 'that', 'that man', etc. Although different utterances of such expressions may have different *semantical values*, we are not forced to conclude that they have variable *linguistic meanings*. This is something that Russell apparently saw:

> The word 'this' appears to have the character of a proper name, in the sense that it merely designates an object without in any degree describing it ... the word 'this' is one word, which has, *in some sense*, a constant meaning. But if we treat it as a mere name, it cannot have in any sense a constant meaning, for a name means merely what it designates, and the designatum of 'this' is continually changing ... (Russell 1948, pp. 103–4).

Although Russell was close to distinguishing between meaning and value here, he does not seem to be guided by any general considerations reflecting the distinction between expression-types and particular utterances of expressions. Rather, he is concerned with the fact that demonstratives seem to be a bit like ordinary names (they refer without describing) and a bit like descriptions (they may be associated with different individuals on different occasions of utterance), but are really neither.[10] However, from the perspective I am adopting, the distinction should be seen as a reflex of the distinction between expression-types and particular utterances of expressions.

In simple formal languages like the first-order predicate calculus, there is neither room nor need to distinguish between meaning and value. Not until we introduce context-dependent expressions does the relevant gap open up. Following Strawson (1950), we might say that mastery of the linguistic meaning of an indexical referring expression consists in the mastery of some sort of *rule* or *recipe for referring* that takes into account the situation of utterance. The linguistic meaning of such an expression might be *identified* with this rule. For instance, since the referent of an utterance of 'I' is simply whoever is speaking, the rule for 'I' might be characterized as: *the referent is the individual speaking.* (To characterize the linguistic meaning of 'I' in this way is not, of course, to say that 'I' and 'the individual speaking' have the same linguistic meaning.) And since the referent of an utterance of 'you' is whoever is being addressed by the speaker, the rule for 'you' might say something like: *the referent is whoever is being addressed.*

Such proposals have been implemented by taking the linguistic meaning of an indexical expression to be a function from contexts to semantical values.[11] On this accounts, a context C can be represented as an ordered n-tuple, the elements of which are features of the situation of utterance relevant to determining semantical value. For example, on a simple model, C might be represented as a quadruple $\langle s, a, t, p \rangle$, where $s = $ the speaker, $a = $ the addressee, $t = $ the time of utterance, and $p = $ the place of utterance. Following Lewis (1972), let's call the particular features that make up C "contextual coordinates." Using $[\![\zeta]\!]$ to represent the function that is the linguistic meaning of an expression ζ, we can formulate some elementary rules:

$$[\![I]\!](\langle s, a, t, p \rangle) = s$$

$$[\![you]\!](\langle s, a, t, p \rangle) = a$$

$$[\![now]\!](\langle s, a, t, p \rangle) = t$$

$$[\![here]\!](\langle s, a, t, p \rangle) = p.$$

In contrast to these "pure indexicals," Kaplan (1977) has suggested that genuinely demonstrative uses of the demonstrative pronouns 'this' and 'that', the personal pronouns 'he', 'she', 'him', 'his', and 'her', and demonstrative descriptions like 'this man', and 'that woman', require accompanying "demonstrations," and that the rule for a genuine demonstrative specify that *the referent is the object of that demonstration.* To capture this we can construe a context as an ordered quintuple

$$\langle s, a, \langle d_1, \ldots, d_n \rangle, t, p \rangle$$

where $d_1, \ldots, d_n$ are the objects of any demonstrations $\delta_1, \ldots, \delta_n$ in the utterance.[12]

It is important to see that indexical pronouns like 'I' and 'you', demonstrative expressions like 'this', 'that', 'this vase', and 'that man', and demonstrative occurrences of personal pronouns like 'he' and 'she' are genuine referring expressions—a fact that is sometimes overlooked because of their context-sensitivity. As Kaplan (1977) has emphasized, once we distinguish the situation of utterance from the actual or counter-factual situation at which the proposition expressed is to be evaluated for truth or falsity, the intrinsically rigid nature of demonstratives is plain to see. Suppose I point to someone and say to you

(1) That man is a spy.

The referent of my utterance of the demonstrative 'that man' is the person I am demonstrating in the situation of utterance. However, we do not want to say that the definite description 'the man I am demonstrating' determines the referent of (this particular utterance of) 'the man'. The proposition expressed by my (actual) utterance of (1) is true at some worlds in which I fail to point during my lifetime. And descriptions such as 'the man I am talking about' or 'the man I have in mind' will not do because the proposition expressed by my (actual) utterance to (1) is true at some worlds in which (e.g.) I never utter a word or think about anyone. It is clear, then, that a sentence of the form 'that F is G' is semantically very different from a sentence of the form 'the F is G'. An utterance of the former expresses an object-dependent proposition; an utterance of the latter expresses an object-independent proposition.

Under certain reasonable assumptions to do with compositionality, a corollary of the distinction between the meaning of a referring expression b and the value (i.e., referent) of a particular utterance of b is a distinction between the meaning of a sentence 'b is G' and the value of (i.e., the proposition expressed by) an utterance of 'b is G'. This comes out clearly when we turn to *understanding*. Suppose I have a room in which I keep nothing but a private vase collection. One day, I let a friend into the room and leave him there to browse. After a few minutes he calls out to me

(2) This vase is broken.

There is a clear sense in which I cannot grasp the proposition expressed by his utterance unless I establish the referent of "this vase." (This, of course follows on the assumption that the demonstrative phrase 'this vase' is a genuine referring expression; see above.) But there is an equally clear sense in which I know the *meaning* of the sentence uttered, simply by virtue of my knowledge of English—that is, by virtue of my knowledge of the meanings of the words of which the sentence is composed, and my ability to project the meanings of phrases on the basis of the meanings of their parts and their syntactical organization. We might say that although I do not know *which* proposition my friend has expressed, I know the *sort of* proposition he has expressed. He has said *of* some particular vase or other—which I have yet to identify—that it is broken. Another way of putting this is to say that although I do not come to entertain an object-dependent proposition concerning any particular vase, I come to entertain an object-independent proposition to the effect that one of my vases is broken.

(Consider the following nonlinguistic analogy. My friend says nothing while he is in the room, but after a few minutes I hear a crash. I deduce that he has broken one of my vases. It is in virtue of the fact that some particular vase broke that I heard what I heard, and that I came to believe what I came to believe. However, I only came to have an object-*in*dependent belief to the effect that one of my vases was broken, not an object-dependent belief concerning any particular vase.)

Precisely the same considerations apply in the case of pure indexicals. Suppose I return home at 7:30 P.M. and find the following message on my answering machine: "Guess what? I just flew in from London and I want to take you out for dinner tonight. I'll pick you up at eight." The voice is female and sounds familiar, but owing to the poor quality of the machine I cannot recognize it. Since I fail to establish the referent of "I," I fail to establish the proposition expressed. But I know the *sort of* proposition expressed: that's why I take a shower rather than start cooking.

It is important to see that quantifiers, including descriptions, may contain indexical expressions as constituents:

every *currently* registered Democrat
the *present* king of France
the first person *I* saw this morning
a woman who came to see *you*
the men who delivered *your* sofa
the girl who made *this* vase
most philosophers *I* have met
my mother
that woman's car.

Now it would be quite inappropriate to object to the Theory of Descriptions on the grounds that the implication of uniqueness is not honored by a sentence containing an indexical description. It is worth running through an example just to see how an indexical description like 'my mother' works. For Russell the semantical value—what he would call the "meaning"—of an utterance of a referring expression 'b' is just its referent; and the semantical value of an utterance of a sentence 'b is G' is an object-dependent proposition. An utterance of a definite description, by contrast, will not take an object as its semantical value, because a description is a quantifier not a referring expression. The semantical value of an utterance of 'the F is G' is a descriptive proposition to the effect that there is one and only one thing that is F and that one thing is G. There is no object for which the grammatical subject 'the F' stands that is a genuine constituent of that proposition. Before looking at 'my mother', let's look at 'Stephen Neale's mother'. An utterance of

(3) Stephen Neale's mother is English

expresses the proposition we can represent as

(4) [the x: x mother-of Stephen Neale] (x is English)

which invokes the relational property *being mother of Stephen Neale*, i.e., (λx) (x mother-of Stephen Neale).[13] But what property gets into the proposition expressed by an utterance of

(5) My mother is English

made by me? The same relational property. This does not mean that the relational description 'Stephen Neale's mother', and the indexical description 'my mother', have the same linguistic meaning. On the contrary, they have quite different rules of use. Only *I* can use the latter to invoke the property of being mother of *me*. However, you may use 'My mother' to invoke the property of being mother of *you*. The fact that the denotation of 'my mother' changes from speaker to speaker poses no threat to the Russellian implication of uniqueness. When I utter 'My mother is English', unique motherhood is relative to *me*; when you utter it, it is relative to you.[14]

It is not, then, the *sentence* 'the F is G' that carries any *particular* implication of uniqueness, but particular dated utterances of that sentence. The linguistic meaning of the sentence is just a rule for use that, among other things, specifies that the description is being used correctly only if there is, relative to the particular context $\langle s, a, \langle d_1, \ldots, d_n \rangle, t, p \rangle$, just one object satisfying the description in question. It is clear, then, that the Theory of Descriptions is not threatened by the existence of descriptions containing indexical components. Rather, this gives the Theory of Descriptions yet more expressive power (the importance of indexical descriptions will come out in sections 5 and 7).

In this section, I have made the common assumption that the proposition expressed by an utterance u of a sentence ϕ bears a tight relationship to the linguistic meaning of ϕ. To the extent that this relationship *is* tight, there is also a tight connection between understanding ϕ and understanding an utterance u of ϕ. But as we saw, there are several respects in which the linguistic meaning of ϕ may underdetermine the proposition expressed by u because of the various parameters left open by indexical expressions, parameters that must be pinned down by u's contextual coordinates.

Notice that knowledge of the language to which ϕ belongs together with knowledge of the relevant contextual coordinates will not necessarily put a hearer H in position to grasp the proposition expressed by u. The existence of lexical and structural ambiguity means that a particular string of sounds may satisfy the phonological criteria for being a tokening of sentence ϕ or of sentence ϕ^* ("Visiting relatives can be a nuisance"). Then there are the interpretive problems raised by (e.g.) names and pronouns. Consider an utterance of

(6) Nicola thinks she should become a banker.

H will need to assign referents to 'Nicola' and to the pronoun 'she', which may or may not be anaphoric on 'Nicola'.[15] H is surely seeking the reading that S *intended*. Indeed, if H assigns to 'Nicola' a referent other than the one S had in mind, it is clear that H has not grasped the proposition expressed.[16]

For a referring expression 'b' and a monadic predicate '( ) is G', the identity of the proposition expressed by a particular utterance of 'b is G' is dependent upon the identity of the object b referred to by 'b'. The utterance expresses a true proposition just in case b is G. The proposition in question is object-dependent in the sense that it simply could not be expressed, or even entertained, if b did not exist.

The connection with contemporary talk of *truth conditions* can be made explicit by focusing on what it means to understand a proposition. To understand an object-dependent proposition, one must have identifying knowledge of the thing the proposition is about. In addition, one must know what property is being ascribed to that object. Thus we reach the position advanced by Wittgenstein, in the *Tractatus*, that understanding a proposition involves knowing what is the case if it is true.[17] And by extension we might therefore say that understanding an utterance (of a sentence) involves knowing its truth conditions—indeed its truth conditions in actual and counterfactual situations—and that a specification of the semantical value of an utterance (of a sentence) consists, at least in part, in a specification of its truth-conditions.

4 PROPOSITIONS EXPRESSED AND PROPOSITIONS MEANT

It is clear that a hearer *H* may gather a lot more from an utterance than the proposition it expresses. Quite different thoughts may come to *H*'s mind. Let's begin with some trivial examples of the sort we shall *not* be concerned with. I am in a restaurant in San Francisco; the waitress asks me if I'd like an aperitif and I reply,

(1) I'd like a gin and tonic, please.

On the basis of certain acoustic properties of my utterance, the waitress may come to believe that I am English, or that I have a cold or hay fever. Such propositions are irrelevant to the communicative act performed, as are other propositions that are, in some sense, *made available* by my speech act but that may not spring immediately to mind, such as the proposition that I can speak English or the proposition that I am not dead.

Of considerably more importance for current concerns is the fact, emphasized by Grice (1961, 1967), that there are speech acts involving, in some communicatively *relevant* way, propositions other than the proposition strictly and literally expressed. A speaker may express a particular proposition by means of an utterance yet at the same time *communicate* something beyond this. Consider the following example due to Grice (1961). You are writing a letter of recommendation for one of your students who has applied for a position teaching philosophy at another institution. You write

(2) Jones has beautiful handwriting and is always very punctual.

The people who read this letter will surely conclude that you do not rate Jones very highly as a philosopher. And if so, you have succeeded in communicating a proposition to that effect. There is an intuitive distinction here between the proposition you expressed by the utterance and the proposition (or propositions) you sought to *convey* by it, what we might call the *proposition(s) meant*.

There is no temptation to say that the proposition that you do not rate Jones very highly as a philosopher is (or is a consequence of) the proposition expressed by your utterance. There is no specifiable method of correlating this proposition with the proposition determined by the linguistic meaning of (2) together with the contextual coordinates of the utterance. The sentence has a clear linguistic meaning based on the meanings of its parts and their syntactical arrangement, a meaning that has nothing to do with your assessment of Jones' philosophical abilities, even when the relevant contextual coordinates are plugged in. On the other hand, we might say that *you mean*, by your utterance of (2), that you do not rate Jones very highly. This is something that *you* have implied or suggested by uttering (2) in this particular context.

It is clear, then, that there may, on occasion, be a divergence between the proposition (or propositions) strictly and literally expressed by an utterance and the proposition(s) meant. (In the case we just considered, they might well be disjoint; in other cases they might not be; see below.) Indeed, there seems little doubt that any plausible account of the way language works in communication will have to appeal to a distinction of this sort.

We have reached the familiar Gricean view, then, that at least three different notions need to be distinguished when talking about the "meaning" of a sentence ϕ as uttered by a speaker S on a given occasion: (i) the linguistic meaning of the sentence ϕ; (ii) the semantical value of ϕ relative to the context of utterance (the proposition expressed); and (iii) what S meant by uttering ϕ (the proposition(s) meant). But we need to get a lot clearer about the notion in (iii) and its relation to the notion in (ii) before we can use either with any confidence in our investigation.

In the simplest cases we might say that the proposition *expressed* is meant, and that in many such cases the proposition expressed *exhausts* the proposition(s) meant. But, of course, in Grice's letter of recommendation example this is not the case at all. How, then, might we characterize when a proposition is meant? One constraint that comes to mind is the following: For a particular utterance u of ϕ made by a speaker S to a hearer H, a proposition P is meant only if, on the basis of uttering ϕ, S

intends H to entertain *P*. But we can go further than this. Borrowing from Grice's (1957, 1967) seminal work in this area, we might impose the following constraint on what it is for *S* to mean the *p* by uttering ϕ:

(G1) By uttering ϕ, *S* means that *p* only if for some audience *H*,
      S utters ϕ intending:
      (1) *H* to actively entertain the thought that *p*, and
      (2) *H* to recognize that *S* intends (1).

Consider the restaurant scene again, where the waitress learns from certain acoustic properties of my utterance of

(1) I'd like a gin and tonic, please

that I am English (or that I have a cold or hay fever). All *I mean* by my utterance is that I'd like a gin and tonic; I do *not* mean that I am English (or that I have a cold or hay fever). The first intention mentioned in (1) prevents such communicatively irrelevant propositions from being classed as part of what I mean because I do not *intend* the waitress to entertain the thought that I am English (or the thought that I have a cold or hay fever).

A modification of the same example will explain the role of the intention mentioned in (2). Suppose I do actually intend the waitress to realize that I have a cold (in order to get sympathy), or to realize that I am English (because I think I will get better service as a tourist), but I don't want her to realize that this is my intention. Intuitively, we don't want to say that *I mean* that I have a cold (or that I am English). The intention in (1) allows these propositions through. But I do not intend the waitress to *realize* that I intend her to think that I have a cold (or that I am English), so the intention in (2) prevents these propositions from being classed as a part of what I mean by my utterance.[18]

With the aid of this tentative constraint on when a proposition is meant, let's now turn to Grice's theory of *conversational implicature*. As Kripke (1977) and others have emphasized, several of Grice's proposals have a direct bearing on how we might characterize the uses of descriptions in various types of communicative settings. I shall therefore spend a little time going over certain features of Grice's general picture before putting it to use in the area of main interest.

On Grice's (1967) account, conversation is a characteristically purposeful and cooperative enterprise governed by what he calls the *Cooperative Principle*:

(CP) Make your conversational contribution such as is required, at the stage at which it occurs, by the accepted purpose or direction of the talk exchange in which you are engaged.

Subsumed under this general principle, Grice distinguishes four categories of more specific maxims and submaxims enjoining truthfulness, informativeness, relevance, and clarity.

Maxim of Quantity: Make your contribution as informative as is required (for the current purposes of the exchange). Do not make your contribution more informative than is required.
Maxim of Quality: Try to make your contribution one that is true. Specifically: Do not say what you believe to be false; do not say that for which you lack adequate evidence.
Maxim of Relation: Be relevant.
Maxim of Manner: Be perspicuous. Specifically: Be brief and orderly, avoid ambiguity and obscurity.

Of central concern to us is Grice's claim that there is a systematic correspondence between the assumptions required in order to preserve the supposition that the Cooperative Principle and attendant maxims are being observed and a certain class of propositions meant, what Grice calls *conversational implicatures*. The letter of recommendation case discussed earlier is a good example of a case that seems to involve a deliberate and flagrant violation of the Cooperative Principle, or at least one or more of the maxims. On Grice's account, by writing "Jones has wonderful handwriting and is always very punctual," (in this context) you appear to have violated the maxim enjoining relevance—since Jones is one of your students, you must know more of relevance than *this*. Furthermore, you know that more information than this is required in this particular context. Not surprisingly, the reader is naturally led to believe that you are attempting to convey something else, perhaps something you are reluctant to express explicitly. This supposition is plausible only on the assumption that you think Jones is no good at philosophy. And this is what you have *conversationally implicated*. In general, a speaker S conversationally implicated that which S must be assumed to believe in order to preserve the assumption that S is adhering to the CP and maxims.[19]

Grice contrasts this case with one in which there is supposed to be "no obvious violation" of the Cooperative Principle. Suppose H is standing by an obviously immobilized car and is approached by S. H says to S, "Where can I buy some gas?" S replies, "There is a gas station around the next corner." If *S* did not think, or think it possible, that the gas station was open and had gas for sale, his remark would not be properly relevant; thus he may be said to conversationally *implicate* that it is open and has gas for sale. That is, *S* implicates that which he must be assumed to believe in order to preserve the assumption that he is adhering to the CP, in particular, the maxim enjoining relevance.

On Grice's account, a necessary condition for an implication to count as a conversational implicature is that it be *cancellable*, either explicitly or contextually, without literal contradiction, or at least without linguistic transgression.[20] For instance, in the letter case you might have continued with "Moreover, in my opinion he is the brightest student we have ever had here." This addition might be odd, but it would not give rise to any literal contradiction. Notice that it might well be the case that in this example only what is implicated is meant (i.e., backed by your communicative intentions). You may have no idea what Jones' handwriting is like because he has only shown you typed manuscripts of his work (or because he has never shown you anything), and you may have no opinion as to whether or not he is punctual. Here the proposition implicated *supplants* the proposition expressed with respect to being meant.[21] The truth-values of the proposition expressed and the proposition(s) implicated may of course differ. Jones may have quite atrocious handwriting, and you may know this; but given the relevance of the proposition implicated, you may care very little whether the proposition expressed is true. That is, the primary message (what you *meant*) may not be calculable at the level of the proposition expressed but only at the level of the proposition implicated, in the sense that it is the latter that has the backing of your communicative intentions. (In the stranded motorist case, the propositions implicated seem to *supplement* (rather than supplant) the proposition expressed.)

Although cancellability is taken by Grice to be a necessary condition of an implication's being classed as a conversational implicature, rather more importance is attached to derivability:[22]

... the final test for the presence of a conversational implicature ha[s] to be, as far as I [can] see, a derivation of it. One has to produce an account of how it could have arisen and why it is there. And I am very much opposed to any kind of sloppy use of this philosophical tool, in which one does not fulfil this condition (Grice 1981, p. 187).

Let's call this the *Justification Requirement*. On Grice's account, whenever there is a conversational implicature, one should be able to reason somewhat as follows:

(a) S has expressed the proposition that p.

(b) There is no reason to suppose that S is not observing the CP and maxims.

(c) S could not be doing this unless he thought that q.

(d) S knows (and knows that I know that he knows) that I can see that he thinks the supposition that he thinks that q is required.

(e) S has done nothing to stop me thinking that q.

(f) S intends me to think, or is at least willing to allow me to think, that q.

(g) And so, S has implicated that q.

In each of the cases we have considered, it is possible to justify the existence of the implicature in question in this sort of way.[23]

So far, we have only looked at cases involving what Grice calls *particularized* conversational implicature. The presence and content of a particularized conversational implicature depend in a very transparent way upon facts about the particular context of utterance. Of rather more philosophical interest are those implicatures the presence and general form of which seem to have very little to do with the particular details of a given context of utterance, so-called "generalized" conversational implicatures. It is tempting to characterize the syntactician as that philosopher of language whose job it is to provide a finite, systematic characterization of a proprietary body of intuitions concerning such things as syntactical well-formedness, i.e., grammaticality. Analogously, we might view the semanticist as that philosopher of language who does the same thing for intuitions of truth, falsity, entailment, contradiction, and so on. In effect, the semanticist's aim is to construct a theory that will, among other things, yield predictions in accord with these intuitions. But great care must be taken when appealing to semantical intuitions. An initial judgment of truth or falsity, or of entailment or contradiction, might have to be reevaluated in the light of further considerations or a little tutoring of one form or another. For instance, what at first sight may seem like a semantical entailment may, upon further reflection, turn out to be something quite different.[24]

Grice (1961, 1967) argues that there has been a tendency among some linguistically oriented philosophers to overcharacterize the linguistic meanings of certain linguistic expressions. Let ζ be such an expression. According to Grice, certain conversational implicatures that typically attach to uses of ζ have been treated, mistakenly, as part of ζ's meaning. Semantical claims about certain "intentional" verbs (e.g., 'seem', 'try', 'intend', 'know', and 'remember') and about the linguistic counterparts to some of the formal devices of quantification theory (e.g., 'and', 'or', 'if . . . then . . . ', 'the', and 'a') were some of Grice's philosophically important targets. Indeed, for Grice, conversational implicature is a powerful philosophical tool with which to investigate the logical forms of certain philosophical claims and also clarify the relationship between formulae of quantification theory and sentences of natural language.

For example, *pace* Strawson (1952, p. 79ff.), it is at least arguable that many of the apparently divergent implications that seem to be present when the English word 'and' is used to conjoin sentences are not attributable to any sort of lexical ambiguity in the word but can be understood as conversational implicatures of one form or another, there being no difference in meaning between 'and' and the & of classical logic.[25] Compare the following sentences:

(1) The moon goes around the earth and the earth goes around the sun
(2) Jack and Jill got married and Jill gave birth to twins
(3) The President walked in and the troops jumped to attention.

One feature of & is that it is commutative (p & q is equivalent to q & p). This does not seem to create a problem for the view that the occurrence of 'and' in (1) has the force of &. But in (2) the conjuncts describe events and, in the normal course of things, someone who uttered this sentence would be taken to imply that Jack and Jill got married *before* Jill gave birth to twins. Indeed, if the order of the conjuncts is reversed, so is the implication. And in (3) there seems to be an implication not just of temporal priority but of causal connection.

On the basis of facts like these, one might be led to the view that 'and' is at least three ways ambiguous. Now the fact that the truth of 'p and$_{(3)}$ q' guarantees the truth of 'p and$_{(2)}$ q', which guarantees the truth of 'p and$_{(1)}$ q' might well make one wonder whether the postulation of such ambiguity is not a little extravagant. Indeed, on Grice's account, there is another, perhaps preferable avenue that might be explored. It is good methodological practice, Grice (1967) suggests, to subscribe to what he calls *Modified Occam's Razor: Senses are not to be multiplied beyond necessity*. Given the viability of a broadly Gricean distinction between the proposition expressed and the proposition(s) meant, if a pragmatic explanation is available of why a particular expression appears to diverge in meaning in different linguistic environments (or in different conversational settings) then *ceteris paribus* the pragmatic explanation is preferable to the postulation of a semantical ambiguity.

As Grice observes, pragmatic explanations of what is going on in (2) and (3) do seem to be available. The implication of temporal sequence might be explicable in terms of the fact that each of the conjuncts describes an event (rather than a state) and the presumption that the speaker is observing the Maxim of Manner, in particular the submaxim enjoining an orderly delivery.[26] And the implication of causal connection in (3) might be explicable in terms of the presumption that the speaker is being relevant. Again the conjuncts describe events and it is natural to seek some sort of connection between them since the speaker has mentioned them both in the same breath. The idea, then, is that these implications are cases of *generalized* conversational implicature. I am not going to present a serious defense of the view that 'and' *always* means & (even if restricted to cases where it conjoins pairs of sentences rather than pairs of noun phrases or pairs of verb phrases); I just want to outline the form a pragmatic explanation of the alleged ambiguity is supposed to take.[27]

The reasons for preferring pragmatic explanations over the postulation of semantical ambiguities are, of course, economy and generality. A pragmatic explanation is, in some sense, *free*: the machinery that is appealed to is needed anyway. In any particular case, this may not in itself constitute an overwhelming objection to a theory that posits an ambiguity; but in the case of 'and' the generality lost by positing several readings is considerable. Grice makes three relevant observations here. First, there is the fact that implications of (e.g.) temporal priority and causal connection attach to uses of the counterparts of 'and' across unrelated languages. One could, of course, posit parallel ambiguities in these languages; but the phenomenon is more readily explained as the product of general pragmatic considerations. Second, it is not unreasonable to assume that implications of the same sorts would arise even for speakers of a language containing an explicitly truth-functional connective &. Third, the same implications that attach to a particular utterance of p & q would attach to an utterance of the two sentence sequence $p. q$. It seems clear, then, that on *methodological* grounds the pragmatic account of the temporal and causal implications in (2) and (3) is preferable to an account that makes essential use of a semantical ambiguity. Of course, there may well be uses of the English word 'and' that resist a truth-functional semantics, but I do not take myself to arguing for the view that the word has just one meaning; my purpose is to illustrate Grice's point that where semantical and pragmatic accounts handle *the same range of data*, the pragmatic account is preferable.

It will be convenient now to focus on an example of generalized conversational implicature that involves the use of the determiner 'some'. (This will put us on course for a detailed discussion of the determiner 'the' in the next section.) Suppose two journalists S and H are discussing a recent demonstration in a notoriously repressive country. There was some violence at the demonstration and several of the demonstrators were killed, allegedly by the police. S was present at the demonstration and he knows that some of the deaths were accidental because he saw two demonstrators accidentally run over by a car full of other demonstrators. H knows that S dislikes the repressive regime, but he also knows that S is a very honest reporter. When H quizzes S about the deaths, S says,

(4) Some of the deaths were accidental.

In this situation, S would very likely be taken to endorse the truth of, or at least entertain the possibility of the truth of (5):

(5) Some of the deaths were not accidental.

But we don't want to say that 'some Fs are Gs entails 'some Fs are not Gs', or even that (4) entails (5). Nor do we want to say that 'some' is ambiguous, that on one reading 'some Fs are Gs' entails 'some Fs are not Gs' and that on another it does not. At least, not if a pragmatic explanation is available of how (4) may be used to convey a proposition that differs from the proposition it would be taken to express on its standard quantificational reading.

And of course a pragmatic explanation *is* available. Intuitively, the proposition expressed by (4) is "weaker" than the one expressed by

(6) All of the deaths were accidental.

And since in a typical communicative setting it would be more appropriate (informative, straightforward, relevant) to make the stronger claim (if it were believed true), a speaker who makes the weaker claim (in such a setting) will, *ceteris paribus*, conversationally implicate that he or she does not subscribe to the stronger claim. Now if S does not subscribe to the view that all of the deaths were accidental, S must be willing to entertain the possibility that some of the deaths were not accidental.[28] Using a Gricean justification schema,

(a) S has expressed the proposition that some of the deaths were accidental.
(b) There is no reason to suppose that S is not observing the CP and maxims.

(c) S could not be doing this unless he were willing to entertain the possibility that some of the deaths were *not* accidental. (Gloss: On the assumption that S is adhering to the Maxim of Quantity, if he thought that *all* of the deaths were accidental he would have said so. Therefore S is willing to entertain the possibility that some of the deaths were not accidental. [On the assumption that S is adhering to the Maxim of Quality, he does not think that *none* of the deaths were accidental, since he has said that some of them *were*.])

(d) S knows (and knows that I know that he knows) that I can see that he thinks the supposition that he is willing to entertain the possibility that some of the deaths were not accidental is required.

(e) S has done nothing to stop me thinking that he is willing to entertain the possibility that some of the deaths were not accidental.

(f) S intends me to think, or is at least willing to allow me to think, that he is willing to entertain the possibility that some of the deaths were not accidental.

(g) And so, S has implicated that he is willing to entertain the possibility that some of the deaths were not accidental.

It seems to me that we should resist the temptation to formulate *pragmatic rules* with which to derive certain standard cases of generalized conversational implicature. For instance, it might be suggested that a pragmatic theory contain a rule like the following:

(7) [some x: Fx] $(Gx) \gg \Psi$ [some x: Fx] $\neg (Gx)$

where $\gg$ stands for something like 'conversationally implicates unless there is good evidence to the contrary', and Ψ stands for something like 'the speaker is willing to entertain the possibility that'. In one very important respect, nothing could be further from the spirit of Grice's theory than the construction of such an avowedly singular pragmatic rule. For Grice, the conversational implicatures that attach to a particular utterance must be justifiable given the CP and maxims, construed as quite *general* antecedent assumptions about the rational nature of conversational practice. It is important not to be misled by Grice's intuitive distinction between particularized and generalized implicatures into thinking that instances of the latter do not have to satisfy the Justification Requirement. To label a certain range of implicatures "generalized" is not to bestow upon them some special status, it is simply to acknowledge the fact that the presence of the implicatures is relatively independent of the details of the particular conversational context.

We now have enough of a framework in place to begin addressing the issues raised by so-called referential uses of descriptions.

5   THE REFERENTIAL CHALLENGE REVISITED

As I mentioned in section 2, we can, I believe, ascribe to those who see the need for a semantically distinct referential interpretation of definite descriptions the following thesis:

(A1)   If a speaker S uses a definite description 'the F' referentially in an utterance u of 'the F is G', then 'the F' functions as a referring expression and the proposition expressed by u is *object-dependent* (rather than descriptive).

But what does it mean to say that a definite description is being used *referentially* on a given occasion? (Or, to use the alternative terminology of Kripke (1977) and Donnellan (1978), what does it mean to say that a particular use of a definite description is *accompanied by speaker reference?*)

This question is addressed by Donnellan (1978). Consider S's utterance u of the sentence 'The strongest man in the world can lift at least 450lbs.' Donnellan claims, quite rightly in my opinion, that it is not enough for S's use of 'the strongest man in the world' to be classified as referential that there exist some object b such that S knows (or believes) that b is the strongest man in the world. On such an account, the referentialist would be committed to the fantastic view that whenever S knows (or thinks he or she knows) who or what satisfies some description or other, S can no longer use that description nonreferentially. This would, indeed, be a peculiar consequence: the existence or nonexistence of a particular semantical ambiguity in a speaker's idiolect would be based solely on the speaker's epistemological history.[29]

Donnellan also claims, again correctly in my opinion, that it is not enough for S's use of 'the strongest man in the world' to be classified as referential that there exist some object b such that the grounds for S's utterance are furnished by the object-dependent belief that b is the strongest man in the world and the object-dependent belief that b can lift 450lbs.[30] What is characteristic of a referential use, Donnellan suggests, is the nature of "the intentions of the speaker toward his audience" (p. 50).

In the light of the discussions in sections 2 and 5, we might suggest that a speaker S uses a definite description 'the F' referentially in an utterance *u* of 'the *F* is *G*' if and only if there is some object *b* such that *S* means by *u* that *b* is *G*. But this is not quite strong enough. Suppose it is common knowledge between *S* and *H* that the tallest man in the world, whoever he is, is spending the weekend with Nicola. Suppose that there is no individual *b* such that either *S* or *H* believes of *b* that *b* is the tallest man in the world; however, it is common knowledge between *S* and *H* that the tallest man in the world (whoever he is) is very shy and that Nicola will take him with her wherever she goes this weekend. *S* and *H* are at a party on Saturday and it is a matter of some interest to *S* and *H* whether Nicola is present. *S* overhears a conversation during which someone says "The tallest man in the world is here." *S* goes over to *H* and says "The tallest man in the world is here" intending to communicate that *Nicola* is here. In this example there clearly is some object *b* (viz., Nicola) such that *S* means by *u* that *b* is here; but equally clearly, *S*'s utterance does not involve a referential use of 'the tallest man in the world'. We seem to need something more like this:

(A2)   A speaker *S* uses a definite description 'the *F*' referentially in an utterance *u* of 'the *F* is *G*' iff there is some object *b* such that *S* means by *u* that *b* is the *F* and that *b* is *G*.[31]

The debate between the Russellian-Gricean and the referentialist can now be summarized as follows. The referentialist endorses (A1) and (A2); the Russellian (to the extent that he or she believes that it is possible to provide a clear account of referential usage) endorses (A2) and (A3):

(A3)   If a speaker *S* uses a definite description 'the *F*' referentially in an utterance *u* of 'the *F* is *G*', 'the *F*' still functions as a quantifier and the proposition expressed by *u* is the object-independent proposition given by [the *x*: *Fx*](*Gx*).

In short, then, the Russellian-Gricean sees referential usage as an important fact about *communication* to be explained by general pragmatic principles not something of *semantical* import. Let us now examine this position.

As Evans (1982) observes, there are two rather different cases of referential usage to take into account, according as the putative referential description is supposed to be functioning like a *name* or like a *demonstrative*. Suppose that you and I both know Harry Smith and it is common knowledge between us that Harry is the present Chairman of the Flat Earth Society. Harry calls me up and informs me that he will be arriving in San Francisco next Saturday. Later that day I see you in the street and I say,

(1) The Chairman of the Flat Earth Society is coming to San Francisco next Saturday

fully intending to communicate to you the object-dependent proposition that Harry Smith is coming to San Francisco next Saturday, rather than (or rather than *just*) a descriptive proposition concerning the unique satisfier of a certain descriptive condition. I utter (1) intending you (a) to actively entertain the (object-dependent) proposition that Harry Smith is coming to San Francisco next Saturday, and (b) to recognize that I intend you to actively entertain that proposition (see (G1)). And I feel confident that these intentions can be fulfilled because I believe (i) that you have identifying knowledge of Harry Smith, (ii) that you take Harry Smith to uniquely satisfy the description 'the Chairman of the Flat Earth Society', and (iii) that you can infer from the fact that I have used this description that I wish to convey something to you about Harry Smith. There would appear to be no barrier, then, to saying that (part of) what *I mean* by my utterance of (1) is that Harry Smith is coming to San Francisco next Saturday; the object-dependent proposition that Harry Smith is coming to San Francisco next Saturday is (one of) the *propositions(s) meant*.

Now it is clear that I might have conveyed to you that Harry Smith is coming to San Francisco next Saturday by uttering (2) instead of (1):

(2) Harry Smith is coming to San Francisco next Saturday.

Consequently, one might consider interpreting the description (as it occurs in this utterance) as something akin to a proper name. Let's say that in this case the description is used *referentially$_N$* ('*N*' for 'name').

Let's now turn to a rather different example of the sort exploited by Donnellan (1966). We are at a party together; in one corner of the room is a man, *x*, wearing a top hat; I notice that *x* is trying to attract your attention, so I say to you,

(3) The man wearing a top hat is trying to attract your attention

fully intending to communicate to you an object-dependent proposition (about *x*), rather than (or rather than *just*) a descriptive proposition concerning the unique satisfier of the descriptive condition. I utter (3) intending you (a) to actively entertain the (object-dependent) proposition that *x* is trying to attract your attention, and (*b*) to recognize that I intend you to actively entertain proposition that proposition. And I feel confident that these intentions can be fulfilled because I believe (i) that you have identifying knowledge of x, (ii) that you take x to uniquely satisfy the description 'the man wearing a top hat', and (iii) that you can infer from the fact that I have used this description that I wish to convey something to you about x. There would appear to be no barrier, then, to saying that (part of) what I *mean* by my utterance of (3) is that x is trying to attract your attention; the object-dependent proposition that x is trying to attract your attention is (one of) the *proposition(s) meant*.

Now it is clear that I might have conveyed to you the same object-dependent proposition by uttering

(4) That man is trying to attract your attention

accompanied by some sort of demonstration or gesture. Consequently, one might consider interpreting the description (as it occurs in this utterance) as something akin to a demonstrative. Let's call this a *referential$_D$* use of a description ('D' for 'demonstrative').[32]

The question for the semanticist here is whether we need semantically distinct non-Russllian interpretations of the descriptions in (1) and (3) in order to make sense of the scenarios just constructed.

There are good methodological reasons to resist a complication of the semantics of the definite article in this way. The first thing to remember is that the phenomenon of referential usage is not something peculiar to definite descriptions. Consider the following example adapted from Wilson (1978). You and I both see Harris lurking around at the party; we both know (and know that the other knows) that Harris is a convicted embezzler; later in the evening I see Harris flirting with you sister so I come up to you and say,

(5) A convicted embezzler is flirting with your sister

fully intending to communicate to you the object-dependent proposition that Harris is flirting with your sister. I utter (5) intending you (a) to actively entertain the (object-dependent) proposition that Harris is is flirting with your sister, and (b) to recognize that I intend you to actively entertain that proposition. There would appear to be no barrier, then, to saying that (part of) what I *mean* by my utterance of (5) is that Harris is flirting with your sister; the object-dependent proposition that Harris is flirting with your sister is (one of) the *proposition(s) meant*.

It is clear that I might have conveyed to you that Harris is flirting with you sister by uttering (6) instead of (5):

(6) Harris is flirting with your sister.

We appear to have here something approximating a referential$_N$ use of an *indefinite* description (modifications to (A2) would capture this).

It is, of course, open to the referentialist to claim that indefinite descriptions are also ambiguous between Russellian and referential *interpretations*.[33] But the Gricean-Russellian will claim that some sort of important communicative generalization is being missed by proceeding in this way. Indeed, as Sainsbury (1979) emphasizes, the case for an ambiguity in the definite article weakens considerably once it is realized that sentences containing all sorts of quantifiers may be used to convey object-dependent propositions. Suppose it is common knowledge that Smith is the only person taking Jones' seminar. One evening, Jones throws a party and Smith is the only person who turns up. A despondent Jones, when asked the next morning whether his party was well attended, says,

(7) Well, everyone taking my seminar turned up

fully intending to inform me that only Smith attended. The possibility of such a scenario, would not lead us to complicate the semantics of 'every' with an ambiguity; i.e., it would not lead us to posit semantically distinct quantificational and referential interpretations of 'everyone taking my seminar'.

We find a similar situation with plural quantifiers.[34] Suppose that Scott Soames, David Lewis, and I are the only three people in Lewis's office. Soames has never played cricket and knows that I know this. In addition, Soames wants to know whether Lewis and I have ever played cricket, so I say

(8) Most people in this room have played cricket

fully intending to communicate to Soames that Lewis and I have both played cricket. There is surely no temptation to complicate the semantics of 'most' with an ambiguity, no temptation to posit a semantically distinct referential interpretation of 'most people in this room'. The natural thing to say is that given his background beliefs and given the quantificational proposition expressed by my utterance in the context in question, Soames was able to *infer* the truth of a particular object-dependent proposition (or two object-dependent propositions). I was thus able to convey an object-dependent proposition by uttering a sentence of the form 'most Fs are Gs'. (Similar cases can be constructed using 'all senators', 'many Americans', 'few Stanford women', 'five of us', 'a convicted embezzler', 'some politicians' 'the man wearing a top hat', 'the women who work for Martha', and so on.)

Thus the Gricean-Russellian views the referential use of definite descriptions as an instance of a more general phenomenon associated with the use of quantified noun phrases. Of course, definite descriptions are particularly susceptible to referential usage because of their own particular semantics. As Klein (1980) points out, if S is observing the Maxim of Quality, S will typically believe that one an only one object satisfies the description used. (The complications introduced by so-called *incomplete* descriptions like 'the table', 'the cat' and so on are discussed in section 7.) And quite often S will believe this because S knows of some particular object b that b is uniquely F. The beginnings of an explanation of the quite general phenomenon of communicating object-dependent propositions using quantified sentences surely lie in the fact that the grounds for a quantificational assertion are very often object-dependent beliefs of one form or another. (By (A1), object-dependent grounds do not suffice for referential usage, of course.) I know that some Britons are currently residing in the U.S.A. One reason I know this is that I know that I am British and that I am currently residing here, and I know that John McDowell is British and that he is currently residing here. Thus the grounds for my asserting

(9) Some Britons are currently residing in the U.S.A.

are furnished by object-dependent beliefs about John McDowell and about me. Similar remarks apply to the cricket case discussed a moment ago. Add to this the context of utterance, shared background assumptions, the sorts of inferential abilities we all possess, and the sorts of Gricean considerations that appear to govern rational discourse, and the way is open for a quite general explanation of how it is that we manage to convey object-dependent propositions using quantificational sentences, including, of course, sentences containing descriptions.

Consider the referential$_N$ use of 'the Chairman of the Flat Earth society' in (1) again. Echoing Grice, we might say that

(a) S has expressed the proposition that [the x: Fx](Gx).
(b) There is no reason to suppose that S is not observing the CP and maxims.
(c) S could not be doing this unless he thought that Gb (where 'b' is a name). Gloss: on the assumption that S is observing the Maxim of Rela-

tion, he must be attempting to convey something beyond the general proposition that whoever is uniquely F is G. On the assumption that S is adhering to the Maxim of Quality, he must have adequate evidence for thinking that the F is G. I know S knows that b is the F, therefore S thinks that Gb.

(d) S knows (and knows that I know that he knows) that I know that b is the F, that I know that S knows that b is the F, and that I can see that S thinks the supposition that he thinks that Gb is required.

(e) S has done nothing to stop me thinking that Gb.

(f) S intends me to think, or is at least willing to allow me to think, that Gb.

(g) And so, S has implicated that Gb.

On a referential$_D$ use of 'the F', (c) might be replaced by

(c′) S could not be doing this unless he thought that Gb (where 'b' is a demonstrative.) Gloss: On the assumption that S is observing the Maxim of Relation, he must be attempting to convey something over and above the general proposition that whoever is uniquely F is G. On the assumption that S is adhering to the Maxim of Quality, he must have adequate evidence for thinking that the F is G. It is not plausible to suppose that he has just general grounds for this belief, therefore he must have object-dependent grounds. I can see that there is someone b in the perceptual environment who could be taken to satisfy the description 'the F', and I can see that S can see this. Therefore the grounds for his assertion that the F is G are plausibly furnished by the belief that Gb.[35]

Although a description 'the F' does not itself refer to any individual, following Kripke (1977) let us say that in situations like those just discussed *the speaker S refers* to an individual, the individual S is interested in communicating a proposition about.

We have reached the situation, then, in which we appear to have a perfectly good explanation of referential uses of definite descriptions that does not appeal to any sort of semantical ambiguity. The Russellian and the ambiguity theorist agree that when a description is used referentially, (one of) the proposition(s) *meant* is object-dependent; they just provide different explanations of this fact. The referentialist complicates the semantics of 'the'; the Russellian appeals to antecedently motivated principles governing the nature of rational discourse and ordinary inference. As far as accounting for the data we have considered, a stalemate appears to have been reached.

But general methodological considerations lend support to the Russellian. Modified Occam's Razor enjoins us not to multiply senses beyond necessity, i.e., to opt for a theory that (*ceteris paribus*) does not have to appeal to a semantical ambiguity. The similarity with the case of 'and' (discussed in section 4) is striking. First, the phenomenon of referential usage is not something specific to English, nor even to Indo-European languages. Second, as already noted, the phenomenon is not even specific to definite descriptions, it arises with quantifiers quite generally. Third, as Kripke (1977) has pointed out, there is no good reason to suppose that speakers of a language who are taught explicitly Russellian truth conditions for sentences containing definite and indefinite descriptions would not come to use such phrases referentially. Furthermore, speakers of a version of first-order logic without descriptions might still succeed in referring to particular individuals by using existential quantifications of the form 'there is exactly one F and whatever is F is G.' Indeed, as Kripke (1977, p. 17 [399 in this vol.]) observes, on occasion one can even get away with this sort of thing in English:

(10)   Exactly one person is drinking champagne in that corner and I hear he is romantically linked with Jane Smith.

On methodological grounds, then, if attention is restricted to basic cases (section 2), a unitary Russellian theory seems to be preferable to a theory that posits a semantical ambiguity.[36]

6   THE ARGUMENT FROM MISDESCRIPTION

Up to now, discussion of referential usage has been restricted to what I earlier called the *basic case*. I want now to turn to the first of several arguments that are often appealed to by some of those who reject (A3) in favor of (A2), the Argument from Misdescription. This argument comes in two forms. What I shall call the "standard" form of the argument is due to Donnellan (1966) and goes something like this. Consider a referential$_D$ use of 'Smith's murderer'. Now suppose Smith was not in fact murdered but died of natural causes. On Russell's account, the definite description 'Smith's murderer' will be nondenoting, therefore the proposition expressed will be false (it is not the case that there exists some unique x such that x murdered Smith). But this, Donnellan claims, is just incorrect. For suppose the man S *meant*, viz., Jones, *is* insane. Then, surely S will have said something true of that man. The moral we are supposed to draw is that "... using a definite description referentially, a speaker may say something true even though the description applies to nothing" (p. 207 [375]). And the conclusion we are encouraged to accept is that when a description is used referentially, it is the object S wishes to convey something about rather than the descriptive condition used to get at this object that is of semantical relevance. The proposition expressed is therefore object-dependent rather than descriptive.[37]

The problem with this argument is that it relies on the existence of a clear intuition that the proposition expressed is still true despite the fact that neither Jones nor anyone else satisfies the description 'Smith's murderer'. But this is simply not so. We feel an uneasy tension when we are presented with such cases. As several authors have noted, we want to say that S did something right but *also* that S did something *wrong*. After all, the description he used *failed to fit* the person S wanted to "talk about," and to that extent the speech act was defective.[38]

The referentialist can say nothing useful here, but the Russellian can provide a theoretical explanation of the aforementioned tension: What has been left out by the referentialist is the Gricean distinction between the proposition expressed and the proposition(s) meant. Indeed, one of the earliest overt defenses of the Theory of Descriptions in the face of the Argument from Misdescription was the one sketched by Grice (1969) himself. According to Grice, "what, in such a case, a speaker has *said* may be false, what he *meant* may be true" (p. 142). The proposition expressed by an utterance of 'the F is G' is still descriptive, but the speaker may exploit the fact that both speaker and hearer are willing to entertain the idea that some particular individual b is uniquely F in order to communicate an object-dependent proposition about b. Again, the proposition that b is G may well be part of what is *meant* but it is not the proposition expressed, nor is it implied by it.[39] Applied to Donnellan's example, the proposition expressed by my utterance of 'Smith's murderer is insane' is false; but the proposition I intended to communicate is true (if Jones is indeed insane). Thus the Russellian-Gricean has, if only in a rudimentary way, an account of the conflicting pretheoretic intuitions we typically have when presented with cases involving misdescription. The possibility of misdescription does not advance the case for a semantically referential interpretation in the least; indeed, the unitary Russellian analysis has the edge here.

More or less the same is true with what we can call the *inverted* form of the Argument from Misdescription, due to Hornsby (1977). Consider again a referential$_D$ use of 'Smith's murderer is insane'. Now suppose that the man I *meant* was not insane, and moreover that he did not murder Smith. But suppose that the man who did murder Smith is insane. On Russell's account, the proposition expressed is true, since the unique individual who murdered Smith is insane. But according to Hornsby this is a mistake. I was talking about that man there in the dock, and since he is not insane my utterance cannot be true. We should conclude, Hornsby suggests, that on this occasion, 'Smith's murderer' functions as a genuine referring expression.

The problem with this form of the argument is that is relies on the existence of a clear intuition that the proposition expressed is false, despite the fact that the unique individual that does in fact satisfy 'Smith's murderer' is insane. But this is simply not so. As with the standard form of the argument, we feel an uneasy tension when we are presented with such cases, a tension the Russellian-Gricean can explain.[40]

I doubt these sorts of considerations can be worked up into knock-down arguments against a semantically distinct referential interpretation. However, Salmon (1982) argues that related counterfactual considerations cast serious doubt on the viability of a referential interpretation. Occurrences of 'Smith's murderer' that are semantically referential will be rigid designators. Consequently, if I utter the sentence 'Smith's murderer is insane' in a context C, with the intention that 'Smith's murderer' refer to Jones, then the proposition expressed by my utterance is true with respect to any counterfactual situation in which Jones is insane, even those in which Jones does not murder Smith, those in which Smith is not murdered, those in which Smith does not exist, and those in which there are no murders. And this, Salmon maintains, is quite unacceptable.

Salmon's argument can also be inverted. If I utter the sentence 'Smith's murderer is insane' in a context C, with the intention that 'Smith's murderer' refer to Jones, then the proposition expressed by my utterance is false with respect to any counterfactual situation in which Jones exists but is not insane, even those in which Smith is murdered and the person who murdered him is insane. I must admit I am sympathetic to Salmon's reaction to such results, but I doubt that it is possible to arrive at judgments of truth or falsity that are not to some extent clouded by either one's initial position on the debate or one's views about the bearers of truth or falsity.[41] My own conclusion—a conclusion I am perfectly happy with—is that cases involving misdescription simply provide no evidence for a semantically referential interpretation of descriptions.

7   THE ARGUMENT FROM INCOMPLETENESS

In section 3, we established that the propositions expressed by utterances containing indexical descriptions like 'my mother' or 'the philosopher I most admire' are partially determined by context. But it is not just overtly indexical descriptions that are context-sensitive. This can be illustrated with the help of the following passage from Strawson's "On Referring":

Consider the sentence, 'The table is covered with books'. It is quite certain that in any normal use of this sentence, the expression 'the table' would be used to make a unique reference, i.e. to refer to some one table. It is a quite strict use of the definite article, in the sense in which Russell talks on p. 30 of *Principia Mathematica*, of using the article "strictly, so as to imply uniqueness." On the same page Russell says that a phrase of the form "the so-and-so," used strictly, "will only have an application in the event of there being one so-and-so and no more." Now it is obviously quite false that the phrase 'the table' in the sentence 'the table is covered with books', used normally, will "only have an application in the event of there being one table and no more" (1950, pp. 14–15 [chap. 16, pp. 347–8 herein]).

There is an important truth in this passage. A speaker may use a definite description when, strictly speaking, it is quite clear that there is no object that uniquely satisfies it. And, on the face of it, this seems to pose a problem for Russell. If I say to you right now

(1) The table is covered with books

I would not normally be understood as committing myself to the existence of one and only one table. But a naïve application of the Theory of Descriptions appears to have precisely this unwelcome consequence. And since there does not seem to be any good reason for doubting that a determinate proposition is expressed by an utterance of (1), *prima facie* the Russellian is under some obligation to specify its content. By contrast, a theory that postulates a semantically distinct referential interpretation of descriptions seems to provide a natural account of what is going on in (1): the description functions as a referring expression.

Let's call a description 'the *F*' that appears to have a legitimate application even if there is more than one *F* an *incomplete* or *improper* description.[42]

The first thing to notice about incompleteness is that it is neither a necessary nor a sufficient condition for referential usage, an observation made explicit by Peacocke. That incompleteness is not necessary:

If you and I visited the Casino at Monte Carlo yesterday, and saw a man break the bank ... and it is common knowledge that this is so, then the description:

"The man who broke the bank at Monte Carlo yesterday"

as it occurs in a particular utterance *today* of

"The man who broke the bank at Monte Carlo yesterday had holes in his shoes"

may well be satisfied by just one object in the universe but it is here [referential] (1975, p. 117).

That incompleteness is not sufficient:

[Suppose] two school inspectors [are] visiting an institution for the first time: one may say to the other, on the basis of the activities around him, "The headmaster doesn't have much control of the pupils." Here there is no object such that the school inspector has said of it that it doesn't have much control over the pupils. One cannot say that the headmaster is such an object, since what the inspector (*actually*) said would be true even if someone else were headmaster (*ibid.*).[43]

Whenever we find some phenomenon associated with the use of definite descriptions, we should look for corresponding phenomena associated with the uses of other quantifiers. This tactic served us well in section 5 when we examined how someone might convey an object-dependent proposition while expressing (only) an object-independent proposition, and it serves us equally well here. Suppose I had a dinner party last night. In response to a question as to how it went, I say to you

(2) Everyone was sick.

Clearly I do not mean to be asserting that everyone in existence was sick, just that everyone *at the dinner party I had last night* was. In some fashion or other, this is discernible from the context of utterance.[44] Similar examples can be constructed using 'no', 'most', 'just one', 'exactly eight', and, of course, 'the' (as it occurs with both singular and plural complements). Indeed, the problem of incompleteness has nothing to do with the use of definite descriptions *per se*; it is a quite general fact about the use of quantifiers in natural language.[45] What is needed, then, is not just an account of incomplete descriptions, but a quite general account of incomplete quantifiers. It seems unlikely, therefore, that incompleteness raise any special problems for a quantificational analysis of descriptions that do not have to be faced in any event by quantificational analyses of other quantifiers.[46]

There are two main approaches to incompleteness in the literature, what we might call the *explicit* and the *implicit* approaches. According to the explicit approach, incomplete quantifiers are *elliptical* for proper quantifiers. As Sellars puts it, the descriptive content is "completed" by context. According to the implicit approach, the context of utterance delimits the domain of quantification and leaves the descriptive content untouched.[47] Consider sentence (2) again. On the explicit approach, the quantifier 'everybody' (as it is used on this occasion) is elliptical for 'everybody at the dinner party I had last night', or some such "narrower" quantifier. On the implicit approach, the domain of quantification is understood as restricted to some favored class of individuals (or to some favored part of the world).[48]

On the assumption that one (or both) of these approaches (or something very similar to one or other of them) will play a role in any complete theory of natural language quantification, any theory that treats definite descriptions as quantifiers is at liberty to appeal to either when incompleteness arises. Consider again Strawson's example

(1) The table is covered with books.

On the explicit approach (taken by, e.g., Sellars 1954), a particular utterance of 'the table' might be elliptical for (e.g.) 'the table *over there*'.[49] On the implicit approach, the domain of quantification might be restricted to (e.g.) objects in the immediate shared perceptual environment. The mere fact that we find incomplete descriptions in discourse does not *by itself*, then, give us any reason to abandon Russell's quantificational analysis of descriptions.[50]

Nonetheless, some philosophers have argued that there are intrinsic problems with one or other of these approaches to incompleteness, and that instead of being contextually completed, some occurrences of incomplete descriptions simply have to be provided with semantically referential interpretations.

Let's suppose that an incomplete description is elliptical for a proper (i.e., uniquely-denoting) description recoverable from the context of utterance. As a general account of incomplete descriptions, this type of proposal has come under fire from Donnellan (1968), Hornsby (1977), Wettstein (1981), and Recanati (1986).[51] In his brief discussion of incomplete descriptions, Donnellan is quite willing to accept the elliptical proposal for descriptions used nonreferentially:

Without considering the two uses of descriptions, the reply [to Strawson's comments cited above] one is inclined to make on Russell's behalf is that in the loose way of everyday speech the context is relied upon to supply further qualifications on the description to make it unique. This seems a plausible reply when considering attributive uses. Suppose someone says, "The next President will be a dove on Viet Nam," and the context easily supplies the implicit "of the United States" (1968, p. 204, note 5).

But Donnellan does not think that this will work for incomplete descriptions used referentially:

But where one has a very "indefinite" [i.e., incomplete] definite description, with many things in the world satisfying the actual description, the reply is not so plausible. These are commonly, I believe, referential uses. A speaker wants to refer to some object and uses an "indefinite" definite description. Asked to make his description more precise, he may have to think about how best to do it. Several further descriptions may come to mind, not all of which are actually correct. Which, then, shall we say is the full but implicit one? Once we see the function of a referential description, however, we need not suppose that there is any one description recoverable from the speech act that is supposed uniquely to apply to the object referred to. The audience may through the partial description and various clues and cues know to what the speaker refers without being in possession of a description that uniquely fits it and which was implicit all along in the speaker's speech act (*ibid*).

Donnellan is not, then, arguing *from* incompleteness *to* referentiality; rather he seems to be claiming that the method of contextual supplementation is implausible *if the description in question is being used referentially*. Wettstein (1981) suggests that we have here the basis of a knock-down argument for a semantically distinct referential interpretation of descriptions. For according to Wettstein, in many cases where an incomplete description is used there will simply be *no* adequate way of contextually deriving a complete description. And the only plausible way out, he suggests, is to concede that in such a case the description is functioning as a *demonstrative* referring expression and that consequently the proposition expressed in object-dependent rather than descriptive. On this account, then, the description takes as its semantical value the object the speaker intended to communicate something about (in the sense of section 5).

To fix ideas, let's consider Wettstein's argument as applied to one of his own examples. Suppose, on a particular occasion of utterance, 'the table' is taken to be elliptical for 'the table in room 209 of Camden Hall at [time] t_1.' According to Wettstein, this proposal is unworkable because there are a number of nonequivalent ways of filling out the descriptive condition to make it uniquely applicable and no principled way to choose between the resulting descriptions. For instance, 'the table on which Wettstein carved his name at [time] t_2' might well be satisfied by, and only by, the unique object that satisfies the descriptive condition 'table in room 209 of Camden Hall at t_1'. Since it is the descriptive condition rather than the denotation that makes it into the proposition expressed, on Russell's account the particular choice of uniquely-denoting description seems to be crucial: a different description means a different proposition. And this apparently leaves the Russellian with the embarrassing task of deciding which of these nonequivalent descriptions is the correct one.

According to Wettstein, it is "implausible in the extreme" to suppose that the situation of utterance somehow enables the hearer to recover the correctly completed description, viz., the one the speaker intended. In many cases, there will simply be no such indication. Moreover, in many cases it doesn't even make sense to ask which of a batch of nonequivalent, codenoting descriptions is *the correct one*. What criterion would one use in deciding which description is the correct one? The one that figures in the speaker's intentions?

> In many cases ... the speaker will have no such determinate intention. If the speaker is asked which Russellian description(s) was implicit in his utterance of 'the table' he will not ordinarily be able to answer. 'Although I meant to refer to that table' our speaker may well reply, 'I don't think I meant to refer to it *as* the table in in room 209 of Camden Hall at t_1 as opposed to, say, *as* the table at which the author of *The Persistence of Objects* is sitting at t_1. Nor did I intend to refer to it *as* the table in 209 *and* the table at which the author ... as opposed to, say, just *as* the table in 209' (1981, p. 247).

If we can't, even by enlisting the help of the speaker, determine which complete description the incomplete description is elliptical for, Wettstein argues, it doesn't make sense to say that there *is* some such correct, complete description.

According to Wettstein, the entire problem can be sidestepped by endorsing the neo-Russellian conception of object-dependent proposition and treating the description as a referring expression that contributes just an object to the proposition expressed. In short the description is to be viewed as a device of *demonstrative reference*. Embarrassing questions about the complete descriptive content are then circumvented, as it is the *object itself*, rather than any particular descriptive condition, that makes it into the proposition expressed. We can call this the Argument from Incompleteness for a referential interpretation of description.

The first sign that something is amiss here is the fact that the argument seems to go through just as well with other quantifiers and with descriptions used *non*referentially. Consider again the sentence

(2) Everyone was sick

uttered in response to a question about last night's dinner party. On the explicit approach, the quantifier 'everyone' (as it is used on this occasion) might be viewed as elliptical for 'everyone at my dinner party last night', 'everyone who ate at my house last night', or some other quantifier of the form 'every *F*' that denotes everyone who came to the dinner party I had last night. Since the descriptive content is different in each case, the precise character of the proposition expressed depends upon which of these codenoting quantifiers is selected. It is clear, then, that Wettstein has put his finger on a very important fact about elliptical analyses of incomplete quantifiers (and perhaps ellipsis quite generally); but it is beginning to look as though no real support for a referential interpretation of descriptions is going to come out of this.

Ironically, this becomes much clearer when we take into account Wettstein's own remarks on incomplete descriptions used *non*referentially. Consider the case of the detective who comes across Smith's body and has no idea who killed him. Rather than uttering 'Smith's murderer is insane' or 'The man who murdered Smith is insane', the detective simply says,

(3) The murderer is insane.

According to Wettstein,

As in the cases of referential use ... there will be any number of ways to fill out the description so as to yield a Russellian description (e.g., 'Harry Smith's murderer', 'the murderer of Joan Smith's husband', 'the murderer of the junior senator from New Jersey in 1975') and in many cases there will be nothing about the circumstances of utterance or the intentions of the speaker which would indicate that any of these Russellian descriptions is the correct one (1981, p. 250–1).

As Wettstein observes, here he is in conflict with Donnellan, who suggests that the elliptical proposal *will* work for descriptions used nonreferentially. Indeed, Wettstein concedes, on Russellian grounds, that the objection he has raised cannot be overcome by treating *this* occurrence of 'the murderer' as a device of demonstrative reference: "One fully understands the proposition without having any idea who murdered Smith" (p. 251). We seem to be stuck:

[1] 'the murderer' is not elliptical for some Russellian description, and [2] no appeal to the referent of 'the murderer' will account for propositional determinacy (1981, p. 251).

Given his endorsement of [1], Wettstein then makes a very odd suggestion. Although this occurrence of the description 'the murderer' is not referential, Wettstein suggests that demonstrative reference still plays a role in a proper characterization of its content:

For in uttering, 'the murderer is insane' in the presence of the mutilated body, the speaker relies on the context to reveal *whose* murder is in question. The speaker, that is, makes an *implicit* reference to the victim (*ibid.*).

Recall that Wettstein's own account of descriptions used referentially is supposed to be immune to the problem of codenoting, nonequivalent descriptions that he has raised for the Russellian. The reason, of course, is that Wettstein explicitly endorses the neo-Russellian conception of an object-dependent proposition: it is the object itself (rather than any descriptive condition or sense) that gets into the proposition expressed. But on this conception of an object-dependent proposition, in the example we are considering there is simply no difference between saying that there is an "implicit reference" to the victim and saying that the incomplete description 'the murderer' is elliptical for a uniquely denoting description, such as 'the murderer of *that man*' (where 'that man' refers to the victim), or 'the murderer of him' (where 'him' refers to the victim), or '*his* murderer' (where 'his' refers to the victim), all of which contribute the same thing to the proposition expressed, viz., the descriptive condition *murderer-of-b* where *b* is the victim himself rather than some description of *b*. Wettstein is just mistaken in claiming that 'the murderer' is "not elliptical for some Russellian description" (*ibid*); the proposition expressed by (3) is given by (4):

(4) [the *x*: *x* murdered *b*] (*x* is insane).

It is unclear why Wettstein thinks the description in (4) is non-Russellian. One possibility is that he has conflated (a) the notion of a *referential description* (i.e., a description that is interpreted referentially), and (b) the notion of *a description containing a referential component*. An alternative diagnosis is that he is unwilling to countenance descriptions containing relational predicates like 'murderer-of-b', where 'b' is a referential term. But this is certainly not a constraint the *Russellian* is obliged to work under.[52] If 'R' is a binary relational predicate, 'b' is a name, and 'x' is a variable, then 'Rbx' is an open sentence, and '[the *x*: Rbx]' is a perfectly good definite description. Perhaps Wettstein is just unwilling to allow the Russellian access to descriptions containing context-sensitive elements such as demonstratives or indexicals. But again, there is no reason to constrain the Russellian in this way. (As Grice (1970) observes, one of Russell's (1905) own examples of a definite description is 'my son'.) To the extent that one countenances idexical and demonstrative referring expressions—and Wettstein certainly does—if 'b' is an indexical or demonstrative, then '[the x: Rbx]' is a perfectly good Russellian description, albeit one with an indexical or demonstrative component. I submit, then, that if descriptions may contain overtly referential components (including indexical and demonstrative components), then there is nothing to prevent the ellipsed elements of incomplete descriptions from being referential. And this is very different from saying that the *description* is interpreted referentially.[53]

The completion of incomplete descriptions with referential components is implicit in Evans' discussion of incompleteness:

... travelling in a car through the United states, I might pass through a town whose roads are particularly bumpy, and in consequence say "They ought to impeach the mayor." I do not intend my audience to identify the object spoken about as one of which he has information; I intend merely that he take me to be saving that the mayor of this town, through which we are passing, ought to be impeached, and this statement is adequately represented quantificationally (1982, p. 324).

Evans is surely right to claim that in his example there is no intention to identify any individual—and hence no temptation to regard this particular utterance of the incomplete description 'the mayor' as referential. Moreover, Evans suggests that he (the speaker) *would* be able to complete the description in a uniquely appropriate way, and supplies a plausible completion using referential rather than descriptive material. As the neo-Russllian would put it, it is the *town itself* rather than some descriptive characterization of the town that gets into the descriptive condition and thereby into in proposition expressed.

There is no reason, of course, why descriptions used referentially should not also be completed using referential material, thus avoiding the problem raised by nonequivalent codenoting descriptions. As Soames (1986) remarks, this suggestion is very natural for descriptions such as 'the Mayor' or 'the murderer', where an additional argument place can be made available for a particular individual specified by the context of utterance. But with examples like 'the table' (which Strawson originally used to attack Russell, and upon which Wettstein fastens in mounting his own attack) it is true that there is no natural argument position to be made available. However, the contextual coordinates of an utterance provide further nondescriptive material. One way of construing Sellars's (1954) original proposal for dealing with 'the table' is that reference is made to the spatial coordinate. On Sellars's account, an utterance of 'the table' is treated as elliptical for (e.g.) 'the table *over here*', or 'the table *over there*', both which of course contain indexicals sensitive to the spatial coordinate p rather than additional descriptive material.[54] Wettstein's own list of complete descriptions for which 'the table' might be viewed as elliptical includes only sentences containing descriptions completed with additional *descriptive* material ('the table in room 209 of Camden Hall at t_1', 'the table at which the author of *The Persistence of Objects* is sitting at t_1', and so on). This is the weak point in his discussion. The semanticist who regards (utterances of) incomplete quantifiers—including incomplete descriptions—as elliptical for complete quantifiers is under no obligation to treat the ellipsed material as free of referring expressions and indexicals.

An account of how incomplete descriptions are to be treated is not required solely to ward off the Argument from Incompleteness. First, incompleteness affects descriptions used *non*referentially, so a general account of the phenomenon cannot be based on a referential interpretation. Second, incompleteness affects quantifiers more generally, not just definite descriptions. And to that extent, appeals to contextual coordinates and ellipsed material are independently required by any adequate theory of natural language quantification.[55]

It should be noted that the problem of incompleteness can also emerge with descriptions used *anaphorically*, as in (5) and (6):

(5) I bought *a donkey* and a horse last week. For some reason *the donkey* will not eat anything.

(6) *Three women* and *a man* arrived in a large truck. *The women* got out and began dancing in the road while *the man* played the accordian.

In these cases, it is plausible to suppose (as Evans (1977) has argued) that the descriptions in question are completed using material from the clause containing their antecedents.

CONCLUDING REMARKS

We have seen that the Theory of Descriptions in not threatened by the fact that context plays important and complex roles in the way sentences containing descriptions are understood. First, indexicality is a pervasive feature of natural language, and the fact that quantifiers, including definite descriptions, may contain indexical components does nothing to undermine either the schematic theory of quantification or the place of the Theory of Descriptions within that theory. Second, the fact that a speaker may use a definite description to convey an object-dependent proposition poses no threat to this picture; in particular it provides no support for the view that descriptions are ambiguous between Russellian and referential interpretations. Again, the phenomenon is one that is not specific to descriptions but something we find with quantifiers quite generally. Once one takes into account (a) a very natural distinction between the proposition expressed and the proposition(s) meant, (b) the nature and role of context, (c) communicative aims or goals, and (d) our abilities to make certain elementary inferences, the general form of an explanation of this phenomenon comes clearly into view. Finally, no support for a referential interpretation of descriptions can be derived from the fact that quantifiers may be superficially incomplete.

Notes

1. Mitchell (1962, pp. 84–85) writes:

Definite descriptions occurring as the subjects of sentences, have at least two distinct functions, which may be illustrated by two sets of examples:

1. a. 'The Prime Minister presides at Cabinet meetings'
   b. 'The Sovereign of Great Britain is the head of the Commonwealth'
   c. 'The man who wrote this unsigned letter had a bad pen'
2. a. 'The Prime Minister has invited me to lunch'
   b. 'The Queen made a tour of the Commonwealth'
   c. 'The author of *Waverley* limped'.

It is not difficult to see that the grammatical subjects of the sentences quoted in List 1 are not used—as proper names, for instance, are used—to refer uniquely. For 'The Prime Minister' and 'the Sovereign' we can substitute, without change of meaning, 'Whoever is Prime Minister' and 'Whoever is Sovereign'.... With the sentences in List 2 the case is different. The subject phrases serve to identify individuals, and what is predicated in each case is predicated of the individuals so identified.

2. Construed as a general account of such readings, the position has been falsified by Cartwright (1968) and Kripke (1977), both of whom produce example whose *de re* readings are not correctly captured by referential interpretations.

3. It is tempting to think of Donnellan as simply labeling Mitchell's distinction (see, e.g., Davies, 1981). However, I do not think this is quite right. First, Mitchell seems to think that his two "functions" of descriptions are tied to the particular sentences used, whereas Donnellan argues that the same sentence may be used with either an attributive or a referential "reading" of the description it contains. Second, Mitchell's (1c)—see note 1—is very like the sorts of examples Donnellan uses to illustrate his attributive use in that the proposition expressed seems to be "about" an individual only under a description. However, (1a) and (1b) seem to be "about" a particular role or position that may be filled by different individuals on different occasions. Thus I am not much inclined to see Mitchell's non-identificatory function as a genuine precursor of Donnellan's attributive use. In

particular, it seems to me that an utterance of (1b) could be true even if there were not, at the time of utterance, a Sovereign of Great Britain. Suppose the Queen dies and for various complex reasons a constitutional crisis ensues that somehow prevents Prince Charles or anyone else from taking the throne. A true utterance of (1b) might still be made.

François Recanati has pointed out to me that something very close to Donnellan's distinction can be found in the work of the seventeenth-century French philosopher Antoine Arnauld, author of the *Port-Royal Logic*. See Dominicy (1984), pp. 123–27.

4. Grice also echoes the point, made by Mitchell (1962) and Donnellan (1966), that in case (1), one may legitimately insert 'whoever he may be' after the definite description. In view of certain worries pointed out by Searle (1979), I have not emphasized this characteristic of case (1).

5. This is also the view of Hampshire (1959), Geach (1962), Kripke (1972, 1977), Wiggins (1975, 1980), Castañeda (1977), Sainsbury (1979), Searle (1979), Klein (1980), Davies (1981), Evans (1982), Salmon (1982), Davidson (1986), and Soames (1986). There are important differences of detail in these proposals, but at the same time there is a consensus that the phenomenon of referential usage does not warrant the postulation of a semantical ambiguity in the definite article. (My indebtedness to the detailed discussions by Kripke, Sainsbury, Searle, and Davies will become clear as this chapter unfolds.)

6. This way of characterizing the alleged semantical significance of referential usage is explicit in (e.g.) Peacocke (1975), Hornsby (1977), and Kaplan (1978); it also seems to be what Donnellan (1978) has in mind. As both Kripke (1977) and Searle (1979) emphasize, for those who advocate a *semantical* distinction between Russellian and referential descriptions, there is still the problem of providing an account of *when*, exactly, a definite description *is* referential (see section 5). The importance of this fact seems to be recognized by Donnellan (1978).

7. The argument implicit in this remark is unpacked in note 36. In places, Donnellan (1966) suggests that he is highlighting a "pragmatic" rather than a semantical ambiguity. But as Searle (1979) quite rightly points out, it is quite unclear what a "pragmatic ambiguity" is supposed to be:

"I went to the bank" is semantically ambiguous. "Flying planes can be dangerous" is syntactically ambiguous. But what is a pragmatic ambiguity? Is "You are standing on my foot" supposed to be pragmatically ambiguous because in some contexts its utterance can be more than just a statement of fact? If so, then every sentence is indefinitely "pragmatically ambiguous." If we had a notion of "pragmatic ambiguity" we would also have a notion of "pragmatic univocality" but in fact neither notion has any clear sense at all (Searle, 1979, p. 150, note 3).

All things considered, it seems to me that the (semantical) ambiguity thesis is held by Rundle (1965), Donnellan (1966, 1968, 1978), Stalnaker (1972), Partee (1972), Peacocke (1975), Hornsby (1977), Kaplan (1978), Devitt (1981), Wettstein (1981), Recanati (1981, 1986, 1989), Fodor and Sag (1982), and Barwise and Perry (1983), among others. Recanati (1989) explicitly denies that his view entails a semantical ambiguity; I disagree. For discussion, see note 36.

A parallel semantical thesis for *indefinite* descriptions appears to be held by (e.g.) Partee (1972), Chastanin (1975), Donnellan (1978), Wilson (1978), Fodor and Sag (1982), Barwise and Perry (1983), and Stich (1986), among others. For discussion, see King (1988) and Ludlow and Neale (1991).

8. An expression ζ occurs in a nonextensional context just in case ζ is within the scope of a nonextensional operator. For present concerns, we can say that a unary, sentential, sentence-forming operator O is extensional just in case the truth-value of '$O(\phi)$' depends only upon the truth-value of the embedded sentence ϕ. Thus, the contexts created by modal operators and attitude verb frames are nonextensional.

9. I was tempted to borrow Kaplan's (1977) technical terms "character" and "content." However, any suggestion of commitment to Kaplan's intensional machinery is best be avoided by using different terminology. I have, however, drawn on Kaplan's informal remarks on indexicals and demonstratives in which his character-content distinction is introduced.

10. In the period with which I am primarily concerned (1905–1919) Russell came to view the class of genuine names as restricted to just (e.g.) 'this' and 'that', which makes his (albeit later) talk of demonstratives as not "mere" names rather misleading in the present context.

11. See (e.g.) Montague (1968), Lewis (1975), and Kaplan (1977).

12. Further contextual coordinates may be required to capture other essential features of context. For discussion, see Lewis, (1975) p. 175.

13. $(\lambda X)\zeta$ represents a function from objects of the type over which X ranges to objects of the same type as ζ. The Russellian could take the semantical value of a description [the x: Fx] to be the function denoted by (λP) ([the x: Fx] (Px)), i.e., as a function from properties to propositions. See Montague (1970, 1973).

14. We can construct analogous cases for a description such as 'your mother', which contains an element sensitive to the addressee coordinate a; 'that man's mother', which is sensitive to the demonstration coordinate d; 'the current U.S. President', sensitive to the temporal coordinate t; and 'the woman who was just sitting here', sensitive to the temporal and spatial coordinates t and p.

15. It is open to argue that (6) is actually ambiguous according as the pronoun is to be given an anaphoric or nonanaphoric (e.g., demonstrative) reading (see Evans (1977) for discussion). The general form of the problem the hearer is faced with is the same.

16. As argued by Sperber and Wilson (1986), even if we anchor indexicals, assign referents, and fully disambiguate an utterance, very often H will *still* not be able to properly characterize the proposition expressed because of vagueness, ellipsis, and so on. As they put is, sentence meaning *radically* underdetermines the proposition expressed.

17. Wittgenstein, *Tractatus Logico-Philosophicus*, 4.024.

18. Part of Grice's project involves providing an analysis of meaning that does not presuppose any linguistic or otherwise semantical concepts, so (G1) is not a

genuine Gricean condition because ϕ is implicitly understood to be a *sentence*. More appropriate would be the following:

(G2) By producing u, S means that p only if for some audience H, S produced u intending:

    (1) H to actively entertain the thought that p, and

    (2) H to recognize that S intends (1)

where u is any piece of behavior the production of which is a candidate for meaning something. For the purposes of this essay, (G1) will suffice because (a) I am not attempting any sort of reductive analysis, and (b) the examples I am most concerned with all involve linguistic utterances. In cases where u is an utterance of the sentence ϕ, I see no harm (for present purposes) in treating as interchangeable the locutions "by producing u, S means that p" and "by uttering ϕ, S means that p."

Grice's attempts to provide necessary and sufficient conditions for utterer's meaning make use of a third intention designed to rule out cases where some feature of the utterance in question makes it completely obvious that p. Grice was worried by cases like the following: (i) Herod presents Salome with the head of St. John the Baptist on a charger; (ii) in response to an invitation to play squash, Bill displays his bandaged leg. According to Grice, we do not want to say that Herod *meant* that St. John the Baptist was dead. Nor do we want to say that Bill *meant* that his leg was bandaged. (We may well want to say that he meant that he could not play squash, or even that he had a bad leg, but not that his leg was bandaged.) Thus Grice suggests the addition of a third clause, the rough import of which is that S intend H's recognition of S's first intention to function as a reason for H to actively entertain the thought that p. Candidate conditions of the form of (G2) are therefore superseded by conditions of the form of (G3):

(G3) By producing u, S means that p only if for some audience H, S produced u intending:

    (1) H to actively entertain the thought that p,

    (2) H to recognize that S intends (1), and

    (3) H's recognition that S intends (1) to function, at least in part, as a reason for (1).

It is not clear to me that the additional constraint in (3) is necessary. The same degree of manifestness seems to be present in certain cases involving properly linguistic utterances. Consider an utterance of, e.g., 'I can speak English', or an utterance of 'I can speak in squeaky voice' said in a squeaky voice (I owe this example to Neil Smith), or an utterance of 'I am over here' bawled across a crowded room at someone known to be looking for the utterer (this example is due to Schiffer (1972)). In none of these cases is there a temptation to say that the speaker did not *mean* what he or she said. As I have stated it, I am not sure whether clause (3) really blocks such cases, but in any event, in the light of the similarities between these cases and those that worried Grice, I do not feel the need for an additional constraint on utterer's meaning, such as (3), that is supposed to prevent (e.g.) Herod from meaning that St. John the Baptist was dead, or Bill from meaning that his leg was bandaged. On this matter, see also Schiffer (1972) and Sperber and Wilson (1986).

19. Grice's wording suggests that a particular maxim or submaxim concerns only what is said (e.g., 'Do not say what you believe to be false') while another concerns, perhaps, what is *meant* (e.g., 'Be relevant'). (I owe this observation to Deirdre Wilson.) However, except for those submaxims under Manner (perhaps) that apply only to what is said, I think we must interpret Grice as allowing a violation of a maxim at the level of what is said to be over-ridden by adherence to that maxim at the level of what is implicated. This seems to me to be the only way to make sense of his account of flouting; i.e., blatantly violating a maxim at the level of what is said but adhering to it at the level of what is implicated does not involve a violation of the CP.

A variety of complications for Grice's theory are discussed by Sperber and Wilson (1981, 1986) and Wilson and Sperber (1981, 1986), who utilize some of Grice's insights in their *relevance*-based approach to utterance interpretation. Since writing the body of this chapter, I have come to believe (mostly through conversations with Dan Sperber) that my own discussion might well have been facilitated had I made use of Sperber and Wilson's theory rather than Grice's.

20. Consider an utterance of 'She is poor and she is honest. Moreover, I don't think she's honest'. The linguistic transgression here is not of the order of an outright contradiction; rather it is more like an instance of Moore's paradox. Nor will contradiction ensue in cases involving an attempted cancellation of what Grice calls *conventional* implicature. Unlike conversational implicatures, conventional implicatures arise regardless of context and are (at least in part) attributable to linguistic convention. To borrow one of Grice's (1961) examples, there is no truth-conditional difference between 'She is poor and honest' and 'She is poor but honest', but we are still inclined to say that these sentences differ in meaning. On Grice's account, an assertion of the latter would involve an additional "non-central" speech act indicating the speaker's (or perhaps someone else's) attitude towards the propositional content of the central speech act (i.e., the assertion that she is poor and honest), an attitude of unexpectedness or contrast. This Grice calls a *conventional* implicature.

There are complex issues involved in spelling out Grice's remarks on this topic, in particular the extent to which the precise content of a given conventional implicature is conversationally determined, i.e., established by recourse to the maxims of conversation and not just to linguistic meaning. As Grice (1961, p. 127) observes, in the example just discussed there is no prospect of characterizing the conventional implicature as a "presupposition" in any interesting sense of this much abused term: even if the implicature were false, i.e., even if there were no reason on Earth to suppose that poverty and honesty contrasted in any way, what is asserted could still be false, say if she were *rich* and honest. I am here indebted to discussion with Paul Grice.

21. In such a case, Grice would say that you "made as if to say" that *p*, and implicated that *q*, as long as you had no intention of inducing (or activating) in your interlocutor the thought that *p*.

22. Cancellability cannot be a sufficient condition because of ambiguity. Consider the following exchange. *A* and *B* meet in the street:

A Where are you going?
B I am going down to the bank to get some money.
A Who do you bank with?
B I'm sorry, I don't understand.
A You said you were going down to the bank to get some money.
B And so I am; I keep my money buried in a chest down by the river.

One might be tempted to argue that *B*'s first utterance carries with it the implication that *B* is about to visit some sort of financial institution, and that his third utterance succeeds in cancelling this implication. Of course, no one would be tempted to argue that 'bank' is unambiguous in English; but since Grice wanted to account for certain alleged ambiguities of philosophical importance in terms of conversational implicature rather than lexical (or syntactical) ambiguity, he cannot (and does not) take cancellability as a sufficient condition for implicature.

23. As pointed out by (e.g.) Sperber and Wilson (1986), since *q* is simply introduced without explanation in step (c), this schema cannot be construed as a characterization of any sort of method for actually *calculating* implicatures, but only as a method for establishing whether or not a particular implication qualifies as a conversational implicature.

24. As Chomsky has emphasized, the syntactician is in a very similar position with respect to intuitions concerning well-formedness (grammaticality). And as Rawls (1971) has pointed out, more or less the same considerations carry over from syntax to ethics.

25. I shall restrict attention to cases where 'and' conjoins sentences for the simple reason that it seems unlikely, to me at least, that all occurrences of 'and' that conjoin (e.g.) noun phrases can be analysed in terms of logical conjunction. While a sentence like

(i)   Russell and Whitehead lived in Cambridge

might be analysable in terms of the conjunction of (ii) and (iii),

(ii) Russell lived in Cambridge

(iii) Whitehead lived in Cambridge

such a proposal is quite unsuitable for

(iv) Russell and Whitehead wrote *Principia Mathematica*.

We have here yet another problem raised by sentences involving plural noun phrases that admit of collective readings.

26. The results of some psycholinguistic experiments suggest that an "order-of-mention" strategy is applied fairly blindly in the earlier stages of language acquisition by children confronted with utterances containing the words 'before' and 'after'. In particular, children appear to grasp '*A* before *B*' and 'After *A*, *B*' before they grasp 'Before *B*, *A*' and '*B* after *A*'. See Clark (1971) and Johnson (1975).

27. Even if it is possible to treat the temporal and causal implications that attach to utterances in which 'and' is conjoining sentences in terms of conversational implicature, Carston (1988) points out that it is not at all clear how to extend the proposal to sentences like

(i) Tell me a secret and I'll tell you one

(ii) Shout at me again and I'll quit

in which 'and' seems to have the force of 'if . . . then'.

Carston proposes a way of holding onto the idea that 'and' is unambiguous while at the same time allowing for a difference between the proposition expressed by 'p and q' and 'p & q' on the grounds that linguistic meaning underdetermines the proposition expressed. Carston's approach may well inherit the positive characteristics of Grice's approach without inheriting many of its problems.

28. According to (e.g.) Gazdar (1979), an utterance of a sentence of the form 'some Fs are Gs' gives rise to a generalized conversational implicature to the effect that the speaker knows that some Fs are not Gs. But as Soames (1981, pp. 533–37) points out, it is more plausible to suppose that the generalized implicature is really that the speaker does not know whether all Fs are Gs, an additional particularized implicature to the effect that the speaker knows (or believes) that some Fs are not Gs, arising if the speaker can be presumed to know whether or not all Fs and Gs. In order to avoid getting immersed in the details of this type of example, I have deliberately refrained from saying that the speaker conversationally implicates that some of the deaths were not accidental, or that the speaker believes (or knows) that some of the deaths were not accidental, opting instead for talk of the speaker implicating that he or she is willing to entertain the possibility that some Fs are not Gs.

29. Furthermore, as Martin Davies has pointed out to me, parity of reasoning would require that if S knew of a, b, c, d, and e that they were all of the Fs in existence, S could not use 'all Fs' as a quantifier. The real force of this point will emerge once we turn to referential uses of other quantifiers.

30. The existence of certain object-dependent beliefs on the part of the speaker is sometimes taken to suffice for a "referential" or "specific" use of an *indefinite* description in the literature on this topic (see, e.g., Fodor and Sag (1982)). In my opinion, this leads to considerable confusion. For discussion, see Ludlow and Neale (1991).

31. Although there are counterexamples to (A2), I shall ignore them in what follows. The type of patching that is required would take us too far astray, and after all, I am only trying to provide the referentialist with a workable account of referential usage that can be utilized in conjunction with (A1), I am not trying to present a watertight conceptual analysis. The conjunction of (A1) and (A2) provides the referentialist with *a far more plausible position* than does the conjunction of (A1) with any alternative characterization of referential usage I have seen. (As Kripke (1977) and Searle (1979) observe, Donnellan's (1966) positive characterizations of referential and attributive usage lead to a classification that is neither exclusive nor exhaustive and problematic borderline cases can easily be con-

structed (on this point, see also Davies, 1981). No doubt the sorts of considerations that Kripke and Searle adduce could also be used to undermine (A2), but it still seems to me to provide the referentialist with the most reasonable position available.)

32. In conversation, it has more than once been suggested that the distinction between referential$_D$ and referential$_N$ uses is pedantic since the claim made by the referentialist is just the broad claim that descriptions used referentially function as referring expressions. But the distinction can only seem pedantic to those who presuppose a neo-Russellian conception of an object-dependent proposition. To someone who is as sensitive as Evans to the important differences between names and demonstratives, the distinction between referential$_D$ and referential$_N$ uses of descriptions will be vital if a semantically distinct referential interpretation turns out to be necessary. I do not want to presuppose any particular account of object-dependence; my reasons for adhering to the distinction concern satisfaction of the Justification Requirement.

33. Such an ambiguity is argued for by Chastain (1975), Wilson (1978), Donnellan (1978), Fodor and Sag (1982), Barwise and Perry (1983), and Stich (1986). For problems with this view, see King (1988) and Ludlow and Neale (1991). As Kripke (1977) points out, many of the considerations that favor a unitary Russellian account of definite descriptions carry over *mutatis mutandis* to indefinite descriptions.

34. This point is made by Sainsbury (1979), Davies (1981), and Blackburn (1984). The example I have used is based on an example due to Davies.

35. To the extent that such schemata seem to be adequate for many cases involving referential uses of descriptions, and to the extent that purely descriptive grounds for an assertion that the *F* is *G* are the exception rather than the rule, we might view such schemata as having the status of interpretive heuristics. More or less this suggestion is made by Klein (1980), though he does not distinguish between referential$_N$ and referential$_D$ uses.

36. This view has been contested by Recanati (1989) on the grounds that one can endorse (A1) and (A2) without being committed to an ambiguity in the definite article. I am baffled by this claim. Recanati explicitly assumes something akin to a three-way Gricean distinction between (a) the linguistic meaning of a sentence ϕ, (b) the proposition expressed by a particular utterance u of ϕ by a speaker S, and (c) the proposition(s) S meant by u. By analogy with the semantics of indexical and demonstrative referring expressions, Recanati suggests that a difference in the proposition expressed by distinct utterances of 'the *F* is *G*' does not correspond to distinct linguistic meanings of this sentence (or to linguistic meanings of the description 'the F' or two linguistic meanings of the definite article 'the').

    To fix ideas, let's return to the semantics of demonstratives. If I point to Recanati and say

(i) That man is French

I express a true object-dependent proposition about Recanati. If I point to David Lewis and utter (i) I express a false object-dependent proposition about Lewis. Of course, we do not have to say that (i) is ambiguous. It has a unique linguistic meaning; but because it contains an indexical component sensitive to a contextual coordinate, it may be used on different occasions to express different object-dependent propositions. In cases in which the proposition expressed exhausts the proposition(s) meant, we get the following picture (F1):

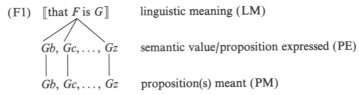

(F1) $[\![\text{that } F \text{ is } G]\!]$ linguistic meaning (LM)

$Gb, Gc, \ldots, Gz$ semantic value/proposition expressed (PE)

$Gb, Gc, \ldots, Gz$ proposition(s) meant (PM)

where each chain represents a distinct utterance of 'that F is G'.

I have assumed until now that the referential use of a description 'the F' may be captured in one of two ways, which might be pictured as follows:

(F2) Russellian

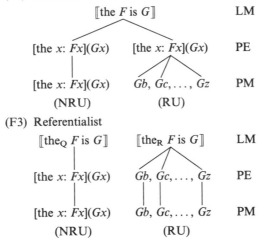

$[\![\text{the } F \text{ is } G]\!]$ LM

[the x: Fx](Gx)   [the x: Fx](Gx)   PE

[the x: Fx](Gx) $Gb, Gc, \ldots, Gz$ PM

(NRU)   (RU)

(F3) Referentialist

$[\![\text{the}_Q F \text{ is } G]\!]$ $[\![\text{the}_R F \text{ is } G]\!]$ LM

[the x: Fx](Gx) $Gb, Gc, \ldots, Gz$ PE

[the x: Fx](Gx) $Gb, Gc, \ldots, Gz$ PM

(NRU)   (RU)

where 'NRU' and 'RU' signify nonreferential and referential usage, respectively. For the Russellian 'the F is G' has one linguistic meaning, represented as $[\![\text{the } F$ is $G]\!]$; for the referentialist it has two linguistic meanings, represented as $[\![\text{the}_Q F$ is $G]\!]$ and $[\![\text{the}_R F$ is $G]\!]$.

Underlying the picture of the referentialist's position given in (F3) is the following argument: (i) if a particular utterance u of 'the F is G' expresses the object-independent proposition that whoever or whatever is uniquely F is also G, and a distinct utterance u^* of 'the F is G' expresses the object-dependent proposition that b is G, then the sentence 'the F is G' is semantically ambiguous, i.e., the sentence has two (or more) linguistic meanings (in the sense of §3); (ii) if the sentence 'the F is G' is ambiguous and the predicate 'is G' is unambiguous, then the definite description 'the F' is ambiguous, i.e., the description has two (or more) linguistic meanings; (iii) if the description 'the F' is ambiguous and the predicate 'F'

is unambiguous, then the definite article 'the' is ambiguous, i.e., the article has two (or more) linguistic meanings.

It appears to be Recanati's view that descriptions can be treated on this model of indexicals and demonstratives, i.e, on the model of (F1) rather than (F3). That is, the sentence 'the *F* is *G*' does *not* have two linguistic meanings; rather, it is "indexical" and expresses either an *object-dependent* or an object-independent proposition according as the description is used referentially or nonreferentially. Recanati is, then, advocating the following picture:

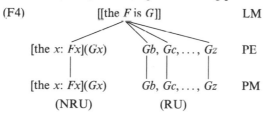

(F4)   [[the *F* is *G*]]   LM

[the *x*: *Fx*](*Gx*)   *Gb*, *Gc*, ..., *Gz*   PE

[the *x*: *Fx*](*Gx*)   *Gb*, *Gc*, ..., *Gz*   PM
         (NRU)   (RU)

I find this proposal puzzling. The word 'I' is unambiguous because it always refers to the speaker; a simple sentence of the form 'I am *G*' is unambiguous because it always expresses an *object-dependent* proposition about the speaker. The demonstrative expression 'that *F*' is unambiguous because it always refers to the object of the speaker's demonstration and a simple sentence of the form 'the *F* is *G*' is unambiguous because it always expresses an *object-dependent* proposition about the object of the speaker's demonstration. On Recanati's proposal, not only may different utterances of 'the *F* is *G*' express different *object-dependent* propositions, but other utterances of this same sentence may express the *object independent* proposition that whatever is uniquely *F* is *G*. It all depends on whether the description is used referentially or nonreferentially.

It seems to me highly artificial to say that 'the *F* is *G*', 'the *F*' and 'the' are "unambiguous" on this proposal. On some occasions of use 'the *p*' refers (or is supposed to *refer*) to some contextually determined individual and the proposition expressed by 'the *F* is *G*' is object-dependent, whereas on other occasions of use 'the *F*' does *not* refer (and is not even intended to refer), and the proposition expressed is a complex quantificational affair. Since two utterly distinct *types* of proposition may be expressed, I fail to see how a theory with such flexibility can fail to be a theory that is postulating a semantical ambiguity. Despite Recanati's remarks to the contrary, it seems to me that his claim that 'the *F*' is unambiguous within his theory is close to being on a par with the claim that the noun 'bank' is unambiguous: on some occasions it is used for ground alongside a river and on others it is used for a type of financial institution.

Of course, even if Recanati is right that one can endorse (A1) and (A2) without postulating a genuine lexical ambiguity, a unitary Russellian theory of descriptions is still simpler than a theory that allows the proposition expressed to be either object-independent or object-dependent depending upon the context of utterance. Furthermore, the putative coherence of such a theory would not demonstrate that (A1) is true and (A3) is false. (There are also problems internal to Recanati's own positive proposed that I shall not address here.)

37. The general observation that one may succeed in conveying something about an individual by using a description that the individual does not satisfy is due to Hampshire (1959), p. 203. (See also Geach, 1962, and Linsky, 1963, 1966.) Indeed, Hampshire's brief discussion of descriptions (pp. 201–4) appears to anticipate quite a lot of subsequent discussion that appeals to misdescription and the distinction between the proposition expressed and the proposition(s) meant.

38. See (e.g.) Kripke (1977), Sainsbury (1979), Searle (1979), Davies (1981), Evans (1982), and Blackburn (1984). As pointed out by Kripke and Searle we find a similar tension in cases where a proper name is misapplied. To borrow Kripke's example, suppose two people A and B see Smith in the distance but mistake him for Jones. A says "Jones is up early." B replies "Yes, he's hard at work too." Devitt (1981) points out some further troubling features of this sort of example that suggest that the distinction between the proposition expressed and the proposition(s) meant will not clear up all of its complexities.

39. Responses to the Argument from Misdescription in the same vein are also presented by Wiggins (1975), and in rather more detail by Kripke (1977), Sainsbury (1979), Searle (1979), and Davies (1981). For remarks that anticipate the Gricean response to the Argument from Misdescription, see Hampshire (1959), pp. 201–4, and Geach (1962), p. 8.

40. Up to now, I have considered only cases in which the speaker is genuinely mistaken about who or what satisfies the description that is being employed. But as Donnellan (1966) points out, one might perfectly well use a description 'the F' referentially without being sure that the individual one has in mind is the F; indeed, as Hampshire (1959), Donnellan (1966), Grice (1981), and others have pointed out, conceivably one might use the description 'the F' while being quite sure that it does *not* apply to the individual one has in mind, or to any individual at all. The possibility of such cases does not force us to alter the general picture that has emerged so far, though it certainly adds interesting complications in providing an exact specification of when a description is being used referentially.

If the hearer is intended to reason as before, then such cases are no different from the ones we have been considering, except that [the x: Fx] $(x = b)$, and very like [the x: Fx](Gx), will no longer furnish the speaker's grounds for his or her utterance. On the other hand, the speaker may be well aware that the hearer does not believe that b is the F, yet still think it possible to communicate a singular proposition to the effect that b is G by uttering 'the F is G'. (For example, Donnellan considers a case in which both speaker and hearer are aware that the description 'the king' does not strictly apply to the individual being referred to because that individual is a usurper; but they continue to use this description because they are fearful of reprisals. Another example: it may become the practice of the members of a certain group of individuals to use the description 'the F' when they wish to say something about a certain individual. Of course, at a certain point one might well be inclined to treat this description as a name on a par with 'The Holy Roman Empire' or 'The Evening Star'.) A variety of interesting cases can be constructed by tinkering with speakers' and hearers' beliefs about the satisfiers of descriptions and with beliefs about each others' beliefs, but the complexities involved do not seem to provide any insurmountable problems for the Russellian. Indeed, as Kripke (1977, p. 24 [pp. 409–10], note 22) points out, if anything, the fact that many of these cases— for instance, Donnellan's king/usurper case—look a lot like cases involving irony or "inverted commas" seems to actually *weaken* the case for a semantical ambiguity. After all, we want a pragmatic account of irony, not an account that appeals to distinct literal and ironical meanings of expressions. (Once again, these considerations seem to carry over *mutatis mutandis* to other quantifiers, especially indefinite descriptions. On this matter, see Ludlow and Neale (1991).)

41. Wettstein (1981) suggests that Salmon's argument turns on the mistaken assumption that a sentence relativized to a context of utterance C can be evaluated for truth or falsity at a possible world w, when in fact truth or falsity are properly predicated of the proposition expressed. But if Salmon is assuming a standard possible worlds semantics, it is unclear to me what technical or philosophical error Wettstein claims to have discovered in Salmon's discussion.

42. There seems to be no generally agreed upon label. Such phrases are known variously as *incomplete*, *improper*, *imperfect*, or *indefinite* definite descriptions.

43. According to Devitt (1981), incomplete descriptions "... are ones that are unsuitable for attributive use because only someone with crazy beliefs would use them: it is obvious that they do not denote" (p. 521). Peacocke's example is a clear counterexample to Devitt's claim, as are the examples from Donnellan (1968) and Evans (1982) quoted below.

44. This point is made by Quine (1940), Sellars (1954), Sainsbury (1979), Davies (1981), and Blackburn (1984).

45. Following Barwise and Cooper (1981), let's say that a quantifier $[Dx: Fx]$ is persistent just in case the following is a valid inference:

$$[Dx: Fx](Gx)$$
$$\underline{[\text{every } x: Fx](Hx)}$$
$$[Dx: Hx](Gx)$$

for arbitrary G and H. Strictly speaking, the particular problem concerning incompleteness that I am addressing surfaces only with nonpersistent quantifiers, though a derivative problem surfaces for persistent quantifiers. A precise generalization does not seem to be possible here because of complex issues to do with predication, but very roughly we can say the following. For nonpersistent quantifiers the problem is that $[Dx: Fx](Gx)$ might be false while $[Dx: Fx \& Hx](Gx)$ is true; for persistent quantifiers the problem is that $[Dx: Fx](Gx)$ might be true while $[Dx: Fx \& Hx](Gx)$ to false.

46. There seems to be an even more general issue here. As (e.g.) Sellars (1954) and Sperber and Wilson (1986) have stressed, in many cases the linguistic meaning of a sentence—or sentence fragment—radically underdetermines the proposition it is used to express on a given occasion. We have already considered the sort of contextual supplementation that is required where an utterance contains overtly indexical or demonstrative components; but context-sensitivity does not end there.

Suppose I ask *S* how old he is and he replies, "Twenty-five." We want to say that *S* has expressed the proposition that he is twenty-five years old. Or take the sentence 'This cup is mine'. Here there is no obvious ellipsis but depending upon the context of utterance I might use this sentence to express the proposition that (e.g.) this cup is owned by me, or that it is being drunk from by me, or that it is being used by me, or that it has been assigned to me.

47. One could, of course, maintain that incompleteness is of no consequence once one takes into account the distinction between the proposition expressed and the proposition(s) meant. The idea here would be that my utterance of 'everybody was sick' expresses the manifestly false proposition that everybody was sick, but in the particular conversational setting it is very clear that I am attempting to *convey* the proposition that everybody who came to the dinner party I had last night was sick (standard forms of Gricean reasoning explaining the leap from the proposition expressed to the proposition meant). I know of no knock-down argument against this approach to incompleteness, but in view of the fact that context-dependence is such a ubiquitous feature of the use of natural language, it seems likely that the explicit and implicit methods yield predictions more in accordance with our intuitive ascriptions of truth and falsity.

48. When all is said and done, the explicit and implicit methods might turn out to be notational variants of one another. For remarks that suggest otherwise, see Davies (1981) and Soames (1986).

49. For similar suggestions, see also Quine (1940), Vendler (1967), Lewis (1973), Cresswell (1973), and Grice (1981).

50. As noted at the outset, the problem of incompleteness affects plural as well as singular descriptions. In what follows, I shall restrict attention to singular descriptions, though nearly everything I shall have to say ought to carry over *mutatis mutandis* to plurals.

51. Even Kripke (1977) and Evans (1982), both of whom are very sympathetic to a unitary Russellian interpretation of descriptions, suggest that incompleteness may be just enough of a problem for the Russellian to warrant the postulation of a referential interpretation.

52. This has been noted by, e.g., Sellars (1954), Grice (1970, 1981), Evans (1982), Salmon (1982), and Soames (1986). After the bulk of the present chapter was completed, Nathan Salmon drew my attention to a recent paper by Blackburn (1988) in which the same point is made in the context of a discussion of Wettstein's argument.

53. To be more precise, saying that a Russellian description '[the *x*: *Rbx*]' may contain a referential component '*b*' is very different from saying that the description is referential (in the intended sense) *as long as R is not the identity relation*. A phrase of the form '[the *x*: *x* = *b*]' is technically a Russellian definite description; but the claim that referential uses of descriptions do not require distinctive non-Russellian interpretations would indeed be hollow if the Russellian position could be maintained only by employing the identity relation to concoct descriptions of this form (e.g., '[the *x*: *x* = that]'). There is nothing in the present work to suggest

that descriptions of this form are required to account for referential usage. I am here indebted to Martin Davies.

54. The coordinates of a simple context $\langle s, a, \langle d_1, \dots, d_n \rangle, t, p \rangle$ will not systematically supply a correct completion. Consider the incomplete description 'the President'. Suppose we are in the middle of a conversation right now somewhere in the U.S.A. and I say to you

(i) The President is very ill.

The fact that the utterance takes place in the U.S.A. does not guarantee that the description 'the President' is elliptical for 'the U.S. President'. For suppose our entire conversation has been about the health of French politicians and I was in fact "talking about" the French President.

It may, at this stage, be tempting to add further coordinates to the formal notion of a context to cover such things as the *topic of discourse* and so on (see, e.g., Lewis, 1975). Husserl (1913, p. 85) suggests that "When a contemporary German speaks of 'the Emperor', he means the present German Emperor." A literal reading of this remark suggests that one's nationality is the relevant coordinate! In section 4, I argued that we should not expect to be able to provide a formal specification of those features of context that play a role in the calculation of (e.g.) conversational implicatures. (This is not to say, of course, that one cannot attempt to provide a specification of the sorts of principles hearers bring to bear on the interpretation process.) For essentially the same reasons, I think it quite unlikely that an expansion of the formal notion of a context will be of much help in pinning down those factors that, on a given occasion of utterance, may play a role in the full specification of the content of on incomplete description. The important point to note here is that there is absolutely no requirement that a semantical theory be able to provide an account of which contextual features will be drawn upon in order to complete an incomplete description in any given scenario. It is enough if a semantical theory provide the general mechanisms with the aid of which actual complete contents can be specified.

55. In addition to the referential use of descriptions, it is possible to isolate several others.

Appositive use   Searle (1979), and Barwise and Perry (1983) observe that descriptions may be used *appositively*, as in

(i)   John Smith, the man who threw strawberry ice cream at the Pope, was today sentenced to 50 years hard labor.

This example does not seem to present any sort of additional problem for Russell that will not have to be faced in any event by a semantical theory of apposition. One approach to (i) that might be explored is an analysis in terms of the conjunction of (ii) and (iii).

(ii)   John Smith was today sentenced to 50 years hard labor

(iii)   John Smith was the man who threw strawberry ice cream at the Pope.

Another approach that might be explored is to treat the subject of (i) as a complex definite description [the x: $x =$ John Smith & x threw ice cream at the Pope]. Of course, these suggestions need to be investigated in detail before we can feel comfortable with either of them. Unlike the former proposal, the latter seems to carry over naturally to an example like

(iv) The sculptor John Smith died today.

Predicative use   No new problems are presented by an example like

(v) John Smith is the man who threw strawberry ice cream at the Pope.

Indefinite use   Tom Wasow has noted examples such as

(vi) Look it up in the dictionary!

(vii) Let's go to the beach.

These examples are (perhaps) best seen as idiomatic.

Bibliography

Barwise, J., and J. Perry (1983). *Situations and Attitudes*. Cambridge, Mass.: MIT Press.

Blackburn, S. (1984). *Spreading the Word: Groundings in the Philosophy of Language*. Oxford: Clarendon Press.

Blackburn, W. (1988). Wettstein on Definite Descriptions. *Philosophical Studies* 53, 263–278.

Cartwright, R. (1968). Some Remarks on Essentialism. *Noûs* 2, 229–246.

Castañeda, H. N. (1967). Indicators and Quasi-indicators. *American Philosophical Quarterly* 4, 85–100.

Chastain, C. (1975). Reference and Context. In K. Gunderson (ed.), *Minnesota Studies in the Philosophy of Science, vol. VII: Language, Mind, and Knowledge*. Minneapolis: University of Minnesota Press, 194–269.

Chomsky, N. (1970). Remarks on Nominalization. In *Studies on Semantics in Generative Grammar*. The Hague: Mouton, 1972, 11–61.

Chomsky, N. (1975). Questions of Form and Interpretation. *Linguistic Analysis* 1, 75–109.

Chomsky, N. (1981). *Lectures on Government and Binding*. Dordrecht: Foris.

Chomsky, N. (1986). *Knowledge of Language*. New York: Praeger.

Church, A. (1942). Review of Quine's "Whitehead and the Rise of Modern Logic." *Journal of Symbolic Logic* 7, 100–101.

Church, A. (1943). Review of Quine's "Notes on Existence and Necessity." *Journal of Symbolic Logic* 8, 45–47.

Clark, E. (1971). On the Acquisition of the Meaning of "before" and "after." *Journal of Verbal Learning and Verbal Behavior* 10, 266–275.

Davidson, D. (1986). A Nice Derangement of Epitaphs. In R. Grandy and R. Warner (eds.), *Philosophical Grounds of Rationality, Intentions, Categories, Ends*. Oxford: Clarendon Press, 157–174.

Davies, M. (1981). *Meaning, Quantification, Necessity*. London: Routledge and Kegan Paul.

Devitt, M. (1981). Donnellan's Distinction. In P. A. French, T. E. Uehling, Jr., and H. K. Wettstein (eds.), *Midwest Studies in Philosophy VI*. Minneapolis: University of Minnesota Press, 511–524.

Dominicy, M. (1984). *La Naissance de la Grammaire Moderne: Langage, Logique et Philosophie à Port Royal*. Bruxelles: Pierre Mardags Editeur.

Donnellan, K. (1966). Reference and Definite Descriptions. *Philosophical Review* 77, 281–304. [Chap. 17 in this vol.]

Donnellan, K. (1968). Putting Humpty Dumpty Back Together Again. *Philosophical Review* 77.

Donnellan, K. (1978). Speaker Reference, Descriptions, and Anaphora. In P. Cole (ed.), *Syntax and Semantics, vol. 9: Pragmatics*. New York: Academic Press, 47–68.

Evans, G. (1977). Pronouns, Quantifiers and Relative Clauses (I). *Canadian Journal of Philosophy* 7, 467–536. (Reprinted in Evans (1985), 76–152.)

Evans, G. (1982). *The Varieties of Reference*. Oxford: Clarendon Press.

Fodor, J. D., and I. Sag (1982). Referential and Quantificational Indefinites. *Linguistics and Philosophy* 5, 355–398. [Chap. 20 in this vol.]

Gazdar, G. (1979). *Pragmatics: Presupposition, Implicature, and Logical Form*. New York: Academic Press.

Geach, P. (1962). *Reference and Generality*, Ithaca, NY: Cornell University Press.

Grice, H. P. (1957). Meaning. *Philosophical Review* 66, 377–388.

Grice, H. P. (1961). The Causal Theory of Perception. *Proceedings of the Aristotelian Society*, suppl. vol. 35, 121–52.

Grice, H. P. (1967). Logic and Conversation. (William James Lectures.) In *Studies in the Way of Words*. Cambridge, Mass.: Harvard University Press, 1989. (Lectures II and III published as Grice (1975) and Grice (1978).)

Grice, H. P. (1969). Vacuous Names. In D. Davidson and J. Hintikka (eds.), *Words and Objections*. Dordrecht: Reidel, 118–145.

Grice, H. P. (1970). Lectures on Logic and Reality. University of Illinois at Urbana. (Lecture IV published as Grice (1981).)

Grice, H. P. (1981). Presupposition and Conversational Implicature. In P. Cole (ed.), *Radical Pragmatics*. New York: Academic Press, 1981, 183–198.

Hampshire, S. (1959). *Thought and Action*. New York: Viking Press.

Hornsby, J. (1977). Singular Terms in Contexts of Propositional Attitude. *Mind* 86, 31–48.

Husserl, E. (1913). *Logische Untersuchungen, Zweiter Band*. 2nd ed., Halle: Niemeyer. English tr. by J. N. Findlay, London: Routledge and Kegan Paul, 1970.

Johnson, H. (1975). The Meaning of "before" and "after" for Preschool Children. *Journal of Experimental Child Psychology* 19, 88–99.

Kaplan, D. (1977). Demonstratives. In J. Almog, J. Perry, and H. Wettstein (eds.), *Themes from Kaplan*. New York: Oxford University Press, 1989, 481–563.

Kaplan, D. (1978). Dthat. In P. Cole (ed.), *Syntax and Semantics, vol. 9: Pragmatics*. New York: Academic Press, 221–243. [Chap. 28 in this vol.]

King, J. (1988). Are Indefinite Descriptions Ambiguous? *Philosophical Studies* 53, 417–440.

Klein, E. (1980). Defensible Descriptions. In F. Heny (ed.), *Ambiguities in Intensional Contexts*. Dordrecht: Reidel, 1981, 83–102.

Klima, E. (1964). Negation in English. In J. Fodor and J. Katz (eds.), *The Structure of Language*. Englewood Cliffs, NJ: Prentice Hall, 246–323.

Kripke, S. A. (1972). Naming and Necessity. In D. Davidson and G. Harman (eds.), *Semantics of Natural Language*. Dordrecht: Reidel, 253–355, and 763–769.

Kripke, S. A. (1977). Speaker Reference and Semantic Reference. In P. A. French, T. E. Uehling, Jr., and H. K. Wettstein, *Contemporary Perspectives in the Philosophy of Language*. Minneapolis: University of Minnesota Press, 6–27. [Chap. 18 in this vol.]

Lewis, D. (1972). General Semantics. In D. Davidson and G. Harman (eds.), *Semantics of Natural Language*. Dordrecht: Reidel, 169–218.

Lewis, D. (1973). *Counterfactuals*. Cambridge, Mass.: Harvard University Press.

Lewis, D. (1975). Adverbs of Quantification. In E. Keenan (ed.), *Formal Semantics of Natural Language*, Cambridge: Cambridge University Press, 3–15.

Ludlow, P., and S. Neale (1991). Indefinite Descriptions: In Defense of Russell. *Linguistics and Philosophy* 14, 171–202. [Chap. 21 in this vol.]

Marcus, R. (1962). Modalities and Intensional Languages. *Synthese* 27, 303–322. (Reprinted in I. M. Copi and J. A. Gould (eds.), *Contemporary Philosophical Logic*. New York: St. Martin's Press, 1978, 257–272.)

Mitchell, D. (1962). *An Introduction to Logic*. London: Hutchison.

Montague, R. (1968). Pragmatics. In R. Thomason (ed.), *Formal Philosophy: Selected Papers of Richard Montague*. New Haven: Yale University Press, 1974, 95–118.

Montague, R. (1970). English as a Formal Language. In R. Thomason (ed.), *Formal Philosophy: Selected Papers of Richard Montague*. New Haven: Yale University Press, 1974, 188–221.

Montague, R. (1973). The Proper Treatment of Quantification in Ordinary English. In R. Thomason (ed.), *Formal Philosophy: Selected Papers of Richard Montague*. New Haven: Yale University Press, 1974, 247–270.

Neale, S., and P. Ludlow (1989). Russellian Indefinites, Russellian Anaphors. Abstract in *Journal of Symbolic Logic* 54, 666–7.

Partee, B. (1972). Opacity, Coreference and Pronouns. In D. Davidson and G. Harman (eds.), *Semantics of Natural Language*. Dordrecht: Reidel, 415–441.

Peacocke, C. (1975). Proper Names, Reference, and Rigid Designation. In S. Blackburn (ed.), *Meaning, Reference, and Necessity*. Cambridge: Cambridge University Press, 109–132.

Quine, W. V. (1940). *Mathematical Logic*. Cambridge, Mass.: Harvard University Press, revised edition 1951.

Rawls, J. (1971). *A Theory of Justice*. Cambridge, Mass.: Harvard University Press.

Recanati, F. (1981). On Kripke on Donnellan. In H. Parrett, M. Sbisa, and J. Verschueren (eds.), *Possibilities and Limitations of Pragmatics*. Amsterdam: John Benjamins, 595–630.

Recanati, F. (1986). Contextual Dependence and Definite Descriptions. *Proceedings of the Aristotelian Society* 87, 57–73.

Recanati, F. (1989). Referential/Attributive: A Contextualist Proposal. *Philosophical Studies* 56, 217–249.

Rundle, B. (1965). Modality and Quantification. In R. J. Butler (ed.), *Analytical Philosophy, Second Series*. Oxford: Blackwell, 27–39.

Russell, B. (1905). On Denoting. *Mind* 14, 479–493. (Reprinted in R. C. Marsh (ed.), *Logic and Knowledge*. London: George Allen and Unwin, 1956, 41–56.)

Russell, B. (1948). *An Inquiry into Meaning and Truth*. Harmondsworth: Penguin.

Russell, B. (1959). Mr. Strawson on Referring. In *My Philosophical Development*. London: George Allen and Unwin, 238–245.

Sainsbury, R. M. (1979). *Russell*. London: Routledge and Kegan Paul.

Salmon, N. (1980). *Reference and Essence*. Princeton: Princeton University Press.

Salmon, N. (1982). Assertion and Incomplete Definite Descriptions. *Philosophical Studies* 42, 37–45.

Schiffer, S. (1972). *Meaning*. Oxford: Clarendon Press.

Searle, J. (1979). Referential and Attributive. *The Monist* 62, 140–208. (Reprinted in *Expression and Meaning*. Cambridge: Cambridge University Press, 1983, 137–161.)

Sellars, W. (1954). Presupposing. *Philosophical Review* 63, 197–215.

Soames, S. (1986). Incomplete Definite Descriptions. *Notre Dame Journal of Formal Logic* 27, 349–375.

Sperber, D., and D. Wilson (1981). Irony and the Use-mention Distinction. In P. Cole (ed.), *Radical Pragmatics*. New York: Academic Press, 295–318.

Sperber, D., and D. Wilson (1986). *Relevance*. Oxford: Blackwell.

Stalnaker, R. (1972). Pragmatics. In D. Davidson and G. Harman (eds.), *Semantics of Natural Language*, Dordrecht: Reidel, 380–397.

Stich, S. (1986). Are Belief Predicates Systematically Ambiguous? In R. J. Bogdan (ed.), *Belief*. Oxford: Clarendon Press, 119–147.

Strawson, P. F. (1950). On Referring. *Mind* 59, 320–344. (Reprinted in Strawson (1971), 1–27.) [Chap. 16 in this vol.]

Strawson, P. F. (1952). *Introduction to Logical Theory*. London: Methuen.

Vendler, Z. (1967), Singular Terms. In *Linguistics in Philosophy*. Ithaca, NY: Cornell University Press.

Wettstein H. (1981). Demonstrative Reference and Definite Descriptions. *Philosophical Studies* 40, 241–257.

Wiggins, D. (1975). Identity, Designation, Essentialism, and Physicalism. *Philosophia* 5, 1–30.

Wilson, D., and D. Sperber (1981). On Grice's Theory of Conversation. In P. Werth (ed.), *Conversation and Discourse*. London: Croom Helm, 155–178.

Wilson, D., and D. Sperber (1986). On Defining Relevance. In R. Grandy and R. Warner (eds.), *Philosophical Grounds of Rationality*. Oxford: Clarendon Press, 243–258.

Wilson, G. (1978). On Definite and Indefinite Descriptions. *Philosophical Review* 87, 48–76.

Chapter 20

Referential and Quantificational Indefinites

Janet Dean Fodor and Ivan A. Sag

1 INTRODUCTION

We are going to present what we believe to be conclusive evidence for a semantic ambiguity in indefinite noun phrases, over and above any scope ambiguities they may exhibit in appropriate contexts. Sentence (1), for example, contains no opaque verbs, no modals or negation, and no other quantifiers with which its indefinite noun phrase could interact.

(1) A student in the syntax class cheated on the final exam.

We will argue that (1) is nevertheless ambiguous. Its indefinite noun phrase may be semantically interpreted in two distinct ways. One semantic interpretation is that of a quantified expression such as *each student* or *few students*; the other interpretation is that of a referring expression such as a proper name or demonstrative phrase.

At the end of this paper we will attempt a formal characterization of this ambiguity. Meanwhile we will simply refer to the two interpretations of an indefinite as the *referential interpretation* and the *quantifier interpretation*. The quantifier interpretation is really a family of interpretations because of the scope ambiguities exhibited by all quantifiers. Thus sentences like (2) and (3) each have *three* interpretations, one with a narrow scope quantifier corresponding to the indefinite, one with a wide scope quantifier, and one on which the indefinite is referential.

(2) Every professor met a student in the syntax class.

(3) Jones believes that a student in the syntax class was cheating.

First appeared in *Linguistics and Philosophy* 5 (1982): 355–398. Reprinted with kind permission from Kluwer Academic Publishers.

An indefinite interpreted referentially is not a scoped element and therefore does not exhibit any scope ambiguities in these contexts.[1] We believe that a comparable semantic ambiguity can be demonstrated for numerical determiners such as *two*, *three*, *seventeen*, and so on, and also for *some*, *several* and *many* (though *every*, *all*, *each*, *most*, *few*, *no* and the null plural determiner appear to have only a quantifier interpretation).[2] For simplicity we will limit our arguments here to the singular indefinite article *a*.

The idea that an indefinite can be understood either referentially or quantificationally is not a novel one. (See, for example, Chastain, 1975; Wilson, 1978). It is a familiar observation that a sentence like (1) has two uses in discourse. To put it roughly, we could say that someone who utters (1) might be intending to assert merely that the set of students in the syntax class who cheated on the final exam is not empty; or he might be intending to assert of some particular student, whom he does not identify, that this student cheated.

Though this pragmatic distinction has often been drawn, there has never, to our knowledge, been any convincing demonstration that it is associated with a genuine semantic ambiguity. Those who doubt the semantic ambiguity claim are presumably distrustful of what we are calling the referential interpretation. The quantifier interpretation is widely acknowledged by linguists and philosophers, and it seems to be undeniable in view of the fact that indefinites show exactly the same kinds of scope ambiguities as other quantified phrases. The question, then, is whether the referential *use* of an indefinite rests on a referential *interpretation*, or whether it can be satisfactorily explained on the assumption that pragmatic principles can assign a referential use to the quantifier interpretation (specifically, the widest scope quantifier interpretation).

Methodologically, the cards are stacked against the semantic ambiguity claim. It does not recommend itself on the grounds of parsimony, for even if the referential/quantifier ambiguity is assumed, it will still be necessary to appeal to pragmatic principles to predict which indefinites, in which contexts, lend themselves naturally to which of the two interpretations.

What makes the situation even worse is that the putative referential reading is logically equivalent to a wide scope quantifier reading.[3] If some particular student has cheated, then the set of students who have cheated is not empty; and if the set of students who have cheated is not empty, then some particular student must have cheated. What we are claiming, in other words, is that a sentence such as (1) has two distinct semantic analyses that are associated with the same truth conditions.

There are some precedents for this kind of claim. The sentence *I told a story about John* has two distinct syntactic analyses, each with its own semantic interpretation, but it happens that both interpretations will be true under the same conditions. The sentence *The door was shut* also has two interpretations (which are readily recognizable in *I know the door was shut at 9 o'clock but I don't know when it was shut*; see Jespersen, 1931, p. 98), whose truth conditions are very similar and distinguishable only with respect to certain odd circumstances (e.g. a door built in closed position and never opened since).

It is important to bear in mind the nature of the evidence for such ambiguity claims. There are general principles, needed to account for the meanings of other sentences, which will automatically (i.e unless specifically constrained) assign two semantic analyses to the sentence *I told a story about John*; and there are general principles, needed to account for the truth conditions of other sentences, which will automatically (i.e. unless specifically constrained) assign identical truth conditions on the basis of the two different semantic analyses. Economy considerations thus support the assumption of ambiguity in this case, even in the absence of clear intuitive evidence for it.

For indefinites, there has been no comparably clear demonstration of the semantic divergence and the truth conditional convergence of the referential and quantifier interpretations. For one thing, there is no reason to believe that the two interpretations are associated with distinct syntactic structures. The ambiguity, we will claim, is a lexical ambiguity, comparable to the lexical ambiguity of *bank* rather than to the syntactic ambiguity of *old men and women* or *visiting relatives*. For another thing, there appear to be no other sentences, not contatining indefinites, which motivate general interpretive rules from which it would follow that indefinites should be ambiguous in just this way. For example, since the ambiguity is not a scope ambiguity, it could not be argued to follow automatically from a general theory of scope based on the semantic behavior of other quantifiers and logical operators.

It is our belief that no definitive argument for the ambiguity of a simple sentence like (1) can be established by reference to facts about (1) itself. The evidence derives, as we will show, from multi-clause constructions involving islands and VP Deletion. For these constructions, the assumption that indefinites have only a quantifier interpretation would necessitate complex and *ad hoc* additions to the general theory of scope and variable binding. These problems disappear, however, if an indefinite is assumed to have a referential interpretation as well.

Once this point is established, it reflects back on the simple examples like (1). If indefinites exhibit a referential/quantifier ambiguity in the complex examples, then the same ambiguity must be acknowledged in the simple examples, even if it is not immediately apparent there. The reason is that there is no non-arbitrary way of preventing the semantic principles that apply to the complex examples from applying with the same effect to the simple ones. In this respect our argument resembles the argument for ambiguity in *I told a story about John*, even though in the case of indefinites there are no comparable unambiguous examples to appeal to.

In the next section we will lay out a number of facts about indefinites which any adequate theory must accommodate. We will contrast our semantic ambiguity theory with what we will call the quantifier-interpretation-only theory (QIO). This theory, which maintains that any ambiguities in indefinite phrases are merely the scope ambiguities exhibited by all quantified phrases, looks at first sight, as we have already indicated, to be the more economical of the two. What we will show is that its greater economy is purchased at the expense of insensitivity to the facts. There are observations about indefinites which are incompatible with the simplest and most straightforward version of QIO, and which could be accommodated only by complicating the theory considerably. When the full range of data is taken into account, it is the semantic ambiguity theory which emerges as the more economical of the two.

2   EMPIRICAL DEMANDS ON A THEORY OF INDEFINITES

We have grouped the observations that follow roughly in accord with the demands they make on a theory of indefinites. The points in Section 2.1 are consistent with QIO together with appropriate pragmatic principles. The points in Section 2.2 show that QIO would have to be augmented with special stipulations about *a* as a quantifier in order to accommodate some interesting differences between indefinites and the familiar examples of quantified phrases. The points in Section 2.3 are decisive in our view. They cannot be handled by QIO at all, unless we are prepared to abandon all of the generally accepted principles governing quantifier scope and variable binding. They are easily explained, however, on the assumption that indefinites have a referential as well as a quantificational interpretation.

To avoid prejudging the issue at the outset, we will make use of the term *referential understanding* in what follows. This is intended to be neutral between *referential interpretation* (semantic) and *referential use* (pragmatic).[4]

2.1 Familiar facts

There are a number of factors which favor either a quantificational or a referential understanding of an indefinite. Both theories would need to be supplemented with pragmatic principles which explain why these factors have the effect that they do.

A   The content of the noun phrase, or of the remainder of the sentence, can be relevant. For example, the indefinites in sentences (4) and (5) are more likely to be understood referentially than the descriptively vaguer *someone* in (6).

(4) A student that Betty used to know in Arkansas cheated on the exam.

(5) A friend of mine cheated on the exam.[5]

(6) Someone cheated on the exam.

Also, the indefinite in (7) is more likely to be understood referentially than the identical phrase in (8).

(7) A man just proposed to me in the orangery (though I'm much too embarrassed to tell you who it was).

(8) A man is in the women's bathroom (but I haven't dared to go in there to see who it is).

These contrasts make some sense. For example, the lengthy description in (4) reveals a certain amount of knowledge on the part of the speaker, and it's easy to imagine that this is just part of still greater knowledge, especially as the knowledge the speaker reveals is the kind he is most likely to have come by by knowing who cheated. And if he knows, then it's at least possible and perhaps even probable that he intends to refer. The vague *someone* in (6) *might* be backed up by considerable knowledge, but nothing indicates that it is and so the pure quantifier understanding is plausible. In the case of (7) and (8), it is less likely that the speaker will be unaware of who proposed than of who is in the bathroom. As the parenthesized continuations suggest, the most plausible reason why the speaker did not specify who it was is different in the two cases.

Another indication of this correlation between descriptive richness and referential understanding is the loss of narrow scope quantifier interpretations for indefinites with detailed descriptive content. Any theory, we presume, would prohibit a referential understanding of an indefinite that is construed as being within the scope of another logical operator. Thus the indefinites in (9) and (10) are not as readily construed as being within the scope of the negation and universal quantifier, respectively, as the indefinites in (11) and (12), because they are more naturally construed as referential.

(9) Sandy didn't see a squirrel that was chasing its tail around the oak tree.

(10) Everyone hates a particularly obnoxious student in the syntax class who shouts at the instructor and hogs the discussion.

(11) Sandy didn't see a squirrel.

(12) Everyone hates a student in the syntax class.

B Topicalization and Left Dislocation, as in (13), strongly favor the referential understanding (though perhaps the Yiddish-influenced variety of Topicalization is more neutral).

(13) A Frenchman that I met in Tokyo, I went and had dinner with (him) in New York last week.

This observation too could be expected to fall into place given a suitable theory of pragmatics. If one is talking *about* a particular person, then that person might well be the topic of what is said. But if one is merely asserting that two sets of persons intersect and wishes to focus attention on one of the sets, then a more appropriate kind of topicalization would be as in (14) or (15).

(14) As for Frenchmen that I met in Tokyo, one of them is a linguist.

(15) Of the Frenchmen that I met in Tokyo, at least one is a linguist.

C The referential understanding is strongly, perhaps uniquely, favored by the use of the colloquial non-demonstrative *this*, as in (16) (see Prince, 1981).

(16) This girl in the syntax class cheated on the exam. (uttered with no such girl in the immediate neighborhood)

This, too, makes sense. Normal demonstrative *this* is as referential as anything can be, and so we're not too surprised to find it pressed into service to mark the referential understanding of an indefinite.

D *There*-insertion constructions, such as (17) and (18), are characteristically used to assert the non-emptiness of a set.

(17) There are black swans.

(18) There was someone smoking behind the woodshed.

A *there*-insertion construction would therefore be expected to be more compatible with the quantifier understanding of an indefinite than with the referential understanding. This seems to be so. Sentence (18) is most naturally construed as asserting the non-emptiness of the set of people smoking behind the woodshed. In sentence (19), unlike (18), the indefinite has a rich descriptive content which would itself favor the referential understanding, and as expected the sentence sounds somewhat odd.

(19) There's a man that Kim used to go to school with in the late sixties in Arkansas smoking behind the woodshed.

However, *there*-insertion constructions appear to have another characteristic use in discourse, which is not often mentioned in the literature, and in this use they do tolerate indefinites used referentially. For example, (20) is naturally construed as about a particular girl, rather than as a mere denial of the emptiness of the set of girls in the class who cheated.

(20) There's a girl in our syntax class who cheated on the exam.

Clear evidence for a referential understanding here comes from the fact that even non-demonstrative *this* is tolerated, as in (21).

(21) There's this girl in our syntax class who cheated on the exam.

Notice also that though a purely existential *there* construction like (18) can be denied by saying *No there wasn't*, this form of denial would be quite bizarre in response to (21).

It seems, then, that *there*-insertion does have an effect on how an indefinite is likely to be construed, but the effect does not amount to a straightforward superficial correlation since it depends on how the *there* construction is itself construed in the context.

E Any relative clause modifying an indefinite adds to its descriptive content and thus tends to favor a referential understanding, but the effect is even more pronounced for non-restrictive relatives than for restrictive relatives. The indefinite in (23), for example, can only naturally be understood referentially.

(22) A student in the syntax class who has a Ph.D. in astrophysics cheated on the exam. (restrictive).

(23) A student in the syntax class, who has a Ph.D. in astrophysics, cheated on the exam. (non-restrictive).

This observation is unsurprising in view of the fact that non-restrictive relatives occur freely with definite referring expressions, as in (24), but are quite unacceptable with unambiguously quantified heads, as in (25) and (26).[6]

(24) $\left\{ \begin{array}{l} \text{John} \\ \text{This student} \end{array} \right\}$, who has a Ph.D. in astrophysics, cheated on the exam.

(25) *$\left\{ \begin{array}{l} \text{No} \\ \text{Few} \end{array} \right\}$ students in the syntax class, who have Ph.D.'s in astrophysics, cheated on the exam.

(26) *$\left\{ \begin{array}{l} \text{Every} \\ \text{Each} \end{array} \right\}$ student in the syntax class, who has a Ph.D. in astrophysics, cheated on the exam.

F The modifiers *certain* and *particular*, as in (27) and (28), favor a referential understanding of an indefinite.

(27) I accused a certain student of cheating.

(28) A (one) particular claim in this paper is false.

The stronger claim is sometimes made that *certain* and *particular* force maximally wide scope interpretations of a quantifier with respect to higher predicates, negation, and so forth. It is pointed out, for example, that sentence (29) has only a *de re* (specific) interpretation.

(29) Sandy believes that a certain boy has been accused of cheating.

If this were so, it might conceivably help to explain why these modifiers tend to pick out a referential understanding of an indefinite when there are no other scoped elements in the sentence. (For example, it might be proposed that to understand an indefinite as referential is to understand it as having scope over an implicit 'performative verb' such as *assert*, and that *certain* forces maximally wide scope even relative to this implicit verb.) However, it seems clear to us that sentence (30) can have an interpretation which implies that Sandy, but not Tom, has a boy in mind.

(30) Tom said that Sandy believes that a certain boy has been cheating.

(But (30), like (29), cannot easily be assigned a *fully* non-specific reading.)

The semantics of modifiers like *certain* is completely obscure, and our impression is that these modifiers correlate with scope in only a very rough way. In fact this rather clearly must be so, for the full range of scope relations cannot be distinguished in terms of any binary distinction (see Fodor, 1970, Ch. 2) but the presence or absence of *certain* is a binary distinction. It looks to us as if *certain* is used in discourse as a loose cue to the fact that an identification of a relevant individual could be given by *someone*, either by the speaker or by one of the people whose propositional attitudes are being reported. This would explain both its effect on (29) and (30), and its association with the referential understanding of (27).

G The numerals, though they apparently do permit a referential understanding, tend to favor a quantificational understanding more strongly than the indefinite article does. Thus (31) and (32) incline more strongly than (1) and (33) do towards a non-referential understanding of the subject.

(31) One student in the syntax class cheated on the exam.

(32) Seven students in the syntax class cheated on the exam.

(1) A student in the syntax class cheated on the exam.

(33) Some (i.e. [sm]) students in the syntax class cheated on the exam.

We are not quite sure why this should be so, but we suspect that explicit mention of the number of individuals may, by Gricean principles, implicate that their number is more significant than their identity.

We will not attempt to lay out in detail here the pragmatic principles that would predict which understanding of an indefinite a hearer is likely to arrive at. The facts we have listed need to be borne in mind when constructing arguments based on more complex examples, and they must ultimately be incorporated into a complete theory of the role of indefinites in discourse. But we are not relying on these facts as support for our theory at the expense of QIO. The indications are that the relevant pragmatic principles will not be particularly difficult to formulate, whether one assumes QIO or the semantic ambiguity theory.

In addition to these factors that determine the preferred understanding of an indefinite in various contexts, there are some interesting consequences of which understanding is chosen. For example, the accuracy of the descriptive content of an indefinite noun phrase seems to be more important when it is understood quantificationally than when it is understood referentially. Thus if we construe (34) as making merely an existence claim, it matters whether the student who cheated was indeed an anthropology major rather than, say, a sociology major.

(34) An anthropology major in the syntax class cheated on the exam.

If it turned out that the student who cheated was a sociology major, we would be very inclined to say that the sentence was false. But if the speaker intended to make an assertion about a particular person, and was so understood by the hearer, then in Donnellan fashion (see Donnellan, 1966, 1968) the hearer might well be able to divine which student the speaker had in mind, and might be prepared to overlook the inaccuracy and judge the assertion to be substantially true.

Donnellan formulated this distinction for definite descriptions as a difference between a *referential* and an *attributive* use. A definite description used attributively can typically be paraphrased with *whoever* or *whatever*, as in (35).

(35) The person who murdered Smith is insane ≡ Whoever murdered
      Smith is insane.

Since *whoever* seems to be related to *everyone who* (or *anyone who*), it appears that Donnellan's distinction is closely related to our distinction between a referential and a quantificational use of an indefinite. In support of this we can note that noun phrases containing quantifiers such as *every* and *few*, which cannot be understood referentially in our sense, also cannot be understood as referential in Donnellan's sense; they do not exhibit the characteristic indifference to accuracy of the descriptive content.[7] Thus (36) and (37) seem to be false, however generous a hearer might be inclined to be, if the speaker has mistaken sociology majors for anthropology majors.

(36) Every anthropology major in the syntax class was accused of
      cheating.

(37) Few anthropology majors in the syntax class were accused of cheating.

However, Donnellan's distinction re-emerges if we substitute numerals which do permit both a referential and a quantifier understanding in our sense.

(38) Three anthropology majors in the syntax class were accused of cheating.

Just as for the other facts we have mentioned, there seem to be good pragmatic reasons for this difference in the importance of descriptive accuracy. The descriptive content of a referential phrase functions as a practical instrument for getting the hearer to recognize who is being referred to (cf. Strawson, 1964) and thus would be expected to be subject to the practical attitude associated with all tools—it may or may not be optimally chosen for the job (getting the can open, getting the hearer to realize who is being referred to), but in one sense it succeeds as long as it gets the job done. But the descriptive content of a quantified phrase functions as a criterion that individuals must meet if they are to fall within the domain of the quantifier; and there is in general little tolerance for inappropriately formulated criteria, especially if there is taken to be some connection between an individual's satisfying the criterion and its satisfying the remainder of the sentence. (Notice the oddity of saying *Whoever murdered Smith is insane* if one's grounds for saying it are not that murdering Smith is a sign of insanity, or even that there is evidence that whoever trampled the tulip bed is insane and evidence that whoever trampled the tulip bed murdered Smith, but simply that Jones murdered Smith and Jones has long been known to be insane. The descriptive content of *whoever murdered Smith* is not, in this last case, being used as a criterion, and this is apparently what makes the use of the quantified sentence odd.)

We are going to claim that this pragmatic difference between the two understandings of an indefinite rests on a true semantic ambiguity, but we see no reason to doubt that QIO could also give a satisfactory account of it in purely pragmatic terms. Thus, none of the observations we have made so far discriminates decisively between the two theories.

2.2 Suggestive facts

Indefinites, considered as quantifiers, have unusual scope properties. In particular, they favor wider scope readings than paradigmatic examples of quantified phrases containing *every*, *each*, *few* and so on.

When a sentence contains two quantified noun phrases (at the same clausal level), the preferred interpretation is generally the one on which the first quantifier in the syntactic structure takes wide scope over the second (unless the first is more deeply embedded than the second). Thus sentence (39) favors an EVERY MANY reading, while (40) favors a MANY EVERY reading.

(39) Every actor in our company admires many producers.

(40) Many producers admire every actor in our company.

Only for *each*, which is notorious for its predilection for wide scope, is this general trend reversed. Thus an EACH MANY interpretation is quite natural for (41).

(41) Many producers admire each actor in our company.

An indefinite can also be very naturally assigned a 'crossed' scope interpretation. Thus it is not difficult to read sentence (42) with an A MANY interpretation.

(42) Many producers admire an actor in our company.

This is true, however, only when the indefinite is of the kind that favors a referential use. Sentence (43), with the quite inexplicit *someone*, does not lend itself naturally to a crossed interpretation; the MANY A interpretation is strongly preferred.

(43) Many producers admire someone.

Indefinites apparently lend themselves readily to wide scope readings in negative contexts also. Thus, in (44) and (45), *a friend of mine from Texas* is most naturally construed as outside the scope of *not* and of *scarcely anyone*, though in (46) and (47) the corresponding phrases with *many*, *every* and even *each* are much more naturally construed as within the scope of the negative element.

(44) John does not respect a friend of mine from Texas.

(45) Scarcely anyone respects a friend of mine from Texas.

(46) John does not respect many friends of mine from Texas.

(47) Scarcely anyone respects $\left\{ \begin{array}{l} \text{every} \\ \text{each} \end{array} \right\}$ friend of mine from Texas.

A complete discussion of negation and scope would require consideration of negative polarity items, 'internal' and 'external' negation, and so forth, and would lead us too far afield here. As far as we can see, however, the interactions between indefinites and negation parallel those between indefinites and quantifiers.

If it is assumed that *a* has only a quantifier interpretation, then *a* must be classed with *each* as a quantifier that favors wide scope. The relevance of the descriptive content of the noun phrase then demands the further assumption that for *a* (though not for *each*), this general preference for wide scope can be offset by an opposite preference for narrow scope when the descriptive content is minimal. These assumptions are not necessary if it is acknowledged that an indefinite also has a referential interpretation. A referential noun phrase does not enter into scope interactions with quantifiers. Sentence (48), for example, is unambiguous.

(48) Many producers admire that actor.

However, a referential interpretation at least entails a wide scope existential. Therefore, the crossed reading of a sentence such as (42) or (45) does not have to be attributed to the scope preferences of quantifiers. Instead of assuming that the A MANY interpretation of (42) is due to a quantifier interpretation of *a* with wide scope over *many*, we could assume that it is due to the referential interpretation of *a*.

At this point, then, the semantic ambiguity theory is in competition with a version of QIO which classes *a* with *each* as favoring wide scope over quantifiers and negations, and which adds the condition that the descriptive content of the noun phrase should be compatible with wide scope.

Similar observations can be made about the scope of indefinites with respect to higher verbs. A quantified noun phrase in a complement clause is scope-ambiguous with respect to the matrix predicate, but the preferred interpretation is generally the one on which the quantifier has scope only over the complement clause. For example, the more natural interpretation of (49) is the BELIEVE QUANTIFIER one, rather than the QUANTIFIER BELIEVE one.[8]

(49) This producer believes that every actor in our company is too fat to appear in public.

Only for *each* is the reading with wide scope over a higher predicate favored. Thus (50) is likely to be taken as saying that the producer believes of each actor in our company that he is too fat to appear in public.

(50) This producer believes that each actor in our company is too fat to appear in public.

But even for *each*, the availability of the wide scope reading is sensitive to a number of factors. For (51), for example, the wide scope reading is much less salient than for (50).

(51) This producer believes that each actor in our company speaks two
      languages.

Kroch (1976) observed that *each*, unlike *every* and *all*, occurs most naturally only where there is a potential scope ambiguity to be resolved. It is natural in *Each person lifted a rock*, where it picks out the wide scope reading of the universally quantified noun phrase, but it is unnatural in *Each man was hungry*, since this contains nothing for the universal quantifier to have distinctive scope over. This is apparently what is responsible for the naturalness of the reading of (50) in which *each actor* has scope over *believes*. Since there is nothing in the complement clause whose scope needs to be disambiguated relative to the universal quantifier, the use of *each* rather than *every* or *all* can be justified only on the assumption that it has wide scope over the matrix clause. But in (51), the use of *each* can be justified as a means of disambiguating the quantifier scope ambiguity in the complement clause, and there is correspondingly less pressure for *each* to be construed as having scope over the matrix.

An indefinite in a complement clause can also be naturally interpreted with wide scope over the matrix predicate. Thus (52) is ambiguous between a specific and a nonspecific interpretation of the indefinite, and the specific reading (the A BELIEVE reading) is at least as natural as the nonspecific reading (the BELIEVE A reading).

(52) This producer believes that an actor in our company is too fat to
      perform in public.

Note that the availability of the specific reading does not depend on the sorts of factors that are revelant to *each*; the specific reading is as salient in (53) as it is in (52).

(53) This producer believes that an actor in our company speaks two
      languages.

But the wide scope reading of the indefinite, like the crossed reading with respect to other quantifiers in the same clause, does vary in accessibility with the descriptive richness of the noun phrase. Sentence (54), with the descriptively vague *someone*, is much less likely to be interpreted as about a specific person than (52) and (53).

(54) This producer believes that someone despises him.

However, when the indefinite does contain a detailed description, the wide scope reading relative to the matrix clause seems to be even more natural than the wide scope reading for *each*. It is much more likely that sentence (55), for example, will be read as specific than as nonspecific.

(55) This producer believes that an actor in our company that he used to know in Arkansas before the war despises him.

These observations, like those about crossed scope with respect to other quantifiers, could be accounted for either on the assumption that an indefinite has a referential interpretation which entails a maximally wide scope quantifier interpretation, or on the assumption that it has only a quantifier interpretation with a strong tendency towards wide scope. There is, however, the beginning of a suspicion that the wide scope reading for *a*, when the descriptive content is rich enough to support a referential use, is more robust than for any other quantifier in the language, including the rather unusual *each*.

An even stronger indication of the unusual scope properties of an indefinite, considered as a quantifier, is provided by the fact that the scope of a quantifier within certain types of syntactic constituent is restricted to that constituent. We will call such constituents *scope islands*. All that is needed for our argument about indefinites is that there exist some scope islands. It is completely irrelevant, except for expository purposes, which constituents do function as scope islands and which do not. Some people may consider all subordinate clauses to be scope islands, so that they reject the wide scope quantifier interpretations of (49) and (50) above. For most speakers, however, scope islands are highly correlated with syntactic extraction islands (see Lakoff, 1970; Postal, 1974; Rodman, 1976; May, 1977; Vanlehn, 1978). For example, an object complement or extraposed subject complement is not a scope island, but an unextraposed sentential subject is, and so is a complement to a noun, and a relative clause.[9] Thus despite the wide scope preference of *each*, neither (56) nor (57) can be interpreted with *each* taking scope over the matrix predicate. (Note that it cannot be the definiteness of the head NP *the rumor* that blocks wide scope of *each*, because of examples like *Someone spoke to the father of each student*.)

(56) John overheard the rumor that each of my students had been called before the dean.

(57) John thinks that for each of my students to be called before the
     dean would be preposterous.

So far, *a* has differed only marginally in its scope preferences from *each*,
but with respect to scope islands there is a striking difference. Every other
quantifier, including *each*, has its scope constrained by island boundaries,
but *a* does not. Thus (58) and (59) contrast with (56) and (57) in permitting the indefinite to be interpreted with scope over the highest clause.

(58) John overheard the rumor that a student of mine had been called
     before the dean.

(59) John thinks that for a student I know to be called before the dean
     would be preposterous.

Other examples of the 'island-escaping' behavior of indefinites involve
conditional clause islands, as in (60).

(60) If a friend of mine from Texas had died in the fire, I would have
     inherited a fortune.

It seems clear that this can be understood as about a particular friend of
the speaker, rather than about all of his friends from Texas. Thus the
continuation (61) is consistent with (60), though it would not be if the
indefinite in (60) could only fall within the scope of the *if*.

(61) But if his brother, who is also from Texas and a friend of mine,
     had died instead, I wouldn't have inherited anything.

However, *if* clauses are scope islands for paradigm examples of quantified
phrases, as in (62) and (63).

(62) If each friend of mine from Texas had died in the fire, I would have
     inherited a fortune.

(63) If no friend of mine from Texas had died in the fire, I would have
     inherited a fortune.

Sentence (62) cannot mean that each friend of the speaker is such that if
he had died the speaker would have inherited; and (63) cannot mean that
there is no friend of the speaker such that if he had died the speaker would
have inherited (even though, pragmatically, this would have made somewhat more sense than the actual interpretation of (63)).

If we suppose that *a* has only a quantificational interpretation, then it is
clearly a very unusual quantifier. Its ability to 'escape' from scope islands
must be recorded in the grammar as an exception to the general principles

governing quantifier scope. If, however, an indefinite is also assigned a referential interpretation, there is no need to attribute any exceptional characteristics to *a* as a quantifier. The island constraints on quantifiers could remain completely general, and the apparent island-escaping interpretations of sentences like (58), (59) and (60) could be attributed to the referential interpretation. Since a referential noun phrase isn't a scoped element, there is no question of its scope being constrained by island boundaries.

We should note that attempts have been made to explain away the island-escaping readings of indefinites. Cooper (1979) discusses them at length. In some cases he denies that sentences can be understood in this way.[10] He argues, for example, that (64) can be understood with both *a man* and *a green pick-up truck* as non-specific, or with both of them as specific, but not with *a man* as non-specific and *a green pick-up truck* as specific.

(64) John is looking for a man who stole a green pick-up truck.

The latter understanding would amount to assigning *a green pick-up truck* wider scope than the complex noun phrase island in which it appears. It is rarely instructive simply to announce one's contradictory intuitions, but we do consider that (64) has this understanding (even though it presupposes, implausibly, that the same green truck was stolen by a number of men). There are other examples, such as (65), where the island-escaping reading is not at odds with pragmatic expectations and is clearer still.

(65) John needs to speak to someone who can tell him how to register
     for an introductory statistics class that Professor Smith is giving,
     that he has to take in order to qualify as an MA candidate.

For other sentences, such as those in (66), Cooper admits that there are island-escaping understandings but suggests that only a narrow scope, island-bound, interpretation is assigned by the semantics; the wide scope understanding is classed as a secondary effect, due to an inference based on knowledge of the world.

(66) a. Ford recalled all the '75 models which were put out by <u>a factory
        of theirs in Detroit</u>.
     b. John wants to date every girl who goes out with <u>a professor who
        flunked him out of Linguistics 101</u>.
     c. Mary dates every man who knows <u>a producer I know</u>.

Of these examples Cooper writes:

> It seems that the underlined NP in each of these can be given wider scope than
> *every* . . . . These sentences, however, are not really counter-examples [to the island
> constraints—JDF, IAS]. Certainly they appear to be consistent with a world
> where Ford has only one factory in Detroit, John was only flunked out of Lin-
> guistics 101 by one professor or there is only one producer I know for whom it is
> true that Mary dates every man who knows him. But then the narrow scope
> reading [where the indefinite is island-bound—JDF, IAS] is also consistent with
> such a world . . . . There seems to be no reason *a priori* for us to suppose that the
> English sentences are ambiguous between a wide scope and a narrow scope read-
> ing, since the narrow scope reading will always give truth in those worlds where
> the wide scope reading gives truth. The narrow scope reading will cover all the
> cases we require. It may well be that [(66a)] and [(66b)] seem to make more sense if
> there is just one factory or just one professor with the appropriate properties but
> this is just because it seems unlikely that Ford would have more than one factory
> in Detroit or that John would flunk out of Linguistics 101 more than once. Thus
> what appears to be a preferred wide scope reading we may take to be a narrow
> scope reading which is restricted by our knowledge of the world. (pp. 141–142).

If this suggestion were adequate, it would undercut the need to say anything special at all about indefinites within scope islands; they would not
need to be assigned *either* a referential interpretation or an island-escaping
quantifier interpretation. But Cooper's proposal will not work.

The general idea is plausible enough. It is that a sentence with interpretation I_1 (e.g. narrow scope of the indefinite in (66b)) may be understood by a hearer as if it had interpretation I_2 (e.g. wide scope of the
indefinite in (66b)) just in case (i) I_1 entails I_2, and (ii) the hearer has
empirical knowledge (or belief) which renders inapplicable to the real
world all entailments of I_1 other than I_2. In the case of (66b), it is not out
of the question that a hearer might focus on the weaker (wide scope indefinite) understanding, and overlook the stronger (narrow scope indefinite)
literal interpretation. And it is quite understandable that his tendency to
do so should be greatly reinforced if he knew or believed that only one
professor in fact flunked John out of Linguistics 101, i.e. that the sentence
was in fact 'about' only one professor. In these circumstances, the hearer
might well leave the conversational exchange thinking that he had been
told only about the relation between John, girls, and this one professor—
even though, according to the conventions of the language, he was in fact
told something much more general (which would prove relevant if he
turned out to be wrong about how many professors had flunked John out
of class).

But though this story is plausible, it does not fit the facts (at least for these examples; for all we know, it might be true of some quite different examples not involving indefinites). Note that the wide scope, island-escaping reading of the indefinite is also available in examples like (67) and (68).

(67) John wants to date exactly half the girls who go out with a professor who flunked him out of Linguistics 101.

(68) Mary dates at least five men who know a producer I know.

But neither (67) nor (68) satisfies condition (i), that the literal interpretation of the sentence entails the understanding that the hearer arrives at. For (67), there is no entailment relation in either direction between the two; for (68), there is an entailment relation but it is in the opposite direction.

Condition (ii) also turns out to be irrelevant. Certainly, a hearer who knew that there was only one professor or only one producer with the specified properties would detect no practical difference in import between the narrow scope and wide scope readings in any of these examples. But it is clear that the wide scope understanding is also available to a hearer who does *not* know this, and even to a hearer who knows it to be false. Thus Cooper's example (66c) can easily be understood as about a particular producer, even though there is no special reason for believing that the speaker knows only one producer. (Incidentally, for a hearer who does *not* have access to an empirical premise which makes the two readings effectively equivalent, the various examples we have given would have nothing in common under Cooper's analysis. Such a hearer might know enough to judge (66c) to be false on its literal narrow scope interpretation but true on its secondary wide scope understanding; but he might know enough to judge (68) to be true on its literal narrow scope interpretation but false on its secondary wide scope understanding.)

We are left, then, without any general principles to predict when a hearer will think he has been told something other than what he has in fact (i.e. in accord with the grammatical rules) been told. Sometimes he will arrive at an understanding that is weaker than the literal interpretation, and sometimes he will arrive at an understanding that is stronger. Sometimes the understanding he arrives at is fostered by his knowledge of the world, and sometimes it is not. It seems highly doubtful that a coherent set of pragmatic principles could be formulated which would account for the illusion of a wide scope reading of the indefinite in all of these cases. The one thing they have in common is that the indefinite phrase appears within a constituent that is a scope island for other quantifiers, but its scope is not bounded by the island. Since the availability of this island-indifferent understanding is constant across all examples, it looks as if it must after all be acknowledged as a legitimate interpretation assigned by the semantic rules of the grammar.

We are back, therefore, to a choice between accounting for this interpretation as a referential interpretation, and accounting for it as a quantificational interpretation that is exceptional in not being subject to island constraints. And it should be noted that by this stage in our argument, the difference in formal economy between the semantic ambiguity theory and QIO is much less extreme. QIO has escalated from the theory that *a* is a normal quantifier to the theory that it is an exceptional, island-escaping, quantifier. Thus *both* theories have to say something special about *a*, to distinguish it from paradigm quantifiers like *every*, *many*, *each*. The choice between the theories on the basis of parsimony is thus no longer clear cut.

2.3   Critical facts

In principle, one could continue to complicate the specification of *a* as a quantifier in response to observations about its idiosyncratic behavior. But we turn now to cases for which this tactic, compared with the alternative of recognizing a non-quantifier reading, would be quite implausible. A QIO account of these facts would be completely *ad hoc*; besides being unnecessarily complex, it would miss significant parallels between the behavior of indefinites and that of definite referential phrases. The fact is that all the respects in which *a* does not behave like paradigmatic quantifiers are respects in which it does behave like paradigmatic referential phrases.

Our first observation is that an island-escaping interpretation of an indefinite does not exhibit the full range of scope relations that would be predicted on the assumption that the indefinite is a scoped element whose scope is immune to island constraints. In particular, an indefinite that escapes from an island has *maximally* wide scope with respect to any quantifiers or logical operators outside the island.

Sentences (69) and (70) are identical to (58) and (59) respectively, except that a quantified phrase has been substituted for the highest subject *John*.

(69) Each teacher overheard the rumor that a student of mine had been called before the dean.

(70) Each teacher thinks that for a student I know to be called before the dean would be preposterous.

The theory that *a* is a quantifier unconstrained by scope islands predicts three readings for each of these sentences, one in which the scope of the indefinite is restricted to the island, one in which it escapes the island and has scope over the matrix clause but is inside the scope of *each*, and one in which it has scope over all of the matrix clause including *each*. For sentences (69), these three predicted readings are represented informally in (71).

(71) a. (each teacher: x) [x overheard the rumor that [(a student of mine: y) [y had been called before the dean]]]
   b. (each teacher: x) [(a student of mine: y) [x overheard the rumor that [y had been called before the dean]]]
   c. (a student of mine: y) [(each teacher: x) [x overheard the rumor that [y had been called before the dean]]]

It seems clear to us that neither (69) nor (70) has the intermediate scope reading (b). Either the indefinite is fully nonspecific (i.e., takes scope only over the complement clause), or else it is both specific and independent of the scope of the universal quantifier (i.e., has maximally wide scope in the sentence). It may help to induce agreement on this judgment if (69) and (70) are compared with a simple object complement construction such as (72), where for most people there is no scope island.

(72) Each teacher thinks that a student of mine was called before the dean.

All three readings seem to be legitimate here, including the (b) reading which attributes a *different* specific belief to each teacher.

Some readers may perhaps find the contrast between (69) and (72) less than compelling, but this is to be expected for anyone to whom the context *a rumor that* ... is not an absolute scope island for quantifier readings. The clearest example of an absolute scope island that we know of is a sentence-initial *if* clause (see Section 2.2), and here the absence of the intermediate reading is unquestionable. Thus (73) can be about a particular student, or can be equivalent to *If any student* ..., but it cannot mean that for each professor there is some different but nevertheless specific student such that if that student cheats, that professor will be fired.

(73) If a student in the syntax class cheats on the exam, every professor
     will be fired.

This missing-reading observation is a clear indication that the 'island-
escaping' interpretation of an indefinite is *not* in fact an instance of a
quantifier that manages to escape the island, but is an instance of something very like a proper name or demonstrative which *does not participate
in the network of scope relations* between true quantifiers, negation, higher
predicates, and the like. For example in (74), the interpretation of the
demonstrative phrase *this student* is totally unaffected by the presence of
a quantifier elsewhere in the sentence.

(74) If this student cheats on the exam, every professor will be fired.

A true referential phrase doesn't so much escape from a scope island as
shine right through it; and it also shines right through any scoped elements in the sentence. It is precisely for this reason that the existential
entailment (or presupposition) of a referential phrase is a maximally wide
scope existential. Exactly the same seems to be true of the referential
understanding of the indefinite phrases in (69), (70) and (73).

QIO, even if it assumes that there can be island-escaping quantifiers,
offers no explanation at all for the absence of the intermediate scope
readings in such examples. The normal principles governing quantifier
scope would have to be considerably complicated in order to account for
this observation, and the fact that these complications correlate exactly
with the properties of referential phrases would not be captured.

A quite different observation points to the same conclusion. Sag (1976a,
1976b) and Williams (1977) have observed that VP Deletion is subject to
a semantic identity condition, and in particular that a verb phrase cannot
be deleted if its antecedent contains a quantified phrase whose scope is
wide than the verb phrase.[11] Example (75), for instance, is unacceptable
if *everyone* has wide scope over the subject *someone* in the antecedent,
though it is acceptable if *everyone* has narrow scope.

(75) Someone loves everyone. Chris knows that someone does.

Notice that example (76) is acceptable even if *everyone* is interpreted as
having scope over *someone* in the antecedent, because in this case a larger
VP is deleted and the scope of *everyone* does not have to extend beyond
this larger VP in order to include *someone*.

(76) Sandy thinks that someone loves everyone. Chris does too.

However, deletion of just the lower VP is impossible, as predicted, on the EVERY SOME reading; (77) can only be interpreted with *everyone* within the scope of *someone*.

(77) Sandy thinks that someone loves everyone. Chris thinks that someone does too.

This condition on VP Deletion also predicts, of course, that neither the higher nor the lower VP can be deleted if *everyone* in these examples is interpreted as having scope over the matrix clause. This is apparently correct. Neither (76) nor (77) is acceptable if the first sentence is taken to mean that every person is such that Sandy thinks that someone loves that person. Even *each* behaves as predicted. Neither continuation in (78) is acceptable if *each* is taken to have scope over *Sandy thinks*.

(78) Sandy thinks that someone loves each of my friends.

Chris $\left\{ \begin{array}{c} \text{does} \\ \text{thinks that someone does} \end{array} \right\}$ too.

However, an indefinite noun phrase of the kind that favors a referential understanding is *not* subject to this condition. Example (79), with either continuation, can quite easily be understood as ascribing to Sandy a belief about a particular person that the speaker beat at chess.

(79) Sandy thinks that every student in our class plays chess better than a guy I beat this morning. Chris $\left\{ \begin{array}{c} \text{does} \\ \text{thinks that every student does} \end{array} \right\}$ too.

This observation about indefinites is strong evidence that what look like wide scope quantificational interpretations are in some instances referential interpretations. A quantificational analysis of (79) cannot account for its acceptability. To explain why this is so we must consider the nature of the semantic condition on VP Deletion. The precise formulation of this condition depends heavily on the details of the logical representation language for natural language sentences, over which it is defined. We do not have space here to present all the formal details; interested readers should consult the papers by Sag and by Williams. All we will do here is to sketch the general outlines of the theory and indicate how it applies to quantified sentences.

The general condition on VP Deletion that Sag proposes is given in approximate form in (80). It covers examples (75)–(79), and many other

kinds of examples as well (including sloppy identity sentences, multiple
WH sentences, *tough* constructions, and so on).

(80) A verb phrase may be deleted only if its logical translation is an
      alphabetic variant of an expression in the logical translation of the
      surrounding discourse.

The SOME EVERY interpretation of (77) satisfies this condition, but the
EVERY SOME interpretation does not. Very roughly, the reason is this.

If the EVERY SOME reading of the second sentence of (77) is represented
in the logical language with the universal quantifier outside of the existential quantifier, then since the existential *someone* is not part of what is
deleted, the universal quantifier cannot be part of the logical translation
of the deleted VP. The translation of the deleted VP will, however, include
the variable that is bound by this universal quantifier. Since the translation of what is deleted contains the universally quantified variable but
not its quantifier, the variable is in effect a *free* variable within the translation of the deleted material. The translation of *someone loves everyone*
in the first sentence in (77) will be identical, up to the identity of its bound
variables, with the translation of the corresponding clause of the second
sentence. The translation of the antecedent VP for the deletion will
therefore also contain what is in effect a free variable. The translation
principles do not guarantee the absolute identity of the variables in the
translation of the two sentences. Since expressions containing distinct *free*
variables are not alphabetic variants, the antecedent and the deleted VP
will not meet the identity condition (80). Therefore, deletion is not possible.

By contrast, on the SOME EVERY interpretation of (77), the universal
quantifier can be construed as within the translation of the lower VP, and
hence as within the translation of what deletes. The translation of the
deleted material will thus include both the universally quantified variable
and its quantifier; the translation of the antecedent will likewise contain
both a universally quantified variable and its quantifier; the variable will
therefore be a *bound* variable, in the translation of both the deleted VP
and its antecedent; these translation will therefore qualify as alphabetic
variants; and the deleted VP and its antecedent will satisfy the condition
(80). Hence deletion of the lower VP is permitted on the SOME EVERY
interpretation.

Deletion is also permitted in example (76) on both the SOME EVERY and
the EVERY SOME interpretations. In (76) the whole matrix VP is deleted,
and the translation of this VP includes both the universal quantifier and

its bound variable, even on the EVERY SOME interpretation. Thus condition (80) will be satisfied.

Exactly similar predictions are made for the examples in (79) with an indefinite noun phrase in the lower VP. When the indefinite takes narrow scope, either VP should be deletable. When it takes wide scope over other elements in the complement clause, the higher VP should be deletable but not the lower one. And when it takes wide scope over the whole sentence, neither VP should be deletable. But we have observed that this latter prediction, which does hold for quantifiers such as *every* and *each*, is false for indefinites. The consequence for QIO, which must assume that the indefinite in (79) is a quantified expression on all interpretations, is inevitably a considerable complication of condition (80). By contrast, our assumption that this indefinite can be interpreted as referential allows us to retain (80) in its fully general form. Referential expressions are terms, not variable binding operators. There will therefore be no free variables in the translation of either the matrix VPs or the embedded VPs in (79), and condition (80) will allow either the matrix VP or the embedded VP in the second sentence to delete.

It should be noted that this argument is completely independent of the island-escaping behavior of indefinites. Even given that a quantifier interpretation of a indefinite can take maximally wide scope in (79), this quantifier interpretation does not provide a basis for explaining the acceptability of VP Deletion, or even for describing it economically. It is only if we give up the assumption that all indefinites are to be analyzed as quantifiers binding variables that it is possible to subsume their behavior with respect to VP Deletion under generally motivated principles.[12]

3   CHARACTERIZING THE AMBIGUITY

The observations in Section 2.3 show that an indefinite cannot with any plausibility be held to have only a quantifier interpretation. Its apparently extraordinary behavior with respect to island boundaries and VP Deletion is exactly what would be expected if it had, in addition to its various island-bound quantifier interpretations, an interpretation as an unscoped element which does not bind variables and is insensitive to island boundaries, but which happens to entail a maximally wide scope quantifier reading.

We have labelled this unscoped interpretation *referential*, because on this interpretation an indefinite patterns exactly like definite referential phrases such as proper names, demonstratives, and (non-attributive) definite descriptions. These definite referential phrases are also immune to the constraints on VP Deletion, as shown by the acceptability of both continuations in (81); they are immune to island constraints, as shown by the interpretation of (82); and they entail (or presuppose) maximally wide scope existentials.

(81) Sandy thinks that everyone loves $\left\{ \begin{array}{c} \text{John} \\ \text{that woman} \end{array} \right\}$.

Chris $\left\{ \begin{array}{c} \text{does} \\ \text{thinks that everyone does} \end{array} \right\}$ too.

(82) Each teacher overheard a rumor that $\left\{ \begin{array}{c} \text{John} \\ \text{this student} \end{array} \right\}$ had been called before the dean.

To assimilate the unscoped interpretation of an indefinite to these definite referentials is thus the most economical move compatible with the data.

As we have noted, this conclusion commits us to the claim that even a simple sentence like (1) above is semantically ambiguous. It is not always valid to argue from the ambiguity of a phrase in one context to its ambiguity in another. It would obviously be incorrect, for example, to argue from the specific/nonspecific ambiguity of an indefinite in an opaque context (e.g., *John wants to catch a fish*) to the conclusion that an indefinite in a transparent context (e.g., *John caught a fish*) must be ambiguous in the same way. In general, whenever an ambiguity is a matter of the relative scope of two elements in a sentence, removing one of the elements will remove the ambiguity. (Thus the specificity ambiguity is a matter of the scope of the indefinite with respect to the matrix verb, and removing the matrix verb removes the specificity ambiguity). However, this is *not* the way things stand for the referential/quantifier ambiguity of indefinites, for the referential reading is identifiable precisely by the fact that it does *not* exhibit relational interactions with other elements in a sentence.[13] What we have, then, is a simple binary lexical ambiguity between a variably-scoped element and a non-scoped element. And (unlike the relational ambiguities that the scoped element can exhibit) this lexical ambiguity between the scoped and non-scoped readings is of just the kind which, having been demonstrated in one context, should be present in other contexts as well—in *all* other contexts, except those in which it is excluded by incompatibility with some other property of the sentence (as the social event reading of *ball* is excluded by incompatibility in *John punched the ball*, and the nonspecific reading of *a fish* is excluded by incompatibility in *John wants to catch a fish and* IT *wants to catch* HIM).

What we must do, therefore, is to characterize the referential interpretation of an indefinite in a way that distinguishes it from a wide scope existential quantifier interpretation, even though it entails a wide scope existential. We want this characterization to capture the intuition that a referential indefinite can be used for the purpose of making an assertion *about* an individual, even though the individual in question is not identified by the speaker. We also want this characterization to reveal the similarity between referential indefinites and referential definites. It turns out that there are interesting comparisons to be made among the referential definites which suggest exactly what sort of semantic gap in the language the referential indefinites are filling.

It is a familiar observation that a proper name or (singular) definite description used in discourse often does not apply to only a single individual. A speaker may say *the man at the cafe yesterday* even though there were many men at the cafe, or *Albert* even though there are lots of people called Albert. All being well, however, a hearer will be aware of the implicit limits on the domain of the discourse, and by taking these into account he will have no trouble in determining who the speaker is referring to. Communication may even have been better served than if the speaker had attempted, tediously, to provide a truly unique name or description.

We could say that the *ideal* name or singular definite description is such that it applies to a unique individual, but that in normal use it achieves this ideal only in conjunction with restrictions on the discourse domain. However, the use of a proper name, or of *the* with a singular description, flags the fact that the speaker is at least aspiring to the ideal case. And he can't stray too far from this ideal. If the descriptive content of a definite noun phrase is not rich enough to give the hearer at least a good chance of identifying the intended referent, then the definite noun phrase is not being properly used and it is within the hearer's rights to protest.

For demonstrative phrases, by contrast, there is no requirement, even in the ideal case, that the descriptive content should be uniquely identifying. Indeed, there may be no descriptive content at all; *this* and *that* can be used alone, unlike *the*. The uniqueness condition for a singular demonstrative relates to the conjunction of the descriptive content, if any, and the accompanying pointing gesture (or its contextual surrogate) which indicates which individual, within the domain of discourse, is being referred to. Just as for *the*, this ideal may not always be achieved, but the use of *this* or *that* is nevertheless a signal to the hearer that the speaker is at least aspiring to this ideal. If the speaker were simply to point from a distance to a large multi-colored mural on the wall and say *That splotch is cerulean blue*, his behavior would quite properly be objected to as a flagrant violation of the ideal which his use of *that* commits him to.

Now suppose that somebody wished to make an assertion about an individual but the circumstances prevented him from approaching either of these two ideals. He cannot use *this* or *that* with a minimal description, because the individual is not available for ostensive identification. (Or, the individual happens to be available to the speaker but the hearer, being blind or at the other end of a telephone line, could not observe the pointing.) He cannot use *the*, because a description rich enough to distinguish the individual from all others even within the limited domain of discourse would be hopelessly long and distracting. (Or, the speaker could easily provide a uniquely identifying description but the hearer, lacking relevant background information, would be unable to use it to pick out the referent.) Clearly, what this speaker needs is some form of words which allows him to make an assertion about the individual he has in mind, without ostension, and without providing a full description, but also without rendering himself culpable. This is just what a referential indefinite allows him to do.

If this is correct, it suggests that a referential indefinite is more like a demonstrative than like a definite description, since the demands on its descriptive content are very weak. The determiner *a* cannot occur alone without a noun, but a noun that applies to many other individuals in addition to the intended referent is technically quite sufficient (even though a richer description often facilitates disambiguation of the referential interpretation from the quantifier interpretation for the hearer, as noted above). In fact, the closest analogue to a referential indefinite is a demonstrative phrase accompanied by a pointing gesture which is not visible to the hearer, a 'private' pointing gesture within the mind of the speaker. Of course, when a demonstrative is used the pointing is *supposed* to be public, for the hearer is supposed to be able to decide who or what the speaker is referring to. But the conventions for use of a referential indefinite do not demand that the hearer should be able to identify the referent, even in the ideal case. (He may in fact be able to, on the basis of what he knows about the speaker and about what the speaker knows, but this is certainly not essential to the proper use of an indefinite.) Thus it is not just that the hearer cannot *in fact* observe the speaker's 'private pointing', but that he knows that he is not intended to observe it and need not trouble himself to try to identify the referent.

From the hearer's point of view, then, a referential indefinite conveys no more information than an existential statement would have—except for the prospect that, if it became relevant to the conversation, the speaker *could* specify which individual his assertion was about. [14] But the hearer can also presume that the identity of the referent probably *isn't* relevant to the conversation, at least in the opinion of the speaker; for if it were, then general principles of conversational cooperation would have required the speaker to make whatever effort would have been necessary to identify the referent publicly. (A referential indefinite is surely sometimes used when public identification would be quite easy but the speaker does not want the hearer to know who he is talking about. Without denying that this is a convenient and common use of referential indefinites, we would suggest that in a fully cooperative conversation a referential indefinite should be used only when the nuisance involved in identifying the referent would outweigh any advantages to the hearer of knowing who is being referred to.)

Notice that in the typical case the hearer will not know (and will understand that he is not intended to know) exactly what the speaker is asserting, and he will therefore not be in a position to judge whether what is asserted is true, though he may be in a position to judge that it is not true. That is, if he knows that the corresponding existential statement is false, he will know that the referential statement is not true even without knowing who is referred to. But if he knows, or is prepared to accept, that the existential statement is true, he will be unable to tell whether or not the speaker's assertion was true.

This may seem odd, but it is not a serious drawback for the hearer. If we are right about the cooperation conditions on referential indefinites, then it should be unimportant whether or not the speaker's assertion was true, i.e., whether what he said was true of the person he was referring to or only of somebody else. And if it should turn out to be important, then the issue could be elucidated in the subsequent discussion. There's nothing, after all, to stop the hearer asking the speaker who he was referring to (though he would have to rely on the speaker to be honest about the answer).

Incidentally, this helps to explain why a speaker might *want* to assert something using a referential indefinite, rather than to make a mere existential assertion, even though the net information exchanged would be much the same in both cases. If he makes a referential statement, he is signalling that he knows more than a mere existential, and thus he paves the way for the hearer to ask for more information if he has a mind to. The speaker will also have set things up so that he can take the credit for having made a true assertion if the question of who he was referring to does arise later in the conversation. It should be noted that we are assuming here that the referential statement is stronger than an existential statement and are thus departing from our earlier, approximate, characterization of the referential interpretation of an indefinite as logically equivalent to a wide scope quantifier interpretation. We are claiming now that a referential indefinite entails or presupposes a wide scope existential statement, but not vice versa; the truth of the existential statement guarantees that *some* referential statement must be true, but it does not guarantee the truth of any particular referential.[15] Note that if the existential statement is false, the consequence will be comparable to the results of reference failure for definite referentials (i.e., no assertion will have been made at all, or an assertion will have been made that lacks a truth value, or a false assertion will have been made, depending on what turns out to be the correct account of reference failure in general).[16]

We would emphasize that nothing that we have said implies that there is no fact of the matter about whether the speaker's referential assertion was true or false. We assume that the referent on a particular occasion is fixed by the speaker's intentions, and that even if the speaker is unwilling or unable to be articulate about his intentions, they stand in a determinate relationship to his mind/brain states.[17] It is quite beside the point, of course, that, given the current status of psychology, only God knows how to make the appropriate identification on the basis of the state of the speaker's brain.

It should also be observed that it would be unrealistic to impose the very strong condition that a determinate assertion is made only if the referent can in practice be distinguished by hearers without reference to the psychology of the speaker, for this would also rule out many uses of definite referentials as anomalous. The referent of a demonstrative is fixed by the ostensive gesture, but it is rarely possible to establish what a person is pointing at without appealing to some hypothesis about his mental state. Looking only at his finger won't help to distinguish between his pointing at the vase, at the front surface of the vase, at the color of the vase, the shape of the vase, and so on. (Cf. Wittgenstein, 1953, Section

33). For a definite description, it is usually necessary to take account of the discourse content to establish the referent. But the discourse context is not defined (only) by what is physically present; it depends in large part on what the speaker considers the topic of conversation to be, what he believes the hearer to consider the topic of conversation to be, and so on. Thus for all three phrase types (indefinite, definite, and demonstrative), the nonverbal context which fixes the referent must be construed broadly enough to include the psychological states of the speaker. Referential indefinites are just more flagrant about this than referential definites are.

4 FORMAL SEMANTICS FOR REFERENTIAL AND QUANTIFICTIONAL NOUN PHRASES

A formal semantics for referential indefinites will not subsume all of the observations of the previous section, but it should at least be compatible with them. What we have argued is that a referential indefinite resembles a demonstrative without the associated overt pointing or other public identification of the referent. A demonstrative phrase carries the presupposition that its descriptive content and its associated ostension are compatible (see Kaplan (ms), on pointing to a man and saying *that flower*), and that the two together pick out a unique referent. Likewise, a referential indefinite carries the presupposition that its descriptive content is compatible with the speaker's 'private ostension'. Its denotation will be the individual the speaker 'has in mind', as long as the descriptive content is true of that individual. Thus a referential indefinite can be regarded as an indexical phrase, where the function that determines its referent depends both on its descriptive content and on its context of use, and the latter is taken to include the psychological state of the speaker and perhaps also the history of his causal interaction with the world.

In the absence of a developed theory of these aspects of the context and the way in which they fix the denotation either of demonstratives or of referential indefinites, we will set about the task of giving a formal semantics for referential indefinites by adapting Kaplan's formal treatment of demonstratives. Kaplan's system extends standard model theoretic principles to the analysis of indexcal terms such as *I*, *now*, *that man*, whose denotation depends on the context of utterance. This, of course, requires the specification of such contextual parameters as who is speaking, who the audience is, what the time and place of utterance are, and so forth.

In Kaplan's system a sentence is not simply true or false with respect to a specified world and time (and assignment to variables), but is true or false with respect to a specified world and time (and assignment to variables) *when taken in a certain context* (i.e., when taken to have been uttered in that context). Formally, the metalanguage statement $\models_{cftw} \phi$ says that sentence ϕ is true at time t and world w, under the variable assignment function f, when taken in context c. Similarly, $\|\alpha\|_{cftw}$ is used to designate the denotation of an expression α with respect to time t and world w, under the variable assignment function f, when taken in context c.

A Kaplan-context includes a specification of the agent (speaker) of the utterance, c_{Ag}; the audience, c_{Aud}; the time of utterance, c_T; the world in which the utterance occurred, c_w; and the place of utterance c_p.[18] Simple denotation rules as in (83) can then assign appropriate denotations to certain indexical terms. (Boldface items are the logical translations of the corresponding English expressions.)

(83) $\|\mathbf{I}\|_{cftw} = c_{Ag}$ $\|\mathbf{you}\|_{cftw} = c_{Aud}$ $\|\mathbf{here}\|_{cftw} = c_p$.

Truth rules for sentences containing these indexicals can then be given. For example, the English sentence *I am happy* will translate into the logical formula $\mathbf{happy(I)}$, and the truth rules stipulate that this is true when taken in context c just in case c_{Ag} is an element of the denotation of $\mathbf{happy}$ at time c_T and world c_W.[19]

Notice that relative to a given context the denotations of these indexical expressions are constant. Even if they occur within the scope of an intensional operator, their denotations do not depend on the interpretation of this operator but only on the context of utterance. Thus in the sentence *You will say that I am wrong*, the denotation of *I* is unaffected by the future tense operator; it is simply c_{Ag}, the **present** speaker. Thus, though expressions like *I* and *now* are not rigid designators, since their denotations vary with the context of utterance, they nevertheless share with rigid designators the property of being immune to scoped elements in the sentence. In the informal terms of our earlier discussion, they 'shine through' the scope of quantifiers, negation, modal operators and the like, and do not participate in the network of scope relations holding between these scoped elements.[20]

Proper names and referential definite descriptions can be incorporated into the system quite straightforwardly. For their 'ideal' use, nothing need be added to the specification of a context. The denotation of a name such as *Tom* will be the unique individual named Tom at the time and world of the context; if there is no such unique individual, the denotation will be undefined. Kaplan uses the dagger symbol † to denote 'a completely alien entity', not in the denotation domain of the model, which represents the 'undefined' value of a function. Thus the denotation of *Tom* will be † in case there is no individual, or more than one individual, named Tom at the time and world of the context. The denotation of a singular referential definite description of the form *the N ϕ* will be the unique individual which satisfies both N and ϕ at the time and world of the context, if there is such an individual; otherwise it will be †. Formal denotation rules are given in (84). We assume that a singular referential definite phrase such as *the man who runs* will translate as $(\mathbf{the_r}\ x\colon \mathbf{man}(x) \wedge \mathbf{run}(x))$, and in general the translation of a referential description will have the form $(\mathbf{the_r}\ \alpha\colon \phi)$ where α is a variable that occurs freely in ϕ, and f_i^{α} is the variable assignment function just like f except for the possible difference that it assigns α the value i.[21]

(84) (i) If N is a name whose intension is $\mathscr{I}_N$, then $\|N\|_{cftw} =$ the unique individual $i \in \mathscr{U}$ ($\mathscr{U} =$ the set of individuals in the model) such that $i \in \mathscr{I}_N(c_w, c_T)$ if there is such; otherwise †.

　　(ii) $\|(\mathbf{the_r}\ \alpha\colon \phi)\|_{cftw} =$ the unique individual $i \in \mathscr{U}$ such that $\models_{cf_i^{\alpha}c_Tc_w} \phi$, if there is such; otherwise †.[22]

To deal with the more realistic uses of proper names and definite descriptions, which are intended to pick out a unique individual only from among the individuals in the domain of discourse at the time of utterance, we need to add to the specification of a context a set $c_D \subseteq \mathscr{U}$ whose members are the individuals in $\mathscr{U}$ which are in the domain of discourse. Then the denotation rules in (84) will be modified to refer not to a unique individual in $\mathscr{U}$, but to a unique individual in c_D.[23]

Demonstrative expressions demand a further enrichment of the definition of a context. It must include not only a specification of the agent of the utterance, but also a specification of the activities of the agent at the time of utterance, specifically his ostensive gestures. (We will concentrate here on singular demonstratives. We will also not discuss the difference between demonstrative phrases with *this* and with *that*, nor the use of demonstrative expressions unaccompanied by ostensive gestures.)[24] Let us use c_O to designate a subset of $\mathscr{U}$ whose members are the individuals in $\mathscr{U}$ being ostended by the agent at the time of the context. Notice that this allows for 'ambiguity' in the ostension; several individuals could qualify as being pointed to in the same gesture. Ultimately, c_O will have to be refined to allow for different ostensive gestures to be associated with different demonstrative phrases in the same sentence (e.g. *That box is bigger than that one*). We will not bother with this here, but simply note that it will in any case be necessary to allow the context to change during the utterance of a sentence in order to allow for examples like *I want you, you and you to guard the candy supply*, or *The bomb will go off ... right ... NOW*.[25]

The denotation of a simple singular demonstrative *that* can now be defined as the unique individual in c_O, if there is such; otherwise †. We assume that a singular demonstrative phrase such as *that man* or *that man who runs* will have a translation of the form (**that** α: ϕ) where α is a variable that occurs freely in ϕ. For example, the translation of *that man who runs* will be (**that** x: **man**$(x) \wedge$ **run**(x)). The denotation of such an expression will be the unique individual i in c_O such that $\models_{cf_i^{\alpha}c_Tc_W} \phi$, if there is such; otherwise †. Clearly, this denotation rule could be collapsed with the denotation rule for simple demonstratives with no associated nominal.

If we wish to allow for the intentionality of ostension, we could substitute c_{IO} for c_O in the specification of the context, where c_{IO} is the individual in $\mathcal{U}$ that the agent of the utterance intends to identify ostensively at the time of utterance.[26] (The specification of c_{IO} raises some difficult and interesting questions that have been discussed in the literature. See, for example, Nunberg (1977), Stern (1979), and Sag (1980). It may be proper to allow for uses of demonstratives without any ostensive gesture, and for cases of deferred ostension in which what is pointed to is not the intended referent but is associated with it in some way. But the definition of c_{IO} must not be so weak as to permit a pointing gesture which is *totally* unrelated to the individual that the speaker intends to identify as the referent.)

We can now give a denotation rule for singular referential indefinites, which resemble demonstratives except that there is no overt ostensive gesture, and the denotation depends exclusively on who the speaker intends to refer to and the descriptive content of the phrase he uses. We will assume that a singular indefinite noun phrase on its referential interpretation translates as an expression of the form ($\mathbf{a}_r$ α: ϕ) where α is a variable that occurs freely in ϕ.[27] For example, *a man I know* will have the translation ($\mathbf{a}_r$ x: **man**$(x) \wedge$ **know**$(x)(\mathbf{I})$). We will add to the specification of a context an element of $\mathcal{U}$, c_{IR}, which is the individual that the speaker intends to refer to at the time of utterance—specifically, at the time of utterance of the indefinite noun phrase. The denotation of an expression of the form ($\mathbf{a_r}$ α: ϕ) will be the unique individual i such that $i = c_{IR}$ and $\models_{cf_i^{\alpha}c_Tc_W} \varnothing$, if there is such; otherwise †.

The important feature of these denotation rules for demonstratives and referential definite and indefinite phrases is that the denotation depends only on the context of the utterance and not on the sentential context in which the phrase appears. Like *I*, *you*, *here* and so on, these phrases are thus immune to the usual effects of scoped elements in the sentence. They may appear within the **syntactic** scope of a quantifier or tense operator or intensional verb, but their denotations will be exactly the same as if they had not. They therefore need not be treated as scoped elements themselves. That is, there is no need for the translation rules to assign them a special position relative to scoped elements in the sentence in order to capture the fact that they have wide scope existential presuppositions; they can be assigned positions which reflect their role in the predicate-argument structure of the sentence, even if they are deeply embedded, and their wide scope presuppositions will nevertheless be predicted.

For proper names and demonstratives, the denotation rules we have given so far are sufficient, for these phrases are apparently always construed referentially. But definite and indefinite phrases have another interpretation as scoped elements. For example, sentence (85) implies that the vice-president in 1992 will be someone who is now a stupid man.

(85) In 1992 that stupid man will be vice-president.

Sentence (86) can be interpreted in this way, but it can also be interpreted as implying that the vice-president in 1992 will be someone who is a stupid man in 1992 (but who might be an intelligent woman now).

(86) In 1992 a stupid man will be vice-president.

Similarly, sentence (87) has an interpretation on which it implies that the vice-president in 1992 will be smeone who is now the stupidest man in the United States, but it also has an interpretation on which it implies that the vice-president in 1992 will be someone who is the stupidest man in the United States in 1992 (because, for example, all stupider men leave the United States before 1992).

(87) In 1992 the stupidest man in the United States will be vice-president.

De dicto (non-specific) interpretations for indefinite noun phrases in opaque contexts can be accommodated, as is usual, by translating *a* as an existential quantifier. For the sake of formal parallelism we will symbolize this quantifier not as $\exists$, but as $\mathbf{a}_q$. The phrase *a man*, on its non-referential interpretation, will translate as $(\mathbf{a}_q\ x\colon \mathbf{man}(x))$, and this will be an operator that binds the variable x in the translation of the remainder of the sentence. Thus *A man will run* will be assigned the translations in (88), where $\mathbf{F}$ is the future tense operator.

(88) i. $\mathbf{F}[\mathbf{run}((\mathbf{a}_r(x)\colon \mathbf{man}(x)))]$
   ii. $(\mathbf{a}_q(x)\colon \mathbf{man}(x))\ [\mathbf{F}[\mathbf{run}(x)]]$
   iii. $\mathbf{F}[(\mathbf{a}_q(x)\colon \mathbf{man}(x))\ [\mathbf{run}(x)]]$

The referential interpretation of the indefinite is represented by (88i), in which the indefinite is translated as a term.[28] The wide scope quantificational reading of the indefinite is represented in (88ii), and the narrow scope quantificational reading in (88iii). The truth rule for formulae with $\mathbf{a}_q$ will be (89), which parallels the rules for other quantifiers.

(89) $\models_{cftw} (\mathbf{a}_q\ \alpha\colon \phi)[\psi]$ iff there is an individual $i \in \mathcal{U}$ such that $\models_{cf_i^{\alpha}tw} [\phi \wedge \psi]$.

It follows from this that the wide scope quantificational interpretation of an indefinite will be distinct from its referential interpretation, though it will be presupposed by the referential interpretation. This analysis thus captures exactly the relation between the referential and quantificational interpretations that we outlined in the previous section.

We have not discussed definite noun phrases in any great detail in this paper, but we will now suggest that their analysis parallels the analysis of indefinites very closely. In order to capture the full range of *de dicto* readings for a definite description we will analyze it as a quantified expression. On this point our semantics diverges significantly from Kaplan's system.

Kaplan allows for *de dicto* interpretations by translating definite descriptions as terms whose denotations are determined not by reference to the context of utterance but by reference to the sentential context in which they appear. The relevant rules (reformulated slightly for expository purposes) are given in (90).

(90) i. If π is a primitive n-place predicate, then $\models_{cftw} \pi(\alpha_1, \ldots, \alpha_n)$ iff $\langle \|\alpha_1\|_{cftw}, \ldots, \|\alpha_n\|_{cftw}\rangle$ is in the denotation of π at t and w.
   ii. $\models_{cftw} \mathbf{F}[\phi]$ iff $\models_{cft'w} \phi$, where $t' > t$.
   iii. $\|(\mathbf{the}\colon \alpha\colon \phi)\|_{cftw} =$ the unique individual $i \in \mathcal{U}$ such that $\models_{cf_i^{\alpha}tw} \phi$, if there is such; otherwise $\dagger$.

The effect of these rules is to assign as denotation to the phrase *the stupidest man in the United States* in (87), on its non-referential interpretation, the individual who is the stupidest man in the United States at the future, not the present, time.

This is quite appropriate for sentence (87), but for other examples, such as (91), Kaplan's treatment misses one legitimate interpretation.

(91) It was predicted last year that the stupidest man in the United States would be vice-president in 1992.

On its referential interpretation, the denotation of the definite description will depend only on the context of utterance; it will be the stupidest man in the United States at the time of speaking. On its non-referential interpretation, the denotation specified by Kaplan's rules will be the stupidest man in the United States in 1992. These are both legitimate readings of (91), but there is also another reading on which the definite phrase denotes the stupidest man in the United States last year. On this reading the denotation depends on the past tense operator in the main clause but not on the embedded future operator.

In Kaplan's system a definite description always translates as a term. The only ambiguity is a matter of whether its denotation is determined solely by the context of utterance, or whether it depends on any time- or world-changing operators that have scope over the term in the sentence. In the latter case the term is treated, in effect, as having narrow scope relative to *all* such operators. This is adequate for a sentence like (87) because (87) contains only one such operator. But (91) and other similar examples show that where there is more than one operator the definite description can vary in its scope; it can be interpreted relative to only the highest operator, or relative to the highest two operators, and so forth. In this respect definite noun phrases behave exactly like quantified expressions, and like indefinite noun phrases on their quantificational interpretations. The formal semantics must reflect this fact.[29]

We can modify Kaplan's system by replacing his term $(\mathbf{the}\ \alpha : \phi)$ with a variable binding operator $(\mathbf{the_q}\ \alpha : \phi)[\ \equiv (\exists!\alpha : \phi)]$ which is comparable to $(\mathbf{a_q}\ \alpha : \phi)[\ \equiv (\exists\alpha : \phi)]$ for indefinites. (Note that we retain the **term** $(\mathbf{the_r}\ \alpha : \phi)$ for **referential** definites; this does the work of Kaplan's **dthat** $(\mathbf{the}\ \alpha : \phi)$.) Thus the translation of *The man runs*, interpreted non-referentially, will not be (92) but (93).

(92) **run** $(\mathbf{the}\ x : \mathbf{man}(x))$

(93) $(\mathbf{the_q}\ x\colon \mathbf{man}(x))\ [\mathbf{run}(x)]$.

Like other quantifiers $(\mathbf{the_q}\ \alpha\colon \phi)$ will be allowed to appear in the logical translation of an English sentence either at the level corresponding to the clause in which the definite noun phrase appears in the phrase marker, or at any higher clausal level (subject to scope island constraints). Sentence (91) will therefore receive the three quantificational translations in (94), and the truth rule (95) will assign the appropriate truth conditions to each.[30]

(94) i. $(\mathbf{the_q}\ x\colon \mathbf{S}(x))\ [\mathbf{P}[\mathbf{W}[\mathbf{V}(x)]]]$
    ii. $\mathbf{P}[(\mathbf{the_q}\ x\colon \mathbf{S}(x))\ [\mathbf{W}[\mathbf{V}(x)]]]$
    iii. $\mathbf{P}[\mathbf{W}[(\mathbf{the_q}\ x\colon \mathbf{S}(x))\ [\mathbf{V}(x)]]]$

    where $\mathbf{S} = $ *stupidest man in the U.S.*, $\mathbf{V} = $ *vice-president*, $\mathbf{P} = $ *it was predicted last year that*, and $\mathbf{W} = $ *it will be the case in 1992 that*.

(95) i. $\models_{cftw} (\mathbf{the_q}\ \alpha\colon \phi)\ [\psi]$ iff there is a unique individual $i \in c_D$ such that $\models_{cf_i^{\alpha}tw}\ \phi$, and $\models_{cf_i^{\alpha}tw}\ \psi$.
    ii. $\not\models_{cftw}(\mathbf{the_q}\ \alpha\colon \phi)\ [\psi]$ iff there is a unique individual $i \in c_D$ such that $\models_{cf_i^{\alpha}tw}\ \phi$, and $\not\models_{cf_i^{\alpha}tw}\ \psi$.

Two points are worth making about this analysis. One is that the quantificational status of the singular definite determiner would follow automatically if it were translated, on its non-referential interpretation, in the same way as *all one*, as suggested by Fodor (1970), Chomsky (1975), Cushing (1976). The semantics must in any case provide an analysis of phrases such as *all three men, all five books* which accommodates the presupposition that there are exactly three men, or exactly five books, in the domain of discourse. If *the man* on its non-referential use were taken to fill the gap represented by **all one man*, the uniqueness presupposition would follow from the meaning of *one*, and the fact that the phrase enters into scope relations with other logical operators would follow from the presence of the explicit quantifier *all*.

The second point is that once a quantificational interpretation for *the* has been acknowledged, either the referential interpretation must be dropped, or else an ambiguity is predicted comparable to the ambiguity we have discussed at length for indefinite phrases. Thus sentence (91) will be assigned the translation (96), as well as the three translations in (94); and (96) will be logically equivalent to (94i).

(96) $\mathbf{P}[\mathbf{W}[\mathbf{V}(\mathbf{the_r}\ x\colon \mathbf{S}(x))]]$.

We have no direct evidence in favor of retaining (96) as well as (94i), but the idea is interesting not just because of the parallelism with indefinites but also because this 'redundancy' in the semantics corresponds exactly to Donnellan's referential/attributive distinction for definite noun phrases. This distinction has often been taken to be purely pragmatic, just as the distinction between referential and quantificational indefinites has been taken (incorrectly) to be purely pragmatic. Attempts to relate it to a semantic distinction have generally been based on the assumption that it must be a scope distinction, and have foundered on the fact that (unless a higher performative verb is introduced into the analysis) there need be no element in the sentence with respect to whose scope the scope of the definite description could vary.[31] The rules that we have given, however, characterize the referential/attributive distinction as a binary lexical ambiguity, where the definite description is interpreted either as a referring term or as a quantified expression. This has the advantage of permitting a completely general treatment, applicable to both definites and indefinites, of the consequences of descriptive inaccuracy (see Section 2.1).

5   CONCLUSION

The formal semantics that we have proposed for definite and indefinite descriptions analyzes them both as variable-binding operators and as referring terms. It is the referential analysis which makes it possible to account for the facts outlined in Section 2, e.g. for the purely 'instrumental' role of the descriptive content; for the appearance of unusually wide scope readings relative to other quantifiers, higher predicates, and island boundaries; for the fact that the island-escaping readings are always equivalent to *maximally* wide scope quantifiers; and for the appearance of violations of the identity conditions on variables in deleted constituents. We would emphasize that this is not a random collection of observations. They cohere naturally with each other, and with facts about other phrases that are unambiguously referential.

We conceded at the outset of this paper that the referential *use* of an indefinite noun phrase does not, by itself, motivate the postulation of a referential *interpretation*. Our argument has been that the behavior of indefinites in complex sentences cannot be economically described, and certainly cannot be explained, unless a referential interpretation is assumed. It could be accounted for in pragmatic terms only if the whole theory of scope relations and of conditions on deletion could be eliminated from the semantics and incorporated into a purely pragmatic theory. But this seems unlikely.

Notes

This paper is a blend of unpublished manuscripts by the authors: Section 1 of 'Indefinite Noun Phrases and the Mental Representation of Quantifiers' by Fodor, prepared for the Workshop on Indefinite Reference at the University of Massachusetts, December 1978; and 'A Non-scopal Analysis of Specific Indefinite NP's' by Sag. It was written in Spring, 1980 while Fodor was a Visiting Scholar at Stanford University and an ACLS research fellow. An earlier draft appeared in Barwise and Sag (1980).

1. In the formal treatment sketched in Section 4, we represent a referential indefinite as a term, not as a quantifier binding a variable. But see note 28.

2. It is not clear what the distinguishing characteristic is. It may have to do with whether the determiner has a 'relative' or an 'absolute' interpretation. *Every*, *most*, and so on have a relative interpretation, since the number of individuals picked out by *every man* or *most trees* depends on how many men or trees there are. Numerals such as *three* obviously have an absolute interpretation. It seems that *many* and *several* can be construed either as relative or as absolute. (On the relative interpretation, more atoms would have to be green for it to be true that many atoms are green, than apples would have to be green for it to be true that many apples are green.) The suggestion is that a referential interpretation is possible for a noun phrase only if its determiner is construed as absolute. But we are not sure that this is so. (Can the phrase *many friends of ours*, for example, be understood referentially if it means a large *proportion* of our friends or only if it means a large *number* of our friends?) Some other property of determiners may prove to be the crucial one, for example, the *persistence* property of Barwise and Cooper (1981).

3. This is not quite true, as we will argue in Section 3 below. But it is close enough to the truth to serve for present purposes.

4. The term *understanding* is borrowed from Sadock (1975).

5. Phrases of the form *a N of NP's* (e.g., *a friend of mine*, *a student of yours*) are particularly susceptible to referential understandings, even when their descriptive content is not especially detailed. We don't know why this should be so, though it may be relevant that these phrases have partitive interpretations. In general, partitive phrases (which can also have the form *one of the Ns*) seem more likely to be understood referentially than corresponding non-partitive phrases (of the form *a N*), possibly because they contain a referential phrase.

6. Explaining this latter fact is not our primary business here, but it presumably has to do with the fact, often noted (see, for example, Thompson, 1971), that a non-restrictive relative is roughly equivalent semantically to a clause conjoined at the level of the matrix clause. It therefore cannot have the role of narrowing the set of individuals that the noun phrase denotes, but must instead contribute additional information about the individuals that have independently been picked out by the head noun phrase and any restrictive modifiers it carries. This accounts for

the acceptability of (24) and the unacceptability of (25). The *every* example in (26) probably suffers from a conflict of number agreement, since its only acceptable conjunctive paraphrase would be something along the lines of: *Every student in the syntax class cheated on the exam, and they all have Ph.D.'s in astrophysics.* The doubtful acceptability of the *each* example in (26) correlates with the marginal status of: *Each student in the syntax class was accused of cheating on the exam, and he has a Ph.D. in astrophysics.* However, this raises new problems, since there are other examples with a singular back-reference to an *each* phrase which are considerably more acceptable, e.g., *Each student in the syntax class cheated on the exam, and he was reprimanded by the dean.*

7. A sentence such as (i) looks like a counterexample to this generalization, since the subject phrase is clearly quantified and yet a charitable Donnellan-type construal seems possible—if in fact the men are drinking water from martini glasses, the hearer might nevertheless understand the speaker's intent and judge his assertion to be true.

(i) Most of the men over there drinking martinis are millionaires.

But it should be noted that *most of the men* contains a referential expression. It is apparently this which renders the descriptive inaccuracy tolerable. In (ii), where the quantifier *most* is not accompanied by a referential noun phrase, the descriptive content must be taken literally in judgements of truth or falsity.

(ii) Most men who drink martinis are millionaires.

8. Descriptive adequacy seems to demand that quantifiers be allowed to bind variables within opaque contexts (e.g., for sentences such as *Jack believes Jill met everyone she didn't meet*) despite the doubts that have been raised as to whether there is a coherent semantics for such constructions (see, for example, Quine (1966), Dennett (1980), and references therein).

9. We would emphasize that the semantic constraints are squishier than the constraints on syntactic extractions. But any reader who disagrees with our judgements here has two recourses: to find *some* construction which is truly, for him, a scope island, and recast everything that follows in terms of that construction; or to recast our observations in terms of preferred and less preferred readings rather than possible and impossible readings.

10. Cooper maintains, and we would agree, that 'pure' quantifiers such as *every*, *any*, *no* and *each* do not escape islands, and that all the apparent counterexamples to the island constraints come from proper names, definite descriptions and indefinite descriptions. For the definite and indefinite description examples he resists the conclusion that the semantics must supply an island-escaping interpretation, but for the proper name examples he accepts the conclusion and proposes a solution which is essentially the same as the solution we will propose for all of these examples, i.e., that they have an interpretation as unscoped elements. (We will discuss the definite description examples in Sections 3 and 4 below.)

There is one datum that concerns Cooper that we will have nothing to say about. This is the existence of anaphoric relations between noun phrases and pronouns that are apparently not within their scope, as in *Every girl who ate a steak enjoyed it* when *a steak* is assigned a narrow scope, island-bound, interpretation. This problem cannot be solved simply by acknowledging a referential interpretation for indefinites.

11. For convenience, we have couched our exposition here in terms of Sag's deletion analysis rather than William's interpretive analysis. In Sag (1981), the ideas developed here are integrated into a semantically based account of verb phrase ellipsis where null surface VPs are directly generated.

12. For this argument to go through, it is important that the continuation *Chris thinks that every student does too* in (79) should not be acceptable if *a guy I beat this morning* is interpreted as nonspecific with respect to *Sandy thinks* but as having wide scope over *every student*. If (79) were acceptable on this interpretation, it might be possible to maintain that VP Deletion is allowed as long as the interpretation of undeleted constituents is not *affected by* deleted constituents. The interpretation of *everyone* within the scope of an existential quantifier (unlike the interpretation of *someone* within the scope of a universal quantifier) is no different from its interpretation when no other quantifiers are present; in both cases it picks out the set of all people. Thus even though (79) does not satisfy condition (80) under QIO, the acceptability of (79) might nevertheless be explicable.

However, careful examination of the examples indicates that the intermediate scope reading of the antecedent is in fact incompatible with this kind of continuation. It may seem to be possible in some cases, but only if this intermediate scope reading is confusable with the narrow scope reading. For example, in (i) the intermediate scope reading implies that Sandy thinks the same note was sent by everyone, which is plausible only if the sending was a collective action, i.e., if the note was sent by a *group* of students.

(i) Sandy thinks that everyone in our class sent a note to the teacher. Chris thinks that everyone did, too.

Though the semantics of collectivities is poorly understood at present, it seems that the noun phrase *everyone* here does not have its normal role of quantifying over individuals, but picks out a single entity, viz. the whole collection of students in the class. In that case, there is no necessity to assume that the existential quantifier of *a note* has anything but narrowest scope. Note that in example (ii) a group reading is not plausible; as predicted, there is not even any temptation to think that (ii) has the intermediate scope reading.

(ii) Sandy thinks that two Italians married a Frenchwoman. Chris thinks that two Italians did, too.

13. This shows that the referential interpretation of an indefinite must be acknowledged even in simple contexts where it is equivalent to a (wide scope) quantifier interpretation. It might, of course, be proposed instead that these examples are unambiguous because the *quantifier* interpretation is absent. But this would be very odd. It would mean that indefinites, unlike all other quantified phrases, can have any scope *except* maximally wide scope.

14. Perry (1980) has observed that the speaker may in fact be able to give only the very vaguest account of who he was referring to, an account which would not

allow anyone else, or even the speaker himself, to recognize the person concerned. The speaker's intention may nevertheless be well-defined. See note 17.

15. One of the reviewers of this paper has suggested that even this may be too strong for incomplete worlds, such as a soap opera world in which it has been determined that someone shot JR but not yet written into the script *who* shot JR.

16. In the formal semantic analysis of the next section we will follow Kaplan (ms.) in assuming that existential statements are logically presupposed by referential phrases. If a non-presuppositional semantics could be shown to be more adequate, this would not affect the fundamental distinction we are drawing between referential and quantificational phrases.

17. Mind/brain states alone may not be sufficient. Perry's point is that the intended referent may be identifiable only by appeal to the relation between the psychological state of the speaker and the causal determinants of that state. Thus someone might encounter a certain actress and subsequently intend to refer to her, even though by then he has only a hazy conception of her, as long as his conviction that there is such a person can be traced back via a causal chain to the encounter.

18. Kaplan includes $c_A (=$ our $c_{Ag})$ in his formal system, but not c_{Aud}. However, he indicates that in a complete system an audience specification would be needed, as would something like the term c_o that we introduce below.

19. For ease of exposition we are assuming a first order system here and throughout. All the essential points of our analysis could be incorporated into a higher order system, e.g. that of Montague (1970). See also note 28.

20. One of the reviewers of this paper has reminded us of examples like *Necessarily I am here now*, which might be thought to exhibit a scope ambiguity between *necessarily* and the indexical terms that follow. The reviewer suggests that quotation rather than scope may be what is at the heart of this ambiguity. For detailed discussion, see Kaplan (ms.).

21. Our formalism departs here from Kaplan's. Kaplan uses *the* without our subscript **r** (**r** = referential) to capture the *non*-referential interpretation of a definite, and then adds the operator *dthat* to convert a non-referential term into a referential term. In a logic like Kaplan's, in which relevant aspects of the situation are made explicit and accessible to the denotation rules, we do not see that the *dthat* operator makes an essential contribution; but it does increase the difference between English syntax and the syntax of the logical language into which English sentences are translated. We will therefore use just **the**$_r$ and **the**$_q$ (**q** = quantification), and the parallel **a**$_r$ and **a**$_q$.

We have also, for simplicity, ignored Kaplan's distinction between positions, and individuals other than positions.

22. We take for granted here and throughout (and assume that Kaplan does too) that in a completely felicitous case of referring, the actual referent is identical with the individual that the speaker intends to refer to. To distinguish cases where this is so from cases (like some of Donnellan's) where it is not, it would be necessary to add to the Kaplan context a specification of the speaker's referential intentions.

Note, incidentally, that we take the actual referent in such a case to be the individual, if any, that is in fact picked out by the descriptive content of the phrase. Charitable Donnellan-type construals of who has been referred to are regarded as derivative; they are a matter not of the formal semantics of the language but of the hearer's ability to make inferences about the speaker's beliefs and intentions.

23. Limits on the domain of discourse are relevant to referential phrases but not to pure quantified phrases. If, for example, the discourse concerns just the members of the Doe family, then the phrase *the boys* can be understood to refer to just the boys in the Doe family, and hence *all the boys* can too. But *all boys* will still be understood to range over all boys in the world. See Barwise (1981) and Barwise and Perry (1981) for discussion of a semantics making use of partial models.

24. In fact there are all sorts of complications that we will ignore in this oversimplified treatment. Demonstratives can be used to refer to individuals identified only by prior sentences of the discourse, or to an individual picked out by an ostensive gesture by another participant in the discourse, and so on.

25. Unwelcome though the conclusion may be, such examples make it clear that a logic for discourse must allow, in principle, for a different Kaplan-context to be associated with each word (syllable? phoneme?) of an utterance. Quite apart from ostensive gestures and time references, there will be a constant updating of the domain of discourse in response to the content of what is said and to passing events such as people entering the room, the ceiling falling in, and so forth.

26. This definition of c_{IO} will suffice for singular phrases. For plurals it may prove necessary to define c_{IO} as a subset of $\mathcal{U}$.

27. Syntactically $\mathbf{a}_r$ functions exactly like the ϵ operator of Hilbert and Bernays (1939), and the η operator of Reichenbach (1947). However, the semantics that we associate with $\mathbf{a}_r$ differs from these earlier treatments.

28. Note that scope relations are not defined for terms, in a first order system of the kind we are assuming here. The formalism thus corresponds quite directly to our informal characterization of referential noun phrases as non-scoped elements. However, this is not the only way in which the referential/quantifier distinction can be formally captured. In a higher order system of the kind developed by Montague (1970) and others, a referential noun phrase could be rendered as, say, $PP\{(\mathbf{a}_r : \phi)\}$ (where the interpretation of $\mathbf{a}_r$ remains unaltered). The empirical facts we have considered in this paper do not distinguish, as far as we can see, between these two formal approaches, since both acknowledge a reading which is insensitive to the presence of operators which are known to affect the interpretation of true quantifiers.

29. Note that our intent here is simply to rectify Kaplan's analysis within the general framework that he adopts. Since writing this paper, we have become acquainted with Enç (1981), which presents examples that threaten to undermine the whole theory of scope relations as an explication of the multiple interpretation possibilities of sentences containing quantifiers, tense operators and similar expressions. In Enç is right, then the whole framework of our analysis of quantifier readings would need to be revised.

30. Note that the truth conditions on the three understandings of (91) identified here are quite different. We are assuming that these understandings (like all scope-differentiated understandings) cannot be accounted for as purely pragmatic phenomena but must be distinguished as separate semantic interpretations.

We should also make it clear that we don't intend the representations in (94) to make any claims about the logic of tense and time relations in natural languages. We have assumed what is obviously an oversimplified treatment of tense here since our goal is merely to illustrate, with a minimum of distractions, the scope distinctions for quantificational definite descriptions.

31. Partee (1972) made the opposite suggestion, viz. that the ambiguity of quantified phrases in opaque contexts is not a scope ambiguity but a binary ambiguity related to the binary referential/attributive distinction. She noted, however, that there are 'some fundamental inadequacies' in this approach. The major problem is that only one non-referential reading is predicted for a noun phrase embedded more than one clause down within a complement construction (e.g., *John believes that Betty knows that Sam wants to catch a fish*).

This vacillation in the literature between recognizing a binary ambiguity in noun phrases and recognizing the multiple ambiguity of scope distinctions is resolved by our demonstration that **both** ambiguities are present.

Bibliography

Barwise, J.: 1981, 'Scenes and Other Situations', *Journal of Philosophy* LXXVIII, 369–397.

Barwise, J., and R. Cooper: 1981, 'Generalized Quantifiers and Natural Languages', *Linguistics and Philosophy* 4, 159–219.

Barwise, J., and J. Perry: 1981, 'Semantic Innocence and Uncompromising Situations', *Midwest Studies in Philosophy* VI, 387–403.

Barwise, J., and I. A. Sag: 1980, *Stanford Working Papers in Semantics*, Vol. 1 (Stanford University, California).

Chastain, C.: 1975, 'Reference and Context', in K. Gunderson (ed.), *Language, Mind and Knowledge*, Vol. 7 of the *Minnesota Studies in the Philosophy of Science* (University of Minnesota press, Minneapolis).

Chomsky, N.: 1975, 'Questions of Form and Interpretation', *Linguistic Analysis* 1, 75–109.

Cooper, R.: 1979, 'Variable Binding and Relative Clauses', in F. Guenthner and S. J. Schmidt (eds.), *Formal Semantics and Pragmatics for Natural Languages* (Reidel, Dordrecht, Holland).

Cushing, S.: 1976, *The Formal Semantics of Quantification* (doctoral dissertation, UCLA, reproduced by the Indiana University Linguistics Club).

Dennett, D. C.: 1981, 'Beyond Belief', in A. Woodfield (ed.), *Thought and Object* (Oxford University Press, Oxford, England).

Donnellan, K.: 1966, 'Reference and Definite Descriptions', *Philosophical Review* 75, 281–304. [Chap. 17 in this vol.]

Donnellan, K.: 1968, 'Putting Humpty Dumpty Together Again', *Philosophical Review* 77, 203–215.

Enç, M.: 1981, 'Tense Without Scope: An Analysis of Nouns As Indexicals', (University of Wisconsin, Madison).

Fodor, J. D.: 1970, *The Linguistic Description of Opaque Contexts*, Ph.D. dissertation, MIT (Published by Garland Publishing, Inc., New York, 1979).

Fodor, J. D.: 1982, 'The Mental Representation of Quantifiers', in S. Peters and E. Saarinen (eds.), *Processes, Beliefs and Questions* (Reidel, Dordrecht, Holland).

Hilbert, D., and P. Bernays: 1939, *Grundlagen der Mathematik*, Vol. II (Springer, Berlin).

Jespersen, V.: 1931, *A Modern English Grammar on Historical Principles*, Part IV, *Syntax*, Third Volume (Heidelberg, Carl Winters Universitätsbuch handlung).

Kaplan, D.: (ms.), 'Demonstratives' (unpublished manuscript, UCLA).

Kroch, A.: 1974, *The Semantics of Scope in English*, Ph.D. dissertatation, MIT (Published by Garland Publishing, Inc., New York, 1979).

Lakoff, G.: 1970, 'Repartee', *Foundations of Language* 7, 389–422.

May, R.: 1977, *The Grammar of Quantification*, doctoral dissertation, MIT (reproduced by the Indiana University Linguistics Club).

Morgan, J.: 1973, *Presupposition and the Representation of Meaning*, Ph.D. dissertation (University of Chicago).

Nunberg, G.: 1977, *The Pragmatics of Reference*, unpublished Ph.D. dissertation, C.U.N.Y. Graduate Center (distributed by Indiana University Linguistics Club).

Partee, B. H.: 1972, 'Opacity, Coreference, and Pronouns', in D. Davidson and G. Harman (eds.), *Semantics of Natural Language* (D. Reidel, Dordrecht, Holland).

Perry, J.: 1980, 'A Problem About Continued Belief', *Pacific Philosophical Quarterly* 61, 317–332.

Postal, P. M.: 1974, 'On Certain Ambiguities', *Linguistic Inquiry* 5, 367–424.

Prince, E.: 1981, 'On the Inferencing of Indefinite-*this* NP's', in A. Joshi, I. A. Sag and B. L. Webber (eds.), *Linguistic Structure and Discourse Setting* (Cambridge University Press, Cambridge, England).

Reichenbach, H.: 1947, *Elements of Symbolic Logic*, (Macmillan, New York).

Rodman, R.: 1976, 'Scope Phenomena, 'Movement Transformations', and Montague Grammar', in B. H. Partee, (ed.), *Montague Grammar* (Academic Press, New York), pp. 165–176.

Quine, W. V. O.: 1966, 'Quantifiers and Propositional Attitudes'', in W. V. O. Quine, *Ways of Paradox* (Random House, New York).

Sadock, J.: 1975, 'The Soft Interpretive Underbelly of Generative Semantics', in P. Cole and J. Morgan (eds.), *Speech Acts*, Vol. 3 of the *Syntax and Semantics* series (Academic Press, New York).

Sag. I. A.: 1976a, 'A Logical Theory of Verb Phrase Deletion', in S. Mufwene et al. (eds.), *Papers from the Twelfth Regional Meeting of the Chicago Linguistic Society* (University of Chicago).

Sag, I. A.: 1976b, *Deletion and Logical Form*, Ph.D. dissertation, MIT (Published by Garland Publishing, Inc., New York, 1980).

Sag, I. A.: 1980, 'Formal Semantics and Extralinguistic Context', in P. Cole (ed.), *Radical Pragmatics*, Vol. 13 of the *Syntax and Semantics* series (Academic Press, New York).

Sag, I. A.: 1981, 'Partial Variable Assignment Functions, Verb Phrase Ellipsis, and the Dispensability of Logical Form', unpublished manuscript, Stanford University.

Stern, J.: 1970, *Metaphor as Demonstrative: A Formal Semantics for Demonstratives and Metaphors*, unpublished Ph.D. dissertation (Columbia University).

Strawson, P. F.: 1964, 'Identifying Reference and Truth-values', *Theoria* 30, 96–118.

Thompson, S. A.: 1971, 'The Deep Structure of Relative Clauses', in C. J. Fillmore and D. T. Langendoen (eds.), *Studies in Linguistic Semantics* (Holt, Rinehart and Winston, New York).

Vanlehn, K.: 1978, 'Determining the Scope of English Quantifiers, (Technical report, Artificial Intelligence Laboratory, MIT).

Williams, E.: 1977, 'Discourse and Logical Form', *Linguistic Inquiry* 8, 101–140.

Wilson, G.: 1978, 'On Definite and Indefinite Descriptions', *Philosophical Review* LXXXVII, 48–76.

Wittgenstein, L.: 1953, *Philosophical Investigations*, transl. by G. E. M. Anscombe (Blackwell, Oxford).

Chapter 21

Indefinite Descriptions: In Defense of Russell

Peter Ludlow and Stephen Neale

According to Bertrand Russell (1905, 1919), definite descriptions (phrases of the form 'the *F*') and indefinite descriptions (phrases of the form 'an *F*') are devices of *quantification* rather than *reference*. However, under the influence of P. F. Strawson (1950, 1952), many philosophers and linguists appear to be exercised by the fact that, on some occasions of use, descriptions appear to function rather more like referring expressions than quantified noun phrases. Indeed, it is now widely held that definite and/or indefinite descriptions are semantically *ambiguous* between quantificational and referential *interpretations*.

It must be conceded by the Russellian that definite descriptions admit of referential *uses*. But as Saul Kripke (1977) has stressed, it is far from clear that referential uses of definite descriptions are reflexes of semantically referential *interpretations*. With the help of an independently motivated, Gricean distinction between what a speaker *says* and what a speaker *means*,[1] Kripke provides a plausible non-semantic analysis of referential usage that obviates the need to posit a semantical ambiguity. In passing, Kripke suggests that some of his points might carry over *mutatis mutandis to indefinite* descriptions. In our opinion, Kripke's suggestion has been insufficiently appreciated; and in this paper we shall attempt to amplify several of his points and provide further reasons for advocating a unitary Russellian analysis of indefinite descriptions. By doing this, we put ourselves in direct opposition to a number of philosophers and linguists who argue for a semantically significant referential interpretation of indefinites.[2] It is our view that the literature on this topic contains no convincing argument for a referential interpretation of

First appeared in *Linguistics and Philosophy* 14 (1991): 171–202. Reprinted with kind permission from Kluwer Academic Publishers.

indefinite and that methodological considerations favor a unitary Russellian theory.

In Section 1, we spell out Russell's arguments for the existential analysis of indefinite descriptions, pointing out some important connections with his theory of definite descriptions. In Section 2, we distinguish various uses of indefinites that have been labelled 'referential', and argue that none of these uses needs to be regarded as reflecting anything semantical in nature. Section 3 concerns ambiguities of scope involving indefinites. We find no syntactical or semantical evidence for a referential interpretation. Section 4 concerns pronouns anaphoric on indefinite descriptions. We argue that Russell's theory is perfectly compatible with what is currently known about the syntax and semantics of pronominal anaphora.

1 RUSSELL'S THEORY OF INDEFINITES

1.1 Singular and general propositions

On Russell's account, a referring expression 'b' may be combined with a (monadic) predicate expression to express a proposition which simply could not be entertained or expressed if the entity referred to by 'b' did not exist.[3] Russell often puts this by saying that the referent of 'b' is a constituent of such a proposition; it will be convenient to follow him in this, but nothing in the present paper turns on this conception of a so-called *singular* proposition.

A sentence consisting of a definite description 'the F' combined with a (monadic) predicate phrase does not express a singular proposition; it expresses a *general* proposition, a proposition that is not *about* any entity, in the sense that the proposition is not contingent upon the existence of any entity in particular. Specifically, it does not contain as a constituent the object which in fact satisfies 'the F' (if anything does).

For Russell, the distinction between singular and general propositions reflects a certain theory of thought at the heart of which is the following principle: It is not possible for a subject to think about (e.g. have a belief about, make a judgment about) something unless he knows which particular individual he is thinking about.[4] For Russell there are two ways of cashing out *knowing which*: (i) one may be directly acquainted with (or have a memory of being directly acquainted with) the individual in question; (ii) one may think of the individual as the unique satisfier of some definite description or other.[5] In an intuitive sense, there are clearly some entities with which we can be directly acquainted: ourselves, objects in our perceptual fields, and objects with which we have recently come into epistemic contact. This intuitive notion appears to have been what Russell had in mind in 'On Denoting'.[6] The center of mass of the solar system on April 19th, 1905, the candidate who gets most votes at the next general election, the first person born in the twenty-first century, and the man with the iron mask are examples of things known to us only by *description*. Now there is a sense in which knowledge of something by description is not really knowledge *about* an individual at all:

I shall say that an object is 'known by description' when we know that it is 'the so-and-so', i.e. when we know that there is one object, and no more, having a certain property (1911, p. 159).

The point of this remark is that knowing something by description is a species of knowing *that* rather than knowing *which*. To put it another way, it is sufficient for knowledge of something by description that one know a purely general proposition; to know something by description it is not necessary to be acquainted with the object which in fact answers to the description one knows it under. So on Russell's account, where we have a thought *about* a particular individual, we entertain a singular proposition; where we only have a thought to the effect that a unique individual satisfies some description, we entertain a general proposition.

The insight behind the Theory of Descriptions is simply the following: One can perfectly well understand an utterance of 'the *F* is *G*' without knowing who or what answers to the description 'the *F*'; indeed, independently of whether or not anything actually satisfies 'the *F*'. Neither failure to be acquainted with the denotation of 'the *F*'—by which Russell means the individual it *describes*—nor absence of a denotation are barriers to understanding the proposition expressed. For the proposition expressed is just the general proposition that there is exactly one *F* and that thing is also *G* (that is, the truth conditions of 'the *F* is *G*' are given by '$(\exists x)(Fx \,\&\, (\forall y)(Fy \supset y = x) \,\&\, Gx))$'). For referring expressions this is simply not so. If '*b*' is a referring expression it is necessary to identify the referent of '*b*' in order to understand the proposition expressed by an utterance of '*b* is *G*'.[7]

1.2   Indefinite descriptions

Russell's treatment of indefinite descriptions may be stated as follows: If 'an *F*' is an indefinite description and '____ is *G*' is a predicate phrase, then the proposition expressed by an assertion of 'An *F* is *G*' is the same as the one expressed by an assertion of 'Some Fs are Gs'.[8] Thus the logical form of an utterance of 'An F is G' is captured by the formula

$(\exists x)(Fx \ \& \ Gx)$.

Or, in a more perspicuous restricted quantifier notation:

$[\text{an } x: Fx](Gx)$.

Russell's reasons for denying that indefinite descriptions are referring expressions are most clearly stated in Chapter XVI of his *Introduction to Mathematical Philosophy* [chap. 15 in this vol.]:

> Our question is: What do I really assert when I assert "I met a man"? Let us assume, for the moment, that my assertion is true, and that in fact I met Jones. It is clear that what I assert is not "I met Jones." I may say "I met a man, but it was not Jones"; in that case, though I lie, I do not contradict myself, as I should do if when I say I met a man I really mean that I met Jones. It is clear also that the person to whom I am speaking can understand what I say, even if he is a foreigner and has never heard of Jones.
>
> But we may go further: not only Jones, but no actual man enters into my statement. This becomes obvious when the statement is false, since then there is no more reason why Jones should be supposed to enter into the proposition than why anyone else should. Indeed the statement would remain significant though it could not possibly be true, even if there were no man at all.

Russell is presenting three separate arguments against treating indefinite descriptions as referring expressions.

(a) The first argument is based on what, at first sight, looks like a plausible test: If one can assert the conjunction of *S1* and $\ulcorner \neg S2 \urcorner$ without contradiction, then the truth of *S1* does not guarantee the truth of *S2*.[9] We might reconstruct the argument as follows. Suppose I met Jones last night; Jones is from York, and I know he is. I now utter (1):

(1) I met a man from York last night.

If the indefinite description 'a man from York' refers to Jones, then I would have contradicted myself if, instead of (1), I had uttered (2):

(2) I met a man from York last night but I did not meet Jones last night.

But clearly I would not have contradicted myself had I uttered (2). Therefore 'a man from York' is not a referring expression.[10] Russell is clearly onto something here, but his argument is flawed in numerous ways. At best it shows that 'a man from York' does not *always* refer to

Jones. It certainly does not show that 'a man from York' is not a referring expression, nor even that this particular occurrence of 'man from York' is not a referring expression.[11]

(b)   The second argument has important connections with Russell's theory of thought. We might spell it out as follows. Suppose I say to someone 'A man from York died last night," and, in fact, a man from York did die last night, a man named Jones. All that can be asked of the competent speaker/hearer of English by way of *understanding* my utterance, is that he grasp the general proposition that some man from York died last night. The hearer is in no way required to establish that Jones died last night, even if, in fact, a singular belief about Jones furnishes the grounds for my utterance. (If I had uttered 'Jones died last night," the situation would be very different. 'Jones' is a genuine referring expression, and by Russell's Principle, it is necessary to establish the referent of 'Jones' in order to understand the proposition expressed.)

This would seem to point to a substantial difference between indefinite descriptions and genuine referring expressions.

(c)   Russell's third argument is based on a strategy he also employs in arguing for his theory of definite descriptions, a strategy we shall also use. Suppose there are no men from York. Then clearly my utterance of 'A man from York died last night' was not about Jones or anybody else. But if 'a man from York' is interpreted as a referring expression then no proposition was expressed: there is no object answering to the descriptive condition and hence no object to make it into any proposition. Yet my utterance still expresses a perfectly determinate proposition. In fact, the proposition expressed by my utterance is false. A proposition is expressed independently of whether the denoting phrase actually denotes. With a referring expression, however, if there is no referent then no proposition is expressed.

2   REFERENTIALITY, SPECIFICITY, DEFINITENESS

In order that we may evaluate the claim that some indefinites are semantically referential, we want to present a partial taxonomy of the uses of such phrases (or at least a partial taxonomy of the types of situations in which one might use such phrases). Ultimately, we think that such a taxonomy is of importance to pragmatics rather than semantics; we provide it as a means to establishing how best to understand the claim that indefinite descriptions admit of referential interpretations.

2.1 Purely quantificational uses

Suppose I receive a telegram from the IRS informing me that an auditor is coming to see me today, and on the basis of this I come to have the general belief that an auditor is coming to see me today. Seeing me looking more despondent that usual, a friend asks me if I'm feeling all right. I respond by uttering (1):

(1) An auditor is coming to see me today.

Let's use SG ("speaker's grounds") for the proposition that is the object of the most relevant belief furnishing the grounds for an utterance. In this example, SG is a general proposition that [an x: auditor x](x is coming to see me today). And the proposition I *intend to communicate* to my friend is the same general proposition. Let's use PM ("propositions meant") to label the proposition(s) a speaker *intends to communicate*. What we have here, then, is a case where SG = PM. What about the *proposition expressed* (PE) by my utterance? On Russell's account, PE will just be [an x: auditor x] (x is coming to see me today) and there seems to be little point in contesting this for the example we are considering.

However, a sentence of the form 'An F is G' may be used to *communicate* something other than an existential proposition; that is, indefinite descriptions may be *used* in a different setting to communicate different things. Let's now look at some of these other uses of indefinites and see if we can find any evidence for the view that indefinites are ambiguous between quantificational and non-quantificational interpretations.

2.2 Referential uses

People seem to have meant various things when they have talked about referential interpretations of indefinite descriptions. To make matters clear, we want to distinguish between what we shall call *referential, specific, and definite* uses.[12] We begin with the referential use.

Consider a case where SG and PM are both singular. Suppose we notice Jones, whom we both know to be a convicted embezzler, lurking around at a function we are attending. Seeing Jones flirting with you sister, I say to you

(2) A convicted embezzler is flirting with your sister.[13]

The grounds for my assertion are furnished by a singular belief concerning Jones, that Jones is flirting with your sister. And what I intend to communicate is the singular proposition that Jones is flirting with your sister. Thus SG = PM.[14]

In other cases, I might use the indefinite to highlight an object in the perceptual environment. Suppose we are sitting by a window overlooking your garden. I look out of the window and I see a man uprooting your prize turnips. I utter (3):

(3) Look! A man is uprooting your turnips

Here I intend to communicate to you a singular proposition about that man in the garden.[15] For present purposes, let's define a referential use of an indefinite as follows:

An indefinite description 'an F' is being used *referentially* in an utterance of 'An F is G' if, and only if, (i) the speaker intends to communicate something about a particular individual b, and (ii) the speaker is using 'an F' intending that his audience shall realize that it is b that he intends to communicate something about.

The claim that referential usage (as we define it) is a reflex of something semantical is nothing short of the claim that, on occasion, indefinites have the characteristic properties of genuine referring expressions. But this claim does not stand up to serious scrutiny. Recall that a noun phrase b is a referring expression just in case its bearer is a constituent of the proposition expressed by an utterance of a sentence containing b. If the indefinites in (2) and (3) are interpreted referentially they should pass Russell's tests with flying colors. In order to understand an utterance of a sentence with a referring expression as subject, one must know which object the expression refers to. Consider the following pairs:

(4) a. Jones is flirting with your sister
     b. A convicted embezzler is flirting with your sister

(5) a. That man is uprooting your turnips
     b. A man is uprooting your turnips

Names and demonstratives are *bona fide* referring expressions. So, if a speaker S utters (4a) to hearer H, and H does not know who Jones is, then, by Russell's Principle, H will be unable to grasp the proposition expressed by the utterance. Although S would express a perfectly determinate proposition, H would be unable to recover it.[16]

Now suppose S is using 'a convicted embezzler' referentially in an utterance of (4b). S intends to *communicate* something about Jones, and is using 'a convicted embezzler' intending that H shall realize that it is Jones that he intends to communicate something about—because, for example, S thinks (i) that H knows Jones, (ii) that H knows that Jones is a convicted embezzler and (iii) that H can infer from the fact that S is using the indefinite description 'a convicted embezzler', that it is Jones that S intends to communicate something about. But now let us suppose that, contrary to S's expectations, H is not in a position to determine who S has in mind (at least one of (i), (ii), and (iii) fails to hold). Would H thereby be deprived of the possibility of grasping the proposition expressed by S's utterance?

Intuition suggest not. So if the Russellian analysis is to be undermined, the semantical ambiguity theorist must present an argument to the effect that H would be so deprived. As far as we know, no ambiguity theorist has even attempted to provide such an argument. We find ourselves in agreement with Russell and ordinary intuition here: if S speaks clearly, at an audible volume, and if H is a competent English speaker and is paying attention, then H will have a shot at grasping the proposition expressed, namely the proposition that a convicted embezzler is flirting with his sister. Performing the inference S expects him to perform is surely no part of what is required of H in order for him to grasp the proposition expressed by an utterance of (4b).

An analogous point can be made with respect to (5). Suppose S utters (5a) but H is some way prevented from seeing who S demonstrates; then H simply cannot be said to have understood S's remark. Failure to identify the referent of the demonstrative 'that man', results in failure to grasp the proposition expressed.

Suppose S is using 'a man' referentially in an utterance of (5b). S intends to communicate something about that man in the garden, and is using 'a man' intending that H should realize that it is that man he inters to communicate something about—because, for example, S thinks that H has a clear view of the garden and that H can infer from the fact that S used 'a man' that it is that very man in the garden that he intends to communicate something about. But now suppose, contrary to S's expectations, H is prevented from seeing just who it is that S intends to communicate something about. Does it follow that H cannot grasp the proposition expressed, viz., that a man is uprooting his turnips?

Again, intuition sides with Russell; and again it is incumbent upon the theorist who maintains that the indefinite is a referring expression to produce some sort of argument for that view. In both (4b) and (5b) then, treating the indefinite as a referring expression just seems to lead to a counter-intuitive conclusion.

With respect to example (4), Russell's second diagnostic is even more telling. I see Jones, whom we both take to be a convicted embezzler, flirting with your sister. I decide to inform you of this fact. It takes me several minutes to find you, and during this time, and unknown to me, Jones leaves the party. However, Smith, also a convicted embezzler, starts flirting with your sister. By the time I find you, it is no longer true that Jones is flirting with your sister, but it is true that Smith is. I utter (4b) with the intention of informing you that Jones is flirting with your sister. I am again using 'a convicted embezzler' referentially. Here the Russellian and the referentialist make divergent predictions concerning the truth value of the utterance of (4b). The Russellian predicts that (4b) will be true. The referentialist predicts that it will be false. Intuition again sides with Russell: I spoke truly albeit by accident.

Finally, whatever the force of these arguments *against* a referential interpretation of indefinites, we should note that there is an observation (due to Grice (1975) and Kripke (1977)) that undercuts a number of arguments *for* such an interpretation. Suppose we find a linguistic community whose members speak a language L with the surface syntax of some version of first-order logic with equality. Assume, further, that each member of this community knows and uses an explicit first-order semantics to interpret L. Would the members of this linguistic community be unable to communicate singular propositions using existentially quantified sentences? Surely there is no reason to think they would be subject to such a limitation.[17]

We suggest that the following characterizes the example we just considered, involving a referential use of 'a convicted embezzler':

SG: flirting-with-your-sister(Jones)
PE: [an x: convicted-embezzler x](x is flirting-with-your-sister)
PM: flirting-with-your-sister(Jones)

The speaker's grounds are singular. What the speaker intends to communicate is a singular proposition; but the proposition expressed is just a general proposition. The mere existence of a referential use of indefinites does not warrant the postulation of a semantical ambiguity. The phenomenon in question can (and we believe *should*) be accounted for non-semantically, as part of more general theory of communication and inference of the sort pioneered by Grice.

2.3   Specific uses

There is another use of indefinite descriptions. closely related to the referential use, but sufficiently different to warrant independent discussion. The rough and ready way of characterizing this use makes use of the idea of "having an individual in mind." Consider the following modification of the tax auditor case discussed in 2.1. Suppose I was audited by the IRS last year, by a man called Bill Beastly. Mr. Beastly caused me untold misery for three days, at the end of which he ruled that I owed the IRS a further two dollars. I receive a letter from the IRS informing me that Mr. Beastly will be coming to see me again this year, in fact today, and so come to have the singular belief that Mr. Beastly is coming to see me today. In response to a question about my look of gloom, I answer, as before, by uttering (6):

(6) An auditor is coming to see me today.

Now let's suppose I have no reason to expect you (my addressee) to know of Mr. Beastly, or to know that I was audited by the IRS last year. All I intend to communicate is the general proposition that an auditor is coming to see me today. We have here, then, a case where SG and PM do not coincide:

SG: *Fa, Ga*
PM: [an *x*: *Fx*](*Gx*)

When the speaker has singular grounds for an assertion of the form 'An *F* is *G*' but no intention of communicating a singular proposition, let us say that the indefinite description 'an *F*' is used *specifically*.

We can distinguish two types of cases involving a specific use of an indefinite. In the case just discussed, you (the hearer) would probably not deduce that I (the speaker) had singular grounds for my assertion. But now consider the following example of a specific use. You and I are driving through a village and you notice a smashed store window. "I wonder who did that?" you ask. I reply with (7):

(7) A colleague I had coffee with last night did it.

I have a singular belief concerning some particular colleague I had coffee with last night, but I do not intend or expect you to identify who it was (I may or may not intend you *not* to be able to identify who it was.) However, you would undoubtedly take me to have singular grounds for this assertion. Although I do not expect you to have identifying knowledge of the colleague I had coffee with last night, upon reflection I would expect you to realize that a singular belief furnishes the grounds for my utterance. Let's call this a *strongly* specific use of an indefinite and the previous case of the tax auditor a *weakly* specific use of an indefinite, the difference being that in the latter there is no reason to expect the hearer to think that the speaker has singular grounds for the assertion.[18]

A question now emerges: Is there any reason to suppose that the existence of specific uses of indefinites requires postulating a non-Russellian interpretation?

The general form of the argument against treating a referential use of an indefinite as a reflex of a referential interpretation (see Section 2.2) also holds for the specific use.[19] To claim that when I utter (7) the indefinite 'a colleague' receives a referential interpretation is tantamount to claiming that my epistemic history can prohibit me from making a purely existential assertion by my use of a sentence of the form 'An F is G'. We should rightly reject this. (Indeed, purely existential grounds for an existential assertion must be quite the exception.) Thus the semanticist who thinks that there is a non-Russellian interpretation of the indefinite description in (7) will be forced to argue that the proposition expressed is neither the existential proposition provided by Russell's analysis nor a singular proposition about some particular colleague, but some other proposition.

What, on this view, would be the proposition expressed? It might be argued that *two* propositions are expressed: the existential proposition and the proposition that the speaker has singular grounds for his assertion (or the *conjunctive* proposition obtained from these). This proposal may or may not involve some sort of self-reflexive paradox: an utterance u of 'An F is G' made by S at time t will express the proposition that [an x: Fx] (Gx) and the proposition that S's grounds for u are singular. But even if this side of the proposal is unproblematic, the Gricean/Kripkean methodological considerations tell against it. Not only is it difficult to see why a language community that knew and used a Russellian semantics for 'An F is G' would be incapable of communicating something other than a purely existential proposition by uttering 'An F is G', it is unclear how, given the meaning or 'had coffee with x' one could *fail* to do so by uttering this sentence (given the meaning and attendant epistemological justification necessary for a correct utterance of 'I had coffee with x').

2.4 Definite uses

Suppose that many people in a certain wealthy village have had their jewelry stolen over the last two months. The police are convinced that the thefts were all carried out by a single individual. They issue a warning about "the local jewelry thief." One morning, one of the villagers comes back from a walk to find his house has been broken into. The ground floor of the house has been completely ransacked and his jewelry has been stolen. Later in the day he meets a friend who asks him why he is so upset. The villager replies as follows:

(8) A jewelry thief paid me a visit this morning

Let us suppose that the villager's grounds for his utterance are furnished by the non-singular belief that the local jewelry thief paid him a visit this morning. That is, the grounds for his assertion are furnished by a general belief concerning the unique satisfier of some definite description. It is also this descriptive proposition he wishes to communicate to his friend. Here we get the following breakdown:

SG: [the x: jewelry thief x](paid-me-a-visit x)
PE: [an x: jewelry thief x](paid-me-a-visit x)
PM: [the x: jewelry thief x](paid-me-a-visit x)

(where '[the x: Fx](Gx)' is the restricted quantifier rendering of '$(\exists x)(Fx \,\&\, \forall y) (Fy \supset y = x) \,\&\, Gx))$'). Let's call this a definite use of an indefinite description:

A description 'an F' is used *definitely* in an utterance of 'An F is G' if, and only if, (i) the speaker's grounds for his utterance are furnished by the non-singular belief that the unique F is G, and (ii) the speaker intends to communicate that the F is G (or at least intends to communicate that some such non-singular belief furnishes the grounds for his utterance).

The claim that definiteness is a semantical phenomenon amounts to the claim that the proposition expressed in this example is of the form [the x: Fx](Gx). This is an odd claim. Consider the case where there is not a single jewelry thief, but rather two. Under such circumstances the semantical account entails that what was *said* in (8) was false, for what was said (on such a view) was that there is a unique jewelry thief and he paid a visit. We find such a result highly counter-intuitive, for we think it clear that under such circumstances, the speaker of (8) said something quite true.

The conclusion we draw from this section is that nothing about the *use* of indefinite descriptions warrants the postulation of a semantically referential interpretation. In the next section, we address the question of whether there is anything about *linguistic structure* that warrants such an interpretation.

3   INDEFINITES AND SCOPE

3.1   Kripke's observations

In 'On Denoting' Russell points out that sentences containing definite descriptions and verbs of propositional attitude give rise to so-called *de re–de dicto* ambiguities that his quantificational analysis of descriptions captures in terms of scope permutations. For instance, (1) is ambiguous between (2) and (3):

(1) John thinks that the man who lives upstairs is crazy

(2) [the x: man x & x lives upstairs] (John thinks that (x is crazy))

(3) John thinks that ([the x: man x & x lives upstairs] (x is crazy))

Many people have been attracted to the idea of accounting for the *de re* reading of (1) in terms of a referential interpretation. But as Kripke (1971, 1977) has argued, this idea is misguided. Suppose John has a singular belief concerning the man who lives upstairs, that he is crazy. I may correctly report this state of affairs by uttering (1) with the definite description 'the man who lives upstairs' understood *de re*. But this does not mean that I have used this description *referentially* (or even *specifically*). *I* may entertain no relevant singular proposition about the man in question nor any intention to communicate such a proposition. Russell captures this reading by giving the definite description wide scope over 'John thinks that' as in (2).

Kripke also points out that no binary distinction can replace Russell's notion of scope. A sentence like:

(4) Mary doubts that John thinks that the man who lives upstairs is a spy

is *three* ways ambiguous according as the description is given wide, intermediate, or narrow scope with respect to 'Mary doubts that' and 'John thinks that'.

It is clear, then, that definite descriptions understood *de re* cannot, in general, be identified with descriptions understood referentially, and that a semantical ambiguity between Russellian and referential interpretations of definite descriptions cannot replace either the *de re–de dicto* distinction or the wide-scope/narrow-scope distinction, as it shows up in attitude contexts. So even if one could provide a good argument for a referential interpretation of the description in (1), *we would still need the wide scope reading* given by (2).

In passing, Kripke (1977) notes that parallel considerations apply to *indefinite* descriptions in attitude contexts.[20] But for some reason the ramifications of this fact have been insufficiently appreciated in the literature. Sentence (5) is ambiguous between (6) and (7):

(5) John thinks a student of mine cheated.

(6) [an x: student of mine x] (John thinks that (x cheated))

(7) John thinks that ([an x: student of mine x] (x cheated))

First, the wide scope reading given by (6) cannot be emulated by a reading in which the indefintie is treated referentially. Suppose someone tells me that a student of mine is such that John thinks of him that he cheated but does not know of him that he is one of students. Suppose further that I am not informed of the identity of the student in question. If someone who knows John but is otherwise completely unconnected with my school asks me why I look so upset, I might utter (5), and my utterance would be true on the wide scope reading given by (6). But a semantically referential interpretation of 'a student of mine' would be incorrect here. I have not even *used* the phrase 'a student of mine' referentially. I don't know the identity of the student, nor do I have any intention to get you to identify any particular student. In short, if the indefinite description in (5) is provided with a referential interpretation it will express a *singular* proposition; but the wide scope reading given by (6) expresses a *general* proposition. (Similarly, the condition necessary for a specific use of the indefinite is not satisfied because I do not have singular grounds for my utterance: I do not know the identity of the student in question. However, there is something interesting about this sort of case, viz. that the indefinite is used in what we might call an *agent-specific* fashion.)

Second, even if one could demonstrate conclusively that indefinite descriptions have referential interpretations, as Kripke points out the referentialist would still have to appeal to Russell's notion of scope in order to capture the intermediate scope reading in a sentence like the following

(8) Hoover charged that the Berrigans plotted to kidnap a high American official

which is three ways ambiguous.

These facts demonstrate that indefinite descriptions understood *de re* cannot, in general, be identified with indefinite descriptions understood referentially, and that a semantical ambiguity between Russellian and referential interpretations of indefinite descriptions cannot replace either the *de re-de dicto* distinction or the wide-scope/narrow-scope distinction, as it shows up in attitude contexts. So even if one could provide a good argument for a referential interpretation of the description in (5), *we would still need the wide scope reading* given by (6).[21]

3.2 Fordor and Sag's Observations

In the light of Kripke's observations it is somewhat surprising to find that facts about the scope possibilities of indefinite descriptions have been appealed to in attempts to undermine a unitary Russellian analysis. Fordor and Sag (1982), for example, devote a very large part of their paper to this enterprise, and claim that the behavior of indefinites in so-called *scope islands* shows decisively that indefinites have semantically distinct referential interpretations. In particular, Fordor and Sag argue that (i) if a unitary quantificational analysis of indefinites is to be maintained, the Russellian must attribute to these phrases exceptional 'island-escapting" properties that other quantified phrases do not have, and (ii) that a semantically distinct referential interpretation captures all of the relevant data. Of course, since referential interpretations of descriptions cannot replace wide scope readings, Fordor and Sag simply *cannot* establish claim (ii). At most, they can hope to provide us with a catalog of facts about the scope possibilities of indefinites. However, some of the data Fordor and Sag bring up are quite interesting, and it seems to us important to clarify the issues they raise.

Embedded clauses such as those introduced by attitude verbs and relative clauses are supposed to create, or at least contribute to the creation of, scope islands. For example, there does not seem to be a reading of (9) in which 'every British detective' takes wide scope over 'a man in Bermuda':

(9) A man in Bermuda thinks that every British detective is after him.

But now consider:

(10) Every man in Bermuda thinks that a British detective is after him.

Here the indefinite description appears to be able to take wide scope. This suggests to Fodor and Sag that the scope of 'every British detective' in (9) can be no larger than the sentence embedded under the attitude verb, whereas no such restriction applies to indefinite descriptions. They conclude that either indefinite descriptions are quantifiers with exceptional scope properties or else they admit of referential interpretations; they opt for the latter.

There are several points to take issue with here. Let's begin by laying out both the legitimate and illegitimate scope possibilities for the embedded quantifiers in (9) and (10):

(9) a. [an x: man-in-Bermuda (x)] (x thinks that ([every y: British detective (y)] (y is after x)))

b. [an x: man-in-Bermuda (x)] ([every y: British detective (y)] (x thinks that (y is after x)))

c. [every y: British detective (y)] ([an x: man-in-Bermuda (x)] ((x thinks that (y is after x)))

(10) a. [every x: man-in-Bermuda (x)] (x thinks that ([a y: British detective (y)] (y is after x)))

b. [every x: man-in-Bermuda (x)] ([a y: British detective (y)] (x thinks that (y is after x)))

c. [a y: British detective (y)] ([every x: man-in-Bermuda (x)] (x thinks that (y is after x)))

The first point is that, for reasons already given, a reading of (10) in which 'a British detective' is referential (or specific) cannot replace (10c); so the fact that (10c) is a legitimate reading of (10), while (9c) is not a legitimate reading of (9), does not advance the case for a referential interpretation in the least. This can be made clear with the help of an example like

(11) Mary wonders whether Jane doubts that every man in Bermuda thinks that a British detective is after him

in which the indefinite may take wide scope over 'every man in Bermuda' without taking widest possible scope. The fact that this reading is available, and the fact that (10) admits of reading (10b), both falsify Fodor and Sag's claim that 'an indefinite that escapes from an island has *maximally* wide scope with respect to any quantifiers or logical operators outside the island'' (p. 374 [494 in this vol.]).

Second, the behavior of 'a British detective' is not exceptional. Wide scope reading for 'several detectives', 'three detectives', and 'some detectives' are available in the same environment.

Third, if (9c) is blocked because unexceptional quantifiers cannot escape from sentences embedded under attitude verbs, how can the acceptability of the intermediate reading (9b)—not to mention (10b)—be explained? The fact that (9b) is a perfectly good reading of (9) shows that the unexceptional quantifier 'every British detective' must be allowed to escape from the sentence embedded under the attitude verb. The unacceptability of (9c) as a reading of (9) must be explained in some other way.[22]

Fodor and Sag base their main argument for a referential interpretation of indefinites on the scope possibilities of sentences like (12):

(12) Each teacher overheard the rumor that a student of mine cheated.

According to Fodor and Sag, 'a student of mine' in (12) can be understood as taking maximally wide scope but not as taking intermediate scope, and this fact, they argue, undermines scope-based explanations of the "wide scope" readings. If all scope readings were available for (12) we would have the following possibilities:

(12) a. [each x: teacher x] ([the y: rumor-that-([a z: student-of-mine z] (z cheated))(y)] (x overhead y))

  b. [each x: teacher x] ([a z: student-of-mine z] ([the y: rumor-that-(z cheated)(y)] (x overheard y)))

  c. [the y: rumor-that-([a z: student-of-mine z] (z cheated))(y)] ([each x: teacher x] (x overheard y))

  d. [a z: student-of-mine z] ([each x: teacher x] ([the y: rumor-that-(z cheated)y] (x overheard y)))[23]

It is reading (12b) that Fodor and Sag object to. Now even if they are right that this is not a legitimate reading of (12)—and it is not at all clear that they are[24]—this would show merely that *not all scope possibilities are permissible*. This is a far cry from showing that (12d) must be replaced by a referential reading of the indefinite description! (And in any case, Kripke's observations stymie any chance of such a replacement).

Another argument offered by Fodor and Sag, indirectly related to the behavior of indefinites in nonextensional environments, is an argument from certain facts about VP deletion. They claim (following Sag (1976) and Williams (1977)) that VP deletion fails if a quantifier in the deleted VP has wide scope. So for example in (13), we cannot interpret the NP 'everyone' in the first sentence as having wide scope:

(13) Someone loves everyone and Chris knows that someone does.

With indefinites, however, it appears that VP deletion is possible when the indefinite has wide scope. Thus:

(14) Everyone loves a woman I dated and Chris knows that everyone does.

However, indefinites are not the only quantifiers that can exhibit this property. Hirschbühler (1982) observes that the same phenomenon occurs with 'every' in examples like the following:

(15) An American flag flew over every house and a Canadian one did too.

(16) An American flag flew over every house and Sal knows that a Canadian one did too.

The universally quantified noun phrase must be taking wide scope in these sentences. (One could sincerely utter such sentences without committing oneself to the existence of a single gigantic flag flying over every house.) Moreover, if a universal quantifier can take wide scope here, why should it be surprising if a quantificational indefinite can do the same?

4   INDEFINITES AND ANAPHORA

Facts involving pronominal anaphora appear to have convinced some philosophers and linguists that a unitary Russellian treatment of indefinite descriptions cannot be maintained. In this section we shall explain why we believe that Russell's proposal is quite consistent with what is know about the semantics of anaphoric pronouns.

4.1   Bound vs unbound anaphora

It is a familiar point that many occurrences of pronouns that are anaphoric on quantified NPs can be treated as variables bound by those quantifiers:

(1) Every Frenchman loves his mother.

(2) A woman was teaching her son how to ski.

(3) A man from Texas thought he had lost his wallet.

However, in the light of the work on pronouns by Evans (1977, 1980), it is clear that some pronouns anaphoric on quantified NPs cannot be interpreted as bound variables. To see this, let's back up a bit and focus on Strawson's (1952) observation that an indefinite description in one sentence may function as the antecedent of an anaphoric pronoun in a subsequent sentence as in

(4) A man walked into the room. He fell over.

Strawson sees this type of cross-sentential anaphora as a problem for Russell's existential analysis of 'a man': surely the pronoun 'he' refers to the man who walked into the room, i.e. to whoever 'a man' refers to; but on Russell's account 'a man' has no referent.

The naive Russellian response to this sort of objection goes back to Geach (1962): we should treat 'he' in the second sentence as a bound pronoun. The logical form of (4) can thus be represented as

(5) [an x: man x] (walked-into-the-room x & fell-over x),

preserving the insight that the indefinite is quantificational.

However, Evans (1977) has exposed some serious defects in this proposal. First, notice that the bound variable treatment doesn't extend to other quantifiers. If the pronoun 'them' in (6) is treated as a variable bound by 'some men', the logical form of (6) is given by (7):

(6) Some men walked-into-the-room. They fell over.

(7) [some x: man x] (walked-into-the-room x & fell-over x).

As Evans points out, this is quite wrong. First, (7) will be true as long as some of the men that walked into the room fell over; but on its most natural reading, the truth of (6) requires *all* of them to fall over. Thus the bound proposal delivers the wrong truth conditions.

Second, there is a syntactical reason for thinking that the pronouns in (4) and (6) are not bound by their antecedents: the pronouns are not *c-commanded* by the quantified NPs that are supposed to be binding them.[25] Indeed, detailed investigation reveals that it is only when the NP does not c-command the pronoun that the previous problem occurs.[26]

Third, because it incorrectly extends the scope of the quantifier to bind a pronoun in an adjacent sentence, the bound variable analysis wrongly predicts that the nonsensical 'No men came in and they fell over' will be synonymous with the perfectly intelligible 'No men came in and fell over'.[27]

It is clear, then, that an alternative to the bound variable analysis is required for pronouns not c-commanded by their antecedents. So what is the Russellian to say about unbound anaphora? Let's begin by returning to Strawson's problem. Consider the following examples:

(8) *A convicted embezzler* is flirting with your sister; *he's drunk.*

(9) Look! *A man* is uprooting your turnips; *he* looks hungry.

Let's assume that these sentences are uttered under the circumstances we described in Section 2. In both (8) and (9), it is claimed, the occurrence of 'he' in the second sentence is anaphoric on the indefinite description in the first. Since (it is assumed) the pronoun is a referring expression, and since the pronoun "picks up" its reference from the indefinite antecedent, the conclusion we are to draw is that the indefinite must be a referring expression.

There are two interesting premises in this argument: (i) the pronouns in question refer; (ii) the pronouns "pick up" their references from the antecedent indefinite noun phrases. Premise (i) ignores the possibility (later suggested by Cooper (1979) and Parsons (1978)) that some unbound pronouns are interpreted as definite descriptions.[28] On such an account, (8) might be interpreted as

(8') *A convicted embezzler* is flirting with your sister; *the convicted embezzler that is flirting with your sister* is drunk

with the pronoun 'he' cashed out as the definite description 'the convicted embezzler that is flirting with your sister'. If this proposal succeeds, then premise (i) is false as definite descriptions are not referring expressions but quantifiers.[29]

Premise (ii) ignores the possibility (later suggested by Kripke and Lewis) that some apparently anaphoric pronouns refer to individuals raised to salience in one way or another.[30] As Lewis puts it:

I may say 'A cat is on the lawn' under circumstances in which it is apparent to all parties to the conversation that there is some one particular cat that is responsible for the truth of what I say, and for my saying it. Perhaps I am looking out of the window, and you rightly presume that I said what I did because I saw a cat; and further (since I spoke in the singular) that I saw only one. What I said was an existential quantification; hence strictly speaking, it involves no reference to any particular cat. Nevertheless it raises the salience of the cat that made me say it . . .

Thus although indefinite descriptions—that is, idioms of existential quantification—are not themselves referring expressions, they may raise the salience of particular individuals in such a way as to pave the way for referring expressions that follow. (p. 243)

On this sort of account, pronouns like those in the above examples would not pick up their respective contents from their indefinite "antecedents", but would function as genuine referring expressions. In (9) for example, the pronoun would not inherit its content from 'a man', but would simply refer to an individual assumed by the speaker to be in the shared perceptual environment. On this account, the pronoun is referential even though its antecedent is quantificational.

If an unbound pronoun is to be treated as a definite description let's say it is a *D-type* anaphor; and if it is to be treated as a referring expression let's say it is an *A-type* anaphor.[31] It is clear that Russell's treatment of indefinite descriptions is compatible with both D-type and A-type accounts of pronouns anaphoric on such phrases. One interesting empirical question, then, is which approach provides the most plausible and general account of unbound anaphora in natural language. We should stress immediately that there is no reason to rule out an overall theory that makes room for both D-type *and* A-type anaphors. That is, perhaps the rules of language dictate only that an unbound pronoun anaphoric on a quantifier must be interpreted as a referring expression *or* a description. It would then be a question for pragmatics exactly how any particular unbound anaphor is interpreted.[32]

We are inclined to think that the D-type approach is more likely to provide the basis of a general theory of unbound anaphora; but we are also inclined to think that a reasonable case can be made for the view that, on occasion, pronouns anaphoric on indefinite descriptions receive A-type interpretations. We are not going to present the details of a theory of D-type anaphora here because that would require addressing a variety of questions about the interpretation of definite descriptions that would take us too far astray.[33] We shall however, address several problems that may arise in the interpretation of purportedly D-type pronouns that are anaphoric on indefinite descriptions.

Let us take the position that if *P* is a pronoun anaphoric on a quantified NP that does not *c*-command *P*, then *P* is interpreted as a definite description. As pointed out by Evans (1977, 1980), it would seem that the content of such a pronoun is systematically related to the content of the sentence containing its antecedent:

(4)   A man walked into the room. He fell over.

(10) Only one man walked into the room and he looked very frightened.

(6)   Some men walked into the room. They fell over.

In (4) and (10), the pronoun is plausibly interpreted as the singular definite description 'the man who walked into the room'; in (6), the pronoun 'them' is plausibly interpreted as the plural definite description 'the men who walked into the room'. At this point, we might propose the following rough generalization:

(P)   If x is a pronoun that is anaphoric on, but not c-commanded by a quantifier '$[Dx: Fx]$' that occurs in an antecedent clause '$[Dx: Fx]$ (Gx)', then x is interpreted as '$[$the $x: Fx$ & $Gx]$'.

Assume a Russellian semantics for singular definite descriptions: if F is singular then '$[$the $x: Fx$ & $Gx]$' is true iff every F is G and there is exactly one F (that is, where F is singular '$[$the $x: Fx$ & $Gx]$' is the restricted quantifier rendering of '$(\exists x)(Fx$ & $(\forall y)(Fy \supset y = x)$ & $Gx))$'). Extending Russell's theory in the manner suggested by Chomsky (1975), if F is plural then '$[$the $x: Fx$ & $Gx]$' is true iff every F is G and there are at least two Fs.[34]

The relevant question now is whether the conjunction of (P) and Russell's semantics for indefinite descriptions succeeds once we get beyond the simple cases discussed so far.

4.2   D-type content

A   Uniqueness implications   Consider the following example:

(11) Socrates kicked a dog and it bit him.

Geach has objected to any implication of uniqueness generated by a theory that analyzes 'it' in (11) as (or via) a Russellian description, on the grounds that it would be perfectly coherent to utter the conjunction of (11) and (12):

(12) Socrates kicked another dog and it did not bite him.

But all Geach's example really shows is that the problem of so-called "incomplete" definite descriptions—a problem that Strawson (1950) first brought up for Russell's (1905) quantificational analysis of definite descriptions—recurs for D-type pronouns (indeed, it would be most odd if the problem did not recur). There are two points here. (i) All sorts of quantifiers ('the dog', 'no men', 'most politicians', etc.) must either have their contents completed by contextual means (using e.g., additional descriptive material or temporal parameters) or have their domains of quantification contextually delimited if our intuitive ascriptions of truth and falsity are to hold; thus it is no objection to Russell's quantificational analysis that many occurrences of definite descriptions are incomplete. (ii) As we would expect, the phenomenon of underspecified D-type pronouns is not restricted to cases involving anaphora on singular indefinite descriptions. Consider (13) and (14):

(13) Harry bought some books. He put them in his office with some other books he bought.

(14) Several politicians entered the room. They went straight over and talked to several other politicians who entered the room.

The moral here is surely that rote applications of (P) will not always deliver the full descriptive content of a D-type pronoun; sometimes a degree of contextual flexibility is required in spelling it out.[35]

B Donkey anaphora   According to Heim (1982), both Russell's analysis of indefinites and broadly D-type approaches to unbound anaphora are undermined by so-called donkey anaphora as exemplified in sentences like (15) and (16):[36]

(15) Every man who buys a donkey vaccinates it

(16) If a man buys a donkey he vaccinates it

Let's focus on (15). The problem here is that if the pronoun 'it' is treated as going proxy for a singular description, (15) will come out as (17)

(17) Every man who buys a donkey vaccinates the donkey he bought

(with 'he' bound by 'every man who buys a donkey'). But then on Russell's account of definite descriptions (17) is false if any man buys more that one donkey.

This type of example is widely regarded as thwarting descriptive approaches to unbound anaphora; but it is our belief that there is not very much of a problem here at all.

One idea might be to follow a suggestion made by Parsons (1978) and Cooper (1979) and claim that there really is an implication of uniqueness in examples of the form of (15), and then back up this claim by pointing to an example like the following:

(18) Every man who has a daughter thinks she is the most beautiful girl in the world.

It is not really possible to evaluate this proposal without a detailed discussion of the semantics-pragmatics distinction, so we shall simply leave it open as possibility to be explored.

A second idea would be to appeal to the existence of D-type pronouns that are silent on the matter of semantical number, an idea suggested in passing by Parsons (1978) and Davies (1981) and developed in detail by Neale (1990). The idea here would be that some D-type pronouns anaphoric on quantifiers that do not give rise to cardinality implications—e.g. 'every donkey', 'each donkey', 'some donkey', 'a donkey'—might be interpreted as descriptions that are neither singular or plural. On this account, (15) would be interpreted as

(19) Every man who bought a donkey vaccinated the donkey or donkeys he bought.

A third idea would be to appeal to event or situation quantifiers that are implicit in many sentences, an idea explored by Berman (1987), Heim (1990), and by Ludlow (1994). On such an account, a paraphrase of (16) might be something like "For every event e, if e is a buying of a donkey by a man, then there is a related event f which is a vaccinating of the unique donkey bought in e by the man who bought that donkey in e."

None of these options need involve a radical departure from the D-type approach to unbound anaphora, and to that extent donkey anaphora does not seem to present the Russellian with any insurmountable obstacles.

C Pronominal contradiction   Consider the following dialogue, adapted from Strawson (1952):

(20) A: A man fell in front of the train.
     B: He didn't fall, he was pushed.

This is a perfectly coherent dialogue, but if we cash out the anaphoric pronoun using (P) we get something that is always false:

(21) The man who fell in front of the train didn't fall, he was pushed.

Following a suggestion made by Davies (1981), the D-type theorist might say that the pronoun in (20) has an ironical character that can be captured by marking off its descriptive content with scare quotes. Thus *B*'s utterance in (20) might be interpreted in exactly the same way as:

(21) The man who "fell in front of the train" didn't fall, he was pushed.

The logical form of (21) might be cashed out as (22):

(22) [the *x*: man *x* & *x* is said to have fallen in front of the train]
      (*x* didn't fall) &
      [the *x*: man *x* & *x* is said to have fallen in front of the train]
      (*x* was pushed)

One helpful way to think about this proposal is to suppose that the speaker may know that the hearer is deluded about certain facts—for example, that someone was pushed in front of the train—and will *humor* the hearer by assuming a descriptive content that comports with the hearer's until such time that the hearer can be straightened out. Thus the speaker "ironically" assumes a certain descriptive content.

Notice that there are ironic uses of *explicit* definite descriptions in discourse. For example imagine a case where man posing as a Green Peace representative comes to ask me for a contribution. I give the man fifty dollars and tell you about it later that day. But you know the "Green Peace representative" to be a con man and you reply:

(23) The "Green Peace representative" you speak of was a con man and just conned you out of fifty dollars.

Again, to the extent we find this phenomenon with overt descriptions, we ought to expect it with D-type pronouns.

D A-type anaphors? We mentioned earlier that there is no reason in principle to rule out a theory of unbound anaphora that makes room for both D-type *and* A-type pronouns. Indeed, if it is true that pragmatic factors determine the content of any particular D-type anaphor then it is not really much of a modification to the theory to say that an unbound pronoun may receive *objectual* rather than descriptive content.

What do we mean by this? The overarching idea would be that the interpretation of an unbound pronoun is not determined by semantical rule; rather it is fixed by contextual factors. Very often descriptive material from preceding utterances is used, but on occasion it may just be so obvious which object or objects the speaker has in mind that the pronoun can be interpreted referentially. A useful strategy in thinking about the semantical content of a particular occurrence of a pronoun (e.g.) 'he' in an utterance, is to think about how the speaker might respond to a question like 'Who did you mean by 'he'?" Let's go back to the tax auditor case. I say to you "A tax auditor is coming to see me today. He will probably need to see my credit card receipts." You then ask "Who did you mean by 'he'?" I reply "The tax auditor who is coming to see me today." Contrast this with a case in which the indefinite description is being used referentially. We are sitting by a window overlooking your garden. I notice a man uprooting your prize turnips, and I say "Look! A man is uprooting your turnips; he looks angry." You ask "Who did you mean by 'he'? Now it is true that I could reply by saying "The man who is uprooting your turnips." But an equally reasonable answer under the circumstances would be "Him; that man over there," perhaps accompanied by some sort of gesture or demonstration. This suggests that some unbound anaphors might be interpreted referentially. Of course, one might just maintain that the D-type pronoun is being used referentially too and that this creates the illusion of a referential interpretation in the same way as it does for referential uses of overt definite descriptions and, of course, indefinite descriptions.

There is no need for us to adjudicate between these proposals here. The main point is that Russell's account of indefinites is compatible with either a comprehensive D-type account of unbound anaphora or with a theory that allows for both D-and A-type anaphors.

We have attempted to show that the existence of so-called referential uses of indefinites, the possibility of indefinites taking maximally wide scope in complex syntactical constructions, and the possibility of cross-sentential anaphora on indefinites can all be handled without postulating a semantically distinct referential interpretation. And to this extent it is our hope that talk of the semantical relevance of so-called "specific," "definite," or "referential" indefinites, and the ensuing confusion that such talk ultimately creates, can be avoided.

Notes

Thanks to Irene Heim for detailed comments and to Sylvian Bromberger, Martin Davies, Saul Kripke, Richard Larson, Trip McCrossin, John Perry, François Recanati, Ivan Sag, and Scott Soames for valuable discussion.

1. See Grice (1968, 1975). The Gricean/Kripkean strategy for dealing with referential uses of *definite* descriptions is defended in detail in Neale (1990) in the context of a general defense of Russell's theory. That work and the present paper borrow from one another here and there in their mutually supporting projects.

2. See, e.g., Partee (1972), Chastain (1975), Donnellan (1978), Wilson (1978), Fodor and Sag (1982), Barwise and Perry (1983), and Stich (1983, 1986).

3. For discussion, see Evans (1982) chapters 2 and 4.

4. See Russell (1911) p. 159; Russell (1912) p. 58.

5. Russell (1905) pp. 41–2, pp. 55–6, Russell (1912) ch. V.

6. Russell later came to hold a far more restricted view, according to which we are acquainted only with sense-data, universals, and (perhaps) ourselves. It is clear, however, that the semanticist can perfectly coherently endorse the Theory of Descriptions without commitment to this idea. For discussion see Neale (1990) Chapter 2.

7. This is not the place to address the philosophical problem of identification. For discussion, see Evans (1982).

8. Russell (1919) p. 171 [326 in this vol.].

9. A similar test—the so-called "cancellability test"—is proposed by Grice (1975) to distinguish conversational implicatures from genuine entailments. Grice's test appears to have more or less the same defects as Russell's diagnostic, in that it fails to distinguish cases where an implicature is present from cases where there is a genuine ambiguity of some sort. For discussion, see Sadock (1978).

10. Kaplan (1971) presents more or less the same argument in defense of Russell.

11. Once one distinguishes between (a) sentence meaning, (b) what is said, and (c) what is communicated, this argument can be cleaned up considerably, but we shall not be appealing to it in what follows.

12. In this section, we are indebted to John Perry for pointing out that the distinction between the speaker's *grounds* and the speaker's *intentions* that is central to much of the discussion of referential uses of definite descriptions—see Kripke (1977), Donnellan (1978), Davies (1981), Evans (1982), and Neale (1990)—ought to carry over (with modification) to the study of indefinite descriptions.

13. This example is adapted from Wilson (1978).

14. Strictly speaking, it is not necessary that my grounds be furnished by this singular belief at all. I may not actually believe that Jones is flirting with your sister, I may just want to get Jones into more trouble by getting you to believe he is. Nothing in our presentation higher on the possibility of insincere assertion, and for the sake of simplicity we shall ignore it.

15. From the point of view of spelling out a theory of singular thought there is an important difference between these two cases of referential usage, due to the fact that we may have discriminating knowledge of individuals in various ways. This, however, is not our concern in this essay. For discussion, see Evans (1982) and Neale (1990).

16. *H* may, of course, recover some "weaker" proposition, for instance that someone named 'Jones' is flirting with *H*'s sister.

17. Grice's way of making the point officially concerns the logical particles & and ∨, and their natural language counterparts, but it comports well with his remarks

against a referential interpretation of definite descriptions in Grice (1969). Kripke's (1977) way of making the point is directed specifically at the idea of a referential interpretation of definite descriptions, but as he points out, it ought to carry over *mutatis mutandis* to indefinites.

18. Both of these cases may be contrasted with the following (adapted from Fodor and Sag, 1982) in which the speaker *intends* to convey that he has singular grounds for his assertion. Suppose I am about to give back some examination papers that I have just graded. And suppose that I have been informed by somebody not in the class that Henry cheated. Before I hand back the papers, I say "A student in this class cheated on the examination", intending full well to convey that I know of one of the students that he cheated. Once again we have a case involving a strongly-specific use of an indefinite, but in addition it is part of my communicative intention to convey that I have singular grounds for my assertion. It would seem, then, that specificity is a graded phenomenon, increasing in strength as information about speakers grounds is made available.

19. Many writers seem to think that an indefinite description use specifically should be interpreted as a referring expression. Fodor and Sag (1982), for example, claim that in

(i) A student in the syntax class cheated on the final exam

"[the] indefinite noun phrase may be semantically interpreted in two distinct ways. One semantic interpretation is that of a quantified expression such as *each student* or *few students*; the other interpretation is that of a referring expression such as proper name or demonstrative phrase" (p. 355 [475 herein]). But then they go on to say that the indefinite in (i) will be a referring expression even if the speaker "does not identify" the person he knows to be the cheater, (p. 356 [476]) i.e. even if the sentence is used specifically, and not referentially. Fodor and Sag seem to be suggesting that the indefinite in such examples is just like a name for which the hearer does not know the referent. It is true, of course, that we sometimes use a name in circumstances where our addressee turns out to be unable to identify the referent, and it is just as surely true that this fact does not mean that the names uttered cannot be referring expressions. But with names it is plausible to suppose that the reference is fixed by some sort of historical, or information-based chain, or by the common practice of a community of language users. (See Kripke (1972) and Evans (1973) for discussion.) Whatever the merits of such accounts of naming, it is obvious that they do not provide (nor are they *intended* to provide) any sort of account of reference for indefinite descriptions. (Nor, of course, does talk of *demonstration* help in the case we are considering.) It is quite unnecessary for a hearer *H* to establish exactly who I had coffee with last night in order to understand my utterance of (7).

The difference between the quantificational interpretation and the specific interpretation—whatever it is—cannot, then, be cashed out in terms of the difference between a general and a singular proposition. Although Fodor and Sag do not overtly invoke Russellian singular and general propositions, they are clearly under the same relevant obligations as theorists who do, because they explicitly follow Kaplan when they emphasize the special role of the *bearer* of a referring expression *vis-a-vis* the semantics of so-called referential indefinites and appeal to his technical apparatus in spelling out the formal details. However, one cannot be at all sure about the point of this appeal because Fodor and Sag appear to part company with Kaplan at critical points, for instance, when they assert what "... expressions like *I* and *now* are not rigid designators, since their denotations vary with the context of utterance, ..." (1982, p. 385 [506]).

20. See also Higginbotham (1988).

21. That we are not dealing with a phenomenon that is confined to definite and indefinite descriptions is made clear by a sentence like:

(i) John thinks that everyone who lives on the twentieth floor is a spy.

A wide scope reading of 'everyone who lives on the twentieth floor' is needed to capture the fact that there is a reading of (i) which could be true if John has singular beliefs concerning each person who lives on the twentieth floor that that person is a spy but does not know that the persons in question live on the twentieth floor. In such a situation, a referential or specific interpretation of 'everyone who lives on the twentieth floor' would not be appropriate.

22. This might suggest that attitude verbs *do* impose a constraint on the interpretation of quantifiers contained in sentences they embed, but a weaker one than is usually assumed: a quantifier in a sentence embedded under an attitude verb may not take wider scope than a quantifier not so embedded. Such a constraint would rule out (9c) while allowing (9a) and (9b) as readings of (9). One attracted to this idea might then propose that (10c) is not a genuine reading of (10), and offer a pragmatic account of why the truth of (10c) might be inferred. When (10) is read as (10b), in suitable circumstances one might reasonably conclude that every man in Bermuda has the same detective in mind. So even if the indefinite cannot take wide scope—which, of course, we have not assumed—it might still present the *illusion* of taking wide scope. This seems to be more or less the position taken by Cooper (1979).

23. Fodor and Sag do not represent the possibilities quite like this, but the differences are not important for present purposes. (The main difference is that Fodor and Sag ignore the fact that, for the Russellian, 'the rumor that ...' is a definite description, and hence a quantifier. Consequently they do not get (12c), which is in any case equivalent to (12a).)

24. It is worth mentioning that many of our informants actually disagree with Fodor and Sag's intuitions that (12b) is not a genuine reading of (12). Consider the following sentences:

(i)   Each teacher overheard seven rumors that a student of mine cheated

(ii) Each teacher overheard many rumors that a student of mine cheated.

These sentences exhibit the same structure as (12), yet the intermediate understanding for 'a student of mine' is fine. For example, in (i) we can imagine a situation in which each teacher overheard rumors about one of my students (perhaps not the same student that the other teachers heard rumours about), and in every case the teacher overheard seven distinct rumors. These examples can be improved further. The term 'rumor' here is problematic, as it is hard to discriminate rumors on the basis of the way they are told. For example one person might report to the teacher of hearing that Jackie wrote the answers on her sleeve, and another person might report (second hand) that Jackie wrote the answers on a stick of chewing gum. Given two such reports, it is not clear whether the teacher has heard one rumor of cheating or two. A much better example would be one with *reports* or *exclamations* (construed as utterance events):

(iii) Each teacher overheard seven reports that a student of mine cheated.

(iv) Each teacher overheard many exclamations that a student of mine cheated.

If there is an intermediate understanding of the indefinite in these examples, there seem to be two obvious ways of accounting for it. First, one might reject the view that attitude verbs create scope islands. Alternatively, one might opt for a pragmatic explanation. Suppose every teacher comes to overhears several reports communicating a unique singular proposition, but each teacher overhears the communication of a different singular proposition. That there is a unique singular proposition communicated is not what was expressed in examples (iii) to (iv), but it is something we might be tempted to infer in appropriate circumstances.

Consider now the intermediate reading of (12) given by (12b). This is simply the case in which each teacher overheard a different rumor but each rumor was about a particular student, and an analogous pragmatic explanation could be constructed. It interesting to note that Fodor and Sag appear to back off a bit when they say (p. 375 [495]) that some may find their judgments about example (12) "less than compelling," and suggest that conditionals containing indefinites might be more persuasive. We find no reason to dispute the received view that a conditional sentence is composed of two sub-sentences and a binary sentential connective, and to that extent we too assume that a quantifier in the antecent or consequent of a conditional cannot take wide scope over the entire conditional; so, in effect, we are quite prepared to go along with Fodor and Sag in viewing conditionals as what they call 'scope islands." Now Fodor and Sag note that

(v) If a student on the syntax exam cheats every professor will be fired

cannot mean that for every professor there is a student such that if the student cheats the professor will be fired. But as King (1988) has observed, the missing intermediate reading in this example has an explanation, namely that to generate it, it would be necessary for the universally quantified NP 'every professor' to escape the consequent clause of the conditional, i.e. it would be necessary for it to violate a scope island.

25. Following Reinhart (1976) we will say that a noun phrase x c-commands a noun phrase y if, and only if, the first branching node dominating x also dominates y, and neither x nor y dominates the other.

26. See Evans (1980), Davies (1981) and Neale (1990).

27. It is also arguable that the bound variable analysis does considerable violence to our intuitive ascriptions of truth and falsity. When uttering a sequence of sentences like those in (2) and (3) it seems reasonable to suppose that a perfectly determinate claim has been expressed after the first sentence has been uttered. But if we are to take Geach's proposal seriously, we would have to say that a complete

claim has not been made until the second sentence has been uttered. Indeed, a complete claim will not have been made until the speaker is through using pronouns that are anaphoric on the indefinite.

28. Evans (1977) was the first to present a comprehensive account of unbound anaphors in terms of definite descriptions. Parsons (1978) and Cooper (1979) suggest that unbound pronouns go proxy for definite descriptions, a view Evans rejects in favor of the view that descriptive pronouns (*E-type* pronouns, as he calls them) have their references *fixed* by description in the sense of Kripke (1972).

29. It will not do to contest this conclusion on the grounds that definite descriptions might be referring expressions. For the purposes of this essay we are entitled to assume that *some* occurrences of definite descriptions can be analysed as quantified NPs. Even *if* one holds (as we do not, see Neale (1990)) that some occurrences of English definite descriptions are referential, the point still stands. The crucial idea is that these pronouns may well have descriptive content, which is just to say that they are quantificational. Whether or not English descriptions are *always* quantificational is irrelevant here.

30. See Kripke (1977) and Lewis (1979).

31. These labels are borrowed very loosely from Sommers (1982). Whereas Evans' (1977) E-type pronouns have their references fixed by description, D-type pronouns go proxy for definite descriptions. Unlike E-type pronouns, D-type pronouns may therefore enter into scope interactions with other operators. The ramifications of this difference are explored in Davies (1981) and Neale (1990).

32. With respect to unbound pronouns anaphoric on definite descriptions, a related idea is mentioned briefly by Kripke (1977).

33. For extended discussion, see Neale (1990).

34. We shall not attempt to defend this proposed semantics for singular and plural descriptions here. See Neale (1990).

35. For a detailed discussion of these points, see Davies (1981) chap. VII and Neale (1990) chap. 3 [chap. 19 herein] and chap. 6.

36. On the first point, see also Kamp (1981).

References

Barwise, J. and J. Perry: 1983, *Situations and Attitudes*, MIT Press, Cambridge.

Berman, S.: 1987, 'Situation-based Semantics for Adverbs of Quantification', *UMass. Occasional Papers in Linguistics*, 12.

Chastain, C.: 1975, 'Reference and Context', in K. Gunderson (ed.), *Minnesota Studies in the Philosophy of Science, vol. VII: Language, Mind, and Knowledge*, University of Minnesota Press, Minneapolis.

Chomsky, N.: 1975, 'Questions of Form and Interpretation', *Linguistic Analysis* 1.

Cooper, R.: 1979, 'The Interpretation of Pronouns', in F. Heny and H. Schnelle (ed.), *Syntax and Semantics, Vol. 10*, Academic Press, New York.

Davies, M.: 1981, *Meaning, Quantification, Necessity*, Routledge and Kegan Paul, London.

Donnellan, K. S.: 1978, 'Speaker Reference, Descriptions, and Anaphora', in P. Cole (ed.), *Syntax and Semantics 9: Pragmatics*, Academic Press, New York.

Evans, G.: 1973, 'The Causal Theory of Names', *Proceedings of the Aristotelian Society*, Supplementary Volume 47. [Chap. 26 in this vol.]

Evans, G.: 1977, 'Pronouns, Quantifiers and Relative Clauses (I)', *Canadian Journal of Philosophy*, 7. Reprinted in Evans (1985).

Evans, G.: 1980, 'Pronouns', *Linguistic Inquiry* 11. Reprinted in Evans (1985).

Evans, G.: 1982, *The Varieties of Reference*, Clarendon Press, Oxford.

Evans, G.: 1985, *Collected Papers*, Clarendon Press, Oxford.

Fodor, J. D., and I. Sag: 1982, 'Referential and Quantificational Indefinites', *Linguistics and Philosophy* 5. [Chap. 20 in this vol.]

Geach, P.: 1962, *Reference and Generality*, Cornell University Press, Ithaca, NY.

Grice, H. P.: 1969, 'Vacuous Names', In D. Davidson and J. Hintikka (eds.), *Words and Objections*, Reidel, Dordrecht.

Grice, H. P.: 1975, 'Logic and Conversation', in J. Cole and J. Morgan (eds.), *Syntax and Semantics, Vol 3: Speech Acts*, Academic Press, New York.

Heim, I.: 1982, *The Semantics of Definite and Indefinite Noun Phrases*, Garland Press, New York.

Heim, I.: 1990, 'E-type Pronouns and Donkey Anaphora', *Linguistics and Philosophy* 13.

Higginbotham, J.: 1988, 'Is Semantics Necessary?', *Proceedings of the Aristotelian Society*.

Hirschbühler, P.: 1982, 'VP Deletion and Across-the-board Quantifier Scope', NELS XII, Graduate Linguistics Student Association, Amherst.

Kamp, H.: 1981, 'A Theory of Truth and Semantical Interpretation', in J. Groenendijk et al. (eds.), *Formal Methods in the Study of Natural Language*, Amsterdam Centre.

Kaplan, D. 1971, 'What is Russell's Theory of Descriptions?', in D. F. Pears (ed.), *Bertrand Russell: A Collection of Critical Essays*, Doubleday Anchor, Garden City, NY.

Kaplan, D.: 1977, 'Demonstratives', in J. Almog, J. Perry, and H. Wettstein (eds.), *Themes from Kaplan*, Oxford University Press, New York.

King, J.: 1988, 'Are Indefinite Descriptions Ambiguous?', *Philosophical Studies*, 53.

Kripke, S.: 1971, 'Identity and Necessity', in M. K. Muntitz (ed.), *Identity and Individuation*, New York University Press, New York.

Kripke, S.: 1972, 'Naming and Necessity', in D. Davidson and G. Harman (eds.), *Semantics of Natural Language*, Reidel, Fordrecht.

Kripke, S.: 1977, 'Speaker's Reference and Semantic Reference', in French, Uehling, and Wettstein (eds.), *Contemporary Perspectives in the Philosophy of Language*, University of Minnesota Press, Minneapolis. [Chap. 18 in this vol.]

Lewis, D.: 1979, 'Scorekeeping in a Language Game', *Journal of Philosophical Logic* 8.

Ludlow, P.: 1994, 'Conditionals, Events, and Unbound Pronouns'. *Lingua e Stile* 29.

Neale, S.: 1990, *Descriptions*, MIT Press, Cambridge.

Parsons, T.: 1978, 'Pronouns as Paraphrases', manuscript, University of Massachusetts, Amherst.

Partee, B.: 1972, 'Opacity, Coreference and Pronouns', in D. Davidson and G. Harman (eds.), *Semantics of Natural Language*. Reidel, Dordrecht.

Reinhart, T.: 1976, 'The Syntactic Domain of Anaphora', Ph.D. dissertation, MIT.

Russell, B.: 1905, 'On Denoting', *Mind* 14.

Russell, B.: 1911, 'Knowledge by Acquaintance and Knowledge by Description', Proceedings of the Aristotelian Society 1910–11. Reprinted in Russell's *Mysticism and Logic*. George Allen and Unwin, London.

Russell, B.: 1912, *The Problems of Philosophy*, Oxford University Press, Oxford.

Russell, B.: 1919, *Introduction to Mathematical Philosophy*, George Allen and Unwin, London.

Sadock, J.: 1978, 'On Testing for Conversational Implicature', in P. Cole (ed.), *Syntax and Semantics, Vol 9: Pragmatics*, Academic Press, New York.

Sag, I.: 1976, *Deletion and Logical Form* Ph.D. dissertation, MIT.

Sommers, F.: 1982, *The Logic of Natural Language*, Clarendon Press, Oxford.

Stich, S.: 1983, *From Folk Psychology to Cognitive Science*, MIT Press, Cambridge, Mass.

Stich, S.: 1986, 'Are Belief Predicates Systematically Ambiguous?', in R. J. Bogdan (ed.), *Belief*, Clarendon Press, Oxford.

PART IV
NAMES

INTRODUCTION

In part III we saw the importance of the distinction between singular and general terms for the theory of descriptions. As it turns out, that distinction is also important in the theory of proper names.

Just as we can contentfully use nonreferring descriptions like 'the present King of France', it appears that we can also contentfully use nonreferring singular terms like 'Pegasus' and 'Zeus'. One suggestion, *apparently* advanced by Gottlob Frege in "On Sense and Reference" is that despite failing to have a reference, these terms nevertheless have senses, which allows us to use them contentfully.[1] Of course, this solution runs into the same epistemological problems with senses that we saw in Part I: it is completely unclear how we can stand in any interesting relation to objects like senses, which stand outside of space and time.

Another solution, advanced by Bertrand Russell in "On Denoting," was that proper names might be definite descriptions in disguise. So, for example, a name like 'Pegasus' might be shorthand for 'the white winged horse ...'. John Searle adopts this general strategy, but with some modifications designed to make the proposal more serviceable. For example, is it really part of the meaning of 'Pegasus' that *all* of the properties attributed to him in Greek mythology should hold? Or consider a name like 'Socrates'. Is it really part of the meaning of that name that it's bearer drank hemlock, taught Plato, and did all of the other things that we are told he did when we study the history of philosophy? Searle suggests that we needn't associate the meaning of a name with a description that contains all of these elements—it might be enough that most of them hold or that a suitably weighted combination of them hold.

In addition to descriptive theories of proper names, there is the line, advocated by Willard Van Orman Quine, that names might be simple predicates rather than genuine referring expressions. In "Reference and

Proper Names" Tyler Burge develops this idea, suggesting that a name like 'Socrates' might in fact have a form akin to 'the x: x is a Socrates'. As Burge notes, there is much grammatical evidence to recommend this analysis. We can say things like 'Fred is a Jones' and 'No Kennedy I know would say that', suggesting that at the very minimum names *can* function as predicates.

In spite of the merits of proposals like those offered by Russell, Searle, and Quine, Saul Kripke notes that there are serious drawbacks to such proposals—indeed, *any* proposal that does not take names to be rigid designators. As Kripke argues in *Naming and Necessity*, descriptive theories of names fail to account for the behavior of names in modal environments. For example, even if we concede that Socrates did all the things he was supposed to have done, it is still true that Socrates need not have done any of the things he did. He could have forsaken philosophy for other pursuits. He could have been run over by a chariot at age 2. But then how do we make sense of a descriptive name in a sentence like (1)?

(1) It might have been the case that Socrates was run over by a chariot at age two.

If the description is unpacked, we get something like (2):

(2) It might have been the case that the philosopher who taught Plato, drank hemlock, . . ., was run over by a chariot at age two.

And this looks like a claim that is necessarily false.

If names like 'Socrates' do not get their content by virtue of being descriptions, how do they get their contents? Clearly, Socrates is not in our perceptual environment, so it is no good to say that the objectual content of the name 'Socrates' is fixed by some sort of demonstration. Kripke proposes that there is a causal chain, linking our use of 'Socrates' with an initial baptism of Socrates over 2000 years ago.

In "The Causal Theory of Names," Gareth Evans takes aim at the causal account of names offered by Kripke and others. For Evans, if we keep an eye on questions of semantic competence—on our knowledge of meaning—then the causal story makes little sense. For Evans, there has to be some sort of information-theoretic chain linking the name 'Socrates' with the original bearer of that name.

This may seem like a strange place for me to leave the discussion of names, since, unlike other parts of this reader, there has been no development of a clear linguistic investigation of proper names. That may be in part due to the profound influence of Kripke's critique of descriptive theories of proper names. However, I think that the pieces are in place to launch a serious linguistic investigation into the nature of names.

In the first place, there are the undeniable facts about names that are discussed in the reading from Burge. Names take determiners like 'a' and 'the' (indeed, in some languages they routinely do so), which suggests that they are behaving more like nouns than like saturated referring expressions. A widespread linguistic analysis of names is that they have possibly empty determiner positions, so that a name like Socrates has at a minimum the following structure: $[_{DP}[_{Det} \varnothing][_N$ Socrates$]]$. It is not a long step to the supposition that the default interpretation of the null element is as the definite determiner 'the'. But what about the interaction of names with modals? Here too there are things to be said.

For example, in *Frege: The Philosophy of Language*, Michael Dummett makes the off-hand proposal that perhaps the behavior of names in modal contexts could be accounted for as due to names taking wide scope (see —Russell, "Descriptions," chapter 15). So, for example, perhaps the sensibility of (1) above is actually due to the possibility of quantifier raising, which yields the following:

(3) $[_{DP}[_{Det}(\text{the})][_N$ Socrates$]]x$ It might have been the case that x was run over by a chariot at age two

Kripke discusses this possibility briefly in the introduction to *Naming and Necessity*, holding that this move overlooks the fact that we can take a sentence that is free of modals (e.g. 'Socrates was run over by a chariot at age two') and evaluate that sentence in counterfactual situations.

Of course, this isn't to say that the theory of direct reference for names is in trouble or that an alternative theory is soon to emerge, but look at where the debate is heading. On the one hand, there will be serious questions about the fine structure of determiner phrases—in particular, about whether they are structured more like quantifier expressions or whether they are logically simple expressions. Then there is the issue of whether it makes sense to extend the theory of quantifier raising to names and whether one can account for the wide-scope-taking behavior of names. Finally, there is the modal question, which looks like it will be embedded within the general questions about the theory of meaning that we began addressing in Part II,—questions about the kinds of properties that we would expect a robust theory of meaning to have. All of these questions have an empirical flavor to them, and all of them will have to be addressed as the philosophy of language continues to investigate the nature of proper names.

Note

1. But see "The Causal Theory of Names" by Gareth Evans (chapter 26) for doubts about this interpretation of Frege on sense and nonreferring expressions.

Further Reading for Part IV

Burge, T. 1974. "Truth and Singular Terms." *Noûs* 8:309–325.

Devitt, M. 1980. *Designation*. New York: Columbia University Press.

Devitt, M., and K. Sterelny. 1987. *Language and Reality: An Introduction to the Philosophy of Language*. Chapters 3–4. Cambridge: MIT Press.

Donnellan, K. "Speaking of Nothing." *Philosophical Review* 83:3–32.

Dummett, M. 1981. *Frege: Philosophy of Language*. 2nd edition. Cambridge: Harvard University Press.

Evans, G. 1982. *The Varieties of Reference*. Oxford: Oxford University Press.

Kripke, S. 1980. *Naming and Necessity*. Harvard: Harvard University Press.

Larson, R., and G. Segal. 1995. *Knowledge of Meaning: An Introduction to Semantic Theory*. Chapter 5. Cambridge: MIT Press.

McDowell, J. 1977. "On the Sense and Reference of a Proper Name." *Mind* 86:159–185.

Russell, B. 1905. "On Denoting." *Mind* 14:479–493.

Chapter 22

On Sense and Reference

Gottlob Frege

Translated by Max Black

Equality[1] gives rise to challenging questions which are not altogether easy to answer. Is it a relation? A relation between objects, or between names or signs of objects? In my *Begriffsschrift*[2] I assumed the latter. The reasons which seem to favour this are the following: $a = a$ and $a = b$ are obviously statements of differing cognitive value; $a = a$ holds a priori and, according to Kant, is to be labelled analytic, while statements of the form $a = b$ often contain very valuable extensions of our knowledge and cannot always be established a priori. The discovery that the rising sun is not new every morning, but always the same, was one of the most fertile astronomical discoveries. Even to-day the identification of a small planet or a comet is not always a matter of course. Now if we were to regard equality as a relation between that which the names 'a' and 'b' designate, it would seem that $a = b$ could not differ from $a = a$ (i.e. provided $a = b$ is true). A relation would thereby be expressed of a thing to itself, and indeed one in which each thing stands to itself but to no other thing. What is intended to be said by $a = b$ seems to be that the signs or names 'a' and 'b' designate the same thing, so that those signs themselves would be under discussion; a relation between them would be asserted. But this relation would hold between the names or signs only in so far as they named or designated something. It would be mediated by the connexion of each of the two signs with the same designated thing. But this is arbitrary. Nobody can be forbidden to use any arbitrarily producible event or object as a sign for something. In that case the sentence $a = b$ would no longer refer to the subject matter, but only to its mode of designation; we

This translation first appeared in *The Philosophical Review* 57 (1948): 207–230. In the public domain.

would express no proper knowledge by its means. But in many cases this is just what we want to do. If the sign '*a*' is distinguished from the sign '*b*' only as object (here, by means of its shape), not as sign (i.e. not by the manner in which it designates something), the cognitive value of $a = a$ becomes essentially equal to that of $a = b$, provided $a = b$ is true. A difference can arise only if the difference between the signs corresponds to a difference in the mode of presentation of that which is designated. Let a, b, c be the lines connecting the vertices of a triangle with the midpoints of the opposite sides. The point of intersection of a and b is then the same as the point of intersection of b and c. So we have different designations for the same point, and these names ('point of intersection of a and b,' 'point of intersection of b and c') likewise indicate the mode of presentation; and hence the statement contains actual knowledge.

It is natural, now, to think of there being connected with a sign (name, combination of words, letter), besides that to which the sign refers, which may be called the reference of the sign, also what I should like to call the *sense* of the sign, wherein the mode of presentation is contained. In our example, accordingly, the reference of the expressions 'the point of intersection of a and b' and 'the point of intersection of b and c' would be the same, but not their senses. The reference of 'evening star' would be the same as that of 'morning star,' but not the sense.

It is clear from the context that by 'sign' and 'name' I have here understood any designation representing a proper name, which thus has as its reference a definite object (this word taken in the widest range), but not a concept or a relation, which shall be discussed further in another article.[3] The designation of a single object can also consist of several words or other signs. For brevity, let every such designation be called a proper name.

The sense of a proper name is grasped by everybody who is sufficiently familiar with the language or totality of designations to which it belongs;[4] but this serves to illuminate only a single aspect of the reference, supposing it to have one. Comprehensive knowledge of the reference would require us to be able to say immediately whether any given sense belongs to it. To such knowledge we never attain.

The regular connexion between a sign, its sense, and its reference is of such a kind that to the sign there corresponds a definite sense and to that in turn a definite reference, while to a given reference (an object) there does not belong only a single sign. The same sense has different expressions in different languages or even in the same language. To be sure, exceptions to this regular behaviour occur. To every expression belonging to a complete totality of signs, there should certainly correspond a definite sense; but natural languages often do not satisfy this condition, and one must be content if the same word has the same sense in the same context. It may perhaps be granted that every grammatically well-formed expression representing a proper name always has a sense. But this is not to say that to the sense there also corresponds a reference. The words 'the celestial body most distant from the Earth' have a sense, but it is very doubtful if they also have a reference. The expression 'the least rapidly convergent series' has a sense; but it is known to have no reference, since for every given convergent series, another convergent, but less rapidly convergent, series can be found. In grasping a sense, one is not certainly assured of a reference.

If words are used in the ordinary way, what one intends to speak of is their reference. It can also happen, however, that one wishes to talk about the words themselves or their sense. This happens, for instance, when the words of another are quoted. One's own words then first designate words of the other speaker, and only the latter have their usual reference. We then have signs of signs. In writing, the words are in this case enclosed in quotation marks. Accordingly, a word standing between quotation marks must not be taken as having its ordinary reference.

In order to speak of the sense of an expression '*A*' one may simply use the phrase 'the sense of the expression "*A*"'. In reported speech one talks about the sense, e.g., of another person's remarks. It is quite clear that in this way of speaking words do not have their customary reference but designate what is usually their sense. In order to have a short expression, we will say: In reported speech, words are used *indirectly* or have their *indirect* reference. We distinguish accordingly the *customary* from the *indirect* reference of a word; and its *customary* sense from its *indirect* sense. The indirect reference of a word is accordingly its customary sense. Such exceptions must always be borne in mind if the mode of connexion between sign, sense, and reference in particular cases is to be correctly understood.

The reference and sense of a sign are to be distinguished from the associated idea. If the reference of a sign is an object perceivable by the senses, my idea of it is an internal image,[5] arising from memories of sense impressions which I have had and acts, both internal and external, which I have performed. Such an idea is often saturated with feeling; the clarity of its separate parts varies and oscillates. The same sense is not always connected, even in the same man, with the same idea. The idea is subjective: one man's idea is not that of another. There result, as a matter of course, a variety of differences in the ideas associated with the same sense. A painter, a horseman, and a zoologist will probably connect different ideas with the name 'Bucephalus'. This constitutes an essential distinction between the idea and the sign's sense, which may be the common property of many and therefore is not a part of a mode of the individual mind. For one can hardly deny that mankind has a common store of thoughts which is transmitted from one generation to another.[6]

In the light of this, one need have no scruples in speaking of *the* sense, whereas in the case of an idea one must, strictly speaking, add to whom it belongs and at what time. It might perhaps be said: Just as one man connects this idea, and another that idea, with the same word, so also one man can associate this sense and another that sense. But there still remains a difference in the mode of connexion. They are not prevented from grasping the same sense; but they cannot have the same idea. *Si duo idem faciunt, non est idem.* If two persons picture the same thing, each still has his own idea. It is indeed sometimes possible to establish differences in the ideas, or even in the sensations, of different men; but an exact comparison is not possible, because we cannot have both ideas together in the same consciousness.

The reference of a proper name is the object itself which we designate by its means; the idea, which we have in that case, is wholly subjective; in between lies the sense, which is indeed no longer subjective like the idea, but is yet not the object itself. The following analogy will perhaps clarify these relationships. Somebody observes the Moon through a telescope. I compare the Moon itself to the reference; it is the object of the observation, mediated by the real image projected by the object glass in the interior of the telescope, and by the retinal image of the observer. The former I compare to the sense, the latter is like the idea or experience. The optical image in the telescope is indeed one-sided and dependent upon the standpoint of observation; but it is still objective, inasmuch as it can be used by several observers. At any rate it could be arranged for several to use it simultaneously. But each one would have his own retinal image. On account of the diverse shapes of the observers' eyes, even a geometrical congruence could hardly be achieved, and an actual coincidence would be out of the question. This analogy might be developed still further, by assuming *A*'s retinal image made visible to *B*; or *A* might also see his own retinal image in a mirror. In this way we might perhaps show how an idea can itself be taken as an object, but as such is not for the observer what it directly is for the person having the idea. But to pursue this would take us too far afield.

We can now recognize three levels of difference between words, expressions, or whole sentences. The difference may concern at most the ideas, or the sense but not the reference, or, finally, the reference as well. With respect to the first level, it is to be noted that, on account of the uncertain connexion of ideas with words, a difference may hold for one person, which another does not find. The difference between a translation and the original text should properly not overstep the first level. To the possible differences here belong also the colouring and shading which poetic eloquence seeks to give to the sense. Such colouring and shading are not objective, and must be evoked by each hearer or reader according to the hints of the poet or the speaker. Without some affinity in human ideas art would certainly be impossible; but it can never be exactly determined how far the intentions of the poet are realized.

In what follows there will be no further discussion of ideas and experiences; they have been mentioned here only to ensure that the idea aroused in the hearer by a word shall not be confused with its sense or its reference.

To make short and exact expressions possible, let the following phraseology be established:

A proper name (word, sign, sign combination, expression) *expresses* its sense, *stands for* or *designates* its reference. By means of a sign we express its sense and designate its reference.

Idealists or sceptics will perhaps long since have objected: 'You talk, without further ado, of the Moon as an object; but how do you know that the name 'the Moon' has any reference? How do you know that anything whatsoever has a reference?' I reply that when we say 'the Moon,' we do not intend to speak of our idea of the Moon, nor are we satisfied with the sense alone, but we presuppose a reference. To assume that in the sentence 'The Moon is smaller that the Earth' the idea of the Moon is in question, would be flatly to misunderstand the sense. If this is what the speaker wanted, he would use the phrase 'my idea of the Moon'. Now we can of course be mistaken in the presupposition, and such mistakes have indeed occurred. But the question whether the presupposition is perhaps always mistaken need not be answered here; in order to justify mention of the reference of a sign it is enough, at first, to point out our intention in speaking or thinking. (We must then add the reservation: provided such reference exists.)

So far we have considered the sense and reference only of such expressions, words, or signs as we have called proper names. We now inquire concerning the sense and reference for an entire declarative sentence. Such a sentence contains a thought.[7] Is this thought, now, to be regarded as its sense or its reference? Let us assume for the time being that the sentence has reference. If we now replace one word of the sentence by another having the same reference, but a different sense, this can have no bearing upon the reference of the sentence. Yet we can see that in such a case the thought changes; since, e.g., the thought in the sentence 'The morning star is a body illuminated by the Sun' differs from that in the sentence 'The evening star is a body illuminated by the Sun.' Anybody who did not know that the evening star is the morning star might hold the one thought to be true, the other false. The thought, accordingly, cannot be the reference of the sentence, but must rather be considered as the sense. What is the position now with regard to the reference? Have we a right even to inquire about it? Is it possible that a sentence as a whole has only a sense, but no reference? At any rate, one might expect that such sentences occur, just as there are parts of sentences having sense but no reference. And sentences which contain proper names without reference will be of this kind. The sentence 'Odysseus was set ashore at Ithaca while sound asleep' obviously has a sense. But since it is doubtful whether the name 'Odysseus', occurring therein, has reference, it is also doubtful whether the whole sentence has one. Yet it is certain, nevertheless, that anyone who seriously took the sentence to be true or false would ascribe to the name 'Odysseus' a reference, not merely a sense; for it is of the reference of the name that the predicate is affirmed or denied. Whoever does not admit the name has reference can neither apply nor withhold the predicate. But in that case it would be superfluous to advance to the reference of the name; one could be satisfied with the sense, if one wanted to go no further than the thought. If it were a question only of the sense of the sentence, the thought, it would be unnecessary to bother with the reference of a part of the sentence; only the sense, not the reference, of the part is relevant to the sense of the whole sentence. The thought remains the same whether 'Odysseus' has reference or not. The fact that we concern ourselves at all about the reference of a part of the sentence indicates that we generally recognize and expect a reference for the sentence itself. The thought loses value for us as soon as we recognize that the reference of one of its parts is missing. We are therefore justified in not being satisfied with the sense of a sentence, and in inquiring also as to its reference. But now why do we want every proper name to have not only a sense, but also a reference? Why is the thought not enough for us? Because, and to the extent that, we are concerned with its truth value. This is not always the case. In hearing an epic poem, for instance, apart from the euphony of the language we are interested only in the sense of the sentences and the images and feelings thereby aroused. The question of truth would cause us to abandon aesthetic delight for an attitude of scientific investigation. Hence it is a matter of no concern to us whether the name 'Odysseus', for instance, has reference, so long as we accept the poem as a work of art.[8] It is the striving for truth that drives us always to advance from the sense to the reference.

We have seen that the reference of a sentence may always be sought, whenever the reference of its components is involved; and that this is the case when and only when we are inquiring after the truth value.

We are therefore driven into accepting the *truth value* of a sentence as constituting its reference. By the truth value of a sentence I understand the circumstance that it is true or false. There are no further truth values. For brevity I call the one the True, the other the False. Every declarative sentence concerned with the reference of its words is therefore to be regarded as a proper name, and its reference, if it has one, is either the True or the False. These two objects are recognized, if only implicitly, by everybody who judges something to be true—and so even by a sceptic. The designation of the truth values as objects may appear to be an arbitrary fancy or perhaps a mere play upon words, from which no profound consequences could be drawn. What I mean by an object can be more exactly discussed only in connexion with concept and relation. I will reserve this for another article.[9] But so much should already be clear, that in every judgment,[10] no matter how trivial, the step from the level of thoughts to the level of reference (the objective) has already been taken.

One might be tempted to regard the relation of the thought to the True not as that of sense to reference, but rather as that of subject to predicate. One can, indeed, say: 'The thought, that 5 is a prime number, is true.' But closer examination shows that nothing more has been said than in the simple sentence '5 is a prime number.' The truth claim arises in each case from the form of the declarative sentence, and when the latter lacks its usual force, e.g., in the mouth of an actor upon the stage, even the sentence 'The thought that 5 is a prime number is true' contains only a thought, and indeed the same thought as the simple '5 is a prime number.' It follows that the relation of the thought to the True may not be compared with that of subject to predicate. Subject and predicate (understood in the logical sense) are indeed elements of thought; they stand on the same level for knowledge. By combining subject and predicate, one reaches only a thought, never passes from sense to reference, never from a thought to its truth value. One moves at the same level but never advances from one level to the next. A truth value cannot be a part of a thought, any more than, say, the Sun can, for it is not a sense but an object.

If our supposition that the reference of a sentence is its truth value is correct, the latter must remain unchanged when a part of the sentence is replaced by an expression having the same reference. And this is in fact the case. Leibniz gives the definition: '*Eadem sunt, quae sibi mutuo substitui possunt, salva veritate.*' What else but the truth value could be found, that belongs quite generally to every sentence if the reference of its components is relevant, and remains unchanged by substitutions of the kind in question?

If now the truth value of a sentence is its reference, then on the one hand all true sentences have the same reference and so, on the other hand, do all false sentences. From this we see that in the reference of the sentence all that is specific is obliterated. We can never be concerned only with the reference of a sentence; but again the mere thought alone yields no knowledge, but only the thought together with its reference, i.e. its truth value. Judgments can be regarded as advances from a thought to a truth value. Naturally this cannot be a definition. Judgment is something quite peculiar and incomparable. One might also say that judgments are distinctions of parts within truth values. Such distinction occurs by a return to the thought. To every sense belonging to a truth value there would correspond its own manner of analysis. However, I have here used the word 'part' in a special sense. I have in fact transferred the relation between the parts and the whole of the sentence to its reference, by calling the reference of a word part of the reference of the sentence, if the word itself is a part of the sentence. This way of speaking can certainly be attacked, because the whole reference and one part of it do not suffice to determine the remainder, and because the word 'part' is already used in another sense of bodies. A special term would need to be invented.

The supposition that the truth value of a sentence is its reference shall now be put to further test. We have found that the truth value of a sentence remains unchanged when an expression is replaced by another having the same reference: but we have not yet considered the case in which the expression to be replaced is itself a sentence. Now if our view is correct, the truth value of a sentence containing another as part must remain unchanged when the part is replaced by another sentence having the same truth value. Exceptions are to be expected when the whole sentence or its part is direct or indirect quotation; for in such cases, as we have seen, the words do not have their customary reference. In direct quotation, a sentence designates another sentence, and in indirect quotation a thought.

We are thus led to consider subordinate sentences or clauses. These occur as parts of a sentence complex, which is, from the logical standpoint, likewise a sentence—a main sentence. But here we meet the question whether it is also true of the subordinate sentence that its reference is a truth value. Of indirect quotation we already know the opposite. Grammarians view subordinate clauses as representatives of parts of sentences and divide them accordingly into noun clauses, adjective clauses, adverbial clauses. This might generate the supposition that the reference of a subordinate clause was not a truth value but rather of the same kind as the reference of a noun or adjective or adverb—in short, of a part of a sentence, whose sense was not a thought but only a part of a thought. Only a more thorough investigation can clarify the issue. In so doing, we shall not follow the grammatical categories strictly, but rather group together what is logically of the same kind. Let us first search for cases in which the sense of the subordinate clause, as we have just supposed, is not an independent thought.

The case of an abstract[11] noun clause, introduced by 'that', includes the case of indirect quotation, in which we have seen the words to have their indirect reference coinciding with what is customarily their sense. In this case, then, the subordinate clause has for its reference a thought, not a truth value; as sense not a thought, but the sense of the words 'the thought, that ...,' which is only a part of the thought in the entire complex sentence. This happens after 'say', 'hear', 'be of the opinion', 'be convinced', 'conclude', and similar words.[12] There is a different, and indeed somewhat complicated, situation after words like 'perceive', 'know', 'fancy', which are to be considered later.

That in the cases of the first kind the reference of the subordinate clause is in fact the thought can also be recognized by seeing that it is indifferent to the truth of the whole whether the subordinate clause is true or false. Let us compare, for instance, the two sentences 'Copernicus believed that the planetary orbits are circles' and 'Copernicus believed that the apparent motion of the Sun is produced by the real motion of the Earth.' One subordinate clause can be substituted for the other without harm to the truth. The main clause and the subordinate clause together have as their sense only a single thought, and the truth of the whole includes neither the truth nor the untruth of the subordinate clause. In such cases it is not permissible to replace one expression in the subordinate clause by another having the same customary reference, but only by one having the same indirect reference, i.e. the same customary sense. If somebody were to conclude: The reference of a sentence is not its truth value, for in that case it could always be replaced by another sentence of the same truth value; he would prove too much; one might just as well claim that the reference of 'morning star' is not Venus, since one may not always say 'Venus' in place of 'morning star'. One has the right to conclude only that the reference of a sentence is not *always* its truth value, and that 'morning star' does not always stand for the planet Venus, viz. when the word has its indirect reference. An exception of such a kind occurs in the subordinate clause just considered which has a thought as its reference.

If one says 'It seems that ...' one means 'It seems to me that ...' Or 'I think that ...' We therefore have the same case again. The situation is similar in the case of expressions such as 'to be pleased', 'to regret', 'to approve', 'to blame', 'to hope', 'to fear'. If, toward the end of the battle of Waterloo,[13] Wellington was glad that the Prussians were coming, the cause for his joy was a conviction. Had he been deceived, he would have been no less pleased so long as his illusion lasted; and before he became as convinced he could not have been pleased that the Prussians were coming—even though in fact they might have been already approaching. Just as a conviction or a belief is the ground of a feeling, it can, as an inference, also be the ground of a conviction. In the sentence: Columbus inferred from the roundness of the Earth that he could reach India by travelling towards the west,' we have as the reference of the parts two thoughts, that the Earth is round, and that Columbus by travelling to the west could reach India. All that is relevant here is that Columbus was convinced of both, and that the one conviction was a ground for the other. Whether the Earth is really round, and whether Columbus could really reach India by travelling to the west, are immaterial to the truth of our sentence; but it is not immaterial whether we replace 'the Earth' by 'the planet which is accompanied by a moon whose diameter is greater than the fourth part of its own.' Here also we have the indirect reference of the words.

Adverbial final clauses beginning 'in order that' also belong here; for obviously the purpose is a thought; therefore: indirect reference for the words, subjunctive mood.

A subordinate clause with 'that' after 'command', 'ask', 'forbid', would appear in direct speech as an imperative. Such a clause has no reference but only a sense. A command, a request, are indeed not thoughts, yet they stand on the same level as thoughts. Hence in subordinate clauses depending upon 'command', 'ask', etc., words have their indirect reference. The reference of such a clause is therefore not a truth value but a command, a request, and so forth.

The case is similar for the dependent question in phrases such as 'doubt whether', 'not to know what'. It is easy to see that here also the words are to be taken to have their indirect reference. Dependent clauses expressing questions and beginning with 'who', 'what', 'where', 'when', 'how', 'by what means', etc., seem at times to approximate very closely to adverbial clauses in which words have their customary references. These cases are distinguished linguistically [in German] by the mood of the verb. With the subjunctive, we have a dependent question and indirect reference of the words, so that a proper name cannot in general be replaced by another name of the same object.

In the cases so far considered the words of the subordinate clauses had their indirect reference, and this made it clear that the reference of the subordinate clause itself was indirect, i.e. not a truth value but a thought, a command, a request, a question. The subordinate clause could be regarded as a noun, indeed one could say: as a proper name of that thought, that command, etc., which it represented in the context of the sentence structure.

We now come to other subordinate clauses, in which the words do have their customary reference without however a thought occurring as sense and a truth value as reference. How this is possible is best made clear by examples.

Whoever discovered the elliptic form of the planetary orbits died in misery.

If the sense of the subordinate clause were here a thought, it would have to be possible to express it also in a separate sentence. But this does not work, because the grammatical subject 'whoever' has no independent sense and only mediates the relation with the consequent clause 'died in misery'. For this reason the sense of the subordinate clause is not a complete thought, and its reference is Kepler, not a truth value. One might object that the sense of the whole does contain a thought as part, viz. that there was somebody who first discovered the elliptic form of the planetary orbits; for whoever takes the whole to be true cannot deny this part. This is undoubtedly so; but only because otherwise the dependent clause 'whoever discovered the elliptic form of the planetary orbits' would have no reference. If anything is asserted there is always an obvious presupposition that the simple or compound proper names used have reference. If one therefore asserts 'Kepler died in misery,' there is a presupposition that the name 'Kepler' designates something; but it does not follow that the sense of the sentence 'Kepler died in misery' contains the thought that the name 'Kepler' designates something. If this were the case the negation would have to run not

Kepler did not die in misery

but

Kepler did not die in misery, or the name 'Kepler' has no reference.

That the name 'Kepler' designates something is just as much a presupposition for the assertion

Kepler died in misery

as for the contrary assertion. Now languages have the fault of containing expressions which fail to designate an object (although their grammatical form seems to qualify them for that purpose) because the truth of some sentences is a prerequisite. Thus it depends on the truth of the sentence:

There was someone who discovered the elliptic form of the planetary orbits

whether the subordinate clause

Whoever discovered the elliptic form of the planetary orbits

really designates an object or only seems to do so while having in fact no reference. And thus it may appear as if our subordinate clause contained as a part of its sense the thought that there was somebody who discovered the elliptic form of the planetary orbits. If this were right the negation would run:

Either whoever discovered the elliptic form of the planetary orbits did not die in misery or there was nobody who discovered the elliptic form of the planetary orbits.

This arises from an imperfection of language, from which even the symbolic language of mathematical analysis is not altogether free; even there combinations of symbols can occur that seem to stand for something but have (at least so far) no reference, e.g. divergent infinite series. This can be avoided, e.g., by means of the special stipulation that divergent infinite series shall stand for the number 0. A logically perfect language (*Begriffsschrift*) should satisfy the conditions, that every expression grammatically well constructed as a proper name out of signs already introduced shall in fact designate an object, and that no new sign shall be introduced as a proper name without being secured a reference. The logic books contain warnings against logical mistakes arising from the ambiguity of expressions. I regard as no less pertinent a warning against apparent proper names having no reference. The history of mathematics supplies errors which have arisen in this way. This lends itself to demagogic abuse as easily as ambiguity—perhaps more easily. 'The will of the people' can serve as an example; for it is easy to establish that there is at any rate no generally accepted reference for this expression. It is therefore by no means unimportant to eliminate the source of these mistakes, at least in science, once and for all. Then such objections as the one discussed above would become impossible, because it could never depend upon the truth of a thought whether a proper name had a reference.

With the consideration of these noun clauses may be coupled that of types of adjective and adverbial clauses which are logically in close relation to them.

Adjective clauses also serve to construct compound proper names, though, unlike noun clauses, they are not sufficient by themselves for this purpose. These adjective clauses are to be regarded as equivalent to adjectives. Instead of 'the square root of 4 which is smaller than 0', one can also say 'the negative square root of 4'. We have here the case of a compound proper name constructed from the expression for a concept with the help of the singular definite article. This is at any rate permissible if the concept applies to one and only one single object.[14]

Expressions for concepts can be so constructed that marks of concept are given by adjective clauses as, in our example, by the clause 'which is smaller than 0'. It is evident that such an adjective clause cannot have a thought as sense or a truth value as reference, any more than the noun clause could. Its sense, which can also be expressed in many cases by a single adjective, is only a part of a thought. Here, as in the case of the noun clause, there is no independent subject and therefore no possibility of reproducing the sense of the subordinate clause in an independent sentence.

Places, instants, stretches of time, are, logically considered, objects; hence the linguistic designation of a definite place, a definite instant, or a stretch of time is to be regarded as a proper name. Now adverbial clauses of place and time can be used for the construction of such a proper name in a manner similar to that which we have seen in the case of noun and adjective clauses. In the same way, expressions for concepts bringing in places, etc., can be constructed. It is to be noted here also that the sense of these subordinate clauses cannot be reproduced in an independent sentence, since an essential component, viz. the determination of place or time, is missing and is only indicated by a relative pronoun or a conjunction.[15]

In conditional clauses, also, there may usually be recognized to occur an indefinite indicator, having a similar correlate in the dependent clause. (We have already seen this occur in noun, adjective, and adverbial clauses.) In so far as each indicator refers to the other, both clauses together form a connected whole, which as a rule expresses only a single thought. In the sentence

If a number is less than 1 and greater than 0, its square is less than 1 and greater than 0

the component in question is 'a number' in the conditional clause and is in the dependent clause. It is by means of this very indefiniteness that the sense acquires the generality expected of a law. It is this which is responsible for the fact that the antecedent clause alone has no complete thought as its sense and in combination with the consequent clause expresses one and only one thought, whose parts are no longer thoughts. It is, in general, incorrect to say that in the hypothetical judgment two judgments are put in reciprocal relationship. If this or something similar is said, the word 'judgment' is used in the same sense as I have connected with the word 'thought', so that I would use the formulation: 'A hypothetical thought establishes a reciprocal relationship between two thoughts.' This could be true only if an indefinite indicator is absent;[16] but in such a case there would also be no generality.

If an instant of time is to be indefinitely indicated in both conditional and dependent clauses, this is often achieved merely by using the present tense of the verb, which in such a case however does not indicate the temporal present. This grammatical form is then the indefinite indicator in the main and subordinate clauses. An example of this is: 'When the Sun is in the tropic of Cancer, the longest day in the northern hemisphere occurs.' Here, also, it is impossible to express the sense of the subordinate clause in a full sentence, because this sense is not a complete thought. If we say: 'The Sun is in the tropic of Cancer,' this would refer to our present time and thereby change the sense. Just as little is the sense of the main clause a thought; only the whole, composed of main and subordinate clauses, has such a sense. It may be added that several common components in the antecedent and consequent clauses may be indefinitely indicated.

It is clear that noun clauses with 'who' or 'what' and adverbial clauses with 'where', 'when', 'wherever', 'whenever' are often to be interpreted as having the sense of conditional clauses, e.g. 'who touches pitch, defiles himself.'

Adjective clauses can also take the place of conditional clauses. Thus the sense of the sentence previously used can be given in the form 'The square of a number which is less than 1 and greater than 0 is less than 1 and greater than 0.'

The situation is quite different if the common component of the two clauses is designated by a proper name. In the sentence:

Napoleon, who recognized the danger to his right flank, himself led his guards against the enemy position

two thoughts are expressed:

1. Napoleon recognized the danger to his right flank
2. Napoleon himself led his guards against the enemy position.

When and where this happened is to be fixed only by the context, but is nevertheless to be taken as definitely determined thereby. If the entire sentence is uttered as an assertion, we thereby simultaneously assert both component sentences. If one of the parts is false, the whole is false. Here we have the case that the subordinate clause by itself has a complete thought as sense (if we complete it by indication of place and time). The reference of the subordinate clause is accordingly a truth value. We can therefore expect that it may be replaced, without harm to the truth value of the whole, by a sentence having the same truth value. This is indeed the case; but it is to be noticed that for purely grammatical reasons, its subject must be 'Napoleon', for only then can it be brought into the form of an adjective clause belonging to 'Napoleon'. But if the demand that it be expressed in this form be waived, and the connexion be shown by 'and', this restriction disappears.

Subsidiary clauses beginning with 'although' also express complete thoughts. This conjunction actually has no sense and does not change the sense of the clause but only illuminates it in a peculiar fashion.[17] We could indeed replace the conditional clause without harm to the truth of the whole by another of the same truth value; but the light in which the clause is placed by the conjunction might then easily appear unsuitable, as if a song with a sad subject were to be sung in a lively fashion.

In the last cases the truth of the whole included the truth of the component clauses. The case is different if a conditional clause expresses a complete thought by containing, in place of an indefinite indicator, a proper name or something which is to be regarded as equivalent. In the sentence

If the Sun has already risen, the sky is very cloudy

the time is the present, that is to say, definite. And the place is also to be thought of as definite. Here it can be said that a relation between the truth values of conditional and dependent clauses has been asserted, viz. such that the case does not occur in which the antecedent stands for the True and the consequent for the False. Accordingly, our sentence is true if the Sun has not yet risen, whether the sky is very cloudy or not, and also if the Sun has risen and the sky is very cloudy. Since only truth values are here in question, each component clause can be replaced by another of the same truth value without changing the truth value of the whole. To be sure, the light in which the subject then appears would usually be unsuitable; the thought might easily seem distorted; but this has nothing to do with its truth value. One must always take care not to clash with the subsidiary thoughts, which are however not explicitly expressed and therefore should not be reckoned in the sense. Hence, also, no account need be taken of their truth values.[18]

The simple cases have now been discussed. Let us review what we have learned.

The subordinate clause usually has for its sense not a thought, but only a part of one, and consequently no truth value as reference. The reason for this is either that the words in the subordinate clause have indirect reference, so that the reference, not the sense, of the subordinate clause is a thought; or else that, on account of the presence of an indefinite indicator, the subordinate clause is incomplete and expresses a thought only when combined with the main clause. It may happen, however, that the sense of the subsidiary clause is a complete thought, in which case it can be replaced by another of the same truth value without harm to the truth of the whole—provided there are no grammatical obstacles.

An examination of all the subordinate clauses which one may encounter will soon provide some which do not fit well into these categories. The reason, so far as I can see, is that these subordinate clauses have no such simple sense. Almost always, it seems, we connect with the main thoughts expressed by us subsidiary thoughts which, although not expressed, are associated with our words, in accordance with psychological laws, by the hearer. And since the subsidiary thought appears to be connected with our words of its own accord, almost like the main thought itself, we want it also to be expressed. The sense of the sentence is thereby enriched, and it may well happen that we have more simple thoughts than clauses. In many cases the sentence must be understood in this way, in others it may be doubtful whether the subsidiary thought belongs to the sense of the sentence or only accompanies it.[19] One might perhaps find that the sentence

Napoleon, who recognized the danger to his right flank, himself led his guards against the enemy position

expresses not only the two thoughts shown above, but also the thought that the knowledge of the danger was the reason why he led the guards against the enemy position. One may in fact doubt whether this thought is merely slightly suggested or really expressed. Let the question be considered whether our sentence be false if Napoleon's decision had already been made before he recognized the danger. If our sentence could be true in spite of this, the subsidiary thought should not be understood as part of the sense. One would probably decide in favour of this. The alternative would make for a quite complicated situation: We would have more simple thoughts than clauses. If the sentence

Napoleon recognized the danger to his right flank

were now to be replaced by another having the same truth value, e.g.

Napoleon was already more than 45 years old

not only would our first thought be changed, but also our third one. Hence the truth value of the latter might change—viz. if his age was not the reason for the decision to lead the guards against the enemy. This shows why clauses of equal truth value cannot always be substituted for one another in such cases. The clause expresses more through its connexion with another than it does in isolation.

Let us now consider cases where this regularly happens. In the sentence:

Bebel mistakenly supposes that the return of Alsace-Lorraine would appease France's desire for revenge

two thoughts are expressed, which are not however shown by means of antecedent and consequent clauses, viz.:

(1) Bebel believes that the return of Alsace-Lorraine would appease France's desire for revenge
(2) the return of Alsace-Lorraine would not appease France's desire for revenge.

In the expression of the first thought, the words of the subordinate clause have their indirect reference, while the same words have their customary reference in the expression of the second thought. This shows that the subordinate clause in our original complex sentence is to be taken twice over, with different reference, standing once for a thought, once for a truth value. Since the truth value is not the whole reference of the subordinate clause, we cannot simply replace the latter by another of equal truth value. Similar considerations apply to expressions such as 'know', 'discover', 'it is known that'.

By means of a subordinate causal clause and the associated main clause we express several thoughts, which however do not correspond separately to the original clauses. In the sentence: 'Because ice is less dense than water, it floats on water' we have

(1) Ice is less dense than water;
(2) If anything is less dense than water, it floats on water;
(3) Ice floats on water.

The third thought, however, need not be explicitly introduced, since it is contained in the remaining two. On the other hand, neither the first and third nor the second and third combined would furnish the sense of our sentence. It can now be seen that our subordinate clause

because ice is less dense than water

expresses our first thought, as well as a part of our second. This is how it comes to pass that our subsidiary clause cannot be simply replaced by another of equal truth value; for this would alter our second thought and thereby might well alter its truth value.

The situation is similar in the sentence

If iron were less dense than water, it would float on water.

Here we have the two thoughts that iron is not less dense than water, and that something floats on water if it is less dense than water. The subsidiary clause again expresses one thought and a part of the other.

If we interpret the sentence already considered

After Schleswig-Holstein was separated from Denmark, Prussia and Austria quarrelled

in such a way that it expresses the thought that Schleswig-Holstein was once separated from Denmark, we have first this thought, and secondly the thought that at a time, more closely determined by the subordinate clause, Prussia and Austria quarrelled. Here also the subordinate clause expresses not only one thought but also a part of another. Therefore it may not in general be replaced by another of the same truth value.

It is hard to exhaust all the possibilities given by language; but I hope to have brought to light at least the essential reasons why a subordinate clause may not always be replaced by another of equal truth value without harm to the truth of the whole sentence structure. These reasons arise:

(1) when the subordinate clause does not stand for a truth value, inasmuch as it expresses only a part of a thought;
(2) when the subordinate clause does stand for a truth value but is not restricted to so doing, inasmuch as its sense includes one thought and part of another.

The first case arises:

(a) in indirect reference of words
(b) if a part of the sentence is only an indefinite indicator instead of a proper name.

In the second case, the subsidiary clause may have to be taken twice over, viz. once in its customary reference, and the other time in indirect reference; or the sense of a part of the subordinate clause may likewise be a component of another thought, which, taken together with the thought directly expressed by the subordinate clause, makes up the sense of the whole sentence.

It follows with sufficient probability from the foregoing that the cases where a subordinate clause is not replaceable by another of the same value cannot be brought in disproof of our view that a truth value is the reference of a sentence having a thought as its sense.

Let us return to our starting point.

When we found '$a = a$' and '$a = b$' to have different cognitive values, the explanation is that for the purpose of knowledge, the sense of the sentence, viz., the thought expressed by it, is no less relevant than its reference, i.e. its truth value. If now $a = b$, then indeed the reference of 'b' is the same as that of 'a', and hence the truth value of '$a = b$' is the same as the of '$a = a$'. In spite of this, the sense of 'b' may differ from that of 'a', and thereby the sense expressed in '$a = b$' differs from that of '$a = a$'. In that case the two sentences do not have the same cognitive value. If we understand by 'judgment' the advance from the thought to its truth value, as in the above paper, we can also say that the judgments are different.

Notes

1. I use this word strictly and understand '$a = b$' to have the sense of 'a is the same as b' or 'a and b coincide'.

2. Trans. note: The reference is to Frege's *Begriffsschrift, eine der arithmetischen nachgebildete Formelsprache des reinen Denkens* (Halle, 1879).

3. Trans. note: See his 'Ueber Begriff und Gegenstand', *Vierteljahrsschrift für wissenschaftliche Philosophie*, 16 (1892), 192–205.

4. In the case of an actual proper name such as 'Aristotle' opinions as to the sense may differ. It might, for instance, be taken to be the following: the pupil of Plato and teacher of Alexander the Great. Anybody who does this will attach another sense to the sentence 'Aristotle was born in Stagira' than will a man who takes as the sense of the name: the teacher of Alexander the Great who was born in Stagira. So long as the reference remains the same, such variations of sense may be tolerated, although they are to be avoided in the theoretical structure of a demonstrative science and ought not to occur in a perfect language.

5. We can include with ideas the direct experiences in which sense-impressions and acts themselves take the place of the traces which they have left in the mind. The distinction is unimportant for our purpose, especially since memories of sense-impressions and acts always help to complete the perceptual image. One can also understand direct experience as including any object, in so far as it is sensibly perceptible or spatial.

6. Hence it is inadvisable to use the word 'idea' to designate something so basically different.

7. By a thought I understand not the subjective performance of thinking but its objective content, which is capable of being the common property of several thinkers.

8. It would be desirable to have a special term for signs having only sense. If we name them, say, representations, the words of the actors on the stage would be representations; indeed the actor himself would be a representation.

9. Trans. note: See his 'Ueber Begriff und Gegenstand', *Vierteljahrsschrift für wissenschaftliche Philosophie*, 16 (1892), 192–205.

10. A judgment, for me is not the mere comprehension of a thought, but the admission of its truth.

11. Trans. note: A literal translation of Frege's 'abstracten Nennsätzen' whose meaning eludes me.

12. In 'A lied in saying he had seen B', the subordinate clause designates a thought which is said (1) to have been asserted by A (2) while A was convinced of its falsity.

13. Trans. note: Frege uses the Prussian name for the battle—'Belle Alliance'.

14. In accordance with what was said above, an expression of the kind in question must actually always be assured of reference, by means of a special stipulation, e.g. by the convention that 0 shall count as its reference, when the concept applies to no object or to more than one.

15. In the case of these sentences, various interpretations are easily possible. The sense of the sentence, 'After Schleswig-Holstein was separated from Denmark, Prussia and Austria quarrelled' can also be rendered in the form 'After the separation of Schleswig-Holstein from Denmark, Prussia and Austria quarrelled.' In this version, it is surely sufficiently clear that the sense is not to be taken as having as a part the thought that Schleswig-Holstein was once separated from Denmark, but that this is the necessary presupposition in order for the expression 'after the separation of Schleswig-Holstein from Denmark' to have any reference at all. To be sure, our sentence can also be interpreted as saying that Schleswig-Holstein was once separated from Denmark. We then have a case which is to be considered later. In order to understand the difference more clearly, let us project ourselves into the mind of a Chinese who, having little knowledge of European history, believes it to be false that Schleswig-Holstein was ever separated from Denmark. He will take our sentence, in the first version, to be neither true nor false but will deny it to have any reference, on the ground of absence of reference for its subordinate clause. This clause would only apparently determine a time. If he interpreted our sentence in the second way, however, he would find a thought expressed in it which he would take to be false, beside a part which would be without reference for him.

16. At times an explicit linguistic indication is missing and must be read off from the entire context.

17. Similarly in the case of 'but', 'yet'.

18. The thought of our sentence might also be expressed thus: 'Either the Sun has not risen yet or the sky is very cloudy'—which shows how this kind of sentence connexion is to be understood.

19. This may be important for the question whether an assertion is a lie, or an oath a perjury.

Chapter 23

Proper Names

John R. Searle

Do proper names have senses? Frege[1] argues that they must have senses, for, he asks, how else can identity statements be other than trivially analytic? How, he asks, can a statement of the form $a = b$, if true, differ in cognitive value from $a = a$? His answer is that though 'a' and 'b' have the same reference they have or may have different *senses*, in which case the statement is true, though not analytically so. But this solution seems more appropriate where 'a' and 'b' are both non-synonymous definite descriptions, or where one is a definite description and one is a proper name, than where both are proper names. Consider, for example, statements made with the following sentences:

(a) 'Tully = Tully' is analytic.

But is

(b) 'Tully = Cicero' synthetic?

If so, then each name must have a different sense, which seems at first sight most implausible, for we do not ordinarily think of proper names as having a sense at all in the way that predicates do; we do not, e.g. give definitions of proper names. But of course (b) gives us information not conveyed by (a). But is this information about words? The statement is not about words.

For the moment let us consider the view that (b) is, like (a), analytic. A statement is analytic if and only if it is true in virtue of linguistic rules alone, without any recourse to empirical investigation. The linguistic rules for using the name 'Cicero' and the linguistic rules for using the name 'Tully' are such that both names refer to, without describing, the same

First appeared in *Mind* 67 (1958): 166–173. Reprinted by permission of Oxford University Press.

identical object; thus it seems the truth of the identity can be established solely by recourse to these rules and the statement is analytic. The sense in which the statement is informative is the sense in which any analytic statement is informative; it illustrates or exemplifies certain contingent facts about words, though it does not of course describe these facts. On this account the difference between (a) and (b) above is not as great as might at first seem. Both are analytically true, and both illustrate contingent facts about our use of symbols. Some philosophers claim that (a) is fundamentally different from (b) in that a statement using this form will be true for any arbitrary substitution of symbols replacing 'Tully'.[2] This, I wish to argue, is not so. The fact that the same mark refers to the same object on two different occasions of its use is a convenient but contingent usage, and indeed we can easily imagine situations where this would not be the case. Suppose, e.g., we have a language in which the rules for using symbols are correlated not simply with a type-word, but with the order of its token appearances in the discourse. Some codes are like this. Suppose the first time an object is referred to in our discourse it is referred to by 'x', the second time by 'y', etc. For anyone who knows this code '$x = y$' is trivially analytic, but '$x = x$' is senseless. This example is designed to illustrate the similarity of (a) and (b) above; both are analytic and both give us information, though each gives us different information, about the use of words. The truth of the statements that Tully = Tully and Tully = Cicero both follow from linguistic rules. But the fact that the words 'Tully = Tully' are used to express this identity is just as contingent as, though more universally conventional in our language than, the fact that the words 'Tully = Cicero' are used to express the identity of the same object.

This analysis enables us to see how both (a) and (b) could be used to make analytic statements and how in such circumstances we could acquire different information from them, without forcing us to follow either of Frege's proposed solutions, i.e. that the two propositions are in some sense about words (*Begriffsschrift*) or his revised solution, that the terms have the same reference but different senses (*Sinn und Bedeutung*). But though this analysis enables us to see how a sentence like (b) *could* be used to make an analytic statement it does not follow that it could not also be used to make a synthetic statement. And indeed some identity statements using two proper names are clearly synthetic; people who argue that Shakespeare was Bacon are not advancing a thesis about language. In what follows I hope to examine the connexion between proper names and their referents in such a manner as to show how both kinds of identity statement are possible and in so doing to show in what sense a proper name has a sense.

I have so far considered the view that the rules governing the use of a proper name are such that it is used to refer to and not to describe a particular object, that it has reference but not sense. But now let us ask how it comes about that we are able to refer to a particular object by using its name. How, for example, do we learn and teach the use of proper names? This seems quite simple—we identify the object, and, assuming that our student understands the general conventions governing proper names, we explain that this word is the name of that object. But unless our student already knows another proper name of the object, we can only *identify* the object (the necessary preliminary to teaching the name) by ostension or description; and, in both cases, we identify the object in virtue of certain of its characteristics. So now it seems as if the rules for a proper name must somehow be logically tied to particular characteristics of the object in such a way that the name has a sense as well as a reference; indeed, it seems it could not have a reference unless it did have a sense, for how, unless the name has a sense, is it to be correlated with the object?

Suppose someone answers this argument as follows: 'The characteristics located in teaching the name are not the rules for using the proper name: they are simply pedagogic devices employed in teaching the name to someone who does not know how to use it. Once our student has identified the object to which the name applies he can forget or ignore these various descriptions by means of which he identified the object, for they are not part of the sense of the name; the name does not have a *sense*. Suppose, for example, that we teach the name "Aristotle" by explaining that it refers to a Greek philosopher born in Stagira, and suppose that our student continues to use the name correctly, that he gathers more information about Aristotle, and so on. Let us suppose it is discovered later on that Aristotle was not born in Stagira at all, but in Thebes. We will not now say that the meaning of the name has changed, or that Aristotle did not really exist at all. In short, explaining the use of a name by citing characteristics of the object is not giving the rules for the name, for the rules contain no descriptive content at all. They simply correlate the name to the object independently of any descriptions of it.'

But is the argument convincing? Suppose most or even all of our present factual knowledge of Aristotle proved to be true of no one at all, or of several people living in scattered countries and in different centuries?

Would we not say for this reason that Aristotle did not exist after all, and that the name, though it has a conventional sense, refers to no one at all? On the above account, if anyone said that Aristotle did not exist, this must simply be another way of saying that 'Aristotle' denoted no objects, and nothing more; but if anyone did say that Aristotle did not exist he might mean much more than simply that the name does not denote any-one.[3] If, for example, we challenged his statement by pointing out that a man named 'Aristotle' lived in Hoboken in 1903, he would not regard this as a relevant countercharge. We say of Cerberus and Zeus that neither of them ever existed, without meaning that no object ever bore these names, but only that certain kinds (descriptions) of objects never existed and bore these names. So now it looks as though proper names do have a sense necessarily but have a reference only contingently. They begin to look more and more like shorthand and perhaps vague descriptions.

Let us summarize the two conflicting views under consideration: the first asserts that proper names have essentially a reference but not a sense—proper names denote but do not connote; the second asserts that they have essentially a sense and only contingently a reference—they refer only on the condition that one and only one object satisfies their sense.

These two views are paths leading to divergent and hoary metaphysical systems. The first leads to ultimate objects of reference, the substances of the scholastics and the *Gegenstände* of the *Tractatus*. The second leads to the identity of indiscernibles, and variables of quantification as the only referential terms in the language. The subject-predicate structure of the language suggests that the first must be right, but the way we use and teach the use of proper names suggests that it cannot be right: a philo-sophical problem.

Let us begin by examining the second. If it is asserted that every proper name has a sense, it must be legitimate to demand of any name, 'What is its sense?'. If it is asserted that a proper name is a kind of shorthand description then we ought to be able to present the description in place of the proper name. But how are we to proceed with this? If we try to present a complete description of the object as the sense of a proper name, odd con-sequences would ensue, e.g. that any true statement about the object using the name as subject would be analytic, any false one self-contradictory, that the meaning of the name (and perhaps the identity of the object) would change every time there was any change at all in the object, that the name would have different meanings for different people, etc. So sup-pose we ask what are the necessary and sufficient conditions for applying a particular name to a particular object. Suppose for the sake of argument that we have independent means for locating an object; then what are the conditions for applying a name to it; what are the conditions for saying, e.g. 'This is Aristotle'? At first sight these conditions seem to be simply that the object must be identical with an object originally christened by this name, so the sense of the name would consist in a statement or set of statements asserting the characteristics which constitute this identity. The sense of 'This is Aristotle' might be, 'This object is spatio-temporally continuous with an object originally named "Aristotle"'. But this will not suffice, for, as was already suggested, the force of 'Aristotle' is greater than the force of 'identical with an object named "Aristotle"', for not just any object named 'Aristotle' will do. 'Aristotle' here refers to a particular object named 'Aristotle', not to any. 'Named "Aristotle"' is a universal term, but 'Aristotle', is a proper name, so 'This is named "Aristotle"' is at best a necessary but not a sufficient condition for the truth of 'This is Aristotle'. Briefly and trivially, it is not the identity of this with any object named 'Aristotle', but rather its identity with Aristotle that constitutes the necessary and sufficient conditions for the truth of 'This is Aristotle'.

Perhaps we can resolve the conflict between the two views of the nature of proper names by asking what is the unique function of proper names in our language. To begin with, they mostly refer or purport to refer to particular objects; but of course other expressions, definite descriptions and demonstratives, perform this function as well. What then is the difference between proper names and other singular referring expressions? Unlike demonstratives, a proper name refers without presupposing any stage settings or any special contextual conditions surrounding the utterance of the expression. Unlike definite descriptions, they do not in general *specify* any characteristics at all of the objects to which they refer. 'Scott' refers to the same object as does 'the author of *Waverley*', but 'Scott' specifies none of its characteristics, whereas 'the author of *Waverley*' refers only in virtue of the fact that it does specify a characteristic. Let us examine this difference more closely. Following Strawson[4] we may say that referring uses of both proper names and definite descriptions presuppose the existence of one and only one object referred to. But as a proper name does not in general specify any characteristics of the object referred to, how then does it bring the reference off? How is a connexion between name and object ever set up? This, which seems the crucial question, I want to answer by saying that though proper names do not normally assert or specify any characteristics, their referring uses nonetheless presuppose that the object to which they purport to refer has certain characteristics. But which ones? Suppose we ask the users of the name 'Aristotle' to state what they regard as certain essential and established facts about him. Their answers would be a set of uniquely referring descriptive statements. Now what I am arguing is that the descriptive force of 'This is Aristotle' is to assert that a sufficient but so far unspecified number of these statements are true of this object. Therefore, referring uses of 'Aristotle' presuppose the existence of an object of whom a sufficient but so far unspecified number of these statements are true. To use a proper name referringly is to presuppose the truth of certain uniquely referring descriptive statements, but it is not ordinarily to assert these statements or even to indicate which exactly are presupposed. And herein lies most of the difficulty. The question of what constitutes the criteria for 'Aristotle' is generally left open, indeed it seldom in fact arises, and when it does arise it is we, the users of the name, who decide more or less arbitrarily what these criteria shall be. If, for example, of the characteristics agreed to be true of Aristotle, half should be discovered to be true of one man and half true of another, which would we say was Aristotle? Neither? The question is not decided for us in advance.

But is this imprecision as to what characteristics exactly constitute the necessary and sufficient conditions for applying a proper name a mere accident, a product of linguistic slovenliness? Or does it derive from the functions which proper names perform for us? To ask for the criteria for applying the name 'Aristotle' is to ask in the formal mode what Aristotle is; it is to ask for a set of identity criteria for the object Aristotle. 'What is Aristotle?' and 'What are the criteria for applying the name "Aristotle"?' ask the same question, the former in the material mode, and the latter in the formal mode of speech. So if we came to agreement in advance of using the name on precisely what characteristics constituted the identity of Aristotle, our rules for using the name would be precise. But this precision would be achieved only at the cost of entailing some specific predicates by any referring use of the name. Indeed, the name itself would become superfluous for it would become logically equivalent to this set of descriptions. But if this were the case we would be in the position of only being able to refer to an object by describing it. Whereas in fact this is just what the institution of proper names enables us to avoid and what distinguishes proper names from descriptions. If the criteria for proper names were in all cases quite rigid and specific then a proper name would be nothing more than a shorthand for these criteria, a proper name would function exactly like an elaborate definite description. But the uniqueness and immense pragmatic convenience of proper names in our language lie precisely in the fact that they enable us to refer publicly to objects without being forced to raise issues and come to agreement on what descriptive characteristics exactly constitute the identity of the object. They function not as descriptions, but as pegs on which to hang descriptions. Thus the looseness of the criteria for proper names is a necessary condition for isolating the referring function from the describing function of language.

To put the same point differently, suppose we ask, 'Why do we have proper names at all?' Obviously, to refer to individuals. 'Yes, but descriptions could do that for us.' But only at the cost of specifying identity conditions every time reference is made: suppose we agree to drop 'Aristotle' and use, say, 'the teacher of Alexander', then it is a necessary truth that the man referred to is Alexander's teacher—but it is a contingent fact that Aristotle ever went into pedagogy (though I am suggesting it is a necessary fact that Aristotle has the logical sum, inclusive disjunction, of properties commonly attributed to him: any individual not having at least some of these properties could not be Aristotle).

Of course it should not be thought that the only sort of looseness of identity criteria for individuals is that which I have described as peculiar to proper names. Referring uses of definite descriptions may raise problems concerning identity of quite different sorts. This is especially true of past tense definite descriptions. 'This is the man who taught Alexander' may be said to entail, e.g. that this object is spatio-temporally continuous with the man teaching Alexander at another point in space-time: but someone might also argue that this man's spatio-temporal continuity is a contingent characteristic and not an identity criterion. And the logical nature of the connexion of such characteristics with the man's identity may again be loose and undecided in advance of dispute. But this is quite another dimension of looseness than that which I cited as the looseness of the criteria for applying proper names and does not affect the distinction in function between definite descriptions and proper names, viz. that definite descriptions refer only in virtue of the fact that the criteria are not loose in the original sense, for they refer by telling us what the object is. But proper names refer without so far raising the issue of what the object is.

We are now in a position to explain how it is that 'Aristotle' has a reference but does not describe, and yet the statement 'Aristotle never existed' says more than that 'Aristotle' was never used to refer to any object. The statement asserts that a sufficient number of the conventional presuppositions, descriptive statements, of referring uses of 'Aristotle' are false. Precisely which statements are asserted to be false is not yet clear, for what precise conditions constitute the criteria for applying 'Aristotle' is not yet laid down by the language.

We can now resolve our paradox: does a proper name have a sense? If this asks whether or not proper names are used to describe or specify characteristics of objects, the answer is 'no'. But if it asks whether or not proper names are logically connected with characteristics of the object to which they refer, the answer is 'yes, in a loose sort of way'. (This shows in part the poverty of a rigid sense-reference, denotation-connotation approach to problems in the theory of meaning.)

We might clarify these points by comparing paradigmatic proper names with degenerate proper names like 'The Bank of England'. For these latter, it seems the sense is given as straightforwardly as in a definite description; the presuppositions, as it were, rise to the surface. And a proper name may acquire a rigid descriptive use without having the verbal form of a description: God is just, omnipotent, omniscient, etc., *by definition* for believers. Of course the form may mislead us; the Holy Roman Empire was neither holy, nor Roman, etc., but it was nonetheless the Holy Roman Empire. Again it may be conventional to name only girls 'Martha', but if I name my son 'Martha' I may mislead, but I do not lie.

Now reconsider our original identity, 'Tully = Cicero'. A statement made using this sentence would, I suggest, be analytic for most people; the same descriptive presuppositions are associated with each name. But of course if the descriptive presuppositions were different it might be used to make a synthetic statement; it might even advance a historical discovery of the first importance.

Notes

1. Gottlob Frege, *Philosophical Writings*, translated by Geach and Black, pp. 56 ff. [chap. 22 in this vol.].
2. W. V. Quine, *From a Logical Point of View*, esp. chap. 2.
3. Cf. Wittgenstein, *Philosophical Investigations*, para. 79.
4. 'On Referring', *Mind* (1950) [chap. 16 in this vol.].

Chapter 24

Reference and Proper Names

Tyler Burge

It is perhaps surprising that one needs to theorize about proper names.[1] They seem to present a straightforward, uncomplicated example of how language relates to the world. During the last eighty years, however, there has been considerable disagreement on issues surrounding them. The disagreement has centered on three broad questions: (a) the question of how to explicate the conditions under which a proper name designates an object; (b) the question of how best to speak (semantically and pragmatically) about nondesignating proper names; and (c) the question of the logical role of proper names in a formal theory of language.

In this paper I will be primarily concerned with the third of these questions, although I shall touch briefly on the other two. In particular, I will be concerned with the logical role of proper names in a semantical account of natural languages. The semantical framework within which I shall be working is Tarskian truth theory as applied to the sentences of a person at a time. But most of what I have to say will hold for other semantical approaches.

At the outset I want to place a condition of adequacy on our approach. This is the condition that the theory of truth be *fully formalized*—that is, that the sense and reference (if any) of every expression of the theory should be unambiguously determinable from its form.[2] Interpretation of the truth theory should depend on no contextual parameter other than the inescapable one: the symbols of the theory are to be construed as symbols in the language of the theorist. So much context must be presupposed. But natural languages intuitively exhibit two further sorts of context-dependence: dependence on context for determination of the intended reference of token-reflexive constructions, and dependence on context for

First appeared in *The Journal of Philosophy* 70 (1973): 425–439. Reprinted by permission of Tyler Burge and *The Journal of Philosophy*.

determination of the intended reading of ambiguous words and grammatical constructions. An effect of the conditions is to rule out use of demonstratives or ambiguous constructions in a truth theory to account for use of demonstratives or ambiguous constructions by the person whose sentences are being studied. The motivation for the condition is simply that theories of language should be no less general and precise (where feasible) than mathematical or physical theories.

It is possible to distinguish two major positions on the question of the role that proper names play in a formal semantical theory. One is the view that proper names play the role of constant, noncomplex singular terms. The other is the view of Russell, elaborated by Quine, that they play the role of predicates.[3]

To my knowledge there are no arguments in the literature for thinking that proper names are individual constants. But the intuitive considerations that seem to support this position lie right on the surface: In their most ordinary uses proper names are singular terms, purporting to pick out a unique object; they appear to lack internal semantical structure; they do not seem to describe the objects they purportedly designate, as definite descriptions do; and in some sense they specify the objects they purportedly designate, as demonstratives do not. It is probably true to say that most philosophers, linguists, and logicians have on these grounds accepted an individual-constants view of proper names.

The traditional predicate view has been prompted by a sense of the clarity and simplicity that results in one's theory of reference if one treats proper names as abbreviated or manufactured descriptions. Whatever its philosophical virtues, this view has been widely regarded as having the vice of artificiality, at least insofar as it is supposed to give analyses of sentences in natural languages.

The view I shall maintain is, roughly speaking, a modified predicate view. The main body of the paper will be devoted to setting out my view with explicit reference to the predicate approach of Russell and Quine. In sections II and III I shall relate that view briefly to the questions about application conditions and about failures of designation. I shall conclude in section IV by criticizing the treatment of proper names as individual constants.

I

I remarked that the traditional predicate view was widely thought to have the disadvantage of artificiality. In fact, there are three points at which the Russellian approach has been held to do violence to ordinary preconceptions. The first is its treatment of proper names as abbreviated or manufactured descriptions. The violated preconception here is simply the notion that names do not describe. Appeals to abbreviation or manufacture are transparently *ad hoc*. The second point at which Russell's approach has seemed artificial is its elimination of definite descriptions (including proper names) as incomplete symbols. In this case, the violated preconception is the notion that names play the semantical and grammatical role of singular terms. The third alleged element of artificiality is the closing of apparent truth-value gaps. And the violated preconception here is that some sentences that involve failures of designation are neither true nor false.

These points are, of course, recognized by Russell and Quine. Russell tends to regard the cited preconceptions as indefensible confusions. Quine sees them as relevant evidence for understanding natural language, but irrelevant to, or dispensable in the face of, his purpose of constructing a smooth logical theory suitable for the general use of natural science. Since we are concerned with understanding natural languages, we need not take exception to Quine's view of the matter here. Our grammatical and semantical preconceptions are evidence for a theory of natural language; their bearing on the development of logical theory for general scientific use is a further question.

I intend to postpone the issues regarding the elimination of definite descriptions and the closing of so-called truth-value gaps, and concentrate on the first source of artificiality in the traditional predicate view: the claim that proper names are abbreviated or manufactured descriptions.

There are two ways in which a proper name has been seen to function as an abbreviation. One is that it abbreviates a string of descriptive general terms that the language-user would employ—or abbreviates an artificial predicate like 'Aristotelizes'. The other is that a proper name abbreviates into one symbol the semantical roles of operator and predicate which, in definite descriptions, are usually represented separately by at least two symbols: the 'the' (or an analogous construction) and the general term. In explaining my view I shall deal consecutively with these two senses of abbreviation. I shall argue first that proper names do not abbreviate predicates but are predicates in their own right. Then I shall argue that they do not abbreviate the roles of predicate and operator, but that in some of their uses they play the roles of predicate and demonstrative.

Russell sometimes holds that a proper name abbreviates the descriptions the speaker associates with the putative designation of the name. Since this view has been criticized in detail elsewhere,[4] I will not take the time to discuss the difficulties with it here. Suffice it to say that proper names ordinarily have at best a tenuous logical relation to the descriptions that language users associate with them, certainly not the relation of abbreviation.[5]

In one passage, Russell suggests that a proper name abbreviates the description 'the object called "PN"', where 'PN' stands for the proper name.[6] I think that there is something to be said for this suggestion, and we shall return to it later. But one may say against it that it is needlessly counterintuitive and that it leads to unnecessary theoretical complications. Intuitively, proper names simply do not describe. Theoretically, it is undesirable to postulate abbreviation rules if they can be avoided. I think that they can be.

A proper name is a predicate true of an object if and only if the object is given that name in an appropriate way. There is and need be no claim that a proper name abbreviates *another* predicate, even a roughly coextensive predicate such as 'is an entity called "PN"'. A proper name is a predicate in its own right.[7]

Failure to appreciate this point has stemmed largely from concentrating on singular, unmodified uses of proper names:

Alfred studies in Princeton.

But proper names take the plural:

There are relatively few Alfreds in Princeton.

They also take indefinite and definite articles:

An Alfred Russell joined the club today.

The Alfred who joined the club today was a baboon.

And quantifiers:

Some Alfreds are crazy; some are sane.

Proper names are usually used in singular and unmodified form. But there is nothing ungrammatical about the above sentences.[8] Moreover, the occurrences of proper names in them are literal and not metaphoric or ironic. Contrast these uses with the metaphoric use in

George Wallace is a Napoleon.

George Wallace is not literally one of the Napoleons—he has not been given the name 'Napoleon' in a socially accepted way. Rather, he is like the most famous Napoleon in significant respects.

The modified proper names in the examples just given have the same conditions for literal application to an object that singular, unmodified proper names have. This point is confirmed by such sentences as

(1) Jones is a Jones.

which is an obvious truth under normal conditions of use.

Now one might claim that the uses I have cited are "special" uses of proper names, and that they should not be taken as throwing light on the usual uses. Vendler, for example, notes that there is "something unusual" about noun phrases like 'the Joe in our house':

Such phrases do occur and we understand them. It is clear, however, that such a context is fatal to the name as proper name, at least for the discourse in which it occurs. The full context, explicit or implicit, will be of the following sort:

The Joe in our house is not the one you are talking about ... As the noun replacer, *one*, makes abundantly clear, the name here simulates the status of a count noun. There are two Joe's presupposed in the discourse, and this is, of course, inconsistent with the idea of a logically proper name. *Joe* is here really equivalent to something like *person called Joe*, and because this phrase fits many individuals, it should be treated as a general term by the logician.[9]

We may agree with Vendler that modified occurrences of ordinary names are in a sense not "proper" to any one object. But it would be a mistake to think that the passage provides any reason to hold that modified and unmodified occurrences of ordinary proper names are semantically independent of each other. For no reason is given to believe that ordinary names are ever "logically proper names" (presumably individual constants). In a limited context, proper names may be—and often are—assumed to apply to a unique object. But a semantical theory (like ours) that is applicable to a language without restrictions on the context in which sentences of the language may be used, cannot commit itself to such an assumption.

Postulation of special uses of a term, semantically unrelated to what are taken to be its paradigmatic uses, is theoretically undesirable—particularly if a straightforward semantical relation between these different uses can be found. We have already indicated what this relation is: A proper name is (literally) true of an object just in case that object is given that name in an appropriate way.

In holding that a name applies to an object just in case the object bears a certain pragmatic relation to that name, I am suggesting that the name itself enters into the conditions under which it is applicable. In this respect, proper names differ from many other predicates. Take, for example, the predicate 'is a dog'. An object could be a dog even if the word 'dog' were never used as a symbol. But an object could not be a Jones unless someone used 'Jones' as a name. This mild self-referential element in the application conditions of proper names can be further illustrated by comparing

(2) Jones is necessarily a Jones.

with

(3) This entity called 'Jones' is necessarily an entity called 'Jones'.

To obtain (3) we have substituted for 'Jones' in (2) the roughly coextensive predicate expression 'entity called "Jones"'. Not surprisingly, both sentences come out false on any occasion of use. Thus, proper names are like ordinary predicates containing quotation marks in their intuitively clear failure to be necessarily true of objects to which they apply.

Our predicate view of proper names avoids one source of artificiality in the views of Russell and Quine. It does not involve the claim that proper names abbreviate any descriptive predicates, nor does it involve the manufacture of predicates that are not present in ordinary natural languages. Our account also seems to meet the charge, often raised against the abbreviated-description view, that proper names do not convey information about, or attribute characteristics to, the named object. I do claim that, when a speaker uses the name 'Aristotle' (taken literally), he purports to convey the information that the object of which he speaks, if any, is called 'Aristotle'. But this does not seem to be something anyone would want to deny.

So far I have held that although in surface grammar proper names function sometimes as singular terms and sometimes as general terms, they play the semantic role of predicates—usually true of numerous objects—on all occurrences. How then are we to represent unmodified occurrences, where proper names function as singular terms? This question brings us to the second sense in which proper names may be said to be abbreviations on the Russell-Quine view—abbreviations in one symbol of the semantic roles of a uniqueness operator and a predicate.

Consider the sentence 'Aristotle is human'. On the Russell-Quine view, this sentence would be analyzed as

(4) $(\exists x) ((y) (\text{Aristotle } (y) \leftrightarrow y = x) \ \& \ \text{Is-Human } (x))$

or in unexpanded form:

(5) $\text{Is-Human } (\imath x) (\text{Aristotle } (x))$

It has frequently been pointed out that, in order for the Russell-Quine analysis to be strictly correct, the predicate 'Aristotle' must be uniquely true of the designated object (if any). But it is not: there are many Aristotles. The usual answer to this point is that we ordinarily rely on context to resolve the ambiguities of ordinary language.[10] But although it is perfectly in order for natural-language *users* to rely on context to clarify intended reference, the condition that we placed on our discussion at the outset prevents the *theorist* from relying on context in a like manner to clarify intended references in his analyses of truth conditions. Most of the proper names that a person is capable of using at a given time will be true of more than one object. We should therefore reject the claim that proper names in singular unmodified form abbreviate the roles of the uniqueness operator and a predicate.

They play instead the roles of a demonstrative and a predicate. Roughly, singular unmodified proper names, functioning as singular terms, have the same semantical structure as the phrase 'that book'. Unlike other predicates, proper names are usually (though, as we have seen, not always) used with the help of speaker-reference and context, to pick out a particular. For this reason demonstratives are not ordinarily attached to proper names, although, of course, they may be so attached. In general, modifications of proper names occur when the speaker is not relying on them, unsupplemented, to pick out a particular. But whether or not the speaker's act of reference is explicitly supplemented with a demonstrative like 'this' is semantically irrelevant.

Evidence for the view that proper names in singular unmodified form involve a demonstrative element emerges when one compares sentences involving such names with sentences involving demonstratives. Apart from speaker-reference or special context, both

Jim is 6 feet tall.

and

That book is green.

are incompletely interpreted—they lack truth value. The user of the sentences must pick out a particular (e.g., a particular Jim or book) if the sentences are to be judged true or false. It is this conventional reliance on extrasentential action or context to pick out a particular which signals the demonstrative element in both sentences.

Further evidence for the view that proper names functioning as singular terms involve a demonstrative element derives from the fact that such proper names usually take widest possible scope. In this respect they are like demonstratives and descriptions governed by demonstratives.[11] Note, for example, that it is hard to hear a reading of either (2) or (3) under which the scope of the singular terms is small and the sentence comes out true.

Object-language formalizations of sentences containing proper names that function as singular terms are open sentences. 'Aristotle is human', for example, receives the analysis

(6) Is-Human ($[x_i]$ Aristotle (x_i))

Our logic includes the uniqueness operator, and we adjust our formation rules to allow open singular terms of the form

(i) $[x_i]A_{j^n}(x_1 \ldots x_i \ldots x_n)$

The bracketed 'x_i' marks the free variable in the term which represents the demonstrative governing the whole scope of the term. '$[x_i]$' is *not* an operator for binding the variable 'x_i'. (i) is to be understood as equivalent to

(ii) $(\imath y) (A_{j^n}(x_1 \ldots y \ldots x_n) \ \& \ y = x_i)$

I prefer the form (i) to the more usual form (ii) because it seems to me to represent better the syntax of English. Since 'x_i' is a *free* variable as it occurs in (i), it may be quantified from outside the term—just as 'x_i' can in (ii).

An open sentence like (6) takes on truth value only if the user of the sentence carries out an act of reference in the process of using the sentence, and thereby performs extrasententially a task analogous to that which the iota operator performs in classical logical theory.

Whereas the language user himself relies on extrasentential action or context to designate the object, the truth-theorist is barred by our initial condition from doing the same in his metalanguage. The object referred to by the language user (if any) is specified in the truth theory by means of a set of reference clauses:

(7) $(x) (y)$ (Reference (x), & By (x, p) & $At(x, t)$ & With $(x,$ 'Aristotle$_1$', 'Aristotle is human') & To $(x, y) \rightarrow$ ('Aristotle is human' is true with respect to p at $t \leftrightarrow$ Human ($[y]$ Aristotle (y)))))

Read: For all x and y, if x is an act of reference by person p at time t to y with the first occurrence of 'Aristotle' in 'Aristotle is human', then 'Aristotle is human' is true with respect to p at t just in case the object which is y and is an Aristotle is human. Here is not the place to expand on the analysis.[12] For our purposes what is important is the contrast between the context-dependence of the object-language representation (6) and the *analysis of context* that occurs in the account of truth conditions (7).

So far I have argued (a) that proper names do not abbreviate other predicates but are themselves predicates, and (b) that in their most common uses proper names involve a demonstrative element. Before arguing against the individual-constants approach to the semantical role of proper names, I want in sections II and III to place our predicate approach in the context of the two other traditional issues regarding proper names: the question of the conditions under which they designate an object, and the question of how to account for them when they fail to designate.

II

I have suggested that a proper name functioning as a singular term designates an object only if the object is given that name in an appropriate way. Despite its intended vagueness, this suggestion provides an explication for the fact that we talk of the normal or literal use of proper names. Literal use contrasts with metaphorical use. Unlike metaphorical uses ("George Wallace is a Napoleon'), literal uses of proper names—whether or not in singular unmodified form—involve application only to objects that bear them.

It is not always desirable to identify the designation of a proper name functioning as a singular term with the reference a speaker makes in using the name. Unlike the object that a speaker designates, the object that the proper name itself designates can only be an object that bears that name. The point is perhaps most evident in the case of misidentifications.[13] Suppose a novice is fooled into thinking that he is speaking to Hilbert at the Convention for Aggregative Psychology. Afterwards he reports, "Hilbert spoke more about mental mechanisms than about syntax." Now if the man at the convention to whom he speaks is not called "Hilbert," the name does not designate that man, although the novice does. This is because 'Hilbert' is not true of the aggregative psychologist: he is not a Hilbert (literally, as well as metaphorically). The novice thinks that he is, but the novice is wrong. Intuitively, one might want to say that what the novice reported was true of what the novice designated, but false of what the name designated.

Of course, one might hold that, since the novice used the name to designate the psychologist, it *did* designate the psychologist. Speakers often use singular terms in ways other than their normal or literal uses—whether by mistake or by design (lying, irony)—in order to designate an object other than an object that the terms would normally be expected to designate. Having noted this special sense in which names "designate" objects, I propose to ignore it. It seems entirely parasitic on the use of 'designate' to signify a relation between a person and an object, and so can be passed over without loss. When we use 'designate' to signify a relation between a proper name and an object, we shall be concerned with a relation between names and those objects which the names normally or literally apply to.

The relation of designation between proper name (functioning as singular term) and object is definable by means of 'refers to' (speaker-designation) and 'is-true-of': A proper name occurring in a sentence used by a person at a time designates an object if and only if the person refers to that object at that time with that proper name, and the proper name is true of that object. On this usage, when the language user (e.g., the novice) refers to an object (e.g., the psychologist) and mistakenly calls the object by a proper name ('Hilbert') which not it but some other (intended) object bears, we shall not say that the proper name designates that other object at that time. But the proper name *is* true of the intended object. And the language user will normally refer to objects of which the name is true when he uses sentences containing the name. The element of predication in singular unmodified proper names accounts for the intuition that one can speak of normal or literal applications of a proper name and contrast them, in some cases, with the object designated or referred to by the speaker.

I have held that a proper name designates an object only if the object is given that name in an appropriate way. I do not intend to define 'given' or 'appropriate way'. It is not incumbent on us (as truth theorists) to define the conditions under which proper names, or any other predicates, are true of objects. The vague necessary and sufficient application condition for proper names which I have offered may be regarded as a mere stand-in for a full-fledged empirical account of how objects get proper names attached to them. Baptism, inheritance, nicknaming, brand-naming, labeling may all be expected to enter into such an account. Semantics, however, need not await the full returns of sociology. Rules like the following are sufficient: 'O'Hara' is true of any object y just in case y is an O'Hara.

The demonstrative-references that occur with the use of singular, unmodified proper names seem often to occur when there is some causal-like relation between named object and language user. But this point does not go very far. At most, it is the bare beginning of a sociological account of the designation conditions of proper names. Moreover, even in this vague form, the point is not fully generalizable. Sometimes names lack designations. Either the proper name is true of nothing or the language user refers to nothing that it is true of. Sometimes names are introduced as surrogates for definite descriptions even when the introducer is not causally related to the named object. Here the demonstrative in our analysis, which is usually represented by a free variable, is not a device for referring to an extra-linguistic object, but is a pronominal place marker whose antecedent is the definite description. (Cf. note 11.) Thus: "The shortest spy in the 21st century will be Caucasian. Call him 'Bertrand'. (That) Bertrand will also be bald." There are other cases in which the demonstrative acts as a bound variable—as when we say, "Someone cast the first stone. Whoever he was, call him 'Alfred'. (That) Alfred was a hyprocrite." In neither of these cases need there be a causal relation between language user and named object.

III

A full account of the semantics and pragmatics of nondesignating proper names is beyond the scope of this paper. But it may help illuminate our treatment of proper names as predicates to make some brief remarks on the subject. Let us consider the sentence

(8) It is not the case that Pegasus exists.

as uttered at a particular time by me, where the utterance is to be construed as a denial of what believers in the existence of an ancient winged horse might assert. The proper name is functioning as a singular term. So the logical form of (8) is the same as

(9) It is not the case that that Pegasus exists.

where the second occurrence of 'that' is read as a demonstrative. The truth-theoretic biconditional for (8) is roughly

(10) (x) (y) (Reference (x) & By (x, TB^*) & At $(x, 4/23/1970/11$ AM EST$)$
& With $(x, \text{'Pegasus}_1\text{'}, \text{'Pegasus does not exist'})$ & To $(x, y) \to$
('Pegasus does not exist' is true with respect to TB* at $4/23/1970/$
11 AM EST $\leftrightarrow \sim(\exists z)$ $(z = [y]$ Pegasus$)$ $(y))))$

('TB*' represents a complete canonical specification of me.)

In the case of proper names that designate an object, the person's act of reference provides the open singular term representing the proper name with an interpretation and the containing sentence with a truth value. The effect of such an act on the truth condition of the sentence is specified metalinguistically in sentences like (10). But what of the case in which the proper name designates nothing —as in (8)? According to our definition of designation in the previous section, this case will be realized if and only if either the proper name is true of nothing or the language user refers to nothing that it is true of.

Now the failure of 'Pegaus' to designate in my utterance of (8) does not follow from a failure of 'Pegasus' to be true of anything. There are plenty of Pegasi; Richard Gale, for example, has a dog by that name. Hence the failure of 'Pegasus' to designate in my utterance of (8) follows from the fact that I referred to nothing that the proper name is true of. We are assuming that there was an act of reference by me at 4/23/1970/11 AM EST with 'Pegasus'. So I could refer to nothing that the proper name is true of only if one of two cases holds. On the one hand, it might be that 'Pegasus' in (8) failed to designate because I referred to something that is not a Pegasus:

(11) $(\exists x)(\exists z)$ (Reference (x) & By (x, TB^*) & With $(x, \text{'Pegasus}_1\text{'},$
'Pegasus does not exist') & At $(x, 4/23/1970/11$ AM EST$)$ & To (x, z)
& $\sim$ Pegasus $(z))$

On the other hand, it might be that I *referred* but referred to nothing at all, so *a fortiori* to no Pegasus:

(12) $(\exists x)$ (Reference (x) & By (x, TB^*) & With $(x, \text{'Pegasus}_1\text{'}, \text{'Pegasus}$
does not exist') & At $(x, 4/23/1970/11$ AM EST$)$ & $\sim(\exists z)$ To $(x, z)))$

In the first case, I might be referring to the events that began the Pegasus myth. In the second case my reference would have spatio-temporal direction toward the ur-events of the myth. But it would have no referred-to object. It is clear that sentences like (11) sometimes hold. Such sentences are useful in explaining misidentifications of the sort the novice made. Whether sentences like (12) ever hold is perhaps debatable, though

I am inclined to think that they probably do. Fortunately, our formalization in (10) does not force us to take a stand on the issue. The failure of 'Pegasus' to designate in my utterance of (8)—and the truth of the utterance itself—may be explicated by either (11) or (12).[14]

IV

I want to close by making some derogatory remarks about the individual-constants view of the semantical role of proper names. One disadvantage of the view has already been brought out. Our account covers plural and modified occurrences as well as singular, unmodified ones. A constants view not only is more complicated in that it must give a different semantics for these different occurrences (and fail to account as neatly for the obviousness of (1)). But it is also faced with the task of justifying its disunification. Appeal to "special" uses whenever proper names clearly do not play the role of individual constants is flimsy and theoretically deficient.

A second disadvantage of the individual-constants view emerges from reflecting on the respective accounts of the "ambiguity" of proper names. If proper names are treated as ambiguous individual constants, then occurrences designating different objects will have to be differentiated (indexed) in the truth theory for a person at a time. Otherwise, the truth conditions of sentences treated by the theory would be ambiguous; and our initial condition would be violated. But such differentiation poses a problem. There is no evident limit on the number of objects that bear a given name. So there is no way to know how many indexes to provide, much less what denotations to provide them with.

A proponent of the constants view may wish to avoid this problem by claiming that the number of objects that a person at a given time knows to correlate with any given name is probably delimitable and manageable. Thus, the claim would be that one need only provide a denotation for each indexed name for which a person has a denotation in his ken.

This position is not as simple as it may seem. In the first place, a name like 'John' would complicate the semantical theory considerably. Whereas the individual-constants approach would have to provide a large number of denotation rules for the name (say, four hundred), our predicate approach provides a single satisfaction rule for it, plus the set of primitive reference clauses applicable to all occurrences of demonstratives (implicit or explicit) in sentences. In the second place, the truth theorist for the idiolect of a person at a time would be presented with the awesome task of actually tracking down and specifying each of the Johns that a person has in his ken in order to complete his theory. Quite apart from the practical difficulties involved—difficulties that would have no analog in any other part of the theory—there are unpleasant theoretical problems in deciding what objects fall within a person's ken at a given time. None of these problems arises on the predicate approach.

A sophisticated variant of the multi-indexed individual-constants treatment of proper names would be to parse them as fully interpreted constants only when they are being used and as dummy constants otherwise.[15] Such a view would allow for the fact that unmodified occurrences of proper names receive their semantical interpretation in and through a person's actually using them. If it were to avoid the previously mentioned problems in specifying the denotations of (used) proper names, the view would have to invoke something like the apparatus that we utilized in our analysis (7). The "denotation" of the proper name would be determined in the context of use by the reference of the language user. Such an approach would treat proper names as very like free variables—a treatment with which I would have considerable sympathy. The disadvantage of the approach is that it would ignore the conventional predicative element, the element of literalness or factuality, in the application conditions of proper names. For example, it would fail to give a semantical representation to the fact that a given name—whether used or unused (at a given time) applies to some objects and not others. As a result, the approach would fail to give a unified account of modified and unmodified occurrences of proper names (cf. (1)).

Our account's handling of the foregoing problems is simple. Proper names are predicates. One need not distinguish truth-theoretically the objects of which they are true. When a proper name occurs in singular-term position, the object designated by the name (if any) is picked out by the language user's reference. And the truth theory specifies that object in a context-independent manner. The designative indefiniteness or "ambiguity" of proper names is reflected by the variable in formal representations. Insofar as proper names exemplify a fundamental way in which language relates to the world, they provide reason to focus not on individual constants, but on variables—and not the variables of quantification, but free variables which represent demonstratives and which receive their interpretation extralinguistically, through the referential actions of language users.

Notes

I am indebted to Keith Donnellan, Richard Grandy, Gilbert Harman, Edwin Martin, and John Wallace for comments on earlier versions of this paper. An abbreviated version was presented at the meetings of the American Philosophical Association, Eastern Division, in December, 1971.

1. In what follows I shall use 'proper name' in an intuitive way. Intuitively, proper names are nouns that do not describe the objects, if any, to which they apply, and which may in natural language function without modification as singular terms. I exclude from present considerations certain names—"canonical names" such as '0'—which are perhaps best represented as individual constants. Roughly, such names carry a uniqueness presupposition at all their occurrences that is sufficiently global for them to figure in our most comprehensive, context-free theories. Like 'proper name', the term 'designate' is to be construed intuitive—until defined.

2. For expressions of this notion of a formal system, see Gottlob Frege, "On Sense and Reference," in *Translations from the Philosophical Writings of Gottlob Frege*, P. Geach and M. Black, eds. (Oxford: Blackwell's, 1966), p. 58; and Alfred Tarski, "The Concept of Truth in Formalized Languages," in *Logic, Semantics, Metamathematics* (New York: Oxford, 1956), pp. 165–166.

3. For an example of the constants view, see H. P. Grice, "Vacuous Names," in *Words and Objections*, Donald Davidson and Jaakko Hintikka, eds. (Dordrecht: Reidel, 1969). Chief sources of the predicate view are Bertrand Russell, "Knowledge by Acquaintance and by Description," *Proceedings of the Aristotelian Society*, XI (1911):108–128; "The Philosophy of Logical Atomism" (1918) in *Logic and Knowledge*, Robert Charles Marsh, ed. (London: Macmillan 1956), esp. pp. 241–254; W. V. O. Quine, "On What There Is," in *From a Logical Point of View* (New York: Harper, 1953), p. 6; first published 1948; and *Methods of Logic* (New York: Holt, 1950), pp. 218–219 (in 3d ed., 1972, pp. 228–230).

4. Keith S. Donnellan, "Proper Names and Identifying Descriptions," *Synthese*, XXI, 3/4 (October, 1970): 335–358; Saul Kripke, "Naming and Necessity," in Donald Davidson and Gilbert Harman, eds., *Semantics of Natural Languages* (Dordrecht: Reidel, 1972), pp. 253–355.

5. Some philosophers have held that a proper name does not abbreviate, but rather presupposes a set of descriptions uniquely true of the designated object (if any). Cf. John Searle, "Proper Names," *Mind*, LXVII, 266 (April 1958): 166–173, [chap. 23 herein]; P. F. Strawson, *Individuals* (New York: Doubleday, 1959), p. 20. This view faces a number of difficulties, but it is compatible with various positions on the semantical role of proper names, so there is no pressing reason to discuss it here.

6. "The Philosophy of Logical Atomism," *op. cit.*

7. Calling proper names "predicates" slurs a distinction which for present purposes is unimportant but which is worth bearing in mind. Strictly speaking, proper names are general terms which, together with a copula and an indefinite article on some occurrences, are parsed as predicates in a formal semantical theory.

8. Worth mentioning here is the syntactic theory of Clarence Sloat, "Proper Nouns in English," *Language*, XLX (1969): 26–30, which Edwin Martin and Barbara Partee called to my attention. Sloat gives a neat account of proper names which treat them on a close analogy to common nouns. Clearly, such a syntactical account is congenial with our predicate view of the semantical role of proper names—and uncongenial with an individual-constants view.

9. "Singular Terms," in *Linguistics in Philosophy* (Ithaca, N.Y.: Cornell, 1967), pp. 40–41. I have eliminated one of Vendler's examples and adjusted the grammar to accommodate the elimination.

10. Cf. Quine, *Methods of Logic, op. cit.*, p. 216 (3d ed., p. 227).

11. There are pronominal occurrences of demonstratives and demonstrative-governed singular terms which do not take widest scope if their antecedents do not. These occurrences will be ignored for present purposes. It should be mentioned, however, that in such occurrences proper names sometimes play an abbreviative rather than an independently predicative role.

12. Fuller discussion occurs in my dissertation *Truth and Some Referential Devices* (Princeton University, 1971). As a result of a suggestion by David Kaplan, the bracket notation replaced a less perspicuous predecessor. Note that the quantifier 'y' binds the variably 'y' both as it occurs in 'To (x, y)' and as it occurs in '$[y]$ Aristotle (y)'. The subscript on 'Aristotle' marks a particular occurrence of the term in the sentence. (One might use the term more than once in a given sentence to refer to more than one object.) All positions in sentence (7) are fully extensional. The formulation of the antecedent owes something to Donald Davidson's treatment of action verbs; cf. his "The Logical Form of Action Sentences," in Nicholas Rescher, ed., *The Logic of Action and Decision* (Pittsburgh, Pa.: University Press, 1967), pp. 81–95 [chap. 11 herein].

13. Other aspects of misidentifications are given valuable discussion by Donnellan in "Proper Names and Identifying Descriptions," *op. cit.*; and "Reference and Definite Descriptions," *Philosophical Review*, LXXV, 3 (July 1966): 281–304 [chap. 17 herein].

14. It should be noted that, if (12) is chosen as the explication, an additional axiom is needed to prevent (10) from being uninformative because the condition laid down by the antecedent is unfulfilled. But supplying such an axiom is not difficult.

15. Dummy constants are discussed in Rudolf Carnap, *The Logical Syntax of Language* (London: Routledge & Kegan Paul, 1937), pp. 189–195; first published, 1934. (Carnap does not propose the view of proper names I am here constructing.) It should be noted that in some free logics Carnap's way of distinguishing dummy constants and free variables breaks down.

Chapter 25

Lecture II of *Naming and Necessity*

Saul A. Kripke

Last time we ended up talking about a theory of naming which is given by a number of theses here on the board.

(1) To every name or designation expression 'X', there corresponds a cluster of properties, namely the family of those properties ϕ such that A believes 'ϕX'.

(2) One of the properties, or some conjointly, are believed by A to pick out some individual uniquely.

(3) If most, or a weighted most, of the ϕ's are satisfied by one unique object y, then y is the referent of 'X'.

(4) If the vote yields no unique object, 'X' does not refer.

(5) The statement, 'If X exists, then X has most of the ϕ's' is known *a priori* by the speaker.

(6) The statement, 'If X exists, then X has most of the ϕ's' expresses a necessary truth (in the idiolect of the speaker).

(C) For any successful theory, the account must not be circular. The properties which are used in the vote must not themselves involve the notion of reference in such a way that it is ultimately impossible to eliminate.

(C) is not a thesis but a condition on the satisfaction of the other theses. In other words, Theses (1)–(6) cannot be satisfied in a way which leads to a circle, in a way which does not lead to any independent determination of reference. The example I gave last time of a blatantly circular attempt to satisfy these conditions was a theory of names mentioned by William Kneale. I was a little surprised at the statement of the theory when I was reading what I had copied down, so I looked it up again. I looked it up in the book to see if I'd copied it down accurately. Kneale *did* use the past tense. He said that though it is not trifling to be told that Socrates was the greatest philosopher of ancient Greece, it is trifling to be told that Socrates was called 'Socrates'. Therefore, he concludes, the name 'Socrates' must simply mean 'the individual called "Socrates"'. Russell, as I've said, in some places gives a similar analysis. Anyway, as stated using the past tense, the condition wouldn't be circular, because one certainly could decide to use the term 'Socrates' to refer to whoever was called 'Socrates' by the Greeks. But, of course, in that sense it's not at all trifling to be told that Socrates was called 'Socrates'. If this is any kind of fact, it might be false. Perhaps we know that *we* call him 'Socrates'; that hardly shows that the Greeks did so. In fact, of course, they may have pronounced the name differently. It may be, in the case of this particular name, that transliteration from the Greek is so good that the English version is not pronounced *very* differently from the Greek. But that won't be so in the general case. Certainly it is not trifling to be told that Isaiah was called 'Isaiah'. In fact, it is false to be told that Isaiah was called 'Isaiah'; the prophet wouldn't have recognized this name at all. And of course the Greeks didn't call their country anything like 'Greece'. Suppose we amend the thesis so that it reads: it's trifling to be told that Socrates is called 'Socrates' by us, or at least, by me, the speaker. Then in some sense this is fairly trifling. I don't think it is necessary or analytic. In the same way, it is trifling to be told that horses are called 'horses', without this leading to the conclusion that the word 'horse', simply *means* 'the animal called a "horse"'. As a theory of the reference of the name 'Socrates' it will lead immediately to a vicious circle. If one was determining the referent of a name like 'Glunk' to himself and made the following decision, 'I shall use the term "Glunk" to refer to the man that I call "Glunk"', this would get one nowhere. One had better have some independent determination of the referent of 'Glunk'. This is a good example of a blatantly circular determination. Actually sentences like 'Socrates is called "Socrates"' are very interesting and one can spend, strange as it may seem, hours talking about their analysis. I actually did, once, do that. I won't do that, however, on this occasion. (See how high the seas of language can rise. And at the lowest points too.) Anyway this is a useful example of a violation of the noncircularity condition. The theory will satisfy all of these statements, perhaps, but it satisfies them only because there is some independent way of determining the reference independently of the particular condition: being the man called 'Socrates'.

I have already talked about, in the last lecture, Thesis (6). Theses (5) and (6), by the way, have converses. What I said for Thesis (5) is that the statement that if X exists, X has most of the ϕ's, is *a priori* true for the speaker. It will also be true under the given theory that certain converses of this statement hold true also *a priori* for the speaker, namely: if any unique thing has most of the properties ϕ in the properly weighted sense, it is X. Similarly a certain converse to this will be *necessarily* true, namely: if anything has most of the properties ϕ in the properly weighted sense, it is X. So really one can say that it is both *a priori* and necessary that something is X if and only if it uniquely has most of the properties ϕ. This really comes from the previous Theses (1)–(4), I suppose. And (5) and (6) really just say that a sufficiently reflective speaker grasps this theory of proper names. Knowing this, he therefore sees that (5) and (6) are true. The objections to Theses (5) and (6) will *not* be that some speakers are unaware of this theory and therefore don't know these things.

What I talked about in the last lecture is Thesis (6). It's been observed by many philosophers that, if the cluster of properties associated with a proper name is taken in a very narrow sense, so that only one property is given any weight at all, let's say one definite description to pick out the referent—for example, Aristotle was the philosopher who taught Alexander the Great—then certain things will seem to turn out to be necessary truths which are not necessary truths—in this case, for example, that Aristotle taught Alexander the Great. But as Searle said, it is not a necessary truth but a contingent one that Aristotle ever went into pedagogy. Therefore, he concludes that one must drop the original paradigm of a single description and turn to that of a cluster of descriptions.

To summarize some things that I argued last time, this is not the correct answer (whatever it may be) to this problem about necessity. For Searle goes on to say,

> Suppose we agree to drop 'Aristotle' and use, say, 'the teacher of Alexander', then it is a necessary truth that the man referred to is Alexander's teacher—but it is a contingent fact that Aristotle ever went into pedagogy, though I am suggesting that it is a necessary fact that Aristotle has the logical sum, inclusive disjunction, of properties commonly attributed to him. . . .[1]

This is what is not so. It just is not, in any intuitive sense of necessity, a necessary truth that Aristotle had the properties commonly attributed to him. There is a certain theory, perhaps popular in some views of the philosophy of history, which might both be deterministic and yet at the same time assign a great role to the individual in history. Perhaps Carlyle would associate with the meaning of the name of a great man his achievements. According to such a view it will be necessary, once a certain individual is born, that he is destined to perform various great tasks and so it will be part of the very nature of Aristotle that he should have produced ideas which had a great influence on the western world. Whatever the merits of such a view may be as a view of history or the nature of great men, it does not seem that it should be trivially true on the basis of a theory of proper names. It would seem that it's a contingent fact that Aristotle ever did *any* of the things commonly attributed to him today, *any* of these great achievements that we so much admire. I must say that there is *something* to this feeling of Searle's. When I hear the name 'Hitler', I do get an illusory 'gut feeling' that it's sort of analytic that that man was evil. But really, probably not. Hitler might have spent all his days in quiet in Linz. In that case we would not say that then this man would not have been Hitler, for we use the name 'Hitler' just as the name of that man, even in describing other possible worlds. (This is the notion which I called a *rigid designator* in the previous talk.) Suppose we do decide to pick out the reference of 'Hitler', as the man who succeeded in having more Jews killed than anyone else managed to do in history. That is the way we pick out the reference of the name; but in another counterfactual situation where some one else would have gained this discredit, we wouldn't say that in that case that other man would have been Hitler. If Hitler had never come to power, Hitler would not have had the property which I am supposing we use to fix the reference of his name. Similarly, even if we define what a meter is by reference to the standard meter stick, it will be a contingent truth and not a necessary one that that particular stick is one meter long. If it had been stretched, it would have been longer than one meter. And that is because we use the term 'one meter' rigidly to designate a certain length. Even though we fix what length we are designating by an accidental property of that length, just as in the case of the name of the man we may pick the man out by an accidental property of the man, still we use the name to designate that man or that length in all possible worlds. The property we use need not be one which is regarded in any way as necessary or essential. In the case of a yard, the original way this length was picked out was, I think, the distance when the arm of King Henry I of England was outstretched from the tip of his finger to his nose. If this was the length of a yard, it nevertheless will not be a necessary truth that the distance between the tip of his finger and his nose should be a yard. Maybe an accident might have happened to foreshorten his arm;

that would be possible. And the reason that it's not a necessary truth is not that there might be other criteria in a 'cluster concept' of yardhood. Even a man who strictly uses King Henry's arm as his one standard of length can say, counterfactually, that if certain things had happened to the King, the exact distance between the end of one of his fingers and his nose would not have been exactly a yard. He need not be using a cluster as long as he uses the term 'yard' to pick out a certain fixed reference to be that length in all possible worlds.

These remarks show, I think, the intuitive bizarreness of a good deal of the literature on 'transworld identification' and 'counterpart theory'. For many theorists of these sorts, believing, as they do, that a 'possible world' is given to us only qualitatively, argue that Aristotle is to be 'identified in other possible worlds', or alternatively that his counterparts are to be identified, with those things in other possible worlds who most closely resemble Aristotle in his most important properties. (Lewis, for example, says: 'Your counterparts ... resemble you ... in important respects ... more closely than do the other things in their worlds ... weighted by the importance of the various respects and by the degrees of the similarities.'[2]) Some may equate the important properties with those properties used to identify the object in the actual world.

Surely these notions are incorrect. To me Aristotle's most important properties consist in his philosophical work, and Hitler's in his murderous political role; both, as I have said, might have lacked these properties altogether. Surely there was no logical fate hanging over either Aristotle or Hitler which made it in any sense inevitable that they should have possessed the properties we regard as important to them; they could have had careers completely different from their actual ones. *Important* properties of an object need not be essential, unless 'importance' is used as a synonym for essence; and an object could have had properties very different from its most striking actual properties, or from the properties we use to identify it.

To clear up one thing which some people have asked me: When I say that a designator is rigid, and designates the same thing in all possible worlds, I mean that, as used in *our* language, it stands for that thing, when *we* talk about counterfactual situations. I don't mean, of course, that there mightn't be counterfactual situations in which in the other possible worlds people actually spoke a different language. One doesn't say that 'two plus two equals four' is contingent because people might have spoken a language in which 'two plus two equals four' meant that seven is even. Similarly, when we speak of a counterfactual situation, we speak of it in English, even if it is part of the description of that counterfactual situation that we were all speaking German in that counterfactual situation. We say, 'suppose we had all been speaking German' or 'suppose we had been using English in a nonstandard way'. Then we are describing a possible world or counterfactual situation in which people, including ourselves, did speak in a certain way different from the way we speak. But still, in describing that world, we use *English* with *our* meanings and *our* references. It is in this sense that I speak of a rigid designator as having the same reference in all possible worlds. I also don't mean to imply that the thing designated exists in all possible worlds, just that the name refers rigidly to that thing. If you say 'suppose Hitler had never been born' then 'Hitler' refers here, still rigidly, to something that would not exist in the counterfactual situation described.

Given these remarks, this means we must cross off Thesis (6) as incorrect. The other theses have nothing to do with necessity and can survive. In particular Thesis (5) has nothing to do with necessity and it can survive. If I use the name 'Hesperus' to refer to a certain planetary body when seen in a certain celestial position in the evening, it will not therefore be a necessary truth that Hesperus is ever seen in the evening. That depends on various contingent facts about people being there to see and things like that. So even if I should say to myself that I will use 'Hesperus' to name the heavenly body I see in the evening in yonder position of the sky, it will not be necessary that Hesperus was ever seen in the evening. But it may be *a priori* in that this is how I have determined the referent. If I have determined that Hesperus is the thing that I saw in the evening over there, then I will know, just from making that determination of the referent, that if there is any Hesperus at all it's the thing I saw in the evening. This at least survives as far as the arguments we have given up to now go.

How about a theory where Thesis (6) is eliminated? Theses (2), (3), and (4) turn out to have a large class of counterinstances. Even when Theses (2)–(4) are true, Thesis (5) is usually false; the truth of Theses (3) and (4) is an empirical 'accident', which the speaker hardly knows *a priori*. That is to say, other principles really determine the speaker's reference, and the fact that the referent coincides with that determined by (2)–(4) is an 'accident', which we were in no position to know *a priori*. Only in a rare class of cases, usually initial baptisms, are all of (2)–(5) true.

What picture of naming do these Theses ((1)–(5)) give you? The picture is this. I want to name an object. I think of some way of describing it uniquely and then I go through, so to speak, a sort of mental ceremony: By 'Cicero' I shall mean the man who denounced Catiline; and that's what the reference of 'Cicero' will be. I will use 'Cicero' to designate rigidly the man who (in fact) denounced Catiline, so I can speak of possible worlds in which he did not. But still my intentions are given by first, giving some condition which uniquely determines an object, then using a certain word as a name for the object determined by this condition. Now there may be some cases in which we actually do this. Maybe, if you want to stretch and call it description, when you say: I shall call that heavenly body over there 'Hesperus'.[3] That is really a case where the theses not only are true but really even give a correct picture of how the reference is determined. Another case, if your want to call this a name, might be when the police in London use the name 'Jack' or 'Jack the Ripper' to refer to the man, whoever he is, who committed all these murders, or most of them. Then they are giving the reference of the name by a description.[4] But in many or most cases, I think the theses are false. So let's look at them.[5]

Thesis (1), as I say, is a definition. Thesis (2) says that one of the properties believed by A of the object, or some conjointly, are believed to pick out some individual uniquely. A sort of example people have in mind is just what I said: I shall use the term 'Cicero' to denote the man who denounced Catiline (or first denounced him in public, to make it unique). This picks out an object uniquely in this particular reference. Even some writers such as Ziff in *Semantic Analysis*, who don't believe that names have meaning in any sense, think that this is a good picture of the way reference can be determined.

Let's see if Thesis (2) is true. It seems, in some *a priori* way, that it's got to be true, because if you don't think that the properties you have in mind pick out anyone uniquely—let's say they're all satisfied by two people— then how can you say which one of them you're talking about? There seem to be no grounds for saying you're talking about the one rather than about the other. Usually the properties in question are supposed to be some famous deeds of the person in question. For example, Cicero was the man who denounced Catiline. The average person, according to this, when he refers to Cicero, is saying something like 'the man who denounced Catiline' and thus has picked out a certain man uniquely. It is a tribute to the education of philosophers that they have held this thesis for such a long time. In fact, most people, when they think of Cicero, just think of *a famous Roman orator*, without any pretension to think either that there was only one famous Roman orator or that one must know something else about Cicero to have a referent for the name. Consider Richard Feynman, to whom many of us are able to refer. He is a leading contemporary theoretical physicist. Everyone *here* (I'm sure!) can state the contents of one of Feynman's theories so as to differentiate him from Gell-Mann. However, the man in the street, not possessing these abilities, may still use the name 'Feynman'. When asked he will say: well he's a physicist or something. He may not think that this picks out anyone uniquely. I still think he uses the name 'Feynman' as a name for Feynman.

But let's look at some of the cases where we do have a description to pick out someone uniquely. Let's say, for example, that we know that Cicero was the man who first denounced Catiline. Well, that's good. That really picks someone out uniquely. However, there is a problem, because this description contains another name, namely 'Catiline'. We must be sure that we satisfy the conditions in such a way as to avoid violating the noncircularity condition here. In particular, we must not say that Catiline was the man denounced by Cicero. If we do this, we will really not be picking out anything uniquely, we will simply be picking out a pair of objects A and B, such that A denounced B. We do not think that this was the only pair where such denunciations ever occurred; so we had better add some other conditions in order to satisfy the uniqueness condition.

If we say Einstein was the man who discovered the theory of relativity, that certainly picks out someone uniquely. One can be sure, as I said, that everyone *here* can make a compact and independent statement of this theory and so pick out Einstein uniquely; but many people actually don't know enough about this stuff, so when asked what the theory of relativity is, they will say: 'Einstein's theory', and thus be led into the most straightforward sort of vicious circle.

So Thesis (2), in a straightforward way, fails to be satisfied when we say Feynman is a famous physicist without attributing anything else to Feynman. In another way it may not be satisfied in the proper way even when it is satisfied: If we say Einstein was 'the man who discovered relativity theory', that does pick someone out uniquely; but it may not pick him out in such a way as to satisfy the noncircularity condition, because the theory of relativity may in turn be picked out as 'Einstein's theory'. So Thesis (2) seems to be false.

By changing the conditions ϕ from those usually associated with names by philosophers, one could try to improve the theory. There have been various ways I've heard; maybe I'll discuss these later on. Usually they think of famous achievements of the man named. Certainly in the case of famous achievements, the theory doesn't work. Some student of mine once said, 'Well, Einstein discovered the theory of relativity'; and he determined the reference of 'the theory of relativity' independently by referring to an encyclopedia which would give the details of the theory. (This is what is called a transcendental deduction of the existence of encyclopedias.) But it seems to me that, even if someone has heard of encyclopedias, it really is not essential for his reference that he should know whether this theory is given in detail in any encyclopedia. The reference might work even if there had been no encyclopedias at all.

Let's go on to Thesis (3): If most of the ϕ's, suitably weighted, are satisfied by a unique object y, then y is the referent of the name for the speaker. Now, since we have already established that Thesis (2) is wrong, why should any of the rest work? The whole theory depended on always being able to specify unique conditions which are satisfied. But still we can look at the other theses. The picture associated with the theory is that only by giving some unique properties can you know who someone is and thus know what the reference of your name is. Well, I won't go into the question of knowing who someone is. It's really very puzzling. I think you *do* know who Cicero is if you just can answer that he's a famous Roman orator. Strangely enough, if you know that Einstein discovered the theory of relativity and nothing about that theory, you can both know who Einstein is, namely the discoverer of the theory of relativity, and who discovered the theory of relativity, namely Einstein, on the basis of this knowledge. This seems to be a blatant violation of some sort of non-circularity condition; but it is the way we talk. It therefore would seem that a picture which suggests this condition must be the wrong picture.

Suppose most of the ϕ's are in fact satisfied by a unique object. Is that object necessarily the referent of 'X' for A? Let's suppose someone says that Gödel is the man who proved the incompleteness of arithmetic, and this man is suitably well educated and is even able to give an independent account of the incompleteness theorem. He doesn't just say, 'Well, that's Gödel's theorem', or whatever. He actually states a certain theorem, which he attributes to Gödel as the discoverer. Is it the case, then, that if most of the ϕ's are satisfied by a unique object y, then y is the referent of the name '*X*' for *A*? Let's take a simple case. In the case of Gödel that's practically the only thing many people have heard about him—that he discovered the incompleteness of arithmetic. Does it follow that whoever discovered the incompleteness of arithmetic is the referent of 'Gödel'?

Imagine the following blatantly fictional situation. (I hope Professor Gödel is not present.) Suppose that Gödel was not in fact the author of this theorem. A man named 'Schmidt', whose body was found in Vienna under mysterious circumstances many years ago, actually did the work in question. His friend Gödel somehow got hold of the manuscript and it was thereafter attributed to Gödel. On the view in question, then, when our ordinary man uses the name 'Gödel', he really means to refer to Schmidt, because Schmidt is the unique person satisfying the description, 'the man who discovered the incompleteness of arithmetic'. Of course you might try changing it to 'the man who *published* the discovery of the incompleteness of arithmetic'. By changing the story a little further one can make even this formulation false. Anyway, most people might not even know whether the thing was published or got around by word of mouth. Let's stick to 'the man who discovered the incompleteness of arithmetic'. So, since the man who discovered the incompleteness of arithmetic is in fact Schmidt, we, when we talk about 'Gödel', are in fact always referring to Schmidt. But it seems to me that we are not. We simply are not. One reply, which I will discuss later, might be: You should say instead, 'the man to whom the incompleteness of arithmetic is commonly attributed', or something like that. Let's see what we can do with that later.

But it may seem to many of you that this is a very odd example, or that such a situation occurs rarely. This also is a tribute to the education of philosophers. Very often we use a name on the basis of considerable misinformation. The case of mathematics used in the fictive example is a good case in point. What do we know about Peano? What many people in this room may 'know' about Peano is that he was the discoverer of certain axioms which characterize the sequence of natural numbers, the so-called 'Peano axioms'. Probably some people can even state them. I have been told that these axioms were not first discovered by Peano but by Dedekind. Peano was of course not a dishonest man. I am told that his footnotes include a credit to Dedekind. Somehow the footnote has been ignored. So on the theory in question the term 'Peano', as we use it, really refers to—now that you've heard it you see that you were really all the time talking about—Dedekind. But you were not. Such illustrations could be multiplied indefinitely.

Even worse misconceptions, of course, occur to the layman. In a previous example I supposed people to identify Einstein by reference to his work on relativity. Actually, I often used to hear that Einstein's most famous achievement was the invention of the atomic bomb. So when we refer to Einstein, we refer to the inventor of the atomic bomb. But this is not so. Columbus was the first man to realize that the earth was round. He was also the first European to land in the western hemisphere. Probably none of these things are true, and therefore, when people use the term 'Columbus' they really refer to some Greek if they use the roundness of the earth, or to some Norseman, perhaps, if they use the 'discovery of America'. But they don't. So it does not seem that if most of the ϕ's are satisfied by a unique object y, then y is the referent of the name. This seems simply to be false.[6]

Thesis (4): If the vote yields no unique object the name does not refer. Really this case has been covered before—has been covered in my previous examples. First, the vote may not yield a *unique* object, as in the case of Cicero or Feynman. Secondly, suppose it yields *no* object, that nothing satisfies most, or even any, substantial number, of the ϕ's. Does that mean the name doesn't refer? No: in the same way that you may have false beliefs about a person which may actually be true of someone else, so you may have false beliefs which are true of absolutely no one. And these may constitute the totality of your beliefs. Suppose, to vary the example about Gödel, no one had discovered the incompleteness of arithmetic—perhaps the proof simply materialized by a random scattering of atoms on a piece of paper—the man Gödel being lucky enough to have been present when this improbable event occurred. Further, suppose arithmetic is in fact complete. One wouldn't really expect a random scattering of atoms to produce a correct proof. A subtle error, unknown through the decades, has still been unnoticed—or perhaps not actually unnoticed, but the friends of Gödel. ... So even if the conditions are not satisfied by a unique object the name may still refer. I gave you the case of Jonah last week. Biblical scholars, as I said, think that Jonah really existed. It isn't because they think that someone ever was swallowed by a big fish or even went to Nineveh to preach. These conditions may be true of no one whatsoever and yet the name 'Jonah' really has a referent. In the case above of Einstein's invention of the bomb, possibly no one really deserves to be called the 'inventor' of the device.

Thesis 5 says that the statement 'If X exists, then X has most of the ϕ's', is *a priori* true for A. Notice that even in a case where (3) and (4) *happen* to be true, a typical speaker hardly knows *a priori* that they are, as required by the theory. I *think* that my belief about Gödel *is* in fact correct and that the 'Schmidt' story is just a fantasy. But the belief hardly constitutes *a priori* knowledge.

What's going on here? Can we rescue the theory?[7] First, one may try and vary these descriptions—not think of the famous achievements of a man but, let's say, of something else, and try and use that as our description. Maybe by enough futzing around someone might eventually get something out of this;[8] however, most of the attempts that one tries are open to counterexamples or other objections. Let me give an example of this. In the case of Gödel one may say, 'Well, "Gödel" doesn't mean "the man who proved the incompleteness of arithmetic"'. Look, all we really know is that most people *think* that Gödel proved the incompleteness of arithmetic, that Gödel is the man to whom the incompleteness of arithmetic is commonly attributed. So when I determine the referent of the name 'Gödel', I don't say to myself, 'by "Gödel" I shall mean "the man who proved the incompleteness of arithmetic, whoever he is"'. That might turn out to be Schmidt or Post. But instead I shall mean 'the man who most people *think* proved the incompleteness of arithmetic'.

Is this right? First, it seems to me that it's open to counterexamples of the same type as I gave before, though the counterexamples may be more recherché. Suppose, in the case of Peano mentioned previously, unbeknownst to the speaker, most people (at least by now) thoroughly realize that the number-theoretic axioms should not be attributed to him. Most people don't credit them to Peano but now correctly ascribe them to Dedekind. So then even the man to whom this thing is commonly attributed will still be Dedekind and not Peano. Still, the speaker, having picked up the old outmoded belief, may still be referring to Peano, and hold a false belief about Peano, not a true belief about Dedekind.

But second, and perhaps more significantly, such a criterion violates the noncircularity condition. How is this? It is true that most of us think that Gödel proved the incompleteness of arithmetic. Why is this so? We certainly say, and sincerely, 'Gödel proved the incompleteness of arithmetic'. Does it follow from that that we believe that Gödel proved the incompleteness of arithmetic—that we attribute the incompleteness of arithmetic to this man? No. Not just from that. We have to be *referring to Gödel* when we say 'Gödel proved the incompleteness of arithmetic'. If, in fact, we were always referring to Schmidt, then we would be attributing the incompleteness of arithmetic to Schmidt and not to Gödel—if we used the sound 'Gödel' as the name of the man whom I am calling 'Schmidt'.

But we do in fact refer to Gödel. How do we do this? Well, not by saying to ourselves, 'By "Gödel" I shall mean the man to whom the incompleteness of arithmetic is commonly attributed'. If we did that we would run into a circle. Here we are all in this room. Actually in this institution[9] some people have met the man, but in many institutions this is not so. All of us in the community are trying to determine the reference by saying 'Gödel is to be the man to whom the incompleteness of arithmetic is commonly attributed'. None of us will get started with any attribution unless there is some independent criterion for the reference of the name other than 'the man to whom the incompleteness of arithmetic is commonly attributed'. Otherwise all we will be saying is, 'We attribute this achievement to the man to whom we attribute it', without saying who that man is, without giving any independent criterion of the reference, and so the determination will be circular. This then is a violation of the condition I have marked '*C*', and cannot be used in any theory of reference.

Of course you might try to avoid circularity by passing the buck. This is mentioned by Strawson, who says in his footnote on these matters that one man's reference may derive from another's.

The identifying description, though it must not include a reference to the speaker's own reference to the particular in question, may include a reference to another's reference to that particular. If a putatively identifying description is of this latter kind, then, indeed, the question, whether it is a genuinely identifying description, turns on the question, whether the reference it refers to is itself a genuinely identifying reference. So one reference may borrow its credentials, as a genuinely identifying reference, from another; and that from another. But this regress is not infinite.[10]

I may then say, 'Look, by "Gödel" I shall mean the man Joe thinks proved the incompleteness of arithmetic'. Joe may then pass the thing over to Harry. One has to be very careful that this doesn't come round in a circle. Is one really sure that this won't happen? If you could be sure yourself of knowing such a chain, and that everyone else in the chain is using the proper conditions and so is not getting out of it, then maybe you could get back to the man by referring to such a chain in that way, borrowing the references one by one. However, although in general such chains do exist for a living man, you won't know what the chain is. You won't be sure what descriptions the other man is using, so the thing won't go into a circle, or whether by appealing to Joe you won't get back to the right man at all. So you cannot use this as your identifying description with any confidence. You may not even remember from whom you heard of Gödel.

What is the true picture of what's going on? Maybe reference doesn't really take place at all! After all, we don't really know that any of the properties we use to identify the man are right. We don't know that they pick out a unique object. So what *does* make my use of 'Cicero' into a name of *him*? The picture which leads to the cluster-of-descriptions theory is something like this: One is isolated in a room; the entire community of other speakers, everything else, could disappear; and one determines the reference for himself by saying—'By "Gödel" I shall mean the man, whoever he is, who proved the incompleteness of arithmetic'. Now you can do this if you want to. There's nothing really preventing it. You can just stick to that determination. If that's what you do, then if Schmidt discovered the incompleteness of arithmetic you *do* refer to him when you say 'Gödel did such and such'.

But that's not what most of us do. Someone, let's say, a baby, is born; his parents call him by a certain name. They talk about him to their friends. Other people meet him. Through various sorts of talk the name is spread from link to link as if by a chain. A speaker who is on the far end of this chain, who has heard about, say Richard Feynman, in the market place or elsewhere, may be referring to Richard Feynman even though he can't remember from whom he first heard of Feynman or from whom he ever heard of Feynman. He knows that Feynman is a famous physicist. A certain passage of communication reaching ultimately to the man himself does reach the speaker. He then is referring to Feynman even though he can't identify him uniquely. He doesn't know what a Feynman diagram is, he doesn't know what the Feynman theory of pair production and annihilation is. Not only that: he'd have trouble distinguishing between Gell-Mann and Feynman. So he doesn't have to know these things, but, instead, a chain of communication going back to Feynman himself has been established, by virtue of his membership in a community which passed the name on from link to link, not by a ceremony that he makes in private in his study: 'By "Feynman" I shall mean the man who did such and such and such and such'.

How does this view differ from Strawson's suggestion, mentioned before, that one identifying reference may borrow its credentials from another? Certainly Strawson had a good insight in the passage quoted;

on the other hand, he certainly shows a difference at least in emphasis from the picture I advocate, since he confines the remark to a footnote. The main text advocates the cluster-of-descriptions theory. Just because Strawson makes his remark in the context of a description theory, his view therefore differs from mine in one important respect. Strawson apparently requires that the speaker must *know* from whom he got his reference, so that he can say: 'By "Gödel" I mean the man *Jones* calls "Gödel"'. If he does not remember how he picked up the reference, he cannot give such a description. The present theory sets no such requirement. As I said, I may well not remember from whom I heard of Gödel, and I may think I remember from which people I heard the name, but wrongly.

These considerations show that the view advocated here can lead to consequences which actually *diverge* from those of Strawson's footnote. Suppose that the speaker has heard the name 'Cicero' from Smith and others, who use the name to refer to a famous Roman orator. He later thinks, however, that he picked up the name from Jones, who (unknown to the speaker) uses 'Cicero' as the name of a notorious German spy and has never heard of any orators of the ancient world. Then, according to Strawson's paradigm, the speaker must determine his reference by the resolution, 'I shall use "Cicero" to refer to the man whom Jones calls by that name', while on the present view, the referent will be the orator in spite of the speaker's false impression about where he picked up the name. The point is that Strawson, trying to fit the chain of communication view into the description theory, relies on what the speaker *thinks* was the source of his reference. If the speaker has forgotten his source, the description Strawson uses is unavailable to him; if he misremembers it, Strawson's paradigm can give the wrong results. On our view, it is not how the speaker thinks he got the reference, but the actual chain of communication, which is relevant.

I think I said the other time that philosophical theories are in danger of being false, and so I wasn't going to present an alternative theory. Have I just done so? Well, in a way; but my characterization has been far less specific than a real set of necessary and sufficient conditions for reference would be. Obviously the name is passed on from link to link. But of course not every sort of causal chain reaching from me to a certain man will do for me to make a reference. There may be a causal chain from our use of the term 'Santa Claus' to a certain historical saint, but still the children, when they use this, by this time probably do not refer to that saint. So other conditions must be satisfied in order to make this into a really rigorous theory of reference. I don't know that I'm going to do this because, first, I'm sort of too lazy at the moment; secondly, rather than giving a set of necessary and sufficient conditions which will work for a term like reference, I want to present just a *better picture* than the picture presented by the received views.

Haven't I been very unfair to the description theory? Here I have stated it very precisely—more precisely, perhaps, than it has been stated by any of its advocates. So then it's easy to refute. Maybe if I tried to state mine with sufficient precision in the form of six or seven or eight theses, it would also turn out that when you examine the theses one by one, they will all be false. That might even be so, but the difference is this. What I think the examples I've given show is not simply that there's some technical error here or some mistake there, but that the whole picture given by this theory of how reference is determined seems to be wrong from the fundamentals. It seems to be wrong to think that we give ourselves some properties which somehow qualitatively uniquely pick out an object and determine our reference in that manner. What I am trying to present is a better picture—a picture which, if more details were to be filled in, might be refined so as to give more exact conditions for reference to take place.

One might never reach a set of necessary and sufficient conditions. I don't know, I'm always sympathetic to Bishop Butler's 'Everything is what it is and not another thing'—in the nontrivial sense that philosophical analyses of some concept like reference, in completely different terms which make no mention of reference, are very apt to fail. Of course in any particular case when one is given an analysis one has to look at it and see whether it is true or false. One can't just cite this maxim to oneself and then turn the page. But more cautiously, I want to present a better picture without giving a set of necessary and sufficient conditions for reference. Such conditions would be very complicated, but what is true is that it's in virtue of our connection with other speakers in the community, going back to the referent himself, that we refer to a certain man.

There may be some cases where the description picture is true, where some man really gives a name by going into the privacy of his room and saying that the referent is to be the unique thing with certain identifying properties. 'Jack the Ripper' was a possible example which I gave. Another was 'Hesperus'. Yet another case which can be forced into this description is that of meeting someone and being told his name. Except for a belief in the description theory, in its importance in other cases, one probably wouldn't think that that was a case of giving oneself a description, i.e., 'the guy I'm just meeting now'. But one can put it in these terms if one wishes, and if one has never heard the name in any other way. Of course, if you're introduced to a man and told, 'That's Einstein', you've heard of him before, it may be wrong, and so on. But maybe in some cases such a paradigm works—especially for the man who first gives someone or something a name. Or he points to a star and says, 'That is to be Alpha Centauri'. So he can really make himself this ceremony: 'By "Alpha Centauri" I shall mean the star right over there with such and such coordinates'. But in general this picture fails. In general our reference depends not just on what we think ourselves, but on other people in the community, the history of how the name reached one, and things like that. It is by following such a history that one gets to the reference.

More exact conditions are very complicated to give. They seem in a way somehow different in the case of a famous man and one who isn't so famous. For example, a teacher tells his class that Newton was famous for being the first man to think there's a force pulling things to the earth; I think that's what little kids think Newton's greatest achievement was. I won't say what the merits of such an achievement would be, but, anyway, we may suppose that just being told that this was the sole content of Newton's discovery gives the students a false belief *about Newton*, even though they have never heard of him before. If, on the other hand,[11] the teacher uses the name 'George Smith'—a man by that name is actually his next door neighbor—and says that George Smith first squared the circle, does it follow from this that the students have a false belief about the teacher's neighbor? The teacher doesn't tell them that Smith is his neighbor, nor does he believe Smith first squared the circle. He isn't particularly trying to get any belief *about the neighbor* into the student's heads. He tries to inculcate the belief that there was a man who squared the circle, but not a belief about any particular man—he just pulls out the first name that occurs to him—as it happens, he uses his neighbor's name. It doesn't seem clear in that case that the students have a false belief about the neighbor, even though there is a causal chain going back to the neighbor. I am not sure about this. At any rate more refinements need to be added to make this even begin to be a set of necessary and sufficient conditions. In that sense it's not a theory, but is supposed to give a better picture of what is actually going on.

A rough statement of a theory might be the following: An initial 'baptism' takes place. Here the object may be named by ostension, or the reference of the name may be fixed by a description.[12] When the name is 'passed from link to link', the receiver of the name must, I think, intend when he learns it to use it with the same reference as the man from whom he heard it. If I hear the name 'Napoleon' and decide it would be a nice name for my pet aardvark, I do not satisfy this condition.[13] (Perhaps it is some such failure to keep the reference fixed which accounts for the divergence of present uses of 'Santa Claus' from the alleged original use.)

Notice that the preceding outline hardly *eliminates* the notion of reference; on the contrary, it takes the notion of intending to use the same reference as a given. There is also an appeal to an initial baptism which is explained in terms either of fixing a reference by a description, or ostension (if ostension is not to be subsumed under the other category).[14] (Perhaps there are other possibilities for initial baptisms.) Further, the George Smith case casts some doubt as to the sufficiency of the conditions. Even if the teacher does refer to his neighbor, is it clear that he has passed on his reference to the pupils? Why shouldn't their belief be about any other man named 'George Smith'? If he says that Newton was hit by an apple, somehow his task of transmitting a reference is easier, since he has communicated a common misconception about Newton.

To repeat, I may not have presented a theory, but I do think that I have presented a better picture than that given by description theorists.

I think the next topic I shall want to talk about is that of statements of identity. Are these necessary or contingent? The matter has been in some dispute in recent philosophy. First, everyone agrees that descriptions can be used to make contingent identity statements. If it is true that the man who invented bifocals was the first Postmaster General of the United States—that these were one and the same—it's contingently true. That is, it might have been the case that one man invented bifocals and another was the first Postmaster General of the United States. So certainly when you make identity statements using descriptions—when you say 'the x such that ϕx and the x such that ψx are one and the same'—that can be a contingent fact. But philosophers have been interested also in the question of identity statements between names. When we say 'Hesperus is Phosphorus' or 'Cicero is Tully', is what we are saying necessary or contingent? Further, they've been interested in another type of identity statement, which comes from scientific theory. We identify, for example, light with electromagnetic radiation between certain limits of wavelengths, or with a stream of photons. We identify heat with the motion of molecules;

sound with a certain sort of wave disturbance in the air; and so on. Concerning such statements the following thesis is commonly held. First, that these are obviously contingent identities: we've found out that light is a stream of photons, but of course it might not have been a stream of photons. Heat is in fact the motion of molecules; we found that out, but heat might not have been the motion of molecules. Secondly, many philosophers feel damned lucky that these examples are around. Now, why? These philosophers, whose views are expounded in a vast literature, hold to a thesis called 'the identity thesis' with respect to some psychological concepts. They think, say, that pain is just a certain material state of the brain or of the body, or what have you—say the stimulation of C-fibers. (It doesn't matter what.) Some people have then objected, 'Well, look, there's perhaps a *correlation* between pain and these states of the body; but this must just be a contingent correlation between two different things, because it was an empirical discovery that this correlation ever held. Therefore, by "pain" we must mean something different from this state of the body or brain; and, therefore, they must be two different things.'

Then it's said, 'ah, but you see, this is wrong! Everyone knows that there can be contingent identities.' First, as in the bifocals and Postmaster General case, which I have mentioned before. Second, in the case, believed closer to the present paradigm, of theoretical identifications, such as light and a stream of photons, or water and a certain compound of hydrogen and oxygen. These are all contingent identities. They might have been false. It's no surprise, therefore, that it can be true as a matter of contingent fact and not of any necessity that feeling pain, or seeing red, is just a certain state of the human body. Such psychophysical identifications can be contingent facts just as the other identities are contingent facts. And of course there are widespread motivations—ideological, or just not wanting to have the 'nomological dangler' of mysterious connections not accounted for by the laws of physics, one to one correlations between two different kinds of thing, material states, and things of an entirely different kind, which lead people to want to believe this thesis.

I guess the main thing I'll talk about first is identity statements between names. But I hold the following about the general case. First, that characteristic theoretical identifications like 'Heat is the motion of molecules', are not contingent truths but necessary truths, and here of course I don't mean just physically necessary, but necessary in the highest degree—whatever that means. (Physical necessity, *might* turn out to be necessity in the highest degree. But that's a question which I don't wish to prejudge.

At least for this sort of example, it might be that when something's physically necessary, it always is necessary *tout court*.) Second, that the way in which these have turned out to be necessary truths does not seem to me to be a way in which the mind-brain identities could turn out to be either necessary or contingently true. So this analogy has to go. It's hard to see what to put in its place. It's hard to see therefore how to avoid concluding that the two are actually different.

Let me go back to the more mundane case about proper names. This is already mysterious enough. There's a dispute about this between Quine and Ruth Barcan Marcus.[15] Marcus says that identities between names are necessary. If someone thinks that Cicero is Tully, and really uses 'Cicero' and 'Tully' as names, he is thereby committed to holding that his belief is a necessary truth. She uses the term 'mere tag'. Quine replies as follows, 'We may tag the planet Venus, some fine evening, with the proper name "Hesperus". We may tag the same planet again, some day before sunrise, with the proper name "Phosphorus". When we discover that we have tagged the same planet twice our discovery is empirical. And not because the proper names were descriptions.'[16] First, as Quine says when we discovered that we tagged the same planet twice, our discovery was empirical. Another example I think Quine gives in another book is that the same mountain seen from Nepal and from Tibet, or something like that, is from one angle called 'Mt. Everest' (you've heard of that); from another it's supposed to be called 'Gaurisanker'. It can actually be an empirical discovery that Gaurisanker is Everest. (Quine says that the example is actually false. He got the example from Erwin Schrödinger. You wouldn't think the inventor of wave mechanics got things that wrong. I don't know where the mistake is supposed to come from. One could certainly imagine this situation as having been the case; and it's another good illustration of the sort of things that Quine has in mind.)

What about it? I wanted to find a good quote on the other side from Marcus in this book but I am having trouble locating one. Being present at that discussion, I remember[17] that she advocated the view that if you really have names, a good dictionary should be able to tell you whether they have the same reference. So someone should be able, by looking in the dictionary, to say that Hesperus and Phosphorus are the same. Now this does not seem to be true. It does seem, to many people, to be a consequence of the view that identities between names are necessary. Therefore the view that identity statements between names are necessary has usually been rejected. Russell's conclusion was somewhat different. He did think there should never be any empirical question whether two names have the same reference. This isn't satisfied for ordinary names, but it is satisfied when you're naming your own sense datum, or something like that. You say, 'Here, this, and that (designating the same sense datum by both demonstratives).' So you can tell without empirical investigation that you're naming the same thing twice; the conditions are satisfied. Since this won't apply to ordinary cases of naming, ordinary 'names' cannot be genuine names.

What should we think about this? First, it's true that someone can use the name 'Cicero' to refer to Cicero and the name 'Tully' to refer to Cicero also, and not know that Cicero is Tully. So it seems that we do not necessarily know *a priori* that an identity statement between names is true. It doesn't follow from this that the statement so expressed is a contingent one if true. This is what I've emphasized in my first lecture. There is a very strong feeling that leads one to think that, if you can't know something by *a priori* ratiocination, then it's got to be contingent: it might have turned out otherwise; but nevertheless I think this feeling is wrong.

Let's suppose we refer to the same heavenly body twice, as 'Hesperus' and 'Phosphorus'. We say: Hesperus is that star over there in the evening; Phosphorus is that star over there in the morning. Actually, Hesperus is Phosphorus. Are there really circumstances under which Hesperus wouldn't have been Phosphorus? Supposing that Hesperus is Phosphorus, let's try to describe a possible situation in which it would not have been. Well, it's easy. Someone goes by and he calls two *different* stars 'Hesperus' and 'Phosphorus'. It may even be under the same conditions as prevailed when we introduced the names 'Hesperus' and 'Phosphorus'. But are those circumstances in which Hesperus is not Phosphorus or would not have been Phosphorus? It seems to me that they are not.

Now, of course I'm committed to saying that they're not, by saying that such terms as 'Hesperus' and 'Phosphorus', when used as names, are rigid designators. They refer in every possible world to the planet Venus. Therefore, in that possible world too, the planet Venus is the planet Venus and it doesn't matter what any other person has said in this other possible world. How should *we* describe this situation? He can't have pointed to Venus twice, and in the one case called it 'Hesperus' and in the other 'Phosphorus', as we did. If he did so, then 'Hesperus is Phosphorus' would have been true in that situation too. He pointed maybe neither time to the planet Venus—at least one time he didn't point to the planet Venus, let's say when he pointed to the body he called 'Phosphorus'. Then in that case we can certainly say that the name 'Phosphorus' might not have referred to Phosphorus. We can even say that in the very position when viewed in the morning that we found Phosphorus, it might have been the case that Phosphorus was not there—that something else was there, and that even, under certain circumstances it would have been *called* 'Phosphorus'. But that still is not a case in which Phosphorus was not Hesperus. There might be a possible world in which, a possible counterfactual situation in which, 'Hesperus' and 'Phosphorus' weren't names of the things they in fact are names of. Someone, if he did determine their reference by identifying descriptions, might even have used the very identifying descriptions we used. But still that's not a case in which Hesperus wasn't Phosphorus. For there couldn't have been such a case, given that Hesperus is Phosphorus.

Now this seems very strange because in advance, we are inclined to say, the answer to the question whether Hesperus is Phosphorus might have turned out either way. So aren't there really two possible worlds—one in which Hesperus was Phosphorus, the other in which Hesperus wasn't Phosphorus—in advance of our discovering that these were the same? First, there's one sense in which things might turn out either way, in which it's clear that that doesn't imply that the way it finally turns out isn't necessary. For example, the four color theorem might turn out to be true and might turn out to be false. It might turn out either way. It still doesn't mean that the way it turns out is not necessary. Obviously, the 'might' here is purely 'epistemic'—it merely expresses our present state of ignorance, or uncertainty.

But it seems that in the Hesperus-Phosphorus case, something even stronger is true. The evidence I have before I know that Hesperus is Phosphorus is that I see a certain star or a certain heavenly body in the evening and call it 'Hesperus', and in the morning and call it 'Phosphorus'. I know these things. There certainly is a possible world in which a man should have seen a certain star at a certain position in the evening and called it 'Hesperus' and a certain star in the morning and called it 'Phosphorus'; and should have concluded—should have found out by empirical investigation—that he names two different stars, or two different heavenly bodies. At least one of these stars or heavenly bodies was not Phosphorus, otherwise it couldn't have come out that way. But that's true. And so it's true that given the evidence that someone has antecedent to his empirical investigation, he can be placed in a sense in exactly the same situation, that is a qualitatively identical epistemic situation, and call two heavenly bodies 'Hesperus' and 'Phosphorus', without their being identical. So in that sense we can say that it might have turned out either way. Not that it might have turned out either way as to Hesperus's being Phosphorus. Though for all we knew in advance, Hesperus wasn't Phosphorus, that couldn't have turned out any other way, in a sense. But being put in a situation where we have exactly the same evidence, qualitatively speaking, it could have turned out that Hesperus was not Phosphorus; that is, in a counterfactual world in which 'Hesperus' and 'Phosphorus' were not used in the way that we use them, as names of this planet, but as names of some other objects, one could have had qualitatively identical evidence and concluded that 'Hesperus' and 'Phosphorus' named two different objects.[18] But we, using the names as we do right now, can say in advance, that if Hesperus and Phosphorus are one and the same, then in no other possible world can they be different. We use 'Hesperus' as the name of a certain body and 'Phosphorus' as the name of a certain body. We use them as names of those bodies in all possible worlds. If, in fact, they are the *same* body, then in any other possible world we have to use them as a name of that object. And so in any other possible world it will be true that Hesperus is Phosphorus. So two things are true: first, that we do not know *a priori* that Hesperus is Phosphorus, and are in no position to find out the answer except empirically. Second, this is so because we could have evidence qualitatively indistinguishable from the evidence we have and determine the reference of the two names by the positions of two planets in the sky, without the planets being the same.

Of course, it is only a contingent truth (not true in every other possible world) that the star seen over there in the evening is the star seen over there in the morning, because there are possible worlds in which Phosphorus was not visible in the morning. But that contingent truth shouldn't be identified with the statement that Hesperus is Phosphorus. It could only be so identified if you thought that it was a necessary truth that Hesperus is visible over there in the evening or that Phosphorus is visible over there in the morning. But neither of those are necessary truths even if that's the way we pick out the planet. These are the contingent marks by which we identify a certain planet and give it a name.

Notes

1. Searle, 'Proper Names', in Caton, *Philosophy and Ordinary Language*, p. 160 [chap. 23, p. 591 herein].

2. D. Lewis, 'Counterpart Theory and Quantified Modal Logic' (*Journal of Philosophy* 65 [1968]), pp. 114–15.

3. An even better case of determining the reference of a name by description, as opposed to ostension, is the discovery of the planet Neptune. Neptune was hypothesized as the planet which caused such and such discrepancies in the orbits of certain other planets. If Leverrier indeed gave the name 'Neptune' to the planet before it was ever seen, then he fixed the reference of 'Neptune' by means of the description just mentioned. At that time he was unable to see the planet even through a telescope. At this stage, an *a priori* material equivalence held between the statements 'Neptune exists' and 'some one planet perturbing the orbit of such and such other planets exists in such and such a position', and also such statements as 'if such and such perturbations are caused by a planet, they are caused by Neptune' had the status of *a priori* truths. Nevertheless, they were not *necessary* truths, since 'Neptune' was introduced as a name rigidly designating a certain planet. Leverrier could well have believed that if Neptune had been knocked off its course one million years earlier, it would have caused no such perturbations and even that some other object might have caused the perturbations in its place.

4. Following Donnellan's remarks on definite descriptions, we should add that in some cases, an object may be identified, and the reference of a name fixed, using a description which may turn out to be false of its object. The case where the reference of 'Phosphorus' is determined as the 'morning star', which later turns out not to be a star, is an obvious example. In such cases, the description which fixes the reference clearly is in no sense known *a priori* to hold of the object, though a more cautious substitute may be. If such a more cautious substitute is available, it is really the substitute which fixes the reference in the sense intended in the text.

5. Some of the theses are sloppily stated in respect of fussy matters like use of quotation marks and related details. (For example, Theses (5) and (6), as stated, presuppose that the speaker's language is English.) Since the purport of the theses is clear, and they are false anyway, I have not bothered to set these things straight.

6. The cluster-of-descriptions theory of naming would make 'Peano discovered the axioms for number theory' express a trivial truth, not a misconception, and similarly for other misconceptions about the history of science. Some who have conceded such cases to me have argued that there are *other* uses of the same proper names satisfying the cluster theory. For example, it is argued, if we say, 'Gödel proved the incompleteness of arithmetic,' we are, of course, referring to Gödel, not to Schmidt. But, if we say, 'Gödel relied on a diagonal argument in this step of the proof,' don't we here, perhaps, refer to *whoever proved the theorem*? Similarly, if someone asks, 'What did Aristotle (or Shakespeare) have in mind here?', isn't he talking about the author of the passage in question, whoever he is? By analogy to Donnellan's usage for descriptions, this might be called an ''attributive' use of proper names. If this is so, then assuming the Gödel-Schmidt story, the sentence 'Gödel proved the incompleteness theorem' is false, but 'Gödel used a diagonal argument in the proof' is (at least in some contexts) true, and the reference of the name 'Gödel' is ambiguous. Since some counterexamples remain, the cluster-of-descriptions theory would still, in general, be false, which was my main point in the text; but it would be applicable in a wider class of cases than I thought. I think, however, that no such ambiguity need be postulated. It is, per-

haps, true that sometimes when someone uses the name 'Gödel', his main interest is in whoever proved the theorem, and *perhaps*, in some sense, he 'refers' to him. If I mistake Jones for Smith, I may *refer* (in an appropriate sense) to Jones when I say that Smith is raking the leaves; nevertheless I do not use 'Smith' ambiguously, as a name sometimes of Smith and sometimes of Jones, but univocally as a name of Smith. Similarly, if I erroneously think that Aristotle wrote such-and-such passage, I may perhaps sometimes use 'Aristotle' to *refer* to the actual author of the passage, even though there is no ambiguity in my use of the name. In both cases, I will withdraw my original statement, and my original use of the name, if apprised of the facts. Recall that, in these lectures, 'referent' is used in the technical sense of the thing named by a name (or uniquely satisfying a description), and there should be no confusion.

7. It has been suggested to me that someone might argue that a name is associated with a 'referential' use of a description in Donnellan's sense. For example, although we identify Gödel as the author of the incompleteness theorem, we are talking about him even if he turns out not to have proved the theorem. Theses (2)–(6) could then fail; but nevertheless each name would abbreviate a description, though the role of description in naming would differ radically from that imagined by Frege and Russell. As I have said above, I am inclined to reject Donnellan's formulation of the notion of referential definite description. Even if Donnellan's analysis is accepted, however, it is clear that the present proposal should not be. For a referential definite description, such as 'the man drinking champagne', is typically withdrawn when the speaker realizes that it does not apply to its object. If a Gödelian fraud were exposed, Gödel would no longer be called 'the author of the incompleteness theorem' but he would still be called 'Gödel'. The name, therefore, does not abbreviate the description.

8. As Robert Nozick pointed out to me, there is a sense in which a description theory must be trivially true if any theory of the reference of names, spelled out in terms independent of the notion of reference, is available. For if such a theory gives conditions under which an object is to be the referent of a name, then it of course uniquely satisfies these conditions. Since I am not pretending to give any theory which eliminates the notion of reference in this sense, I am not aware of any such trivial fulfillment of the description theory and doubt that one exists. (A description using the notion of the reference of a name is easily available but circular, as we saw in our discussion of Kneale.) If any such trivial fulfillment were available, however, the arguments I have given show that the description must be one of a completely different sort from that supposed by Frege, Russell, Searle, Strawson and other advocates of the description theory.

9. Princeton University.

10. Strawson, *Individuals*, p. 182 n.

11. The essential points of this example were suggested by Richard Miller.

12. A good example of a baptism whose reference was fixed by means of a description was that of naming Neptune in n. 3, above. The case of a baptism by ostension can perhaps be subsumed under the description concept also. Thus

the primary applicability of the description theory is to cases of initial baptism. Descriptions are also used to fix a reference in cases of designation which are similar to naming except that the terms introduced are not usually called 'names'. The terms 'one meter', '100 degrees Centigrade', have already been given as examples, and other examples will be given later in these lectures. Two things should be emphasized concerning the case of introducing a name via a description in an initial baptism. First, the description used is not synonymous with the name it introduces but rather fixes its reference. Here we differ from the usual description theorists. Second, most cases of initial baptism are far from those which originally inspired the description theory. Usually a baptizer is acquainted in some sense with the object he names and is able to name it ostensively. Now the inspiration of the description theory lay in the fact that we can often use names of famous figures of the past who are long dead and with whom no living person is acquainted; and it is precisely these cases which, on our view, cannot be correctly explained by a description theory.

13. I can transmit the name of the aardvark to other people. For each of these people, as for me, there will be a certain sort of causal or historical connection between my use of the name and the Emperor of the French, but not one of the required type.

14. Once we realize that the description used to fix the reference of a name is not synonymous with it, then the description theory can be regarded as presupposing the notion of naming or reference. The requirement I made that the description used not itself involve the notion of reference in a circular way is something else and is crucial if the description theory is to have any value at all. The reason is that the description theorist supposes that each speaker essentially uses the description he gives in an initial act of naming to determine his reference. Clearly, if he introduces the name 'Cicero' by the determination, 'By "Cicero" I shall refer to the man I call "Cicero",' he has by this ceremony determined no reference at all.

Not all description theorists thought that they were eliminating the notion of reference altogether. Perhaps some realized that some notion of ostension, or primitive reference, is required to back it up. Certainly Russell did.

15. Ruth Barcan Marcus, 'Modalities and Intensional Languages' (comments by W. V. Quine, plus discussion) *Boston Studies in the Philosophy of Science*, volume I, Reidel, Dordrecht, Holland, 1963, pp. 77–116.

16. p. 101.

17. p. 115.

18. There is a more elaborate discussion of this point in the third lecture, where its relation to a certain sort of counterpart theory is also mentioned.

Chapter 26

The Causal Theory of Names

Gareth Evans

1

In a paper which provides the starting-point of this enquiry Saul Kripke opposes what he calls the Description Theory of Names and makes a counter-proposal of what I shall call the Causal Theory.[1] To be clear about what is at stake and what should be the outcome in the debate he initiated seems to me important for our understanding of talk and thought about the world in general as well as for our understanding of the functioning of proper names. I am anxious therefore that we identify the profound bases and likely generalizations of the opposing positions and do not content ourselves with counter-examples.

I should say that Kripke deliberately held back from presenting his ideas as a theory. I shall have to tighten them up, and I may suggest perhaps unintended directions of generalization; therefore his paper should be checked before the Causal Theory I consider is attributed to him.

There are two related but distinguishable questions concerning proper names. The first is about what the name denotes upon a particular occasion of its use when this is understood as being partly determinative of what the speaker strictly and literally said. I shall use the faintly barbarous coinage: *what the speaker denotes* (upon an occasion) for this notion. The second is about *what the name denotes*; we want to know what conditions have to be satisfied by an expression and an item for the first to be the, or a, name of the second. There is an entirely parallel pair of questions concerning general terms. In both cases it is ambiguity which

First appeared in *Aristotelean Society*, suppl. vol. 47 (1973): 187–208. Reprinted by courtesy of the Aristotelean Society. © 1973.

prevents an easy answer of the first in terms of the second; to denote x it is not sufficient merely to utter something which is x's name.

Consequently there are two Description Theories, not distinguished by Kripke.[2] The Description Theory of speaker's denotation holds that a name 'NN' denotes x upon a particular occasion of its use by a speaker S just in case x is uniquely that which satisfies all or most of the descriptions ϕ such that S would assent to 'NN is ϕ' (or '*That* NN is ϕ'). Crudely: the cluster of information S has associated with the name determines its denotation upon a particular occasion by *fit*. If the speaker has no individuating information he will denote nothing.

The Description Theory of what a name denotes holds that, associated with each name as used by a group of speakers who believe and intend that they are using the name with the same denotation, is a description or set of descriptions cullable from their beliefs which an item has to satisfy to be the bearer of the name. This description is used to explain the role of the name in existential, identity, and opaque contexts. The theory is by no means committed to the thesis that every user of the name must be in possession of the description; just as Kripke is not committed to holding that every user of the expression 'one metre' knows about the metre rod in Paris by saying that its reference is fixed by the description 'Length of stick S in Paris'. Indeed in the description is arrived at in the manner of Strawson[3]—averaging out the different beliefs of different speakers— it is most unlikely that the description will figure in every user's name-associated cluster.

The direct attack in Kripke's paper passes this latter theory by; most conspicuously the charge that the Description Theory ignores the social character of naming. I shall not discuss it explicitly either, though it will surface from time to time and the extent to which it is right should be clear by the end of the paper.

Kripke's direct attacks are unquestionably against the first Description Theory. He argues:

(a) An ordinary man in the street can denote the physicist Feynman by using the name 'Feynman' and say something true or false of him even though there is no description uniquely true of the physicist which he can fashion. (The conditions aren't necessary.)

(b) A person who associated with the name 'Gödel' merely the description 'prover of the incompleteness of Arithmetic' would none the less be denoting Gödel and saying something false of him in uttering 'Gödel proved the incompleteness of Arithmetic' even if an unknown Viennese by the name of Schmidt had in fact constructed the proof which Gödel had subsequently broadcast as his own. (If it is agreed that the speaker does not denote Schmidt the conditions aren't sufficient; if it is also agreed that he denotes Gödel, again they are not necessary.)

The strong thesis (that the Description Theorist's conditions are sufficient) is outrageous. What the speaker denotes in the sense we are concerned with is connected with saying in that strict sense which logicians so rightly prize, and the theory's deliverance of strict truth conditions are quite unacceptable. They would have the consequence, for example, that if I was previously innocent of knowledge or belief regarding Mr Y, and X is wrongly introduced to me as Mr Y, then I must speak the truth in uttering 'Mr Y is here' since X satisfies the overwhelming majority of descriptions I would associate with the name and X is there. I have grave doubts as to whether anyone has ever seriously held this thesis.

It is the weaker thesis—that some descriptive identification is necessary for a speaker to denote something—that it is important to understand. Strictly, Kripke's examples do not show it to be false since he nowhere provides a convincing reason for not taking into account speakers' possession of descriptions like 'man bearing such-and-such a name'; but I too think it is false. It can be seen as the fusion of two thoughts. First: that in order to be saying something by uttering an expression one must utter the sentence with certain intentions; this is felt to require, in the case of sentences containing names, that one be aiming at something with one's use of the name. Secondly—and this is where the underpinning from a certain Philosophy of Mind becomes apparent—to have an intention or belief concerning some item (which one is not in a position to demonstratively identify) one must be in possession of a description uniquely true of it. Both strands deserve at least momentary scrutiny.

We are prone to pass too quickly from the observation that neither parrots nor the wind *say* things to the conclusion that to say that p requires that one must intend to say that p and therefore, so to speak, be able to identify p independently of one's sentence. But the most we are entitled to conclude is that to say something one must intend to say something by uttering one's sentence (one normally will intend to say what it says). The application of the stricter requirement would lead us to relegate too much of our discourse to the status of mere mouthing. We constantly use general terms of whose satisfaction conditions we have but the dimmest idea. 'Microbiologist', 'chlorine' (the stuff in swimming-pools), 'nicotine' (the stuff in cigarettes); these, and countless other words, we cannot define nor offer remarks which would distinguish their meaning from that of closely related words. It is wrong to say that we say nothing by uttering sentences containing these expressions, even if we recoil from the strong thesis, from saying that what we do say is determined by those hazy ideas and half-identifications we would offer if pressed.

The Philosophy of Mind is curiously popular but rarely made perfectly explicit.[4] It is held by anyone who holds that S believes that a is F and only if

$$\exists\phi[(S \text{ believes } \exists x(\phi x \& (\forall y)(\phi y \to x = y) \& Fx))$$
$$\& \phi a \& (\forall y)(\phi y \to y = a)]$$

Obvious alterations would accommodate the other psychological attitudes. The range of the property quantifier must be restricted to exclude such properties as 'being identical with a', otherwise the criterion is trivial.[5] The situation in which a thinking, planning or wanting human has some item which is the object of his thought, plan or desire is represented as a species of essentially the same situation as that which holds when there is no object and the thought, plan or desire is, as we might say, purely general. There are thoughts, such as the thought that there are eleven-fingered men, for whose expression general terms of the language suffice. The idea is that when the psychological state involves an object, a general term believed to be uniquely instantiated and in fact uniquely instantiated by the item which is the object of the state will figure in its specification. This idea may be coupled with a concession that there are certain privileged objects to which one may be more directly related; indeed such a concession appears to be needed if the theory is to be able to allow what appears an evident possibility; object-directed thoughts in a perfectly symmetrical or cyclical universe.

This idea about the nature of object-directed psychological attitudes obviously owes much to the feeling that there must be something we can say about what is believed or wanted even when there is no appropriate object actually to be found in the world. But it can also be seen as deriving support from a Principle of Charity: so attribute objects to beliefs that true belief is maximized. (I do not think this is an acceptable principle; the acceptable principle enjoins minimizing the attribution of *inexplicable* error and therefore cannot be operated without a theory of the causation of belief for the creatures under investigation.)

We cannot deal comprehensively with this Philosophy of Mind here. My objections to it are essentially those of Wittgenstein. For an item to be the object of some psychological attitude of yours may be simply for you to be placed in a context which relates you to that thing. What makes it one rather than the other of pair of identical twins that you are in love with? Certainly not some specification blueprinted in your mind; it may be no more than this: it was one of them and not the other that you have met. The theorist may gesture to the description 'the one I have met' but can give no explanation for the impossibility of its being outweighed by other descriptions which may have been acquired as a result of error and which may in fact happen to fit the other, unmet, twin. If God had looked into your mind, he would not have seen there with whom you were in love, and of whom you were thinking.

With that I propose to begin considering the Causal Theory.

2

The Causal Theory as stated by Kripke goes something like this. A speaker, using a name 'NN' on a particular occasion will denote some item x if there is a causal chain of *reference-preserving links* leading back from his use on that occasion ultimately to the item x itself being involved in a name-acquiring transaction such as an explicit dubbing or the more gradual process whereby nicknames stick. I mention the notion of a reference-preserving link to incorporate a condition that Kripke lays down; a speaker S's transmission of a name 'NN' to a speaker S' constitutes a reference-preserving link only if S intends to be using the name with the same denotation as he from whom he in his turn learned the name.

Let us begin by considering the theory in answer to our question about speaker's denotation (i.e., at the level of the individual speaker). In particular, let us consider the thesis that it is *sufficient* for someone to denote x on a particular occasion with the name that this use of the name on that occasion be a causal consequence of his exposure to other speakers using the expression to denote x.

An example which might favorably dispose one towards the theory is this. A group of people are having a conversation in a pub, about a certain Louis of whom S has never heard before. S becomes interested and asks: 'What did Louis do then?' There seems to be no question but that S denotes a particular man and asks about him. Or on some subsequent occasion S may use the name to offer some new thought to one of the participants: 'Louis was quite right to do that.' Again he clearly denotes whoever was the subjects of conversation in the pub. This is difficult to reconcile with the Description Theory since the scraps of information which he picked up during the conversation might involve some distortion and fit someone else much better. Of course he has the description 'the man they were talking about' but the theory has no explanation for the impossibility of its being outweighed.

The Causal Theory can secure the right answer in such a case but I think deeper reflection will reveal that it too involves a refusal to recognize the insight about contextual determination I mentioned earlier. For the theory has the following consequence: that at any future time, no matter how remote or forgotten the conversation, no matter how alien the subject-matter and confused the speaker, S will denote one particular Frenchman—perhaps Louis XIII—so long as there is a causal connection between his use at that time and the long-distant conversation.

It is important in testing your intuitions against the theory that you imagine the predicate changed—so that he says something like 'Louis was a basketball player' which was not heard in the conversation and which arises as a result of some confusion. This is to prevent the operation of what I call the 'mouthpiece syndrome' by which we attach sense and reference to a man's remarks only because we hear someone else speaking through him; as we might with a messenger, carrying a message about matters of which he was entirely ignorant.

Now there is no knock-down argument to show this consequence unacceptable; with pliant enough intuitions you can swallow anything in philosophy. But notice how little *point* there is in saying that he denotes one French king rather than any other, or any other person named by the name. There is now nothing that the speaker is prepared to say or do which relates him differentially to that one king. This is why it is so outrageous to say that he believes that Louis XIII is a basketball player. The notion of saying has simply been severed from all the connections that made it of interest. Certainly we did not think we were letting ourselves in for this when we took the point about the conversation in the pub. What has gone wrong?[6]

The Causal Theory again ignores the importance of surrounding context, and regards the capacity to denote something as a magic trick which has somehow been passed on, and once passed on cannot be lost. We should rather say: in virtue of the context in which the man found himself the man's dispositions were bent towards one particular man—Louis XIII—whose states and doings alone he would count as serving to verify remarks made in that context using the name. And of course that context can persist, for the conversation can itself be adverted to subsequently. But it can also disappear so that the speaker is simply not sensitive to the outcome of any investigations regarding the truth of what he is said to have said. And at this point saying becomes detached, and uninteresting.

(It is worth observing how ambivalent Kripke is on the relation between denoting and believing; when the connection favours him he uses it; we are reminded for example that the ordinary man has a false belief about Gödel and not a true belief about Schmidt. But it is obvious that the results of the 'who are they believing about?' criterion are bound to come dramatically apart from the results of the 'who is the original bearer of the name?' criterion, if for no other reason than that the former must be constructed to give results in cases where there is no name and where the latter cannot apply. When this happens we are sternly reminded that 'X refers' and 'X says' are being used in *technical* senses.[7] But there are limits. One could regard the aim of this paper to restore the connection which must exist between strict truth conditions and the beliefs and interests of the users of the sentences if the technical notion of strict truth conditions is to be of interest to us.)

Reflection upon the conversation in the pub appeared to provide one reason for being favourably disposed towards the Causal Theory. There is another connected reason we ought to examine briefly. It might appear that the Causal Theory provides the basis for a general non-intentional answer to the Problem of Ambiguity. The problem is clear enough: What conditions have to be satisfied for a speaker to have said that p when he utters a sentence which may appropriately be used to say that q and that r and that s in addition? Two obvious alternative answers are:

(a) the extent to which it is reasonable for his audience to conclude that he was saying that p
(b) his intending to say that p

and neither is without its difficulties. We can therefore imagine someone is hoping for a natural extension of the Causal Theory to general terms which would enable him to explain for example how a child who did not have determinative intentions because of the technical nature of the subject-matter may still say something determinate using a sentence which is in fact ambiguous.

I touch upon this to ensure that we are keeping the range of relevant considerations to be brought to bear upon the debate as wide as it must be. But I think little general advantage can accrue to the Causal Theory from thus broadening the considerations. The reason is that it simply fails to have the generality of the other two theories; it has no obvious application, for example, to syntactic ambiguity or to ambiguity produced by attempts to refer with nonunique descriptions, or pronouns. It seems inconceivable that the general theory of disambiguation required for such cases would be inadequate to deal with the phenomenon of shared names and would require *ad hoc* supplementation from the Causal Theory.

I want to stress how, precisely because the Causal Theory ignores the way context can be determinative of what gets *said*, it has quite unacceptable consequences. Suppose, for example, on a TV quiz programme I am asked to name a capital city and I say 'Kingston is the capital of Jamaica'; I should want to say that I had said something strictly and literally true even though it turns out that the man from whom I had picked up this scrap of information was actually referring to Kingston upon Thames and making a racist observation.

It may begin to appear that what gets said is going to be determined by what name is used, what items bear the name, and general principles of contextual disambiguation. The causal origin of the speaker's familiarity with the name, save in certain specialized 'mouthpiece cases', does not seem to have a critical role to play.

This impression may be strengthened by the observation that a causal connection between my use of the name and use by others (whether or not leading back ultimately to the item itself) is simply not necessary for me to use the name to say something. Amongst the Wagera Indians, for example, 'newly born children receive the names of deceased members of their family according to strict rules ... the first born takes on the name of the paternal grandfather, the second that of the father's eldest brother, the third that of the maternal grandfather'.[8] In these and other situations (names for streets in US cities etc.) a knowledgeable speaker may excogitate a name and use it to denote some item which bears it without any causal connection whatever with the use by others of that name.

These points might be conceded by Kripke while maintaining the general position that the denotation of a name in a community is still to be found by tracing a causal chain of reference preserving links back to some item. It is to this theory that I now turn.

3

Suppose a parallel theory were offered to explain the sense of general terms (not just terms for natural kinds). One would reply as follows:

'There aren't two fundamentally different mechanisms involved in a word's having a meaning: one bringing it about that a word acquires a meaning, and the other—a causal mechanism—which operates to ensure that its meaning is preserved. The former processes are operative all the time; whatever explains how a word gets its meaning also explains how it preserves it, if preserved it is. Indeed such a theory could not account for the phenomenon of a word's changing its meaning. It is perfectly possible for this to happen without anyone's intending to initiate a new practice with the word; the causal chain would then lead back too far.'

Change of meaning would be decisive against such a theory of the meaning of general terms. Change of denotation is similarly decisive against the Causal Theory of Names. Not only are changes of denotation imaginable, but it appears that they actually occur. We learn from Isaac Taylor's *Names and their History* (1898):

In the case of 'Madagascar' a hearsay report of Malay or Arab sailors misunderstood by Marco Polo ... has had the effect of transferring a corrupt form of the name of a portion of the African mainland to the great African Island.

A simple imaginary case would be this: two babies are born, and their mothers bestow names upon them. A nurse inadvertently switches them and the error is never discovered. It will henceforth undeniably be the case that the man universally known as 'Jack' is so called because a woman dubbed some other baby with the name.

It is clear that the Causal Theory unamended is not adequate. It looks as though, once again, the intentions of the speakers to use the name to refer to something must be allowed to count in determination of what it denotes.

But it is not enough to say that and leave matters there. We must at least sketch a theory which will enable 'Madagascar' to be the name of the island yet which will not have the consequence that 'Gödel' would become a name of Schmidt in the situation envisaged by Kripke, nor 'Goliath' a name of the Philistine killed by David. (Biblical scholars now suggest that David did not kill Goliath, and that the attribution of the slaying to Elhannan the Bethlehemite in 2 Sam. 21: 19 is correct. David is thought to have killed a Philistine but not Goliath.)[9] For although this has never been explicitly argued I would agree that even if the 'information' connected with the name in possession of an entire community was merely that 'Goliath was the Philistine David slew' this would still not mean that 'Goliath' referred in that community to that man, and therefore that the sentence expressed a truth. And if we simultaneously thought that the name *would* denote the Philistine slain by Elhannan then both the necessity and sufficiency of the conditions suggested by the Description Theory of the denotation of a name are rejected. This is the case Kripke should have argued but didn't.

4

Before going on to sketch such a theory in the second part of this paper let me survey the position arrived at and use it to make a summary statement of the position I wish to adopt.

We can see the undifferentiated Description Theory as the expression of two thoughts.

(a) The denotation of a name is determined by what speakers intend to refer to by using the name.
(b) The object a speaker intends to refer to by his use of a name is that which satisfies or fits the majority of descriptions which make up the cluster of information which the speaker has associated with the name.

We have seen great difficulties with (a) when this is interpreted as a thesis at the micro-level. But consideration of the phenomenon of a name's getting a denotation, or changing it, suggests that there being a community of speakers using the name with such-and-such as the intended referent is likely to be a crucial constituent in these processes. With names as with other expressions in the language, what they signify depends upon what we use them to signify; a truth whose recognition is compatible with denying the collapse of saying into meaning at the level of the individual speaker.

It is in (b) that the real weakness lies: the bad old Philosophy of Mind which we momentarily uncovered. Not so much in the idea that the intended referent is determined in a more or less complicated way by the associated information, but the specific form the determination was supposed to take: *fit*. There is something absurd in supposing that the intended referent of some perfectly ordinary use of a name by a speaker could be some item utterly isolated (causally) from the user's community and culture simply in virtue of the fact that it fits better than anything else the cluster of descriptions he associates with the name. I would agree with Kripke in thinking that the absurdity resides in the absence of the causal relation between the item concerned and the speaker. But it seems to me that he has mislocated the causal relation; the important causal relation lies between that item's states and doings and the speaker's body of information—not between the item's being dubbed with a name and the speaker's contemporary use of it.

Philosophers have come increasingly to realize that major concepts in epistemology and the philosophy of mind have causality embedded within them. Seeing and knowing are both good examples.

The absurdity in supposing that the denotation of our contemporary use of the name 'Aristotle' could be some unknown (n.b.) item whose doings are causally isolated from our body of information is strictly parallel to the absurdity in supposing that one might be seeing something one has no causal contact with solely upon the ground that there is a splendid match between object and visual impression.

There probably is some *degree of fit* requirement in the case of seeing which means that after some amount of distortion or fancy we can no longer maintain that the causally operative item was still being seen. And I think it is likely that there is a parallel requirement for referring. We learn, for example, from E. K. Chambers's *Arthur of Britain* that Arthur had a son Anir 'whom legend has perhaps confused with his burial place'. If Kripke's notion of reference fixing is such that those who said Anir was a burial place of Arthur might be denoting a person it seems that it has little to commend it, and is certainly not justified by the criticism he makes against the Description Theory. But the existence or nature of this 'degree of fit' requirement will not be something I shall be concerned with here.

We must allow, then, that the denotation of a name in the community will depend in a complicated way upon what those who use the term intend to refer to, but we will so understand 'intended referent' that typically a *necessary* (but not sufficient) condition for x's being the intended referent of S's use of a name is that x should be the source of causal origin of the body of information that S has associated with the name.

5

The aim I have set myself, then, is modest; it is not to present a complete theory of the denotation of names. Without presenting a general theory to solve the problem of ambiguity I cannot present a theory of speaker's denotation, although I will make remarks which prejudice that issue. I propose merely to sketch an account of what makes an expression into a name for something that will allow names to change their denotations.

The enterprise is more modest yet for I propose to help myself to an undefined notion of speaker's reference by borrowing from the theory of communication. But a word of explanation.

A speaker may have succeeded in *getting it across* or in *communicating* that p even though he uses a sentence which may not appropriately be used to say that p. Presumably this success consists in his audience's having formed a belief about him. This need not be the belief that the speaker intended to say in the strict sense that p, since the speaker may succeed in getting something across despite using a sentence which he is known to know cannot appropriately be used to say that p. The speaker will have referred to a, in the sense that I am helping myself to, only if he has succeeded in getting it across that Fa (for some substitution F). Further stringent conditions are required. Clearly this notion is quite different from the notion of denotation which I have been using, tied as denotation is to saying in the strict sense. One may refer to x by using a description that x does not satisfy; one may not thus denote x.

Now a speaker may know or believe that there is such-and-such an item in the world and intend to refer to it. And this is where the suggestion made earlier must be brought to bear, for *that* item is not (in general) the satisfier of the body of information the possession by the speaker of which makes it true that he knows of the existence of the item; it is rather that item which is causally responsible for the speaker's possession of that body of information, or dominantly responsible if there is more than one. (The point is of course not specific to this intention, or to intention as opposed to other psychological attitudes.) Let us then, very briefly, explore these two ideas: source and dominance.

Usually our knowledge or belief about particular items is derived from information-gathering transactions, involving a causal interaction with some item or other, conducted ourselves or is derived, maybe through a long chain, from the transactions of others. Perception of the item is the main but by no means the only way an item can impress itself on us; for example, a man can be the source of things we discover by rifling through his suitcase or by reading his works.

A causal relation is of course not sufficient; but we may borrow from the theory of knowledge and say something like this. X is the source of the belief S expresses by uttering 'Fa' if there was an episode which caused S's belief in which X and S were causally related in a type of situation apt for producing knowledge that something F-s($\exists x(Fx)$)—a type of situation in which the belief that something F-s would be caused by something's F-ing. That it is a way of producing knowledge does not mean that it cannot go wrong; that is why X, by smoking French cigarettes, can be the source of the belief S expresses by 'a smokes Greek cigarettes'.

Of course some of our information about the world is not so based; we may deduce that there is a tallest man in the world and deduce that he is over 6 feet tall. No man is the source of this information; a name introduced in relation to it might function very much as the unamended Description Theory suggested.

Legend and fancy can create new characters, or add bodies of source-less material to other dossiers; restrictions on the causal relation would prevent the inventors of the legends turning out to be the sources of the beliefs their legends gave rise to. Someone other than the ϕ can be the source of the belief S expresses by 'a is the ϕ'; Kripke's Gödel, by claiming the proof, was the source of the belief people manifested by saying 'Gödel proved the incompleteness of Arithmetic', not Schmidt.

Misidentification can bring it about that the item which is the source of the information is different from the item about which the information is believed. I may form the belief about the wife of some colleague that she has nice legs upon the basis of seeing someone else—but the girl I saw is the source.

Consequently a cluster or dossier of information can be dominantly *of* [10] an item though it contains elements whose source is different. And we surely want to allow that persistent misidentification can bring it about that a cluster is dominantly of some item other than that it was dominantly of originally.

Suppose I get to know a man slightly. Suppose then a suitably primed identical twin takes over his position, and I get to know him fairly well, not noticing the switch. Immediately after the switch my dossier will still be dominantly of the original man, and I falsely believe, as I would acknowledge if it was pointed out, that *he* is in the room. Then I would pass through a period in which neither was dominant; I had not mis-identified one as the other, an asymmetrical relation, but rather confused them. Finally the twin could take over the dominant position; I would not have false beliefs about who is in the room, but false beliefs about, for example, when I first met the man in the room. These differences seem to

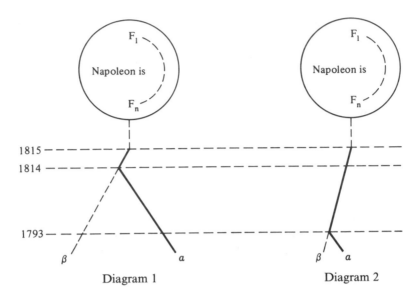

Diagram 1   Diagram 2

reside entirely in the differences in the believer's reactions to the various discoveries, and dominance is meant to capture those differences.

Dominance is not simply a function of *amount* of information (if that is even intelligible). In the case of persons, for example, each man's life presents a skeleton and the dominant source may be the man who contributed to covering most of it rather than the man who contributed most of the covering. Detail in a particular area can be outweighed by spread. Also the believer's reasons for being interested in the item at all will weigh.

Consider another example. If it turns out that an impersonator had taken over Napoleon's role from 1814 onwards (post-Elba), the cluster of the typical historian would still be dominantly of the man responsible for the earlier exploits (α in Diagram 1) and we would say that they had false beliefs about who fought at Waterloo. If however the switch had occurred much earlier, it being an unknown Army Officer being impersonated, then their information would be dominantly of the later man (β in Diagram 2). They did not have false beliefs about who was the general at Waterloo, but rather false beliefs about that general's early career.

I think we can say that *in general* a speaker intends to refer to the item that is the dominant source of his associated body of information. It is important to see that this will not change from occasion to occasion depending upon subject-matter. Some have proposed[11] that if in case 1 the historian says 'Napoleon fought skilfully at Waterloo' it is the imposter β who is the intended referent, while if he had said in the next breath '... unlike his performance in the Senate' it would be α. This seems a mistake; not only was what the man said false, what he intended to say was false too, as he would be the first to agree; it wasn't Napoleon who fought skilfully at Waterloo.

With this background, then, we may offer the following tentative definition:

'NN' is a name of x if there is a community C
1. in which it is common knowledge that members of C have in their repertoire the procedure of using 'NN' to refer to x (with the intention of referring to x)
2. the success in reference in any particular case being intended to rely on common knowledge between speaker and hearer that 'NN' has been used to refer to x by members of C and not upon common knowledge of the satisfaction by x of some predicate embedded in 'NN'.[12]

(In order to keep the definition simple no attempt is made to cover the sense in which an unused institutionally approved name is a name.)

This distinction (between use-because-(we know)-we-use-it and use upon other bases) is just what is needed to distinguish dead from live metaphors; it seems to me the only basis on which to distinguish referential functioning of names, which may grammatically be descriptions, from that of descriptions.[13]

The definition does not have the consequence that the description 'the man we call "NN"'' is a name, for *its* success as a referential device does not rely upon common knowledge that *it* is or has been used to refer to x.

Intentions alone don't bring it about that a name gets a denotation; without the intentions being manifest there cannot be the common knowledge required for the practice.

Our conditions are more stringent than Kripke's since for him an expression becomes a name just so long as someone has dubbed something with it and thereby caused it to be in common usage. This seems little short of magical. Suppose one of a group of villagers dubbed a little girl on holiday in the vicinity 'Goldilocks' and the name caught on. However suppose that there were two identical twins the villagers totally fail to distinguish. I should deny that 'Goldilocks' is the name of either— even if by some miracle each villager used the name consistently but in no sense did they fall into two coherent sub-communities. (The name might denote the girl first dubbed if for some peculiar reason the villagers were deferential to the introducer of the name—of this more below.)

Consider the following case. An urn is discovered in the Dead Sea containing documents on which are found fascinating mathematical proofs. Inscribed at the bottom is the name 'Ibn Khan' which is quite naturally taken to be the name of the constructor of the proofs. Consequently it passes into common usage amongst mathematicians concerned with that branch of mathematics. 'Khan conjectured here that ...' and the like. However suppose the name was the name of the scribe who had transcribed the proofs much later; a small '*id scripsit*' had been obliterated.

Here is a perfect case where there is a coherent community using the name with the mathematician as the intended referent and a consequence of the definition would be that 'Ibn Khan' would be one of his names. Also, 'Malachi' would have been the name of the author of the biblical work of the same name despite that its use was based upon a misapprehension ('Malachi' means my messenger).[14]

Speakers within such traditions use names under the misapprehension that their use is in conformity with the use of other speakers referring to the relevant item. The names would probably be withdrawn when that misapprehension is revealed, or start a rather different life as 'our' names for the items (cf. 'Deutero Isaiah' etc.). One might be impressed by this, and regard it as a reason for denying that those within these traditions spoke the literal truth in using the names. It is very easy to add a codicil to the definition which would have this effect.

Actually it is not a very good reason for denying that speakers within such traditions are speaking the literal truth.[15] But I do not want to insist upon any decision on this point. This is because one can be concessive and allow the definition to be amended without giving up anything of importance. First: the definition with its codicil will still allow many names to change their denotation. Secondly: from the fact that, in our example, the community of mathematicians were not denoting the mathematician it obviously fails to follow that they were denoting the scribe and were engaged in strictly speaking massive falsehood of him.

Let me elaborate the first of these points.

There is a fairly standard way in which people get their names. If we use a name of a man we expect that it originated in the standard manner and this expectation may condition our use of it. But consider names for people which are obviously nicknames, or names for places or pieces of music. Since there is no standard way in which these names are bestowed subsequent users will not in general use the name under any view as to its origin, and therefore when there is a divergence between the item involved in the name's origin and the speakers' intended referent there will be no *mis*apprehension, no latent motive for withdrawing the name, and thus no bar to the name's acquiring a new denotation even by the amended definition. So long as they have no reason to believe that the name has dragged any information with it, speakers will treat the revelation that the name had once been used to refer to something different with the same sort of indifference as that with which they greet the information that 'meat' once meant groceries in general.

We can easily tell the story in case 2 of our Napoleon diagram so that α was the original bearer of the name 'Napoleon' and it was transferred to the counterfeit because of the similarity of their appearances and therefore without the intention on anyone's part to initiate a new practice. Though this is not such a clear case I should probably say that historians have used the name 'Napoleon' to refer to β. They might perhaps abandon it, but that of course fails to show that they were all denoting α. Nor does the fact that someone in the know might come along and say 'Napoleon was a fish salesman and was never at Waterloo' show anything. The relevant question is: 'Does this contradict the assertion that was made when the historians said "Napoleon was at Waterloo"?' To give an affirmative answer to this question requires the prior determination that they have all along been denoting α.

We need one further and major complication. Although standardly we use expressions with the intention of conforming to the general use made of them by the community, sometimes we use them with the *overriding* intention to conform to the use made of them by some other person or persons. In that case I shall say that we use the expression *deferentially* (with respect to that other person or group of persons). This is true of some general terms too: 'viol', 'minuet' would be examples.

I should say, for example, that the man in the conversation in the pub used 'Louis' deferentially. This is not just a matter of his ignorance; he could, indeed, have an opinion as to who this Louis is (the man he met earlier perhaps) but still use the expression deferentially. There is an important gap between

intending to refer to the ϕ and believing that $a = $ the ϕ;

intending to refer to a

for even when he has an opinion as to who they are talking about I should say that it was the man they were talking about, and not the man he met earlier, that he intended to refer to.

Archaeologists might find a tomb in the desert and claim falsely that it is the burial place of some little known character in the Bible. They could discover a great deal about the man in the tomb so that he and not the character in the Bible was the dominant source of their information. But, given the nature and point of their enterprise, the archaeologists are using the name deferentially to the authors of the Bible. I should say, then, that they denote that man, and say false things about him. Notice that in such a case there is some point to this characterization.

The case is in fact no different from any situation in which a name is used with the overriding intention of referring to something satisfying such-and-such a description. Kripke gives the example of 'Jack the Ripper'. Again, after the arrest of a man a not in fact responsible for the crimes, a can be the dominant source of speakers' information but the intended referent could well be the murderer and not a. Again this will be productive of a whole lot of falsehood.

We do not use all names deferentially, least of all deferentially to the person from whom we picked them up. For example, the mathematicians did not use the name 'Ibn Khan' with the *overriding* intention of referring to whoever bore that name or was referred to by some other person or community.

We must thus be careful to distinguish two reasons for something that would count as 'withdrawing sentences containing the name'

(a) the item's not bearing the name 'NN' ('Ibn Khan', 'Malachi')
(b) the item's not being NN (the biblical archaeologists).

I shall end with an example that enables me to draw these threads together and summarize where my position differs from the Causal Theory.

A youth A leaves a small village in the Scottish highlands to seek his fortune having acquired the nickname 'Turnip' (the reason for choosing a nickname is I hope clear). Fifty or so years later a man B comes to the village and lives as a hermit over the hill. The three or four villagers surviving from the time of the youth's departure believe falsely that this is the long-departed villager returned. Consequently they use the name 'Turnip' among themselves and it gets into wider circulation among the younger villagers who have no idea how it originated. I am assuming that the older villagers, if the facts were pointed out, would say 'It isn't Turnip after all' rather than 'It appears after all that Turnip did not come from this village.' In that case I should say that they use the name to refer to A, and in fact, denoting him, say false things about him (even by uttering 'Here is Turnip coming to get his coffee again').

But they may die off, leaving a homogeneous community using the name to refer to the man over the hill. I should say the way is clear to its becoming his name. The story is not much affected if the older villagers pass on some information whose source is A by saying such things as 'Turnip was quite a one for the girls', for the younger villagers' clusters would still be dominantly of the man over the hill. But it is an important feature of my account that the information that the older villagers gave the younger villagers could be so rich, coherent, and important to them that A could be the dominant source of their information, so that they too would acknowledge 'That man over the hill isn't Turnip after all.'

A final possibility would be if they used the name deferentially towards the older villagers, for some reason, with the consequence that no matter who was dominant they denote whoever the elders denote.

6   CONCLUSION

Espousers of both theories could reasonably claim to be vindicated by the position we have arrived at. We have secured for the Description Theorist much that he wanted. We have seen that for at least the most fundamental case of the use of names (non-deferentially used names) the idea that their denotation is fixed in a more or less complicated way by the associated bodies of information that one could cull from the users of the name turns out not to be so wide of the mark. But of course that the fix is by causal origin and not by fit crucially affects the impact this idea has upon the statement of the truth conditions of existential or opaque sentences containing names. The theorist can also point to the idea of dominance as securing what he was trying, admittedly crudely, to secure with his talk of the 'majority of' the descriptions, and to the 'degree of fit requirement' as blocking consequences he found objectionable.

The Causal Theorist can also look with satisfaction upon the result, incorporating as it does his insight about the importance of causality into a central position. Further, the logical doctrines he was concerned to establish, for example the non-contingency of identity statements made with the use of names, are not controverted. Information is individuated by source; if *a* is the source of a body of information nothing else could have been. Consequently nothing else could have been *that a*.

The only theorists who gain no comfort are those who, ignoring Kripke's explicit remarks to the contrary,[16] supposed that the Causal Theory could provide them with a totally *non-intentional* answer to the problem posed by names. But I am not distressed by their distress.

Our ideas also point forward; for it seems that they, or some close relative, must be used in explaining the functioning of at least some demonstratives. Such an expression as 'That mountaineer' in 'That mountaineer is coming to town tonight' may avert to a body of information presumed in common possession, perhaps through the newspapers, which fixes its denotation. No one can be *that* mountaineer unless he is the source of that information no matter how perfectly he fits it, and of course someone can be that mountaineer and fail to fit quite a bit of it. It is in such generality that defence of our ideas must lie.

But with these hints I must leave the subject.

Notes

1. S. A. Kripke, 'Naming and Necessity', in D. Davidson and G. Harman (eds), *Semantics of Natural Language* (Dordrecht: Reidel, 1972), pp. 253–355 (+ Appendix). [Lecture II appears as chap. 25 in this vol.]

2. This can be seen in the way the list of theses defining the Description Theory alternate between those mentioning a speaker and those that don't, culminating in the uneasy idea of an idiolect of one. The Description Theorists of course do not themselves distinguish them clearly either, and many espouse both.

3. P. F. Strawson, *Individuals* (London: Methuen, 1959), p. 191.

4. See, e.g., J. R. Searle, *Speech Acts* (Cambridge: Cambridge University Press, 1969), p. 87; E. Gellner, 'Ethics and Logic', *Proceedings of the Aristotelian Society* 55 (1954–5), pp. 157–78; B. Russell, *Problems of Philosophy* (Oxford: Oxford University Press, paperback 1976), p. 29. E. Sosa criticizes it in 'Quantifiers Belief and Sellars', in J. W. Davis, D. J. Hockney, and W. K. Wilson (eds), *Philosophical Logic* (Dordrecht: Reidel, 1969), p. 69.

5. I owe this observation to G. Harman.

6. Kripke expresses doubts about the sufficiency of the conditions for this sort of reason, see op. cit., p. 303.

7. Ibid., p. 348 fn.

8. E. Delhaise, 'Les Wagera', *Monogr. Ethnogr.* (1909).

9. H. W. Robinson, *The History of Israel* (London: Duckworth, 1941), p. 187.

10. The term is D. Kaplan's, see 'Quantifying In', in D. Davidson and J. Hintikka (eds), *Words and objections* (Dordrecht: Reidel, 1969): I think there are clear

similarities between my notion of a dominant source and notions he is there sketching. However I want nothing to do with vividness. I borrow the term 'dossier' from H. P. Grice's paper 'Vacuous Names' in the same volume.

11. K. S. Donnellan, 'Proper Names and Identifying Descriptions', in Davidson and Harman (eds), op. cit., p. 371.

12. For the notion of 'common knowledge', see D. K. Lewis, *Convention* (Cambridge, Mass.: Harvard University Press, 1969) and the slightly different notion in S. R. Schiffer, *Meaning* (Oxford: Clarendon Press, 1972). For the notion of 'a procedure in the repertoire' see H. P. Grice 'Utterer's Meaning, Sentence Meaning, Word Meaning', *Foundations of Language* (1968). Clearly the whole enterprise owes much to Grice but no commitment is here made to any specific version of the theory of communication.

13. And if Schiffer is right much more as well—see *Meaning*, chap. V.

14. See O. Eissfeldt, *The Old Testament: An Introduction* (Oxford: Oxford University Press, 1965), p. 441.

15. John McDowell has persuaded me of this, as of much else. He detests my conclusions.

16. Kripke, op. cit., p. 302.

PART V
DEMONSTRATIVES

INTRODUCTION

Demonstratives are expressions like 'this', 'that', 'him', 'her', etc. What is characteristic about demonstratives is that their content is highly context-sensitive. So, for example, every time I use the name 'Winston Churchill', it has the same content, but virtually every time I use the demonstrative 'that', it has a different content, and its content will depend on which object I demonstrate.

In part I we encountered a number of readings that suggested that the most promising way to achieve a theory of meaning is via some form of a Davidsonian T-theory. For some reason, many commentators have supposed that T-theories cannot easily accommodate demonstrative expressions, and by extension, extremely context-sensitive expressions. Where this idea comes from is completely opaque to me, as an account of demonstrative expressions in a T-theoretic framework already appears in Davidson's "Truth and Meaning" (chapter 5 in this volume). A more detailed account is provided in Scott Weinstein's "Truth and Demonstratives." As work like Weinstein's shows, there is really no serious controversy as to whether the context-sensitive nature of demonstratives can be accommodated by T-theories (it can).

Another issue about demonstratives is also pretty much uncontroversial—the issue of whether they are rigid designators (they are). In the past there have been proposals to try an assimilate demonstratives to descriptions ("the object at which I now point"), but as David Kaplan argues in "Dthat," demonstratives, like names, are in fact rigid designators.

So far we seem to have two uncontroversial things that we know about demonstratives, but the area is hardly free from controversy. One of the most contentious issues turns on the nature of the "character" or "role" of demonstratives and the consequences for semantic theory. Character (or role) is that part of the meaning of a demonstrative that is constant between uses. There is something we know about the meaning of 'that',

that isn't enough to fix the content of the demonstrative but takes us from various contexts to the appropriate contents. This is not a trivial thing.

The question is, What is the semantic nature of this constant meaning? Frege, in "The Thought" (chapter 1 in this volume) appears to think the constant meaning can be assimilated to sense, but John Perry argues that the Fregean solution will not do. To illustrate this problem I'll borrow a story from another of Perry's papers.

John is shopping in the supermarket, aimlessly pushing his grocery cart up and down the aisles. At a certain point he sees a trail of sugar, no doubt spilling from some poor shopper's cart. Let's suppose that John forms the following belief.

(1) The person pushing that cart is making a mess.

Being a good citizen, John decides to find the person spilling the sugar and begins following the trail. He follows the trail around to the next aisle, down past the canned vegetables, around the next corner up the aisle, and then suddenly notices that the trail of sugar has become thicker. He looks down and sees that *he* is spilling sugar. John suddenly forms a new belief.

(2) *I* am making a mess.

Notice that both propositions (1) and (2) are about John, but notice that when John knows (2), he knows something that he didn't know when he knew only (1).

One might object here that the knowledge expressed in (1) is not really about John but is really an example of knowledge by description. That is fair enough. But the objection can be recast without recourse to definite descriptions. The following example (I believe) is from Howard Wettstein.

Suppose that I am in an unfamiliar building and I see a man about to be attacked by a ferocious dog. I think (3):

(3) Oh no, that poor man is about to be attacked by a dog.

But unknown to me, this is a house of mirrors, and the mirrors are arranged so that I am actually looking at myself. I soon discover the unfortunate truth, and come to know (4):

(4) Oh no, *I* am about to be attacked by a dog.

Again, when I know (4), I know much more than I knew when I knew only (3), even though each piece of knowledge is *about* the same individual, namely me. The word 'I' is an indexical like 'that', and like 'that' it has a certain character distinct from the content of the expression. But can it be assimilated to some sort of descriptive content? Perry argues that it cannot.

In "Understanding Demonstratives" Gareth Evans takes issue with Perry's claim, suggesting that it was never supposed that character could be assimilated to a *description*. Evans also takes issue with how Perry wants to individuate demonstrative thoughts, and asks whether it is so obvious that the same demonstrative thought cannot be grasped in different ways.

There really is an issue of how this extra element of demonstratives might be incorporated into an empirical investigation of language—particularly one of the form discussed in the end of part I. But as Evans points out, there does not appear to be a conceptual barrier to developing such theories.

There are other issues that will have to be taken seriously in any genuine attempt to naturalize the investigation of demonstratives. As Martin Davies notes, one of the properties of demonstratives is that they generally appear as fairly complex expressions ("that guy eating chips over there," "that denigrator of Smith," etc.). The facts surveyed by Davies suggest that there is much work to be done even on the question of the structure of demonstrative expressions.

Further Reading for Part V

Almog, J., J. Perry, and H. Wettstein (eds). 1989. *Themes from Kaplan.* New York: Oxford University Press.

Barwise, J., and J. Perry. 1983. *Situations and Attitudes.* Cambridge: MIT Press.

Castañeda, H.-N. 1966. "'He': A Study in the Logic of Self-Consciousness." *Ratio* 8:130–157.

Castañeda, H.-N. 1967. "Indicators and Quasi-indicators." *American Philosophical Quarterly* 4:85–100.

Kaplan, D. 1979. "On the Logic of Demonstratives." *Journal of Philosophical Logic* 8:81–98.

Perry, J. 1993. *The Problem of the Essential Indexical and Other Essays.* New York: Oxford University Press.

Recanati, F. 1993. *Direct Reference: From Language to Thought.* Oxford: Blackwell.

Stalnaker, R. 1981. "Indexical Belief." *Synthese* 49:129–151.

Taylor, B. 1980. "Truth-Theory for Indexical Languages." In M. Platts (ed.) *Reference, Truth, and Reality*, pp. 182–198. London: Routledge & Kegan Paul.

Yourgrau, P. (ed.). 1990. *Demonstratives.* Oxford: Oxford University Press.

Chapter 27

Truth and Demonstratives

Scott Weinstein

Recently, various philosophers have argued that there is a close connection between a theory of truth for a language and a theory of meaning
for that language (e.g., [1]). Even if we do not wish to equate the two, I
believe we must agree that a necessary component of an adequate theory
of meaning is a theory of truth. We might require a complete semantical
theory of a language to do many things, but it should at least give us a
systematic account of the conditions under which the sentences of that
language are true.

If we grant that provision of a truth definition is a condition of adequacy on a theory of meaning for some language, then we are faced with
a difficulty when we embark on the project of framing semantical theories
for natural languages. These languages contain what Quine has called
non-eternal sentences, i.e., sentences whose truth value may vary from
one occasion of utterance to another. The linguistic devices which make
for the non-eternality of sentences containing them are the so-called indicator words: the personal pronouns "I", "he", "she", the demonstrative
pronouns "this", "that", tensed verbs, etc. The problem about sentences
containing these devices is that they are, from a semantical point of view,
incomplete expressions. Frege noted that "the mere wording [of a sentence containing indicator words] . . . is not the complete expression of the
thought, but the knowledge of certain accompanying conditions of utterance, which are used as means of expressing the thought, are needed for
its correct apprehension" ([2]: 24). Consider, for example, the sentence,

(1) I stood on that.

First appeared in *Noûs* 8 (1974): 179–184. Reprinted by permission of Blackwell Publishers,
Inc.

Let someone utter (1) and let "T" name his utterance. Then, T is true if and only if the utterer of T stands at some time prior to uttering T on the object he indicates while uttering T. The consideration of sentences containing indicator words suggests that a theory of truth for a natural language will have to treat of the conditions under which utterances and not sentences are true. In addition, such a theory will have to give a systematic account of how the truth conditions of utterances depend upon features of the contexts in which they occur.

To illustrate how such a theory may be constructed, let us consider a simple language, L, whose only indicator word is the demonstrative pronoun "that". (Our treatment of this simple language can easily be extended to languages containing further indicator words by enriching the vocabulary of the metalanguage in order to describe other features of the context in which an utterance may occur. E.g., in order to handle the first person pronoun, we would require a relation in the metalanguage which matches an utterance with its utterer.) We specify the syntax of L as follows:

terms: the demonstrative pronoun "that" is a term; all the variables in the following infinite list are terms: "v_0", "v_1", $\ldots$;

predicates: "is a cat" is a predicate;

atomic formulae: if P is a predicate and t is a term, then $t^\cap P$ is an atomic formula;

operations of formula formation: if A and B are formulae and v is a variable, then "($"^\cap A^\cap$" $\vee$ "$^\cap B^\cap$")", "$\neg$"$^\cap$ "($"^\cap A^\cap$")", and "$\exists$"$^\cap v^\cap$ "($"^\cap A^\cap$")" are formulae.

The set of formulae of L is the smallest set which contains all the atomic formulae and is closed under the operations of formula formation.

We want to construct a truth definition for utterances of sentences of L. Before we do so, we ought to ask what the condition of adequacy on such a definition is, so that we will know if our project succeeds. Tarski stated a condition of adequacy on truth definitions which reads as follows: an adequate definition of truth for a language L' must have as consequences all instances of the schema, $T(s) \leftrightarrow P$, where "T" is the truth predicate for L', "s" is a place holder for a structural descriptive name of some sentence of L', and "P" is a place holder for the translation of that sentence into the metalanguage, i.e., the language in which the truth predicate for L' is being defined ([3]). This condition of adequacy must be modified if we are to apply it to a truth definition for utterances of the language L described above. As we have already remarked, some of the sentences of L (those which contain occurrences of the demonstrative pronoun) are incomplete expressions, and the conditions under which utterances of such sentences are true will depend on features of the contexts in which they occur. Therefore, I propose the following as a condition of adequacy on a truth definition for the language L described above: an adequate definition of truth for the language L must have as consequences all instances of the schema,

(DT)   If u is an utterance of s and the referents of the demonstrative
       pronouns occurring in u are $w_0, \ldots, w_n$, then $T(u) \leftrightarrow P$,

where "w_0",...,"w_n" are the first $n + 1$ variables of the metalanguage, "u" is a variable of the metalanguage distinct from each of these, "s" is a place holder for a structural descriptive name of a sentence of L, "T" is the truth predicate for utterances of sentences of L, "T" is the truth predicate for utterances of sentences of L, and "P" is a placeholder for a translation into the metalanguage of the (perhaps) open sentence obtained from s by replacing the ith occurrence of the demonstrative pronoun in s by the ith variable of L and relettering the bound variables of s so as to avoid binding any of the variables introduced by the substitution. (It is understood as a convention that if a formula of L contains a free occurrence of the ith variable of L, then its translation contains a free occurrence of the ith variable of the metalanguage in the corresponding place.)

Let us now proceed to construct a definition of truth for utterances of sentences of L and to prove that it meets the condition of adequacy stated above. We give our truth theory in an informal metalanguage. In a more formal treatment our truth theory would be constructed in an extension of first-order arithmetic in which the syntactical relations we use would be represented by certain arithmetical formulae via some Gödel numbering of the symbols of L. In addition, we make implicit use of a theory of finite sequences. The structure of our truth theory is as follows. First, we define satisfaction for the eternal formulae of L, i.e., those formulae which contain no occurrences of the demonstrative pronoun, in a standard way. Then, we define truth for utterances of sentences of L in terms of the satisfaction of certain eternal formulae by specified sequences of objects. We state the axioms of our truth theory followed by an explanation of the notations that occur therein:

Axioms of the theory of satisfaction for eternal formulae of L:
(1) x SAT "v_i is a cat" $\leftrightarrow x(i)$ is a cat.
(2) x SAT disj$(s, s') \leftrightarrow x$ SAT $s \lor x$ SAT s'.
(3) x SAT neg$(s) \leftrightarrow \neg x$ SAT s.
(4) x SAT eq$(i, s) \leftrightarrow \exists x' (\forall j (j \neq i \rightarrow x'(j) = x(j)) \land x'$ SAT $s)$.

Additional axiom defining truth for utterances:
(5) u UT $p \land x$ OC $u \land x$ REF $x' \rightarrow (T(u) \leftrightarrow x'$ SAT $F(p))$.

"x" and "x'" are variables ranging over finite sequences. "i" and "j" are variables ranging over natural numbers. "$x(i)$" denotes the ith term of the sequence x if i is less than the length of x, and "$x(i)$" denotes the (length of $x - 1$)-th term of x if i is greater than or equal to the length of x. (This fails to define $x(i)$ when x is the null sequence, i.e., the unique sequence whose length is 0. We don't care.) "SAT" is a relation between sequences and eternal formulae of L: its intended interpretation is the satisfaction relation for eternal formulae of L. "disj(s, s')", "neg(s)", and "eq(i, s)" denote respectively the disjunction of s and s', the negation of s, and the existential quantification of s with respect to the ith variable of L. ""v_i is a cat"" denotes the formula of L which results from concatenating the ith variable of L with the predicate symbol "is a cat". "u" is a variable which ranges over utterances of expressions of L (an expression of L is any finite sequence of symbols of L). "p" is a variable which ranges over eternal and non-eternal sentences, i.e., closed formulae, of L. "u UT y" is a relation between utterances and expressions of l whose intended interpretation is: u is an utterance of y. "x OC u" is a relation between sequences and utterances whose intended interpretation is: there exists an i such that i is the number of occurrences of the demonstrative pronoun in u, and i is equal to the length of x, and for every j, if j is less than i, then $x(j)$ is the jth occurrence of the demonstrative pronoun in u. "x REF x'" is a relation between sequences whose intended interpretation is: the length of x is equal to the length of x', and for every i, $x(i)$ is an utterance of the demonstrative pronoun and $x'(i)$ is the referent of $x(i)$. "$T(u)$" is a predicate of utterances whose intended interpretation is: u is true. "$F(p)$" denotes the formula of L obtained from the sentence p by substituting the ith variable of L for the ith occurrence of the demonstrative pronoun in p and, if necessary, relettering the bound variables of p in some systematic manner so as to avoid binding any of the variables introduced by the substitution.

  We proceed to sketch a proof that our truth theory satisfies the condition of adequacy stated above, i.e., that it has as consequences all instances of the schema (DT), which, in our current notation, reads as follows:

$$u \text{ UT } r \wedge x \text{ OC } u \wedge x \text{ REF } x' \rightarrow (T(u) \leftrightarrow R(x'(0), \ldots, x'(n))),$$

where "r" stands in place of a structural descriptive name of a sentence of L, and "$R(x'(0), \ldots, x'(n))$" stands in place of the translation into the metalanguage of $F(r)$ with "$x'(i)$" substituted for all free occurrences of the ith variable of the metalanguage in the translation of $F(r)$. The proof makes use of the fact that all instances of the schema,

$$(S) \quad x \text{ SAT } q \leftrightarrow Q(x(i_i), \ldots, x(i_n))$$

(where "q" stands in place of a structural descriptive name of an *eternal formula* of L, and "$Q(x(i_1), \ldots, x(i_n))$" stands in place of the translation of that formula into the metalanguage with the indicated substitutions) are consequences of our truth theory. This is true in virtue of the standardness of our definition of satisfaction for the eternal formulae of L. The proof is completed by observing that $F(r)$ is always an eternal formula and consequently that for each sentence r of L, the instance of the schema (DT) for r is derivable from axiom (5) and the instance of the schema (S) for $F(r)$.

We conclude with a brief remark about some of the primitive notions of our theory. According to our theory, in order to determine the condition under which an utterance is true, we must determine what sentence it is an utterance of and what the referents of any demonstratives which occur in that utterance are. That is, we must determine whether a certain phonological and a certain semantical (or, if you prefer, pragmatical) relation hold. We have made no attempt to say anything informative about these relations in our theory.

Note

I would like to thank Professor Donald Davidson for many helpful discussions and constant encouragement without which this paper would not have been written. I am indebted to Michael Bratman for pointing out an error in an earlier version of this paper.

References

[1] Donald Davidson, "Truth and Meaning," *Synthese* 17 (1967): 304–23. [Chap. 5 in this vol.]

[2] Gottlob Frege, "The Thought: A Logical Inquiry," in *Philosophical Logic*, ed. by P. F. Strawson (London: Oxford University Press, 1967). [Chap. 1 in this vol.]

[3] Alfred Tarski, "The Concept of Truth in Formalized Languages," in *Logic, Semantics, Metamathematics* (London: Oxford University Press, 1956): 152–278.

Chapter 28
Dthat

David Kaplan

Donnellan, in 'Reference and Definite Descriptions' says, 'Using a definite description referentially a speaker may say something true even though the description correctly applies to nothing.'[1] His example—taken from Linsky[2]—has someone saying of a spinster:

Her husband is kind to her.

after having had Mr Jones—actually the spinster's brother—misintroduced as the spinster's husband. And—to fill it out—having noticed Jones's solicitous attention to his sister. The speaker used the non-denoting description 'Her husband' to refer to Mr Jones. And so, what he said was true.

There are a lot of entities associated with the utterance of 'Her husband is kind to her' which are commonly said to have been said: tokens, types, sentences, propositions, statements, etc. The something-true-said, Donnellan calls a *statement*.

On the other hand, 'If ... the speaker has just met the lady and, noticing her cheerfulness and radiant good health, made his remark from his conviction that these attributes are always the result of having good husbands, he would be using the definite description attributively.'[3]

After pointing out that 'in general, whether or not a definite description is used referentially or attributively is a function of the speaker's intentions in a particular case',[4] he mentions a function to Russell's theory of descriptions, the use of *the* ϕ might be thought of as involving reference 'in a very weak sense ... to *whatever* is the one and only one ϕ, if there is any such'.[5] Donnellan then concludes:

First appeared in P. Cole (ed.), *Pragmatics*, Syntax and Semantics, no. 9 (New York: Academic Press, 1978). Reprinted by permission of Academic Press.

Now this is something we might well say about the attributive use of definite descriptions ... But this lack of particularity is absent from the referential use of definite descriptions precisely because the description is here merely a device for getting one's audience to pick out or think of the thing to be spoken about, a device which may serve its function even if the description is incorrect. More importantly, perhaps, in the referential use as opposed to the attributive, there is a right thing to be picked out by the audience, and its being the right thing is not simply a function of its fitting the description.[6]

Donnellan develops his theory by adducing a series of quite plausible examples to help him answer certain theoretical questions, e.g. are there sentences in which the contained definite description can only be used referentially (or only attributively)?, can reference fail when a definite description is used referentially?, etc.

In my own reading and rereading of Donnellan's article I always find it both fascinating and maddening. Fascinating, because the fundamental distinction so clearly reflects an accurate insight into language use, and maddening, because, first, the examples seem to me to alternate between at least two clearly discriminable concepts of *referential use*; second, the notion of *having someone in mind* is not analysed but used; and third, the connections with the developed body of knowledge concerning intensional logics—their syntax and semantics—are not explicitly made, so we cannot immediately see what Donnellan and intensional logic have to offer each other, if anything.

As one of the body developers, I find this last snub especially inexcusable. This is not a divergent perception for those of my ilk. Hintikka remarks (plaintively?), 'The only thing I miss in Donnellan's excellent paper is a clear realization that the distinction he is talking about is only operative in contexts governed by propositional attitudes or other modal terms.'[7]

Hintikka's remark is at first surprising, since none of Donnellan's examples seems to have this form. But the remark falls into place when we recognize that Donnellan is concerned essentially with a given speaker who is *asserting* something, *asking* something, or *commanding* something. And thus if we pull back and focus our attention on the sentence *describing* the speech act:

John asserted that Mary's husband is kind to her.

the intensional operator appears.

Probably Hintikka wanted to argue that the sentence:

Her husband is kind to her.

is not itself ambiguous in the way that, say:

Every boy kissed a girl.

is. The fact that an ambiguous sentence is produced by embedding ϕ in some sentential context (for example, an intensional or temporal operator) should not be construed to indicate an ambiguity in ϕ. For were it so, (almost?) all sentences would be ambiguous.

Donnellan's distinction is a contribution to the redevelopment of an old and commonsensical theory about language which—at least in the philosophical literature—has rather been in a decline during the ascendency of semantics over epistemology of the 1930s, 1940s, and 1950s. The common-sense theory is one that Russell wrestled with in *The Principles of Mathematics*[8] but seemed to reject in 'On Denoting'.[9] This theory asserts roughly that the correct analysis of a typical speech act, for example:

John is tall.

distinguishes *who* is being talked about, i.e. the individual under consideration—here, John—from *how* he is being characterized—here, as tall.

Russell's analysis of the proposition expressed by

John is tall.

provides it with two components: the property expressed by the predicate is tall, and the individual John. That's right, John himself, right there, trapped in a proposition.

During the Golden Age of Pure Semantics we were developing a nice homogeneous theory, with language, meanings, and entities of the world each properly segregated and related one to another in rather smooth and comfortable ways. This development probably came to its peak in Carnap's *Meaning and Necessity*.[10] Each *designator* has both an intension and an extension. Sentences have truth-values as extensions and propositions as intensions, predicates have classes as extensions and properties as intensions, terms have individuals as extensions and *individual concepts* as intensions, and so on. The intension of a compound is a function of the intensions of the parts and similarly the extension (except when intensional operators appear). There is great beauty and power in this theory.

But there remained some nagging doubts: proper names, demonstratives, and quantification into intensional contexts.

Proper names may be a practical convenience in our mundane transactions, but they are a theoretician's nightmare. They are like bicycles. Everyone easily learns to ride, but no one can correctly explain how he does it. Completely new theories have been proposed within the last few years, in spite of the fact that the subject has received intense attention throughout this century, and in some portions of Tibet people have had proper names for even longer than that.

The main difficulty has to do, I believe, with the special intimate relationship between a proper name and its bearer. Russell said that in contrast with a common noun, like 'unicorn', a proper name *means* what it names. And if it names nothing, it means nothing. In the case of 'unicorn' we have a meaning, perhaps better a *descriptive meaning*, which we make use of in looking for such things. But in the case of the name 'Moravcsik' there is just Moravcsik. There is no basis on which to ask whether Moravcsik exists. Such a question is—for Russell—meaningless. But people persist in asking this question. Maybe not this very question, but analogous ones like:

Does Santa Claus exist?

There were other apparent difficulties in Russell's theory. The astronomical discovery that Hesperus was identical with Phosphorus became a triviality. The sentence expressing it expressed the same proposition as 'Hesperus is identical with Hesperus.' Furthermore, although the bearer of a given proper name is the be-all and end-all of the name's semantic relata, almost every proper name has dozens of bearers.

And then there are the unforgivable distortions of the minimal descriptive content of proper names. We all know of butchers named 'Baker' and dogs named 'Sir Walter'. The ultimate in such perversity occurs in titles of the top administrative officers at UCLA. We have four vice-chancellors at UCLA, one of whom has the title 'The Vice-Chancellor'.

All in all, proper names are a mess and if it weren't for the problem of how to get the kids to come in for dinner, I'd be inclined to just junk them.

At any rate, the attempt during the Golden Age was to whip proper names into line. In fact into the line of common nouns. People do ask:

Does Santa Claus exist?

So that must mean something like:

Does a unicorn exist?

They do ask:

Is Hesperus identical with Phosphorus?

So that must mean something like:

Are bachelors identical with college graduates?

Thus was waged a war of attrition against proper names. Many were unmasked as disguised descriptions, e.g. 'Aristotle' means *the student of Plato and teacher of Alexander who* ... —not an unreasonable proposal.

However, some of these exposés did seem a bit oppressive, e.g. Russell's suggestion that:

Scott is Sir Walter.

really means:

The person named 'Scott' is the person named 'Sir Walter'.

followed by his nonchalant remark: 'This is a way in which names are frequently used in practice, and there will, as a rule, be nothing in the phraseology to show whether they are being used in this way or as names.'[11] But at least they isolated the few real trouble-makers—who turned out not to be our good old proper names at all but a handful of determined outside demonstratives: 'this', 'that', etc.

In summary, the technique was first to expose a proper name as a disguised description (sometimes on tenuous and unreliable evidence) and then ruthlessly to eliminate it.

We thus reduce the exciting uncertainties of:

Socrates is a man.

to the banality of:

All men are mortal.

The demonstratives were still there, but they were so gross they could be ignored.

Lately, under the pressure of the new interest in singular propositions generated by intensional logic, the verities of the Golden Age are breaking down. Once logicians became interested in formalizing a logic of necessity, belief, knowledge, assertion, etc., traditional syntactical ways quickly led to formulas like

John asserted that x is a spy.

with free 'x' and then with 'x' bound to an anterior operator. Under what circumstances does a given individual, taken as value of 'x', satisfy this formula? Answer: If the appropriate singular proposition was the content of John's assertive utterance.

It seems that in at least certain speech acts, what I am trying to express can't quite be put into words. It is that proposition of Russell's with John trapped in it.

The property of being tall is exactly expressed by 'is tall', and the concept of the unique spy who is shorter than all other spies is exactly expressed by 'the shortest spy'; but no expression exactly expresses John. An expression may express a concept or property that, in reality, only John satisfies. There are many such distinct concepts; none of which is John himself.

I would like to distinguish between the kind of propositions which were considered by Aristotle (*all S is P, some S is not-P*, etc.) and the kind of proposition considered by the early Russell. I call the former *general propositions* and the latter *singular propositions*. Suppose, just for definiteness, that we fix attention on sentences of simple subject-predicate form. The following are examples:

(1) A spy is suspicious.

(2) Every spy is suspicious.

(3) The spy is suspicious.

(4) John is suspicious.

Now let us think of the proposition associated with each sentence as having two components. Corresponding to the predicate we have the property of being suspicious; and corresponding to the subject we have either what Russell in 1903 called a *denoting concept* or an individual. Let us take the proposition to be the ordered couple of these two components.

Again, to fix ideas, let us provide a possible-world style of interpretation for these notions. We think of each total or complete possible state of affairs as a possible world. The possible worlds are each constituents through time and may in fact overlap at certain times. For example, a possible world may agree with the actual world up to the time at which some individual made a particular decision; the possible world may then represent an outcome of a decision other than the one actually taken. (In science fiction, such cases are called *alternate time lines*.)

Within this framework we can attempt to represent a number of the semantic notions in question. We might represent the property of *being suspicious* by that function P which assigns to each possible world w and each time t the set of all those individuals of w which, in w, are suspicious at t. We might represent the denoting concepts expressed by the denoting phrases 'A spy', 'Every spy', and 'The spy' as, say, the ordered couples: $\langle$'A', $S\rangle$, $\langle$'Every', $S\rangle$, $\langle$'The', $S\rangle$ where S is the property (represented as above) of *being a spy*.[12] The fact that the logical words 'A', 'Every', and 'The' are just carried along reflects our treatment of them as *syncategorematic*, i.e. as having no independent meaning but as indicators of how to combine the meaning-bearing parts (here 'spy' and the predicate) in determining the meaning of the whole. For (1), (2), and (3) the corresponding propositions are now represented by:

(5) $\langle\langle$'A', $S\rangle, P\rangle$

(6) $\langle\langle$'Every', $S\rangle, P\rangle$

(7) $\langle\langle$'The', $S\rangle, P\rangle$

It should be clear that each of (5)–(7) will determine a function which assigns to each possible world w and time t a truth-value. And in fact the truth-value so assigned to any w and t will be exactly the truth-value in w at t of the corresponding sentence. For example: (6) determines that function which assigns truth to a given w and t if and only if every member of $S(w, t)$ is a member of $P(w, t)$. Notice that the function so determined by (6) also correctly assigns to each w and t the truth-value in w at t of (2). (For the purpose of (7), let us take * to be a 'truth-value' which is assigned to w and t when $S(w, t)$ contains other than a single member.)

The proposition corresponding to (4) would be:

(8) $\langle$John, $P\rangle$

not $\langle$'John', $P\rangle$ mind you, but $\langle$John, $P\rangle$. And (8) will determine that function F which assigns Truth to w and t if and only if John is a member of $P(w, t)$. If John is an individual of w at the time t (i.e. John exists in w and is alive at t) but is not a member of $P(w, t)$, then $F(w, t)$ is falsehood; and if John is not an individual of w at the time t, then $F(w, t)$ is *.

This brief excursion into possible-world semantics is only to fix ideas in a simple way within that framework (I will later make further use of the framework) and is not put forward as an ideal (in any sense: generalizability, elegance, etc.) representation of the semantic notions of property, proposition, denoting concept, etc. My main motivation is to present a representation which will clearly distinguish singular and general propositions.

It would, of course, have been possible to supply a representation of the proposition expressed by (4) which is, in a sense, formally equivalent to (8) and which blurs the distinction I wish to emphasize. I do it now lest anyone think that the possibility is a relevant refutation of my later remarks. Let us clearly depart from Russell by associating a denoting concept:

(9) $\langle$'Proper Name', $J\rangle$

where J is what we might call *John's essence*, the property of *being John*, namely, that function which assigns to each possible world w and time t the set {John} if John is an individual of w and is alive in w at t and the empty set otherwise. The analogue to (8) is now

(10) $\langle\langle$'Proper Name', $J\rangle, P\rangle$

It will be noted that we have now treated the proper name 'John' rather like the definite description 'The John', in which the proper name plays the role of a common noun. Accordingly the function from possible worlds and times to truth values which is determined by (10) is identical with that determined by:

(11) $\langle\langle$'The', $J\rangle, P\rangle$

There are certainly other representations of these propositions which ally various subgroups. In fact, once any formal structure is established, the production of isomorphic structure satisfying specified 'internal' conditions is largely a matter of logical ingenuity of the 'pure' kind.[13]

To return to the point, I have represented propositions in a way which emphasizes the singular—general distinction, because I want to revive a view of language alternate to that of the Golden Age. The view of the Golden Age is, I believe, undoubtedly correct for a large portion of language behaviour, in particular communication by means of general propositions. But the alternate view accounts for a portion of language behaviour not accommodated by the view of the Golden Age.

The alternate view is: *that some or all of the denoting phrases used in an utterance should not be considered part of the content of what is said but should rather be thought of as contextual factors which help us interpret the actual physical utterance as having a certain content.* The most typical of such contextual factors is the fact that the speaker's utterance is to be taken as an utterance of some specific language, say, English. When I utter 'yes' in English and *no* in Knoh, you must know I am speaking Knoh to know I have said *no*. It is no *part* of what I have said that I am speaking Knoh, though Knoh being a complete tongue, I could add that by uttering 'I am speaking English.' Such an utterance is of doubtful utility in itself; but, fortunately, there are other means by which this fact can be ascertained by my auditor, e.g. by my general physical appearance, or, if I am not a native Knoh, by my pointing to Knoh on a celestial globe. A homelier example has a haberdasher utter to a banker, 'I am out of cheques.' Whether the utterance takes place in the store or at the bank will help the banker determine what the haberdasher has said. In either case it is no *part* of what was said that the haberdasher used 'cheques' to mean bank cheques rather than suits with a chequered pattern. Of course the haberdasher could go on, if he desired, so to comment on his past performance, but that would be to say something else. Still closer to home is my wife's utterance: 'It's up to you to punish Jordan for what happened today.' It is by means of various subtle contextual clues that I understand her to be charging me to administer discipline to our son and not to be calling on me to act where the United Nations has failed. Again, should I exhibit momentary confusion she might, by a comment, a gesture, or simply some more discourse on the relevant naughtiness, assist me in properly decoding her first utterance so that I could understand what she was, in fact, saying. There are other ways—more controversial than the intentional resolution of the reference of a proper name among the many persons so dubbed—in which contextual factors determine the content of an utterance containing a proper name; but I am reserving all but the most blatantly obvious remarks for later.

Now let us narrow our attention to utterances containing *singular denoting phrases* (i.e. denoting phrases which purport to stand for a unique individual, such as 'the spy', 'John', '$\sqrt{2}$', etc.).[14]

How can contextual factors determine that part of the content of an utterance which corresponds to a singular denoting phrase? Two ways have already been mentioned: by determining what language is being spoken and by determining which of the many persons so dubbed a proper name stands for. But the most striking way in which such contextual factors enter is in connection with *demonstratives*: 'this', 'this spy', 'that book', etc. In at least some typical uses of these phrases, it is required that the utterance be accompanied by a *demonstration*— paradigmatically, a pointing—which indicates the object for which the phrase stands.[15] I will speak of a *demonstrative* use of a singular denoting phrase when the speaker intends that the object for which the phrase stands be designated by an associated demonstration.[16]

Now we can add another example of a subject-predicate sentence to those of (1)–(4):

(12) He [the speaker points at John] is suspicious.

I am adopting the convention of enclosing a description of the relevant demonstration in square brackets immediately following each denoting phrase which is used demonstratively.[17]

What shall we take as the proposition corresponding to (12) (which I also call the *content* of the *utterance* (12))? In line with our programme of studying contextual factors which are not *part* of what is said but whose role is rather to help us interpret the utterance as *having* a certain content, we shall take the component of the proposition which corresponds to the demonstrative to be the individual demonstrated. Thus the varying *forms* which such a demonstration can take are not reflected in the content of the utterance (i.e. the proposition). The demonstration 'gives us' the element of the proposition corresponding to the demonstrative. But *how* the demonstration gives that individual to us is here treated as irrelevant to the content of the utterance; just as the different *ways* by which I might have come to understand which Jordan was relevant to my wife's utterance, or the different *ways* by which one might come to understand that a speaker is speaking Knoh rather than English, do not alter the content of those utterances. Thus, for example, the utterances (in English):

(13) He [the speaker points at John, as John stands on the demonstration platform nude, clean shaven, and bathed in light] is suspicious.

(14) He [the speaker points at John, as John lurks in shadows wearing a trench-coat, bearded, with his hat pulled down over his face] is suspicious.

are taken, along with other refinements of (12), as expressing the same proposition, namely:

(15) $\langle$John, $P\rangle$

It should immediately be apparent that we are in store for some delightful anomalies. Erroneous beliefs may lead a speaker to put on a demonstration which does not demonstrate what he thinks it does, with the result that he will be under a misapprehension as to *what* he has said. Utterances of identity sentences containing one or more demonstratives may express necessary propositions, though neither the speaker nor his auditors are aware of it. In fact, we get extreme cases in which linguistic competence is simply insufficient to determine completely the content of what is said. Of course this was already established by the case of the Knoh-English translation problem, but the situation is more dramatic using the demonstratives.

The present treatment is not inevitable. An alternative is to incorporate the demonstration in the proposition. We would argue as follows: Frege's *sense and denotation* distinction[18] can be extended to all kinds of indicative devices. In each case we have the object indicated (the 'denotation') and the manner of indication (the 'sense'). It is interesting to note that (at least in Feigl's translation) Frege wrote of 'the sense (connotation, meaning) of the sign in which is contained the *manner and context* of presentation of the denotation of the sign'.[19] I think it reasonable to interpret Frege as saying that the sense of a sign is what is grasped by the linguistically competent auditor, and it seems natural to generalize and say that it is the 'sense' of the demonstration that is grasped by the competent auditor of utterances containing demonstratives. Thus we see how the drawn-out English utterance:

(16)   That [the speaker points at Phosphorus in early morning] is the same planet as that [the speaker points at Hesperus in the early evening].

could be both informative and true.

Let us call the preceding a *Fregean treatment of demonstratives*. It is worth developing (which means primarily working on the ontology (metaphysics?) of demonstrations and the semantics of demonstration descriptions) but, I believe, will ultimately be unsatisfactory. For now I'll just outline some of the reasons. The demonstrative use of demonstratives plays an important role in language learning, in general, in the learning and use of proper names, in our misty use of *de re* modalities, in our better grounded use of what Quine calls the *relational* senses of epistemic verbs (i.e. the senses of those intensional verbs that permit quantification in).[20] And, in general, I believe that we can sharpen our epistemological insights in a number of areas by taking account of what I call the demonstrative use of expression. Such uses are far more widespread than one imagined.

I earlier called the Fregean treatment of demonstratives 'unsatisfactory'. I would be more cautious in saying that it was wrong. (However I do think an empirical argument from linguistic behaviour could be developed to show that it is wrong. I take Donnellan's study of the phenomenology of what he calls referential use to be an excellent start in that direction.) What I am confident of is that if we force all phenomena that suggest a special *demonstrative* use of language, along with what I regard as a corresponding feature—a special *singular* form of proposition—into the Fregean mould of linguistic elements with a sense and a denotation, the sense being the element which appears in the proposition (thus leaving us with only general propositions), then important insights will be lost. I don't deny that on a phenomenon-by-phenomenon basis we can (in some sense) keep stretching Frege's brilliant insights to cover. With a little ingenuity I think we *can* do that. But we shouldn't.

Now let me offer a slightly different and somewhat a priori justification for studying the phenomena of demonstrative uses of expressions and singular propositions. I leave aside the question whether we have correctly analysed any actual linguistic behaviour, whether concerned with the so-called demonstrative *phrases* or otherwise.

Having explained so clearly and precisely what such a use of language would amount to, in terms of a possible-world semantics, I can simply resolve so to use the word 'that' in the future. At a minimum I could introduce the *new* word 'dthat' for the demonstrative use of 'that'. Couldn't I? I can, and I will. In fact I do.

I like this intentional (i.e. stipulative) way of looking at the use of 'dthat' because I believe that in many cases where there are competing Fregean and demonstrative analyses of some utterances or class of utterances the matter can be resolved simply by the intentions of the speaker (appropriately conveyed to the auditor?). Thus in the ease of proper names (to which I will return below) I might simply resolve to use them demonstratively (i.e. as demonstrating the individual whom they are a name *of* in the nomenclature of an earlier paper[21]) on certain occasions and in a Fregean way[22] on other occasions. Of course, one who did not have a clear understanding of the alternatives might have difficulty in characterizing his own use, but once we have explored each choice there is nothing to prevent us from choosing either, 'unnatural' though the choice may be.

It should probably be noted that despite the accessibility of the semantics of 'dthat' our *grasp* of the singular propositions so expressed is, in John Perry's apt phrase, a bit of *knowledge by description* as compared with our rather more direct acquaintance with the general propositions expressed by non-demonstrative utterances.

Armed with 'dthat' we can now explore and possibly even extend the frontiers of demonstrations.

When we considered the Fregean analysis of demonstrations, we attempted to establish parallels between demonstrations and descriptions.[23] In so far as this aspect of the Fregean programme is successful, it suggests the possibility of a demonstrative analysis of descriptions. *If pointing can be taken as a form of describing, why not take describing as a form of pointing?* Note that our demonstrative analysis of demonstrations need not, indeed should not, deny or even ignore the fact that demonstrations have both a sense and a demonstratum. It is just that according to the demonstrative analysis the sense of the demonstration does not appear in the proposition. Instead the sense is used only to fix the demonstratum which itself appears directly in the proposition. I propose now to do the same for descriptions. Instead of taking the sense of the description as the subject of the proposition, we use the sense only to fix the denotation which we then take directly as the subject component of the proposition. I now take the utterance of the description as a demonstration and describe it with the usual quotation devices, thus:

(17) Dthat ['the spy'] is suspicious.

For fixity of ideas, let us suppose, what is surely false, that in fact, actuality, and reality there is one and only one spy, and John is he. We might express this so:

(18) 'the spy' denotes John.[24]

In the light of (18), (17) expresses:

(19) $\langle$John, $P\rangle$

(also known as '(8)' and '(15)').

Recollecting and collecting we have:

(3)   The spy is suspicious.

(4)   John is suspicious.

(7) $\langle\langle$'The', $S\rangle, P\rangle$

(12) He [the speaker points at John] is suspicious.

or as we might now write (12):

(20) Dhe [the speaker points at John] is suspicious.[25]

Earlier we said that an utterance of (3) expresses (7), and only an utterance of (12) [i.e. (20)] or possibly (4) expresses (19). I have already suggested that an utterance of (4) may sometimes by taken in a Fregean way to express something like (7), and now I want to point out that for want of 'dthat' some speakers may be driven to utter (3) when they intend what is expressed by (17).

If an utterance of (3) may indeed sometimes express (19), then Donnellan was essentially correct in describing his referential and attributive uses of definite descriptions as a 'duality of function'. And it might even be correct to describe this duality as an *ambiguity* in the sentence type (3). I should note right here that my demonstrative use is not quite Donnellan's referential use—a deviation that I will expatiate on below—but it is close enough for present purposes.

The ambiguity in question here is of a rather special kind. For under no circumstances could the choice of disambiguation for an utterance of (3) affect the truth-value. Still there are two distinct propositions involved, and even two distinct functions from possible worlds and times to truth-values, determined by the two propositions.

Before continuing with the ambiguity in (3), it would be well to interject some remarks on sentence types and sentence tokens (of which utterances are one kind) especially as they relate to demonstratives.

Sentence types vary considerably in the degree to which they contain implicit and explicit references to features of the context of utterance. The references I have in mind here are those that affect the truth-value of the sentence type on a particular occasion of utterance. At one extreme stand what Quine (in *Word and Object*) called *eternal sentences*: those in which the feature linguists call *sense* does not really reflect a perspective from some point in time, which contain no *indexicals* such as 'now', 'here', 'I', etc., and whose component names and definite descriptions are not understood to require contextual determination as did the 'Jordan' of our earlier example. Quine describes such sentences as 'those whose truth value stays fixed through time and from speaker to speaker'.[26] But I prefer my own vaguer formulation: *those sentences which do not express a perspective from within space-time*. Quine and I would both count 'In 1970 American women exceed American men in wealth' as eternal; he would (presumably) also count 'The UCLA football team always has, does, and will continue to outclass the Stanford football team' as eternal. I would not.

Truth-values are awarded directly to eternal sentences without any relativization to time, place, etc.[27] But for the fugitive sentence no stable truth-value can be awarded. Let us consider first tensed sentences, e.g.:

(21) American men will come to exceed American women in intelligence.

Without disputing the facts, if (21) were true at one time, it would fail to be true at some later time. (Since one doesn't come to exceed what one already exceeds.)

Now let's dredge up the possible worlds. We associated with (21) a function which assigns to each possible world and time a truth-value. Such a function seems to represent, for reasons which have been much discussed, at least part of the meaning of (21) or part of what we grasp when we understand (21).[28] There is another kind of 'content' associated with a fugitive sentence like (21), namely, the content of a particular utterance of (21). In a sense, any particular utterance (token) of a fugitive sentence (type) is an *eternalization* of the fugitive sentence. The relativization to time is fixed by the time of utterance. We can associate with each utterance of a fugitive sentence the same kind of function from possible worlds to truth-values that we associate directly with eternal sentences.

Before becoming completely lost in vague nomenclature, let me make some stipulations. I will call the function which assigns to a time and a possible world the truth-value of a given fugitive sentence (type) at that time in that world the *meaning* of the given sentence. The meaning of a sentence is what a person who is linguistically competent grasps, it is common to all utterances of the sentence, and it is one of the components which goes into determining the *content* of any particular utterance of the sentence. The *content* of an utterance is that function which assigns to each possible world the truth-value which the utterance would take if it were evaluated with respect to that world. There is some unfortunate slack in the preceding characterizations, which I will try to reduce.[29]

Let ϕ be a fugitive sentence like (21); let $\bar{\phi}$ be the meaning of ϕ, let W be the set of possible worlds; let T be the set of times (I assume that all possible worlds have the same temporal structure and, in fact, the very same times, i.e. a given time in one world has a unique counterpart in all others); let U be the set of possible utterances; for $u \in U$ let $S(u)$ be the sentence uttered in u; let $T(u)$ be the time of u (when only $S(u)$ and $T(u)$ are relevant; we might identify u with $\langle S(u), T(u) \rangle$ and let $\bar{u}$ be the content of u. The relation between the meaning of a sentence (whose only fugitive aspect is its temporality) and the content of one of its possible utterances can now be concisely expressed as follows:

(22) $\forall u \in U \; \forall w \in W(\bar{u}(w) = \overline{S(u)}(T(u), w))$

or, identifying u with $\langle S(u), T(u) \rangle$:

(23) $\forall w \in W \ \forall t \in T(\overline{\langle \phi, t \rangle}(w) = \phi(t, w))$

To put it another way, an utterance of ϕ fixes a time, and the content of the utterance takes account of the truth value of ϕ in all possible worlds but *only at that time*.

From (22) and (23) it would appear that the notions of meaning and content are interdefinable. Therefore, since we already have begun developing the theory of meaning for fugitive sentences (see especially the work of Montague),[30] why devote any special attention to the theory of content? Is it not simply a subtheory of a definitional extension of the theory of meaning? I think not. But the reasons go beyond simple examples like (21) and take us, hopefully, back to the main track of this paper. It is worth looking more deeply into the structure of utterances than a *simple* definition of that notion within the theory of meaning would suggest. (I stress *simple* because I have not yet really investigated sophisticated definitions.)

First we have problems about the counterfactual status of possible utterances: are utterances *in* worlds, are they assumed to occur in worlds in which their content is being evaluated, or are they extra-worldly, with their content evaluated independent of their occurrence? Consider the infamous 'I am here now', or perhaps more simply:

(24) An utterance is occurring.

Is the meaning of (24) to assign to a time and world the truth-value which an utterance of (24) *would* take *were* it to occur in that world at that time? Or does it assign simply the truth-value of (24) in that world at that time? Presumably the latter. But this is to assume that utterances come complete, with the value of all of their contextually determined features filled in (otherwise the utterance alone—without being set in a world— would not have a content). I do not want to make this assumption since I am particularly interested in the *way* in which a demonstration, for example, picks out its demonstratum.

And now we are back to the ambiguity in (3). I would like to count my *verbal* demonstration, as in (17), as part of the sentence type. Then it seems that an utterance of such a sentence either must include a world, or else, what is more plausible, must be in a world. I guess what I want to say, what I should have said, is that an utterance has to occur *somewhere*, in some world, and the world in which it occurs is a crucial factor in determining what the content is. This really says something about how (I think) I want to treat (possible) demonstrations. I want the same (possible) demonstrations (e.g. ['the spy']) to determine different demonstrata in different worlds (or possibly even at different times in the same world). Now I see why I was so taken with the Fregean treatment of demonstrations. We should be able to represent demonstrations as something like functions from worlds, times, etc., to demonstrata. Thus, *just like the meaning of a definite description!* The difference lies in how the content of a particular utterance is computed.

I realize that the foregoing is mildly inconsistent, but let us push on. Let u be an utterance of (17) in w at t, and let u' be an utterance of (3) in w at t. Let's not worry, for now, about the possibility of a clash of utterances. If we look at the content of u and the content of u' we will see that they differ—though they will always agree in w. The content of u is like what I earlier called a singular proposition (except that I should have fixed the time), whereas the content of u' is like what I earlier called a general proposition. For the content of u to assign truth to a given world w', the individual who must be suspicious in w' at t is not the denotation of 'the spy' in w' at t, but rather the denotation of 'the spy' in w at t. The *relevant individual* is determined in the world in which the utterance takes place, and then that same individual is checked for suspicion in all other worlds, whereas for the content of u', we determine a (possibly) new relevant individual in each world.[31]

What is especially interesting is that these two contents must agree in the world w, the world in which the utterance took place.

Now note that the verbal form of (3) might have been adopted by one who lacked 'dthat' to express what is expressed by (17). We seem to have here a kind of *de dicto–de re* ambiguity in the verbal form of (3) and without benefit of any intensional operator. No question of an utterer's intentions has been brought into play. *There is no question of an analysis in terms of scope, since there is no operator.* The two sentence types (3) and (17) are such that when uttered in the same context they have different contents but always the same truth-value where uttered. Donnellan vindicated! (Contrary to my own earlier expectations.)

I am beginning to suspect that I bungled things even worse than I thought in talking about meanings, contents, etc. The meaning of a sentence type should probably be a function from utterances to *contents* rather than from something like utterances to truth-values. If this correction were made then we could properly say that (13) and (17) differ in meaning.

It would also give a more satisfactory analysis of a sentence type like:

(25) Dthat ['the morning star'] is identical with dthat ['the evening star'].

Although (25) expresses a true content on some possible occasions of use and a false content on others, it is not simply contingent, since on all possible occasions its content is either necessary or impossible. (I am assuming that distinct individuals don't merge.) Even one who grasped the meaning of (25) would not of course know its truth-value simply on witnessing an utterance. Thus we answer the question how an utterance of an identity sentence can be informative though *necessary!*

Another example on the question of necessity. Suppose I now utter:

(26) I am more than thirty-six years old.

What I have said is true. Is it necessary? This may be arguable. (*Could* I be younger than I am at this very same time?) But the fact that the sentence, if uttered at an earlier time or by another person, could express something false is certainly irrelevant. The point is: simply to look at the spectrum of *truth-values* of different utterances of (25) and (26) and not at the spectrum of *contents* of different utterances of (25) and (26) is to miss something interesting and important.

I earlier said that my demonstrative use is not quite Donnellan's referential use, and I want now to return to that point. When a speaker uses an expression demonstratively he *usually* has in mind—so to speak—an intended demonstratum, and the demonstration is thus *teleological.* Donnellan and I disagree on how to bring the intended demonstratum into the picture. To put it crudely, Donnellan believes that for most purposes we should take the demonstratum to be the intended demonstratum. I believe that these are different notions that may well involve different objects.

From my point of view the situation is interesting precisely because we have a case here in which a person can fail to say what he intended to say, and the failure is not a linguistic error (such as using the wrong word) but a factual one. It seems to me that such a situation can arise only in the demonstrative mode.

Suppose that without turning and looking I point to the place on my wall which has long been occupied by a picture of Rudolf Carnap and I say:

(27) Dthat [I point as above] is a picture of one of the greatest
      philosophers of the twentieth century.

But unbeknownst to me, someone has replaced my picture of Carnap with one of Spiro Agnew. I think it would simply be wrong to argue an 'ambiguity' in the demonstration, so great that it can be bent to my intended demonstratum. I have said of a picture of Spiro Agnew that it pictures one of the greatest philosophers of the twentieth century. And my speech and demonstration suggest no other natural interpretation to the linguistically competent public observer.

Still, it would be perhaps equally wrong not to pursue the notion of the intended demonstratum. Let me give three reasons for that pursuit:

1. The notion is epistemologically interesting in itself.
2. It may well happen—as Donnellan has pointed out—that we succeed in communicating what we intended to say in spite of our failure to say it (E.g. the mischievous fellow who switched pictures on me would understand full well what I was intending to say.)
3. There are situations where the demonstration is sufficiently ill-structured in itself so that we would regularly take account of the intended demonstratum as, *within limits*, a legitimate disambiguating or vagueness removing device.

I have two kinds of examples for this third point. First, there are the case of vague demonstrations by a casual wave of the hand. I suppose that ordinarily we would allow that a demonstration had been successful if the intended object were *roughly* where the speaker pointed. That is, we would not bring out surveying equipment to help determine the content of the speaker's assertion; much more relevant is what he intended to point at. Second, whenever I point at something, from the surveyor's point of view I point at many things. When I point at my son (and say 'I love dthat'), I may also be pointing at a book he is holding, his jacket, a button on his jacket, his skin, his heart, and his dog standing beside him—from the surveyor's point of view. *My* point is that if I intended to point at my son and it is true that I love him, then what I said is true. And the fact that I do not love his jacket does not make it equally false. There are, of course, limits to what can be accomplished by intentions (even the best of them). No matter how hard I intend Carnap's picture, in the earlier described case, I do not think it reasonable to call the content of my utterance true.

Another example where I would simply distinguish the content asserted and the content intended is in the use of 'I'.[32] A person might utter:

(2) I am a general.

intending—that is 'having in mind'—de Gaulle, and being under the delusion that he himself was de Gaulle. But the linguistic constraints on the possible demonstrata of 'I' will not allow anyone other than de Gaulle so to demonstrate de Gaulle, no matter how hard they try.

All this familiarity with demonstratives has led me to believe that I was mistaken in 'Quantifying In' in thinking that the most fundamental cases of what I might now describe as a person having a propositional attitude (believing, asserting, etc.) towards a singular proposition required that the person be *en rapport* with the subject of the proposition. It is now clear that I can assert *of* the first child to be born in the twenty-first century that *he* will be bald, simply by assertively uttering,

(29) Dthat ['the first child to be born in the twenty-first century'] will be bald.

I do not now see how the requirement of being *en rapport* with the subject of a singular proposition fits in. Are there two kinds of singular propositions? Or are there just two different ways to know them?

EXCITING FUTURE EPISODES

1. Making sense out of the foregoing.
2. Showing how nicely (3) and (17) illustrate an early point about the possibility of incorporating contextual factors (here, a demonstration) as part of the content of the utterance. Another example compares uses of 'the person at whom I am pointing' as demonstration and as subject.
3. Justifying calling (17) a *de re* form by showing how it can be used to explicate the notion of modality *de re* without depending on scope.
4. Extending the demonstrative notion to *in*definite descriptions to see if it is possible so to explicate the $\pm$ specific idea. (It isn't.)
5. Improving (by starting all over) the analysis of the relation between Montague's treatment of indexicals and my treatment of demonstratives.
6. Showing how the treatment of proper names in the Kripke–Kaplan–Donnellan way (if there is such) is akin (?) to demonstratives.
7. Discussing the role of common noun phrases in connection with demonstratives, as in:

(30) Dthat coat [the speaker points at a boy wearing a coat] is dirty.

8. Quine's contention that the content of any utterance can also be expressed by an eternal sentence. Is it true?

9. Much more to say about the phenomenology of intending to demonstrate *x*, and also about the truth conditions of '*y* intends to demonstrate *x*'.

10. Demonstratives, dubbings, definitions, and other forms of language learning. Common nouns: what they mean and how we learn it. This section will include such pontifications as the following:

It is a mistake to believe that normal communication takes place through the encoding and decoding of general propositions, by means of our grasp of *meanings*. It is a more serious mistake, because more pernicious, to believe that other aspects of communication can be accounted for by a vague reference to 'contextual features' of the utterance. Indeed, we first learn the meanings of almost all parts of our language by means quite different from those of the formal definitions studied in metamathematics; and the means used for first teaching the meanings of words, rather than withering away, are regularly and perhaps even essentially employed thereafter in all forms of communication.

Notes

This chapter appeared originally in its present form with the following warning: 'This paper was prepared for and read at the 1970 Stanford Workshop on Grammar and Semantics. Peter Cole has persuaded me—against my better judgement— that it has aged long enough to be digestible. The paper has not been revised other than to remove the subtitle comment "[Stream of Consciousness Draft: Errors, confusions, and disorganizations are not to be taken seriously]."' That injunction must still be strictly obeyed. Some parts of this ramble are straightened out in the excessive refinements of "Bob and Carol and Ted and Alice" which appeared in the proceedings for which this was destined: J. Hintikka, J. Moravcsik, and P. Suppes (eds.), *Approaches to Natural Language* (Dordrecht, 1973). A more direct presentation of the resulting theory along with some of its applications is to be found in "Demonstratives" (mimeo, Los Angeles: Dept. of Philosophy, 1977). An intermediate progress report occurs in "On the Logic of Demonstratives", *The Journal of Philosophical Logic*, 8 (1979), 81–98; reprinted in N. Salmon and S. Soames (eds.), *Propositions and Attitudes* (New York: Oxford University Press, 1988).

'DTHAT' is pronounced as a single syllable.'

1. K. S. Donnellan, 'Reference and Definite Descriptions', *Philosophical Review*, 75 (1966), 298 [p. 375 in this vol.].

2. L. Linsky, 'Reference and Referents', in C. Caton (ed.), *Philosophy and Ordinary Language* (Urbana, 1963).

3. Donnellan, 'Reference and Definite Descriptions', p. 299 [375].

4. Ibid. 297 [374].

5. Ibid. 303 [379].

6. Ibid.

7. J. Hintikka, 'Individual, Possible Worlds, and Epistemic Logic', *Noûs*, 1 (1967), 47.

8. B. Russell, *The Principles of Mathematics* (Cambridge, 1903).

9. B. Russell, 'On Denoting', *Mind*, 14 (1905), 479–93.

10. R. Carnap, *Meaning and Necessity* (Chicago, 1947).

11. B. Russell, *Introduction to Mathematical Philosophy* (London, 1920), 174.

12. Both 'denoting concept' and 'denoting phrase' are Russell's terms used in Russell's way.

13. An e.g. is the possibility of producing set theoretical representations of the system of natural numbers which make all even numbers alike in certain set theoretical features (distinct from such numerical features as divisibility by 2) and all odd numbers alike in other set theoretical features, or which provide simple and elegant definitions (i.e. representations) of certain basic numerical operations and relations such as *less than* or *plus*, etc.

14. It's not too easy to single out such phrases without the help of some theory about logical form or some semantical theory. I suppose what I am after is what linguists call syntactical criteria. But I have had difficulty in finding one which will not let in phrases like 'a spy'. Another difficulty is concerned with phrases like 'John's brother' which seem to vary in their uniqueness suppositions. 'John's brother is the man in dark glasses' carries, for me, the supposition that John has just one brother; whereas 'The man in dark glasses is John's brother' does not. In fact the latter seems the most natural formulation when suppositions about the number of John's brothers are completely absent, since both 'The man in dark glasses in one of John's brothers' and 'The man in dark glasses is a brother of John' suppose, for me, that John has more than one brother.

15. The question whether all uses of demonstratives are accompanied by demonstrations depends on a number of factors, some empirical, some stipulative, and some in the twilight zone of theoretical ingenuity. The stipulative question is whether we use 'demonstrative' to describe certain phrases which might also be described by enumeration or some such syntactical device, e.g. all phrases beginning with either 'this' or 'that' and followed by a common noun phrase; or whether we use 'demonstrative' to describe a certain characteristic *use* of such phrases. In the latter case it may be stipulatively true that an utterance containing a demonstrative must be accompanied by a demonstration. In the former case, the question turns both on how people in fact speak and on how clever our theoretician is in producing recherché demonstrations to account for apparent counterexamples.

16. This formulation probably needs sharpening. Don't take it as a definition.

17. It should not be supposed that my practice indicates any confidence as to the nature and structure of what I call *demonstrations* or the proper form for a

demonstration–description to take. Indeed, these are difficult and important questions which arise repeatedly in what follows.

18. G. Frege, 'Ueber Sinn und Bedeutung', *Zeitschrift für Philosophie und philosophische Kritik*, trans. (by Feigl) in H. Feigl and W. Sellars (eds.), *Readings in Philosophical Analysis* (New York, 1949). Also trans. (by Black) in P. Geach and M. Black. (eds.), *Translations from the Writings of Gottlob Frege*, (Oxford, 1966).

19. Ibid., emphasis added.

20. W. V. Quine, 'Quantifiers and Propositional Attitudes', *Journal of Philosophy*, 53 (1956), 177–87.

21. D. Kaplan, 'Quantifying In', *Synthese*, 19 (1968), 178–214. I will attempt later to press the case that this use of proper names, which involves no waving of hands or fixing of glance, may be assimilated to the more traditional forms of demonstrative use.

22. 'In the case of genuinely proper names like "Aristotle" opinions as regards their sense may diverge. As such it may, e.g., be suggested: Plato's disciple and the teacher of Alexander the Great. Whoever accepts this sense will interpret the meaning of the statement "Aristotle was born in Stagira" differently from one who interpreted the sense of "Aristotle" as the Stagirite teacher of Alexander the Great' (from Feigl's translation of Frege's 'Ueber Sinn und Bedeutung').

23. A third kind of indicative device is the picture. Consideration of pictures, which to me lie somewhere between pointing and describing, may help drive home the parallels—in terms of the distinction between the object indicated and the manner of indication   between description, depiction, and demonstration.

24. That all utterances are in English is a general and implicit assumption except where it is explicitly called into question.

25. 'Dhe' is really a combination of the demonstrative with a common noun phrase. It stands for 'dthat male'. More on such combinations later.

26. W. V. Quine, *Word and Object* (Cambridge, Mass., 1960), 193.

27. There are, of course, 2 hidden relativizations involved even for eternal sentences. One is to a *language*, i.e. an association of meanings with words. The Knoh-English example was meant to dramatize this relativization. The other is to a possible world. There is always the implicit reference to the actual world when we use just the expression 'true'. If the analogy between moments of time and possible worlds holds—as some philosophers think—then maybe we should begin our classification of sentences not with explicitly dated eternal sentences like 'in 1970 ...' but with 'perfect' sentences like 'In the possible world Charlie in 1970 ...'.

28. Rather than talking directly of these functions, I should really talk of entities like $\langle \langle \text{'The'}, S \rangle, P \rangle$ and only derivatively of the functions. I will do so in the next draft.

29. This is aside from the inadequacy mentioned in the previous footnote, which continues to bother me.

30. The most relevant works are 'Pragmatics' (1968) and 'Pragmatics and Inten-sional Logic' (1970), both reprinted in R. Montague, *Formal Philosophy* (New Haven, 1974).

31. I am still bothered by the notion of an utterance at *t* in *w*, where there is no utterance at *t* in *w*.

32. 'I' is, of course, a demonstrative; as opposed, e.g., to 'the person who is uttering this utterance', which contains only the demonstrative 'this utterance'. Let us compare utterances of: (i) I am exhausted; (ii) The person who is uttering this utterance is exhausted. Both are uttered by *s* on the same occasion (!). To find the truth-value of the content of (ii) in *w'* we must first locate the same utterance in *w'* (if it exists there at all) and see who, if anyone, is uttering it. Since *s* could well be exhausted silently in *w'*, the two contents are not the same.

Bibliographic Postscript

This paper was written (if that is the right word for it) in early 1970. Since that time I have written (really written, and even published) several papers in which the ideas of the present work are expounded and developed. These words are:

'On the Logic of Demonstratives', *The Journal of Philosophical Logic*, 8 (1979), 81–98; reprinted in N. Salmon and S. Soames (eds.), *Propositions and Attitudes* (New York: Oxford University Press, 1988).

'Demonstratives: An Essay on the Semantics, Logic, Metaphysics, and Epis-temology of Demonstratives and other Indexicals', in J. Almog, J. Perry, and H. K. Wettstein (eds.), *Themes from Kaplan* (New York: Oxford University Press, 1989), 481–563.

'Afterthoughts' in J. Almog, J. Perry, and H. K. Wettstein (eds.), *Themes from Kaplan* (New York: Oxford University Press, 1989), 565–614.

And to some extent:

'Bob and Carol and Ted and Alice' in J. Hintikka *et al.* (eds.), *Approaches to Natural Language* (Dordrecht: Reidel, 1973), 490–518.

'Opacity', in L. Hahn (ed.), *The Philosophy of W. V. Quine*, The Library of Living Philosophers (Open Court, 1986), La Salle, Ill.: 229–89. See especially section 7.

Chapter 29

Frege on Demonstratives

John Perry

In "The Thought," Frege briefly discusses sentences containing such demonstratives as "today," "here," and "yesterday," and then turns to certain questions that he says are raised by the occurrence of "I" in sentences (T, 24–26 [15–17]).[1] He is led to say that, when one thinks about oneself, one grasps thoughts that others cannot grasp, that cannot be communicated. Nothing could be more out of the spirit of Frege's account of sense and thought than an incommunicable, private thought. Demonstratives seem to have posed a severe difficulty for Frege's philosophy of language, to which his doctrine of incommunicable senses was a reaction.

In the first part of the paper, I explain the problem demonstratives pose for Frege, and explore three ways he might have dealt with it. I argue that none of these ways provides Frege with a solution to his problem consistent with his philosophy of language. The first two are plausible as solutions, but contradict his identification of the sense expressed by a sentence with a thought. The third preserves the identification, but is implausible. In the second part, I suggest that Frege was led to his doctrine of incommunicable senses as a result of some appreciation of the difficulties his account of demonstratives faces, for these come quickly to the surface when we think about "I." I argue that incommunicable senses won't help. I end by trying to identify the central problem with Frege's approach, and sketching an alternative.

I

Before explaining the problem posed by demonstratives, certain points about Frege's philosophy of languages need to be made.

First appeared in *Philosophical Review* 86 (1977): 474–497. Reprinted by permission of *Philosophical Review* and John Perry. © 1977 Cornell University.

In "On Sense and Reference," Frege introduces the notion of sense, in terms of the cognitive value of sentences. He then goes on to make two key identifications. First, he identifies the sense of a sentence with the thought it expresses. Then, he identifies the thought expressed by a sentence, and so the sense it has, with the indirect reference of the sentence in the scope of a cognitive verb.

The phrases "the sense of a sentence," "the thought expressed by a sentence," and "the indirect reference of a sentence," are not mere synonyms. They have different senses, though, if Frege's account is correct, they have the same reference. In particular, each is associated, as Frege introduces it, with a separate criterion of difference.

Sense

In the beginning of "On Sense and Reference," Frege introduces the notion of sense as a way of accounting for the difference in cognitive value of the senses of "$a = a$" and "$a = b$," even when both are true, and so made up of coreferential expressions (SR, 56–58 [563–565]). So a criterion of difference for sense is,

If S and S' have differing cognitive value, then S and S' have different senses.

Dummett's explanation of sense will help us to convert this to something more helpful. He emphasizes that sense is linked to understanding and truth. The sense of an expression is "what we know when we understand it," and what we know when we understand it is something like an ideal procedure for determining its reference. (F, 293, 589ff.) In the case of a sentence, whose reference is a truth value, the sense is that we know when, roughly, we know what would have to be done—whether or not this is humanly possible—to determine whether or not it is true.

What Frege seems to have in mind at the beginning of "On Sense and Reference," then, is a situation in which some person A who understands both "$a = a$" and "$a = b$," accepts the first while rejecting, or being unsure about, the second. The assumption seems to be, that if A associated just the same ideal procedures with both sentences, he would accept the second if he accepted the first. So he must not associate the same ideal procedures with both sentences, and so, since he understands them, their senses differ. So we have:

If A understands S and S', and accepts S as true while not accepting S', then S and S' have different senses.

This criterion of difference allows that sentences might have different senses, though provably or necessarily equivalent. A complex true mathematical equation might be provably equivalent to "$2 + 3 = 5$," and yet a perfectly competent speaker might accept the latter and reject the former, having made an error in calculation. To know an ideal procedure for determining reference, is not necessarily to have carried it out, or even to be able to.

Thought

"Thought" is not just a term introduced by Frege as another way of saying, "sense of a sentence." The notion derived from Frege's untangling of the jumbled notion of a judgment, into act, thought, and truth value. The thought is, first and foremost, "that for which the question of truth arises" (T, 20–22 [11–13]). This is clearly intended to be a criterion of difference for thoughts:

If S is true and S' is not, S and S' express different thoughts.

Indirect reference

Consider a report of a belief: "Copernicus believed that the planetary orbits are circles." On Frege's analysis, this is relational. "Believed that" stands for a relation, which is asserted to hold between Copernicus and whatever it is that "the planetary orbits are circles" refers to as it occurs in this sentence. Standing alone, "the planetary orbits are circles" would refer to the False, but here it clearly does not have that ordinary reference. If it did, the substitution of any false sentence at all should preserve truth of the whole report (SR, 66–67 [570]). The notion of the indirect reference of "the planetary orbits are circles," is just whatever it is, that this sentence has as reference here. (The phrase is first used in connection with indirect discourse (SR, 59 [565]).) Now if "$a\,R\,b$" is true, and "$a\,R\,c$" is not, b is not c. So we have a clear criterion of difference:

If 'A believes S' is true, and 'A believes S'' is not, then S and S' do not have the same indirect reference.

So we have three separable criterion of difference. But Frege, as noted, identifies the sense of S the thought expressed by S, and the indirect reference of S. So we are led to a further principle:

S and S' have different senses, if and only if they express different thoughts, and if and only if they have different indirect references.

Sense completers

Frege takes the structure of language as a suggestive guide to the structure of senses and objects. Just as he views the sentence,

two plus two equals four

as the result of combining the complete

two

with the incomplete

( ) plus two equals four,

so he sees the sense of "two plus two equals four" as determined by the sense of "two" and the sense of "( ) plus two equals four." The sense of the latter is incomplete; the sense of the former completes it, to yield the complete sense of "two plus two equals four."

"( ) plus two equals four" could also be made into a sentence by writing "something" in the blank; similarly the sense of "( ) plus two equals four" can be completed with the sense of "something." The sense of "something," however, unlike the sense of "two," is itself also incomplete. Where "two" refers to an object, "something" refers to a concept. Two appropriately related incomplete senses can combine to form a complete sense; two complete senses cannot combine at all (CT, 538).

Thus the class of *sense completers* for a given incomplete sense is hybrid, containing both complete and incomplete senses. But the term will be useful in what follows.

Sense had and sense expressed

The structure of language is not always a sure guide to the structure of senses. Not everything we count as a sentence has a complete sense. Consider (1),

(1) Russia and Canada quarrelled when Nemtsanov defected.

"Russia and Canada quarrelled," as it occurs as a clause in (1), does not have a complete sense (SR, 71 [581]; T, 37 [28]). It refers to a concept of times and thus must have an incomplete sense. "When Nemtsanov defected" refers to a time; the sentence is true if the time referred to falls under the concept referred to. Thus the sense of "when Nemtsanov defected" is a sense completer for the sense of "Russia and Canada quarrelled."

So the sense of the sentence "Russia and Canada quarrelled" is not a thought. Not any sentence, but only a sentence "complete in every respect" expresses a thought (T, 37 [28]).

Now "Russia and Canada quarrelled" could be used, without a dependent clause, to express a thought. If it appeared alone, we might take it to express, *on that occasion*, the sense of

At some time or other, Russia and Canada quarrelled.

In another setting, for example after the question, "What happened when Nemtsanov defected?", the sentence would express the sense of (1). So we must, even before considering demonstratives, distinguish between the sense a sentence *has* on each occasion of use and the senses it *expresses* on various occasions of use. For an "eternal" sentence, one that really is "complete in every respect," the two will be the same; for a sentence like "Russia and Canada quarrelled," the sense *had* is incomplete; the sense *expressed* on a given occasion will be the result of completing that sense, with some sense completer available from the context of utterance. It is clearly only the sense expressed on such occasions, that Frege wants to identify with a thought.

The problem posed by demonstratives

We are now in a position to see why demonstratives pose a problem for Frege.

I begin by quoting the passage in "The Thought" in which Frege discusses demonstratives in general.

> often ... the mere wording, which can be grasped by writing or the gramophone, does not suffice for the expression of the thought ... If a time indication is needed by the present tense [as opposed to cases in which it is used to express timelessness, as in the statement of mathematical laws] one must know when the sentence was uttered to apprehend the thought correctly. Therefore, the time of utterance is part of the expression of the thought. If someone wants to say the same today as he expressed yesterday using the word 'today', he must replace this word with 'yesterday'. Although the thought is the same its verbal expression must be different so that the sense, which would otherwise be affected by the differing times of utterance, is readjusted. The case is the same with words like 'here' and 'there'. In all such cases the mere wording, as it is given in writing, is not the complete expression of the thought, but the knowledge of certain accompanying conditions of utterance, which are used as means of expressing the thought, are needed for its correct apprehension. The pointing of fingers, hand movements, glances may belong here too. The same utterance containing the word 'I' will express different thoughts in the mouths of different men, of which some may be true, others false. (T, 24 [15]).

Consider (2),

(2) Russia and Canada quarrelled today.

The sentence "Russia and Canada quarrelled" has in (2), as in (1), only an incomplete sense. So presumably "today" in (2) must somehow do what "when Nemtsanov defected" does in (1), and supply us with a completing sense. But it does not seem to do this at all.

If I uttered (2) on August 1, I expressed something true, on August 2, something false. If "today" had the same sense on August 1 as on August 2, then (2) in its entirety must have had the same sense on both occasions. If so, the sense of (2) must be incomplete, for if it were complete, its truth value could not change.

So, if "today" provides a completing sense on both days, its sense must change just at midnight. But what we know when we understand how to use "today" doesn't seem to change from day to day.

When we understand a word like "today," what we seem to know is a rule taking us from an occasion of utterance to a certain object. "Today" takes us to the very day of utterance, "yesterday" to the day before the day of utterance, "I" to the speaker, and so forth. I shall call this the *role* of the demonstrative. I take a context to be a set of features of an actual utterance, certainly including time, place, and speaker, but probably also more. Just what a context must include is a difficult question, to be answered only after detailed study of various demonstratives. The object a demonstrative takes us to in a given context, I shall call its value in that context or on that occasion of use. Clearly, we must grant "today" a role, the same on both occasions of use. And we must, as clearly, give it different values on the two occasions.

Any reasonable account has to recognize that demonstratives have roles. The role of a demonstrative does not seem reducible to other notions available from Frege's philosophy. Senses do not carry us from context to references, but directly to references, the same on each occasion of use. One might suppose that "yesterday" could be thought to have just the sense of "the day before." But,

(3) Russia and Canada quarrelled the day before

does not have the same sense as (4).

(4) Russia and Canada quarrelled yesterday.

If I ask on August 5, "Did Russia and Canada quarrel August 2?," (3) would imply that they quarrelled on August 1, (4) that they quarrelled on August 4. If (3) were uttered when no day had already been mentioned, it would not express anything complete, but simply give rise to the question, "before what?" An utterance of (4) would still be fully in order.

Frege recognizes that demonstratives have roles, or at least that the context of utterance is crucial when dealing with demonstratives. He does not talk about the sense of "today" or "I" so he also seems to have recognized that the role of a demonstrative is not just a sense, as he has explained senses.

But Frege clearly thinks that, given knowledge of the accompanying conditions of utterance, we can get from an utterance of a sentence like (2) or (4) to a thought. He must have thought, then, that the demonstrative provides us not simply with an object—its value on the occasion of utterance—but with a *completing sense*. This is puzzling. Neither the unchanging role of "today," or its changing value, provides us with a completing sense. A day is not a sense, but a reference corresponding to indefinitely many senses (SR, 71 [581]). There is no route back from reference to sense. So how do we get from the incomplete sense of "Russia and Canada quarrelled," the demonstrative "today," and the context to a thought? This is the problem demonstratives pose for Frege.

I shall first describe two options Frege might have taken, which would have excused him from the necessity of finding a completing sense. I shall argue that Frege did not take these options, and could not, given his identification of sense expressed and thought.

Sense as Roles?

Let $S(d)$ be a sentence containing a demonstrative d. Without the demonstrative, we have something, $S(\ )$, that has an incomplete sense, and so refers to a concept. This may actually still be a sentence, as when we remove "today" from (2), or it may look more like it should, as when we remove the "I" from "I am wounded."

The following scheme gives us a rule for getting from a particular context, to a truth value, for any such sentence $S(d)$.

$S(d)$ is true when uttered in context c, if and only if the value of d in c falls under the concept referred to by $S(\ )$.[2]

Such a rule is the *role of $S(d)$*. It is just an extension of the notion of the role of a demonstrative. Roles take us from contexts to objects. In the case of a sentence, the object is a truth value.

Thus (4) is true as uttered on August 2, if and only if August 1 is a day that falls under the concept referred to by "Russia and Canada quarrelled." "I am ill" as uttered by Lauben is true if and only if Lauben falls under the concept referred to by "( ) is ill."

The role of a sentence containing a demonstrative is clearly analogous in many ways to the sense of a sentence not containing a demonstrative. The role is a procedure for determining truth value, just as the sense is. The difference is that the role is a procedure which starts from a context.

This analogy suggests an option, which Frege might have taken. He might have identified the sense expressed by a sentence containing a demonstrative with its role. This would amount to a generalization of the notion of sense. On this view, an incomplete sense like that of "Russia and Canada quarrelled," could be completed in two ways. A sense completer, such as the sense of "when Nemtsanov defected," gives us a complete sense of the old sort. A demonstrative, like "today," yields a sense of the new sort, a role. No complete sense of the old sort is involved at all in the utterance of a sentence containing a demonstrative, so no completing sense need be found.

But this cannot have been Frege's view. For it is clear that he thinks a thought has been expressed in the utterance of a sentence containing a demonstrative. The role of the sentence cannot be identified with the thought, for a sentence could express the same role on different occasions while having different truth-values. So by the criteria of difference for thoughts, roles are not thoughts. By the identification of the sense expressed by a sentence and the thought expressed, roles are not the senses expressed by a sentence.

Thoughts as information

We can put the problem this way. (2), as uttered on August 1st, with the role of "today" fully mastered, seems to yield just this information:

(i) an incomplete sense, that of "Russia and Canada quarrelled;"
(ii) an object, the day August 1st, 1976.

(i) and (ii) do not uniquely determine a thought, but only an equivalence class of thoughts. Belonging to this equivalence class will be just those thoughts obtainable by completing the sense of "Russia and Canada quarrelled" with a sense completer which determines, as reference, August 1st, 1976. I shall call thoughts related in this manner *informationally equivalent*.[3]

The second option I shall discus, is introducing a new notion of a thought, corresponding to such a class of informationally equivalent thoughts. Since the information in (i) and (ii) is sufficient to identify such a class, without identifying any one of its members, this would explain how we can get from (i) and (ii) to a thought, without needing a completing sense.

On this view, an utterance of $S(d)$ in context c, and $S'(d')$ in context c', will express the same thought if the (incomplete) senses of $S(\ )$ and $S'(\ )$ are the same, and if the value of d in c is the same as the value of d' in c'. Thus (2), uttered on August 1, and (4), uttered on August 2, would express the same thought. Dummett interprets Frege in this way (F, 384).

If someone wants to say the same today as he expressed yesterday using the word 'today', he must replace this with 'yesterday'. Although the thought is the same its verbal expression must be different....

But this cannot have been Frege's view. This criterion actually introduces a new kind of thought, corresponding to informationally equivalent classes of thoughts of the old kind. The thought expressed by Lauben when he says "I am wounded" to Leo Peter, cannot be identified with the thought expressed by any nondemonstrative completion of the same incomplete sense in which the singular term refers to Lauben, such as

The man born on the thirteenth of September, 1875, in N.N. is wounded.

The only doctor who lives in the house next door to Rudolf Lingens is wounded.

These express different thoughts, so the thought Lauben expresses with "I am wounded" cannot be identified with *the* thought they both express; there just isn't any such thought. There is no more reason to identify it with the one than with the other, or with any other such thought. Nor can thoughts of this new type be identified with classes of thoughts of the old, for in different possible circumstances the pair, Dr. Lauben and the incomplete sense of "( ) am ill," would correspond to different sets of Fregean thoughts. If Lauben had moved, the two Fregean thoughts in question would not be informationally equivalent. We have here a radically new kind of thought, of which Frege would not have approved, even if he had seen its necessity. We have in effect made the value of the demonstrative a part of the thought. But Frege insists that only senses can be parts of senses.

Dummett remarks,

It is, of course, quite unnecessary to suppose that a thought expressible by the utterance on a particular occasion of a sentence containing a token reflexive expression can also be expressed by some 'eternal' sentence containing no such expressions. (F, 384)

But it is not only unnecessary, but impossible, on this account, that the thought should be expressed by an eternal sentence. It is not the right kind of thought for an eternal sentence to express.

Second, and closely related, this notion of a thought would violate the criteria of difference.

Suppose I am viewing the harbor from downtown Oakland; the bow and stern of the aircraft carrier *Enterprise* are visible, though its middle is obscured by a large building. The name "*Enterprise*" is clearly visible on the bow, so when I tell a visitor, "This is the *Enterprise*," pointing towards the bow, this is readily accepted. When I say, pointing to the stern clearly several city blocks from the bow, "That is the *Enterprise*," however, she refuses to believe me. By the criterion of difference, a different sense was expressed the first time than the second. On the present suggested criterion of identity for thoughts, the same thought was expressed; the incomplete sense was the same in both cases, and the value of the demonstratives was the *Enterprise* in both cases. To adopt this notion of a thought, Frege would have to give up the identification of sense expressed and thought expressed.

This is, of course, simply a variation on Frege's own Morning Star example. Suppose I point to Venus in the morning, and again in the evening, saying "That's the Morning Star." My listener may accept what I say the first time, and continue to think I was right, while rejecting what I say the second time. Here the *same* sentence has a different cognitive value at different times—for my listener has not changed her mind. The sentence does not have different cognitive values because the words have undergone a change of meaning, but because the sentence alone does not express the complete sense. Some supplementation is needed; here the gestures toward Venus provide it. But just what supplementation do they provide? If the supplementation were merely taken to be Venus itself—which is what the present proposal amounts to—then the sense of the sentence would have been supplemented in the same way on both occasions. But then we would have the same sense expressed in both occasions, in violation of the criterion of difference for senses.

Frege does not explicitly mention the demonstratives "this" and "that." So it is worth pointing out that examples can be constructed using demonstratives he does mention. For example, I might accept what you say at 11:15 p.m. when you utter "Russia and Canada quarrelled today," but disbelieve you at 12:15 a.m. when you utter "Russia and Canada quarrelled yesterday," having lost track of time.

Of course, Frege may have meant to introduce such a new notion of a thought at this point. That he does not explain it, counts against this interpretation. And what he goes on to say, in the next paragraphs, seems to make it totally implausible. There he discusses proper names, and arrives at a point where he has all the materials for this notion of a thought in his hand, so to speak, and yet passes up the opportunity to mold them into the new notion. He describes a situation in which two men express different thoughts with the sentence "Gustav Lauben has been wounded," one knowing him as the unique man born a certain day, the other as the unique doctor living in a certain house. He recognizes that these different thoughts are systematically equivalent:

The different thoughts which thus result from the same sentence correspond in their truth-value, of course; that is to say, if one is true then all are true, and if one is false then all are false.

But he insists,

Nevertheless their distinctness must be recognized.

His reason here is clearly a complex example he has just constructed, in which sentences expressing such informationally equivalent thoughts have different cognitive value:

It is possible that Herbert Garner takes the sense of the sentence 'Dr. Lauben has been wounded' to be true while, misled by false information, taking the sense of 'Gustav Lauben has been wounded' to be false. Under the assumptions given these thoughts are therefore different. (T, 25 [17])

If demonstratives had driven Frege, three paragraphs before this, to the introduction of a class of thoughts, corresponding to a class of informationally equivalent thoughts of the old sort, I think he would have employed it, or at least mentioned it, here.

Senses, considered to be roles, cannot be thoughts. Thoughts, considered as information, cannot be senses. If Frege is to keep his identification of sense expressed by a sentence, with thought expressed by a sentence, he must find, somewhere, a completing sense.

Demonstratives as providing a completing sense

How can we extract from a demonstrative, an appropriate completing sense? Such a sense, it seems, would have to be intimately related to, the sense of a unique description of the value of the demonstrative in the context of utterance. But where does such a description come from?

"Today" seems to get us only to a day. And a day does not provide a particular description of itself.

In the case of proper names, Frege supposes that different persons attach different senses to the same proper name. To find the sense a person identifies with a given proper name, we presumably look at his beliefs. If he associates the sense of description D with Gustav Lauben, he should believe,

Gustav Lauben is D.

Perhaps, with demonstratives too, Frege supposes that speakers and listeners, in grasping the thought, provide the demonstrative with an appropriate sense. To understand a demonstrative, is to be able to supply a sense for it on each occasion, which determines as reference the value the demonstrative has on that occasion.[4] This is, I think, as near as we are likely to come to what Frege had in mind.

There is a problem here, with no analog in the case of proper names. One can attach the same sense to a proper name, once and for all. But, since the demonstrative takes a different value on different occasions, different senses must be supplied. So the demonstrative could not be regarded as an abbreviation, or something like an abbreviation, for some appropriate description.

But still, can we not say that for each person, the sense of the demonstrative "today" for that person on a given day, is just the sense of one of the descriptions D (or some combination of all the descriptions) such that on that day he believes,

Today is D.

One objection to this, is that we seem to be explaining the senses of sentences containing demonstratives in terms of beliefs whose natural expressions contain demonstratives. But there are three more serious problems.

The first problem might be called the *irrelevancy of belief*.[5] The sense I associate with my use of a demonstrative, do not determine the thought expressed by a sentence containing that demonstrative.

Suppose I believe that today is the fourteenth of October, 1976. From that it does not follow that, when I utter

Today is sunny and bright

I express the thought

The fourteenth of October is sunny and bright.

For suppose today is really the fifteenth, cloudy, and dull. Then what I have said is wrong, whatever the weather was like on the fourteenth.

The second problem, we might call the *non-necessity of belief.* I can express a thought with "Today is sunny and bright"—that is, say something for which the question of truth arises—whether or not I associate any correct sense at all with "today." I may have no idea at all what day it is, and not be able, without recourse to "today" or other demonstratives, to say anything about today at all, that does not describe dozens of other days equally well.

Both of these problems are illustrated by Rip Van Winkle. When he awakes on October 20, 1823, and says with conviction,

Today is October 20, 1803

the fact that he is sure he is right doesn't make him right, as it would if the thought expressed were determined by the sense he associated with "today." And, what is really the same point from a different angle, he doesn't fail to be wrong, as would be the case if "today" had to be associated with a completing sense which determined the value of "today" as reference, before the question of truth arose for sentences in which it occurs.

To state my third objection, the *nonsufficiency of belief,* I shall shift to an example using the demonstrative "I." I do so because the objection is clearest with respect to this demonstrative, and because some awareness of this problem might help explain how consideration of "I" led Frege to incommunicable senses.

Let us imagine David Hume, alone in his study, on a particular afternoon in 1775, thinking to himself, "I wrote the *Treatise.*" Can anyone *else* apprehend the thought he apprehended by thinking this? First note that what he thinks is true. So no one could apprehend the same thought, unless they apprehended a true thought. Now suppose Heimson is a bit crazy, and thinks himself to be David Hume. Alone in his study, he says to himself, "I wrote the *Treatise.*" However much his inner life may, at that moment, resemble Hume's on that afternoon in 1775, the fact remains: Hume was right, Heimson is wrong. Heimson cannot think the very thought to himself the Hume thought to himself, by using the very same sentence.

Now suppose Frege's general account of demonstratives is right. Then it seems that, by using the very same sense that Hume supplied for "I,"

Heimson should be able to think the same thought, without using "I," that Hume did using "I." He will just have to find a true sentence, which expresses the very thought Hume was thinking, when he thought to himself, "I wrote the *Treatise*." But there just does not seem to be such a thought.

Suppose Heimson thinks to himself, "The author of the *Inquiries* wrote the *Treatise*." This is true, for the sense used to complete the sense of "( ) wrote the *Treatise*" determines Hume not Heimson as reference. But it seems clear that Hume could acknowledge "I wrote the *Treatise*" as true, while rejecting, "The author of the *Inquiries* wrote the *Treatise*." He might have forgotten that he wrote the *Inquiries*; perhaps Hume had episodes of forgetfulness in 1775. But then the thought Heimson thinks, and the one Hume apprehended, are not the same after all, by the identification of thoughts with senses, and the criterion of difference for senses.

One might suppose that, while there is no particular sentence of this sort that must have had, for Hume, the same cognitive value as "I wrote the *Treatise*," there must be some such sentence or other that would have had the same cognitive value for him.

But I see no reason to suppose this is so. For now we have reached just the point where the first objection takes hold. There is no reason to believe we are on each occasion each equipped with some nondemonstrative equivalent of the demonstratives we use and understand. This goes for "I" as well as "today." After all, as I am imagining Heimson, he does not have any correct demonstrative free description of himself at hand. Every correct demonstrative free description he is willing to apply to himself refers to Hume instead. I'm not at all sure that I have one for myself.

To keep the identification between thought and sense intact, Frege must provide us with a completing sense. But then his account of demonstratives becomes impausible.

II

Frege follows his general discussion of demonstratives by saying that "I" gives rise to certain questions. He then makes the point, with the examples concerning Dr. Lauben discussed above, that various persons might associate various senses with the same proper name, if the person were presented to them in various ways. This discussion seems intended to prepare the way for the startling claim about thoughts about ourselves,

Now everyone is presented to himself in a particular and primitive way, in which he is presented to no-one else. So, when Dr. Lauben thinks that he has been wounded, he will probably take as a basis this primitive way in which he is presented to himself. And only Dr. Lauben himself can grasp thoughts determined in this way. But now he may want to communicate with others. He cannot communicate a thought which he alone can grasp. Therefore, if he now says 'I have been wounded', he must use the 'I' in a sense which can be grasped by others, perhaps in the sense of 'he is speaking to you at this moment', by doing which he makes the associated conditions of his utterance serve for the expression of his thought. (T, 25–26 [17])

Frege's doctrine appears to be this. When I use "I" to communicate, it works like other demonstratives, and perhaps could even be replaced by some phrase which included only other demonstratives. The sense would be completed in whatever way is appropriate for sentences containing these demonstratives. When I use "I" to think about myself, however, it has an incommunicable sense.

This is not quite right, for Frege would not have thought it necessary, in order to think about myself, to use language at all. It is at this point that Frege makes his famous remark, about how the battle with language makes his task difficult, in that he can only give his readers the thought he wants them to examine dressed up in linguistic form.

Nevertheless, it seems clear that Frege thinks there are senses, for each of us, that determine us as reference, which are incommunicable, and which would be the natural sense to associate with "I" if it did happen to be used, not merely to communicate with others, but think about oneself.

I suggest this doctrine about "I" is a reaction to the problems just mentioned, the third in particular. I am not at all certain that this is so. Philosophers have come to hold somewhat similar views about the self, beliefs about oneself, and "I," without thinking as rigorously as Frege did about these matters. Perhaps Frege had adopted some such view independently of his thinking about demonstratives, and simply wished to show he could accommodate it. It seems to me more likely, however, that Frege was led to this view by his own philosophical work, in particular by some realization of the problems I have discussed for his general account, as they apply particularly to "I." All three problems turned on the failure to find a suitable description for the value of the demonstrative, whose sense would complete the sense of the sentence in just the right way. If the sense we are looking for is private and incommunicable, it is no wonder the search was in vain.

But the appeal to private and incommunicable senses cannot, I think, be a satisfactory resolution of the problem.

In the first place, I see no reason to believe that "everyone is presented to himself in a particular and primitive way." Or at least, no reason to accept this, with such a reading that it leads to incommunicable senses.

Suppose M is the private and incommunicable sense, which is to serve as the sense of "I" when I think about myself. M cannot be a complex sense, resulting from the compounding of simpler, generally accessible senses. For it seems clear that it is sufficient, to grasp the result of such compounding, that one grasp the senses compounded. So M will have to be, as Frege says, primitive.

A sense corresponds to an aspect or mode of presentation (SR, 57, 58 [564–565]). There are, I hope, ways in which I am presented to myself, that I am presented to no one else, and aspects of me that I am aware of, that no one else is aware of. But this is not sufficient for Frege's purposes.

Suppose that only I am aware of the scratchiness of a certain fountain pen. Still, "thing which is scratchy" does not uniquely pick out this pen; this pen may not be the only one which falls under the concept this phrase stands for, though perhaps the only one of which I am aware. Similarly, just because there is some aspect, such that only I am aware that I have it, and M is the sense corresponding to that aspect, it does not follow that M determines as reference a concept that only I fall under, or that *the M*, (by which I mean the result of combining the sense of "the" with M), is a sense which determines just me as reference, and can appropriately be associated with my utterances of "I."

What is needed is a primitive aspect of me, which is not simply one that only I am aware of myself as having, but that I alone have. While there are doubtless complex aspects that only I have, and primitive aspects, that only I am aware of myself as having, I see no reason to believe there are primitive aspects, that only I have. Even if there were, if they were incommunicable, I should have no way of knowing there were, since I hardly ask others if they happened to have *mine*. So I shouldn't know that *the M* determined me as reference. But I do know that I am thinking about me, when I use the word "I" in thinking to myself.

My second point in opposition to incommunicable senses, is that the third objection does not merely apply to "I," but to at least one other demonstrative, "now." However one may feel about one's private and unique aspects, Frege's doctrine must appear less plausible when it is seen that it must be extended to other demonstratives.

Suppose the department meeting is scheduled for noon, September 15, 1976. Then only at that time could we say something true with (5).

(5) The meeting starts now.

Now consider any of the informationally equivalent thoughts we might have had the day before, for example (6).

(6) The meeting starts at noon, September 15, 1976.

It seems that one could accept this day before, and continue to accept it right through the meeting, without ever accepting (5), and even rejecting it firmly precisely at noon, simply by completely losing track of time. So (5) and (6) express different senses, and so different thoughts. And it seems this would be true, no matter what nondemonstrative informational equivalent we came up with instead of (6). So with "now," as with "I," it is not sufficient, to grasp the thought expressed with a demonstrative, to grasp an informational equivalent with a complete sense. Frege will have to have, for each time, a primitive and particular way in which it is presented to us at that time, which gives rise to thoughts accessible only at that time, and expressible, at it, with "now." This strikes me as very implausible. An appeal to incommunicable senses won't serve to patch up Frege's treatment.

I will conclude by sketching an alternative treatment of these problems. I try to show just how these recent examples motivate a break between sense and thought, and how, once that break is made, senses can be treated as roles, thoughts as information, and the other examples we have discussed handled.

III

Consider some of the things Hume might have thought to himself,

I am David Hume
This is Edinburgh
It is now 1775.

We would say of Hume, when he thought such things, that he knew *who* he was, *where* he was, and *when* it was. I shall call these self locating beliefs. The objections, posed in the last section to Frege's account of demonstratives, may be put in the following way: Having a self locating belief does not consist in believing a Fregean thought.

We can see that having such beliefs *could* not consist *wholly* in believing Fregean thoughts. Consider Frege's timeless realm of generally accessible thoughts. If Hume's knowing he was Hume, consisted in his believing certain true thoughts in this realm, then it would seem that anyone else could know that *he* was Hume, just by believing those same thoughts. But only Hume can know, or even truly believe, that he is Hume. Analogous remarks apply to his knowing where he was, and when it was.

Either there are some thoughts only Hume can apprehend, and his believing he is Hume consists in believing those thoughts, or self locating knowledge does not consist wholly in believing some true subset of the Fregean thoughts. Frege chose the first option; let's see what happens when we choose the second.

We accept that there is no thought only Hume can apprehend. Yet only he can know he is Hume. It must not just be the thought that he thinks, but the way that he thinks it, that sets him apart from the rest of us. Only Hume can think a true thought, by saying to himself,

I am Hume.

Self locating knowledge, then requires not just the grasping of certain thoughts, but the grasping of them via the senses of certain sentences containing demonstratives.

To firmly embed in our minds the importance that thinking a thought via one sense rather than another can have, let us consider another example. An amnesiac, Rudolf Lingens, is lost in the Stanford library. He reads a number of things in the library, including a biography of himself, and a detailed account of the library in which he is lost. He believes any Fregean thought you think might help him. He still won't know who he is, and where he is, no matter how much knowledge he piles up, until that moment when he is ready to say,

This place is aisle five, floor six, of Main Library, Stanford.
I am Rudolf Lingens.

If self locating knowledge consists not merely in believing certain thoughts, but believing them by apprehending certain senses, then senses cannot be thoughts. Otherwise it would make no sense to say that Hume and Heimson can apprehend all the same thoughts, but Hume can do so by apprehending different senses.

Let us then see how things begin to resolve themselves when this identification is given up. Let us speak of *entertaining* a sense, and apprehending a thought. So different thoughts may be apprehended, in different contexts, by entertaining the same sense (without supposing that it is an incomplete sense, somehow supplemented by a sense completer in the context), and the same thought, by entertaining different senses.

By breaking the connection between senses and thoughts, we give up any reason not to take the options closed to Frege. We can take the sense of a sentence containing a demonstrative to be a role, rather than a Fregean complete sense, and thoughts to be the new sort, individuated by object and incomplete sense, rather than Fregean thoughts. Though senses considered as roles, and thoughts considered as information, cannot be identified, each does its job in a way that meshes with the other. To have a thought we need an object and an incomplete sense. The demonstrative in context gives us the one, the rest of the sentence the other. The role of the entire sentence will lead us to Truth by leading us to a true thought, that is just in case the object falls under the concept determined as reference by the incomplete sense.[6]

Let us see how some of the examples we have discussed are handled.

We must suppose that both Hume and Heimson can entertain the same senses, and think the same thoughts. The difference between them is that they do not apprehend the same thoughts when they entertain the same senses. When Heimson entertains the sense of "I am the author of the *Treatise*" he apprehends the thought consisting of Heimson and the sense of "( ) is the author of the *Treatise*." This thought is false. When Hume entertains the same sense, he apprehends the thought consisting of Hume and the sense of "( ) is the author of the *Treatise*," which is true. Hume is right, Heimson is crazy.

Similarly, only at twelve noon can someone think the thought consisting of noon and the sense of "The meeting starts at ( )" by entertaining the sense of "the meeting starts now."

Why should we have a special category of self locating knowledge? Why should we care how someone apprehends a thought, so long as he does? I can only sketch the barest suggestion of an answer here. We use senses to individuate psychological states, in explaining and predicting action. It is the sense entertained, and not the thought apprehended, that is tied to human action. When you and I entertain the sense of "A bear is about to attack me," we behave similarly. We both roll up in a ball and try to be as still as possible. Different thoughts apprehended, same sense entertained, same behavior. When you and I both apprehend the thought that I am about to be attacked by a bear, we behave differently. I roll up in a ball, you run to get help. Same thought apprehended, different sense entertained, different behavior. Again, when you believe that the meeting begins on a given day at noon by entertaining, the day before, the sense of "the meeting begins tomorrow at noon," you are idle. Apprehending the same thought the next day, by entertaining the sense of "the meeting begins now," you jump up from your chair and run down the hall.

What of the indirect reference? Is the indirect reference of a sentence containing a demonstrative in the scope of such a cognitive verb, the sense or the thought?

It seems, a priori, that the "believes that" construction (to pick a particular verb) could work either way. That is,

A believes that S

might be designed to tell us the sense A entertains, or the thought A apprehends. The first seems a little more efficient. If we know the sense entertained, we can compute the thought apprehended, given the believer's context.

Nevertheless, it is surely the thought apprehended that is the indirect reference of a sentence containing a demonstrative in the scope of "believes." Consider (7), (8), and (9),

(7) I believe that Russia and Canada quarrelled today.

(8) Mary believed that Russia and Canada quarrelled today.

(9) Mary believed that Russia and Canada quarrelled yesterday.

Suppose Mary utters (7) on August 1, and I want to report the next day on what she believed. If I want to report the sense entertained, I should use (8). But this gives the wrong result. Clearly I would use (9). To get from the sentence embedded in (9), to the thought Mary apprehended, we take the value of the demonstrative in the context of the belief reporter, not in the context of the believer.

It has been suggested that we try to use the sense entertained by the believer in reporting his belief, whenever possible. What we have just said does not conflict with this. The point is simply that the function of thought identification dominates the function of sense identification, and when we use demonstratives, there is almost always a conflict.

There will be no conflict, when one is dealing with eternal sentences, or when one is reporting one's own current beliefs. The need for distinguishing sense from thought will not be forced to our attention, so long as we concentrate on such cases.

Let us now consider the Morning Star example.

Mary says "I believe that is the Morning Star" in the morning while pointing at Venus, and "I believe that is not the Morning Star" at night while pointing at Venus. It seems that Mary, though believing falsely, has not changed her mind, and does not believe a contradiction.

As long as we think of thoughts as senses, it will seem that anyone who understands the relevant sentences, will not believe both a thought and its negation. So long as we think of senses as thoughts, we shall think that anyone who accepts a sense at one time, and its negation at another, must have changed her mind. The correct principle is simply that no thoughtful person will accept a sense and its negation in the same context, since just by understanding the language, she should realize that she would thereby believe both a thought and its negation.

We should take "believing a contradiction," in the sense in which thoughtful people don't do it, to mean accepting senses of the forms S and not-S, relative to the same context of utterance. Mary doesn't do this; she accepts S in the morning, not-S in the evening. Has she then changed her mind? This must mean coming to disbelieve a thought once believed. We shouldn't take it to mean coming to reject a sense once accepted. I can reject "Today is sunny and bright" today, though I accepted it yesterday, without changing my mind about anything. So Mary hasn't changed her mind, either.

What she does do, is believe a thought and its negation. (Here we take the negation of a thought consisting of a certain object and incomplete sense, to be the thought consisting of the same object, and the negation of the incomplete sense.) I am inclined to think that only the habit of identifying sense and thought makes this seem implausible.

I have tried to suggest how, using the concepts of sense, thought, and indirect reference in a way compatible with the way Frege introduced them, but incompatible with his identifications, sentences containing demonstratives can be handled. I do not mean to imply that Frege could have simply made these alterations, while leaving the rest of his system intact. The idea of individuating thoughts by objects, or sequences of objects, would be particularly out of place in his system. The identification of thought with complete sense was not impulsive, but the result of pressure from many directions. I do not claim to have traced the problems that come to surface with demonstratives back to their ultimate origins in Frege's system.

IV

I have argued that Frege's identification of senses of sentences with thoughts leads to grave problems when sentences containing demonstratives are considered. The utterance of such a sentence in a context seems to yield only an incomplete sense and an object, not a complete sense of the sort a Fregean thought is supposed to be. He probably supposed that context supplies not just an object, but somehow a completing sense. There seems no place for such a sense to be found, save in the mind of the person who apprehends the thought expressed by the sentence. But to understand such a sentence, it is neither necessary nor sufficient to have grasped, and associated with the value of the demonstrative, any such sense. Frege's appeal to incommunicable senses in the case of "I," is probably an implausible attempt to deal with these problems. What is needed is to give up the identification of sense expressed with thought expressed. This would allow us to see the sense as a procedure for determining reference from a context, and the thought as identified by the incomplete sense and the value of the demonstrative. The identification of the thought, with the indirect reference of the sentence is the scope of a cognitive verb, need not be given up.[7]

Notes

1. The following abbreviations are used for works cited in the text. 'T' for Gottlob Frege "The Thought: A Logical Inquiry," reprinted in P. F. Strawson *Philosophical Logic* (Oxford, 1967), 17–38. This translation, by A. M. and Marcelle Quinton, appeared originally in *Mind*, Vol. 65 (1956), pp. 289–311. The original, "Der Gedanke. Eine logische Untersuchung," appeared in *Beiträge zur Philosophie des deutschen Idealismus*, I (1918), 58–77. 'SR' for Frege "On Sense and Reference," in Max Black and Peter Geach (eds.), *Translations from the Philosophical Writings of Gottlob Frege* (Oxford, 1960). Translated by Max Black. The original, "Über Sinn und Bedeutung," appeared in *Zeitschrift für Philosophie und philosophische Kritik*, L (1892), 25–50. 'CT' for "Compound Thoughts," in E. D. Klemke (ed.), Essays on Frege. Translated by R. H. Stoothoff. The original, "Gedankenfuge," appeared in *Beiträge zur Philosophie des deutschen Idealismus*, III (1923), 36–51. 'F' for Michael Dummett, *Frege* (London, 1973). [T appears as chap. 1 in this vol. SR appears as chap. 22. Page references to this vol. appear in brackets.]

2. Here and elsewhere I assume, for the sake of simplicity of exposition, that we are considering sentences containing no more than one demonstrative. Given the

notion of a sequence of objects, there would be no difficulties in extending various suggestions and options for the general case. In some of the examples I use, additional demonstratives are really needed. 'Lauben is wounded', for example, still needs a time indication.

3. This notion is taken from A. W. Burks, "Icon, Index, and Symbol," *Philosophy and Phenomenological Research*, Vol. IX, (1949), p. 685. In this pioneering and illuminating work on demonstratives, Burks emphasizes the ineliminability of demonstratives.

4. This interpretation was suggested to me by Dagfinn Føllesdal.

5. In the three problems that follow, and the balance of the paper, I am much in debt to a series of very iluminating papers by Hector-Neri Castañeda. The fullest statement of his view is in "Indicators and Quasi-Indicators," *American Philosophical Quarterly*, Vol. 4 (1967): 85–100. See also "He': A Study in the Logic of Self-Consciousness," *Ratio*, VIII (1966): 130–157, and "On the Logic of Attributions of Self-Knowledge to Others," *Journal of Philosophy*, LXV (1968): 439–456. All the examples of what I later call "self locating knowledge" are adaptations from Castañeda, and the difficulties they raise for Frege's account are related to points Castañeda has made.

6. The notions of the role of a sentence, and of a thought as information, are similar to the concepts of *character* and *context* in David Kaplan's "On the logic of Demonstratives," xeroxed, UCLA Department of Philosophy. This is no accident, as my approach to these matters was formed, basically, as a result of trying to extract from this work of Kaplan's, and Kaplan himself, answers to questions posed by Castañeda's work. One should not assume that Kaplan would agree with my criticisms of Frege, my treatment of self locating knowledge, or the philosophical motivation I develop for distinguishing between sense and thought.

7. Discussions of these issues with Robert Adams, Michael Bratman, Tyler Burge, Keith Donnellan, Dagfinn Føllesdal, Alvin Goldman, Holly Goldman, David Kaplan, and Julius Moravcsik were enormously helpful. This paper was written while I was a Guggenheim Fellow, and on sabbatical leave from Stanford University. I thank both institutions for their support.

Chapter 30

Understanding Demonstratives

Gareth Evans

I

It has recently been claimed that the use of demonstrative or indexical expressions like 'today', 'yesterday', 'here', 'I', 'you', 'this', etc., resists incorporation into a Fregean theory of meaning.[1] I have two reasons for attempting to show that this claim is not true. First, the reasoning seems to me to rest upon a common view of Frege's notions of sense and reference which is neither attractive nor required by the text, and second, because I believe that a Fregean approach to demonstrative expressions is essentially correct.

The argument which is supposed to show that demonstratives provide an insuperable problem for Frege runs like this. Consider the sentence:

(1) Today is fine

as uttered upon a particular day, *d*. Now, the concept expression '(ξ) is fine' has (on that occasion) a sense, but if the whole sentence is to have (on that occasion) a sense—express a Fregean thought—the expression 'today' must have (on that occasion) a sense as well as a referent, namely *d*. Now, the expression-type, 'today' certainly has a meaning, which does not vary from occasion to occasion, which Kaplan[2] calls its character and Perry calls its role. But that cannot by itself provide a completing sense, if for no other reason than that a 'thought' which is a function of these unchanging senses could no more be assigned a truth value than can the sentence-type 'Today is fine'. But equally, the referent, *d*, cannot be regarded as providing a completing sense. So:

First appeared in H. Parret and J. Bouveresse (eds.), *Meaning and Understanding* (Berlin: W. de Gruyter, 1981). Copyright Ms. Antonia Phillips. Reprinted by kind permission of the Trustees of the Gareth Evans Memorial Trust.

Neither the unchanging role of 'today' (its constant meaning) nor its changing value, provides us with a completing sense. A day is not a sense but a reference corresponding to indefinitely many different senses. So how do we get from the incomplete sense of '(ξ) is fine', the demonstrative 'today', and the context to a thought? This is the problem demonstratives pose for Frege.[3]

Obviously, if a Fregean approach to this utterance is to be sustained, the demonstrative in context must have a sense, and a different sense in different contexts. To this, Perry replies:

How can we extract from a demonstrative an appropriate completing sense? Such a sense, it seems, would have to be intimately related to the sense of a unique description of the value of the demonstrative in the context of utterance. But where does such a description come from? 'Today' seems only to get us to a day.[4]

Perry then goes on to show rather convincingly that no unique description can serve the purpose, for no thought about a day expressible with the use of a definite description true of that day is the same as the thought expressed with the use of a demonstrative; one can always take different epistemic attitudes towards them if one does not know that the day in question satisfies the description.

As far as I can make out, this is the main case against a Fregean approach to demonstrative expressions, and it rests, quite plainly, upon the view that a Fregean sense of any singular term must be either the sense of a definite description or 'intimately related' to such a sense. This assumption is quite unwarranted, and when this is realized, the case collapses. In order to establish this, I need to explain what I take to be essential to Frege's notion of sense.

II

I am attracted by the following, very abstract, account of the inter-relations between Fregean concepts of sense and reference—an account which owes considerably to Michael Dummett.[5]

The heart of a semantic theory for a language constructed on Fregean lines will be a *theory of reference*: a theory which assigns to each meaningful expression of the language something that can be regarded as that expression's reference or semantic value. Such a theory will proceed by discerning structure in the complex expressions of the language, and assigning references to those expressions upon the basis of assignments of references to their parts. A Fregean theory of reference will observe the principle of the compositionality: the reference of a complex expression is a function of the reference of its parts. Frege himself advocated a theory of reference according to which the references, or semantic values, of sentences and singular terms are truth values and objects, respectively, but neither of these choices is required by the adoption of the general conception. The only fixed point is this: an understanding of the language must be capable of being regarded as involving knowledge of the semantic values of expressions. In the case of sentences this knowledge can be regarded as more or less explicit, but for sub-sentential expressions, knowledge of their semantic values will simply be a logical construction out of the knowledge of the semantic values of the sentences in which they occur.

Before you object that one can understand a sentence without knowing its truth value, I hasten to remind you that the references of expressions can be thought of, or identified, in many different ways. One is thinking of the value True both when one thinks of it as the value True, and as the value of the thought that snow is white, though one may not know that one is thinking of the same thing. Similarly, the function which is the semantic value of the concept expression '(ξ) is bald' can either be thought of as the function which yields truth given as inputs the objects ... (here follows a list of the bald men) or as the function which yields truth given any object if and only if that object is bald. Frege's idea was that to understand an expression, one must not merely think of the reference that it is the reference, but that one must, in so thinking, think of the reference *in a particular way*. The way in which one must think of the reference of an expression in order to understand it is that expression's *sense*. No substantial, or positive theory of the notion of a way of thinking of something is presupposed by this conception of sense. If the intuitive notion needs to be supplemented, we can appeal to the general idea of an account of what makes it the case that a thought is about the object which it is about; two people will then be thinking of an object in the same way if and only if the account of what makes the one person's thought about that object is the same as the account of what makes the other person's thought about that object.[6]

Although a theory of meaning for a language must give the senses of expressions, we are not to think of the theory of sense as a separate tier, additional to and independent of the theory of reference. If sense is a way of thinking of reference, we should not expect to be given the sense of an expression save in the course of being given the reference of that expression. Rather than look for a theory quite independent of the theory of reference, we must take one formulation of the theory of reference—the formulation of the theory which identifies the references of expressions in the way in which one must identify them in order to understand the language—and make it *serve as* a theory of sense. Thus, the clauses:

(2) The reference of 'Hesperus' = Hesperus

(3) The reference of 'Hesperus' = Phosphorus

are equivalent as clauses in the theory of reference, but only (2) can occur in a theory of reference which is to serve as a theory of sense, for it alone identifies the reference of the name in a way which *shows*, or *displays*, its sense. The use of the *Tractatus* metaphor to make this point is due to Dummett:

> Indeed, even when Frege is purporting to give the sense of a word or symbol, what he actually *states* is what the reference said: and, for anyone who has not clearly grasped the relation between sense and reference, this fact makes his hold on the notion of sense precarious. The sense of an expression is the mode of presentation of the referent; in saying what the reference is, we have to choose a particular way of saying this.... In a case in which we are concerned to convey, or stipulate, the sense of the expression, we shall choose that means of stating what the referent is which displays the sense: we might here borrow a famous pair of terms from the *Tractatus*, and say that, for Frege, we *say* what the referent of a word is, and thereby *show* what its sense is.[7]

As I have already said, Frege quite generally regarded the referent of a singular term as its semantic value. Therefore, on the present conception, the sense of a singular term is a way of thinking about a particular object: something that obviously could not exist if that object did not exist to be thought about. If we take seriously Frege's metaphor of sense as a mode of presentation of reference, we shall not expect to be provided with specifications of sense save by means of specifications of reference, and therefore, if we remember Frege's equation of the reference of a singular term with its referent, we apparently discover at the heart of Frege's semantical system singular terms whose sense depends upon their having a referent—singular terms we more typically regard as Russellian than Fregean. But what makes a Fregean recognition of Russellian singular terms so much more sophisticated than Russell's own is that it allows such terms to have a sense as well as a reference. Russell himself did not grasp this possibility:

> For the name itself is merely a means of pointing to the thing ... so that, if one thing has two names, you make exactly the same assertion whichever of the

two names you use, provided that they really are names and not truncated descriptions.[8]

The semantic difference between two such Russellian terms which have the same referent can be acknowledged, with all the benefits which Frege derived from that acknowledgement. The theory of reference will state their references like this:

(4) The reference of 'a' $= a$

(5) The reference of 'b' $= b$.

These clauses *show* the different senses which the two terms possess, but at the same time they could not truly be stated if the terms had no referent.[9]

Attractive though this possibility may be, various things that Frege explicitly says seem to rule it out as an interpretation of his views. Frege says in several places that empty singular terms may have a sense, and, what would be a consequential inconsistency with the conception outlined, he also says that sentences containing empty singular terms may have a sense (express a thought) even though they have no reference (no truth value). How can we attribute to Frege the view that sense is a mode of presentation of reference, is a way of thinking of reference, when he seems to say things explicitly inconsistent with it? However, before abandoning this interpretation of Frege's ideas, which does incorporate much that Frege says, and which takes into account his willingness to apply the distinction between sense and reference to linguistic expressions quite generally, we should examine carefully what Frege actually says about empty singular terms. For, though he does say that they, and sentences containing them, may have a sense, other things that he says in the same connection make it clear that this is far less the unequivocal rejection of the conception I have outlined than it might at first appear.

In the first place, it is clear that Frege regarded empty singular terms as *defective*, in the same way, and indeed for the same reason, as he regarded vague concept-expressions as defective. His picture of the functioning of atomic sentences required them to be composed of expressions of two kinds: one (or more) which signified an object, and one which signified a function which mapped objects (or *n*-tuples of objects) on to truth values. If any expression in an atomic sentence failed to refer to an entity of an appropriate kind, the possibility would be open that no further truth value would be determined for the sentence, and it is clear that Frege regarded this as a defect in a sentence of a quite fundamental kind—

which he was quite right to do.[10] With this picture in mind, Frege was simply prepared to insist that concept-expressions must be precise; there is no concession that vague concept-expressions may nevertheless have a sense of a kind appropriate for concept-expressions, or that a sentence which has no truth value on account of vagueness may nevertheless express a thought. He did not make quite the same uncompromising statements about empty singular terms, despite the fact that the motivation is precisely the same—indeed Frege frequently treats the two cases together—because of his willingness to regard empty singular terms *as fictional* (or *mythical*). Instead of simply saying: 'Proper names must have a reference', he says: 'Myth and fiction aside, proper names must have a reference', or 'For scientific purposes, proper names must have a reference'. Frege was well aware that language could be used in fiction, story-telling, and drama, and he appeared to be willing to regard the serious use of an empty singular term as of this kind; he says that the speaker has 'lapsed into the sphere of fiction', without knowing it. The following is one of the many passages in which he takes this line:

But if my intention is not realized, if I only think I see without really seeing, if on that account the designation 'That lime tree' is empty, then I have gone astray into the sphere of fiction without knowing it or wanting to.[11]

So, Frege regarded serious utterances containing empty singular terms as belonging with the fictional use of language, and however much we may deplore this idea, it forces us to turn to Frege's account of fiction for our understanding of his views on empty singular terms. The most extended treatment is in the material for a book on Logic which Frege never finished dated around 1897.[12]

Names that fail to fulfil the usual role of a proper name, which is to name something, may be called mock proper names. Although the tale of William Tell is a legend and not history and the name 'William Tell' is a mock proper name, we cannot deny it a sense. But the sense of the sentence 'William Tell shot an apple off his son's head' is no more true than is that of the sentence 'William Tell did not shoot an apple off his son's head'. I do not say that this sense is false either, but I characterize it as fictitious.

Instead of speaking of 'fiction' we could speak of 'mock thoughts'. Thus, if the sense of an assertoric sentence is not true, it is either false or fictitious, and it will generally be the latter if it contains a mock proper name. (Footnote: We have an exception where a mock proper name occurs within a clause in indirect speech.) ... Assertions in fiction are not to be taken seriously: they are only mock assertions. Even the thoughts are not to be taken seriously as in the sciences; they are only mock thoughts. If Schiller's *Don Carlos* were to be regarded as a piece of history, then to a large extent the drama would be false. But a work of fiction is not meant to be taken seriously in this way at all: it's all play.

The logician does not have to bother with mock thoughts, just as a physicist, who sets out to investigate thunder, will not pay any attention to stage-thunder. When we speak of thoughts in what follows we mean thoughts proper, thoughts that are either true or false.[13]

This passage makes it clear that Frege's claim that empty singular terms, and sentences containing them, have a sense, expressed briefly elsewhere, is much more complex and qualified than is usually realized. We might gloss it as follows. Yes: a sentence containing an empty singular term can have a sense, in that it does not necessarily have to be likened to a sentence containing a nonsense-word, but no: it does not *really* have a sense of the kind possessed by ordinary atomic sentences because it does not function properly, it is only *as if* it functions properly. Frege's use of the notion of fiction wrongly directs our attention to just one case in which it is *as if* a singular term refers to something, namely when we are engaged in a pretence that it does, but there are others, and if we think of them we will perhaps speak of apparent, rather than mock or pretend, thoughts.

However indefensible Frege's idea of unwitting lapses into fiction may be, and however much his treatment of fiction depends upon a slide from 'mock assertions' to 'mock thoughts', his intention in this passage is clearly to deny that sentences containing empty singular terms really express thoughts, and is therefore one which makes it not at all impossible that he held the conception of the relations between sense and reference which I have outlined. (Indeed, the idea of 'mock', or anyway 'apparent', thoughts indicates a further direction in which Russell's conception of Russellian singular terms needs to be extended if it is to have any plausibility.)

I want to stress that the idea of sense as a mode of presentation of reference is not *by itself* inconsistent with the quite unqualified ascription of sense to empty singular terms. Even if a Fregean went along with Russell and hived off definite descriptions for treatment as quantifiers, he might want to recognize a category of 'descriptive names'—names introduced by means of, and governed by, a 'reference-fixing' stipulation like: 'Let 'α' refer to whatever is ϕ'—whose sense is thereby guaranteed to be independent of whether or not it has a referent.[14] But for names such as these the equation of reference with referent would have to be given up. One formally adequate possibility would be to take the reference, i.e. the semantic value, of such a name to be a set, determined by the rule:

(6) $(x)(x \in \text{Reference of '}\alpha\text{' iff } \phi(x))$

with corresponding adjustments to the semantic values of concept-expressions. When nothing is ϕ, the name 'α' has no *referent*, but its *reference* is the empty set.[15]

I have tried to show that on a perfectly possible understanding of Frege's semantic theory, he recognized only Russellian singular terms—terms whose customary sense depends upon their having a referent. Although this seems to me to be the correct position, I am aware that many will regard it as highly controversial. It is therefore important to emphasize that the argument of this paper depends only upon a much weaker claim, namely: that there is at least nothing to prevent Frege recognizing Russellian singular terms: i.e. that there is no difficulty in ascribing to such terms a Fregean sense. Since this claim is the basis of my defence of Frege against Perry's attack, it is as well to work through the argument in detail.

The essential use to which Frege puts the ascription of sense to singular terms is to explain the differing cognitive values of the sentences A(t) and A(t') when t and t' refer to the same thing. (The difference between $t = t$ and $t = t'$ is just a special case of this phenomenon.) Now, to say that two sentences differ in cognitive value is to say that it is possible for anyone who understands them correctly to coherently take different epistemic attitudes towards them—to accept one sentence as true and to reject, or to be unsure about the other sentence.

Suppose now that to ascribe a Fregean sense to a singular term is to say that there is a particular way in which its referent must be thought of (as the referent) if the term is to be understood. If two co-referring Russellian singular terms have different senses, different ways of thinking of their common referent are required in order to understand them. We have linked the idea of a way of thinking of something to an account that may be offered of what makes a subject's thought about its object, and certainly no argument can be based upon this idea alone to the conclusion that senses can be grasped in the absence of a referent.

Now if the assignment of senses to singular terms t and t' is to explain the differing cognitive values of the sentences A(t) and A(t'), it must be the case that if the singular terms t and t' have different senses the sentences will have different cognitive values—i.e. it must be possible for anyone who understands the sentences to take different epistemic attitudes towards them. And this will be so, provided the following very plausible principle is true:

(P) If the account of what makes a subject's thought T_1 (about x to the effect that it is F) about x is different from the account of what makes his thought T_2 (about x to the effect that it is F) about x, it is possible for the subject coherently to take, at one and the same time, different epistemic attitudes towards the thoughts he entertains in T_1 and in T_2.

At no point is it necessary for Frege to adopt any substantial theory of what form these accounts must take. In particular it is not necessary for him to suppose that ways of thinking of objects can always be given by giving some definite description uniquely true of the object, or to make any other supposition which would lead to 'existence-independent' senses. It is not necessary, because it is not plausible to suggest that the only kind of account of what makes a subject's thought about an object which is capable of making (P) true is one which relies upon the subject's possessing a unique description of the object.

The initial 'if' in (P) can be strengthened to an 'if and only if' without loss of a plausibility and if this strengthening is acceptable Frege is entitled to his equation of the sense of a singular sentence and a thought, when this is understood to be the object of propositional attitudes. An equation can be made between the senses of a singular sentence and a thought only if it is not possible for someone who has understood two singular sentences which agree in sense to take different attitudes to them, but on Frege's view this will not be possible. A difference in attitude would require a difference in the ways the subject thought of the object referred to (by the strengthening of (P)), and this would conflict with the hypothesis of an identity of sense, given that sense is a way of thinking of the referent.

Thus, we see that far from the Fregean sense of a singular term being restricted to the sense of some definite description (and therefore being 'existence-independent'), it is perfectly possible for there to be 'existence-dependent' Fregean senses—the Fregean senses of Russellian singular terms. I have in fact suggested that we should re-examine those passages in which Frege showed himself willing to ascribe sense to empty singular terms, but in any case, I know of no passage in which Frege can be construed as insisting that singular terms *must* have an existence-independent sense. In view of this we can appreciate how wrong-headed it is to consider a Fregean sense as necessarily *intermediary* between thinker and referent, as something which must, from a certain point of view, *get in the way*, or anyway render indirect what might be direct. A way of thinking of an object is no more obliged to get in the way of thinking of an object, or to render thinking of an object indirect, than is a way of dancing liable to get in the way of dancing, or to render dancing somehow indirect.[16] And, finally, we can appreciate how baseless it is to maintain that an extension of a Fregean theory to demonstrative singular terms *must* involve assigning to them the sense of, or anything like the sense of, some definite description. So Perry's argument against Frege collapses.

III

Let us return to the problem of demonstratives. We have seen that Perry's demonstration that there can be no 'completing sense' for 'today' is unsound, but something must be said about what such a completing sense might be.

'Today', as uttered on *d*, has a completing sense, if and only if there is some particular way in which one must think of the referent, *d*, in order to understand the utterance containing it. And of course there is. Even if *d* is the first day after my last lecture, I shall not have understood the utterance of (1) if I think of *d* only as the first day after my last lecture, thereby coming to believe that the utterance is true if and only if the first day after my last lecture is fine, perhaps not realizing that today is the first day after my last lecture. In order to understand (1) I must think of *d* as the current day, thereby coming to have the thought which I might express in the words: 'What the speaker said is true if and only if it is fine today.'[17] Now, what makes a man's thought about a day when he thinks of it as the current day—as 'today'—is not something which it is incumbent upon Frege to explain. It is indeed a difficult question. I myself would say something like this.

To give an account of how a thought concerns an object is to explain how the subject knows which object is in question. In the case of 'today', the subject, of course, knows which day is in question, but this knowledge at least partly consists in a disposition to judge the thoughts (which depend upon this knowledge) as true or false according to how things observably are upon that day which in no way rests upon his capacity to identify that day as meeting some antecedently given condition, but depends only upon his being alive on that day. There should be no mystery here; we can test very easily whether or not someone, in his interpretation of a sentence, is thinking of the day in the right way by seeing if he is disposed to judge the sentence as true or false according to how things observably are on that day. Similarly, I should want to place in a central position in any account of what makes a man's thought concern a particular place in the way which is required for understanding sentences containing the term 'here', a knowledge of which place is in question which at least partly consists in a disposition to judge that thought as true or false according to how things observably are at that place—a disposition which he can have *vis-à-vis* just one place in the universe in virtue of his occupying it, and which in no way depends upon his capacity to recognize that place as the unique satisfier of some description. If these accounts are on anything like the right lines, it is very easy to understand how these 'ways of thinking' are irreducible to any other, since no other way of knowing which object is in question, certainly no 'descriptive' way, can guarantee the existence of the relevant dispositions.

However, these are speculations which need to be embedded in a general theory of thought if they are to carry conviction. All that a Fregean needs from his opponent is an acknowledgement that those thoughts about a day which we typically express with the use of 'today' do involve a particular way of thinking about a day; if this is granted, he can explain how 'today', in a context, had a 'completing sense'.

Therefore, in order to understand the utterance of (1) made on *d*, one must have, on *d*, the thought which one might express in words by:

(7) What the speaker said is true if it is fine *today*.

It seems reasonable to say that such a statement is capable of showing the sense which the sentence has on that occasion. However, there might appear to be a difficulty here. A theory of reference was conceived to be a finite set of principles from which the references of complex expressions, particularly sentences, could be derived. When we think of the principles from which (7) might be derived, we naturally think of the general statement:

(8) For all days *d*, 'today' as uttered on *d* refers to *d*.

But now, this universally quantified principle cannot be thought to show these sense of any particular use of the expression, nor does it appear to issue exclusively in theorems of the form (7), which can. After all,

(9) What the speaker said in uttering 'Today is fine' on my birthday is true if it is fine on my birthday

is equally a consequence of (8), but it apparently does not show the sense which that sentence had on that occasion.

Our interest in theories of reference and of sense is ultimately to better understand the capacity of speakers to speak and understand their language, and when we remember this interest, the present difficulty will be seen as spurious. Speakers do not literally deduce the truth conditions which sentences have from certain universally quantified principles, whose precise form we must endeavour to establish. Speakers judge the truth conditions of particular sentences, and in so doing they exercise complex and interconnected dispositions in which their understanding of the individual atoms of the language may be taken to consist. We are therefore not required to attribute to speakers the general belief that any token of 'today' refers to the day on which it is uttered—and then wonder what form that belief takes, or how they derive the right kind of judgement of truth conditions from it. We are rather ascribing to speakers a *propensity to form particular beliefs*, of particular tokens of 'today', that they refer to the day of utterance, identified in a particular way, the exercise of which yields thoughts of the form of (7). The inclusion in a theory of reference of a general principle like (8) is a gesture in the direction of identifying the relevant propensity, and it certainly requires supplementation. But this point, though it needs to be borne in mind in interpreting systematic theories of meaning, is irrelevant to a Fregean theory of the sense and reference of 'today'. What matters for that theory is that tokens of 'today' should have a sense as well as a reference, not that the sense of all tokens of the expression should be capable of being shown in a single principle of the theory of reference.

Thus we have found no reason to depart from Frege's view:

[The thought, for example, that this tree is covered with green leaves will surely be false in six months' time. No, for it is not the same thought at all. The words, 'This tree is covered with green leaves' are not sufficient by themselves for the utterance, the time of utterance is involved as well. Without the time indication this gives we have no complete thought, i.e. no thought at all] . . . the same words, on account of the variability of language with time, take on another sense, express another thought.[18]

IV

In understanding the sentence 'Today is fine', said on d_1, one can be regarded as having a Fregean thought, but is it a thought which one can have on any other day? Frege appears to have thought that it is:

If someone wants to say the same today as he expressed yesterday using the word 'today', he must replace this word with 'yesterday'.[19]

Frege appears to have held that to have on d_2 just the thought which one has when one thinks 'Today is fine' on d_1, one must think 'Yesterday was fine'. Presumably this means that it is possible for someone reading yesterday's newspaper to understand sentences like:

(10) The Prime Minister is holding a cabinet meeting today

by realizing that it is true if the Prime Minister held a cabinet meeting the day before. Now, many philosophers, commenting on this passage, have concluded that Frege intended to abandon a notion of 'what is said', or 'the thought expressed' which was 'psychologically real' in the sense of being the object of propositional attitudes, and was giving expression to the idea that two people would express the same thought provided that they refer to the same object (in whatever way) and say the same thing about it.[20] Such a conception of *what is said*, or *the thought expressed* is so wholly antagonistic to the theory of language ushered in by the distinction between sense and reference, and is otherwise so wholly absent from his work, that it seems to me to be doubtful that the passage has been correctly interpreted. It is clear, for example, that Frege would have been willing to continue the passage:

... he must replace this word with 'yesterday', or 'my birthday', or any other expression designating the same day?

Might Frege not have had in mind an idea of a thought the grasp of which, on a later day, requires just as specific a way of thinking of a day as does its grasp on an earlier day—namely as the preceding day? Pursuing this suggestion, we discover that, far from abandoning the 'psychologically real' notion of a thought in favour of a psychologically quite uninteresting equivalence class of thoughts, Frege may well have glimpsed what results when the notion is extended to the sphere of human thinking which depends upon the position human beings have in space and time.

We must agree that, if a subject thinks on d_1, about d_1, to the effect that it is fine by thinking 'Today is fine', and thinks on d_2, about d_1, to the effect that it is fine, by thinking 'Yesterday was fine', there is some level of description at which he is thinking of the same day in different ways—the account of what makes his thoughts about d_1 in the two cases will not be entirely the same. And it is natural to think that this difference in ways of thinking can be exploited to produce the possibility of differing epistemic attitudes to the thoughts, which would then preclude their being the same thought, if thoughts are intended to be the object of propositional attitudes.

However, the natural suggestion is not correct; there is no headlong collision between Frege's suggestion that grasping the same thought on different days may require different things of us, and the fundamental criterion of difference of thoughts which rests upon the principle that it is not possible coherently to take different attitudes towards the same thought. For that principle, properly stated, precludes the possibility of coherently taking different attitudes towards the same thought *at the same time*. Consider S, who accepted the sentence 'Today is fine' when uttered on d_1, and who rejects the sentence 'Yesterday was fine' when uttered on d_2, perhaps because he has misremembered the weather, or because he has 'lost track of time'. Now, in order to apply the criterion of difference in this situation, we must first make a decision as to what it would be for S to have exactly the same thought on d_2 as he had when he thought on d_1 'Today is fine'. Because its application requires a prior decision on this question, the criterion for difference cannot by any means be the whole story of the identity and distinctness of thoughts, and it is powerless to upset Frege's suggestion. For, either we hold that it is possible to think again the thought entertained on d_1 or we do not. If we hold that it *is* possible, no better account than Frege's can be given of the circumstances under which it is possible. (If this is not obvious, some merits of his account will be given below.) Hence, on this alternative, to think 'Yesterday was fine' *is* to think the same thought again, and so no possibility opens up, on d_2, of coherently assenting to the same thought as one accepted when one judged on d_1 'Today is fine', and of dissenting from the thought 'Yesterday was fine'. To hold, on the other hand, that it is not possible to have on d_2 the very same thought as one had on d_1, while not at all a ridiculous proposal, obviously precludes use of the criterion of difference against Frege's contrary view. Some other consideration must be appealed to.

Frege's idea is that being in the same epistemic state may require different things of us at different times; the changing circumstances force us to change in order to keep hold of a constant reference and a constant thought—we must run to keep still. From this point of view, the acceptance on d_2 of 'Yesterday was fine', given an acceptance on d_1 of 'Today is fine' can manifest the *persistence* of a belief in just the way in which acceptance of different utterances of the same sentence 'The sun sets in the West' can. Are there any considerations which can be advanced in favour of this way of looking at matters?

To answer this question, we must contrast Frege's conception with the opposing conception, according to which the thoughts associated with sentences containing temporal indexicals cannot be grasped at later times. On this atomistic conception, what Frege regards as a persistence of a belief is really a succession of different but related beliefs concerning the same time. It must of course be acknowledged that these patterns, or sequences, of beliefs are very commonly to be met with—that human beings do have a general propensity, on forming one belief in this series, later to have the other beliefs in the series, but this fact by itself does not settle the issue. Admittedly it is not clear what account can be given of this succession of belief on the atomistic conception. One belief cannot give rise to another by any *inference*, since the identity belief that would be required to underwrite the inference is not a thinkable one; no sooner does one arrive in a position to grasp the one side of the identity than one has lost the capacity to grasp the other. But one can be suspicious of the atomistic conception for other, deeper, reasons.

On the atomistic conception, whether there are later elements in the series, and whether or not they concern the same object is quite irrelevant to the subject's capacity to entertain one of the atoms. The atom must be a perfectly coherent unit of thought by itself, even if it is entertained by one who has not the least propensity to form the other members of the series. But this, Frege might well have thought, is wrong. No one can be ascribed at t a belief with the content 'It is now ψ', for example, who does not have the propensity as time goes on to form beliefs with the content 'It was ψ just a moment ago', 'It was ψ earlier this morning', 'It was ψ this morning', 'It was ψ yesterday morning', etc., though of course this propensity can be counteracted by new evidence. Frege might be credited with the insight that a capacity to keep track of the passage of time is not an optional addition to, but a precondition of, temporal thought. If this is so, the thought-units of the atomist are not coherent, independent, thoughts at all, but so to speak, cross-sections of a persisting belief state which exploits our ability to keep track of a moment as it recedes in time.

The metaphor of 'keeping track of something' originates in connection with another kind of thought about an object, and it provides a useful, if only partial, parallel. Suppose that one is watching a scene in which there are several similar objects moving about fairly rapidly, but not so rapidly as to prevent one's keeping track of one in particular. In such a situation, one can think about one of these objects rather than any other, but any such thought rests upon a skill we possess of keeping track of an object in a visual array over time. Our eyes and our heads move, perhaps we are also obliged to turn or move our bodies, but these changes are required to maintain contact with the same object over time. So, one's thought *at* a time is dependent upon an ability which is necessarily manifested only *over* time. One might begin the period with the belief of an object that it is valuable, and end it with a belief of the same object that it is valuable. Now, a move parallel to the one which Frege made in connection with 'today' and yesterday', would be to hold that one belief has persisted over time, despite the local differences which the changing circumstances have imposed upon one. And there is a parallel, opposing, atomistic move which would regard the subject as holding a *sequence* of different beliefs over the relevant period of time, altering as the subject's relation to the object altered. And the objection to the atomistic position here is the same as in the earlier case. If the atomistic position were correct, it ought to be possible to have just one of the members of the sequence no matter which others accompanied it, i.e. in the absence of any capacity to keep track of the object. But if that ability is missing, it is not possible for a subject to have a thought about an object in this kind of situation at all. Now Frege himself did not give this parallel, but he did write, after the passage just quoted: 'The case is the same with "here" and "there".' Indeed it is; our ability to think of a place as 'here' is dependent upon our general ability to keep track of places as we move about (which requires, in general, the ability to know when we are moving), so, once again, there could not be thoughts interpretable as 'It's ψ here', if they were not entertained by a subject who had the propensity to entertain, as he moves about, thoughts expressible in the words 'It's ψ there'.

These examples suggest that we have to regard the static notion of 'having hold of an object at t' as essentially an abstraction from the dynamic notion of 'keeping track of an object from t to t''. And the grasp, at t, of a thought of the kind suggested by the passage from Frege, a *dynamic* Fregean thought, requires a subject to possess at t an ability to keep track of a particular object over time. It is not precluded that one should have only a momentary grasp of a dynamic Fregean thought, for it is not precluded that, after an object has engaged with one's capacity to keep track of objects of that kind, one should lose track of it, and with it, the thought. Indeed, it is an aspect of the capacity that the subject will, in general, know when this has happened. The capacities upon which certain kinds of thought rest can only be described in dynamic terms; it does not follow that any exercise of those capacities must be extended over time.

Consequently, the *way of thinking of an object* to which the general Fregean conception of sense directs us is, in the case of a dynamic Fregean thought, a *way of keeping track of an object*. This permits us to say after all that a subject on d_2 is thinking of d_1 *in the same way* as on d_1, despite lower level differences, because the thought-episodes on the two days both depend upon the same exercise of a capacity to keep track of a time.[21]

V

In discussing thoughts expressed with the use of the pronoun 'I' Frege wrote:

Now, everyone is presented to himself in a particular and primitive way in which he is presented to no one else.[22]

Replacing Frege's metaphor of 'being presented with an object' with the notion of 'thinking of' which underlies it, Frege appears to be saying that each person thinks about himself in a way which is primitive and available to no one else. Since this way of thinking about oneself would be neither primitive nor available to anyone else if it exploited one's knowledge that one uniquely satisfied some description, the passage appears to provide the clearest possible evidence that Frege did not hold that all ways of thinking of objects must involve thinking of those objects as uniquely satisfying some description. It is not unreasonable to suppose, on the strength of this passage, that Frege hand noticed the irreducibility of 'I'-thoughts to any other kind of thought fifty years before Castañeda made it part of the philosopher's stock in trade.[23]

However, Perry holds that Frege's conception of a thought was such that to have an 'I'-thought could not possibly be to have a Fregean thought. One of his reasons is that Frege held that thoughts are 'generally accessible'.

We can see that having such beliefs *could* not consist *wholly* in believing Fregean thoughts. Consider Frege's timeless realm of generally accessible thoughts.[24]

Since it is an immediate consequence of what Frege said about 'I'-thoughts that they are *not* 'generally accessible', Perry appears to be arguing that a Fregean approach to 'I'-thoughts must be inadequate by citing a supposed requirement upon Fregean thoughts—that they be generally accessible—which Frege appears to have shown himself free of precisely in what he says about 'I'-thoughts. Presumably Perry would justify his line of criticism by arguing that the shareability of thoughts was such a central Fregean doctrine that nothing recognizably Fregean could exist in its absence:

Nothing could be more out of the spirit of Frege's account of sense and thought than an incommunicable, private thought.[25]

I do not believe that this is true. It is true that Frege stresses that it is *possible* for thoughts to be grasped by more than one person; were this not so, neither communication nor disagreement would be possible. But this point requires only that thoughts are not by their very nature precluded from being grasped by more than one person, not that every single thought must be capable of being grasped by more than one person. What *is* absolutely fundamental to Frege's philosophy of language is that thoughts should be *objective*—that the existence of a thought should be independent of its being grasped by anyone, and hence that thoughts are to be distinguished from *ideas* or the contents of a particular consciousness. When Frege stresses that thoughts can be grasped by several people, it is usually to emphasize that it is not like an idea:

A true thought was true before it was grasped by anyone. A thought does not have to be owned by anyone, the same thought can be grasped by several people.[26]

His most extended treatment of the nature of thoughts—'The Thought'—makes it clear that it is the inference from shareability to objectivity which is of paramount importance to Frege, rather than shareability itself. Since an unshareable thought can be perfectly objective—can exist and have a truth value independently of anyone's entertaining it—there is no clash between what Frege says about 'I'-thoughts and this, undeniably central, aspect of his philosophy. Although Frege does tend to speak without qualification of thoughts as graspable by more than one person, I do not myself see why this should be regarded as an indispensable tenet, rather than a slight overstatement, of his position. Perry certainly does not tell us why he attaches such importance to it.

Perry makes clear that, quite independently of any question of Fregean scholarship, he thinks that fatal objections can be raised to the idea of an unshareable thought. This might seem a bit steep, coming after a criticism of Frege based upon his supposed insistence that all thoughts be 'generally accessible'. However Perry will explain that the peculiarities of 'I'-thoughts can be accommodated on his system without recognizing unshareable thoughts. On Perry's system, both you and I can grasp the thought you express when you say 'I am hot', only we grasp it *in different ways.* However, I try to show in the next section that this is just a notational variant of Frege's theory.

It is true that Perry has other reasons for saying that an 'I'-thought cannot be a Fregean thought, for he thinks that objection can be raised to a Fregean treatment of 'I'-thoughts even if Frege is allowed the 'private senses' to which he so desperately resorted. The argument here contains no surprises, for the difficulties result from the excessively wooden interpretation which Perry places on Frege's notion of 'way of being presented to oneself' as a result of trying to force it into the mould of descriptive identification.[27] He does point out that thoughts about times expressible with 'now' are also irreducible to description, and therefore if Frege's strategy is general:

> Frege will have to have, for each time, a primitive and particular way in which it is presented to us at that time, which gives rise to thoughts accessible only at that time, and expressible at it, with 'now'. This strikes me as very implausible.[28]

In fact we have seen that Frege does not appear to hold that such thoughts are only graspable at one time (Part IV), but even if we ignore this, I do not see that the approach can be so easily dismissed. What is so absurd about the idea that there are thoughts which one can have only because one occupies a particular position in space, or time, or because one is currently perceiving an object? This is just to say that there are ways of thinking about objects which require one to stand in a specific spatial, temporal, or causal relation to the object, and rather than deserving dismissal as implausible, the point seems to me to be worthy of the greatest respect. And to say that the ways of thinking are primitive is to say that they are not reducible to any other, particularly not to any which exploit knowledge of a description of the object, and this too is a point which Perry should applaud, figuring as it does so extensively in his own work.

Perhaps the implausibility is supposed to lie in the consequence of there being an infinite number of distinct, primitive, and particular ways of thinking of objects—one for each time—but alarm at this idea can only rest upon a confusion. A way of thinking about an object is given by an account of what makes some thinking about that object. In the case of a particular 'I'-thought, for example, I envisage statements of the form

(11) S is thinking of S' at t because R_1 (S, S', t)

where R_1 is an as yet unspecified relation which can only be satisfied by a triple of S, S', and t if $S = S'$. In terms of this idea, we can make perfectly good sense of the claim that different people think of different things (i.e. themselves) *in the same way*; we do not hold that precisely the same account can be given of what makes each of their thoughts have the object that it does, but that the same *type* of account can be given—namely in terms of the relation R_1. While it would no doubt be implausible to suppose that there are an infinite number of different *types* of accounts, I see no difficulty whatever in the idea of as many different *particular* accounts as there are times and persons.

VI

A Fregean thought of the kind associated with a sentence 'Today is F' said on d can be equated with the ordered pair of the sense which 'Today' has on d and the sense of the concept-expression '(ξ) is F', thus:

(12) $\langle$Sense on d of 'today', Sense of '(ξ) is F'$\rangle$.

One grasps the sense of 'today' on d if and only if one thinks of d as the current day—i.e. in virtue of one's satisfying some relational property λx $(R_2(x, d))$—so we may equivalently equate the Fregean thought with the ordered pair:

(13) $\langle \lambda x(R_2(x, d))$, Sense of '($\xi$) is F'$\rangle$.

One entertains the object (13) if one thinks of a day in virtue of one's satisfying the first component, to the effect that it is F. If we wished to bring out the way in which any two utterances of (1) are similar, we might, equivalently, equate the thought with the triple:

(14) $\langle d, \lambda x \lambda y(R_2(x, y))$, Sense of '($\xi$) is F'$\rangle$;

one entertains (14) if one thinks of the first member, in virtue of oneself and the first member, satisfying the second member, to the effect that it is F. In this construction the second and third components of the sense of an utterance of (1) are always the same, though the sense which 'today' has on d can be equated with neither the first member, nor the second member, taken singly, but only with the pair. Then, when Hume thinks 'I am hot' he entertains:

(15) $\langle$Hume, $\lambda x \lambda y(R_1(x, y))$, Sense of '($\xi$) is hot'$\rangle$,

and when I think that I am hot, I entertain:

(16) $\langle$G.E., $\lambda x \lambda y(R_1(x, y))$, Sense of '($\xi$) is hot'$\rangle$.

We know that Perry thinks that it is necessary to abandon the notion of a Fregean thought when dealing with sentences containing demonstratives, but with what would he replace it? He introduces a notion of thought according to which the sentence $F(t)$ uttered in context c, and the sentence $F(t')$ uttered in c' express the same thought provided the referent of t in c is the same as the referent of t' in c'. Let us call a thought of this kind a 'P-thought'; a P-thought can be identified with an equivalence class of Fregean thoughts, or alternatively with an ordered pair of an object and a sense of a concept expression ('... a thought consisting of a certain object and an incomplete sense ...').[29] It is the introduction of thoughts of this kind that Perry claims to be his greatest departure from Frege: 'The idea of individuating thoughts by objects or sequences of objects would be particularly out of place in (Frege's) system'.[30] However, for Perry, when we entertain a thought, we do not just stand in a certain relation to a P-thought; we entertain a P-thought *in a certain way*. When Hume thinks 'I am F' and then thinks 'That man is F' (indicating himself in a mirror), he entertains the same P-thought, but in a different way. Perry has a positive proposal about ways of entertaining thoughts, one which links them to the 'roles' of meanings of demonstrative expressions of natural language. I shall come to this aspect of his position in a moment, but what concerns me now is to see whether, the positive characterization apart, Perry is putting forward anything other than a notational variant of Frege's position.

Perry frequently speaks as though P-thoughts are the objects of propositional attitudes; this is, indeed, what their name would suggest. This means, I take it, that a belief-ascription asserts a relation between a subject and a P-thought. If this is Perry's intention, then his position is not a notational variant of Frege's, since although Frege can say everything Perry can say (using the equivalence class to Fregean thoughts) the converse is not the case. (This is generally true when the ontology of a theory T_1 is less 'fine-grained' than the ontology of theory T_2.) Frege, for example, can consistently describe the belief system of a subject S who understands and accepts, in context c, the sentence $F(t)$, and who understands, and neither accepts nor rejects, in context c', the sentence $F(t')$ when t in c refers to what t' in c' refers to. S believes one Fregean thought, and neither believes nor disbelieves another Fregean thought. If belief is simply a relation to a P-thought, this situation cannot be described.[31]

If Perry is to be able to report S's epistemic situation, his belief reports must be more complex than just a simple relational statement between a subject and a P-thought: the way in which the thought is apprehended must come in as well. Perry uses locutions like 'By entertaining the sense of "I", S apprehended the thought consisting of Hume and the sense of "(ξ) is hot"', and so perhaps he has in mind some such construction as:

(17) S apprehends-in-way-w $\langle x$, Sense of '(ξ) is F'$\rangle$.

But surely this is now a notational variant of Frege's approach, at best. Where Frege would write:

(18) S believes $\langle x, w$, Sense of '(ξ) is F'$\rangle$.

Perry will write:

(19) S believes-in-way-w $\langle x$, Sense of '(ξ) is F'$\rangle$.

or 'S believes, by apprehending such-and-such a sense, the thought consisting of x and the sense of "(ξ) is hot"'.

So, finally, we can come to examine Perry's positive proposals about the various ways of thinking about objects which are involved in the understanding of sentences containing demonstratives, clear in our minds that they are not opposed, but supplementary to any views of Frege's. If Perry has succeeded in making these ways of thinking clear, if he has explained the various R-relations upon which they depend, all other Fregeans have reason to be grateful. For as I have said, Frege left these ways of thinking of objects quite uncharacterized, and so the nature of the senses of these expressions is unknown, even if their existence is not. Furthermore, it has seemed that such an account must presuppose some of the profoundest philosophy. In the case of 'I' for example, one might think that an account of the relation R_1 which explicates 'self-identification' must incorporate the insights, as well as illuminate the struggles, of Descartes, Kant, and Wittgenstein, and many others. One might have expected an account of self-identification—of the way in which we know, when we think of ourselves, which object is in question—would have to relate it to our special ways of gaining knowledge of ourselves, both mental and physical, both past and present. (At the very least, Hume's realizing that he is Hume must involve appreciating the bearing of the knowledge he can gain in these special ways to the truth value of very many thoughts that Hume is F.) In this way, the 'immunity to error through misidentification' of these ways of gaining knowledge would be explained.[32] And one might have thought that an explanation of one's capacity to grasp indefinitely many thoughts about oneself which one does not know to be true—thoughts about one's remote past, or one's future—could be provided only when the role of conceptions of personal identity in self-identification had been made clear.[33]

Similarly, one might have thought that an account of demonstrative identification, which underlies the thoughts we might express in (certain uses of) sentences like 'This table is round' would have to show how thought can depend upon perception, at least in such a way that we would know what kind of perception can sustain demonstrative identification. Can one demonstratively identify a man when one sees him in a mirror, on a television, in a photograph, in an X-ray? Can one demonstratively identify a man when one hears his footsteps, when one hears him on the telephone, on the radio, on a record? Can one demonstratively identify a city when one perceives only the inside of a room located within it?[34]

Perry's answers to these profound questions have an appealing simplicity. In the case of a 'self-conscious' thought, for example, he writes:

We accept that there is no thought only Hume can apprehend. Yet only he can know that he is Hume. It must not just be the thought that he thinks, but the way that he thinks it, that sets him apart from the rest of us. Only Hume can think a true thought, by saying to himself

I am Hume

Self-locating knowledge, then, requires not just the grasping of certain thoughts, but the grasping of them via the senses of certain sentences containing demonstratives.[35]

By 'entertaining' the meaning or role of the demonstrative 'I', Hume thinks of himself. Similarly, by entertaining the meaning or role of the demonstrative 'here', Hume thinks of a particular place.

Simple though it is, I find that the proposal evades me. The role of a demonstrative was explained as that aspect of the meaning of the expression which was constant from occasion to occasion—presumably a (constant) function from contexts of utterance to objects. So to 'entertain the role' of the demonstrative 'I', for example, would presumably be to have this function in mind in some way. The function is determined by the rule that in any context of utterance the value of the function is the speaker in that context, so I suppose that in a derivative sense one could be said to have the function in mind, and so to be entertaining the role of the demonstrative, if one had in mind the description 'the person speaking', or 'the person who utters the token of "I"'. Since Perry insists that the meaning of 'I' is not a complete Fregean sense, and that different people entertain precisely the same meaning, perhaps we should think of this as like a description containing a free variable:

(20) The person who utters x and x is a token of 'I'.

But, leaving aside the question of how reference is achieved to a particular token—which is an aspect of the same general problem with which we are concerned—what has the idea in (20) got to do with one's capacity to think of oneself self-consciously? The problem is this. No one can give an account of the constant meaning (= role) of a demonstrative without mentioning some relational *property* (relating an object to a context of utterance) which an object must satisfy if it is to be the referent of the demonstrative in that context of utterance, but the idea of this property plays no part in an explanation of what makes a subject's *thought* about himself, or the place he occupies, or the current time.

It seems clear that we are on the wrong track: these suggestions must be as far from capturing what Perry intended by 'entertaining the role of a demonstrative' as they are from answering the questions with which we began. An alternative interpretation is suggested by Perry's remark: 'Only Hume can think a true thought by *saying to himself* "I am Hume"'.[36] Perhaps 'entertaining the sense of "I am Hume"' is to be understood along the lines of 'mentally uttering "I am Hume"', or 'saying in one's heart "I am Hume"'. But this would be to suggest that self-conscious thought depends upon the interior exploitation of the conventional meaning of certain public linguistic devices, which is surely neither necessary nor sufficient for it. It could not be suggested that self-conscious thought would be beyond the reach of those who spoke a language which had no first person pronoun, and who had to refer to themselves with their own names, or that one's capacity to think about the place one occupies is dependent upon one's language possessing a device with the meaning of 'here'. These suggestions would surely get things exactly the wrong way round.

Perhaps Perry has no sympathy with these suggestions. Perhaps, contrary to first impressions, he intended by his use of the phrase 'entertaining the sense of' not to characterize, but merely to label these ways of thinking. Perry has adopted a terminology according to which one can grasp the same thought in different ways, and when Perry speaks of Hume's grasping the thought ⟨Hume, sense of '(ξ) is Hume'⟩ 'by entertaining the sense of "I am Hume"', perhaps he means simply Hume's self-consciously thinking that he is Hume—however that is ultimately to be characterized.[37] Whether or not this last suggestion is correct, it seems clear that all good Fregeans must live in hope of a yet profounder philosophy.

Notes

The present paper rests on an idea of John McDowell's. Quite a few years ago, and more recently in 'On Sense and Reference of a Proper Name' (*Mind* 86 (1977), pp. 159–85), he argued that it was possible to ascribe Fregean sense to singular terms which I describe in this paper as 'Russellian'. The present paper is an attempt to apply this basic idea of McDowell's to demonstratives, though in the course of doing so I develop it in ways for which he must not be held responsible, particularly by tying sense to a way of *thinking of* a reference. Reading through Frege's works, I became convinced that the position McDowell argued for as a possibility is one to which he is in fact committed. (For similar views of McDowell's, see 'Truth-value Gaps' in *Logic, Methodology and Philosophy of Science VI* (Amsterdam: North-Holland, 1982).) In my interpretation of Frege I am much indebted to Dummett, whose writings I follow closely. I somehow seem to end up at a quite different place.

1. J. Perry, 'Frege on Demonstratives', *Philosophical Review* 86 (1977), pp. 474–97. [Chap. 29 in this vol.]

2. D. Kaplan, 'Demonstratives' (unpublished mimeo Los Angeles: UCLA, 1977).

3. Perry, op. cit., p. 480 [p. 699 in this vol.] (I have changed the example.)

4. Ibid., p. 485 [pp. 703–704].

5. M. Dummett, *Frege: Philosophy of Language* (London: Duckworth, 1973), chaps. 5–7, 12.

6. I should explain the main point of departure from Dummett's account of Frege's views. Dummett is impressed, to my mind overly impressed, by the fact that one can understand a sentence without knowing its truth value. To take account of this, he regards sense, not as a way of thinking of reference, but as a way of *determining* reference—possibly by means which only a being with superior powers is capable of employing. To think of the sense of a singular term as a procedure for recognizing an object as the referent generates just the idea of sense as independent of the existence of a referent which is resisted in this paper.

7. Dummett, op. cit., p. 227. This passage of Dummett's seems to me to contain the answer to those who argue, like Wallace (see 'Logical Form, Meaning, Translation', in F. Guenther and M. Guenther-Reutter (eds.), *Meaning and Translation* (London: Duckworth), pp. 45–58), that Davidsonian theories of meaning are inadequate because they do not state the meanings of sentences. The similarity between a Davidsonian conception of the theory of meaning as a theory of truth, and a Fregean conception of a theory of sense as a theory of reference should be particularly striking. Davidson lightens the ontological load, but the general idea is the same. I should explain that I am ignoring in this

brief presentation the distinction between 'model-theoretic' and 'truth-theoretic' approaches to semantics—a Fregean theory of reference, with its ontological weight, should really be regarded as exemplifying the former approach. I have tried to explain the relation between these approaches in 'Semantic Structure and Logical Form', in G. Evans and J. H. McDowell (eds.), *Truth and Meaning* (Oxford: Clarendon Press, 1976).

8. B. Russell, *Lectures on Logical Atomism*, ed. D. Pears (London Fontana, 1972), p. 103.

9. The significance of clauses like (4) and (5) as providing a formal recognition of the possibility of ascribing Fregean sense to Russellian singular terms is first elaborated in J. McDowell, 'On the Sense and Reference of a Proper Name', in *Mind* 86 (1977), pp. 159–85.

10. See Dummett, op. cit., p. 342–8.

11. G. Frege, 'The Thought', p. 300 (trans. by A. and M. Quinton), *Mind* 65 (1956), p. 287–311 [chap. 1 in this vol.]. A similar use of the notion of fiction is made on almost all of the occasions on which Frege discusses empty singular terms. See, for example, 'On Sense and Reference' (pp. 62–3), '*Grundgesetze*' (p. 167), and the review of Schröder (p. 104), in *Translations from the Philosophical Writings of Gottlob Frege*, trans. and ed., P. T. Geach and M. Black (Oxford: Blackwell, 1970) and many places in *Posthumous Writings* eds. J. Hermes, F. Kambartel, F. Kaulbach (trans. P. Long and R. White) (Oxford: Blackwell, 1979), e.g., pp. 118, 122, 129–30, 191, 225, 232.

12. 'Logic', in *Posthumous Writings*, pp. 126–51.

13. *Posthumous Writings*, p. 130. I am grateful to Dagfinn Føllesdal for pointing this passage out to me. I have followed the translation of Peter Long and Roger White, save in retaining the traditional translation of 'Bedeutung' as 'reference'.

14. The idea of a reference-fixing stipulation is Kripke's, see 'Naming and Necessity', in D. Davidson and G. Harman (eds.), *Semantics of Natural Language* (Dordrecht: Reidel, 1972), pp. 253–355. I am presuming that ϕ is incapable of being satisfied by more than one thing. I have discussed the semantics of descriptive names in 'Reference and Contingency', *Monist* 62 (1979).

15. Here and elsewhere I rely upon the verbal distinction between 'referent' and 'reference' introduced by Dummett, op. cit., pp. 409 ff. Were we accustomed to Long and White's translation of 'Bedeutung' as 'meaning', the position adopted in the text would have stood out as a possibility more clearly.

16. I have in mind here several remarks of Kaplan's, who advocates 'the semantics of direct reference ... theories of meaning according to which certain singular terms refer directly without the mediation of a Fregean *Sinn* as meaning' (Kaplan, 'Demonstratives', p. 1). See also Kaplan, 'How to Russell a Frege-Church', *Journal of Philosophy* 72 (1975), pp. 716–29.

17. It is therefore not true that 'today' only gets us to a day.

18. Frege, 'The Thought', pp. 309–10 [p. 28 in this vol.].

19. Ibid., p. 296 [p. 15].

20. See, for example, Kaplan, 'Demonstratives', p. 43. Dummett comes close to this in *Frege*, p. 384, although there, other expressions which can be used to express the same thought are restricted to other *demonstrative* expressions with the same referent.

21. Kaplan briefly raises the possibility sketched in this section, under the heading 'cognitive dynamics', but dismisses it: 'Suppose that yesterday you said, and believed it, "It is a nice day today". What does it mean to say, today, that you have retained *that* belief? ... Is there some obvious standard adjustment to make to the character, for example, replacing *today* with *yesterday*? If so, then a person like Rip van Winkle, who loses track of time, can't retain any such beliefs. This seems strange.' I see no more strangeness in the idea that a man who loses track of time cannot retain beliefs than in the idea that a man who loses track of an object cannot retain the beliefs about it with which he began. If one has in fact lost track of time without knowing it, then one could think that one had retained one's beliefs when one has not. But, since in general thoughts associated with Russellian singular terms are such that the subject cannot infallibly know that he has one, we should not jib at denying the subject infallible knowledge of when he has the same one.

22. Frege, 'The Thought', p. 298 [p. 17].

23. See H.-N. Castañeda, ' "He": A Study in the Logic of Self-Consciousness', *Ratio* 8 (1966), pp. 130–57, and in many other papers.

24. Perry, op. cit., p. 492 [p. 693].

25. Ibid., p. 474 [p. 693].

26. *Posthumous Writings*, p. 251.

27. Perry, op. cit., p. 491 [p. 710].

28. Ibid.

29. Cf. ibid., p. 496 [p. 713].

30. Ibid., p. 496 [p. 713].

31. Perry makes life too easy for himself by considering only the case where S rejects $F(t')$ in c'; this he can, and does, describe as S's believing the different P-thought, concerning the object, that it is not F (op. cit., pp. 495–6 [p. 713]). The importance of the case of agnosticism was noticed by Kaplan in 'Quantifiying In', in D. Davidson and J. Hintikka (eds), *Words and Objections* (Dordrecht: Reidel, 1969), pp. 206–42.

32. S. Shoemaker, 'Self-Knowledge and Self-Identification', *Journal of Philosophy* 65 (1968), pp. 555–68.

33. For two papers that help to bring out the profundity of the question, see L. Wittgenstein, 'Notes for a Lecture on Private Experience', *Philosophical Review* 77 (1968), pp. 275–320 and G. E. M. Anscombe, 'The First Person', in *Mind and Language*, S. Guttenplan (ed.) (Oxford: Clarendon Press, 1975), pp. 45–65.

34. For a discussion of this latter question, see G. E. Moore, 'Some Judgements of Perception', *Philosophical Papers* (London: Routledge & Kegan Paul, 1922), pp. 220–53.

35. Perry, op. cit., p. 492 [p. 710].

36. Perry, op. cit., p. 492 [p. 710]. Emphasis added.

37. This is certainly all I am able to understand by Kaplan's parallel talk of Hume's thinking of himself 'under the character of "I"'. He gives evidence of the intention to be enlightening about 'the particular and primitive way in which each person is presented to himself' ('Demonstratives', p. 65), but I can derive no more enlightenment from the literal meaning of the phrase, 'under the character' than I can from 'entertaining the role', and further elucidation is not to be found.

Chapter 31

Individuation and the Semantics of Demonstratives

Martin Davies

> Obsessed by the cases where things go wrong, we pay too little attention to the vastly more numerous cases where they go right, and where it is perhaps easier to see that the descriptive content of the expression concerned is wholly at the service of this function [of identifying reference], a function which is complementary to that of predication and contains no element of predication in itself (Strawson [1974], p. 66).

SECTION 0

In this paper, I am concerned with two semantic questions about demonstratives; particularly about *complex* rather than *bare* demonstratives. The first, very general, question is this. What is the function of the expression 'man' in 'that man', or the expression 'man wearing a carnation' in 'that man wearing a carnation', or the expression 'admirer of Mary's' in 'that admirer or Mary's'? In short, what is the semantic function of the *matrix* of a complex demonstrative?

I was moved to ask this general question by a concern with a second, more specific, question; a question about the semantic coherence or incoherence of sentences of a rather peculiar kind. It is not, perhaps, a question that will grip the imagination of every philosopher of language. In the sentence

Mary loathes that admirer of Mary's (of hers)

the name 'Mary' occurs twice. Are these positions open to quantification? That is, can we form such a sentence as

($\exists y$) [y loathes that admirer of y's]

First appeared in *Journal of Philosophical Logic* 11 (1982): 287–310. Reprinted with kind permission from Kluwer Academic Publishers.

a sentence which presumably would surface as

Some woman loathes *that admirer of hers*?

More generally, given a sentence of the form

$$\Phi(a, (\text{That } x)\Psi(x, a))$$

(where 'That' is a variable binding operator used in the formation of complex demonstratives), can we quantify into the position occupied by 'a' (particularly, into the position occupied by 'a' within the matrix of the complex demonstrative) to yield a quantified sentence of the form

$$(Qy)[\Phi(y, (\text{That } x)\Psi(x, y))]?$$

As Barry Taylor has shown, the answer to this second question is related to a choice between two ways of providing a truth theory for a language containing demonstratives. He calls them 'the method of conditional assignment of truth-conditions' and 'the method of scope-distinction'.[1]

I do not ask these two semantic questions because I think that answers to them will shed light upon the philosophy of mind; upon the nature of demonstrative thoughts, for example. On the contrary, I begin from an idea of Christopher Peacocke's about perceptual demonstrative thoughts,[2] and use that to motivate answers to the semantic questions. I reach that starting point towards the end of Section 2. Thereafter, my strategy is as follows. I use Peacocke's idea to motivate an initial account of the use of perceptual demonstratives in communication: an account of the contents of the thoughts expressed and of the assertions made (Section 3). I then use that account to argue for a choice in favour of the method of conditional assignment of truth conditions in a truth theory for bare demonstratives, and for complex demonstratives (Section 4). The initial account can be extended to give a more complete answer to our first question in any of three ways (Section 5). A choice between these three ways, and the prior choice of the method of conditional assignment of truth conditions, jointly determine the answer to our second question. As it turns out, the quantification is coherent only if the surface form of demonstrative sentences is massively misleading as to underlying semantic structure. Since there is no independent reason to suppose that this is so, I conclude that the quantification is indeed incoherent (Section 6). Finally, I note some empirical evidence that seems to support my conclusion, and make some brief remarks about the relation between syntax and semantics (Section 7).

SECTION 1

My starting point is an idea of Christopher Peacocke's about *perceptual* demonstrative thoughts. I shall reach it towards the end of Section 2. First, I shall summarise some familiar ideas about *indexical* demonstrative thoughts.

Associated with indexical expressions, such as 'I', 'now', and 'here', are *ways of thinking* of objects (or *modes of presentation* of objects). In an 'I'-thought one thinks of an object, namely oneself, in a way in which one can think only of oneself, and in which no one else can think of one. Let us call this way of thinking '[I]'. And what goes for 'I', the way of thinking [I], and the thinker, goes *mutatis mutandis* for 'now', the way of thinking [now], and the time of the thought, and for 'here', the way of thinking [here], and the place of the thought.

Suppose two thinkers *a* and *b* think thoughts which each would express by 'I am hot', What is in common between the two token thought events can be represented by the ordered pair

$\langle$[I], *being hot*$\rangle$.

I shall say that their thoughts have the same *intrinsic content*. But *a*'s and *b*'s thoughts are thoughts concerning different objects. They have different truth conditions, and perhaps different truth values. This difference is reflected in the difference between these ordered pairs:

$\langle a, being\ hot \rangle$.

$\langle b, being\ hot \rangle$.

I shall say that the thoughts have different *referential contents*. The ordered pair

$\langle\langle a, [I] \rangle, being\ hot \rangle$.

brings together elements from the intrinsic and referential contents of *a*'s thought. I shall call it the *extrinsic content* of his thought.[3]

There is no shortage of terminology surrounding these intuitive distinctions. In Perry's scheme, intrinsic content corresponds to the sentence or text *accepted*, while referential content corresponds to what is *believed*. Extrinsic content corresponds to believing something *in a certain way*, to believing something *by* accepting a certain text. Likewise, the way of thinking associated with an indexical demonstrative corresponds to Perry's *role*.[4] In his more recent scheme, explicitly tied to situation semantics, [I] corresponds to the linguistic meaning (cf. Kaplan's character), and the object *a* corresponds to the *interpretation* in a discourse situation.[5] In Evans's scheme, extrinsic content corresponds to a *Fregean thought*. [I] corresponds to a *way of thinking*, to a *type of account* that can be given of what makes the thought have the object it does, and consequently to some *relation* $\lambda x \lambda y R(x, y)$. $\langle a, [I] \rangle$ corresponds to the *sense* of 'I' in the mouth of *a*, to *a particular account* of what makes the thought have the object it does, and consequently to some *relational property* $\lambda x R(x, a)$.[6] In Peacocke's scheme, also, extrinsic content corresponds to a Fregean thought. [I] corresponds to a *type* of mode of presentation, and $\langle a, [I] \rangle$ to a *token* mode of presentation.[7]

These differences in terminology correspond *inter alia* to different views about Frege. Thus, while Evans believed 'that a Fregean approach to demonstrative expressions is essentially correct', Perry thinks that 'Fregean sense [is] a confusing mixture of interpretation and meaning'.[8] But, for present purposes, that difference is less important than a point that is not disputed. Of the two components of the pair $\langle a, [I] \rangle$, the way of thinking [I] is 'on the side of the mind' and the object *a* is 'on the side of the world'. What is not in dispute is that, in the context of a token thought event, the component that is on the side of the mind determines, or fixes, the component that is on the side of the world. Equivalently, the intrinsic content, and the causal and more generally contextual relations in which the token thought event stands, jointly determine the referential, and consequently the extrinsic, content. Thus, for example, '... character or role ... takes us from the subject's identity and position in the world to reference' (Perry); 'A way of thinking about an object is given by an account of what makes some thinking about that object' (Evans); 'there cannot, for a given person at a given time, be token [modes of presentation] which he can employ in his thought, and which differ only in respect of the objects which index the type [modes of presentation]' (Peacocke).[9]

SECTION 2

Let us now turn to perceptual demonstrative thoughts. It is not plausible to hold that there is a (type of) way of thinking *W* associated with the bare demonstrative 'that' or with the complex demonstrative 'that man' (used in perceptual confrontation with objects) such that the intrinsic content of all perceptual demonstrative thoughts expressible by 'that is hot' or 'that man is hot' is captured by the ordered pair

$\langle W,\ being\ hot \rangle$.

For objects may present themsclves perceptually in different modes (visually, aurally etc.), and may present themselves differently even in a single mode. I shall concentrate on visual perception. A (type of) way of thinking, or (type of) mode of (visual) presentation must include, at least, an element corresponding to a type of (visual) perceptual experience. (Cf. Perry on 'ways of seeing'.[10]) I shall use 'Π' for such an element.

The relevant kind of experience is not merely an experience (as) of seeing a certain scene. It is rather an experience (as) of seeing a scene and having a particular feature of the scene or (loosely speaking) a particular object in the scene psychologically salient for one. The nature of this salience will be made clearer by the role that such experiential elements of thought play in what follows. For now it may help to imagine having one's eye upon (in the sense of fixating) a certain feature, or (what is not quite the same) having one's attention fixed upon a certain feature, although neither of these is strictly necessary.[11] (Cf. Kaplan's 'picture with a little arrow pointing to the relevant subject'.[12])

But such an experiential element is not itself a way of thinking. For, in the context of a token thought event, it does not yet determine an object as the object thought about. Such an element, and the contextual relations in which the token thought event stands (particularly, the casual relations between the thinker and the scene before his eyes), jointly leave several objects with competing claims to be the object thought about. In general, these competing claims correspond to varying evaluations of the thought for truth or falsity.

To the extent that Π, and the context of a's thought at t, jointly determine a man d to be the object of a's thought they also jointly determine as the object of that thought a temporal slice of a man, a front surface of a man, a mereological union of parts of a man, an aggregate of molecules constituting a man, and doubtless various other objects of more or less recherché sorts, objects which are not identical with the man d. And in general these differences matter for truth evaluation. Perhaps d will still exist tomorrow although the temporal slice of d will not exist tomorrow. Perhaps d is heavy although the front surface of d is not heavy. Perhaps d will one day have a finger cease to exist and yet go on existing himself although the mereological union of d's parts will not endure through that finger's ceasing to exist. Perhaps d has been here before although the aggregate of molecules constituting d has not been here before.

If a (type of) mode of (visual) presentation is to determine an object relative to a context, then that mode of presentation must include a conceptual, as well as an experiential, element. What determines an object is not merely Π, but Π plus a concept C of a sort of spatio-temporal object (a sortal concept).[13] This is why we were speaking loosely when we spoke of a particular object being salient; apart from the sortal concept C, several objects of various sorts are equally salient. I shall represent a (type of) mode of visual presentation, or way of thinking of an object visually presented, by an ordered pair $\langle \Pi, C \rangle$. Thus, the intrinsic content of a particular thought might be

$$\langle\langle \Pi, \text{ } being \text{ } a \text{ } man \rangle, \text{ } being \text{ } hot \rangle$$

for some Π, and the referential content might be

$$\langle d, \text{ } being \text{ } hot \rangle.$$

In that case, the extrinsic content would be

$$\langle\langle d, \langle \Pi, \text{ } being \text{ } a \text{ } man \rangle\rangle, \text{ } being \text{ } hot \rangle.$$

Here we have a fairly full representation of the content of a perceptual demonstrative thought, concerning a visually presented man d, expressible by 'That man is hot'.

In such a thought concerning d, the two concepts *being a man* and *being hot* are employed in very different roles. Let us say that the concept *being a man* is employed in an *individuative role*, while the concept *being hot* is employed in a *predicative role*. Clearly, the individuative role cannot be assimilated to the predicative role. To do so is to forgo any account of what makes the man d the object of a particular thought with that intrinsic content. If a thinker is to secure an object for his thought, then he must employ in the thought a concept in an individuative role.

We have reached the promised starting point, in the following idea about perceptual demonstrative thoughts.[14]

The notation '$\langle\langle d, \langle \Pi, \text{ } being \text{ } a \text{ } man \rangle\rangle, \text{ } being \text{ } hot \rangle$' provides a sense in which in the thought 'that man is hot', the concept of a man does not serve to make a predication of something already identified in thought, but serves to assist in the identification of the object thought about.

This account of perceptual demonstrative thoughts is very different from description theories of such thoughts. The heart of the difference lies in Burge's distinction between thoughts which are fully conceptualised and thoughts which are not fully conceptualised but 'whose correct ascription places the [thinker] in an appropriate nonconceptual, contextual relation to objects the [thought] is about'.[15] According to Peacocke's account, perceptual demonstrative thoughts are irreducibly different from fully conceptualised, descriptive thoughts; they are irreducibly *de re*. According to description theories, such demonstrative thoughts are just descriptive thoughts; the term '*de re*' does not mark a distinctive kind of thought but, at most, a distinctive kind of ascription of thoughts. A further difference is that, according to Peacocke's account, special significance attaches to the class of sortal concepts. For sortal concepts are especially suited to resolve the indeterminacy left by the nonconceptual, contextual (in particular, perceptual) relations, as to which object is being thought about. Thus, sortal concepts are especially suited to play an individuative role in thought. According to description theories, no special significance attaches to the class of sortal concepts.

SECTION 3

Let us now take some steps in the direction of an idea about the use of perceptual demonstratives in communication, analogous to Peacocke's idea about perceptual demonstrative thoughts. The doctrine that in successful communication the hearer (audience) comes to have a thought with the same content as the thought expressed by the speaker obviously needs to be complicated in the case of communication using demonstratives. We need to consider the speaker's intentions, and then the notion of the content of an assertion.

Suppose that a speaker a assertorically utters 'I am hot' to express his thought, whose extrinsic content is

$\langle\langle a, [\text{I}]\rangle, \textit{being hot}\rangle.$

He does not intend that his audience b should come to have a thought with that same extrinsic content, nor even a thought with the same intrinsic content. One thing that a intends is that b should have a thought, concerning a, to the effect that he is hot. He may, in addition, have intentions about the way in which b is to think of him. Another thing that a intends is that b should recognise that a has a thought whose intrinsic content is

$\langle [\text{I}], \textit{being hot}\rangle.$

These two intentions are not unrelated. It is very plausible that a intends or expects (à la Grice) that b's recognition of a's thought should be part of *b*'s reason for his own thought, concerning *a*, to the effect that he is hot. If that recognition is to be part of that reason then, it seems, *b* must recognise *a* as the object of *a*'s 'I'-thought. And, if that is so, it is plausible that, at some point in the communicative transaction, *b* has some such thought as

The object of *a*'s 'I'-thought is hot.

But it is not *a*'s primary intention that *b* should have such a thought; *b*'s having such a thought is not sufficient for a successful communicative transaction.[16]

We should not identify the content of the assertion that *a* performed with the extrinsic content of the thought that *a* expressed.[17] Rather, we should take as the content of the assertion what is, as a matter of linguistic convention, in common between the thought that *a* expressed and the thought that *b* was intended to arrive at ultimately. Whether, on this account, there is more to the content of the assertion than the referential content $\langle a, being\ hot \rangle$ is not a question we need to pursue. But there is certainly no reason to think that the content of the assertion will involve the concept *being the object of a's 'I'-thought*, or the concept *being the object referred to by 'I'*.

Analogous points about speaker's intentions and about the content of assertions can be made in the case of communication using perceptual demonstratives. If an object *d* is (visually) presented to *a* in a way $\langle \Pi, C \rangle$ then, even if *b* employs the same concept *C* in an individuative role, that same object *d* will, in general, be presented to *b* in a different way $\langle \Pi', C \rangle$, where Π' differs from Π as a result of *b*'s different point of view upon the world. Thus, if speaker *a* assertorically utters 'That man is hot' to express his thought whose extrinsic content is

$\langle\langle d, \langle \Pi,\ being\ a\ man \rangle\rangle,\ being\ hot \rangle$

then he does not, in general, intend that his audience *b* should come to have a thought with that very same content. One thing that *a* intends is that *b* should have a (perceptual demonstrative) thought, concerning *d*, to the effect that he is hot. But we can say more. For it is surely a conventional feature of the use of the complex demonstrative 'That man' that the speaker intends the audience to employ the concept *being a man* in an individuative role. So *a*'s primary intention is that, for some Π' (perhaps differing from Π as a result of *b*'s different point of view upon the world), *b* should have a thought

$$\langle\!\langle d, \langle \Pi', \text{ } being\text{ } a\text{ } man\rangle\!\rangle, \text{ } being\text{ } hot\rangle.$$

Another thing that a intends is that b should recognise that a has a (perceptual demonstrative) thought, concerning d individuated under the concept *being a man*, to the effect that he is hot. It is plausible that a intends or expects that b's recognition of a's thought should be part of b's reason for his own thought. If that recognition is to occur then, it seems, b must recognise d as the object of a's thought (individuated under the concept *being a man*). And, if that is so, it is plausible that, at some point in the communicative transaction, b has some such thought as

The object individuated by a under the concept *being a man* is hot.

But it is not a's primary intention that b should have such a thought; b's having such a thought is not sufficient for a successful communicative transaction.

Here again, we should take as the content of the assertion what is, as a matter of linguistic convention, in common between the content of the thought that a expressed and the content of the thought that b was intended to arrive at ultimately. Certainly, the two thoughts have the same referential content. But, further, as a matter of linguistic convention, the same concept *being a man* is employed in an individuative role in both thoughts. So, we can represent the content of the assertion by an ordered triple

$$\langle d, being\text{ } a\text{ } man, being\text{ } hot\rangle.^{18}$$

There is certainly no reason to think that the content of the assertion involves the concept *being the object individuated by a under the concept being a man*, or the concept *being the object referred to by 'than man'*, or the concept *being demonstrated (as a man) by a*. (This will be important in Section 4, below.)

Consider now the following example. A thinker a is gazing upon the scene before him and starts attending to a particular feature of the scene (in fact, a man/temporal slice of a man/front surface of a man/mereological union of parts of a man/aggregate of molecules constituting a man). He individuates the man d in question by employing the concept *being a man* in an individuative role. Continuing to fix his attention upon d thus individuated, a comes to believe d to be hot. Furthermore, a wants to communicate this belief to his audience b who is standing beside him. What a has to do is to direct b's attention to the man d and then get b to have a thought with the same content as a's thought (since, in this case, a

and b share a point of view upon the world). The audience b is gazing upon the same scene as a is, but without attending to the same feature. An utterance by a of 'that' accompanied by an act of pointing may at least direct b's attention in the right direction. ('The scene is selectively enlivened by the conspicuous intrusion of a finger in the foreground of a chosen subject, or by the motion of a finger outlining a chosen region.'[19]) Pointing indicates angle but not range. But because of shared beliefs about the features of scenes to which human attention is most easily directed, a's utterance of 'that' accompanied by an act of pointing directs b's attention to the right feature. It does not, by itself, direct b's attention to the right object. For b also needs to employ a concept in an individuative role. An utterance by a of 'that man' accompanied by an act of pointing would serve both to direct b's attention to the right feature and to arm b with a concept by employing which his attention could be fixed upon the right object d. An assertoric utterance by a of 'That man is hot' would serve to communicate a's thought to b.

Here we have reached an idea about the use of perceptual demonstratives in communication, analogous to the idea about perceptual demonstrative thoughts. The concept *being a man* does not serve to make a predication of something already identified in the communicative exchange, but serves to assist in the identification of the object communicated about. (I sacrifice elegance to highlight the analogy.)

SECTION 4

It is clear that, in a theory about the nature of perceptual demonstrative thoughts concerning spatio-temporal objects, we must concern ourselves with complex demonstratives rather than with the bare demonstrative 'that'. For in such thoughts the employment of concepts in individuative roles is ineliminable. But it is equally clear that in a semantic theory for a natural language such as English we must make room for the use of the bare demonstrative. Speakers of English do sometimes succeed in directing the attention of an audience to a particular object of a particular sort by an utterance of the bare demonstrative 'that' accompanied, perhaps, by an act of pointing. It is not difficult to see how this might be achieved. We have a greater (human) interest in men than in temporal slices of men, in tomatoes than in front surfaces of tomatoes, in cars than in mereological unions of car parts, and in cats than in aggregates of molecules constituting cats. Once an audience's attention has been directed towards the right feature the audience will naturally tend to fix his attention upon an object of a sort in which he has a greater interest rather than an object of a sort in which he has a lesser interest. And it is common knowledge that all this is so. Such common knowledge as this, together with common knowledge about, for example, the preceding discourse, may remove the need for use of a complex demonstrative in an utterance. An utterance of 'That is heavy' in an appropriate context may have quite determinate truth conditions. The truth of the utterance may depend, for example, upon how things are with a particular demonstrated man, tomato, car or cat.

Let us fix upon a first-order language L which contains some one-place predicates including 'P' and some names including 'm' along with connectives and quantifiers. Suppose that 'P' has the sense of 'is hot', that 'm' names our man d, and that LI extends L by allowing the occurrence of indexed bare demonstratives $\ulcorner that_i \urcorner$ in name positions. There are several ways of providing a truth theory for LI; the way I opt for is familiar enough.[20] The truth predicate 'Tr' is relativised to contexts. The axiom for 'P' is

$$(\forall c)(\forall \pi)(\forall x)\, [\mathrm{Ref}(c, \pi, x) \rightarrow (\mathrm{Tr}(c, \ulcorner P\pi \urcorner) \leftrightarrow x \text{ is hot})]$$

in which '$(\forall c)$' ranges over contexts, '$(\forall \pi)$' ranges over both names and demonstratives, and the language parameter is suppressed. The axiom for 'm' is simply

$$(\forall c)\, \mathrm{Ref}(c, \text{'}m\text{'}, d).$$

Connectives and quantifiers in LI are treated exactly as in a truth theory for L, save for the presence of the additional parameter for contexts.

In this truth theory for LI we use what Barry Taylor calls 'the method of conditional assignment of truth-conditions'.[21] The sentence '$P(that_1)$' is not true relative to a context c unless there is an object x such that both $\mathrm{Ref}(c, \text{'}that_1\text{'}, x)$ and x is hot. The speaker in a context needs to secure a reference (relative to that context) for his demonstrative. But a truth condition specification along the lines of

$$\mathrm{Tr}(c, \text{'}P(that_1)\text{'}) \leftrightarrow (\exists x)(\mathrm{Ref}(c, \text{'}that_1\text{'}, x) \,\&\, x \text{ is hot})$$

invites trouble when taken together with the obvious truth theoretic treatment of the negation operator '$\sim$'. For we find ourselves with

$$\mathrm{Tr}(c, \text{'}\sim P(that_1)\text{'}) \leftrightarrow \sim(\exists x)(\mathrm{Ref}(c, \text{'}that_1\text{'}, x) \,\&\, x \text{ is hot}).$$

And this, together with a theory of utterances which relates truth of sentences and truth of utterances, suggests or even entails that an utterance of '$\sim P(\text{that}_1)$' can be true (correct) in virtue of the speaker's failing to secure a reference (relative to the context of utterance) for the demonstrative 'that$_1$'. Yet it is surely a precondition for the truth (indeed, even for the truth evaluability) of an utterance of '$\sim P(\text{that}_1)$', just as much as for the truth of an utterance of '$P(\text{that}_1)$', that a reference be secured for the demonstrative. The method of conditional assignment of truth conditions respects this precondition. What it delivers for '$\sim P(\text{that}_1)$' is just

$$\text{Ref}(c, \text{'that}_1\text{'}, x) \to (\text{Tr}(c, \text{'}\sim p(\text{that}_1)\text{'}) \leftrightarrow \sim(x \text{ is hot})).$$

Taylor acknowledges the *prima facie* attraction of the method of conditional assignment of truth conditions. But he suggests, and ultimately opts for, a different method of skirting around the problems presented by negation. This second method is 'the method of scope-distinction'.[22] By treating indexed demonstratives as variable binding devices of the same syntactic category as the familiar quantifiers '$\forall$' and '$\exists$', we can distinguish between the externally negated sentence '$\sim(\text{That}_1 \ v_1)Pv_1$' and the internally negated sentence '$(\text{That}_1 \ v_1) \sim Pv_1$'. The externally negated sentence has the semantic property that it is made true by reference failure.

$$\text{Tr}(c, \text{'}\sim(\text{That}_1 \ v_1)Pv_1\text{'}) \leftrightarrow \sim(\exists x)(\text{Ref}(c, \text{'That}_1 \ v_1\text{'}, x) \ \& \ x \text{ is hot})$$

On the other hand, the internally negated sentence requires successful reference for its truth.

$$\text{Tr}(c, \text{'}(\text{That}_1 \ v_1) \sim Pv_1\text{'}) \leftrightarrow (\exists x)(\text{Ref}(c, \text{'That}_1 \ v_1\text{'}, x) \ \& \ \sim(x \text{ is hot}))$$

We shall come, in due course, to Taylor's reason for preferring this second method. (See below, at the end of Section 6.) But there seems to me to be a very strong reason for preferring the first method; a reason which is not exhausted by noting that the scope-distinctions of the second method correspond to no intuitive distinction at the level of surface syntax.

In the specification of truth conditions by the second method, the distinction between the externally and internally negated sentences corresponds to a distinction between occurrences of the reference predicate inside and outside the scope of the negation operator. But if we consider the content of the assertion made, in an utterance of the un-negated sentence (written '$P(\text{that}_1)$' or $(\text{That}_1 v_1)Pv_1$') we find that the concept of reference, like the concept of demonstration and the concept of individuation under a concept, does not enter that content. If the object demonstrated in an utterance of the un-negated sentence is n, and it is clear from the context that the concept C is employed by the speaker (and is to be employed by the audience) in an individuative role, then the content of the assertion is represented by the ordered triple

$\langle n, C, being\ hot \rangle$

or, if the contextually furnished concept C is deemed not to be involved in the content of the assertion, by the ordered pair

$\langle n, being\ hot \rangle$.

In either case, it is the latter ordered pair that determines the truth conditions of the assertion. So there is nothing in the assertoric content of an utterance of '$P(\text{that}_1)$' (or '$(\text{That}_1\ v_1)Pv_1$'), nothing in what ought, in virtue of that content, to be regarded as the truth condition of such an utterance, and consequently nothing in what ought to be regarded as the truth condition, relative to the context of utterance, of the sentence uttered, which would allow for the two different semantic interactions with negation. Indeed, the method of scope-distinction seems to require that the assertoric content of utterances of the un-negated sentence should be something like

The reference of 'that' (or: the demonstrated object) is hot.

Many of these reflections upon the language LI containing indexed bare demonstratives carry over to the language LJ which contains, instead, indexed complex demonstratives. Let us suppose that L contains a one-place sortal predicate 'J' expressing the sortal concept *being a man*. Then the language LJ contains *inter alia* complex demonstratives $\ulcorner(\text{That}_i\ v_j)Jv_j\urcorner$. According to the method of conditional assignment of truth conditions, a truth theory for LJ will contain such theorems as the following.

$(\forall c)[\text{Ref}(c, \text{'}(\text{That}_1\ v_1)Jv_1\text{'}, x) \rightarrow (\text{Tr}(c, \text{'}P(\text{That}_1\ v_1)Jv_1\text{'}) \leftrightarrow x\ \text{is hot})]$

If, for a particular context of utterance c,

$\text{Ref}(c, \text{'}\text{That}_1\ v_1)Jv_1\text{'}, d)$

then an utterance in that context of

$P(\text{That}_1\ v_1)Jv_1$

has an assertoric content which can be represented by the ordered triple

$\langle d, being\ a\ man, being\ hot \rangle$.

It is clear enough what the semantic function of the matrix of the complex demonstrative is in such cases. The predicate '*J*' expresses a concept employed by the speaker, and to be employed by the audience, in an individuative role. This concept serves to individuate in thought the object upon whose being hot the truth of the utterance (and of the sentence relative to the context) depends. Thus with respect to such simple cases, we can answer the first of the two semantic questions with which we began.

SECTION 5

We need to extend our answer to the first semantic question to cover two more difficult kinds of case.

(i)   In the first kind of case, the concept expressed by the matrix of a complex demonstrative is neither an ultimate sortal concept nor a concept which is sortal entailing: it is a *sortal indifferent* concept. Examples might be the concepts *being an object*, *being blue*, and *being an object that John likes*.

We have already considered (at the beginning of Section 4) what is really the limiting case of a matrix expressing a sortal indifferent concept, namely the case in which there is no matrix at all. What I said there can be generalised. From the way in which the employment of concepts in individuative roles was introduced (in Section 2), it is clear that if a perceptual demonstrative thought whose intrinsic content is

$\langle\langle \Pi,\ C \rangle, being\ Q \rangle$

is to have an object, then the concept C must at least be sortal entailing. But speakers of English do sometimes succeed in directing the attention of an audience to a particular object of a particular sort without explicitly expressing that sortal concept in their utterance. For a speaker may trade upon various kinds of common knowledge while expressing a sortal indifferent concept: common knowledge about greater and lesser human interests, common knowledge about the preceding discourse, and even common knowledge about the sorts of objects that John likes.[23]

There will remain questions over cases in which the unexpressed but implicit sortal concept individuates an object which does not fall under the explicitly expressed sortal indifferent concept: cases where 'things go wrong'. But such questions must be answered along with corresponding questions about the use of complex demonstratives whose matrices contain a sortal predicate together with an (apparently) restrictive relative clause; and, more importantly, along with questions about the use of such complex demonstratives in cases where 'things go right'.

(ii) In the second kind of case, then, the concept expressed by the matrix is not an ultimate sortal concept but is *sortal entailing*. Examples of such far-from-ultimate sortal concepts might be the concepts *being a tall man*, *being a tree with a bird in it*, and *being a philosopher*. Such examples prompt questions concerning the semantic function of the matrix to the extent that it expresses 'excess' conceptual material.

There seem to be three possible accounts of the thought expressed by an utterance containing such a complex demonstrative. Thus, consider an utterance of the sentence

That man wearing a carnation is hot

made to express a thought concerning a man d who is, indeed, wearing a carnation. According to account (1), the concept expressed by the matrix is employed in an individuative role and the extrinsic content of the thought is (for some Π)

$$\langle\!\langle d, \langle \Pi, being\ a\ man\ wearing\ a\ carnation \rangle\!\rangle, being\ hot \rangle.^{24}$$

According to account (2), only the entailed ultimate sortal concept is employed in an individuative role. The concept expressed by the matrix is itself semantically irrelevant and the extrinsic content of the thought is

$$\langle\!\langle d, \langle \Pi, being\ a\ man \rangle\!\rangle, being\ hot \rangle.$$

According to account (3), only the entailed ultimate sortal concept is employed in an individuative role. The concept expressed by the matrix is itself employed in a predicative role and the extrinsic content of the thought is

$$\langle\!\langle d, \langle \Pi, being\ a\ man \rangle\!\rangle, (being\ a\ man)\ wearing\ a\ carnation\ being\ hot \rangle.$$

The three accounts yield differing descriptions of communication involving the use of complex demonstratives. The descriptions yielded by accounts (1) and (2) are rather similar.

In order to direct an audience's attention to an object, a speaker has to indicate to his audience a direction, a range, and a sort of object. In very simple cases (in particular, when the matrix itself expresses an ultimate sortal concept) an act of pointing indicates direction and (with the help of some background common knowledge) range, while the matrix of the complex demonstrative indicates a sort of object. But if, for example, there are several men (several objects of the relevant sort) in roughly the same direction and at roughly the same range then it may be that by his act of pointing the speaker succeeds only in directing the audience's attention to a feature of the scene before him from which he can individuate several different men (several different objects of the relevant sort). In such a case, what is needed is that the matrix should express extra conceptual material to assist in directing the audience's attention to the right object.

The difference between the descriptions yielded by accounts (1) and (2) is this. According to account (1), the extra conceptual material is employed in an individuative role. The matrix of the complex demonstrative arms the audience with a richer concept which he can employ in an individuative role in order to individuate the right man d even if (because of the vagueness of pointing) his attention is directed to a feature of the scene before him from which several different men can be individuated. According to account (2) on the other hand, only the entailed ultimate sortal concept is employed in an individuative role. The provision of the extra conceptual material is to be assimilated to more accurate pointing, ensuring that the audience's attention is directed to a narrower feature of the scene from which the ultimate sortal concept can individuate the right man d. The occurrence in the matrix of the restrictive relative clause serves a pragmatic rather than a semantic function.

Account (3) yields a very different description of communication involving the use of complex demonstratives. According to that account, only the entailed ultimate sortal concept is employed in an individuative role. The extra conceptual material is employed in a predicative role. The (apparently restrictive) relative clause '(who is) wearing a carnation', for example, serves exactly the same kind of communicative function as the grammatical predicate 'is hot', and assists in the identification of the object communicated about only in the very derivative way that the predicate 'is hot' also so assists, namely *via* the audience's expectation that the speaker is saying something true.

We need not pause to spell out the consequent descriptions of cases of (attempted) communication in which 'things go wrong'. Obviously, what we say about such cases is heavily constrained by our choice between the three accounts.

SECTION 6

Clearly enough, our initial answer to the first semantic question could be developed into a more comprehensive answer along the lines of any one of the accounts (1), (2), or (3). But, before making a choice between the accounts, we should note the consequences of each of the three accounts for the second (the more specific) semantic question. According to account (1), the concept expressed by the matrix of a complex demonstrative is employed by the speaker, and is to be employed by the audience, in an individuative role. The concept assists in securing an object for the thought to be about, and this is logically prior to the evaluation of the thought for correctness (truth). Similarly, on the side of communication, the semantic function of the matrix is to express a concept which has a role in securing a reference for the complex demonstrative. This is something logically prior to the evaluation of the utterance, or of the sentence uttered, for truth; indeed, logically prior even to the assignment of truth conditions. Thus, there can be no question of quantifying into name positions within a matrix from outside the matrix so as to construct sentences of the form

$$(Qy)[\Phi(y, (\text{That } x)\Psi(x, y))].$$

According to account (2), the entailed ultimate sortal concept has the kind of role that, according to account (1), the concept expressed by the whole matrix has. The concept expressed by the matrix is, to the extent that it goes beyond the entailed ultimate sortal concept, semantically irrelevant. Thus, to fix ideas, if the matrix is made up of a sortal predicate plus a restrictive relative clause, then the sortal predicate has the semantic function which, according to account (1), the whole matrix has; and the restrictive relative clause has no semantic function at all. But then, there can be no question of quantifying into name positions within a matrix. For either the considerations of account (1) apply, or else the name position is in a part of the matrix that is semantically irrelevant.

According to account (3) on the other hand, there is no problem over quantifying into name positions within a matrix from outside the matrix. The sentence

$$(\exists y)(y \text{ likes } (\text{That } x) (x \text{ is a man who admires } y))$$

is true, relative to a context in which the reference of the demonstrative is the man d, just in case there is some y such that both y likes d and d

admires y. For, according to account (3), the occurrence, in the matrix of a complex demonstrative, of a complex predicate containing an apparently restrictive relative clause is massively misleading as to underlying semantic structure. The sentence

Mary likes (That x) (x is a man who admires Mary)

would be far less misleadingly represented as

Mary likes (That x) (x is a man) & (That x) (x is a man) admires Mary.

There is clearly no problem over quantifying into the two positions occupied by the name 'Mary' to form the sentence

$(\exists y)(y$ likes (That x) (x is a man) & (That x) (x is a man) admires $y)$.

In Section 3, I gave an initial account of the use of perceptual demonstratives in communication. That account motivated a choice of the method of conditional assignment of truth conditions, and it yielded an initial answer to our first semantic question. What we have just seen is that quantification into the matrix of a complex demonstrative from outside the matrix can be seen as semantically coherent only if the initial answer is developed along the lines of account (3). The formal analogue of this point is that, if we adopt the method of conditional assignment of truth conditions, then the truth theory cannot deal with sentences involving such quantification (unless, of course, the appearance of such quantification in the surface form is massively misleading as to the form to be assigned to the sentences at the level of input to the truth theory).[25] Since we lack any independent reason for supposing that account (3) is correct, I conclude that such quantification is indeed semantically incoherent.

As for the choice between accounts (1) and (2), I shall say only that in the absence of any argument to show that only ultimate sortal concepts can be employed in individuative roles, account (1) seems to me to be the more natural of the two. It avoids any difficulty that may be raised by the question whether a speaker will always know what the entailed ultimate sortal concept is. And it takes more seriously the syntactic form of complex demonstratives.[26]

I have now returned answers to the two semantic questions with which I began. But there is one loose end to be tied up. The initial account of the use of perceptual demonstratives in communication motivated the choice of the method of conditional assignment of truth conditions. But I did not, at that point (in Section 4), consider Taylor's own reason for choosing instead the method of scope-distinction. So there is room for a nagging worry that his reason might also oblige us to abandon even our initial account.

In fact we need not worry. Taylor's reason for preferring the method of scope-distinction is precisely that it enables him to deal with sentences involving the controversial kind of quantification. According to that method, the sentence

Someone loathes that denigrator of his

is true, relative to a context in which the demonstrated object is the man d, just in case there is some y such that both (i) y loathes d, and (ii) d is demonstrated as a denigrator of y (or d is individuated under the concept *being a denigrator of y*).[27] But, of course, that cannot be a reason for abandoning an account according to which the sentences in question are semantically incoherent.

SECTION 7

Some of the claims of this paper seem to gain support (however limited) from empirical facts about the reactions of language users to sentences of the dubious kind when it is made clear that the demonstratives are supposed to be interpreted as perceptual demonstratives. Here are three claims:

(i) account (3) is not correct;
(ii) the content of assertions does not involve such concepts as reference, demonstration, or individuation;
(iii) quantification into the matrix of a complex demonstrative would be coherent only if account (3) were correct.

Now consider the sentence

Someone loathes that denigrator of his.

Whatever this first sentence means, it does not mean anything very different from

Someone loathes that man who denigrates him.

According to claim (iii), that second sentence is semantically coherent only if what is apparently a restrictive relative clause occurring within the matrix of a complex demonstrative is, in semantic reality, a non-restrictive relative clause, so that the sentence is equivalent to

Someone both loathes and is denigrated by that man.

When language users are presented with the first sentence they typically regard it as bizarre. (That supports claim (i).) They do not impose upon the sentence an interpretation involving such concepts as reference, demonstration, or individuation. (That supports claim (ii).) Rather, to the extent that they are able to impose any interpretation upon it at all, they interpret it as equivalent to the third sentence. (That supports claim (iii).)[28]

The semantic claims I have made in this paper are claims about perceptual demonstratives; that is to say, about demonstrative expressions used as perceptual demonstratives. But demonstrative expressions also have semantically quite different uses. Consequently, nothing in the paper requires the claim that such a string as

Some woman likes *that* left-handed man who admires her

is not a well-formed sentence of English. On the contrary, that is a well-formed sentence, and it could occur quite naturally in the following linguistic context.

For every woman there are several left-handed men who admire her, and amongst those left-handed men one is the most ardent. Some woman likes *that* left-handed man who admires her.

This *anaphoric* use of 'that' results in a sentence whose semantic value in that linguistic context is just that of

Some woman likes *the most ardent* left-handed man who admires her.

Similarly, and indeed more simply, nothing in the paper requires the claim that such a string as

Most women like *that* man (*those* men) who most ardently admires (admire) them

is not a well-formed sentence of English. On the contrary, it could occur quite naturally in any context in which 'that' (or 'those') was heard as equivalent to 'the'.

Syntax need not distinguish between the anaphoric 'that' and the 'that' which shades into 'the' on the one hand, and the perceptual demonstrative 'that' on the other. But semantically they are quite different. Here is one more point at which syntax and semantics do not go neatly in step.

Notes

Many of the ideas in this paper were picked up from lectures, seminars, and conversations involving Tyler Burge, Gareth Evans, Lloyd Humberstone, David Kaplan, Brian Loar, Christopher Peacocke, John Perry, Stephen Schiffer, and Barry Taylor. My debts to the papers by Peacocke [1981] and Taylor [1980] are enormous.

An earlier version of the paper was written during an enjoyable year spent as a Research Fellow at the University of Melbourne.

1. Taylor [1980].

2. Peacocke [1981].

3. My choice of terminology was influenced by McGinn [1982].

4. Perry [1977], [1979], [1980a], [1980b].

5. Perry [1982], Kaplan [1977].

6. Evans [1981], pp. 298–299 [pp. 735–736 in this vol.].

7. Peacocke [1981], p. 189.

8. Evans [1981], p. 280 [p. 717 in this vol.], Perry [1982].

9. Perry [1980b], p. 320, Evans [1981], p. 298 [735], Peacocke [1981], p. 195.

10. Perry [1982].

11. I am indebted here to Francis Dauer and Christopher Peacocke.

12. Kaplan [1977].

13. My use of the notion of a sortal concept is supposed to conform to that of Strawson [1959] and Wiggins [1980].

14. Peacocke [1981], p. 201; I have altered the example and the notation.

15. Burge [1977], p. 346. Cf. Schiffer [1981].

16. Brian Loar and Christopher Peacocke helped me to get clearer about the points of this paragraph and the next few. When considering the speaker's intentions about the audience's thought, it is instructive to consider the use of 'you'.

17. Cf. the argument against the *Principle of Expressibility* in Schiffer [1981].

18. The referential content is already enough to determine the truth conditions of the assertion. The extra component in the assertoric content is relevant not to the truth or falsity of the assertion, but to the characterisation of the associated beliefs of the speaker and the audience. This is, indeed, a feature of any account of the contents of assertions which cuts those contents more finely than truth conditional equivalence. I am indebted here to Stephen Schiffer and Barry Taylor. Note that Schiffer [1981] takes the referential content as the content of the assertion.

19. Quine [1974], p. 44.

20. For a different way, see Weinstein [1974].

21. Taylor [1980], p. 188.

22. *ibid.*

23. I do not deny that sometimes, when there is no risk of a difference in truth value, a speaker may leave the reference of his demonstrative partially indeterminate.

24. The employment of the concept *being a man wearing a carnation* in an individuative role will be accompanied by a willingness to judge concerning that man *d* that he is wearing a carnation; and in that judgement the concept *wearing a carnation* is employed in a predicative role. This fact is relevant in cases where 'things go wrong'.

25. See Taylor [1980], p. 195.

26. Christopher Peacocke has suggested to me that we can find reasons for favouring account (1), if we consider non-visual examples. In some such examples, it seems that if a thought is to have an object then non-sortal material must play an individuative role.

27. Taylor [1980], p. 195.

28. In fact there is a complication here, for language users have even greater difficulty with the sentence

No one loathes that denigrator of his.

I suspect that this extra difficulty may be related to the fact that, to the extent that the sentence is interpreted in such a way that 'his' belongs in a non-restrictive relative clause, the position occupied by the quantifier does not govern the position occupied by the pronoun 'his'. Consequently it is difficult to interpret the pronoun as bound by the quantifier. A different interpretation of the pronoun is possible when its antecedent is 'someone' but not when its antecedent is 'no one'. This complication can be corrected for, if we consider the sentence

Someone is such that he loathes that denigrator of his

and the corresponding sentence with 'no one'.

References

Burge, T.: 1977, 'Belief *De Re*', Journal of Philosophy 74, 338–362.

Evans, G.: 1981, 'Understanding Demonstratives', in H. Parret and J. Bouveresse (eds.), *Meaning and Understanding*, de Gruyter, pp. 280–303. [Chap. 30 in this vol.]

Kaplan, D.: 1977, *Demonstratives*, Draft #2, mimeo, UCLA.

McGinn, C.: 1982, 'The Structure of Content', in A. Woodfield (cd.) *Thought and Object*, Oxford University Press, pp. 207–258.

Peacocke, C.: 1981, 'Demonstrative Thought and Psychological Explanation', *Synthese* 49, 187–217.

Perry, J.: 1977, 'Frege on Demonstratives', *Philosophical Review* 86, 474–497. [Chap. 29 in this vol.]

Perry, J.: 1979, 'The Problem of the Essential Indexical', *Noûs* 13, 3–21.

Perry, J.: 1980a, 'Belief and Acceptance', in P. A. French, *et al.* (eds.) *Midwest Studies in Philosophy Volume V: Studies in Epistemology*, University of Minnesota Press, pp. 533–542.

Perry, J.: 1980b, 'A Problem about Continued Belief', *Pacific Philosophical Quarterly* 61, 317–332.

Perry, J.: 1982, 'Perception, Action, and the Structure of Believing', to appear in a *Festschrift* for Paul Grice edited by Richard Grandy and Richard Warner.

Quine, W. V. O.: 1974, *The Roots of Reference*, Open Court.

Schiffer, S.: 1981, 'Indexicals and the Theory of Reference', *Synthese* 49, 43–100.

Strawson, P. F.: 1959, *Individuals*, Methuen.

Strawson, P. F.: 1974, *Subject and Predicate in Logic and Grammar*, Methuen.

Taylor, B.: 1980, 'Truth-theory for Indexical Languages', in M. Platts (ed.) *Reference, Truth and Reality*, Routledge & Kegan Paul, pp. 182–198.

Weinstein, S.: 1974, 'Truth and Demonstratives', *Noûs* 8, 179 184. [Chap. 27 in this vol.]

Wiggins, D.: 1980, *Sameness and Substance*, Blackwell.

PART VI
ATTITUDE REPORTS

INTRODUCTION

One area where the extrusion of philosophy into linguistics has been quite marked has been in the analysis of sentences that report psychological attitudes. Attitude reports pose particular problems for semantic theory, because it is unclear what semantic value should be assigned to the embedded clause of an attitude report. For example, consider sentence (1):

(1) [s Galileo believed that [s the Earth moves]]

Intuitively, (1) expresses a relation between Galileo and some sort of object, but what sort of object? Clearly (as Frege noted) the semantic value of the embedded clause can't be its truth value here, for then its semantic value is simply the True, and that would mean that (1) expresses the same thing as (1'), which also has a true embedded clause:

(1') [s Galileo believed that [s the Moon moves]]

One possible proposal is that (1) expresses a relation between Galileo and the clause itself—in other words, between Galileo and (2).

(2) [s the Earth moves]

But this seems implausible, since the clause itself does not carry as much information as the belief report intuitively does. For example, pointing at the moon, I might utter (3):

(3) [s Galileo believed that [s that moves]]

But I might also utter (3) when pointing at the sun. The problem is that if the object of Galileo's belief is simply the syntactic object in (4), then these two belief attributions are not distinguished in the semantics.

(4) [s that moves]

There have been many responses to this problem in the semantic literature over the last 50 years, but the field can perhaps be divided into two approaches to the problem. According to the first camp, one must utilize the resources of possible worlds to account for the behavior of these environments. For example, one approach to the problem, articulated by Jaakko Hintikka, Richard Montague, and others, has been to hold that an attitude report expresses a relation between an agent and a set of possible worlds. So, for example, a belief report like (3) expresses a relation between Galileo and the set of possible worlds in which the Earth moves. According to the other camp, this move isn't necessary. Attitudes need merely express relations between agents and Russellian propositions, or perhaps sentencelike entities.

The stage for this debate is set in the papers by Rudolph Carnap and Israel Sheffler. In *Meaning and Necessity*, which may be thought of as a precursor to possible-world analyses of attitudes, Carnap introduces the notion of a "state description," which can be thought of as a description of a possible state of affairs. This resource is serviceable enough for modal environments ("necessarily p" could be treated as "p is true in all possible state descriptions"), but it runs into difficulties with sentences that report attitudes. The problem with Carnap's proposal is that state descriptions are too "course-grained" to handle treatments of the attitudes, since they do not distinguish the belief that p from the belief that (p & q), where q is some complex logical truth.

Carnap saw that it would be necessary to introduce potential objects of the attitudes that are more fine-grained. His response was to propose that state descriptions had to be structured in a certain way. The idea was that a belief that p could be distinguished from the belief that p & q on the grounds that the two objects of belief are structured differently and hence are not "intensionally isomorphic." (More recent efforts to run possible-world theories of attitudes, for example Cresswell 1984, have executed similar strategies.)

According to Sheffler, Carnap's proposal for the attitudes, while somewhat fine-grained, will still not be fine-grained enough, since how we distinguish attitudes will be highly sensitive to matters such as the terms we use under certain circumstances. Indeed, Sheffler speculates that any theory fine-grained enough to distinguish propositional attitudes will be too course-grained in some circumstances. Sheffler thus lays out an important challenge to anyone who hopes to construct a successful theory of the attitudes: finding potential objects of the attitudes that are fine-grained enough to reflect the sensitivity of our attitude reporting to factors such as choice of word yet at the same time course-grained enough for other circumstances.

The selection from Quine's *Word and Object*, "Vagaries of Reference," shows both an interesting approach to the problem of the attitudes and some powerful syntactic insights into the structure of attitude verbs like 'seeks' (Quine reanalyzes 'seeks' as 'trying to find' and thus as a propositional attitude in disguise). For Quine, appeal to intensions à la Carnap is just not a possible way out (given Quine's general philosophical stance that intensions are "creatures of darkness").

Donald Davidson shares Quine's aversion to intensional logics but takes a somewhat different route in his handling of attitude reports. Davidson proposes that a report like 'Johns said that the Earth moves' really has a logical form akin to (5).

(5) John said that. The Earth moves.

Clearly, on Davidson's analysis any attempt to substitute within the embedded clause will radically alter the truth conditions of the construction as a whole, yet no intensional resources are required to get this effect.

With the solution to the problem of the attitudes proffered by Quine and Davidson we begin to see a deep philosophical dispute emerging in the analysis of attitude environments. On the one hand, there are those, like Carnap, who see attitude contexts as a species of intensional phenomena in natural language. On the other hand, with Quine and Davidson there begins to emerge a view that is skeptical of treatments regarding these phenomena as intensional and that rather treats the phenomena as owing to some form of reference to a sentencelike object.

The dispute is no trivial matter. In part I we considered arguments that model-theoretic semantics in general and possible-world semantics in particular are not well suited for delivering meaning theories that state the relation between language and the world. So it appeared that possible worlds and like resources could be dispensed with. Here, however, there is a challenge to the effect that possible worlds might be needed to handle certain natural-language constructions like attitude reports.

With this concern in the background, the selection from Barbara Partee becomes particularly interesting. On the one hand, her paper pursues part of the rich domain of facts surrounding the scopal interactions of quantified expressions with attitude environments. On the other hand, it offers a profound challenge to the sententialists. As Partee notes, there are numerous kinds of attitude reports, but not all of them can be characterized as being sentential in character. For example, there are certain linguistic reasons for supposing that there are intensional transitive verbs ('seeks', 'looks for', etc.) that don't have clausal complements and for which a Quinean "hidden clause" analysis seems implausible (for example, these verbs don't evince the adverb-attachment ambiguity we would expect if they had clausal complements). Partee concludes that intensionality must be a quite general property of natural languages, and is quite out of reach of sententialist accounts of the attitudes. If Partee's observations pose problems for sententialist theories of the attitudes, such theories (in particular Davidson's theory) come under additional fire in the excerpt from Stephen Schiffer's *Remnants of Meaning* ("Sententialist Theories of Belief"), which catalogs several objections to sententialist theories.

Seeking a nonsententialist alternative to possible-world theories of the attitudes, a number of philosophers have maintained that the objects of the attitudes are Russellian propositions. The idea is that the utterance of a sentence like (3) above might express a relation between Galileo and a singular proposition that consists of the Earth itself and the property of moving. The virtue of this approach is that one needn't invoke possible worlds to account for the attitudes—the semantic value of a 'that' clause is simply an object that consists of an individual and a property. No possible worlds are required.

In addition to skirting the need for possible worlds, Russellian solutions have another advantage over Carnapian and possible-world analyses of the attitudes. Russellian propositions are fine-grained enough so that a belief that p will be distinguished from a belief that p & q, where q is some tautology. Likewise, on the hypothesis that being a cordate is a different property from being a renate, such theories can distinguish a belief that x is a cordate from a belief that x is a renate—hence they are quite fine-grained in this respect. There are, however, problems with such theories. In the first place, it is far from clear how such accounts are to be extended to other kinds of attitude reports—in particular, the ones that Partee thinks will require full-blown intensional languages. Second, one might well wonder about the status of the properties that are constituents in these propositions. What exactly are they, and what are their individuating conditions? But finally, there is the matter of coreferring names and Kripke's puzzled Pierre (in "A Puzzle about Belief").

Pierre, while in France, assents to 'Londres est jolie.' We report him as believing that London is pretty. Following a strange set of circumstances,

Pierre ends up in an ugly part of London, not knowing it as "Londres." He now affirms 'London is not pretty', so we report him as believing that London is not pretty. It appears that Pierre both believes and doesn't believe that London is pretty.

What can be done about this problem? There appear to be two routes one can take. Either one can argue that attitude reports can be distinguished despite the fact that their propositional constituents are identical, or one can argue that these propositions have constituents that will help us to distinguish them. As an example of the former route, Scott Soames argues that attending to the distinction between the proposition expressed and the information conveyed by an attitude report can help us distinguish reports that have the same propositional constituents. Mark Crimmins and John Perry, providing an example of the latter route, argue that propositional objects must also contain "notions," which are privately individuated contents that do the work that modes of presentation did for Frege.

Do these solutions work? I'm a player in this game, so it would be unfair to pass judgment here, but I can at least note in passing that there are worries about both approaches. The hard line, taken by Soames, appears to conflict with our intuitions about what the truth values of certain reports actually are. Perhaps pragmatic theories can be enlisted to explain how our intuitions stray, but not everyone has been satisfied with the pragmatic stories developed thus far. As for enlisting ideas like notions, this solution appears to collide with the concerns that initially drove Frege to reject psychologism over 100 years ago—if notions are private psychological states, exactly how is communication about these states possible?

One rather large worry about notions, and indeed the use of properties in Russellian propositions, is the fact that our grasp on the identity of notions and properties and like entities is no better than the linguistic resources we have for speaking about them. No one has every actually seen a notion, so how do we know that there are two separate notions for Venus? Well, someone may assent to a belief attribution that contains the name 'Hesperus' yet dissent from one that contains the name 'Phosphorus'. No one has ever seen a property, so how do we know that there are separate properties for 'woodchuck' and 'groundhog'? Well, we have different ways of speaking about that species of genus *Marmota*. It begins to appear that how we distinguish the attitudes may have more to do with our lexicon than with anything else, and this is precisely the intuition that motivates ILF theories of attitudes.

In recent literature a number of authors have suggested a proposal in which the semantic problems arising with propositional-attitude verbs might be resolved by taking such verbs to express relations between agents and interpreted logical forms (ILFs). ILFs are phrase markers whose nodes are paired with semantic values.

For example, the ILF for 'The Earth moves' would include the syntactic phrase marker for that sentence (abstracting from detail here):

(6)

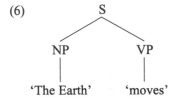

It would also have semantic values assigned to each node of the tree. We might therefore represent the ILF of 'The Earth moves' as follows, where each node is paired with its semantic value:

(7)

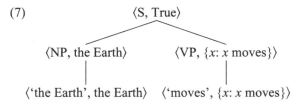

Such objects in effect represent a semantic value together with its linguistic "mode of presentation." Unlike the naive syntactic theory discussed above, ILF theories, by including semantic values, can distinguish both of the beliefs reported as 'Galileo said that that moves', because the two different acts of pointing pick out different semantic values (the Moon in one case and the Sun in the other). Thus, in the case where I point at the Moon, we get the ILF in (8). In the case where I point at the Sun, we get the ILF in (9).

(8)

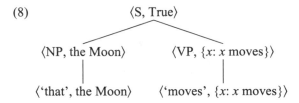

(9)

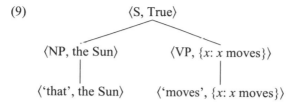

ILF theories thus provide an alternative to treatments of propositional-attitude constructions that traditionally make use of possible-world semantics, Russellian propositions, or Fregean senses.

Despite the appeal of such theories, there is still Partee's observation that many attitude reports cannot be construed as having clausal constituents. Or can they? Marcel den Dikken, Richard Larson, and I argue that there actually is good syntactic evidence that all of the examples that exercised Partee in fact have covert clausal constituents, and hence that ILF-type analyses trivially extend to them.

By closing with some of my collaborative work, I don't mean to imply that those papers represent the end of the problem of the attitudes. Quite the contrary. Rather, I think it is instructive to note how the debate has taken a decidedly linguistic turn—in particular as regards the question of whether sentimentalist accounts can be extended to verbs like 'seeks'. Here are some very delicate linguistic questions about the nature of natural language, and I think it is fair to say that the debate has only just begun.

Further reading for Part VI

Possible-world analyses of the attitudes
Cresswell, M. 1984. *Structured Meanings*. Cambridge: MIT Press.

Hintikka, J. 1962. *Knowledge and Belief*. Ithaca: Cornell University Press.

Montague, R. 1974. *Formal Philosophy*. New Haven: Yale University Press.

Partee, B. 1982. "Belief Sentences and the Limits of Semantics." In S. Peters and E. Saarinen (eds.), *Processes, Beliefs, and Questions*. Dordrecht: D. Reidel.

Stalnaker, R. 1987. *Inquiry*. Cambridge: MIT Press.

Davidsonian analyses of attitudes
Lepore, E., and B. Loewer. 1989. "You Can Say That Again." In P. French, T. Uehling, and H. Wettstein (eds.), *Contemporary Perspectives in the Philosophy of Language, II*, Midwest Studies in Philosophy no. 14. Notre Dame: University of Notre Dame Press.

Lepore, E. 1986. *Truth and Interpretation: Perspectives on the Philosophy of Donald Davidson*. Oxford: Blackwell.

Solutions that employ Russellian propositions

Salmon, N. 1986. *Frege's Puzzle*. Cambridge: MIT Press.

Salmon, N., and S. Soames (eds.). 1988. *Propositions and Attitudes*. Oxford: Oxford University Press.

Richard, M. 1990. *Propositional Attitudes*. Cambridge: Cambridge University Press.

On ILF theories

Higginbotham, J. 1986. "Linguistic Theory and Davidson's Program." In E. Lepore and B. MacLaughlin (eds.), *Truth and Interpretation: Perspectives on the Philosophy of Donald Davidson*. Oxford: Blackwell.

Higginbotham, J. 1991. "Belief and Logical Form." *Mind and Language* 6:344–369.

Larson, R., and G. Segal. 1995. *Knowledge of Meaning: An Introduction to Semantic Theory*. Cambridge: MIT Press.

Segal, G. 1989. "A Preference for Sense and Reference." *Journal of Philosophy* 86:73–89.

Chapter 32

The Method of Intension

Rudolph Carnap

SENTENCES ABOUT BELIEFS

We study sentences of the form 'John believes that ...'. If here the sub-sentence '...' is replaced by another sentence L-equivalent to it, then it may be that the whole sentence changes its truth-value. Therefore, the whole belief-sentence is neither extensional nor intensional with respect to the subsentence '...'. Consequently, an interpretation of belief-sentences as referring either to sentences or to propositions is not quite satisfactory. For a more adequate interpretation we need a relation between sentences which is still stronger than L-equivalence. Such a relation will be defined in the next section.

We found that '... ∨ - - -' is extensional with respect to the subsentence indicated by dots, and that 'N(...)' is intensional. Can there be a context which is neither extensional nor intensional? This would be the case if (but not only if) the replacement of a subsentence by an L-equivalent one changed the truth-value and hence also the intension of the whole sentence. In our systems this cannot occur; every sentence in S_1 (and likewise in S_3, to be explained later) is extensional, and every sentence in S_2 is either extensional or intensional. However, it is the case for a very important kind of sentence with psychological terms, like 'I believe that it will rain'. Although sentences of this kind seem to be quite clear and unproblematic at first glance and are, indeed, used and understood in everyday life without any difficulty, they have proved very puzzling to logicians who have tried to analyze them. Let us see whether we can throw some light upon them with the help of our semantical concepts.

In order to formulate examples, we take here, as our object language S, not a symbolic system but a part of the English language. We assume that

First appeared in *Meaning and Necessity* (Chicago: University of Chicago Press, 1947; 2nd ed., 1956), pp. 53–64. Reprinted by permission of the University of Chicago Press.

S is similar in structure to S_1 except for containing the predicator '.. believes that - -' and some mathematical terms. We do not specify here the rules of S; we assume that the semantical rules of S are such that the predicator mentioned has its ordinary meaning; and, further, that our semantical concepts, especially 'true', 'L-true', 'equivalent', and 'L-equivalent', are defined for S in accord with our earlier conventions. Now we consider the following two belief-sentences; 'D' and 'D''' are here written as abbreviations for two sentences in S to be explained presently:

(i) 'John believes that D'.

(ii) 'John believes that D'''.

Suppose we examine John with the help of a comprehensive list of sentences which are L-true in S; among them, for instance, are translations into English of theorems in the system of *Principia Mathematica* and of even more complicated mathematical theorems which can be proved in that system and therefore are L-true on the basis of the accepted interpretation. We ask John, for every sentence or for its negation, whether he believes what it says or not. Since we know him to be truthful, we take his affirmative or negative answer as evidence for his belief or non-belief. Among the simple L-true sentences, there will certainly be some for which John professes belief. We take as 'D' any one of them, say 'Scott is either human or not human'. Thus the sentence (i) is true. On the other hand, since John is a creature with limited abilities, we shall find some L-true sentences in S for which John cannot profess belief. This does not necessarily mean that he commits the error of believing their negations; it may be that he cannot give an answer either way. We take as 'D''' some sentence of this kind; that is to say, 'D''' is L-true but (ii) is false. Thus the two belief-sentences (i) and (ii) have different truth-values; they are neither equivalent nor L-equivalent. Therefore, the definition of interchangeability and L-interchangeability lead to the following two results:

(1) The occurrence of 'D' within (i) is not interchangeable with 'D'''.

(2) The occurrence of 'D' within (i) is not L-interchangeable with 'D'''.

   'D' and 'D''' are both L-true; therefore:

(3) 'D' and 'D''' are equivalent and L-equivalent.

Examining the first belief-sentence (i) with respect to its subsentence 'D', we see from (1) and (3) that the condition of extensionality is not fulfilled;

and we see from (2) and (3) that the condition of intensionality is not fulfilled either:

(4) The belief-sentence (i) is *neither extensional nor intensional* with respect to its subsentence 'D'.

Although 'D' and 'D''' have the same intension, namely, the L-true or necessary proposition, and hence the same extension, namely, the truth-value truth, their interchange transforms the first belief-sentence (i) into the second (ii), which does not have the same extension, let alone the same intension, as the first.

The same result as (4) holds also if any other sentence is taken instead of 'D', in particular, any factual sentence.

Let us now try to answer the much-discussed question as to how a sentence reporting a belief is to be analyzed and, in particular, whether such a sentence is about a proposition or a sentence or something else. It seems to me that we may say, in a certain sense, that (i) is about the sentence 'D', but also, in a certain other sense, that (i) is about the proposition that D. In interpreting (i) with respect to the sentence 'D', it would, of course, not do to transform it into 'John is disposed to an affirmative response to the sentence "D"', because this might be false, although (i) was assumed to be true; it might, for instance, be that John does not understand English but expresses his belief in another language. Therefore, we may try the following more cautious formulation:

(iii) 'John is disposed to an affirmative response to some sentence in some language, which is L-equivalent to "D"'.

Analogously, in interpreting (i) with respect to the proposition that D, the formulation 'John is disposed to an affirmative response to any sentence expressing the proposition that D' would be wrong because it implies that John understands all languages. Even if the statement is restricted to sentences of the language or languages which John understands, it would still be wrong, because 'D''', for example, or any translation of it, likewise expresses the proposition that D, but John does not give an affirmative response to it. Thus we see that here again we have to use a more cautious formulation similar to (iii):

(iv) 'John is disposed to an affirmative response to some sentence in some language which expresses the proposition that D'.

However, it seems to me that even the formulations (iii) and (iv), which are L-equivalent, should not be regarded as anything more than a first approximation to a correct interpretation of the belief-sentence (i). It is true that each of them follows from (i), at least if we take 'belief' here in the sense of 'expressible belief', leaving aside the problem of belief in a wider sense, interesting though it may be. However, (i) does not follow from either of them. This is easily seen if we replace 'D' by 'D''. Then (iii) remains true because of (3); on the other hand, (i) becomes (ii), which is false. It is clear that we must interpret (i) as saying as much as (iii) but something more; and this additional content seems difficult to formulate. If (i) is correctly interpreted in accord with its customary meaning, then it follows from (i) that there is a sentence to which John would respond affirmatively and which is not only L-equivalent to 'D', as (iii) says, but has a still stronger relation to 'D'—in other words, a sentence which has something more in common with 'D' than the intension. The two sentences must, so to speak, be understood in the same way; they must not only be L-equivalent in the whole but consist of L-equivalent parts, and both must be built up out of these parts in the same way. If this is the case, we shall say that the two sentences have the same intensional structure. This concept will be explicated in the next section and applied in the analysis of belief sentences in the section after next.

INTENSIONAL STRUCTURE

If two sentences are built in the same way out of designators (or designator matrices) such that any two corresponding designators are L-equivalent, then we say that the two sentences are *intensionally isomorphic* or that they have the same *intensional structure*. The concept of L-equivalence can also be used in a wider sense for designators in different language systems; and the concept of intensional isomorphism can then be similarly extended.

We shall discuss here what we call the analysis of the intensional structures of designators, especially sentences. This is meant as a semantical analysis, made on the basis of the semantical rules and aimed at showing, say for a given sentence, in which way it is built up out of designators and what are the intensions of these designators. If two sentences are built in the same way out of corresponding designators with the same intensions, then we shall say that they have the same intensional structure. We might perhaps also use for this relation the term 'synonymous', because it is used in a similar sense by other authors (e.g., Langford, Quine, and Lewis), as we shall see in the next section. We shall now try to explicate this concept.

Let us consider, as an example, the expressions '2 + 5' and 'II sum V' in a language S containing numerical expressions and arithmetical functors.

Let us suppose that we see from the semantical rules of S that both '+' and 'sum' are functors for the function Sum and hence are L-equivalent; and, further, that the numerical signs occurring have their ordinary meanings and hence '2' and 'II' are L-equivalent to one another, and likewise '5' and 'V'. Then we shall say that the two expressions are *intensionally isomorphic* or that they have *the same intensional structure*, because they not only are L-equivalent as a whole, both being L-equivalent to '7', but consist of three parts in such a way that corresponding parts are L-equivalent to one another and hence have the same intension. Now it seems advisable to apply the concept of intensional isomorphism in a somewhat wider sense so that it also holds between expressions like '2 + 5' and 'sum (II, V)', because the use in the second expression of a functor preceding the two argument signs instead of one standing between them or of parentheses and a comma may be regarded as an inessential syntactical device. Analogously, if '>' and 'Gr' are L-equivalent, and likewise '3' and 'III', then we regard '5 > 3' as intensionally isomorphic to 'Gr(V, III)'. Here again we regard the two predicators '>' and 'Gr' as corresponding to each other, irrespective of their places in the sentences; further, we correlate the first argument expression of '>' with the first of 'Gr', and the second with the second. Further, '2 + 5 > 3' is isomorphic to 'Gr[sum(II, V), III]', because the corresponding expressions '2 + 5' and 'sum(II, V)' are not only L-equivalent but isomorphic. On the other hand, '7 > 3' and 'Gr[sum(II, V), III]' are not isomorphic; it is true that here again the two predicators '>' and 'Gr' are L-equivalent and that corresponding argument expressions of them are likewise L-equivalent, but the corresponding expressions '7' and 'sum(II, V) are not isomorphic. We require for isomorphism of two expressions that the analysis of both down to the smallest subdesignators lead to analogous results.

We have said earlier that it seems convenient to take as designators in a system S at least all those expressions in S, but not necessarily only those, for which there are corresponding variables in the metalanguage M. For the present purpose, the comparison of intensional structures, it seems advisable to go as far as possible and take as designators all those expressions which serve as sentences, predicators, functors, or individual expressions of any type, irrespective of the question of whether or not M contains corresponding variables. Thus, for example, we certainly want to regard as isomorphic '$p \lor q$' and 'Apq', where 'A' is the sign of disjunction (or alternation) as used by the Polish logicians in their parenthesis-free notation, even if M, as is usual, does not contain variables of the type of connectives. We shall then regard '$\vee$' and 'A' as L-equivalent connectives because any two full sentences of them with the same argument expressions are L-equivalent.

Frequently, we want to compare the intensional structures of two expressions which belong to different language systems. This is easily possible if the concept of L-equivalence is defined for the expressions of both languages in such a way that the following requirement is fulfilled, in analogy to our earlier conventions: an expression in S is L-equivalent to an expression in S' if and only if the semantical rules of S and S' together, without the use of any knowledge about (extra-linguistic) facts, suffice to show that the two expressions have the same extension. Thus, L-equivalence holds, for example, between 'a' in S and 'a''' in S' if we see from the rules of designation for these two individual constants that both stand for the same individual; likewise between 'P' and 'P''', if we see from the rules alone that these predicators apply to the same individuals; between two functors '+' and 'sum', if we see from the rules alone that they assign to the same arguments the same values—in other words, if their full expressions with L-equivalent argument expressions (e.g., '2 + 5' and 'sum(II, V)') are L-equivalent; for two sentences, if we see from the rules alone that they have the same truth-value (e.g., 'Rom ist gross' in German, and 'Rome is large' in English). Thus, even if the sentences '2 + 5 > 3' and 'Gr[sum(II, V), III]' belong to two different systems, we find that they are intensionally isomorphic by establishing the L-equivalence of corresponding signs.

If variables occur, the analysis becomes somewhat more complicated, but the concept of isomorphism can still be defined. We shall not give here exact definitions but merely indicate, with the help of some simple examples, the method to be applied in the definitions of L-equivalence and isomorphism of matrices. Let 'x' be a variable in S which can occur in a universal quantifier '(x)' and also in an abstraction operator '(λx)', and 'u' be a variable in S' which can occur in a universal quantifier 'Πu', and also in an abstraction operator '$\hat{u}$'. If 'x' and 'u' have the same range of values (or, more exactly, of value intensions), for example, if both are natural number variables (have natural number concepts as value intensions), we shall say that 'x' and 'u' are L-equivalent, and also that '(x)' and 'Πu' are L-equivalent, and that '(λx)' and '$\hat{u}$' are L-equivalent. If two matrices (sentential or other) or degree n are given, one in S and the other in S', we say that they are L-equivalent with respect to a certain correlation between the variables, if corresponding abstraction expressions are L-equivalent predicators. Thus, for example, '$x > y$' in S and 'Gr(u, v)' in S' are L-equivalent matrices (with respect to the correlation of 'x' with 'u' and 'y' with 'v') because '$(\lambda xy) [x > y]$' and '$\hat{u}\hat{v}[\mathrm{Gr}(u, v)]$' are L-equivalent predicators. Intensional isomorphism of (sentential or other) matrices can then be defined in analogy to that of closed designators, so that it holds if the two matrices are built up in the same way out of corresponding expressions which are either L-equivalent designators or L-equivalent matrices. Thus, for example, the matrices '$x + 5 > y$' and 'Gr$[\mathrm{sum}(u, \mathrm{V}), v]$' are not only L-equivalent but also intensionally iso-morphic; and so are the (L-false) sentences '$(x)(y)[x + 5 > y]$' and '$\Pi u\Pi v[\mathrm{Gr}[\mathrm{sum}(u, \mathrm{V}), v]]$'.

These considerations suggest the following definition, which is recursive with respect to the construction of compound designator matrices out of simpler ones. It is formulated in general terms with respect to designator matrices; these include closed designators and variables as special cases. The definition presupposes an extended use of the term 'L-equivalent' with respect to variables, matrices, and operators, which has been indi-cated in the previous examples but not formally defined. The present defi-nition makes no claim to exactness; an exact definition would have to refer to one or two semantical systems whose rules are stated completely.

(1) *Definition of intensional isomorphism*
    a. Let two designator matrices be given, either in the same or in two different semantical systems, such that neither of them contains another designator matrix as proper part. They are intensionally isomorphic $=_{\mathrm{Df}}$ they are L-equivalent.
    b. Let two compound designator matrices be given, each of them consisting of one main submatrix (of the type of a predicator, functor, or connective) and n argument expressions (and possibly auxiliary signs like parentheses, commas, etc.). The two matrices are intensionally isomorphic $=_{\mathrm{Df}}$ (1) the two main submatrices are intensionally isomorphic, and (2) for any m from 1 to n, the mth argument expression within the first matrix is intensionally isomorphic to the mth in the second matrix ('the mth' refers to the order in which the argument expressions occur in the matrix).
    c. Let two compound designator matrices be given, each of them consisting of an operator (universal or existential quantifier, abstraction operator, or description operator) and its scope, which is a designator matrix. The two matrices are intensionally isomorphic $=_{\mathrm{Df}}$ (1) the two scopes are intensionally isomorphic

with respect to a certain correlation of the variables occurring in them, (2) the two operators are L-equivalent and contain correlated variables.

In accord with our previous discussion of the explicandum, rule b in this definition takes into consideration the order in which argument expressions occur but disregards the place of the main subdesignator. For the intensional structure, in contrast to the merely syntactical structure, only the order of application is essential, not the order and manner of spelling.

APPLICATIONS OF THE CONCEPT OF INTENSIONAL STRUCTURE

The concept of intensional structure is compared with the concepts of synonymity discussed by Quine and Lewis. The concept is then used for giving an interpretation of belief sentences that seems more adequate than the interpretations discussed earlier. Further, the same concept helps in solving the so-called paradox of analysis.

It has often been noticed by logicians that for the explication of certain customary concepts a stronger meaning relation than identity of intension seems to be required. But usually this stronger relation is not defined. It seems that in many of these cases the relation of intensional isomorphism could be used. For example, if we ask for an exact translation of a given statement, say the exact translation of a scientific hypothesis or of the testimony of a witness in court from French into English, we should usually require much more than agreement in the intensions of the sentences, that is, L-equivalence of the sentences. Even if we restrict our attention to designative (cognitive) meaning—leaving aside other meaning components like the emotive and the motivative, although they are often very important even for the translation of theoretical texts—L-equivalence of sentences is not sufficient; it will be required that at least some of the component designators be L-equivalent, in other words, that the intensional structures be alike or at least similar.

Quine explains, without giving a definition, a concept of synonymity which is different from and presumably stronger than L-equivalence. He says: "The notion of synonymity figures implicitly also whenever we use the method of indirect quotations. In indirect quotation we do not insist on a literal repetition of the words of the person quoted, but we insist on a synonymous sentence; we require reproduction of the *meaning*. Such synonymity differs even from logical equivalence; and exactly what it is remains unspecified."[1] We might perhaps think of an explicatum of this concept of synonymity similar to our concept of intensional isomorphism. Quine himself seems to expect that the explication will be found not in semantics but in what we would call pragmatics, because he says that the concept of synonymity "calls for a definition or a criterion in psychological and linguistic terms."

C. I. Lewis[2] gives a definition for the concept of synonymity which shows a striking similarity to our concept of intensional isomorphism, although the two concepts have been developed independently. Since it is interesting to see the points of agreement and of difference, I will quote his explanations at length. "Not every pair of expressions having the same intension would be called synonymous; and there is good reason for this fact. Two expressions are commonly said to be synonymous (or in the case of propositions, equipollent) if they have the same intension, and *that intension is neither zero nor universal*. But to say that two expressions with the same intension have the same meaning, without qualification, would have the anomalous consequence that any two analytic propositions would then be equipollent, and any two self-contradictory propositions would be equipollent." In order to overcome this difficulty, Lewis introduces a new concept: "Two expressions are *equivalent in analytic meaning*, (1) if at least one is elementary [i.e., not complex] and they have the same intension, or (2) if, both being complex, they can be so analyzed into constituents that (a) for every constituent distinguished in either, there is a corresponding constituent in the other which has the same intension, (b) no constituent distinguished in either has zero intension or universal intension, and (c) the order of corresponding constituents is the same in both, or can be made the same without alteration of the intension of either whole expression." As examples, Lewis states that "round excision" and "circular hole" are equivalent in analytic meaning, while "equilateral triangle" and "equiangular triangle" are not, although they have the same intension. He continues: "We shall be in conformity with good usage if we say that two expressions are synonymous or equipollent, (1) if they have the same intension and that intension is neither zero nor universal, or (2) if, their intension being either zero or universal, they are equivalent in analytic meaning."

Thus Lewis' concept of synonymity is very similar to our concept of intensional isomorphism except for one point: He applies this stronger relation only to the two extreme cases of intension, for example, in the field of sentences, only to L-determinate and not to factual sentences. This discrimination seems to me somewhat arbitrary and inadvisable. Let us consider the following examples (in a language which, in distinction to S_1, also contains expressions for finite cardinal numbers and for relations and properties of them):

(i) 'two is an even prime number';

(ii) 'two is between one and three';

(iii) 'the number of books on this table is an even prime number';

(iv) 'the number of books on this table is between one and three'.

The sentences (i) and (ii) have the same intension but are not equivalent in analytic meaning (intensionally isomorphic). The same holds for (iii) and (iv). Now, according to Lewis' definition, (i) and (ii) are not synonymous because they are L-true, analytic; while (iii) and (iv) are synonymous because they are factual, synthetic. It seems to me that it would be more natural to regard (iii) and (iv) also as nonsynonymous, since the difference between them is essentially the same as that between (i) and (ii). The logical operation which leads from (i) to (ii) is the same as that which leads from (iii) to (iv); it is the transformation of 'n is an even prime number' into 'n is (a cardinal number) between one and three'.

Now let us go back to the problem of the analysis of belief-sentences, and let use see how the concept of intensional structure can be utilized there. It seems that the sentence 'John believes that D' in S can be interpreted by the following semantical sentence:

(1) 'There is a sentence $\mathfrak{S}_i$ in a semantical system S' such that (a) $\mathfrak{S}_i$ in S' is intensionally isomorphic to 'D' in S and (b) John is disposed to an affirmative response to $\mathfrak{S}_i$ as a sentence of S'.'

This interpretation may not yet be final, but it represents a better approximation than the interpretations discussed in the first section. As an example, suppose that John understands only German and that he responds affirmatively to the German sentence 'Die Anzahl der Einwohner von Chicago ist grösser als 3,000,000' but neither to the sentence 'Die Anzahl der Einwohner von Chicago ist grösser als $2^6 \times 3 \times 5^6$' nor to any intensionally isomorphic sentence, because he is not quick enough to realize that the second sentence is L-equivalent to the first. Then our interpretation of belief-sentences, as formulated in (1), allows us to assert the sentence 'John believes that the number of inhabitants of Chicago is greater than three million' and to deny the sentence 'John believes that the number of inhabitants of Chicago is greater than $2^6 \times 3 \times 5^6$'. We can do so without contradiction because the two German sentences, and likewise their English translations just used, have different intensional structures. [By the way, this example shows another disadvantage of Lewis' definition of equivalence in analytic meaning. According to part (1) of his definition, the two German sentences are equivalent in analytic meaning if we take '3,000,000' as one sign.] On the other hand, the interpretation of belief-sentences in terms of propositions as objects of beliefs (like (iv) two sections ago) would not be adequate in this case, since the two German sentences and the two English sentences all express the same proposition.

An analogous interpretation holds for other sentences containing psychological terms about knowledge, doubt, hope, fear, astonishment, etc., with 'that'-clauses, hence generally about what Russell calls propositional attitudes and Ducasse epistemic attitudes. The problem of the logical analysis of sentences of this kind has been much discussed,[3] but a satisfactory solution has not been found so far. The analysis here proposed is not yet a complete solution, but it may perhaps be regarded as a first step. What remains to be done is, first, a refinement of the analysis in terms of linguistic reactions here given and, further, an analysis in terms of dispositions to nonlinguistic behavior.

The concept of intensional structure may also help in clarifying a puzzling situation that has been called "the paradox of analysis". It was recently stated by G. E. Moore,[4] and then discussed by C. H. Langford,[5] Max Black,[6] and Morton White.[7] Langford[8] states the paradox as follows: "If the verbal expression representing the analysandum has the same meaning as the verbal expression representing the analysans, the analysis states a bare identity and is trivial; but if the two verbal expressions do not have the same meaning, the analysis is incorrect." Consider the following two sentences:

'The concept Brother is identical with the concept Male Sibling.'
'The concept Brother is identical with the concept Brother.'

The first is a sentence conveying fruitful information, although of a logical, not a factual, nature; it states the result of an analysis of the analysandum, the concept Brother. The second sentence, on the other hand, is quite trivial. Now Moore had been puzzled by the following fact: If the first sentence is true, then the second seems to make the same statement as the first (presumably because, if two concepts are identical, then a reference to the one means the same as a reference to the other, and hence the one expression can be replaced by the other); "but it is obvious that these two statements are not the same", he says. Black tries to show that the two sentences do not express the same proposition; he supports this assertion by pointing to the fact that the first sentence, or rather a paraphrasing he gives for it ('the concept Brother is the conjunct of the concept Male and the concept Sibling') refers to a certain nonidentical relation (the triadic relation Conjunct), while the second is a mere identity. White replies that this is not a sufficient reason for the assertion. None of the four authors states his criterion for the identity of "meaning", "statement", or "proposition"; this seems the chief cause for the inconclusiveness of the whole discussion. If we take, as in the terminology used in this book, L-equivalence as the condition for the identity of propositions, then White is certainly right; since the two sentences are L-true and hence L-equivalent to each other, they express the same proposition in our sense. On the other hand, Black feels correctly, like Moore and Langford, that there is an important difference in meaning between the two sentences, because of a difference in meaning between the two expressions for the analysandum ('the concept Brother') and the analysans ('the concept Male Sibling'). The paradox can be solved if we can state exactly what this difference in meaning is and how it is compatible with the identity of meaning in another sense. The solution is quite simple in terms of our concepts: The difference between the two expressions, and, consequently, between the two sentences is a difference in intensional structure, which exists in spite of the identity of intension. Landford saw the point at which the difference lies; he says[9] that the analysans is more articulate than the analysandum, it is a grammatical function of more than one idea; the two expressions are not synonymous but "cognitive equivalent in some appropriate sense". It seems to me that this cognitive equivalence is explicated by our concept of L-equivalence and that the synonymity, which does not hold for these expressions, is explicated by intensional isomorphism.

Notes

1. W. V. Quine, "Notes on Existence and Necessity", *Journal of Philosophy* 40 (1943), p. 120.

2. C. I. Lewis, "The Modes of Meaning", *Philosophy and Phenomenological Research* 4 (1943–1944), pp. 245 f. Other concepts used by Lewis will be discussed in the next section.

3. Russell, *An Inquiry into Meaning and Truth* (New York, 1940), gives a detailed discussion of the problem in a wider sense, including beliefs not expressed in language; he investigates the problem under both an epistemological and a logical aspect (in our terminology, both a pragmatical and a semantical aspect), not always distinguishing the two clearly. For C. J. Ducasse's conception see his paper "Propositions, Opinions, Sentences, and Facts", *Journal of Philosophy*, 37 (1940), 701–11.

4. *The Philosophy of G. E. Moore*, ed. P. Schilpp (1942), pp. 660–67.

5. "The Notion of Analysis in Moore's Philosophy", *ibid.*, pp. 321–42.

6. *Mind*, 53 (1944), 263–67 and 54 (1945), 272 f.

7. *Mind*, 54 (1945), 71 f. and 357–61.

8. "The Notion of Analysis in Moore's Philosophy", p. 323.

9. "The Notion of Analysis in Moore's Philosophy", p. 326.

Chapter 33

On Synonymy and Indirect Discourse

Israel Scheffler

The notion of synonymy has recently been severely criticized, and its replacement by graded, continuous notions of one or another sort urged on general grounds.[1] At the same time, it has usually been assumed both by critics and defenders of the notion, that synonymy and indirect discourse are in the same boat, that analyzing the latter, for instance, requires no more than an acceptable decision on the former while it requires at least that. Defenders of synonymy have thus though it sufficient to apply their interpretations of this idea to indirect discourse, while opponents have not thought to attack such application save by way of an attack on synonymy.

Contrary to this common assumption, I shall here urge the fruitfulness of considering indirect discourse independently,[2] arguing that the case for a graded conception of such discourse holds even granted a generally adequate intensional explication of synonymy. Since Professor Carnaps' explication in terms of intensional isomorphism[3] seems to me the clearest and most explicit recent attempt at a joint analysis of synonymy and indirect discourse, my discussion will center on his treatment, though directed toward the general point just stated.

That Carnap's "intensional isomorphism" is inapplicable in a direct way to natural languages seems clear,[4] and it is this which has given much point to the general critique of synonymy. Bypassing this issue in line with our present thesis, however, suppose we do have languages enabling application of Carnap's concept. Imagine, e.g, some sentence N, indirectly referred to by a sentence Q ("John believes [or says] that W"), such that N and "W" (hereafter called the that-content of Q) are parts of languages

First appeared in *Philosophy of Science* 22 (1955): 39–44. Reprinted by permission of *Philosophy of Science*.

whose semantical rules are completely stated. Yet Carnap's analysis of Q is not intended as merely nominal, but rather as an explication of pre-systematic usage.[5] Its adequacy may therefore be tested by reference to such usage. The following discussion will attempt to show that intensional isomorphism is too rigid to reflect the presystematic variability of the relation between N's and their corresponding that-contents in true Q's, i.e., that this relation in indirect discourse is often narrower and often wider than intensional isomorphism.

Carnap's motive for using "intensional isomorphism" in analyzing indirect discourse is the need for a narrower relation than L-equivalence. His reasoning here may be indicated by a consideration of the following sentences:

(i)   "John believes that D."

(ii) "John believes that D'."

(iii) "John is disposed to an affirmative response to some sentence in some language, which is L-equivalent to 'D'."

With an appropriate list of L-true sentences, we proceed to examine John. Says Carnap (p. 53 [780 in this vol.]), "We ask John, for every sentence or for its negation, whether he believes what it says or not. Since we know him to be truthful, we take his affirmative or negative answer as evidence for his belief or nonbelief." Assume 'D' to be a sentence which John affirms under questioning, and 'D''' to be one which he fails to affirm. Though L-equivalent, since both L-true, their interchange alters the truth of (i) to the falsity of (ii). This shows (iii) to be a faulty analysis of (i), since it remains true under the very same interchange, i.e., "John is disposed to an affirmative response to some sentence in some language, which is L-equivalent to 'D'''" remains as true as (iii), John being affirmatively disposed to 'D', which is L-equivalent to 'D'''.

The nub of (iii)'s inadequacy is that it compels us to say that John believes both that D and that D', provided he affirms 'D', while pre-systematically (as determined by our questioning procedure) John may very well be said to believe that D but not that D'. Hence Carnap suggests using the narrower relation of intensional isomorphism, in which (p. 55 [782]) "The two sentences must, so to speak, be understood in the same way; they must not only be L-equivalent in the whole but consist of L-equivalent parts, and both must be built up out of these parts in the same way." The suggested alternative to (iii) we write here in similar form to facilitate comparison:

(iv) "John is disposed to an affirmative response to some sentence in some language, which is intensionally isomorphic to 'D'."

The advantage of (iv) over (iii) is that it no longer compels us always to say that John believes that D and that D', when he affirms 'D'. For when they are L-equivalent (but not intensionally isomorphic), their interchange not only turns the true (i) into the false (ii), but also the true (iv) into the false "John is disposed to an affirmative response to some sentence in some language, which is intensionally isomorphic to 'D'''."

But how can we rule out the possibility that the latter sentence may be true after all because John affirms some third sentence which is intensionally isomorphic to 'D''', even though he fails to affirm the latter? It seems generally curious that Carnap's treatment omits consideration of the possibility that 'D' and 'D''' in his example may be intensionally isomorphic as well as L-equivalent, and that his argument may be extended to disqualify (iv) just as (iii) was disqualified. Suppose, e.g., that 'T' is intensionally isomorphic to 'D', but that John fails to affirm 'T' while affirming 'D' under questioning. Thus (i) is true, but the following sentence is false:

(v) "John believes that T."

Though 'D' and 'T' are intensionally isomorphic, their interchange alters (i)'s truth to (v)'s falsity. However, it also exposes the inadequacy of (iv) which remains true under the identical interchange. That is, "John is disposed to an affirmative response to some sentence in some language, which is intensionally isomorphic to 'T'" is just as true as (iv), since John affirms 'D' which is intensionally isomorphic to 'T'.

The nub of (iv)'s inadequacy is that it forces us to say that John believes both that D and that T, provided he affirms 'D', while presystematically (as determined by our questioning procedure) John may perfectly well be said to believe that D but not that T. Now it might be argued that our example of John's believing one sentence and yet not believing another sentence intensionally isomorphic to it is impossible or at least implausible. For, so it might be said, such sentences are, as Carnap puts it, "understood in the same way", since built in the same way out of L-equivalent parts. But "understood" is here crucially ambiguous. Carnaps' treatment of "intensional isomorphism" refers throughout to purely linguistic entities and not at all to pragmatics, i.e., to the psychological reactions of persons to sentences. Hence, "being understood in the same way" refers to some semantic characteristic, and no inference may be drawn from the intensional isomorphism of two sentences to the nature of the psychological reactions to them. To exclude the possibility that John may truly be said to believe one and not the other is to express a *psychological* theory as well as a *semantical* one, and a highly improbable one at that. For the same limitations which prevent John from seeing that a sentence is *L*-equivalent to another may prevent his seeing that one sentence is intensionally isomorphic to another.[6] Psychological abilities are continuous and not likely to follow sharp semantical boundaries. Generalizing now, if our notion of the relation between an indirectly mentioned *N* and some appropriate that-content is to be faithful to presystematic use and psychologically plausible, then no matter how semantically narrow this relation is conceived, short of identity, it will be too wide for some cases.[7]

Psychological considerations support an analogous conclusion in the other direction as well, i.e., human abilities are graded upward as well as downward from the ability to respond equivalently to intensionally isomorphic sentences. Hence, on general grounds, it seems implausible to hold that only a relation as narrow as intensional isomorphism will do for all contexts. Suppose, e.g., we question not John but Russell, using *L*-true sentences from *Principia*. Secondly, there are cases where the pragmatic context does not require so narrow a relation but only some obvious extensional connection. A witness, let us suppose,[8] is asked to identify the culprit (Lightfingered Larry) among seven suspects on the police lineup and, not knowing his proper name, declares truly, "The third man from the left is the culprit". Reporting in indirect mode, the attendant states, "The witness says that Lightfingered Larry is the culprit." Though the witness' *N* and the attendant's that-content are hardly construable systematically as intensionally isomorphic, the latter's *Q* is surely true, even if the witness fails to affirm its that-content under questioning. Generally, where our purpose is to pick out or identify, we may be satisfied with less than intensional isomorphism.

Finally, the use of indicator phrases[9] cannot be generally formalized and systematically referred to in terms of intensional isomorphism. Since such phrases are nevertheless employed within that-contents of indirect discourse, intensional isomorphism cannot reflect such presystematic discourse with indicators. The point about indicators is that their designata must be determined by reference to the contexts of the inscriptions themselves, e.g., we do not know the designatum of a particular '*I*'-inscription without knowledge of some feature of its context, in this case, its producer. Since a replica of a particular indicator-inscription may differ in context, it may differ as to designata.

Now Carnap's specification of "intensional isomorphism" depends on "L-equivalent", explained (p. 14) as follows: "Let 'P' and 'Q' be two predicators of degree one in S_I ... They are equivalent if and only if '$P \equiv Q$' is true, hence,... if and only if '$(x)(Px \equiv Qx)$' is true, hence if 'P' holds for the same individuals as 'Q'." If, in addition, the truth of '$(x)(Px \equiv Qx)$' can be established without referring to facts by merely using the semantical rules of S_I, then this sentence is L-true. If so, 'P' and 'Q' are L-equivalent in S_I. We cannot, however, test indicators thus, i.e., by putting them into sentences of the form '$(x)(Px \equiv Qx)$'; we cannot literally re-employ a given indicator-inscription with spatio-temporal boundaries, while to use a replica of it is not necessarily to discourse about the same designata. Thus, we can establish neither the L-equivalence nor the intensional isomorphism of indicators. This is not to deny that an appropriate nonindicator may often replace an indicator. But such a replacing term cannot itself be intensionally isomorphic to the original; it can at most agree with it by some extensional criteria. Also, such replacement, often undeniably convenient, neither alters nor explains the fact that indicators are employed in presystematic cases of indirect discourse where intensional isomorphism is out of the question for systematic representation.[10]

If the considerations adduced are relevant, then "intensional isomorphism" is too inflexible to serve adequately for the analysis of indirect discourse,[11] even granted its general adequacy in explicating synonymy, and independently of the issue of its direct applicability to natural languages. An analogous judgment seems plausible for other explications of synonymy.[12] For defenders of synonymy, such considerations would seem to indicate a revised, independent analysis of indirect discourse, while for critics, who favor graded, and perhaps frankly psychological conceptions of likeness of meaning, an independent reinforcement of their position seems available here.

Notes

I am deeply indebted to Prof. N. Goodman for comments on an earlier form of this paper, and for discussion of related topics. Thanks are also due Prof. C. G. Hempel and Mr. A. N. Chomsky for helpful comments and suggestions.

1. See for example Goodman's "On Likeness of Meaning", *Analysis*, Vol. 10, pp. 1–7, White's "The Analytic and the Synthetic: An Untenable Dualism" in

John Dewey: Philosopher of Science and Freedom, ed. S. Hook, Dial, 1950, and Quine's *From A Logical Point of View*, Harvard, 1953.

2. In a different connection, some aspects of such a consideration are discussed in the writer's "An Inscriptional Approach to Indirect Quotation", *Analysis*, Vol. 14, pp. 83–90.

3. In Carnap, R. *Meaning and Necessity*, Univ. of Chicago Press, 1947. [Portions appear as chap. 32 in this vol.]

4. See his remark, ibid., p. 58 [785 in this vol.], "The present definition makes no claim to exactness; an exact definition would have to refer to one or two semantical systems whose rules are stated completely."

5. See his statement, ibid., p. 53 [779], "Although sentences of this kind ... are, indeed, used and understood in everyday life without any difficulty, they have proved very puzzling to logicians who have tried to analyze them. Let us see whether we can throw some light upon them with the help of our semantical concepts."

6. See Goodman's argument in "On a Pseudo-Test of Translation", *Phil. Studies*, Vol. III, pp. 81–82, that *knowing* of a specified kind can be only a pseudo-test of translational equivalence. Perhaps one motivation for offering this pseudo-test is precisely the notion disputed in the present paper, that synonymy must be explicated so as to apply to indirect discourse, e.g., "John *knows* that ____", so that if interchangeability fails here, synonymy is precluded.

See also White's suggestion in "Ontological Clarity and Semantic Obscurity", *Jour. Phil.*, Vol. 48, p. 379, of the need for a psychological analysis of even synonymy. For our limited consideration of indirect discourse directly referring to reactions like stating, believing, etc., the point seems even clearer, in favor of some pragmatic requirement.

7. This criticism of (iv) seems more general than Mates' point in "Synonymity", *Univ. of Calif. Pub. in Phil.*, Vol. 25, 1950, "that, for any pair of intensionally isomorphic sentences—let them be abbreviated by 'D' and 'D''—if anybody even doubts that whoever believes that D believes that D', then Carnap's explication is incorrect." His argument assumes that the sentences:

(1) Whoever believes that D believes that D.

(2) Whoever believes that D believes that D'.

are intensionally isomorphic, and since nobody doubts (1), if anybody doubts (2), Carnap's analysis is faulty. Putnam, in "Synonymity and the Analysis of Belief Sentences", *Analysis*, Vol. 14, pp. 114–122, has tried to meet this argument by revising the notion "intensional isomorphism" to include identical logical structure, and hence to render (1) and (2) nonsynonymous. But, since Putnam's criterion *does* allow some different sentences to be intensionally isomorphic in his revised sense, (say 'D' and 'T' in our treatment above), his proposal, even if it meets Mates' objection, fails to upset our criticism of (iv) above, which does not depend on Carnap's omission of logical structure from his explanation of intensional isomorphism. Further, as Chomsky suggests, this point can be used to formulate an example analogous to that of Mates which seems difficult even for

Putnam's revision: Suppose 'A', 'B', and 'C' all intensionally isomorphic. Then the sentences:

(3) Whoever believes that A believes that B.

(4) Whoever believes that A believes that C.

are intensionally isomorphic even for Putnam's revision. Yet how is the factual possibility ruled out that nobody doubts that (3) but someone doubts that (4), or that John believes that (3) but not that (4)?

8. This example was suggested to me by Dr. Goodman, in conversation.

9. For a general, inscriptional treatment of indicators, see Ch. XI of Goodman's *The Structure of Appearance*, Harvard, 1951.

10. The point made here seems applicable generally to theories of indirect discourse depending on senses or rules of terms. Frege, e.g., in "Ueber Sinn und Bedeutung", translated in Feigl and Sellars *Readings in Philosophical Analysis*, says that in such discourse, "words have their indirect nominata which coincide with what are ordinarily their sense." What is the ordinary sense of an indicator term?

11. In "An Inscriptional Approach to Indirect Quotation" (see Note 2. above), concerned with the structure rather than the basic terms for analyzing indirect discourse, I used the term "rephrasal" rather than "intensional isomorphism" for the relation between the that-content of a true Q and its appropriate N. There, the issue of structure is independent of choice of term. Here, in criticizing Carnap's term, I make no claim to be able to *define* any alternative like "rephrasal". But if my arguments in the present paper are well-taken, any alternative will need to be conceived as graded and contextually variable with purpose, perhaps with the particular verb introducing the indirect mode, etc., such variable relation being at times tighter than synonymy or translation, at times considerably weaker. To suggest these characteristics which appear to me necessary, I use the term "rephrasal".

12. The present paper was accepted for publication prior to the appearance of Professor A. Church's "Intensional Isomorphism and Identity of Belief" (*Phil. Stud.*, V, 5, October 1954, pp. 65–73), but the editors have been kind enough to allow me space for the following comments:

(A) Church proposes to replace intensional isomorphism by synonymous isomorphism as a "criterion of identity of belief," illustrating his rejection of the former by appeal to the historical difficulty of finding a proof of Fermat's Last Theorem (and hence the possibility of believing its denial while disbelieving an obviously false counterpart which, assuming Fermat's claim correct, is intensionally isomorphic to this denial).

But if the history of belief-responses to sentences is held relevant in controlling proposals for identity-criteria, must we not reject synonymous isomorphism too? If someone (apparently confused by the terms "optician," "oculist," "optometrist," and "ophthalmologist") says "I believe that eye-doctors are eye-doctors but not that eye-doctors are oculists," ought we not, in a perfectly good sense of "belief," take him literally at his word, especially in view of the patent history of confusion of these terms in the popular mind?

(B) Church seeks to rebut Mates' conclusion with respect to synonymous isomorphism by denying that one of the latter's illustrative sentences (see n. 7 above) is really doubted while the other is not. Instead, Church construes the purported doubt as applying to an equivalent (but not synonymously isomorphic) metalinguistic sentence.

But this strategy can (with slight modification) be applied equally to save intensional isomorphism as well, i.e. to reconstrue ostensible divergence in belief-response to intensionally isomorphic pairs as holding actually of equivalent but not intensionally isomorphic sentences. Thus, e.g. suppose 'A' and 'B' to be intensionally isomorphic. Then " 'B' is true" is intensionally isomorphic to neither, and can be taken to be the real object of doubt in every case where it is claimed that 'A' is believed and 'B' doubted. Why, in sum, does Church draw the line just between intensional and synonymous isomorphism, when his argument from history can be applied *against* the latter and his reconstruction of doubt can be used *for* the former?

(C) As support for his rebuttal of Mates, Church cites a case where translation of Mates' pair results in identical sentences in a different language, while translation of the associated metalinguistic sentence preserves its distinctness. Now if intensionally as well as synonymously isomorphic sentences may ever be said to translate each other, then analogous support could be found for a resolution to save intensional isomorphism. If translation is, however, synonymous isomorphism, then Church's argument restates simply the original case of divergent beliefs about synonymous sentences, which Mates began with. To one who is willing to accept such a case, the translation argument offers no new deterrent. If, finally, Church's point concerns not the differing truth-values of "Mates doubts that (15) but not that (14)" and its German translation, but depends rather on the assumption that both represent the same reasoning while only the second is self-contradictory, then is not the assumption that translatability implies identity of reasoning itself a (partial) criterion of identity of belief, which is precisely what is at issue?

Chapter 34

Vagaries of Reference

Willard Van Orman Quine

REFERENTIAL OPACITY

Definite singular terms may shift in reference with occasions of use, either through ambiguity or through the peculiar functions of 'the', 'this', and 'that'. Under some circumstances the term may simply fail of reference, through there being no object of the required sort. And there is a further kind of variation: in sentences there are positions where the term is used as a means simply of specifying its object, or purporting to, for the rest of the sentence to say something about, and there are positions where it is not. An example of the latter sort is the position of 'Tully' in:

(1) 'Tully was a Roman' is trochaic.

When a singular term is used in a sentence purely to specify its object, and the sentence is true of the object, then certainly the sentence will stay true when any other singular term is substituted that designates the same object. Here we have a criterion for what may be called *purely referential position:* the position must be subject to the *substitutivity of identity*.[1] That the position of 'Tully' in (1) is not purely referential is reflected in the falsity of what we get by supplanting 'Tully' in (1) by 'Cicero'.

If we understand the sentence:

(2) The commissioner is looking for the chairman of the hospital board

in such a way as to be prepared to affirm it and yet to deny:

(3) The commissioner is looking for the dean

even though, by recent appointment and unknown to the commissioner,

First appeared in *Word and Object* (Cambridge: MIT Press, 1960), pp. 138–156. Reprinted by permission of the MIT Press.

(4) The dean = the chairman of the hospital board,

then we are treating the position to the right of 'looking for' as not purely referential. On the other hand if, aware of the commissioner's persistent avoidance of the dean, we are still constrained by (2) and (4) to treat (3) as true, then we are indeed treating the position as purely referential.

Example (2), even if taken in the not purely referential way, differs from (1) in that it still seems to have far more bearing on the chairman of the hospital board, dean though he be, than (1) has on Tully. Hence my cautious phrase 'not purely referential', designed to apply to all such cases and to affirm no distinction among them. If I omit the adverb, the motive will be brevity.

An illustration of purely referential position is the position of singular terms under predication. For, the predication is true so long merely as the predicated general term is true of the object named by the singular term; hence the substitution of a new singular term that names the same object leaves the predication true. In particular the question whether to take the main singular-term positions in (2) as purely referential is the question whether to treat (2) as a predication of a relative term 'looking for'.

The positions that we have been classifying into purely referential and other are positions of singular terms relative to sentences that contain them. Now it is convenient to extend the concept to apply also to positions of singular terms relative to singular terms that contain them. Thus, take quotation marks: applied to any sort of expression, what they produce is a singular term (naming, as it happens, the expression inside). It is convenient to be able to speak of the personal name in (1) as having non-referential position not only in the sentence (1), but equally in the singular term, of quotational form, that is the grammatical subject of (1). Indeed, it is rather the quotation than (1) as a whole that is primarily in point here; the personal name has non-referential position in (1) simply because of the quotation.

As a criterion of referential position, substitutivity of identity works as well for positions within singular terms as for positions within sentences. For positions in sentences, what it says is that the containing sentence keeps its truth value when the contained singular term is supplanted by any other having the same reference. For positions in singular terms, what it says is that the containing singular term keeps its reference when the contained singular term is so supplanted. Thus what shows the position of the personal name in the quotation:

(5) 'Tully was a Roman'

to be non-referential is that, though Tully = Cicero, yet

'Tully was a Roman' ≠ 'Cicero was a Roman'.

Quotation, we see, gives rise to non-referential positions. Now this is not true of an alternative device to the same purpose as quotation, viz. *spelling*. Instead of (5) we can as well say:

tee⌢yu⌢ell⌢ell⌢wye⌢space⌢doubleyu⌢ay⌢ess⌢space⌢ay⌢space⌢ar⌢oh⌢em⌢ay⌢en,

thus using explicit names of the letters and an arch (following Tarski) to indicate concatenation. The shift from quotation to spelling has an independent advantage, but incidentally it is instructive as stressing that any non-referential occurrences caused by quotation are surface appearances, dispelled by an easy change in notation.

Also apart from quotation there are frequent cases where a not purely referential occurrence of a singular term can be banished by paraphrase. But there is no compulsion upon us to banish all non-referential occurrences of singular terms, nor to reduce them to quotation. We are not unaccustomed to passing over occurrences that somehow "do not count" —'mary' in 'summary', 'can' in 'canary'; and we can allow similarly for all non-referential occurrences of terms, once we know what to look out for.

One and the same occurrence of a term may have purely referential position with respect to its immediate surroundings and not with respect to a broader context. For example, the personal name has purely referential position in the sentence.

(6) Tully was a Roman.

and yet in neither of the more extended expressions (1) and (5). Quotation, which thus interrupts the referential force of a term, may be said to fail of referential *transparency*.[2]

Referential transparency has to do with constructions; modes of containment, more specifically, of singular terms or sentences in singular terms or sentences. I call a mode of containment Φ referentially transparent if, whenever an occurrence of a singular term t is purely referential in a term or sentence $\psi(t)$, it is purely referential also in the containing term or sentence $\Phi(\psi(t))$. Take $\Phi(\psi(t))$ as (5), $\psi(t)$ as (6), and t as the personal name, and you have the referential opacity of quotation.

Alternation, in contrast, is referentially transparent. That is, if a sentence is compounded of component sentences by means of 'or', all purely referential positions in the component sentences qualify still as purely referential positions in the compound. Clearly any truth function is referentially transparent.

General terms predicatively used may be looked on as constructions: modes of containment of the subject singular terms in sentences. As constructions they are referentially transparent; for this is simply to say, what was remarked above, that the subject position in a predication is purely referential.

Again the construction 'looking for' counts as transparent if adjacent term positions are treated as referential, and not otherwise. In the one case 'look for' is a genuine relative term; in the other not.

A construction that may be transparent or opaque is the belief construction, '*a* believes that *p*'. Thus suppose that though

(7) Tom believes that Cicero denounced Catiline,

he is ill-informed enough to think that the Cicero of the orations and the Tully of *De Senectute* were two. Faced with his unequivocal denial of 'Tully denounced Catiline', we are perhaps prepared both to affirm (7) and to deny that Tom believes that Tully denounced Catiline. If so, the position of 'Cicero' in (7) is not purely referential. But the position of 'Cicero' in the part 'Cicero denounced Catiline', considered apart, is purely referential. So 'believes that' (so conceived) is opaque.

At the same time there is an alternative way of construing belief that is referentially transparent.[3] The difference is as follows. In the opaque sense of belief considered above, Tom's earnest 'Tully never denounced Catiline' counts as showing that he does not believe that Tully denounced Catiline, even while he believes that Cicero did. In the transparent sense of belief, on the other hand, Tom's earnest 'Cicero denounced Catiline' counts as showing that he does believe that Tully denounced Catiline, despite his own misguided verbal disclaimer.

'Cicero' has purely referential occurrence in (7) or not according as 'believes' is taken transparently or not. If belief is taken transparently, then (7) expresses an outright relation between the men Tom and Cicero, viz. the relation of deeming denouncer of Catiline; if belief is taken opaquely, then (7) expressly relates Tom to no man.

There will be more to say of the distinction between transparent and opaque belief. But note meanwhile that the distinction is unrelated to the familiar quirk of English usage whereby 'x does not believe that p' is equated to 'x believes that not p' rather than to 'It is not the case that x believes that p'. I have been avoiding the concatenation 'does not believe', lest this incidental idiomatic complication seem to figure in the reasoning.

It would be wrong to suppose that an occurrence of a term within an opaque construction is barred from referential position in every broader context. Examples to the contrary are provided by the occurrences of the personal name in:

(8) 'Tully was a Roman' is true,

(9) 'Tully' refers to a Roman.

Despite the opacity of quotation, these occurrences of the personal name are clearly subject to substitutivity of identity *salve veritate*, thanks to the peculiarities of the main verbs involved. On this account 'non-transparent' would be more suggestive than 'opaque'; but the term would be cumbersome, and it is rather a fine point.

OPACITY AND INDEFINITE TERMS

Since indefinite singular terms do not designate objects,we have had only definite singular terms in mind in our considerations of referential position. The terms that we replace by others of like designation, in testing for substitutivity of identity, are definite singular terms. Still, what we are testing are positions, and indefinite singular terms can be put into them. Let us see with what effect.

We saw that the position after 'The commissioner is looking for' might or might not be taken as purely referential, with unlike effects. But if we put an indefinite singular term in it, say 'someone', we cease to be free to choose between two interpretations. To make proper sense of 'The commissioner is looking for someone' we have to think of the position as purely referential. For, who is this person the commissioner is looking for? The chairman of the hospital board, i.e., the dean. In the sense of 'looking for' in which the commissioner can be said to be looking for someone, (3) of the previous section. Has to be reckoned true along with (2). The treatment that would count (2) as true and (3) as false makes the truth value of such statements depend on what epithet is used in designating the sought person; and such a distinction is inapplicable in 'The commissioner is looking for someone', where the sought person is not designated at all. To put the point paradoxically, indefinite singular terms need referential position because they do not refer.

The same consideration would seem to suggest that for purposes of 'Tom believes that someone denounced Catiline' we must take 'believes' transparently; i.e., take the position of 'someone' as referential. But this case is complicated by a second, intersecting ambiguity: a question of the scope of the indefinite singular term. According as that scope is taken as narrow or wide, the sentence is explained by one or the other of:

(1) Tom believes that someone (is such that he) denounced Catiline,

(2) Someone is such that Tom believes that he denounced Catiline.

Surely (1) is likelier than (2) to do justice to 'Tom believes that someone denounced Catiline'; the words 'is such that he' in (1) are indeed immediately felt as superfluous. But in (1), unlike 'The commissioner is looking for someone', we remain quite free to take the position of 'someone' as referential or not as we please. This is because 'someone' obviously and unequivocally occupies referential position in the subsidiary sentence 'someone denounced Catiline' considered alone. And just because the subsidiary sentence makes sense in any event, (1) does too. In short, therefore, the denouncing position in (1) can freely be taken as referential or non-referential in (1) as a whole. In other words, belief can be construed transparently or opaquely; (1) makes sense either way.

Not so (2), which may be put more idiomatically as 'There is (or was) someone whom Tom believes to have denounced Catiline'. Here it is that those reflections apply that applied to 'The commissioner is looking for someone'. For, who is this person whom Tom believes to have denounced Catiline? Cicero, i.e., Tully. In the sense of 'believes' in which there can be said to be someone whom Tom believes to have denounced Catiline, 'Tom believes that Tully denounced Catiline' has to be reckoned true along with 'Tom believes that Cicero denounced Catiline'. In short, belief must be taken transparently to make proper sense of (2), though it can be taken either way for (1).

The two interpretations of 'I believe he saw a letter of mine' are on this score quite like (1) and (2). Where transparency matters in relation to indefinite singular terms is that there must not be a pronominal cross-reference from inside an opaque construction to an indefinite singular term outside the construction. Such is the lesson of (2). Parallel considerations show also that there must not be a pronominal cross-reference from inside an opaque construction to a 'such that' outside the construction. Adapted to variables the maxim is this: an indefinite singular term outside an opaque construction does not bind a variable inside the construction.

The need of cross-reference from inside a belief construction to an indefinite singular term outside is not to be doubted. Thus see what urgent information the sentence 'There is someone whom I believe to be a spy' imparts, in contrast to 'I believe that someone is a spy' (in the weak sense of 'I believe there are spies'). The one corresponds to (2), the other to (1). Surely, therefore, the transparent sense of belief is not to be lightly dismissed. Yet let its urgency not blind us to its oddity. "Tully," Tom insists, "did not denounce Catiline. Cicero did." Surely Tom must be acknowledged to believe, in every sense, that Tully did not denounce Catiline and that Cicero did. But still he must be said also to believe, in the referentially transparent sense, that Tully *did* denounce Catiline. The oddity of the transparent sense of belief is that it has Tom believing that Tully did and that he did not denounce Catiline. This is not yet a self-contradiction on our part or even on Tom's, for a distinction can be reserved between (a) Tom's believing that Tully did and that Tully did not denounce Catiline, and (b) Tom's believing that Tully did and did not denounce Catiline. But the oddity is there, and we have to accept it as the price of saying such things as (2) or that there is someone whom one believes to be a spy.

Certainly we are not to blame the oddity on Tom's mere misunderstanding of a proper name, for there are parallel examples without names. Thus instead of having Tom say, "Tully did not denounce Catiline; Cicero did," have him say, "The dean is not married, but the chairman of the hospital board is," not appreciating that they are one.

Now if this much oddity on the part of the transparent sense of belief is tolerable, more remains that is not. Where 'p' represents a sentence, let us write 'δp' (following Kronecker) as short for the description:

the number x such that $((x = 1)$ and $p)$ or $((x = 0)$ and not $p)$.

We may suppose that poor Tom, whatever his limitations regarding Latin literature and local philanthropies, is enough of a logician to believe a sentence of the form '$\delta p = 1$' when and only when he believes the sentence represented by 'p'. But then we can argue from the transparency of belief that he believes everything. For, by the hypotheses already before us,

(3) Tom believes that δ (Cicero denounced Catiline) $= 1$.

But, whenever 'p' represents a true sentence,

$\delta p = \delta$ (Cicero denounced Catiline).

But then, by (3) and the transparency of belief,

Tom believes that $\delta p = 1$,

from which it follows, by the hypothesis about Tom's logical acumen, that

(4) Tom believes that p.

But 'p' represented any true sentence. Repeating the argument using the falsehood 'Tully did not denounce Catiline' instead of the truth 'Cicero denounced Catiline', we establish (4) also where 'p' represents any falsehood. Tom ends up believing everything.[4]

Thus in declaring belief invariably transparent for the sake of (2) and 'There is someone whom I believe to be a spy', we would let in too much. It can sometimes best suit us to affirm 'Tom believes that Cicero denounced Catiline' and still deny 'Tom believes that Tully denounced Catiline', at the cost—on *that* occasion—of (2). In general what is wanted is not a doctrine of transparency or opacity of belief, but a way of indicating, selectively and changeably, just what positions in the contained sentence are to shine through as referential on any particular occasion.

A way of doing that is to agree to localize the failure of transparency regularly in the 'that' of 'believes that' and the 'to' of 'believes to', and not in the 'believes'. Thus we may continue to write 'Tom believes that Cicero denounced Catiline' when we are content to leave the occurrences of 'Cicero' and 'Catiline' nonreferential, but write rather:

(5) Tom believes Cicero to have denounced Catiline

if we want to bring 'Cicero' into referential position.[5] Similarly we can get 'Catiline' into referential position thus:

(6) Tom believes Catiline to have been denounced by Cicero.

If we want to get both into referential position, we are driven to something like:

(7) Tom believes Cicero and Catiline to be related as denouncer and denounced.

On this convention 'believes that' is unequivocally opaque and (2) therefore simply goes by the board as a bad formulation involving cross-reference from inside an opaque construction to an indefinite singular term outside. What was offered before as an idiomatic equivalent of (2) remains legitimate, however: 'There is (or was) someone whom Tom believes to have denounced Catiline'.

Here as usual we can revise the relative clauses at will into 'such that' clauses; thus '... whom Tom believes to ...' and '... which I believe to ...' become '... such that Tom believes him to ...' and '... such that I believe it to ...', without ever disturbing the insides of the opaque 'to' construction. Note that the 'that' of 'such that' is referentially transparent; it is only the 'that' of 'believes that', and the 'to' of 'believes to', that our convention counts opaque.

The constructions 'believes that', 'says that', 'wishes that', 'endeavors that', 'urges that', 'fears that', 'is surprised that', etc., are what Russell calls expressions of *propositional attitude*.[6] What has been observed of the first of them in recent pages applies equally to the lot. The contortions of (5)–(7) strain ordinary language in varying degrees when applied to the rest of the verbs of propositional attitude. 'Wishes', 'urges', and 'fears' fit (5)–(7) as naturally as 'believes' (except that 'urges' is inappropriate to our particular example on account of the past tense). 'Says' falls into place with no great violence. 'Endeavors' and 'is surprised' have to be reworded in some such fashion as 'endeavors-to-cause' and 'is surprised-to-learn' when fitted to those positions.

An opaque construction is one in which you cannot in general supplant a singular term by a *codesignative* term (one referring to the same object) without disturbing the truth value of the containing sentence. In an opaque construction you also cannot in general supplant a general term by a *coextensive* term (one true of the same objects), nor a component sentence by a sentence of the same truth value, without disturbing the truth value of the containing sentence. All three failures are called failures of *extensionality*. A reason for stressing the first is that one rightly expects substitutivity of identity in discourse about the identical object, whereas no such presumption is evident for full extensionality. A related reason is that the first failure is what disallows cross-reference from inside opaque constructions. Frege was bound to stress all three failures, for he treated general terms and sentences as naming classes and truth values; all failures of extensionality became failures of substitutivity of identity.[7] Failures of substitutivity of identity, moreover, were in Frege's view unallowable; so he nominally rectified them by decreeing that when a sentence or term occurs within a construction of propositional attitude or the like it ceases to name a truth value, class, or individual and comes to name a proposition, attribute, or "individual concept." (In some ways this account better fits Church, who has sharpened and elaborated the doctrine.[8]) I make none of these moves. I do not disallow failure of substitutivity, but only take it as evidence of non-referential position; nor do I envisage shifts or reference under opaque constructions.

OPACITY IN CERTAIN VERBS

We have hit upon a convenient trick of so phrasing our statements of propositional attitude as to keep selected positions referential and others not. The device does not yet apply to our earlier example:

(1) The commissioner is looking for the chairman of the hospital board,

since this example contains no expression of propositional attitude. But it can be made to do so by expanding 'look for' into 'endeavor to find':

(2) The commissioner is endeavoring that the commissioner finds the chairman of the hospital board.

The point of the bad English is to stress the parallel of 'Tom believes that Cicero denounced Catiline'. Now if we carry over the convention of two pages back, the term 'the chairman of the hospital board' has non-referential position in (2). Sentence (2) expands (1) in a way that counts 'looking for . . .' opaque. To get an expansion of (1) in a transparent sense, we must operate on (2) to bring 'the chairman of the hospital board' out from under the opaque 'endeavoring that'. The desired operation on (2) is precisely the operation which, applied to 'Tom believes that Cicero denounced Catiline', gave 'Tom believes Cicero to have denounced Catiline'. Applied to (2), the operation delivers:

(3) The commissioner is endeavoring (-to-cause) the chairman of the hospital board to be found by the commissioner.

Note that the opaque 'to' of (3) is the one after 'board' and not the one in parentheses; the parenthetical expression is for our purposes merely part of the inflection of 'endeavor'. (See end of the last section.)

So (2) construes (1) with opaque 'looking for . . .', and (3) construes (1) with transparent 'looking for . . .'. Thus (2) construes (1) in such a way that substituting 'someone' for 'the chairman of the hospital board' produces nonsense; (3) construes (1) in such a way that substituting 'someone' makes sense. Again (2) construes (1) in such a way that substitution of 'the dean' produces falsity; (3) construes (1) in such a way that substitution of 'the dean' preserves truth.

In both (2) and (3), the first occurrence of 'the commissioner' has referential position and the second has not. Thus (1), no matter whether we take its 'looking for . . .' in the opaque manner of (2) or in the transparent manner of (3), is a sentence whose single grammatical subject implicitly plays two roles, a referential one and a non-referential one. An example in which this same phenomenon of two-role subject comes out more vividly is:

(4) Giorgione was so-called because of his size,

which anyone is ready enough to paraphrase into:

Giorgione was called 'Giorgione' because of his size.

Taking (4) as it stands, we have of course to reckon the position of the subject as not (purely) referential, because of the non-referential character of one of its two implicit roles. And the same conclusion emerges by the direct substitutivity criterion: substitution in (4) according to the identity 'Giorgione = Barbarelli' yields a falsehood.

'The commissioner' in (1) is likewise found to resist substitutivity, if (1) is construed as (2) or (3). Thus suppose the commissioner, for all his self-importance, is the least competent of the county officials. Substitution in (1) according to this identity would give 'The least competent official is endeavoring that the least competent official finds etc.', if we construe (1) as (2); and this, with opaque 'endeavoring that', is doubtless to be adjudged false. The case is similar when we construe (1) as (3).

Now the account of (4) was unexceptionable, but this parallel account of (1) is certainly a distortion.[9] Surely, on a fair account, 'the commissioner' should have referential position in (1), and be replaceable by 'the least competent official' *salva veritate.*

The non-referential status of the subject position in (4) excludes 'someone' from that position, and rightly; 'Someone was so-called because of his size' is nonsense. But the non-referential status of the subject position in (1) would likewise exclude 'someone' from that position; whereas we must surely insist on saying 'Someone is looking for the chairman of the hospital board'.

The upshot of these reflections is that (1) is wrongly construed in both (2) and (3). We must bring the second occurrence of 'the commissioner' into referential position by an additional twist, analogous to the one used on 'Cicero' in (5) or (7) of the last section. The proper account of (1) with opaque 'looking for ...' is not (2) above, but rather this analogue of (5) of the last section.

(5) The commissioner is endeavoring (-to-cause) himself to find the chairman of the hospital board.

The proper account of (1) with transparent 'looking for ...' is not (3) above, but rather this analogue of (7) of the last section:

(6) The commissioner is endeavoring (-to-cause) himself and the chairman of the hospital board to be related as finder and found.

Sentences (2) and (3) remain all right in themselves, but not as versions of (1).

If (1) were construed as (2) or (3), which would be indefensible, and again if (1) is construed as (5), which is one of two admissible interpretations, the verb 'is looking for' does not count as a relative term; not as a term at all, but an opaque verb whose function is explained by the overall paraphrase. If (1) is construed as (6), on the other hand, 'is looking for' qualifies as a relative term. Subject and object in (1) have referential position when (1) is construed as (6). This does not make (6) preferable to (5). Sentence (5) explains (1) with 'looking for' taken as opaque and hence not as a term, and (6) explains (1) with 'looking for' taken as transparent and hence as a term; and both uses of 'looking for' have their place.

The constrast between the two uses of 'looking for' is the same as the contrast between hunting lions in the abstract and hunting or stalking known ones. For, observe how lion-hunting turns out. Just as looking for is endeavoring to find, so hunting is endeavoring to shoot or capture. The difference between the two cases of 'Ernest is hunting lions' is *prima facie* a difference in scope:

(7) Ernest is endeavoring that some lion is such that Ernest shoots it,

(8) Some lion is such that Ernest is endeavoring that Ernest shoots it.

This symmetrical pair of formulations brings the contrast of scopes instructively to the fore, but we shall not want to leave them thus. Sentence (7), to begin with, can as well be put more concisely:

(9) Ernest is endeavoring that Ernest shoots a lion.

And (8) is simply wrong under the convention of the previous section, for that convention counts 'is endeavoring that' unequivocally as opaque.

Sentence (8) is like (2) of the last section in involving a cross-reference from inside an opaque construction to an indefinite singular term outside. Correcting (8), we have:

There is a lion which Ernest is endeavoring (-to-cause) to be shot by Ernest,

or, if we feel we can keep the intended scope of the indefinite singular term in mind with less extravagant aids,

(10) Ernest is endeavoring (-to-cause) a (certain) lion to be shot by Ernest.

Now note that (9) and (10) have the same forms as (2) and (3) of the present section, except that they use an indefinite singular term instead of a definite one. Consequently the objection to (2) and (3) as versions of (1) applies equally to (9) and (10) as versions of 'Ernest is hunting lions': they fail to give 'Ernest' purely referential position at its second occurrences. Rather, just as we dropped (2) and (3) (as versions of (1)) in favor of (5) and (6), so we must drop (9) and (10) (as versions of 'Ernest is hunting lions) in favor of:

(11) Ernest is endeavoring (-to-cause) himself to shoot a lion,

(12) Ernest in endeavoring (-to-cause) himself and a (certain) lion to be related as shooter and shot.

When 'Ernest is hunting lions' is construed as (12), 'hunt' qualifies as a straightforward relative term. 'Hunt' is so used in 'man-hunting', as applied to the police; not as applied to man-hunting lions. 'Hunt' in the latter use, and in 'unicorn-hunting' and in the commonest use of 'lion-hunting', is not a term; it is an opaque verb whose use is clarified by the paraphrase (11).

What we have been remarking of 'hunt' or 'look for' and 'endeavor' applies *mutatis mutandis* to 'want' and 'wish'; for to want is to wish to have. 'I want a sloop' in the opaque sense is parallel to (11): 'I wish myself to have a sloop (to be a sloop owner)'; 'I want a sloop' in the transparent sense, 'There is a sloop I want', comes out parallel to (12). Only in the latter sense is 'want' a relative term, relating people to sloops. In the other or opaque sense it is not a relative term relating people to anything at all, concrete or abstract, real or ideal. It is a shortcut verb whose use is set forth by 'I wish myself to have a sloop', wherein 'have' and 'sloop' continue to rate as general terms as usual but merely happen to have an opaque construction 'wish to' overlying them. This point needs to be noticed by philosophers worried over the nature of objects of desire.

Whenever sentences capable of containing 'want' or 'hunt' or 'look for' in an opaque sense are up for consideration in an at all analytic vein, it behooves us forthwith to paraphrase them into the more explicit idiom of propositional attitude. The question of transparency thereupon stands forth and can be settled, now as in (5) and (11) and now as in (6) and (12), in clear view of the alternative commitments and consequences. In general it is a good rule thus to try by paraphrase to account for non-referential positions by explicitly opaque constructions. And in the present instances there is also another benefit from the paraphrase: it exposes a structure startlingly unlike what one usually associates with the grammatical form of 'Ernest is hunting lions' and 'I want a sloop' (cf. 'I hear lions').

When 'hunt lions' and the like are meant rather in the transparent way, there is seldom call to paraphrase them into the idiom of propositional attitudes; for here the verb is a well-behaved relative term as it stands. Usually we are well enough off with 'There is a lion that Ernest is hunting', 'There is a sloop I want'; nothing is gained by expanding it in the grotesque manner of (12), except for purposes of comparisons of the sort in which we have just now been engaged. Our paraphrases, aimed at bringing out the distinction between referential and non-referential positions, have been cumbersome at best; but the most cumbersome ones are the ones least needed.

Notes

1. The concept and its criterion are due essentially to Frege, "On sense and reference," in his *Philosophical Writings* [chap. 22 in this vol.]. But there is much in his associated theory that I do not adopt.

2. The term is from Whitehead and Russell, *Principia Mathematica*, 2d ed., vol. 1, p. 665.

3. This is apparent from an example of Goodman cited by Scheffler, "On synonymy and indirect discourse," *Philosophy of Science* 22 (1955), p. 42 [p. 796 in this vol.].

4. See Church's review of Carnap's *Introduction to Semantics* (*Philosophical Review* 52 [1943], pp. 298–304) for a related argument in another connection.

5. Davidson points out to me that the rearrangement 'By Tom, Cicero is believed to have denounced Catiline' has, along with the drawback of unnaturalness, the virtue of being more graphic than (5) in two respects: it unifies the opaque 'believe to', and it displays the referential positions before mentioning belief. Similar rearrangements work for (6) and (7).

6. *Inquiry into Meaning and Truth*, p. 210. See also Reichenbach, *Elements of Symbolic Logic* (1947), pp. 277 ff.

7. Even apart from this special doctrine, the following connection between referential transparency and extensionality can be established: if a construction is transparent and allows substitutivity of concretion, it is extensional. The argument is obvious, but see Church's review of "On Frege's way out" *Journal of Symbolic Logic* (ca. 1960) for exposure of a fallacy in my adaptation of it to Whitehead and Russell's theory.

8. Church, "A formulation of the logic of sense and denotation," in Paul Henle, H. M. Kallen, and S. K. Langer, *Structure, Method, and Meaning* (New York: liberal Arts, 1951).

9. I am indebted here to a remark of Davidson's.

Chapter 35

On Saying That

Donald Davidson

'I wish I had said that', said Oscar Wilde in applauding one of Whistler's witticisms. Whistler, who took a dim view of Wilde's originality, retorted, 'You will, Oscar; you will'.[1] This tale reminds us that an expression like 'Whistler said that' may on occasion serve as a grammatically complete sentence. Here we have, I suggest, the key to a correct analysis of indirect discourse, an analysis that opens a lead to an analysis of psychological sentences generally (sentences about propositional attitudes, so-called), and even, though this looks beyond anything to be discussed in the present paper, a clue to what distinguishes psychological concepts from others.

But let us begin with sentences usually deemed more representative of *oratio obliqua*, for example 'Galileo said that the earth moves' or 'Scott said that Venus is an inferior planet'. One trouble with such sentences is that we do not know their logical form. And to admit this is to admit that, whatever else we may know about them, we do not know the first thing. If we accept surface grammar as guide to logical form, we will see 'Galileo said that the earth moves' as containing the sentence 'the earth moves', and this sentence in turn as consisting of the singular term 'the earth', and a predicate, 'moves'. But if 'the earth' is, in this context, a singular term, it can be replaced, so far as the truth or falsity of the containing sentence is concerned, by any other singular term that refers to the same thing. Yet what seem like appropriate replacements can alter the truth of the original sentence.

The notorious apparent invalidity of this move can only be apparent, for the rule on which it is based no more than spells out what is involved

First appeared in *Synthese* 19 (1968): 130–146. Reprinted with kind permission from Kluwer Academic Publishers.

in the idea of a (logically) singular term. Only two lines of explanation, then, are open: we are wrong about the logical form, or we are wrong about the reference of the singular term.

What seems anomalous behaviour on the part of what seem singular terms dramatizes the problem of giving an orderly account of indirect discourse, but the problem is more pervasive. For what touches singular terms touches what they touch, and that is everything: quantifiers, variables, predicates, connectives. Singular terms refer, or pretend to refer, to the entities over which the variables of quantification range, and it is these entities of which the predicates are or are not true. So it should not surprise us that if we can make trouble for the sentence 'Scott said that Venus is an inferior planet' by substituting 'the Evening Star' for 'Venus', we can equally make trouble by substituting 'is identical with Venus or with Mercury' for the coextensive 'is an inferior planet'. The difficulties with indirect discourse cannot be solved simply be abolishing singular terms.

What should we ask of an adequate account of the logical form of a sentence? Above all, I would say, such an account must lead us to see the semantic character of the sentence—its truth or falsity—as owed to how it is composed, by a finite number of applications of some of a finite number of devices that suffice for the language as a whole, out of elements drawn from a finite stock (the vocabulary) that suffices for the language as a whole. To see a sentence in this light is to see it in the light of a theory for its language, a theory that gives the form of every sentence in that language. A way to provide such a theory is by recursively characterizing a truth predicate, along the lines suggested by Tarski.[2]

Two closely linked considerations support the idea that the structure with which a sentence is endowed by a theory of truth in Tarski's style deserves to be called the logical form of the sentence. By giving such a theory, we demonstrate in a persuasive way that the language, though it consists in an indefinitely large number of sentences, can be comprehended by a creature with finite powers. A theory of truth may be said to supply an effective explanation of the semantic role of each significant expression in any of its appearances. Armed with the theory, we can always answer the question, 'What are these familiar words doing here?' by saying how they contribute to the truth conditions of the sentence. (This is not to assign a 'meaning', much less a reference, to every significant expression.)

The study of the logical form of sentences is often seen in the light of another interest, that of expediting inference. From this point of view, to give the logical form of a sentence is to catalogue the features relevant to its place on the logical scene, the features that determine what sentences it is a logical consequence of, and what sentences it has as logical consequences. A canonical notation graphically encodes the relevant information, making theory of inference simple, and practice mechanical where possible.

Obviously the two approaches to logical form cannot yield wholly independent results, for logical consequence is defined in terms of truth. To say a second sentence is a logical consequence of a first is to say, roughly, that the second is true if the first is no matter how the non-logical constants are interpreted. Since what we count as a logical constant can vary independently of the set of truths, it is clear that the two versions of logical form, though related, need not be identical. The relation, in brief, seems this. Any theory of truth that satisfies Tarski's criteria must take account of all truth-affecting iterative devices in the language. In the familiar languages for which we know how to define truth the basic iterative devices are reducible to the sentential connectives, the apparatus of quantification, and the description aperture if it is primitive. Where one sentence is a logical consequence of another on the basis of quantificational structure alone, a theory of truth will therefore entail that if the first sentence is true, the second is. There is no point, then, in not including the expressions that determine quantificational structure among the logical constants, for when we have characterized truth, on which any account of logical consequence depends, we have already committed ourselves to all that calling such expressions logical constants could commit us. Adding to this list of logical constants will increase the inventory of logical truths and consequence-relations beyond anything a truth definition demands, and will therefore yield richer versions of logical form. For the purposes of the present paper, however, we can cleave to the most austere interpretations of logical consequence and logical form, those that are forced on us when we give a theory of truth.[3]

We are now in a position to explain our aporia over indirect discourse: what happens is that the relation between truth and consequence just sketched appears to break down. In a sentence like 'Galileo said that the earth moves' the eye and mind perceive familiar structure in the words 'the earth moves'. And structure there must be if we are to have a theory of truth at all, for an infinite number of sentences (all sentences in the indicative, apart from some trouble over tense) yield sense when plugged into the slot in 'Galileo said that ____'. So if we are to give conditions of truth for all the sentences so generated, we cannot do it sentence by sentence, but only by discovering an articulate structure that permits us to treat each sentence as composed of a finite number of devices that make a stated contribution to its truth conditions. As soon as we assign familiar structure, however, we must allow the consequences of that assignment to flow, and these, as we know, are in the case of indirect discourse consequences we refuse to buy. In a way, the matter is even stranger than that. Not only do familiar consequences fail to flow from what looks to be familiar structure, but our common sense of language feels little assurance in any inferences based on the words that follow the 'said that' of indirect discourse (there are exceptions).

So the paradox is this: on the one hand, intuition suggests, and theory demands, that we discover semantically significant structure in the 'content-sentences' of indirect discourse (as I shall call sentences following 'said that'). On the other hand, the failure of consequence-relations invites us to treat contained sentences as semantically inert. Yet logical form and consequence relations cannot be divorced in this way.

One proposal at this point is to view the words that succeed the 'said that' as operating within concealed quotation marks, their sole function being to help refer to a sentence, and their semantic inertness explained by an account of quotation. One drawback of this proposal is that no usual account of quotation is acceptable, even by the minimal standards we have set for an account of logical form. For according to most stories, quotations are singular terms without significant semantic structure, and since there must be an infinite number of different quotations, no language that contains them can have a recursively defined truth predicate. This may be taken to show that the received accounts of quotation must be mistaken—I think it does. But then we can hardly pretend that we have solved the problem of indirect discourse by appeal to quotation.

Perhaps it is not hard to invent a theory of quotation that will serve: the following theory is all but explicit in Quine. Simply view quotations as abbreviations for what you get if you follow these instructions: to the right of the first letter that has opening quotation marks on its left write right-hand quotation marks, then the sign for concatenation, and then left-hand quotation marks, in that order; do this after each letter (treating punctuation signs as letters) until you reach the terminating right-hand quotation marks. What you now have is a complex singular term that gives what Tarski calls a structural description of an expression. There is a modest addition to vocabulary: names of letters and of punctuation signs, and the sign for concatenation. There is a corresponding addition to ontology: letters and punctuation signs. And finally, if we carry out the application to sentences in indirect discourse, there will be the logical consequences that the new structure dictates. For two examples, each of the following will be entailed by 'Galileo said that the earth moves':

$(\exists x)$ (Galileo said that 'the ea'$^\frown x^\frown$'th moves')

and (with the premise 'r = the 18th letter in the alphabet'):

Galileo said that 'the ea'$^\frown$'the 18th letter of the alphabet$^\frown$'th moves'

(I have clung to abbreviations as far as possible.) These inferences are not meant in themselves as criticism of the theory of quotation; they merely illuminate it.

Quine discusses the quotational approach to indirect discourse in *Word and Object*,[4] and abandons it for what seems, to me, a wrong reason. Not that there is not a good reason; but to appreciate *it* is to be next door to a solution, as I shall try to show.

Let us follow Quine through the steps that lead him to reject the quotational approach. The version of the theory he considers is not the one once proposed by Carnap to the effect that 'said that' is a two-place predicate true of ordered pairs of people and sentences.[5] The trouble with this idea is not that it forces us to assimilate indirect discourse to direct, for it does not. The 'said that' of indirect discourse, like the 'said' of direct, may relate persons and sentences, but be a different relation; the former, unlike the latter, may be true of a person, and a sentence he never spoke in a language he never knew. The trouble lies rather in the chance that the same sentence may have different meanings in different languages—not too long a chance either if we count ideolects as languages. To give an example, the sounds 'Empedokles liebt' do fairly well as a German or an English sentence, in one case saying that Empedokles loved and in the other telling us what he did from the top of Etna. If we analyse 'Galileo said that the earth moves' as asserting a relation between Galileo and the sentence 'The earth moves', we do not have to assume that Galileo spoke English, but we cannot avoid the assumption that the words of the content-sentence are to be understood as an English sentence.[6]

Calling the relativity to English an assumption may be misleading; perhaps the reference to English is explicit, as follows. A long-winded version of our favourite sentence might be 'Galileo spoke a sentence that meant in his language what "The earth moves" means in English'. Since in this version it needs all the words except 'Galileo' and 'The earth moves' to do the work of 'said that', we must count the reference to English as explicit in the 'said that'. To see how odd this is, however, it is only necessary to reflect that the English words 'said that', with their built-in reference to English, would no longer translate (by even the roughest extensional standards) the French 'dit que'.

We can shift the difficulty over translation away from the 'said that' or 'dit que' by taking these expressions as three-place predicates relating a speaker, a sentence, and a language, the reference to a language to be supplied either by our (in practice nearly infallible) knowledge of the language to which the quoted material is to be taken as belonging, or by a demonstrative reference to the language of the entire sentence. Each of these suggestions has its own appeal, but neither leads to an analysis that will pass the translation test. To take the demonstrative proposal, translation into French will carry 'said that' into 'dit que', the demonstrative reference will automatically, and hence perhaps still within the bounds of strict translation, shift from English to French. But when we translate the final singular term, which names an English sentence, we produce a palpably false result.

These exercises help bring out important features of the quotational approach. But now it is time to remark that there would be an anomaly in a position, like the one under consideration, that abjured reference to propositions in favour of reference to languages. For languages (as Quine remarks in a similar context in *Word and Object*) are at least as badly individuated, and for much the same reasons, as propositions. Indeed, an obvious proposal linking them is this: languages are identical when identical sentences express identical propositions. We see, then, that quotational theories of indirect discourse, those we have discussed anyway, cannot claim an advantage over theories that frankly introduce intensional entities from the start; so let us briefly consider theories of the latter sort.

It might be thought, and perhaps often is, that if we are willing to welcome intensional entities without stint—properties, propositions, individual concepts, and whatever else—then no further difficulties stand in the way of giving an account of the logical form of sentences in *oratio obliqua*. This is not so. Neither the languages Frege suggests as models for natural languages nor the languages described by Church are amenable to theory in the sense of a truth definition meeting Tarski's standards.[7] What stands in the way in Frege's case is that every referring expression has an infinite number of entities it may refer to, depending on the context, and there is no rule that gives the reference in more complex contexts on the basis of the reference in simpler ones. In Church's languages, there is an infinite number of primitive expressions; this directly blocks the possibility of recursively characterizing a truth predicate satisfying Tarski's requirements.

Things might be patched up by following a leading idea of Carnap's *Meaning and Necessity* and limiting the semantic levels to two: extensions and (first-level) intensions.[8] An attractive strategy might then be to turn Frege, thus simplified, upside down by letting each singular term refer to its sense or intension and providing a reality function (similar to Church's delta function) to map intensions on to extensions. Under such treatment our sample sentence would emerge like this: 'The reality of Galileo said that the earth moves.' Here we must suppose that 'the earth' names an individual concept which the function referred to by 'moves' maps on to the proposition that the earth moves; the function referred to by 'said that' in turn maps Galileo and the proposition that the earth moves on to a truth value. Finally, the name 'Galileo' refers to an individual concept which is mapped, by the function referred to by 'the reality of' on to Galileo. With ingenuity, this theory can perhaps be made to accommodate quantifiers that bind variables both inside and outside contexts created by verbs like 'said' and 'believes'. There is no special problem about defining truth for such a language: everything is on the up and up, purely extensional save in ontology. This seems to be a theory that might do all we have asked. Apart from nominalistic qualms, why not accept it?

My reasons against this course are essentially Quine's. Finding right words of my own to communicate another's saying is a problem in translation. The words I use in the particular case may be viewed as products of my total theory (however vague and subject to correction) of what the originating speaker means by anything he says: such a theory is indistinguishable from a characterization of a truth predicate, with his language as object language and mine as metalanguage. The crucial point is that there will be equally acceptable alternative theories which differ in assigning clearly non-synonymous sentences of mine as translations of his same utterance. This is Quine's thesis of the indeterminacy of translation.[9] An example will help bring out the fact that the thesis applies not only to translation between speakers of conspicuously different languages, but also to cases nearer home.

Let someone say (and now discourse is direct), 'There's a hippopotamus in the refrigerator'; am I necessarily right in reporting him as having said that there is a hippopotamus in the refrigerator? Perhaps; but under questioning he goes on, 'It's roundish, has a wrinkled skin, does not mind being touched. It has a pleasant taste, at least the juice, and it costs a dime. I squeeze two or three for breakfast.' After some finite amount of such talk we slip over the line where it is plausible or even possible to say correctly that he said there was a hippopotamus in the refrigerator, for it becomes clear he means something else by at least some of his words than I do. The simplest hypothesis so far is that my word 'hippopotamus' no longer translates his word 'hippopotamus'; my word 'orange' might do better. But in any case, long before we reach the point where homophonic translation must be abandoned, charity invites departures. Hesitation over whether to translate a saying of another by one or another of various non-synonymous sentences of mine does not necessarily reflect a lack of information: it is just that beyond a point there is no deciding, even in principle, between the view that the Other has used words as we do but has more or less weird beliefs, and the view that we have translated him wrong. Torn between the need to make sense of a speaker's words and the need to make sense of the pattern of his beliefs, the best we can do is choose a theory of translation that maximizes agreement. Surely there is no future in supposing that in earnestly uttering the words 'There's a hippopotamus in the refrigerator' the Other has disagreed with us about what can be in the refrigerator if we also must then find ourselves disagreeing with him about the size, shape, colour, manufacturer, horsepower, and wheelbase of hippopotami.

None of this shows there is no such thing as correctly reporting, through indirect discourse, what another has said. All that the indeterminacy shows is that if there is one way of getting it right there are other ways that differ substantially in that nonsynonymous sentences are used after 'said that'. And this is enough to justify our feeling that there is something bogus about the sharpness questions of meaning must in principle have if meanings are entities.

The lesson was implicit in a discussion started some years ago by Benson Mates. Mates claimed that the sentence 'Nobody doubts that whoever believes that the seventh consulate of Marius lasted less then a fortnight believes that the seventh consulate of Marius lasted less than a fortnight' is true and yet might well become false if the last word were replaced by the (supposed synonymous) words 'period of fourteen days', and that this could happen no matter what standards of synonymy we adopt short of the question-begging 'substitutable everywhere *salva veritate*.[10] Church and Sellars responded by saying the difficulty could be resolved by firmly distinguishing between substitutions based on the speaker's use of language and substitutions coloured by the use attributed to others.[12] But this is a solution only if we think there is some way of telling, in what another says, what is owed to the meanings he gives his words and what to his beliefs about the world. According to Quine, this is a distinction that cannot be drawn.

The detour has been lengthy; I return now to Quine's discussion of the quotational approach in *Word and Object*. As reported above, Quine rejects relativization to a language on the grounds that the principle of the individuation of languages is obscure, and the issue when languages are identical irrelevant to indirect discourse. He now suggests that instead of interpreting the content-sentence of indirect discourse as occurring in a language, we interpret it as voiced by a speaker at a time. The speaker and time relative to which the content-sentence needs understanding is, of course, the speaker of that sentence, who is thereby indirectly attributing a saying to another. So now 'Galileo said that the earth moves' comes to mean something like 'Galileo spoke a sentence that in his mouth meant what "The earth moves" now means in mine'. Quine makes no objection to this proposal because he thinks he has something simpler and at least as good in reserve. But in my opinion the present proposal deserves more serious consideration, for I think it is nearly right, while Quine's preferred alternatives are seriously defective.

The first of these alternatives is Scheffler's inscriptional theory.[12] Scheffler suggests that sentences in indirect discourse relate a speaker and an utterance: the role of the content-sentence is to help convey what sort of utterance it was. What we get this way is, 'Galileo spoke a that-the-earth-moves utterance'. The predicate 'x is-a-that-the-earth-moves-utterance' has, so far as theory of truth and of inference are concerned, the form of an unstructured one-place predicate. Quine does not put the matter quite this way, and he may resist my appropriation of the terms 'logical form' and 'structure' for purposes that exclude application to Scheffler's predicate. Quine calls the predicate 'compound' and describes it as composed of an operator and a sentence. These are matters of terminology; the substance, about which there may be no disagreement, is that on Scheffler's theory sentences in *oratio obliqua* have no logical relations that depend on structure in the predicate, and a truth predicate that applies to all such sentences cannot be characterized in Tarski's style. The reason is plain: there is an infinite number of predicates with the syntax 'x is-a-____-

utterance' each of which is, in the eyes of semantic theory, unrelated to the rest.

Quine has seized one horn of the dilemma. Since attributing semantic structure to content-sentences in indirect discourse apparently forces us to endorse logical relations we do not want, Quine gives up the structure. The result is that another desideratum of theory is neglected, that truth be defined.

Consistent with his policy of renouncing structure that supports no inferences worth their keep, Quine contemplates one further step; he says, '... a final alternative that I find as appealing as any is simply to dispense with the objects of the propositional attitudes'. Where Scheffler still saw 'said that' as a two-place predicate relating speakers and utterances, though welding content-sentences into one-piece one-place predicates true of utterances, Quine now envisions content-sentence and 'said that' welded directly to form the one-place predicate 'x said-that-the-earth-moves', true of persons. Of course some inferences inherent in Scheffler's scheme now fall away: we can no longer infer 'Galileo said something' from our sample sentence, nor can we infer from it and 'Someone denied that the earth moves' the sentence 'Someone denied what Galileo said'. Yet as Quine reminds us, inferences like these may fail on Scheffler's analysis too when the analysis is extended along the obvious line to belief and other propositional attitudes, since needed utterances may fail to materialize. The advantages of Scheffler's theory over Quine's 'final alternative' are therefore few and uncertain; this is why Quine concludes that the view that invites the fewest inferences is 'as appealing as any'.

This way of eliminating unwanted inferences unfortunately abolishes most of the structure needed by the theory of truth. So it is worth returning for another look at the earlier proposal to analyse indirect discourse in terms of a predicate relating an originating speaker, a sentence, and the present speaker of the sentence in indirect discourse. For that proposal did not cut off any of the simple entailments we have been discussing, and it alone of recent suggestions promised, when coupled with a workable theory of quotation, to yield to standard semantic methods. But there is a subtle flaw.

We tried to bring out the flavour of the analysis to which we have returned by rewording our favourite sentence as 'Galileo uttered a sentence that meant in his mouth what "The earth moves" means now in mine'. We should not think ill of this verbose version of 'Galileo said that the earth moves' because of apparent reference to a meaning ('what "The earth moves" means'); this expression is not treated as a singular term in the theory. We are indeed asked to make sense of a judgement of synonymy between utterances, but not as the foundation of a theory of language, merely as an unanalysed part of the content of the familiar idiom of indirect discourse. The idea that underlies our awkward paraphrase is that of *samesaying*: when I say that Galileo said that the earth moves, I represent Galileo and myself as samesayers.[13]

And now the flaw is this. If I merely *say* we are samesayers, Galileo and I, I have yet to *make* us so; and how am I to do this? Obviously, by saying what he said; not by using his words (necessarily), but by using words the same in import here and now as his then and there. Yet this is just what, on the theory, I cannot do. For the theory brings the content-sentence into the act sealed in quotation marks, and on any standard theory of quotation, this means the content-sentence is mentioned and not used. In uttering the words 'The earth moves' I do not, according to this account, say anything remotely like what Galileo is claimed to have said; I do not, in fact, say anything. My words in the frame provided by 'Galileo said that ____' merely help refer to a sentence. There will be no missing the point if we expand quotation in the style we recently considered. Any intimation that Galileo and I are same-sayers vanishes in this version:

Galileo said that 'T'⌒'h'⌒'e'⌒' '⌒'e'⌒'a'⌒'r'⌒'t'⌒'h'⌒' '⌒'m'⌒'o'⌒'v'⌒'e'⌒'s'

We seem to have been taken in by a notational accident, a way of referring to expressions that when abbreviated produces framed pictures of the very words referred to. The difficulty is odd; let's see if we can circumvent it. Imagine an altered case. Galileo utters his words 'Eppur si muove', I utter my words, 'The earth moves'. There is no problem yet in recognizing that we are samesayers; an utterance of mine matches an utterance of his in purport. I am not now using my words to help refer to a sentence; I speak for myself, and my words refer in their usual way to the earth and to its movement. If Galileo's utterance 'Eppur si muove' made us samesayers, then some utterance or other of Galileo's made us samesayers. The form '($\exists x$) (Galileo's utterance x and my utterance y makes us samesayers)' is thus a way of attributing any saying I please to Galileo provided I find a way of replacing 'y' by a word or phrase that refers to an appropriate utterance of mine. And surely there is a way I can do this: I need only produce the required utterance and replace 'y' by a reference to it. Here goes:

The earth moves.

$(\exists x)$ (Galileo's utterance x and my last utterance makes us samesayers).

Definitional abbreviation is all that is needed to bring this little skit down to:

The earth moves.
Galileo said that.

Here the 'that' is a demonstrative singular term referring to an utterance (not a sentence).

This form has a small drawback in that it leaves the hearer up in the air about the purpose served by saying 'The earth moves' until the act has been performed. As if, say, I were first to tell a story and then add, 'That's how it was once upon a time'. There's some fun to be had this way, and in any case no amount of telling what the illocutionary force of our utterances is going to insure that they have that force. But in the present case nothing stands in the way of reversing the order of things, thus:

Galileo said that.
The earth moves.

It is now safe to allow a tiny orthographic change, a change without semantic significance, but suggesting to the eye the relation of introducer and introduced: we may suppress the stop after 'that' and the consequent capitalization:

Galileo said that the earth moves.

Perhaps it should come as no surprise to learn that the form of psychological sentences in English apparently evolved in much the way these ruminations suggest. According to the *Oxford English Dictionary*,

The use of *that* is generally held to have arisen out of the demonstrative pronoun pointing to the clause which it introduces. Cf. (1) He once lived here: we all know *that*: (2) *That* (now *this*) we all know: he once lived here; (3) We all know *that* (or *this*): he once lived here; (4) We all know *that* he once lived here ...[14]

The proposal then is this: sentences in indirect discourse, as it happens, wear their logical form on their sleeves (except for one small point). They consist of an expression referring to a speaker, the two-place predicate 'said', and a demonstrative referring to an utterance. Period. What follows gives the content of the subject's saying, but has no logical or semantic connection with the original attribution of a saying. This last point is no doubt the novel one, and upon it everything depends: from a semantic point of view the content-sentence in indirect discourse is not contained in the sentence whose truth counts, i.e. the sentence that ends with 'that'.

We would do better, in coping with this subject, to talk of inscriptions and utterances and speech acts, and avoid reference to sentences.[15] For what an utterance of 'Galileo said that' does is announce a further utterance. Like any utterance, this first may be serious or silly, assertive or playful; but if it is true, it must be followed by an utterance synonymous with some other. The second utterance, the introduced act, may also be true or false, done in the mode of assertion or of play. But if it is as announced, it must serve at least the purpose of conveying the content of what someone said. The role of the introducing utterance is not unfamiliar: we do the same with words like 'This is a joke', 'This is an order', 'He commanded that', 'Now hear this'. Such expressions might be called performatives, for they are used to usher in performances on the part of the speaker. A certain interesting reflexive effect sets in when performatives occur in the first-person present tense, for then the speaker utters words which if true are made so exclusively by the content and mode of the performance that follows, and the mode of this performance may well be in part determined by that same performative introduction. Here is an example that will also provide the occasion for a final comment on indirect discourse.

'Jones asserted that Entebbe is equatorial' would, if we parallel the analysis of indirect discourse, come to mean something like, 'An utterance of Jones' in the assertive mode had the content of this utterance of mine. Entebbe is equatorial.' The analysis does not founder because the modes of utterance of the two speakers may differ; all that the truth of the performative requires is that the second utterance, in whatever mode (assertive or not), match in content an assertive utterance of Jones. Whether such an asymmetry is appropriate in indirect discourse depends on how much of assertion we read into the concept of saying. Now suppose I try: 'I assert that Entebbe is equatorial.' Of course by saying this I may not assert anything; mood of words cannot guarantee mode of utterance. But if my utterance of the performative is true, then do I say something in the assertive mode that has the content of my second utterance—I do, that is, assert that Entebbe is equatorial. If I do assert it, an element in my success is no doubt my utterance of the performative, which announces an assertion; thus performatives tend to be self-fulfilling. Perhaps it is this feature of performatives that has misled some philosophers into thinking that performatives, or their utterances, are neither true nor false.

On the analysis of indirect discourse here proposed, standard problems seem to find a just solution. The appearance of failure of the laws of extensional substitution is explained as due to our mistaking what are really two sentences for one: we make substitutions in one sentence, but it is the other (the utterance of) which changes in truth. Since an utterance of 'Galileo said that' and any utterance following it are semantically independent, there is no reason to predict, on grounds of form alone, any *particular* effect on the truth of the first from change in the second. On the other hand, if the second utterance had been different in any way at all, the first utterance *might* have had a different truth value, for the reference of the 'that' would have changed.

The paradox, that sentences (utterances) in *oratio obliqua* do not have the logical consequences they should if truth is to be defined, is resolved. What follows the verb 'said' has only the structure of a singular term, usually the demonstrative 'that'. Assuming the 'that' refers, we can infer that Galileo said something from 'Galileo said that'; but this is welcome. The familiar words coming in the train of the performative of indirect discourse do, on my account, have structure, but it is familiar structure and poses no problem for theory of truth not there before indirect discourse was the theme.

Since Frege, philosophers have become hardened to the idea that content-sentences in talk about propositional attitudes may strangely refer to such entities as intensions, propositions, sentences, utterances, and inscriptions. What is strange is not the entities, which are all right in their place (if they have one), but the notion that ordinary words for planets, people, tables, and hippopotami in indirect discourse may give up these pedestrian references for the exotica. If we could recover our pre-Fregean semantic innocence, I think it would seem to us plainly incredible that the words 'The earth moves', uttered after the words 'Galileo said that', mean anything different, or refer to anything else, than is their wont when they come in other environments. No doubt their role in *oratio obliqua* is in some sense special; but that is another story. Language is the instrument it is because the same expression, with semantic features (meaning) unchanged, can serve countless purposes. I have tried to show how our understanding of indirect discourse does not strain this basic insight.

Notes

1. From H. Jackson, *The Eighteen-Nineties*, 73.
2. A. Tarski, 'The Concept of Truth in Formalized Languages', in his *Logic, Semantics, Metamathematics*.

3. For further defence of a concept of logical form based on a theory of truth, see *Essays on Actions and Events*, 137–46.

4. W. V. Quine, *Word and Object*, Ch. 6.

5. R. Carnap, *The Logical Syntax of Language*, 248. The same was in effect proposed by P. T. Geach in *Mental Acts*.

6. The point is due to A. Church, 'On Carnap's Analysis of Statements of Assertion and Belief', *Analysis* 10 (1950), 97–9.

7. G. Frege, 'On Sense and Reference', in his *Philosophical Writings*. A. Church, 'A Formulation of the Logic of Sense and Denotation', in *Structure, Method, and Meaning*, ed. P. Henle, H. M. Kallen, and S. K. Langer.

8. The idea of an essentially Fregean approach limited to two semantic levels has been suggested by M. Dummett in *Frege: Philosophy of Language*. Ch. 9.

9. My assimilation of a translation manual to a theory of truth is not in Quine.

10. B. Mates, 'Synonymity', in *Semantics and the Philosophy of Language*, ed. L. Linsky. The example is Church's.

11. A. Church, 'Intensional Isomorphism and Identity of Belief', *Philosophical Studies* 5 (1954), 65–73. W. Sellars, 'Putnam on Synonymity and Belief', *Analysis* 15 (1955), 117–20.

12. I. Scheffler, 'An Inscriptional Approach to Indirect Quotation', *Analysis* 10 (1954), 83–90.

13. Strictly speaking, the verb 'said' is here analysed as a three-place predicate which holds of a speaker (Galileo), an utterance of the speaker ('Eppur si muove'), and an utterance of the attributer ('The earth moves'). This predicate is from a semantic point of view a primitive. The fact that an informal paraphrase of the predicate appeals to a relation of sameness of content as between utterances introduces no intentional entities or semantics. Some have regarded this as a form of cheating, but the policy is deliberate and principled. For a discussion of the distinction between questions of logical form (which is the present concern) and the analysis of individual predicates, see 'Truth and Meaning', in my *Truth and Interpretation*. It is also worth observing that radical interpretation, if it succeeds, yields an adequate concept of synonymy as between utterances. [Footnote added in 1982.]

14. J. A. H. Murray *et al.* (eds.), *The Oxford English Dictionary*, 253. Cf. C. T. Onions, *An Advanced English Syntax*, 154–6. I first learned that 'that' in such contexts evolved from an explicit demonstrative in J. Hintikka, *Knowledge and Belief*, 13. Hintikka remarks that a similar development has taken place in German and Finnish. I owe the *OED* reference to Eric Stiezel.

15. I assume that a theory of truth for a language containing demonstratives must apply strictly to utterances and not to sentences, or will treat truth as a relation between sentences, speakers, and times.

Chapter 36
Opacity and Scope

Barbara Partee

The purpose of this paper is to contrast two views of opacity; more specifically, two views as to how opaque contexts arise. One view, which is expressed or implicit in the work of many philosophers[1] and linguists,[2] is that opacity results from the embedding of a sentence into a construction headed by a modal (construed widely) verb, adjective, or adverb, such as *necessarily*, *believes that*, *must*, or *certain*. On this view, wherever there is an opaque context, it is a context of a sentence; grammatical relations internal to sentences such as verb plus object or adverb plus verb never create opacity. The second view, suggested by the work of Montague,[3] is that opacity is one aspect of intensionality, and that intensionality is more the norm than the exception for grammatical relations. On this view any noun phrase position is liable to be opaque, and will be unless the construction it occurs in happens to be extensional. I will describe these two views a little more explicitly, discuss some of the cases where they suggest different syntactic analyses, and compare their attractions. I will try to show that while the first view makes a stronger theoretical claim and would be preferable if it could be substantiated, it runs into some serious descriptive problems with constructions which the second view can handle in a straightforward way.

0   SOME PRELIMINARY DEFINITIONS

A context in which a term phrase can occur is an *opaque context* (or *referentially opaque context*) if substitution of a coreferential term phrase

First appeared in Munitz and Unger (eds.), *Semantics and Philosophy* (New York: NYU Press, 1974), pp. 81–101. Reprinted by permission of NYU Press.

does not always preserve truth. The italicized term phrase in (1), for example, is in an opaque context:

(1) Mary believes that *the man who lives upstairs* is insane.

A context which is not (referentially) opaque is (*referentially*) *transparent*, as, for example, the context of the italicized term phrase in (2).

(2) The police who arrested *the man who lives upstairs* behaved badly.

Sentences in which a term phrase occurs in an opaque context are generally ambiguous; there will in general be both a *referential reading* (loosely called the "transparent reading"), on which the term phrase is used purely referentially and substitution of a coreferential term phrase does preserve truth, and a *nonreferential reading* (more accurately called a *not-purely-referential reading*; loosely called the "opaque reading"), on which substitution of a coreferential term phrase may happen to but often does not preserve truth. Thus a context is opaque if it *permits* of a not-purely-referential reading; but it will almost always permit a purely referential reading as well. The two readings of (1) are approximately paraphrased below:

(1-ref.)   Mary believes of a certain individual, namely the man who lives upstairs, that he is insane.

(1-nonref.) Mary believes that whoever it is that lives upstairs is insane.

The opacity of sentence (1) evidently results from the verb *believes* in construction with its *that*-clause: any term phrase[4] in a *that*-clause embedded under *believes* has a nonreferential reading, while the subject of *believes*, for example, does not. As we look at various kinds of grammatical constructions, and alternative analyses of them, we will distinguish between *extensional* and *intensional* constructions, always relative to a particular analysis. We will say, following Carnap (1947), that a grammatical construction is *extensional*, relative to a certain syntactic and semantic analysis, if the extension of the whole is a function of the extensions of the parts. And we will say that a grammatical construction is *intensional*, relative to a certain syntactic and semantic analysis, if the extension of the whole is a function of the intensions of one or more parts and the extensions of he remaining parts. Following the standard treatment of possible-world semantics,[5] we take the extension of a sentence to be a truth value, and its intension to be a function from possible worlds to truth values (the intension of a sentence is called a *proposition*); the extension of a one-place predicate is taken to be a set of individuals, and its intension, called a *property*, is taken to be a function from possible worlds to sets of individuals. On the matter of term phrases, the usual interpretation is that the extension is an individual and the intension is a function from possible worlds to individuals; but Montague suggests a different analysis which gives a uniform treatment of term phrases and quantifier phrases, which we describe briefly below before turning to the central issues.

1   TERMS AND QUANTIFIER PHRASES

On the classical view of logical structure, individual variables, proper names, and definite descriptions are grammatically treated as terms and can stand as arguments of predicates, while quantifier phrases with *all* and *some* are not treated as unitary phrases at all. Thus a representation of

(3) John walks

in ordinary predicate logic is as in (3′)

(3′) walk(j)

where *John* appears as a term. But in the representation of (4) as (4′):

(4) Every man walks

(4′) $(\forall x)(\text{man}(x) \rightarrow \text{walk}(x))$

there is no single constituent corresponding to *every man*; what corresponds to *every man* is the whole frame (4″):

(4″) $(\forall x)(\text{man}(x) \rightarrow \ldots (x))$

which is not itself a well-formed formula. From the point of view of predicate logic, it is an accident that expressions like *some man* and *every man* behave as noun phrases in ordinary language. Montague (1973) proposes an analysis which treats quantifier phrases as terms, but it involves a departure from the usual semantics of terms. Instead of taking the extension of a term to be an individual, he takes it to be a set of properties. In the case of a proper name like *John*, the link between the name "John" and the individual, John, is not taken to be direct designation; rather, "John" denotes the set of all of those properties whose extension includes John. Translating English into an intensional logic which includes an individual constant j which does denote John, this gives:

(5) John: $\lambda P^{\vee}P(j)$

where P is a variable over properties, and $^{\vee}$ is the extension operator. Then a sentence like (3) is analyzed not as asserting simply that the individual John is in the set of entities that walk, but as asserting that the property of walking is included in John's property-set; but this is logically equivalent to the former interpretation. ($^{\wedge}$ is the intension operator.)

(6) *John walks*:
   John($^{\wedge}$ walk)
   $\lambda P^{\vee}P(j)(^{\wedge}$ walk)
   $^{\wedge\vee}$ walk (j)
   walk (j)

Given this analysis of terms as designating property-sets, *every man* and *some man*, as well as *the man*, can be treated as terms, since they can also be interpreted as designating sets of properties.

(7) *every man*: $\lambda P(\forall x)(\mathrm{man}(x) \to P(x))$

(8) *some man*: $\lambda P(\exists x)(\mathrm{man}(x) \wedge P(x))$

(9) *the man*: $\lambda P(\exists y)[(\forall x)(\mathrm{man}(x) \leftrightarrow x = y) \wedge {}^{\vee}P(y)]$

A sentence like *every man walks* is then analyzed as saying that the property of walking is in the property-set for *every man*, that is, is in the set of those properties which every man has. This can be shown to be equivalent to the standard interpretation:

(10) *every man walks*:
   $\lambda P(\forall x)(\mathrm{man}(x) \to {}^{\vee}P(x))(^{\wedge}\mathrm{walk})$
   $(\forall x)(\mathrm{man}(x) \to {}^{\vee\wedge}\mathrm{walk}(x))$
   $(\forall x)(\mathrm{man}(x) \to \mathrm{walk}(x))$

Nothing new is being said about the interpretation of the particular sentence, *every man walks*; but the treatment of *every man* as a term-phrase constituent of the sentence allows for a more direct connection between the syntax and semantics of English than is possible if *every man* is viewed as a peculiar natural-language shorthand for a complex sentential matrix. This unification of natural language noun phrases as logical term phrases is central to the alternative account of intensional constructions, as we shall see below.

One more aspect of Montague's treatment of term phrases needs to be mentioned. In the examples above, a term phrase was combined directly with a verb to form a sentence. Term phrases are introduced directly in a variety of grammatical constructions—transitive verb plus object, preposition plus object, and so on. Among the term phrases, in addition to proper names and quantifier phrases, are free variables, x_1, x_2, ... In order to represent the bound variable interpretation of pronouns and to represent scope ambiguities in sentences with more than one quantifier, there is a rule which allows a term phrase to be introduced into a sentence via substitution for a free variable. Any term phrase may be introduced in this way—not only a quantifier phrase, but also a proper noun or another free variable. The rule is given in a rough form below.

Sentence-scope quantification: If α is a term and ϕ is a formula, then for any n, $F_n(\alpha, \phi)$ is a formula, where F_n is as illustrated in the following example:

(11) $F_3(a\ fish,\ John\ caught\ x_3\ and\ ate\ x_3) = John\ caught\ a\ fish\ and\ ate\ it.$

The semantic interpretation of the rule is as follows: if α is interpreted as α', and ϕ', then the interpretation of $F_n(\alpha, \phi)$ is $\alpha'(\hat{x}_n \phi')$, where $\hat{x}_n$ is an intensional abstraction operator, that is, $^\wedge x_n$. Thus the interpretation of example (11) is as in (12) (with some parts left uninterpreted).

(12) $\lambda P(\exists x)(\text{fish}(x) \wedge {}^\vee P(x))(\hat{x}_3(\text{John caught } x_3 \text{ and ate } x_3))$

2   OPAQUE CONTEXTS

Now we return to an examination of a variety of constructions that create opaque contexts. In trying to account for the opacity of these constructions, we will consider alternative syntactic analyses and the alternative semantic representations they support. In each case, at least one of the suggested analyses will follow the classical view that attributes opacity to be the embedding of a sentence under some sort of modal operator; in a number of cases, Montague's approach allows the possibility of a more "local" analysis of opacity.

a   *That*-clauses

The clearest and least controversial cases are those where there is clearly an embedded sentence. Embedded *that*-clauses are almost always opaque contexts, as the following sample illustrates.

(13) Mary believes that the man in the raincoat is a spy.

(14) Tom is certain that a student in my class is a spy.

(15) That the bank president works in the bank is obvious.

(16) That John's favorite uncle works in the bank is obvious.

(17) It appears that a child has been writing on the walls.

The following example is transparent, but that need not contradict the generalization that the construction it exemplifies is opaque, since the transparency is deducible from the meaning of the word *true*, and thus could be accounted for by a special meaning postulate for that lexical item.

(18) It is true that the bank president is a spy.

For opaque constructions of this sort there is general agreement that the distinction between the referential and the nonreferential reading is simply a matter of the scope of the quantifier of the term phrase in question. The referential reading of (14) can be represented as in (14a) and the nonreferential reading as in (14b).

(14a) $(\exists x)(x$ is a student in my class $\wedge$ Tom is certain that x is a spy)

(14b) Tom is certain that $(\exists x)(x$ is a student in my class $\wedge$ x is a spy)

Such embedded constructions are generally thought of as the paradigm case of opaque contexts; controversy only arises over the question of whether all types of opacity are to be analyzed as deriving ultimately from constructions of this type.

b   Sentence adverbs and modal auxiliaries

In sentences (19) and (20), the subject is in an opaque context even though overtly it appears to be in a simple, unembedded sentence.

(19) Smith's murderer is probably insane.

(20) Smith's murderer may be insane.

Since it is the sentence adverb *probably* in (19) and the modal auxiliary *may* in (20) that is responsible for the opacity, the obvious solution (and the standard one) is to treat such adverbs and auxiliaries as taking a sentence in their scope. There are at least two ways to do this. One solution, which assimilates these cases totally to the preceding type, would represent the underlying form of (19) and (20) as (19a) and (20a), with a transformational rule to delete *it is* and *true*, and move the adverb or auxiliary into what then becomes the main clause.

(19a) It is probably true that Smith's murderer is insane.

(20a) It may be true that Smith's murderer is insane.

However, about the only virtue of this approach is the uniformity of opaque contexts it provides. Syntactically, it leaves unanswered the question of how *probably* and *may* got into (19a) and (20a), since *it is probably true that* and *it may be true that* are presumably not unanalyzed atomic expressions, and it is hard to imagine a nonregressing source for *probably* and *may* in (19a) and (20a) that could not be invoked for (19) and (20) directly.

The second solution is more direct syntactically and departs only slightly from the model of the embedded *that*-clause. That is to treat sentence adverbs and modal auxiliaries both as sentence operators: expressions which combine with a sentence to form a new sentence, as indicated in (19b) and (20b).

(19b) $_S$[probably $_S$[Smith's murderer is insane]]

(20b) $_S$[may $_S$[Smith's murderer is insane]]

The only difficulty this analysis faces is in the case of the modal auxiliaries, where some kind of syntactic mechanism must be invoked to prevent iteration, since only one modal auxiliary can appear in a sentence. In either of these analyses, the distinction between the two readings can be represented as a matter of whether the quantifier has the whole sentence or only the inner sentence in its scope, so the basic mechanism is the same as in the case of *that*-clauses.

c Infinitives

The alternatives become a little more distinct and disputable when we consider embedded infinitive phrases, as in (21)–(23), all of which are opaque and have the usual two interpretations.

(21) John is trying to find a gold watch.

(22) Sam is afraid to talk to a professor in the department.

(23) It would be wise to read an article by Russell.

On the view that seems to be most prevalent among philosophers, these infinitive phrases are to be analyzed as abbreviations of *that*-clauses:[6] for (21), for instance, the source would be (21a):

(21a) John is trying (endeavoring) that he find a gold watch.

The advantage of such a structure is that it provides an embedded sentence which the quantifier can take as its scope on the nonreferential reading, as in (21b).

(21b) John is endeavoring that $(\exists x)(x$ is a gold watch and he find $x)$.

From the point of view of a theory of natural language which is concerned with both syntax and semantics, the semantic neatness of such an analysis must be weighed against the fact that it leaves unexplained the syntax of English verbs like *try*, which never in fact take *that*-clause complements. It would be desirable to find an analysis which offered some explanation for the existence of a distinction between *that*-clauses and infinitives.[7]

For sentence (22), the analysis is somewhat worse, since the putative source would be (22b).

(22b) Sam is afraid that he talk to a professor in the department.

The problem here is that *afraid* does take *that*-clauses, thought not normally in the subjunctive, but *afraid that* is clearly distinct in meaning from *afraid to*. It will not do to simply view the two *afraids* as homonyms, since parallel differences between the meanings of *that*-complements and *to*-complements are found with a wide range of emotive adjectives, such as *happy, sorry*, and so on. Perhaps the difference can be pinned on the subjunctive/indicative distinction, but that requires some analysis of the subjunctive. In the case of (23) above, a *that*-clause produces either ungrammaticality or a meaning change or both, with the added difficulty that some subject must be provided for the embedded clause, and it is not clear that there is any choice available that would not do violence to the meaning of the original sentence.

Montague's treatment, because it allows for quantifier phrases to be inserted like other term phrases directly into term-phrase positions, allows infinitive phrases to be analyzed directly as opaque contexts. A verb such as *try to* is treated as taking a verb phrase to make a new verb phrase, and semantically it is the intension of the embedded verb phrase that contributes to the extension of the whole.

In (21), the distinction between the two readings can be represented as the distinction between *a gold watch* having been introduced directly as object of the embedded transitive verb *find*, as in (21c), giving the nonreferential reading, versus substitution of *a gold watch* for a free variable at the sentence level, leading to the referential interpretation (21d).

(21c) John (^ try to (^ find a gold watch)

(21d) (a gold watch)($\hat{x}_1$ John (^ try to (^ find x_1)))

One serious difficulty encountered by Montague's analysis and not by the analysis mentioned earlier is exemplified by sentence (24).

(24) John tried to be easy to please.

Here there is no opacity to worry about; the problem is a syntactic one. The analysis of *try to* as taking verb phrases directly is satisfactory for simple verb phrases, but *be easy to please* is a paradigm example of the sort of phrase for which transformational derivation from a full sentence (in which *easy* is the predicate and *to please* a subpart of the subject) can be very strongly argued for. For such reasons I have proposed elsewhere[8] that Montague's system be augmented by the addition of transformational rules, which can be done within the ground rules of his theory as long as it is possible to associate a unique semantic interpretation rule with each transformation. For infinitive complements, the relevant transformation is one which maps sentences having a free variable as subject into verb phrases (this rule, which I call the Derived Verb-Phrase Rule, has no direct counterpart in standard transformational grammar because there transformations always convert sentences [with their associated structure] into sentences). The rule is illustrated in (25).

(25) a. *x* finds a gold watch $\Rightarrow$ find a gold watch
      b. *x* is easy to please $\Rightarrow$ be easy to please

The semantic interpretation is simply predicate abstraction: if the sentence ϕ is interpreted as ϕ', the derived verb phrase is interpreted as $\hat{x}_i\phi'$, where x_i is the deleted variable. Then given an ordinary transformational derivation of the sentence "*x* is easy to please," we have a derivation and an interpretation of the verb phrase "be easy to please." We can then insert such a verb phrase as the complement of *try to*. In fact, if we like, we can require that all infinitives be derived via abstraction using the derived verb-phrase rule, and if we did that, we would have the advantages of both the two preceding analyses: infinitives would be kept syntactically distinct from *that*-clauses, but would be derived from sentential forms. The distinction between nonreferential and referential readings would then still be representable as a difference in quantifier scope: the scope would be the embedded sentence or the whole sentence, as in (21e) and (21f).

(21e) John ($^\wedge$ try to ($\hat{y}$) ($\exists x$)(x is a gold watch $\wedge$ y finds x)))

(21f) ($\exists x$)(x is a gold watch $\wedge$ John ($^\wedge$ try to ($\hat{y}$ (y finds x)))))

This analysis is very similar syntactically to the usual transformational analysis of infinitive complements, except that it makes use of the derived verb-phrase rule, with its interpretation as abstraction over a free variable, in place of the usual Equi-Noun-Phrase Deletion Rule. Semantically it is equivalent to Montague's analysis. As for the account of opacity, the analysis I have ended up with here supports both of the views that I am comparing: the verb-plus-infinitive phrase construction is intensional, but it is also possible to view all infinitive phrases as deriving from sentences, although the underlying sentences must be open sentences and hence not full sentences semantically. Thus, although several accounts of opacity in infinitives are possible, the one that seems most adequate is neutral on the central issue.

d   Verb phrase adverbs

Assuming that we can, at least in clear cases, make a distinction between sentence adverbs and verb-phrase adverbs,[9] we find that verb-phrase adverbs can create opaque contexts in the verb phrases they modify, though not in subject position (this being one of the distinguishing criteria between the two types of adverbs). For example, the term phrases in the verb phrases of the following examples have both a purely referential and a not purely referential[10] reading.

(26) Big Mack intentionally shot a student.

(27) Mary reluctantly bet on the best horse.

(28) Sam willingly invited the robber into his house.

The major alternatives in representing the construction so as to account for its opacity are, as in the preceding case, either to find an appropriate underlying structure in which a whole sentence falls under the scope of the adverb, or to represent the construction directly as modification of a verb phrase by an adverb, but bring the intension of the verb phrase into the corresponding semantic interpretation.

On the first alternative, the problem is to find a suitable paraphrase to serve a plausible underlying form. The most promising line seems to be to make use of the corresponding adjectives, *intentional*, *willing*, and so on, since many of the adverbs of this category which create opacity are of the *Adj-ly* form (though not all: *on purpose*, *with malice aforethought*, and so on). I am convinced that no such suitable paraphrases exist, but it is virtually impossible to argue conclusively for such a point. The following might seem to be appropriate first tries, but note that not only are they not good paraphrases, but they involve infinitives which in turn would have to be reanalyzed as sentences to maintain the first view.

(26a) It was intentional of Big Mack to shoot a student.

(27a) Mary was reluctant to bet on the best horse.

(28a) Sam was willing to invite the robber into his house.

A considerably closer paraphrase can be gotten by conjoining such sentences with the original sentences minus their adverbs, since part of what is missing in the (a) paraphrases is the factivity of the originals. (26a) does appear to be factive as it stands; it would be more parallel to the others if we used the verb *intend*.

(26b) Big Mack intended to shoot a student, and Big Mack shot a student.

(27b) Mary was reluctant to bet on the best horse, and Mary bet on the best horse.

(28b) Sam was willing to invite the robber into his house, and Sam invited the robber into his house.

Now the (b) sentences do seem to be implied by the original sentences, and in an informal way help elucidate the dual referential and non-referential role played by the term phrases in the verb phrases of the originals. But for the implication to go the other way it would be necessary to establish identity of some appropriate sort between the verb phrases in the two conjuncts in each (b) sentence. And since in each case the first conjunct has an intensional construction and the second conjunct an extensional one, it is hard to imagine what an appropriate sort of identity would be; perhaps it is with good reason that the verb-phrase adverb constructions of the originals manage to make double use of a single occurrence of the verb phrase.

As I indicated above, I don't take my argument as conclusive refutation of an embedded-sentence analysis of verb-phrase adverbs, since all I have done is point out problems for what seems to me the most plausible approach to such an analysis. I am sure, in fact, that such an analysis can be maintained by invoking abstract predicates whose meanings are appropriate by fiat and which trigger obligatory transformations to insure that they end up as verb-phrase adverbs.[11] But let me turn instead to the analysis suggested by Montague, in which verb-phrase adverbs are analyzed as verb-phrase adverbs. Montague's analysis agrees semantically with the proposal of Thomason and Stalnaker (1973).

On the Montague analysis, a verb-phrase adverb combines with a verb phrase to give a new verb phrase; as with the verbs like *try to*, in the semantic interpretation the adverb is interpreted as a function which takes the intension of the verb phrase as its argument. Also as in the *try to* case, the transformational extensions that I mentioned earlier make it possible for verb-phrase adverbs to be applied to sententially derived verb phrases as well as (26c) and (26d) if we apply Montague's system directly. If we were to require that verb-phrase adverbs apply only to verb phrases derived via abstraction, we would end up with (26e) and (26f) instead; but these are logically equivalent to (26c) and (26d), respectively, though that may not be apparent from my loose notation.

(26c) Big Mack (^ intentionally (^ shoot (^ a student)))

(26d) $(\exists x)(x$ is a student and Big Mack (^ intentionally (^ shoot (x)))))

(26e) Big Mack (^ intentionally
$(\hat{y}((\exists x)(x$ is a student and y (^ shoot(x)))))))

(26f) $(\exists x)(x$ is a student and
Big Mack (^ intentionally $(\hat{y}(y($^ shoot(x)))))))

On the analysis which is like Montague's with the addition of the derived verb-phrase rule, the generalizations that emerge are the same as for the infinitive complement case. On the one hand, we have an intensional construction of adverb plus verb phrase; on the other hand, the verb phrase can be taken to be derivative from a sentence, though again it is necessarily an open sentence. Note that in both of the last two constructions examined, it is only the transformationally complex verb phrases that need to be derived via the derived verb-phrase rule; there is no syntactic reason to require all verb phrases entering these constructions to be derived via that rule, and the only reason for doing so would be to preserve the generalization that all opaque contexts be contexts of sentences. In the next section, I will turn to the class of constructions for which the two approaches have the most sharply divergent consequences.

3 THE OPACITY OF *LOOK FOR*

There are a few verbs whose direct objects can be interpreted nonreferentially.

(29) John is looking for a unicorn.

(30) You owe me a Coke.

(31) Mary offered John a cigar.

(32) Janice advertised for a cook.

On Montague's approach these are analyzed directly as transitive verb plus object; semantically, the verb is analyzed as a function from intensions of term phrases to extensions of verb phrases. They thus fall under the generalization that grammatical relations in general are to be interpreted in a function-argument way, with the argument in general an intension. This generalization can be shown most naturally with the notation of categorial grammar: taking t as sentence, T as term phrase, IV as verb phrase, and CN as common noun phrase, the major grammatical relations can be sketched as follows (see Partee, 1972b, for a fuller explication).

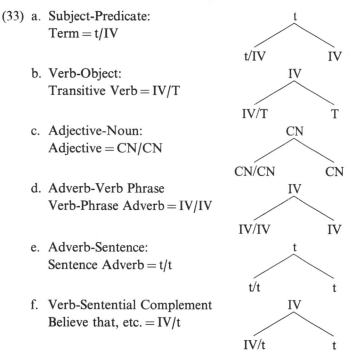

(33) a. Subject-Predicate:
Term = t/IV

b. Verb-Object:
Transitive Verb = IV/T

c. Adjective-Noun:
Adjective = CN/CN

d. Adverb-Verb Phrase
Verb-Phrase Adverb = IV/IV

e. Adverb-Sentence:
Sentence Adverb = t/t

f. Verb-Sentential Complement
Believe that, etc. = IV/t

In each case, if the semantic interpretation of the A/B constituent is α and the interpretation of the B constituent is β, the semantic interpretation of the resulting A-phrase is taken to be $\alpha(^{\wedge}\beta)$. Thus in each case it is the intension of the B constituent which enters into the semantic interpretation of the result.

Of the constructions listed above, only the subject-predicate construction appears to be always extensional;[12] the other constructions turn out to be sometimes intensional and sometimes extensional, depending on which lexical items of the *A/B* classes are involved. Since the extension can be determined from the intension (plus the way the world is) but not vice versa, Montague takes the intensional case as fundamental and adds meaning postulates for the lexical items whose associated functions are extensional. Among the adjectives, for example, *good, alleged, famous*, and *large* are intensional, while *blue, oval, dead*, and *four-footed* are extensional, so a meaning postulate would be added for the adjectives of the latter class. For the subject-predicate construction, either a meaning postulate can be added for the construction as a whole, or it can be reanalyzed to start with as $\alpha(\beta)$ rather than $\alpha(^\wedge\beta)$.

Looking at this range of constructions, it is the extensionality of the subject-predicate construction rather than the intensionality of (some cases of) the verb-object construction which appears to be exceptional. It is not surprising that the opposite has generally been assumed, since (a) the subject-predicate construction is a central one, and in the simplest sentences is the only one; it has been canonized in the $P(a)$ notation of logic; (b) logicians have been concerned primarily with "scientific discourse," which can be restricted to extensional constructions with very little loss, and have been concerned with intensional constructions only when they bear on matters of philosophical relevance, as *necessarily* and *believe* do but *look for* and such cases presumably do not; (c) a direct analysis of verb-object constructions is not feasible without something like Montague's treatment of quantifiers as term phrases.

The two interpretations of (29) in Montague's system can be represented grossly as (29a), the nonreferential reading, and (29b), the referential reading.

(29a) [John (^ look for (^ a unicorn))]

(29b) [(a unicorn)($\hat{x}$(John(^ look for(x))))]

Expanding the interpretation of a *unicorn* into its analysis as the set of all properties which some unicorn has, that is, the union of the sets of properties of individual unicorns, (29a) and (29b) become (29c) and (29d), respectively.

(29c) [John (^ look for (^$\lambda P(\exists y)$(unicorn(y) $\wedge^\vee P(y)$)))]

(29d) [($\lambda P (\exists y)$(unicorn (y) $\wedge^\vee P(y)$))($\hat{x}$(John(^ look for (x))))]

(29d) is equivalent in turn to (29e).

(29e) $(\exists y)(\text{unicorn}(y) \wedge \text{John} (^\wedge \text{ look for } (y)))$

In the nonreferential interpretation, *look for* is a relation between John and the property of being a property of a unicorn; in the referential interpretation, *look for* is a relation between John and an individual unicorn. The same kind of analysis applies to *owe, offer, advertise for, hunt for, guard against, listen for, need, demand* (although probably not to *worship* or *conceive*, for which Montague also intended it).

Now let us consider the approach which tries to preserve the generalization that opacity is a property of sentence contexts. On this approach, a transitive verb like *look for* cannot be regarded as lexically basic, but must be viewed as lexically decomposable into a complex expression like *try to find*, where there infinitive in turn is derived from a sentence. The decomposition of *look for* into *try to find* was first proposed by Quine (1960), was argued for linguistically by Bach (1968), and has become generally accepted within the generative semantics framework.

Support for this view can be found in the existence of a considerable range of verbs which can be used either as transitive verbs or with embedded complements; *need, want, demand, ask for, insist on, wish for, hope for* and *expect*, for example. In their use as transitive verbs, furthermore, a good paraphrase can almost always be found by forming a complement with the verb *have*, so that the transitive verb use can be regarded as resulting from *have*-deletion.

(34) John needs a winter coat.

(35) John needs to have a winter coat.

Expect does not always have paraphrases with *have*; with *company* or *a letter* or *a train*, a more suitable candidate for deletion might be *arrive*. *Offer* and *promise* when used as two-object verbs generally have paraphrases with *give*.

But a number of verbs which can have nonreferential objects do not double as complement-taking verbs, and for such verbs, including *look for*, an underlying complement form must be specified individually for each one. This would not be a very heavy price to pay if a good paraphrase could be found for each such verb, since it would allow the generalization of opacity as a property of sentence contexts to be maintained.

But there are at least two serious problems in trying to maintain the lexical decomposition view for *look for* and related verbs. The first problem is that *look for, search for, seek, hunt for, hunt, ransack . . . for, rummage about for*, and several other expressions all share *try to find* as a part of their meaning, but they are not synonymous with each other, and so *try to find* can be the lexical decomposition for at most one of them; it is doubtful that it is a fully adequate paraphrase for any of them. This problem is central to the lexical decomposition approach; if there are no perfect paraphrases which have the appropriate complement structure and which consist entirely of actual English lexical items, then the decomposition analysis must posit abstract (one is tempted to say fictitious) lexical items in the underlying structure, for example, *try-to-find*-LOOKINGLY, *try-to-find*-SEARCHINGLY, or the like. In this kind of case, unlike the somewhat stronger arguments for abstract CAUSE, DO, and he like (see Lakoff [1970], Ross [1972]), there is no independent evidence, either syntactic or semantic, for the elements in question; they are simply an unexplained semantic residue that must be invoked to maintain the analysis, in this case to maintain the generalization that opacity always involves sentence embedding.

The second problem with the decomposition analysis of such items as *look for* is a syntactic one. This problem is similar to one of the objections raised by Fodor (1970) to the analysis of *kill* as CAUSE *to die*.

Consider first the verbs like *need, want, demand, promise*, which double as transitive verbs and complement-taking verbs. There is some fairly strong syntactic evidence that the transitive use of these verbs *is* derived from the complement use, and I will show below that this same type of evidence can be turned against the decomposition analysis of *look for*, and the like.[13] This evidence concerns the occurrence of various types of adverbial modifiers with transitive verbs.

(36) John wanted my car until next Tuesday.

(37) The foundation has demanded a report by next month.

(38) I expected you tomorrow.

(39) Sally asked for the typewriter for two hours.

Sentences (36)–(38) are well formed, and sentence (39) is ambiguous, whereas similarly constructed sentences with other transitive verbs are not; cf. (40)–(43).

(40) *John washed my car until next Tuesday.

(41) *The foundation has written a report by next month.

(42) *I saw you tomorrow.

(43)   Sally used the typewriter for two hours. (unambiguous)

The differences are predictable on the hypothesis that (36)–(39) are derived from (44)–(47), respectively.

(44) John wanted to have my car until next Tuesday.

(45) The foundation has demanded to have a report by next month.

(46) I expected you to arrive (come) tomorrow.

(47) Sally asked to have the typewriter for two hours.

The adverbs in the first three examples must be analyzed as associated with the embedded verb phrases; the last one can be associated with either verb. A simple lexically governed transformation which deletes the embedded *to have* (or *to arrive*, with *expect*), can then produce (36)–(39).

Other constructions which are peculiar to *have*, or nearly so, can show up with transitive *want*, *need*, and the like, further bolstering their derivation from complement structures. For instance, corresponding to the construction *have it ready* is sentence (48):

(48) I want it ready by 5.

If (48) were not derived from a source containing "to have", it would be necessary to add another kind of basic structure for *want*, namely object plus adjectival complement. Such examples can be proliferated, strongly supporting the contention that the infinitival complement construction underlies the superficially transitive verb-plus-object construction with the verbs like *want*, *need*, *expect*, which occur in both types of construction.

But such tests give negative results for the putative derivation of *look for*, *hunt for*, and so on, from *try to find* (with or without an added abstract element like LOOKINGLY or the like). Corresponding to (49), we would expect (50) to be well formed, but it is not.

(49)   Martha is trying to find an apartment by Saturday.

(50)   *Martha is looking for an apartment by Saturday.

Similarly, since *alone* is an acceptable complement to *find*, (51) is ambiguous, but (52) does not share the ambiguity.

(51) I tried to find you alone.

(52) I looked for you alone.

Sentence (53) is likewise ambiguous, and again the corresponding sentence with *look for* does not share the ambiguity.

(53) Fred was trying to find the minutes before the meeting began.

(54) Fred was looking for the minutes before the meeting began.

This kind of evidence seems to me particularly strong, since it discriminates among transitive verbs, supporting a decompositional analysis for some and arguing against it for others.[14] And while it supports the idea that the opacity of sentences like (55) is traceable to a sentential context (or at least to an embedded verb phrase), it disconfirms that idea for sentences like (56) with *look for* and other similar verbs.

(55) John wants a paper that's classified "Top Secret".

(56) John is looking for a paper that's classified "Top Secret".

It seems to me both surprising and unfortunate that the choice between two such large-scale hypotheses about the nature of opacity should come down to the fine-grained analysis of a handful of verbs. As far as I know, there aren't more than one or two dozen verbs like *look for*; I have only been able to find *look for, search for, seek, hunt for, hunt, ransack ... for, rummage about for, advertise for, listen for, guard against,* and *owe*. If these verbs were missing from the language, or if their syntax were slightly different, then there would seem to be no empirical difference between the theory that all opacity results from sentence-embedding and the theory that intensions are centrally involved in the semantic interpretation of all or most grammatical relations. Since these two hypotheses are linked with very different views about the degree of abstractness needed in syntax for natural languages, basic questions about the relation between syntax and semantics in natural language are at issue. Although I believe I have shown that the balance of the available evidence goes against the hypothesis that all opaque contexts are sentential contexts and in favor of basic grammatical relations being intensional, it is certainly to be hoped that clearer kinds of evidence on the question will eventually be discovered.

Notes

1. Quine, the father of opacity, is probably the primary source of this view, although he also includes the embedding of terms and other nonsentential stretches within quotation marks as a source of opacity. See Quine (1960). Most of the philosophical attention to opacity has centered on verbs of propositional attitude and modal operators.

2. This idea can be found in Bach (1968) and is particularly clear in the work of Lakoff and McCawley, where opaque constructions are analyzed in terms of "higher predicates," that is, predicates one of whose arguments is a sentence. See Lakoff (1970), (1972), McCawley (1970), for example.

3. This view comes out most clearly in Montague's last work, Montague (1973).

4. If we accept the analysis of Kripke (1972), of proper names as rigid designators, then proper names are exceptions to this claim, which should then be more carefully worded in terms of term-phrase positions.

5. See Kripke (1963) and subsequent work of Kripke, Montague, Dana Scott, David Kaplan, Richmond Thomason, and others.

6. See Quine (1960), section 32 [pp. 810–814 in this vol.], which is the source of this view. Bach (1968) and other linguists have argued for the inclusion of such analyses in transformational grammars.

7. There is a spurious objection that is sometimes raised to analyses like (21b) on semantic grounds, which perhaps need to be mentioned here. The objection usually runs something like this: "The representation (21b), unlike the original sentence (21), entails that John is endeavoring to make there exist a gold watch, so (21b) cannot possibly be a paraphrase of (21)." But this is fallacious, since the quantifier has the whole conjoined sentence as its scope, and thus the supposed entailment is invalid.

8. Partee (1972a), Partee (1972b).

9. See Thomason and Stalnaker (1973).

10. Since all there adverbs are "standard" in the sense that the entailment (a) below holds for them,

(a) *a β*-ly VP'ed → *a* VP'ed

the distinction between "not purely referential" and "nonreferential" is particularly important here. In each of sentences (26)–(28), the term phrase in question has a particular referent if the sentence is true, even on the not-purely-referential reading, but the substitution of another description of the same referent will not necessarily preserve truth on that reading.

11. Lakoff, in fact, proposed something of this sort in Lakoff (1970), where he suggests structures such as:

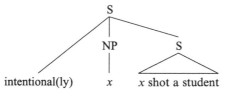

This gives verb-phrase adverbs like *intentionally* the same underlying structure as verbs like *try*, with the differences between them represented as differences in the rules they undergo: *try* triggers infinitive formation and ends up as the main verb of the sentence, whereas *intentionally* undergoes "adverb-lowering" and ends up embedded in the lower sentence. The same structure would, with different transformations, yield sentences like "It was intentional of John to shoot a student."

12. Montague (1973) regards even some subject-predicate constructions as intensional, for example, sentence (a) below, because of the invalidity of inferences like that from (a) and (b) to (c).

(a) The temperature is rising.

(b) The temperature is ninety.

(c) Ninety is rising.

But the "intensionality" of verbs like *rise, change, increase* relates only to the time coordinate of the ⟨time, world⟩ pairs in Montague's semantics, and not to opacity of the usual sort. Furthermore, his analysis of the (b) sentence as a simple equational sentence is open to question.

There are other sentences which appear on the surface to be instances of a nonextensional subject-predicate construction, such as (d) below.

(d) A unicorn appears to be approaching.

Montague suggests that such a sentence should not be generated directly, but treated "indirectly as a paraphrase," which agrees with the common transformational view that (d) should be derived from (e) which in turn derives from (f).

(e) It appears that a unicorn is approaching.

(f) *That a unicorn is approaching appears.

13. This argument emerged during informal conversation some invited speakers at the University of Massachusetts in April, 1973, and was not included in the oral presentation of this paper. Unfortunately, I no longer remember whether the idea was mine or was developed jointly, and I am not sure who I was talking with, though I suspect it was Richmond Thomason and/or Lauri Karttunen, whom I hereby tentatively thank.

14. Incidentally, some of the verbs for which such tests support a decompositional analysis require a considerably more abstract decomposition than just an added "to have" or the like; Lakoff pointed out in a La Jolla English syntax conference some years ago such evidence for decomposition of *lend, borrow*, and similar verbs, with sentences such as (i) and (ii).

(i) I lent John my bicycle until next Saturday.

(ii) I have rented this house until September.

What the underlying forms should be is much less clear for these examples. It is still not out of the question that these examples do not in fact force a decompositional analysis; it is possible that adverbs such as *until September* can co-occur not only with certain tenses, whatever the verb, but also with certain verbs, whatever the tense. For example, *last* is a verb that clearly seems to co-occur with durative adverbs, so perhaps *lend, rent*, and so on also have an inherently durative feature that would be sufficient to account for (i) and (ii). That is in part why I have included above evidence from complements like *have NP ready, find NP above*, and the like, as well as from time adverbials.

Bibliography

Bach, Emmon (1968). "Nouns and Noun Phrases," in E. Back and R. Harms, eds., *Universals in Linguistic Theory*. New York: Holt, Rinehart and Winston.

Carnap, Rudolph (1947). *Meaning and Necessity: A Study in Semantics and Modal Logic*. Chicago: University of Chicago, Phoenix Books (paper, 1967).

Fodor, Jerry (1970). "Three Reasons for Not Deriving 'Kill' from 'Cause to Die'," *Linguistic Inquiry*, 1.4, 429–438.

Kripke, Saul (1963). "Semantical Considerations on Modal Logic," *Acta Philosophica Fennica*, Fasc. 16, 83–94.

Kripke, Saul (1972). "Naming and Necessity," in D. Davidson and G. Harman, eds., *Semantics of Natural Language*. Dordrecht: Reidel.

Lakoff, George (1970). *Irregularity in Syntax*. New York: Holt, Rinehart and Winston.

Lakoff, George (1972). "Linguistics and Natural Logic," in Davidson and Harman (1972) (*op. cit.*)

McCawley, James D. (1970). "Where Do Noun Phrases Come From?," in R. Jacobs and P. Rosenbaum, eds., *Readings in English Transformational Grammar*. Waltham, Mass.: Ginn and Co.

Montague, Richard (1973). "The proper treatment of quantification in ordinary English," in K. J. J. Hintikka, J. M. E. Moravcsik, and P. Suppes, eds., *Approaches to Natural Language: Proceedings of the 1970 Stanford Workshop on Grammar and Semantics*. Dordrecht: Reidel.

Partee, Barbara H. (1972a). "Some transformational extensions of Montangue grammar," in R. Rodman, ed., *Papers in Montague Grammar*. UCLA Occasional Papers in Linguistics #2, Los Angeles.

Partee, Barbara H. (1972b). "Montague Grammar and Transformational Grammar" (draft).

Quine, Willard V. O. (1960). *Word and Object*. Cambridge, Mass.: MIT Press.

Ross, John Robert (1972). "Act," in Davidson and Harman (1972) (*op. cit.*).

Thomason, Richmond, and R. C. Stalnaker (1973). "A Semantic Theory of Adverbs," *Linguistic Inquiry*, 4.2, 195–220.

Chapter 37

Sententialist Theories of Belief

Stephen Schiffer

DAVIDSON ON SAYING THAT

Davidson does not *explicitly* offer what we are in search of, a relational theory of propositional attitudes that tells us what propositional attitudes are relations to. But in his article "On Saying That" he does propose such a relational account of one kind of propositional attitude, that ascribed in sentences of the form '*x* said that *p*'; and a partial account of the logical form of all propositional-attitude ascriptions is offered that would at least greatly constrain answers to the question we have been concerned with. Actually, one problem that I shall raise is about the way Davidson intends his theory of saying-that to generalize to believing and the other propositional attitudes. Consequently, my most perspicuous strategy is first to describe Davidson's theory of saying-that and then to raise problems for it that would challenge the claim that that account provides the basis for a generalization applicable to all propositional attitudes.

The classic sententialist took belief ascriptions to contain (as it were) a two-place predicate 'believes that' and two singular terms, one denoting an alleged believer and the other—the sequence of words following 'that' —denoting itself. Switching from believing to another propositional attitude, this theorist would represent the logical form of

[1] Galileo said that the earth moves

as

S(Galileo, 'the earth moves').

First appeared in *Remnants of Meaning* (Cambridge: MIT Press, 1987), pp. 122–138. Reprinted by permission of the MIT Press.

In other words, 'said' (or 'said that') in [1] expresses a two-place relation that, if [1] is true, relates Galileo to the sentence-type 'the earth moves'. This relation will obtain by virtue of the meaning of the content sentence 'the earth moves' but is consistent with Galileo's having been a monolingual speaker of Italian.

Davidson, too, is eager to account for the logical form of [1]; he would like, that is, an account that leads us "to see the semantic character of the sentence—its truth or falsity—as owed to how it is composed, by a finite number of applications of some of a finite number of devices that suffice for the language as a whole, out of elements drawn from a finite stock (the vocabulary) that suffices for the language as a whole" (1968, p. 94) [p. 818 in this vol.]. For if Davidson could not give such an account, this would call into question his Tarskian program, which requires that there be such an account. This is one connection for Davidson between the theory of meaning and saying-that; another, of course, is that the theory of meaning has as its concern language understanding, and that consists precisely in the ability to know what speakers of a language are saying when they utter sentences of the language. Consequently, an account of saying-that must be part of any complete account of language understanding.

But while Davidson shares the need to account truth-theoretically for the logical form of [1], and while he would applaud the classic sententialist's eschewal of propositions as referents of 'that'-clauses, he would still find fault with that theorist's representation of [1] on the following two counts. First, sharing an objection already made, Davidson would object to taking the relatum of the saying-that relation to be a sentence "both because ... the reference [to a sentence] would then have to be relativized to a language, since a sentence may have different meanings in different languages; but also ... because the same sentence may have different truth values in the same language" (1975, pp. 165–166). Second, Davidson would raise an objection not raised in the last section, one that he would also raise against the Fregean: both the Fregean and the classic sententialist assign to the content sentence in [1], 'the earth moves', a semantic role that is radically different from its normal one. They construe it (qualifications aside) as the larger part of a *singular term*, 'that the earth moves', which refers in [1] to what Galileo said—to a proposition, for the Fregean, to the sentence 'the earth moves' for the classic sententialist. Here, Davidson is well aware, both theorists are motivated by failures of coextensional substitutions in the content sentence to preserve truth value. Even so, Davidson would prefer a theory in which the content sentence had only its old familiar semantic properties. At the same time, Davidson recognizes the need for a relational theory of propositional-attitude verbs to cohere with his Tarskian conception of a compositional semantics.

Thus Davidson wants a theory of [1] that satisfies the following desiderata:

a. 'Said' in [1] is represented as a two-place relational predicate.[1]

b. The things in the range of that relation have truth values but are neither propositions nor sentences.

c. A relatum of that relation *chez* Galileo (i.e., something to which Galileo stands in the saying relation of indirect discourse) is referred to in [1].

d. The content sentence 'the earth moves' has in [1] its normal and familiar semantic properties, its normal sense and reference. It is not part of any singular term; the only reference of 'the earth' is the earth, and the only extension determined for 'the earth moves' is its truth value. Sub-stitutivity *savla veritate* in the content sentence applies as usual.

Davidson's terrifically ingenious solution is well known. What we have in [1] is an instance of parataxis. Semantically speaking, the utterance of [1] is not the utterance of one sentence that contains 'the earth moves' as a part, but rather utterances of two sentences paratactically joined, some-thing best represented as

Galileo said that. The earth moves.

Here 'the earth moves' is seen to occur, not as part of a single sentence that contains the 'said' construction, but as an autonomous utterance with its predictable sense and reference: this utterance is true iff the earth moves. At the same time, the word 'that' in the first utterance occurs as a *demonstrative*, whose referent is the utterance that follows it; and the first utterance is true just in case Galileo stands in the saying relation of indi-rect discourse to the referent of 'that', i.e., to the utterance in question of 'the earth moves'. And he will stand in that relation, Davidson tells us— not as part of his account of the logical form of [1], but as an intuitive and informal gloss of it—provided that he himself produced an utterance that matches in content the speaker of [1]'s utterance of 'the earth moves'. This explains why it is that, although the occurrence of a content sentence is autonomous, it is typically not *asserted*: the speaker produces it not to express his own opinion but so that he will have produced an utterance that itself has a content that can be exploited to reveal the content of some utterance, no doubt in Italian, of Galileo's.

In this way the above desiderata are achieved.

We achieve (a) because 'said' is in effect represented as

[2] $S(x, u)$,

that is, as a two-place relation between a speaker x and any *actual* utterance u that matches some utterance of x's in content.[2]

We achieve (b) because these utterances have truth values.

We achieve (c) because 'that' in [1] is a singular term that refers to an utterance—viz., the utterance of the sentence following it—to which Galileo stands in the saying-that relation.

And we achieve (d) because the "analysis accounts for the usual failure of substitutivity in attributions of attitude without invoking any nonstandard semantics, for the reference of the 'that' changes with any change in the following utterance" (Davidson 1979, p. 119).[3]

Davidson is aware that his theory must be importantly revised in order to account for quantifications into 'that'-clauses; because as his theory now stands, it has no way of making sense of an utterance such as

Galileo said of a certain person that she baked terrific lasagna.

Nor, relatedly, can it account for the ambiguity, induced by possibilities pertaining to Galileo's knowledge or ignorance of who baked terrific lasagna, of

Galileo said that his mother baked terrific lasagna.

The problems raised by these "*de re*" issues are formidable, and I am aware of no very plausible solution available to Davidson. But these familiar problems are not ones that I shall press.

Another problem with Davidson's theory of saying-that with which I shall not be concerned but which I do feel compelled just to mention (partly because, to my amazement, I have never seen it raised before), is this: it is by no means clear what the application of Davidson's theory to *French* would be. For it is essential to at least the initial *plausibility* of Davidson's theory *as applied to English* that the word 'that' does have a use as a free-standing demonstrative; otherwise the suggestion that 'that' in [1] ('Galileo said that the earth moves') is a demonstrative would be worse than bizarre. But now consider the French translation of [1]:

[1'] Galilei a dit que la terre bouge.

The word 'que' in French has no use as a demonstrative. So what could possibly be the application of Davidson's theory to [1']? (To be sure, Davidson could restate his theory in a way that did not entail that 'that' in [1] was a singular term. He would then probably have to say that 'that' was not occurring as a genuine semantical unit but was an orthographic part of the semantically primitive verb 'to say that'. But then there would be no term in [1] that carried the reference to the utterance of 'the earth moves', and one may wonder about the plausibility of the paratactic account without the attendant claim about 'that'.)

At all events, it is a few other problems that I want now to raise for Davidson's theory of saying-that, and for the extension of it to belief ascriptions.

THREE PROBLEMS

I shall now describe three problems for Davidson's theory, each of which seems to require, at best, that the theory be revised in some important way. In each case I shall mention a possible or mandatory revision, but I shall not dwell on them or draw dire conclusions until the end, when the conclusion reached will have application to any sententialist position.

First problem

Davidson intends his account of the logical form of [1] to be the basis for a general account of the logical form of propositional-attitude ascriptions, and his account of saying-that would be of only marginal interest if this were not the case. How, then, does Davidson intend his theory to be extended to the other attitudes, and to believing in particular?

Consider this utterance:

[3] Galileo believed that the earth moves.

Davidson has made it clear (in, for example, Davidson 1975) that he intends the analysis of the logical form of [3] to have this much in common with that of [1]: First, the logical form of [3] is that of two utterances paratactically joined, and thus best represented as

Galileo believed that. The earth moves.

Second, as in [1], 'that' in [3] is a demonstrative, its referent the utterance following it of 'the earth moves'. Third, 'believes' is thus a two-place relational predicate, and the range of the belief relation—the values of 'y' in the schema 'x believes y'—includes actual utterances.

But now we come to an important *dissimilarity*, and with it the first problem. For whereas the saying-relation of [1] could plausibly be represented as [2]—that is, as a relation to *actual utterances*—the believing-relation of [3] cannot be correctly represented as a two-place relation,

$$B(x, u),$$

which relates a believer x to an *actual utterance u*. The representation of the saying-that relation as [2] is plausible because if

Galileo said something

is true, then there can be no barrier to inferring

$$(\exists u)S(\text{Galileo}, u),$$

for there is always Galileo's own utterance to be an utterance to which he stands in the saying-relation as portrayed in [2]. But if

Galileo believed something

is true, then there *is* a barrier to inferring

$$(\exists u)B(\text{Galileo}, u);$$

namely, that there may not be any actual utterance that gives the content of Galileo's belief. (Cf. Loar 1976a, p. 148; Leeds 1979, p. 51.) He may never have expressed his belief, and it may be that no one ever produced an utterance that conveys the content of his belief. Believing could be represented as a relation to actual utterances only if one could be assured that for every belief there was some actual utterance that gave the content of that belief; but of course one cannot be so assured.

Well, what things are available to Davidson to be the objects in the range of the belief relation, that is, the values of 'y' in 'x believes y'? There are two moves that might be entertained by way of answering this question. One is still within the bounds of *sententialist* theories of the belief relation, while the other jumps those bounds and regresses to the theory that believing is a relation, not to any sort of *public-language* entity, but to a mental representation, in this case, a belief state-token.

The nonsententialist move seeks to press an analogy with the analysis of the saying-that relation. According to Davidson, an utterance of [1] ('Galileo said that the earth moves') is true provided that some utterance-token of Galileo's had the same content as the speaker of [1]'s utterance of 'the earth moves'. Why not say, then, that an utterance of [3] ('Galileo believed that the earth moves') is true provided that some belief state-token of Galileo's had the same content as the speaker of [3]'s utterance of 'the earth moves'? And if one can say that, then why not say, further, that believing is a relation between a person and a belief state-token? Anything is a *candidate* for being a value of 'y' in 'x believes y' if it has a truth value, and the neural state-tokens that are beliefs have them: if neural state-token n is my present belief that worms do not have noses, then that state, being a belief that worms do not have noses, is true if and only if worms do not have noses. The state n, is a *mental representation*: since it has the truth condition it has, it represents the state of affairs that worms do not have noses. It may seem a little strange to say that believing is a relation to beliefs, but we can get over that. And if we do say that, then there is no trouble with representing 'Galileo believed something'. That becomes just what we might expect,

$(\exists x)B(\text{Galileo}, x)$,

the value of 'x' that makes this true being any belief state-token Galileo happened to be in.

The preceding chapter may already have discredited the view that believing is a relation to a mental representation; I shall ignore this possibility, however, and raise three problems that might be raised by someone who had not read that chapter.

1. On Davidson's theory of saying-that, [1] first gives way to

Galileo said that. The earth moves.

And then the logical form of the first utterance is represented as

$S(\text{Galileo}, \text{that})$.

As a representation of *logical form*, this is satisfying. Among other virtues, the form, thus represented, nicely mirrors the sentence's surface structure; for example, although '$S(\text{Galileo}, \text{that})$' gets *analyzed* as

$(\exists x)(x$ was an utterance & x was by Galileo
& x had the same content as that),

nothing about sameness of content enters into the representation of logical form. From the point of view of logical form, 'says' is a semantical primitive that happens to be roughly explicable in a certain way.

But now let us consider the required treatment of [3] if believing is a relation to belief states. As with [1], [3] first gives way to

Galileo believed that. The earth moves.

But a big difference emerges at the next stage, in the representation of the logical form of 'Galileo believed that'. That cannot be represented as

B(Galileo, that),

for the referent of 'that' is an utterance, and brain states, not utterances, constitute the range of the belief relation on the present hypothesis. The representation of logical form must either be

$(\exists x)(B$(Galileo, x) & x had the same content as that),

at best, or

$(\exists x)(x$ was a belief state & Galileo was in x
& B(Galileo, x) & x had the same content as that),

at worst. Either representation would be a very significant departure from the neatness of Davidson's original idea, and a great deal of work would have to be done before it could be made plausible as a representation of logical form.

2. If neural state-token n is a belief that worms do not have noses, then it has content: it has the content ascribed in the 'that'-clause, 'that worms do not have noses'. On most views, 'that'-clauses do not refer to beliefs— that is, to the neural state-tokens that are beliefs—but to entities which have truth values and other content-determining features that *determine* the content of beliefs. Thus, for the propositionalist, n's having its content just is its standing in the relevant belief relation to the proposition that worms do not have noses; and for the sententialist, n's having its content just is its standing in the relevant belief relation to a certain linguistic entity with the relevant content. For the propositionalist and the sententialist, then, one needs no *independent* account of the content of beliefs; the theory of belief content *just is* the theory of content for the objects of belief. That one needs no independent account of the content of belief state-tokens is part of the attraction of these views. But on the view being proposed, according to which believing is a relation to belief state-tokens, *one would need an independent account of the content of belief state-tokens.* If my utterance of [3] means that Galileo believed some belief state-token of his that had the same content as my utterance of 'the earth moves', then we are owed some independent account of the content-determining features of that belief state-token that would show this to be true. And what might such an account look like? Davidson seems not to have addressed this question.

3. Moreover, it is not even clear that it could make sense for Davidson to say that a belief b had the same content as an utterance u. For how is the sameness-in-content relation invoked in the representation of the logical form of [3] to be spelled out? We could not without circularity say that b and u had the same content if, for one and the same such-and-such, b was a belief that such-and-such while u was a statement that such-and-such. Evidently, the claim that b and u had the same content would have to mean that there was some content-determining feature Φ such that b had Φ and u had Φ.[4] But for Davidson the content-determining features of utterances are to be unpacked in terms of what gets ascribed in theorems of a Tarksian truth theory for the language to which the utterance belongs, which truth theory satisfies certain formal and empirical constraints. Mental representations, are cheaply purchased: we have them if brain states are beliefs. But would Davidson want to be committed to the view that brain states are, or involve, sentences of a neural language that enjoys a Tarskian description?

So much for the retrograde nonsententialist answer to the question of what for Davidson might be the values of 'y' in 'x believes y', given that those values cannot be utterance-tokens. *Our* present interest in Davidson, fueled by the theory of content, is in what *sententialist* theory of the belief relation he may have to offer. And the only remaining sententialist answer, it would appear, is that believing is a relation to *utterance-kinds*, or possible utterances (I think that for our purposes we can take these as coming to the same thing). Because kinds can be uninstantiated, this revision would not be subject to the difficulty that infected the theory that believing was a relation to utterance-tokens.

But if Davidson is constrained to say that believing is a relation to an utterance-kind, then this will have for him the following problematic features.

1. Davidson's theory of propositional attitudes is driven by his need to find a theory of them that coheres with his account of the form that a meaning theory for a particular language should take. Now the hallmark of his famous Tarskian proposal about the form that a meaning theory should take is that it is *extensional*; not for Davidson is a compositional semantics whose theorems relate sentences to intensions, but rather one that issues in the well-understood extensionality of

'Snow is white' is true iff snow is white.

Now the problem with the only apparent extension of Davidson's account of saying-that to believing is just this: *How is one to square a quantification over utterance-kinds with this extensionalist program*? On the face of it, utterance-kinds are universals; if one has them, one has properties, propositions, and the lot, and no need to worry then about achieving an extensionalist semantics (cf. Leeds 1979, p. 51). (Utterance-kinds cannot be construed as sets, for then all beliefs whose contents had never been expressed would have, unacceptably, the same object, viz., the empty set.)

2. If Davidson is constrained to say that believing is a relation to an utterance-kind, then an utterance-kind, and not an actual utterance, should be represented as the relatum of the belief relation that is referred to in [3], 'Galileo believed that the earth moves'. Davidson, in other words has misrepresented his position on the logical form of [3] if he is constrained to say that believing is a relation to utterance-kinds. The logical form of 'Galileo believed that' in [3] should not be represented as

B(Galileo, that),

where 'that' refers to the actual utterance of 'the earth moves', but should be represented as, say,

B(Galileo, the utterance-kind to which that belongs).[5]

In still other words, the skit involved in the utterance of [3] should be portrayed thus:

[4] The earth moves.
   Galileo believed that kind of utterance.

3. Unfortunately, one cannot just say that believing is a relation to an utterance-kind; one has to say what *sort* of utterance-kind. The issue here can be illuminated by noticing the glaring inadequacy of [4]: the utterance of 'the earth moves' will be of *many* kinds. Which one, then, is being referred to in [3]? Presumably, the kinds would have to be individuated by the *contents* of the utterances they subsume. Perhaps, then, a better version of the skit involved in the utterance of [3] would be

The earth moves.
Galileo believed the utterance-kind to which an utterance belongs just in case it has the same content as my last utterance.

But even this will not do as it stands. One reason (another comes later) is that 'content' is a term of art in this context, and we really have not been told what is being referred to in [3] as the relatum of the belief relation *chez* Galileo until we have been given an account of what the content-determining features of an utterance are. This is not the tired old objection that Davidson's account of saying-that relies on an unexplicated notion of sameness of content. *That* objection is a bad one; for Davidson's account of the logical form of saying-that sentences relies on no such notion. On Davidson's theory, 'says' of indirect discourse is a *semantically primitive* predicate that relates a person to an actual utterance, and it is further consistent with his theory to hold that the relation expressed is not strictly definable. Talk of "sameness of content" is intended merely as an informal gloss on conceptual connections that the saying-that relation bears to other of our semantic concepts—as " 'an expository and heuristic device': an aid in instructing novices in the use of the saying primitive" (McDowell 1980, p. 231; the inner quotation is from Davidson 1976, p. 177). But the point that I am making is that the role of "content" in Davidson's theory cannot be comfortably trivialized in this way *on the revision being entertained*. On the required revision, 'that' may still be seen as referring to an actual utterance, but now it will no longer enjoy a primary occurrence. Its occurrence will be ensconced in an implicit occurrence of the singular term 'the kind of utterances having the same content as that', and my point is that we will not know the *reference* of that singular term until we know what notion of content is here intended.

But is there really a problem here? Is not the needed sense of 'sameness of content' already available in Davidson's theory of the form that a meaning theory for a particular language should take? We are shortly to see that the answer to this question is no.

Second problem

The objection here, which I owe to Brian Loar (in conversation), is that Davidson's theory of saying-that is in conflict with a certain correct principle about the function of singular terms in content sentences. Before this principle can be stated, we need the following definition:

An occurrence of a singular term in a sentence is a *primary* occurrence iff that occurrence is not properly contained within the occurrence of some other singular term.

Thus, the occurrence of 'that car' in

That car is blue

is primary, whereas in

George's car is blue

only 'George's car' has a primary occurrence; 'George' has a secondary occurrence.

Now I can state the principle alluded to, which is this:

[P] If the occurrence of the singular term t in ⌜So-and-so said that ... t ...⌝ is primary and refers to x, then that sentence is true only if so-and-so also referred to x.

Thus, suppose I say,

Ralph said that she drove that car,

myself referring to a certain woman and a certain car. Then my utterance is true only if Ralph also referred to that woman and that car. The reason for the restriction to primary references is this. Consider my utterance of

Ralph said that she drove George's car,

where I again refer to a certain woman and a certain car. In order for my last utterance to be true, Ralph must have referred somehow to George's car; but he need not have referred to George, for he need not have referred to the car as George's car. Perhaps the utterance of Ralph's that makes us samesayers is his utterance of 'She drove that car'.

We can see the problem for Davidson in all this if we now consider

[5] Laplace said that Galileo said that the earth moves.

It follows from Davidson's theory that the second occurrence of 'that' in [5] is the primary occurrence of a singular term whose referent is the utterance following it of 'the earth moves'. Whence we have the following argument in refutation of Davidson:

1. [P].
2. If Davidson's theory is correct, the second occurrence of 'that' in [5] is a primary occurrence, whose referent is the occurrence in [5] of 'the earth moves'.
3. But [5] can be true even though Laplace did not refer to that utterance.
4. Ergo, Davidson's theory is not correct.

This argument is valid, and the only premise Davidson could conceivably challenge is (1). But how is the strategy of denying [P] to be pursued? Davidson cannot with any degree of plausibility simply claim that the uses of 'that' in question constitute the sole exception to [P]. He must either (a) discredit the principle independently of its present application or else (b) give a *principled* explanation of why the occurrences of 'that' in question constitute an exception to [P]. But I am doubtful that either of these strategies can be pursued successfully. It seems to me that the more promising way out for Davidson would be to revise his theory just enough to bring it in line with [P]. The needed revision turns out to be the one he is already committed to if his paratactic theory is both to accommodate belief ascriptions and to remain a sententialist theory of the belief relation. The idea is to construe 'that' as really having a secondary occurrence in the implicit singular term 'the kind of utterances having the same content as that'. This would plainly square [5] with [P], but it would also, alas, encounter the difficulties we have just finished rehearsing in the first problem.

Third problem

This, I think, is the really urgent problem. Succinctly put, the objection is as follows: Davidson's representation of

[a] Sam PAs that flounders snore.

as

[b] Sam PAs that. Flounders snore.

cannot be right, for (1) one cannot know the *assertion made*, the truth stated, by [a] without knowing *what* Sam PAs, the *content* of his PA; but (2) one can know the assertion made by [b] without knowing what Sam PAs, the content of his PA.

Now (1) seems correct. If in uttering 'Sam said that flounders snore' you assert truly that Sam said that flounders snore, and if I know what truth you asserted in your utterance, then I know that Sam said that flounders snore. And if I know this, then I certainly know the content of Sam's statement. I know that what Sam said is about flounders and snoring; and I know, especially, that what he said is true just in case flounders snore. Davidson, if he acknowledges (2), is evidently constrained to maintain either that I can know the truth you asserted without knowing that Sam said that flounders snore, or that knowing that does not carry with it any knowledge whatever of the content of Sam's statement. What basis can he have for pursuing either of these disjuncts other than the need to be consistent with his theory?

But (2) is just as certainly correct. To see this clearly, let us start with the following dialogue:

Pierre La neige est blanche.
Donald Tarski said that.

The relevant point about this is that it is a consequence of Davidson's theory that one can know what Donald asserted without knowing the content of Pierre's utterance, and thus without knowing the content of Tarski's saying. For one can know that some utterance of Tarski's had the same content as Pierre's utterance without knowing the content of either utterance.

With this in mind, let us now consider the Davidsonian representation of

[6] Sam said that flounders snore,

which, of course, is

[7] Sam said that. Flounders snore.

Here the only *assertion* made is made by the first utterance, 'Sam said that'. What this asserts, according to Davidson, is that some utterance of Sam's has the same content as the foregoing utterance of 'Flounders snore'. But this, as (2) correctly notes, can be known without knowing the content of either utterance. So, on Davidson's account, one can know the assertion made by [6], namely, the assertion made by the first utterance in [7], without knowing the content of what Sam said. To be sure, one who knows English and hears the whole of [7] will know the content of Sam's statement because he knows the meaning of 'flounders snore'; but that hardly controverts (2). For if *all that one knew* was what was *asserted* by the first utterance of [7], then one would not know what Sam said.

Here is what I take to be another, but non-epistemic, way of making essentially the same objection (to forestall a certain reply, I have changed the example from saying to believing): (1) The sentence

[i] Sam believes that flounders snore

entails

[ii] Sam believes something that is true iff flounders snore

in this sense: there is no possible world in which Sam believes that flounders snore but does not believe something that is true iff flounders snore. (2) But [ii] would not be entailed by [i] if Davidson's theory were correct. For if that theory were correct, then [i] would be representable as

Flounders snore.
Sam believes that.

And from this one cannot in any sense infer [ii] without the further, contingent premise

That (i.e., the preceding utterance of 'Flounders snore') is true iff flounders snore.

Is there any way Davidson's theory can be revised to avoid this objection? Perhaps. At least there is a line to be explored, an extension of the revision already seen to be required by the preceding two objections.

On Davidson's original, unrevised theory, [6] got represented as

S(Sam, that),

the referent of 'that' being the utterance in [6] of 'flounders snore'. Then we noticed that if Davidson is to avoid the first two of our objections, he would do better to represent [6] as

[8] *S*(Sam, the utterance-kind to which an utterance belongs just in case it has the same content as that),

'that' construed as before, only now having a secondary, rather than a primary, occurrence.

But even [8] will not escape our third objection; for someone could know the assertion made by [8] without knowing the content of the utterance referred to by 'that'. What is needed is to get a specification of the actual content of the content sentence 'flounders snore' into the reference to the utterance-kind.

Recall Mme S's utterance 'Monsieur, votre fille a mordu mon singe encore une fois'. To understand her utterance, we have noted, is to know what she said in it. Suppose that one knows that she did say something in producing her utterance. What *more* would one have to know in order to know what she said and thereby to understand her utterance? Intuitively, one wants to answer: the *content* of her utterance. Earlier I described the compositional semanticist's thought that there is some feature of Mme S's utterance such that if one knew that the utterance had it, then one would be in a position to interpret Mme S's utterance, that is, to know what she said in producing it. Suppose that utterances have such content-determining features and that Φ is that feature for the utterance of the content sentence 'flounders snore'. This, to repeat, would be to say that if someone were to utter 'Flounders snore' assertively, then a hearer would be in a position to interpret that utterance—to know what the utterer said—if the hearer knew that that utterance had Φ. Then one could entertain avoiding our third objection by revising Davidson's theory in such a way as to yield the following representation of the skit performed in uttering [6]:

[9] Sam said the kind of utterances that are Φ, like that. Flounders
      snore.

In short, if Davidson is to have a theory of propositional-attitude
ascriptions that avoids the three objections raised, then he will have to
find content-determining features of utterances and construe propositional attitudes as relations to *utterance-kinds as individuated by those
features*, in the way indicated by [9].

There are, I think, several problems with this entertained way out,
but here is the most serious of them: In order for there to be content-
determining features that enter into propositional-attitude ascriptions
in the way indicated in [9], such features will obviously have to be within
the ken of ordinary people; but the only content-determining features that
are even prima facie available do not enter into anyone's propositional
knowledge.

This objection brings us back to Davidson's theory of the nature of
meaning theories for particular languages, and to the curious feature of
the theory that whereas, on Davidson's theory [MT], every sentence of a
language has a content-determining feature, no one who understands the
language knows, for any sentence σ and its content-determining feature
Φ, that σ has Φ. For suppose that Sam utters, assertively and literally, the
sentence

[10] Flounders snore,

and that Carla knows this. Is there any feature Φ of [10] such that if Carla
also knew that [10] had Φ, then she would be able to interpret Sam's
utterance—be able, that is, to know that in uttering [10] Sam said that
flounders snore? Now Davidson, we know, does hold that there is such a
feature. For his theory of meaning commits him to holding that

It will suffice for Carla to interpret Sam's utterance of [10] if (refinements aside)
she knows (a) that [10] is true iff flounders snore, (b) that that fact is entailed by a
correct, finitely axiomatized, extensional, Tarski-style truth theory for the language to which [10] belongs, and (c) that that truth theory satisfies ___ empirical
constraints.

(Imagine the blank filled by a specification of the empirical constraints
forthcoming from Davidson's finished theory.)

But we have already noticed the main problem with this as regards
our present concern. Even if it were true, the content-determining features
specified are not ones that enter into anyone's propositional knowledge.
If there are Davidsonian content-determining features, then they are not

within the ken of plain folk. This means that we cannot construe propositional attitudes as relations to utterance-kinds as specified by such content-determining features; for that proposal makes sense only if plain people know that these features are features of utterances.

Now the point just made about Davidsonian content-determining features remains true no matter how the blank in (c) is filled: the knowledge required by (b) already secures that whatever content-determining features are determined by a specification of empirical constraints will be beyond the ken of plain folk. This means that if there are any extensionalist content-determining features, then they, too, will be beyond the ken of plain people. If there is *any* extensionalist meaning theory for a language L that explicitly states something knowledge of which would suffice for interpreting utterances in L, then no one knows what that theory states.

SOME CONSEQUENCES

I conclude that there can be no correct sententialist theory of propositional attitudes for at least this reason. Any such theory would require that the values of 'y' in

x PAs y

be utterance-kinds individuated by features that are content-determining, within the ken of plain folk, and consonant with the extensionalist account of compositional semantics. But no such features will ever materialize.

Since there can be no correct sententialist theory of propositional attitudes, I also conclude that there can be no correct extensionalist account of compositional semantics for natural languages. For we saw that the extensionalist with respect to compositional meaning theories was constrained to be a sententialist with respect to propositional attitudes. This conclusion, however, is about to be swallowed by the larger conclusion that there can be no correct account of compositional semantics of any kind.

Earlier chapters argued that there can be no correct nonsententialist account of believing. As this one concludes that there can be no correct sententialist account, I further conclude, by elimination, that the relational theory of propositional attitudes is false: nothing is available to constitute the range of values of 'y'.

I thus conclude that various phenomena that would appear to support the relational theory must not really support it. For example, one would think that if John believes that snow is white and Mary believes that snow is white, then there is something that John and Mary both believe. But if the relational theory is false, then the last conditional is false—either that or the ostensible quantification in its consequent over things believed is not all that, to a Quinean eye, it might appear to be.

I further conclude that no natural language has a correct compositional truth-theoretic semantics; for if they did, then the relational theory of propositional attitudes would be correct.

I further conclude that no natural language has a correct compositional meaning theory; for I cannot see how such a theory could fail to be a truth-theoretic semantics.

So I must also conclude that compositional semantics are not needed to explain language understanding, or anything else.

Notes

1. This ignores complexities arising from quantification into the position of the content sentence. The next note introduces a further possible qualification.

2. Although this is the official position in the text of Davidson 1968, it is evidently denied in a footnote added in 1982. In that note Davidson says of his analysis of 'Galileo said that the earth moves', "Strictly speaking, the verb 'said' is here analysed as a three-place predicate which holds of a speaker (Galileo), an utterance of the speaker ('Eppur si muove'), and an utterance of the attributer ('The earth moves')" (p. 104 [831 in this vol.]). But this seems not to be true. Davidson's account of 'Galileo said that' commits him to holding (a) that 'that' refers to an utterance of 'the earth moves' and (b) that the ascription is true if Galileo uttered some sentence (e.g. 'Eppur si move') with the same content as the referent of 'that'. Yet this certainly does not entail that 'said' is a three-place relation; one can certainly have a two-place relation that is defined in terms of a three-place relation (e.g., 'x photocopied y'). Clearly, the surface grammer of 'Galileo said that' favors construing 'said' as a two-place relation, as there is no grammatical slot for a third singular term (with Davidson I am ignoring implicit temporal references), and parity with 'believes' favors the dyadic construal. But nothing important turns on this issue.

3. Davidson's point, of course, is that all of the positions in, say,

Galileo said that. The earth moves.

are extensional, but that substitutions in the second sentence can change the truth value of the first because it will change the reference of 'that'.

4. It should be noticed that it is completely irrelevant to remark that the sameness-in-content relation may be taken as primitive in the construction of a theory

of logical form for belief sentences. Of course that is so; but that is consistent with knowing that in the *theory of content* the relation is to be explicated in terms of nonrelative content-determining features. Surely any plausible theory of content will understand 'x has the same content as y' on the model of 'x has the same weight as y'.

5. 'That' still refers to an actual utterance, but it now no longer refers to that which Galileo believes; rather than having a primary occurrence, 'that' now has a secondary occurrence in another (implicit) singular term which does refer to what Galileo believes—the utterance-kind. Notice, too, how easily the Fregean can accept the paratactic aspect of Davidson's account: he can represent the logical form of [3] as

B(Galileo, the proposition expressed by that).

References

Davidson, D. (1968). "On Saying That." *Synthese* 19, 130–146. (Chapter 35 in this volume.)

Davidson, D. (1975). "Thought and Talk." In S. Guttenplan (ed.), *Mind and Language*. Oxford: Oxford University Press.

Davidson, D. (1976). "Reply to Foster." In G. Evans and J. McDowell (eds.), *Truth and Meaning*. Oxford: Oxford University Press.

Davidson, D. (1979). "Moods and Performances." In A. Margalit (ed.), *Meaning and Use*. Dordrecht: D. Reidel.

Leeds, S. (1979). "Church's Translation Argument." *Canadian Journal of Philosophy* 9, 43–51.

Loar, B. (1976). "Two Theories of Meaning." In G. Evans and J. McDowell (eds.), *Truth and Meaning*. Oxford: Oxford University Press.

McDowell, J. (1980). "Quotation and Saying That." In M. Platts (ed.), *Truth and Reality*. London: Routledge and Kegan Paul.

Chapter 38

A Puzzle about Belief

Saul A. Kripke

In this paper I will present a puzzle about names and belief. A moral or two will be drawn about some other arguments that have occasionally been advanced in this area, but my main thesis is a simple one: that the puzzle *is* a puzzle. And, as a corollary, that any account of belief must ultimately come to grips with it. Any speculation as to solutions can be deferred.

The first section of the paper gives the theoretical background in previous discussion, and in my own earlier work, that led me to consider the puzzle. The background is by no means necessary to *state* the puzzle: As a philosophical puzzle, it stands on its own, and I think its fundamental interest for the problem of belief goes beyond the background that engendered it. As I indicate in the third section, the problem really goes beyond beliefs expressed using names, to a far wider class of beliefs. Nevertheless, I think that the background illuminates the genesis of the puzzle, and it will enable me to draw one moral in the concluding section.

The second section states some general principles which underlie our general practice of reporting beliefs. These principles are stated in much more detail than is needed to comprehend the puzzle; and there are variant formulations of the principles that would do as well. Neither this section nor the first is necessary for an intuitive grasp of the central problem, discussed in the third section, though they may help with fine points of the discussion. The reader who wishes rapid access to the central problem could skim the first two sections lightly on a first reading.

In one sense the problem may strike some as no puzzle at all. For, in the situation to be envisaged, all the relevant facts can be described in *one*

First appeared in A. Margalit (ed.), *Meaning and Use* (Dordrecht: D. Reidel, 1979), pp. 239–283. Reprinted with kind permission from Kluwer Academic Publishers.

terminology without difficulty. But, in *another* terminology, the situation seems to be impossible to describe in a consistent way. This will become clearer later.

I PRELIMINARIES: SUBSTITUTIVITY

In other writings,[1] I developed a view of proper names closer in many ways to the old Millian paradigm of naming than to the Fregean tradition which probably was dominant until recently. According to Mill, a proper name is, so to speak, *simply* a name. It *simply* refers to its bearer, and has no other linguistic function. In particular, unlike a definite description, a name does not describe its bearer as possessing any special identifying properties.

The opposing Fregean view holds that to each proper name, a speaker of the language associates some property or (conjunction of properties) which determines its referent as the unique thing fulfilling the associated property (or properties). This property(ies) constitutes the 'sense' of the name. Presumably, if '...' is a proper name, the associated properties are those that the speaker would supply if asked, "Who is '...'?" If he would answer "... is the man who ___", the properties filling the second blank are those that determine the reference of the name for the given speaker and constitute its 'sense.' Of course, given the name of a famous historical figure, individuals may give different, and equally correct, answers to the "Who is '...'?" question. Some may identify Aristotle as the philosopher who taught Alexander the Great, others as the Stagirite philosopher who studied with Plato. For these two speakers, the sense of "Aristotle" will differ: in particular, speakers of the second kind, but not of the first kind, will regard "Aristotle, if he existed, was born in Stagira" as analytic.[2] Frege (and Russell)[3] concluded that, strictly speaking, different speakers of English (or German!) ordinarily use a name such as 'Aristotle' in different senses (though with the same reference). Differences in properties associated with such names, strictly speaking, yield different idiolects.[4]

Some later theorists in the Frege-Russellian tradition have found this consequence unattractive. So they have tried to modify the view by 'clustering' the sense of the name (e.g. Aristotle is the thing having the following long list of properties, or at any rate most of them), or, better for the present purpose, socializing it (what determines the reference of 'Aristotle' is some roughly specified set of *community-wide* beliefs about Aristotle).

One way to point up the contrast between the strict Millian view and Fregean views involves—if we permit ourselves the jargon—the notion of propositional content. If a strict Millian view is correct, and the linguistic function of a proper name is completely exhausted by the fact that it names its bearer, it would appear that proper names of the same thing are everywhere interchangeable not only *salva veritate* but even *salva significatione*: the proposition expressed by a sentence should remain the same no matter what name of the object it uses. Of course this will not be true if the names are 'mentioned' rather than 'used': "'Cicero' has six letters" differs from "'Tully' has six letters" in truth value, let alone in content. (The example, of course, is Quine's.) Let us confine ourselves at this stage to *simple* sentences involving no connectives or other sources of intensionality. If Mill is completely right, not only should "Cicero was lazy" have the same *truth value* as "Tully was lazy", but the two sentences should express the same *proposition*, have the same content. Similarly, "Cicero admired Tully", "Tully admired Cicero", "Cicero admired Cicero", and "Tully admired Tully" should be four ways of saying the same thing.[5]

If such a consequence of Mill's view is accepted, it would seem to have further consequences regarding 'intensional' contexts. Whether a sentence expresses a necessary truth or a contingent one depends only on the proposition expressed and not on the words used to express it. So any simple sentence should retain its 'modal value' (necessary, impossible, contingently true, or contingently false) when 'Cicero' is replaced by 'Tully' in one or more places, since such a replacement leaves the content of the sentence unaltered. Of course this implies that coreferential names are substitutable in modal contexts *salva veritate*: "It is necessary (possible) that Cicero ..." and "It is necessary (possible) that Tully ..." must have the same truth value no matter how the dots are filled by a simple sentence.

The situation would seem to be similar with respect to contexts involving knowledge, belief, and epistemic modalities. Whether a given subject believes something is presumably true or false of such a subject no matter how that belief is expressed; so if proper name substitution does not change the content of a sentence expressing a belief, coreferential proper names should be interchangeable *salva veritate* in belief contexts. Similar reasoning would hold for epistemic contexts ("Jones knows that ...") and contexts of epistemic necessity ("Jones knows *a priori* that ..."), and the like.

All this, of course, would contrast strongly with the case of definite descriptions. It is well known that substitution of coreferential descriptions in simple sentences (without operators), on any reasonable conception of 'content,' *can* alter the content of such a sentence. In particular, the modal value of a sentence is not invariant under changes of coreferential descriptions: "The smallest prime is even" expresses a necessary truth, but "Jones's favourite number is even" expresses a contingent one, even if Jones's favourite number happens to be the smallest prime. It follows that coreferential descriptions are *not* interchangeable *salva veritate* in modal contexts: "It is necessary that the smallest prime is even" is true while "It is necessary that Jones's favourite number is even" is false.

Of course there is a *'de re'* or 'large scope' reading under which the second sentence is true. Such a reading would be expressed more accurately by "Jones's favourite number is such that it is necessarily even" or, in rough Russellian transcription, as "One and only one number is admired by Jones above all others, and any such number is necessarily even (has the property of necessary evenness)." Such a *de re* reading, if it makes sense at all, by definition must be subject to a principle of substitution *salva veritate*, since necessary evenness is a property of the *number*, independently of how it is designated; in this respect there can be no contrast between names and descriptions. The contrast, according to the Millian view, must come in the *de dicto* or "small scope" reading, which is the *only* reading, for belief contexts as well as modal contexts, that will concern us in this paper. If we wish, we can emphasize that this is our reading in various ways. Say, "It is necessary that: Cicero was bald" or, more explicitly, "The following proposition is necessarily true: Cicero was bald", or even, in Carnap's 'formal' mode of speech[6] "'Cicero was bald' expresses a necessary truth". Now the Millian asserts that all these formulations retain their truth value when 'Cicero' is replaced by 'Tully,' even though 'Jones's favourite Latin author' and 'the man who denounced Catiline' would *not* similarly be interchangeable in these contexts even if they are codesignative.

Similarly for belief contexts. Here too *de re* beliefs—as in "Jones believes, *of* Cicero (or: *of* his favourite Latin author) that he was bald" do *not* concern us in this paper. Such contexs, if they make sense, are by definition subject to a substitutivity principle for both names and descriptions. Rather we are concerned with the *de dicto* locution expressed explicitly in such formulations as, "Jones believes that: Cicero was bald" (or: "Jones believes that: the man who denounced Catiline was bald").

The material after the colon expresses the *content* of Jones's belief. Other, more explicit, formulations are: "Jones believes the proposition-that-Cicero-was-bald", or even in the 'formal' mode, "The sentence 'Cicero was bald' gives the content of a belief of Jones". In all such contexts, the strict Millian seems to be committed to saying that codesignative names, but not codesignative descriptions, are interchangeable *salva veritate*.[7]

Now it has been widely assumed that these apparent consequences of the Millian view are plainly false. First, it seemed that sentences can alter their *modal* values by replacing a name by a codesignative one. "Hesperus is Hesperus" (or, more cautiously: "If Hesperus exists, Hesperus is Hesperus") expresses a necessary truth, while "Hesperus is Phosphorus" (or: "If Hesperus exists, Hesperus is Phosphorus"), expresses an empirical discovery, and hence, it has been widely assumed, a contingent truth. (It might have turned out, and hence might have been, otherwise.)

It has seemed even more obvious that codesignative proper names are not interchangeable in belief contexts and epistemic contexts. Tom, a normal speaker of the language, may sincerely assent to "Tully denounced Catiline", but not to "Cicero denounced Catiline". He may even deny the latter. And his denial is compatible with his status as a normal English speaker who satisfies normal criteria for using both 'Cicero' and 'Tully' as names for the famed Roman (without knowing that 'Cicero' and 'Tully' name the same person). Given this, it seems obvious that Tom believes that: Tully denounced Catiline, but that he does not believe (lacks the belief) that: Cicero denounced Catiline.[8] So it seems clear that codesignative proper names are not interchangeable in belief contexts. It also seems clear that there must be two distinct propositions or contents expressed by 'Cicero denounced Catiline' and 'Tully denounced Catiline'. How else can Tom believe one and deny the other? And the difference in propositions thus expressed can only come from a difference in *sense* between 'Tully' and 'Cicero'. Such a conclusion agrees with a Fregean theory and seems to be incompatible with a purely Millian view.[9]

In the previous work mentioned above, I rejected one of these arguments against Mill, the modal argument. 'Hesperus is Phosphorus', I maintained, expresses just as necessary a truth as 'Hesperus is Hesperus'; there are no counterfactual situations in which Hesperus and Phosphorus would have been different. Admittedly, the truth of 'Hesperus is Phosphorus' was not known *a priori*, and may even have been widely disbelieved before appropriate empirical evidence came in. But these epistemic questions should be separated, I have argued, from the metaphysical question of the necessity of 'Hesperus is Phosphorus'. And it is a consequence of my conception of names as 'rigid designators' that codesignative proper names are interchangeable *salva veritate* in all contexts of (metaphysical) necessity and possibility; further, that replacement of a proper name by a codesignative name leaves the modal value of any sentence unchanged.

But although my position confirmed the Millian account of names in modal contexts, it equally appears at first blush to imply a *non-Millian* account of epistemic and belief contexts (and other contexts of propositional attitude). For I presupposed a sharp contrast between epistemic and metaphysical possibility: Before appropriate empirical discoveries were made, men might well have failed to know that Hesperus was Phosphorus, or even to believe it, even though they of course knew and believed that Hesperus was Hesperus. Does not this support a Fregean position that 'Hesperus' and 'Phosphorus' have different 'modes of presentation' that determine their references? What else can account for the fact that, before astronomers identified the two heavenly bodies, a sentence using 'Hesperus' could express a common belief, while the same context involving 'Phosphorus' did not? In the case of 'Hesperus' and 'Phosphorus', it is pretty clear what the different 'modes of presentation' would be: one mode determines a heavenly body by its typical position and appearance, in the appropriate season, in the evening; the other determines the same body by its position and appearance, in the appropriate season, in the morning. So it appears that even though, according to my view, proper names would be *modally* rigid—would have the same reference when we use them to speak of counterfactual situations as they do when used to describe the actual world—they would have a kind of Fregean 'sense' according to how that rigid reference is fixed. And the divergences of 'sense' (in this sense of 'sense') would lead to failures of interchangeability of codesignative names in contexts of propositional attitude, though not in modal contexts. Such a theory would agree with Mill regarding modal contexts but with Frege regarding belief contexts. The theory would not be *purely* Millian.[10]

After further thought, however, the Fregean conclusion appears less obvious. Just as people are said to have been unaware at one time of the fact that Hesperus is Phosphorus, so a normal speaker of English apparently may not know that Cicero is Tully, or that Holland is the Netherlands. For he may sincerely assent to 'Cicero was lazy', while dissenting from 'Tully was lazy', or he may sincerely assent to 'Holland is a beautiful country', while dissenting from 'The Netherlands is a beautiful country'.

In the case of 'Hesperus' and Phosphorus', it seemed plausible to account for the parallel situation by supposing that 'Hesperus' and 'Phosphorus' fixed their (rigid) references to a single object in two conventionally different ways, one as the 'evening star' and one as the 'morning star'. But what corresponding *conventional* 'sense,' even taking 'senses' to be 'modes of fixing the reference rigidly', can plausibly be supposed to exist for 'Cicero' and 'Tully' (or 'Holland' and 'the Netherlands')? Are not these just two names (in English) for the same man? Is there any special *conventional, community-wide* 'connotation' in the one lacking in the other?[11] I am unaware of any.[12]

Such considerations might seem to push us toward the extreme Frege-Russellian view that the senses of proper names vary, strictly speaking, from speaker to speaker, and that there is no community-wide sense but only a community-wide reference.[13] According to such a view, the sense a given speaker attributes to such a name as 'Cicero' depends on which assertions beginning with 'Cicero' he accepts and which of these he regards as *defining*, for him, the name (as opposed to those he regards as mere factual beliefs 'about Cicero'). Similarly, for 'Tully'. For example, someone may define 'Cicero' as 'the Roman orator whose speech was Greek to Cassius', and 'Tully' as 'the Roman orator who denounced Catiline'. Then such a speaker may well fail to accept 'Cicero is Tully' if he is unaware that a single orator satisfied both descriptions (if Shakespeare and history are both to be believed). He may well, in his ignorance, affirm 'Cicero was bald' while rejecting 'Tully was bald', and the like. Is this not what actually occurs whenever someone's expressed beliefs fail to be indifferent to interchange of 'Tully' and 'Cicero'? Must not the source of such a failure lie in two distinct associated descriptions, or modes of determining the reference, of the two names? If a speaker does, as luck would have it, attach the same identifying properties both to 'Cicero' and to 'Tully,' he *will*, it would seem, use 'Cicero' and 'Tully' interchangeably. All this appears at first blush to be powerful support for the view of Frege and Russell that in general names are peculiar to idiolects, with 'senses' depending on the associated 'identifying descriptions'.

Note that, according to the view we are now entertaining, one *cannot* say, "Some people are unaware that Cicero is Tully." For, according to this view, there is no single proposition denoted by the 'that' clause, that the community of normal English speakers expresses by 'Cicero is Tully'. Some—for example, those who define both 'Cicero' and 'Tully' as 'the author of *De Fato*'—use it to express a trivial self-identity. Others use it to express the proposition that the man who satisfied one description (say, that he denounced Catiline) is one and the same as the man who satisfied another (say, that his speech was Greek to Cassius). There is no single fact, 'that Cicero is Tully', known by some but not all members of the community.

If I were to assert, "Many are unaware that Cicero is Tully", *I* would use 'that Cicero is Tully' to denote the proposition that *I* understand by these words. If this, for example, is a trivial self-identity, I would assert falsely, and irrelevantly, that there is widespread ignorance in the community of a certain self-identity.[14] I *can*, of course, say, "Some English speakers use both 'Cicero' and 'Tully' with the usual referent (the famed Roman) yet do not assent to 'Cicero is Tully.'"

This aspect of the Frege-Russellian view can, as before, be combined with a concession that names are rigid designators and that hence the description used to fix the reference of a name is not synonymous with it. But there are considerable difficulties. There is the obvious intuitive unpalatability of the notion that we use such proper names as 'Cicero', 'Venice', 'Venus' (the planet) with differing 'senses' and for this reason do not 'strictly speaking' speak a single language. There are the many well-known and weighty objections to any description or cluster-of-descriptions theory of names. And is it definitely so clear that failure of interchangeability in belief contexts implies some difference of sense? After all, there is a considerable philosophical literature arguing that even word pairs that are straightforward synonyms if any pairs are—"doctor" and "physician," to give one example—are not interchangeable *salva veritate* in belief contexts, at least if the belief operators are iterated.[15]

A minor problem with this presentation of the argument for Frege and Russell will emerge in the next section: if Frege and Russell are right, it is not easy to state the very argument from belief contexts that appears to support them.

But the clearest objection, which shows that the others should be given their proper weight, is this: the view under consideration does not in fact account for the phenomena it seeks to explain. As I have said elsewhere,[16] individuals who "define 'Cicero'" by such phrases as "the Catiline denouncer", "the author of *De Fato*", etc. are relatively rare: their prevalence in the philosophical literature is the product of the excessive classical learning of some philosophers. Common men who clearly use 'Cicero' as a name for Cicero may be able to give no better answer to "Who was Cicero?" than "a famous Roman orator", and they probably would say the same (if anything!) for 'Tully'. (Actually, most people probably have never heard the name 'Tully'.) Similarly, many people who have heard of both Feynman and Gell-Mann would identify each as 'a leading contemporary theoretical physicist'. Such people do not assign 'senses' of the usual type to the names that uniquely identify the referent (even though they use the names with a determinate reference). But to the extent that the *indefinite* descriptions attached or associated can be called 'senses', the 'senses' assigned to 'Cicero' and 'Tully', or to 'Feynman' and 'Gell-Mann', are *identical*.[17] Yet clearly speakers of this type can ask, "Were Cicero and Tully one Roman orator, or two different ones?" or "Are Feynman and Gell-Mann two different physicists, or one?" without knowing the answer to either question by inspecting 'senses' alone. Some such speaker might even conjecture, or be under the vague false impression, that, as he would say, 'Cicero was bald but Tully was not'. The premiss of the argument we are considering for the classic position of Frege and Russell—that whenever two codesignative names fail to be interchangeable in the expression of a speaker's beliefs, failure of interchangeability arises from a difference in the 'defining' descriptions the speaker associates with these names—is, therefore, false. The case illustrated by 'Cicero' and 'Tully' is, in fact, quite usual and ordinary. So the apparent failure of codesignative names to be everywhere interchangeable in belief contexts in not to be explained by differences in the 'senses' of these names.

Since the extreme view of Frege and Russell does not in fact explain the apparent failure of the interchangeability of names in belief contexts, there seems to be no further reason—for present purposes—not to give the other overwhelming *prima facie* considerations against the Frege-Russell view their full weight. Names of famous cities, countries, persons, and planets are the common currency of our common language, not terms used homonymously in our separate idiolects.[18] The apparent failure of codesignative names to be interchangeable in belief contexts remains a mystery, but the mystery no longer seems so clearly to argue for a Fregean view as against a Millian one. Neither differing public senses nor differing private senses peculiar to each speaker account for the phenomena to be explained. So the apparent existence of such phenomena no longer gives a *prima facie* argument for such differing senses.

One final remark to close this section. I have referred before to my own earlier views in "Naming and Necessity". I said above that these views, inasmuch as they make proper names rigid and transparent[19] in modal contexts, favour Mill, but that the concession that proper names are not transparent in belief contexts appears to favour Frege. On a closer examination, however, the extent to which these opacity phenomena really support Frege against Mill becomes much more doubtful. And there are important theoretical reasons for viewing the 'Naming and Necessity' approach in a Millian light. In that work I argued that ordinarily the real determinant of the reference of names of a former historical figure is a chain of communication, in which the reference of the name is passed from link to link. Now the legitimacy of such a chain accords much more with Millian views than with alternatives. For the view supposes that a learner acquires a name from the community by determining to use it with the same reference as does the community. We regard such a learner as using "Cicero is bald" to express the same thing the community expresses, regardless of variations in the properties different learners associate with 'Cicero', as long as he determines that he will use the name with the referent current in the community. That a name can be transmitted in this way accords nicely with a Millian picture, according to which only the reference, not more specific properties associated with the name, is relevant to the semantics of sentences containing it. It has been suggested that the chain of communication, which on the present picture determines the reference, might thereby itself be called a 'sense'. Perhaps so—if we wish[20]—but we should not thereby forget that the legitimacy of such a chain suggests that it is just preservation of reference, as Mill thought, that we regard as necessary for correct language learning.[21] (This contrasts with such terms as 'renate' and 'cordate', where more than learning the correct extension is needed.) Also, as suggested above, the doctrine of rigidity in modal contexts is dissonant, though not necessarily inconsistent, with a view that invokes anti-Millian considerations to explain propositional attitude contexts.

The spirit of my earlier views, then, suggests that a Millian line should be maintained as far as is feasible.

II   PRELIMINARIES: SOME GENERAL PRINCIPLES

Where are we now? We seem to be in something of a quandary. On the one hand, we concluded that the failure of 'Cicero' and 'Tully' to be interchangeable *salva veritate* in contexts of propositional attitude was by no means explicable in terms of different 'senses' of the two names. On the other hand, let us not forget the initial argument against Mill: If reference is *all there is* to naming, what semantic difference can there be between 'Cicero' and 'Tully'? And if there is no semantic difference, do not 'Cicero was bald' and 'Tully was bald' express exactly the same proposition? How, then, can anyone believe that Cicero was bald, yet doubt or disbelieve that Tully was?

Let us take stock. Why do we think that anyone can believe that Cicero was bald, but fail to believe that Tully was? Or believe, without any logical inconsistency, that Yale is a fine university, but that Old Eli is an inferior one? Well, a normal English speaker, Jones, can sincerely assent to 'Cicero was bald' but not to 'Tully was bald'. And this even though Jones uses 'Cicero' and 'Tully' in standard ways—he uses 'Cicero' in this assertion as a name for the Roman, not, say, for his dog, or for a German spy.

Let us make explicit the *disquotational principle* presupposed here, connecting sincere assent and belief. It can be stated as follows, where '*p*' is to be replaced, inside and outside all quotation marks, by any appropriate standard English sentence: "*If a normal English speaker, on reflection, sincerely assents to 'p', then he believes that p.*" The sentence replacing '*p*' is to lack indexical or pronominal devices or ambiguities that would ruin the intuitive sense of the principle (e.g. if he assents to "You are wonderful", he need not believe that *you*—the reader—are wonderful).[22] When we suppose that we are dealing with a normal speaker of English, we mean that he uses all words in the sentence in a standard way, combines them according to the appropriate syntax, etc.: in short, he uses the sentence to mean what a normal speaker should mean by it. The 'words' of the sentence may include proper names, where these are part of the common discourse of the community, so that we can speak of using them in a standard way. For example, if the sentence is "London is pretty", then the speaker should satisfy normal criteria for using 'London' as a name of London, and for using 'is pretty' to attribute an appropriate degree of pulchritude. The qualification "on reflection" guards against the possibility that a speaker may, through careless inattention to the meaning of his words or other momentary conceptual or linguistic confusion, assert something he does not really mean, or assent to a sentence in linguistic error. "Sincerely" is meant to exclude mendacity, acting, irony, and the like. I fear that even with all this it is possible that some astute reader—such, after all, is the way of philosophy—may discover a qualification I have overlooked, without which the asserted principle is subject to counter-example. I doubt, however, that any such modification will affect any of the uses of the principle to be considered below. Taken in its obvious intent, after all, the principle appears to be a self-evident truth. (A similar principle holds for sincere affirmation or assertion in place of assent.)

There is also a strengthened 'biconditional' form of the disquotational principle, where once again any appropriate English sentence may replace '*p*' throughout: *A normal English speaker who is not reticent will be disposed to sincere reflective assent to '*p*' if and only if he believes that p.*[23] The biconditional form strengthens the simple one by adding that failure to assent indicates lack of belief, as assent indicates belief. The qualification about reticence is meant to take account of the fact that a speaker may fail to avow his beliefs because of shyness, a desire for secrecy, to avoid offence, etc. (An alternative formulation would give the speaker a sign to indicate lack of belief—not necessarily disbelief—in the assertion propounded, in addition to his sign of assent.) Maybe again the formulation needs further tightening, but the intent is clear.

Usually below, the simple disquotational principle will be sufficient for our purposes, but once we will also invoke the strengthened form. The simple form can often be used as a test for disbelief, provided the subject is a speaker with the modicum of logicality needed so that, at least after appropriate reflection, he does not hold simultaneously beliefs that are straightforward contradictions of each other—of the forms '*p*' and '$\sim p$'.[24] (Nothing in such a requirement prevents him from holding simultaneous beliefs that jointly *entail* a contradiction.) In this case (where '*p*' may be replaced by any appropriate English sentence), the speaker's assent to the negation of '*p*' indicates not only his disbelief that *p* but also his failure to believe that *p*, using only the simple (unstrengthened) disquotational principle.

So far our principle applies only to speakers of English. It allows us to infer, from Peter's sincere reflective assent to "God exists", that he believes that God exists. But of course we ordinarily allow ourselves to draw conclusions, stated in English, about the beliefs of speakers of any language: we infer that Pierre believes that God exists from his sincere reflective assent to "*Dieu existe*". There are several ways to do this, given conventional translations of French into English. We choose the following route. We have stated the disquotational principle in English, for English sentences; an analogous principle, stated in French (German, etc.) will be assumed to hold for French (German, etc.) sentences. Finally, we assume the *principle of translation: If a sentence of one language expresses a truth in that language, then any translation of it into any other language also expresses a truth (in that other language).* Some of our ordinary practice of translation may violate this principle; this happens when the translator's aim is not to preserve the content of the sentence, but to serve—in some other sense—the same purposes in the home language as the original utterance served in the foreign language.[25] But if the translation of a sentence is to mean the same as the sentence translated, preservation of truth value is a minimal condition that must be observed.

Granted the disquotational principle expressed in each language, reasoning starting from Pierre's assent to '*Dieu existe*' continues thus. First, on the basis of his utterance and the French disquotational principle we infer (in French):

Pierre croit que Dieu existe.

Form this we deduce,[26] using the principle of translation:

Pierre believes that God exists.

In this way we can apply the disquotational technique to all languages.

Even if I apply the disquotational technique to English alone, there is a sense in which I can be regarded as tacitly invoking a principle of translation. For presumably I apply it to speakers of the language other than myself. As Quine has pointed out, to regard others as speaking the same language as I is in a sense tacitly to assume a *homophonic* translation of their language into my own. So when I infer from Peter's sincere assent to or affirmation of "God exists" that he believes that God exists, it is arguable that, strictly speaking, I combine the disquotational principle (for Peter's idiolect) with the principle of (homophonic) translation (of Peter's idiolect into mine). But for most purposes, we can formulate the disquotational principle for a single language, English, tacitly supposed to be the common language of English speakers. Only when the possibility of individual differences of dialect is relevant need we view the matter more elaborately.

Let us return from these abstractions to our main theme. Since a normal speaker—normal even in his use of 'Cicero' and 'Tully' as names—can give sincere and reflective assent to "Cicero was bald" and simultaneously to "Tully was not bald", the disquotational principle implies that he believes that Cicero was bald and believes that Tully was not bald. Since it seems that he need not have contradictory beliefs (even if he is a brilliant logician, he need not be able to deduce that at least one of his beliefs must be in error), and since a substitutivity principle for coreferential proper names in belief contexts would imply that he does have contradictory beliefs, it would seem that such a substitutivity principle must be incorrect. Indeed, the argument appears to be a *reductio ad absurdum* of the substitutivity principle in question.

The relation of this argument against substitutivity to the classical position of Russell and Fege is a curious one. As we have seen, the argument can be used to give *prima facie* support for the Frege-Russell view, and I think many philosophers have regarded it as such support. But in fact this very argument, which has been used to support Frege and Russell, cannot be stated in a straightforward fashion if Frege and Russell are right. For suppose Jones asserts, "Cicero was bald, but Tully was not". If Frege and Russell are right, I cannot deduce, using the disquotational principle:

(1) Jones believes that Cicero was bald but Tully was not,

since, in general, Jones and I will not, strictly speaking, share a common idiolect unless we assign the same 'senses' to all names. Nor can I combine disquotation and translation to the appropriate effect, since homophonic translation of Jones's sentence into mine will in general be incorrect for the same reason. Since in fact I make no special distinction in sense between 'Cicero' and 'Tully'—to me, and probably to you as well, these are interchangeable names for the same man—and since, according to Frege and Russell, Jones's very affirmation of (1) shows that for him there *is* some distinction of sense, Jones must therefore, on Frege-Russellian views, use one of these names differently from me, and homophonic translation is illegitimate. Hence, if Frege and Russell are right, we *cannot* use this example in the usual straightforward way to conclude that proper names are not substitutable in belief contexts—even though the example, and the ensuing negative verdict on substitutivity, has often been thought to support Frege and Russell!

Even according to the Frege-Russellian view, however, *Jones* can conclude, using the disquotational principle, and expressing his conclusion in his own idiolect:

(2) I believe that Cicero was bald but Tully was not.

I cannot endorse this conclusion in Jones's own words, since I do not share Jones's idiolect. I *can* of course conclude, "(2) expresses a truth in Jones's idiolect". I can also, if I find out the two 'senses' Jones assigns to 'Cicero' and 'Tully', introduce two names 'X' and 'Y' into my own language with these same two senses ('Cicero' and 'Tully' have already been preempted) and conclude:

(3) Jones believes that X was bald and Y was not.

All this is enough so that we can still conclude, on the Frege-Russellian view, that codesignative names are not interchangeable in belief contexts. Indeed this can be shown more simply on this view, since codesignative descriptions plainly are not interchangeable in these contexts, and for Frege and Russell names, being essentially abbreviated descriptions, cannot differ in this respect. Nevertheless, the simple argument, apparently free of such special Frege-Russellian doctrinal premisses (and often used to support these premisses), in fact cannot go through if Frege and Russell are right.

However, if, *pace* Frege and Russell, widely used names are common currency of our language, then there no longer is any problem for the simple argument, using the disquotational principle, to (2). So, it appears, on pain of convicting Jones of inconsistent beliefs—surely an unjust verdict—we must not hold a substitutivity principle for names in belief contexts. If we used the *strengthened* disquotational principle, we could invoke Jones's presumed lack of any tendency to assent to 'Tully was bald' to conclude that he does not believe (lacks the belief) that Tully was bald. Now the refutation of the substitutivity principle is even stronger, for when applied to the conclusion that Jones believes that Cicero was bald but does not believe that Tully was bald, it would lead to a straightout contradiction. The contradiction would no longer be in Jones's beliefs but in our own.

This reasoning, I think, has been widely accepted as proof that codesignative proper names are not interchangeable in belief contexts. Usually the reasoning is left tacit, and it may well be thought that I have made heavy weather of an obvious conclusion. I wish, however, to question the reasoning. I shall do so without challenging any particular step of the argument. Rather I shall present—and this will form the core of the present paper—an argument for a paradox about names in belief contexts that invokes *no* principle of substitutivity. Instead it will be based on the principles—apparently so obvious that their use in these arguments is ordinarily tacit—of disquotation and translation.

Usually the argument will involve more than one language, so that the principle of translation and our conventional manual of translation must be invoked. We will also give an example, however, to show that a form of the paradox may result within English alone, so that the only principle invoked is that of disquotation (or, perhaps, disquotation plus *homophonic* translation). It will intuitively be fairly clear, in these cases, that the situation of the subject is 'essentially the same' as that of Jones with respect to 'Cicero' and 'Tully'. Moreover, the paradoxical conclusions about the subject will parallel those drawn about Jones on the basis of the substitutivity principle, and the arguments will parallel those regarding Jones. Only in these cases, no special substitutivity principle is invoked.

The usual use of Jones's case as a counter-example to the substitutivity principle is thus, I think, somewhat analogous to the following sort of procedure. Someone wishes to give a *reductio ad absurdum* argument against a hypothesis in topology. He does succeed in refuting this hypothesis, but his derivation of an absurdity from the hypothesis makes essential use of the unrestricted comprehension schema in set theory, which he regards as self-evident. (In particular, the class of all classes not members of themselves plays a key role in his argument.) Once we know that the unrestricted comprehension schema and the Russell class lead to contradiction by themselves, it is clear that it was an error to blame the earlier contradiction on the topological hypothesis.

The situation would have been the same if, after deducing a contradiction from the topological hypothesis plus the 'obvious' unrestricted comprehension schema, it was found that a similar contradiction followed if we replaced the topological hypothesis by an apparently 'obvious' premiss. In both cases it would be clear that, even though we may still not be confident of any specific flaw in the argument against the topological hypothesis, blaming the contradiction on that hypothesis is illegitimate: rather we are in a 'paradoxical' area where it is unclear *what* has gone wrong.[27]

It is my suggestion, then, that the situation with respect to the interchangeability of condesignative names is similar. True, such a principle, when combined with our normal disquotational judgments of belief, leads to straightforward absurdities. But we will see that the 'same' absurdities can be derived by replacing the interchangeability principle with our normal practices of translation and disquotation, or even with disquotation alone.

The particular principle stated here gives just one particular way of 'formalizing' our normal inferences from explicit affirmation or assent to belief; other ways of doing it are possible. It is undeniable that we *do* infer, from a normal Englishman's sincere affirmation of 'God exists' or 'London is pretty', that he believes, respectively, that God exists or that London is pretty; and that we would make the same inferences from a Frenchman's affirmation of *'Dieu existe'* or *'Londres est jolie'*. Any principles that would justify such inferences are sufficient for the next section. It will be clear that the particular principles stated in the present section are sufficient, but in the next section the problem will be presented informally in terms of our inferences from foreign or domestic assertion to belief.

III   THE PUZZLE

Here, finally(!), is the puzzle. Suppose Pierre is a normal French speaker who lives in France and speaks not a word of English or of any other language except French. Of course he has heard of that famous distant city, London (which he of course calls *'Londres'*), though he himself has never left France. On the basis of what he has heard of London, he is inclined to think that it is pretty. So he says, in French, *"Londres est jolie"*.

On the basis of his sincere French utterance, we will conclude:

(4) Pierre believes that London is pretty.

I am supposing that Pierre satisfies all criteria for being a normal French speaker, in particular, that he satisfies whatever criteria we usually use to judge that a Frenchman (correctly) uses *'est jolie'* to attribute pulchritude and uses *'Londres'*—standardly—as a name of London.

Later, Pierre, through fortunate or unfortunate vicissitudes, moves to England, in fact to London itself, though to an unattractive part of the city with fairly uneducated inhabitants. He, like most of his neighbours, rarely ever leaves this part of the city. None of his neighbours know any French, so he must learn English by 'direct method', without using any translation of English into French: by talking and mixing with the people he eventually begins to pick up English. In particular, everyone speaks of the city, 'London', where they all live. Let us suppose for the moment—though we will see below that this is not crucial—that the local population are so uneducated that they know few of the facts that Pierre heard about London in France. Pierre learns from them everything they know about London, but there is little overlap with what he heard before. He learns, of course—speaking English—to call the city he lives in 'London'.

Pierre's surroundings are, as I said, unattractive, and he is unimpressed with most of the rest of what he happens to see. So he is inclined to assent to the English sentence:

(5) London is not pretty.

He has *no* inclination to assent to:

(6) London is pretty.

Of course he does not for a moment withdraw his assent from the French sentence, "*Londres est jolie*"; he merely takes it for granted that the ugly city in which he is now stuck is distinct from the enchanting city he heard about in France. But he has no inclination to change his mind for a moment about the city he still calls '*Londres*'.

This, then, is the puzzle. If we consider Pierre's past background as a French speaker, his entire linguistic behaviour, on the same basis as we would draw such a conclusion about many of his countrymen, supports the conclusion ((4) above) that he believes that London is pretty. On the other hand, after Pierre lived in London for some time, he did not differ from his neighbours—his French background aside—either in his knowledge of English or in his command of the relevant facts of local geography. His English vocabulary differs little from that of his neighbours. He, like them, rarely ventures from the dismal quarter of the city in which they all live. He, like them, knows that the city he lives in is called 'London' and knows a few other facts. Now Pierre's neighbours would surely be said to use 'London' as a name for London and to speak English. Since, as an English speaker, he does not differ at all from them, we should say the same of him. But then, on the basis of his sincere assent to (5), we should conclude:

(7) Pierre believes that London is not pretty.

How can we describe this situation? It seems undeniable that Pierre *once* believed that London is pretty—at least before he learnt English. For at that time, he differed not at all from countless numbers of his countrymen, and we would have exactly the same grounds to say of him, as of any of them, that he believes that London is pretty: if any Frenchman who was both ignorant of English and never visited London believed that London is pretty, Pierre did. Nor does it have any plausibility to suppose, because of his later situation *after* he learns English, that Pierre should *retroactively* be judged *never* to have believed that London is pretty. To allow such *ex post facto* legislation would, as long as the future is uncertain, endanger our attributions of belief to *all* monolingual Frenchmen. We would be forced to say that Marie, a monolingual who firmly and sincerely asserts, "*Londres est jolie*", may or may not believe that London is pretty depending on the *later* vicissitudes of her career (if later she learns English and . . .). No: Pierre, like Marie, believed that London is pretty when he was monolingual.

Should we say that Pierre, now that he lives in London and speaks English, no longer believes that London is pretty? Well, unquestionably Pierre *once* believed that London is pretty. So we would be forced to say that Pierre has *changed his mind, has given up his previous belief*. But has he really done so? Pierre is very set in his ways. He reiterates, with vigour, every assertion he has ever made in French. He says he has not changed his mind about anything, has *not* given up any belief. Can we say he is wrong about this? If we did not have the story of his living in London and his English utterances, on the basis of his normal command of French we would be *forced* to conclude that he *still* believes that London is pretty. And it does seem that this is correct. Pierre has neither changed his mind nor given up any belief he had in France.

Similar difficulties beset any attempt to deny him his new belief. His French past aside, he is just like his friends in London. Anyone else, growing up in London with the same knowledge and beliefs that he expresses in England, we would undoubtedly judge to believe that London is not pretty. Can Pierre's French past nullify such a judgement? Can we say that Pierre, because of his French past, does not believe that (5)? Suppose an electric shock wiped out all his memories of the French language, what he learnt in France, and his French past. He would then be *exactly* like his neighbours in London. He would have the *same* knowledge, beliefs, and linguistic capacities. We then presumably would be forced to say that Pierre believes that London is ugly if we say it of his neighbours. But surely no shock that *destroys* part of Pierre's memories and knowledge can *give* him a new belief. If Pierre believes (5) *after* the shock, he believed it before, despite his French language and background.

If we would deny Pierre, in his bilingual stage, his belief that London is pretty *and* his belief that London is not pretty, we combine the difficulties of both previous options. We still would be forced to judge that Pierre once believed that London is pretty but does not longer, in spite of Pierre's own sincere denial that he has lost any belief. We also must worry whether Pierre would *gain* the belief that London is not pretty if he totally forgot his French past. The option does not seem very satisfactory.

So now it seems that we must respect both Pierre's French utterances and their English counterparts. So we must say that Pierre has contradictory beliefs, that he believes that London is pretty *and* he believes that London is not pretty. But there seem to be insuperable difficulties with this alternative as well. We may suppose that Pierre, in spite of the unfortunate situation in which he now finds himself, is a leading philosopher and logician. He would *never* let contradictory beliefs pass. And surely anyone, leading logician or no, is in principle in a position to notice and correct contradictory beliefs if he has them. Precisely for this reason, we regard individuals who contradict themselves as subject to greater censure than those who merely have false beliefs. But it is clear that Pierre, as long as he in unaware that the cities he calls 'London' and '*Londres*' are one and the same, is in no position to see, by logic alone, that at least one of his beliefs must be false. He lacks information, not logical acumen. He cannot be convicted of inconsistency: to do so is incorrect.

We can shed more light on this if we change the case. Suppose that in France Pierre, instead of affirming "*Londres est jolie*", had affirmed, more cautiously, "*Si New York est jolie, Londres est jolie aussi*", so that he believed that *if* New York is pretty, so is London. Later Pierre moves to London, learns English as before, and says (in English) "London is not pretty". So he now believes, further, that London is *not* pretty. Now from the two premises, both of which appear to be among his beliefs ((a) If New York is pretty, London is, and (b) London is not pretty), Pierre should be able to deduce by *modus tollens* that New York is not pretty. But no matter how great Pierre's logical acumen may be, *he cannot in fact make any such deduction as long as he supposes that 'Londres' and 'London' may name two different cities*. If he *did* draw such a conclusion, he would be guilty of a fallacy.

Intuitively, he may well suspect that New York is pretty, and just this suspicion may lead him to suppose that '*Londres*' and 'London' probably name distinct cities. Yet, if we follow our normal practice of reporting the beliefs of French and English speakers, *Pierre has available to him (among his beliefs) both the premises of a* modus tollens *argument that New York is not pretty*.

Again, we may emphasize Pierre's *lack* of belief instead of his belief. Pierre, as I said, has no disposition to assent to (6). Let us concentrate on this, ignoring his disposition to assent to (5). In fact, if we wish we may change the case: Suppose Pierre's neighbours think that since they rarely venture outside their own ugly section, they have no right to any opinion as to the pulchritude of the whole city. Suppose Pierre shares their attitude. Then, judging by his failure to respond affirmatively to "London is pretty," we may judge, from Pierre's behaviour as an *English* speaker, that he lacks the belief that London is pretty: never mind whether he disbelieves it, as before, or whether, as in the modified story, he insists that he has no firm opinion on the matter.

Now (using the *strengthened* disquotational principle), we can derive a contradiction, not merely in Pierre's judgements, but in our own. For on the basis of his behaviour as an English speaker, we concluded that he does *not* believe that London is pretty (that is, that it is not the case that he believes that London is pretty). But on the basis of his behaviour as a *French* speaker, we must conclude that he *does* believe that London is pretty. This is a contradiction.[28]

We have examined four possibilities for characterizing Pierre while he is in London: (a) that at that time we no longer respect his French utterance ('*Londres est jolie*'), that is that we no longer ascribe to him the corresponding belief; (b) that we do not respect his English utterance (or lack of utterance); (c) that we respect neither; (d) that we respect both. Each possibility seems to lead us to say something either plainly false or even downright contradictory. Yet the possibilities appear to be logically exhaustive. This, then, is the paradox.

I have no firm belief as to how to solve it. But beware of one source of confusion. It is no solution in itself to observe that some *other* terminology, which evades the question whether Pierre believes that London is pretty, may be sufficient to state all the relevant facts. I am fully aware that complete and straightforward descriptions of the situation are possible and that in this sense there is no paradox. Pierre is disposed to sincere assent to '*Londres est jolie*' but not to 'London is pretty'. He uses French normally, English normally. Both with '*Londres*' and 'London' he associates properties sufficient to determine that famous city, but he does not realize that they determine a single city. (And his uses of '*Londres*' and 'London' are historically (causally) connected with the same single city, though he is unaware of that.) We may even give a rough statement of his beliefs. He believes that the city he calls '*Londres*' is pretty, that the city he calls 'London' is not. No doubt other straightforward descriptions are possible. No doubt some of these are, in a certain sense, *complete* descriptions of the situation.

But none of this answers the original question. Does Pierre, or does he not, believe that London is pretty? I know of no answer to *this* question that seems satisfactory. It is no answer to protest that, in some *other* terminology, one can state 'all the relevant facts'.

To reiterate, this is the puzzle: Does Pierre, or does he not, believe that London is pretty? It is clear that our normal criteria for the attribution of belief lead, when applied to *this* question, to paradoxes and contradictions. One set of principles adequate to many ordinary attributions of belief, but which leads to paradox in the present case, was stated in Section II; and other formulations are possible. As in the case of the logical paradoxes, the present puzzle presents us with a problem for customarily accepted principles and a challenge to formulate an acceptable set of principles that does not lead to paradox, is intuitively sound, and supports the inferences we usually make. Such a challenge cannot be met simply by a description of Pierre's situation that evades the question whether he believes that London is pretty.

One aspect of the presentation may misleadingly suggest the applicability of Frege-Russellian ideas that each speaker associates his own description or properties to each name. For as I just set up the case Pierre learnt one set of facts about the so-called '*Londres*' when he was in France, and *another* set of facts about 'London' in England. Thus it may appear that 'what is really going on' is that Pierre believes that *the city* satisfying *one* set of properties *is* pretty, while he believes that *the city* satisfying *another* set of properties *is not* pretty.

As we just emphasized, the phrase 'what is really going on' is a danger signal in discussions of the present paradox. The conditions stated may—let us concede for the moment—describe 'what is really going on'. But they do not resolve the problem with which we began, that of the behaviour of names in belief contexts: Does Pierre, or does he not, believe that London (not the city satisfying such-and-such descriptions, but *London*) is pretty? No answer has yet been given.

Nevertheless, these considerations may appear to indicate that descriptions, or associated properties, are highly relevant somehow to an ultimate solution, since at this stage it appears that the entire puzzle arises from the fact that Pierre originally associated different identifying properties with 'London' and '*Londres*'. Such a reaction may have some force even in the face of the now fairly well-known arguments against 'identifying descriptions' as in any way 'defining', or even 'fixing the reference', of names. But in fact the special features of the case, as I set it out, are misleading. The puzzle can arise even if Pierre associates exactly the same identifying properties with both names.

First, the considerations mentioned above in connection with 'Cicero' and 'Tully' establish this fact. For example, Pierre may well learn, in France, '*Platon*' as the name of a major Greek philosopher, and later, in England, learn 'Plato' with the same identification. Then the same puzzle can arise: Pierre may have believed, when he was in France and was monolingual in French, that Plato was bald (he would have said, "*Platon était chauve*"), and later conjecture, in English, "Plato was not bald", thus indicating that he believes or suspects that Plato was *not* bald. He need only suppose that, in spite of the similarity of their names, the man he calls '*Platon*' and the man he calls 'Plato' were two distinct major Greek philosophers. In principle, the same thing could happen with 'London' and '*Londres*'.

Of course, most of us learn a *definite* description about London, say 'the largest city in England'. Can the puzzle still arise? It is noteworthy that the puzzle can still arise even if Pierre associates to '*Londres*' and to 'London' *exactly* the same *uniquely identifying* properties. How can this be? Well, suppose that Pierre believes that London is the largest city in (and capital of) England, that it contains Buckingham Palace, the residence of the Queen of England, and he believes (correctly) that these properties, conjointly, uniquely identify the city. (In this case, it is best to suppose that he has never seen London, or even England, so that he uses *only* these properties to identify the city. Nevertheless, he has learnt English by 'direct method'.) These uniquely identifying properties he comes to associate with 'London' after he learnt English, and he expresses the appropriate beliefs about 'London' in English. Earlier, when he spoke nothing but French, however, he associated *exactly* the same uniquely identifying properties with '*Londres*'. He believed that '*Londres*', as he called it, could be uniquely identified as the capital of England, that it contained Buckingham Palace, that the Queen of England lived there, etc. Of course he expressed these beliefs, like most monolingual Frenchmen, in French. In particular, he used '*Angleterre*' for England, '*le Palais de Buckingham*' (pronounced '*Bookeengam*'!) for Buckingham Palace, and '*la Reine d'Angleterre*' for the Queen of England. But if any Frenchman who speaks no English can ever be said to associate *exactly* the properties of being the capital of England etc. with the name '*Londres*', Pierre in his monolingual period did so.

When Pierre becomes a bilingual, *must* he conclude that 'London' and '*Londres*' name the same city, because he defined each by the same uniquely identifying properties?

Surprisingly, no! Suppose Pierre had affirmed, '*Londres est jolie*'. If Pierre has any reason—even just a 'feeling in his bones', or perhaps exposure to a photograph of a miserable area which he was told (in English) was part of 'London'—to maintain 'London is not pretty', he need not contradict himself. He need only conclude that 'England' and '*Angleterre*' name two different countries, that 'Buckingham Palace' and '*le Palais de Buckingham*' (recall the pronunciation!), name two different palaces, and so on. Then he can maintain *both* views without contradiction, and regard *both* properties as uniquely identifying.

The fact is that the paradox reproduces itself on the level of the 'uniquely identifying properties' that description theorists have regarded as 'defining' proper names (and *a fortiori*, as fixing their references). Nothing is more reasonable than to suppose that if two names, A and B, and a single set of properties, S, are such that a certain speaker believes that the referent of A uniquely satisfies all of S and that the referent of B also uniquely satisfies all of S, then that speaker is committed to the belief that A and B have the same reference. In fact, the identity of the referents of A and B is an easy *logical consequence* of the speaker's beliefs.

From this fact description theorists concluded that names can be regarded as synonymous, and hence interchangeable *salva veritate* even in belief contexts, provided that they are 'defined' by the same uniquely identifying properties.

We have already seen that there is a difficulty in that the set S of properties need not in fact be uniquely identifying. But in the present paradoxical situation there is a surprising difficulty even if the supposition of the description theorist (that the speaker believes that S is uniquely fulfilled) in fact holds. For, as we have seen above, Pierre is in no position to draw ordinary logical consequences from the conjoint set of what, when we consider him separately as a speaker of English and as a speaker of French, we would call his beliefs. He cannot infer a contradiction from his separate beliefs that London is pretty and that London is not pretty. Nor, in the modified situation above, would Pierre make a normal *modus tollens* inference from his beliefs that London is not pretty and that London is pretty if New York is. Similarly here, if we pay attention only to Pierre's behaviour as a French speaker (and at least in his monolingual days he was no different from any other Frenchmen), Pierre satisfies all the normal criteria for believing that '*Londres*' has a referent uniquely satisfying the properties of being the largest city in England, containing Buckingham Palace, and the like. (If Pierre did not hold such beliefs, no

Frenchman *ever* did.) Similarly, on the basis of his (later) beliefs expressed in English, Pierre also believes that the referent of 'London' uniquely satisfies these same properties. But Pierre cannot combine the two beliefs into a single set of beliefs from which he can draw the normal conclusion that 'London' and '*Londres*' must have the same referent. (Here the trouble comes not from 'London' and '*Londres*' but from 'England' and '*Angleterre*' and the rest.) Indeed, if he *did* draw what would appear to be the normal conclusion in this case and any of the other cases, Pierre would in fact be guilty of a logical fallacy.

Of course the description theorist could hope to eliminate the problem by 'defining' '*Angleterre*', 'England', and so on by appropriate descriptions also. Since in principle the problem may rear its head at the next 'level' and at each subsequent level, the description theorist would have to believe that an 'ultimate' level can eventually be reached where the defining properties are 'pure' properties not involving proper names (nor natural kind terms or related terms, see below!) I know of no convincing reason to suppose that such a level can be reached in any plausible way, or that the properties can continue to be uniquely identifying if one attempts to eliminate all names and related devices.[29] Such speculation aside, the fact remains that Pierre, judged by the *ordinary* criteria for such judgements, *did* learn both '*Londres*' and 'London' by *exactly* the same set of identifying properties; yet the puzzle remains even in this case.

Well, then, is there any way out of the puzzle? Aside from the principles of disquotation and translation, only our normal practice of translation of French into English has been used. Since the principles of disquotation and translation seem self-evident, we may be tempted to blame the trouble on the translation of '*Londres est jolie*' as 'London is pretty,' and ultimately, then, on the translation of '*Londres*' as 'London.'[30] Should we, perhaps, permit ourselves to conclude that '*Londres*' should not, 'strictly speaking' be translated as 'London'? Such an expedient is, of course, desperate: the translation in question is a standard one, learnt by students together with other standard translations of French into English. Indeed, '*Londres*' is, in effect, introduced into French as the French version of 'London'.

Since our backs, however, are against the wall, let us consider this desperate and implausible expedient a bit further. If '*Londres*' is *not* a correct French version of the English 'London,' under what circumstances can proper names be translated from one language to another?

Classical description theories suggest the answer: Translation, strictly speaking, is between idiolects; a name in one idiolect can be translated into another when (and only when) the speakers of the two idiolects associate the same uniquely identifying properties with the two names. We have seen that any such proposed restriction, not only fails blatantly to fit our normal practices of translation and indirect discourse reportage, but does not even appear to block the paradox.[31]

So we still want a suitable restriction. Let us drop the references to idiolects and return to '*Londres*' and 'London' as names in French and English, respectively—the languages of two communities. If '*Londres*' is not a correct French translation of 'London', could any other version do better? Suppose I introduced another word into French, with the stipulation that *it* should always be used to translate 'London'. Would not the same problem arise for this word as well? The only feasible solution in this direction is the most drastic: decree that no sentence containing a name can be translated except by a sentence containing the phonetically identical name. Thus when Pierre asserts '*Londres est jolie*', we English speakers can at best conclude, if anything: Pierre believes that *Londres* is pretty. Such a conclusion is, of course, not expressed in English, but in a word salad of English and French: on the view now being entertained, we cannot state Pierre's belief in *English* at all.[32] Similarly, we would have to say: Pierre believes that *Angleterre* is a monarchy, Pierre believes that *Platon* wrote dialogues, and the like.[33]

This 'solution' appears at first to be effective against the paradox, but it is drastic. What is it about sentences containing names that makes them—a substantial class—intrinsically untranslatable, express beliefs that cannot be reported in any other language? At best, to report them in the other language, one is forced to use a word salad in which names from the one language are imported into the other. Such a supposition is both contrary to our normal practice of translation and very implausible on its face.

Implausible though it is, there is at least this much excuse for the 'solution' at this point. Our normal practice with respect to some famous people and especially for geographical localities is to have different names for them in different languages, so that in translating sentences we translate the names. But for a large number of names, especially names of people, this is not so: the person's name is used in the sentences of all languages. At least the restriction in question merely urges us to mend our ways by doing *always* what we presently do *sometimes*.

But the really drastic character of the proposed restriction comes out when we see how far it may have to extend. In 'Naming and Necessity' I suggested that there are important analogies between proper names and natural kind terms, and it seems to me that the present puzzle is one instance where the analogy will hold. Putnam, who has proposed views on natural kinds similar to my own in many respects, stressed this extension of the puzzle in his comments at the Second Jerusalem Philosophical Encounter (April 1976). Not that the puzzle extends to all translation from English to French. At the moment, at least, it seems to me that Pierre, if he learns English and French separately, without learning any translation manual between them, *must* conclude, if he reflects enough, that 'doctor' and '*médecin*', and '*heureux*' and 'happy', are synonymous, or at any rate, coextensive;[34] any potential paradox of the present kind for these word pairs is thus blocked. But what about '*lapin*' and 'rabbit', or 'beech' and '*hêtre*'? We may suppose that Pierre is himself neither a zoologist nor a botanist. He has learnt each language in its own country, and the example he has been shown to illustrate '*les lapins*' and 'rabbits,' 'beeches' and '*les hêtres*' are distinct. It thus seems to be possible for him to suppose that '*lapin*' and 'rabbit,' or 'beech' and 'hêtre', denote distinct but superficially similar kinds or species, even though the differences may be indiscernible to the untrained eye. (This is especially plausible if, as Putnam supposes, an English speaker—for example, Putnam himself— who is not a botanist may use 'beech' and 'elm' with their normal [distinct] meanings, even though he cannot himself distinguish the two trees.[35] Pierre may quite plausibly be supposed to wonder whether the trees which in France he called '*les hêtres*' were beeches or elms, even though as a speaker of French he satisifies all usual criteria for using '*les hêtres*' normally. If beeches and elms will not serve, better pairs of ringers exist that cannot be told apart except by an expert.) Once Pierre is in such a situation, paradoxes analogous to the one about London obviously can arise for rabbits and beeches. Pierre could affirm a French statement with '*lapin*', but deny its English translation with 'rabbit.' As above, we are hard pressed to say what Pierre *believes*. We were considering a 'strict and philosophical' reform of translation procedures which proposed that foreign proper names should always be appropriated rather than trans- lated. Now it seems that we will be forced to do the same with all words for natural kinds. (For example, on price of paradox, one must not trans- late '*lapin*' as 'rabbit'!) No longer can the extended proposal be defended, even weakly, as 'merely' universalizing what we already do sometimes. It is surely too drastic a change to retain any credibility.[36]

There is yet another consideration that makes the proposed restriction more implausible: Even this restriction does not really block the paradox. Even if we confine ourselves to a single language, say English, and to phonetically identical tokens of a single name, we can still generate the puzzle. Peter (as we may as well say now) may learn the name 'Paderewski' with an identification of the person named as a famous pianist. Naturally, having learnt this, Peter will assent to 'Paderewski had musical talent'', and *we* can infer—using 'Paderewski', as we usually do, to name the Polish musician and statesman:

(8) Peter believes that Paderewski had musical talent.

Only the disquotational principle is necessary for our inference; no translation is required. Later, in a different circle, Peter learns of someone called 'Paderewski' who was a Polish nationalist leader and Prime Minister. Peter is sceptical of the musical abilities of politicians. He concludes that probably two people, approximate contemporaries no doubt, were both named 'Paderewski'. Using 'Paderewski' as a name for the *statesman*, Peter assents to, "Paderewski had no musical talent". Should we infer, by the disquotational principle.

(9) Peter believes that Paderewski had no musical talent

or should we not? If Peter had not had the past history of learning the name 'Paderewski' in another way, we certainly would judge him to be using 'Paderewski' in a normal way, with the normal reference, and we would infer (9) by the disquotational principle. The situation is parallel to the problem with Pierre and London. Here, however, no restriction that names should not be translated, but should be phonetically repeated in the translation, can help us. Only a single language and a single name are involved. If any notion of translation is involved in this example, it is homophonic translation. Only the disquotational principle is used explicitly.[37] (On the other hand, the original 'two languages' case had the advantage that it would apply even if we spoke languages in which all names must denote uniquely and unambiguously.) The restriction that names must not be translated is thus ineffective, as well as implausible and drastic.

I close this section with some remarks on the relation of the present puzzle to Quine's doctrine of the 'indeterminacy of translation', with its attendant repudiation of intensional idioms of 'propositional attitude' such as belief and even indirect quotation. To a sympathizer with these doctrines the present puzzle may well seem to be just more grist for a familiar mill. The situation of the puzzle seems to lead to a breakdown of our normal practices of attributing belief and even of indirect quotation. No obvious paradox arises if we describe the same situation in terms of Pierre's sincere assent to various sentences, together with the conditions under which he has learnt the name in question. Such a description, although it does not yet conform to Quine's strict behaviouristic standards, fits in well with his view that in some sense direct quotation is a more 'objective' idiom than the propositional attitudes. Even those who, like the present writer, do not find Quine's negative attitude to the attitudes completely attractive must surely acknowledge this.

But although sympathizers with Quine's view can use the present examples to support it, the differences between these examples and the considerations Quine adduces for his own scepticism about belief and translation should not escape us. Here we make no use of hypothetical exotic systems of translation differing radically from the usual one, translating '*lapin*', say, as 'rabbit stage' or 'undetached part of a rabbit'. The problem arises entirely within our usual and customary system of translation of French into English; in one case, the puzzle arose even within English alone, using at most 'homophonic' translation. Nor is the problem that many different interpretations or translations fit our usual criteria, that, in Davidson's phrase,[38] there is more than one 'way of getting it right'. The trouble here is not that many views as to Pierre's beliefs get it right, but that they all definitely get it *wrong*. A straightforward application of the principles of translation and disquotation to all Pierre's utterances, French and English, yields the result that Pierre holds inconsistent beliefs, that logic alone should teach him that one of his beliefs is false. Intuitively, this is plainly incorrect. If we refuse to apply the principles to his French utterances at all, we would conclude that Pierre never believed that London is pretty, even though, before his unpredictable move, he was like any other monolingual Frenchman. This is absurd. If we refuse to ascribe the belief in London's pulchritude only after Pierre's move to England, we get the counterintuitive result that Pierre has changed his mind, and so on. But we have surveyed the possibilities above: the point was not that they are 'equally good', but that all are *obviously wrong*. If the puzzle is to be used as an argument for a Quinean position, it is an argument of a fundamentally different kind from those given before. And even Quine, if he wishes to incorporate the notion of belief even into a 'second level' of canonical notation,[39] must regard the puzzle as a real problem.

The alleged indeterminacy of translation and indirect quotation causes relatively little trouble for such a scheme for belief; the embarrassment it presents to such a scheme is, after all, one of riches. But the present puzzle indicates that the usual principles we use to ascribe beliefs are apt, in certain cases, to lead to contradiction, or at least, patent falsehoods. So it presents a problem for any project, Quinean or other, that wishes to deal with the 'logic' of belief on any level.[40]

IV CONCLUSION

What morals can be drawn? The primary moral—quite independent of any of the discussion of the first two sections—is that the puzzle *is* a puzzle. As any theory of truth must deal with the Liar Paradox, so any theory of belief and names must deal with this puzzle.

But our theoretical starting point in the first two sections concerned proper names and belief. Let us return to Jones, who assents to "Cicero was bald" and to "Tully was not bald". Philosophers, using the disquotational principle, have concluded that Jones believes that Cicero was bald but that Tully was not. Hence, they have concluded, since Jones does not have contradictory beliefs, belief contexts are not 'Shakespearean' in Greach's sense: codesignative proper names are not interchangeable in these contexts *salva veritate*.[41]

I think the puzzle about Pierre shows that the simple conclusion was unwarranted. Jones's situation strikingly resembles Pierre's. A proposal that 'Cicero' and 'Tully' *are* interchangeable amounts roughly to a homophonic 'translation' of English into itself in which 'Cicero' is mapped into 'Tully' and *vice versa*, while the rest is left fixed. Such a 'translation' can, indeed, be used to obtain a paradox. But should the problem be blamed on this step? Ordinarily we would suppose without question that sentences in French with '*Londres*' should be translated into English with 'London'. Yet the same paradox results when we apply this translation too. We have seen that the problem can even arise with a single name in a single language, and that it arises with natural kind terms in two languages (or one: see below).

Intuitively, Jones's assent to both 'Cicero was bald' and 'Tully was not bald' arises from sources of just the same kind as Pierre's assent to both 'Londres est jolie' and 'London is not pretty.'

It is wrong to blame unpalatable conclusions about Jones on substitutivity. The reason does not lie in any specific fallacy in the argument but rather in the nature of the realm being entered. Jones's case is just like Pierre's: both are in an area where our normal practices of attributing belief, bases on the principles of disquotation and translation or on similar principles, are questionable.

It should be noted in this connection that the principles of disquotation and translation can lead to 'proofs' as well as 'disproofs' of substitutivity in belief contexts. In Hebrew there are two names for Germany, transliteratable roughly as 'Ashkenaz' and 'Germaniah'—the first of these may be somewhat archaic. When Hebrew sentences are translated into English, both become 'Germany'. Plainly a normal Hebrew speaker analogous to Jones might assent to a Hebrew sentence involving 'Ashkenaz' while dissenting from its counterpart with 'Germaniah'. So far there is an argument *against* substitutivity. But there is also an argument *for* substitutivity, based on the principle of translation. Translate a Hebrew sentence involving 'Ashkenaz' into English, so that 'Ashkenaz' goes into 'Germany'. Then retranslate the result into Hebrew, this time translating 'Germany' as 'Germaniah'. By the principle of translation, both translations preserve truth value. So: the truth value of any sentence of Hebrew involving 'Ashkenaz' remains the same when 'Ashkenaz' is replaced by 'Germaniah'—a 'proof' of substitutivity! A similar 'proof' can be provided wherever there are two names in one language, and a normal practice of translating both indifferently into a single name of another language.[42] (If we combine the 'proof' and 'disproof' of substitutivity in this paragraph, we could get yet another paradox analogous to Pierre's: our Hebrew speaker both believes, and disbelieves, that Germany is pretty. Yet no amount of pure logic or semantic introspection suffices for him to discover his error.)

Another consideration, regarding natural kinds: Previously we pointed out that a bilingual may learn 'lapin' and 'rabbit' normally in each respective language yet wonder whether they are one species or two, and that this fact can be used to generate a paradox analogous to Pierre's. Similarly, a speaker of *English* alone may learn 'furze' and 'gorse' normally (separately), yet wonder whether these are the same, or resembling kinds. (What about 'rabbit' and 'hare'?) It would be easy for such a speaker to assent to an assertion formulated with 'furze' but withhold assent from the corresponding assertion involving 'gorse'. The situation is quite analogous to that of Jones with respect to 'Cicero' and 'Tully'. Yet 'furze' and 'gorse', and other pairs of terms for the same natural kind, are normally thought of as *synonyms*.

The point is *not*, of course, that codesignative proper names *are* interchangeable in belief contexts *salva veritate*, or that they *are* interchangeable in simple contexts even *salva significatione*. The point is that the absurdities that disquotation plus substitutivity would generate are exactly paralleled by absurdities generated by disquotation plus translation, or even 'disquotation alone' (or: disquotation plus homophonic translation). Also, though our naïve practice may lead to 'disproofs' of substitutivity in certain cases, it can also lead to 'proofs' of substitutivity in some of these same cases, as we saw two paragraphs back. When we enter into the area exemplified by Jones and Pierre, we enter into an area where our normal practices of interpretation and attribution of belief are subjected to the greatest possible strain, perhaps to the point of breakdown. So is the notion of the *content* of someone's assertion, the *proposition* it expresses. In the present state of our knowledge, I think it would be foolish to draw any conclusion, positive or negative, about substitutivity.[43]

Of course nothing in these considerations prevents us from observing that Jones can sincerely assert both "Cicero is bald" and "Tully is not bald", even though he is a normal speaker of English and uses 'Cicero' and 'Tully' in normal ways, and with the normal referent. Pierre and the other paradoxical cases can be described similarly. (For those interested in one of my own doctrines, we can still say that there was a time when men were in no epistemic position to assent to 'Hesperus is Phosphorus' for want of empirical information, but it nevertheless expressed a necessary truth.)[44] But it is no surprise that quoted contexts fail to satisfy a substitutivity principle within the quotation marks. And, in our *present* state of clarity about the problem, we are in no position to apply a disquotation principle to these cases, nor to judge when two such sentences do, or do not, express the same 'proposition.'

Nothing in the discussion impugns the conventional judgment that belief contexts are 'referentially opaque,' if 'referential opacity' is construed so that failure of coreferential *definite descriptions* to be interchangeable *salva veritate* is sufficient for referential opacity. No doubt Jones can believe that the number of planets is even, without believing that the square of three is even, if he is under a misapprehension about the astronomical, but not the arithmetical facts. The question at hand was whether belief contexts were 'Shakespearean', not whether they were 'referentially transparent'. (Modal contexts, in my opinion, are 'Shakespearean' but 'referentially opaque'.)[45]

Even were we inclined to rule that belief contexts are not Shakespearean, it would be implausible at present to use the phenomenon to support a Frege-Russellian theory that names have descriptive 'senses' through 'uniquely identifying properties'. There are the well-known arguments against description theories, independent of the present discussion; there is the implausibility of the view that difference in names is difference in idiolect: and finally, there are the arguments of the present paper that differences of associated properties do not explain the problems in any case. Given these considerations, and the cloud our paradox places over the notion of 'content' in this area, the relation of substitutivity to the dispute between Millian and Fregean conclusions is not very clear.

We repeat our conclusions: Philosophers have often, basing themselves on Jones's and similar cases, supposed that it goes virtually without saying that belief contexts are not 'Shakespearean'. I think that, at present, such a definite conclusion in unwarranted. Rather Jones's case, like Pierre's, lies in an area where our normal apparatus for the ascription of belief is placed under the greatest strain and may even break down. There is even less warrant at the present time, in the absence of a better understanding of the paradoxes of this paper, for the use of alleged failures of substitutivity in belief contexts to draw any significant theoretical conclusion about proper names. Hard cases make bad law.[46]

Notes

1. 'Naming and Necessity', in D. Davidson and G. Harman (eds.) *The Semantics of Natural Languages* (Dordrecht: Reidel, 1971), 253–355 and 763–9. (Also as a separate monograph published by Harvard University Press and Basil Blackwell, 1972, 1980). 'Identity and Necessity', in M. Munitz (ed.), *Identity and Individuation* (New York University Press, 1971), 135–64. Acquaintance with these papers is not a prerequisite for understanding the central puzzle of the present paper, but is helpful for understanding the theoretical background.

2. Frege gives essentially this example as the second footnote of 'On Sense and Reference' [n. 4, p. 582 in this vol.]. For the "Who is ...?" to be applicable one must be careful to elicit from one's informant properties that he regards as defining the name and determining the referent, not mere well-known facts about the referent. (Of course this distinction may well seem fictitious, but it is central to the original Frege–Russell theory.)

3. For convenience Russell's terminology is assimilated to Frege's. Actually, regarding genuine or 'logically proper' names, Russell is a strict Millian: 'logically proper names' *simply* refer (to immediate objects of acquaintance). But, according to Russell, what are ordinarily called 'names' are not genuine, logically proper names but disguised definite descriptions. Since Russell also regards definite descriptions as in turn disguised notation, he does not associate any 'senses' with descriptions, since they are not genuine singular terms. When all disguised notation is eliminated, the only singular terms remaining are logically proper names, for which no notion of 'sense' is required. When we speak of Russell as assigning 'senses' to names, we mean ordinary names and for convenience we ignore his view that the descriptions abbreviating them ultimately disappear on analysis.

On the other hand, the explicit doctrine that names are abbreviated definite descriptions is due to Russell. Michael Dummett, in his recent *Frege* (Duckworth and Harper and Row, 1973), 110–11, denies that Frege held a description theory of sense. Although as far as I know Frege indeed makes no explicit statement to that effect, his examples of names conform to the doctrine, as Dummett acknowledges. Especially his 'Aristotle' example is revealing. He defines 'Aristotle' just as Russell would; it seems clear that in the case of a famous historical figure, the 'name' is indeed to be given by answering, in a uniquely specifying way, the 'who is' question. Dummett himself characterizes a sense as a 'criterion ... such that the referent of the name, if any, is whatever object satisfies that criterion'. Since presumably the satisfaction of the criterion must be unique (so a unique referent is determined), does not this amount to defining names by unique satisfaction of properties, *i.e.*, by descriptions? *Perhaps* the point is that the property in question need not be expressible by a usual predicate of English, as might be plausible if the referent is one of the speaker's acquaintances rather than a historical figure. But I doubt that even Russell, father of the explicitly formulated description theory, ever meant to require that the description must always be expressible in (unsupplemented) English.

In any event, the philosophical community has generally understood Fregean senses in terms of descriptions, and we deal with it under this usual understanding. For present purposes this is more important than detailed historical issues. Dummett acknowledges (p. 111) that few substantive points are affected by his (allegedly) broader interpretation of Frege; and it would not seem to be relevant to the problems of the present paper.

4. See Frege's footnote in 'On Sense and Reference' mentioned in n. 2 above and especially his discussion of 'Dr Gustav Lauben' in *'Der Gedanke'*. (In the recent Geach-Stoothoff translation, 'Thoughts', in *Logical Investigations* [Oxford: Blackwell, 1977], 11–12 [pp. 16–17 in this vol.]).

5. Russell, as a Millian with respect to genuine names, accepts this argument with respect to 'logically proper names'. For example, taking for the moment 'Cicero' and 'Tully' as 'logically proper names', Russell would hold that if I judge that Cicero admired Tully, I am related to Cicero, Tully, and the admiration relation in a certain way: since Cicero *is* Tully, I am related in exactly the same way to Tully, Cicero, and admiration; therefore I judge that Tully admired Cicero. Again,

if Cicero *did* admire Tully, then according to Russell a single fact corresponds to all of 'Cicero admired Tully', 'Cicero admired Cicero', etc. Its constituent (in addition to admiration) is the man Cicero, taken, so to speak, twice.

Russell thought that 'Cicero admired Tully' and 'Tully admired Cicero' are in fact obviously not interchangeable. For him, this was one argument that 'Cicero' and 'Tully' are *not* genuine names, and that the Roman orator is no constituent of propositions (or 'facts' or 'judgements') corresponding to sentences containing the name.

6. Given the arguments of Church and others, I do not believe that the formal mode of speech is synonymous with other formulations. But it can be used as a rough way to convey the idea of scope.

7. It may well be argued that the Millian view implies that proper names are *scopeless* and that for them the *de dicto–de re* distinction vanishes. This view has considerable plausibility (my own views on rigidity will imply something like this for *modal* contexts), but it need not be argued here either way: *de re* uses are simply not treated in the present paper.

Christopher Peacocke ('Proper Names, Reference, and Rigid Designation', in S. Blackburn [ed.], *Meaning, Reference, and Necessity* [Cambridge, 1975]; see Section I), uses what amounts to the equivalence of the *de dicto–de re* constructions in *all* contexts (or, put alternatively, the lack of such a distinction) to characterize the notion of rigid designation. I agree that for *modal* contexts, this is (roughly) equivalent to my own notion, also that for proper names Peacocke's equivalence holds for temporal contexts. (This is roughly equivalent to the 'temporal rigidity' of names.) I also agree that it is very plausible to extend the principle to all contexts. But, as Peacocke recognizes, this appears to imply a substitutivity principle for codesignative proper names in belief contexts, which is widely assumed to be false. Peacocke proposes to use Davidson's theory of intensional contexts to block this conclusion (the material in the 'that' clause is a separate sentence). I myself cannot accept Davidson's theory; but even if it were true, Peacocke in effect acknowledges that it does not really dispose of the difficulty (p. 127, first paragraph). (Incidentally, if Davidson's theory does block any inference to the transparency of belief contexts with respect to names, why does Peacocke assume without argument that it does not do so for modal contexts, which have a similar grammatical structure?) The problems are thus those of the present paper; until they are resolved I prefer at present to keep to my earlier more cautious formulation.

Incidentally, Peacocke hints a recognition that the received platitude—that codesignative names are not interchangeable in belief contexts—may not be so clear as is generally supposed.

8. The example comes from Quine, *Word and Object* (MIT Press, 1960), 145 [804 in this vol.]. Quine's conclusion that 'believes that, construed *de dicto* is opaque has widely been taken for granted. In the formulation in the text I have used the colon to emphasize that I am speaking of belief *de dicto*. Since, as I have said, belief *de dicto* will be our *only* concern in this paper, in the future the colon will usually be suppressed, and all 'believes that' contexts should be read *de dicto* unless the contrary is indicated explicitly.

9. In many writings Peter Geach has advocated a view that is non-Millian (he would say 'non-Lockean') in that to each name a sortal predicate is attached by definition ('Geach', for example, by *definition* names a man). On the other hand, the theory is not completely Fregean either, since Geach denies that any definite description that would identify the referent of the name among things of the same sort is analytically tied to the name. (See e.g. his *Reference and Generality* (Cornell, 1962), 43–5.) As far as the present issues are concerned, Geach's view can fairly be assimilated to *Mill*'s rather than Frege's. For such ordinary names as 'Cicero' and 'Tully' will have both the same reference and the same (Geachian) sense (namely, that they are names of a man). It would thus seem that they ought to be interchangeable everywhere. (In *Reference and Generality*, Greach appears not to accept this conclusion, but the *prima facie* argument for the conclusion will be the same as on a purely Millian view.)

10. In an unpublished paper, Diana Ackerman urges the problem of substitutivity failure against the Millian view and, hence, against my own view. I believe that others may have done so as well. (I have the impression that the paper has undergone considerable revision, and I have not seen recent versions.) I agree that this problem is a considerable difficulty for the Millian view, and for the Millian *spirit* of my own views in 'Naming and Necessity'. (See the discussion of this in the text of the present paper.) On the other hand I would emphasize that there need be no *contradiction* in maintaining that names are *modally* rigid and satisfy a substitutivity principle for modal contexts. While denying the substitutivity principle for belief contexts. The entire apparatus elaborated in 'Naming and Necessity' of the distinction between epistemic and metaphysical necessity, and of giving a meaning and fixing a reference, was meant to show, among other things, that a Millian substitutivity doctrine for modal contexts can be maintained even if such a doctrine for epistemic contexts is rejected. 'Naming and Necessity' never asserted a substitutivity principle for epistemic contexts.

It is even consistent to suppose that differing modes of (rigidly) fixing the reference is responsible for the substitutivity failures, thus adopting a position intermediate between Frege and Mill, on the lines indicated in the text of the present paper. 'Naming and Necessity' may even perhaps be taken as suggesting, for some contexts where a conventional description rigidly fixes the reference ('Hesperus-Phosphorus'), that the mode of reference fixing is relevant to epistemic questions. I knew when I wrote 'Naming and Necessity' that substitutivity issues in epistemic contexts were really very delicate, due to the problems of the present paper, but I thought it best not to muddy the waters further. (See nn. 43–4.)

After this paper was completed, I saw Alvin Planting's paper 'The Boethian Compromise', *American Philosophical Quarterly* 15 (1978), 129–38. Plantinga adopts a view intermediate between Mill and Frege, and cites substitutivity failures as a principal argument for his position. He also refers to a forthcoming paper by Ackerman. I have not seen this paper, but it probably is a descendant of the paper referred to above.

11. Here I use 'connotation' so as to imply that the associated properties have an *a priori* tie to the name, at least as rigid reference fixers, and therefore must be true of the referent (if it exists). There is another sense of 'connotation,' as in 'The

Holy Roman Empire', where the connotation need not be assumed or even believed to be true of the referent. In some sense akin to this, classicists and others with some classical learning may attach certain distinct 'connotations' to 'Cicero' and 'Tully'. Similarly, 'The Netherlands' may suggest low altitude to a thoughtful ear. Such 'connotations' can hardly be thought of as community-wide; many use the names unaware of such suggestions. Even a speaker aware of the suggestion of the name may not regard the suggested properties as true of the object; cf. 'The Holy Roman Empire.' A 'connotation' of this type neither gives a meaning nor fixes a reference.

12. Some might attempt to find a difference in 'sense' between 'Cicero' and 'Tully' on the grounds that "Cicero is called 'Cicero'" is trivial, but "Tully is called 'Cicero'" may not be. Kneale, and in one place (probably at least implicitly) Church, have argued in this vein. (For Kneale, see 'Naming and Necessity', p. 283.) So, it may be argued, being called 'Cicero' is part of the sense of the name 'Cicero', but not part of that of 'Tully'.

I have discussed some issues related to this in 'Naming and Necessity', pp. 283–6. (See also the discussions of circularity conditions elsewhere in 'Naming and Necessity'.) Much more could be said about and against this kind of argument; perhaps I will sometime do so elsewhere. Let me mention very briefly the following parallel situation (which may be best understood by reference to the discussion in 'Naming and Necessity'). Anyone who understands the meaning of 'is called' and of quotation in English (and that 'alienists' is meaningful and grammatically appropriate), knows that "alienists are called 'alienists'" expresses a truth in English, even if he has no idea what 'alienists' means. He need *not* know that "psychiatrists are called 'alienists'" expresses a truth. None of this goes to show that 'alienists' and 'psychiatrists' are not synonymous, or that 'alienists' has *being called 'alienists'* as part of its meaning when 'psychiatrists' does not. Similarly for 'Cicero' and 'Tully'. There is no more reason to suppose that being so-called is part of the meaning of a name than of any other word.

13. A view follows Frege and Russell on this issue, even if it allows each speaker to associate a cluster of descriptions with each name, provided that it holds that the cluster varies from speaker to speaker and that variations in the cluster are variations in idiolect. Searle's view thus is Frege-Russellian when he writes in the concluding paragraph of 'Proper Names' (*Mind* 67 [1958], 166–73 [592 in this vol.]), "'Tully = Cicero' would, I suggest, be analytic for most people; the same descriptive presuppositions are associated with each name. But of course if the descriptive presuppositions were different it might be used to make a synthetic statement."

14. Though here I use the jargon of propositions, the point is fairly insensitive to differences in theoretical standpoints. For example, on Davidson's analysis, I would be asserting (roughly) that many are unaware-of-the-content-of the following *utterance* of mine: Cicero is Tully. This would be subject to the same problem.

15. Benson Mates, 'Synonymity', *University of California Publications in Philosophy* 25 (1950), 201–26; reprinted in *Semantics and the Philosophy of Language*, L. Linsky (ed.) (University of Illinois Press, 1952). (There was a good deal of subsequent discussion. In Mates's original paper the point is made almost paren-

thetically.) Actually, I think that Mates's problem has relatively little force against the argument we are considering for the Fregean position. Mates's puzzle in no way militates against some such principle as: If one word is synonymous with another, then a sufficiently reflective speaker subject to no linguistic inadequacies or conceptual confusions who sincerely assents to a simple sentence containing the one will also (sincerely) assent to the corresponding sentence with the other in its place.

It is surely a crucial part of the present 'Fegean' argument that codesignative names may have distinct 'senses', that a speaker may assent to a simple sentence containing one and deny the corresponding sentence containing the other, even though he is *guilty of no conceptual or linguistic confusion, and of no lapse in logical consistency*. In the case of two straightforward synonyms, this is not so.

I myself think that Mates's argument is of considerable interest, but that the issues are confusing and delicate and that, if the argument works, it probably leads to a paradox or puzzle rather than to a definite conclusion. (See also nn. 23, 28. and 46.)

16. 'Naming and Necessity', pp. 291–3.

17. Recall also n. 12.

18. Some philosophers stress that names are not words of a language, or that names are not *translated* from one language to another. (The phrase 'common currency of our common language' was meant to be neutral with respect to any such alleged issue.) Someone may use 'Mao Tse-Tung', for example, in English, though he knows not one word of Chinese. It seems hard to deny, however, that "*Deutschland*", "*Allemagne*", and "Germany", are the German, French, and English names of a single country, and that one translates a French sentence using "*Londres*" by an English sentence using "London". Learning these facts *is* part of learning German, French, and English.

It would appear that *some* names, especially names of countries, other famous localities, and some famous people, *are* thought of as part of a language (whether they are called 'words' or not is of little importance). Many other names are not thought of as part of a language, especially if the referent is not famous (so the notation used is confined to a limited circle), or if the same name is used by speakers of all languages. As far as I can see, it makes little or no *semantic* difference whether a particular name is thought of as part of a language or not. Mathematical notation such as '$<$' is also ordinarily not thought of as part of English, or any other language, though it is used in combination with English words in sentences of mathematical treatises written in English. (A French mathematician can use the notation though he knows not one word of English.) 'Is less than', on the other hand, *is* English. Does this difference have any semantic significance?

I will speak in most of the text as if the names I deal with are part of English, French, etc. But it matters little for what I say whether they are thought of as parts of the language or as adjuncts to it. And one need not say that a name such as '*Londres*' is 'translated' (if such a terminology suggested that names have 'senses', I too would find it objectionable), as long as one acknowledges that *sentences* containing it are properly translated into English using 'London'.

19. By saying that names are transparent in a context, I mean that codesignative names are interchangeable there. This is a deviation for brevity from the usual terminology, according to which the *context* is transparent. (I use the usual terminology in the paper also.)

20. But we must use the term 'sense' here in the sense of 'that which fixes the reference', not 'that which gives the meaning', otherwise we shall run afoul of the rigidity of proper names. If the source of a chain for a certain name is in fact a given object, we use the name to designate that object even when speaking of counterfactual situations in which some *other* object originated the chain.

21. The point is that, according to the doctrine of 'Naming and Necessity', when proper names are transmitted from link to link, even though the beliefs about the referent associated with the name change radically, the change is not to be considered a linguistic change in the way it *was* a linguistic change when 'villain' changed its meaning from 'rustic' to 'wicked man'. As long as the reference of a name remains the same, the associated beliefs about the object may undergo a large number of changes without these changes constituting a change in the language.

If Geach is right, an appropriate sortal must be passed on also. But see footnote 58 of 'Naming and Necessity'.

22. Similar appropriate restrictions are assumed below for the strengthened disquotational principle and for the principle of translation. Ambiguities need not be excluded if it is tacitly assumed that the sentence is to be understood in one way in all its occurrences. (For the principle of translation it is similarly assumed that the translator matches the *intended* interpretation of the sentence.) I do not work out the restrictions on indexicals in detail, since the intent is clear.

Clearly, the disquotational principle applies only to *de dicto*, not *de re*, attributions of belief. If someone sincerely assents to the near triviality, "The tallest foreign spy is a spy", it follows that he believes that: the tallest foreign spy is a spy. It is well known that it does *not* follow that he believes, *of* the tallest foreign spy, that he is a spy. In the latter case, but not in the former, it would be his patriotic duty to make contact with the authorities.

23. What if a speaker assents to a sentence, but fails to assent to a synonymous assertion? Say, he assents to "Jones is a doctor", but not to "Jones is a physician". Such a speaker either does not understand one of the sentences normally, or he should be able to correct himself "on reflection". As long as he confusedly assents to 'Jones is a doctor' but not to 'Jones is a physician', we *cannot* straightforwardly apply disquotational principles to conclude that he does or does not believe that Jones is a doctor, because his assent is not "reflective".

Similarly, if someone asserts, "Jones is a doctor but not a physician", he should be able to recognize his inconsistency without further information. We have formulated the disquotational principles so they need not lead us to attribute belief as long as we have grounds to suspect conceptual or linguistic confusion, as in the cases just mentioned.

Note that if someone says, "Cicero was bald but Tully was not", there need be *no* grounds to suppose that he is under *any* linguistic or conceptual confusion.

24. This should not be confused with the question whether the speaker simultaneously believes *of* a given object, both that it has a certain property and that it does not have it. Our discussion concerns *de dicto* (notional) belief, not *de re* belief.

I have been shown a passage in Aristotle that appears to suggest that *no one* can really believe both of two explicit contradictories. If we wish to use the *simple* disquotational principle as a test for disbelief, it suffices that this be true of *some* individuals, after reflection, who are simultaneously aware of both beliefs, and have sufficient logical acumen and respect for logic. Such individuals, if they have contradictory beliefs, will be shaken in one or both beliefs after they note the contradiction. For such individuals, sincere reflective assent to the negation of a sentence implies disbelief in the proposition it expresses, so the test in the text applies.

25. For example, in translating a historical report into another language, such as "Patrick Henry said, 'Give me liberty or give me death!'", the translator may well translate the quoted material attributed to Henry. He translates a presumed truth into a falsehood, since Henry spoke English; but probably his reader is aware of this and is more interested in the content of Henry's utterance than in its exact words. Especially in translating fiction, where truth is irrelevant, this procedure is appropriate. But some objectors to Church's 'translation argument' have allowed themselves to be misled by the practice.

26. To state the argument precisely, we need in addition a form of the Tarskian disquotation principle for truth: For each (French or English) replacement for 'p', infer "'p' is true" from "p", and conversely. (Note that "'p' is true" becomes an English sentence even if 'p' is replaced by a French sentence.) In the text we leave the application of the Tarskian disquotational principle tacit.

27. I gather that Burali-Forti originally thought he had 'proved' that the ordinals are not linearly ordered, reasoning in a manner similar to our topologist. Someone who heard the present paper delivered told me that König made a similar error.

28. It is not possible, in this case, as it is in the case of the man who assents to "Jones is a doctor" but not to "Jones is a physician", to refuse to apply the disquotational principle on the grounds that the subject must lack proper command of the language or be subject to some linguistic or conceptual confusion. As long as Pierre is unaware that 'London' and '*Londres*' are codesignative, he need not lack appropriate linguistic knowledge, nor need he be subject to any linguistic or conceptual confusion when he affirms '*Londres est jolie*' but denies 'London is pretty'.

29. The 'elimination' would be most plausible if we believed, according to a Russellian epistemology, that all my language, when written in unabbreviated notation, refers to constituents with which I am 'acquainted' in Russell's sense. Then no one speaks a language intelligible to anyone else; indeed, no one speaks the same language twice. Few today will accept this.

A basic consideration should be stressed here. Moderate Fregeans attempt to combine a roughly Fregean view with the view that names are part of our common language, and that our conventional practices of interlinguistic translation and interpretation are correct. The problems of the present paper indicate that it is very difficult to obtain a requisite socialized notion of sense that will enable such a program to succeed. Extreme Fregeans (such as Frege and Russell) believe that in general names are peculiar to idiolects. They therefore would accept no general rule translating '*Londres*' as 'London,' nor even translating one person's use of 'London' into another's. However, if they follow Frege in regarding senses as 'objective', they must believe that in principle it makes sense to speak of two people using two names in their respective idiolects with the same sense, and that there must be (necessary and) sufficient conditions for this to be the case. If these conditions for sameness of sense are satisfied, translation of one name into the other is legitimate, otherwise not. The present considerations (and the extension of these below to natural kind and related terms), however, indicate that the notion of sameness of sense, if it is to be explicated in terms of sameness of identifying properties and if these properties are themselves expressed in the languages of the two respective idiolects, presents interpretation problems of the same type presented by the names themselves. Unless the Fregean can give a method for identifying sameness of sense that is free of such problems, he *has no sufficient conditions for sameness of sense, nor for translation to be legitimate.* He would therefore be forced to maintain, contrary to Frege's intent, that not only in practice do few people use proper names with the same sense but that *it is principle meaningless to compare sense.* A view that the identifying properties used to define senses should always be expressible in a Russellian language of 'logically proper names' would be one solution to this difficulty but involves a doubtful philosophy of language and epistemology.

30. If any reader finds the term 'translation' objectionable with respect to names, let him be reminded that all I mean is that French sentences containing '*Londres*' are uniformly translated into English with 'London'.

31. The paradox would be blocked if we required that they define the names by the same properties expressed in the same words. There is nothing in the motivation of the classical description theories that would justify this extra clause. In the present case of French and English, such a restriction would amount to a decree that neither '*Londres*', nor any other conceivable French name, could be translated as 'London'. I deal with this view immediately below.

32. Word salads of two languages (like ungrammatical 'semisentences' of a single language) need not be unintelligible, though they are makeshifts with no fixed syntax. "If God did not exist, Voltaire said, *il faudrait l'inventer.*" The meaning is clear.

33. Had we said, "Pierre believes that the country he calls '*Angleterre*' is a monarchy", the sentence would be English, since the French word would be mentioned but not used. But for this very reason we would not have captured the sense of the French original.

34. Under the influence of Quine's *Word and Object*, some may argue that such conclusions are not inevitable: perhaps he will translate '*médecin*' as 'doctor stage', 'undetached part of a doctor'! If a Quinean sceptic makes an empirical prediction that such reactions from bilinguals as a matter of fact can occur, I doubt that he

will be proved correct. (I do not know what Quine would think, but see *Word and Object*, p. 74, first paragraph.) On the other hand, if the translation of 'médecin' as 'doctor' rather than 'doctor part' in this situation *is*, empirically speaking, inevitable, then even the advocate of Quine's thesis will have to admit that there is something special about one particular translation. The issue is not crucial to our present concerns, so I leave it with these sketchy remarks. But see also n. 36.

35. Putnam gives the example of elms and beeches in "The Meaning of 'Meaning'" (in *Language, Mind, and Knowledge* (University of Minnesota Press, 1975) also reprinted in Putnam's *Philosophical Papers*, ii (Cambridge University Press, 1975). See also Putnam's discussion of other examples on pp. 139–43; also my own remarks on 'fool's gold', tigers, etc. in 'Naming and Necessity', pp. 316–23.

36. It is unclear to me how far this can go. Suppose Pierre hears English spoken only in England, French in France, and learns both by direct method. (Suppose also that no one else in each country speaks the language of the other.) Must he be sure that 'hot' and '*chaud*' are coextensive? In practice he certainly would. But suppose somehow his experience is consistent with the following bizarre—and of course, false!—hypothesis: England and France differ atmospherically so that human bodies are affected very differently by their interaction with the surrounding atmosphere. (This would be more plausible if France were on another planet.) In particular, within reasonable limits, things that feel cold in one of the countries feel hot in the other, and *vice versa*. Things don't change their *temperature* when moved from England to France, they just *feel* different because of their effects on human physiology. Then '*chaud*', in French, would be true of the things that are called 'cold' in English! (Of course the present discussion is, for lack of space, terribly compressed. See also the discussion of 'heat' in 'Naming and Necessity'. We are simply creating, for the physical property 'heat', a situation analogous to the situation for natural kinds in the text.)

If Pierre's experiences were arranged somehow so as to be consistent with the bizarre hypothesis, and he somehow came to believe it, he might simultaneously assent to '*C'est chaud*' and 'This is cold' without contradiction, even though he speaks French and English normally in each country separately.

This case needs much more development to see if it can be set up in detail, but I cannot consider it further here. Was I right in assuming in the text that the difficulty could not arise for '*médecin*' and 'doctor'?

37. One might argue that Peter and we do speak different dialects, since in Peter's idiolect 'Paderewski' is used ambiguously as a name for a musician and a statesman (even though these are in fact the same), while in our language it us used unambiguously for a musician-statesman. The problem then would be whether Peter's dialect can be translated homophonically into our own. Before he hears of 'Paderewski-the-statesman', it would appear that the answer is affirmative for his (then unambiguous) use of 'Paderewski', since he did not differ from anyone who happens to have heard of Paderewski's musical achievements but not of his statesmanship. Similarly for his later use of 'Paderewski', if we ignore his earlier use. The problem is like Pierre's, and is essentially the same whether we describe it in terms of whether Peter satisfies the condition for the disquotational principle to

be applicable, or whether homophonic translation of his dialect into our own is legitimate.

38. D. Davidson, 'On Saying That', in D. Davidson and J. Hintikka (eds.), *Words and Objections* Dordreect: Reidel, 1969), 166 [824 in this vol.].

39. In *Word and Object*, p. 221, Quine advocates a second level of canonical notation, "to dissolve verbal perplexities or facilitate logical deductions", admitting the propositional attitudes, even though he thinks them "baseless" idioms that should be excluded from a notation "limning the true and ultimate structure of reality".

40. In one respect the considerations mentioned above on natural kinds show that Quine's translation apparatus is insufficiently sceptical. Quine is sure that the native's *sentence* "Gavagai!" should be translated "Lo, a rabbit!", provided that its affirmative and negative stimulus meanings for the native match those of the English sentence for the Englishman; scepticism sets in only when the linguist proposes to translate the *general term* 'gavagai' as 'rabbit' rather than 'rabbit stage', 'rabbit part', and the like. But there is another possibility that is independent of (and less bizarre than) such sceptical alternatives. In the geographical area inhabited by the natives, there may be a species indistinguishable to the nonzoologist from rabbits but forming a distinct species. Then the 'stimulus meanings', in Quine's sense, of 'Lo, a rabbit!' and 'Gavagai!' may well be identical (to nonzoologists), especially if the ocular irradiations in question do not include a specification of the geographical locality. ('Gavagais' produce the same ocular irradiation patterns as rabbits.) Yet 'Gavagai!' and 'Lo, a rabbit!' are hardly synonymous; on typical occasions they will have opposite truth values.

I believe that the considerations about names, let alone natural kinds, emphasized in 'Naming and Necessity' go against any simple attempt to base interpretation solely on maximizing agreement with the affirmations attributed to the native, matching of stimulus meanings, etc. The 'principle of Charity' on which such methodologies are based was first enunciated by Neil Wilson in the special case of proper names as a formulation of the cluster-of-descriptions theory. The argument of 'Naming and Necessity' is thus directed against the simple 'Principle of Charity' for that case.

41. Geach introduced the term 'Shakespearean' after the line, "A rose/By any other *name*, would smell as sweet".

Quine seems to define 'referentially transparent' contexts so as to imply that coreferential names and definite descriptions must be interchangeable *salva veritate*. Geach stresses that a context may be 'Shakespearean' but not 'referentially transparent' in this sense.

42. Generally such cases may be slightly less watertight than the 'London'/'Londres' case. '*Londres*' just is the French version of 'London', while one cannot quite say that the same relation holds between '*Ashkenaz*' and '*Germaniah*'. Nevertheless:

(a) Our standard practice in such cases is to translate both names of the first language into the single name of the second.

(b) Often no nuances of 'meaning' are discernible differentiating such names as 'Ashkenaz' and 'Germaniah', such that we would not say either that Hebrew would have been impoverished had it lacked one of them (or that English is impoverished because it has only one name for Germany), any more than a language is impoverished if it has only one word corresponding to 'doctor' and 'physician'. Given this, it seems hard to condemn our practice of translating both names as 'Germany' as 'loose'; in fact, it would seem that Hebrew just has two names for the same country where English gets by with one.

(c) Any inclinations to avoid problems by declaring, say, the translation of 'Ashkenaz' as 'Germany' to be loose should be considerably tempered by the discussion of analogous problems in the text.

43. In spite of this official view, perhaps I will be more assertive elsewhere.

In the case of 'Hesperus' and 'Phosphorus' (in contrast to 'Cicero' and 'Tully'), where there is a case for the existence of conventional community-wide 'senses' differentiating the two—at least, two distinct modes of 'fixing the reference of two rigid designators'—it is more plausible to suppose that the two names are definitely not interchangeable in belief contexts. According to such a supposition, a belief that Hesperus is a planet is a belief that a certain heavenly body, rigidly picked out as seen in the evening in the appropriate season, is a planet; and similarly for Phosphorus. One may argue that translation problems like Pierre's will be blocked in this case, that 'Vesper' must be translated as 'Hesperus,' not as 'Phosphorus'. As against this, however, two things:

(a) We should remember that sameness of properties used to fix the reference does *not* appear to guarantee in general that paradoxes will not rise. So one may be reluctant to adopt a solution in terms of reference-fixing properties for this case if it does not get to the heart of the general problem.

(b) The main issue seems to me here to be—how essential is a particular mode of fixing the reference to a correct learning of the name? If a parent, aware of the familiar identity, takes a child into the fields in the morning and says (pointing to the morning star), "That is called 'Hesperus'", has the parent mistaught the language? (A parent who says, "Creatures with kidneys are called 'cordates', definitely has mistaught the language, even though the statement is extensionally correct.) To the extent that it is *not* crucial for correct language learning that a particular mode of fixing the reference be used, to that extent there is no 'mode of presentation' differentiating the 'content' of a belief about 'Hesperus' from one about 'Phosphorus'. I am doubtful that the original method of fixing the reference *must* be preserved in transmission of the name.

If the mode of reference fixing *is* crucial, it can be maintained that otherwise identical beliefs expressed with 'Hesperus' and with 'Phosphorus' have definite differences of 'content', at least in an epistemic sense. The conventional ruling against substitutivity could thus be maintained without qualms for some cases, though not as obviously for others, such as 'Cicero' and 'Tully'. But it is unclear to me whether even 'Hesperus' and 'Phosphorus' do have such conventional 'modes of presentation'. I need not take a definite stand, and the verdict may be different for different particular pairs of names. For a brief related discussion, see 'Naming and Necessity', p. 331, first paragraph.

44. However, some earlier formulations expressed disquotationally such as "It was once unknown that Hesperus is Phosphorus" are questionable in the light of the present paper (but see the previous note for this case). I was aware of this question by the time 'Naming and Necessity' was written, but I did not wish to muddy the waters further than necessary at that time. I regarded the distinction between epistemic and metaphysical necessity as valid in any case and adequate for the distinctions I wished to make. The considerations in this paper are relevant to the earlier discussion of the 'contingent *a priori*' as well; perhaps I will discuss this elsewhere.

45. According to Russell, definite descriptions are not genuine singular terms. He thus would have regarded any concept of 'referential opacity' that includes definite descriptions as profoundly misleading. He also maintained a substitutivity principle for 'logically proper names' in belief and other attitudinal contexts, so that for him belief contexts were as 'transparent', in any philosophically decent sense, as truth-functional contexts.

Independently of Russell's views, there is much to be said for the opinion that the question whether a context is 'Shakespearean' is more important philosophically— even for many purposes for which Quine invokes his own concept—than whether it is 'referentially opaque'.

46. I will make some brief remarks about the relation of Benson Mates's problem (see n. 15) to the present one. Mates argued that such a sentence as (*) 'Some doubt that all who believe that doctors are happy believe that physicians are happy', may be true, even though 'doctors' and 'physicians' are synonymous, and even though it would have been false had 'physicians' been replaced in it by a second occurrence of 'doctors'. Church countered that (*) could not be true, since its translation into a language with only one word for doctors (which would translate both 'doctors' and 'physicians') would be false. If *both* Mates's and Church's intuitions were correct, we might get a paradox analogous to Pierre's.

Applying the principle of translation and disquotation to Mates's puzzle, however, involves many more complications than our present problem. First, if someone assents to 'Doctors are happy', but refuses assent to 'Physicians are happy', *prima facie* disquotation does not apply to him since he is under a linguistic or conceptual confusion. (See n. 23.) So there are as yet no grounds, merely because this happened, to doubt that all who believe that doctors are happy believe that physicians are happy.

Now suppose someone assents to 'Not all who believe that doctors are happy believe that physicians are happy'. What is the source of his assent? If it is failure to realize that 'doctors' and 'physicians' are synonymous (this was the situation Mates originally envisaged), then he is under a linguistic or conceptual confusion, so disquotation does not clearly apply. Hence we have no reason to conclude from this case that (*) is true. Alternatively, he may realize that 'doctors' and 'physicians' are synonymous; but he applies disquotation to a man who assents to 'Doctors are happy' but not to 'Physicians are happy', ignoring the caution of the previous paragraph. Here he is not under a simple linguistic confusion (such as failure to realize that 'doctors' and 'physicians' are synonymous), but he appears to be under a deep conceptual confusion (misapplication of the disquotational principle). Perhaps, it may be argued, he misunderstands the 'logic of belief'. Does his conceptual confusion mean that we cannot straightforwardly apply disquotation to his utterance, and that therefore we cannot conclude form his behaviour that (*) is true? I think that, although the issues are delicate, and I am not at present completely sure what answers to give, there is a case for an affirmative answer. (Compare the more extreme case of someone who is so confused that he thinks that someone's *dissent* from 'Doctors are happy' implies that he believes that doctors are happy. If someone's utterance, 'Many believe that doctors are happy', is based on such a misapplication of disquotation, surely we in turn should not apply disquotation to it. The utterer, at least in this context, does not really know what 'belief' means.)

I do *not* believe the discussion above ends the matter. Perhaps I can discuss Mates's problem at greater length elsewhere. Mates's problem is perplexing, and its relation to the present puzzle is interesting. But it should be clear from the preceding that Mates's argument involves issues even more delicate than those that arise with respect to Pierre. First, Mates's problem involves delicate issues regarding iteration of belief contexts, whereas the puzzle about Pierre involves the application of disquotation only to affirmations of (or assents to) *simple* sentences. More important, Mates's problem would not arise in a world where no one ever was under a linguistic or a conceptual confusion, no one ever thought anyone else was under such a confusion, no one ever thought anyone ever thought anyone was under such a confusion, and so on. It is important, both for the puzzle about Pierre and for the Fregean argument that 'Cicero' and 'Tully' differ in 'sense', that they would still arise in such a world. They are entirely free of the delicate problem of applying disquotation to utterances directly or indirectly based on the existence of linguistic confusion. See nn. 15 and 28, and the discussion in the text of Pierre's logical consistency.

Another problem discussed in the literature to which the present considerations may be relevant is that of 'self-consciousness', or the peculiarity of 'I'. Discussions of this problem have emphasized that 'I', even when Mary Smith uses it, is not interchangeable with 'Mary Smith', nor with any other conventional singular term designating Mary Smith. If she is 'not aware that she is Mary Smith', she may assent to a sentence with 'I', but dissent from the corresponding sentence with 'Mary Smith'. It is quite possible that any attempt to clear up the logic of all this will involve itself in the problem of the present paper. (For this purpose, the present discussion might be extended to demonstratives and indexicals.)

The writing of this paper had partial support from a grant from the National Science Foundation, a John Simon Guggenheim Foundation Fellowship, a Visiting Fellowship at All Souls College, Oxford, and a sabbatical leave from Princeton University. Various people at the Jerusalem Encounter and elsewhere, who will not be enumerated, influenced the paper through discussion.

Chapter 39

Direct Reference, Propositional Attitudes, and Semantic Content

Scott Soames

I

What do we want from a semantic theory? A plausible answer is that we want it to tell us what sentences say. More precisely, we want it to tell us what sentences say relative to various contexts of utterance. This leads to the view that the meaning of a sentence is a function from contexts of utterance to what is said by the sentence in those contexts. Call this the propositional attitude conception of semantics.

Another semantic picture that has enjoyed considerable popularity is the truth conditional conception. According to it, the job of a semantic theory is to tell us what the truth conditions of sentences are. On this view, the meaning of sentence can be thought of as a function from contexts of utterance to truth conditions of the sentence as used in those contexts.

Suppose now that we put the propositional attitude and the truth conditional conceptions together. If we do this, it is virtually irresistible to conclude that what is said by a sentence in a context consists in its truth conditions relative to the context. But what are truth conditions?

One natural idea, embraced by the ruling semantic paradigm, is that the truth conditions of a sentence, relative to a context, are the metaphysically possible worlds in which the sentence, as used in the context, is true. Such truth conditions can be specified by a recursive characterization of truth relative to a context and a world. This characterization implicitly associates with each sentence a function representing its meaning. The value of the function at any context as argument is the set of

First appeared in *Philosophical Topics* 15 (1987): 44–87. Reprinted by permission of Scott Soames.

metaphysically possible worlds in which the sentence, as used in the context, is true. It is this that is identified with what is said by the sentence in the context, when the propositional attitude conception of semantics is combined with this version of the truth conditional conception.

This identification is, of course, highly problematic. The first difficulty one notices is that if S and S' are necessarily equivalent relative to a context, then they are characterized as saying the same thing, relative to the context. However, it is highly counterintuitive to hold that all necessary truths say the same thing, that the conjunction of a sentence with any necessary consequence of it says the same thing as the sentence itself, and so on.

A plausible pragmatic principle extends this difficulty to the propositional attitudes of speakers:

(1) A sincere, reflective, compent speaker who assertively utters S in a context C says (or asserts), perhaps among other things, what S says in C.

This principle reflects an incipient relational analysis of the attitude of saying, or asserting—an analysis that sees it as a relation between speakers and things which serve as the semantic contents of sentences. Once this analysis is accepted, it is a short step to view propositional attitude reports in accord with (2) and (3):

(2) An individual i satisfies ⌜x says (asserts) that S⌝ relative to a context C iff i stands in a certain relation R to the semantic content of S in C.

(3) An individual i satisfies ⌜$x\,v$'s that S⌝ (where $v = $ 'believes', 'knows', 'proves', 'expects', etc.) relative to a context C iff i stands in a certain relation R' to the semantic content of S in C.

But now our difficulties are surely unmanageable. Let us characterize distribution over conjunction and closure under necessary consequence as follows:

Distribution over conjunction
If an individual i satisfies ⌜$x\,v$'s that P & Q⌝ relative to C, then i satisfies ⌜$x\,v$'s that P⌝ and ⌜$x\,v$'s that Q⌝ relative to C. (For example, anyone who asserts that P & Q asserts that P and asserts that Q.)

Closure under necessary consequence
If an individual i satisfies ⌜$x\,v$'s that P⌝ relative to C, and if every possible world in which P is true relative to C is a possible world in which Q

is true relative to C, then i satisfies $\ulcorner x v$'s that $Q \urcorner$ relative to C. (For example, anyone who asserts that P asserts everything that necessarily follows from P.)

The second main difficulty with our combined truth conditional and propositional attitude conception of semantics is that it equates distribution of a propositional attitude verb over conjunction with closure of the attitude under necessary consequence. For if Q is a necessary consequence of P, then the set of metaphysically possible worlds in which $\ulcorner P$ & $Q \urcorner$ is true is the same as the set of worlds in which P is true. Given the identification of truth conditions with semantic content, this means that their semantic contents are the same. But then, a relational semantics of propositional attitude reports together with distribution over conjunction will yield closure under necessary consequence.

The problem is that for many propositional attitude verbs distribution over conjunction is a fact whereas closure under necessary consequence is not. My four-year-old son Greg has said many things, and whenever he says that P & Q he says that P and he says that Q. However, there are lots of necessary consequences of things he has said that he has left unasserted, for example that $2^9 = 512$, that first order logic is complete but undecidable, and that stones are made up of molecules.

A third difficulty with our semantic conception takes this problem one step further. The same considerations that lead to the view that beliefs and assertions are closed under necessary consequence lead to the view that no one has ever believed or asserted anything that could not have been true (in any metaphysically possible world). Since every Q is a necessary consequence of an impossible P, anyone who believes or asserts what P expresses believes or asserts everything. And surely, no one ever has, or could have, done that.

The semantic assumptions that lead to these difficulties can be summarized as follows:

(A1a)   The semantic content of sentence (relative to a context) is the collection of circumstances supporting its truth (as used in the context).

(A1b)   The collection of circumstances supporting the truth of a sentence (as it is used in a context) = the set of metaphysically possible worlds in which it is true (relative to the context).

(A2)   Propositional attitude sentences report relations to the semantic contents of their complements—i.e. an individual i satisfies $\ulcorner x v$'s that $S^\lnot$ (relative to a context C) iff i bears R to the semantic content of S (relative to C).

(A3)   Many propositional attitude verbs, including 'say', 'assert', 'believe', 'know', and 'prove' distribute over conjunction.

Since these assumptions lead to unacceptable results, one or more of them must be rejected.

The crucial assumptions are (A1) and (A2), which, in turn, are direct descendants of the two conceptions of semantics mentioned earlier. (A1a and b) represent the truth conditional conception, with metaphysically possible worlds taken as truth conditions. (A2) represents the propositional attitude conception, with the relational analysis of 'say' and 'assert' extended to propositional attitude reports generally. The need to give up one or the other of these assumptions makes it necessary to rethink the fundamental issues underlying these semantic conceptions.

I will focus on the truth conditional conception. Much of the support it has enjoyed comes from the familiarity of the possible worlds machinery plus the fact that the semantic content of a sentence (relative to a context) should determine the possible worlds in which it is true. However, there is a big difference between admitting that semantic content determines such truth conditions and claiming that it should be identified with them. What we need is some conception of semantics in which the content of a sentence determines, but is not determined by, the metaphysically possible worlds in which it is true.

There are two main ways in which such a conception might be developed. One way is to retain the basic assumption (A1a) of the truth conditional conception, while rejecting the characterization of truth conditions, or truth-supporting circumstances, as metaphysically possible worlds. The idea is to try and find some more finely grained circumstances that will distinguish among sentences true in the same worlds. The second way in which an appropriate semantic account might be developed is to give up (A1a) thereby abandoning the fundamental tenet of the truth conditional conception. In its place, one might substitute a conception of semantic contents as complex objects that encode much of the structure of the sentences that express them, and that determine sets of truth-supporting circumstances, without being identified with them.

In what follows, I shall argue for the second approach. The heart of my argument involves the interaction of propositional attitudes with the phenomenon of direct reference. Let us say that a singular term is directly referential iff its semantic content relative to a context (and assignment of values to variables) is its referent relative to the context (and assignment). Variables are the paradigm examples of such terms. In recent years, a number of arguments have been given for treating names and indexicals as directly referential as well. Later, I will show how this view can be defended against certain objections based on the behavior of such terms in propositional attitude ascriptions. To begin with, however, I wish to note the destructive consequences it has when added as a fourth assumption to (A1)–(A3):

(A4) Names, indexicals, and variables are directly referential.

This expanded set of assumptions has a number of clearly unacceptable consequences. Suppose, for example, that Mary assertively utters (4a), while pointing at me. On the assumptions we are considering, she cannot correctly be reported to believe, or to have said, that I am David Kaplan:[1]

(4a) He is David Kaplan (said pointing at Scott).

(4b) Mary says (believes) that he (Scott) is David Kaplan.

The reason for this is that the semantic content of the complement sentence, relative to the context, is taken to be the set of metaphysically possible worlds in which two distinct objects are absolutely identical with one another—that is, the empty set. But then the third difficulty noted above—the impossibility of saying or believing the impossible—comes into play, ruling out the possibility that Mary said or believed what she seemed to say and believe. The same problem arises in a variety of cases, including those in (5):

(5a) John says (believes) that Ruth Marcus is Ruth Barcan's sister.

(5b) Martin says (believes) that this table is made up of atomic particles with properties, P, Q, and R (where it is later discovered that nothing made of such particles could be a table).

The significance of these difficulties is not that they mar an otherwise unproblematic account of the attitudes. As we have seen, the conjunction of (A1)–(A3) is problematic in its own right. Nevertheless, the difficulties arising from the addition of (A4) are special.

I shall argue that these difficulties are intractable for theories that identify semantic contents of sentences with sets of truth-supporting circumstances. Although many of the problems encountered in standard, truth-theoretic accounts of the attitudes can be avoided by substituting fine-grained circumstances for metaphysically possible worlds, those posed by names and indexicals cannot. Not only do these problems resist such treatment, they remain even when assumptions (A2), (A3), and (A4) are weakened substantially. In effect, directly referential singular terms can be used to show that semantic contents of sentences (relative to contexts) cannot be sets of truth-supporting circumstances, no matter how fine-grained.

The reason for this is that such terms require the introduction of structure into semantic contents. After establishing this, I shall consider two different ways in which such structure might be constructed—one based on a modified version of the truth-theoretic approach, the other based on the introduction of structured, Russellian propositions. Although considerations involving directly referential singular terms are insufficient to decide between these alternatives, I shall argue that additional factors favour the Russellian approach. Thus, the end result is an argument for an expanded conception of semantics that includes Russellian propositions as semantic contents of sentences, over and above standard, truth-theoretic intensions and extensions.

II

Let us begin with the strategy of substituting fine-grained truth-supporting circumstances for metaphysically possible worlds. These circumstances can be thought of as arising from the relaxation of certain constraints that hold for such worlds. Taking a cue from Carnap's notion of a state description, we can describe these constraints in terms of their role in constructing a semantics for a language L.

Let D be the set of individuals L is used to talk about, and B be the set of properties expressed by simple predicates of L plus their complements.[2] Let us say that a C-description is a set each of whose members consists of an n-place property plus an n-tuple of objects drawn from D (for variable n). A C-description X is complete iff it contains a complete assignment of objects to properties—i.e. iff for every n-place property P in B, and every $o_1, \ldots, o_n$ in D, either $\langle P, o_1, \ldots, o_n \rangle$ is a member of X or $\langle [-P], o_1, \ldots, o_n \rangle$ is a member of X, where $[-P]$ is the complement of P. A C-description X is *consistent* iff no two of its members are negations of one another—i.e. iff for every n-place property P in B, $\langle P, o_1, \ldots, o_n \rangle$ is a member of X only if $\langle [-P], o_1, \ldots, o_n \rangle$ is not a member of X. A C-

description is *metaphysically possible* only if it is metaphysically possible for the objects mentioned in the description to (jointly) instantiate the properties they are paired with in the description.

For present purposes, truth-supporting circumstances might either be identified with C-descriptions, or be taken to correspond to them. The classifications "complete", "consistent", and "metaphysically possible" can then be applied to circumstances.

Metaphysically possible worlds are truth-supporting circumstances that are metaphysically possible, complete, and consistent. Suppose the first of these constraints is relaxed, while retaining the second and third. This allows truth-supporting circumstances corresponding to every consistent and complete C-description. Thus, we allow metaphysically impossible circumstances in which Ruth Marcus is Ruth Barcan's sister, $2^9 \neq 512$, and I am identical with David Kaplan ('=' being treated as a simple, non-logical predicate in the object language). In effect, we substitute what might be called "logically possible" worlds or circumstances for "metaphysically possible" worlds or circumstances.

However, the structure of the semantic theory remains the same as before. It continues to be a recursive characterization of truth relative to a context and circumstance, with the recursive clauses retaining their standard specifications. The semantic content of a sentence relative to a context is identified with the set of circumstances in which it is true. But since these circumstances are more finely grained than metaphysically possible worlds, we no longer have the results that metaphysically equivalent sentences have the same semantic content, that distribution of a propositional attitude verb over conjunction requires closure of the attitude under metaphysically necessary consequence, or that no one can believe or assert the metaphysically impossible. In this way, substitution of (A1b′) for (A1b) might be seen as alleviating the original difficulties with (A1)–(A4):

(A1b′) The collection of circumstances supporting the truth of a
   sentence (relative to a context) = the set of *logically possible
   worlds* in which it is true (relative to the context).

It does, of course, remain true on this view that logically equivalent sentences have the same semantic content, that distribution of a propositional attitude verb over conjunction requires closure of the attitude under logical consequence, and that no one can believe or assert the logically impossible. However, with another weakening of the constraints even these results can be avoided.

Suppose we give up the requirement that truth-supporting circumstances be complete. Instead we allow circumstances to correspond to (and, in effect, be exhausted by) any consistent C-description. Such circumstances are more like "logically possible facts" than "logically possible worlds". For example, one such circumstance may consist entirely of my being human.

The introduction of partial circumstances has import for certain logical constructions, most notably negation. In order to make semantic use of partiality, one must distinguish between it not being the case that in C an individual o has the basic property P, and it being the case that in C, o has the property of not being P. The latter is a truth-supporting circumstance for the negation of the atomic sentence that predicates P of o; the former is not. Full fledged negation, applied to sentences of arbitrary complexity, as well as related constructions like material implication, raise complications that we need not go into. However, other constructions are straightforward. For example, the recursive clauses governing conjunction, disjunction, and existential generalization are exactly those used in standard, truth-theoretic accounts.

The semantic content of a sentence relative to a context is, as usual, the set of circumstances supporting its truth, as used in the context. However, since circumstances are partial, the semantic contents of logically equivalent sentences are no longer identified. For example, the content of (6a) is not the same as the content of (6b), because the former includes "facts" that are, so to speak, silent about radioactivity:

(6a) Plymouth Rock is in Massachusetts.

(6b) Plymouth Rock is in Massachusetts & (Plymouth Rock is
      radioactive ∨ Plymouth Rock is not radioactive).

This is significant, since, it might be argued, a person lacking the concept of radioactivity might believe that which is expressed by (6a) without believing that which is expressed by (6b). Certainly, it would seem that someone could assert the former without asserting the latter. One way of accounting for this within the framework of (A1–A4) is to substitute (A1b″) for (A1b′):

(A1b″) The collection of circumstances supporting the truth of a
        sentence (relative to a context) = the set of *logically possible
        facts* that would make it true (as used in the context).

This strategy is followed by Jon Barwise and John Perry in their book *Situations and Attitudes*. However, they take it one step further, allowing truth-supporting circumstances to be inconsistent, as well as incomplete and metaphysically impossible. If one ignores complications involving time, tense, and spatio-temporal location, one can take their "abstract situations" to be arbitrary C-descriptions.[3] Allowing these circumstances to be inconsistent, and substituting (A1s) for (A1b″), makes it possible to correctly characterize certain agents as believing and asserting contradictions—e.g. as believing and asserting that London is pretty and London is not pretty.

(A1s)   The collection of circumstances supporting the truth of a sentence (relative to a context) = the set of *abstract situations* which would make it true (as used in the context).

Logically complex constructions are characterized along familiar truth-theoretic lines. For example, we have:

(7a)   The semantic content of a conjunction (relative to a context) is the intersection of the semantic contents of the conjuncts (relative to the context).

(7b)   The semantic content of a disjunction (relative to a context) is the union of the semantic contents of the disjuncts (relative to the context).

(7c)   The semantic content of an existential generalization ⌜For some x: Fx⌝ (relative to a context) is the set of circumstances E such that for some object o in E, o "is F" in, or relative to, E (and the context).[4]

(7d)   The semantic content of ⌜F[an x: Gx]⌝ (relative to a context) is the set of circumstances E such that for some object o in E, o "is G" and o "is F" in, or relative to, E (and the context).

(7e)   The semantic content of ⌜F[the x: Gx]⌝ (relative to a context) is the set of circumstances E such that for exactly one object o in E, o "is G" in, or relative to, E (and the context); and, moreover, o "is F" in, or relative to, E (and the context).

The invariance of these principles across different choices of truth-supporting circumstances reflects the fact that no matter what one's conception of circumstances, the circumstances that make a conjunction true are those that make the conjuncts true; the circumstances that make a disjunction true are those that make either disjunct true; and so on. Indeed, we may take the principles in (7) to be partially constitutive of the view that the semantic content of a sentence consists in the circumstances that support its truth. As such, they may be regarded as corollaries of assumption (A1a).

There is, then, a whole range of possible theories within the standard, truth conditional framework that adopt the same basic approach to the problems posed by various kinds of propositional attitudes. The central idea is to relax the constraints on truth-supporting circumstances. This results in more finely grained semantic contents being attached, in the first instance, to atomic sentences. Logically complex constructions are given the usual recursive treatment, resulting in semantic contents for complex sentences along the lines of (7).

This approach can be seen as an attempt to save the truth conditional conception of semantic content, while countenancing direct reference and continuing to take semantic contents of sentences to be objects of propositional attitudes. Although not without plausibility, it is, I believe, fundamentally flawed. Its chief virtue is its recognition that if assumptions (A2), (A3), and (A4), plus an elementary principle of compositionality,[5] are to be retained, then semantic contents must be more fine-grained than sets of metaphysically possible worlds. Its chief error is its failure to recognize that if these assumptions are retained, then no conception of truth-supporting circumstances validating (7) can do the job, no matter how fine-grained.

III

A number of different arguments can be used to show this. For example, consider (8):

(8a) The ancients believed (asserted) that 'Hesperus' referred to Hesperus and 'Phosphorus' referred to Phosphorus.

(8b) The ancients believed (asserted) that 'Hesperus' referred to Hesperus and 'Phosphorus' referred to Hesperus (from (A2), (A4), and compositionality in the complement).

(8c) The ancients believed (asserted) that 'Hesperus' referred to Hesperus and 'Phosphorus' referred to Hesperus and for some x, 'Hesperus' referred to x and 'Phosphorus' referred to x (from (A1a) and (A2)).

(8d) The ancients believed (asserted) that for some x, 'Hesperus' referred to x and 'Phosphorus' referred to x (where the quantifier is inside the scope of the propositional attitude verb). (From (A3).)

Since (8d) is tantamount to the claim that the ancients believed and asserted that the terms 'Hesperus' and 'Phosphorus' were coreferential, it is false. Since (8a) can be regarded as true, at least one of the principles used in going from (a) to (d) must be rejected.

The first thing to note is that these principles do not include (A1b), (A1s), or any other specific characterization of truth-supporting circumstance. The only use made of truth-supporting circumstances was the appeal to (7a) and (7c) in the move from (b) to (c) in the argument. Since these principles are corollaries of (A1a), acceptance of the other assumptions in the argument requires rejection of the claim that the semantic content of a sentence (relative to a context) is the set of circumstance supporting its truth (as used in the context).

The same point can be made using definite descriptions instead of existential quantification. For example, consider (9):

(9a) y believes (asserts) that Hesperus = the x: Fx and Phosphorus = the x: Gx.

(9b) y believes (asserts) that Hesperus = the x: Fx and Hesperus = the x: Gx (from (A2), (A4), and compositionality in the complement).

(9c) y believes (asserts) that Hesperus = the x: Fx and Hesperus = the x: Gx and the x: Fx = the x: Gx (from (A1) and (A2)).

(9d) y believes (asserts) that the x: Fx = the x: Gx (where the descriptions are used attributively and are within the scope of the propositional attitude verb). (From A3.)

The move from (b) to (c) is justified if every circumstance supporting the truth of the complement of (b) supports the truth of the complement of (c). One gets this if circumstances are metaphysically possible worlds, since any world in which o is identical with o' and o'' is a world in which o' and o'' are identical.

However, there is no need to rest the case on special assumptions about circumstances, or identity. By recasting the example one can make use of the semantics (7e) for definite descriptions to construct an argument that applies to all the theories in section II. One simply starts with (9a') instead of (9a):

(9a') y believes (asserts) that Hesperus = the x: Fx and Phosphorus = the x: Gx and the x: Fx = the x: Fx and Hesperus = the x such that Hesperus = x.

It follows from (7a) that a circumstance E will support the truth of the complement of (9a′)) iff it supports the truth of each of its conjuncts. It follows from (7e) that E will support the truth of the final conjunct iff there is exactly one object o such that Hesperus $= o$ in E. Since Hesperus is Phosphorus, this means that o must be both the unique F-er in E and the unique G-er in E. The third conjunct requires that $o = o$ in E. This guarantees that E will be a member of the semantic content of the complement of (9d). Thus, (A2), (A3), (A4), and a principle of compositionality allow one to derive (9d) from (9a′), no matter how finely grained one takes truth-supporting circumstances to be.[6] Since (9d) may be false even when (9a′) is true, acceptance of (A2), (A3), (A4), and the compositionality principle requires rejection of (A1a).

A more startling illustration of this conclusion can be constructed using the examples in (10):

(10a) Mark Twain $=$ Herman Melville and Samuel Clemens $=$ Stephen Crane.

(10b) Mark Twain $=$ the x such that Mark Twain $= x$.

(a) is an embarrassment to standard treatments of the attitudes (encompassing (A2)–(A4)) in which truth-supporting circumstances are taken to be metaphysically possible worlds. Since its semantic content in such systems is the empty set, everything is a semantic consequence of it. Thus, that which it expresses cannot be believed or asserted.

One of the virtues of systems that relax constraints on truth-supporting circumstances is that they avoid this embarrassment. In such systems the semantic content of (10a) is a non-empty set of circumstances in which three distinct individuals are identified. Although such circumstances are metaphysically impossible, they are regarded as semantically legitimate, and hence are available for the construction of semantic contents. Thus, it is perfectly possible, in a system like that of *Situations and Attitudes*, for a person to believe or assert that which is expressed by (10a).

Belief or assertion of that which is expressed by (10b) is unproblematic on any account. However, now consider their conjunction, (10c):

(10c) Mark Twain $=$ Herman Melville and Samuel Clemens $=$ Stephen Crane and Mark Twain $=$ the x such that Mark Twain $= x$.

In order for a circumstance E to be a member of the semantic content of this sentence, E must be a member of the semantic content of each conjunct. In order for E to be a member of the semantic content of the first two conjuncts it must be the case that in E Mark Twain is identified with two distinct individuals. But now E cannot be a member of the semantic content of the third conjunct, since, by (7e), that conjunct requires that Mark Twain be identified with only one object. The semantic content of (10c) is, therefore, the empty set. Thus, the problems posed by (10a) for theories embracing the original (A1)–(A4) are reproduced by (10c) for theories that substitute finer grained truth-supporting circumstances for metaphysically possible worlds.[7]

Although this example is particularly graphic, the basic difficulty is extremely general. It is repeated in (11), where (b) is derived from (a) using the semantics (7d) for indefinite descriptions, and in (12), where a similar derivation uses material implications:[8]

(11a) x believes (asserts) that Mark Twain wrote the greatest American novel and Samuel Clemens was an ignorant illiterate.

(11b) x believes (asserts) that an ignorant illiterate wrote the greatest American novel (where the indefinite description is attributive and inside the scope of the propositional attitude verb).

(12a) x believes (asserts) that Mark Twain is F and if Samuel Clemens is F then S (where F is any predicate and S is any sentence).

(12b) x believes (asserts) that S.

The difficulty common to all these cases is, I suggest, not due to special assumptions about particular constructions (existential quantification, definite descriptions, indefinite descriptions, conjunction, material implication, etc.) Rather, the general assumptions (A1a), (A2), (A3), and (A4) (plus compositionality in the complements of propositional attitude verbs) are jointly incompatible with facts about propositional attitudes and propositional attitude ascriptions. In short, we have established (13):

(13)   If direct reference is legitimate and (some) propositional attitude verbs have a relational semantics ((A4) plus (A2)), then (assuming compositionality and distribution over conjunction) the semantic contents of sentences relative to contexts cannot be sets of truth-supporting circumstances (that validate 7).

This way of putting the matter is, of course, not neutral, since it suggests that the assumption to be rejected is (A1a). This suggestion can be supported by showing that the remaining assumptions are both stronger than needed to refute (A1a) and more plausible than they might initially appear.

IV

First consider (A4). The arguments in section III all involve proper names. Thus, one response to them might be to give up the claim that names are directly referential, thereby blocking substitution of coreferential names in propositional attitude ascriptions. It is important to note that this response is insufficient, since, in each case the problem an be recreated using other terms.

For example, so long as direct reference is retained for demonstratives, (A1a), (A2), (A3), and compositionality will allow one to derive the false (14b) from the potentially true (14a):

(14a) The ancients believed (asserted) that their such-and-such utterance referred to this (pointing in the morning to Venus) and (speaking very slowly) their so-and-so utterance referred to that (pointing in the evening to Venus).

(14b) The ancients believed (asserted) that for some x, their such-and-such utterance referred to x and their so-and-so utterance referred to x.

The same point can be made using variables in place of names and indexicals:

(15a) There is a planet x which is seen in the morning sky and a planet y which is seen in the evening sky and the ancients believed that x was seen in the morning sky and y was seen in the evening sky.
$(\exists x: Px \ \& \ Mx) \ (\exists y: Py \ \& \ Ey) \ (a \ \text{believed that} \ (Mx \ \& \ Ey))$.

(15b) The planet seen in the morning sky is the planet seen in the evening sky.
the $x: (Px \ \& \ Mx) = $ the $y: (Py \ \& \ Ey)$.

(15a) is true iff there is an assignment f which assigns a planet seen in the morning sky to 'x' and a planet seen in the evening sky to 'y' such that the open belief sentence is true with respect to f. From (15b) it follows that the referents of 'x' and 'y' with respect to f are identical. But now (A1)–(A4) can be applied as before to derive the false (15c–d) from the true (15a–b):[9]

(15c) There is a planet x and a planet y such that the ancients believed the following: that x was seen in the morning sky and y was seen in the evening sky and there was something which was (both) seen in the morning sky and seen in the evening sky.
$(\exists x: Px)(\exists y: Py)(a$ believed that $((Mx \, \& \, Ey) \, \& \, \exists z(Mz \, \& \, Ez)))$.

(15d) The ancients believed that there was something which was (both) seen in the morning sky and seen in the evening sky.
$(a$ believed that $\exists z(Mz \, \& \, Ez))$.

Thus, if direct reference is the source of the difficulty, it must be banned entirely—for names, indexicals, and variables. But this is implausible; the arguments for it are too strong, and there are too many cases (where the words of the speaker differ systematically from those of the agent of the attitude) in which it is instrumental in capturing clear semantic intuitions.

There is, however, another way in which one might try to block the problematic arguments. Each of them relies on assumptions—(A2), compositionality, and some version of direct reference—that jointly legitimate the substitution of coreferential terms in propositional attitude ascriptions. It might be thought that such substitution is the source of the problem. As against this, it is worth noting that the difficulty can be recreated without appealing to substitutivity, or the assumptions that give rise to it.

Instead of relying on semantic analyses of propositional attitude statements one can invoke principles underlying our practice of reporting propositional attitudes and ascribing them to individuals. Why, for example, do we ascribe to the ancients the belief and assertion that Hesperus was visible in the evening, while being reluctant (at least initially) to ascribe to them the belief and assertion that Phosphorus was visible in the evening? Probably because they assertively uttered sentences whose English translation is 'Hesperus is visible in the evening', but refused to assertively utter (and indeed dissented from) sentences whose English translation is 'Phosphorus is visible in the evening'. These examples suggest (if we focus on indexical-free sentences and ignore complications involving time and tense) the following principles of propositionat attitude ascription:

(16a) If a competent speaker x of a language L sincerely and reflectively assents to (or assertively utters) an indexical-free sentence s of L, and if p is a proper English translation of s, then x satisfies $\ulcorner y$ believes that $p \urcorner$. (Note that this covers the case in which $L =$ English and $s = p$.)

(16b) If a sincere, reflective, and competent speaker x of a language L assertively utters an indexical-free sentence s of L, and if p is a proper English translation of s, then x satisfies $\ulcorner y$ says (asserts) that $p \urcorner$.

These principles are, of course, modelled after Kripke's principles of (weak) disquotation and translation.[10] With them we can derive the concluion that Kripke's bilingual speaker Pierre believes and asserts both that London is pretty and that London is not pretty. The former follows from his sincere and reflective utterance of 'Londres est jolie', plus (16) and an elementry truth of translation. The latter follows from his equally sincere and reflective utterance of 'London is not pretty', plus either (16) alone, or (16) in conjunction with homophonic translation.

It seems to me that these ascriptions to Pierre are correct. It is, of course, striking that Pierre's beliefs and assertions should be contradictory without his having made any mistake in logic or reasoning. However, this just shows that in certain cases one may be in no position to determined the consistency of one's statements and beliefs.

The point is particularly obvious in the case of what is said or asserted. Imagine Pierre on the telephone talking to a friend in Paris. During the course of the conversation he assertively utters 'Londres est jolie'. After hanging up the phone he says 'London is not pretty' to a visitor who asks his opinion of the city he lives in. What has Pierre said? Clearly, he has said both that London is pretty (to his friend) and that London is not pretty (to the visitor).

Now consider a slight extension of the example. Suppose that there are a number of Frenchmen in London in the same linguistic and epistemic situation as Pierre. When together they converse with one another in French—standard French plus one addition. Since they are unaware that 'Londres' names the city they live in, they use the name 'London' for that purpose. One day Pierre assertively utters 'Londres est jolie et London n'est pas jolie'. I, an English speaker, am asked to report what he said. Since Pierre is competent in his own dialect, I can appeal to (16). Since his dialect is one in which both 'London' and 'Londres' are properly translated into English as 'London', I can report that he said (asserted) that London is pretty and London is not pretty. To avoid puzzling my audience, I will, of course, say more than this. However, the initial report is surely correct. In certain cases two words in one language do have the same translation into a second language (e.g. 'Peking' and 'Bejing' in

English); and assertive utterances by normal, competent speakers can be reported in indirect discourse of the second language.[11]

This fact can be used to reconstruct the arguments of section III without appealing to direct reference, compositionality, or substitutivity at all. In the case at hand, we have used (16b) plus a truth of translation to establish (17):

(17) Pierre said (asserted) that London is pretty and London is not pretty.

To derive (18):

(18) Pierre said (asserted) that London is pretty and London is not pretty and for some x, x is pretty and x is not pretty.

we need only appeal to corollaries (7a) and (7c) of (A1a), plus the following weakened version of (A2):

(A2') An individual i satisfies $\ulcorner x$ v's that $S \urcorner$ (relative to a context C) iff i bears a certain relation R^* to the pair consisting of the content of S (relative to C) and the character of S (i.e. the function from contexts to contents that represents the meaning of S).[12]

(19) follows from (18) by (A3):

(19) Pierre said (asserted) that for some x, x is pretty and x is not pretty.

But (19) is false—Pierre did not assert the proposition that something is both pretty and not pretty. Thus, we have another reductio of (A1a), this time from a considerably weakened set of premisses. Similar reductios can be constructed corresponding to each of the arguments in III.[13]

However, the premisses are still stronger than they need to be. Although (A3) is useful in deriving obviously false conclusions, it is not strictly necessary. (8c), (8c'), (9c), (9c'), (15c), and (18) are all false, and can be derived without (A3):[14]

(8c') The ancients believed (asserted) that 'Hesperus' referred to Hesperus and 'Phosphorus' referred to Phosphorus and for some x, 'Hesperus' referred to x and 'Phosphorus' referred to x.

(9c') y believes (asserts) that Hesperus = the x: Fx and Phosphorus = the x: Gx and the x: Fx = the x: Gx.

Even (A2), and its weakened counterpart (A2'), may give a misleading impression of strength. As presently formulated, they ignore one possible type of semantic information—to wit, information fixing the referent of a name as a matter of linguistic convention. I suspect that arabic numerals are names that carry such information.[15] Some might hold that 'Hesperus' and 'Phosphorus' are, too.[16] If they are, then the weakened principle (A2*) will block substitution of one for the other in propositional attitude ascriptions:[17]

(A2*)   An individual i satisfies $\ulcorner x$ v's that $S \urcorner$ (relative to a context C) iff i bears a certain relation R^{**} to the triple consisting of the content of S (relative to C), the character of S, and an n-tuple of properties $\langle P_1, \ldots, P_n \rangle$, where P_i fixes, as a matter of linguistic convention, the referent of the ith name in S.

However, such a move will not block the reduction of (A1a). First, not all proper names have conventionally associated reference fixing properties. Second, as Kripke has shown, variants of the Pierre case can be constructed in which the names 'London' and 'Londres' *are* associated with the same properties (provided they are not "purely qualitative").[18] Finally, substitution of one term for another is not always required for refutations of (A1a). Suppose, for example, that 'Hesperus' and 'Phosphorus' share the same object as content and the same constant function from contexts to that object as character, but differ in reference fixing properties. Although (A2*) will then block the derivation of (8b) and (8c) from (8a), it will still allow the derivation of (8c'). (The same goes for (15).)[19]

Results like these suggest that the reduction of (A1a) cannot be blocked by any plausible weakening of the subsidiary premises used in the original argument. It is true that those premises jointly give rise to some surprising, and initially counterintuitive, results involving substitution in propositional attitude ascriptions. However, the reductio can be recreated (in a variety of ways) even when those results are avoided, or minimized.

A final illustration of this point is provided by the following example: Professor McX, looking through the open back door of the faculty lounge, sees Y walking down the hall and says to a visitor, "He (pointing to Y) is a professor in the department." A few seconds later Y passes by the front door, and McX says "He (pointing to Y again) is a graduate student in the department." Although McX does not realize that he has pointed twice to the same individual, Y, who has overheard the remarks, can correctly say, "McX said both that I am a professor in the department and that I am a graduate student in the department."

Developing the example further, we can have McX conjoin his remarks:

(20) Who is in the department? Let me see. He (pointing to Y as he passes the back door) is a professor in the department and (turning) he (pointing to Y as he passes the front door) is a graduate student in the department.

On the basis of McX's remark, Y says:

(21) McX said that I am a professor in the department and I am a graduate student in the department.

Y's assertion is unexceptionable. Unlike some other examples we have considered, this one does not require the creation of an unusual situation; it does not involve attributing conflicting statements (or beliefs) to an otherwise rational agent; nor does it raise the suspicion that adherence to otherwise plausible principles forces us to accept a counterintuitive result. Whatever semantic analysis of propositional attitude ascriptions turns out to be correct, Y's report is one that we want, pre-theoretically, to come out true.

This is not the case with (22) (where the quantifier is understood as being inside the scope of the propositional attitude verb):

(22a) Professor McX said (asserted) this: that there is at least one x such that x is a professor in the department and x is a graduate student in the department and I am a professor in the department and I am a graduate student in the department.

(22b) Professor McX said (asserted) that there is at least one x such that x is a professor in the department and x is a graduate student in the department.

These reports are clearly not true.[20]

If this is correct, then the problem for (A1a) is obvious. Corollaries (7a) and (7c) of that principle characterize the complements of (21) and (22a) as having the same content (with respect to the context). But then there will be no semantic value (content, character, or reference fixing properties) differentiating them. As a result, virtually any relational semantics of assertion-ascriptions (e.g. (A2), (A2'), (A2*)) will assign (21) and (22a) the same truth value. (A3) will then extend this error to (22b). Since these results are unacceptable, while relational treatments of assertion and other attitudes remain plausible, (A1a) should be rejected.

V

We have just seen that the impossibility result of section III can be reproduced using (A1a) together with sets of auxiliary premises considerably weaker than the original (A2), (A3), (A4), and compositionality. This constitutes an important reason for taking that result to be a reductio of the assumption that semantic contents of sentences are sets of truth-supporting circumstances. Another reason is that the supplementary assumptions of the original argument are themselves highly justified.

This can be seen by looking at what many regard as the most questionable consequence of those assumptions, namely (23):[21]

(23) If i satisfies $\ulcorner x$ v's that $S\urcorner$ relative to a context C (and assignment f), and if t and t' are names, indexicals, or free variables having the same referent relative to C (and f), then i satisfies $\ulcorner x$ v's that $S'\urcorner$ relative to C (and f), where S' arises from S by substituting one or more occurrences of t' for occurrences of t.

Many seem to think that counterexamples to this principle are easy to come by. In the case of belief ascriptions, they tend to be examples in which a competent speaker assents to S and $\ulcorner I$ believe that $S\urcorner$, while dissenting from S' and $\ulcorner I$ believe that $S'\urcorner$, even though the latter arise from the former by substitution of names or indexicals with the same referent. Such cases tell against (23) only if assent and dissent are reliable guides to what is, and what is not, believed. However, dissent is not reliable in this way.[22]

A recent example of Mark Richard's makes this point quite nicely:[23]

Consider A—a man stipulated to be intelligent, rational, a competent speaker of English, etc.—who both sees a woman, across the street, in a phone booth, and is speaking to a woman through the phone. He does not realize that the woman to whom he is speaking—B, to give her a name—is the woman he sees. He perceives her to be in some danger—a runaway steamroller, say, is bearing down upon her phone both. A waves at the woman; he says nothing into the phone, ... If A stopped and quizzed himself concerning what he believes, he might well sincerely utter:

(3) I believe that she is in danger.

but not

(4) I believe that you are in danger.

Many people, I think, suppose that ... [these sentences] clearly diverge in truth value, (3) being true and (4) being false.... But [this] view ... is, I believe, demonstrably false. In order to simplify the statement of the argument which shows that the truth of (4) follows from the truth of (3), allow me to assume that A is the unique man watching B. Then we may argue as follows:

Suppose that (3) is true, relative to A's context. Then B can truly say that the man watching her—A, of course—believes that she is in danger. Thus, if B were to utter

(5) The man watching me believes that I am in danger

(even through the telephone) she would speak truly. But if B's utterance of (5) through the telephone, heard by A, would be true, then A would speak truly, were he to utter, through the phone

(6) the man watching you believes that you are in danger.

Thus, (6) is true, taken relative to A's context.
But, of course,

(7) I am the man watching you

is true, relative to A's context. [Which is not, of course, to say that A would accept it. My addition.] But (4) is deducible from (6) and (7). Hence, (4) is true, relative to A's context.

In this example, Richard is concerned with substitution of coreferential indexicals. However, the argument seems to generalize. Suppose, for example, that ⌜A believes that Ruth Barcan is F⌝ is true relative to a context. ⌜A believes that I am F⌝ should then be true relative to a corresponding context in which Ruth Barcan (i.e. Ruth Marcus) is the agent (where F is free of first person pronouns). Suppose, in fact, that Ruth utters the sentence in a conversation with someone who knows her as "Ruth Marcus". It would seem that this person can truly report ⌜A believes that she (pointing at Ruth) is F⌝, or even ⌜A believes that Ruth Marcus is F⌝. Thus, substitution of one coreferential name or indexical for another preserves truth value. Since there seems to be nothing special about this example, we have a general argument for (23).[24]

Why, then, does substitution so often provoke resistance? The answer, I think, has to do, at least in part, with the conversational purposes served by propositional attitude ascriptions. For example, suppose that Mary's neighbour, Samuel Clemens, is in the habit of soliciting her opinion of his manuscripts before sending them off to the publisher. Mary thinks they are wonderful, and regards Mr Clemens (whom she knows only under that name) as a great writer. The question is, does she think that Mark Twain is a great writer?

First consider a conversation the purpose of which is to determine Mary's opinion of various authors. The conversational participants, who use the name 'Mark Twain' to refer to the author, want to know Mary's opinion of him. I, knowing Mary's situation, report "Mary thinks that Mark Twain is a great writer." My remark seems perfectly acceptable.

However, now consider a different conversation. Mary, who is a student, has just taken a written examination, and her teacher is explaining why she failed to get a perfect score. The teacher says, "Mary did a good job, but she didn't know that Mark Twain is a writer." In the context of this conversation, the teacher's remark also seems acceptable.

But how can it be? Surely it is not the case that Mary thinks that Mark Twain is a great writer, while not knowing that Mark Twain is a writer at all.[25] To clarify this we need to distinguish between the proposition semantically expressed by a sentence relative to a context, and the information conveyed by an utterance of the sentence in a conversation. In the second conversation, the proposition semantically expressed by the propositional attitude ascription is false, even though the primary information conveyed by the utterance is true—namely, that Mary did not know that 'Mark Twain is a writer' is true; and hence was not able to answer exam questions of the sort, "What is Mark Twain's profession?" The teacher's utterance seems acceptable because the main information it conveys is correct.

This example brings out an important point about the relationship between propositional and sentential attitudes. Attitudes like asserting and believing are relations between individuals and propositions. However, often these attitudes arise in connection with attitudes towards sentences—e.g. uttering and accepting. Although propositional attitude ascriptions report relations to particular propositions, they often suggest corresponding relations to certain sentences. For example, a competent speaker of English typically (though not always) knows that 'Mark Twain is a writer' is true iff he knows that Mark Twain is a writer. Thus, it is natural that the teacher's remark should carry the meta-linguistic suggestion.

It is also natural that in many cases these suggestions should be important to the conversation. As John Perry has emphasized, sentential attitudes are often more significant for explaining action than propositional attitudes are.[26] Think again of Richard's telephone example. Suppose that a third party asks the question "Why doesn't A tell B that she is in danger?" (We assume that A knows his conversational partner under the name 'B' and accepts 'You are B' in the context.) It is tempting to try to explain A's behaviour by saying "A doesn't know that B is in danger." But this, as we have seen, is false. A better explanation is that A does not accept the sentence 'B is in danger'. The reason we are tempted by the propositional attitude ascription is that normally we would expect A to accept the sentence iff he thought that B was in danger. However, in this case the usual correlation between sentential and propositional attitudes breaks down. As a result, the explanation suggested by the propositional attitude ascription is correct, even though the ascription itself is false.

The general thesis, then, is that the substitutivity principle (23) is correct; and that resistance to it is based on a failure to properly distinguish the semantic information expressed by a sentence relative to a context from the information conveyed by an utterance of it in a given conversation.[27] If this is correct, then the main objection to assumptions (A2), (A4), and compositionality is eliminated, and the case against (A1a) is strengthened.

VI

What becomes of the difficulties in III once this assumption is given up? Taking the argument in (8) as a representative example, we see that the move from (8b) to (8c), and ultimately to (8d), is no longer warranted. In order to defend this as the proper response to the difficulty, I must explain how one might believe (or assert) an instance of an existential generalization, without believing (or asserting) the generalization itself. Let us focus in particular on the notion of belief. Then, what must be explained is how an individual might satisfy an open sentence $\ulcorner x$ believes that $R(t,t)\urcorner$, for directly referential t, without satisfying $\ulcorner x$ believes that $R(t,t)$ and for some y, $R(y,y)\urcorner$, or $\ulcorner x$ believes that for some y, $R(y,y)\urcorner$.

It should be noted that the answer is not that the agent may never have actually drawn the relevant conclusion. For the problematic derivation in (8) would proceed from true premises to a false conclusion even if the agents were perfect logicians. Thus, there must be some deeper explanation of how a person might fail to believe the existential generalization of something he already believes.

There are two different aspects of such an explanation. The first is a metaphysical characterization of the nature of belief, specifying the facts in virtue of which belief ascriptions are true. The second is a specification of the objects of belief needed in a semantic theory. I will say a word about each.

Regarding the former, we may think of beliefs as arising from certain kinds of mental states, together with their causal relations to objects in the environment.[28] On this picture, a belief report $\ulcorner x$ believes that $S\urcorner$ characterizes the agent as being in a mental state whose information content is identical with the semantic content of S in the context of the report. For example, an agent who is in a mental state appropriate for believing that a particular object is F will be correctly reported to believe that Phosphorus is F just in case the relevant part of his belief state is causally anchored to Phosphorus. Since Phosphorus is Hesperus, the agent will thereby believe that Hesperus is F.

Suppose the agent believes that Hesperus bears R to Phosphorus. On this picture, he thereby believes of a certain object o that o bears R to o. However, it does not follow that he believes the proposition that something bears R to itself. Since none of the agent's mental states has this as its information content, he does not believe it.

If we restrict our attention to cases in which the agent is a competent speaker of a language, we can make this account less abstract by letting dispositions to assent to sentences play the role of mental states. We then assume something like (24):[29]

(24) If i is a sincere, reflective, and competent speaker, then i satisfies $\ulcorner x$ believes that $S\urcorner$ relative to a context C (and assignment f) iff i is disposed to assent to some sentence S' whose semantic content in the context of assent = the semantic content of S relative to C (and f).

Let us suppose that the agent accepts $\ulcorner R(\text{Hesperus, Phosphorus})\urcorner$ while rejecting $\ulcorner R(\text{Hesperus, Hesperus})\urcorner$ and $\ulcorner$For some $x\ R(x, x)\urcorner$. An impeccable logician, the agent would accept the latter if he accepted any of its instances, $\ulcorner R(a, a)\urcorner$. However, he rejects all of these. Since the semantic content of one of the sentences he accepts is identical with the semantic content of $\ulcorner R(\text{Hesperus, Hesperus})\urcorner$, he believes that Hesperus bears R to Hesperus even though he would not express his belief this way. Since the semantic content of $\ulcorner$For some $x\ R(x, x)\urcorner$ is not identical with the content of any sentence he is disposed to accept, he does not believe that something bears R to itself. Thus, there is a principled way of blocking the move from (8b) to (8d).

What we need now is a conception of semantic content capable of incorporating this point. Given that the move from (8c) to (8d) is unproblematic, we need a conception that blocks the move from (8b) to (8c) by assigning different semantic contents to the complement sentences in these examples. This requires the introduction of structure into contents.

First consider simple sentences:

(25a) R(Hesperus, Phosphorus)

(25b) R(Hesperus, Hesperus)

(25c) R(Hesperus, itself).

Regimenting a bit, we can think of the semantic contents of these examples as being identical with that of certain canonical representations:

(26a) $R(h, p)$

(26b) $R(h, h)$

(26c) $[\lambda x\ R(x, x)]h$.

Where o is the referent of 'Hesperus' and 'Phosphorus' the content of (a) and (b) is, in effect, $\langle\langle o, o\rangle$, the two place property $R\rangle$; the content of (c) is $\langle\langle o\rangle$, the one place property of bearing R to oneself$\rangle$.[30]

Accepting (a) leads to a belief whose object is the first of these semantic contents; accepting (c) leads to a belief whose object is the second such content. Accepting (b) typically leads to a belief in both. The reason for this has to do with the transparent linguistic relationship between (b) and (c). A competent speaker who accepts one will normally be disposed to accept the other, thereby acquiring both beliefs.[31]

Thus, a speaker who satisfies (27a) will standardly satisfy both (27b) and (27c):

(27a) x accepts 'R(Hesperus, Hesperus)'

(27b) x believes that 'R(Hesperus, Hesperus)

(27c) x believes that 'R(Hesperus, itself).

However, not everyone who satisfies (27b) satisfies (27c). Whether or not the latter is satisfied will depend on the manner in which the agent believes that Hesperus bears R to Hesperus. If he believes it in virtue of accepting a sentence of the form '$R(a, a)$' then he can be expected to believe that Hesperus bears R to itself. However, if he believes it in virtue of accepting a sentence of the form '$R(a, b)$', then (27c) may not be satisfied.

The same point holds for (27d):

(27d) x believes that for some y, $R(y, y)$.

A sincere, reflective, competent speaker who accepts $\ulcorner R(a, a)\urcorner$ will typically be disposed to accept $\ulcorner$For some $y\ R(y, y)\urcorner$, and thereby believe that which it expresses. However, someone who accepts $\ulcorner R(\text{Hesperus, Phosphorus})\urcorner$ may satisfy (27b) without satisfying (27d).

In order to reflect this in a semantic theory we must extend our account of structured semantic contents from atomic sentences to compound sentences of arbitrary complexity. This raises the question of how much structure is needed. Where S is an atomic sentence consisting of an n-place predicate plus n occurrences of directly referential terms, its structured semantic content consists of the content of the predicate plus the content of each term occurrence. There are two ways of thinking of this—as a complex made up of the semantic contents of all occurrences of its semantically significant parts, or as a complex made up of the contents of all occurrences of its directly referential terms, plus the content of whatever else is left over. In the case of atomic sentences, these characterizations come to the same thing. However, they generalize in different ways. The first leads to a conception of the semantic contents of sentences as structured Russellian propositions, the second to a conception of contents as partially structured intensions.

For simplicity let us consider the semantic contents of sentences in a first order language with lambda abstraction, a belief predicate, and a stock of semantically simple singular terms, all of which are directly referential. On the Russellian account, the semantic content of a (free) variable v relative to an assignment f of individuals to variables is $f(v)$, and the semantic content of a closed (directly referential) term, relative to a context, is its referent relative to the context. The semantic contents of n-place predicates are n-place properties and relations. The contents of '&' and '−' are functions, CONJ and NEG, from truth values to truth values.[32]

Variable binding operations, like lambda abstraction and existential quantification, can be treated in a number of ways. One of the simplest, semantically, involves the use of propositional functions in place of complex properties as propositional constituents corresponding to certain compound expressions.[33] On this approach, the semantic content of $\ulcorner[\lambda x\, Rx, x]\urcorner$ is the function g from individuals o to propositions that attribute the property expressed by R to the pair $\langle o, o \rangle$. $\ulcorner\exists x\, Rx, x\urcorner$ can then be thought of as "saying" that g assigns a true proposition to at least one object.

(28) uses these ideas to assign Russellian propositions to sentences:

(28a) The proposition expressed by an atomic formula $\ulcorner Pt_1, \ldots, t_n\urcorner$
      relative to a context C and assignment f is $\langle\langle o_1, \ldots, o_n \rangle, P^* \rangle$, where

P^* is the property expressed by P, and o_i is the content of t_i relative to C and f.

(28b)   The proposition expressed by a formula $\ulcorner[\lambda v S]t\urcorner$ relative to C and f is $\langle\langle o \rangle, g\rangle$, where o is the content of t relative to C and f, and g is the function from individuals o' to propositions expressed by S relative to C and an assignment f' that differs from f at most in assigning o' as the value of v.

(28c)   The propositions expressed by $\ulcorner -S\urcorner$ and $\ulcorner S \& R\urcorner$ relative to C and f are $\langle\text{NEG}, \text{Prop } S\rangle$ and $\langle\text{CONJ}, \langle\text{Prop } S, \text{Prop } R\rangle\rangle$ respectively, where Prop S and Prop R are the propositions expressed by S and R relative to C and f, and NEG and CONJ are the truth functions for negation and conjunction.

(28d)   The proposition expressed by $\ulcorner \exists v S\urcorner$ relative to C and f is $\langle\text{SOME}, g\rangle$, where SOME is the property of being a non-empty set, and g is as in (b).

(28e)   The proposition expressed by $\ulcorner t$ believes that $S\urcorner$ relative to C and f is $\langle\langle o, \text{Prop } S\rangle, B\rangle$, where B is the belief relation, o is the content of t relative to C and f, and Prop S is the proposition expressed by S relative to C and f.

(28f)   The proposition expressed by a sentence (with no free variables) relative to a context C is the proposition it expresses relative to C and every assignment f.

In stating clause (d), I have departed slightly from Russellian ideas in favour of a suggestion by Nathan Salmon. A purely Russellian approach would treat SOME as the property of being a propositional function that is "sometimes true". However, since the existential quantifier is an extensional operator, it seems more natural that it should express a property of the extension of its operand (rather than a property of the propositional constituent expressed by the operand, as in the case of 'believe'). On this formulation, $\langle\text{SOME}, g\rangle$ is true relative to a circumstance E iff the set of objects in E that g maps onto propositions true in E is non-empty.

This discussion of truth conditions brings up an important point. Propositional contents do not replace truth-supporting circumstances in a semantic theory; rather, they supplement them with a new kind of semantic value. On this view, the meaning of an expression is a function from contexts to propositional constituents. The meaning of a sentence is a compositional function from contexts to structured propositions.

Intensions (and extensions) of expressions relative to contexts (and circumstances) derive from intensions (and extensions) of propositions and propositional constituents. These, in turn, can be gotten from a recursive characterization of truth with respect to a circumstance, for propositions.

For this purpose, we let the intension of an n-place property be a function from circumstances to sets of n-tuples of individuals (that instantiate the property in the circumstance); we let the intension of an individual be a constant function from circumstances to that individual; and we let the intension of a one place propositional function g be a function from circumstances E to sets of individuals in E that g assigns propositions true in E. Extension is related to intension in the normal way, with the extension of a proposition relative to a circumstance being its truth value in the circumstance, and its intension being the set of circumstances in which it is true (or, equivalently, the characteristic function of that set). Truth relative to a circumstance is defined as follows:

(29a) A proposition $\langle\langle o_1, \ldots, o_n\rangle, P^*\rangle$ is true relative to a circumstance E iff the extension of P^* in E contains $\langle o_r, \ldots, o_n\rangle$.

(29b) A proposition $\langle\langle o\rangle, g\rangle$ is true relative to E (where g is a one place propositional function) iff o is a member of the extension of g in E (i.e. iff $g(o)$ is true in E).

(29c) A proposition $\langle$NEG, Prop $S\rangle$ is true relative to E iff the value of NEG at the extension of Prop S in E is truth (i.e. iff Prop S is not true in E). A proposition $\langle$CONJ, $\langle$Prop S, Prop $R\rangle\rangle$ is true relative to E iff the value of CONJ at the pair consisting of the extension of Prop S in E and the extension of Prop R in E is truth (i.e. iff Prop S and Prop R are true in E).

(29d) A proposition $\langle$SOME, $g\rangle$ is true relative to E (where g is as in (b)) iff the extension of g in E is non-empty (i.e. iff $g(o)$ is true relative to E for some o in E).

(29e) A proposition $\langle\langle o$, Prop $S\rangle, B\rangle$ is true relative to E iff $\langle o$, Prop $S\rangle$ is a member of the extension of B in E (i.e. iff o believes Prop S in E).

According to this theory, the propositions expressed by the complements of (8b) and (8c) are (8b*) and (8c*):

(8b*) $\langle$CONJ, $\langle\langle\langle$'Hesperus', Hesperus$\rangle$, the reference relation$\rangle$, $\langle\langle$'Phosphorus', Hesperus$\rangle$, the reference relation$\rangle\rangle\rangle$

(8c*) $\langle \text{CONJ}, \langle (8b^*), \langle \text{SOME}, g \rangle \rangle \rangle$ (Where g is the function which assigns to any object o the proposition about o corresponding to the proposition (8b*) about Hesperus.)

Although the circumstances supporting the truth of these propositions are the same, the propositions themselves are different. Thus we no longer have the result that anyone who believes the proposition expressed by the complement of (8b) thereby believes the proposition expressed by the complement of (8c). The argument in (8) is, therefore, blocked and the problematic conclusion avoided. Similar results hold for the other arguments in III.

However, this is not the only way these results can be achieved. One of the striking features of Russellian propositions is that they encode a good deal of the syntactic structure of the sentences that express them. Sentences that are negations, conjunctions, or quantifications express propositions which are themselves negative, conjunctive, or quantificational in structure.[34] Although this systematic assignment of structure to semantic contents is appealing, it goes beyond what is required by the interaction of propositional attitudes and directly referential singular terms exhibited in III.

In each of the problematic arguments, the agent accepts, or assertively utters, a sentence of the form (30a), but fails to accept, or assertively utter, a corresponding sentence of the form (30b) (which is true in the same circumstances as (30a)):

(30a) $S(t, t')$

(30b) $S(t, t')$ & R.

In each case, the agent would accept, or assertively utter, (30b) if he knew that the directly referential terms t and t' had the same content (and he continued to accept (30a)). However, he does not know that they have the same content. In order to focus on the special difficulties created by this sort of ignorance, let us suppose, for the sake of argument, that the agent is otherwise semantically omniscient. Thus he knows, for any two expressions not containing directly referential terms, whether or not they have the same intension.

In particular, he knows this about (31a) and (31b):

(31a) $\lambda v, v'[S(v, v')]$

(31b) $\lambda v, v'[S(v, v')$ & $R]$.

If he thought that these expressions had the same intension, then his attitude towards (30a) and (30b) would be the same—he would either accept them both or reject them both. Since, in fact, he accepts one and rejects the other, it follows that (31a) and (31b) have different intensions.

This means that whenever an argument of the sort presented in III can be constructed, its problematic conclusion can be blocked by taking the semantic content of a sentence to be a complex consisting of intensions of all occurrences of its directly referential singular terms, plus an intension determined by the remainder of the sentence. The idea can be carried out using a standard style definition of truth with respect to a context and circumstance. Such a definition allows one to associate both a standard intension and a partially structured intension with every object language sentence. Standard intensions of sentences can be taken to be sets of truth-supporting circumstances. Partially structured intensions are complexes made up in part of the intensions of directly referential terms. If a sentence contains no such terms, then its partially structured intension is identified with its standard intension.

We can make this more precise as follows: let us call an occurrence of a singular term in a sentence S a *structurally sensitive occurrence* iff it is a free occurrence of a variable in S or it is an occurrence of a (constant) directly referential term.[35] Let $\ulcorner \lambda v_1, \ldots, v_n\, S' \urcorner$ arise from S by prefixing $\ulcorner \lambda v_1, \ldots, v_n \urcorner$ and replacing each structure sensitive occurrence of a singular term in S with a variable new to S, distinct variables for distinct occurrences, v_i replacing the ith such occurrence. The extension of $\ulcorner \lambda v_1, \ldots, v_n\, S' \urcorner$ relative to an assignment f, context C, and circumstance E is taken to be the function from n-tuples $\langle o_1, \ldots, o_n \rangle$ to truth values of S' relative to f', C, and E, where f' is just like f except (at most) for assigning o_i, as the value of v_i, for each i. Standard intension is determined from extensions in the normal way. For any (open or closed) sentence S, the *partially structured intension* of S relative to an assignment f and context C is $\langle\langle [t_1], \ldots, [t_n] \rangle, [\lambda v_1, \ldots, v_n\, S'] \rangle$, where $[t_i]$ is the intension of the ith structure sensitive occurrence of a singular term in S, relative to f and C, and $[\lambda v_1, \ldots, v_n\, S']$ is the intension of $\ulcorner \lambda v_i, \ldots, v_n\, S' \urcorner$, relative to f and C. (Closed sentences have the same partially structured intensions—with respect to a context—relative to all assignments.) An individual i satisfies an open sentence $\ulcorner x$ believes that $S \urcorner$, relative to f, C, and E, iff in E i bears the belief relation to the partially structured intension expressed by S relative to f and C.[36]

Conceptually, this approach lies somewhere between the Russellian theory and the familiar truth-supporting circumstance conception. Like the

Russellian theory, it takes propositions to be structured complexes which are both the semantic contents of sentences and the objects of propositional attitudes.[37] However, unlike the Russellian theory, the constituents of these "propositions" are intensions extractable from a conventional truth definition. Moreover, the resulting "propositions" are only partially structured.

For example, the partially structured contents of the complements of (8b) and (8c) are:

(8b#) $\langle\langle$'Hesperus', Hesperus, 'Phosphorus', Hesperus$\rangle, R'\rangle$ (where R' is the intension corresponding to the 4-place relation of x's referring to y and z's referring to v).[38]

(8c#) $\langle\langle$'Hesperus', Hesperus, 'Phosphorus', Hesperus$\rangle, R''\rangle$ (where R'' is the intension corresponding to the 4-place relation of x's referring to y and z's referring to v and there being a common referent of x and z).

Since R' is not identical with R'', these contents are different. The move from (8b) to (8c) is, therefore, blocked and the problematic conclusion (8d) is avoided. Corresponding results hold for other arguments of this type, including those in III.

This approach represents a theoretically minimum response to the difficulties in III. As such it allows us to establish a minimum positive result about the relationship between direct reference and propositional attitudes, corresponding to the impossibility result, (13):[39]

(32) If direct reference is legitimate and (some) propositional attitude verbs have a relational semantics ((A4) plus (A2)), then (assuming compositionality and distribution over conjunction) the semantic content of a sentence, relative to a context and assignment of values to variables, must encode at least as much structure as is determined by occurrences of its directly referential singular terms (including free variables).

Both structured Russellian propositions and partially structured intensions satisfy this requirement.

VII

How then might we decide between these two conceptions of semantic content? Considerations involving the interaction of propositional attitudes and directly referential singular terms will, I believe, take us no further. However, other considerations will.

The first of these involves related expressions which allow the construction of arguments corresponding to those in III. For example, if K and K' are natural kind terms with the same semantic content, the potentially false (12b') can be derived from the potentially true (12a') by an argument paralleling the original (12):

(12a') x believes (asserts) that the G is a K and if the G is a K', then S
       (where S is any sentence and ⌜the G⌝ is any description).

(12b') x believes (asserts) that S.

Both this argument and the original (12) are blocked by requiring the semantic content of a sentence to encode at least as much structure as is determined by occurrences of its directly referential singular terms, *plus* its natural kind terms.

This conclusion can be extended to include every kind of expression that is relevantly similar to directly referential singular terms and natural kind terms. The relevant feature, I suggest, is one that involves linguistic competence—in the sense that linguistic competence is important for determining what is said or believed by a speaker from what is assertively uttered or accepted by the speaker. If it is possible for a competent speaker to fail to recognize cases in which expressions of type T have the same semantic content, then it will be possible to use these expressions to construct arguments of the kind given in III. Blocking these arguments requires ensuring that the structure encoded in semantic contents includes that determined by occurrences of expressions of type T.

This line of reasoning leads to the encoding of more and more structure into semantic contents. However, it might be thought that at least some expressions—including logical constructions plus certain predicates— remain immune from such considerations.[40] If S is a sentence containing only such expressions, then its semantic content, on the partially structured intension approach, will just be a standard intension. If S contains only such expressions plus directly referential singular terms, then its semantic content, on this approach, will be a partially structured intension in the original sense. But this is still problematic.

The difficulties posed by propositional attitude ascriptions for truth conditional approaches to semantics are not limited to cases arising from directly referential singular terms and their ilk. For example, if truth-supporting circumstances are metaphysically possible worlds, then the partially structured intension approach will assign the same semantic contents to the (a) and (b) sentences in the following examples:

(33a) First order logic is complete.

(33b) First order logic is undecidable.

(34a) First order logic is decidable.

(34b) First order logic is decidable and S (for unrelated S).

However, in both cases, many have believed or asserted that which is expressed by (a) without believing or asserting that which is expressed by (b).

Switching to a conception in which truth-supporting circumstances are logically possible worlds only shifts attention to a more restricted, but similarly problematic, class of cases. Like Frege of the *Grundgesetze*, many of us have had the misfortune of satisfying $\ulcorner x$ asserts (believes) that $I \urcorner$, for a some logically impossible I, without thereby satisfying $\ulcorner x$ asserts (believes) that $I \ \& \ S \urcorner$, or $\ulcorner x$ asserts (believes) that $S \urcorner$, for unrelated S.

The problem is, I believe, inherent, in the truth conditional approach, and, hence, cannot be solved by weakening constraints on truth-supporting circumstances still further. For example, consider a system like that of *Situations and Attitudes*, in which truth-supporting circumstances may be metaphysically impossible, incomplete, and inconsistent in the sense defined in II. In such a system, logically equivalent sentences are often assigned different semantic contents, which may be the objects of different propositional attitudes. As with all such approaches, however, the system incorporates principles like (7a–e), which can be extracted from standard, recursive treatments of logical constructions. Inevitably, sentences involving multiple constructions of this kind require psychologically non-trivial computations to determine their "semantic contents". Thus, one can always find psychologically non-equivalent sentences which are true in the same circumstances, and, hence, are assigned the same content.

One simple example of this kind if given in (35):

(35a) $C[\text{the } x: Ax] \ \& \ D[\text{the } x: Cx] \ \& \ C[\text{the } x: Bx]$

(35b) $A[\text{the } x: Bx \lor Cx] \ \& \ B[\text{the } x: Dx \ \& \ Cx] \ \& \ D[\text{the } x: Ax \lor Cx]$

(35c) $B[\text{the } x: Ax] \ \& \ C[\text{the } x: Bx] \ \& \ D[\text{the } x: Cx]$

Although these sentences are assigned the same semantic content by corollaries (7a, b, e) or (A1a), it takes a modest amount of calculation to determined this. Not all agents of propositional attitudes are adept at such calculations. Thus, it is possible to find agents who are willing to accept, or assertively utter, one of these sentences at a certain time, but not the others. Such agents believe, or assert, that which is expressed by the sentence they accept, or assertively utter. However, it is counterintuitive to suppose that they must thereby believe, or assert, what the other sentences express. The Russellian conception of propositions allows one to respect this intuition; the truth-supporting circumstance approach does not.

A related point involves the relationship between propositional attitudes and conjunction. Surely, anyone who believes that (35a), or believes that (35c), believes that (36):[41]

(36) C[the x: Bx].

However, this does not seem to be so with (35b). The reason for this difference is that in one case the move is from a belief in a conjunction to a belief in a conjunct, whereas in the other it is not. Although many logical operations do not preserve belief, it would seem that simplification of conjunction does.

In fact, I think his observation about conjunction and belief is correct. However, it has far-reaching theoretical significance that belies its widespread acceptance. Let us suppose that what are believed are semantic contents of sentences. On the truth-supporting circumstance approach, these contents never have conjunctive structure. At best, they are partially structured intensions, which reflect the structure determined by occurrences of directly referential terms (and related expressions), but obliterate other logical structure. Thus, on this approach, there is no more reason to think that anyone who believes that (35a) (or (35c)) believes that (36) than there is to think that anyone who believes that (35b) does.

Proponents of the truth-supporting circumstance approach can, of course, countenance the move from belief in that which is expressed by a conjunction to belief in that which is expressed by the conjuncts. Indeed, they standardly do. However, the price to be paid is that of countenancing the move from ⌜x believes that S⌝ to ⌜x believes that S'⌝ whenever the set of circumstances suporting the truth of S is included in the set of circumstances supporting the truth of S'. But this just substitutes the generation of unwanted inferences for the failure to capture one that is desired. In short, the truth-supporting circumstance approach does not provide the right options.[42]

The Russellian approach offers a welcome contrast. Given the intuition that whenever an individual satisfies ⌜x believes that A & B⌝ he also satisfies ⌜x believes that A⌝ and ⌜x believes that B⌝, the Russellian approach supplies a plausible explanation. Since objects of belief reflect the logical structure of sentences used to report those beliefs, whenever a belief is correctly reported using a conjunction the agent will believe a conjunctive proposition which includes the propositions expressed by the conjuncts as constituents. Since these constituent propositions are, so to speak, before his mind, no computation is required in order for him to arrive at beliefs in the conjuncts.

We can think of this somewhat less metaphorically as follows: to believe a conjunctive proposition ⟨CONJ, ⟨P, Q⟩⟩ is to be in a belief state whose constituents correspond to its three main components. In the case of CONJ, this correspondence is, presumably, functional. A belief state constituent C represents CONJ only if an individual who is in a "conjunctive belief state" S, in which C relates constituent belief states S1 and S2, is also in—or disposed to be in—S1 and S2. Thus, anyone who believes a conjunction believes both conjuncts.

The point to notice is that with propositions as semantic contents this result does not generalize in unwanted ways. Even though structured propositions determine truth-supporting circumstances, there is no reason to suppose that just because an agent bears the belief relation B to a proposition P, he must also bear B to Q whenever the class of truth-supporting circumstances for P is identical with, or a subclass of, the class of truth-supporting circumstances for Q.

There are, then, good reasons not only for rejecting a strict truth-supporting circumstance conception of semantics, but also for adopting a Russellian approach. The reasons I have stressed rest on commonplace intuitions and assumptions about propositional attitudes. There are, of course, those who regard the attitudes as ill-behaved and problematic, and would, therefore, not accept such intuitions and assumptions. In my opinion, such pessimism is unwarranted.

If I am right, a major reason why propositional attitudes have often seemed intractable is that the basic features of strict truth-theoretic semantics have been incompatible with elementary facts about them. The introduction of structured Russellian propositions, which determine, but are not determined by, sets of truth-supporting circumstance, has the potential to change that.

Notes

This article grew out of work originating in my critique, 'Lost Innocence', *Linguistics and Philosophy* 8.1 (1985), 59–71, of J. Barwise and J. Perry, *Situations and Attitudes* (MIT Press, 1983). It was written in 1983–4 while on leave from Princeton University on the Class of 1936 Bicentennial Preceptorship, and while a guest, first, of The Syntax Research Center at the University of California, Santa Cruz, and, later, of the philosophy department of the University of Washington. Portions of it provided the basis for talks at the University of California at Berkeley, Riverside, and Santa Cruz (1983–4); the University of Illinois (1985); North Carolina State University (1985); the University of Pennsylvania (1985); Princeton University (1984); Simon Fraser University (1983); Stanford University (1984); and the Pacific Division Meetings of the American Philosophical Association (1985). A shortened version of the paper, adapted from the APA talk, will appear in *Themes from Kaplan*, edited by Joseph Almog, John Perry, and Howard Wettstein (Oxford University Press, 1988).

I have benefited considerably in the development of several important points from extensive discussion and correspondence with Joseph Almog, David Kaplan, and Nathan Salmon. I have also profited from discussion with Ali Akhtar Kazmi, Julius Moravcsik, and Mark Richard.

1. I assume here, and in what follows, that the semantic content of the complement sentence in a propositional attitude ascription is compositionally determined from the semantic contents of its parts.

2. For example, the properties of being human and of not being human are complements of one another. I will assume that every property has a (unique) complement and that P is the complement of Q iff Q is the complement of P.

3. The idea of thinking of abstract situations as resulting from relaxing constraints on Carnapian state descriptions was suggested to me by David Kaplan.

4. Thus, the content of an existential generalization is a superset of the contents of instances from which it follows. It should be noted that no formal treatment of existential quantification is provided in *Situations and Attitudes*. Nevertheless, (7c) accords well with the leading ideas of that work. (7a), (7b), (7d) and (7e) are explicitly endorsed.

5. The compositional principle I will appeal to may be understood as applying to sentences free of quotation and opacity-producing operators:

If S and S' are non-intensional sentences with the same grammatical structure, which differ only in the substitution of constituents with the same semantic contents (with respect to their respective contexts and assignments of values to variables), then the semantic contents of S and S' will be the same (with respect to those contexts and assignments).

This principle is presupposed in standard versions of truth-conditional semantics, and is itself a corollary of assumption (A1a).

6. So long as they validate (7a) and (7e). This continues to hold when any two place relation replaces identity.

7. One might, of course, try to avoid this result by tampering with the semantics of definite descriptions. For example, one might try substituting the unlovely (7e') for (7e).

(7e′) The semantic content of ⌜F[the x: Gx]⌝ (relative to a context) is the set of circumstances E such that there is at least one object o in E which is both an F-er and a G-er in E; and moreover, for any other object o′, if o′ is a G-er in E, then o = o′ and o′ = o in E, and, more generally, o and o′ have exactly the same properties (and stand in the same relations to the same objects) in E.

One drawback of this from the point of view of a system like that of *Situations and Attitudes* is that it gives up the view that definite descriptions determine partial functions from circumstances to objects that uniquely satisfy the descriptions in those circumstances. Since this feature of definite descriptions is used extensively in *Situations and Attitudes*, it is not clear that Barwise and Perry would be willing to replace (7e) with (7e′). In any case, such a move would do nothing to remove the problem posed by (9a′).

8. The derivation in (12) depends on the assumption that if E supports the truth of P and also supports the truth of ⌜P → Q⌝, then E supports the truth of Q. This will hold if truth-supporting circumstances are logically possible words and E supports the truth of a material conditional whenever it supports the truth of the consequent or fails to support the truth of the antecedent. When circumstances are allowed to be partial and inconsistent, the situation is no longer straightforward. For example, the system in *Situations and Attitudes* provides no treatment of conditionals, and so is not subject to the argument based on (12).

9. Here, (A1)–(A4) must be understood as relativizing semantic content and associated truth conditions to both contexts and assignments of values to variables:

(A1a) The semantic content of a sentence (relative to a context C and assignment f) is the collection of circumstances supporting its truth (as used in C with respect to f).

(A2)   An individual i satisfies ⌜x v's that S⌝ (relative to C and f) iff i bears R to the semantic content of S (relative to C and f).

(A3)   For many propositional attitude verbs (including 'say', 'assert', and 'believe') if i satisfies ⌜x v's that P & Q⌝ (relative to C and f), then i satisfies ⌜x v's that P⌝ and ⌜x v's that Q⌝ (relative to C and f).

10. S. A. Kripke, 'A Puzzle about Belief' in A. Margalit (ed.), *Meaning and Use* (Reidel: Dordrecht, 1979), 239–75 [chap. 38 in this volume].

11. See 'A Puzzle about Belief' p. 268 [905 in this vol.] and n. 42 for relevant discussion.

12. (A2′) is a consequence of (A2), but not vice versa. If (A2) is true, then R* in (A2′) can be taken to be a relation that an individual i bears to a content-character pair, ⟨y, z⟩, iff i bears the relation R of (A2) to the content y. However, (A2′) might be true even if substitution of complement sentences with the same content failed to preserve truth value, in which case (A2) would be false.

13. The basis for these reductios is partially prefigured in 'A Puzzle about Belief'.

14. In the case of (10), one can use (7e) to derive ⌜x believes that S & P⌝ from ⌜x believes that S⌝, where S is (10c) and P is *any sentence at all*. See, however, the qualification in n. 7.

15. See M. Richard, 'Grammar, Quotation, and Opacity', *Linguistics and Philosophy* 9.3 (1986), 383–403.

16. See 'A Puzzle about Belief', n. 43 for relevant discussion.

17. I am indebted to Joseph Almog for suggesting that I reconstruct my argument using this sort of weakening of (A2).

18. 'A Puzzle about Belief', pp. 260–3 [896–9 in this vol.]. If the properties are not required to pick out a unique referent (e.g. if the property of being a famous Roman is the one associated with both 'Cicero' and 'Tully'), then problematic substitution will go though even when the property is "purely qualitative". See 'A Puzzle about Belief', n. 9.

19. There is another respect in which (A2) and its weakened counterparts may give a misleading impression of strength. They may suggest that the arguments against (A1a) rely crucially on assumptions about the semantics of sentences of the form $\ulcorner x\ v$'s that $S \urcorner$. In fact, such sentences are dispensable.

There are two leading ideas behind the various versions of (A2). The first is that propositional attitudes like saying, asserting, and believing are relations to things that are said, asserted, and believed. The second is that these things are said, or semantically expressed, by sentences. If these ideas are correct, then the arguments against (A1a) can be reconstructed—either directly, in terms of *what sentences say*, or indirectly, using (1) and, if desired, (A3′) to derive conclusions about *what speakers say*.

(A3′) If x says (or asserts) that which is said (expressed) by a conjunction in a context C, then x says (or asserts) that which is said (expressed) by each conjunct in C.

Using these principles, one can derive the incorrect conclusion that x has said (or asserted) that which is expressed by $\ulcorner$ For some $y\ Ryy \urcorner$ from the premiss that x has assertively uttered $\ulcorner R(\text{Hesperus, Phosphorus}) \urcorner$ or $\ulcorner R(\text{Londres, London}) \urcorner$

20. The same point could be made using other logical constructions—for example, indefinite descriptions—in place of existential quantification in the complement sentence.

21. Where S is free of quotation and related constructions.

22. The other main type of putative counterexample to (23) involves cases in which a competent speaker assents to (translations of) $\ulcorner n$ is $F \urcorner$ and $\ulcorner m$ is not $F \urcorner$ in a context in which n and m are coreferential names or indexicals. With (16a) plus translation one gets the result that the agent satisfies $\ulcorner x$ believes that n is $F \urcorner$ and $\ulcorner x$ believes that m is not $F \urcorner$. Substitutivity then results in the ascription of contradictory beliefs, which is sometimes thought to be objectionable in light of the fact that the agent may have made no logical mistakes.

However, Kripke's example of puzzling Pierre shows that this is not a compelling criticism of (23). As we have seen, ascriptions of contradictory statements and beliefs can be derived from (16) plus translation, without any appeal to substitutivity. Moreover, the inconsistency is genuine. Kripke's Pierre really does say and believe both that London is pretty and that London is not pretty. But then, if the statements and beliefs of even the best reasoner can be inconsistent without his being in a position to recognize it, the mere fact that the substitutivity principle can sometimes be used to arrive at ascriptions of such inconsistency does nothing to discredit it.

23. M. Richard, 'Direct Reference and Ascriptions of Belief', *Journal of Philosophical Logic* 12 (1983), 425–52, esp. 439–41.

24. Richard himself does not go this far. For one thing, his semantics for belief ascriptions is silent about sentences containing proper names. More important, however, is a weakening of (23) involving complement sentences containing two or more occurrences of indexicals and/or free variables. Let t and t' be two such terms which have the same content relative to a context C and assignment f. According to Richard, if (i) is true relative to C, f, and a circumstance E, then (ii) must be true relative to C, f, and E, but not vice versa:

(i) x believes that $S(t, t)$

(ii) x believes that $S(t, t')$.

Both this conclusion and the semantic system that leads him to it are, in my opinion, incorrect. Nevertheless, there is an important truth underlying Richard's observations. This truth (first suggested to me by Nathan Salmon) is brought out by (iii):

(iii) a. x believes that t is not identical with t'
    b. x believes that t is not identical with t
    c. x believes that t is not identical with itself
    d. x believes that t is non-self-identical.

It seems evident that (a) can be true when (d) is not. The reason for this is that believing the latter involves attributing the property of non-self-identity to an object, whereas believing the former does not. In light of this, one must block either the move from (a) to (b), or the move from (b) to (c) and (d).

Richard selects the first of these. According to him,

(iv) x believes that S

is true only if the agent believes the proposition (semantic content) expressed by S (relative to the context and assignment). Moreover, the complements of (a) and (b) express the same proposition. Nevertheless, Richard holds that (a) can be true when (b) is false. The reason for this is that on his semantics a belief ascription of the form (iv) not only reports what proposition is believed, but also places constraints on the sentence acceptance of which is responsible for the agent's belief. In the case of (b), the agent must hold the belief in virtue of accepting a sentence containing occurrences of directly referential terms with the same character. (If the account were extended to names it would be more natural to require two occurrences of the same term.) In the case of (a), this is allowed, but not required.

One problem with this account is that it is too restricted. Whatever may be the case regarding ascriptions of the form (iv), some belief ascriptions express straightforward relations to propositions:

(v) a. *x* believes the proposition expressed at the bottom of page 437
    b. The proposition expressed at the bottom of page 437 is the proposition that *P*
    c. Therefore, *x* believes the proposition that *P*.

Given the admission that ⌜*t* is not identical with *t*′⌝ and ⌜*t* is not identical with *t*⌝ express the same proposition, one can use examples of the form (v) to reinstate the very problems that the non-relational semantics of (iv) was designed to avoid.

It seems to me that a better approach is to take all belief ascriptions (with the possible exception of belief *de se*) to express relations to propositions (semantic contents), but to distinguish the proposition expressed by the complements of (iii.a) and (iii.b) from the proposition expressed by the complements of (iii.c) and (iii.d). In this way, one can block the move from (b) to (c), while preserving (23). An account of this kind is presented in VI below.

I am grateful to Mark Richard and Nathan Salmon for discussions of the issues in this note.

25. It might be thought that a theory that took names to be disguised descriptions (associated with them by the speaker) could render the remarks in the two conversations true by appealing to a difference in scope. But this will not work. If the description associated by the teacher with the name 'Mark Twain' is something like 'the author of *The Adventures of Tom Sawyer* and *Huckleberry Finn*', then the teacher's remark will be false no matter what the scope of the description.

26. J. Perry, 'Frege on Demonstratives', *The Philosophical Review*, 86.4 (1977), 474–97 [chap. 29 in this vol.] and 'The Problem of the Essential Indexical', *Noûs* 13 (1979), 3–21.

27. This thesis has recently been championed by several philosophers, most notably Nathan Salmon in *Frege's Puzzle* (MIT Press, 1986). Although I developed the arguments given above independently, I have profited from Salmon's work on the topic.

28. See *Situations and Attitudes* for an articulation of this view.

29. Although this principle is a useful heuristic, it should not be regarded as an analysis of belief. Its most obvious limitation is that it does not apply to believers who are not language users. Even when applied to language users it must be restricted to cases in which the agent, i, the sentence *S′*, and its semantic content (in the context of assent) stand in a certain (as yet not fully analysed) recognition relation. I have in mind examples like 'Newminister 1', in which a proper name is introduced by a reference-fixing description 'the first Tory Prime Minister of Britain elected in the 21st century'. (The example parallels the 'Newman 1' example discussed in K. Donnellan 'The Contingent A Priori and Rigid Designators' in P. A. French, T. E. Uehling, Jr., and H. K. Wettstein (eds.), *Contemporary Perspectives in the Philosophy of Language* (University of Minnesota Press, 1977)). In such a case, the sentence 'Newminister 1 will be conservative' may express a singular proposition involving a certain individual. However, assent to the sentence by a competent speaker is not sufficient for belief in that proposition. Intuitively,

the manner in which the sentence presents the proposition to the agent is too indirect for assent to indicate belief.

It should be noted that the cases discussed in the text ('Hesperus'/'Phosphorus', 'London'/'Londres', etc.) are not like this. In these cases, the agents are acquainted with the referents, they associate names with them, and they grasp the propositions expressed by sentences containing the names. What they do not do is recognize that the same referents are associated with different names, and that the same propositions are expressed by different sentences. But that is not required in order for assent to the sentences to indicate belief in the propositions they express.

Similar points can be made about assertion (except that here the principles involving assent come closer to providing an actual analysis).

(i) An individual i satisfies $\ulcorner x$ says (asserts) that $S \urcorner$ relative to a context C (assignment f) and circumstance E, if there is a sentence S' and context C' corresponding to E with i as agent, such that i assertively utters S' in C', and the content of S' in C' = the content of S in C (relative to f).

(ii) An individual i satisfies $\ulcorner x$ says (asserts) that $S \urcorner$ relative to a context C (assignment f) and circumstance E iff there are sentences S' and S'', and a context C' corresponding to E with i as agent, such that i assertively utters S' in C', S'' is readily inferable from S', and the content of S'' in C' = the content of S in C (relative to f).

If one takes (ii) to be a reasonable approximation of the notion of assertion, one can use it in place of (24) to construct arguments and explanations involving assertions corresponding to those in the text involving beliefs. (Note that (ii) allows contents not expressed by the sentence uttered to be asserted when, but only when, the conversational participants "can't miss them".)

30. The idea for this lambda-treatment of (25c) was suggested to me by Nathan Salmon.

31. Except in situations like Kripke's Paderewski example, in which the agent misconstrues two tokens of the same name (referring to the same individual) for tokens of different (but phonologically identical) names of different individuals ('A Puzzle about Belief', 265–6 [902 in this vol.]). In such cases an agent might accept (b) without accepting (c), or believing what it expresses.

32. On this treatment, '&' and '−' are like directly referential terms in that their semantic contents = their extensions. This is not crucial to the general Russellian conception, which could just as well take the contents of these expressions to be entities—call them operation—which bear a relation to functions analogous to that borne by properties to the objects they apply to. It is even possible to take the contents of truth functional operators to be properties of truth values. The differences between these alternatives do not affect the present discussion.

33. I am indebted to David Kaplan for this Russellian suggestion.

34. It is, of course, possible for sentences of one form to express propositions of another form, as happens in some cases of stipulative definition.

35. I retain here the simplifying assumption that all directly referential terms in the object language are semantically simple.

36. This account has two precursors. The first is the introduction of structured meanings (characters) in Richard's 'Direct Reference and Ascriptions of Belief'. The second is a somewhat different use of structured intensions suggested by David Kaplan (personal correspondence) in response to Richard. The account in the text is designed as an improvement on those treatments intended to capture certain insights that motivated them.

37. One could have versions of these theories in which semantic contents were not objects of the attitudes, but only by foregoing the strong motivation the attitudes provide for these theories.

38. Strictly speaking, the intensions of directly referential terms in (8b) and (8c) should be constant functions from circumstances to objects, rather than objects themselves. However, this does not affect the issues at hand.

39. The significance of this result is enhanced by the defence, in section V, of the consequence (23) of (A2), (A4), and compositionality. However, it should be noted that analogous results involving the encoding of structure in objects of the attitudes can be established using the weakenings in IV.

40. I leave it open whether there are such expressions.

41. Here I am using '(35a)', '(35c)', and '(36)' not as names, but as abbreviations for the sentences they normally name.

42. An analogous argument can be constructed regarding assertion.

Chapter 40

The Prince and the Phone Booth: Reporting Puzzling Beliefs

Mark Crimmins and John Perry

In Mark Twain's *The Prince and The Pauper*, Tom Canty and Edward Tudor decide to change lives for a day, but fate intervenes, and the exchange goes on for a considerable period of time. The whole story turns on what people believe and do not believe about the two boys, and an intelligent reader, unexposed to recent philosophy of language and mind, could probably describe the key facts of the story with some confidence. Such a reader might explain why Miles Hendon, a penniless nobleman who encounters a boy dressed in rags, does not bow to the Prince, by noting:

(1) Miles Hendon did not believe that he was of royal blood.

And such a reader might ward off the implication that Miles was a fool or ignoramus by noting that Miles shared the dominant conception of Edward Tudor:

(2) Miles Hendon believed that Edward Tudor was of royal blood.

One of our main claims in this paper is that such a reader would be right on both counts. In this we depart from a recent trend to explain the apparent truth of statements like (1) as an illusion generated by pragmatic features of such claims. Accounts of belief reporting given by Jon Barwise and John Perry,[1] Scott Soames,[2] and Nathan Salmon[3] have employed this strategy of denying the accuracy of our strong intuitions about truth and falsity. Here, we shall present an account that does not ignore pragmatic features, but assigns to them a more honorable role. They do not create an illusion, but help to identify the reality the report is about. Our account honors the intuition that claims (1) and (2) are true.

First appeared in *The Journal of Philosophy* 86 (1989): 685–711. Reprinted by permission of *The Journal of Philosophy* and the authors.

Since 'Edward Tudor' in (2) and 'he' in (1) both refer to Edward Tudor, this seems to commit us to some version of the doctrine of *opacity*.[4] Specifically, we are committed to the view that, if our reader were to say either of the following, in the same circumstances, he would be incorrect:

(1′) Miles Hendon did not believe that Edward Tudor was of royal blood.

(2′) Miles Hendon believed that he was of royal blood.

The doctrine of opacity has been thought incompatible with two others, to which we also are attracted: the first, *direct reference*, is that the utterance of a simple sentence containing names or demonstratives normally expresses a "singular proposition"—a proposition that contains as constituents the individuals referred to, and not any descriptions of or conditions on them; the second, *semantic innocence*, is that the utterances of the embedded sentences in belief reports express just the propositions they would if not embedded, and these propositions are the contents of the ascribed beliefs.[5]

Direct reference and semantic innocence are well-motivated by many considerations in the philosophy of language. But if direct reference and semantic innocence are correct, then it seems that opacity must not be: the substitution of 'Edward Tudor' for 'he' in (1) [or vice-versa in (2)] should be completely legitimate. The name and the demonstrative refer to the same object. There is just one proposition, belief in which is denied by (1) and affirmed by (2), the "singular" proposition, which we shall represent in this way:

《Being of royal blood; Edward Tudor》

The example is typical of many doxastic puzzle cases in the literature—puzzles because they seem to reveal a conflict among the three very plausible doctrines. We hold all three, however.

I

When we substitute 'Edward Tudor' for 'he', the words change while the proposition expressed by the embedded sentence stays the same. If we think that belief is a relation to propositions and not words, the apparent change in truth value of the whole report seems puzzling. We are likely to focus on the most apparent change, the change in words, as the clue to the mystery.

The most famous doxastic puzzle case, due to Saul Kripke,[6] has nothing to do with substitution, however. Kripke describes a case in which the Frenchman Pierre first hears of London, comes to believe it is pretty, then moves to London, and, not connecting it to the city he has heard about (under the French 'Londres'), comes to believe it is not pretty. He does not change his mind about the city he has heard of, but simply does not connect the "two" cities. We have on sentence

(3) Pierre believes that London is pretty.

that we seem to be able to use, when reflecting on different parts of the story, to say something true and to say something false. The words have not changed. What has?

What changes in this case, and in every other doxastic puzzle case, is what we are talking about. Pierre has two different notions of London, which play very different roles in his beliefs. An assertion of (3) is true if it is about one of them, false if it is about the other. An ordinary doxastic puzzle case uses a change in words to precipitate the change in the subject matter of the utterance. Kripke spells out the details of his case so clearly that our focus gets redirected without a change in the wording of the report. We shall return to these claims about belief reports in the next section.

One of Pierre's beliefs was caused by his acceptance of the stories he heard about London. It has the content that London is pretty, and it leads him to cherish the prospect of someday visiting that city. This belief also causes him to affirm, in French, "Londres est jolie," in discussions about the city he has heard of.

Also, Pierre has a different belief which was caused by his displeasure with his new surroundings, which has the content that London is not pretty and which causes him to affirm, "London is not pretty," in discussions about his home.

It is a commonplace to distinguish these two beliefs. We think it is often not sufficiently appreciated, however, that the beliefs so distinguished are concrete cognitive structures. Focusing on this fact provides the basis for our account of belief and for our solutions to the various doxastic puzzle cases.

These are the key features of our theory of beliefs:

(i) Beliefs are concrete cognitive structures: they are particulars that belong to an agent, come into existence, endure, and go out of existence.
(ii) Beliefs are related to the world and to other cognitive structures

and abilities in a way that allows us to classify them by propositional content.

Beliefs, since they are cognitive particulars or "things in the head," are not things that are believed; they are not in any sense the objects of belief. The propositions believed are the objects of belief. An agent believes some proposition in virtue of having a belief with that content. Many agents can believe the same proposition, so propositions are public; they also are abstract. Beliefs are neither public nor abstract; they are concrete particulars that belong to agents just like arms, headaches, and bouts of the flu. A belief comes into existence when an agent forms it; it is not the sort of thing that is around for the agent to adopt. Agents believe the same thing, a proposition p, when each has a belief with p as its content. This is not an analysis of reports of "believing the same thing"—which are not always so simple to unpack—but a clarification of what we mean by objects of belief.

To countenance beliefs as particulars is not to deny that there are interesting systems of abstract objects which might be used to classify them, such as meanings, Fregean senses, intensions, characters, or the like. But in addition to having these abstract features, beliefs, like other concrete particulars, have lots of other features, both intrinsic and relational, many of which can in some cases be relevant to explaining how we talk about beliefs in belief reports. In particular, we often exploit facts about the causes and effects of beliefs, a point to which we shall return.

There are a number of reasons to allow ourselves to speak of particular beliefs, rather than just of a belief relation between a person and an abstract object of some kind. There is, first, the attraction of having entities that can occupy causal roles with respect to perception, reasoning, and action. As Jerry Fodor and others have argued at length, structured concrete particulars or "token" mental entities go a long way toward explaining the roles of belief, desire, and so on in cognition. There is, second, the fact that the most plausible statements of materialist intuitions about the mind are formulated in terms of particular mental entities. And, third, there is the problem that belief puzzles repeatedly have emphasized: it seems that, for any natural way of classifying beliefs with abstract objects, we can find examples in which a single agent, at a single time, is belief-related to one such abstract object twice over. These are cases, we would like to be able to say, in which an agent, at a time, has two beliefs classified by the same sense, meaning, or whatever. Classifying beliefs only with abstract meanings, senses, and so on is like classifying drops of water only with intrinsic properties. Kant argued against Leibniz that intrinsic properties of particulars will not always provide us with sufficient material for their individuation. Kant took it as obvious that there can be two exactly similar drops of water; the puzzle cases make it clear that there can be two beliefs sharing the abstract features which one or another theory of belief claims to be central.[7]

Beliefs, then, are particulars that bear complex causal relations to an agent's perceptions, actions, and other cognitive structures and abilities. The story of the causal properties of beliefs will be closely bound to the story of how and why beliefs can be classified with propositional content. A belief constrains an agent's reasoning and action in a way that is conducive, if the belief's content is true, to the agent's getting what she wants.

The ground-level facts behind belief are simply the facts of agents having beliefs. There is a basic relation $B(a, b, t)$ that holds of an agent, a belief, and a time just in case b is a belief that belongs to the agent a at time t.

Normally, a belief has a propositional content. So there is a partial function $\text{Content}(b, t)$ that, for a belief b and time t at which b exists, yields the content of b. The content of a belief will be determined by the "internal" structural properties of the belief plus its real connections to things and circumstances in the world and to the agent's other cognitive structures and abilities.

If an agent a at time t has as an object of belief the proposition p, then there is a belief b such that:

$$B(a, b, t) \ \& \ \text{Content}(b, t) = p.$$

So much is all that is really needed for a theory of belief adequate for a broad explanation of the doxastic puzzle cases, and so we are tempted to stick with just the minimal theory of beliefs given so far. The minimal theory is compatible with a wide class of views about beliefs, about propositions (or contents), and about central issues in theories of representation, practical reasoning, and inference. The crucial features of the semantics we give for belief reports, and the resulting solutions for the troubling cases, are therefore to some degree theory-neutral. But we want to present a slightly more detailed, if still simple-minded, theory of beliefs which satisfies the demands of the minimal theory and which yields a sufficiently rich account of just how the puzzling belief reports work.

Beliefs are structured entities that contain ideas and notions as constituents. Ideas and notions, like beliefs, are on our view concrete cognitive particulars. So there is no such thing as agents having the same idea or notion, but only similar ones. Admittedly, the technical use we make of these terms involves a departure from what we ordinarily say about 'ideas' and 'notions', or at least represents a choice among the many different ordinary uses of these terms. On our use of the terms, there are no notions and ideas that agents do not have, any more than there are headaches that no one has. The difference between notions and ideas is the difference between an agent's "ways of thinking" about individuals versus properties. The properties and things of which ideas and notions are ideas and notions we call their *contents*. We shall explain in a moment how the contents of ideas and notions help determine the contents of beliefs.

What determines the content of an idea or notion? For example, what is it about Miles's notion of the poorly-dressed boy which causes it to be a notion of Edward as opposed to another boy? The crucial fact is that it was Edward with whom Miles was confronted when he formed this notion. Edward played the right part in the causal origin of the notion; the notion was formed in order to keep track of information about Edward—that is what makes him its content. So the content of an idea can depend on its external properties, like facts about its origin. The very same notion might have been a notion of a different person, had someone other than Edward figured in its origin.

There is a close parallel between this view of the contents of ideas and causal views of the semantics of names. A speaker can refer to an individual with a name, it is held, because that individual figured, in the right way, in the speaker's adoption of the name as a tool of reference.[8]

The content of an idea is not always fixed once for all by facts about the circumstances of the idea's origin. Some ideas are *context-sensitive*, in that their contents change with changes in the agent's circumstances. The context sensitivity of ideas is analogous to that of demonstratives in language. David Kaplan[9] has proposed that there is associated with each demonstrative a *character*, a function that specifies how the content of a demonstrative depends on the circumstances surrounding its use. The content of a use of the word 'you', for example, is the person being addressed in the circumstances of the utterance. Analogously, an agent a may have an idea I_{addr} of "being the one I am addressing." The property which is the content of this idea changes with changes in circumstances as follows:

In any circumstances in which a person b is being addressed by a, the content of a's idea I_{addr} is the property of being b.

Undoubtedly, each of us has a "you" idea, the content of which is determined functionally in this way. We do not share ideas, but we have ideas with the same *semantic role*. An idea's semantic role is the function that determines the idea's content based on the agent's circumstances. Semantic roles for ideas are a bit like characters of expressions; some ideas have semantic roles that are context-sensitive, others have semantic roles that are constant functions—their contents do not vary with changes in context.

So there are two ways in which an agent's external circumstances might be relevant to determining the content of an idea. First, the facts surrounding the origin of the idea may fix its content once for all. Second, the idea's semantic role may be sensitive to changes in the agent's circumstances—the content of the idea may vary from occasion to occasion. So an idea may exhibit origin sensitivity, context sensitivity, or both.

Miles's idea of red is certainly not context-sensitive. It may be deemed origin-sensitive, whether one supposes that his idea stands for red innately, or because of some original assignment of ideas of colors early in Miles's life. Miles's idea of being past, in contrast stands for different properties as his life unfolds; at each time t, the idea stands for the property of occurring before t. This idea is certainly context sensitive, and may or may not be origin sensitive. And Miles's notion of Prince Edward, formed upon hearing of the newborn Prince, is origin-sensitive, but it is not context-sensitive.

Notions are the things in the mind that stand for things in the world. A notion is a part of each of a collection of beliefs[10] (and of other mental structures, such as desires and intentions) that are internally about the same thing. This is not a definition of 'notion', but just a central fact about notions—sharing a notion is what it is for beliefs to be internally about the same thing. An agent may occasionally (and will in many of the examples) have several notions of a single individual. This can happen in two ways. First, in cases of misrecognition and "failure to place," an agent may have two notions of an individual which he does not link or connect; such an agent is guilty of no internal inconsistency. But also an agent can retain two notions of an individual, while linking them, in the way one does when one recognizes that "two" of one's acquaintances are actually a single individual. Why might two notions be retained when such a recognition takes place? One reason for this would be to allow the possibility of easy revision in case the "recognition" was in error. But an agent can also burn his bridges and merge two notions into a single notion. Two beliefs, then, can be internally about the same thing in two ways: by sharing a notion, and by containing notions that are linked.

For the purposes of this paper, we assume that each belief involves a single k-ary idea and a sequence of k notions.[11] To represent the structure of such a belief, we write:

$$\text{Structure}(b) = \langle \text{Idea}^k, \text{Notion}_1, \dots, \text{Notion}_k \rangle.$$

Each belief has as its content the proposition that the objects its notions are of have the property or stand in the relation, that its idea is of:

$$\text{Content}(b, t) = \langle\!\langle \text{Of}(\text{Idea}^k, t); \text{Of}(\text{Notion}_1, t), \dots, \text{Of}(\text{Notion}_k, t) \rangle\!\rangle.$$

The structures of beliefs are individuated not simply by the ideas and notions involved in them, but also by which argument places of the ideas the various notions fill. Thus the order of the notions in our representation of the structure of the belief reflects an assignment of notions to the argument places of the associated idea.

To be clear about the relation between beliefs and their contents, we need to introduce some new concepts.

A belief b associates an idea I with a notion n at an argument place pl:

Associates (b, I, n, pl)

The belief that Tom fired Mary and the belief that Mary fired Tom differ in which places are associated with which notions, even though the ideas and notions involved are the same.

An argument place of an idea is intimately connected with an argument role of the relation which is the content of the idea, and so with an argument role in the content of the beliefs of which the idea forms a part.[12] If we were to consider complex cases, spelling out this relationship might be a matter of some delicacy, but we shall take it to be straightforward here. We shall say that an argument place pl_I of an idea I generates an argument role r_p of a proposition p (an example below will make this clearer):

Generates(pl_I, r_p)

Finally, a notion is responsible for which object occupies an argument role of the content of a belief, when the belief associates it with an idea at the argument place which generates the argument role in the content of the belief:

$$\text{Responsible}(n, r, b) \Leftrightarrow_{\text{def}} \exists I, pl \; \text{Associates}(b, I, n, pl), \text{ and } \text{Generates}(pl, r)$$

When a notion in a belief is responsible for filling an argument role of the belief's content, it fills the role with its own content, the object of which the notion is a notion.

To give an example: Arthur's belief that Yvain smote Kay involves Arthur's idea for smiting, I_s, and his two notions of Yvain and Kay, call these n_Y and n_K. The idea I_s has two argument places, one (pl_+) for the smiter and one (pl_-) for the smitten. In Arthur's belief (call it b), the notion n_Y is associated with argument place pl_+ of I_s, and n_K is associated with pl_-. The content of b is the proposition p, where:

$$p = \langle\!\langle \text{Smote}; \text{Yvain}, \text{Kay} \rangle\!\rangle$$

The relation "smote" has two argument roles, one (r_+) for the smiter and one (r_-) for the smitten; these are also argument roles of the proposition p. In p, Yvain fills r_+ and Kay fills r_- of the "smote" relation. Since b associates pl_+ with n_Y, and pl_+ (the smiter in I_s) generates r_+ (the smiter in p), we say that, in b, n_Y is responsible for filling r_+ in p. Arthur's notion of Yvain is responsible in b for determining who fills the argument role r_+ in p. And n_Y provides its content, Yvain, to fill that argument role. Figure 1 should make this clear.

Notions and ideas are key figures in our commonsense "folk" model of cognition. The recurring appearance in philosophy of such things as concepts, senses, ways of thinking, names in a language of thought, mental file folders, and other such devices reflects a firm intuition about the mind, namely, that having beliefs about an individual means having beliefs involving an internal something that is one's cognitive "fix" on the individual. As we have said, we think the correct way to express this intuition demands reference to cognitive particulars that are involved in beliefs, desires, and so on. Now, this leaves a great deal open about just what kinds of thing our notions and ideas are. For all we have said, notions and ideas might be—or might have been—particular words in a language of thought, physical objects like file folders, or things with more of a dispositional character, like the process underlying the disposition of an agent to have a specific "pattern of neural activation" in certain circumstances. And, whichever of these kinds of thing our notions and ideas are,

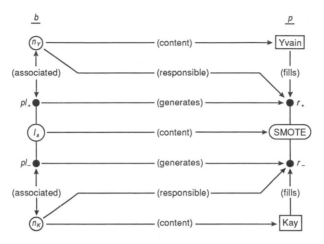

Figure 1
Arthur's belief and its content

they certainly may be classifiable with senses, property clusters, intensions, and so on. We want our "notions and ideas" to capture what is in common among all these very different models of cognition: there are things shared by different beliefs which explain the internal way in which beliefs must be about the same object or property.

On this theory, one can have two beliefs with exactly the same content or with diametrically opposed contents, such that there is no significant causal relation between them—because they involve different notions. This is a feature of all of the problematic examples that we shall consider. There is nothing particularly puzzling about this—and in fact there is nothing particularly puzzling about any of the examples that we discuss, so long as we simply consider the beliefs and not the reporting of them. Nevertheless, it is a good idea to go over the examples in some detail, for it is these details which our semantic account pays more attention to than others of which we know.

Consider the Prince and the Pauper. Miles Hendon has two notions of Edward Tudor. They have quite different circumstances of origin. One Miles has had for a long time. It is associated (in his beliefs) with his ideas as being a Prince of England, being named 'Edward Tudor', being rich, not being a pauper, not looking like a pauper, not being likely to run into (me) on an average day, and the like. The beliefs with this notion as a constituent influence Miles's behavior when confronted with ordinary sorts of information about Edward Tudor. When he reads an article in the

Times, for example, it is beliefs with this notion as a constituent which are affected.

His other notion was formed when he saw Edward being set upon by an angry mob—angry because Edward, dressed in rags, had been proclaiming himself to be Prince. This notion is associated with ideas of being out of his mind, being dressed like a pauper, and not being of royal blood. The beliefs involving this notion, and not those involving his old notion of Edward Tudor, influence Miles's behavior toward Edward and Edward's assertions during the period he is associated with him as a comrade, until that point, toward the end of the story, when Miles merges his two notions and comes to believe that Edward the pauper is Edward the Prince.

Perhaps the ultimate doxastic puzzle case is Mark Richard's [13] puzzle about the woman in the telephone booth:

Consider *A*—a man stipulated to be intelligent, rational, a competent speaker of English, etc.—who both sees a woman, across the street, in a phone booth, and is speaking to a woman through a phone. He does not realize that the woman to whom he is speaking—*B*, to give her a name—is the woman he sees. He perceives her to be in some danger—a run-away steamroller, say, is bearing down upon her phone booth. *A* waves at the woman; he says nothing into the phone (*ibid.*, p. 439).

The man has two distinct, unlinked notions of the woman. Via one, he believes that she is in danger. This is the notion which arose in virtue of his visual perception of her, and which is associated with an idea of being in grave danger. It is this notion which is involved in the beliefs that motivate his waving out the window. The second notion is an older one, assuming the woman is an old acquaintance. It is associated with an idea of being the person addressed, and not associated with ideas of being the person seen or being in danger. Hence, the beliefs involving this notion do not motivate a warning.

Let us return to Kripke's case. Pierre has the same misfortune as Miles and the man on the phone: he has two notions of the same thing. He has one notion of London which is linked to his memories of the stories and to his use of the word 'Londres'. He has another, unconnected notion of London which is influenced by his perceptions and memories about his present surroundings and which influences his use of the word 'London'. He has a belief associating the former notion with his idea of being pretty, but has no belief associating the latter notion with this idea. In fact. Pierre associates an idea of being ugly with the latter notion.

II

Our basic idea is simple: a belief report claims that an agent has a belief with a certain content. But the basic idea, unembellished, will not allow us to hold the family of views we want to defend. For (2) and (2′) would claim that Miles Hendon had at least one belief with the content

《Being of roval blood: Edward Tudor》

while (1) and (1′) would deny this—thus contradicting our truth intuitions and the doctrine of opacity.

But our embellishment is also simple. When we report beliefs, there is always some further condition that a belief with the specified content is claimed to meet. The belief report is true, only if a belief meeting that further condition has the right content. What may be novel is our insistence that this additional requirement is part of the proposition expressed by the belief report. Thus, it is a condition on the truth, not merely the felicity, of the report.

Consider (1). In context, (1) provides an explanation of why Miles Hendon did not treat someone he was looking at in a certain way—a way that would have been compulsory for Miles, given the status of that person. We are interested in the content of only those beliefs which motivated Miles's behavior, the beliefs which involve the notion of Edward which arose when Miles saw him being threatened and which explain Miles's treatment of him. The existence of such a notion is clear from the description of the incident. We know that Miles is perceiving Edward and interacting with him on the basis of what he, Miles, perceives. Our view is that, in reporting beliefs, we quite often are talking about such notions, although our belief reports do not explicitly mention them. The general solution to the puzzles is to allow a condition on particular beliefs, over and above a content condition, to be part of the claim made. The version of this strategy we shall pursue here is to take this further condition always to be a specification of the notions that are supposed to be involved in the ascribed belief.

We shall say that a notion that a belief report is about is an *unarticulated constituent* of the content of the report—it is a propositional constituent that is not explicitly mentioned. We shall distinguish another kind of belief report, and say more about the notion of unarticulated constituents in a moment. But first let us see what the semantics of this sort of belief report looks like.

From our account of beliefs, we have the following concepts:

$B(a, b, t)$: b is a belief that belongs to agent a at time t.

Content $(b, t) = p$: p is the content of belief b at time t.

Responsible (n, r, b): $\exists I, pl$ Associates (b, I, n, pl), and Generates (pl, r).

We take a belief report to be an utterance u of a belief sentence of the form:

A believes that S

where A is a singular term and S is a sentence. We assume a semantics for the use of the embedded sentence, so that $Con(u_S)$ (the content of u_S) is the proposition expressed by the subutterance of u corresponding to S.[14] Where u is a belief report at t which is about notions $n_1, \ldots, n_k$, and $p = Con(u_S)$,

$$Con(u) = \exists b[B(a, b, t) \wedge \text{Content}(b, t) = p \wedge \bigwedge_{r_i \text{ in } p}\text{Responsible}(n_i, r_i, b)]$$

The claim made by the belief report is that the agent a[15] has a belief with the content p, involving the notions $n_i, \ldots, n_k$ (in a certain way).[16] This claim entails the proposition that a has a belief with the content p, but the truth of that proposition is not sufficient for the truth of the report—the report says more than that about the ascribed belief.

We shall say in such cases that the notions that the belief report is about are *provided* by the utterance and its context. Note that the provided constituents of the report's content are not existentially quantified.

Let us see how this theory works with Miles, Edward, and our intelligent reader. We take our reader to be talking about n_{vis}, the notion Miles acquires of Edward from visually perceiving him on the occasion of the rescue. $Con(u_S)$ is just the proposition 《Being of royal blood; Edward》. So our reader is saying with (1) that there is no belief that associates Miles's idea of the property of being of royal blood with Miles's notion n_{vis}. He is not contradicting any proposition that Miles has some other notion of Edward Tudor which is so associated.

And, in fact, a proposition of this latter kind might be just what our reader intends to claim with (2). Imagine the case in which he reads that Miles Hendon is shouting, while treating Edward as a mad fool, "Prince Edward is a man of royal blood, you fool, who would not dress in rags." Our reader might intend to say, of the notion involved in the beliefs that motivate this behavior, that it both is of Edward Tudor and is associated with the idea of being of royal blood.

If so, our reader would surely be consistent, direct, and innocent. On the one hand, the proposition he in turn denies and affirms Miles's belief in is just the singular proposition that contemporary theories of direct reference assign to the utterances of "Edward Tudor is of royal blood" and "He is of royal blood" in the described contexts. On the other, the denial and affirmation are completely consistent.

III

We have claimed that, in belief reports, an n-ary relation is reported with an n-minus-one-place predicate. On our account, the complex relation invoked in belief reports is a four-place relation: an agent believes a proposition at a time relative to a sequence of notions. But there is no argument place in the 'believes' predicate for the sequence of notions. The notions are unarticulated constituents of the content of the report.

Propositions have constituents. The proposition that Yvain smote Kay has Kay as a constituent—Kay himself is in that claim. When Arthur says, "Yvain smote Kay," there is no great mystery about why Kay, rather than someone else, is part of the claim Arthur makes: Arthur uses the name 'Kay', which, as he uses it, refers to Kay. Kay is the content of Arthur's utterance of 'Kay'. This is what it is to be an articulated constituent of the content of a statement.

It is very common in natural languages for a statement to exploit unarticulated constituents. When we consider the conditions under which such a statement is true, we find it expresses a proposition that has more constituents in it than can be traced to expressions in the sentence that was spoken. Each constituent of the content which is not itself the content of some expression in the sentence is an unarticulated constituent of the content of the statement.

We report the weather, for example, as if raining and snowing and sleeting and dark of night were properties of times, but they are one and all relations between times and places. If I say, "it is raining," you understand me as claiming that it rains at that time at some place the context supplies. It often is, but need not be, the place of utterance. If I am talking to a friend in Kansas City on the phone, or watching news reports about the continuing floods in Berkeley, you may understand me to be talking about those places rather than the place where we both are.

The phenomenon of unarticulated constituency is similar to that of indexicality in the reliance on context. But the two phenomena should not be conflated. If we say, "It's raining *here*," an expression in our statement identifies the place. The place is articulated in a context-sensitive way. In the case of indexicals, expression and context share in the job of identifying the constituent, according to the conventional meaning or character of the indexical. In a case of underarticulation, there is no expression to determine the constituent in this way.

It would be misleading, however, to say that, in the case of unarticulated constituents, the context alone does the job. The whole utterance—the context and the words uttered—is relevant to identifying the unarticulated constituent. Thus, a change in wording can affect the unarticulated constituent, even though it is not a change in an expression that designates that constituent. Suppose I am in Palo Alto talking on the phone to someone in London; we both know that it is morning in Palo Alto and evening in London. If I say, "It's exactly 11 A.M.," I will be taken to be talking about the time in Palo Alto; if I had said, in the same context, "It's exactly 8 P.M.," I would be taken to be talking about the time in London.

The important principle to be learned is that a change in wording can precipitate a change in propositional constituents, even when the words do not stand for the constituents.

Unarticulated constituency is one example of the incrementality of language. In the circumstances of an utterance, there always is a great deal of common knowledge and mutual expectation that can and must be exploited if communication is to take place. It is the function of the expression uttered to provide just the last bit of information needed by the hearer to ascertain the intended claim, exploiting this rich background. What is obvious in context we do not belabor in syntax—we do not articulate it.

This is by no means to transgess the intuition of the systematicity of language which is commonly reflected in principles of "compositionality." Since we finite creatures are able to make and understand a potential infinity of claims, there must be systematic features of our statements which explain our infinite abilities in something like a combinatorial fashion—in terms of our more finite abilities to understand the contributions of specific features of statements toward the claims made. But there is no reason to assume that these features of statements must all involve syntactic expressions. It is just as systematic for a form of speech, like a belief report or a report of rain, to *call for* a propositional constituent that meets, say, certain conditions of relevance and salience, as it is for a form of speech to have a syntactic expression *stand for* a propositional constituent.[17]

Consider our practices of reporting velocity. A claim that an object is moving at a certain velocity makes sense only if it is understood with respect to what the velocity is to be assessed. We say that velocity is relative to an observer, or a frame of reference—we must count something as stationary. But we articulate this additional parameter of velocity claims only when it is not obvious what is to count as stationary. We have in English a number of general-purpose constructions for articulating commonly suppressed constituents of a claim. We say, 'with respect to ...' or 'relative to ...' or 'in the sense that ...'. The more likely the unarticulated constituent is to be unclear, the more likely it is that we have a natural way to articulate it.

In the case of belief reports, in which notions are unarticulated, we do have rough and ready ways to clarify just which notions we mean to talk about. We say, for instance, that Miles believes that Edward is a peasant in one way—the way related to the boy in front of him, not in the way related to the Prince. Or we add to the report, "that is, he thinks the boy in front of him, who really is Edward, is a peasant." Or we specify how Miles would or would not "put" his belief. Or we allude to the evidence which led Miles to form the belief, or to the actions it would be likely to bring about. Each of these devices can succeed in distinguishing among the two notions which in context can seem equally relevant, thus eliminating possible confusion about which notion we mean to talk about.

We do not, of course, have a very direct way of specifying the notions we mean to talk about in belief reports. This is due to the fact that it almost always obvious which notion a speaker is talking about. Where it is not, we either use one of the devices just mentioned, or leave the language of belief reporting altogether and talk instead about what the agent would say or would do.

IV

Unarticulated constituency and direct reference are of a single stripe. In fact, if we take the term 'reference' in the ordinary sense in which it does not require a referring expression, unarticulated constituency can be seen to result from a kind of direct reference—perhaps "tacit" reference. When a speaker claims that "it's raining," she is referring to a place and not to a description of, nor a condition on, a place. In the same way, on our view, a belief reporter refers to an agent's notions. We have chosen not to talk this way in our official account only to avoid being read as claiming that notions are referred to by the reporter's words.

A difficult issue facing all views of direct reference, and ours in particular, is the need to make sense of intuitions about truth and falsity in cases of reference failure. This problem is especially acute for our account in some cases of denials. Consider the following example. A blind man is facing in the direction of a distant building. Someone, unaware of the man's blindness, says, "He believes that that building is far away." One normally would take this report to be about the notion the man has as a result of his current visual perception of the building. The speaker is trying to refer (though not with a word) to such a notion, to provide such a notion for the report to be about. But of course there is no such notion in this case. Is this report false, or, owing to a failure of tacit reference, does it fail to express a proposition? Certainly, we ordinarily would respond not by saying, "You have failed to express a proposition," but "He doesn't believe that"—and we have the strong intuition that this denial would be true.

Compare the following case: an astronaut on the moon[18] says, "It's three o'clock." Typically, this sentence would be used to express the claim that it is three o'clock in Z, where Z is the time zone in which the utterance takes place. The confused astronaut thinks that there are time zones on the moon, and he intends to claim that it is three o'clock in "Z," which is the time zone he is in. But there is no such time zone. So he fails to express a proposition. We feel no qualms, however, about denying his claim: "It's not three o'clock. There are no time zones on the moon, you . . . ."

The present difficulties are often discussed in connection with "negative existential" claims. But the same issues arise with respect to all sorts of denials in which the speaker believes there to be reference failure. A child who sincerely asserts, "Santa will come tonight," fails to refer, and therefore, on most direct reference accounts, fails to express a proposition. But the parent who responds, "Santa will not come tonight," explaining that there is no Santa, makes what seems to be a true claim, despite the fact that the use of 'Santa' does not refer.

Note that these examples would present no trouble for descriptional theories of reference. For if in these cases the original speakers are seen, not as attempting to provide a specific thing to be a propositional constituent, but merely as claiming that there is a thing meeting a certain condition (being the generous elf known as 'Santa', being the local time zone, or being the man's perceptual notion of the building), then the claims are straightforwardly false and the denials are true.

The descriptive theories have even more than this kind of extensional correctness going for them; it is because the cited conditions—call them *providing conditions*—are not satisfied that the denials are true. In the child's use of 'Santa', the providing condition, of being the generous elf known as 'Santa', plays a central semantic role, even though it is not the referent of the child's use of the name. It is a condition that the child expects to be filled as a precondition of successful reference. He expects to refer successfully to a thing in virtue of its meeting the providing condition. His supposed ability to refer to a thing by using the name 'Santa' depends on the condition's being satisfied. Similarly, the astronaut takes it that he can talk directly about a time zone, that he can provide one, because it meets the providing condition of being the local time zone. And, we claim, the belief reporter expects to be able to talk directly about a notion because it satisfies the condition of being the man's perceptual notion of the building.[19]

A normal, successful case of direct reference involves a speaker referring to an object in virtue of that object's satisfying a providing condition. Reference failure involves failure of a presupposition, namely, the presupposition that a providing condition is satisfied. Now, expressions like proper names and underarticulated phrases that normally invoke devices of direct reference are sometimes used where there is no presupposition that the relevant providing conditions are satisfied. The denials in the cases of the blind man, the astronaut, and Santa are like this. In each of these denials, the speaker does not presuppose that there is a thing meeting the providing condition that is invoked by the utterance. Instead, we claim, the speaker *raises the providing condition to constituency*—he talks about the condition itself rather than about a supposed thing that meets it. The providing condition now plays a semantic role—as a constituent of the proposition expressed in the denial—more central than its usual auxilliary role of providing a propositional constituent.

In particular, the claim expressed by 'Santa will not come tonight' (in the described circumstances)[20] is to the effect that there is no generous elf known as "Santa" who will come tonight. And the proposition expressed by 'It is not three o'clock' is that there is no local time zone such that it is three o'clock there. And the content of 'He does not believe that that building is far away' is the claim that there is no perceptual notion of the building such that the man has a belief involving that notion, with the content that the building is far away. The denials are thus true, and their truth is consistent with our claim that the assertions they deny strictly speaking fail to make claims.

Of course, for each of the original, claimless assertions, there is a proposition closely related to the kind of proposition the speaker intends to express, which we can for most purposes charitably treat as the content of the statement. Specifically, we can take the speaker to have expressed the claim that there is a thing meeting the invoked providing condition, such that so-and-so. In fact, the speaker of such an assertion is pre-assertively committed to this proposition, in virtue of his commitment to the presuppositions that must be satisfied if he is to make a successful claim in the way he intends.

Above we analyzed our reader's utterance of (2) in an imaginary case in which Miles has been shouting about the Prince. In fact, Miles was not shouting, "Edward Tudor is of royal blood," at the time he encountered the boy. The reader actually has no specific actions on Miles's part to which he can tie such a notion of Prince Edward. It is obvious from the general tenor of the novel, however, that Miles would have such a notion. Every full-witted adult in England at the time has a notion of Prince Edward—one they acquired shortly after he was born which motivates their behavior in regard to the Prince of Wales, such as their use of the phrase 'Prince Edward', their decorum when the royal procession goes by, and the like. Our reader may not be able to pick out anything very specific in Miles's behavior to serve as evidence that he has such a normal notion of the Prince. But he has every right to suppose that he has one.[21]

It may seem implausible to suppose that our reader, in using (2), can directly provide a notion for the report to be about, since the reader is not directly acquainted with such a notion. If this intuition is right—an assumption we shall question in a minute—our machinery gives us a natural way of respecting it: this is a case in which, instead of a notion, a providing condition becomes a propositional constituent. What our reader is claiming with (2) is that there is some normal notion via which Miles believes that Edward is royal; that is, the condition of being a normal notion of the Prince is the unarticulated constituent. The report, on this construal, is an example of a second kind of belief report—in which notions are not provided, but instead are constrained by provided conditions; the report is about those conditions in the sense of "about" appropriate to propositional constituents.

For this (supposed) second kind of belief report we can give the following account. Where u is a belief report at t which is about conditions $C_1, \ldots, C_k$, and $p = Con(u_S)$, where u_S is the subutterance of u corresponding to the object sentence S,

$$Con(u) = \exists b[B(a, b, t) \wedge \text{Content}(b, t) = p$$

$$\wedge\ \exists n_1, \ldots, n_k \bigwedge_{r_i \text{ in } p} (C_i(n_i) \wedge \text{Responsible}(n_i, r_i, b))]$$

So we have room in our framework for two sorts of belief report, corresponding to whether notions are themselves *provided* or merely *constrained* by conditions. Supposing for now that there really are two kinds of belief report, how can we know, for a given report, of which kind it is? One way, surely, is to look at what would happen if the appropriate notions were to fail to exist. If the report would then be false, then it is a case of notion constraint rather than provision; if the report would fail to make a claim, then it is a case of (attempted) notion provision.

Of course, we have seen how, in a case where an attempt to provide a notion fails, a proposition closely related to what the speaker is trying to express takes center stage. This is the false proposition to the effect that the agent has a notion which meets the invoked providing condition and which is involved in a belief with such-and-such content. Given this fact, our intuitions about whether a belief report fails to make a claim or is simply false are in the same boat as our intuitions about the truth value of the child's claim that Santa is coming. The falsity of the closely related propositions, plus the truth of the natural denials of these statements, may well obscure intuitions about the truth of the original claims.

In this paper, we adopt officially the position that there really are belief reports of the second kind (which are about conditions rather than notions). Given our points about providing conditions and propositions to which speakers are pre-assertively committed in cases of direct reference, however, a plausible case can be mounted for the view that, in all successful belief reports, specific notions are provided for the report to be about.[22]

Assuming, now, that there are two classes of belief reports, there is no reason to suspect that all reports will fall clearly into one camp or the other. For example, if our reader simply assumes that Miles must have a normal notion of King Henry and expects his audience to do the same, then it makes little difference whether he claims that Miles has a belief involving that notion (notion provision) or just a belief involving a normal notion (notion constraint). Since it makes little difference, our reader need not go to any pains to indicate which of the claims he is making; his report simply can land between the two claims.[23]

V

With that out of the way, let us turn to our examples.

First, a recap of the semantics of (1) and (2). We shall treat (1) as a case of notion provision. The provided notion is Miles's notion of Edward which is connected with his perception of and actions toward Edward in the mob incident. The reader claims that Miles does not have a belief involving that notion, with the content that Edward is of royal blood.

With (2), the reader provides a condition on notions, the condition of being a normal notion of Prince Edward. The reader claims that Miles has a belief involving some normal notion of Edward, with the content that Edward is of royal blood.

In the Pierre case, the sentence (3) gets used in two reports, first in a discussion of Pierre's initial acquaintance with London through stories, then in a discussion about Pierre's thoughts of his adopted home. Call these reports u_3 and u_3'. Pierre actually has two notions of London, one relevant to each discussion; call the first n and the second n'. The notion n meets the condition C of being a notion germane to the discussion of Pierre's reaction to the stories; the notion n' meets the condition C' of being a notion germane to the discussion of Pierre's new home.

If one of the two analyses is uniquely correct for u_3 and u_3', it is perhaps the account in terms of notion constraint. The speaker of the former report is claiming that Pierre has a belief involving some notion germane to the current conversation about the stories, with the content that London is pretty. The speaker of the latter report requires that the belief involve some notion relevant to the conversation about Pierre's new home.

If the circumstances of u_3 and u_3' are such as to make the notions n and n' clear and present to the speakers and their audiences, then the analysis should be in terms of notion provision. If this is the case, then the speaker of u_3 claims that Pierre has a belief involving the notion n with the content that London is pretty; the speaker of u_3' claims that Pierre has a belief involving the notion n' with the content that London is pretty. If the circumstances of the two reports are less clear-cut, as they often are, then, as noted earlier, the claims made by the speakers might fall between those offered by the notion-provision and notion-constraint accounts. There just might be no saying.

Note, though, that any of these analyses constitutes a solution to the puzzle. The claim made in u_3 is simply true, and the claim made in u_3' is simply false.

Kripke presents the puzzle as arising from a few very plausible principles about belief reports, including:

Disquotation: If a normal English speaker, on reflection, sincerely assents to 'p', then he believes that p (*op. cit.*, pp. 248–9 [885–6 in this vol.]).

Translation: If a sentence of one language expresses a truth in that language, then any translation of it into any other language also expresses a truth (*op. cit.*, p. 250 [886–7]).

On our account of belief reporting, neither of these principles is at all plausible in general. Each principle presupposes that it is belief sentences that are true or false. On our view, a single sentence, like (3), can be used in both true and false reports. Kripke assumes that, because of the lack of obviously context-sensitive words, (3) can be considered more or less "eternal." But words are not the only sources of context-sensitivity; the presence of unarticulated constituents also can widen the gap between a sentence and the proposition expressed by a statement of it. And that is what happens in the Pierre case.

Richard lists three sentences considered as uttered by A watching B in the phone booth:

(4) I believe she is in danger.

(5) I believe you are in danger.

(6) The man watching you believes you are in danger.

A uses (4), clearly, to make a true report. His notion n_{vis} of B which stems from his view out the window, which is associated with his idea of being in peril, and which causes his waving is supplied. It is claimed that A has a belief involving n_{vis} with the content that B is in danger. He in fact has such a belief.

The man would not sincerely use (5) over the phone; if sincere, he certainly would deny (5). The natural intuition, we think, is that a use of (5) in the described circumstances would make a false claim. (It is this reaction which Richard sets out to prove mistaken. The very possibility of our semantics shows that his proof is in error.)

The set-up for (6) is as follows. *B* sees a man, *A*, in a building across the street waving frantically. Amused, she says (over the phone), "the man watching me believes that I'm in danger." Echoing her, *A* utters (6). Surely, *B*'s claim is true. And if so, *A*'s use of (6), which is in explicit agreement with her, is true also.

So we hold that the use of (5) is false while that of (6) is true. But how can this be? The two reports are uttered by the same person in the same circumstances, they ascribe beliefs to the same agent, and they use precisely the same embedded sentence, understood in the same way! The only difference is the way in which the man is referred to—in the one case with 'I', in the other with 'the man watching you'.

Difference enough, we think. The pragmatic principle of self-ascription applies to (5) but not to (6):

Self-Ascription: An utterance of 'I believe that ... τ ...' provides (or, is about) the notion that is connected to the speaker's use of 'τ'.

Using 'I' in (5), *A* thus directs attention to the notion (n_{phone}) that is linked to his use, in (5), of 'you'—the notion of *B* which is associated with his idea of being the one he is addressing[24] and not associated with his idea of being in danger. So *A*'s use of (5) makes the claim that he has a belief involving n_{phone}, which has the content that *B* is in danger. He in fact has no such belief.

In (6), *A* is discussing those beliefs of the man watching *B*, that is, of *A* himself, which explain the frantic gestures directed at *B*. So he claims that the man has a belief involving n_{vis}, the notion linked to his perception out the window and his gestures of warning, which has the content that *B* is in danger. In fact, *A* has such a belief.

Richard's case is especially interesting because it shows how a contextual shift can be brought about by a change in wording outside of the embedded sentence in a belief report. This gives added force to our analysis of substitution worries: the wording changes in the usual cases of reluctance to substitute are responsible, not for changes in meaning or explicitly specified content, but for changes in what is provided by context for the reports to be about.

Our semantics allows that, for a given belief sentence, absolutely any of the agent's notions may be provided—there is no semantic restriction on what notions may be provided in a use of a given sentence. But there are many pragmatic principles, like self-ascription, that constrain which notions can be provided in the normal case. It is semantically but not pragmatically possible for a use of 'I believe I am not me' or (normally) 'S, but I do not believe that S' to be true. Although it is semantically possible, in W. V. O. Quine's example, for an utterance of 'Tom believes that Cicero is Tully' to express a true proposition (say, if Tom's 'Cicero' notion is provided twice over), there may be no very natural use of that sentence which in fact expresses the proposition (although surely we can concoct a Richard-ish example to put this point in doubt). In the normal case, the use of different names for Cicero serves as a strong, though perhaps defeasible, indication that the names have some importance to what's being said over and above just standing for Cicero. Such a difference in names requires a sufficient reason—in this case, a difference in which notions are being provided to play the corresponding roles in the ascribed belief.

VI

The relation of the present proposal to Fregean semantics for belief reports should be relatively clear. The broad similarity consists in the agreement that a belief report specifies, in addition to simply which objects the agent is claimed to have a belief about, also just how the agent is cognitively connected to those objects. On our account, the report specifies (or constrains) the particular notions allegedly involved in the belief. On a Fregean account, "senses" are specified.

Two crucial differences separate the accounts. First, we stress the particularity and unsharability of notions. Since notions are full-fledged particulars immersed in the causal order, they have a great array of different features that we can exploit to provide them in our belief reports. They are involved in beliefs, associated (sometimes) with words, formed in specific circumstances, connected to preceptual situations, reasonings, and actions; they survive the formation and abandonment of beliefs in which they are involved; and so on. We can use each of these kinds of fact to give us a handle on a notion, a way of picking it out. This frees us from a problem often noted about the Fregean strategy: it appears that, on most natural construals of what senses are, we often do not know just what sense an agent attaches to an object (we do not grasp it), and so we cannot know just what we are attributing to the agent with a belief report, which, after all, must be about the agent's ways of thinking.

As we have said, there is nothing in our view incompatible with something like Fregean senses, considered as entities which we can use to classify an agent's notions. A Fregean might well take our talk of "notions" as an account of what it takes for an agent to grasp a sense—agents grasp senses in virtue of having appropriate notions.

The second departure from a Fregean account is in our claim that the agent's way of thinking about things (her notions), though they are specified in a belief report, are not the referents of the words occurring in the embedded sentence. This difference becomes especially important in the analysis of certain kinds of reports: those with content sentences containing devices of underarticulation, and those with no content sentences at all, but which instead are completed with the likes of 'what you said', 'the same thing', and 'Church's Thesis'.

VII

The account of belief reports sketched here closes some doors. If, as we claim, a single belief sentence can be used in both true and false reports, then there can be no simple logic of such sentences. The simplest possible rule,

A believes that S

A believes that S

does not hold in general, as we learn from Kripke's puzzle.

Even a logic of belief sentences restricted to a single context will prove difficult.[25] Although a relativized version of the above rule will certainly hold, this one,

A believes that S (relative to c)
$A = B$ (relative to c)

B believes that S (relative to c)

will not, as we learn from Richard's puzzle.

Also closed is the prospect of a strictly compositional semantics for belief sentences. The semantic values of the subexpressions in a belief report, on our analysis, do not provide all the materials for the semantic value of the report itself. Notions and conditions on notions are not articulated, but end up in the contents of reports; so the semantics of belief reports is in an important way noncompositional.

In addition, our account denies what some have seen as a primary desideratum for theories of belief: that a belief report claims simply that a binary relation holds between an agent and an object of belief.

And, perhaps worst of all, we have given an account on which it appears to be next to impossible to give a complete, systematic account of which claims are made by which belief reports. We have claimed that belief reports are context-sensitive, that they invoke unarticulated constituents, without offering any general method for determining what the relevant contextual factors are, and how they give rise to these unarticulated constituents of belief reports.

Tempted as we are to view each of the above results as an insight rather than a drawback, we realize that we have abandoned many of the issues and goals commonly pursued in this area. But we think the account opens many doors as well.

Whereas there is little possibility of an interesting logic of belief sentences, the logic of beliefs, notions, and ideas is available. Such issues as logical and analytic closure of belief, explicit versus implicit belief, and inferential issues in belief change really belong to the logic of beliefs rather than to the logic of belief sentences. We can explore the logic of the relations we have seen as underlying our ordinary talk about beliefs—but this logic will not be a logic of ordinary language.

Of course, we have explained very little about what beliefs, notions, and ideas are. But we think our partial account of them raises obvious questions in theories of representation, action, perception, and the metaphysics of mind.

Our semantics is not compositional, but there is system in the noncompositional mayhem. The ways in which notions and conditions on notions are provided have yet to be explored to any great extent. But the discussions of the belief puzzles suggest several directions from which to look at these mechanisms.

Last, the move to unarticulated constituents emphasizes the importance of pragmatic facts about language to the study of what seem like purely semantic issues. In order to express claims, we exploit a tremendous variety of facts, conventions, and circumstances, of which the meanings and referents of our terms form just a part. So it is a mistake to relegate pragmatics to matters of felicity and implicature. In the case of belief reports, it is central to understanding content and truth.

Notes

This work was supported in part by the System Development Foundation through a grant to the Center for the Study of Language and Information. We would like to thank the Philosophy of Situation Theory group at CSLI; special thanks to David Israel.

1. *Situations and Attitudes* (Cambridge: MIT, 1983), pp. 253–264.

2. "Substitutivity," in *Essays in Honor of Richard Cartwright* (Cambridge: MIT, 1987), pp. 99–132, and "Direct Reference and Propositional Attitudes," in Almog, Perry, Wettstein, eds., *Themes from Kaplan* (New York: Oxford, 1989).

3. *Frege's Puzzle* (Cambridge: MIT, 1986).

4. *Opacity* is the claim that substitution of coreferring names and demonstratives in belief reports does not necessarily preserve the truth of those reports (definite descriptions are another matter; it is not nearly as controversial that substituting a description for a coreferring name can influence the truth value of a belief report). What "substitution" comes to with respect to utterances (belief reports), as opposed to sentences (belief sentences), is not at all obvious. Our simple notions of substitutivity, opacity, and so on are really useful only if sentences are (wrongly) taken as the bearers of truth and content. Here, we shall adopt an informal notion of substitution in belief reports, such that the reports (1) and (1′), as well as (2) and (2′) are related by substitution.

5. For an important qualification, see n. 14 below.

6. "A Puzzle about Belief," in A. Margalit, ed., *Meaning and Use* (Dordrecht: Reidel, 1979), pp. 239–283 [chap. 38 in this vol.].

7. For a fuller defense of the particularity of beliefs, see Crimmins, *Talk about Beliefs* (Cambridge: MIT, 1992).

8. A speaker can adopt a name (like 'John') more than once, to refer to what may be different individuals. Each such adoption creates a type of use to which the speaker may put the name. So a causal analysis of names should look not at names themselves, but at types of uses of names, as the things for which reference is determined causally. An agent may use 'John' to refer either to John Dupre or to John Etchemendy. What individuates these distinct types of uses of the name 'John'? One answer is that the types of uses of 'John' are tied to distinct notions in the agent.

9. See "Demonstratives," 1977 manuscript reprinted in *Themes from Kaplan*.

10. There is no mystery as to how a single thing can be a part of many different things at the same time (and at different times). One may, for example, be a member of many different committees or clubs.

11. This is to consider only beliefs of a certain kind of composition. In a more thorough presentation, a discussion of other kinds of belief structures, perhaps including general beliefs and complex beliefs, might be called for—although the logical connectives and quantifiers can be accommodated within this simple structure. Also, we have chosen to ignore in this paper many subtleties of time and tense.

12. Roughly, an argument role of a relation is also an argument role of a proposition (at least) when, in that proposition, the role of the relation is occupied by at object.

13. "Direct Reference and Ascriptions of Belief," *Journal of Philosophical Logic*, XII (1983): 425–452.

14. In accord with our simple version of "semantic innocence," we assume throughout that a belief report specifies the content of the ascribed belief by providing a sentence with the same content, as uttered in the report. The puzzle cases that we consider seem to be ones for which this assumption is correct. There are good reasons, however, to think that things do not always work this way. One way of analyzing, "Barbara believes that the Twin Towers are over a foot tall," would involve quantification over contents of beliefs. Other cases of reporting implicit and tacit beliefs might well work similarly. Another case in which a proposition might be "quantified out" is in the use of, "He believes that Russell's yacht is longer than it is." Also, one can use, "Timmy believes that the Tooth Fairy will make him rich," knowing full well that the embedded sentence does not express any proposition (if in fact it does not). These and other cases make us wary of insisting that a content proposition is always specified in a belief report. The present strategy can be extended in relatively simple ways to account for such cases.

15. Yet another simplification: we ignore the fact that many uses of singular terms, including terms in the subject position of belief sentences, are not directly referential. "Attributive" uses of definite descriptions really should be handled differently. Note also that we really should treat the idea in a belief in the same way we treat notions here: though the puzzles considered here do not turn on this, others certainly do.

16. Here one major difference from the "official" belief-report semantics in ch. 10 of Perry's *Situations and Attitudes* (p. 256) is apparent. There, a belief report is true if the agent has any belief with the specified content. There is a further crucial differnce that is not so obvious. Barwise and Perry countenance beliefs as real, concrete things, as we do here. But these beliefs are represented as situations of an agent being related to an anchored belief schema. Belief schemas are abstract objects in which what we have called notions are represented by indeterminates. Although the way this all works is quite complicated, in the end beliefs are individuated by belief schemas—abstract objects—and the things in the world to which the indeterminates in the schemas are anchored. But indeterminates are not notions, and, we think, relations to anchored belief schemas are not quite fine-grained enough to individuate beliefs in the ways needed for belief reports. So we suggest two major changes to the account in *Situations and Attitudes*: we give ourselves the theoretical machinery to talk about notions and ideas directly; we then claim that these things are among the subject matter of belief reports (via the mechanism of unarticulated constituents), and are not merely quantified over.

17. For more on unarticulated constituents, see Perry, "Thought without Representation," *Proceedings of the Aristotelian Society*, suppl. vol. LX (1986): 263–283. There, a systematic semantics for some underarticulated constructions is given, which is connected to a recursive model of syntax in the usual way.

18. John Etchemendy brought up this version of Wittgenstein's example.

19. Just which providing conditions are invoked in a given case depends on a wide range of circumstances. Also, there usually is more than one such condition for

a given use of a term. Providing conditions for a use u of 'here' by speaker A at location l, for instance, include the conditions of being the location of the utterer of u, being where A is, and being l. In the 'Santa' case, we have the conditions of being the referent of the utterance of 'Santa', being the relevant thing known as 'Santa', being the generous elf known as 'Santa', and so on.

20. In circumstances where it is presupposed that the providing condition is met, the denial expresses just the negation of the proposition (if there is one) expressed by the corresponding assertion.

21. What counts as being a normal notion certainly depends, we think, not only on what is common in a community, but also on other aspects of the background of the discourse, including facts about what is relevant to the goals of the discourse. We would expect an account of "being a normal notion" to exhibit many of the same features as an appropriate account of "knowing who b is," which certainly is background-sensitive in many way. See, for example, Böer and Lycan, *Knowing Who* (Cambridge: MIT, 1985).

22. This view is argued in Crimmins, *Talk about Beliefs*, though in the end the argument rests precariously on the fact that none of the examples considered as natural candidates for reports of the "second kind" seems clearly to be as required.

23. There is another way, also, in which a report can land between the notion-provision and the notion-constraint types of report. It is not hard to concoct cases in which one notion is provided and another is constrained; a natural construal of our reader's report "Miles believed that he (Edward in rags) was less noble than Prince Edward" might go along these lines. So in the general case, both notions and conditions may be provided; there are no difficulties in formalizing this along the lines already given for the pure notion-provision and pure notion-constraint analyses.

24. More precisely, with his idea I_{addr}, the idea that has the context sensitive semantic role picking out the person being addressed.

25. Here we mean 'context' in a sense such that various different statements can be made in the same context. One way of taking our claims in this paper would be as denying the general usefulness in semantics of such a restricted notion of context. Taken this way, we have claimed that such things as the words used in a statement can affect the semantically relevant parts of the statement's context.

Chapter 41

Interpreted Logical Forms

Richard K. Larson and Peter Ludlow

In recent semantics literature, a number of authors (including Harman
(1972), Higginbotham (1986, 1991), and Segal (1989)) have suggested
that familiar semantic problems arising with propositional attitude verbs
might be resolved by taking such predicates to express relations between
agents and *interpreted logical forms* (ILFs). ILFs are annotated constituency graphs or phrase-markers whose nodes pair terminal and non-
terminal symbols with a semantic value. Such objects in effect represent a
semantic value together with its linguistic 'mode of presentation'.[1]

In this paper, we present an explicit theory of interpreted logical forms
(ILFs)—their construction and properties—and we argue that classical
questions regarding propositional attitude semantics are indeed illuminated by these means. In Section 1, we introduce ILFs informally and
then go on, in Section 2, to present our formal construction algorithm,
embedding it within a recursive theory of truth for natural language of the
kind advocated by Davidson (1984a). In Sections 3–5, we discuss the
application of ILFs to issues involving substitutivity, demonstratives,
general beliefs, and iterated attitude ascriptions. In Section 6, we briefly
compare the account to other theories. Finally, in Section 7, we explore
the relation of ILFs to belief ascriptions.

1 ILFS AND THE 'PROBLEM OF THE ATTITUDES'

ILFs are advanced in response to a familiar problem for extensional
semantic theories posed by propositional attitude contexts. As noted by

First appeared in *Synthese* 95 (1993): 305–356. Reprinted with kind permission from Kluwer
Academic Publishers.

Frege (1892), such contexts appear to challenge the otherwise quite general principle that the reference of an expression is a function of the references of its subconstituent parts. The pairs in (1) and (2) give a standard example of the problem. Whereas substitution of the coreferring noun phrase *Frances Gumm* for *Judy Garland* preserves truth-value in nonattitudinal contexts like (1a, b), the same is not true in attitudinal contexts like (2a, b):

(1) a. Judy Garland sang "Somewhere Over the Rainbow".
    b. Frances Gumm sang "Somewhere Over the Rainbow".

(2) a. Max believes Judy Garland sang "Somewhere Over the Rainbow".
    b. Max believes Frances Gumm sang "Somewhere Over the Rainbow".

This behavior is observed broadly with expressions occurring in the scope of attitude verbs, and not just with proper names. Thus despite the fact that *xerox* and *photocopy* are coextensive predicates, from (3a) we cannot infer (3b). Similarly, although the common nouns *woodchuck* and *groundhog* refer to exactly the same members of genus *Marmota*, (4a) does not entail (4b):[2]

(3) a. Max believes Mary xeroxed *War and Peace*.
    b. Max believes Mary photocopied *War and Peace*.

(4) a. Max believes there is a woodchuck on the veranda.
    b. Max believes there is a groundhog on the veranda.

The leading idea of the ILF theory is that clausal complement-taking verbs express relations between agents and interpreted phrase-markers, in which each mode has been paired with the semantic value assigned to it under some valuation predicate. These objects provide an account of failures of substitution in attitude contexts. We may illustrate the main idea with example (2a). On the ILF theory, *believe* will express a relation between Max and the ILF for the embedded clause *Judy Garland sang "Somewhere Over the Rainbow"*. (5a) gives a standard syntactic representation for the embedded sentence. Furthermore, under a simple extensional semantic theory, the subparts of this tree might plausibly receive semantic values (or referents) as shown in (5b):

(5) a.

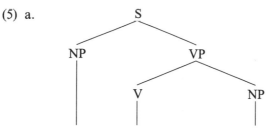

Judy Garland   sang   "Somewhere Over the Rainbow"

b. i. *Judy Garland* refers to Judy Garland.
   ii. [$_{NP}$ *Judy Garland*] refers to Judy Garland.
   iii. "*Somewhere Over the Rainbow*" refers to the song "Somewhere Over the Rainbow".
   iv. [$_{NP}$ "*Somewhere Over the Rainbow*"] refers to the song "Somewhere Over the Rainbow".
   v. *sang* refers (in (5a)) to the pair ⟨Judy Garland, "Somewhere Over the Rainbow"⟩.
   vi. [$_V$ *sang*] refers (in (5a)) to the pair ⟨Judy Garland, "Somewhere Over the Rainbow"⟩.
   vii. [$_{VP}$ *sang "Somewhere Over the Rainbow"*] refers (in (5a)) to Judy Garland.
   viii. [$_S$ *Judy Garland Sang "Somewhere Over the Rainbow"*] refers to t (i.e., the sentence is true).

The ILF for the embedded clause is derived by pairing semantic values with their respective nodes in the syntactic tree, as in (6). Here *j* is the individual Judy Garland/Frances Gumm, and *o* is the song "Somewhere Over the Rainbow". The resulting object is analyzed as the second argument of *believe* in the final statement of truth-conditions, or T-sentence for the example given in (7):[3]

(6)

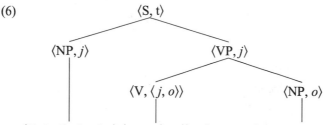

⟨*Judy Garland*, *j*⟩ ⟨*sang*, ⟨*j*, *o*⟩⟩   ⟨"*Somewhere Over the Rainbow*", *o*⟩

(7) *Max believes Judy Garland sang "Somewhere Over the Rainbow"* is true iff Max believes

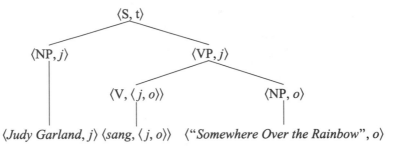

⟨*Judy Garland, j*⟩ ⟨*sang, ⟨j, o⟩*⟩   ⟨*"Somewhere Over the Rainbow", o*⟩

Recall now (2a, b), where the truth of the former, and the coreferentiality of *Judy Garland* and *Frances Gumm*, are insufficient to guarantee the truth of the latter. The ILF theory correctly predicts this result. As we have seen, (2a) receives the T-sentence in (7). By contrast, (2b) receives the T-sentence in (8):

(8) *Max believes Frances Gumm sang "Somewhere Over the Rainbow"* is true iff Max believes

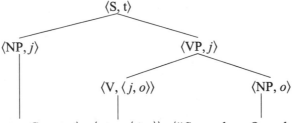

⟨*Frances Gumm, j*⟩   ⟨*sang, ⟨j, o⟩*⟩   ⟨*"Somewhere Over the Rainbow", o*⟩

(7) and (8) are distinct T-sentences whose truth requires Max to stand in the belief-relation to different objects. The former requires that he believe an ILF containing the sub-ILF ⟨*Judy Garland, j*⟩, whereas the latter requires that he believe an ILF containing the sub-ILF ⟨*Frances Gumm, j*⟩. The ILF theory thus correctly distinguishes the two sentences semantically, as desired; neither entails the other.

2   A FORMAL THEORY OF ILFS

We now present an explicit ILF theory of the attitudes, embedding it within a formal semantics for (a subportion of) English. Since ILFs partake of both form and reference, their definition evidently presupposes a syntax and a semantic theory for extensional contexts. We thus begin with a brief sketch of our background assumptions.

2.1 Background assumptions

We assume a syntax embodying the basic tenets of the Extended Standard Theory, as developed in Chomsky (1981, 1986) and a large number of related works. Under this theory each sentence is assigned a pair of labeled phrase-markers representing its surface form (or S-structure) and its logical form (or LF).[4] These two representations are related to one another by means of a movement operation that applies optionally in certain cases and obligatorily in others. For example, the sentence *Judy Garland sings* is assigned the S-structure in (9a), and is associated with two possible LFs according to whether the subject noun phrase optionally raises out of subject position or remains in situ. In the former case, the LF for *Judy Garland sings* is as in (9b); in the latter case, the LF for *Judy Garland sings* is identical to the S-structure (9a). A quantified sentence such as *Every starlet sings* is assigned a similar surface form (10a). However, the derivation of its LF involves obligatory raising of the quantified subject with attachment to S (10b). In both (9b) and (10b), the empty noun phrase in subject position (t_i) is the 'trace' left by raising and represents, in effect, a formal variable bound by the moved quantifier:

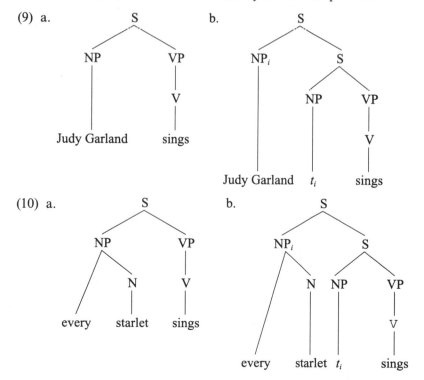

Representations like (9b) and (10b) are analogous to the familiar restricted quantifier form of first-order logic (e.g., [for some x_i: $x_i =$ Judy Garland][Sings(x_i)] and [every x_i: starlet(x_i)][sings(x_i)]). The movement that derives such representations may be viewed as a form of scope assignment.

For our semantic theory, we assume a general approach along the lines initiated by Davidson (1984a, 1984c), and developed by many subsequent authors (for example, Lycan (1984), Higginbotham (1985, 1986), Larson and Segal (1995)). The core of this approach is a recursive theory of material truth, whose axioms assign semantic values to natural language expressions and yield familiar Tarskian T-sentences. We assume that these axioms apply to syntactic LFs as specified above, and have the general form shown in (11). The latter specifies a semantic value α for a constituent $[_X Y_1 \ldots Y_n]$ in terms of semantic values $\beta_1, \ldots, \beta_n$ for its immediate subconstituents $Y_1 \ldots Y_n$ (respectively); as usual, all free variables are understood as universally quantified:

(11) Val(α, $[_X Y_1 \ldots Y_n]$, σ) iff $\ldots$, Val(β_1, Y_1, σ), $\ldots$, Val(β_n, Y_n, σ), $\ldots$

(12) gives sample axioms of this form. (12a) states that any sentence S consisting of a subject NP and a predicate VP has the value t with respect to any sequence σ (i.e., the sentence is true with respect to σ) iff there is some individual x that is a semantic value of both the NP and the VP (wrt σ). (12b) states that an NP node dominating the name *Judy Garland* has the value x (wrt σ) iff x is Judy Garland. (12d) states that a V node dominating the verb *sings* has the value x (wrt σ) iff x sings, and so on:

(12) a. Val(t, $[_S$ NP VP], σ) iff for some x, Val(x, NP, σ) and Val(x, VP, σ).
   b. Val(x, $[_{NP}$ *Judy Garland*], σ) iff $x =$ Judy Garland.
   c. Val(x, $[_{VP}$ V], σ) iff Val(x, V, σ).
   d. Val(x, $[_V$ *sings*], σ) iff x sings.

Using the axioms in (12a–d) we may prove a T-sentence for the LF phrase-marker in (9a). The biconditionals allow us to derive (13a); substitution of identicals then yields the final T-sentence (13b):

(13) a. Val(t, $[_S[_{NP}$ *Judy Garland*]$[_{VP}]_V$ *sings*]]], σ) iff for some x, $x =$ Judy Garland and x sings.
   b. Val(t, $[_S[_{NP}$ *Judy Garland*]$[_{VP}]_V$ *sings*]]], σ) iff Judy Garland sings.

A full set of axioms for interpreting the constructions shown in (9) and (10) is given in the Appendix (see Fragment L_0).[5]

2.2 Semantic axioms for embedded clauses

Our formal proposal for an ILF theory of the attitudes extends the basic framework sketched above by adding three parts: (i) a semantic axiom for VPs containing a clause-embedding verb and a sentential complement, (ii) lexical axioms for clause-selecting verbs such as *believe, claim,* and *think,* and (iii) a recursive definition of ILFs.

The new VP axiom is given in (14). In prose this rule states that an individual x is a value of a VP containing a clause-embedding V and a complement S (wrt σ) iff there is some y such that $\langle x, y \rangle$ is a value of V and y is the ILF of S (wrt σ):

(14) Val$(x, [_{VP} \text{ V S}], \sigma)$ iff for some y, Val$(\langle x, y \rangle, \text{V}, \sigma)$ and
    $y = ⟦S⟧$ wrt σ.

Note that under (14), ILFs (and the intensionality effects they bring) are not introduced by specific predicates, such as those involving thoughts and beliefs; rather they are introduced constructionally. ILFs appear in the truth-conditions whenever one has a VP containing a complement S.

Semantic axioms for clause-embedding verbs like *believe* and *think* are given in) (15a–c). These embody the simple and familiar idea that such predicates are relational. In prose, (15a) states that a pair $\langle x, y \rangle$ is a value of the verb $[_V \textit{believes}]$ (wrt a sequence σ) iff x believes y; and so on:

(15) a. Val$(\langle x, y \rangle, [_V \textit{believes}], \sigma)$ iff x believes y.
    b. Val$(\langle x, y \rangle, [_V \textit{thinks}], \sigma)$ iff x thinks y.
    c. Val$(\langle x, y \rangle, [_V \textit{claims}], \sigma)$ iff x claims y.

In the T-sentence derivation for a sentence containing one of these verbs, x will be the agent of the attitude and y will be an ILF.

Finally, (16) gives the general inductive definition of the *ILF of α with respect to a sequence σ* (abbreviated $⟦\alpha⟧$ wrt σ):[6]

(16) *Definition*: Let α be a phrase-marker with root S, let σ be a sequence, and let β be a sub-phrase-marker of α. Then:
    (i) If there is an x such that Val(x, β, σ) is provable from Val(t, α, σ) under the axioms of L_0, and for all y, Val(y, β, σ) is provable from Val(t, α, σ) iff $y = x$, and:
        (a) β is a terminal node, then $⟦\beta⟧ = \langle \beta, x \rangle$.
        (b) β is $[_\gamma \delta_1 \delta_2 \ldots \delta_n]$ for $n \geqslant 1$, then
            $⟦\beta⟧ = [_{\langle \gamma, x \rangle} ⟦\delta_1⟧ \ ⟦\delta_2⟧ \ldots ⟦\delta_n⟧]$.

(ii) If there is no x as defined in clause (i), and:

    (a) β is a terminal node, then $\ulcorner \beta \urcorner = \langle \beta \rangle$.

    (b) β is $[_\gamma\, \delta_1 \delta_2 \ldots \delta_n]$ for $n \geqslant 1$, then

       $\ulcorner \beta \urcorner = [_{\langle \gamma \rangle}\, \ulcorner \delta_1 \urcorner\, \ulcorner \delta_2 \urcorner \ldots \ulcorner \delta_n \urcorner]$.

The underlying idea here is just the one introduced informally above: we assume a prior syntactic theory assigning structures to sentences, and a prior semantic theory assigning values to sentences and their subparts under the condition of truth. Assuming the truth of the sentence α whose ILF is to be constructed—that is, assuming Val(t, α, σ)—we can actually prove various subphrases of α to have specific values. The ILF for α is then defined recursively using the structure and the values so assigned. ILFs for simplex lexical items are defined in clause (i.a); ILFs for more complex phrases are then built up from the former inductively, as specified in clause (i.b).

Clause (ii) appears in the definition of ILFs to accommodate expressions that either fall outside the domain of Val, and hence receive no value in L_1, or else fail to receive a unique value assignment (with respect to a given sequence σ). Such elements demand some specific convention for construction of their ILFs, and here we claim that when an expression β fails to receive any value, or fails to receive a unique value, then the ILF for β is just the singleton sequence containing the expression β itself. We discuss applications of clause (ii) in detail in Section 3.2.

2.3 A sample T-sentence derivation

The content of these assumptions is most easily seen by considering a sample T-sentence derivation for the sentence *Max believes Judy Garland sings*, under the LF structure in (17):

(17)

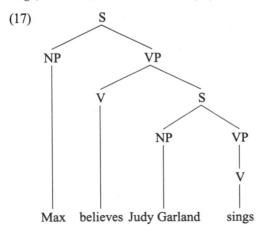

Using axioms from (12), (14), and (15) we proceed as follows:

(18) a. Val(t, [$_S$ [$_{NP}$ *Max*][$_{VP}$ [$_V$ *believes*][$_S$ *Judy Garland sings*]]], σ)
iff for some x, Val(x, [$_{NP}$ *Max*], σ) and
Val(x, [$_{VP}$ [$_V$ *believes*][$_S$ *Judy Garland sings*]], σ).   (by (12a))

  b. Val(x, [$_{NP}$ *Max*], σ) iff $x =$ Max.   (by the counterpart of (12b))

  c. Val(x, [$_{VP}$ [$_V$ *believes*][$_S$ *Judy Garland sings*]], σ) iff for some y,
Val($\langle x, y \rangle$, [$_V$ *believes*], σ) and
$y - $ □ [$_S$ *Judy Garland sings*] □ wrt σ.   (by (14))

  d. Val($\langle x, y \rangle$, [$_V$ *believes*], σ) iff x believes y.   (by (15a))

  e. Val(x, [$_S$ [$_{NP}$ *Max*][$_{VP}$ [$_V$ *believes*][$_S$ *Judy Garland sings*]]], σ)
iff for some x, y, $x =$ Max, x believes y, and
$y =$ □ [$_S$ *Judy Garland sings*] □ wrt σ.   (by (18a d))

  f. Val(x, [$_S$ [$_{NP}$ *Max*][$_{VP}$ [$_V$ *believes*][$_S$ *Judy Garland sings*]]], σ)
iff Max believes □ [$_S$ *Judy Garland sings*] □ wrt σ.

(by (18e) and Substitution of Identicals)

To complete this T-sentence we must determine the ILF □[$_S$ *Judy Garland sings*]□, applying the recursive definition in (16). We begin by using the results obtained in (12) and (13) for the embedded sentence *Judy Garland sings*:

(19) a. Val(t, [$_S$ [$_{NP}$ *Judy Garland*][$_{VP}$ [$_V$ *sings*]]], σ) iff for some x,
Val(x, [$_{NP}$ *Judy Garland*], σ) and Val(x, [$_{VP}$ [$_V$ *sings*]], σ).

(by (12a))

  b. Val(x, [$_{NP}$ *Judy Garland*], σ) iff $x =$ Judy Garland.   (by (12b))

  c. Val(x, [$_{VP}$ [$_V$ *sings*]], σ) iff Val(x, [$_V$ *sings*], σ).   (by (12c))

  d. Val(x, [$_V$ *sings*], σ) iff x sings.   (by (12d))

(19a–d) are all biconditionals stating the values that various expressions take when their containing sentence is true. Accordingly, these expressions can be associated with definite values under the assumption that S is in fact true. This assumption allows us to formally prove the following:

(20) a. Val(t, [$_S$ [$_{NP}$ *Judy Garland*][$_{VP}$ [$_V$ *sings*]]], σ).

  b. Val(Judy Garland, [$_{NP}$ *Judy Garland*], σ).

  c. Val(Judy Garland, [$_{VP}$ [$_V$ *sings*]], σ).

  d. Val(Judy Garland, [$_V$ *sings*], σ).

We now derive the ILF for [$_S$ [$_{NP}$ *Judy Garland*][$_{VP}$ [$_V$ *sings*]]], recursively pairing the component expressions of S with the values that have been proved for them according to the algorithm in (16):

(21)

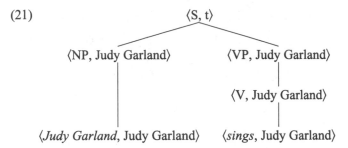

This allows us to complete the derivation, obtaining the desired T-sentence for the matrix sentence:

(22) Val(t, [s [NP *Max*][VP [V *believes*][S *Judy Garland sings*]]], σ)
      iff Max believes

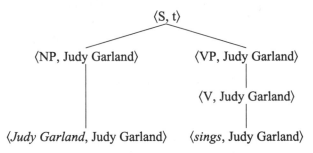

3   EQUIVALENCE OF ATTITUDE REPORTS

The assumption that ILFs are composed of linguistic forms and extra-linguistic objects yields straightforward individuation criteria for ILFs: two ILFs will be distinct whenever they contain distinct forms or distinct objects. This in turn yields straightforward criteria for distinguishing attitude reports. Two attitude reports will be logically nonequivalent whenever their complement clauses are associated with ILFs that differ in either form or content.

3.1   Attitudes distinguished by form

Under the recursive definition in (16), the linguistic components of an ILF derive from the syntactic phrase-marker that is used to construct it. In current linguistic theory, phrase-markers include a variety of information concerning the gross and fine structure of lexical forms, their identity, the hierarchical structures into which they are arrayed, and dependency relations of various kinds that hold between them. Under the ILF theory, then, it follows that all of these syntactic features are potentially relevant for distinguishing the truth-conditions of attitude reports.

Examples of attitude reports distinguished by the gross shape of words have already been encountered with (2)–(4); and (23) is analogous. These are pairs that differ in the lexical items appearing in their complement clauses, but not in the semantic values of these items. The ILF theory correctly distinguishes their truth-conditions:

(23) a. Kelly believes [St. Petersburg swings].
     b. Kelly believes [Leningrad swings].

Examples involving more subtle aspects of word form are also available. Linguistic theory views the lexical items in phrase-markers as including information about their segmental and supersegmental phonology.[7] Since this phonological information is present, the ILF theory predicts it can give rise to distinct ILFs. Discussion of examples like (24) by Ludlow (1985) supports this prediction. Ludlow notes that the truth or falsity of (24) might easily depend on the pronunciation given to the word *Harvard*. Thus consider the case of an individual Jason, who is from New York and unfamiliar with Bostonian dialect patterns. The truth of (24) might well depend on how *Harvard* is pronounced, with (25a) true and (25b) false:

(24) Jason believes [Harvard is a fine school].

(25) a. Jason believes that [[harvard] is a fine school].
     b. Jason believes that [[hahvahd] is a fine school].

The articulation of morphemes into words and syntactic phrases is also a prominent feature of phrase-markers, and thus is also predicted to be able to distinguish the truth-conditions of attitude reports. This prediction is verified straightforwardly by examples like (26) and (28). The truth of (26) may evidently depend on whether the subconstituent words of the complement clause are grouped as in (27a) or (27b). Similarly, the truth of (28) may depend on whether the subconstituent morphemes of the word *unlockable* are grouped as in (29a) or (29b):

(26) Max believes old men and women are vulnerable.

(27) a. Max believes [[[old men] and women] are vulnerable].
     b. Max believes [[old [men and women]] are vulnerable].

(28) Kathrin thinks this door is unlockable.

(29) a. Kathrin thinks [this door is [un[lockable]]]].
     b. Kathrin thinks [this door is [[unlockable]].

Under (29a), Kathrin is asserted to think that the door in question cannot be locked, whereas with (29b) she is asserted to think that the door can be unlocked.

Various dependency relations, including relations of antecedence and binding, are also widely assumed to be encoded in phrase-markers. Thus consider an example like (30); such sentences (discussed by Geach (1962)) are well known to possess two distinct interpretations according to whether John is asserted to be the only 'John's-mother-lover' or the only 'own-mother-lover'. In current syntactic theory, these two readings correspond to two distinct formal representations that differ according to whether the pronoun *his* is understood as bound by *John* or *only John*. This binding relation is indicated by coindexation as in (31), where (31a, b) correspond to the 'John's-mother-lover' and 'own-mother-lover' readings (respectively):[8]

(30) Only John loves his mother.

(31) a. [Only John$_i$]$_j$ [t_j loves his$_i$ mother].
     b. [Only John$_i$]$_j$ [t_j loves his$_j$ mother].

Since these numeral 'diacritics' are a part of syntactic representation, we predict that they may figure in the truth-conditions of attitude reports; and, once again, this prediction appears correct. Clearly, (32) may have different truth-values depending on whether Mary is taken to believe that John is the only 'John's-mother-lover' or the only 'own-mother-lover'. Under the ILF this difference of truth-conditions follows from the formal difference in ILFs in the two cases (33a, b):[9]

(32) Mary believes only John loves his mother.

(33) a. Val(t, *Mary believes* [[*only John$_i$*]$_j$ [t_j *loves his$_i$ mother*]], σ)
        iff Mary believes ⌐[[*only John$_i$*]$_j$ [t_j *loves his$_i$ mother*]]⌐.
     b. Val(t, *Mary believes* [[*only John$_i$*]$_j$ [t_j *loves his$_j$ mother*]], σ)
        iff Mary believes ⌐[[*only John$_i$*]$_j$ [t_i *loves his$_j$ mother*]]⌐.

The formal features relevant to the truth-conditions of attitude reports also plausibly include those distinguishing the identity of homophonous morphemes or lexical items. Consider the following examples:

(34) Max believes [that is a bank].

(35) Max believes [Bill is a flier].

Evidently, we want to differentiate (34) as an assertion that Max believes some object to be a savings institution from (34) as an assertion that Max believes some object to be a fluvial embankment. Similarly, we will want to distinguish the the assertion that Max believes Bill to be an individual who flies, from the assertion that Max believes Bill to be an advertising circular (35). In a lexicon or dictionary, the relevant difference of sense would in each case correspond to a formal distinction: the words *bank* and *flier* would each receive two distinct lexical entries. This yields four formally distinct lexical objects, which we might represent with diacritics as $bank_I$, $bank_{II}$, $flier_I$, and $flier_{II}$. As part of the syntactic representation of a lexical item, these markings will be present in phrase-markers and so serve to discriminate the corresponding attitudes. That is, we will have four distinct ILFs in (34) and (35) according to whether $bank_I$ vs. $bank_{II}$ or $flier_I$ vs. $flier_{II}$ appears.

We believe that syntactic discrimination between homophones may furnish a plausible account of certain interesting cases noted by Kripke (1979). Consider the example of a single individual Paderewski, who is known by another individual, Ralph, in two distinct contexts: as the famous, flamboyant, symphony conductor, and as Ralph's reclusive upstairs neighbor. Ralph knows that both have the name *Paderewski*; what he does not know is that the two are one and the same individual. Under these circumstances it seems possible for both of the following to be true.

(36) a. Ralph believes [Paderewski is shy].
     b. Ralph does not believe [Paderewski is shy].

The objects appearing in the ILFs for (36a, b) will be the same in both cases since *Paderewski* refers to a single individual. Hence if these attitude reports are to be distinguished at all, it seems their ILFs must be distinguished formally. We suggest the (36a, b) represent a case of homophony between what are in fact two syntactically distinct objects. That is, we suggest that there are actually two names here, $Paderewski_I$ and $Paderewski_{II}$, and that the reports in (36) are distinguished analogously to those in (35).

Richard (1990) entertains a suggestion similar to this one but rejects it on grounds that *Paderewski* is surely unambiguous in our public language, the language of the belief report, and that Ralph's dialect is arguably identical with our own.[10] Either of these assumptions may be challenged. Presumably, the grammar in which the report is couched can accommodate the general situation of a single entity bearing more than one name (*Frances Gumm/Judy Garland; Hesperus/Phosphorus/Venus*). Furthermore, given our discussion of (35), it presumably also has the resources to discriminate syntactically between homophones, say, through 'diacritics' like those distinguishing *bank*$_I$ and *bank*$_{II}$. Taken together it then follows that the grammar of the report will have resources that allow a single entity to bear several names, all homophonous, but formally distinct. Accordingly, even if the name *Paderewski* is univocal for both the belief reporter and the interlocutor, we will nonetheless have the linguistic wherewithal to assign T-sentences to (36a, b) that do not amount to an assertion and its negation.

3.2   Attitudes distinguished by content

A simple case of attitude reports that are logically nonequivalent by virtue of containing distinct extralinguistic objects is the pair in (37a, b). Although the second sentence in each is identical in form, it is nonetheless possible for one to be true and the other false. Once again, the ILF theory correctly yields this result. The embedded complement in the second sentence of (37a) will receive the ILF in (38a), whereas the embedded complement in (37b) receives the ILF in (38b):[11]

(37) a. Hans is brawny. Arnold believes he works out. (*he* refers to Hans)

     b. Franz is brawny. Arnold believes he works out. (*he* refers to Franz)

(38) a. Val(t, *Arnold believes he works out, σ*) iff Arnold believes

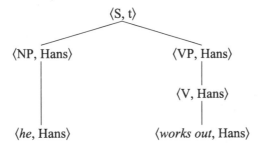

b. Val(t, *Arnold believes he works out σ*) iff Arnold believes

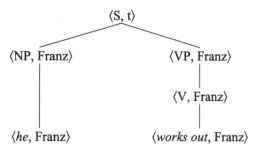

These are distinct T-sentences; neither logically entails the other.[12]

We believe that certain interesting examples involving demonstratives may also represent cases of attitude reports distinguished by content. Consider the following two situations in which it is dusk and I am standing with a friend and facing west.[13] In the first situation, I point to the planet Venus, uttering the sentence in (39) at a normal rate, and gesturing twice. In the second, I point to Venus and utter the portion of (39) up to the first occurrence of *that planet*, but then proceed to speak very slowly so that, in the interval, the night passes and Venus once again becomes visible in the morning sky. I finish the sentence, gesturing now at the newly arisen planet.

(39) Max believes that that planet is that planet.

It seems intuitively clear that, in the two situations just described, the truth-conditions of (39) should be distinguished analogously to the familiar pair in (40a, b) involving proper names for Venus. In the first, we ascribe to Max little more than a grasp of self-identity, whereas in the second, we ascribe to him belief about a significant empirical truth:

(40) a. Max believes that Hesperus is Hesperus.
b. Max believes that Hesperus is Phosphorus.

What is wanted is a way of distinguishing the complement of (39) qua a statement of self-identity and the complement of (39) qua a statement of significant empirical truth.

It is clear that to draw such a distinction, the ILF for the demonstrative *that planet* must be richer than what is given in (41a). Specifically, the ILF must involve some additional representational content α (41b), for example, a representation of sensory information: the-appearance-of-Venus-at-dusk or the-appearance-of-Venus-at-dawn, etc. Alternatively, the ILF for *that planet* must involve additional objectual content β (41c) (where 'v' denotes the planet Venus):[14]

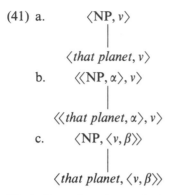

(41) a. $\langle NP, v \rangle$

         $\langle that\ planet, v \rangle$

   b. $\langle\langle NP, \alpha \rangle, v \rangle$

         $\langle\langle that\ planet, \alpha \rangle, v \rangle$

   c. $\langle NP, \langle v, \beta \rangle\rangle$

         $\langle that\ planet, \langle v, \beta \rangle\rangle$

We believe that the analysis of demonstratives proposed in Burge (1974) offers a promising approach along the line of (41c). In brief, Burge argues that the axioms for demonstrative constructions must accommodate the act or event of demonstration. For example, the T-sentence Burge assigns to *That dog is an animal* is as paraphrased in (42):[15]

(42) For any e, p, x, t, if e is an act of reference by p to x at time t with *that* in *That dog is an animal*, then *That dog is an animal* is true wrt p and t iff the object that is x and that is a dog is an animal.

Abstracting from details, what is crucial to note in (42) is the presence of the event variable e, which ranges over acts of demonstration or reference by the speaker. Under Burge's account, the semantic value of a demonstrative NP like *that dog* involves not only an object x but also an event e; that is, such expressions are relational, taking pairs $\langle x, e \rangle$ as their semantic values.[16] Given this reanalysis of the semantic value for demonstratives, distinct T-sentences for (39) can now be assigned in the two situations described above. These will involve sub-ILFs for the demonstratives that do not differ in their linguistic form (*that planet*), or in the object demonstrated (Venus); but do differ in the second member of the pair $\langle x, e \rangle$. Each demonstrative will involve a different event, corresponding to a different act of demonstration:[17]

(43) a. $\langle NP, \langle v, e \rangle\rangle$ b. $\langle NP, \langle v, e' \rangle\rangle$

         $\langle that\ planet, \langle v, e \rangle\rangle$ $\langle that\ planet, \langle v, e' \rangle\rangle$

If this proposal is on the right track, then examples like (39) represent another case of attitudes distinguished by content.

3.3 Logically equivalent attitude reports

Although (14)–(16) impose rather strict conditions on the logical equivalence of attitude reports, equivalence nonetheless is still possible in certain cases within the ILF theory. In particular, two distinct attitude reports α and β will be logically equivalent when the following two conditions are met: (i) the values assigned to the subparts of the complement clauses of α and β are identical (that is, α and β differ at most in the forms of (some of) their subconstituent parts); and (ii) α and β are evaluated under structures in which their formally distinct (but coreferring) subparts are given scope out of the complement clauses, beyond the highest attitude verb. We illustrate once again with (2a, b). In the discussion above we considered LF representations of sentences in which their proper name subjects were confined to the subordinate clause. Suppose, however, that these sentences are assigned LFs in which the subordinate subject is optionally given broad scope:

(44) a. [NP Judy Garland]$_1$[Max believes [t_1 sang "Somewhere Over the Rainbow"]].
    b. [NP Frances Gumm]$_1$[Max believes [t_1 sang "Somewhere Over the Rainbow"]].

The clausal complements are now formally identical, both having the form: t_1 *sang "Somewhere Over the Rainbow"*. Furthermore, the semantic value assigned to the trace t_1 will be the same in both cases: t_1 will denote the individual Judy Garland/Frances Gumm. Accordingly, the T-sentences for (2a) and (2b) will be identical, requiring Max to stand in the believe-relation to one and the same object (45):[18]

(45)

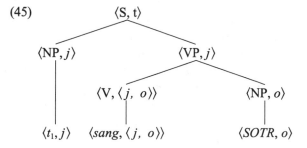

Hence under these structures, in which formally distinct but coreferring phrases are scoped out of the complement clause, the truth-conditions of (44a, b) are the same.

The scopal mechanism for producing truth-conditionally equivalent attitude reports will of course be constrained by whatever independent syntactic limitations exist on what can be 'moved' at LF and the distances such moved phrases may traverse. Under current syntactic theory, the possibilities for such movements are in fact quite limited. Thus although NPs like those in (2) are subject to movement over potentially large amounts of syntactic context, predicates like those in (3) are not.[19] This means that (3a, b) are not predicted to have truth-conditions that are logically equivalent in virtue of *xerox* and *photocopy* having been scoped out of the complement clause:

(46) a. $[_V \text{xerox}]_1 [\text{Max believes } [\text{Mary } t_1 \text{ } War \text{ } and \text{ } Peace]]$.
      b. $[_V \text{photocopy}]_1 [\text{Max believes } [\text{Mary } t_1 \text{ } War \text{ } and \text{ } Peace]]$.

Thus although a mechanism is available within the ILF theory that will yield equivalent T-sentences for distinct attitude reports, its purview is in fact quite restricted, given independent syntactic principles.

4 PURE SYNTACTIC BELIEF: GENERAL NPS AND EMPTY NAMES

On the theory proposed here, the ILF for an attitude report like (2a) (repeated below) contains specific individuals—in this case, the person Judy Garland, and the song "Somewhere Over the Rainbow":

(2a) Max believes Judy Garland sang "Somewhere Over the Rainbow".

Our account thus implicitly accepts that the truth-conditions of such singular attitude reports—reports whose content clause contains a referring term—are object-dependent, in the sense that without the individuals the report could not have the truth-conditions that it does.[20] Under the ILF theory, without the individuals there could be no ILFs containing them, and hence no corresponding ILFs for agents to believe, think, claim, etc.

The object-dependence of (2a) evidently distinguishes it from examples like (47a), where *Judy Garland* is replaced by the general NP *some starlet* (and the latter is understood as being within the scope of the attitude verb), and from examples like (47b), where *Judy Garland* is replaced by the empty proper name *Orpheus*:

(47) a. Max believes [some starlet performed].

  b. Max believes [Orpheus performed].

Intuitively, we know that Max may believe that some starlet performed without holding beliefs about any particular individual: no particular starlet need exist for (47a) to be true. Likewise, since Orpheus was a mythological character, we know that Max simply cannot have beliefs about a particular individual for (47b) to be true. It is thus natural to ask how the ILF theory treats object-independence in attitude reports such as those involving quantificational NPs and empty proper names.[21]

Our general answer to this question is given through clause (ii) of the ILF formation rule in (16). When expressions of a complement clause are nonreferring, or nonuniquely referring, then their ILFs will involve only linguistic material and no objectual content. The attitude verb will thus relate an agent to a purely syntactic object. The case of general NPs may be illustrated with the T-sentence for (47a), assuming narrow scope for the quantifier *some starlet*:

(48) Val(t, *Max believes some starlet performed*, σ) iff Max believes

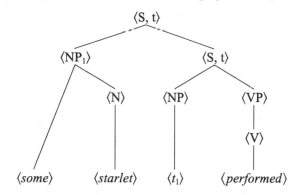

We assume a standard Tarskian account of quantification in which certain expressions are assigned no semantic values (i.e., are syncategorematic) and others are assigned values that vary in a systematic way.[22] Instances of the former include quantified NPs and determiners like *some*; these are interpreted only in construction with other elements, and so fall outside the domain of Val as given by our axioms. By the algorithm in (16) (clause (ii)), they receive ILFs containing only linguistic material and no objectual content (specifically, ⟨NP₁⟩, ⟨*some*⟩). Instances of the latter include the remaining expressions in (47). Under our axioms, the truth-conditions for the embedded complement in (47a) involve calculation over alternative sequences. The latter fix the values of various sentence constituents, including the formal variable t_1, the common noun (*starlet*), the verb phrase (*performed*), and the verb (*performed*). As the sequences vary, so do the values assigned to these expressions; hence the latter receive no unique semantic value under the assumption that Val(t, S, σ). This means that their ILFs are also provided under (16) clause (ii).

Empty proper names yield a result similar to general NPs as illustrated by the T-sentence for (47b):

(49) Val(t, *Max believes Orpheus performed*, σ) iff Max believes

(49)

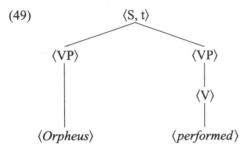

Like syncategorematic elements, empty names such as *Orpheus* or *Prof. Moriarty* fall outside the domain of Val as given by our axioms, and hence are associated with no objects. The semantic value of β, assuming Val(t, S, σ), is thus simply undefined for such expressions β. This entails that their ILFs (and the ILFs of expressions whose own values depend on them) are given through clause (ii) of (16).

These results yield truth-conditions for a general belief-report like (47a), and for a report involving an empty name like (47b); the truth of such examples is correctly represented as object-independent. Note, moreover, that they also entail commitment to the proposal made earlier that we be able to distinguish syntactically between otherwise homophonic names. Thus consider the case of a language containing two empty names, both pronounced *Cerberus*. The first purports to refer to a mythological three-headed dog guarding Hades. The second purports to refer to another nonexisting creature, say, a talking aardvark.[23] Intuitively, (50a) could be either true or false depending on which Cerberus was intended, hence two distinct ILFs must be made available. However, because the valuation predicate assigns neither name a semantic value, the ILFs cannot be distinguished by objectual content. The ILF theory may accommodate this result by assuming that the lexicon contains two formally distinct names, *Cerberus*$_I$ and *Cerberus*$_{II}$, and that the relevant ILFs are distinguished syntactically (50b, c):

(50) a. John believes [Cerberus talks].
    b. John believes [Cerberus$_I$ talks].
    c. John believes [Cerberus$_{II}$ talks].

This will yield two distinct ILFs, as in the case of *Paderewski* discussed above.

5 ITERATED ATTITUDE REPORTS

The algorithm for ILF construction given in (16) is fully recursive, successfully iterating with sentences that involve multiply embedded attitude reports. Furthermore, the resulting T-sentences appear to account correctly for familiar inferential properties of such examples.

To illustrate, a sentence like *Bill thinks Max believes Judy Garland sang "Somewhere Over the Rainbow"* receives the T-sentence shown in (51):

(51) Val(t, *Bill thinks Max believes Judy Garland sang "Somewhere Over the Rainbow"*, σ) iff Bill thinks

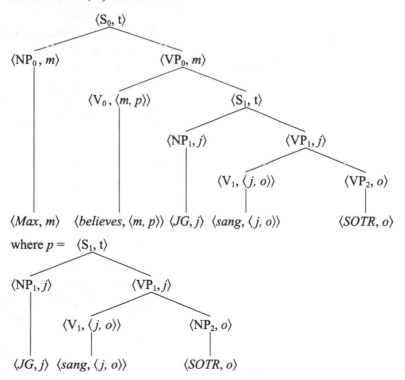

Observe that the ILF for the larger embedded clause *Max believes Judy Garland sang "Somewhere Over the Rainbow"* contains the ILF for the smaller embedded clause *Judy Garland sang "Somewhere Over the Rainbow"* twice over. The latter appears as part of the value for the second argument of *thinks*: it is a subpart of the ILF for the larger embedded clause. But the ILF for *Judy Garland sang "Somewhere Over the Rainbow"* also appears as the value for the second argument of *believes*: it is the value *p* for the embedded verb.

This is the (weak) sense in which our version of the ILF theory encodes a 'hierarchy of senses' in multiply embedded attitude contexts. It does so not by producing 'ILFs of ILFs', but rather by using a given ILF a number of times. The ILFs for multiply embedded clauses appear both as the value for the second argument of their immediately embedding propositional attitude verb, and then as part of the value of the second argument of each higher embedding propositional attitude verb.[24]

The T-sentences resulting from this theory correctly predict inference paradigms like (52a, b) that are sometimes thought to raise problems for accounts that don't yield a hierarchy of senses stronger than that available here. The observation is that singly embedded attitude contexts like (52a) permit substitution of a proper name for a clausal complement when the former refers to the sense (here the ILF) of the latter; however, the same substitution is not licit in doubly embedded contexts like (52b). This result appears to suggest a distinction between senses in singly vs. multiply embedded contexts; i.e., a distinction between senses, senses of senses, and so on.

(52) Suppose Val(x, *Henry*, σ) iff $x = $ ⟦*Judy Garland sang SOTR*⟧

a. Max believes Judy Garland sang SOTR
   ―――――――――――――――――――――――――――
   Max believes Henry

b. Bill thinks Max believes Judy Garland sang SOTR
   ―――――――――――――――――――――――――――――――――
   # # Bill thinks Max believes Henry

As it turns out, the ILF theory predicts these paradigms directly without appeal to a sense hierarchy. Assuming that *Judy Garland sang SOTR* and *Henry* are associated semantically with the very same ILF (the former by the lexical axiom in (52), the latter by the definition in (16)), it follows that *Max believes Judy Garland sang SOTR* is true only if *Max believes Henry* is true.[25] On the other hand, the inference in (52b) will be excluded in the by now familiar way: Bill simply believes different ILFs in thc two cascs. If thc first sentence is truc, he believes the ILF given earlier in (51); if the second sentence is true, he believes the ILF given in (53). The inference is thus correctly blocked:

(53) Val(t, *Bill thinks Max believes Henry*, σ) iff Bill thinks

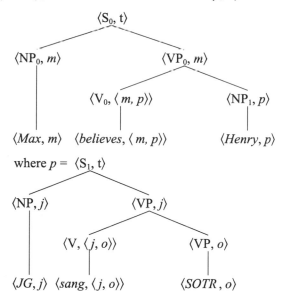

$\langle S_0, t \rangle$

$\langle NP_0, m \rangle$ $\langle VP_0, m \rangle$

$\langle V_0, \langle m, p \rangle \rangle$ $\langle NP_1, p \rangle$

$\langle Max, m \rangle$ $\langle believes, \langle m, p \rangle \rangle$ $\langle Henry, p \rangle$

where $p = \langle S_1, t \rangle$

$\langle NP, j \rangle$ $\langle VP, j \rangle$

$\langle V, \langle j, o \rangle \rangle$ $\langle VP, o \rangle$

$\langle JG, j \rangle$ $\langle sang, \langle j, o \rangle \rangle$ $\langle SOTR, o \rangle$

6   RELATION TO OTHER THEORIES

The ILF theory shares features with other analyses of propositional attitude constructions that have been advanced in the literature. Like quotational accounts, it takes the objects of the attitudes to contain linguistic forms. Hence it shares with them the prediction that the truth-conditions of propositional attitude reports may be at least as finely individuated as the linguistic means that express them. This prediction appears correct given cases like (2a, b), where reference is constant, but its linguistic expression is not. On the other hand, unlike quotational theories, the ILF analysis also takes the objects of the attitudes to contain nonlinguistic items—things. Hence it makes the further prediction, unavailable under strictly quotational views, that the truth-conditions of propositional attitude reports may be at least as fine-grained as the things referred to in those reports. This further prediction is confirmed by cases like (37a, b), where linguistic expression is constant, but reference is not.[26]

The ILF theory also shares features with the account of propositional attitude contexts advanced in Frege (1892). As is well known, failures of substitutivity like those in (2)–(4) led Frege to introduce the notion of senses, which he took to have the following central properties:

(i) Senses are expressed by phrases.

(ii) Senses are compositionally derived (that is, the sense expressed by a phrase is a function of the sense expressed by its parts).

(iii) Senses determine the referent of their associated phrase.

(iv) Senses constitute a mode of presentation of their associated referent.

Frege proposed that in embedded contexts, expressions take on different semantic values and refer to their (customary) senses, rather than their usual referents. The logical nonequivalence of pairs like (2)–(4) is then explained by saying that substitution yields different semantic values for the substituted parts. In (2a), *Judy Garland* contributes its sense, which is a mode of presentation of the individual Judy Garland. By contrast, in (2b), *Frances Gumm* contributes its sense, which is presumably a distinct mode of presentation of the same individual Judy Garland. ILFs resemble Fregean senses in some respects, and explain failures of equivalence with attitude reports in a roughly analogous way. ILFs can be seen as being expressed by their associated phrases in the sense of being built out of them (together with their values); and under the formal theory presented above ILFs are also fully compositional, being defined in terms of the ILFs of their subconstituents. Furthermore, ILFs can be seen as giving a mode of presentation of a referent insofar as they pair that referent with a particular expression that linguistically 'presents it'. This latter feature entails that the different names *Frances Gumm* and *Judy Garland* will make different semantic contributions to the complement clauses in (2a, b), and hence yield nonequivalent attitude reports.[27]

Finally, the ILF theory is also related to the account of propositional attitude contexts proposed by Russell (1956), and its more modern versions elaborated in Barwise and Perry (1983), Salmon (1986a), Soames (1987), and Richard (1990).[28] Russell took verbs like *believe, think, say*, etc., to express relations between agents and propositions, where the latter are abstract objects containing predicable and nonpredicable individuals. On this view, the sentential complements in (3a) and (3b) (repeated below) would be associated with the propositions in (54a) and (54b), respectively, where $\mathscr{R}_{xerox}$ is the relation (i.e., the particular universal) of xeroxing and $\mathscr{R}_{photocopy}$ is the relation of photocopying:

(3)   a. Max believes Mary xeroxed *War and Peace*.
      b. Max believes Mary photocopied *War and Peace*.

(54) a. ⟨Mary, $\mathscr{R}_{\text{xerox}}$, *War and Peace*⟩.
      b. ⟨Mary, $\mathscr{R}_{\text{photocopy}}$, *War and Peace*⟩.

Since $\mathscr{R}_{\text{xerox}}$ and $\mathscr{R}_{\text{photocopy}}$ are different relations, the respective propositions containing them are different as well. This permits failures of substitutivity like those in (3) and (4) to be explained by saying that the two attitude reports express relations to different propositions. Standing in the believe-relation to one thus does not entail standing in the believe-relation to the other. ILFs resemble Russellian propositions in containing extralinguistic objects as constitutents. And like propositions, ILFs are distinguished in virtue of containing distinct objects. This yields an account of (certain) substitution failures in attitude reports similar to that in the Russellian theory.

The most important difference between Russellian propositions and ILFs is that the former contain nonpredicable individuals and particular universals, whereas the latter contain nonpredicable individuals and linguistic forms.[29] Two points appear noteworthy in this regard. First, the ILF theory does not appear to suffer in virtue of its more restrictive ontology. The responsibilities borne by properties and relations in the richer ontology of Russellian propositions seem to be discharged equally well by appeal to more homey entities such as words. The ILF theory successfully separates the truth-conditions of (3a, b) by reference to the different predicates *xerox* and *photocopy* that appear in each. No further entities such as $\mathscr{R}_{\text{xerox}}$ and $\mathscr{R}_{\text{photocopy}}$ need be invoked.[30]

Second, the more restrictive ontology of the ILF theory is not an arbitrary feature of the account but rather reflects the important conceptual dependence of its treatment of intensional contexts on its treatment of extensional contexts. The recursive algorithm in (16) has the effect of ensuring that the nonlinguistic objects appearing in ILFs, and hence the ontology of nonlinguistic objects appealed to in the analysis of (hyper)intensional contexts, can be no richer than that required for the portion of the grammar that excludes them. Under these proposals, then, the analysis of propositional attitudes cannot introduce anything new into the ontology; it must be semantically 'innocent' in the sense of Davidson (1984b). To justify introducing primitive properties and relations into ILFs would require first justifying their introduction in the account of the simple parts of language falling outside the attitudes. At present, the grounds for such a move do not appear secure to us.

7   EQUIVALENCE AND CONTENT

As a result of its fine-grained individuation criteria for ILFs, the ILF theory entails the logical nonequivalence of many attitude reports. Attitude reports from a given language whose logical forms contain different expressions in the complement clause (55a, b) will always differ in truth-conditions, since these will involve distinct ILFs (cf. (56a) and (56b)):[31]

(55) a. Galileo believed the Earth moves.
b. Galileo believed the Earth is nonstationary.

(56) a. Val(t, *Galileo believed the Earth moves*, σ) iff Galileo believed

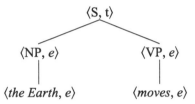

b. Val(t, *Galileo believed the Earth is nonstationary*, σ) iff Galileo believed

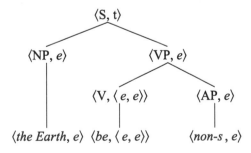

Similarly, attitude reports from different languages (57a, b) will always be logically nonequivalent, since, once again, their truth-conditions will involve relations to distinct ILFs (cf. (56a) and (58)):

(57) a. Galileo believed the Earth moves.
b. Galileo glaubte daß die Erde sich bewegte.

(58) Val(t, *Galileo glaubte daß die Erde sich bewegte*, σ) iff Galileo believed

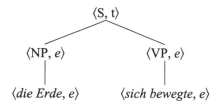

$$\langle S, t \rangle$$

$$\langle NP, e \rangle \qquad \langle VP, e \rangle$$

$$\langle die\ Erde, e \rangle \qquad \langle sich\ bewegte, e \rangle$$

These results raise an important general question for the ILF theory. It is arguable that one of the main charges of any semantic theory is to give (or at least contribute to) an account of the content of a given utterance: semantic theories should characterize what is said in uttering a given sentence S, and what is grasped in understanding it. In a truth-conditional theory, such as the ILF theory, content is ostensibly captured through the truth-conditions that are assigned; hence the fact that pairs like (55) and (57) receive different truth-conditions entails that they are ascribed different content by this account. Nonetheless, in many communicative contexts, and for many communicative purposes, speakers of English would very clearly regard these pairs as reporting the same beliefs—more generally, as 'saying the same thing'. For example, if one wished to report what someone had said in uttering (55a), then (55b) would be a natural choice for most purposes. Similarly, if one wished to report in English what a speaker of German said in uttering (57b), then in most cases it would be very natural to employ (57a). Evidently, logical equivalence of attitude reports, as defined by the ILF theory, does not mirror the notion of 'same-saying' or 'same communicative content' that figures in everyday attitude ascriptions. The simple question arises, then, as to how we may square the two.

Broadly speaking, we see two ways of doing this: on the one hand, we may adjust the truth-conditions delivered by the ILF theory so as to bring its relation of logical equivalence into closer agreement with the informal relation of same-saying or same-content. Alternatively, we may leave the truth-conditions of the ILF theory intact and propose an auxiliary theory specifying when two sentences, despite different truth-conditions and hence different content, might nonetheless be used to report the same propositional attitudes.

7.1 Similarity/same-saying

One way to adjust the ILF theory so as to reflect sameness of content is to import this notion directly into the truth-conditions that it assigns. Broadly speaking, this is the approach advocated by Davidson (1984b),

Lepore and Loewer (1989), and Higginbotham (1986), who propose introducing a relation of *same-saying* or *similarity* that would serve to relate either events of saying/believing/thinking, etc., or ILFs.[32] Thus suppose our lexical axioms in (15) are replaced with the ones in (15'):[33]

(15') a. Val($\langle x, y \rangle$, [v *believes*], σ) iff x believes some ILF similar to y.
   b. Val($\langle x, y \rangle$, [v *thinks*], σ) iff x thinks some ILF similar to y.
   c. Val($\langle x, y \rangle$, [v *claims*], σ) iff x claims some ILF similar to y.

This revision 'loosens' the truth-conditions for attitude reports insofar as an agent is no longer required to stand in relation to an ILF defined through the complement clause, but only to one similar to it. This in turn allows reports containing formally distinct complement clauses to nonetheless come out logically equivalent. For example, under the revised VP axiom, sentences (55a, b) receive the T-sentences in (59a, b) (respectively):

(59) a. Val(t, *Galileo believed the Earth moves*, σ) iff Galileo believed some ILF similar to

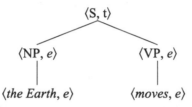

   b. Val(t, *Galileo believed the Earth is nonstationary*, σ) iff Galileo believed some ILF similar to

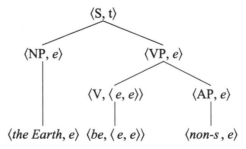

Supposing that the ILFs given here are indeed similar (with respect to some set of features F), the two sentences will come out equivalent despite the formal differences in their complement clauses. An analogous result holds for (57a, b). Assuming similarity (wrt some features F) between the relevant ILFs containing English and German words, the English and the

German sentences will be truth-conditionally equivalent under the ILF theory.[34]

Introduction of the similarity relation relaxes the conditions on equivalence of attitude reports; where we previously required strict identity of ILFs we now require only similarity. Nonetheless it is important to observe that appeal to similarity does not lose the fine-grained distinctions among attitude reports available through ILFs: these distinctions still delimit the *potential* individuation of attitude reports. Recall that the predicate *similar* is a three-place relation of the general form $R(x, y, F)$: one object x is similar to another y with respect to some features F. It follows that in the similarity theory, equivalence of attitude reports will turn crucially on the features F by which ILFs are compared. For example, if the feature is objectual content, then the ILFs for (2a, b) will be grouped as similar, but those for (37a, b) will not. By contrast, if the feature is linguistic content, then the ILFs for (37a, b) will be grouped as similar, but those (2a, b) will not.[35] Finally, if the features are objectual and linguistic content taken together, then neither of the pairs in (2) and (37) will count as having similar ILFs, and the attitude reports will all be truth-conditionally distinct. The upshot is that while the similarity relation allows us to assimilate the content of ILFs in certain circumstances, the underlying distinctions among ILFs remain, and their full individuating power can be exploited through choice of the features F.[36]

An ILF theory, relativized by means of the similarity (or same-saying) relation, is attractive in certain respects. It retains the virtues of the original ILF theory, while also permitting an approach to the issue of content. Furthermore, through the context-dependence of *similar* it captures the fact that equivalence of attitude reports often varies pragmatically according to the goals and assumptions of the agent, attitude reporter, and/or attitude reportee. Nonetheless, as discussed by Segal (1989), the theory also has an important drawback. Segal observes that in a T-sentence like (59a) or (59b), the *believe* occurring in the metalanguage on the right-hand side of the biconditional cannot be the English word *believe*. To see why this is so, the following example may be helpful.

Imagine a language English* that is like English except that the English* word *kick* in an English* sentence like *Max kicked Smith* has a meaning that we would express in English as 'x kicked something that resembles y'. So, for example, if Smith resembles Jones, and someone kicks Jones but not Smith, one may truly assert the English* sentence *Someone kicked Smith*. Now suppose that a semanticist who is a monolingual speaker of English* offers the following axiom for the English* word *kicks*:

(60) Val($\langle x, y \rangle$, *kicks*, σ) iff x kicks something that resembles y.

In fact, this will not be a legitimate axiom for the English* semanticist. The problem is that it relies on a word that is not part of English*, namely, the English word *kicks* on the right-hand side of the biconditional.[37] Such an axiom therefore does not give the semantic value of the object language expression in the language that the semanticist understands.

What should the English* semanticist do? Segal observes that one of two options is open. Either the semanticist must provide some explication of the new, nonEnglish* word *kick* appearing on the right-hand side of the biconditional in (60) or, alternatively, he or she should simply replace (60) with an axiom like the following:

(61) Val($\langle x, y \rangle$, *kicks*, σ) iff x kicks y.

Here the English* semanticist would be relying on the meaning of the English* word *kicks* to give the semantic value of the object language expression.

Segal argues that English propositional attitude verbs like *believe, think, claim*, etc., are analogous to the hypothetical English* word *kick* in that whenever we stand in an attitude relation to a given ILF we stand in the same relation to ILFs similar to it. It follows, then, that when analyzing these predicates we are in essentially the same position as the English* semanticist, and when we appeal to axioms like (15'a–c), we encounter the same problem encountered with the English* axiom (60). (15'a–c) do not use the English expressions *believe, think*, and *claim* on the right-hand side of the axiom, but rather expressions of a language that we do not understand. The same two options are then open to us. We must provide some explication of the new, non-English words appearing in our axioms. Alternatively, we must simply replace (15'a–c) with our original (15a–c), relying on the English expressions *believe, think, claim*, etc., to give the semantic values of the corresponding object language expressions.

Appeal to (61) is clearly the simplest course of action for our English* semanticist with regard to English* *kick*. Nonetheless, it is perhaps plausible that he or she might come up with the technical notion 'kick$^+$' required for the right-hand side of (60). This notion 'kicks$^+$' would in fact just be the familiar notion of 'kick' in English, hence (59) would be reconstructed as (61):

(62) $\text{Val}(\langle x, y \rangle, kicks, \sigma)$ iff x kicks$^+$ something that resembles y where x kicks$^+$ y iff ...

However, in the case of *believe* and the English semanticist, Segal argues that the prospects for the latter move are dim. Evidently, we would have to replace (15′a), for example, with an axiom like (63), where the new, technical notion 'believes$^+$' is given some explicit definition in English:

(63) $\text{Val}(\langle x, y \rangle, believes, \sigma)$ iff x believes$^+$ some ILF similar to y where x believes$^+$ y iff ...

Segal points out that the content of this definition is anything but clear. Segal concludes that, like the English* semanticist, we are better off adopting the simplest course. We should dispense with the foreign verb *believes$^+$* and the similarity predicate, relying on the use of the English verb *believes* in the metalanguage to give the semantic value of the corresponding object language expression. In short, we are best off relying on the original axioms (15a–c).

7.2 ILFs and belief ascription

If, as Segal (1989) argues, the ILF theory should retain the simple truth-conditions given by axioms (15a–c), then our view must be that although speakers use sentence pairs like (55) and (57) to report the same propositional attitudes in certain cases, these sentences nonetheless always express different content. Accordingly, the ILF theorist is committed to the view that similarity or same-saying in such cases is fundamentally a matter of *usage* and not content, and that the correct account of these phenomena falls outside the domain of semantics proper and into pragmatics.

Although we believe that the responsibility for explaining when two propositional attitude sentences can be used to report the same attitude is a pragmatic matter, we believe that the general shape of such a pragmatic account is fairly clear. Our picture of this account rests on the view that the ability to use language to ascribe beliefs is a complex ability relying on a rich system of tacit knowledge. The precise nature of this system of tacit knowledge is a matter of empirical enquiry, and much work needs to be done to illuminate it. Nonetheless, we believe that a full account of this system will involve at least the following three components:

I.   The theory of belief tacitly held by speakers.
II. The theory of the goals of belief ascription tacitly held by speakers.
III. The theory of belief ascription 'logistics' tacitly held by speakers.

To illustrate, consider speaker S, who wishes to ascribe a propositional attitude to agent A for the benefit of hearer H. In order for S to succeed, S and H must share a theory of what beliefs are, for it is the shared ontology of beliefs that will guide the way in which beliefs are ascribed. S must also have tacit knowledge of the goals of belief ascription. That is, S must have a theory that allows him or her to determine what features of A's belief will assist H in the relevant way. Finally, S must have a tacit theory that allows him or her to deliver the kind of ascription that will be helpful to H.

Component I will state the properties that speakers tacitly ascribe to beliefs, including their relations to other components of thought and to action. For example, in ascribing beliefs, speakers and hearers would standardly assume that beliefs are formed on the basis of knowledge and experience, that they interact together, that they are relatively stable over time, that they can be shared or mistaken, and that they can and often do correspond to the world. Philosophers have often discussed this theory under the heading of 'folk psychology', which they take to be the theory of psychology used by individuals to explain the actions of other agents. Philosophical explications of folk psychology have been helpful, but full elaboration of the common-sense theory of belief will doubtless require systematic study on the model of work investigating common-sense physics (see Hobbs and Moore 1985) and common-sense biology (Carey 1988). Fortunately, much work is currently being done in this area, particularly in regards to the child's theory of mind (see Astington, Harris, and Olson (1988) and Frye and Moore (1991) for surveys).

Component II will state the theory a speaker deploys in determining a hearer's interest. With propositional attitude ascriptions, the goal of a speaker S is typically to cause a hearer H to form a certain theory about the belief structure of an agent A. Unless S has duplicitous motives, S will be attempting to assist H in forming a theory of A's psychology. What H finds helpful will of course depend on H's interests. Sometimes H will want a theory that allows him or her to predict the behavior of A. Other times H will want a theory of what A knows, so that H may modify his or her behavior accordingly. For example, H may need to know whether to inform A of something, ask A something, or otherwise act in the knowledge that A has the proper information. A theory of this ability is a species of a more general family of cognitive abilities studied under the guise of 'planning' and the theory of action (see, for example, Georgeff and Lansky (1986)).

Finally, component III will state which expressions may be used in a given context to achieve specific belief ascription goals. This theory interacts with ILFs directly on our view, and will incorporate the knowledge required for determining which ILF should be used in reporting a given attitude. For example, depending on H's interests, it is sometimes the referential component of an ILF and sometimes the syntactic component that will be important to the goals of ascription. We can identify several rules of thumb in characterizing which component of an ILF will be relevant in a given belief report. For example, if H is interested in information that A has about the world (for example, the distance to the Venus), then the objectual component of the ILF will be of primary importance to the goals of belief ascription. H will therefore be indifferent to the choice of *The Morning Star* vs. *The Evening Star* in an attitude ascription concerning Venus. By contrast, if H is interested in explaining or predicting A's behavior, for example, whether A will assent to an utterance of *The Morning Star is The Evening Star*, or whether A will act in a way compatible with the knowledge that the Morning Star is the Evening Star, then H may well be interested in the syntactic expressions that S uses to characterize A's belief.

In cases of the latter kind, where prediction or explanation of behavior is the goal, we envision the speaker's choice of syntactic constituents in an ILF to involve a two-stage process vis-à-vis the hearer H. First, S determines the way in which H models A's belief structure. Then S 'negotiates' with H the expressions to be used in speaking of the components of that model. Both steps involve complex subprocesses. For example, in inferring H's model of A's belief structure, S would appear to draw at least on all of the following:

- S's knowledge of H's interests;
- General principles of common-sense psychology that S supposes that H believes;
- Knowledge that S knows H to have about A.

Suppose that S knows H to be interested in the behavior of A—for example, in whether A will train his or her telescope on a particular region of the dawn sky. Then by general principles of common-sense psychology, which S supposes H to share, S may infer that H will deploy a fine-grained model of A's psychology—one that distinguishes Morning Star-beliefs from Evening Star-beliefs. S may also rely on information supplied directly by H or some other source. For example, S may learn that H knows that A is unaware that the Morning Star is the Evening Star.

In the second stage of selecting an ILF, S and H must agree on expressions used to speak of the components of H's model of A's belief structure. We speculate that expressions used in attitude ascriptions will be tacitly 'negotiated' by participants in the discourse, following quite general principles holding of discourses of all kinds. The general process by which discourse participants negotiate a way to speak of objects (sometimes called 'entrainment' by psychologists) is currently the subject of research in psycholinguistics (e.g., by Brennan and Clarke 1992). Ultimately, we believe this work must be extended to the study of the way states of mind come to be described, and why subtle differences in expression will have great consequences for the truth of the attitude ascription.

If our perspective differs from most other theories of attitude ascription it is in our emphasis on the relation between the ascription and the hearer, rather than on the relation between the ascription and the agent to whom the attitude is ascribed. In our view, it is studying the former relationship that will yield the biggest dividends in the understanding of belief ascription.

APPENDIX: FRAGMENTS FOR THE LANGUAGES L_0 AND L_1

1 The language L_0 (names, predicates, connectives, and quantifiers)

Terminal Nodes:

(1) a. Val(x, *Judy Garland*, σ) iff $x =$ Judy Garland.
     Val(x, *Frances Gumm*, σ) iff $x =$ Frances Gumm.
     Val(x, *Somewhere Over the Rainbow*, σ) iff $x =$ "Somewhere Over the Rainbow".
     Val(x, *Max*, σ) iff $x =$ Max.
     Val(x, t_i, σ) iff $x = \sigma(i)$ for $i \geqslant 1$.
   b. Val(x, *starlet*, σ) iff x is a starlet.
     Val(x, *girl*, σ) iff x is a girl.
   c. Val(x, *agrees*, σ) iff x agrees.
     Val(x, *walks*, σ) iff x walks.
   d. Val($\langle x, y \rangle$, *sang*, σ) iff x sang y.
     Val($\langle x, y \rangle$, *admires*, σ) iff x admires y.

Nonterminal Nodes:

(2) a. Val (t, [$_S$ NP VP], σ) iff for some x, Val(x, NP, σ) and
Val(x, VP, σ).

b. Val(x,[$_{VP}$ V NP], σ) iff for some y, Val($\langle x, y \rangle$, V, σ) and
Val(y, NP, σ).

c. Val(x,[$_\alpha$ β], σ) iff Val(x, β, σ) (where α ranges over categories, and
β ranges over categories and lexical items).

(3) a. Val(t, [$_S$ S_1 *and* S_2], σ) iff it is both the case that Val(t, S_1, σ) and
Val(t, S_2, σ).

b. Val(t, [$_S$ S_1 *or* S_2], σ) iff either Val(t, S_1, σ) or Val(t, S_2, σ).

c. Val(t, [$_S$ *it is not the case that* S_1], σ) iff it is not true that
Val(t, S_1, σ).

(4) a. Val(t, [$_S$ [$_{NPi}$ *every* N] S_1], σ) iff for every $\sigma' \approx_i \sigma$ such that
Val($\sigma'(i)$, N, σ), Val(t, S_1, σ').

b. Val(t, [$_S$ [$_{NPi}$ *some* N] S_1], σ) iff for some $\sigma' \approx_i \sigma$ such that
Val($\sigma'(i)$, N, σ), Val(t, S_1, σ').

c. Val(t, [$_S$ NP_i S_1], σ) iff for $\sigma' \approx_i \sigma$ such that Val($\sigma'(i)$, NP, σ),
Val(t, S_1, σ').

Definitions:

(i) For any sequence σ, $\sigma(i)$ is the ith element of σ.

(ii) For any sequences σ, σ', $\sigma' \approx_i \sigma$ iff σ' differs from σ at most on $\sigma'(i)$.

(iii) Val(t, S) iff Val(t, S, σ) for all sequences σ.

2   The language L_1 (L_0 + intensional contexts)

Terminal Nodes (Lexical Items):

(1) Val ($\langle x, y \rangle$, *believes*, σ) iff x believes y.
Val ($\langle x, y \rangle$, *thinks*, σ) iff x thinks y.
Val ($\langle x, y \rangle$, *claims*, σ) iff x claims y.

Nonterminal Nodes:

(2) Val(x, [$_{VP}$ V S], σ) iff for some y, Val($\langle x, y \rangle$, V, σ) and $y = \llbracket S \rrbracket$ wrt σ.

Definition   Let α be a phrase-marker with root S, let σ be a sequence,
and let β be a sub-phrase-marker of α.

(i) If there is an x such that Val(x, β, σ) is provable from Val(t, α, σ)
under the axioms of L_0, and for all y, Val(y, β, σ) is provable from
Val(t, α, σ) iff $y = x$, and:

(a) β is a terminal node, then $\llbracket\beta\rrbracket = \langle\beta, x\rangle$.

(b) β is $[_\gamma\delta_1\delta_2\ldots\delta_n]$ for $n \geqslant 1$, then $\llbracket\beta\rrbracket = [_{\langle\gamma,x\rangle}\llbracket\delta_1\rrbracket\;\llbracket\delta_2\rrbracket\ldots\llbracket\delta_n\rrbracket]$.

(ii) If there is no x as defined in clause (i), and:

(a) β is a terminal node, then $\llbracket\beta\rrbracket = \langle\beta\rangle$.

(b) β is $[_\gamma\delta_1\delta_2\ldots\delta_n]$ for $n \geqslant 1$, then $\llbracket\beta\rrbracket = [_{\langle\gamma\rangle}\llbracket\delta_1\rrbracket\;\llbracket\delta_2\rrbracket\ldots\llbracket\delta_n\rrbracket]$.

We call $\llbracket\alpha\rrbracket$ wrt σ *the ILF of α with respect to σ*.

Notes

Earlier versions of this work were presented at the 2nd annual Irvine Workshop in Theoretical Linguistics, the University of Massachusetts (Amherst), Cornell University, and the University of California (Berkeley). For comments and helpful discussion, we are grateful to Mark Aronoff, Max Cresswell, Mark Crimmins, Donald Davidson, Irene Heim, James Higginbotham, Jaakko Hintikka, Norbert Hornstein, Ernest Lepore, Robert May, Stephen Neale, Paul Pietroski, Barry Schein, and Gabriel Segal.

1. Accounts of propositional attitudes similar to the ILF theory have been developed by Burdick (1982) and Richard (1990). Each stresses the importance of including lexical material in the objects of propositional attitudes.

2. For an extended defense of this observation see Burge (1978).

3. The T-sentences in (7) and (8) pair a sentence of the object language containing a verb and a sentential complement with a sentence of the metalanguage containing a verb and a noun phrase complement (here, a description of an ILF). The theory is thus nonhomophonic, but note that this involves no violation of the grammar of the metalanguage. As is well known, propositional attitude verbs routinely accept nominal complements in uses like those in (i):

(i) Max believed/said/wanted $\begin{cases} \text{that} \\ \text{the very same thing} \end{cases}$

4. This discussion simplifies considerably for the purposes of exposition. In modern versions of the EST theory, sentences are in fact associated with a quadruple of syntactic representations including a D-structure, an S-structure, a Phonetic Form, and a Logical Form. D-structure is a pure representation of grammatical and thematic relations, and Phonetic Form is the input to phonological interpretation. We ignore these additional representations here, since they are irrelevant to semantic interpretation. For fuller discussion see Chomsky (1986), and the helpful summary in Sells (1985).

5. The axioms collected in our fragments all satisfy a general compositionality principle that can be stated as follows:

Compositionality If α is an expression, $\beta_1, \beta_2, \ldots, \beta_n$ are immediate constituents of α, and for some $x, y_1, y_2, \ldots, y_n$, Val(x, α), Val(y_1, β_1), Val(y_2, β_2), ..., Val(y_n, β_n), then for some function f, $x = f(y_1, y_2, \ldots, y_n)$.

A number of objections to compositionality have been advanced in Hintikka (1983) and Hintikka and Sandu (1989). See Larson and Segal (1995) for a discussion of these objections and a general defense of compositionality.

6. We are grateful to Stuart Shieber for pointing out an important problem with an earlier version of this definition and to Irene Heim for helpful comments.

7. Lexical information also specifies syntactic category, and subcategorization and selectional features. The content of lexical items assumed in current syntactic theory is discussed in Radford (1988) and Haegeman (1991). For recent theoretical discussion see Baker (1988) and DiSciullo and Williams (1987).

8. Phrases containing *only* are standardly analyzed as quantifiers, hence the LFs for (31a, b) involve a trace in subject position. This analysis of the ambiguity in (30) in terms of binding by *John* or the full quantifier phrase *only John* is first proposed (to our knowledge) in Evans (1977), using a slightly different notational system. Evans employs (i.a, b) in place of our (31a, b) (respectively):

(i) a. [Only [John]] loves his mother.

     b. [Only [John]] loves his mother.

For interesting extensions of this analysis to a number of other constructions, see Higginbotham (1980, 1991).

9. This account follows the general line of Higginbotham (1991) in response to similar issues raised by Salmon (1986b) and Soames (1989–90). Soames observes that (i) may be understood as reporting two quite different thoughts on the part of Mary. On the one hand, she may believe John to be an 'own-mother-lover'; on the other hand, she may believe him to be a 'John's-mother-lover'. Higginbotham (1991) observes that this observation can be accommodated within an ILF type theory if the complements are distinguished syntactically as shown in (ii):

(i)   Mary thinks John loves his mother.

(ii) a. Mary thinks John loves his mother.

     b. Mary thinks John loves his mother.

Higginbotham here adopts the "chain" notation of Evans (1977, 1980) to indicate antecedence in place of numerical indices.

10. See Richard (1990, pp. 181–82) for discussion.

11. Norbert Hornstein and Robert May have drawn our attention to the following variants of the paradigm in (15):

(i) a. Judy Garland was cute. Max believes she sang "Somewhere Over the Rainbow". (*she* refers to JG/FG)
     b. Frances Gumm was cute. Max believes she sang "Somewhere Over the Rainbow". (*she* refers to JG/FG)

They observe that the second sentences in (ia) and (ib) may actually differ in truth-value despite the fact that the pronouns refer to the same individual, namely, to

Judy Garland/Frances Gumm. The question arises as to how the ILF theory can distinguish these cases given that both the form and the values in the associated ILFs appear to be the same.

We suggest that the pronoun in these cases is behaving as a "pronoun of laziness" (Geach 1962) going proxy for its antecedent expression *Judy Garland* and *Frances Gumm*, respectively. On our view, the LFs for these sentences will actually contain the names in place of the pronouns, and hence their ILFs will be those given earlier in (7) and (8). Similar issues arise with the paradigm in (37) when *Hans* and *Franz* are fictional names.

12. We should note that although ILFs containing distinct expressions of the object language will be distinct ILFs, ILFs that are described using distinct expressions of the metalanguage will *not* be distinct. That is, on our view (i.a, b) constitute the same ILF, where 'JG' and 'FG' are expressions of the metalanguage both referring to Judy Garland:

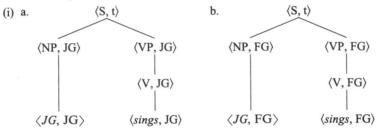

This position reflects the standard assumption that scientific laws and results are not sensitive to the way in which they are expressed in the metalanguage of investigation. Thus, in stating the results of astronomical inquiry, it is irrelevant whether we chose the metalanguage expression *Luna* or *the Moon* to refer to Earth's only satellite:

(ii) a. Luna is approximately 248,000 miles distant from the Earth.

  b. The Moon is approximately 248,000 miles distant from the Earth.

Similarly, in stating the results of semantic inquiry it is irrelevant whether we chose the metalanguage expression *Frances Gumm* or *Judy Garland* to refer to the individual Judy Garland.

13. We understand that this example is due originally to David Kaplan.

14. For simplicity, we ignore the internal syntactic structure of demonstratives here.

15. We are grateful to Barry Schein for bringing this work to our attention.

16. Other parameters in Burge's T-sentence such as *p* (the speaker) and *t* (the time of utterance) need not be regarded as parameters in the semantic value of the demonstrative itself, although see Enc (1983) and Larson (1983) for arguments that noun phrases are in fact generally relativized to times and spatial locations.

17. It is an interesting consequence of Burge's account that a sentence like (i.a) will differ in informativeness from a sentence like (i.b) even when it involves two demonstrations of the same object) (where N ranges over common nouns):

(i) a. That N is that N. (e.g., *That man is that man*)
    b. That N is self-identical. (e.g., *That man is self-identical*)

Whereas statements like *That man is self-identical* will be necessarily true and un-informative, statements like *That man is that man* will be necessarily true and informative. This is because distinct occurrences of a demonstrative will involve distinct demonstrations and hence distinct semantic values $\langle x, e \rangle$.

These remarks appear to leave open certain important questions about the logical equivalence of attitude reports containing demonstratives. Suppose that Max and John are both at Edwards Air Force Base observing the landing of the Space Shuttle. At the moment it appears in the sky, both individuals utter (ii.a) while making distinct gestures accompanying their distinct utterances of the demonstrative *that*. I report this situation with (ii.b):

(ii) a. That is the space shuttle.
     b. John said what Max said.

There is a clear intuition that I have spoken truly with (ii.b). Nonetheless, on the version of Burge's account urged here, John stands in the say-relation to a different ILF than Max—one distinguished by its different event of demonstration. We believe that a correct understanding of (ii.b) turns crucially on a correct account of similarity of actions and events generally; we take up this point in Section 7.

18. It is of course a familiar view of de re attitude reports that successful sub-stitution of coextensive expressions X and Y involves assigning the latter scope broader than their embedding attitude verbs (see, e.g., Buridan (1966, pp. 126–27), Harman (1972)). The representations in (44), and analogous ones for quanti-fied examples such as *John believes everyone in the neighborhood is a spy*, have been asserted to be ruled out on syntactic grounds by Hornstein (1987). Hornstein suggests that such representations would violate the so-called Empty Category Principle (ECP) of Chomsky (1986), and concludes that de dicto/de re ambiguities are not a matter of scope at LF. Hornstein's syntactic claim is highly dubious, however. Other movements that are similar to QR, but syntactically overt, show configurations of the kind Hornstein asserts to be excluded. For example, consider Topicalization, as illustrated in (i.a). According to Lasnik and Saito (1984), this operation involves syntactic movement of a referential phrase with adjunction to S (i.b). this is analogous to QR as described earlier, except that it involves overt movement at Surface Form instead of covert movement at Logical Form (iia, b):

(i)   a. Judy Garland, Max admires.   Surface Form
    b. $[_S [_{NP}$ Judy Garland$]_i [_S$ Max admires $t_i]]$.   Logical Form

(ii) a. Max admires every starlet.   Surface Form
    b. $[_S [_{NP}$ every starlet$]_i [_S$ Max admires $t_i]]$.   Logical Form

Notice now that covert movements of the kind postulated for QR in (44) are *overtly* available with Topicalization (iii.a, b):

(iii) a. Judy Garland, Max believes sang "Somewhere Over the Rainbow".
     b. "Somewhere Over the Rainbow", Max believes Judy Garland sang.

We conclude that such movements will be available with QR as well.

Topicalization and QR do show a difference with respect to the paradigm in (iv) that might be thought significant in this context. Observe that whereas overt Topicalization of an embedded subject is impossible when the complementizer *that* appears (iv.a), scopal movement of the subject at LF must be possible if (iv.b, c) are to have equivalent truth-conditions under one reading:

(iv) a. *Judy Garland, Max believes that sang "Somewhere Over the Rainbow".
   b. Max believes that Judy Garland sang "Somewhere Over the Rainbow".
   c. Max believes that Frances Gumm sang "Somewhere Over the Rainbow".

In fact this difference is a superficial one. Lasnik and Saito (1984) argue that (iv.a) is excluded by a syntactic constraint holding at Surface Form and that at LF semantically empty elements like *that* are deleted from syntactic representation. It follows that at the level of LF, (iv.b, c) are not analogous to (iv.a), where *that* appears, but rather to (iii.a), where *that* has been omitted. Hence movement of the names is possible with (iv.b, c) for the same reason it is possible with (iii.a). For further discussion of LF movement out of tensed complements, see Ludlow and Neale (1991).

19. In modern versions of the Extended Standard Theory (Chomsky 1989), representations like (46a, b) are excluded by the Empty Category Principle (ECP).

20. In the terms of Davies (1981), individuals are *truth-conditionally salient* under this theory. For further discussion, see McDowell (1980), Davies (1981), and Evans (1982).

21. We are indebted to Stuart Shieber for criticism and teachnical advice on this section.

22. We believe that a more adequate analysis of natural language quantification would ultimately involve binary or generalized quantifiers (Barwise and Cooper 1981; Higginbotham and May 1981; Sher 1991). Under a binary quantifier analysis, determiners like *every*, *no*, etc., are categorematic and express relations between sets; thus in *every starlet smiled*, *every* denotes the subset relation between the set of individuals given by the quantifier restriction (the set of starlets) and the set of individuals given by the predicate (the set of smilers). We adopt a classical quantification theory here mainly for expository convenience. For further discussion of binary quantifiers in the current framework, see Davies (1981) and Larson and Segal (1995).

23. There is in fact a current comic book whose main character, named *Cerebus*, is a (rather ill-tempered) talking aardvark. The spelling of the name apparently represents an error on the part of the comic's authors, who had intended the same name as the mythological canine guardian of Hades (see Sim 1981). But for this error, English would in fact have contained the two empty names described in the text.

24. The ILF analysis appears to embody a 'one-level' theory of sense, in the terminology of Parsons (1981). Burge (1979) has argued that multi-level sense theories are in fact necessary to account for the properties of intensional contexts, however, our account appears to fall outside the scope of Burge's argument in

adopting what he would view as a nonextensional analysis of the $[_{VP} \text{ V S}]$ configuration. Recall that under our axioms, the extension of the latter is not a function of the extensions of V and S; specifically, it is a not a function of the extension of S, but rather its ILF.

25. The inference in (25a) thus follows under the same reasoning that yields (i):

(i) Suppose Val$(x, \textit{Tully}, \sigma)$ iff $x = \text{Cicero}$, then

John saw Tully

John saw Cicero

26. This limitation on quotational theories is also discussed in Partee (1979). See also Cresswell (1980).

27. The most important difference between ILFs and Fregean senses is that the former contain extralinguistic objects, whereas the latter do not.

28. The ILF theory is also similar in this regard to the theory of Cresswell (1984), which derives from suggestions by Carnap (1956) and Lewis (1972). On Cresswell's account, the object of a propositional attitude verb is a "structured meaning": a graph that is partially to fully isomorphic to the syntactic structure of the complement clause, and with intensions (understood as functions from possible worlds to values) as its terminal and nonterminal nodes. As in most Russellian theories, but unlike ILF theories, Cresswell assumes that no lexical material appears in the 'structured meaning', but only semantic values.

Cresswell (1984) is one of a large number of analyses of propositional attitude constructions involving central appeal to possible worlds. For lack of space, we will not attempt to address these analyses here; for representative literature the reader is referred to Hintikka (1962, 1969), Lewis (1972), Cresswell (1973), Montague (1974), and Stalnaker (1987).

29. One neo-Russellian theory bears a number of similarities to the ILF theory—Richard's (1990) theory in which Russellian Annotated Matrices (RAMs) are introduced as the objects of the attitudes. RAMs, like ILFs, include lexical formatives and at least some linguistic structure. Nevertheless, there are significant differences between the proposals. First, the linguistic forms introduced into ILFs are much richer than those found in RAMs. ILFs, as noted earlier, include complete syntactic phrase-markers, including diacritics (e.g., variables and indices). A more important and more fundamental difference between these proposals, however, is that RAMs include properties among their constituents, whereas ILFs contain only objects and linguistic forms.

30. An account of (3a, b) involving primitive relations $\mathscr{R}_{\text{xerox}}$ and $\mathscr{R}_{\text{photocopy}}$ appears objectionable on at least two grounds. First, such an analysis appears to require very different accounts of nonequivalence for semantically similar elements in propositional attitude contexts. Note that while an analysis assuming distinct reference for *xerox* and *photocopy* is possible for (3), this view is not possible for (i), in which *Judy Garland* and *Frances Gumm* refer to the same individual. A 'primitive relations' account therefore cuts across the uniform status of the relevant items in (3) and (i) as rigid designators (Kripke 1972; Putnam 1975), and is forced to treat the two cases quite differently:

(i) a. Max believes Judy Garland is a starlet.

   b. Max believes Frances Gumm is a starlet.

Furthermore, the very possibility of an account of (3) involving distinct reference appears to trade on a familiar 'weakness' in our understanding of properties vs. other individuals, namely, on the fact that whereas our grasp on the identity of persons and dinner plates goes beyond our linguistic resources, our grasp on the identity of properties appears no stronger than the words we use to express them. It is precisely because we lack language-independent criteria for identifying properties that we feel free to postulate distinct properties in (3), given the presence of distinct words. And it is precisely because we possess such language-independent criteria for persons that we cannot make such a proposal for (i), despite the presence of different words. These general points are of course familiar from Quine (1961a, 1961b).

31. Axioms yielding the result in (56b) would include the following:

Val($\langle x, y \rangle, be, \sigma$) iff $x = y$.

Val($x, nonstationary, \sigma$) iff x is nonstationary.

Val($x, [_{VP} \text{ V AP}], \sigma$) iff for some y, Val ($\langle x, y \rangle, \text{V}, \sigma$) and Val($y$, AP, σ).

32. Davidson (1984b) analyzes only constructions involving the English verb *say*; Lepore and Loewer (1989) extend Davidson's analysis to the general class of propositional attitude verbs. Higginbotham (1986) introduces similarity in relation to ILFs.

33. An alternative, and more efficient way to introduce similarity into the truth-conditions of the ILF theory, would be to alter, not the lexical items in (15), but rather the general composition axiom in (14):

(14′) Val($x, [_{VP} \text{ V S}], \sigma$) iff for some y such that y is similar to ⟦S⟧ wrt σ,
     Val($\langle x, y \rangle, \text{V}, \sigma$).

This avoids the redundancy in the lexical specifications of (15′), allowing us to locate similarity in a single axiom. We appeal to the revision in (15′) in virtue of the points made below in connection with Segal (1989). Note that Segal's criticisms of the similarity theory go through equally with the axiom in (14′).

34. The same general account could be offered for sentences purporting to attribute propositional attitudes to humans at a prelinguistic stage, or to nonhuman species that do not display extensive linguistic capacities:

(i) a. Vicky thinks it's time to eat. (said of a baby)

   b. Jubilation thinks it's time for a walk. (said of a dog)

Presumably, to the extent that such reports are not metaphor or anthropomorphizing, they implicitly ascribe to the infant or dog some representational system—however rudimentary—in which the beliefs are given—a 'language of thought' as it were. What is then required by the ILF theory is that the ILF for *It's time to eat* or *It's time for his walk* be similar (in relevant features) to one definable with respect to the representational system of the child or animal. Again, it is not necessary that they stand in relation to an ILF containing English words.

It is perhaps useful here to point out a pseudoproblem that also appears to be addressed by the similarity theory. We noted earlier that the ILF account represents attitude reports like those in (55) and (57) as *object-dependent*, since their truth requires the existence of ILFs that in turn demand the existence of certain individuals. Equally, however, this theory represents such reports as *language-dependent*, since their truth requires the existence of ILFs that in turn demand the existence of certain English expressions. It is tempting to see this latter result as raising a problem that is eased by the similarity theory. One might worry that although Galileo's belief reported in (55) is dependent on the existence of the planet Earth, it is implausible to take it to be dependent on the existence of English. Surely, Galileo could have had the attitudes he did even if, causally, he were entirely isolated from English. Introduction of similarity would appear to ease this problem by not requiring Galileo to stand in relation to an ILF containing English expression but only one similar to it, and so on.

It is important to recognize that the apparent problem sketched above and the apparent solution just considered rest on a confusion between two quite different assertions:

(ii) a. If English failed to exist, the English sentence *Galileo believed that the Earth moved* could not be assigned truth-conditions.
    b. If English failed to exist, Galileo could not have had the beliefs he did (specifically, he could not have believed that the Earth moved).

The first assertion is trivially true. One cannot give truth-conditions for nonexistent languages. The second assertion is surely false, and does not follow under the ILF theory. The latter (as a semantic theory) addresses only the truth-conditions of sentences involving *believe, think, assert,* etc., it does not address the beliefs, thoughts, and assertions of persons. The 'problem' referred to above rests on a confusion, and does not require the introduction of similarity to solve it. (We are grateful to Gabriel Segal for discussion on this point.)

35. The pair in (i) gives a natural case in which we might want to talk about people having the same attitudes in virtue of being related to linguistically similar ILFs:

(i) a. John believes his favorite actress will receive an Oscar.
    b. Max believes his favorite actress will receive an Oscar.

Supposing that John and Max have different favorite actresses, and supposing that each pronoun refers back to its respective subject, the ILFs for the complements of (i.a, b) will contain different individuals. Nonetheless, for certain purposes it is clear that we might still want to report the two men as having the same belief.

36. This result has an interesting consequence for pairs like (2a, b) (repeated). Note that under the similarity theory, such pairs can be truth-conditionally equivalent in either of two very different ways:

(2) a. Max believes Judy Garland sang "Somewhere Over the Rainbow".
    b. Max believes Frances Gumm sang "Somewhere Over the Rainbow".

On the one hand, the proper names may remain with scope within the complement clause, with equivalence obtained by appropriate choice of similarity features, despite different ILFs (e.g, as discussed in the text, the two can be equivalent if F is the feature 'objectual content'). Alternatively, the proper names may be assigned scope outside the complement clauses (as discussed in (44) above) yielding identical ILFs. Equivalence will then obtain independently of similarity feature choice. This result shows that de re equivalence (equivalence in virtue of broad scope) can be distinguished even in a theory employing similarity. De re equivalence of attitude reports is the case where equivalence obtains without regard to choice of similarity features.

37. Notice that if (60) does utilize the the English* word *kicks* on the right-hand side, then it will assign the wrong truth-conditions; for then *Someone kicked Smith* will mean that someone kicked something that resembles something that resembles Smith.

References

Astington, J., P. Harris, and D. Olson (eds.) 1988, *Developing Theories of Mind*, Cambridge University Press, Cambridge.

Baker, M.: 1988, *Incorporation*, University of Chicago Press, Chicago.

Barwise, J., and R. Cooper: 1981, 'Generalized Quantifiers and Natural Language', *Linguistics and Philosophy* 4, 159–220.

Barwise, J., and J. Perry: 1983, *Situations and Attitudes*, Bradford Books/MIT Press, Cambridge, Massachusetts.

Brennan, S. E., and H. Clark: 1992, 'Lexical Choice and Local Convention', Stanford University and SUNY/Stony Brook, unpublished.

Buridan, J.: 1966, *Sophisms on Meaning and Truth*, trans. T. K. Scott, Appleton-Century-Crofts, New York.

Burdick, H.: 1982, 'A Logical Form for the Propositional Attitudes', *Synthese* 52, 185–230.

Burge, T.: 1974, 'Demonstrative Constructions, Reference and Truth', *The Journal of Philosophy* 71, 205–23.

Burge, T.: 1978, 'Belief and Synonymy', *The Journal of Philosophy* 75, 119–38.

Burge, T.: 1979, 'Frege and the Hierarchy', *Synthese* 40, 265–81.

Carey, S.: 1988, *Conceptual Change in Childhood*, Bradford Books/MIT Press, Cambridge, Massachusetts.

Carnap, R.: 1956, *Meaning and Necessity*, 2nd ed., University of Chicago Press, Chicago.

Chomsky, N. 1976, 'Conditions on Rules of Grammar', *Linguistic Analysis* 2, 303–51.

Chomsky, N.: 1981, *Lectures on Government and Binding*, Foris, Dordrecht.

Chomsky, N.: 1986, *Knowledge of Language*, Praeger, New York.

Chomsky, N.: 1989, 'Notes on Economy of Derivation and Representation', in I. Laka and A. Mahajan (eds.), *MIT Working Papers in Linguistics Volume 10: Functional Heads and Clause Structure*, MIT, Cambridge, Massachusetts.

Cresswell, M.: 1973, *Logics and Languages*, Methuen, London.

Cresswell, M.: 1980, 'Quotational Theories of Propositional Attitudes', *Journal of Philosophical Logic* 9, 17–40.

Cresswell, M.: 1984, *Structured Meanings*, MIT Press, Cambridge, Massachusetts.

Davidson, D.: 1984a, 'Truth and Meaning', in *Inquiries into Truth & Interpretation*, Clarendon Press, Oxford, pp. 17–36 (originally published: 1967). [Chap. 5 in this vol.]

Davidson, D.: 1984b, 'On Saying That', in *Inquiries into Truth & Interpretation*, Clarendon Press, Oxford, pp. 93–108 (originally published: 1968). [Chap. 35 in this vol.]

Davidson, D.: 1984c, 'Semantics for Natural Language', in *Inquiries into Truth & Interpretation*, Clarendon Press, Oxford, pp. 55–64 (originally published: 1970).

Davies, M. 1981, *Meaning, Quantification, Necessity*, Routledge and Kegan Paul, London.

DiSciullo, A., and E. Williams: 1987, *On the Definition of Word*, MIT Press, Cambridge, Massachusetts.

Enc, M.: 1982, 'Tense Without Scope', Ph.D. Dissertation, University of Wisconsin, Madison, unpublished.

Evans, G.: 1977, 'Pronouns, Quantifiers and Relative Clauses (I)', *Canadian Journal of Philosophy* 3, 467–536.

Evans, G.: 1980, 'Pronouns', *Linguistic Inquiry* 11, 337–62.

Evans, G.: 1982, *The Varieties of Reference*, Clarendon Press, Oxford.

Frege, G.: 1892, 'Sinn und Bedeutung', *Zeitschrift für Philosophie und philosophische Kritik* 100, 25–50 (published as 'Sense and Reference', in P. Geach and M. Black (eds.): 1952, *Translations from the Philosophical Writings of Gottlob Frege*, Blackwell, Oxford, pp. 56–78). [Chap. 22 in this vol.]

Frye, D., and C. Moore (eds.): 1991, *Children's Theories of Mind: Mental States and Social Understanding*, Lawrence Erlbaum Associates, Hillsdale, New Jersey.

Geach, P.: 1962, *Reference and Generality*, Cornell University Press, Ithaca.

Georgeff, M., and A. Lansky (eds.): 1986, *The 1986 Workshop on Reasoning about Actions and Plans*, Morgan Kaufmann, Los Altos, California.

Haegeman, L.: 1991, *Introduction to Government & Binding Theory*, Blackwell, New York.

Harman, G.: 1972, 'Logical Form', *Foundations of Language* 9, 38–65.

Higginbotham, J.: 1980, 'Anaphora and GB', in J. Jensen (ed.), *Proceedings of the Tenth Annual Meeting of NELS* (*Cahiers linguistiques d'Ottawa 9.4*), Dept. of Linguistics, University of Ottawa, Ontario, pp. 223–36.

Higginbotham, J.: 1985, 'On Semantics', *Linguistic Inquiry* 16, 547–93.

Higginbotham, J.: 1986, 'Linguistic Theory and Davidson's Program', in E. Lepore (ed.), *Truth and Interpretation: Perspectives on the Philosophy of Donald Davidson*, Blackwell, Oxford, pp. 29–48.

Higginbotham, J.: 1991, 'Belief and Logical Form', *Mind and Language* 6, 344–69.

Higginbotham, J., and R. May: 1981, 'Questions, Quantifiers and Crossing', *The Linguistic Review* 1, 41–80.

Hintikka, J.: 1962, *Knowledge and Belief*, Cornell University Press, Ithaca.

Hintikka, J.: 1969, 'Semantics for Propositional Attitudes', in J. Davis et al. (eds.), *Philosophical Logic*, D. Reidel, Dordrecht, pp. 21–45.

Hintikka, J.: 1983, *The Game of Language*, D. Reidel, Dordrecht.

Hintikka, J., and G. Sandu: 1989, 'Informational Independence as a Semantical Phenomenon', in J. E. Fenstad et al. (eds.), *Logic, Methodology and the Philosophy of Science VIII*, North-Holland, Amsterdam, pp. 571–89.

Hobbes, J., and B. Moore (eds.): 1985, *Theories of the Commonsense World*, Ablex, Norwood, New Jersey.

Hornstein, N.: 1987, 'Levels of Meaning', in J. Garfield (ed.), *Modularity in Knowledge Representation and Natural-Language Understanding*, Bradford Books/MIT Press, Cambridge, Massachusetts, pp. 133–50.

Kaplan, D.: 1969, 'Quantifying In', in D. Davidson and J. Hintikka (eds.), *Words and Objections*, D. Reidel, Dordrecht, pp. 206–42.

Kripke, S.: 1972, 'Meaning and Necessity', in D. Davidson and G. Harman (eds.), *Semantics of Natural Language*, D. Reidel, Dordrecht, pp. 253–355, 763–69.

Kripke, S.: 1979, 'A Puzzle About Belief', in A. Margalit (ed.), *Meaning and Use*, D. Reidel, Dordrecht, pp. 239–83. [Chap. 38 in this vol.]

Larson, R.: 1983, 'Restrictive Modification: Relative Clauses and Adverbs', Ph.D. Dissertation, University of Wisconsin, Madison, unpublished.

Larson, R., and G. Segal: 1995, *Knowledge of Meaning: Semantic Value and Logical Form*, Bradford Books/MIT Press, Cambridge, Massachusetts.

Lasnik, H., and M. Saito: 1984, 'The Nature of Proper Government', *Linguistic Inquiry* 15, 235–89.

Lepore, E., and B. Loewer: 1989, 'You can Say *That* Again', in P. French, T. Uehling, and H. Wettstein (eds.), *Midwest Studies in Philosophy XIV: Contemporary Perspectives in the Philosophy of Language II*, University of Notre Dame Press, Notre Dame, pp. 338–56.

Lewis, D.: 1972, 'General Semantics', in D. Davidson and G. Harman (eds.), *Semantics of Natural Language*, D. Reidel, Dordrecht, pp. 169–218.

Ludlow, P.: 1985, 'The Syntax and Semantics of Referential Attitude Reports', Ph.D. Dissertation, Columbia University, New York, unpublished.

Ludlow, P., and S. Neale: 1991, 'Indefinite Descriptions: In Defense of Russell', *Linguistics and Philosophy* 14, 171–202. [Chap. 21 in this vol.]

Lycan, W.: 1984, *Logical Form in Natural Language*, MIT Press/Bradford Books, Cambridge, Massachusetts.

May, R.: 1977, 'The Grammar of Quantification', Ph.D. Dissertation, MIT, Cambridge, Massachusetts, unpublished.

May, R.: 1985, *Logical Form: Its Structure and Derivation*, MIT Press, Cambridge, Massachusetts.

McDowell, J.: 1980, 'On the Sense and Reference of a Proper Name', in M. Platts (ed.), *Reference, Truth and Reality*, Routledge and Kegan Paul, London, pp. 141–66.

Montague, R.: 1974, *Formal Philosophy*, Yale University Press, New Haven.

Parsons, T.: 1981, 'Frege Hierarchies', in P. French, T. Uehling, and H. Wettstein (eds.), *Midwest Studies in Philosophy VI: The Foundations of Analytic Philosophy*, University of Minnesota Press, Minneapolis, pp. 37–57.

Partee, B.: 1979, 'Semantics: Mathematics or Psychology?', in R. Bäuerle, U. Egli, and A. von Stechow (eds.), *Semantics from Different Points of View*, Springer-Verlag, Berlin, pp. 1–14.

Putnam, H.: 1975, 'The Meaning of "Meaning"', in K. Gunderson (ed.), *Language, Mind, and Knowledge, Minnesota Studies in the Philosophy of Science, Vol. VII*, University of Minnesota, Minneapolis, pp. 131–93.

Quine, W. V. O.: 1961a, 'On What There Is', in *From a Logical Point of View*, Harper & Row, New York, pp. 1–19.

Quine, W. V. O.: 1961b, 'Logic and the Reification of Universals', in *From a Logical Point of View*, Harper & Row, New York, pp. 102–29.

Radford, A.: 1988, *Transformational Grammar*, Cambridge University Press, Cambridge.

Richard, M.: 1990, *Propositional Attitudes*, Cambridge University Press, Cambridge.

Russell, B.: 1956, 'The Philosophy of Logical Atomism', in R. C. Marsh (ed.), *Logic and Knowledge*, George Allen and Unwin, London, pp. 175–281.

Salmon, N.: 1986a, *Frege's Puzzle*, Bradford Books/MIT Press, Cambridge, Massachusetts.

Salmon, N.: 1986b, 'Reflexivity', *Notre Dame Journal of Formal Logic* 27, 401–29.

Salmon, N. and S. Soames (eds.): 1988, *Propositions and Attitudes*, Oxford University Press, Oxford.

Sher, G.: 1991, *The Bounds of Logic: A Generalized Viewpoint*, MIT Press, Cambridge, Massachusetts.

Segal, G.: 1989, 'A Preference for Sense and Reference', *The Journal of Philosophy* 86, 73–89.

Sells, P.: 1985, *Lectures on Contemporary Syntactic Theories*, CSLI Lecture Notes, Standford.

Sim, D.: 1981, *Swords of Cerebus*, Aardvark Vanaheim Press, Toronto.

Soames, S.: 1987, 'Direct Reference, Propositional Attitudes, and Semantic Content', *Philosophical Topics* 15, 47–87. [Chap. 39 in this vol.]

Soames, S.: 1989–90, 'Pronouns and Propositional Attitudes', *Proceedings of the Aristotelian Society* 90, 191–212.

Stalnaker, R.: 1987, *Inquiry*, MIT Press, Cambridge, Massachusetts.

Chapter 42

Intensional "Transitive" Verbs and Concealed Complement Clauses

Marcel den Dikken, Richard K. Larson, and Peter Ludlow

Harman (1972), Higginbotham (1986), Segal (1989), Larson and Ludlow (1993), and Larson and Segal (1995) have argued that the object of a propositional attitude report (e.g., 'Ralph believes that snow is white') is an interpreted logical form (ILF), i.e., a syntactic representation of the complement clause combined with the semantic values that are assigned to various parts of that clause.[1]

One of the questions facing ILF theories has been how they can be extended to natural-language constructions that are known to be intensional but do not appear to have clausal constituents. Famous examples include (1) to (3):

(1) John wants a donkey.

(2) John seeks a donkey.

(3) John looks for a donkey.

Clearly these examples induce intensional environments—John may just as easily want or seek or look for a unicorn—so how can this be reconciled with the fact that there are no apparent clausal constituents in (1) to (3)?

One possible response is to extend the ILF construction algorithm of Larson and Ludlow (1993) so that ILFs can be constructed from smaller constituents, such as NPs. While there may be no inherent barrier to such a move, in our view it is unnecessary. On independent evidence, we believe that examples like (1) to (3) in fact have implicit clausal con-

Abridged from a version to appear in *Rivista di Linguistica* 8 (1996), no. 2.

stituents. In effect, examples (1) to (3) are propositional attitude reports in disguise, and the ILF theory trivially extends to such cases.

The view that "intensional transitive constructions" involve a covert clausal complement has previously been argued in the linguistics literature on a number of grounds.[2] As noted by McCawley (1974), Karttunen (1976), and Ross (1976), many of these constructions show an ambiguity with adverb construal, which strongly suggests the presence of a covert predicate. Consider the following examples.

(4) John will want a hippogriff tomorrow.

(5) John is hoping for a fish tomorrow.

For example, (4) is ambiguous between a reading in which the adverb modifies the matrix verb ('Tomorrow John will want a hippogriff') and a reading in which the adverb modifies an implicit verb with approximately the meaning of 'have' ('John will want (perhaps later today) that tomorrow he have a hippogriff'). Notice that such ambiguities are not found with simple transitive verbs such as 'kick' or 'eat', which take no clausal complement:

(6) John will kick a hippogriff tomorrow.

(7) John will eat a fish tomorrow.

If there is an implicit clause with 'want' and 'hope for', then the ambiguity can be viewed straightforwardly as reflecting a simple difference of attachment site for the adverb, analogous to (8a) versus (8b):

(8) a. John will [want [PRO to have a hippogriff tomorrow]]
    b. John will [want [PRO to have a hippogriff] tomorrow]

It is interesting to note that the so-called intensional transitive verbs are all capable of appearing with *overt* clausal complementation, as in (9) to (11):

(9) John wants [Mary to buy a donkey]

(10) John seeks [PRO to discover the solution]

(11) John imagined [that a hippogriff was approaching]

This suggests that there is a very close connection indeed between clausal complementation and intensional environments.

If so-called intensional transitive constructions are actually clausal, then the ILF analysis of propositional attitudes will extend to them directly.[3] The syntactic form of (1), for example, will be broadly as in (12):

(12)

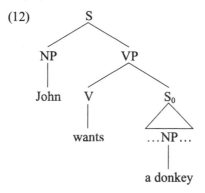

The ILF formation algorithm of Larson and Ludlow (1993) will operate on S0 just like any other clausal complement, and S0 will thus undergo ILF formation. The net result will be that the NP 'a donkey' will be correctly predicted to show intensionality effects.

Semantically, the ILF analysis of these constructions will be trivial. Still, a number of significant questions arise about the form and interpretation of the concealed clause. For example:

• What precisely is the form of the embedded S0?
• What precisely is the semantics of the predicate contained in the concealed clause?
• Why is it that some intensional transitive predicates fail to show all the earmarks of concealed complementation?

All of these questions will need to be taken up. We begin with the issue of the form of the concealed clause.

THE FORM OF CONCEALED COMPLEMENT CLAUSES

Intuitively, the simplest possible syntactic hypothesis about concealed complements is that the only thing distinguishing them from overt complements is that they are unpronounced. This embodies two basic ideas.

• Concealed complements will show the same general range of forms available with overt complements.
• Embedded concealed predicates will show the same general range of interactions with their matrix verb as do embedded overt predicates.

Let us consider the consequences of the assumption of the simplest possible syntactic theory. If (so-called) intensional transitive constructions are actually clausal, we would then expect essentially three different underlying forms, corresponding to whether NP is the object of a concealed clause, as in (13a), the subject of a concealed clause, as in (13b), or the subject of a "small clause," as in (13c):

(13) a. John wants [PRO to have a donkey]
          John wants [PRO VERB$_2$ a donkey]

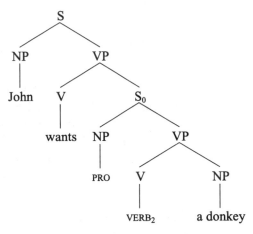

      b. John wants [a donkey to appear]
          John wants [a donkey VERB$_1$]

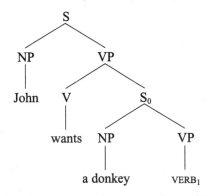

      c. John wants [a donkey in the audience]
          John wants [a donkey PRED]

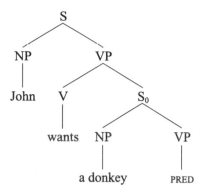

We think that the simplest theory is in fact the right theory—that we can distinguish three basic types of concealed complements corresponding to the three possibilities given above.

THE INTERPRETATION OF THE CONCEALED PREDICATES

One general question facing a theory of the kind embraced here lies in the vagueness of the concealed predicate. In some cases, concealed clauses can be paraphrased relatively accurately and uniformly with overt forms. For example, 'John wants a high-performance off-shore power boat' can be paraphrased as 'John wants to have a high-performance off-shore power boat'.

In the majority of cases, however, concealed clause structures can be paraphrased with any number of different predicates, depending on context. For example, Decarrico (1983) has stressed that 'hopes for a bus' may be paraphrased as 'hopes a bus will arrive' or 'hopes to receive a bus', etc. This raises the question as to what kinds of semantic axioms are going to be introduced for empty predicates.

We suggest a general answer to this question using the theory of events initially proposed by Davidson (1967) and developed by Parsons (1990), Higginbotham (1989), and Schein (1993), among many others. Under this analysis, verbs are analyzed as unary predicates of events, whose nominal arguments are related to the "core" event by binary thematic relations. For example 'hit' receives the axiom in (14), where $Val(X, Y, Z)$ is read as "X is the semantic value of Y with respect to assignment Z."

(14) $Val(\langle x, y, e \rangle, \text{'hit'}, \sigma)$ iff
e is a hitting and x is the agent of e and y is the theme of e

We suggest that the empty verbs and predicates in concealed clauses be analyzed in these terms. Specifically, we propose that the semantic axioms for empty verbs depart from those of lexical verbs in the following ways: (1) the former lack a core event predicate, and (2) the relevant thematic relations for the empty verbs will be somewhat less specific (for example, instead of the agent relation, we will speak of a more general "participant" relation). We propose the following axioms for VERB$_2$, VERB$_1$, and PRED.

(15) Val$\langle x, y, e\rangle$, 'VERB$_2$', σ) iff
      e is an event in which x is a participant and y is the theme

(16) Val($\langle x, e\rangle$, 'VERB$_1$', σ) iff
      e is an event in which x is a participant

(17) Val($\langle x, e\rangle$, 'PRED', σ) iff
      e is an event in which x is the theme

Notice that this analysis captures "what is said" when one says, for example, that one wants a hippogriff. We may be able to infer more—for example, that the hippogriff is desired for a collection or perhaps for dinner—but such knowledge need not make it into the content of what is expressed by the speaker. (Strictly speaking, the actual role may be somewhat stronger than mere participant. For current purposes, the relation needs to be at least that strong. If a stronger role can be identified, then so much the better.)

WHY IS IT THAT SOME INTENSIONAL TRANSITIVE PREDICATES FAIL TO SHOW ALL THE EARMARKS OF CONCEALED COMPLEMENTATION?

Consider the following examples.

(18) John seeks a narwhal.

(19) John looks for a tile fish.

(20) John hunts a grouper.

Clearly, the verbs in each of (18) to (20) induce an intensional environment, yet verbs like these do not appear to be candidates for the concealed-clause analysis. Specifically, it appears that these verbs fail to evince an ambiguity when an adverb is appended. Consider (21) to (23):

(21) John seeks a narwhal tomorrow.

(22) John looks for a tile fish tomorrow.

(23) John hunts a grouper tomorrow.

In (21), for example, the seeking occurs tomorrow. There is no reading in which one seeks today and has the narwhal tomorrow.

Although it has been suggested by Partee (1974) and others that these facts argue against the thesis that there is implicit clausal structure in these examples, we find such conclusions altogether too hasty. All that follows from there being implicit clausal structure is that there be two adjunction sites for the adverb. It does not immediately follow that the two possible adjunction sites will give rise to two possible interpretations. Consider the following example, in which the second clause is a kind of result clause.

(24) I will kick a ball into the net with the result that I score a goal tomorrow.

It is difficult to force an ambiguity in this example, and the reason is that the events of kicking and scoring must spatiotemporally overlap. They are perhaps the same event under different descriptions. You cannot kick the ball into the net on Monday and score on Tuesday. Whether the adverb modifies the kicking or the scoring, it is ultimately modifying the same event.

Events need not be identical for this sort of result to occur. It might be that one event is properly contained in the other. For example,

(25) I raced the 100 meters full throttle with the goal of finishing first yesterday.

The finishing must be contained spatiotemporally within the racing, so if the finishing occurs yesterday, at least some of the racing does as well.

Similar considerations apply to sentences with complement clauses (like 'John will be trying to find a unicorn tomorrow') and in particular to sentences with concealed complement clauses. Events like seekings and lookings are much like the cases discussed above. While you can seek something today with the goal of finding it *by* tomorrow, you cannot seek something today with the goal of finding it tomorrow. If you seek something, look for something, etc., and you obtain the object as the result of your search, the time of your obtaining the object must overlap with the time of your search.

The following thought experiment supports this claim. Suppose that a plane goes down in the amazon jungle and we are interested in finding the survivors. Suppose further that an oracle tells us that we will not find the survivors today but that if we search diligently today, we will be rewarded by finding the survivors tomorrow. If we believe the oracle and go out today, are we really searching, or are we merely going through the motions? Just going through the motions, in our judgement.

Concerns of a different nature have been raised about the plausibility of the intensional verb 'fears' taking a propositional complement. Specifically, Kaplan claims that if I fear unicorns, I need not fear that they should harm me, nor indeed do anything. I might just fear them simpliciter.

When a hunting accident so traumatizes Ctesias that he comes to fear unicorns (not, to fear that there are unicorns or that he will encounter a unicorn, but to have a true unicorn phobia—one that has begun to 'generalize' to take in horses and antelopes), what propositional attitude will capture his psychological state? "What is it you fear will happen?" we ask Ctesias. "Nothing," he replies. "I just don't like unicorns." (Kaplan 1986, 267)

It is interesting that Kaplan slides from using the term 'fears' to using the term 'phobia'. Ctesias might fear sharks, but it would be odd if he would fear a shark in an aquarium. And if, upon seeing a shark in an aquarium, Ctesias is gripped with fear, we would probably say that he is not afraid so much as phobic. Strictly speaking, he does not fear sharks, but sharks are the occasion for an emotional reaction by Ctesias.

The upshot, we think, is that if you truly fear sharks, you fear that they will do something. Moreover, it is clear that 'fears' passes all the tests for having an implicit clausal complement. Notice that 'fears' admits of scope ambiguities and even evinces an adverb attachment ambiguity. For example, (26) can mean either that John fears a particular drunken sailor or that he may fear that a drunken sailor may accost him (if, for example, he wanders in Marseille):

(26) John fears a drunken sailor.

Sentence (27) shows us that a temporal adverb need not modify the event of fearing but may modify an implicit event of the storm's arrival:

(27) Until he heard the updated weather report, John feared a storm tomorrow.

We conclude that 'fears', like 'seeks', falls neatly into the same paradigm as 'wants' and 'desires'.

THE THREE TYPES OF CONCEALED PROPOSITIONAL COMPLEMENTS AND HOW TO DIFFERENTIATE BETWEEN THEM: SOME PRELIMINARY SYNTACTIC INVESTIGATIONS

Clearly, the proposal put forward thus far is programmatic. It is one thing to propose that there are implicit clauses but quite another to investigate their structure in detail. What makes any such investigation challenging, of course, is that so much of the material in these clauses is unpronounced. We have, so to speak, entered into an investigation of a largely "invisible" world, and just as investigations into the nature of the invisible have prompted other sciences to develop new tools and methods, we will need to develop certain linguistic tools to probe the nature of invisible clauses. In the remainder of this paper, we consider one such linguistic tool—the study of passive constructions—and use it to gain some insight into the nature of concealed clauses.

PASSIVIZATION

To aid our discussion, let's label the three types of complement clauses in (13a), (13b), and (13c) 'type 1', 'type 2', and 'type 3' cases, respectively. Thus, type 1 cases will be those in which there is a PRO subject and a transitive verb: [PRO VERB₂ [NP]]. In both the type 2 and type 3 cases, the NP will be in subject position: [[NP] VERB₁/PRED].

According to widely attested observations about passivization, a matrix passive involving raising of the embedded object in an explicit type 1 case should be blocked, while passivization from the subject position of a type 2 case should generally be unproblematic. Thus, in the *explicit* cases, we have the contrast between an explicit type 1 case like (28) and an explicit type 2 case like (29):

(28) a.   John is expecting to see a bus.
     b. *A bus is expected to see (by John).

(29) a.   John is expecting a bus to arrive.
     b. A bus is expected to arrive (by John).

Can we use this distinction to purchase any insight into the structure of invisible complement clauses? One fact is clear. As (30) shows, passivization of the so-called intensional transitive verb is possible.

(30) A bus is expected by John.

The key question is what underlying form does (30) come from? According to the assumptions we have made above, the passive form in (30) should be possible, but it must be derived from the underlying type 2 case, 'expects [[a bus] VERB]', and not from the underlying type 1 case, 'expects [PRO VERB [a bus]]'. But what sort of probes will tell us what the source structure of (30) must be?

As a first attempt, we might ask which of the following is the more plausible meaning for (30):

(31) John is expecting to see a bus.

(32) John is expecting a bus to arrive.

A somewhat more refined test turns on the meaning that our theory assigns to VERB$_2$ and VERB$_1$. Recall that the axioms for these elements differed in that the semantics for VERB$_2$ dictated that the controller of PRO (in this case John) is a participant in the described event, while in the case of VERB$_1$ John need not be a participant—the NP ('a bus') is simply the theme of the described event. (Note that John is not *prohibited* from being a participant; (32) is simply mute on John's involvement.)

Thus, it is possible to distinguish the type 1 and type 2 cases by asking whether it is necessary that the matrix subject be a participant in the downstairs event. In the case under discussion, (30), we can ask whether John is expecting some event to unfold in which he is an active participant or whether he simply expects that a bus may arrive when he is miles from the scene. Our intuitions are clear on this matter; in (30) there need be no expectation that John is a participant in the described downstairs event. Hence we conclude that the evidence points to a type 2 source for the passive form in (30)—exactly as the theory predicts.

Bear in mind that the implicit-clause cases should track the explicit ones, so for those verbs in which passivization from a type 2 source is blocked, we predict that there should be no passive form available. Consider 'wants', for example. As (33) to (34) show, passivization from both a type 1 and a type 2 structure is blocked.

(33) a.   John wants to have a hippogriff.
      b.   *A hippogriff is wanted to have (by John).

(34) a.   John wants a hippogriff to appear.
      b.   *A hippogriff is wanted to appear (by John).

Thus we predict, correctly it seems, that the passive in the implicit-clause case (as in (35)) will be greatly degraded.

(35) a. John wants a hippogriff.
     b. ?A hippogriff is wanted (by John).

To the extent that (35b) is acceptable, it appears to trade on on the "wanted poster" construction: 'Smith is wanted by the law'. Some informants find this construction productive, suggesting to us that the underlying form for the passive in such cases may be the type 3 (implicit small clause) construction. So, for example, even in the wanted-poster case, we have 'wanted dead or alive'. Presumably, those individuals that find (35b) acceptable also find (36) acceptable:

(36) ?A hippogriff is wanted dead or alive (by John).

CONCLUDING REMARKS

This single probe is not intended to be the last word on ways of investigating the structure of invisible clauses; indeed, it may not even be the best tool for carrying out such an investigation. Our interest in introducing it is to provide some hint as to what kinds of investigations into the internal structure of these clauses are possible. Internal probes are not the only avenues of investigation open to us, however. One of the very strong empirical predictions of this theory is that, barring grammatical constraints to block their appearance, invisible clauses should be available wherever we find overt clauses. The following example should illustrate what we have in mind.

(37) An apple a day keeps the doctor away.

As (38) shows, it is possible to have a full clause as the subject of this construction:

(38) [PRO eating an apple a day] keeps the doctor away

Thus we predict that an invisible clause may appear here as well, basically following the structure in (39):

(39) [PRO VERB an apple a day] keeps the doctor away

Does (39) reflect the actual syntactic form of (37)? It certainly seems to reflect the fact that it is not apples themselves that are asserted to do good in (37) but rather the eating of apples. Sentence (39) also seems to reflect the fact that the verb does not agree in number with the NP, as (40) shows, which strongly suggests that the actual argument is a clause, and not the plural NP.

(40) [PRO VERB 3 apples a day] keep*/keeps the doctor away

In sum, there are plenty of avenues of investigation to be pursued, both into the internal structure of invisible clauses and (as (37) to (40) show) into the distribution of these clauses within sentences. We reiterate, however, that these investigations are preliminary and programmatic. While it is far too early to draw strong conclusions about the hidden-clause analysis, the evidence accumulated thus far appears to support such an analysis. Given the very strong empirical predictions of such an analysis, the positive evidence is all the more encouraging—certainly encouraging enough to motivate further research into the nature and distribution of invisible complement clauses, as well as into the interaction of the analysis with the rest of grammatical theory. The results are also encouraging for strict ILF accounts of intensionality in natural language. If the evidence available so far is correct, then the extension of ILF theories to intensional transitive constructions will be unproblematic.

Notes

Earlier versions of this material have been presented at the University of California at Irvine, the University of Amsterdam, the University of Delaware, and the University of Potsdam (Berlin). In addition to the audiences at these talks, we are indebted to Anna Cardinaletti, Dan Finer, and Chris Wilder for helpful discussion.

1. See, for example, Harman 1972, Higginbotham 1986, Segal 1989, Larson and Ludlow 1993, and Larson and Segal 1995.

2. Of course, it has also been discussed in the philosophical literature by Quine (1960), Montague (1960), and even by the medieval logician Buridan (1966).

3. Indeed, Ludlow (1985) argues that the ILF analysis works more smoothly with covert propositional attitudes than with overt ones.

References

Buridan, J. 1966. *Sophisms on Meaning and Truth*. Trans. T. K. Scott. New York: Appleton-Century-Crofts.

Davidson, D. 1967. "The Logical Form of Action Sentences." in N. Rescher (ed.), *The Logic of Decision and Action*. Pittsburgh: University of Pittsburgh Press, 1984. Reprinted in Davidson 1980, pp. 105–148. [Chap. 11 in this vol.]

Davidson, D. 1980. *Essays on Actions and Events*. Oxford: Oxford University Press.

Decarrico, J. 1983. "On Quantifier Raising." *Linguistic Inquiry* 14:343–346.

Harman, G. 1972. "Logical Form." *Foundations of Language* 9:38–65.

Higginbotham, J. 1986. "Linguistic Theory and Davidson's Program in Semantics." In Ernest LePore (ed.), *Truth and Interpretation: Perspectives on the Philosophy of Donald Davidson*. Oxford: Basil Blackwell.

Higginbotham, J. 1989. "Elucidations of Meaning." *Linguistics and Philosophy* 12:465–518. [Chap. 8 in this vol.]

Kaplan, D. 1986. "Opacity." In L. E. Hahn and P. A. Schilpp (ed.), *The Philosophy of W. V. Quine*. La Salle: Open Court.

Karttunen, L. 1976. "Discourse Referents." In McCawley (ed.), *Notes from the Linguistic Underground*, Syntax and Semantics, no. 7. New York: Academic Press.

Larson, R., and P. Ludlow. 1993. "Interpreted Logical Forms." *Synthese* 95:305–355. [Chap. 41 in this vol.]

Larson, R., and G. Segal. 1995. *Knowledge of Meaning: An Introduction to Semantic Theory*. Cambridge: MIT Press.

Ludlow, P. 1985. *The Syntax and Semantics of Referential Attitude Reports*. Ph.D. thesis, Columbia University. Reprinted, University of Indiana Linguistics Club, Bloomington, 1986.

McCawley, J. 1974. "On Identifying the Remains of Deceased Clauses." *Language Research* 9:73–85. Reprinted in *Adverbs, Vowels, and Other Objects of Wonder*. Chicago: University of Chicago Press, 1979.

Montague, R. 1960. "On the Nature of Certain Philosophical Entities." *Monist* 53:159–194. Reprinted in Montague, *Formal Philosophy*.

Montague, R. 1974. *Formal Philosophy*. Ed. by R. Thomason. New Haven: Yale University Press.

Parsons, T. 1990. *Events in the Semantics of English*. Cambridge: MIT Press.

Partee, B. 1974. "Opacity and Scope." In Munitz and Unger (eds.), *Semantics and Philosophy*. New York: NYU Press. [Chap. 36 in this vol.]

Quine, W. V. O. 1960. *Word and Object*. Cambridge: MIT Press.

Ross, J. R. 1976. "To Have and to Have Not." In Polome et al. (eds.), *Linguistic and Literary Studies in Honor of Archibald Hill*. Lisse: Peter de Ridder.

Schein, B. 1993. *Plurals and Events*. Cambridge: MIT Press.

Segal, G. 1989. "A Preference for Sense and Reference." *Journal of Philosophy* 86:73–89.

Index of Names

Page numbers in italics refer to chapters in this volume by the author in question.

Ackerman, D., 910 (n. 10)
Adams, R., 715 (n. 7)
Almog, J., 956, 958 (n. 17)
Anscombe, G. E. M., 743 (n. 33)
Aristotle, 359
Arnauld, A., 457 (n. 3)
Aronoff, M., 1028
Astington, J., 1024, 1036
Austin, J. L., 107 (n. 17), 220, 232 (n. 3)

Bach, E., 126 (n. 1), 277 (n. 1), 278, 313
    (& n. 17), 414 (n. 35), 847, 851 (nn. 2, 6),
    853
Baker, J., 1029 (n. 7), 1036
Bar-Hillel, Y., 107 (n. 12)
Barwise, J., 6, 290–291, 312 (n. 6), 313, 457
    (n. 7), 458 (n. 6), 463 (n. 33), 467 (n. 44),
    468 (n. 55), 470, 514 (n. 2), 518 (n. 23),
    519, 549 (n. 2), 553, 661, 928, 955, 957
    (n. 7), 963, 990 (n. 16), 1016, 1032 (n. 22)
Bealer, G., 157, 177
Bell, J. M., 413 (n. 35)
Bentham, J. van, 312 (n. 6), 313
Berman, S., 546, 553
Bernays, P., 518 (n. 27)
Beth, E., 107 (n. 12)
Biro, J., (n. 1)
Black, M., 6, 789–790
Blackburn, S., 463 (n. 34), 466 (n. 38),
    467 (n. 44), 468 (n. 52), 470
Borer, H., 285, 313
Bratman, M., 667, 715 (n. 7)
Brennan, S. E., 1026, 1036
Bromberger, S., 548
Burdick, H., 1028 (n. 1), 1036
Burge, T., 176 (nn. 2, 4), 177, 560, 562, 593–
    608, 715 (n. 7), 750, 765 (& n. 15), 766,
    1008, 1028 (n. 2), 1030 (nn. 16, 17),
    1032 (n. 24), 1036

Buridan, J., 1031 (n. 18), 1036, 1052 (n. 2)
Burks, A. W., 715 (n. 3)

Canfield, J., 379
Cardinaletti, A., 1052
Carey, S., 1024, 1036
Cargile, J., 252, 255 (n. 21)
Carlson, L., 127 (n. 11)
Carlyle, T., 611–612
Carnap, R., 57, 101, 203, 608 (n. 15), 671,
    690 (n. 10), 771–772, 779–791, 793–797,
    798 (nn. 3, 7), 799 (n. 11), 814 (n. 4), 823,
    831 (n. 5), 834, 853, 878, 926, 1033 (n. 28),
    1036
Cartwright, R., 456 (n. 2), 470
Casteñeda, H. N., 457 (n. 5), 470, 661,
    715 (nn. 5, 6), 733, 743 (n. 23)
Caton, C. S., 380 (n. 7)
Chastain, C., 458 (n. 6), 463 (n. 33), 470,
    476, 519, 549 (n. 2), 553
Chierchia, G., 6, 157, 175, 176, 177
Chisolm, R., 57, 223–224, 226, 232 (n. 5)
Chomsky, N., xvii, 100, 106 (n. 4), 107
    (n. 13), 157, 176, 177 (n. 7), 177, 205, 206,
    277 (n. 1), 278, 282–285, 287, 307–309,
    311 (n. 1), 313, 314, 461 (n. 24), 470, 512,
    519, 544, 553, 797, 798 (n. 7), 1028 (n. 4),
    1032 (n. 19), 1036
Church, A., 105, 470, 799–800 (n. 12), 810,
    814 (n. 4), 815 (nn. 7, 8), 822–823, 825,
    831 (nn. 6, 7, 10), 909 (n. 6), 911 (n. 12),
    914 (n. 25), 919 (n. 46), 1031 (n. 18)
Clark, E., 461 (n. 26), 470
Clarke, H., 1026, 1036
Cole, P., 689
Cooper, R., 290–291, 298, 312 (n. 6), 313
    (& n. 13), 467 (n. 45), 314, 491–493, 514
    (n. 2), 515 (n. 10), 519, 542, 545, 551
    (n. 22), 553 (n. 28), 1032 (n. 22), 1036

Cresswell, M. J., 109, 126 (nn. 2, 3), 168, 177, 468 (n. 49), 772, 777, 1028, 1033 (nn. 26, 28), 1037
Crimmins, M., 775, *963–991*, 989 (n. 7), 991 (n. 22), 1028
Croft, W., 164, 177
Croker, L., 385
Cushing, S., 512, 519

Davidson, D., 4, 57, *89–107*, 119, 125 (n. 1), 126 (nn. 4, 5), 134–136, 144–150, 163–165, 171, 178, 179, 197 (nn. 1, 9), 203–205, *217–232*, 233–236, 238–242, 244, 247, 252–253, 254 (nn. 1–4, 6–7), 255 (n. 19), 268–273, 278, 281, 457 (n. 5), 470, 608 (n. 12), 659, 667, 741 (n. 7), 773–774, 814 (n. 5), 815 (n. 9), *817–831*, 855–870, 872 (nn. 2, 3), 873 (& n. 5), 903, 909 (n. 7), 911 (n. 14), 917 (n. 38), 993, 998, 1017, 1019, 1028, 1034 (n. 32), 1037, 1045, 1052
Davies, M., 6, 456 (n. 3), 457 (n. 5), 462 (n. 29), 463 (nn. 31, 34), 466 (nn. 38, 39), 467 (n. 44), 468 (n. 48), 469 (n. 53), 471, 546, 458, 552 (n. 26), 553 (nn. 31, 35), 554, *745–767*, 1032 (nn. 20, 22)
Decarrico, J., 1045, 1052
Delhaise, E., 654 (n. 8)
Den Dikken, M., *1041–1053*
Dennett, D., 515 (n. 8), 519
Descartes, 738
Devitt, M., xvii, 322, 457 (n. 7), 466 (n. 38), 467 (n. 43), 471, 562
DiSciullo, A., 1029 (n. 7), 1037
Domincy, M., 457 (n. 3), 470
Donellan, K. S., 320–322, *361–381*, 383–388, 390–394, 396–401, 403–406, 407 (n. 1–5), 408 (nn. 8–10, 13–14), 409 (nn. 20, 22), 410, (n. 25), 411 (n. 28), 412–413 (n. 32), 414 (nn. 37–38), 416–417, 437, 438, 444–445, 449–450, 452, 456 (n. 3), 457 (nn. 3, 4, 6, 7), 462 (n. 31), 463 (n. 33), 466 (n. 40), 467 (nn. 40, 43), 471, 484–485, 513, 515 (n. 7), 517–518 (n. 22), 519–520, 549 (nn. 2, 12), 554, 562, 607 (& n. 4), 608 (n. 13), 632 (n. 3), 633 (n. 7), 655 (n. 11), 669–671, 679, 685–688, 689 (nn. 1, 3), 715 (n. 7), 960 (n. 29)
Dowty, D., 6, 177 (n. 10), 178
Ducasse, C. J., 789, 791 (n. 3)
Dummett, M. A. E., 5, 126 (n. 6), *129–155*, 176 (n. 3), 254 (n. 4), 561, 562, 594, 701, 718, 720, 741 (& nn. 5–7), 742 nn. 10, 15), 743 (n. 20), 831 (n. 8), 908 (n. 3)

Eissfeldt, O., 655 (n. 14)

Enç, M., 518 (n. 29), 520, 1030 (n. 16), 1037
Ernst, T., 177 (n. 9), 178
Etchemendy, J., 206, 990 (n. 18)
Evans, G., 4–5, 6, 7, 204–205, *233–256*, 313 (n. 17), 314, 319, 322, 438, 454–455, 457 (n. 5), 458 (n. 15), 463 (n. 32), 466 (n. 38), 467 (n. 43), 468 (nn. 51, 52), 471, 541, 543, 549 (nn. 3, 7, 12, 15), 560 (n. 19), 552 (n. 26), 553 (nn. 28, 31), 554, 560, 562 (n. 1), *635–655*, *717–744*, 748, 765 (& nn. 8, 9), 766, 1029 (n. 8), 1032 (n. 20), 1037

Feigel, H., 679
Field, H., 120–121, 128 (n. 44)
Fiengo, R., 286, 314
Fillmore, C. J., 165–166, 277 (n. 1), 278
Finer, D., 1052
Fodor, J. A., 126 (nn. 7, 16), 848, 853, 966
Fodor, J. D., 126 (n. 8), 313 (n. 19), 314, 321–322, 457 (n. 7), 458 (n. 6), 462 (n. 30), 463 (n. 33), 471, *475–521*, 483, 512, 514, 520, 537–539, 549 (n. 2), 550–551 (n. 19), 551 (nn. 23, 24), 552 (n. 24), 554
Føllesdall, D., 715 (nn. 4, 7), 742 (n. 13)
Foster, J., 197 (n. 9)
Frege, G., 3, *9–30*, 34, 89–93, 100, 105, 190, 253, 268–269, 281, 306, 384–388, 404, 559, 562 (n. 1), *563–583*, 581 (n. 2), 583 (nn. 11, 13), 585–586, 592 (n. 1), 607 (n. 2), 633 (nn. 7, 8), 659, 662, 667 (n. 2), 679–680, 691 (n. 18), 693–714, 714 (n. 1), 715 (nn. 5, 6), 717–738, 741 (& n. 6), 742 (nn. 11, 18), 743 (n. 22), 742 (nn. 11, 18), 743 (n. 22), 748, 771, 775, 799 (n. 10), 809, 814 (n. 1), 822–823, 876, 880–884, 888–889, 907 (n. 2), 908 (nn. 3, 4), 910 (nn. 9, 10), 911 (n. 13), 915 (n. 29), 994, 1016, 1037
Frye, D., 1024, 1037
Fukui, N., 177 (n. 7), 178

Gazdar, G., 462 (n. 28), 471
Geach, P. T., 278, 359 (n. 2), 412 (n. 31), 457 (n. 5), 466 (n. 37), 471, 541, 544, 552 (n. 27), 554, 831 (n. 5), 910 (n. 9), 913 (n. 21), 917 (n. 41), 1004, 1030 (n. 11), 1037
Gellner, E., 654 (n. 4)
Georgeff, M., 1025, 1037
George, A., 176 (ack. n.)
Gettier, E., 139
Gilbert, M., 414 (n. 41)
Gödel, K., 255 (n. 12)
Goldman, A., 715 (n. 7)
Goldman, H., 715 (n. 7)

Goodman, N., 797 (& n. 1), 798 (n. 6), 799 (n. 8), 814 (n. 3)
Grice, H. P., 4, 6, *59–88*, 155, 321, 394–396, 408 (n. 16), 416–418, 427–436, 445, 453, 457 (n. 4), 459 (n. 18), 460 (nn. 19–21), 461 (n. 22), 462 (n. 27), 466 (n. 40), 468 (n. 49), 468 (nn. 49, 52), 471, 523, 531–532, 548, 549 (nn. 9, 17), 554, 607 (n. 3), 655 (nn. 10, 12), 751

Haegeman, L., 1029 (n. 7), 1037
Hale, K., 159, 163, 178
Halvorsen, P.-K., 312 (n. 10), 314
Hampshire, S., 466 (nn. 37, 39, 40), 471
Harman, G., 121, 126 (n. 9), 205, *257–279*, 607, 654 (n. 5), 993, 1031 (n. 18), 1037, 1041, 1052 (n. 1)
Harris, P., 1024, 1036
Heim, I., 313 (n. 18), 314, 545–546, 548, 554, 1028, 1029 (n. 6)
Hempel, C. G., 797
Higginbotham, J., xvii, 5, 6, *157–178*, 157, 159, 164, 173, 175, 178, 197 (n. 8), 287–288, 300, 302–304, 312 (nn. 3, 6, 11), 313 (n. 17), 314, 551 (n. 20), 554, 778, 993, 998, 1020, 1028, 1029 (nn. 8, 9), 1032 (n. 22), 1034 (n. 32), 1037, 1041, 1045, 1052 (n. 1), 1053
Higgins, E., 177 (n. 11), 178
Hilbert, D., 518 (n. 27), 520
Hintikka, J., 114, 126 (n. 10), 127 (n. 11), 128 (n. 4), 402, 671, 690 (n. 7), 771, 777, 831 (n. 14), 1028, 1029 (n. 5), 1033 (n. 28), 1038
Hirschbühler, P., 540, 554
Hobbs, J., 1024, 1038
Hoji, H., 207
Hornsby, J., 445–446, 449, 457 (nn. 6, 7), 471
Hornstein, N., xvi, xvii, 207, 1028, 1029 (n. 11), 1031 (n. 18), 1038
Huang, C.-T. J., 207, 299–300, 314
Humberstone, L., 765
Husserl, E., 468 (n. 54), 471

Isaacson, D., 254
Israel, D., 988

Jackendoff, R., 109, 127 (n. 12), 307, 314
Jackobson, P., 304, 314
Jaeggli, O., 284, 314
Jespersen, V., 520
Johnson, H., 461 (n. 26), 472

Kamp, H., 553 (n. 36), 554
Kant, I., 563, 738, 966

Kaplan, D., 408 (n. 10), 422–423, 457 (nn. 6, 7), 458 (n. 9, 11), 472, 505–507, 510–511, 517 (nn. 16, 18, 20–22), 518 (n. 25), 518 (n. 29), 520, 549 (n. 10), 550–551 (n. 19), 554, 608 (n. 12), 654 (n. 10), 659, 661, *669–692*, 688, 715 (nn. 6, 7), 717, 741 (n. 2), 742 (n. 16), 743 (nn. 20, 21, 31), 744 (n. 37), 748–749, 765 (& n. 12), 766, 851 (n. 5), 956 (& n. 3), 962 (n. 36), 968, 1030 (n. 13), 1038, 1053
Karttunen, L., 273, 278, 408 (n. 7), 413 (n. 35), 691 (n. 21), 852 (n. 13), 1042
Katz, J., 109–112, 117, 127 (n. 13–18), 128 (n. 42), 408 (n. 12), 411 (n. 27), 1048, 1053
Kazmi, A. A., 956
Kenny, A., 219–220, 223, 225–227, 230, 232 (nn. 1, 2, 4)
Keyser, S., 159, 163, 178
King, L., 322, 458 (n. 6), 463 (n. 33), 472, 552 (n. 24), 554
Kiss, K., 312 (n. 7), 314
Klein, E., 442, 457 (n. 5), 463 (n. 35), 472
Klima, E., 472
Kneale, W., 609–610, 633 (n. 8), 911 (n. 12)
Koopman, H., 287, 314
Kripke, S. A., 114, 127 (nn. 19, 20), 138, 321–322, *383–414*, 429, 437, 443–444, 456 (n. 2), 457 (nn. 5, 6), 462 (n. 31), 463 (n. 31), 466 (n. 38, 39), 467 (n. 40), 468 (n. 51), 472, 523, 531, 535–537, 539, 542, 458, 550 (n. 19), 553 (nn. 28, 30, 32), 554–555, 560–561, 562, 607 (n. 4), *609–634*, 635–637, 639, 641–645, 647, 649, 652, 654 (& nn. 1, 6), 655 (n. 16), 688, 742 (n. 14), 774, 851 (nn. 4, 5), 853, 936, 938, 957 (n. 10), 958 (n. 22), 961 (n. 31), 973, 984, 987, 1033 (n. 30), 1038
Kroch, A., 488, 520

Ladusaw, W., 291–292, 314
Lakoff, G., 127 (n. 21), 264, 277 (n. 1), 278, 312 (n. 4), 314, 489, 520, 848, 851 (nn. 2, 11), 852 (n. 14), 853
Langford, C. H., 782, 789–790
Lansky, A., 1025, 1037
Larson, R., xv, xvi, 5, 6, 176 (ack. n.), *179–199*, 548, 562, 778, *993–1039*, 998, 1029 (n. 5), 1030 (n. 16), 1032 (n. 22), 1038, *1041–1053*, 1041, 1043, 1052 (n. 1), 1053
Lasnik, H., 176, 313 (n. 17), 314, 1031–1032 (n. 18), 1038
Leeds, S., 860, 864, 873
Leibniz, G. W., 352, 570, 966
Leonardo, P., xvii
Lepore, E., 5, 6, *109–128*, 206, 777, 1020, 1028, 1034 (n. 32), 1038

Levin, B., 164–166, 178
Lewis, C. I., 782, 786–789, 790 (n. 2)
Lewis, D., 6, 109, 114, 127 (nn. 24, 25), 174,
    178, 255 (nn. 16, 20), 458 (nn. 11, 12),
    468 (n. 49), 472, 542, 555, 613, 631 (n. 1),
    655 (n. 12), 1033 (n. 28), 1038
Lindstrom, P., 248, 255 (n. 13)
Linsky, L., 322, 375–376, 378, 380
    (nn. 8, 9), 381 (n. 13), 385, 466 (n. 37),
    669, 689 (n. 2)
Loar, B., 765 (n. 16), 860, 865, 873
Loewer, B., 127 (n. 23), 777, 1020, 1034
    (n. 32), 1038
Ludlow, P., 207, 313 (n. 21), 321–322, 458
    (n. 6), 462 (n. 30), 463 (n. 33), 467 (n. 40),
    472, 523–555, 546, 555, 993–1039, 1003,
    1032 (n. 18), 1038, 1041–1053, 1041,
    1043, 1052 (nn. 1, 3), 1053
Lycan, W., 6, 125 (n. 1), 206, 991 (n. 21),
    998, 1038
Lyons, J., 127 (n. 26)

Marcus, R. B., 416, 472, 628, 634 (n. 15)
Martin, E., 607, 608 (n. 8)
Mates, B., 101, 107 (n. 14), 798 (n. 7), 799–
    800 (n. 12), 824, 831 (n. 10), 911–912
    (n. 15), 919–920 (n. 46)
May, R., xvi, 205, 207, 281–315, 284–286,
    288, 294, 302–304, 312 (n. 3), 313 (n. 13),
    314, 315, 489, 520, 1028, 1029 (n. 11),
    1032 (n. 22), 1039
McCawley, J. D., 127 (nn. 27, 28), 172, 176
    (ack. n.), 177 (nn. 10, 13), 178, 262, 277
    (n. 1), 278, 851 (n. 2), 853, 1042, 1053
McConnell-Ginet, S., 6, 168–169, 170, 176
    (ack. n.), 177 (nn. 8, 9), 178
McCrossin, T., 548
McDowell, J. H., 6, 153, 254, 562, 655
    (n. 15), 741, 742 (n. 9), 865, 873, 1032
    (n. 20), 1039
McGinn, C., 765 (n. 3), 766
Meinong, A. von, 324
Mill, J. S., 876–880, 884, 910 (nn. 9, 10)
Millar, R., 633 (n. 11)
Mitchell, D., 416, 456 (nn. 1, 3), 457 (n. 4),
    472
Montague, R., 6, 114–118, 121, 123–125,
    127 (n. 29–31), 203, 246, 254 (n. 9), 255
    (n. 18), 308, 315, 458 (nn. 11, 13), 472,
    517 (n. 19), 518 (n. 28), 685, 688, 777,
    835–837, 840–842, 844–847, 851
    (nn. 3, 5), 852 (n. 12), 853, 1039, 1052
    (n. 2), 1053
Moore, B., 1024, 1038
Moore, C., 1024, 1037
Moore, G. E., 346, 412 (n. 30), 460 (n. 20),
    743 (n. 34), 772, 789–790, 833

Moravcsik, J., 715 (n. 7), 956
Morgan, J., 520
Mostowski, A., 248, 255 (n. 13)

Nagel, R., 127 (n. 17)
Neale, S., xvii, 319, 321–322, 415–474, 458
    (n. 6), 462 (n. 30), 463 (n. 33), 467 (n. 40),
    472, 523–555, 546, 548 (n. 1), 549
    (nn. 6, 12, 15), 552 (n. 26), 553
    (nn. 29, 31, 33–35), 555, 1028, 1032
    (n. 18), 1038
Nozick, R., 633 (n. 8)
Nunberg, G., 508, 520

Olsen, D., 1024, 1036

Parsons, T., 164, 178, 206, 308, 315, 542,
    545–546, 1032 (n. 24), 1039, 1045, 1053
Partee, B. H., 6, 109, 118, 120–121, 127
    (n. 32), 128 (nn. 42, 43), 408 (n. 8), 472,
    519 (n. 31), 520, 549 (n. 2), 555, 608 (n. 8),
    845, 851 (n. 8), 853, 1033 (n. 26), 1047
Peacocke, C. A. B., 447–448, 457 (nn. 6, 7),
    458 (n. 6), 467 (n. 43), 473, 746–748, 765
    (& nn. 2, 7, 9, 11, 16), 766 (n. 26), 766,
    773–774, 777, 833–853, 909 (n. 7), 1039,
    1053
Perry, J., 6, 457 (n. 7), 458 (n. 6), 463 (n. 33),
    468 (n. 55), 470, 516 (n. 14), 517 (n. 17),
    518 (n. 23), 520, 548, 549 (n. 12), 659,
    661, 680, 693–715, 717–718, 724, 726,
    733–735, 737–740, 741 (nn. 1, 3), 743
    (nn. 24, 27, 31), 744 (nn. 35, 36), 747–749,
    765 (& nn. 4, 5, 8–10), 766, 775, 928, 955,
    957 (n. 7), 960 (n. 26), 963–991, 963, 990
    (nn. 16, 17), 1016, 1036
Peters, S., 6
Pietroski, P., 1028
Plantinga, A., 910 (n. 10)
Plato, 3
Platts, M., 6
Postal, P., 127 (n. 18), 277 (n. 1), 278 (n. 6),
    278, 489, 520
Potts, T., 128 (n. 33)
Prince, E., 520
Putnam, H., 6, 162, 798–799 (n. 7), 901, 916
    (n. 35), 1033 (n. 30), 1039

Quine, W. V. O., 4, 49–57, 95, 98, 106
    (nn. 7, 11), 107 (n. 15), 107 (n. 18), 130,
    149, 162, 178, 249, 255 (n. 17), 278 (n. 8),
    279, 412 (n. 30), 467 (n. 44), 468 (n. 49),
    473, 515 (n. 8), 520, 559–560, 592 (n. 2),
    594–595, 598–599, 607 (n. 3), 608 (n. 10),
    628, 662, 679, 682, 688, 691 (n. 26), 765
    (n. 19), 767, 773, 782, 786–787, 790 (n. 1),
    801–815, 820–823, 825–826, 831 (nn. 4, 9),

847, 850 (n. 1), 851 (n. 6), 853, 876, 887,
902–904, 909 (n. 8), 915 (n. 34), 916
(n. 34), 917 (nn. 39–41), 986, 1034 (n. 30),
1039, 1052 (n. 2), 1053

Radford, A., 1029 (n. 7), 1039
Rawls, J., 461 (n. 24), 473
Recanati, F., 322, 449, 457 (n. 3), 463–
465 (n. 36), 473, 548, 661
Reichenbach, H., 226–230, 232 (n. 10),
518 (n. 27), 520, 815 (n. 6)
Reinhart, T., 287, 312 (n. 2), 315, 552 (n. 25),
555
Richard, M., 778, 940–942, 956, 958 (n. 15),
959 (nn. 23, 24), 962 (n. 36), 973, 984–
985, 987, 1016, 1028 (n. 1), 1029 (n. 10),
1033 (n. 29), 1039
Robinson, H. W., 654 (n. 9)
Rodman, R., 489, 520
Ross, J., 277 (n. 1), 278 (n. 6), 279, 413
(n. 35), 848, 853, 1042, 1053
Rouveret, A., 283, 315
Rundle, B., 416, 457 (n. 7), 473
Russell, B., 203, 206, 209, 281, 319–322,
323–333, 336–340, 342–345, 347–349,
352, 355, 358–359, 361–364, 370–374,
376, 378–379, 380 (n. 5), 383–395,
397–400, 404, 406, 415, 417, 419–421,
425, 444, 446–447, 449–450, 453, 458
(n. 3), 473, 523–531, 533, 535, 537,
540–541, 543–545, 548 (& n. 1), 549
(nn. 4–6, 8–10), 555, 559–561, 562, 594–
596, 598–599, 607 (n. 3), 610, 628, 633
(nn. 7, 8), 634 (n. 14), 669, 671–674, 690
(nn. 8, 9, 11, 12), 723, 742 (n. 8), 789, 791
(n. 3), 809, 814 (n. 2), 815 (n. 7), 876, 881–
883, 888–890, 908 (nn. 3, 5), 911 (n. 13),
915 (n. 29), 919 (n. 45), 1016, 1039
Ryle, G., 255 (n. 22), 654 (n. 4)

Saarinen, E., 128 (n. 34)
Sadock, J., 514 (n. 4), 520, 549 (n. 9), 555
Safir, K., 287, 315
Sag, I., 292, 313 (n. 19), 315, 321–322, 457
(n. 7), 458 (n. 6), 462 (n. 30), 463 (n. 33),
471, 475–521, 496–497, 508, 514, 516
(n. 11), 521, 537–540, 548, 549 (n. 2), 550
(nn. 18, 19), 551 (nn. 23, 24), 552 (n. 24),
554, 555
Sainsbury, R. M., 206, 442, 457 (n. 5), 463
(n. 34), 466 (nn. 38, 39), 467 (n. 44), 473
Saito, M., 1031–1032 (n. 18), 1038
Salmon, N., 322, 446, 457 (n. 5), 467 (n. 41),
468 (n. 52), 473, 778, 947, 956, 959–960
(n. 24), 960 (n. 27), 961 (n. 30), 963, 1016,
1029 (n. 9), 1039

Sanchez-Valencia, V., 207
Sandu, G., 1029 (n. 5), 1038
Scheffler, I., 226, 232 (n. 8), 772, 793–800,
814 (n. 3), 825–826, 831 (n. 12)
Schein, B., xvii, 164, 178, 206, 1028, 1030
(n. 15), 1045, 1053
Schieber, S., 1029 (n. 6), 1032 (n. 21)
Schiffer, S., xvii, 6, 67–68, 70, 87, 88,
322, 459 (n. 18), 473, 655 (nn. 12, 13),
765 (nn. 15, 17, 18), 767, 855–873
Scott, D., 851 (n. 5)
Searle, J. R., 72–74, 88, 457 (n. 4), 457
(n. 5–7), 462 (n. 31), 466 (nn. 38, 39),
468 (n. 55), 473, 559–560, 585–592, 611–
612, 631 (n. 2), 633 (n. 8), 654 (n. 4), 774,
911 (n. 13)
Segal, G., xv, 5, 6, 176 (ack. n.), 179–199,
778, 993, 998, 1021–1023, 1028, 1029
(n. 5), 1032 (n. 22), 1035 (n. 33), 1038,
1039, 1041, 1052 (n. 1), 1053
Sellars, W., 448–449, 454, 467 (nn. 44, 46),
468 (n. 52), 473, 825, 831 (n. 11)
Sells, P., 1028 (n. 4), 1039
Seuren, P. A. M., 277 (n. 1), 279
Sharvey, R., 322
Sher, G., 1032 (n. 22), 1038
Shoemaker, S., 379, 743 (n. 32)
Sim, D., 1032 (n. 23), 1039
Sloat, C., 608 (n. 8)
Smiley, T., 379
Smith, N., 459 (n. 18)
Smullyan, A. F., 278 (n. 7), 279
Smullyan, R. M., 279
Soames, S., 322, 454, 457 (n. 5), 462 (n. 28),
468 (n. 48), 468 (n. 52), 473, 548, 775,
921–962, 963, 1016, 1029 (n. 9), 1038,
1039
Sommers, F., 553 (n. 31), 555
Sosa, E., 654 (n. 4)
Sperber, D., 458 (n. 16), 460 (nn. 18, 19),
461 (n. 23), 467 (n. 46), 473
Sportiche, D., 287, 314
Sproat, R., 164, 177 (n. 14), 178
Stalnaker, R., 128 (n. 35), 169, 408 (n. 8),
457 (n. 7), 473, 661, 777, 844, 851 (n. 9),
1033 (n. 28), 1039
Stampe, D. W., 67
Steizel, E., 831 (n. 14)
Stern, J., 508, 521
Stich, S., 458 (n. 6), 463 (n. 33), 473, 549
(n. 2), 555
Strawson, P. F., 67–68, 88, 154, 254 (n. 11),
319–320, 335–359, 361–364, 367, 370–
376, 380 (nn. 5, 7, 9, 10), 381 (nn. 11, 13),
383–384, 404, 433, 473, 607 (n. 5), 621–
623, 633 (nn. 8, 10), 767

Tarski, A., 94–95, 98–101, 106 (n. 6), 119,
    123, 128 (n. 36), 134, 197 (n. 1), 229, 235,
    269–270, 306, 421, 447, 449, 454, 474,
    521, 523, 541–542, 544, 546, 593, 607
    (n. 2), 654 (n. 3), 664, 667 (n. 3), 745,
    765 (n. 13), 803, 818–820, 822–823, 825,
    830 (n. 2)
Taylor, B., 254, 485, 746, 755–756,
    762–763, 765 (& nn. 1, 18, 21), 766
    (nn. 25, 27), 767
Thomason, R., 118, 121–122, 124–125, 128
    (n. 37), 169, 177 (n. 14), 178, 844, 851
    (nn. 5, 9), 852 (n. 13), 853
Thompson, S. A., 514 (n. 6), 521
Toman, J., 313 (n. 16), 315
Twain, M., 963

Urmson, J. O., 66

Van Fraassen, B., 114, 127 (n. 38)
Vanlehn, K., 521
Vendler, Z., 246, 468 (n. 49), 474, 597, 608
    (n. 9)
Vergnaud, J. R., 283
Vermazen, B., 107 (n. 13), 109, 128 (n. 39)
Vlach, F., 164, 178
Von Wright, G. H., 224–226, 228, 232 (n. 6)

Wall, R., 6
Wallace, J., 125 (n. 1), 262, 278 (n. 7), 279,
    607, 741 (n. 7)
Weinstein, S., 107 (n. 16), 176 (ack. n.), 659,
    663–667, 767
Wettstein, H., 322, 414 (n. 41), 449–455, 457
    (n. 7), 467 (n. 41), 468 (n. 52), 474, 659
Wheeler, S. C., 254 (n. 5)
White, M., 789–790, 797 (n. 1), 798 (n. 6)
Whitehead, A. N., 814 (n. 2), 815 (n. 7)
Wiggins, D., 457 (n. 5), 466 (n. 39), 474,
    765 (n. 13), 767
Wilder, C., 1052
Williams, E., 176, 292, 315, 496–497, 516
    (n. 11), 521, 1029 (n. 7), 1037
Wilson, D., 458 (nn. 6, 16), 460 (nn. 18, 19),
    461 (n. 23), 467 (n. 46), 473
Wilson, G., xvii, 322, 440, 463 (n. 33), 474,
    476, 521, 549 (nn. 2, 12)
Wilson, N., 917 (n. 40)
Wittgenstein, L., 3–4, *31–47*, 203, *209–215*,
    458 (n. 17), 504, 521, 592 (n. 3), 639, 738,
    743 (n. 33), 990 (n. 18)
Wright, C., 7

Yu, P., 125 (n. 1)

Ziff, P., 6, 615

Index of Subjects

Action(s), 44–45, 78, 164–173, 217–232, 253, 711–712, 1024
  as the bringing about of an event, 225–226
  as events, 222–228, 252
  and intention, 220–221, 223–224, 226, 231–232
  logical form of sentences about, 217–232, 270–273
  quantification over (Davidson), 220, 227–232, 271–273
Agent/agency, 175, 220–223, 225, 231–232, 253
Ambiguity, 461 (n. 22), 464–465 (n. 36)
  in definite article, 416, 441, 463 (n. 36)
  lexical, 418, 426, 433, 461 (n. 22), 465 (n. 36), 477, 500
  pragmatic explanation of semantic ambiguity, 433–436, 457 (n. 7)
  semantic, 392–394, 401–403, 406–407 (& n. 3), 408 (n. 14), 410 (n. 22), 411 (n. 28), 412 (n. 29), 413 (n. 35), 418–419, 433–434, 337, 441, 443–444, 457 (nn. 5, 7), 463–465 (n. 36), 467 (n. 40), 511–512, 536
  syntactic, 266, 406, 461 (n. 22), 477
Analyticity, 103, 163, 563, 585–586
Anaphora, 301–303, 305, 419, 426, 455, 458 (n. 15), 515 (n. 10), 524, 540–548, 553 (n. 28, 32), 764
Apprehension (Frege), 25–26, 28–29, 30 (nn. 5, 6)
Artificial language, 204, 246. *See also* Formal/formalized language
Assertion, 13–14, 348–349, 364–365, 388, 396, 448, 502–503, 504, 574, 577, 583 (nn. 12, 19), 922–925, 929, 931–939, 949, 952, 962 (n. 42), 1005. *See also* Utterance(s)
  content of, 752–753, 756–758, 763, 765 (n. 18), 906

of existence, 347, 358, 399, 442, 527–529, 533–534
  grounds of, 527–529, 533–535, 550 (n. 18)

Begriffsschrift (Frege), 575, 582 (n. 4)
Belief attribution, 731, 771, 794–795, 888–896, 903–904, 906–907, 913 (nn. 22, 23), 993, 935–936, 939, 940–941, 943, 958–959 (n. 22), 959–960 (n. 24), 974–975, 985–986, 1023–1026, 1034–1035 (n. 34). *See also* Thoughts (Frege), individuation of
Belief reports, 771, 860–864, 875, 944–945, 954, 960 (n. 24), 963–988, 989 (nn. 4, 11), 990 (nn. 14, 16), 991 (nn. 22, 23)
  content of, 965–968, 971–972, 974–976, 980–985, 987–988, 990 (n. 14)
  and context, 974–977, 985, 987–988, 991 (n. 25)
  Davidsonian analysis of, 860–863, 868–869
  and direct reference, 964, 976, 978–980, 982
  and disquotational principle (Kripke), 887–890, 895, 903, 905, 920 (n. 46), 936, 984
  Fregean account of, 986–987
  and ideas (Crimmmins, Perry), 967–975, 988, 990 (n. 16)
  logical form of, 862–864
  and notions (Crimmins, Perry), 967–975, 978–983, 986–988, 990 (n. 16), 991 (n. 21)
  and opacity, 964, 974, 989
  pragmatic features/principles, 963, 985, 988
  and principle of translation (Kripke), 887–890, 899–900, 903, 905, 936, 984
  with proper names, 877–880, 882–884, 887–907, 909 (n. 7), 918 (n. 43), 919 (nn. 45, 46), 959 (n. 24), 973, 980, 983, 986

Belief reports (cont.)
propositional analysis of, 781–782, 789, 862, 964–967
and reference failure, 979–980
and semantic innocence, 964, 990 (n. 14)
and semantic theory, 987–988
sentential analysis of, 855, 860, 862
and substitutivity, 964–965, 973, 985, 989 (n. 3)
and unarticulated constituents, 974–978, 980–981, 988, 990 (n. 17)
Belief sentences, 779–782, 788–790, 877–907, 913 (n. 23), 915 (n. 33), 920 (n. 46), 925, 930–937, 941, 952–953, 963–988
and *de re–de dicto* distinction, 878, 909 (nn. 7, 8), 913 (n. 22)
and failure of extensionality, 809–810
with proper names, 877–880, 882–884, 887–907, 909 (n. 7), 918 (n. 43), 919 (nn. 45, 46), 959 (n. 24), 973, 980, 983, 986
and referential opacity vs. transparency, 804–814, 833–834, 906–907, 909 (n. 8), 919 (n. 45), 964
and referential position, 808, 810–814
and scope, 806, 812–813, 1031–1032 (n. 18)
and substitutivity, 809–811, 876–884, 888–901, 904–907, 909 (n. 7), 937–938, 940–941
and translation, 903, 936–937
Brain or brain states, 37–39, 193
and correlation with mental states, 627–628
and intention, 504, 517 (n. 17)

Case grammar, 165
Case properties, 284
Case theory, 283
Causes, 45
Central meaning (Grice), 61
Cognition, 194. *See also* Understanding
Cognitive psychology, xiii
Cognitive science, xiv, 5
Communication, 3, 17, 28, 50, 61, 70, 97, 131, 179, 196, 348, 438, 689, 746, 751–754, 759–761, 775
Connotation, 588, 881, 910–911 (n. 11)
Consciousness, 18, 20, 22–24, 45
Content
of consciousness, 18–20, 22, 24
empirical, 49
of sentences, 13–16, 19
Context principle (Frege), 93
Conventional implicature (Grice), 59, 61, 460 (n. 20)
Convention T, 94, 235, 250

Conversational implicature (Grice), 59, 395, 409 (n. 19), 429–436, 460 (n. 20), 462 (n. 27), 468 (n. 54), 549 (n. 9)
generalized, 432, 434–436, 462 (n. 28)
and justification requirement, 431, 436, 463 (n. 32)
particularized, 432, 436, 462 (n. 28)
pragmatic rules of, 436
Cooperative principle (Grice), 59, 429–431, 503
maxim of manner, 430, 434
maxim of quality, 430, 436, 442–443
maxim of quantity, 430, 436
maxim of relation, 430, 442–443
Criteria, 32
of identity, 591
for use of proper names, 590–591

Deep (D) structure (Chomsky), 205, 283–284, 287, 406, 413 (n. 35), 1028 (n. 4)
as logical form, 257–277
and quantifiers, 263–266
and trees, 257–261, 277 (n. 2)
Definite article, 347, 356–357, 406, 440, 575
ambiguity in, 416, 441, 463 (n. 36)
Definite descriptions, 253, 281, 288, 306, 323–333, 335–414, 415–470, 501, 504–509, 524–525, 527, 535, 559, 585, 589, 591, 594–595, 660, 835, 877, 906, 931, 956 (n. 7), 957 (n. 7)
and anaphora, 419, 426, 455, 458 (n. 15), 542–544, 547, 553 (n. 28, 32)
and context of utterance, 415, 448–450, 454–456, 464–465 (n. 36), 468 (n. 46), 468 (n. 54), 505–513, 517 (n. 21)
and *de re–de dicto* distinction, 387–390, 419, 456 (n. 2), 510–511, 535–536, 878
improper/incomplete, 321, 384, 407 (n. 4), 416, 419, 442, 447–455, 467 (nn. 42, 43), 468 (n. 47), 468 (n. 54), 544–545
introduced, 319–322
and knowledge by acquaintance vs. knowledge by description, 319–320, 524–525
and lexical ambiguity, 418
and linguistic meaning vs. semantic value, 420–428, 463–465 (n. 36), 467 (n. 46)
and misdescription, 444–446
in nonextensional contexts, 419
nonreferring use of, 362–363, 370–371, 437, 468 (n. 55)
nonuniquely referring use of, 358–359
as object-dependent propositions, 420, 423–426, 439–441, 442–443, 445, 447, 453, 456, 463–465 (nn. 32, 36)
as object-independent propositions, 423–424

primary vs. secondary occurrences of
(Russell), 332–333
and proposition meant vs. proposition
expressed, 439–440, 443–456, 456 (n. 3),
458 (n. 16), 463–465 (n. 36), 466 (nn. 37,
38), 467 (n. 41), 468 (nn. 46, 47), 525,
549 (n. 11)
and quantifier scope, 388, 390, 476–478,
482, 485–501, 506, 509–513, 516 (n. 12),
518 (n. 28), 535–536, 878
reference of, 323–333, 335–359, 361–381,
447, 504
referential interpretation of, 320–321, 335–
359, 415–420, 437–470, 523, 550 (n. 17),
553 (n. 29)
referential vs. attributive use of (Donellan),
321, 350, 361–381, 384, 386–393, 396–
397, 400–401, 403, 405–407, 408 (n. 10),
409 (nn. 20, 22), 410 (nn. 22, 25), 411
(nn. 27, 28), 412 (nn. 29, 31, 32), 413
(nn. 34, 35), 414 (n. 35), 416–417, 449–
450, 456 (n. 3), 457 (nn. 5, 6), 484–485,
513, 632 (n. 4), 669–671, 679–680, 682,
686, 990 (n. 15)
rigid/nonrigid, 389–390, 406, 408
(nn. 9, 10), 446
and scope islands (Fodor & Sag), 489–500,
513, 515 (n. 10)
and semantic ambiguity, 392–394, 401–
403, 406–407, 407 (n. 3), 408 (n. 14), 411
(n. 28), 412 (n. 29), 413 (n. 35), 418–419,
433–434, 437, 441, 443–444, 457 (nn. 5, 7),
463–465 (n. 36), 467 (n. 40), 511–512, 536
simple vs. complex designation of (Kripke),
396–397, 401, 405, 411 (nn. 27, 28)
and singular vs. general propositions, 320–
321, 524–525, 527, 535
and speaker's intention, 374, 429–430, 439,
446, 450–452, 456, 459 (n. 18), 504, 535,
549 (n. 12)
and speaker's reference vs. semantic reference, 395–407, 407 (n. 1), 410, (n. 22),
411 (nn. 27, 28), 412 (nn. 31, 32), 413
(nn. 22, 33)
and statements (Donellan), 376–378, 393,
669
uniquely referring use of, 340–357, 453,
501
unitary-quantificational analysis of, 415–
420, 437–470, 523–524, 527, 544–545,
548 (n. 1), 723 (see also Descriptions,
theory of [Russell])
Definition, 352
immanent vs. transcendent (Evans), 234–
235, 240
ostensive, 31–32, 42

Demonstrate/demonstration, 559, 677, 680,
684–685, 687, 690 (n. 15), 763–764, 1008,
1030–1031 (n. 17)
Demonstratives, 349, 406, 415, 421–423,
453–454, 458 (n. 9), 463–465 (n. 36), 475,
481, 501–502, 518 (n. 24), 529, 589, 594–
595, 599–600, 603, 608 (n. 11), 654, 659–
661, 663–667, 673, 677–679, 683–689,
690 (nn. 14, 15, 17), 692 (n. 32), 693–715,
717–744, 745–766, 920 (n. 46), 934, 968,
1007–1009
and ambiguity, 682, 684–685, 687
anaphoric use of, 764
bare, 745–747, 754–755, 757–758
and character, role, constant meaning,
659–661, 683–684, 698–700, 717–718,
739–740, 747–748, 968
and communication, 751–754, 759–760
complex, 745–747, 752, 754–755, 757–763
content of, 659–661, 668, 679, 683–685,
687–688
and context of utterance, 659, 664, 677–
678, 682, 684–686, 688, 697–698, 713–
714, 718, 728, 740, 763
demonstrative use of, 679, 682, 686
denotation/designation/referent of, 667,
679, 685, 740, 763–764, 766 (n. 23)
determination of denotation/reference of,
681, 685, 755, 761
and failure to denote, 686
formal semantics of, 103–104, 400, 507–
513, 659, 663–667, 746–766, 831 (n. 15)
Frege's treatment of, 16–17, 697–714,
715–744, 748
and interpreted logical forms (ILFs), 993,
1007–1009, 1030 (nn. 14, 16, 17)
meaning of, 659–660, 683–684
in modal contexts, 685–686, 688
perceptual, 767, 751–754, 762–764
and quantification, 685, 745–746, 755–757,
761–764, 766 (n. 28)
as rigid designators, 659
sense of, 660, 679, 681–682, 717, 726–744
and speaker's intention, 685–687, 751–754
structure of demonstrative expressions,
661
uniqueness supposition of, 690 (n. 14)
Denotation, 105 (n. 3), 111, 119, 143–145,
166, 371, 450
of a definite description, 507–511, 525
formal rules of, 507–511, 517 (n. 21), 605–
606
of an indefinite description, 508–511
of an indexical, 505–506
of a name, 270, 506, 588
vs. referring, 319, 371

De re–de dicto distinction, 387–390, 419,
    456 (n. 2), 482, 509–511, 535–537, 878,
    909 (nn. 7, 8), 913 (n. 22), 1031 (n. 18)
Descriptions, 188, 323–333, 335–359
 as arguments (Frege), 281
 ambiguity of, or ambiguous, 321, 326
Descriptions, theory of (Russell), 323–333,
    336–340, 342–345, 347–349, 352, 355,
    358–359, 361–364, 370–374, 376, 378–
    379, 380 (n. 5), 383–395, 397–400, 404,
    406, 415–420, 425–426, 447, 455, 465
    (n. 36), 525, 527, 544, 549 (n. 6), 669, 919
    (n. 45). *See also* Definite descriptions,
    unitary-quantificational analysis of
 introduced, 319–320
Descriptive functions (Russell), 323, 333
Designator/designation, 235, 395–396, 563,
    567, 583 (n. 12). *See also* Denotation;
    Reference
 simple vs. complex use of, 396–397, 401,
    405, 413 (n. 33)
Determiners, 206, 207, 263, 476, 502, 514
    (n. 2)
Disquotational principle (Kripke), 885–890,
    895, 899, 902–906, 913 (nn. 22, 23), 914
    (n. 28), 916 (n. 37), 919–920 (n. 46), 936,
    984
 as test for disbelief, 886, 914 (n. 24)
Dreams, dreaming, 21

Embedded/subordinate clauses, 189, 257,
    262, 264, 266–270, 537–540, 571–582
 abstract noun, 571–576
 adjectival, 571, 577
 adverbial, 571, 575–577
 conditional, 576–580
Empirical semantics, 57
Entailment, 204–205, 219–220, 238
Epistemology, 129, 209, 246, 645, 671
 strong vs. weak accounts of knowledge
    (Hintikka), 402
Essence, 613
Ethics, 461 (n. 24)
Events, 163–175, 217–232, 247, 252–253,
    434, 1045, 1047
 quantification over, 227–232, 271–272
Existence, 326, 332, 353
Experience, 18, 23–24
Extension, 111, 115, 671, 779, 781, 823, 835,
    926, 948, 950

Facts, 26, 247
Fiction and fictional discourse, 346, 722–
    723, 742 (n. 11)
Folk psychology, 1024

Formal/formalized language, 98–99, 204,
    389
Formal semantics, 100, 103, 107
    (nn. 12, 13), 253, 281
Formal validity, 233–254
Functions (Frege), 253

Game-theoretic semantics, 126 (n. 6)
Generative grammar, 206, 283
Generative semantics, 164, 172
Grammar, 283, 295, 310, 324, 351, 461
    (n. 24)
 generative, 206, 283
 of natural language, 281–282
 phrase-structure, 106 (n. 4), 107 (n. 13), 251
 transformational, 106 (n. 4),107 (n. 13),
    257, 282, 840, 851 (n. 6)
 universal, 193–195
 Wittgenstein on, 36–40, 45–46
Grammatical form, 203, 205, 297
 vs. logical form , 337–339
Grammatical representation, 282, 294
Grammatical theory, 206, 296

Homonymity, 164–166

'I', self, 23–24, 705–712, 733–741, 744
    (n. 37), 920 (n. 46)
Ideas vs. thoughts (Frege), 11, 17–25, 565–
    567, 734
Identity, 237, 327, 357, 397, 591
 law of, 329
 psychophysical, 627–628
 substitutivity of identities, 267–269, 801–
    802, 809–811
Identity statements, 397, 585–587, 592, 678
 contingent vs. necessary, 585, 626–631
 involving names, 563–564, 581–582, 627–
    631, 653
Imagination, 34, 42
Implication
 vs. assertion (Strawson), 348
 vs. logical entailment (Strawson), 345–347,
    355, 370–371
Indefinite descriptions, 323–333, 356–357,
    412 (n. 32), 414 (n. 40), 458 (n. 7), 463
    (n. 33), 475–519, 688, 958 (n. 20)
 and anaphora, 515 (n. 10), 524, 540–548
 and context of utterance, 505, 508–509,
    547
 denotation rules of, 508–511
 and *de re–de dicto* distinction, 482, 509–
    510, 537
 descriptive content of, 485, 487, 489, 505,
    513, 514 (n. 5), 545–546

formal semantics of, 505–513
introduced, 319–322
and lexical ambiguity, 477, 500
and negation, 486–487
and pragmatic explanation, 476, 480
and proposition expressed vs. proposition
  meant, 523, 525, 528–534
and quantifier-scope ambiguity, 475–478,
  482–483, 485–501, 504, 509–513, 515
  (nn. 9, 10), 516 (nn. 12, 13), 524, 535–540,
  552 (nn. 21, 22) (see also Indefinite
  descriptions, and scope islands)
referential vs. quantificational interpretation of, 320–321, 475–519, 523–553
referential interpretation of, vs. referential
  use of, 528–532
referential interpretation of, vs. specific use
  of, 532–534
referential interpretation of, vs. definite use
  of, 534–535
and scope islands (Fodor & Sag), 489–497,
  499–500, 513, 537–540, 552 (n. 24)
semantic ambiguity of, 475–478, 484–485,
  500, 523, 530, 532
and singular vs. general propositions, 524–
  525, 529, 531–534, 536, 550 (n. 19), 552
  (n. 24)
and speaker's intention, 484, 504, 516–517
  (nn. 14, 22), 528–534, 536, 549 (n. 12),
  550 (n. 18)
syntactic ambiguity of, 477
uniqueness implications of, 544–546
and verb-phrase (VP) deletion, 477, 496–
  500, 516 (n. 12), 540
Indexicals, 342, 415, 420–426, 447, 453–455,
  458 (nn. 9, 16), 463–465 (n. 36), 661, 688,
  717
formal semantics of, 505–507
in propositional-attitude contexts, 920
  (n. 46), 925 926, 934–935, 959 (n. 24),
  977
Indirect discourse/speech, 63, 786, 793–797,
  799 (nn. 10, 11), 817–830, 903–904, 931–
  937. See also Quotation
content of, 863–865, 867–871, 872 (n. 4)
and context, 796, 937
Davidsonian/paratactic analysis of, 826–
  830, 855–871, 872 (nn. 2, 3)
inscriptional theory of (Scheffler), 825–826
and intensional isomorphism (Carnap),
  793–797, 798–799 (n. 7), 799–800 (n. 12)
L-equivalence of (Carnap), 780–790, 794–
  797
logical form of, 817–821, 823, 831 (n. 13),
  855–857, 859, 861, 872 (n. 4), 873 (n. 5)

and primary vs. secondary occurrence of
  singular term, 865–867, 873 (n. 5)
propositional theory of, 822–823, 856
quotational theory of, 802–805, 820–822,
  825–827
relational analysis of, 855–857, 871–872
sentential analysis of, 856, 859, 867, 871
and synonymy, 793, 797, 798 (n. 6), 799
  (n. 11), 824
and T-theory of meaning, 818–822, 825,
  863, 870
and translation/interpretation, 799–800
  (n. 12), 822–824, 936–937
Inference, 233–254, 818–819, 825
detachment inference, 237–239, 243–244,
  245
in natural language, 297
structurally valid, 233–254
substitution inference, 238
Infinitival-clause separation, 261–262, 266–
  267
Inner world (Frege), 17–18, 21–22, 25–27
Intention, 220–221
and action, 220–221, 223–224, 226, 231–
  232
M-intentions (Grice), 77–81
speaker's, 59–88, 374, 429–430, 437–438,
  446, 450–452, 456, 459 (n. 18), 484, 504,
  516–517 (nn. 14, 22), 528–536, 549 (n. 12),
  550 (n. 18), 599, 602, 637, 641, 643–646,
  648–649, 651–652, 680, 685–687, 701,
  753–754
Intensions, 111, 115, 118, 247, 308, 671, 774,
  779, 781–790, 823, 835, 840, 842, 845,
  863, 926, 947–950, 972
intensional isomorphism (Carnap), 782–
  790, 793–797, 798–799 (n. 7)
intensional sentences, 779, 781
intensional structure, 782–790
Interpretation, 32–34, 37, 196
principle of charity in, 98, 196, 638, 824,
  917 (n. 40)
radical, 98, 824
Interpretational semantics (Evans), 243,
  245–253
Interpreted logical forms (ILFs)
and attitude/belief ascription, 993, 1023–
  1026, 1034–1035 (n. 34)
and clausal complementation, 1042–1052
and demonstratives, 993, 1007–1009,
  1030 (nn. 14, 16, 17)
and empty proper names, 1010–1013
and equivalence of attitude reports, 1002–
  1010, 1018–1023, 1034 (nn. 32, 33), 1035
  (nn. 34, 36)

Interpreted logical forms (ILFs) (cont.)
and intensional transitive constructions,
1041–1052
and iterated attitude reports, 993, 1013–1015
and lexical axioms, 999, 1014, 1020
and object dependence/independence,
1010–1012, 1035 (n. 34)
and passive constructions, 1049–1051
and propositional attitudes, 776–777, 993–
1028, 1028 (nn. 1, 3), 1029–1030 (n. 11),
1030 (n. 12), 1031–1032 (n. 18), 1032
(n. 24), 1033 (n. 28), 1034 (nn. 33, 34),
1035 (nn. 34, 35), 1036 (n. 36), 1041–1042
and quantifier scope, 997, 1011, 1031–1032
(nn. 18, 22)
recursive definition of, 999, 1001
and semantic axioms, 999, 1045–1046
and substitutivity, 993–994, 1005–1006,
1014, 1031 (n. 18)
Intuition
grammatical/syntactic, 432
linguistic, 392, 401–404, 406
semantic, 412 (n. 30), 432

Judgement (Frege), 13, 24, 28, 29 (n. 1), 570,
576, 582, 583 (n. 10)

Knowledge, 22, 25, 140, 144, 563
by acquaintance vs. by description
(Russell), 319–320, 524–525, 660, 680,
914 (n. 29)
a priori, 614, 620, 623 (n. 4), 879
causal theory of, 246
of a language, 95–99, 112, 116, 125, 131–
155, 157–158, 179, 187, 191, 311, 426
of meaning, 131–132, 137–140, 161–162,
187–197, 348, 424, 560, 719
of meaning vs. knowledge of fact, 162
theory of (see Epistemology)

Language acquisition/learning, 4, 50–51, 89,
131, 158, 161, 195–196, 230, 311, 461
(n. 26), 679, 689, 912 (n. 18)
Language games (Wittgenstein), 46
Language mastery, 135, 146–148, 152–153,
157–158, 179, 728, 1023
Language of thought, 194, 971, 1034 (n. 33)
Laws
of logic, 190–191
of mathematics, 15
of thought (Frege), 9–10
L-equivalence (Carnap), 780–790, 794–797
Lexical ambiguity, 418, 426, 433, 461
(n. 22), 465 (n. 36), 477, 500
Linguistic competence, 4–5, 677–678, 952.
See also Language mastery

Linguistic form, 281–282, 284, 310
Linguistic rules/conventions, 351, 412
(n. 30), 585–587
Linguistic theory, xiv, 161–162, 205, 266,
294, 404, 1003
Logic, 9, 103–104, 238, 262–263, 295, 324–
326, 352–353, 433, 595, 600
applied, 352
deontic, 102
erotetic, 102
first-order, 204, 444, 998
formal, 352
free, 608 (n. 15)
imperative, 102
intensional, 123, 670, 673, 772–774, 835
intuitionistic, 238
many-valued, 254 (n. 12)
mathematical, 258
modal, 102
natural, 204
philosophical, 203
predicate, 262, 835, 846
of relations, 262
and semantic theory, 190–191
tense, 104, 519 (n. 30)
Logical consequence, 240, 249, 297, 819–821
Logical constants, 236, 237, 241, 247, 249,
252, 254 (n. 4), 255 (n. 19), 819
Logical entailment, 204
vs. implication (Strawson), 345–347, 355,
370–371
Logical equivalence, 253, 786
Logical form, 203–205, 210, 214, 218–219,
236, 240, 249, 311, 831 (n. 3)
of action sentences, 217–232, 270–273
of causal sentences, 270–273
and deep structure, 257–277
vs. grammatical form, 339
of indirect discourse, 817–821, 823, 831
(n. 13), 855–857, 859, 861, 872 (n. 4), 873
(n. 5)
of natural/ordinary language, 203–206,
281–311, 359
of quantified sentences, 284–310
of sentences about propositional attitudes,
267–270, 855, 859, 1008
of sentences containing descriptions, 323–
333, 355–359
Logical Form (LF), 205, 206, 282, 284–287,
290, 293–311, 312 (n. 4), 997–998, 1000,
1009, 1028 (n. 4), 1031 (n. 18). See also
Interpreted logical forms (ILFs)
movement, 287, 293, 299–300, 304, 306–
308, 310–311
representations of quantified sentences,
284–310

Logical inference, 204–206
Logical structure, 210, 230, 835, 954–955

Machines, 46
Mathematics, 15, 34, 333, 352, 575
Meaning, 31–35, 38–42, 49, 53–57, 89–105,
    129–155, 157–176, 459 (n. 18), 790, 818,
    830
  of action sentences, 217–232
  austere vs. robust/rich theories of
    (Dummett), 5, 153–154
  of demonstratives, 659–660, 683–684
  descriptive (Strawson), 353, 355–356
  disagreements about, vs. disagreements
    about truth, 148–152
  of evaluative sentences/words, 101
  holism about, 93, 146–153
  of identity statements, 357–358
  knowledge of, 131–132, 137–140, 161–162,
    187–197, 348, 424, 560, 719
  linguistic, vs. semantic value, 420–428,
    463–465 (n. 36), 467 (n. 46)
  modest and full-blooded theories of
    (Dummett), 133–137, 152–154
  molecular theory of, 148, 150, 154
  occasion meaning (Grice), 63–65, 88
  of proper names, 328, 338–339, 354, 559–
    560, 587
  and reference, 323–333, 348 (see also
    Reference)
  of a sentence, 89–95, 100, 111–113, 124,
    140–141, 158–161, 167, 187, 191–194,
    424, 685
  as speaker's intention, 59–88, 394–396
  stimulus meaning (Quine), 55–57, 917
    (n. 40)
  theory of, 89–105, 106 (nn. 3, 7), 107
    (n. 13), 129–155, 203–205, 218, 220, 234,
    249, 561, 592, 663, 717, 719, 856, 863–
    864, 870
  timeless (Grice), 62–64
  and translation, 49–57, 97–105, 110–125,
    130–152
  T-theory of, 4–5, 94–105, 109–125, 134–
    152, 179, 187–197, 235–237, 239, 741
    (n. 7)
  and understanding, 114–125, 131–155
  use theory of, 4–5, 35, 37, 41, 342–346
  of a word, 89, 93–95, 121, 157–161, 167,
    195, 268
Meaninglessness, 49, 332
Meanings, 51–52, 89, 92–95, 105–106 (n. 3),
    159–161, 671, 685, 824–825
  as abstract objects, 3
  as classes of stimuli, 3, 55–57

as psychological entities, 3
as speaker's intention, 4, 59–88
Memory, 44
Mental images, 33, 35, 42
Mental processes/activity, 34, 36
Mention/mentioning (Strawson), 336, 341,
    343, 346, 348, 362
Metalanguage, 94, 96, 99–102, 106 (n. 7),
    126 (n. 5), 134, 137, 140, 152, 179, 184–
    185, 187, 197 (n. 4), 236–238, 244, 250,
    506, 600, 664, 783, 823, 1021, 1023,
    1028 (n. 3), 1030 (n. 12)
Mind, 34–37, 45–46
Model-theoretic semantics, 5, 109, 114–125,
    126 (n. 5), 204, 206, 773
Modified Occam's razor (Grice), 433, 444

Names, naming, 33, 353, 355–356, 362, 364,
    377, 379, 396, 409 (n. 20), 421, 426, 458
    (n. 10), 529, 550 (n. 19), 559, 563, 659,
    802–803, 805, 875, 925–926, 935. See also
    Proper names
  theory of, 349, 559
Naturalization
  of philosophy of language, xiii, 203–205,
    412 (n. 30)
  of theory of meaning, 5
Natural kinds, 243, 901, 904–906, 915
    (n. 29), 916 (n. 36), 917 (n. 40), 952
Natural language, 95, 100, 103, 106 (n. 4),
    148, 203–205, 247, 251, 455, 773, 777,
    793, 797, 840, 850. See also Ordinary
    language
  logical form of, 203–206, 281–311, 359
  semantic theory of, 98–105, 107 (n. 12),
    109–125, 130, 188–179, 235–236, 239,
    247, 320, 850
Natural science, 36, 595
Necessity, 388–389, 611–614, 627–631, 686
  epistemic vs. metaphysical, 879–880,
    910 (n. 10), 919 (n. 44)
  physical, 627–628

Object language, 94, 96, 99, 101–103, 106
    (n. 7), 134–135, 137, 140, 144–145, 179,
    184–185, 187, 197 (n. 2), 238, 248, 252,
    256, 779, 823, 1022–1023, 1028 (n. 3),
    1030 (n. 12)
Objects (Frege), 21, 22, 24–25, 563–566,
    569, 575–576
Ordinary language, 37, 100, 107 (n. 13),
    209–212, 331, 336, 809. See also Natural
    language
Opacity, 801–814, 815 (n. 7), 906, 964, 974,
    989 (& n. 4)

Opaque contexts, 833–835, 837–850, 850
    (n. 1)
  embedded-sentence analysis of, 833, 837,
    843, 848
  higher-predicate analysis of, 851 (n. 2)
  and infinitive phrases, 839–842, 844
  intensional analysis of, 833, 840–846, 850,
    851 (n. 12)
  in intensional constructions, 834, 843–846
  as property of sentence contexts, 847–850
  and quantifier scope, 838–841
  quotational analysis of, 801–814, 850 (n. 1)
  referential vs. nonreferential reading of,
    834, 838, 840–843, 846–847, 851 (n. 10)
  and subject-predicate constructions, 846,
    851 (n. 12)
  and *that* clauses, 837–841
  and verb phrases, 840–850, 851 (n. 11), 852
    (n. 14)
Outer world (Frege), 17, 20, 21, 25–27

Pain, 19, 23–25, 627
Paradox of analysis (Moore), 412 (n. 30),
    460 (n. 20), 786, 789–790
Particular vs. universal, 351, 379
Perception, 22
Phrase markers, 181, 282, 512, 993–994,
    997–999, 1002–1005, 1027
Phrase-structure grammar, 106 (n. 4), 107
    (n. 13), 251
Phrase-structure representation, 283–284
Phrase-structure rules, 197 (n. 4)
Phrase-structure trees, 257
Possible-worlds semantics, 121, 675, 680,
    772–774, 834–835, 921–927, 930–931,
    933, 952–953
Predicates, 188, 219, 230, 246, 248, 252–253,
    257, 262, 300, 307, 374, 487
  binary, 165, 172, 174–175
  as functional expressions, 90
  relational, 453
  vague, 247
Principle of compositionality (Frege), 116–
    117, 121, 126 (n. 6), 147, 568–582, 718–
    719, 977, 1028–1029 (n. 5)
Principle of identity of indiscernables, 588
Private/privacy, 46, 776
Pronomialization, 273–277, 405, 407 (n. 1),
    412 (n. 31), 413 (n. 32)
  anaphoric, 540–548
  backwards, 258, 260–261, 265
  cross-referring, 806–807
  obligatory reflexive, 265
  reflective, 262
Proper names, 16–17, 142–144, 153–154,
    188, 306–307, 475, 501, 506–509, 515

  (n. 10), 559–562, 585–592, 593–608, 609–
    634, 635–655, 671–673, 680, 688, 691
    (n. 21), 807, 835–837, 876–907 (& n. 2),
    908 (nn. 3, 5), 909 (n. 7), 910 (nn. 9, 10),
    911 (nn. 11–13), 912 (nn. 15, 18), 913
    (nn. 19–21, 23), 915 (nn. 29–31), 916
    (n. 37), 917 (n. 40–42), 918 (n. 43), 920
    (n. 46), 934
  and ambiguity, 641–642, 646
  in belief contexts, 877–880, 882–884,
    887–907, 909 (n. 7), 918 (n. 43), 919
    (nn. 45, 46), 959 (n. 24), 973, 980, 983,
    986
  causal theory of (Kripke), 560, 622–626,
    635, 639–646, 649, 652–654, 884, 913
    (n. 21), 968, 989 (n. 8)
  change of denotation of, 643, 650
  compound, 575
  conditions/criteria of use/application of,
    588–592, 594, 598, 650–653
  conditions of designating/denoting for,
    593, 601–603, 605–606, 621, 623–624,
    636–637, 639
  as constant noncomplex singular terms,
    594–595, 605–608
  and context of use, 599–600, 606, 636,
    641–642
  descriptive theory of, 390–391, 408 (n. 12),
    559–561, 588–592, 609, 623–626, 632
    (n. 6), 633 (n. 8), 634 (nn. 12, 14), 635–
    637, 640, 644–646, 653, 654 (n. 2), 672–
    673, 676, 876–877, 884, 888–889, 896–
    900, 907 (& n. 2), 908 (n. 3), 911 (n. 13),
    912 (n. 15), 914 (n. 29), 915 (n. 31), 917
    (n. 40), 960 (n. 25), 979–980
  descriptive use of, 327–330, 349, 351, 353,
    386, 390, 397, 401, 403, 409 (n. 20), 410
    (n. 26), 411 (n. 28), 421, 439, 456 (n. 1),
    466 (n. 38), 592, 603, 633 (n. 6)
  determination/fixing of reference/desig-
    nation/denotation of, 609–610, 612–626,
    630, 632 (nn. 3, 4), 634 (nn. 12, 14), 636,
    643–645, 876, 880–882, 884, 896, 898, 907
    (n. 2), 910 (n. 10), 911 (n. 11), 913 (n. 20),
    918 (n. 43), 938–939
  and disquotational principle (Kripke),
    888–890, 899, 902–906, 913 (nn. 22, 23),
    914 (n. 28), 916 (n. 37), 919–920 (n. 46)
  in epistemic contexts, 877, 879–880
  and failures of denotation/designation,
    593–595, 601, 603–605, 608 (n. 13),
    619
  function of, 589, 590–591, 877
  in intensional contexts, 877
  learning/explaining use of, 587, 623, 679
  linguistic analysis of, 561

logically proper names, 338–339, 355, 362, 378, 386–387, 908 (nn. 3, 5), 915 (n. 29)
meaning of, 328, 338–339, 354, 559–560, 587
in modal contexts, 561, 611–631, 877, 879–880, 883–884, 909 (n. 7), 910 (n. 10)
modified uses of, 596–599, 601, 606
occasion of use of, 635–636, 640
ordinary, 353, 355, 597, 908 (n. 3)
ostensive vs. descriptive definition of, 587, 625–626, 632 (n. 3), 633–634 (n. 12), 634 (n. 14)
and principle of translation (Kripke), 888–890, 899, 903–906, 913 (nn. 22, 23), 919 (n. 46)
in propositional-attitude contexts, 884, 925, 928–940, 944–951, 961 (n. 31), 994–998, 1001–1006, 1009–1015, 1029–1030 (n. 11), 1035 (n. 35)
and quantifier scope, 561, 599–600, 638, 878
reference of, 559, 564–583, 585–592, 599, 610–631, 632 (n. 4), 636–655, 722, 835, 881, 884, 898
reference theory of (Mill), 588, 621, 876–880, 883–885, 907, 908 (nn. 3, 5), 909 (n. 7), 910 (nn. 9, 10)
referring use of, 589–592, 603, 649
as rigid designators, 408 (n. 9), 612–615, 629, 851 (n. 4), 880, 882, 909 (n. 7), 910 (nn. 10, 11), 913 (n. 20), 918 (n. 43)
rules for use of, 585–587, 590
in semantic theory, 593–608
sense of, 559, 562, 564–583, 585–588, 592, 704, 706, 876, 879–884, 888–889, 908 (n. 3), 911 (n. 12), 912 (nn. 15, 18), 915 (n. 29), 920 (n. 46)
as simple predicates, 559–560, 594–608
speaker's denotation of, vs. actual denotation of, 601–603, 606, 621, 635–637, 639–641, 644–646, 648, 652
and speaker's intention, 599, 602, 637, 641, 643–646, 648–649, 651–652
and substitutivity, 876–884, 888–901, 904–907, 909 (nn. 5, 7), 910 (n. 10), 913 (n. 19), 917 (n. 41), 918 (nn. 42, 43), 919 (n. 45), 938
syntactic theory of, 608 (n. 8)
and translation, 899–904, 912 (n. 18), 915 (n. 29–34), 916 (nn. 34, 37), 917 (nn. 40, 42)
uniquely referring, 615–617, 619, 624 (& n. 6)
Properties, 613, 674
Propositional-attitude conception of semantics, 921–926

Propositional attitudes, 104, 267–270, 670, 688, 725, 729–730, 737, 772, 789, 817, 826, 830, 855, 857, 903, 917 (n. 39), 922–955, 956 (n. 1), 958 (n. 19), 959–960 (n. 24), 960–961 (n. 29), 962 (n. 39), 992–1028, 1028 (nn. 1, 3). See also Belief reports; Belief sentences; Indirect discourse; Psychological attitudes
ascriptions of, 933–935, 938–943, 952
and context, 1022–1026
Davidsonian analysis of, 826, 830, 855, 857, 859, 863
and direct reference, 924–926, 930, 933–935, 949–952, 954, 961 (nn. 32, 35), 962 (n. 38)
Fregean account of, 986–987, 1016
and intensions, 947–954, 962 (n. 36)
and interpreted logical forms (ILFs), 776–777, 993–1028, 1028 (nn. 1, 3), 1029–1030 (n. 11), 1030 (n. 12), 1031–1032 (n. 18), 1032 (n. 24), 1033 (n. 28), 1034 (nn. 33, 34), 1035 (nn. 34, 35), 1036 (n. 36), 1041–1042
logical form of, 267–270, 855, 859, 1008
propositional analysis of (Russell), 781–782, 789, 862, 964–967, 1016–1017, 1033 (n. 29)
and propositional-attitude conception of semantics, 923–924, 926, 946–949, 951, 954–955
quotational analysis of, 802–805, 903, 1015–1016
and referential opacity vs. transparency, 809–814
and referential position, 809–814
relational account of, 855, 922–924, 933, 939, 951, 960 (n. 24)
reports of, 922–924, 935, 942
and semantic content, 922–933, 939–940, 944–946, 949–955, 956 (nn. 1, 5), 957 (n. 7), 959 (n. 24), 960 (n. 29), 961 (n. 32), 962 (n. 37)
and semantic innocence, 964, 990 (n. 14)
sentential account of, 855
vs. sentential attitudes, 942–943
and substitutivity, 809–811, 934–935, 938, 940–941, 943, 958–959 (n. 22), 993–996, 1005–1006, 1014, 1016–1017, 1031 (n. 18)
and truth-conditional semantics, 923–931, 952–955, 956 (n. 5)
truth conditions of, 923–924, 929–933, 940, 947, 953, 957 (nn. 8, 9)
Propositional content, 877, 966–967
Propositional functions (Russell), 324, 326, 329–331, 333

Propositions, 34, 138, 209–215, 226, 230, 268, 323–333, 335–359, 790, 834, 989 (n. 12)
atomic, 209–212, 215
knowledge of, vs. knowledge of truth, 138–147, 152
object-dependent, 420, 423–426, 439–441, 442–443, 445, 447, 453, 456, 463–465 (nn. 32, 36) (*see also* Propositions, singular vs. general)
object-independent, 423–424
meant vs. expressed (Grice), 415, 418, 420–437, 439–440, 443–456, 456 (n. 3), 458 (n. 16), 463–465 (n. 36), 466 (nn. 37, 38), 467 (n. 41), 468 (nn. 46, 47), 523, 525, 528–534, 549 (n. 11)
singular vs. general, 320–321, 524–529, 531–536, 550 (n. 19), 552 (n. 24), 674–676, 680, 685, 688–689, 774–775 (*see also* Propositions, object-dependent; Propositions, object-independent)
in subject-predicate form, 210–211, 327, 674
Psychological attitudes, 817. *See also* Propositional attitudes
and context, 773
and intensions, 773
individuation of, 772, 774–776
in semantic theory, 771–777
objects of, 772–775
possible-worlds analysis of, 772–774, 777, 834–835, 921–927, 930–931, 933, 952–953
propositional analysis of, 772–775, 777, 809–810
reports of, 771–777, 829
sentential theories of, 774, 777
Psychology, xiii, 191, 504

Quantification, 284–310, 305, 311, 399, 419, 444, 449, 455, 666, 671, 1031–1032 (n. 18)
linguistic knowledge of, 290
logical form of quantified sentences, 284–310
multiple, 294–310
theory, 262, 272, 296, 307, 433, 449, 455
over actions (Davidson), 220, 227–232, 271–273
over events, 227–232, 271–272
Quantificational structure, 286, 819
Quantifiers, 248, 252, 262–267, 269, 273–274, 276, 289–296, 300, 304, 308, 312 (nn. 6, 10), 320, 415, 424–425, 441, 447–449, 451–452, 455, 467 (n. 40), 475–483, 485–501, 540–541, 543, 545–546, 755–756, 835–837, 846

binary (restricted and unrestricted), 302–303, 1032 (n. 22)
embedded, 537–540
incomplete, 448, 452
in natural language, 263, 284–310, 433, 448, 455
numerical, 289
persistent vs. nonpersistent, 467 (n. 45)
plural, 441
and scope islands (Fodor & Sag), 489–497, 499–500, 513, 515 (n. 10), 537–540, 552 (n. 24)
scope of, 388, 390, 475–478, 482–483, 485–501, 504, 506, 509–513, 515 (nn. 9, 10), 516 (nn. 12, 13), 518 (n. 28), 524, 535–540, 552 (nn. 21, 22), 561, 599–600, 638, 806, 812–813, 836–841, 878, 997, 1011, 1031–1032 (nn. 18, 22)
theory of scope of, 477, 513, 518 (n. 29)
Quotation, 820. *See also* Indirect discourse/speech
and referential position, 802–805
and referential opacity vs. transparency, 802–805

Reason, 44–45
Reference, 91–92, 161–162, 241, 304, 564, 593, 757, 818. *See also* Designator/designation; Denotation
of definite descriptions, 323–333, 335–359, 361–381, 447, 504
vs. denotation, 319, 371
direct, 964, 976, 978–980, 982
failure of, 372–373, 504, 574, 756, 801, 979–980
Fregean (*Bedeutung*), 563–583, 679–680, 694–695, 699, 707–708, 717–724, 728–730, 741 (nn. 6, 7, 15)
indirect, 564, 571–573, 578, 580–581, 695, 712
of proper names, 559, 564–583, 585–592, 599, 610–631, 632 (n. 4), 636–655, 722, 835, 881, 884, 898
semantic vs. speaker's, 321
theory of, 95, 154, 407, 718–721, 727–728
of whole vs. part of a sentence, 568–582, 583 (n. 15)
Referential opacity vs. transparency, 801–814, 815 (n. 7), 906
Referential position, 801–814
and substitutivity of identity, 801–802, 805, 809–811
Regimentation of natural language, 253
Rigid/nonrigid designation, 389–390, 406, 408 (nn. 9, 10), 446, 612–615

Rigid/nonrigid designators, 389–390, 408
(n. 9), 410 (n. 25), 446, 506, 612–615, 629,
851 (n. 4), 880, 882, 909 (n. 7), 910
(nn. 10, 11), 913 (n. 20), 918 (n. 43), 1033
(n. 30)
Rule following (Wittgenstein), 41, 43

Saying that. *See* Indirect discourse/speech
Semantic ambiguity, 392–394, 401–403,
406–407 (& n. 3), 408 (n. 14), 410 (n. 22),
411 (n. 28), 412 (n. 29), 413 (n. 35), 418–
419, 433–434, 437, 441, 443 444, 457
(nn. 5, 7), 463–465 (n. 36), 467 (n. 40),
511–512, 536
Semantic competence, 124, 193–194, 560
Semantic consequences, 236–238
Semantic facts/properties, 187–188, 236,
287
Semantic interpretation, 205, 282, 284, 290,
297, 310
Semantic reference vs. speaker's reference,
395–407, 407 (n. 1), 410, (n. 22), 411
(nn. 27, 28), 412 (nn. 31, 32), 413
(nn. 32, 33)
Semantic rules/axioms, 181, 189, 191, 196,
412 (n. 30), 780, 782–784, 794, 797
Semantics, 92–93, 98, 109–125, 158, 160,
163, 167, 169, 179, 187, 234, 241, 671,
746, 764, 836, 840, 871–872
empirical, 57
formal, 100, 103, 107 (nn. 12, 13), 253, 281
game-theoretic, 126 (n. 6)
generative, 164, 172
interpretational (Evans), 243, 245–253
model-theoretic, 5, 109, 114–125, 126
(n. 5), 204, 206, 773
of natural language, 98–105, 107 (n. 12),
109–125, 130, 188–189, 235–236, 239,
247, 320, 850
possible-worlds, 121, 675, 680, 772–774,
834–835, 921–927, 930–931, 933, 952–
953
propositional-attitude conception of, 921–
926
of propositional attitudes, 922–933, 939–
940, 944–946, 949–955, 956 (nn. 1, 5), 957
(n. 7), 959 (n. 24), 960 (n. 29), 961 (n. 32),
962 (n. 37)
speaker's knowledge of, 5, 179, 187–197
structural, 5, 109–114, 116–119, 123,
126 (n. 5)
truth-conditional, 4–5, 94–105, 109–125,
134–152, 179, 187–197, 235–237, 239,
741 (n. 7), 921–927
Semantic structure, 234, 243, 246–247, 249,
251–252, 269, 282, 310
of indirect discourse, 746, 762, 826

of natural language, 281–310
of quantified sentences, 281, 284–310
Semantic theory, 158–161, 226, 239, 241–
242, 297, 921, 1019
handling of attitude reports, 771–777, 921–
962, 993–1028
handling of proper names, 594–608
for a natural language, 109–125, 179–197,
718, 754
Sensation, 17, 18, 22, 40, 566
Sense (Frege), 11, 15, 34, 105 (n. 3), 563–
583, 593, 682, 693–714, 717–741, 742
(n. 16), 799 (n. 10), 971–972, 1016
complete vs. incomplete, 696, 698–703,
706–707, 711–714, 717, 725, 727
criteria for individuation of, 694–695, 702,
703, 705–706, 709, 711–712, 721
of demonstratives, 697–714
of empty singular terms, 721–724, 742
(n. 11)
vs. idea, 565–567
as indirect reference of a sentence, 695
as mode of presentation of reference, 563–
564, 708, 719–721, 723–724, 741 (n. 6),
1016
as private/incommunicable, 693, 705, 708–
709, 714, 733
of a proper name (*see* Proper names, senses
of)
and reference/denotation, 563–583, 679–
680, 694–695, 699, 707–708, 718–724,
728–729
sense had vs. sense expressed, 696, 699–
700, 702
of a sentence, 11–12, 14, 694–697, 700,
702–703
of a sign, 564–566
and truth, 694
of whole vs. part of a sentence (*see*
Principle of compositionality)
Sense data, 549 (n. 6), 629
Sense impressions, 12, 17, 18, 20, 22–23, 25,
27, 565, 582 (n. 5)
Sense perception, 26–27
Sentence(s), 35, 37, 49–50, 52–53, 56–57,
89–105, 109–125, 179–198
about action, 163–175, 217–232, 270–
273
analytic, 103, 236
about causes, 270–272
as complex singular terms, 90
declarative, 113, 298, 568–569
descriptive vs. evaluative, 101
embedded/subordinate, 189, 257, 262, 264,
266–270, 537–540, 571–582
eternal vs. noneternal (Quine), 663–664,
682, 688, 691 (n. 27), 697, 701–702, 712

Sentence(s) (cont.)
about events, 163–175, 230
expressing degree of a quality, 212–213
grammatical vs. logical form of, 337–339
imperative, 12–13, 80
with indexicals, 15–16, 197 (n. 7), 342
indicative, 13–14, 28, 30 (n. 3), 80–83
interrogative, 13, 298–299
logical form of, and syntactic form of,
    281–311
reference of (*see* Reference, of a sentence)
referring use of, 340–347
sense of (Frege) (*see* Sense, of a sentence)
tensed, 27–28, 682
types vs. tokens, 682–685
Signs, 34–36, 45–46, 88, 563–564, 582 (n. 8)
Speaker's meaning vs. word/sentence mean-
    ing (Grice), 394–396
Speaker's reference vs. semantic reference,
    395–407, 407 (n. 1), 410, (n. 22), 411
    (nn. 27, 28), 412 (nn. 31, 32), 413
    (nn. 32, 33)
Speech acts, 73, 104, 370, 393, 427, 445,
    670–671
theory of, 399, 401, 407
Stimulation (Quine), 49–50, 52–56
Stimulus meaning (Quine), 55–57
Structural semantics, 5, 109–114, 116–119,
    123, 126 (n. 5)
Structural validity, 235–254
Substance, 351
Surface (S) structure, 257–258, 262, 283–
    284, 310–311, 312 (nn. 4, 7), 313 (n. 16),
    413 (n. 35), 997, 1028 (n. 4)
movement, 304, 310–311
of quantified sentences, 287, 293–296, 298–
    302
representations, 284–285, 310
Syllogisms, 358
Synonymy, 92, 97, 102, 109–110, 132, 161,
    782, 786–787, 793, 797, 798 (n. 6), 824,
    827, 831 (n. 13)
of sentences, 92, 102, 137, 143, 786
Syntactic ambiguity. *See* Ambiguity,
    syntactic
Syntactic structure, 157–158, 166, 181, 252,
    257, 269, 282, 294, 310
Syntax, 89, 92–93, 158, 209, 253, 282, 297,
    306, 311, 746, 764, 836, 840, 850
extended standard theory of (Chomsky),
    997
rules of, 209, 211, 242, 290, 296
Syntheticity, 163, 585–586

Third realm (Frege), 3, 20, 27, 710
Thought, 34–38, 45–47, 700–714. *See also*
    Thoughts (Frege)

content of, 746–750
and context, 711–713, 748–750
determination of content of, 749–750, 758–
    764
as information (Perry), 700–703, 709–714,
    715 (n. 6), 737–738, 743 (n. 31)
perceptual demonstrative, 746–751, 758–
    764
Thoughts (Frege), 11–29, 568–582, 583
    (nn. 10, 12, 18), 663–714, 717, 719, 722–
    741, 748
vs. ideas, 11, 17–25, 565–567, 734
and indirect reference, 694–695, 713–714
individuation of, 700–706, 709, 711–714,
    718–719, 729–730, 735–737
as private/incommunicable, 693, 710, 733–
    736, 739
Time, 36
Topology, 890
Trace theory, 286, 294, 312 (n. 4)
Transformation, 263–266, 840–844, 849
passive, 258–261
Transformational grammar, 107 (n. 13),
    257, 282, 840, 851 (n. 6)
vs. phrase-structure grammar, 106 (n. 4),
    107 (n. 13)
Transformational mapping, 284, 290
Transformational rules, 257, 263, 284, 841
Translation, 50–52, 55, 102–103, 107
    (n. 18), 112, 130–131, 134–135, 140, 240–
    241, 786, 877, 888–891, 899–902, 914
    (n. 25), 917 (n. 40)
indeterminacy of, 50, 823, 902–904
and meaning (*see* Meaning, and
    translation)
radical, 51, 57, 98, 106 (n. 11), 824
Translation principle (Kripke), 886–890,
    899–900, 903–906, 913 (nn. 22, 23),
    919 (n. 46)
True/False (Frege), 569, 578, 695, 719, 733,
    771
Truth, 10–12, 20, 49, 94–99, 103, 113, 109–
    111, 119, 281, 412 (n. 30)
a priori, 620, 632 (n. 3)
disagreements about, vs. disagreements
    about meaning, 148–152
logic as laws of (Frege), 9–10
necessary, 388–389, 611–614, 627, 632
    (n. 3), 877–879, 922, 1031 (n. 17)
as property/function of utterances, 104, 342
Tarskian definition/theory of, 95–105,
    119–121, 134, 229, 235–236, 269–270,
    593, 818–820, 870
theory of, 236, 240–242, 252, 593–594,
    663–664, 818–820, 826, 830, 831 (n. 25),
    870, 904
timeless (Frege), 20–21, 26–28

Truth-conditional semantics, 4–5, 94–105, 109–125, 134–152, 179, 187–197, 235–237, 239, 741 (n. 7), 921–927

Truth conditions, 109–114, 123, 150, 153, 599, 601, 605, 637, 641, 819–820, 921
of action sentences, 222, 229–230
assignment/determination of, 746, 755–757, 761–764, 765 (n. 18)
of demonstrative utterances, 664–667, 755–757
of psychological/propositional-attitude sentences, 773, 923–924, 929–933, 940, 947, 953, 957 (nn. 8, 9), 995, 1003–1004, 1007, 1010–1012, 1015, 1017, 1019–1021, 1023, 1032 (n. 18), 1036 (n. 37)
of sentences, 93, 96, 99–100, 104, 106 (nn. 9, 10), 122, 130, 150–151, 153, 184–185, 236, 238, 249–251, 728, 921

Truth definition (Tarski), 95, 100–104, 106 (n. 7), 107 (n. 12), 134, 236–237, 663

Truth-value gaps, 595, 599, 721

T-sentence/T-theorem, 131, 142, 145–148, 151, 180–197, 238, 241
for attitude reports, 995–996, 999–1002, 1006–1014, 1020–1021

T-theory, 94–105, 180–186, 203–204
for action sentences, 229–232
and demonstratives, 659, 663–667, 745–766
for indirect discourse, 826–830, 857, 863
and interpreted logical forms (ILFs), 998–999
interpretive, 187–188, 191–197
and proper names, 593–608
as theory of meaning, 4–5, 94–105, 109–125, 134–152, 179, 187–197, 235–237, 239, 741 (n. 7)

Understanding, 33–35, 41–44
formal semantics as a theory of, 114–125
language, 95–99, 112, 116, 125, 131–155, 157–158, 179, 187, 196, 203, 235, 239, 595, 689, 719–720, 728, 856, 870, 872
propositions, 423–424, 427, 525, 719
sentences, 111, 118, 125, 140–141, 144–148, 151, 185–186, 282, 741, 1019
utterances, 426, 527–530, 726–727
theory of meaning as a theory of, 131–155
words, 141–145, 153–154

Universal grammar, 193–195, 284, 287, 311

Universals, 56, 351, 549 (n. 6)

Use, 359 (n. 1)
ascriptive use of a sentence/expression, 350–353
and assertion, 347–349
of definite descriptions (see Definite descriptions)

and explanation, 4
occasions of, 340–341, 686
predicative use of a sentence/expression, 349
of a proper name, 587–592, 635–653
and reference, 341–359
rules/conventions of, 350–351, 353, 355, 425
of a sentence/expression, 340–359
spurious use of a sentence/expression, 346

Use theory of meaning
introduced, 4–5
meaning as use, 35, 37, 41, 342–346

Utterance(s), 59–88, 104, 268, 340–341, 345, 347, 349–351, 393–394, 405, 419, 692 (n. 32), 925. See also Assertion
assertive, 413 (n. 35), 577, 674, 752, 757
of belief sentences (see Belief reports)
content of, 676–679, 683–685–686, 687, 752, 757, 863–865, 867–871, 872 (n. 4), 925
context of, 351–353, 415, 420–437, 448–450, 454–456, 464–465 (n. 36), 468 (nn. 46, 54), 505–513, 517 (n. 21), 547, 599–600, 606, 664, 676–679, 682, 684–685, 688, 697–699, 713, 755–757, 921, 925
of demonstratives, 664–667, 677–688, 690 (n. 15), 697–699, 702–704, 726, 728, 736, 752–758
grounds of, 527–529, 533–534, 549 (n. 12), 550 (n. 18)
imperative form of, 78, 80
indicative form of, 77, 80–83
of indirect discourse, 826–830, 831 (n. 13), 857–870, 873 (n. 5)
of referring expressions, 425–470, 676–677
of sentences containing definite descriptions, 437–440, 457 (n. 3), 524, 535
of sentences containing indefinite descriptions, 477, 529–534, 536
of sentences containing proper names, 589, 600–601, 636–638, 676–677
and speaker's intention, 59–88, 374, 429–430, 439, 446, 450–452, 456, 459 (n. 18), 504, 528–536, 549 (n. 12), 680, 685–687, 701, 753–754
truth conditions of, 427, 664

Verb-phrase (VP) deletion, 477, 496–500, 516 (nn. 11, 12), 540

Visual experiences/imagery/impressions/phenomena, 22–23, 25, 27, 34, 37–40, 42, 209